ASSEMBLY LANGUAGE PROGRAMMING FOR THE INTEL 80XXX FAMILY

THE MACMILLAN PROGRAMMING LANGUAGES SERIES

Hugo D'Alarco and Robert Sutherland, PROBLEM SOLVING WITH PASCAL: ALGORITHM AND PROGRAM DESIGN.

Victor Broquard and J. William Westley, FUNDAMENTALS OF ASSEMBLER LANGUAGE PROGRAMMING FOR THE IBM PC AND XT.

Ralph Cafolla and Daniel A. Kauffman, TURBO PROLOG: STEP BY STEP

Paul Chirlian, PROGRAMMING IN C++.

Paul Chirlian, TURBO PROLOG: AN INTRODUCTION.

Stacey Edgar, ADVANCED PROBLEM SOLVING WITH FORTRAN 77.

Francis Federighi and Edwin Reilly, VAX ASSEMBLY LANGUAGE.

Daniel Friedman and Matthias Felleisen, THE LITTLE LISPER, Third Edition.

William Giles. ASSEMBLY LANGUAGE PROGRAMMING FOR THE INTEL 80XXX FAMILY.

Robert Gray, MACRO ASSEMBLER PROGRAMMING FOR THE IBM-PC AND COMPATIBLES.

Jerry Houston, LOOKING INTO C: A C LANGUAGE TEXTBOOK.

Kip Irvine, ASSEMBLY LANGUAGE FOR THE IBM-PC.

Richard Johnsonbaugh and Martin Kalin, APPLICATIONS PROGRAMMING IN C.

Richard Johnsonbaugh and Martin Kalin, APPLICATIONS PROGRAMMING IN. ANSI C.

Sanford Leestma and Larry Nyhoff, PASCAL: PROGRAMMING AND PROBLEM SOLVING, Third Edition

Sanford Leestma and Larry Nyhoff, PROGRAMMING AND PROBLEM SOLVING IN MODULA-2.

Sanford Leestma and Larry Nyhoff, TURBO PASCAL: PROGRAMMING AND PROBLEM SOLVING.

Nonna Lehmkuhl, FORTRAN 77: A TOP-DOWN APPROACH.

Metrowerks, Inc. METROWERKS MODULA-2 STARTPAK: COMPILER, TUTORIAL AND DOCUMENTATION FOR THE APPLE MACINTOSH.

Michael Marcotty and Henry Ledgard, THE PROGRAMMING LANGUAGE LANDSCAPE: SYNTAX, SEMANTICS, AND IMPLEMENTATION, Second Edition.

Kenneth Morgan, INTRODUCTION TO STRUCTURED PROGRAMMING USING TURBO PASCAL VERSION 5.0 ON THE IBM PC.

Larry Nyhoff and Sanford Leestma, ADVANCED PROGRAMMING IN PASCAL WITH DATA STRUCTURES.

Larry Nyhoff and Sanford Leestma, DATA STRUCTURES AND PROGRAM DESIGN IN MODULA-2.

Larry Nyhoff and Sanford Leestma, FORTRAN 77 FOR ENGINEERS AND SCIENTISTS, Second Edition.

Ross Overbeek and W. E. Singletary, ASSEMBLER LANGUAGE WITH ASSIST AND ASSIST/I, Fourth Edition.

Dan Rollins, IBM-PC: 8088 MACRO ASSEMBLY LANGUAGE PROGRAMMING.

Gregory Wetzel and William Bulgren, PASCAL AND ALGORITHMS: AN INTRODUCTION TO PROBLEM SOLVING.

ASSEMBLY LANGUAGE PROGRAMMING FOR THE INTEL 80XXX FAMILY

William B. Giles

San Jose State University

Macmillan Publishing Company
New York

Collier Macmillan Canada
Toronto

Maxwell Macmillan International
New York   Oxford   Singapore   Sydney

Editors: Ed Moura and John Griffin
Production Supervisor: John Travis
Production Manager: Pam Kennedy

Macmillan Publishing Company
866 Third Avenue, New York, New York 10022

Collier Macmillan Canada, Inc.
1200 Eglinton Avenue, F.
Suite 200
Don Mills, Ontario, M3C 3N1

Library of Congress Cataloging in Publication Data

Giles, William B.
    Assembly language programming for the Intel 80XXX family / William
B. Giles.
        p.   cm.
    Includes bibliographical references.
    ISBN   0-02-342990-9
    1.   Intel 80XXX series microprocessors—Programming.
2.   Assembler language (Computer program language)   I.Title.
QA76.8.I29294G55   1991
005.265—dc20

Printing: 1 2 3 4 5 6 7 8   Year: 1 2 3 4 5 6 7 8 9

To the students at San Jose State, who suffered through a number of versions and whose opinions — sometimes unknowingly and sometimes very explicitly given — helped to determine the ultimate form of this book.

PREFACE

In this book, I attempt to give a reasonably complete and up-to-date account of the assembly language and programming environment of the Intel **80XXX** family of microprocessors. The book evolved from notes used in teaching beginning assembly language courses over the past several years. The students to whom I teach this material have already programmed in a high-level language and, indeed, some programming experience is an essential prerequisite to reading this book. The reader must be familiar with basic programming constructs such as loops, arrays, and stacks. Beyond that, I have tried to make the contents self-contained.

The basic philosophy underlying the book is that the individual instructions in an assembly language are generally quite trivial. For example, if **ax** is known to represent a storage location, then the meaning of an instruction such as

```
mov  ax, 10
```

is surely quite transparent. In fact, the vast majority assembly language instructions are no more complicated than this one!

The real difficulties in using assembly language are of two kinds:

- The sheer number of instructions in even moderately complex assembly language programs makes them hard to write and, at least as important, hard to read.

- Assembly language programs generally deal directly with the operating system and frequently with the hardware, and these interactions can be very complicated.

The first of these problems is attacked early in the book, in Chapter 5, with the help of reusable code modules, which are of enormous assistance in controlling the complexity of assembly language. Both procedures and macro substitutions are introduced. A function library, USER.LIB, is set up in Chapter 5 and augmented throughout the book. These constructs are, of course, not unique to assembly language. They just implement the basic bottom-up ideas of structured programming in an especially transparent context.

Unfortunately, the second major difficulty with assembly language, namely the interactions of programs with the system software and hardware, has no neat, one-chapter solution. The many aspects of this problem can only be dealt with by detailed discussions and examples, which occupy a good portion of this book.

In a programming text, it is important to provide working programs to illustrate the important ideas. As most programmers discover early in their careers, translating a few descriptive lines from a text or manual into working code can require hours of hard work. As soon as even a skeletal working program is available, it serves as a framework for future development, and generally progress is much faster from that point on. The Program Disk distributed with this book contains copies of all the programs shown in the text (and a number of others). I consider the programs to be as important as the expository material in the text, and hope that the reader will study both with equal diligence. The programs vary widely in their level of difficulty and include many examples that are either of considerable contemporary importance or else relate to "classical" computational problems of enduring interest. For example:

- File buffering and the effect of buffer size on speed are examined in Chapter 8.

- It is well-known that **MS-DOS** is a non-reentrant operating system. Many of the most intriguing aspects of programming under **MS-DOS** are concerned with the effects of non-reentrancy on memory-resident programs. This topic is pursued at length in Chapter 15.

- Installable device drivers are an essential ingredient of any modern operating system. They are examined in detail in Chapter 16.

- As an example of an installable device driver, Chapter 16 contains a device driver for a Postscript laser printer. Although this driver is quite primitive, it permits the printing of any ASCII file on a Postscript printer connected to a parallel port.

- To illustrate programming the hardware, Chapter 15 presents the code for an execution profiler. This example shows how to reprogram the **8253** timer chip and, as a bonus, provides a genuinely useful utility.

- This is a time of transition from real mode programming to protected mode programming on the **80286** and later processors. Chapter 18 develops a minimal protected mode kernel allowing a **80386** or **80486** to boot under **MS-DOS**, run a simple application in protected mode, and then return to **MS-DOS**. Of course, this kernel is only adequate for experimental use.

- A number of computational problems have intrigued programmers since the invention of computers. These problems generally concern either very large integers or else the computation of real numbers to high precision. Chapter 11 includes examples of both of these kinds: the computation of 10,000 factorial (a number having 35,660 digits); and computing the real number π to 1000 decimal places.

So far, numerical coprocessors have been installed in only a relatively small percentage of machines using **80XXX** family processors. However, there is every likelihood that this will change in the future since the new graphics interfaces are so computationally demanding and especially since the **80486** has an integrated floating point unit. Looking to the future, I have therefor included, in Chapter 17, a very complete treatment of the **8087/80287/80387** and the FPU of the **80486**.

There is another significant aspect of the contemporary programming world that any assembly language book must acknowledge: nowadays, very few programs are 100% written in assembly language. Writing in assembly language is just too slow, too error prone and, ultimately, too expensive. Consequently, only the most demanding parts of large programs are coded in assembly language, with the major portions of such programs being written in a high-level language, which is usually **C**. This book makes every attempt to prepare the reader for this kind of hybrid programming. Specifically:

- From the very beginning, the stack is used as the default parameter-passing mechanism. While this is not usual in assembly language, it is a standard convention in high-level languages and is an essential component of the mixed-language interface.

- The structure of multi-module programs and the role of **LINK** in building them are discussed at length. The **MAKE** utility is presented as an incredibly elegant method of building such programs.

- Chapter 13 discusses the details of interfacing different languages. Naturally, **C** receives the lion's share of the attention, since, at this point in time, it is far and away the most important applications language. In this chapter, we also explore some of the less well-known aspects of interfacing by considering the problems involved in "raiding" the **C** libraries, i.e., calling **C** from assembly language.

- As always in programming, good examples are mandatory, and I have included a number of substantial programs that are hybrids of **C** and assembly language. Perhaps the most notable of these is the aforementioned execution profiler. This program makes an excellent interfacing example because it capitalizes on the particular abilities of each language.

Next, I would like to explain the organization of this book. First of all, it seemed imperative to include standard **8086/8088** coverage, as well as a solid introduction to the more modern chips. For the foreseeable future, anyone interested in the Intel **80XXX** family must become familiar with the **8086/8088** for two reasons: there are millions of them in existence, and they won't just go away; and the assembly languages of the more advanced chips are (surprisingly modest) extensions of the basic **8086/8088** language.

Granted that this book should discuss, say, the **8088** and the **80386**, the reader may wonder why I chose to scatter the **80386** material through three separated chapters, rather than grouping it all together at the end. The answer is that, as time passes, more and more readers will have access to at least **386SX** machines and will surely want to explore their more exotic features. This explains the locations chosen for the **80386** chapters: each appears at the earliest point at which its contents are meaningful when the book is read linearly.

However, I do realize that the majority of my readers will not yet have access to the more advanced machines and therefore have been scrupulously careful to ensure that, with the exception of the specific **80386** material (Chapters 7, 11, 18, and part of 17), the programs and discussions given in the text are applicable to the **8086/8088**. The reader who is presently constrained to the **8086/8088** world should find it interesting to, at the very least, browse through the **80386** chapters.

This book can be used in at least four different ways:

- As a text for a standard class or self-study program in the **8086/8088** assembly language. It would be appropriate to cover Chapters 1-6, 8, and parts of 10, 14, and 15.

- As a text for a second course using the **8086/8088**. Reasonable coverage would consist of Chapters 12-17.

- As a text for class or self-study situations where the readers are fairly familiar with the **8086/8088** environment and wish to learn about the more recent processors. The corresponding chapters are 7, 11, 17, and 18.

- As a reference book, to supplement and explain the standard manuals. In this light, the most interesting chapters are 10 through 18.

To amplify on the previous paragraph, I would like to be able to boast that the present volume is absolutely complete and the only reference work the reader will ever need. Alas, this is far from the truth. As examples, the *MS-DOS Encyclopaedia* contains nearly 1600 pages, the documentation distributed with **MASM** (the assembler used in this book) runs to 1000 pages, and the applicable **8086-80486** technical manuals add up to perhaps 3000 pages. These publications only deal with various aspects of the software and hardware environment — none of them even pretends to teach you how to program in assembly language. The point is that if you are *really* interested in the Intel **80XXX** family, you will ultimately need to procure a moderately large collection of reference books. In the Bibliography, I have listed the publications that I found most useful in writing this book

Nevertheless, in an effort to make the book self-contained, I have included a number of appendices, which list the details of the **80XXX** family instruction set, together with descriptions of those operating system and hardware features actually needed in the text.

A number of people contributed significantly to this book. In particular, I would like to thank the following reviewers for their penetrating reviews: Kathy Blicharz of Pima College; Myron Calhoun of Kansas State University; Cay Horstmann of San Jose State University; Robert Schneider of Lehman College. I would also like to thank Eileen Burke, John Griffin, Ed Moura, and John Travis of Macmillan Publishing for their continued advice. And last, but not least, I would like to thank my son Stephen for his many contributions to this project.

W.B.G.

CONTENTS

MAJOR CHAPTER DEPENDENCIES

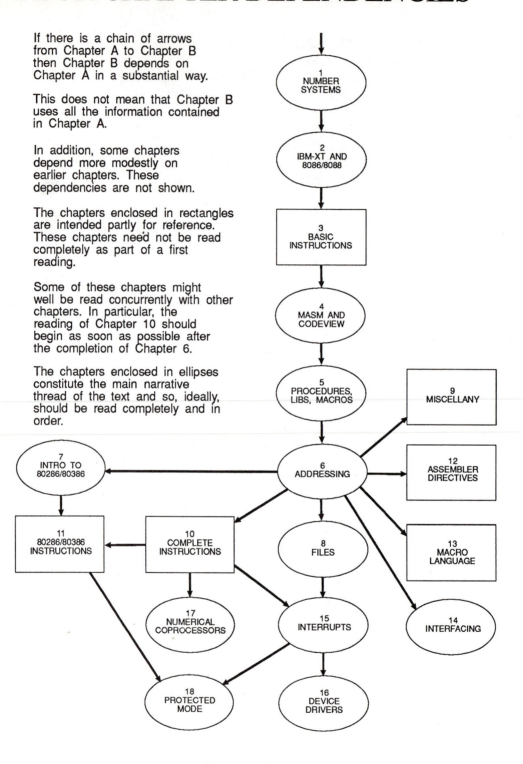

If there is a chain of arrows from Chapter A to Chapter B then Chapter B depends on Chapter A in a substantial way.

This does not mean that Chapter B uses all the information contained in Chapter A.

In addition, some chapters depend more modestly on earlier chapters. These dependencies are not shown.

The chapters enclosed in rectangles are intended partly for reference. These chapters need not be read completely as part of a first reading.

Some of these chapters might well be read concurrently with other chapters. In particular, the reading of Chapter 10 should begin as soon as possible after the completion of Chapter 6.

The chapters enclosed in ellipses constitute the main narrative thread of the text and so, ideally, should be read completely and in order.

1 NUMBER SYSTEMS

2 IBM-XT AND 8086/8088

3 BASIC INSTRUCTIONS

4 MASM AND CODEVIEW

5 PROCEDURES, LIBS, MACROS

9 MISCELLANY

7 INTRO TO 80286/80386

6 ADDRESSING

12 ASSEMBLER DIRECTIVES

11 80286/80386 INSTRUCTIONS

10 COMPLETE INSTRUCTIONS

8 FILES

13 MACRO LANGUAGE

17 NUMERICAL COPROCESSORS

15 INTERRUPTS

14 INTERFACING

18 PROTECTED MODE

16 DEVICE DRIVERS

NOTATIONAL CONVENTIONS

1. In describing **MASM** and **CODEVIEW** command syntax, we often use square brackets [ ] to mean an optional item and curly braces { } to mean one or more repetitions. For example, in the line

   [*instanceName*] *recordName* [*fieldInit* {, *fieldInit*}]

instanceName is an optional item, *recordName* must appear, and the line can optionally include a comma-separated list consisting of one or more appearances of *fieldInit*. This notation is used in many language manuals.

2. In contexts where it is important, we make a distinction between the parameters of a procedure or macro and the corresponding arguments. We use the term *parameter* to mean the variable used in the definition of the procedure or macro (sometimes called a *formal parameter*) and refer to the actual values passed in a given invocation as *arguments* (sometimes called *actual parameters*). Many times this distinction is not significant and we do not always faithfully observe it in such cases.

3. Basically, this book deals with three different architectures: the **8086/8088**, the **80286**, and the **80386/80486**. Nearly always, we use "8088" as a synonym for "8086/8088." Of course, when discussing the differences between these microprocessors, we are always careful to indicate which chip we mean. Likewise, we generally use "80386" as a synonym for "80286/80386/80486" except, again, when distinctions are being made between the different processors.

4. The book contains many memory diagrams. Our standard convention is that such diagrams always appear with addresses increasing either in the downward or rightward direction on the page, depending on the orientation of the drawing. Many of the diagrams consist of a series of boxes, and our convention is that each box contains one byte of data, unless the diagram explicitly states otherwise or represents the hardware stack. In the case of a stack picture, each box represents one word (= two bytes).

5. Even though both **MASM** and **CODEVIEW** are insensitive to the case (lower or upper) used for command input, we often use uppercase in the text to increase readability. (For example, lowercase 'l' (ell) is hard to distinguish from '1' (one).)

CHAPTER 1

POSITIONAL NUMBER SYSTEMS

SECTION 1 PREVIEW

In Section 2, we begin with a discussion of arithmetic in bases other than 10 and state some algorithms used to convert numbers from one base to another. Section 3 contains an introduction to two's complement representations, which are used by the Intel microprocessors (and by many other contemporary processors). The basic properties of two's complement representations are explored and we show why two's complement is a desirable method for storing negatives.

SECTION 2 ARITHMETIC IN DIFFERENT BASES

In the base 10 arithmetic used in everyday computations, 1245, for example, is just a convenient abbreviation for

$$1*10^3 + 2*10^2 + 4*10^1 + 5*10^0$$

and, more generally, $d_n d_{n-1} d_{n-2} \cdots d_2 d_1 d_0$, with each d_i a digit in the range 0 to 9, is an abbreviation for

$$d_n*10^n + d_{n-1}*10^{n-1} + d_{n-2}*10^{n-2} + \cdots + d_2*10^2 + d_1*10^1 + d_0*10^0$$

Of course, base 10 arithmetic is called by that name because the expansion uses powers of 10. Base 10 arithmetic is also called *decimal arithmetic*.

By analogy, arithmetic can be done using any base $b \geq 2$. Most computers use base 2 (*binary*) for their internal arithmetic. As well as base 2, base 16 (*hexadecimal*) and, to a diminishing extent, base 8 (*octal*), play a role in computer arithmetic.

For a fixed integer $b \geq 2$, *the base b representation of an integer $k \geq 0$* just means the expansion

$$k = d_n*b^n + d_{n-1}*b^{n-1} + d_{n-2}*b^{n-2} + \cdots + d_2*b^2 + d_1*b^1 + d_0*b^0$$

of k in powers of b, where each d_i is an integer in the range 0 to $b - 1$. The integers d_i are called the *base b coefficients* of k. The base b representation of k can be abbreviated in any of these three forms:

$$d_n d_{n-1} d_{n-2} \cdots d_2 d_1 d_0$$
$$d_n d_{n-1} d_{n-2} \cdots d_2 d_1 d_0 \,(\text{base } b)$$
$$(d_n d_{n-1} d_{n-2} \cdots d_2 d_1 d_0)_b$$

In many cases, the value of b will be clear from the context, and then we will favor the first of these abbreviations. When the last form is used, it is customary to omit the parentheses.

Here are some simple examples:

$$255_{10} = 11111111_2$$
$$350_{10} = 1010_7$$
$$254_{10} = 376_8$$

Checking any of these equations is easy. For instance, to verify the third:

$$376_8 = (3*8^2 + 7*8^1 + 6*8^0)_{10}$$
$$= (192 + 56 + 6)_{10}$$
$$= 254_{10}$$

One feature of base b expansions is that the coefficients d_i lie in the range from 0 to $b - 1$. If $b \leq 10$, the convention is to use decimal digits from the list

$$0, \; 1, \; 2, \; \cdots, \; b - 2, \; b - 1$$

as the base b coefficients. We have done this implicitly above. But in dealing with bases greater than 10 it is necessary to introduce symbols to represent the "extra" values of the coefficients. The only base greater than 10 that is of interest in computer science is 16, the hexadecimal case. The base 16 coefficients can have values $0, 1, 2, 3, \cdots, 13, 14, 15$ and special names are needed for $10, 11, \cdots, 15$. The letters A, B, $\cdots$, F, either uppercase or lowercase and in that order, are universally used for these coefficients. As an example,

$$1FE_{16} = 1*16^2 + 15*16^1 + 14*16^0 = 510_{10}$$

We will now develop simple algorithms for conversion of integers between different bases, and begin with some examples. First consider the problem of converting 123 to base 2. The goal is to find the values of the coefficients d_i (each being either 0 or 1) and the integer n such that

$$123_{10} = d_n*2^n + d_{n-1}*2^{n-1} + d_{n-2}*2^{n-2} + \cdots + d_2*2^2 + d_1*2^1 + d_0*2^0$$

The first thing to realize is that, since $2^7 = 128 > 123$, the right hand side need not contain any powers with exponents as big as 7. In other words, we may assume that the representation has the form

$$123_{10} = d_6*2^6 + d_5*2^5 + d_4*2^4 + d_3*2^3 + d_2*2^2 + d_1*2^1 + d_0*2^0$$

The d_i can now be found by the method of *undetermined coefficients*. First, divide both sides of the equation by 2. The remainder on the left-hand side is 1. On the right-hand side, 2 divides evenly into every term with the possible exception of d_0, which is 0 or 1. From this we conclude that the remainder on the right-hand side is d_0. Equating remainders gives $d_0 = 1$, and so d_0 has been determined.

Now subtract $d_0 = 1$ from each side and divide by 2 again. The result is

$$61 = d_6*2^5 + d_5*2^4 + d_4*2^3 + d_3*2^2 + d_2*2^1 + d_1*2^0$$

Repeating the process of dividing by 2 and comparing remainders shows that $d_1 = 1$. Again subtract $d_1 = 1$ from both sides, and iterate the process. The final results are

$$d_0 = 1, \quad d_1 = 1, \quad d_2 = 0, \quad d_3 = 1, \quad d_4 = 1, \quad d_5 = 1, \quad d_6 = 1$$

which gives

$$123_{10} = 1111011_2$$

Next convert 123_{10} to base 3. Again, since $3^5 = 243 > 123$, the biggest power of 3 that can enter in is 3^4, and so the expansion really looks like

$$123_{10} = d_4*3^4 + d_3*3^3 + d_2*3^2 + d_1*3^1 + d_0*3^0$$

This computation can now proceed by exactly the same method of dividing by the base, 3 this time, and comparing remainders. The first division shows that $d_0 = 0$. Subtracting $d_0 = 0$ from each side and dividing by 3 reduces the equation to

$$41_{10} = d_4*3^3 + d_3*3^2 + d_2*3^1 + d_1*3^0$$

Repeating the process produces the rest of the d_i and gives

$$123_{10} = 11120_3$$

as the final result.

These computations can be easily formalized into an algorithm, but before doing so let us make an observation. In the examples, we guessed the biggest power needed in the expansion before beginning the computation. Guessing was not really necessary.

In the first case, for example, the occurrence of 2^7 was ruled out because $2^7 > 123$. The fact that $2^7 > 123$ means that 123 divided by 2^7 gives quotient 0. This means that the "stopping condition" can be expressed in terms of the iterated division process: keep dividing by the base only as long as the quotient is non-zero.

Here is the conversion algorithm:

Algorithm 1.1. To convert a decimal integer $k > 0$ to base $b \geq 2$:

    d = k, i = 0.
    while (d ≠ 0)
    {
        Divide d by b, naming the quotient d and the remainder d_i.
        i = i + 1.
    }
    $d_0, d_1, d_2, \cdots$ are the base b coefficients.

Notice that the algorithm generates the base b coefficients in the order $d_0, d_1, d_2, \cdots, d_t$. When using this algorithm in programs, we must frequently invert this order, since the coefficients are normally printed in the order $d_t, \cdots, d_2, d_1, d_0$.

We will now examine the conversion in the opposite direction. Given the expansion in base b, how can the base 10 representation be recovered? On the surface this seems totally trivial — just do the arithmetic!

For example, consider the problem of converting 3234_7 to decimal. From the definition,

$$3234_7 = (3*7^3 + 2*7^2 + 3*7^1 + 4*7^0)_{10}$$

and after performing the arithmetic operations on the right-hand side, we get 152_{10} as the answer. The only objection that can be made to this process is that, if done directly, it is quite inefficient. Computing $3*7^3$ requires three multiplications; $2*7^2$, two multiplications; and $3*7^1$, one multiplication. There are also three additions. Of course, the result of the 7^2 computation could be saved and used in the 7^3 computation, but there is a better way. Rewrite the base 7 expansion in the form

$$3234_7 = ((3*7 + 2)*7 + 3)*7 + 4$$

This decomposition is an example of what is generally called *Horner's rule*. If the arithmetic on the right is done by this scheme, only three multiplications are needed, as well as the three additions. This very simple transformation is the basis for the following algorithm.

Algorithm 1.2. To convert a base b representation $(d_n d_{n-1} d_{n-2} \cdots d_2 d_1 d_0)_b$ to decimal:

```
k = 0.
for (i = n to 1, step -1)
{
        k = b*k + d_i.
}
```
The final value of k is the decimal value.

If the base b happens to be an exact power of 2, then the conversions between base b and base 2 become so trivial that they can be done by inspection. To illustrate this point in the hexadecimal case, consider the problem of converting $3E7F_{16}$ to binary. For demonstration purposes, we will write out the steps of the transformation in detail, and then abstract the general method from the computation:

$$3E7F_{16} = 3*16^3 + 14*16^2 + 7*16^1 + 15*16^0$$

$$
\begin{aligned}
= \quad & (0*2^3 + 0*2^2 + 1*2^1 + 1*2^0)*16^3 \\
+ \quad & (1*2^3 + 1*2^2 + 1*2^1 + 0*2^0)*16^2 \\
+ \quad & (0*2^3 + 1*2^2 + 1*2^1 + 1*2^0)*16^1 \\
+ \quad & (1*2^3 + 1*2^2 + 1*2^1 + 1*2^0)*16^0
\end{aligned}
$$

$$
\begin{aligned}
= \quad & (0*2^{15} + 0*2^{14} + 1*2^{13} + 1*2^{12}) \\
+ \quad & (1*2^{11} + 1*2^{10} + 1*2^9 + 0*2^8) \\
+ \quad & (0*2^7 + 1*2^6 + 1*2^5 + 1*2^4) \\
+ \quad & (1*2^3 + 1*2^2 + 1*2^1 + 1*2^0)
\end{aligned}
$$

This shows that

$$3E7F_{16} = 0011\ 1110\ 0111\ 1111_2$$

The binary display has been printed in blocks of four to emphasize how each block results from a line of the previous display. (As a matter of fact, binary expansions are nearly always printed in this way to enhance readability.) Note that the groups of four binary digits originated as the binary expansions of the hex digits 3, E, 7, and F. The following algorithm formalizes the technique used in the example.

Algorithm 1.3. Conversions between hexadecimal and binary:

To change from hexadecimal to binary, replace each hex digit by the binary four-tuple having the same value. Of course, leading zeros can be deleted from the resulting binary representation.

To change from binary to hex, divide the binary representation into blocks of size four, starting from the right-hand end. (Naturally, the leftmost block may be incomplete.) Replace each block by the hex digit having the same value as the block.

The reader may be wondering why hexadecimal arithmetic is introduced at all. The truth of the matter is that binary arithmetic is for machines and hex is basically for humans. The difficulty with binary representations, from the programmer's point of view, is that they are long and featureless and nearly impossible to remember. In the **8088** architecture the "natural" length of a number is 16 binary digits or, equivalently, four hex digits. A person of normal retentive powers can remember the hex version of such a number for a few minutes — not so the binary version. The reason that the exact base sixteen is chosen is that, as discussed previously, it makes conversions to and from binary trivial because it is power of 2, and to most people it seems just about the right size.

The standard arithmetic operations +, −, *, and / can be done in any base by mimicking the decimal versions, although the last two, even after a lot of practice, are quite trying if done by hand. The essential fact to remember is that the base b plays the role of 10 in generating carries and borrows.

Here is a simple example of hexadecimal addition:

$$1AB74_{16}$$
$$AF23D_{16}$$
$$\overline{}$$
$$C9DB1_{16}$$

This kind of computation is awkward since, unless the hexadecimal addition table has been memorized (which I, for one, have not done), the addition requires a thought process that goes something like this: D is 13 so D + 4 is 17, which means write down 1 and carry 1 (remembering that 16 in this example is the analog of 10 in decimal arithmetic); in the next column, $3 + 7 + $ (the carried 1) is 11, which is B; and so on. Unless the hexadecimal multiplication table has been memorized (Has anyone done this, ever?) the same translation to decimal and back again must be done for each digit-by-digit hex multiplication.

Many of the standard facts about decimal arithmetic have exact analogs in base b. For example, in base 10, appending a zero at the end of a number is equivalent to multiplying it by 10. The corresponding base b fact is that appending a zero multiplies the number by b. It is easy to verify this assertion by looking at the base b representation: adding a zero at the end of the representation effectively increases all the exponents by 1. In base 10, deleting the last digit has the effect of integer division by 10, i.e., dividing by 10 and discarding the remainder. Again, we have the exact analog in base b, and this too is obvious from the power representation. These operations are used often enough that they are given special names. Adding a zero at the end of the base b representation is called *left shifting*, and deleting the last digit is called *right shifting*.

For the rest of this section we will concentrate on the most important case, namely base 2. A useful computation to perform once and for all is finding the decimal value of $111\cdots11_2$, where this binary number contains n 1s. The easiest way to proceed is to first add one to the number. The result is $1000\cdots000_2$, where there are now n 0s at the end. In other words, the result is 1 left shifted n times which, since left shifting in binary multiplies by 2, has value 2^n. Consequently, the original number was equal to $2^n - 1$. The real result of our computation is

- The largest integer that can be stored in n binary digits, using the standard binary representation, is $2^n - 1$.

A single binary digit (0 or 1) is usually called a *bit*. A datum that is stored in 8 bits is called a *byte*. By the result of the last paragraph, the integers that can be stored in a byte, using the standard binary representation, are those in the range from 0 to $2^8 - 1 = 255$.

Each microprocessor has certain storage areas called *registers*. The maximum register size for a particular machine is usually called a *word* on that machine. The size of a word on a machine is of critical importance to the programmer because it also gives the size of the biggest objects for which the machine has internally defined arithmetic operations. In addition, it is related to how much memory the microprocessor can directly supervise (*address*) at one time.

The maximum register size of the **8088** is 2 bytes or 16 bits (which explains why machines using this chip are called *16-bit machines*). Consequently, the range of values that an **8088** register can hold, in the standard binary representation, is from 0 to $2^{16} - 1 = 65535$. This is a hopelessly limited collection of values with which to do arithmetic. As might be suspected, there are ways of getting around this restriction.

Exercise 1-1. Convert these hex integers to decimal:

$$\text{(a)} \;\; 123A \quad \text{(b)} \;\; FFFFABC \quad \text{(c)} \;\; FFFFFFFFFFFE$$

The answers to (b) and (c) each involve a large power of 2, which need not be evaluated.

Exercise 1-2. Convert these decimal integers to hex:

$$\text{(a)} \;\; 1000 \quad \text{(b)} \;\; 30000 \quad \text{(c)} \;\; -30000$$

In (c) the 16-bit two's complement representation should be computed.

Exercise 1-3. Given N = 1ABC and M = 2F (both hex), compute

$$\text{(a)} \;\; N + M \quad \text{(b)} \;\; N - M \quad \text{(c)} \;\; N * M \quad \text{(d)} \;\; N/M$$

Do the computations in hex. Don't convert to decimal to do the computations and then convert back to hex — that is too easy in (c) and (d)!

Exercise 1-4. There is an alternative method for computing the base b expansion from the base 10 representation. As an example, let us convert 200 to base 3. Begin by finding the biggest power of 3 that is less than or equal to 200, which is $3^4 = 81$. Then find the biggest multiple of 3^4 that is less than or equal to 200, namely $2*3^4$. Now replace 200 by 200 − $2*3^4 = 38$ and repeat the process using 38 instead of 200: find the biggest power of 3 that is less than or equal to 38 and then the biggest multiple of this power that is less than or equal to 38. Iterate and collect terms to end up with the base 3 expansion.
a. Finish this example.
b. State the algorithm for arbitrary integer k ≥ 0 and arbitrary base b ≥ 2.
c. Use the algorithm to find 1000 to bases 5, 6, and 7.

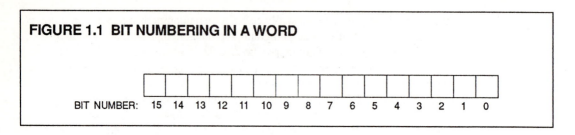

FIGURE 1.1 BIT NUMBERING IN A WORD

BIT NUMBER: 15   14   13   12   11   10   9   8   7   6   5   4   3   2   1   0

Exercise 1-5. Algorithms 1.1 and 1.2 are really more general than we have indicated. In fact, each of these algorithms can be used to convert from base r to base s, where r and s are arbitrary integers ≥ 2.
1. Write versions of both algorithms that change base r to base s.
2. One obvious distinction between these new algorithms is that one uses a division loop while the other uses a multiplication loop. But there is another, more subtle distinction between them. What is this distinction? *Suggestion*: For each algorithm, there is a preferred base in which to actually do the computations. What is that base in each case?

SECTION 3 TWO'S COMPLEMENT REPRESENTATIONS

In many contexts, the maximum size integer that can be stored is even smaller than the upper bound of 65535 given in the previous section. So far, integers have been stored by means of their binary representations, and so only non-negative integers have been considered. But to do arithmetic, both positive and negatives are needed, hence the allowed storage possibilities in a register must be divided between the two. This will obviously decrease the range in either direction. A number of methods are be used to store signed data in binary form so that some of the data can be interpreted as representing positive integers and some negative.

Before proceeding, we introduce one more minor item of notation. In dealing with binary representations, it is customary to number the bits so that they correspond to the powers of two in the binary representation. This means that the rightmost bit is numbered zero, the next bit one, and so on. In dealing with 8 bits of data, the leftmost bit will be number 7, and with 16 bits it will be number 15. In each case, the rightmost bit is called the *low-order bit*, or *low bit*, and the leftmost bit is called the *high-order bit*, or *high bit*. The 16-bit case is illustrated in Figure 1.1.

Perhaps the most natural way of storing positive and negative integers is the *sign-magnitude representation*. Here the high bit is used to represent the sign of the number while the other bits give the binary representation of its magnitude. In the standard encoding, a high-bit value of 0 signifies that the number is ≥ 0, while a high-bit value of 1 means it is ≤ 0. There are two different representation of 0, namely 0000 $\cdots$ and 1000 $\cdots$. This is generally not a problem, but there are other reasons why this is not a terribly desirable storage method.

The approach that is actually used by the **8088** (and many other chips) in dealing with negative integers is a variation of this method, called two's complement representation. It is somewhat more complicated than the sign-magnitude representation but has a number of advantages over it.

In our initial discussion of two's complement representation, we will concentrate on the 8-bit case because it is much easier to do the computations mentally and to write out the resulting bit patterns. Afterwards, we will see that the 16-bit case is totally analogous. The entire discussion will use only decimal and binary integers and, since the context will make it clear which is which, we will not use subscripts to distinguish the different bases.

For an integer n with $0 \leq n \leq 255$, the *8-bit two's complement* of n is defined to be the integer $256 - n$. The *8-bit two's complement representation* stores integers in the range from $+127$ to -128 according to this scheme:

- If $0 \leq n \leq 127$, store n as its binary representation.

- If $-128 \leq n < 0$, store n as the 8-bit two's complement of $-n$, i.e., as $256 - (-n)$ $= 256 + n$.

Of course, slightly more overhead is involved in encoding negatives in the two's complement representation than in the sign-magnitude representation. However, there is a fairly simple method for finding the two's complement representations of negatives, which we will now present. If $0 < m \leq 128$, we would like to determine how the machine stores $-m$. Since $-m$ is in the range $-128 \leq -m < 0$, the preceding rule tells us that it is stored as

```
256 + (−m) = (255 − m) + 1
```

The first expression on the right is easy to compute. $255 = 1111\ 1111$ and so $255 - m$ is obtained from m by replacing all the 0s by 1s and the 1s by 0s. (To check this, write out the computation. The point is that the representation of 255 consists entirely of 1s and so borrows are never needed during the subtraction.) The two's complement is now obtained by adding 1 to $255 - m$.

The quantity $255 - m$ that enters here is called the *8-bit one's complement* of m. It is usually defined directly by saying that it results from "interchanging 1s and 0s in the binary representation of m."

For example, the machine stores -17 as the 8-bit two's complement representation of 17, which can easily be computed by the method just given:

```
2's comp rep.of 17
    = (1s comp of 17)  +  1
    = (1s comp of 0001 0001) + 1
    = 1110 1110 + 1
    = 1110 1111
```

Explicitly, here is how the integers from -128 to 127 are encoded:

```
127      stores as   0111 1111
126      stores as   0111 1110
125      stores as   0111 1101
            .
            .
            .
  2      stores as   0000 0010
  1      stores as   0000 0001
  0      stores as   0000 0000
 -1      stores as   1111 1111
 -2      stores as   1111 1110
            .
            .
            .
-127     stores as   1000 0001
-128     stores as   1000 0000
```

It is easy to summarize the results:

• 0 is encoded as 0000 0000.

• To get the representations of positive integers, "count up" from 0000 0001.

• To get the representations of negative integers, "count down" from 1111 1111.

Two's complement has several features that make it an excellent storage technique for signed integers. Some of these features are shared with the sign-magnitude representation. For example:

1. The most basic requirement is that different integers in the range from -128 to $+127$ should be encoded as different bit patterns, since otherwise we would not be able to recover an integer from its encoding. That this requirement is met follows from the definitions. Indeed, all integers from 0 to 127 are encoded as their bit patterns, which are different from one another, and since each of these integers is $\leq 127 = 0111\ 1111$, each has high bit 0. Similarly, if n is in the range $-128 \leq n < 0$, then n is stored as $256 + n$, and for different ns the quantities $256 + n$ have different bit patterns. In addition, for such an n we have $256 + n \geq 256 - 128 = 128$. Since $128 = 1000\ 0000$ and $256 + n \geq 128$, it follows that all these integers store with high bit 1. This means that we can distinguish ns of the first type from ns of the second on the basis of their high bit.

2. As a spin-off from the computation in 1, it is easy to tell from the two's complement representation whether the integer in storage is positive or negative. Specifically, it is ≥ 0 if the high bit is 0 and is < 0 if the high bit is 1. For this reason, the high bit is also called the *sign bit*.

3. Two's complement works especially well as a vehicle for machine addition and subtraction. The reason is that in doing, say, 8-bit arithmetic (the case we are presently considering), the machine works modulo $2^8 = 256$, i.e., discards all multiples of 256 as it proceeds. We will illustrate this remark with an example.

The **8088** comes complete with "built-in" instructions, which perform a wide variety of arithmetic tasks, and these include the ability to work with unsigned integers and signed integers. For the moment, let us concentrate on the problem of doing 8-bit addition, and suppose we want a version of this addition that will work for unsigned operands and a version that will work for signed operands. The remarkable fact is that, when two's complement representation is used, the *same* built-in machine function will work in both situations. The built-in function just "adds the bit patterns." No matter whether the programmer interprets the operands as signed or unsigned, this gives the right answer. This is a benefit of two's complement that is *not* shared with the sign-magnitude representation.

In the unsigned case, consider the problem of adding 97 and 97. The machine adds the bit patterns and so the computation looks like:

```
 97  =  0110 0001
 97  =  0110 0001
        _____

sum  =  1100 1010  =  194
```

where the resulting bit pattern is interpreted as unsigned to give answer equal to 194.

In the signed case, consider the addition of 10 and -20. The machine again adds the bit patterns:

```
 10  =  0000 1010
-20  =  1110 1100
        _____

sum  =  1111 0110  =  -10
```

This time, the answer is correct if the two's complement interpretation is used throughout.

If this computation is looked at from the right viewpoint, it becomes clear that adding the bit patterns will always work for both kinds of addition. It is obviously the right thing to do in the unsigned case. In the signed case, consider the problem of adding n to $-m$. In terms of two's complement representation, this amounts to adding n to $256 - m$. But if these are added as bit patterns, remembering that the machine throws away multiples of 256, the correct answer is obtained once again.

In these opening illustrations, we are totally ignoring the question of *overflow*, i.e., the possibility that the answer to a computation might be too big or too small to belong to the allowed range of values. This would occur if, for example, 200 and 200 were added as unsigned 8-bit integers, or 100 and 100 were added as signed 8-bit integers. The problem of overflow will be considered in Chapter 3, but will not be completely dealt with until Chapter 10.

Other features (and limitations) of the two's complement representation are explored in the exercises at the end of this section.

The situation with 16-bit two's complement representations is exactly analogous to the 8-bit case with $2^8 = 256$ replaced by $2^{16} = 65536$. We will just state the corresponding results, leaving the details for the reader to check. In the 16-bit two's complement representation, the contents of a 16-bit storage location represent an integer in the range $2^{15} - 1 = 32767$ to $-2^{15} = -32768$. If n is in the range $0 < n \leq 65535$, then the *16-bit two's complement* of n is defined to be $65536 - n$. The *16-bit two's complement representation* of n is defined by the following scheme:

- If $0 \le n \le 32767$, store n as its binary representation.

- If $-32768 \le n < 0$, store n as the 16-bit two's complement of $-n$ or, equivalently, as $65536 + n$.

Exactly as in the 8-bit case, positives and negatives can be distinguished by their sign bits (now bit 15): the integer is ≥ 0 if its sign bit is 0 and is < 0 if its sign bit is 1.

Computing the representation of a negative integer, say $-n$, is easy. First compute the *16-bit one's complement* of n (defined to be $65535 - n$) and then add 1. It is worth stating this result in both the 8-bit and 16-bit cases as

Algorithm 1.4. To compute the k-bit two's complement of n:

Compute the k-bit one's complement by interchanging 0s and 1s.
Add 1 to obtain the two's complement.

Just as the microprocessor performs 8-bit arithmetic operations module 256, it does 16-bit arithmetic module $2^{16} = 65536$. Of course, this is the real reason why two's complement representations are used.

In one of the exercises, we present a much cleverer technique for computing the two's complement representation.

A final question of interest is whether, given the 8-bit two's complement representation of n, there is an easy way to generate the 16-bit two's complement representation. If $n \ge 0$ there is nothing much to do: the two's complement representations are just the binary representations, and so it is only necessary to prepend 8 0s to the 8-bit representation to get the 16-bit representation. If $n < 0$ the situation is more interesting. If n is written as $-m$ with $m > 0$, then the 8-bit representation is $2^8 - m$ and the 16-bit representation is $2^{16} - m$. Consider the following obvious identity:

$$
\begin{aligned}
2^{16} - m &= 2^{16} - 2^8 + 2^8 - m \\
&= 2^8 \ast (2^8 - 1) + (2^8 - m)
\end{aligned}
$$

This shows that to get the 16-bit representation from the 8-bit, the quantity $2^8 \ast (2^8 - 1)$ should be added. But

$$2^8 - 1 = 1111\ 1111$$

and so

$$2^8 \ast (2^8 - 1) = 1111\ 1111\ 0000\ 0000$$

Combining these results, we see that in each case the conversion is achieved by prepending eight copies of the sign bit. This operation is called *sign extension* and arises often enough that it is worth recording it as an algorithm.

Algorithm 1.5. To change the 8-bit two's complement representation of n to the 16-bit two's complement representation:

Perform the operation of sign extension by prepending 8 copies of the sign bit.

Exercise 1-6.
a. Compute the 8-bit two's complement representations of 29, 103, −86, and −125.
b. Compute the 16-bit two's complement representations of 7926, 14329, −16825, and −30133.

Exercise 1-7.
a. Following the pattern given in the text, perform the 8-bit computations

$$20 \ + \ (-10)$$
$$(-20) \ + \ \ \ 10$$

using 8-bit two's complement notation and bitwise addition. Check that the answers are correct when they are given a two's complement interpretation.
b. The number 40000 is too big to fit in the 16-bit two's complement storage range. Its bit pattern has sign bit equal to 1 and so represents a negative number in the two's complement encoding. Check that this negative number is

$$40000 \ - \ 65536 \ = \ -25536$$

Since the microprocessor uses the bit pattern to determine the value, it will interpret 40000 as -25536 in any context where signed numbers are used. This is just another aspect of the microprocessor operating modulo 65536:

- To find the machine interpretation of a quantity that is out of the 16-bit signed or unsigned range, "adjust" it by adding or subtracting a multiple of 65536 to bring it within the appropriate range. (An analogous statement holds in the 8-bit case.)

c. Use 16-bit bitwise addition to compute

$$10000 \ + \ 40000$$

Show that the answer is correct when given either a signed or an unsigned interpretation (using two's complement). To interpret the signed case completely, it is necessary to use the observation made in b.

Exercise 1-8. We showed why both unsigned and signed addition could be implemented by the same machine operation when two's complement notation is used. Show by examples that the corresponding result is not true for multiplication or division.

Exercise 1-9. Discuss 32-bit two's complement representations, imitating the approach used in the text. In particular, find the range of values that can be stored, show that the 32-bit one's complement gives an easy method for computing the two's complement, show that the 32-bit two's complement representation is obtained from the 16-bit or 8-bit two's complement representation by sign extension, and provide some examples.

Exercise 1-10. Suppose that we have a computer that naturally does base 10 arithmetic, so that its basic unit is a decimal digit (a *dit*) rather than a binary digit (a *bit*). Suppose that our machine has registers that will hold 4 dits (a *4-dit machine*). In order to do signed arithmetic we want to use a reasonable analog of two's complement, called (what else?) *ten's complement*.
a. Define the 4-dit ten's complement.
b. What is the range of positive and negative integers that can be stored in a 4-dit register using the ten's complement representation?
c. In two's complement, it is easy to tell whether a stored integer is positive or negative by looking at its sign bit. What is the analogous result for ten's complement?

Exercise 1-11. In the text, we have defined binary representations only for integers, but it is almost as easy to develop binary expansions for arbitrary real numbers. By analogy with the base 10 case, a *mixed binary representation* has the form

$$d_n*2^n + d_{n-1}*2^{n-1} + \cdots + d_1*2^1 + d_0 + c_1*2^{-1} + c_2*2^{-2} + \cdots + c_m*2^{-m}$$

where each d_i and each c_j is either 0 or 1. This expansion will be abbreviated as

$$d_n d_{n-1} \cdots d_1 d_0 . c_1 c_2 ... c_m$$

For example, the mixed binary representation 11.101 is equal to

$$1*2^1 + 1*2^0 + 1*2^{-1} + 0*2^{-2} + 1*2^{-3} = 3\ 5/8$$

a. What is the value of the mixed binary representation 111001.1010101?
b. Find the mixed binary representation of 111 237/256.

Exercise 1-12. Now that we have finite mixed binary representations, can infinite ones be far behind? Again, we should work by analogy with the base 10 case where, for example,

$$1/3 = .3333333\cdots$$

What is the mixed binary representation of 1/3?

Exercise 1-13.

$$.111001001001\cdots$$

where the 001 repeats infinitely often, is the mixed binary representation of what real number?

Exercise 1-14. Here is a different algorithm for finding the two's complement of a non-zero integer. Start with the binary representation of the integer. Scan it from right to left, using the bits to build a new string from right to left, and following these simple rules: as long as zero bits are encountered, copy them unchanged; as soon as a one bit is encountered, also copy it unchanged, but henceforth invert each bit as it is copied.

a. Convince yourself by examples that this method seems to generate the two's complement.

b. Show that it will actually work in all cases.

Suggestion: Let n be an integer whose k-bit two's complement is to be computed. Suppose that the binary representation of n has 0s in bits 0, 1, $\cdots$, $s - 1$ and a 1 in bit s. Then $n = 2^s * t$, where t has a 1 in its low bit. Furthermore,

$$2^k - n = 2^s * (2^{k-s} - t) = 2^s * (((2^{k-s} - 1) - t) + 1)$$

The answer comes from interpreting these formulas correctly.

CHAPTER 2

THE IBM-XT AND THE 8086 MICROPROCESSOR FAMILY

SECTION 1 PREVIEW

We begin this chapter with a general discussion of the **IBM-XT** and its operating system, **MS-DOS**. As the reader probably knows, the vast majority of existing Intel **8086** family microprocessors are used in clones of the **IBM-XT**. For the moment, we will be content to discuss the memory organization of the **IBM-XT**, and how **MS-DOS** is adapted to this organization. A basic understanding of these issues is an essential prerequisite to the study of the **8086** assembly language.

Memory addresses are constructed in an interesting way in the **8086** architecture. Each address consists of two parts, a segment and an offset, and these are combined in a somewhat curious manner to form the final address. Section 3 is devoted to the **8086** addressing scheme.

In Section 4, we formally introduce the **8086** and the **8088**. We do not attempt to analyze their internal construction in detail, mainly because most aspects of their structure are unimportant to the assembly language programmer. Certainly, some facets of their design — most notably the concurrent operation of the execution unit and the bus interface unit and the workings of the prefetch queue — are significant to the programmer, and these are the topics that we discuss in Section 4.

Section 5 gives a survey of the register structure of the **8086**. If the reader is new to assembly language, some of the material in Section 5 may not be completely comprehensible during a first reading. But be assured that these facts will all fall into place as they are examined in detail in later chapters.

The **8086** and the **8088** are the earliest members in a fairly extensive family of microprocessors. In Section 7, we give a brief survey of the later family members, and in the course of this survey explain our selection of the **80386** microprocessor as the subject of the more advanced chapters in this book

SECTION 2 THE IBM-XT AND ITS OPERATING SYSTEM

Since the larger part of this book is directed toward programming the **IBM-XT** and its clones, it is fitting that we should say a few word about the architecture of those machine, and about **MS-DOS**, its standard operating system. Rather than attempting to give a complete account of the workings of the **IBM-XT** or **MS-DOS** in this introductory chapter, we restrict ourselves to information needed to understand the next few chapters. Later, we will need to look carefully at various aspects of the hardware and the operating system in greater detail text, but prefer to present these more technical discussions in context. The interested reader should refer to [10] for an excellent account of the **IBM-XT** hardware, and to [24] for complete information on **MS-DOS**.

A computer needs memory in which to store program instructions and data. Computer memory is generally laid out as a sequence of bytes, each byte receiving a unique number or *address*. In the standard scheme, these addresses are numbered sequentially 0, 1, 2, $\cdots$. A large proportion of the computation that occurs in a typical computer program relates to the manipulation of addresses. The intrinsic structure of any microprocessor limits the range of addresses that can be assigned and supervised efficiently or, as it is usually stated, the amount of *addressable memory that can be supported*. For example, the Intel **8088**, which is the central processor of the **IBM-XT**, can support 2^{20} bytes of addressable memory. Section 3 explains exactly how the **8088** manipulates memory addresses.

Before proceeding, we will introduce some terminology that is universally used in discussing memory. It is easy to check that $2^{10} = 1024$, and, because this quantity is close to 1000, a block of memory of this size is called 1 *kilobyte*, or 1K for short. Since $2^{20} = 2^{10}*2^{10} = 1$ kilobyte * 1 kilobyte, this amount of memory is referred to as 1 *megabyte* or 1 meg or 1M for short. In terms of this new definition, the **8088** can support 1M of addressable memory.

Figure 2.1 shows the *memory map* of the **IBM-XT**. The addresses are shown in hexadecimal to the right of the column display. We will always draw our memory maps so that addresses increase toward the bottom of the page. Each block in the diagram has size 64K and is called a *segment* (for reasons that will emerge later in this chapter). Notice that the highest allowable address is FFFFF.

The amount of memory available for running programs on the **IBM-XT** is much smaller than 1M because the machine hardware and the operating system requisition nearly half of the total for their own uses.

First of all, in the standard **IBM-XT** configuration, all memory above 9FFFF is allocated to various system functions. In other words, the system usurps the highest six segments, leaving only 10 segments, or 640K, of available memory, and we will see

FIGURE 2.1 MEMORY MAP OF IBM-XT

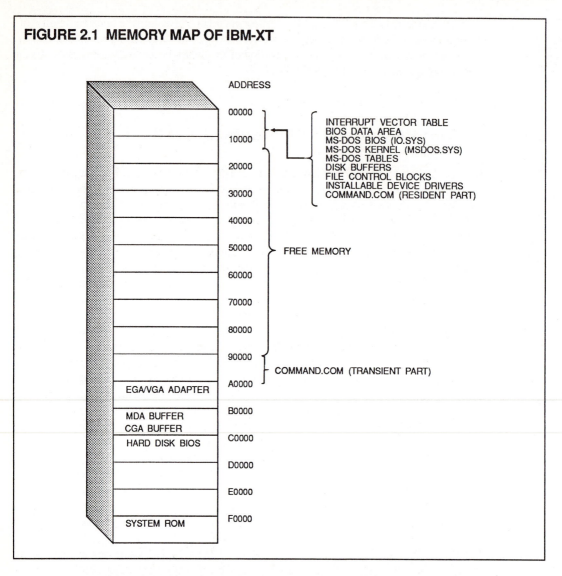

presently that this is not the end of the story. In most machines, not all memory above A0000 is actually used by the system but, unfortunately, **MS-DOS** is so well tailored to the **IBM-XT** architecture that it is incapable of reclaiming any of this memory.

Next, we will briefly explain some of the uses to which high memory is put by the system, but before doing so, will review the distinction between RAM and ROM.

RAM means *random access memory*. From our viewpoint, the most important feature of RAM is that it is *volatile*, which means that it retains its contents only as long as they are *refreshed* by receiving periodic electrical signals. In particular, each time a machine is booted, any information that the system wishes to store in RAM must be reinitialized, usually by reading it into memory from a diskfile.

On the other hand, ROM, or *read-only memory*, holds its contents even when the machine is switched off. The penalty that is paid for this convenience is that ROM is permanent memory — once ROM chips have been programmed, their contents cannot be changed. (This is not strictly true. Some ROM chips can be erased and reused, but these processes require special circuitry.)

When a machine is purchased, and even before the operating system has been loaded into memory, it already contains programs that were supplied by the manufacturer. In light of the above discussion, it is clear that such programs must be contained in ROM. These resident programs are responsible for initializing certain aspects of the machine at boot time and for communication with various hardware devices, such as the keyboard, printer, and disk drives, that may be connected to the machine. They are referred to as the *basic input/output services*, and so the area of memory containing them is called the ROM BIOS. As Figure 2.1 shows, the ROM BIOS is stored at address F0000 (i.e., in the block of memory beginning at address F0000) in the **IBM-XT**.

The **IBM-XT** is not the earliest machine in its family. It is the successor to the **IBM-PC**, the main distinction between the two machines being that the **IBM-XT** can support a hard disk. More precisely, the original **IBM-PC** BIOS was extended with the extra functions needed to service a hard disk. As our memory map shows, the additional BIOS is stored at address C000.

The **IBM-XT** treats the video display differently from most other hardware devices. Hardware devices are generally connected to the **8088** by means of certain *I/O ports*. An I/O port is just a formal address (there can be as many as 64K of them) used for communication between the microprocessor and the hardware. These port addresses have nothing to do with regular memory addresses. For example, a character that is input to the keyboard will arrive at Port 60H. It must be picked up at that port and delivered to the program that will use it. This pick up and delivery is normally performed by the ROM BIOS, although later in the book we will need to substitute programs of our own devising that do these tasks.

The video display, however, is an example of *memory mapped I/O*. This means that, instead of sending data to the video display by means of I/O ports, the information is written to a memory region that has been assigned to the display. An advantage of memory mapped I/O is that it is faster than using I/O ports, especially when large blocks of data are involved, which is the case with the video display. As can be seen from Figure 2.1, the memory region associated with the video display is dependent on the kind of video adapter, monochrome or color, that is attached. The EGA and VGA adapters can make use of more memory than the CGA and MDA.

Adapter cards that are added to the expansion slots of the **IBM-XT** can use additional memory above 640K. A standard example is an *expanded memory board*. Expanded memory is a technique that allows **MS-DOS** to access more than its basic 640K of memory. It works by using a 64K *window* of memory, which can view four independently selectable *pages* of memory, each of size 16K. In this way, an **MS-DOS** system can support a very large amount of memory, although the time penalty involved in switching from one page to another is sizable. Expanded memory boards generally locate the 64K window at address E0000.

So far, we have only chronicled the inroads that the hardware and the BIOS make into the 1M of addressable memory. Unfortunately, a sizable portion of the remaining 640K is also used by the system, and the main culprit here is **MS-DOS** itself. Each version of the operating system is bigger than the last, with the most recent versions requiring about 100K. Figure 2.1 shows exactly how the system uses the low 640K.

We will now give capsule descriptions of the various items named on the left in Figure 2.1. Some of these are complicated enough that they are accorded whole chapters later in this book but, for the moment, here are the basic ideas:

- We have already seen that the **IBM-XT**, like other computers, comes with "built-in" programs to perform a wide range of functions, and that some of these programs are contained in the ROM BIOS. A large number of additional programs are loaded as part of the operating system. Programs of either of these kinds can be used in a variety of ways. Some are meant to be "called" by executing programs, exactly as though they were subroutines or procedures, to perform services such as getting characters from the keyboard or sending characters to the screen. Others are triggered by hardware events, such as a the pressing of a key on the keyboard or the discovery by the machine that a memory cell is defective. These built in programs are called *interrupt handlers*, and the addresses at which the interrupt handlers are stored are themselves stored in the *interrupt vector table*. There can be as many as 100H interrupt handlers and, as we will see later in this chapter, each address requires four bytes of storage. The lowest 400H bytes of memory are reserved for the interrupt vector table.

- The next 200H bytes of memory is called the *BIOS data area*, and is used to hold various pieces of information about the state of the machine. For example, the reader has doubtlessly observed that, even when the machine is busy and cannot accept keyboard input, it is still possible to type a few characters ahead. These characters are stored in a region of the BIOS data area called the *keyboard buffer*. When the keyboard buffer is full, the machine "beeps" and refuses to accept more input. Other locations in the BIOS data area store information about numbers and types of disk drives, the kind of video adapter that is attached, and many other hardware parameters.

- The **MS-DOS** operating system arrives on three different diskfiles. The first part occupies the diskfile called IO.SYS and is called the *MS-DOS BIOS*. The main component of the MS-DOS BIOS is a collection of programs called *resident device drivers*, which are used to interface the computer with external hardware devices. The MS-DOS BIOS is loaded immediately above the BIOS data area.

- The second operating system diskfile is called MSDOS.SYS, and it contains the *MS-DOS KERNEL*, which is loaded into memory next. MS-DOS KERNEL provides most of the operating system services, such as: the code that inputs and outputs characters to the "standard" hardware devices like the screen, keyboard and disk drive; the file system; and the memory management system.

- The MS-DOS TABLES, DISK BUFFERS, and FILE CONTROL BLOCKS are operating system work areas whose names are partially self-explanatory and that are too specialized to be of interest in this introductory survey.

- The third operating system file, COMMAND.COM contains the *MS-DOS SHELL*, which is the "user interface" of the operating system: it presents the **DOS** prompt to the screen; it is responsible for loading user programs and restoring control to the operating system when they terminate; and it is the administrator of the **DOS** batch file language and of the **DOS** *internal commands* such as DIR and COPY.

- The last item on our memory map is of some interest because it demonstrates that shortage of memory is a real concern in **MS-DOS** systems. Our description of the MS-DOS SHELL shows that it is made up of two kinds of information. Most of its contents — the batch file language and internal commands — are not needed while another program is executing. Some parts of the SHELL are needed, notably the code that terminates an application and returns control to **MS-DOS**. Consequently, the operating system undertakes a somewhat bizarre sequence of operations, in order to leave more memory available for executing programs. COMMAND.COM is split into two parts: a smaller *resident portion* consisting of code that must always be present; and a larger *transient portion* consisting of code that can be deleted while another program has control of the machine. The transient portion is copied to the high end of user memory (i.e., to just below location A0000). Programs are now allowed to load just above the resident portion, thereby overwriting the original transient portion. If a user program (or programs) is large enough, it will also obliterate part of the copied transient portion. If a user program is not very large, it will leave the copy of the transient portion undamaged. Each time it terminates a user program, COMMAND.COM runs some consistency checks (technically called *checksums*) to determine whether the copy of the transient portion has been corrupted. If these checks reveal damage, COMMAND.COM renews this copied portion by reloading it from the disk.

SECTION 3 SEGMENTATION

Since address arithmetic is so central to the functioning of any computer, address information must be quickly accessible and easily manipulated by the machine. As we know, the **8086** (like all other processors) has certain storage areas called registers. These registers are very significant because of their fast response time — data can be stored in or retrieved from a register much, much faster than from standard machine memory. This suggests that, in so far as possible, addresses should be stored in registers.

But there is a problem. We have seen that the registers of the **8086** are 16 bits wide. This means that if each byte of memory is given a unique address and all the choices of this address are kept small enough to fit in a single register, then the maximum memory size at most equals the number of different values that can be stored in a 16-bit register. In other words, the machine can support no more than 64K of addressable memory. This is not enough and, indeed, we saw in the previous section that the **IBM-XT** has 1M of addressable memory.

Since a single register will not hold a sufficiently large range of addresses, the solution is clear: use *two* registers to hold each address. The most direct implementation of this strategy would allow addresses to be 32 bits long, storing the high 16 bits in one register and the low 16 bits in another. This is not the solution adopted by the designers of the **8086**. They did indeed break each address into two pieces, a *segment* and an *offset*, and each of these parts is stored in a separate register. But the segment and offset are not combined in the obvious way to give a resulting address. Instead, the following rule is used:

- To recover an address given its segment and offset, multiply the segment by 16 and add the offset.

This representation of addresses is usually referred to as the *Intel segmentation scheme*. Although the reasons for this approach may be puzzling at this moment, the computation is certainly easy to do in binary or hexadecimal. In binary, append four zeros to the segment to effect the multiplication by 16, and then add the offset. In hexadecimal it is even easier: append a single zero to perform the multiplication and then the do the addition. The result of the segment-and-offset computation is usually called a *linear address*, to distinguish it from the Intel segmented form.

The standard notation for an address made up of a given segment and offset pair is *segment:offset*. Here are some examples:

```
1234:1ABC = 12340 + 1ABC = 13DFC
ABCD:0011 = ABCD0 + 0011 = ABCE1
A79C:4321 = A79C0 + 4321 = ABCE1
FFFF:FFFF = FFFF0 + FFFF = 10FFEF
```

The second and third examples illustrate the fact that the same linear address can be represented in the form *segment:offset* in different ways. The fourth example obviously contains the largest linear address that can be represented in this form. It is somewhat larger that the largest five-hex-digit number, FFFFF. Any linear address with five or fewer digits can be represented as *segment:offset* in many different ways. Specifically, given $H_0H_1H_2H_3H_4$, where H_0, H_1, H_2, H_3, and H_4 are hex digits, these are two obvious representations:

$$H_0H_1H_2H_3H_4 = H_0H_1H_2H_3:000H_4$$

and

$$H_0H_1H_2H_3H_4 = H_0H_100:0H_2H_3H_4$$

It is easy to think of a number of analogous alternatives. Since five hex digits convert to 20 binary digits, this result explains why a machine that uses the **8086** can have as much as 1M of addressable memory.

Exercise 2-1. Convert each of the following addresses, given in the form *segment:offset*, to a linear address:

```
3729:FFFF
7373:CDBA
789A:FA9C
```

Exercise 2-2. Write each of the following linear addresses in Intel segmented form in at least six ways:

        1234A
        000F0
        10000

Exercise 2-3. Given a five-hex-digit address

$$H_0 H_1 H_2 H_3 H_4$$

in how many different ways can it be represented as *segment:offset*? Assume that the arithmetic will be done "modulo 100000H", i.e., any multiple of 100000H will be discarded. Equivalently, only the low 20 bits of the result will be retained. Our example from the text

$$FFFF:FFFF = FFFF0 + FFFF = 10FFEF$$

will then end up having value

$$10FFEF - 100000 = FFEF.$$

Is the number of representations the same for all choices of the five hex digits?

Remark. The **8086** does really treat large *segment:offset* values in this way. However, the situation is more complicated with the **80286** and **80386**. First, these processors allow addresses to be wider than 20 bits and so do not discard the high parts of addresses. However, IBM designed the **IBM-AT** to emulate the **IBM-XT** as closely as possible when running **8086** software. Consequently, the **IBM-AT** includes special hardware whose sole purpose is to truncate addresses to 20 bits, and the various **80286** and **80386** clones mimic this behavior. We will need to examine this curious situation in detail in Chapter 18.

SECTION 4 THE 8086 AND 8088 MICROPROCESSORS

In this section, we will briefly consider the Intel **8086** microprocessor, and its very close relative the **8088**, which is used in the **IBM-XT**. Once again, we will discuss only those characteristics that are significant to the assembly language programmer.

Figure 2.2 contains a stylized drawing of the **8086**. A very important feature of this microprocessor is that it consists of two quite independent parts, the *execution unit* (*EU*) and the *bus interface unit* (*BIU*). The names of these elements suggests their functions. The execution unit is responsible for the actual execution of instructions by the microprocessor. The bus interface unit is responsible for sending and receiving information on the *data bus* and the *address bus*. A *bus* is a collection of electrical conductors that transmits signals through the machine. These conductors operate in parallel in the sense that several bits of information can be transmitted at the same time, one along each conductor. For example, a

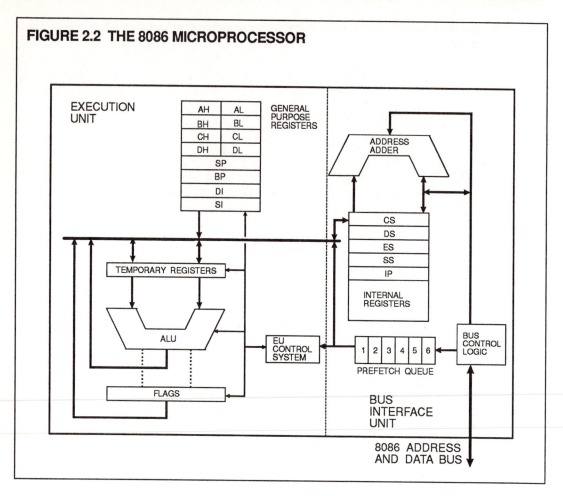

FIGURE 2.2 THE 8086 MICROPROCESSOR

bus that is eight bits wide (i.e., contains 8 conductors) can transmit a byte of information at a time. The address bus of the **8086** is 20 bits wide and the data bus is 16 bits wide. The diagram also shows the registers of the **8088**. We will discuss them in detail in Section 5.

Except for the registers, the various subassemblies of the execution unit are not significant in everyday programming. As a point of general interest, we will mention that the *arithmetic-logic unit* (*ALU*) is ultimately responsible for the computations performed by the microprocessor. **Flags** is one of the registers.

In order to write efficient assembly language programs, the programmer must understand some features of the bus interface unit. Several of the microprocessor registers are associated with the BIU and, again, we will introduce them in Section 5. One of the subassemblies of the BIU is the *address adder*, whose function is to perform the segment arithmetic that we described in the last section: it combines a segment and an offset to build a final address, using the Intel segmentation scheme. It is important to realize that all the information, both code and data, needed to execute an instruction, must be imported to the microprocessor by the BIU. As the BIU brings in code or data, it stores it in a buffer called the *prefetch queue*, where it awaits processing by the EA. If the prefetch queue empties, the EA must wait for the BIU to bring in more code and/or data; if the prefetch queue fills, the BIU must wait for the EA to withdraw some bytes to provide space. The name queue is used here in the same sense as in data structures: it is a first-in/first-out store. The **8086** prefetch queue is six bytes long, but the **8088** queue is only four bytes long.

The division of the microprocessor into EU and BIU is significant because these units can operate *concurrently*, and so, to a large extent, aquisition of data and code from memory and address arithmetic does not add to execution time. Unfortunately, this statement is something of an idealization. To begin with, we will see later that some kinds of address computations *always* increase computation time. (This is the so-called *indirect addressing penalty*, and will be discussed in Chapter 9.)

But beyond this, the division of labor between EA and BIU would work perfectly only if each required the same amount of time to perform its task. This is not always the case because some instructions are fast and some are slow, and some use many bytes of code and data, while others are very modest in size. Furthermore, there is not much correlation between execution time and size of instructions. So the best we can hope for is that, on average, the EA and BIU will require about the same amount of time to complete their duties. The **8086** was designed with this criterion in mind. However, sequences of very fast instructions can easily deplete the prefetch queue, so that the EA must pause and wait before it can begin work again.

One consequence of this dependency on the prefetch queue is that it is very difficult to compute accurate execution times for **8086** programs. We will see later that there are tables giving the time required for each instruction, but that these times are *for execution only*, and make no allowance for bus delays. Consequently, timings computed on the basis of these tables will be lower bounds and will almost definitely be too low.

The physical container that holds the **8086** has 40 *pins*. These pins carry electrical signals between the **8086** to the remainder of the computer and, in particular, connect to the address and data busses. If the designers of the **8086** had allocated separate pins for the address and data busses, a total of 36 of the 40 pins would have been assigned, leaving only 4 pins for all the remaining functions. Since this would have been totally inadequate, they chose to assign 20 pins to the address bus and make 16 of these do double duty by also connecting them to the data bus. The question naturally arises of how the same set of electrical contacts can transmit two different kinds of signals at the same time, and the answer is that they do not. The technique that is used is called *multiplexing* and means that, at different times, the signals on these pins should be interpreted as a datum or an address. Of course, additional information must be provided so that the correct interpretation will always be made. While this is an interesting question, it does not really concern us in this book, and we refer the reader to [10] for a lucid discussion of this and related hardware issues.

The first part of Figure 2.3 shows an idealized drawing of the **8086**. Only the 20 pins that connect to the address bus are shown. They are given their usual names. In particular, notice that the 16 low-numbered pins have a D in their names, as well as an A, because they are also connected to the data bus.

Finally, we are ready to state the principle difference between the **8086** and the **8088**. While the **8088** still uses 20-bit addresses, its data bus that is only 8 bits wide Consequently,

FIGURE 2.3 ADDRESS AND BUS CONNECTIONS

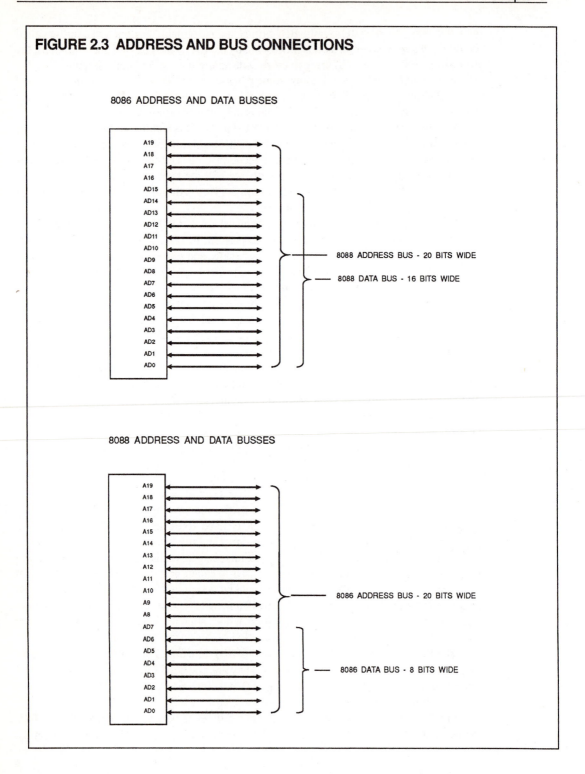

8086 ADDRESS AND DATA BUSSES

8088 ADDRESS BUS - 20 BITS WIDE

8088 DATA BUS - 16 BITS WIDE

8088 ADDRESS AND DATA BUSSES

8086 ADDRESS BUS - 20 BITS WIDE

8086 DATA BUS - 8 BITS WIDE

only the eight lowest address pins need do double duty as data pins. The **8088** configuration is shown in the second part of Figure 8.3.

The **8088** was used in the **IBM-PC** as an economy measure: it is obviously cheaper to use an 8-bit bus than a 16-bit bus. The main economy really resulted from the conditions of microcomputer manufacture at the time (circa 1980). The dominant microprocessors on the market were all 8-bit, with the Intel **8080** being a prime example. Consequently, 8-bit support components were relatively cheap and plentiful and it was definitely advantageous to build a new computer that could use as much existing technology — **8080** technology, in particular — as possible.

Inevitably, using an **8088** rather than an **8086** results in a loss of performance. The EU portions of the chips are identical but the BIU of the **8088** works less efficiently because it imports information only a byte at a time. We have already made the point that, in the **8086**, the EA and BIU are reasonably well balanced and, consequently, in the **8088**, the BIU must lag behind the EA, on average. From our previous discussion, it should be clear that the effect of this lag on the performance of a particular program is dependent on the precise instruction mix in that program. It is probably fair to say that, under typical circumstances, programs run 10%-20% slower on a **8088** machine than on a similar **8086** machine.

SECTION 5 THE REGISTERS OF THE 8086

At this point, we are ready to give a detailed description of the registers of the **8086**. There are a total of 14 registers, some of which are usable in nearly any programming setting, while others are especially adapted to a particular activity, and still others are dedicated to some specific, unchangeable function. To underline these differences, and to make it easier to remember all fourteen of the registers, we divide them into four subsets in the following discussion. This division is illustrated in Figure 2.4.

A. THE FOUR MAIN COMPUTATIONAL REGISTERS

We refer to the registers in this first category as the *main computational registers* because they are used in a wide variety of assembly language contexts. Nevertheless, each of them has its own personality, and there are situations in which a particular one must be used, or at least works better than do the others. Here are the registers:

ax (the *accumulator*). This register is often used in arithmetic. Some operations run faster if **ax** is used, while others, such as multiplication and division, require that it be used.

bx (the *base register*). Again, this register is widely used, but it, too, has a specialty. When **bx** appears in an expression of the form [**bx**], the assembler interprets the value of **bx** not as a datum, but as the offset part of an address. This kind of usage is called *indirect addressing*,

FIGURE 2.4 THE REGISTERS OF THE 8086/8088

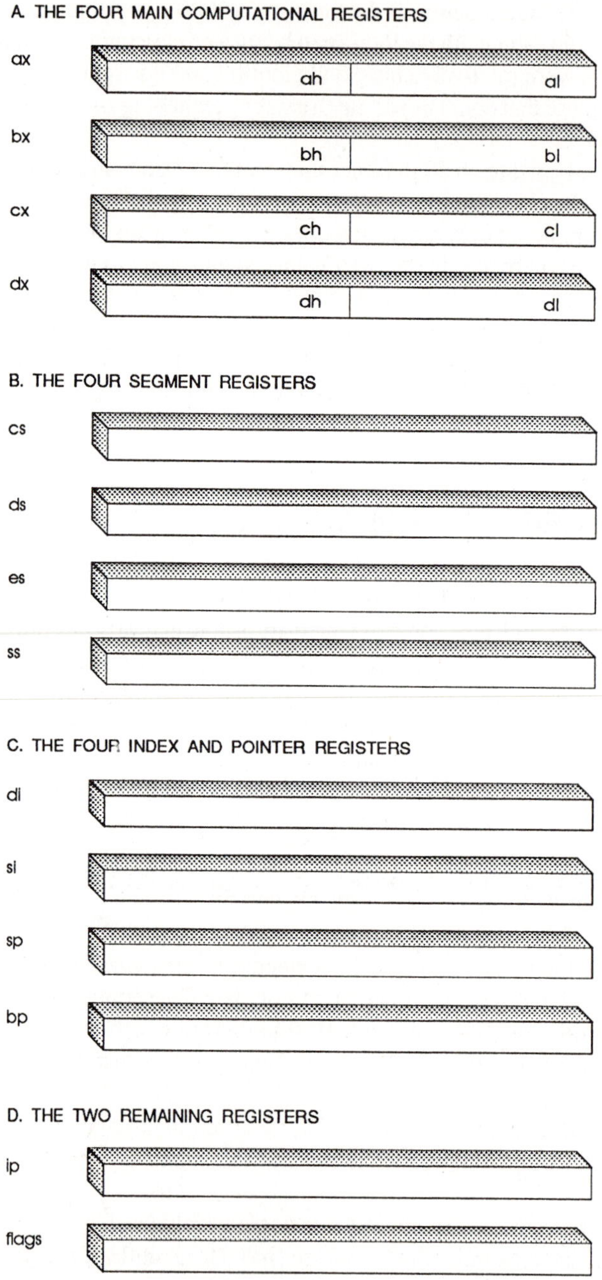

A. THE FOUR MAIN COMPUTATIONAL REGISTERS

ax

| ah | al |

bx

| bh | bl |

cx

| ch | cl |

dx

| dh | dl |

B. THE FOUR SEGMENT REGISTERS

cs

ds

es

ss

C. THE FOUR INDEX AND POINTER REGISTERS

di

si

sp

bp

D. THE TWO REMAINING REGISTERS

ip

flags

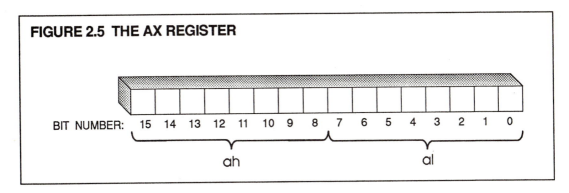

FIGURE 2.5 THE AX REGISTER

and figures prominently in assembly language. It is this application that accounts for the name base register since **bx** frequently contains the base, or starting, offset of a memory region.

cx (the *counter register*). Assembly language, like all programming languages, deals with loops, and loops require counters. As the name suggests, **cx** is used as the default counter in certain looping constructs. Of course, it is also available for general computational use.

dx (the *data register*). This is a sort of catch-all register. It really has no special properties and there seems to be no good explanation for the name *data* — it presumably was the only vaguely applicable name that started with d!

These four registers share an important feature that none of the remaining ten have. Each of them can be used as two separate 8-bit registers, in addition to its use as a single 16-bit register.

The **ax** register is shown in Figure 2.5. As in our previous illustration of the bit pattern of a word, the register is depicted as though the low-order bit occupies the right end and the high-order bit occupies the left end. This is in no way intended to reflect the hardware structure of a register. Just as before, we adopt this convention to conform with the standard method of writing binary representations. The high 8 bits of **ax** are named **ah** and the low 8 bits are named **al**. The pieces of **bx**, **cx**, and **dx** have corresponding names

Being able to address of these four registers as though they were eight different 8-bit registers is especially important because it enables the **8086** to support two different sizes of arithmetic. First, there is the "natural" machine arithmetic, in which operations are done on 16-bit data. For example, two 16-bit objects can be added to give a 16-bit answer. In addition, the **8086** supports an entire set of 8-bit arithmetic operations. These are meant to be used when small data are being considered — for instance, the ASCII codes of characters.

B. THE FOUR SEGMENT REGISTERS

As the name indicates, these registers are used to hold the segment parts of addresses. They are dedicated to this function and are seldom used for anything else. The form of the instruction set almost enforces this "hands off" policy with respect to the segment registers, since most of the instructions will not work if used with a segment register as an operand.

We pause here to introduce some new terminology. So far, the word *segment* has been used in two different contexts: as a name for one of the 64K blocks into which we partitioned the memory space of the **8086** (refer to Figure 2.1); and as part of an address in the Intel segmentation scheme. This second use of the word is not really well chosen — perhaps a name such as *segmentbase* or *segbase* would have been better. With the exception of this usage, a segment always refers to a block of memory. The situation is somewhat clouded by the fact that there are two kinds of segments, which we will now define.

A *physical segment* just means a 64K block of memory with addresses in the range

$$H_0H_1H_2H_3:0000 \ - \ H_0H_1H_2H_3:FFFF$$

for some values of the hex digits H_i. Hence, the segments shown in Figure 2.1 are examples of physical segments.

On the other hand, the term *logical segment* refers to a division of memory that is defined in an assembly language program. The exact method by which programs define the lengths of logical segments is not significant at this juncture. We will discussed it in later chapters.

The code and the data for a program will usually reside in different logical segments, and the appropriate segment registers will be *pointed* at these segments. To *point a segment register to a segment* is the assembly-language idiom for the impossibly clumsy "initialize a segment register so that it contains the segment part of the starting address of a segment." In a moment, we will see that one of the segment registers is called **ds**. If **ds** has been pointed to a logical segment in a program, then that logical segment is the region of memory beginning at address **ds**:0000 and of whatever length the program has decreed. Several different logical segments can overlap and in fact different logical segments can be identical. In nearly all situations where we are talking about physical or logical segments, which we mean will be clear from the context and so we will usually just say "segment."

One of the good features of this assembly language is that it permits the writing of fairly structured code, in the sense of structured programming. For example, a tenet of structured programming is that code and data should not be intermingled. Data can change dynamically (i.e., be altered during program execution) while code should (ideally) never change from its original form. In this assembly language, code and data are kept apart by placing them in different logical segments. While the assembler makes this easy to do, it does not enforce such a division. In fact, we will see later that the so-called .COM format program (somewhat antiquated but, alas, still necessary in a few situations) requires that all parts of the program reside in a single logical segment.

Here are the four segment registers:

cs, (the *code segment register*). In order to execute a program, the microprocessor must be able to find the code in machine memory. The sole function of **cs** is to point to the segment that contains the code for the current instruction.

ds (the *data segment register*). A given program may or may not require data. If it does, then **ds** will normally point to the segment containing the data. We will see that the assembler, in computing addresses for data, will assume that **ds** has been initialized in this way and will frequently generate incorrect code if this initialization has not been performed.

es (the *extra segment register*). As the name implies, this is basically a spare register that acts in the same general way as the other segment registers. Consequently, it gets somewhat less use than other registers, at least in small programs. A program with more than 64K of data must store it data in more than one segment. One method of accessing the data in such a program is to "switch" **ds** repeatedly during execution so that it always points to the segment containing the currently needed data. This switching back and forth will be less frequent if two segment registers are used to address different segments of data, and **es** plays the role of the second register.

ss (the *stack segment register*). Most programs need a *stack*, which is a special area of memory that stores temporary information during program execution. The **ss** register is used to point to the stack. As an example of the use of the stack, consider what happens when a program calls a procedure. The microprocessor stops executing code at the current address and starts executing the instructions from the procedure. At the termination of the procedure, the machine must return control to the calling program and take up where it left off. The address to which it must return is stored temporarily on the stack and retrieved when needed. Other standard uses of the stack are to provide storage space for local variables used by procedures and to provide a mechanism for passing parameters to procedures.

C. THE FOUR INDEX AND POINTER REGISTERS

These are:

si (the *source index register*). This register is often used in general computations, but has special uses in dealing with addresses. For example, it can be used in indirect addressing in a manner that is totally analogous with the use of **bx**: in an expression such as [**si**], the value of **si** is interpreted as the offset part of an address. The **si** register has another special application, which we will mention in the next paragraph.

di (the *destination index register*). Everything said about the **si** register applies equally well to **di**. There is one particular context in which both of these registers play a privileged role, and we will very briefly preview this now. Every processor has its particular strengths and weaknesses, and one of the real strengths of the present family of processors is the *string instructions*. This is a not-very-good name for certain instructions that perform fast operations on blocks of memory. These operations cover the usual programming tasks: move a block from one location to another, compare blocks, search a block, and so on. The **si** and **di** registers must be used with these instructions. In the case of the string-move instruction, for example, **si** contains the offset of the starting location of the memory block to be moved, while **di** contains the offset of the location to which it should be moved. This use explains the names that are attached to these two registers.

sp (the *stack pointer*). As discussed earlier, **ss** contains the segment address of the stack. The **sp** register contains the corresponding offset. More exactly, **ss:sp** is the address of the *top of the stack*, which is the location at which the most recent item was stored on the stack.

bp (the *base pointer*). Like **bx**, **si**, and **di**, the base pointer can be used for indirect addressing but differs from these three in a fundamental way: when **bx**, **si**, or **di** holds an offset, the processor assumes that the corresponding segment is in **ds**; but when **bp** holds an offset, the processor uses **ss** to obtain the corresponding segment value.

In practical terms, this means that **bx**, **si**, and **di** are used to keep track of data, whereas **bp** is used to access the stack. The **bp** register is most commonly used in connection with procedure parameters that have been passed via the stack.

D. THE TWO REMAINING REGISTERS

ip (the *instruction pointer*). The **ip** register holds the offset part of the address of the next instruction that the machine will execute. In other words, the next instruction has address **cs:ip**. From the point of view of the high-level language programmer, the mechanisms by which the machine executes code from procedures and performs gotos may seem mysterious. From the point of view of the assembly language programmer, the situation is incredibly simple. In order to execute the code for a procedure, the processor merely changes the values of **cs** and **ip** so that they contain the address of the beginning of the procedure code. In this assembly language, the **call** instruction is used to transfer control to a procedure, and one of its principle tasks is to modify **cs** and **ip**.

The **flags** register. This register is completely different in its behavior from the other 13 because the individual bits of the **flags** register are interpreted as separate carriers of information. Each of the 16 bits can independently assume the value 0 or 1, and can be used to tell something about the state of the machine. Actually, only 9 of the 16 bits are used by the **8086**, and each of these 9 bits is called a *flag*. A few of the flags are of central importance, others are moderately significant, and some are consulted only under rather special circumstances. Most machine instructions change at least some of the flags, and one of the burdens of learning assembly language is that the programmer must know when these flag changes are important and how to take account of them. The flags register is shown in Figure 2.6.

If a given flag has value 1, it is said to be *on* or *set*; if it has value 0, it is said to be *off* or *cleared* or *reset*. Here is a listing of the 9 flags, with indications of their general meaning:

OF (*overflow flag*). **OF** is set when the machine completes an arithmetic instruction that causes an overflow, i.e., gives a result too large or too small to fit in the space assigned to hold it, when interpreted as an operation on signed data.

DF (*direction flag*). This flag is mainly used in connection with the aforementioned string instructions. It is well known that if a block of data is moved item by item from one location

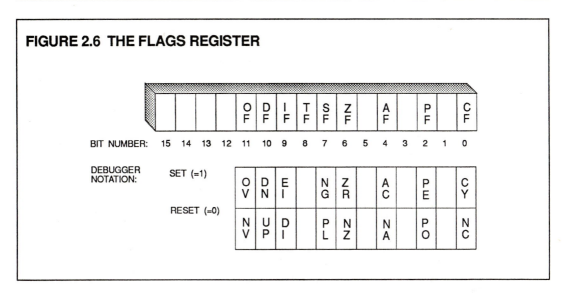

FIGURE 2.6 THE FLAGS REGISTER

to another, and if the source location overlaps the destination, then it is significant whether the moving process starts from the low end and proceeds upwards or is done in the opposite order. (If this is not a familiar fact, think about it and draw some pictures; we will give examples in Chapter 10.) In assembly language, the order in which the elements are moved is controlled by the value of the direction flag.

IF (*interrupt flag*). Certain events are activated by the machine hardware and can interrupt an executing program temporarily. Normally, these *hardware interrupts* are of no significance to the executing program and, in fact, occur many times a second. A hardware interrupt performs some task, such as updating the system clock, and then returns control to the executing program, which continues where it left off. Occasionally, certain critical sections of code should not be interrupted, even for a short period. The interrupt flag provides the programmer with a mechanism for inhibiting hardware interrupts while such sensitive code is executing.

SF (*sign flag*). The sign flag relays information about the outcome of an arithmetic operation whose operands are interpreted as signed integers. It is set if the result is negative and reset if the result is non-negative.

ZF (*zero flag*). The name is self-explanatory. If an arithmetic operation gives zero as answer, this flag is set; otherwise, it is reset. But the zero flag has a significance that goes beyond this. When the machine is asked to compare two quantities, it performs an internal subtraction and sets the flags according to the answer. (This subtraction has no visible effect, other than changing the flags; in particular, it does not affect either of the quantities being compared.) If the quantities are equal, the zero flag is set, and if they are not equal, it is reset. Looking at the zero flag is the *only* way of checking whether a comparison yielded equality or inequality.

AF (*auxiliary flag*) and **PF** (*parity flag*). These are not of general interest. We will make use of the parity flag in Chapter 10, when we examine binary coded decimal arithmetic, which is one of the specialized arithmetic modes of the **8086**.

CF (*carry flag*). The carry flag has the same general significance for unsigned arithmetic that the overflow flag has for signed arithmetic. Namely, it signals an unsigned overflow condition: if, when its operands are interpreted as unsigned quantities, the result of an arithmetic instruction is too large or too small to fit in its destination, then the carry flag is set.

TF (*trap flag*). This flag is of no concern in day-to-day programming, but is of immense value in special applications such as the construction of debuggers. Perhaps the most important thing a debugger can do is to move through code one instruction at a time, stopping and displaying information after each step. An interesting question is how the machine can be induced to stop after every instruction, and the answer is very easy. If the trap flag is set, the machine is in a state called *single-step mode*, and will then (usually!) execute just one program step and stop. Hence a basic requirement in building a debugger is to take control of the trap flag.

Most debuggers (including **CODEVIEW**) show the state of each flag, except that the trap flag is not generally displayed. Standard mnemonics are used to indicate whether each flag is set or reset. For example, in the case of the overflow flag, set is denoted by **OV** because it means that (signed) overflow occurred, while reset is denoted **NV** for the analogous reason. The second part of Figure 2.6 lists the mnemonics that are generally used.

In many discussions of the **8086** register set, the registers in our subsets A and C are lumped together and called the *general-purpose registers*. In other words, the eight general-purpose registers are **ax**, **bx**, **cx**, **dx**, **si**, **di**, **bp**, and **sp**.

Exercise 2-4. Suppose that the registers of the **8088** have the values:

```
ax = DFFF   bx = 300A   cx = 0000   dx = 12F4
cs = 1000   ds = 2000   es = 3000   ss = 4000
di = 0000   si = 0000   sp = 0FFE   bp = 0000
ip = 018F   FLAGS = 0000
```

All values are given in hex.
a. What is the linear address of the next instruction to be executed?
b. What is the linear address of the top of the stack
c. Suppose that the next instruction will add the values of **ax** and **bx** and leave the answer in a 16-bit destination. What will be the values of OF, SF, ZF, and CF immediately after that instruction executes?

FIGURE 2.7 EXAMPLES OF MULTI-BYTE STORAGE

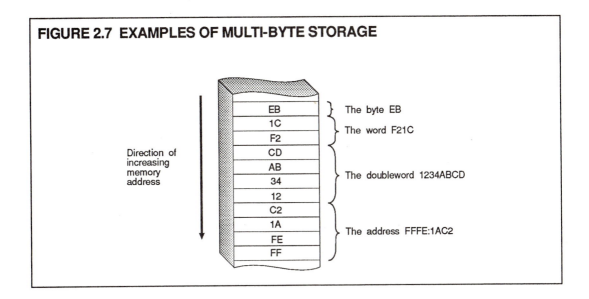

SECTION 6 BYTE ORDER IN MEMORY

Processors in the **8086** family always store multi-byte data in memory with the least significant byte at the lowest memory address and bytes of increasing significance occupying successively higher addresses. For example, when a word is stored in memory, the low byte occurs at the lower memory address and the high byte at the higher address.

This mode of storage is often termed *backwords* because the bytes in a word appear in the wrong order in a memory map that runs across the page with address increasing in the natural left-to-right direction. Not all processors store data with this ordering. For example, the processors in the **68000** series use the opposite approach: they store data with the most significant byte occupying the lowest address.

Figure 2.7 shows a memory map in the format that we will use throughout the book. Each box represents a byte and memory increases in the downward direction. We have shown several data items stored in the correct order. A *doubleword* is a two-word, or four-byte datum. Notice how it is stored: the less significant word comes first, stored "backwords", followed by the more significant word, likewise stored "backwords." The last example in Figure 2.7 is interesting because it shows that addresses are stored in a manner that is consistent with other data. Namely, in the *segment:offset* form, *segment* is clearly the more significant part and *offset* is the less significant. Consequently, *offset* is stored first in memory and *segment* is stored second. Of course, each is stored "backwords."

Throughout the book, we will store multi-word data in a manner that is consistent with the internal architecture. For example, in Chapter 10 we will introduce multiple-precision arithmetic, in which an integer is represented by several words, and will always store these integers in a least-significant-byte-first order.

TABLE 2.1 THE 8086 FAMILY OF MICROPROCESSORS

```
PROCESSOR              FEATURES

8086                   20-bit address bus
                       16-bit data bus

8088                   20-bit addrsssing, 8-bit data bus

8087                   numerical coprocessor for use with 8086/8088

80186                  faster version of 8086, with somewhat
                       improved instruction set

80188                  bears same relationship to 8088 that the
                       80186 bears to the 8086

80286                  major upgrade of 8086 offers:
                               24-bit address bus
                               optional protected mode operation
                               virtual memory management

80287                  numerical coprocessor for use with 80286

80386                  major upgrade of 80286 offers:
                               32-bit registers
                               32-bit data bus
                               32-bit address bus
                               greatly improved instruction set
                               greatly improved addressing modes
                               improved virtual memory support
                               better 8086 emulation than 80286

386SX                  version of 80386 with 16-bit data bus

80387                  numerical coprocessor for use with 80386

80486                  upgrade of 80386 uses same instruction set but:
                               is much faster
                               combines coprocessor functions so that
                               no separate "80487" is needed
                               has integral memory caching unit
```

SECTION 7 THE 8086 FAMILY

Table 2.1 shows the other members of the **8086** family of microprocessors.

The **80186** was a relatively modest extension of the **8086** and was never used widely in computers, although it was (and still is) used in various special purpose applications, such as laser printers.

The **80286** was a major step upward from the **8086**, mainly because its 24-bit addressing capabilities enabled it to control as much as 16 megabytes of memory and because it offered an exciting new method of operation called *protected mode*. We give a preliminary discussion of protected mode in Chapter 11 and devote all of Chapter 18 to it. It is ironic that, until recently, these new features of the **80286** have not been exploited and most machines using the **80286** have been used only as very fast **8086** machines. The reader probably knows that the **80286** is used in the **IBM-AT** and its vast army of clones.

The **80386** represented another huge step upward in the evolution of this family, because it is a full 32-bit microprocessor: its registers and data bus are 32 bits wide, and it supports 32-bit addressing. It offers many enhancements to the basic **8086** instruction set, which we will explore in later chapters. At the moment, most **80386** chips are used in machines whose architecture is essentially identical to the **IBM-AT**, with only the modifications required to support 32-bit operation.

The **386SX** bears the same general relationship to the **80386** that the **8088** bears to the **8086**: it is a 32-bit microprocessor but uses a 16-bit data bus.

The **80486** is, by some measures, a relatively modest advance over the **80386**. It has the same basic instruction set, but executes many instructions much faster than an **80386**. In fact, it appears that the **80486** may be faster by a factor of two or three, on average. The **80486** may ultimately allow the building of somewhat cheaper machines than the **80386** since, as well as replacing the **80386**, it performs the functions of a numerical coprocessor and a memory caching unit and, even now, costs less than the total cost of the three chips it replaces.

This capsule summary of the **8086** family should help to explain the choice of machines used in writing this book. The **8088** is "the common denominator." Millions of machines use this chip, and are not likely to disappear in the near future. Consequently, software will continue to be written and updated for **8088** machines. In addition, the **8086/8088** assembly language is at the core of the extended languages used by the later chips, and so must be learned in any case. It can also be argued that the **8088** is very simple architecturally (by comparison with, say, the **80386**), and so its study is an excellent starting point. For these reasons, we have directed most of this text toward the **8088** and, in particular, toward the ubiquitous **IBM-XT** clones that use it.

Our choice of chip for the advanced chapters was equally easy. The **80386** and **80486** will clearly be the dominant Intel processors for the next few years. Since their assembly languages virtually are identical, it was possible to choose between them on other grounds — the author owns an **80386** but not an **80486**! Therefore, our Chapters 7, 11, and 18 make use of the **80386**, although the interested reader should be able to adapt the 16-bit material from those chapters to run on an **80286** machine without excessive difficulty.

CHAPTER 3

A FIRST LOOK AT THE 8088 INSTRUCTION SET

SECTION 1 PREVIEW

A feature of most assembly languages, including this one, is that the individual instructions are extremely easy to understand. The difficulties attendant to the learning of assembly language do not come from the instructions themselves. They arise from other, more global considerations, which we will begin to address in Chapter 5.

The goals in the present chapter are to acquire familiarity with the general syntax of the **8088** assembly language and to become acquainted with a reasonable subset of the instructions, so that fairly complex programs can be written. Specifically, 22 of the instructions will be presented in this chapter, and these will allow the writing of quite substantial programs. When the other instructions are introduced later, it will become clear that most of them only provide easier or faster ways of doing operations that can already be performed with the basic set.

Chapter 10 contains a detailed study of the entire **8088** instruction set and Chapter 11 discusses the extensions to the basic instruction set that were introduced with the more advanced processors in this series (**80186/80188**, the **80286**, the **80386**, and the **80486**).

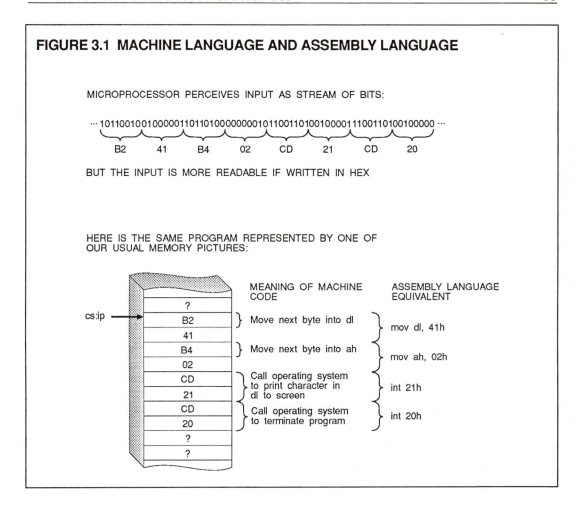

FIGURE 3.1 MACHINE LANGUAGE AND ASSEMBLY LANGUAGE

MICROPROCESSOR PERCEIVES INPUT AS STREAM OF BITS:

··· 1011001001000001101101000000001011001101001000011100110100100000 ···

| B2 | 41 | B4 | 02 | CD | 21 | CD | 20 |

BUT THE INPUT IS MORE READABLE IF WRITTEN IN HEX

HERE IS THE SAME PROGRAM REPRESENTED BY ONE OF
OUR USUAL MEMORY PICTURES:

	MEANING OF MACHINE CODE	ASSEMBLY LANGUAGE EQUIVALENT
?		
B2	} Move next byte into dl	} mov dl, 41h
41		
B4	} Move next byte into ah	} mov ah, 02h
02		
CD	} Call operating system to print character in dl to screen	} int 21h
21		
CD	} Call operating system to terminate program	} int 20h
20		
?		
?		

cs:ip →

SECTION 2 MACHINE LANGUAGE AND ASSEMBLY LANGUAGE

Although the bus that carries information to the central processing unit may carry a byte or word or even larger amounts of data at one time, the processor ultimately interprets its input as a sequence of binary digits. As we indicated in an earlier section, it is easier for the human reader to think of the data in larger pieces such as bytes, and so, whenever possible, we will use a byte as the basic unit in our discussions and diagrams.

The top part of Figure 3.1 shows a complete **8088** program of total length 64 bits. As we will explain later in the present chapter, this program is not self-contained since it relies upon other programs provided by the operating system.

When this program is loaded into machine memory, it will occupy eight contiguous bytes, as shown in the memory picture in the lower half of Figure 3.1. One of the facilities provided by the operating system is the *program loader*. If the name of an executable program is typed at the **DOS** prompt, the loader moves the program into memory and makes various preparations that are necessary for its proper execution. Perhaps the most important of these preparations is initializing **cs:ip** to point to the instruction in the program at which execution should begin.

Figure 3.1 also indicates the meanings of the eight bytes of code in our small program. For example, the microprocessor interprets an instruction byte with value B2 (hex) as a request to move the next byte occurring in its *input stream* into the **dl** register. The meanings of the machine code instructions cannot be logically deduced — the encoding in quite arbitrary and is determined by the circuitry of the microprocessor. We will study this encoding in later chapters. For the moment, the details are of no concern to us, and the reader should take the interpretations given in Figure 3.1 on faith. These interpretations reveal what this program does: since the ASCII code for 'A' is 41H, it prints the letter 'A' to the screen.

Before continuing, we will digress briefly to discuss the mechanics of executing the program. The essential step is to construct a file containing exactly eight bytes of data, with hex values

```
B2 41 B4 02 CD 21 CD 20
```

This is somewhat harder than it looks. A text-editor file consisting of the characters

```
B241B402CD21CD20
```

will actually contain 16 bytes of data, with values the ASCII code for 'B', the ASCII code for '2', and so on. Some text editors allow the user to enter the numeric values of non-printing characters such as B2 (= 178 in decimal) by using the numeric keypad, for example. Since not all readers will have access to such an editor, we have included a utility on the Program Disk that performs this service. This utility is named MAKECOM.EXE and is used in the following way to build the present program. Use a text editor to construct the 16-byte file illustrated above and store it as a disk file. If the file is named PRINTA, for example, then run MAKECOM with the command line

```
makecom printa
```

MAKECOM will produce a new file called PRINTA.COM containing the required eight bytes. (The MAKECOM utility gives its generated file the extension .COM because **MS-DOS** requires that every executable file have extension .COM or .EXE. This is not important to us at the moment.)

PRINTA can now be executed by using the command

```
printa
```

from the **DOS** prompt. If all goes well, the letter 'A' should appear on the screen.

In the exercises, we provide the reader with the opportunity to experiment by constructing other small programs using MAKECOM.

The numeric data stream that is input to the microprocessor, represented in either binary or hex, is usually called *machine language* or *machine code*. We have used only a few instructions in our machine language demonstration, but when one considers that the **8088** instruction set contains over 100 instructions, many having numerous options, the conclusion is inescapable: writing machine language is an incredibly onerous and error-prone activity.

Luckily, in the early days of computing (about 40 years ago), people realized that programming in machine language was an unnecessarily difficult endeavor. Rather than force the programmer to memorize and use the arbitrary machine encodings, why not write a computer program to take care of such details? Thus was born the idea of an assembler and an assembly language.

The term *assembly language* cannot be rigorously defined, but generally it means a programming language that, while not very different from machine language, is much, much easier to use. A program that translates assembly language into machine language is called an *assembler*.

The basic idea behind an assembly language is to replace the machine encodings with short word-descriptions called *mnemonics*. The name mnemonic is used because these descriptions suggest the operations that are being performed: **mov**, **add**, **cmp**, and **div** are examples of mnemonics from the **8088** language.

Figure 3.1 also shows the translation of our sample program into assembly language. Notice how much more readable the mnemonics are than the hex codes. The mnemonic **int** stands for an important machine instruction called *interrupt*, which we will introduce later in this chapter.

Remark. The principle fact needed to work the following two exercises is that if **ah** = 02 and the microprocessor encounters the bytes CD21 in the machine code, then it will print to the screen the character whose ASCII code is in **dl**. By the end of this chapter, the reader will understand the rationale behind these instructions.

Exercise 3-1. Modify PRINTA so that it prints the letter 'A' twice to the screen. Use MAKECOM to build an executable program and test it.

Exercise 3-2. Modify PRINTA so that it prints your name to the screen. Again, test it. A program named HEXDUMP, which we will develop in Chapter 9, is on the Program Disk, and can be used to verify that MAKECOM has generated the correct machine code. In response to the command line

```
hexdump inputFile
```

the HEXDUMP utility will produce a *hex dump* of the file name *inputFile*. This means that it produces a display of the file showing the bytes in the file, 16 to a line, displayed on the left as hex codes and on the right as characters (if they are printable).

Exercise 3-3. If the microprocessor encounters the bytes CD21 in its input stream and **ah** has value 01, then the machine waits for a character to be typed at the keyboard and stores its ASCII code in the **al** register. Bytes 8AD0 occurring in the input stream cause the microprocessor to move the contents of the **al** register to **dl**. Use these facts to write a program that waits for a character to be typed at the keyboard and then echoes it to the screen. Use MAKECOM to test the program. If the program is working correctly, the character should appear twice on the screen, once as it is typed and again (immediately) as it is echoed by the program.

Exercise 3-4. Here are some other machine language codes:

FEC2   Add one to the contents of the **dl** register.
B9XXYY   Move the two-byte quantity occupying bytes
            XX and YY into the **cx** register. Here, as always,
            XXYY is stored "backwords": XX becomes the
            value of **cl** and YY becomes the value of **ch**.
E2XX   Decrements **cx** and then tests its value. If the value
            equals 0, control proceeds to the next instruction.
            Otherwise control "loops" to the location in the code
            XX bytes from the start of this instruction. XX is
            interpreted as a one-byte signed integer, hence its
            allowable range is −128 to +127.

Use these instructions to write a machine language programs that prints the lowercase alphabet to the screen.

SECTION 3 GENERAL FEATURES OF THE INSTRUCTION SET

The form of an assembly language is determined by two general requirements:

- The architecture of the processor mandates which instructions are legal and this strongly affects the structure of the assembly language. The basic **8088** instruction set is shared by the **8086** and is a very large subset of the instruction sets of the more advanced processors in the family.

- The exact syntax of the language is dictated by the assembler being used, and throughout this book we will use **MASM**, the Microsoft Macro Assembler.

The general form of an instruction in this assembly language is

LABEL   MNEMONIC   OPERANDS   COMMENT

LABEL, MNEMONIC, OPERANDS, and *COMMENT* are called the instruction *fields* and need not all be present in any given instruction. *LABEL* represents a named address in the code. As might be suspected, it can be used as the target of the assembly language equivalent of a goto. An identifier is recognized as a label by **MASM** if it is followed by a colon. *COMMENT* is self-explanatory. The simpler of the two comment conventions accepted by **MASM** is that everything on a line beyond the first semicolon is considered as part of a comment and is ignored during the assembly process. We introduced the term *MNEMONIC* in the previous section. *OPERANDS* means the actual objects (constants, register values, or data items stored in memory) on which the instruction operates.

An example of a complete instruction is

```
Start:        mov ax, bx          ;this is a sample instruction
```

The use of spaces and tabs is at the programmer's discretion. **MASM** ignores them, except for the requirement that different tokens be separated by at least one space or tab. A *token* is just a group of characters that is recognized by **MASM** as one of the allowed "words" of the assembly language. Examples of tokens are reserved words such as **mov** or **add**; identifiers that are defined by the user; operators such as '+' or '>'. Replacing the preceding instruction by

```
movax, bx
```

would produce a syntax error, but

```
mov                             ax,bx
```

is an acceptable format.

MASM is also relatively insensitive to the inclusion of empty lines in a source file. The only requirements are that a single instruction cannot span more than one line and a single line cannot contain more than one instruction. But these restrictions are not burdensome since **MASM** is quite liberal in interpreting what constitutes an instruction. For example, starting with an instruction that contains all four fields, it is legal to place the *LABEL* on a line by itself, the *MNEMONIC* and *OPERANDS* on another line, and the *COMMENT* on yet another line. **MASM** will interpret the result as three separate instructions (where, of course, the last one will be entirely ignored).

As a matter of fact, instructions having all four fields on the same line will seldom be used in this book. We believe that white space should be used lavishly in programs, and one manifestation of this policy is that a label will nearly always be written on a separate line, so that our preceding example would actually appear as two instruction lines:

```
Start:

    mov     ax, bx              ;this is a sample instruction
```

In the programs that we write, labels are always set off by inserting an empty line above and below them. However, in the interest of saving space, this nicety will not always be observed in the program reproductions shown in the text.

As we stated earlier, the **8088** assembly language contains about 100 different mnemonics. Some of these require two operands; some, one operand; some, no operands; and some even give a choice of number of operands.

The two-operand mnemonics are the most complex. Consider a two-operand example that is written in the form

```
inst     Operand1, Operand2
```

Such an instruction is always interpreted as

```
inst      Destination, Source
```

and *Destination* is modified in the appropriate way by *Source*, while *Source* remains unchanged. For example,

```
mov       ax, bx
```

moves the value of the **bx** register to **ax**. It preserves **bx** but overwrites **ax** with the value of **bx**, thereby destroying its original contents. Likewise,

```
add       cx, dx
```

replaces the value of **cx** by

```
(value of cx) + (value of dx)
```

and leaves **dx** undisturbed.

Before discussing the allowed formats of operands, we need to give two definitions. In assembly language, the term *immediate data* refers to constant data. More precisely, it means any quantity whose value is known, or can be computed, before the program begins to execute. The real significance of this definition will become clear when we discuss addressing in Chapter 6. *Memory reference* is just the assembly language term for an expression that refers to a location in memory. The simplest example is the name of a user-defined variable, but memory references can have other, more complicated forms, which we will explore in the next few chapters.

The following general rules determine how operands can be used in instructions:

- In most one-operand instruction, the operand must be either a register (8- or 16-bit) or a memory reference. It cannot be immediate data.

- In a two-operand instruction, both operands must be of the same size (i.e., both bytes or both words).

- In a two-operand instruction, one operand must be a register unless the source is immediate, in which case the destination can be either a register or a memory reference. In other words, a two-operand instruction must have one of these forms:

```
inst      Reg, Reg
inst      Reg, Mem
inst      Mem, Reg
inst      Reg, Immed
inst      Mem, Immed
```

There are special rules pertaining to the use of segment registers:

- A segment register can only appear in a **mov**, **push**, or **pop** instruction. (The **push** and **pop** instructions will be introduced soon.)
- An immediate value cannot be moved into a segment register.
- Moves from one segment register to another segment register are forbidden.
- The **cs** register cannot be the destination of a **mov** or a **pop**.

We will now give some examples of these rules, using the **mov** instruction. Suppose that *bData* has been defined as a byte of data and *wData* has been defined as a word of data. (We will show how to define data in the next chapter.) To understand some of the following examples, it is necessary to know that **MASM** will interpret a constant such as 10 as either a byte or as a word, whichever is appropriate for the instruction in question. Consider these instructions:

INSTRUCTION		LEGITIMACY
mov	ax, bx	Legal because at least one operand is a register and both operands have the same size.
mov	ax, bl	Illegal because one operand is a word and one is a byte.
mov	cx, bData	Illegal, again because the operands have different sizes.
mov	dx, 10	Legal. The first operand is a 16-bit register, and so **MASM** interprets 10 as a word.
mov	bData,10	Legal. Since the source is immediate, the destination can be a memory reference. **MASM** interprets 10 to be a byte.
mov	10, bData	Illegal. Not one of the allowed formats. Notice that logically it does not make sense, either, since 10 is a constant. It has not been assigned an address and *bData* cannot be moved to a nonexistent location.
mov	es, 10	Illegal. Immediate data cannot be moved into a segment register.
mov	cs, ax	Illegal since **cs** cannot be the destination of a **mov** instruction.

The restrictions on the use of the segment registers may seem peculiar. But the point is that the segment registers are not intended for general computational purposes, and these restrictions afford some protection against their accidental (or deliberate) misuse. Recall that the microprocessor generally assumes that the **ds** register points to a data segment. If **ds** is changed is some rather arbitrary way, the microprocessor will still make this assumption, and pandemonium will ensue. Some of the restrictions on segment register usage do cause inconvenience on occasion. For example, one of the chores required of most programs is pointing **ds** to the data segment. The segment address of the data segment is available under the name @DATA (if certain standard Microsoft conventions are used) and so the appropriate instruction would seem to be

```
        mov       ds, @DATA
```

But there is a snag — **MASM** views the quantity @DATA as immediate data, and so this instruction is illegal. To circumvent this obstacle, it is necessary to replace this single instruction by two instructions, such as

```
        mov       ax, @DATA
        mov       ds, ax
```

The situation with **cs** is even more delicate. Since **cs** is dedicated to holding the segment part of the address of the current instruction, unscheduled changes in it are inevitably catastrophic. The value of **cs** should only be changed under special circumstances, such as during procedure calls, or when performing the assembly language version of a goto. The protection that is afforded here is to provide special instructions to perform these operations and to basically prohibit the changing of **cs** by any other means.

Only a small subset of the instruction set is needed in order to start writing interesting programs. We will present such a subset now, and these instructions, with a few additions, will suffice to get us through the early chapters.

SECTION 4 SOME ARITHMETIC INSTRUCTIONS

The most basic arithmetic functions are **add** and **sub** . As the names suggest, these perform addition and subtraction. They work with either 8-bit operands or 16-bit operands.

In Chapter 1 we showed that **add** works equally well whether its operands are interpreted as unsigned integers or as signed integers. **Sub** shares this very desirable feature.

One aspect of **add** and **sub** that can be puzzling is their treatment of overflow, and an example will illustrate this point. Suppose that **ah** contains the bit pattern 1111 1111 and the machine executes the instruction

```
        add       ah, ah
```

Exactly what happens? The processor performs addition bitwise, and so the process can be represented diagrammatically as follows:

```
        1111  1111
        1111  1111
      ──────────────
      1 1111  1110
```

The complete answer would require 9 bits of storage since it has a 1 in bit 8, which originates as a carry out of bit 7. Bit 8 contributes 256 to the answer and, since the machine works modulo 256 when doing 8-bit arithmetic, this bit is discarded. This answers the question about what happens: the addition is done as a straight binary addition, and the overflow into bit 8, if there is one, is ignored.

How should the answer be interpreted? This depends on whether the operands are viewed as unsigned or signed.

If the operands are given an unsigned interpretation, then the computation, in decimal, is

```
255 + 255 = 510
```

which gives an outcome that is certainly too big too fit in **ah**, even as an unsigned integer. (Remember that the 8-bit unsigned range is 0 to 255.) Consequently, the machine sets the carry flag to signal that an overflow occurs when the operation is given an unsigned interpretation.

If the operands are interpreted as signed, the equivalent decimal computation is

```
-1 + -1 = -2
```

and so no signed overflow occurs. Hence the machine does not set the overflow flag.

If the possibility of overflow is important in the program, the programmer will presumably have inserted error-checking code after the **add** instruction. If this is an unsigned computation, the carry flag should be checked; otherwise, the overflow flag. Not knowing which interpretation the programmer might make of the computation, the machine assigns the appropriate values to both flags.

It turns out that this example has basically given us the whole story on the carry flag, at least for addition. If there is a carry out of bit 7 in the 8-bit case (or out of bit 15 in the 16-bit case), then the carry flag is set. The situation for subtraction is identical, except that "carry out of" should be replaced by "borrow into."

As we will see, the exact rules that govern the setting of the overflow flag are more involved. We will discuss these rules in detail in Chapter 10, but luckily, under most normal circumstances, the programmer does not need to make any direct use of them.

Multiplication is more complicated than addition or subtraction since, even when using two's complement, it is not possible to interpret the same multiplication operation so that it works with both signed and unsigned operands. As an example to illustrate this point, consider the situation where the 8-bit quantity 1111 1111 is multiplied by itself to get a 16-bit answer. Direct binary multiplication gives

```
1111 1111 * 1111 1111 = 1111 1110 1111 1111
```

(Is there an easy way to verify this answer? Suggestion: 255 = 256 – 1.)

As an unsigned computation, this translates into decimal notation as

```
255 * 255 = 65025
```

On the other hand, if the operands are interpreted as signed, 1111 1111 is the 8-bit representation of –1, and so the corresponding result should be –1 * – 1 = +1 in decimal or, in binary,

```
1111 1111 * 1111 1111 = 0000 0000 0000 0001
```

Since the bit patterns of the answers are not identical, we conclude that multiplication must be done differently on signed and unsigned integers. The machine copes with this unpleasantness by providing separate unsigned and signed versions of multiplication, with different mnemonics for each: **mul** is used for unsigned multiplication and **imul** for signed multiplication. In the present chapter, we will only be concerned with unsigned multiplication.

Even after restricting ourselves to unsigned multiplication, there are still two sizes available. These are illustrated in the first part of Figure 3.2. The *16-bit multiplication* takes two 16-bit operands and multiplies them, recording the answer as a 32-bit integer. The syntax for this multiplication is

```
mul        Operand
```

where, as in all one-operand instructions, *Operand* can be either a register or memory reference, but cannot be immediate. For example,

```
mul        si
```

is a legal instruction but

```
mul        10
```

is not. To multiply by 10 requires a sequence such as

```
mov        si, 10
mul        si
```

When **mul** is used, only one of the factors to be multiplied is written as an operand. The 16-bit **mul** operation assumes that the other factor is contained in the **ax** register. This is a dedicated use of the **ax** register — the other operand *must* be in **ax**. The answer is recorded as a 32-bit integer with the low 16 bits in **ax** and the high 16 bits in **dx**. Again, there is no choice about the answer location. It overwrites the original value in **ax** and — this catches everyone from time to time — it also destroys whatever was in **dx**.

The other **mul** option is called *8-bit multiplication*. It works just like the 16-bit case except that this time two 8-bit quantities are multiplied to give a 16-bit answer. In this version the explicit operand must be an 8-bit register or memory reference, and the other factor is assumed to be in **al**. The answer is recorded as a 16-bit unsigned integer in **ax**.

Division suffers from the same difficulty as multiplication: it requires different machine operations in the unsigned and signed cases. Analogously to the preceding examples, the unsigned case is called **div** and the signed case is called **idiv**. We only need consider the **div** version at the moment.

Like **mul**, **div** has a 16-bit version and an 8-bit version, both of which are illustrated in the second half of Figure 3.2. In 16-bit multiplication, two 16-bit numbers are multiplied to

FIGURE 3.2 MULTIPLICATION AND DIVISION INSTRUCTIONS

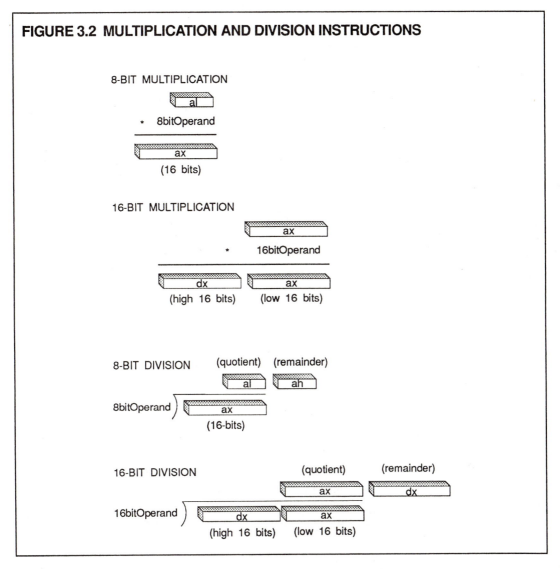

give a 32-bit answer. The division analog is to divide a 32-bit number by a 16-bit number to get a 16-bit quotient and a 16-bit remainder. This is precisely what *16-bit division* does. The syntax is

```
div     Operand
```

where again *Operand* is a 16-bit register or memory reference. The dividend (the numerator in the division) is assumed to be a 32-bit unsigned integer with its high 16 bits in **dx** and its low 16 bits in **ax**. This quantity is divided by *Operand*, and the answer is stored as a 16-bit unsigned integer in **ax** and the remainder as a 16-bit unsigned integer in **dx**.

Unfortunately, in division the sizes may not work out as one would like. In **mul**, if two 16-bit quantities are multiplied, the answer will always fit in 32 bits. (Why?) But if a 32-bit quantity is divided by a 16-bit quantity, the answer may not fit in 16 bits. What if 200000 is divided by 2, for example? When this situation occurs, the response of the machine is rather surprising. Surely, on the basis of our previous discussion, we would expect the machine to signal this kind of overflow by setting the carry flag. But this does not happen and, in fact, the carry flag is in an indeterminate state after a **div** operation. The machine deals with this kind of overflow by using a considerably more exotic mechanism, namely by executing a built-in program called an *exception handler*. Again, it is better to wait until later (Chapter 10) for a detailed discussion. For the moment, we will be content to point out that, when this situation arises, the program is immediately aborted with a curt "Divide Overflow" message.

8-bit division follows exactly the same pattern. The restrictions on the 8-bit operand are the same. The operand is divided into the number in **ax**, the answer is left as an 8-bit unsigned integer in **al**, and the remainder is left in **ah**.

Two other useful instructions are **inc** (meaning *increment* or add one to) and **dec** (*decrement* or subtract one from). These are one-operand instructions and satisfy the usual restrictions on the operand. In the case of **inc**, for example, the syntax is

```
inc      Operand
```

and *Operand* must be a register or memory reference (either 8- or 16-bit). It should be pointed out that **inc** and **dec** are not really essential.

```
add      Operand, 1
```

gives the same result as does

```
inc      Operand
```

(except that, as we will see, they affect the flags somewhat differently). The **inc** instruction is used mainly because it is slightly faster than **add** and, when its operand is a 16-bit register, generates only one byte of machine code.

The final arithmetic instruction needed in the early chapters is **cmp**, the compare instruction. **Cmp** is a two-operand instruction:

```
cmp      Operand1, Operand2
```

It modifies neither of its operands, but it does set the flags as though it had performed the subtraction:

```
Operand1 - Operand2
```

For example, if *Operand1* = *Operand2* the zero flag is set. If *Operand1* = 1 and *Operand2* = 2, the zero flag is cleared, the carry flag is set, and the overflow flag is cleared. It should be clear from the behavior of **cmp** that it is of no value by itself: it must be followed by some other instruction that performs an action based on the condition of the flags as set up by **cmp**. This point will be discussed further in Section 6.

SECTION 5 THE STACK MANIPULATION INSTRUCTIONS

As we stated in Chapter 2, the *stack* is a region of memory used to store temporary data during program execution. The stack is also called the *run-time stack* or the *hardware stack* to distinguish it from other stacks that the programmer may introduce in a program. Its importance can be guessed from the fact that, of the 14 available registers, two are dedicated to the stack (**ss** and **sp**) and a third (**bp**) is used primarily in dealing with it. The three main uses of the stack are to store return address information while procedures are executing, to store local variables that procedures may require, and to pass parameters to procedures.

A stack is always operated as a *last-in first-out (LIFO) store*. In other words, data are retrieved in the reverse order to which they were stored: the most recently stored item is removed first, and so on. Figure 3.3 is a representation of the stack as it is organized in the **8088** architecture.

Some significant features of the stack are

- The actual amount of memory allocated to the stack is under programmer control. In complicated programs, it can be difficult to decide on an efficient yet adequate size for the stack.

- The stack fills from high memory address to low memory address. Hence, if the phrase *top of the stack* refers to the most recent element added to the stack, as it normally does, and if the top of the stack is to be toward the top of the page, then memory diagrams must be drawn so that addresses increase toward the bottom of the page, which is our convention.

- Only word-size data items can be stored on or removed from the stack. Consequently, in a drawing of the stack it is reasonable to have each "memory cell" represent a word. In most other contexts, memory diagrams will be drawn with each cell representing a byte.

There are four instructions that directly manipulate the stack, but only two of these will be needed in our early programs. These have the expected names and functions:

```
        push       Operand
```

loads a copy of *Operand* onto the top of the stack, while

```
        pop        Operand
```

takes the top element from the stack and stores it in *Operand*. The **push** and **pop** instructions automatically do the right things to **sp**. When a push is performed, **sp** is decremented by two (because one word, or two bytes, has been added and the stack is growing toward low memory), and each **pop** causes **sp** to be incremented by two. *Operand* satisfies the usual

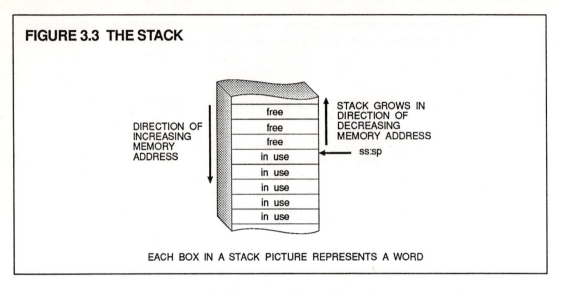

FIGURE 3.3 THE STACK

DIRECTION OF
INCREASING
MEMORY
ADDRESS

free
free
free
in use
in use
in use
in use
in use

STACK GROWS IN
DIRECTION OF
DECREASING
MEMORY ADDRESS

ss:sp

EACH BOX IN A STACK PICTURE REPRESENTS A WORD

restriction associated with one-operand instructions: it must be a register or memory reference. But in this case it must also have size one word.

As well as employing the stack in the standard contexts already mentioned, a programmer can use it casually in various ways. For example, rather than

```
mov     ax, bx
```

the programmer might use the sequence

```
push    bx
pop     ax
```

which has exactly the same effect. There is no good reason to do this since, as the reader can readily verify from a table of instruction times, the **push/pop** sequence is much slower than the **mov** instruction. A more realistic example occurs in moving one segment register to another, say **ds** to **es**. Since direct segment register-to-segment register moves are illegal, a sequence such as

```
mov     ax, ds
mov     es, ax
```

is required. This can be replaced by

```
push    ds
pop     es
```

Again, looking at the timings will show that the second sequence is slower than the first. But another significant point is that the first method involves using a third register, **ax** in our example, and at various points in a program all the registers may be in use. If this were the case, using the first method would require temporarily saving the contents of some register (**ax** would be as good as any) and then restoring it afterwards. The easiest place to store **ax** is on the stack, and so the code sequence would be

```
push    ax
mov     ax, ds
mov     es, ax
pop     ax
```

Under these circumstances, the **push/pop** method looks very attractive indeed.

Exercise 3-5. Suppose that *wData1* and *wData2* are word-size memory variables and that *bData* is a byte-size memory variable. Which of these instructions are legal and which are illegal? Give reasons.

```
a.    mov     wData1, bData
b.    mov     wData1, wData2
c.    mov     wData1, cx
d.    mov     wData1, cs
e.    push    cs
f.    push    wData2
g.    push    bData
h.    push    10
i.    pop     cs
j.    mov     bData, −10
k.    mov     wData, −10
l.    mov     wData, 100000
m.    mov     cs, bl
n.    mov     cs, bx
o.    dec     bData
p.    inc     ax, 2
```

Exercise 3-6. Suppose that *wData1*, *wData2*, *wData3*, ⋯ , *wData10* are one-word memory variables, and we want to assign the present value of *wData1* to wData2, the present value of *wData2* to *wData3*, and so on, and finally assign the present value of *wData10* to *wData1*.
a. Write a sequence of **mov** instructions that will accomplish this.
b. Do the same thing with pushes and pops.

SECTION 6 SOME BASIC PROGRAM CONTROL INSTRUCTIONS

The **8088** normally operates by executing an instruction, then the next in line, then the next, and so on. But there are many times when the instructions should be executed in some different order. Examples: when executing any kind of loop construct, control should jump from the bottom of the loop back to the top (at least some of the time); when a procedure is called, control should transfer to the first instruction of the procedure; when a goto is encountered control should transfer to the target address.

Generically, the instructions that cause a jump in the execution sequence are called *program control instructions*. There are many of these available, although they fall into just a few different categories.

The first of the program control instructions that we will consider is **jmp**, the *unconditional jump* instruction. The form of the instruction is

```
jmp        Target
```

There are several allowed forms for *Target*, but at the moment we need only consider the case where *Target* is a labeled location in the code segment. In our early examples, *Target* will be a label in the sense that labels were introduced earlier in this chapter. The **jmp** instruction is just the assembly language analog of goto. It is called an unconditional jump because the jump is taken under all circumstances.

There are many instructions in assembly language that behave similarly, except that they execute the jump only if some particular condition is true. For this reason, these are called *conditional jumps*. An example of a conditional jump is

```
je        shortTarget
```

The mnemonic **je** is a contraction of *jump if equal* and produces a jump to the destination *shortTarget*, provided some pair of quantities are equal. In practice, **je** nearly always occurs in some context like this:

```
cmp        Op1, Op2
je         Somewhere
```

In this case the jump will be taken if $Op1 = Op2$. Recalling that **cmp** records its results by setting the flags, it becomes clear how **je** *really* works. If the zero flag is set, indicating that the most recent arithmetic operation gave zero as answer, then the jump occurs. Otherwise, it does not. This means that **je** can be used in other situations, for instance

```
add        ax, 0
je         axEquals0
```

As the name of the label suggests, the jump will occur only if the value of ax is 0. (It is hard to imagine actually using these two lines of code in a program — they are only intended to illustrate a point.)

There are 17 different conditional jump instructions, some of which are known by more than one name. As well as **je**, we will need these other conditional jumps in our early chapters:

jne   Jump if not equal; the jump occurs if the operands were not equal
           in the most recent **cmp**.

jge   Jump if greater than or equal to; the jump occurs if the most recent **cmp** showed the first operand to be greater than or equal to the second, when interpreted as signed integers.

jg   Same but with *greater than* instead of *greater than or equal to*.

jle   Same but with *less than or equal to*.

jl   Same but with *less than*.

Of course, just as with **je**, these instructions are not really bound to the **cmp** instruction. They base their decisions on the state of the flags. For example, a **jg** conditional jump will be taken when the carry flag and the overflow flag are either both set or both cleared.

There is one additional aspect of the conditional jumps that must be considered. The careful reader may have noticed that in the case of **jmp** the name *Target* was used to represent the destination, while in the case of **je** the name *shortTarget* was used. These names were chosen to emphasize a restriction imposed on the conditional jumps, namely that a conditional jump cannot have a target that is further ahead in the code than 127 bytes or further back than 128 bytes.

This restriction arises for the following reason. When an instruction such as

```
je        shortTarget
```

is translated into machine code, *shortTarget* is stored as a *distance to be jumped*, or *offset*, from the present location in the code, and this distance is stored as a signed integer in one byte. Hence the range of allowable distances is −128 to +127.

The situation with the **jmp** instruction is more complicated. When an instruction such as

```
jmp       Target
```

is encountered, *Target* is interpreted in a number of different ways, depending on its form. In the case that presently interests us, namely

```
jmp       Label
```

Label is again stored as an offset, but, if necessary, it will be stored as a two-byte signed integer. Hence **jmp** can jump over comparatively large distances.

The short range of conditional jumps is certainly one of the annoyances of the **8088** architecture. The method used to overcome this limitation is direct, though tedious. First of all, programmers do not count bytes of code to find out whether a conditional jump is *out of range*, to use **MASM**'s terminology. Rather, the code is written, ignoring the range restriction, and is repaired if the assembler reports an out-of-range error. The repair runs as follows. Suppose the code contains a sequence like this:

```
je        Dest

      .
      .   (more than 127 bytes of code here)
      .

Dest:
```

After the assembler objects, replace this section of code by

```
jne        madeUpLabel
jmp        Dest

madeUpLabel:
    .
    .        (more than 127 bytes of code here)
    .
    .
Dest:
```

Note that, functionally, this code behaves exactly as before. The difference is that now the conditional jump is over a very short distance and the long distance is covered by a **jmp**. This process is called *jumping over a jump* and can be summarized as follows:

- To repair a conditional jump out-of-range error, replace the conditional jump by three lines of code. The first line is the conditional jump with the logic reversed and has as target a new label, say *madeUpLabel*. The second line is a **jmp** to the original destination. The third line is the defining line for *madeUpLabel*, i.e., consists of the name *madeUpLabel* followed by a ':'.

The basic looping instruction in this language is, reasonably enough, called **loop**. The general format used in **loop** is

```
;initialize cx here

shortLabel:

    .
    .        (code constituting body of loop)
    .
    .
    loop        shortLabel
```

The name *ShortLabel* is used for the same reason that *shortJump* was used earlier: it indicates that the entire extent of the code in the loop cannot be longer than 127 bytes. The **cx** register must be used as the loop counter. It is initialized before the start of the loop (before *shortLabel*). Each time control reaches the line containing the **loop** instruction, **cx** is *automatically decremented by the microprocessor* and the new value of **cx** compared with 0. If the new **cx** value is not equal to 0, control returns to the *shortLabel* line and the loop is traversed again. If **cx** = 0, control "falls through" the loop instruction and execution moves on.

It follows from this description that if **cx** is initialized to a positive integer n, then the loop code will execute exactly n times.

Here is a trivial example:

```
mov        ax, 0
mov        cx, 10
```

```
loopLabel:

    inc     ax
    loop    loopLabel
```

It should be clear that, after this loop terminates, **ax** will have the value 10 and **cx** will have the value 0.

Now comes a sticky point. Suppose that, in the previous example, **cx** had been initialized to 0 rather than 10. Reasonably, the loop should then be traversed 0 times, i.e., not at all. That is, control should immediately fall through the loop. But a quick review of our description of the loop instruction shows that **cx** is always decremented *first* and then checked for equality with 0. This means that if **cx** starts at 0, it is decremented to −1 before it is checked for the first time. More precisely, the loop counter is treated as an unsigned integer by the machine and so, when decremented, the new bit pattern

```
1111 1111 1111 1111
```

is interpreted as 65535. This means that initializing **cx** to 0 causes a lot of iterations of the loop — 65536 to be exact!

This rather undesirable behavior can arise in at least two ways. First, if the initialization of **cx** is forgotten, it will contain some arbitrary value, and a higher than expected proportion of arbitrary values found in a computer are equal to 0. Second, this may be a loop that is supposed to execute a variable number of times, depending on other circumstances, and zero times may be one of the allowed alternatives. For example, in changing a lowercase string to uppercase, a reasonable approach is to set up a loop that processes one character during each traverse. But such a conversion really should work correctly with the empty string as input.

The use of the loop instruction is sufficiently prevalent, and the **cx** = 0 case comes up often enough, that there is a special instruction whose primary use is to circumvent this problem. The instruction in question is

```
    jcxz    shortTarget
```

It is another conditional jump, and, as the name indicates, jumps only if the **cx** register has value 0. Its use is to "jump over" the loop in those cases where **cx** is zero. Now we rewrite our previous example as

```
        mov     ax, 0
        jcxz    endOfLoop

loopLabel:

        inc     ax
        loop    loopLabel

endOfLoop:
```

This fragment of code will do the reasonable thing for any value of **cx**, 0 or not.

The last pair of control instructions that we need are **call** and **ret**. The **call** instruction, like **jmp,** offers many options but, for now, we need only a limited version of the instruction. We will use it in the form

```
call      procName
```

where *procName* is the name of some assembly language procedure. **Call** causes control to transfer to the first instruction in *procName* so that the procedure code starts executing. At the end of *procName*, control should transfer to the point in the calling program immediately beyond the **call** instruction, and this transfer is accomplished by using **ret** (the *return* instruction) as the last instruction in *procName*.

In a nutshell, here is how **call** and **ret** work:

- The **call** instruction pushes the current **cs** and **ip** onto the stack and replaces the values of **cs** and **ip** by a pair of values that point to the code for *procName*.

- The **ret** instruction pops the old **cs** and **ip** off the stack and into the **cs** and **ip** registers.

(This oversimplification ignores the distinction between calls to "far procedures" in which both **cs** and **ip** are changed and calls to "near procedures" in which only **ip** is changed.)

Exercise 3-7. Suppose that *wData1*, *wData2*, *wData3*, and *wData4* are one-word memory variables whose values are interpreted as signed integers. Write a fragment of assembly language code that will put the maximum of these four values into the **ax** register.

Exercise 3-8. Write a code fragment that looks for a factor of the number 31481. If it finds a proper factor (i. e., a factor other than 1 or 31481), it leaves it in **ax**. If it does not, it leaves 0 in **ax**.
Suggestion: Use a loop and try dividing 31481 by 2, 3, 4, ⋯ , stopping as soon as one of these divisions gives remainder 0, because you have then found a factor. If 31481 is reached before the remainder is zero, then there is no proper factor.
Further suggestion: It is not necessary to go nearly as far as 31481 before stopping. If you have not found a factor by the time you have reached the square root of 31481, you never will. (Why not?)

Exercise 3-9. Write a code fragment that translates this pseudocode into assembly language:

```
ax = 0
for (i = 1 to 10, step 1)
     for (j = 1 to 10, step 1)
          add 1 to ax
```

Note that this is a nested double loop. There are various ways of implementing a double loop in assembly language, but this problem is to be done using the **loop** instruction in both the inner and the outer loops. The difficulty with this approach is, of course, that both loops

the outer-loop value of **cx** by pushing it onto the stack before entering the inner loop and popping it after exiting the inner loop.

Exercise 3-10. Let *wData1* and *wData2* be two one-word memory variables. Write a code fragment that leaves a 1 in **ax** if the first variable is greater than or equal to the second and leaves a 0 in **ax** otherwise. Do this by two methods:

a. Write the code in the most direct possible manner.

b. Rewrite it where this time one of the alternatives is assumed to be true at the beginning and the corresponding value is placed in **ax**. Then include code to check the correctness of this assumption. If the assumption is correct, nothing more need be done; if not, fix the value in **ax**.

c. Compare the solutions. (b) should be shorter than (a).

Here is a good rule to remember in assembly language programming:

- If a computation has two possible outcomes, a few lines of code can usually be saved by assuming at the start that one of the outcomes is the right one and then correcting this assumption if necessary.

SECTION 7 THE INTERRUPT INSTRUCTION

Many computer operations require prodigious amounts of programming. This is especially true of those operations that interface the computer with hardware devices such as the keyboard, the screen, and especially the disk drives. Luckily, under most circumstances, it is not necessary to write routines to perform these interfacing tasks. They already exist as part of a large collection of procedures, which are built into the machine and readily accessible to the assembly language programmer.

As we saw in Chapter 2, these prewritten procedures come from two sources. Some, which are usually quite specific to the computer hardware, are part of the ROM BIOS. Others arrive with the operating system. The operating system routines are more generic than the ROM BIOS routines. This means that they are written in a way that is somewhat independent of the hardware and so (ideally) will function on a variety of machines. They have the additional advantage that they can be changed easily — for the price of a new **DOS** version.

The ROM BIOS and **DOS** resources are accessed by the mechanism of *software interrupts*. Software interrupts will be discussed in detail at the proper time, but for the moment it is sufficient to know that a software interrupt is very much like a procedure call, except that the procedure that is being called is usually part of the ROM BIOS or part of **DOS**. Certain conventions must be observed in calling these routines but, for the most part, their precise structure can safely remain opaque to us.

The software interrupts are given integer numbers, usually but not always written in hexadecimal. To call a given interrupt routine, the appropriate instruction is

```
int     XXH
```

where "XX" is the number of the interrupt routine and the trailing 'H' is supplied to tell **MASM** that "XX" is a hex number. For example, the instruction

```
int       10H
```

activates interrupt number 10H (the *video routine*) while

```
int       23H
```

triggers interrupt number 23H (the *control break handler*).

Another example of in interrupt instruction, namely **int 20H**, appeared in our machine language program of Section 2. This particular interrupt invokes operating system code to terminate an executing program. (We will see later that **int 20H** is actually a somewhat archaic method of program termination, and will not use it in the sequel.)

A sampling of the available interrupts is given in Appendix 2. In principle, the **IBM-XT** can support 256 different interrupts, with numbers 00H through 255H, but most of these numbers are not assigned to active interrupts. In Chapter 15, we will show how to augment the existing software interrupts by writing procedures that are installed in memory and accessed through the interrupt mechanism. Of the interrupts that are in use in the standard **IBM-XT** configuration, the code for those interrupts with numbers less than 20H are in the ROM BIOS, and the code for those with numbers 20H or greater are supplied with **MS-DOS**.

By far the most frequently used interrupt is **int 21H,** which is called the *DOS function dispatcher*. It controls a treasure house of functions, which the programmer can use for almost every conceivable programming purpose: to read from the keyboard, to write to the screen, to write to the printer, to read or write or do almost anything else to disk files, to work with disk directories, to find or set the system time or date, and on and on and on. Every version of **DOS** has more functions available than did the previous one. At this point, the reader might profitably spend a few minutes browsing through the partial list of **int 21H** functions given in Appendix 3.

There is a little more involved in accessing the **int 21H** functions than we have stated so far. To begin with, **int 21H** must be told which function is being requested. This information is transmitted by placing the function number in the **ah** register. Depending on the function being used, other information may be needed. For example, suppose that the letter 'A' is to be printed to the screen. Appendix 3 shows that **function 02H** of **int 21H** will perform that task. But **int 21H** must also be told which letter to print and the description says that the ASCII code for the character to be printed must be placed in the **dl** register. **MASM** accepts the name of a character in single quotes as a synonym for its ASCII code, hence these three lines of code are sufficient:

```
mov       dl, 'A'
mov       ah, 02h
int       21h
```

Since the ASCII code for 'A' is 41H, these three instructions are identical with the first three instructions in our machine language program in Section 2, and so we have incidentally explained the essential part of that program.

Exercise 3-11. In Section 4, we remarked that the rules governing the setting of the overflow flag are fairly complicated. Attempt to discover these rules by using the following approach. Do a number of examples of adding and subtracting various combinations of 8-bit signed integers, some with sign bit 1 and some with sign bit 0. In each case, it will be clear from the answer (computed by hand) whether or not the overflow flag should be set. Try to correlate this knowledge with carries into and out of bit 7. The answer to this exercise can be found in Chapter 10.

Exercise 3-12. Although the manipulations is Exercise 3-4 may have seemed somewhat mysterious at the time, you are now in a position to understand them completely. Study your solution to that exercise in light of the material contained in Sections 6 and 7. It should now be clear that the suggested solution is just a machine language implementation of a simple loop controlled by the **loop** instruction.

INTRODUCTION TO MASM AND CODEVIEW

SECTION 1 PREVIEW

Different versions of **MASM** (the Microsoft Macro Assembler) have been released over the years, with each version offering increased speed and more features than the previous ones. Version 5.0 incorporates substantial improvements over earlier versions in a number of areas, two of which are important to us at this point.

First, it allows assembly language programs to be written using what are known as *simplified segment directives*. The result is that many of the technicalities associated with setting up the segment structure of a program can be ignored. The source code need only contain a few, easy-to-remember overhead lines. Based on these lines, **MASM** chooses reasonable default values for the segment parameters.

Of course, the knowledgeable programmer must completely understand the segment organization of programs, and consequently the traditional segment directives will be introduced later in the book. We chose to start with the simplified directives so that the writing of actual programs could begin as soon as possible.

The other great improvement that arrived with Version 5 of **MASM** is **CODEVIEW**, a sophisticated and comparatively easy-to-use debugger. It is our absolute belief that assembly language can be learned thoroughly in only two ways: either by studying it diligently for several years without a debugger or by studying it diligently for several months with a good debugger.

This belief strongly influences the text from this point on. **CODEVIEW** is introduced on an almost equal footing with **MASM**. Even the simplest programs are run through **CODEVIEW** to gain familiarity with its controls. Many examples are given to illustrate its powers (and its quirks).

Section 2 of this chapter contains an introduction to the simplified segment directives. The later sections of the chapter are made up of a series of sample programs of increasing difficulty. Each program is analyzed syntactically, then processed by **MASM** and turned into an executable program, and finally its execution is examined using **CODEVIEW**.

SECTION 2 FORMAT OF THE SOURCE FILE

MASM allows a great deal of flexibility in the format of its input since it is case insensitive (i.e., does not distinguish between uppercase and lowercase letters) and since it permits the copious use of white space (spaces, tabs, carriage returns, linefeeds, and formfeeds). A skillful programmer uses this freedom to make the source code more readable. In general, code with a generous amount of white space is more pleasant to read, and judicious use of uppercase letters can make selected items stand out. There are almost as many formatting systems in use as there are assembly language programmers. Certainly, the most important thing is to adopt a scheme that seems reasonable and use it *consistently*. In this book, we will make various formatting suggestions as we proceed and will use them throughout.

Every source file submitted to **MASM** should contain a number of overhead lines, which **MASM** uses to control various technical aspects of the program. Figure 4.1 shows these basic overhead lines. We will soon give a preliminary discussion of Figure 4.1, but a complete understanding will not come until later in the book. For the moment, it is best to memorize this template and incorporate the appropriate parts of it into each source file.

In general, an assembly language source file contains two kinds of instructions: some intended for the assembler and others that will be executed by the microprocessor. The instructions that are meant for the assembler are called *directives* or *pseudo-operations* (*pseudo-ops*) and convey information on how the assembly process should be conducted. For example, directives are used to tell the assembler what names to use for various segments and to mark the location in the input file at which code execution should begin. We will always use uppercase letters for directives. By contrast, lowercase will be used for actual machine instructions. In Figure 4.1, **DOSSEG** is a pseudo-op, while

```
        mov     ds, ax
```

will be recognized as a machine instruction.

Source files also contain user-defined names. Our convention here will be to use uppercase for the first letter and lowercase for the remaining letters of single-word identifiers. As an example, in Figure 4.1, Start is a user-defined name. The colon following it shows that it is a label for a location in the code. Sometimes it is convenient to use a name that consists of more than one word. For instance, a program that deals with the sizes of several files might use a variable called *first file size*. Since **MASM** does not allow embedded

---

FIGURE 4.1 THE BASIC OVERHEAD LINES

```
TITLE     progName.asm

DOSSEG
.MODEL SMALL

.STACK         100H

.DATA

     (data go here)

.CODE

Start:

     mov     ax, @DATA
     mov      ds, ax

     (code goes here)

     mov     ah, 4ch
     int     21h

END    Start
```

---

spaces in names, this would have to be written *firstfilesize*, but looks much less clumsy and is easier to read if written *firstFileSize*. We will use uppercase in this way for multi-word identifiers.

Here is the general significance of the directives and instructions in Figure 4.1:

The **TITLE** line is optional, but we will always include it, using a name that is appropriate for the program. It is a directive to **MASM** and so has been written in caps. Although it is not mandatory, most programmers use the disk filename as the title. Incidentally, **MASM** requires that the filename of its input file have extension .ASM. As one of its many services, **MASM** prints a very informative listing of the input file after it has been assembled. This is called a listing file and is nicely formatted, with each page heading containing the name that was supplied in the **TITLE** directive.

When different assembly language modules or modules written in different languages are combined, they must use segments that are compatible in terms of names and other properties that we will discuss later. Microsoft has established default values for segment names and for these other properties. Using the **DOSSEG** directive in a source file instructs **MASM** to use these defaults. This is by far the easiest way of handling the segment structure of a program.

In an assembly language program, the code and data can each reside in a single segment or span several segments. The **.MODEL** directive informs **MASM** whether the program will use multiple code and/or data segments. For example,

```
.MODEL SMALL
```

tells the assembler to allow one segment for code and one (different) segment for data.

The directive

```
.STACK      100h
```

informs **MASM** that the program should be allocated a stack of size 100H bytes.

The directive **.DATA** announces the beginning of the data segment. In the next section, we will discuss how data are declared in assembly language. One feature of the simplified directives is that the end of a segment need not be flagged explicitly. The segment is understood to continue until either another segment begins or until the **END** directive (discussed subsequently) is reached.

The directive **.CODE** shows the beginning of the code segment.

As mentioned earlier, *Start* is a label for a location in the code segment. Its function is to mark the point where program execution should begin, and the information that *Start* is the *program entry point* is relayed to **MASM** by its appearance in the directive

```
END         Start
```

This line has another purpose, which is rather obvious: it contains the **END** directive and so notifies **MASM** that this is the end of the input file.

When execution begins, the **ds** register should be initialized to point to the data segment. **@DATA** denotes the segment address of the data segment, and the lines

```
mov       ax, @DATA
mov       ds, ax
```

serve to initialize **ds** to the value **@DATA**.

Finally, consider the lines

```
mov       ah, 4ch
int       21h
```

We know that they contain a call to **function 4CH** of **int 21H**, the **DOS** function dispatcher. From Appendix 3, **function 4CH** terminates a program. A special function is called at program termination in order to finish the program in an orderly way, i.e., to do various housekeeping chores such as closing files and, most importantly, to return control to the operating system.

SECTION 3 A SIMPLE EXAMPLE USING MASM AND CODEVIEW

We will now write our first, rather trivial program and process it with **MASM** and **LINK**. The program is given in Figure 4.2. Nearly all the lines in this program should make sense on the basis of the previous section and Chapter 3.

FIGURE 4.2 A SIMPLE PROGRAM

```
TITLE     Prog4.1.asm

DOSSEG                          ;use Microsoft default segment conventions
.MODEL SMALL                    ;the SMALL MODEL allows one code segment
                                ;  and (at most) one data segment
.STACK 100h                     ;sets the size of the stack

.CODE

Start:                          ;this label is used with the END directive
                                ;  below and so indicate where execution
                                ;     begins
        mov     cx, 1
        mov     ax, 0

There:

        add     ax, cx
        inc     cx
        cmp     cx, 3
        jle     There

        mov     ah, 4ch ;function 4ch of int 21h
        int     21h     ;  terminates a program

    END Start                   ;Start label is program entry point
```

Recall that **MASM** ignores all text from the first semicolon on a line to the end of that line and so the semicolon and linefeed character serve as comment delimiters. We have included a few comments that serve to review our early discussions and have introduced a minor but useful convention relating to comments: if a comment spans more than one line, the text on each line of the comment should be indented a couple of spaces more than the previous line. This gives a nice visual cue that the comment is being continued.

Since this program contains no data, it needs no data segment, and consequently it is not necessary to initialize **ds**. As a matter of fact, the program does not use a stack either. But, as we pointed out in Chapter 2, various background processes called hardware interrupts can occur while a program is executing. Often, these interrupting programs will make use of the stack belonging to the interrupted program. In addition, the **CODEVIEW** debugger uses some space from the stack of the program that is being analyzed. For these reasons, we have included a stack with this program and will do so with every program.

We will now look quickly at the logic of the program. It uses only instructions from the subset introduced in Chapter 3. In this program, the **jle** refers to the result of the **cmp** on the previous line: if **ax** is less than or equal to 3, then the jump occurs; otherwise, control falls through the **jle** instruction and the program terminates. Here is the sequence of events when the program runs:

- **cx** is initialized to 1 and **ax** to 0.

- On each traverse of the loop, the value of **cx** is added to **ax**, **cx** is incremented, and the new value of **cx** is compared with 3.

- As soon as **cx** fails to be less than or equal to 3, the loop terminates.

Consequently, the loop is traversed 3 times, **ax** receives the final value $1 + 2 + 3 = 6$, and **cx** has final value 4.

We will soon process PROG4_1.ASM so that it can actually be run. Of course, running this program is not terribly interesting since it produces no visible output — it just leaves its answer in the **ax** register. To understand the program better, we will follow its execution using **CODEVIEW**.

Before doing this, we must convert PROG4_1 into an executable file, which is a two-step process.

First, PROG4_1.ASM is processed by **MASM**, which completes the assembly process, producing as its output an *object file*, having the default name PROG4_1.OBJ. Object files contain the machine language translation of the source code, although not quite in its final form. They are used because it is often convenient to combine different assembly modules, or even modules written in different languages, to produce a single executable file. Each of the source modules is first converted to object file format, which contains the machine code and extra overhead information required for *linking* the different modules into a single program.

Next, PROG4_1.OBJ is submitted to a utility named **LINK** in order to produce the final executable file, which has default name PROG4_1.EXE. In more complicated cases, **LINK** will be called upon to combine several .OBJ files to produce the final executable program. We will see many examples of this kind later in the book.

Figure 4.3 illustrates this two-step process of building a program.

Both **MASM** and **LINK** provide a bewildering array of options, a number of which will be useful in later chapters. But, for the moment, only a minimal invocation of these utilities is needed.

An appropriate command line to use for invoking **MASM** is

```
masm /zi /z /w2 /Mx prog4_1,,,;
```

Although **MASM** requires that its input file have extension .ASM, it does not require that this extension be explicitly written on the command line. /zi, /z, /w2, and /Mx are command line options that activate some of **MASM**'s special features:

- /zi instructs **MASM** to generate the line-number information needed by **CODEVIEW**.

- /z causes **MASM** to emit complete error messages.

- /w2 triggers **MASM**'s strictest error checking. When the w2 flag is set, MASM not only notifies the user of all serious errors, but also issues "advisory warnings" that pinpoint potential trouble spots in the code. *The w2 flag should always be used and the underlying cause of every warning should be found and repaired.*

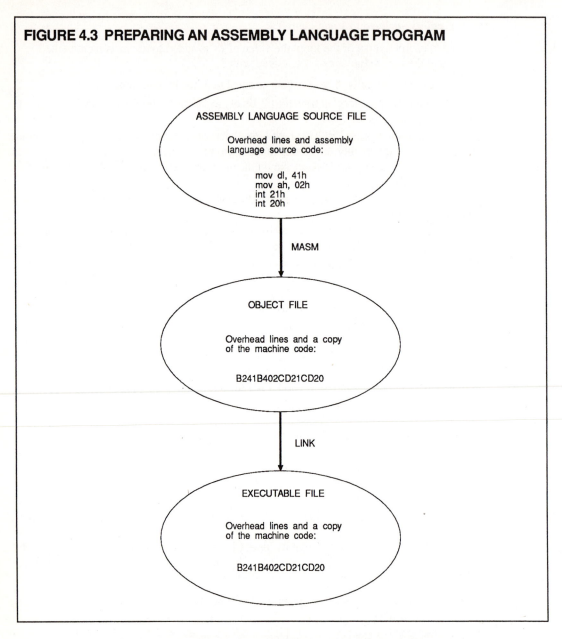

FIGURE 4.3 PREPARING AN ASSEMBLY LANGUAGE PROGRAM

ASSEMBLY LANGUAGE SOURCE FILE

Overhead lines and assembly
language source code:

mov dl, 41h
mov ah, 02h
int 21h
int 20h

MASM

OBJECT FILE

Overhead lines and a copy
of the machine code:

B241B402CD21CD20

LINK

EXECUTABLE FILE

Overhead lines and a copy
of the machine code:

B241B402CD21CD20

- By default, **MASM** converts identifiers to uppercase. The /Mx flag overrides this default and causes **MASM** to retain the case of external variables (defined later). Although this flag is not important in this program, it can be vital when assembly language is mixed with the code from a high-level language that is case sensitive. (**C** is such a language.) Consequently, it is a good idea to build it into our batch files.

Using the optional commas and semicolon causes **MASM** to build two information files, a *listing file* (*.LST file*) and a *cross reference file* (*.CRF file*), and to assign default names to these files rather than prompting the user to supply filenames. As we will see, the listing file is an essential adjunct to serious assembly language programming. The cross reference file is of less significance. (The .CRF file that **MASM** generates is a binary file. To be made intelligible, it must be further processed by the **CREF** utility. For details, we refer the reader to the **MASM** documentation.)

Similarly, a reasonable command line for **LINK** is:

```
link /co prog4_1,,,;
```

The explanations here are similar to those just given; the **/co** command-line switch is needed to generate **CODEVIEW** information.

Typing each of these lines for every program becomes tedious and so the **MS-DOS** batch-file language should be used to automate the process. The Program Disk that accompanies this book contains a batch file named AL.BAT (for *assemble and link*) consisting of these lines:

```
masm /zi /z /w2 /Mx %1,,,;
if errorlevel 1 goto stop
link /co %1,,;
:stop
```

Since the **MS-DOS** batch-file language is peripheral to our concerns, we leave it to the interested ready to pursue it in any of the standard sources. We will be content to present a few ready-made batch files that are adequate for our needs.

If this batch file is in the working directory or on the **PATH**, then the assembly and linking process requires typing only the single line

```
al prog4_1
```

After assembly and linking, PROG4_1 can be run by typing its name at the **DOS** prompt. As expected, nothing perceptible happens — control instantly returns to **DOS**. It is a much more instructive exercise to examine the program execution using **CODEVIEW**. **CODEVIEW** can be invoked and made to load program PROG4_1 by typing the command line

```
cv prog4_1
```

At that point, **CODEVIEW** displays a screen similar to the one in Figure 4.4.

We will now digress to discuss some elementary features of **CODEVIEW**. It is inappropriate for us to try to rewrite the **CODEVIEW** manual here, especially since that manual is quite complete and since **CODEVIEW** has extensive on-line help available. We will be content to introduce the most elementary commands in the next few sections, and from time to time in later chapters to explore some of its more exotic features, which are perhaps not so obvious from the descriptions in the manual.

FIGURE 4.4 THE CODEVIEW SCREEN

```
#File  View  Search  Run  Watch  Options  Language  Calls  Help # F8=Trace F5=Go
############################### prog4_1.ASM ###################################
1:        TITLE      Prog5_1.asm                                   # AX = 0000
2:                                                                 # BX = 0000
3:        DOSSEG               ;use MS segment order/name conventions # CX = 0000
4:        .MODEL SMALL         ;the SMALL MODEL allows one code segment # DX = 0000
5:                             ;  and (at most) one data segment    # SP = 0100
6:        .STACK 100h                                               # BP = 0000
7:                                                                  # SI = 0000
8:        .CODE                                                     # DI = 0000
9:                                                                  # DS = 5696
10:       Start:               ;this label is used with the END directive# ES = 5696
11:                            ;  below to indicate where execution begin# SS = 56A9
12:                                                                 # CS = 56A6
13:                   mov    cx, 1                                  # IP = 0010
14:                   mov    ax, 0                                  #
15:                                                                 #   NV UP
16:       There:                                                    #   EI PL
17:                                                                 #   NZ NA
18:                   add    ax, cx                                 #   PO NC
###############################################################################
Microsoft (R) CodeView (R)  Version 2.2                           #
(C) Copyright Microsoft Corp. 1986-1988.  All rights reserved.    #
>                                                                  #
>                                                                  #
```

Figure 4.4 is a representation of the **CODEVIEW** screen. The source code is displayed in the main window, and the values of the registers are shown on the right. The next instruction to be executed is either highlighted or in a different color, depending on the type of video display being used. In the illustrations in this book, the next instruction will always be shown in boldface. The **NV, UP, ···** at the bottom of the register display gives the state of the flags. (Compare with Figure 2.6.) The window at the bottom of the screen is the *dialog window*, used for entering commands from the keyboard. Various menus are available, as shown at the top of the screen. Holding the alternate key down while pressing the first letter in a menu name causes that menu to pop up. **CODEVIEW** actually presents three user interfaces: pop-up menus, a mouse, and the keyboard, which uses the dialog window. We nearly always use the keyboard interface. Although this is partly prejudice, many of the commands have powerful options that are only available in dialog versions. Instructions for using the mouse and menu variants can be found in the manual or on the help screens.

Here are some basic **CODEVIEW** commands:

F1 (i.e., function key F1) Entry point to the **CODEVIEW** help system. Within the help system, it is possible to navigate from page to page using 'n' or 'p', or to get out using 'c' or the escape key.

F2 Sometimes the register window hides the ends of long lines of code or comments, and sometimes it is just a distraction. F2 toggles the register window on and off.

F3 As well as the *source mode* shown in Figure 4.4, **CODEVIEW** has a *mixed mode*, which shows source code together with assembled code, and an *assembly mode*, which shows only the assembled code. F3 toggles between these alternatives. Figure 4.5 shows our program in assembly mode.

F4 Output generated by the program is sent to a different screen (actually to a different page of video memory). Generally, when output occurs, the screen switches automatically to this output screen. F4 toggles between the screens. Of course, this is of no importance in the present program and is mentioned only to prevent the mystification that could result from accidentally hitting F4!

F5 Makes the program execute. The execution can be modified by inserting "breakpoints" or "tracepoints." The dialog command 'g' (for *go*) has the same effect as F5.

F6 Toggles the cursor between the main window and the dialog window. Commands can still be typed in the dialog window even if the cursor is in the main window. However, only the window that currently shows the cursor can be scrolled.

F8 Causes the microprocessor to *single step* — execute a single instruction and stop.

L (*load*) Loads a new copy of the program being debugged, and is used to restart the debugging process from the beginning. The newly loaded file is displayed starting at its first line, so that the display generally shows the beginning of the data segment. As we will see, this makes it convenient to set up watch windows.

. (*display current instruction*) Repositions the display so that the next instruction to be executed is shown (highlighted) on the screen. This command is useful if the current instruction line has scrolled off the screen.

q (*quit*) Exits **CODEVIEW** and returns to **DOS**.

Now is a good time to try out some of the preceding commands. Although the opportunities offered by the present tiny program are somewhat limited, it is interesting to single-step through it, observing the values in the registers after each instruction. The initial form of the **CODEVIEW** screen is depicted in Figure 4.4. Line 13 is highlighted, indicating that this is the program entry point, i.e., the first instruction to be executed. To single-step through the program, use the F8 key repeatedly, noticing how the **ax** and **cx** registers are changing, as directed by the instructions in the code, and watching how the **ip** register is updated automatically to match the offset of the current instruction.

It is also a good idea to study the assembly listing as given in Figure 4.5. The information seen on the far left of the screen is the location of each instruction in the standard *segment:offset* format. Of course, the segment value will vary from machine to machine since the address at which the code is loaded into memory depends on the exact machine configuration. After the address, the machine code for the instruction is displayed. This information is generally not of interest in everyday assembly language programming, and

FIGURE 4.5 CODEVIEW IN ASSEMBLY MODE

```
#File  View  Search  Run  Watch  Options  Language  Calls  Help # F8=Trace F5=Go
############################## prog4_1.ASM ##################################
START:                                                          # AX = 0000
56A6:0010 B90100            MOV       CX,0001                   # BX = 0000
56A6:0013 B80000            MOV       AX,0000                   # CX = 0000
THERE:                                                          # DX = 0000
56A6:0016 03C1              ADD       AX,CX                     # SP = 0100
56A6:0018 41                INC       CX                        # BP = 0000
56A6:0019 83F903            CMP       CX,+03                    # SI = 0000
56A6:001C 7EF8              JLE       THERE (0016)              # DI = 0000
56A6:001E B8004C            MOV       AX,4C00                   # DS = 5696
56A6:0021 CD21              INT       21                        # ES = 5696
56A6:0023 4E                DEC       SI                        # SS = 56A9
56A6:0024 42                INC       DX                        # CS = 56A6
56A6:0025 3030              XOR       Byte Ptr [BX+SI],DH       # IP = 0010
56A6:0027 92                XCHG      AX,DX                     #
56A6:0028 0000              ADD       Byte Ptr [BX+SI],AL       #   NV UP
56A6:002A 0000              ADD       Byte Ptr [BX+SI],AL       #   EI PL
56A6:002C 0010              ADD       Byte Ptr [BX+SI],DL       #   NZ NA
56A6:002E 0013              ADD       Byte Ptr [BP+DI],DL       #   PO NC
##################################################################
Microsoft (R) CodeView (R)   Version 2.2                        #
(C) Copyright Microsoft Corp. 1986-1988.  All rights reserved.  #
>!                                                              #
>                                                               #
```

in fact this part of the display can be toggled off (by the command ALTERNATE OB). It does show immediately how many bytes of machine code each instruction requires, and a good deal of information about the encoding method can be deduced by studying the assembly mode display in sample programs. Later in the book, we will examine the machine-language encoding in detail.

The assembly listing gives a picture of machine memory and is not sensitive to the boundaries of the program. In Figure 4.5, the code for the program ends with the **int 21H** instruction — the patterns that come after that just happen to be in machine memory at those addresses.

Note that **CODEVIEW** displays the **int** instruction as

          int   21

rather than

          int   21h.

This points out a slightly unpleasant fact: the default radix in **MASM** is 10 but in **CODEVIEW** it is 16. While these defaults can be changed, we have found it more convenient to accept them.

Exercise 4-1. Replace the main code in PROG4_1.ASM with the lines

```
        mov     cx, 3
        mov     ax, 0

There:

        add     ax, cx
        dec     cx
        jne     There
```

Since conditional jumps such as **jne** respond to the state of the flags and since **dec** changes the zero flag, this loop will terminate when **cx** = 0. Consequently, this new version of the program will compute the sum

```
        3 + 2 + 1 = 6
```

and then terminate. In other words, it works just like the original, except that it uses a *count-down* loop rather than a *count-up* loop. However, it does save an instruction since the **dec** replaces the **inc** and the **cmp**. Count-down loops generally offer this advantage.

After you have substituted these lines in PROG4_1.ASM, rebuild the program using **MASM** and **LINK** and trace through it in **CODEVIEW**.

Exercise 4-2. As it stands, PROG4_1 computes the sum

```
        1 + 2 + 3 + 4 + ⋯ + N
```

where N is the initial value placed in **cx**, and leaves this answer in **ax**. Modify PROG4_1 so that, instead of the above sum, it computes

```
        1 + 3 + 5 + 7 + ⋯ + (2*N - 1)
```

i.e., it computes the sum of the first N *odd* integers. This computation is interesting because the new sum has value N^2.

SECTION 4 AN EXAMPLE USING THE LOOP INSTRUCTION

A somewhat more interesting example is PROG4_2.ASM, which is shown in Figure 4.6. PROG4_2.ASM has line numbers, which were added to make it easier to discuss the program in the text. However, **MASM** most emphatically does *not* accept source code containing line numbers. Nearly all the programs in the remainder of the book will be shown with line numbers but none of the programs on the Program Disk have them — they should all be acceptable to **MASM** exactly as written.

We will begin with a discussion of the new features that occur in PROG4_2.ASM.

PROG4_2.ASM has a data segment, and line 10 shows an example of a data declaration. **DB** means *define bytes*. The directive on line 10 asks **MASM** to allocate five contiguous bytes of storage in the data segment, assign the name *Message* to these bytes, and initialize them to the ASCII codes for 'H','E','L','L', and 'O'. When **MASM** assigns a name to a variable such as *Message*, be it a string as in this case or any other kind of variable, the name is really just a label for the starting offset of the memory allocated to that variable. This observation will be amplified considerably in the sequel.

The **DB** statement need not have a string after it. Here are some variants that can be used:

```
M       DB   17
Ary1    DB   3, 4, -7, 14
Ary2    DB   1,'a',"abc",19 DUP(-3),10 DUP(?)
```

These only give an idea of the possibilities. The DUP in 19 DUP(-3) is an abbreviation for *duplication* and has the obvious meaning of initialize 19 bytes, each with value -3. In 10 DUP(?), the ? means allocate the storage but don't bother to initialize it. If this were DUP('?') instead of DUP(?), it would initialize these bytes to the ASCII code for '?'. Strings can be delimited by matching double quotes or matching single quotes. This allows the programmer to embed, say, a single quote in a string by using double quotes as the string delimiters.

As well as the **DB** statement, there are **DW** (*define words*), **DD** (*define doublewords*), and some others, all having the same general syntax.

Another new feature in Figure 4.6 appears on line 26. The [ ] surrounding the **bx** indicates that this is an instance of *indirect addressing* and means that the microprocessor should interpret the value in **bx** as an offset. When this instruction is executed, [bx] refers to the datum whose address is computed as follows: the segment part is the value of the **ds** register and the offset part is the value of **bx**. Therefore, the instruction

```
mov     dl, [bx]
```

moves the byte with address **ds:bx** into **dl**.

The different *addressing modes*, of which indirect addressing is an example, contribute a significant amount to the complexity of assembly language, and we will devote all of Chapter 6 to the subject of addressing. At the moment, it is only important to know that there are severe restrictions on the kinds of expressions that can appear inside the square brackets in indirect addressing. For now, we will use only [bx].

The offset of *Message* was moved into **bx** on line 19, and so [bx] equals the first letter of *Message* when control first reaches line 26. Most assembly language programmers would say that *we have pointed bx to Message*. This usage is consistent with the corresponding terminology for segment registers, which we introduced in Chapter 2. It is also in conformity with many high-level languages, where a *pointer* is a variable that holds an address.

There is one small potential difficulty. Paraphrasing the preceding discussion, [bx] represents the data item with offset **bx**. But the term *data item* is ambiguous. Does it mean the byte beginning at offset **bx** or the word beginning at **bx**? (Or, for that matter, the doubleword or the quadruple word?) Sometimes **MASM** (or **CODEVIEW**) can deduce

FIGURE 4.6 USING THE LOOP INSTRUCTION

```
 1   TITLE Prog4_2.asm
 2
 3   DOSSEG
 4   .MODEL SMALL
 5
 6   .STACK 100h
 7
 8   .DATA
 9
10   Message DB "HELLO"
11
12   .CODE
13
14   Start:
15
16           mov     ax, @DATA            ;ds must be pointed to
17           mov     ds, ax               ;  the data segment
18
19           mov     bx, OFFSET Message
20           mov     cx, 5                ;number of characters to print
21           mov     ah, 02h              ;function 02h of int 21h prints a
22                                        ;  character to the screen
23
24   PrintLabel:
25
26           mov     dl, [bx]             ;example of indirect addressing
27           int     21h
28           inc     bx
29           loop    PrintLabel
30
31           mov     ah, 4ch              ;terminate
32           int     21h
33
34           END     Start
```

which we mean from the context, and sometimes it cannot. The latter situation is called an *anonymous reference*, and we will encounter one quite soon. As a matter of fact, the present situation is *not* an anonymous reference. The instruction in question is

```
mov        dl, [bx]
```

One of the rules for two-operand instructions (see Section 3 of Chapter 3) is that both operands must have the same size. Since the size of the first operand is one byte, **[bx]** must be interpreted as a single byte to make this a legal instruction, and this is the interpretation that **MASM** makes.

Another feature of Figure 4.6 is the use of the **loop** instruction on line 29, and our usage is exactly as described in Chapter 3. Since **cx** was initialized to 5 (line 20), the **loop** instruction causes the code between lines 26 and 29 to execute five times.

Lines 26-27 contain a call to **function 02H** of **int 21H**. As we discussed earlier, that function prints the character in the **dl** register to the screen.

The logic of PROG4_2 should now be clear. The first time through the loop **bx** points to *Message*, and so [**bx**] equals the first letter 'H' in *Message* (or, more precisely, the ASCII code for 'H'). The line

```
        mov     dl, [bx]
```

then moves the 'H' to **dl**, and **int 21H** prints it to the screen. Next, **bx** is incremented so that it points to the 'E' in *Message*, and the program loops back to *printLabel*. The printing process is repeated a total of **cx** = 5 times and, ultimately, all of *Message* is printed.

It is easy to check the execution of PROG4_2. Just assemble and link it using the command

```
        al prog4_2
```

and then execute it by typing its name at the **DOS** prompt.

Once again, it is much more informative to follow the execution in **CODEVIEW**. The standard command line

```
        cv prog4_2
```

activates **CODEVIEW** with the program loaded. Our main interests are to examine the data segment to check that *Message* has been stored correctly and to step through the loop to see indirect addressing in action.

One of the great features of **CODEVIEW** is its ability to "watch" data and other quantities defined in a program and to allow these to be observed *dynamically*, i.e., to have the displayed values change during execution so that they are always current. A basic **CODEVIEW** command in this context is

W*Type Range*

W means *watch* and has the effect of displaying information in a window at the top of the screen, *Type* is a single letter that governs the types and sizes of data to be displayed, and *Range* determines how many items will be displayed. A version of the command that is useful at the moment is

```
        wa Message L 5
```

If 'a' is used for *Type*, data are displayed in ASCII format, which means that they are displayed as characters. The role of *Range* is played by *Message L 5*. **CODEVIEW** interprets this range as follows: begin at *Message*, that is, at the start of the array *Message*; the *L 5* means length 5, so display a total of five data items.

Another extremely useful **CODEVIEW** command is

W? *Expression* [*, Format*]

This is the *watch expression* command and, as the name suggests, it displays the value of an expression. *Expression* can be any one of a large variety of expressions of significance in assembly or other languages. The *Format* specifier permits *Expression* to be displayed in a variety of ways. For example, *Format* specifier 'c' means as a character and 'd' means as a decimal integer. As usual, the [ ] surrounding the *Format* specifier means that this is an optional item; if it is omitted, **CODEVIEW** gives the display in a format that it deems appropriate for the given expression. It is clearly desirable to watch the value of [**bx**] as a character, and so the correct command would seem to be

```
w? [bx], c
```

But, alas, this is not a perfect world. **CODEVIEW** does not always adhere to the [ ] terminology for indirect addressing. Instead, in this instance, it requires a command of the form

```
w? Modifier bx, c
```

where *Modifier* is one of by (meaning byte) or *wo* (meaning word) or *dw* (meaning doubleword). If the *Modifier* is left out, **CODEVIEW** will do the wrong thing entirely — it will show the *value* of the **bx** register formatted as a character, which really means that it will show the low byte of **bx**, and this may well be invisible if it is not the ASCII value of a printable character. Of course, the reason that *Modifier* has one of three values is that this is an anonymous reference: **CODEVIEW** has no way of knowing whether [**bx**] means the byte, word, or doubleword pointed to by **bx**, and must be told which. It might be argued that by looking at the 'c', which presumably connotes a byte of data, **CODEVIEW** should be able to reach the right conclusion. Unfortunately, this does not happen and, in this case, we need to use the command

```
w? by bx,c
```

Figure 4.7 displays the **CODEVIEW** screen after the preceding commands have been entered. Line 16 is highlighted because it is the first instruction that will be executed. The fact that

```
by [bx], c
```

has value '=' is not presently of interest. It means that the byte at address **ds**:0000 (because the value of **bx** is 0 at this point) just happens to have value equal to the ASCII code for '='. This byte does not even represent a location in the data segment since **ds** has not yet been initialized. But the fact that it has value '=' is not just chance. (Explaining this '=' will be the substance of an exercise in a later chapter. An explanation is impossible at this point since a vital fact is missing.)

Figure 4.8 shows the situation after the F8 key has been used enough times to step through the loop once entirely, and as far as line 27 on the second traverse. This time, we

FIGURE 4.7 PROG4_2 IN CODEVIEW

```
#File  View  Search  Run  Watch  Options  Language  Calls  Help # F8=Trace F5=Go
############################### prog4_2.ASM ##################################
0)  message L 5  :  56A8:0008  HELLO                                    # AX = 0000
1)  by bx,c  :  =                                                       # BX = 0000
################################################################### CX = 0000
10:            Message DB "HELLO"                                       # DX = 0000
11:                                                                     # SP = 0100
12:     .CODE                                                           # BP = 0000
13:                                                                     # SI = 0000
14:     Start:                                                          # DI = 0000
15:                                                                     # DS = 5696
16:            mov     ax, @DATA      ;the segment address of D# ES = 5696
17:            mov     ds, ax         ; into the ds register    # SS = 56A9
18:                                                             # CS = 56A6
19:            mov     bx, OFFSET Message  .                    # IP = 0010
20:            mov     cx, 5          ;number of characters to #
21:            mov     ah, 2          ;function 02h of int 21h #    NV UP
22:                                   ;  to the screen          #    EI PL
23:                                                             #    NZ NA
24:     PrintLabel:                                             #    PO NC
####################################################################
>w? by bx,c                                                            #
>                                                                      #
```

chose to display the trace in assembly mode rather than in source mode. A number of points that were made earlier in the text can be verified from Figure 4.8. As examples:

- The current instruction is at address 56A6:001F, and this matches the value of **cs:ip**.
- *Message* begins at offset 0008H, and so the 'E' has offset 0009H. This checks with the information in 1) of the watch window.

One of the features of the starting configuration in this and later displays is peculiar. We will point it out so that the reader can watch for it in future programs. Before **ds** was initialized to contain the segment part of the address of **DATA**, it had value 5696H, as can be seen from Figure 4.7. Afterwards, from Figure 4.8, it had value 56A8H. From the values of **cs** and **ss**, the program is clearly stored in memory in this order: code segment first, then data segment, then stack. In fact, this is the segment order that results from using the **DOSSEG** directive. Looking at the initial value of **ds** shows that, when execution started, it pointed to a location in memory whose segment address was 10H bytes below the program. In other words, this location was 100H bytes below the start of the program. An examination of other programs will suggest that this 100H "hole" is quite standard, and it is natural to ask why it is there. This question will be answered in Chapter 9.

Remarks on the Exercises. Many of the exercises in this book are just variations on other exercises or on programs in the text. In such cases it is unreasonable to start the solution from scratch — begin with a program that fits the requirements as closely as possible and modify it appropriately.

FIGURE 4.8 PROG4_2 IN CODEVIEW: A LATER SCREEN

```
#File  View  Search  Run  Watch  Options  Language  Calls  Help # F8=Trace F5=Go
############################## prog4_2.ASM ##################################
0)  message l 5  :  56A8:0008  HELLO                             # AX = 0248
1)  by bx,c  :  E                                                # BX = 0009
############################################################# CX = 0004
56A6:001F CD21          INT     21                               # DX = 0045
56A6:0021 43            INC     BX                               # SP = 0100
56A6:0022 E2F9          LOOP    PRINTLABEL (001D)                # BP = 0000
56A6:0024 B44C          MOV     AH,4C                            # SI = 0000
56A6:0026 CD21          INT     21                               # DI = 0000
56A6:0028 48            DEC     AX                               # DS = 56A8
56A6:0029 45            INC     BP                               # ES = 5696
56A6:002A 4C            DEC     SP                               # SS = 56A9
56A6:002B 4C            DEC     SP                               # CS = 56A6
56A6:002C 4F            DEC     DI                               # IP = 001F
56A6:002D 4E            DEC     SI                               #
56A6:002E 42            INC     DX                               #   NV UP
56A6:002F 3030          XOR     Byte Ptr [BX+SI],DH              #   EI PL
56A6:0031 B300          MOV     BL,00                            #   NZ NA
56A6:0033 0000          ADD     Byte Ptr [BX+SI],AL              #   PE NC
##########################################################################
>w? by bx,c                                                      #
>                                                                #
>                                                                #
>                                                                #
```

Exercise 4-3. Write a program that uses a loop to print the lowercase alphabet to the screen.

Exercise 4-4. Write a program that uses a loop to print the uppercase alphabet backwards (from 'Z' to 'A') to the screen.

Exercise 4-5. Write a program that prints the word "HELLO" to the screen in letters six rows high. **Suggestion:** Fabricate the letters out of 'l' and '-' characters.

SECTION 5 STRING I/O USING INT 21H

Int 21H provides functions that can be used to input strings from the keyboard and print them to the screen. In the present example, we will show how to use these functions.

We first discuss **function 09H**, which prints a string to the screen. This is a rather irrational function since it uses the '$' character as string terminator. In other words, it starts printing at the beginning of the string and continues until it encounters a '$', at which point it stops without printing the '$'. The function must be told the starting address of the string: it expects to find the offset part of the starting address in the **dx** register and the segment part of the address in **ds**. Normally, the requirement that the segment address be in **ds** is appropriate since the string will likely have been defined by a **DB** statement in the data segment. In Figure 4.9, *Prompt1* and *Prompt2* have the format required by **function 09H**.

Most high-level languages provide a mechanism that allows the programmer to define *symbolic constants*, which means that quantities in a program can be assigned meaningful names and subsequently referred to by those names. **MASM** provides this capability through the **EQUATE** directive. **EQUATE** is abbreviated **EQU**, and its use is illustrated on lines 3 and 4 of Figure 4.9. Symbolic constants are used in assembly language for the same reasons as in high-level languages: they improve readability and make program modification easier. As a matter of fact, we will see that **EQUATE** is really a quite general macro substitution facility and so has many additional uses. In Figure 4.9, line 3 provides the reasonable name CR for 0DH, the ASCII code for carriage return, and line 4 likewise assigns the name LF to 0AH, the code for line feed. The pair {CR,LF} is usually referred to as a *newline* and has the effect of repositioning the cursor at the beginning of the next line. The use of the CR and LF characters in *Prompt1* and *Prompt2* should now be clear.

Another **int 21H** function, number 0AH, is used in Figure 4.9. **Function 0AH** gets a string from the keyboard and stores it in a buffer. The programmer must initialize the first byte of the buffer to a value that equals the maximum capacity of the buffer, including an allowance for a terminating CR. When **function 0AH** executes, it records the actual number of characters that are input, excluding the CR, in the second byte of the buffer, followed by the text of the string, including the CR. The buffer must be long enough to contain all this information. In Figure 4.9, the buffer is defined by

```
Buffer   DB   7, 8 DUP(?)
```

This means that the maximum allowable character count, including the CR, is 7. Notice that 8 additional uninitialized bytes are allocated, one to hold the actual count and 7 for the data. An advantage of this method of storing strings is that the length of the input string is given in the second byte, where it is easily accessible. A disadvantage is that it requires two overhead bytes in addition to the string data.

These functions are quite idiosyncratic and are not used much in serious programming. We will seldom use them after this chapter. A more contemporary form of string storage is the so-called ASCIIZ format, where the string data are followed by a zero byte (called a *null terminator*), which serves as the end-of-string sentinel. This is the format that will be adopted in this text, and in Chapter 5 we will replace **functions 09H** and **0AH** with input and output functions that are tailored to work with ASCIIZ strings.

Only one more point in this program requires detailed explanation, namely the reasoning behind lines 36-40. The characters in the input string will be processed using a loop, and so the loop counter **cx** must be initialized to contain the length of the input string. Lines 36-37 have the obvious effect of pointing **bx** to the actual character count: first point **bx** to the start of the string, then advance it one more byte. It looks as though the instruction

```
mov      cx, [bx]
```

used at this point ought to have the desired effect of moving the actual count to **cx**. Unfortunately, this is not quite right since, by the rules for two-operand instructions, such

FIGURE 4.9 PRINTING A STRING BACKWARDS

```
 1   TITLE Prog4_3.asm
 2
 3   CR     EQU    0dh                           ;ASCII code for carriage return
 4   LF     EQU    0ah                           ;ASCII code for line feed
 5
 6   DOSSEG
 7   .MODEL SMALL
 8
 9   .STACK 100h
10
11   .DATA
12
13         Prompt1  DB    CR, LF, LF, 'Input a string of length <= 6:  $'
14         Prompt2  DB    CR, LF, 'That string written backwards is $'
15         Buffer   DB    7, 8  DUP(?)
16
17   .CODE
18
19   Start:
20
21         mov    ax, @DATA
22         mov    ds, ax
23
24         mov    dx, OFFSET Prompt1     ;use function 09h
25         mov    ah, 09h               ;  of int 21h to print
26         int    21h                   ;    Prompt1 to the screen
27
28         mov    dx, OFFSET Buffer      ;use function 0ah of
29         mov    ah, 0ah               ;  int 21h to get a string
30         int    21h                   ;    string from the keyboard
31
32         mov    dx, OFFSET Prompt2     ;outputting Prompt2
33         mov    ah, 09h
34         int    21h
35
36         mov    bx, OFFSET Buffer      ;point bx to Buffer
37         inc    bx                    ;bx points to actual character count
38         mov    cl, [bx]
39         mov    ch, 0                 ;cx = length of string in Buffer
40         add    bx, cx                ;point bx to end of string in Buffer
41         mov    ah, 02h               ;will use function 02h of int 21h to
42                                      ;  print characters to screen one
43                                      ;    at a time
44   PrintLoop:
45
46         mov    dl, [bx]              ;dl = character to be printed
47         int    21h                   ;print it
48         dec    bx                    ;point to previous character
49         loop   Printloop
50
51         mov    ah, 4ch               ;terminate
52         int    21h
53
54   END Start
```

an instruction is legal only if the second operand is a word. **MASM** always interprets an anonymous reference so that it becomes a legal instruction, if this is possible, and hence in the present case would move the *word* beginning one byte higher in memory than the start of *Buffer* into **cx**. Stated more precisely, **MASM** would build a word, using the byte with offset **bx** as low byte and the next byte in memory as high byte, and move this word into **cx**. This is certainly not what is wanted. For example, if the input string was "12345" then the byte [**bx**] would contribute 5 and the next byte would contain the ASCII code for '1', which is 31H. Hence the value 3105H would be placed in **cx** — rather larger than was bargained for! Figure 4.10 illustrates this scenario.

The way around this problem is not very elegant. Again, we want the byte [**bx**] to become the value of **cx**. But then [**bx**] will occupy only the low half of **cx**, namely **cl**, and **ch** should be 0. This outcome is achieved piecemeal by:

```
mov      cl, [bx]
mov      ch, 0
```

Line 40 holds no particular mystery: **bx** points to the byte immediately *before* the first character in the string and **cx** has value equal to the length of the string. Hence, adding **cx** to **bx** advances **bx** so that it points to the last character in the string. (The reader who doubts this should either draw a picture or else extrapolate from the case where the string length equals one.)

Once again, the best way to appreciate the operation of this program is to follow its execution in **CODEVIEW**. A good watch command to use this time is

```
wb Buffer L 9
```

The *wb* command means *watch bytes*. The effect is to display each byte twice: first as a pair of hex digits and, toward the right, either as a printed character or, if it is not printable, as a period.

Figure 4.11 shows the **CODEVIEW** screen after the watch commands have been typed but before any program steps have been executed. **CODEVIEW** starts with the first executable line positioned on the screen, and this usually means that the data are not visible. Since it is helpful to see the data while setting up the watch window, the simplest thing is to first use the 'L' command, then set up the watch window, and next use the '.' command to display the beginning of the executable code.

Note that the first byte in *Buffer* is 07H, and the remaining bytes are 00H. No particular initialization of these bytes was requested, and 00H is what "happened to be" at those locations. Since 07H and 00H are not printing characters, the right end of this watch line consists of 9 periods. As in the previous program, it is convenient to have the information about [**bx**] displayed and this display is item 1) in the watch window.

If the F8 key is used to step through the program, the display will flip to the user screen after line 30 executes, and the machine will wait for a string to be typed in. In this run, the string consisted of "abcdef" followed by a CR. Figure 4.12 shows the configuration just before line 32 was executed. At that point, *Buffer* contained the originally supplied maximum count, the actual character count, and the text of the string, including the CR. This information was displayed in both hex and character formats.

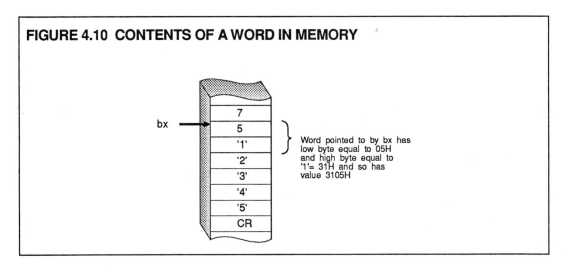

FIGURE 4.10 CONTENTS OF A WORD IN MEMORY

From this point, F8 can be used exactly as before to trace the program. F10 is another key that is useful in this context. It is also designed to single-step through programs. One difference between these keys is that F8 will follow through a loop, iteration by iteration, whereas F10, on encountering a **loop** instruction, immediately completes all remaining iterations and exits the loop. In the present small loop, the F10 key is not especially helpful, but consider a loop that iterates perhaps 1000 times. A reasonable way of checking such a loop would be to use F8 to follow through several iterations, checking that variables are being correctly updated or whatever else is noteworthy in the loop, and then to use F10 to escape from the loop in order to proceed with the analysis of later code.

Exercise 4-6. Use an **EQUATE** of the form

```
maxLen    EQU     6
```

to rewrite PROG4_3.ASM so that the length of the input string is no longer "hard-coded" into the program. That is, replace all occurrences of 6 with *maxLen* and all quantities derived from 6 with the correct quantities derived from *maxLen*. Check that the program runs correctly when reassembled with the 6 in the EQUATE replaced by 10 or some other value.

Exercise 4-7. Modify PROG4_3.ASM so that it prompts for the input of a lowercase string and, instead of reversing the string, prints the string converted to uppercase. **Suggestion:** To convert a lowercase letter to uppercase, add 'A' − 'a'.

Exercise 4-8. Modify PROG4_3.ASM so that, instead of ejecting the user after one line of input, it asks whether or not to continue and, depending on the answer, it either loops back for more input or else exits.

Exercise 4-9. Write a program that draws this beautiful truck on the screen:

FIGURE 4.11 PROGRAM 4_3 IN CODEVIEW: INITIAL SCREEN

```
#File  View  Search  Run  Watch  Options  Language  Calls  Help # F8=Trace F5=Go
############################## prog4_3.ASM ##############################
0)  buffer L 9  :  589A:004C  07 00 00 00 00 00 00 00 00 ........    # AX = 0000
1)  by bx,c  :  =                                                    # BX = 0000
################################################################### CX = 0000
1:       TITLE prog5_3.asm                                           # DX = 0000
2:                                                                   # SP = 0100
3:       CR    EQU   0dh                                             # BP = 0000
4:       LF    EQU   0ah                                             # SI = 0000
5:                                                                   # DI = 0000
6:       DOSSEG                                                      # DS = 5886
7:       .MODEL SMALL                                                # ES = 5886
8:                                                                   # SS = 58A0
9:       .STACK 100h                                                 # CS = 5896
10:                                                                  # IP = 0010
11:      .DATA                                                       #
12:                                                                  #   NV UP
13:              Prompt1  DB   CR, LF, CR, LF, 'Input an string of len#   EI PL
14:              Prompt2  DB   CR, LF, 'That string written backwards #   NZ NA
15:              Buffer   DB   7, 8  DUP(?)                          #   PO NC
####################################################################
>w? by bx,c                                                         #
>.                                                                  #
>L                                                                  #
>                                                                   #
```

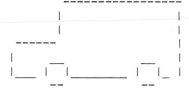

Exercise 4-10. Write a program that prints the string "When a string contains a $ it is somewhat harder to print" to the screen.

SECTION 6 A MORE AMBITIOUS EXAMPLE: USING THE STACK

PROG4_4.ASM, shown in Figure 4.13, is the last example that we will look at in this chapter. It is considerably longer and more complicated than any of our previous programs. It begins to show the power of even the very limited subset of the **8088** instructions that we have introduced. Before reading further, look at the general format of Figure 4.13. We have tried to make the code look neat and orderly. White space was used liberally to set off labels and

FIGURE 4.12 PROG4_3 IN CODEVIEW: A LATER SCREEN

```
#File  View  Search  Run  Watch  Options  Language  Calls  Help # F8=Trace F5=Go
############################### prog4_3.ASM ##################################
0)  buffer L 9  :  589A:004C  07 06 61 62 63 64 65 66 0D ..abcdef.   # AX = 090D
1)  by bx,c  :  !                                                    # BX = 0000
######################################################################## CX = 0000
27:                                                                  # DX = 0028
28:            mov dx, OFFSET Buffer        ;prepare to use          # SP = 0100
29:            mov ah, 0ah                  ;  function 0ah of int 21# BP = 0000
30:            int 21h                      ;    input a string from # SI = 0000
31:                                                                  # DI = 0000
32:            mov dx, OFFSET Prompt2       ;outputting Prompt2      # DS = 589A
33:            mov ah, 09h                                           # ES = 5886
34:            int 21h                                               # SS = 58A0
35:                                                                  # CS = 5896
36:            mov bx, OFFSET Buffer        ;point bx to Buffer      # IP = 0028
37:            inc bx                                                #
38:            mov cl, [bx]                                          #    NV UP
39:            mov ch, 0                    ;cx <- length of string i#    EI PL
40:            add bx, cx                   ;point bx to end of strin#    NZ NA
41:            mov ah, 2                    ;will use function 02h of#    PO NC
############################################################################
>w? by bx,c                                                         #
>.                                                                  #
>L                                                                  #
>                                                                   #
```

loops and to help break the program into logically distinct sections, for example lines 35 through 37. The different fields of the instructions were tabbed neatly into columns. Labels were given suggestive names. The uppercase and lowercase conventions introduced earlier were observed faithfully. Comments were used where they seemed helpful. It is sometimes recommended that every line end with a comment, but littering the code with trivial comments can obscure the important ones.

We will use the same approach in discussing this program as in the previous examples. First, the logic of the program will be analyzed, and then **CODEVIEW** will be used to step through the program in order to check its execution. The title of the program indicates its purpose: the user is prompted to input an integer that is interpreted as base 10 and converted to hex. The program will always print four hex digits, padding with zeros if necessary. For example, 255 will be printed as 00FF.

The most interesting wrinkle in PROG4_4.ASM is the use of the stack. The hex digits are generated using Algorithm1.1. As we observed in Chapter 1, that algorithm generates the digits in right-to-left order, whereas they must be printed in left-to-right order. In this program, the digits are pushed onto the stack as they are produced. Later they are popped off and printed. Pushing and popping gives the required reversal in order. The program, as it stands, is quite primitive, and a number of improvements are suggested in the exercises at the end of this section.

FIGURE 4.13 CONVERTING FROM DECIMAL TO HEX

```
 1    TITLE Prog4_4.asm  Program that converts decimal integer to hex.
 2
 3    DOSSEG
 4    .MODEL SMALL
 5
 6    CR      EQU     0dh
 7    LF      EQU     0ah
 8
 9    .STACK 100h
10
11    .DATA
12
13            Heading    DB     'DECIMAL TO HEX CONVERSION$'
14            Prompt     DB     'Input an integer in the range 0 to 65535: $'
15            ansStr     DB     'The hexadecimal equivalent is $'
16            newLine    DB     CR, LF, '$'
17            inpStr     DB     6, 7 DUP(?)
18
19    .CODE
20
21    Start:
22
23            mov     ax, @DATA              ;initialize ds
24            mov     ds, ax
25
26            mov     dx, OFFSET Heading
27            mov     ah, 09h                ;print to the screen
28            int     21h
29            mov     dx, OFFSET newLine
30            int     21h                    ;print a newline
31            int     21h                    ;  and another
32
33    Print:
34
35            mov     dx, OFFSET Prompt
36            mov     ah, 09h                ;print to the screen
37            int     21h
38
39            mov     dx, OFFSET inpStr
40            mov     ah, 0ah                ;input a string from the keyboard
41            int     21h
42
43            mov     cl, inpStr[1]          ;count of input digits for looping
44            dec     cl
45            mov     ch, 0
46            mov     al, inpStr[2]          ;ASCII code for first input digit
47            mov     ah, 0
48            sub     ax, '0'                ;converted to binary
49            mov     bx, 2                  ;initial index into array InStr
50            jcxz    singleDigit
51            mov     si, 10                 ;multiplier for ASCII-binary
52                                           ;  conversion
53    toBinary:
54
```

```
55              mul     si
56              inc     bx
57              mov     dl, inpStr[bx]          ;get next digit
58              mov     dh, 0
59              sub     dx, 30h                 ;convert to binary
60              add     ax, dx                  ;add it to accumulator
61              loop    toBinary
62
63      singleDigit:
64
65              mov     cx, 3                   ;loop counter
66              mov     si, 16                  ;multiplier for binary-hex
67                                              ; conversion
68
69      toHex:
70
71              mov     dx, 0                   ;msw for 16-bit division
72              div     si
73              push    dx                      ;remainder is next hex digit
74              loop    toHex
75              push    ax                      ;final quotient is last hex digit
76
77              mov     dx, OFFSET newLine      ;print to the screen
78              mov     ah, 09h
79              int     21h
80              mov     dx, OFFSET ansStr
81              int     21h
82
83              mov     cx, 4                   ;number of hex digits to print
84              mov     ah, 02h                 ;will use function 02h
85
86
87      printLoop:
88
89              pop     dx                      ;number to convert really goes into dl
90              add     dl, '0'                 ;convert decimal digit to ascii
91              cmp     dl, '9'                 ;was it a decimal digit?
92              jle     wasDigit
93              add     dl, 'A'-10-'0'          ;if hex digit >= 0ah, must
94                                              ; must make further correction
95      wasDigit:
96
97              int     21h
98              loop    printLoop
99
100             mov     dx, OFFSET newLine
101             mov     ah, 09h                 ;print a total of
102             int     21h                     ; three newlines
103             int     21h                     ;   to the screen
104             int     21h
105             jmp     Print
106
107             mov     ah, 4ch                 ;not actually needed in this
108             int     21h                     ; program since these
109                                             ;  instructions never reached
110                                             ;   must terminate with ^C
111     END     Start
```

THE STRUCTURE OF PROG4_4

Here is a detailed commentary on selected lines of Figure 4.13:

Line 30. We are using **int 21H** to print the string called *newLine* to the screen and are assuming that the **ah** register still contains the value 09H, to which it was set on line 27. In other words, we are tacitly assuming that the complicated code invoked by the **int 21H** instruction on line 28 did not disturb the value in **ah**. This assumption is valid. The functions in **int 21H**, with a few exceptions, save the register values and restore them afterwards. The exceptions stem from the fact that some of the **int 21H** functions return values to the caller in registers, and in these cases the original values of these registers are inevitably lost.

Line 43. The first item of new syntax in the present program is the expression *inpStr[1]*. If *inpStr* is viewed as an array of bytes, then it is natural to think of its elements as *inpStr[0]*, *inpStr[1]*, ···, and **MASM** allows this notation. As in the C language, the indexing of arrays in assembly language starts with 0. **MASM** treats this use of [ ] in the same way as indirect addressing (although technically it is not an example of indirect addressing since there is no register inside the square brackets).

Consequently, **MASM** interprets the expression *inpStr[k]*, where k is an integer, as a reference to the data item whose offset is k bytes larger than the offset represented by *inpStr*. So **MASM** operates by adding offsets, even though the programmer may be thinking in terms of array indexing. The results are consistent as long as the array indexing starts from 0. The **ds** register was used to obtain the segment part of the address, which was correct since *inpStr* was defined in the data segment and **ds** was pointed there.

As well as *inpStr[k]*, where k is an integer, **MASM** allows constructs such as *inpStr[bx]*, and in fact the square brackets can be occupied by any legal indirect addressing expression. The only indirect addressing expression that has been used to date is **bx**, and *inpStr[bx]* is used later in this program (on line 57). If the current value of **bx** is k, then the interpretation of *inpStr[bx]* is identical with the interpretation of *inpStr[k]* given in the last paragraph.

There is one other item of potential confusion, which does not come into this example, but it is good to be prepared. Suppose that *wordAry* was defined by

```
wordAry   DW   10 DUP(?)
```

and we want to use the [ ] notation to index into *wordAry*. The point that must be remembered is that the value occurring inside the [ ] is always interpreted as a displacement in *bytes*. To refer to word number 3 in *wordAry*, where the count starts at 0, it is necessary to advance 6 bytes into *wordAry*. The correct assembly language expression is therefore *wordAry[6]*. This situation is depicted in Figure 4.14. High-level language compilers automatically do this *scaling* by the size of the data item, but in assembly language the programmer must explicitly account for it. Using **bx**, for example, the general rule is

- If *dataAry* is an array of elements of a given size and *dataAry[bx]* is meant to refer to the k-th element of *dataAry*, then **bx** must be given a value equal to k times the size of an array element in bytes.

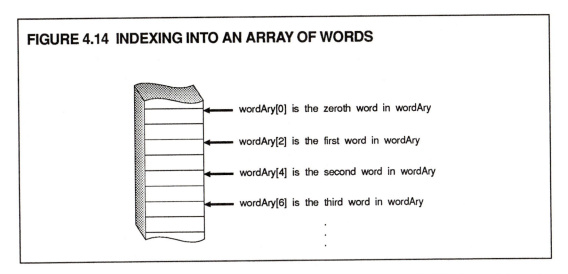

FIGURE 4.14 INDEXING INTO AN ARRAY OF WORDS

wordAry[0] is the zeroth word in wordAry

wordAry[2] is the first word in wordAry

wordAry[4] is the second word in wordAry

wordAry[6] is the third word in wordAry

By now, it should be clear that *inpStr[2]* really represents the first input digit, as the comment on line 46 asserts. We are using **function 0AH** to import the data to *inpStr*. To conform with the conventions used by that function, the initial byte of *inpStr* was initialized to the maximum allowable count (*inpStr[0] = 6* on line 17). The next byte *inpStr[1]* will receive the actual count, and the text of the input string will begin at *inpStr[2]*.

Lines 43-45. The input digits will be processed using a loop that, as we will see, should be iterated one less time than the number of input digits or, equivalently, one less time than the value of the *byte* of data *inpStr[1]*. The problem of initializing **cx** is totally analogous to the one that we faced in the previous program, and the solution is the same:

```
mov     cl, inpStr[1]
mov     ch, 0
```

Of course, **cl** or **cx** must still be decremented.

Lines 46-63. This is an implementation of Algorithm 1.1, where we are converting from decimal to binary and accumulating the answer in the **ax** register. The basic algorithm consists of an initial step of storing the first digit in **ax**, followed by a loop, in each pass of which **ax** is multiplied by 10 and incremented by the value of the next digit.

In lines 46-48, **ax** is initialized to contain the numeric value of the first input digit. The ASCII code for the first digit in the string is stored in *inpStr[2]* and, as before, this byte must be carefully moved into the word-sized register **ax**. In addition, its present value equals the ASCII code for the digit and so must be converted to the corresponding numeric value. The table of ASCII codes shows that the numeric value of a decimal digit can be recovered from its ASCII code by subtracting '0'.

Since the value in **cx** is one less than the number of input digits, the case **cx** = 0 corresponds to a single-digit input, and so the label name used on line 63 is appropriate. Note that falling through the loop is logically the correct thing to do in this case, since **ax** already contains the numeric value of the one-digit input integer.

Next we come to the body of the loop. All the components have been discussed previously: the indirect addressing using *inpStr[bx]*, the 16-bit multiplication using **si** as an operand, and the subtraction of '0' to extract the numeric value of a decimal digit.

Lines 65-75. Now we are implementing Algorithm 1.1 to change the binary value in **ax** to four hex digits. (Technically, this is a slight misrepresentation since Algorithm 1.1, as written, converts *decimal* integers to different bases. However, as we discussed in Exercise 1-5, the method is really independent of the input base.) In the present case, the essential step in Algorithm 1.1 is repeated division by 16. As pointed out previously, the hex digits are pushed onto the stack as they are generated so that they can be easily printed in the opposite order.

Lines 83-98. We pop the four hex digits off the stack and print them immediately. Each digit is popped into **dx** (because **pop** must have a word as operand) but, since the value of a digit is less than 256, its bit pattern lies entirely in **dl**, so effectively it is popped into **dl**.

There is a final complication. Namely, each hex digit lies in the range 0 to 15. A hex digit between 0 and 9 should be printed as the corresponding character '0' through '9', which, as noted earlier, requires adding '0' to its numeric value. But a hex digit between 10 and 15 should be printed as the corresponding character 'A' through 'F', and this requires adding 'A'– 10 to it. The reader can also verify this last statement from the ASCII table. These additions are accomplished on lines 89-93. Specifically, '0' is added in all cases and then, if necessary, a correction factor with value 'A' – 10 – '0' is added as well.

Lines 105-108. Line 105 contains a unconditional jump to a point near the top of the code, effectively making the whole program into an infinite loop. (CONTROL C must be used to break out of this program.) As a consequence, control never reaches lines 107 and 108; hence, they are not really needed in this program. **MASM** will not complain if they are missing, and they are included only as a reminder.

Now that we have analyzed the logic behind the program, we will assemble and link it and check its operation using **CODEVIEW**. The assembly, linking, and entry into **CODEVIEW** are done exactly as before.

PREPARING TO USE CODEVIEW

This program motivates the introduction of some new **CODEVIEW** commands and modes of data display.

After entering **CODEVIEW**, we set up a number of watch commands, as shown in Figure 4.15. Watch item 5) is long, and therefore the register display (toggled by F2) was turned off so that the registers would not hide the right-hand end of the display. Since there were a lot of expressions, the main code window was made as big as possible by moving its lower boundary downward. (CONTROL T moves the lower boundary of the main window down and CONTROL G moves it up.)

Here is a list of the watch commands used. Some of these are new and interesting:

0) wa inpStr L 8. This is analogous to previous examples.

1) w? bx, u. The format specifier 'u' means display as an unsigned decimal integer. Using 'd' or 'i' instead of 'u' causes the value of **bx** to display as a signed decimal integer. Of course, in this particular instance, the value of **bx** is going to be small and positive, and so it is really immaterial which of these three format specifiers is used. The only reason to display **bx** in a watch window in this program is that we have toggled the register display off.

2) w? (&inpStr)[bx],c. Some of **CODEVIEW**'s quirks are annoying, as this expression shows. We want to display *inpStr[bx]*, but this cannot be requested in a direct way. When **CODEVIEW** is asked to index into an array, it must be given the address of the array, and the **CODEVIEW** notation for address is '&'. To make matters worse, '&' has lower operator precedence than [ ] and so parentheses are required around *&inpStr* in the expression "(&inpStr)[bx]". Finally, **CODEVIEW** does not want the [ ] to denote indirect addressing in most other contexts, but requires it here. The format specifier 'c' means display as a character.

Loosely translated, this watch expression says: go to the beginning address of the array, advance a further **bx** bytes, and display the byte found there as a character.

If this were an array of words instead of bytes, the appropriate modification would have to be made to this expression. Specifically, if *wordAry* is an array of words and word number 6 (where, as always, the indexing starts with 0) is to be watched as a signed integer, the correct command is

```
w? (&wordAry)[12], i
```

and if the word whose index is the value of **bx** is to be watched, the command is

```
w? (&wordAry)([(bx)*2]), i
```

An alternate command that displays the same data and is somewhat easier to type is

```
wi &wordAry+bx*2  L 1
```

Our recommendation is that these formats be memorized as part of the process of mastering **CODEVIEW**. Eventually their use will become second nature. We will continue to explore these issues in the text and in the exercises.

3) w? ax, u. The format is just like 1). Even if the register display were on, it would still be convenient to see the value of **ax** as an unsigned decimal integer, since the register display is in hex. It is interesting to watch how **ax** "accumulates" the input and, since the input is given in decimal, the accumulation process can be most easily followed if **ax** is shown in decimal.

FIGURE 4.15 PROG4_4 IN CODEVIEW: FIRST SCREEN

```
#File  View  Search  Run  Watch  Options  Language  Calls  Help # F8=Trace F5=Go
############################## prog4_4.ASM ##################################
0) InpStr L 8  :  58A5:0073  ........                                         #
1) bx,u  :  0                                                                 #
2) (&InpStr)[bx],c  :                                                         #
3) ax,u  :  0                                                                 #
4) sp  :  0x0100                                                              #
5) ss:f0 l 8  :  58AD:00F0  2020 2020 2020 2020 2020 2020 2020 0000           #
###########################################################################
16:                  NewLine    DB     CR, LF, '$'                            #
17:                  InpStr     DB     6, 7 DUP(?)                            #
18:                                                                          #
19:      .CODE                                                               #
20:                                                                          #
21:      Start:                                                              #
22:                                                                          #
23:                  mov     ax, @DATA              ;initialize ds           #
24:                  mov     ds, ax                                          #
25:                                                                          #
26:                  mov     dx, OFFSET Heading                              #
27:                  mov     ah, 09h                ;print to the screen     #
28:                  int     21h                                             #
29:                  mov     dx, OFFSET NewLine                              #
###########################################################################
>                                                                            #
```

4) w? sp. Since **ss:sp** points to the most recent word that was pushed onto the stack, it is a good idea to display the value of **sp**, especially in conjunction with watch number 5).

These watch commands demonstrate another odd feature of **CODEVIEW**, namely its somewhat irrational blend of **MASM** and **C** language syntax. In 4), for example, it uses the **C** convention of prepending numbers with 0x to signal that they are hex, while in 0) and 5) it displays hex quantities in "unadorned" format.

Observe that, if no format specifier is given, the default display format for the w? command is hex.

5) ww ss:f0 L 8. We are going to check that the hex digits are computed and pushed correctly. The basic size of an element on the stack is a word and so the stack should be watched using the ww command, which watches words. If a watch command is issued and only the offset part of the address is supplied, **CODEVIEW** assumes that the reference is to a data item and so uses **ds** to supply the segment part of the address. Here the segment override **ss:** is used to indicate that the stack should be watched. The "L 8" part of the command tells **CODEVIEW** how many items to watch. The number 8 was chosen because only 8 words will fit across the screen. Finally, the activity at the top of the stack should be monitored. Since the stack has size 100H, it occupies offsets 00H-0FFH in the stack segment, and so the top 8 words (= 16 bytes) begin at offset 0F0H. If all goes well, the hex digits should materialize in watch item 5), appearing from right to left as they are pushed.

There is another aspect of working with **CODEVIEW** that is worth mentioning. The typical development cycle of a program runs as follows:

1. Edit, assemble, and link the program.

2. Run the program, subjecting it to a variety of inputs to ensure that it works correctly under all circumstances. If it executes flawlessly, go to 4.

3. Examine program execution in **CODEVIEW**, using inputs that cause the program to misbehave, and setting up appropriate quantities to monitor in the watch window. When it is time to make corrections in the source code, exit **CODEVIEW** and go to 1.

4. Done.

The point is that step 3 may be repeated several times, and on each repetition the quantities to be watched must be reentered into the watch window. As our present program shows, this may involve a lot of typing. It would be ideal if **CODEVIEW** "remembered its parameters" from one use until the next, but unfortunately it does not. There are two ways around this deficiency.

The first solution is the simpler of the two but presents other problems. Instead of exiting **CODEVIEW** after step (3), use the **MS-DOS** shell command. (The '!' dialog command.) This invokes a new copy of COMMAND.COM but leaves **CODEVIEW** resident in memory. From this new **DOS** prompt, call the editor and make the required corrections, then reassemble and relink the program, and finally use the EXIT command to leave the **DOS** shell and fall back into **CODEVIEW**. If the 'L' command is used at that point, a copy of the freshly prepared program will be loaded, and the debugging session can continue. The difficulty with this approach is that there may not be enough memory to go around. When a reasonably large program is being debugged, there probably will not be sufficient memory available for two copies of COMMAND.COM, **CODEVIEW**, **MASM**, and the program under development to coexist in memory. The situation becomes even stickier when mixed language programs are being built, since their construction involves calling various compilers and perhaps other utilities.

The second method is less convenient but can be used in any situation. When **CODEVIEW** is called, certain options can be specified on the command line, for example /C, which allows the user to specify *commands to be executed at startup*. The command line then has the form

cv /C*Commands progName*

Commands represents a command or commands to be executed immediately after **CODEVIEW** receives control. If there are several commands, they should be separated by semicolons; if any of the commands needs white space or if a redirection sign < or > or >> is used in any command, then the whole command sequence should be surrounded by double quotes. The best way to use this option is by means of a batch file. As an example, let us apply this approach to the present program. We write a batch file (a reasonable name for which would be CVBAT44.BAT) that contains only one line:

```
cv /C"wainpStr L 8;w?bx,u;w?(&inpStr)[bx],c;w?ax,u;w?sp;wwss:f0 L 8" prog4_4
```

The simple command

```
cvbat44
```

will now start **CODEVIEW** with the watch window initialized. It is important that the batch file consist of a single line. The only restriction in this method comes from **MS-DOS** — no command line can be longer than 127 characters, which means that the entire contents of the batch file cannot be longer than that, and consequently the startup commands can be no more than 110 characters or so. On the other hand, this is not too much of a restriction since there is a definite limit to how much watch information can be simultaneously viewed on the screen (even in 43-line mode).

There is a variant of this method that circumvents the 127-character command-line limit. Rather than including the list of commands on the **CODEVIEW** command line, it is possible to place them in another file and use **DOS** redirection on the **CODEVIEW** command line in order to invoke them.

To apply this variant efficiently, the author maintains a batch file named CVI.BAT on the PATH, consisting of the following line:

```
cv "/C<cvinput" %1
```

To use this batchfile, save the initialization commands for the program in question in a file called CVINPUT. In the present case, this file might contain the lines

```
wa inpStr L 8
w? bx,u
w? (&inpStr)[bx],c
w? ax,u
w? sp
ww ss:f0 L 8
```

The command

```
cvi Prog4_4
```

can then be used to start **CODEVIEW** with the watch window initialized.

RUN-TIME ANALYSIS OF PROG4_4

CODEVIEW has a complete set of commands for the manipulation of breakpoints. A *breakpoint* is a flag at a location in the code that causes execution to stop when that point is reached. A breakpoint is said to be *taken* if execution actually halts there; otherwise, it is said to be *skipped*. Lines 61 and 74 in the present program are good locations for breakpoints. At line 61, a check can be made on whether the input number is being correctly converted and accumulated in **ax**, and at line 71 the successful arrival of the hex digits onto the stack can be verified.

The syntax for setting a breakpoint is

bp *[Address [Count]["Commands"]]*

Address means the address of the breakpoint. Giving *Count* the value k causes the breakpoint to be skipped the first k − 1 times it is encountered, taken the k-th time, and always taken thereafter. For example, if count is 10, the breakpoint is skipped the first 9 times it is reached and is always taken after that. *Commands* (must be in quotes) is a semicolon-separated list of commands to be executed each time the breakpoint is taken. The particular grouping of the square brackets means that all the items are optional but that *Count* and/or *Commands* can only occur if *Address* is also present. Finally, if *Address* does not appear, the current instruction address is used, and if *Count* does not appear, it is assumed to have value 1.

In line with the preceding discussion, these breakpoint commands might be used:

```
bp .61 2
bp .74 2
```

CODEVIEW accepts '.' as meaning line number. Since the count has been set to 2, the first of these commands will halt execution at the end of the second trip through the *toBinary* loop, while the second breakpoint operates similarly with respect to the *toHex* loop.

A good first command is

```
g.46
```

which allows execution to proceed as far as line 46. The program pauses after line 41 to ask for input. On our trial run, we input the integer 65535. When line 46 is reached, execution stops; the corresponding **CODEVIEW** screen is shown in Figure 4.16. Notice that the buffer does contain 65535. Another item of interest here is that the stack has been changed from its original configuration, even though **sp** has not changed. This is just an example of **CODEVIEW** surreptitiously using the stack, a phenomenon that will be explored in the exercises.

Another 'g' command (or an F5) will take us to the breakpoint set on line 61. The **CODEVIEW** screen at this point is shown in Figure 4.17. Examine this display carefully, especially 3) in the watch window. It contains the result of the computation

$$((6 * 10 + 5) * 10) + 5$$

which is exactly as expected from the *toBinary* loop or from Algorithm 1.1. A reasonable next move is to use F8 to complete the remaining traverses of the *toBinary* loop and then use another 'g' to get to the breakpoint at line 74.

After these operations have been performed, the screen should look like Figure 4.18. Two loops of *toHex* have been completed, and the first two hex digits have shown up at the top of the stack. Again, it would be a good idea to use F8 to step through the *toHex* loop from this point to see how the remaining hex digits get to the stack.

There is nothing new in the code from this point on.

But there is one final exercise that is amusing to do. First, use 'L' to load a new copy of the program and then use

FIGURE 4.16 PROG4_4 IN CODEVIEW: SECOND SCREEN

```
#File  View  Search  Run  Watch  Options  Language  Calls  Help # F8=Trace F5=Go
############################# prog4_4.ASM ###############################
0) inpStr L 8  :  58A5:0073  ..65535.                                       #
1) bx,u  :  0                                                               #
2) (&inpStr)[bx],c  :                                                       #
3) ax,u  :  2573                                                            #
4) sp  :  0x0100                                                            #
5) ss:f0 L 8  :   58AD:00F0   58A5 588C 06EB 271B 0002 003A 589C 0202       #
######################################################################
41:           int    21h                                                   #
42:                                                                         #
43:           mov    cl, inpStr[1]          ;count of input digits for loopi#
44:           dec    cl                                                     #
45:           mov    ch, 0                                                  #
46:           mov    al, inpStr[2]          ;first input digit in ASCII    #
47:           mov    ah, 0                                                  #
48:           sub    ax, 30h                ;converted to binary           #
49:           mov    bx, 2                  ;index into array InStr         #
50:           jcxz   singleDigit                                            #
51:           mov    si, 10                 ;multiplier for ascii-binary    #
52:                                                                         #
53:    toBinary:                                                            #
54:                                                                         #
##############################################################
>                                                                          #
```

bc *

which is the command to cancel all breakpoints, so that they do not halt the execution during the next stage.

Now use the 'e' command. 'e' means *execute* and causes **CODEVIEW** to step through the program at a rate that is (almost) slow enough for the viewer to follow on the screen. Again, the program halts for keyboard input and can be stopped at any time by hitting a key. This demonstrates very clearly how **CODEVIEW** commandeers the stack. As soon as **sp** increments so that a new word on the stack is free, **CODEVIEW** immediately puts it to use!

Exercise 4-11. PROG4_4.ASM does no error checking of its input. Improve this situation so that, at the very least, it complains and aborts if the input string is empty or if it finds a character that is not a bona fide decimal digit.

Exercise 4-12. There is a better way of doing the computations starting on line 87 of PROG4_4.ASM than the method used in the program. The **8088** instructions set contains a rather specialized instruction called **xlat**. It takes no operands and works in the following way. It expects that an array of bytes, say transTable, of any length up to 256, has been defined and that **ds:bx** points to this table. The operation that **xlat** performs is to replace the present value in **al**, call it k, by the k-th entry in transTable.

To apply **xlat** in the present problem, define the table by

```
┌──────────────────────────────────────────────────────────────────────────┐
│  FIGURE 4.17  PROG4_4 IN CODEVIEW: THIRD SCREEN                             │
│                                                                            │
│  #File  View  Search  Run  Watch  Options  Language  Calls  Help # F8=Trace F5=Go │
│  ############################# prog4_4.ASM #################################### │
│  0) inpStr L 8  :   58A5:0073  ..65535.                                  #  │
│  1) bx,u  :  4                                                           #  │
│  2) (&inpStr)[bx],c  :  5                                                #  │
│  3) ax,u  :  655                                                         #  │
│  4) sp  :  0x0100                                                        #  │
│  5) ss:f0 L 8  :  58AD:00F0  58A5 588C 06EB 271B 0041 0058 589C 0202     #  │
│  ############################################################################## │
│  56:            inc    bx                                                #  │
│  57:            mov    dl, inpStr[bx]          ;get next digit           #  │
│  58:            mov    dh, 0                                             #  │
│  59:            sub    dx, 30h                 ;convert to binary        #  │
│  60:            add    ax, dx                  ;add it to accumulator    #  │
│  61:            loop   toBinary                                          #  │
│  62:                                                                     #  │
│  63:     singleDigit:                                                    #  │
│  64:                                                                     #  │
│  65:            mov    cx, 3                   ;loop counter             #  │
│  66:            mov    si, 16                  ;multiplier for binary-hex #  │
│  67:                                           ; conversion              #  │
│  68:                                                                     #  │
│  69:     toHex:                                                          #  │
│  ############################################################################## │
│  >                                                                       #  │
└──────────────────────────────────────────────────────────────────────────┘
```

```
transTable  DB  '0123456789ABCDEF'
```

An application of **xlat** will then replace the value currently in **al** (in the range from 0 to 15) with the corresponding hex digit, either in the range from '0' to '9' or in the range 'A' to 'F', whichever is appropriate.

Rewrite PROG4_4 using the **xlat** instruction.

Exercise 4-13. Write a program that prompts the user to input a string of length ≤ 20 and checks whether or not that string contains a 'b' (lower case), printing a message to the screen indicating whether it does or not.

Exercise 4-14. Write a program that prompts the user to input an integer having no more than 10 digits and checks that it really is an integer (i.e., that each character is a digit). If the input is not an integer, the program should print an appropriate message to the screen and terminate. If it is, the program should use the stack to print the integer in reverse order to the screen.

Exercise 4-15. A string is called a *palindrome* if it reads the same forward and backward. For example,

```
abcba
madamimadam
```

FIGURE 4.18 PROG4_4 IN CODEVIEW: FOURTH SCREEN

```
#File  View  Search  Run  Watch  Options  Language  Calls  Help # F8=Trace F5=Go
############################## prog4_4.ASM ##################################
0) inpStr L 8 :  58A5:0073  ..65535.                                          #
1) bx,u  :  6                                                                 #
2) (&inpStr)[bx],c  :  5                                                      #
3) ax,u  :  255                                                              #
4) sp  :  0x00fc                                                             #
5) ss:f0 L 8  :  58AD:00F0  0FFF 0754 271B 0066 589C 0216 000F 000F          #
#############################################################################
69:     ToHex:                                                              #
70:                                                                         #
71:             mov    dx, 0                    ;msw for 16-bit division     #
72:             div    si                                                    #
73:             push   dx                       ;remainder is next hex digit #
74:             loop   toHex                                                 #
75:             push   ax                       ;final quotient is last hex digi#
76:                                                                         #
77:             mov    dx, OFFSET newline       ;print to the screen         #
78:             mov    ah, 09h                                               #
79:             int    21h                                                   #
80:             mov    dx, OFFSET ansStr                                     #
81:             int    21h                                                   #
82:                                                                         #
#############################################################################
>                                                                           #
```

are palindromes. Write a program that prompts for a string and checks whether or not it is a palindrome, printing a suitable message to the screen. The program should then prompt the user whether or not to do another and should respond correctly to the answer.

Suggestion: The registers **si** and **di** can be used for indirect addressing in exactly the same way as **bx**.

Exercise 4-16. A string is called a *weak palindrome* if it is a palindrome when differences between lowercase and uppercase, spaces, and punctuation are ignored. Famous weak palindromes are

```
Madam, I'm Adam.
A man, a plan, a canal, Panama.
Stop, murder us not, tonsured rumpots.
```

Repeat Exercise 4-15, but this time test for weak palindromes.

Suggestion: Probably the easiest approach is to first copy the input string to another buffer, deleting punctuation and white space characters and changing all letters to lowercase as the string is copied. Then check whether the new string is a palindrome.

Exercise 4-17. Write a program that prompts the user to input an unsigned decimal integer in the range 0 to 65535 and a choice of base between 2 and 16 and prints the representation of the integer to that base.

Exercise 4-18. Write a program that prompts the user to input a string of length ≤ 99 and counts the number of vowels (uppercase or lowercase 'a', 'e', 'i', 'o', or 'u') in the string, printing the answer to the screen. The program should then ask the user whether he or she wishes to do another, and proceed accordingly. Note that the string may have more than 9 vowels.

Exercise 4-19. Same as Exercise 4-18 but this time count the number of double vowels (ae, ai, ao, ⋯) in the string. A triple vowel (⋯xaeiy⋯, for example) adds two to the count and, more generally, a block of k vowels adds k − 1 to the count.

Exercise 4-20. In Chapter 3, we stated that a conditional jump will jump as much as 127 bytes in the forward direction or 128 bytes backward. This is not quite accurate, since the conditional jump instruction itself has length two bytes and these bytes must enter the counting somehow. Do some experiments to decide more precisely what the rules are that govern how many bytes conditional jumps really jump.
Suggestion: It is convenient to use the **nop** (no operation) instruction, which does not perform any action but fills a byte of code space. **MASM** permits the **DB** directive to appear in the code segment, and **nop** has machine code 90H. Hence, an easy way to get, say, 100 of the **nop** instructions into the code segment is

```
DB  100 DUP(90h)
```

Exercise 4-21. Investigate **CODEVIEW**'s use of the stack. This problem is of little practical importance — it is in the spirit of pure detection. Exactly how **CODEVIEW** uses the stack is undocumented, but a few simple experiments will show that it mostly uses it to store register values. The most interesting questions are
1. What items are stored?
2. Are they always stored in the same order?
3. What is the maximum number of words that **CODEVIEW** ever stores simultaneously? Of course, you cannot be completely sure that you have found the maximum under any set of circumstances.
The answer to 3 is of some significance since, if the stack allowance is tight, a program might run correctly under **DOS** but overflow its stack under **CODEVIEW**.

Exercise 4-22. Write a program that runs correctly from the **DOS** command line but misbehaves in some highly visible way when run under **CODEVIEW**.
Suggestion: CODEVIEW initializes some storage areas so that they are filled with zeros.

Exercise 4-23. Write a program that misbehaves in the opposite manner to the program of Exercise 4-22. That is, this program should run perfectly under **CODEVIEW** but should do something unpleasant (say lock up the computer) when it is run from the **DOS** command line.
Suggestion: Same as in the previous problem.

CHAPTER 5

PROCEDURES, LIBRARIES, AND MACROS

SECTION 1 PREVIEW

The real difficulties with assembly language programming are of two kinds. The first stems from the fact that assembly language programs tend to consist of extremely long lists of rather trivial instructions. Reading such programs, whether to understand or to maintain them, can be thoroughly mind-numbing, and hence methods must be devised to structure programs to minimize this problem. The second difficulty relates to the global organization of assembly language programs. This includes things like segmentation, methods of declaring data, addressing modes, the program's interface with **MASM**, and, ultimately, the program's interface with the operating system.

The main goal of the present chapter is to take steps toward controlling the first problem. The techniques that will be introduced include writing procedures, storing these procedures in libraries, and using macros.

To focus better on the issues at hand, we have chosen to keep the programs in this chapter as easy as possible. A simple program is presented in the next section, and variations of it are used throughout the chapter.

In Section 2, we introduce ASCIIZ strings and develop procedures for inputting them from the keyboard and printing them to the screen. In the later sections of the chapter, these procedures are stored in a library, and macros are written to give easier access to them.

It will turn out that only the techniques developed in the chapter are of lasting importance. The actual procedures that we write are based on the early **DOS** functions

(**functions 01H** and **02H**) which, as we will see in Chapter 8, are seriously flawed. These procedures will later be discarded and replaced by better versions.

SECTION 2 ASCIIZ STRINGS

As we stated in Chapter 4, it is not our intention to make much use of **functions 09H** and **0AH** of **int 21H** for input and output of strings. Instead, ASCIIZ strings will be used in nearly all the programs in this book. Recall that in the ASCIIZ format the text of the string is stored followed by a *null terminator*, which is just a byte containing machine zero.

Figure 5.1 shows a program that waits for a string to be input from the keyboard and stores it in ASCIIZ format in the buffer called *String*.

More precisely, the first part of this program takes the input string and stores it exactly as typed, except that the terminating carriage return is converted to a null terminator. The second part of the program echoes the input string to the screen. These two basic operations will be used throughout the chapter.

There are only a few noteworthy items in PROG5_1:

Line 25. The value 01H is moved into **ah** in preparation for using **function 01H** of **int 21H**. This function waits for a character to be input from the keyboard and stores the corresponding ASCII code in the **al** register.

Lines 27-34. This is the main input loop. The **loop** instruction was not used since a value for **cx** was not known in advance. (Later we will encounter a variant of **loop** that could be used.) Instead, we make use of an unconditional jump, from line 34 back to the label *getLoop*.

Such a construction requires an escape hatch, and this is provided by the conditional jump on line 31. The loop logic tests each arriving character for equality with CR. If the character is not equal to CR, it is stored in the next position in String. If it equals CR, it is not stored and control leaves the loop.

Line 38. At this point in the program, the carriage return has arrived and **bx** has already been incremented, hence it is time to store the null terminator. The requisite instruction has the form

```
mov      [bx], 0
```

But, as written, this instruction is an example of an anonymous reference, because it gives **MASM** no clue about whether 0 should be moved into the byte at **ds:bx** or into the word starting at that address or even into some bigger region. To resolve the ambiguity requires writing the instruction as

```
mov      BYTE PTR [bx], 0
```

BYTE PTR is one of the **MASM** *type operators*. Of course, it is needed only because **MASM** does not type pointers in the way that, say, **C** does. The interpretation of this line is

FIGURE 5.1 ASCIIZ STRING HANDLING

```
 1   TITLE Prog5_1.asm   ASCIIZ String Handling
 2
 3
 4   LEN     EQU       10
 5   CR      EQU       0dh
 6   LF      EQU       0ah
 7
 8   DOSSEG
 9   .MODEL SMALL
10
11   .STACK 100h
12
13   .DATA
14
15           String DB (LEN + 1) dup(?)
16
17   .CODE
18
19   Start:
20
21           mov     ax, @DATA
22           mov     ds, ax
23
24           mov     bx, OFFSET String    ;point bx to String
25           mov     ah, 01h              ;prepare to use function 01h
26                                        ; of int 21h
27   getLoop:
28
29           int     21h
30           cmp     al, CR               ;look for a CR in al
31           je      getEnd
32           mov     [bx], al             ;bx points to storage location
33           inc     bx
34           jmp     getLoop
35
36   getEnd:
37
38           mov     BYTE PTR [bx], 0     ;CR is converted to null term.
39
40           mov     ah, 02h              ;these five lines print a
41           mov     dl, CR               ; newline, i.e. a CR
42           int     21h                  ;  followed by a LF
43           mov     dl, LF
44           int     21h
45
46           mov     bx, OFFSET String    ;point bx to start of String
47
48
49   nextChar:
50
51           cmp     BYTE PTR [bx], 0     ;have we reached the null
52           je      endNextChar          ;  terminator yet?
53           mov     dl, [bx]             ;keep printing until
54           int     21h                  ; we reach it
```

```
55              inc     bx
56              jmp     nextChar
57
58   endNextChar:
59
60              mov     ax, 4c00h       ;program termination with 00h in
61              int     21h             ; al as the "return code"
62
63   END    Start
```

the obvious one: view **bx** as a pointer to a byte of data and therefore interpret [**bx**] as a byte. **MASM** will make every effort to resolve references without help. Figure 5.2 shows the effect of using this instruction with **BYTE PTR** and with two commonly used alternatives, **WORD PTR** and **DWORD PTR**.

Rather than using line 38 in its present form we could have initialized **bx** to 0 and then referred to *String[bx]*. If this had been done, **MASM** would have accepted

```
        mov      String[bx], 0
```

without **BYTE PTR**. Why? Because **MASM** keeps a *symbol table*, which contains information about user-defined identifiers. In that symbol table *String* is given type **BYTE** since it was defined using a **DB** statement. **MASM** therefore assumes that a reference such as *String[bx]* refers to a byte location.

Continuing a little further with this aside, suppose that 07H must be moved into *String[0]* and 1FH into *String[1]*. This could be done using two instructions:

```
        mov      String[0], 07h
        mov      String[1], 1fh
```

But it can also be done with the single instruction

```
        mov      WORD PTR String[0], 1f07h
```

WORD PTR is needed here to *override* the defined data size of *String*.

The reader who wishes to see a **MASM** symbol table can easily do so by looking at a .LST file, which is generated as a byproduct of the assembly process. The symbol table is included among the various statistics given at the end of the .LST file.

Line 40. Characters will be printed to the screen using the same **function 02H** of **int 21H** that we used in the previous chapter. Recall that the ASCII code for the character to be printed must be in the **dl** register.

Lines 49-56. This is the basic print-to-the-screen loop. It holds no surprises.

Line 60. The instruction

```
        mov      ax, 4c00h
```

FIGURE 5.2 EFFECT OF TYPING POINTERS

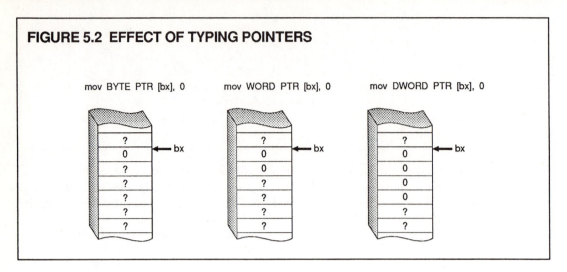

is equivalent to the pair of instructions

```
mov     ah, 4ch
mov     al, 00h
```

The first of these instructions is expected at this point: we are initializing **ah** for a call to **function 4CH** of **int 21H** in order to terminate the program. The second requires explanation.

Function 4CH performs an interesting service that we have not yet mentioned. **DOS** maintains a parameter called the *system error level*, which is useful in communication between different programs. The convention generally used is that a program that success-fully accomplishes its task sets the system error level to 0 at termination; in the contrary case, it sets the system error level to a non-zero value. A program can set the system error level by leaving the desired value in **al** and then exiting by **function 4CH**. Hence lines 60 and 61 are signaling successful completion. 4C00H can be replaced with, say, 4C01H to indicate an unsuccessful termination. Of course, it is not necessary to set an error code in the present program, but it is a good habit to acquire and costs nothing extra.

An example will best illustrate how the error level is really used. Consider the problem of writing a batch file that will call **MASM** and **LINK** to process a .ASM file. This batch file should call **MASM** and then, only if the assembly is successful, it should call **LINK**. It can be written in this way (where for simplicity the **MASM** and **LINK** command-line flags are omitted):

```
masm %1;
if errorlevel 1 goto stop
link %1;
:stop
```

Again, we will not discuss batch-file syntax in detail — the reader should consult any **DOS** reference manual for that information. It suffices to say that we have used the correct format so that the batch-file interpreter will recognize *stop* as a label. This batch file works because **MASM** sets the error level using the convention just introduced. Our example shows the technique used to query the error level from a batch file. There is also (naturally!) a function available in **int 21H** that can be used to determine the value of the error level from within a program.

We made no attempt to do *bounds checking* on strings that are input to PROG5_1. In other words, even though *String*, the storage buffer, is only big enough to hold 10 characters, nothing in the code stops the user from entering a larger number of characters, thereby corrupting memory at addresses above the end of *String*. It certainly would not be hard to add such error-checking code but, in order to keep to the essentials, we have refrained from doing so.

At this point, PROG5_1.ASM should be processed by **MASM** and **LINK** so that its execution can be checked from the **DOS** prompt and, especially, in **CODEVIEW**. There is not enough new material in this program to justify dealing with its **CODEVIEW** trace in detail in the text, but here are a few points to consider.

A good watch command to use is

```
        wb String L b
```

The last 'b' stands for the length to be watched, 0BH or 11 bytes. (There is another slight Microsoft inconsistency here. **MASM** requires that hex numbers begin with a digit and so won't accept BH — it insists on 0BH. On the other hand, the current version of **CODEVIEW** requires that you write B — it will not accept 0B or 0BH. Such is the lot of the programmer.)

When using a debugger, it is sometimes helpful to prefill buffers with some pattern, since this makes it easier to see the new data as it is entered. (This technique has been called *tracks in the snow*.) The **CODEVIEW** command that initializes a region is 'f' (for *fill*) and a reasonable version of the command to use here is

```
        f String L b ff
```

This fills the 11 bytes starting at the beginning of *String* with copies of the hex value 0FFH. The count in the 'f' command is always in bytes.

Here is one final observation on a potentially confusing point. Suppose that PROG5_1 is run under **CODEVIEW** with the 'e' command and that the user plans to input "abcde." After line 29 executes, the program will pause and wait for input, continuing as soon as the 'a' is typed and performing its processing on the 'a'. It will then pause for input until the 'b' is typed, process the 'b', and so on. On the other hand, when run from the **DOS** command line, the program will wait for the whole string "abcde" and the carriage return before it does anything. This difference in behavior has nothing to do with the present program. It arises from the fact that **DOS** buffers command line input. No input typed at the keyboard is forwarded to the program until the carriage return is entered.

Exercise 5-1. Another popular string format stores the string length in the first byte, followed immediately by the text of the string. There is no string terminator and the length of the string is limited to 255 characters. Rewrite PROG5_1.ASM using this alternate format.

Exercise 5-2. Write a program that prompts the user to input a string and counts the number of times "hat" occurs as a substring of the input. You may assume that the length of the input string is less than 80 and that "hat" occurs no more than 9 times.

SECTION 3 PROCEDURES

PROG5_1.ASM contains two blocks of code, one that gets a string from the keyboard and stores it as an ASCIIZ string and another that takes an ASCIIZ string stored in a buffer and prints it to the screen.

These blocks will obviously be useful in many different programs, and so we are faced with the problem of making this code readily available to other programs that needs it. This problem also arises in high-level languages, and the solution is the same. The code is encapsulated in a form called a *procedure*, which can be used as many times as needed. Figure 5.3 shows PROG5_1.ASM rewritten so that the two blocks of code now appear as procedures. We also introduced a third procedure, which prints a newline ({CR,LF} pair) to the screen.

The procedures in Figure 5.3 have the general format:

```
procName        PROC            NEAR

        ;code for the procedure

        ret

procName ENDP
```

procName is a user-defined name for the procedure. **PROC** is a keyword that tells **MASM** that this is a procedure. The code for every procedure should end with the **ret** (*return*) instruction, and the last line in the procedure should be

```
procName ENDP
```

where the directive **ENDP** means *end of procedure*.

We will now discuss the call and return instructions, briefly introduced in Chapter 2, and in the process shed light on the **NEAR** directive. As indicated in Chapter 3, the instruction

```
call    Proc1
```

transfers control to the procedure named *Proc1*. But there are two distinct kinds of procedure calls. In some cases the code that is making the call (the *caller*) resides in the same segment as the procedure being called (the *callee*). This configuration is referred to as a *near call*, and that is what the keyword **NEAR** signifies. In other circumstances, either because the code is too large to fit in one segment, or because the logical structure of the program makes

FIGURE 5.3 USING PROCEDURES

```
 1   TITLE Prog5_2.asm  An Improved Version Using Procedures
 2
 3   LEN     EQU     80
 4   CR      EQU     0dh
 5   LF      EQU     0ah
 6
 7   DOSSEG
 8   .MODEL SMALL
 9
10   .STACK 100h
11
12   .DATA
13
14           Prompt1    DB    "Input a String:", 0
15           Prompt2    DB    "Do another?  ", 0
16           String     DB    (LEN + 1) dup(?)
17
18   .CODE
19
20   ;------------------------------------------------------------
21
22   Start:
23
24           mov     ax, @DATA
25           mov     ds, ax
26
27   Begin:
28
29           mov     bx, OFFSET Prompt1     ;point bx to the string to print
30           call    PutStr
31
32           call    newLine
33           call    newLine
34
35           mov     bx, OFFSET String      ;point bx to the input buffer
36           call    getStr
37
38           call    newLine
39           call    newLine
40
41           mov     bx, OFFSET String
42           call    putStr
43
44           call    newLine
45           call    newLine
46
47           mov     bx, OFFSET Prompt2
48           call    putStr
49
50           mov     bx, OFFSET String
51           call    getStr
52
53           call    newLine
54           call    newLine
```

Figure 5.3 cont.

```
 55
 56          mov     bx, OFFSET String
 57          cmp     BYTE PTR [bx], 'y'
 58          je      Begin
 59
 60          mov     ax, 4c00h
 61          int     21h
 62
 63  ;------------------------------------------------------------
 64
 65  getStr PROC NEAR
 66
 67          mov     ah, 01h             ;prepare to use function 01h
 68                                      ; of int 21h
 69  getLoop:
 70
 71          int     21h
 72          cmp     al, CR              ;look for a CR in al
 73          je      getEnd
 74          mov     [bx], al            ;bx points to storage location
 75          inc     bx
 76          jmp     getLoop
 77
 78  getEnd:
 79
 80          mov     BYTE PTR [bx], 0    ;CR is converted to null term.
 81          ret
 82
 83  getStr  ENDP
 84
 85  ;------------------------------------------------------------
 86
 87  putStr PROC NEAR                    ;expects bx to point to string
 88
 89          mov     ah, 2h              ;prepare to print a char with int 21h
 90
 91  nextChar:
 92
 93          cmp     BYTE PTR [bx], 0h   ;check for null terminator
 94          je      foundEnd            ;when found, exit
 95          mov     dl, [bx]            ;print with int 21h
 96          int     21h
 97          inc     bx                  ;point to next char
 98          jmp     nextChar
 99
100  foundEnd:
101
102          ret
103
104  putStr ENDP
105
106  ;------------------------------------------------------------
107
108  newLine PROC NEAR
109
```

```
110          mov     ah, 02h              ;these five lines give a newline
111          mov     dl, CR               ;   i.e. a CR followed by a LF.
112          int     21h
113          mov     dl, LF
114          int     21h
115
116          ret
117
118  newLine ENDP
119
120  ;-------------------------------------------------------------
121
122  END Start
```

it desirable, or for a variety of other reasons, the caller and the callee may reside in different segments. When this occurs, we have a *far call*, and a procedure of this kind is defined using the keyword **FAR** in place of **NEAR**. Incidentally, it is frequently unnecessary to write either **NEAR** or **FAR**: if neither is written, the default is **NEAR** (at least when the directive **.MODEL SMALL** is used).

In practical terms, the distinction between **NEAR** and **FAR** calls should be clear. In the **NEAR** case only **ip** need be changed in order to point to the code for the procedure, while in the **FAR** case both **cs** and **ip** must be changed. As well, arrangements must be made for the return of control to the instruction just beyond the **call** after completion of the callee. Consequently, the return address must be saved, and this is done by pushing it onto the stack. For a **NEAR** call, only **ip** is pushed; for a **FAR** call both **cs** and **ip** are pushed. In the latter case, it is worth noting that the processor acts in a consistent manner: when it stores any kind of information, the less significant part is stored at the lower memory address. In the present context, this means that **cs** (the more significant part) is pushed first, followed by **ip**, so that **ip** occupies the lower-address position on the stack.

Hence the **call** instruction performs two actions:

• Pushes the return address.

• Transfers control to the callee.

The **ret** instruction undoes these actions:

• Pops the return address.

• Transfers control to that address.

Although there are **retn** (*return near*) and **retf** (*return far*) instructions, they are usually not needed since **MASM** will use the correct return based on whether the procedure was declared **NEAR** or **FAR**.

The formalism of procedure declarations is not essential. It is provided mainly to increase program readability. The line

```
Proc1 PROC NEAR
```

can be replaced with a simple label, say

```
Name:
```

The corresponding line

```
        call    Proc1
```

should then be replaced by

```
        call    Name
```

The transfer of control will occur exactly as before since **MASM** views a procedure name as nothing more than a label. We will see later that it is possible to define **FAR** labels, so that even **FAR** calls can be handled in this way. Why do this? Some programmers use labels because they decrease the number of overhead lines that must be written. But using procedure names does not increase execution time or the size of the machine code, and makes programs somewhat more readable. Hence we will nearly always use the **PROC** directive in this book. But here, as nearly everywhere in programming, it is a good idea to experiment in order to establish the limits of the formalisms being used.

Each of the procedures *getStr* and *putStr* must be given information from the calling program. *getStr* must know the offset of the buffer in which to leave the string, and *putStr* requires the offset of the string that is to be printed. In each case, the offset was passed in the **bx** register. Using registers is a standard technique for passing parameters to assembly language procedures. We have already encountered it several times since it is the method used by the functions in **int 21H**. The pros and cons of this method of parameter passing and the details of another method will be the substance of the next section.

There is not much more to say about PROG5_2. Notice the locations of the procedures. They are all inside the code segment — a requirement enforced by **MASM**. Also, they are not nested, in the sense that no procedure definition begins inside another procedure. That is illegal in the present assembly language and unnecessary because the scope of each procedure is the entire file in which it is defined. To increase readability, we have very visibly divided the code for the different procedures by means of "comments" like the one on line 63.

Finally, the code on line 57 is totally inadequate: the program interprets anything other than 'y' (lowercase) as meaning "no."

Exercise 5-3. Improve PROG5_2 so that it also recognizes 'Y' (uppercase) as an affirmative response and requires the user to repeat the input whenever an inappropriate key is pressed.

Exercise 5-4. Write a program containing two procedures: *toLower*, which is passed the offset of an ASCIIZ in the **bx** register and changes every uppercase letter in that string to lowercase; and *toUpper*, which is the obvious analog. The program should contain a loop that prompts for the input of strings and prints them to the screen after they have been processed by *toLower* and *toUpper*.

Exercise 5-5. Convert your solution to Exercise 5-4 into separate procedures.

Exercise 5-6. Write a program that asks the user to input an integer and checks whether that integer is a multiple of three, printing its conclusion to the screen. The program should work with input integers having as many as 79 digits.

Suggestion: The inputs are potentially much too long to allow the use of machine operations such as **div**. Instead, use the standard fact that an integer is divisible by three only if the sum of its digits is divisible by three. Write a procedure that takes the input integer (formatted as an ASCIIZ string) and adds its digits, returning the answer in **ax**. The caller can then divide **ax** by three (using **div**) and check whether the remainder is zero.

SECTION 4 PASSING PARAMETERS ON THE STACK

There are two standard ways of passing parameters to a procedure: using registers and on the stack. The version of our program in Figure 5.4 uses the second method. The basic idea is simple: the caller pushes the procedure parameter onto the stack and the callee finds it there. When the procedure completes its task, the parameter should be popped from the stack. Here is a basic calling sequence that is typical of several used in Figure 5.4:

```
33      mov     ax, OFFSET String
34      push    ax
35      call    getStr
```

The aim is to push *OFFSET String* onto the stack because *getStr* now expects to find it there. As we pointed out earlier, an offset is a constant, and a constant cannot be the operand of the **push** instruction. Therefore, two instructions such as those on lines 33 and 34 are needed.

The **call** instruction on line 35 pushes the return **ip** onto the stack (only **ip** because it is a **NEAR** call) and transfers control to line 127, the beginning of the code for the *getStr* procedure. The first instructions in *getStr* are

```
129     push    bp
130     mov     bp, sp
```

These lines are critical to the parameter-passing mechanism, and we will include them in every procedure that passes parameters on the stack. To understand their purpose, consider the form of the stack after line 133, as depicted in Figure 5.5.

In general, our stack pictures will only show the part of the stack that pertains to the discussion at hand. Depending on the context, the program may have already stored items at higher addresses on the stack. As is generally the case in a stack picture, each box in Figure 5.5 represents a word. Recall that **sp** is automatically adjusted by the microprocessor so that it always points to the top of the stack.

The explanation for line 129 is easy: we are going to use **bp** in this procedure and so we are saving its value in order to restore it later. The most interesting question here is *what* **bp** will be used for, and the answer involves a discussion of addressing modes. To date, only the expression [**bx**] has been used in indirect addressing. When addressing is discussed in

FIGURE 5.4 PASSING PARAMETERS ON THE STACK

```
 1    TITLE Prog5_3.asm Another Version. Passing Parameters on the Stack.
 2
 3    LEN     EQU    80
 4    CR      EQU    0dh
 5    LF      EQU    0ah
 6
 7    DOSSEG
 8    .MODEL SMALL
 9
10    .STACK 100h
11
12    .DATA
13
14            Prompt1    DB     "Input a string:  ", 0
15            Prompt2    DB     "Do another?  ", 0
16            String     DB     (LEN + 1) dup(?)
17
18    .CODE
19
20    Start:
21
22            mov     ax, @DATA
23            mov     ds, ax
24
25    Begin:
26            mov     ax, OFFSET Prompt1
27            push    ax
28            call    putStr
29
30            call    newLine
31            call    newLine
32
33            mov     ax, OFFSET String
34            push    ax
35            call    getStr
36
37            call    newLine
38            call    newLine
39
40            mov     ax, OFFSET String
41            push    ax
42            call    putStr
43
44            call    newLine
45            call    newLine
46
47            mov     ax, OFFSET Prompt2
48            push    ax
49            call    PutStr
50
51            mov     ax, OFFSET String
52            push    ax
53            call    getStr
54
```

```
55             call    NewLine
56             call    NewLine
57
58             mov     bx, OFFSET String
59             cmp     BYTE PTR [bx], 'y'
60             je      Begin
61
62             mov     ax, 4c00h
63             int     21h
64
65      ;------------------------------------------------------------------
66
67      newLine PROC NEAR
68
69             push    ax
70             push    dx
71
72             mov     ah, 02h                 ;these five lines give a NewLine
73             mov     dl, CR                  ; i.e. a CR followed by a LF.
74             int     21h
75             mov     dl, LF
76             int     21h
77
78             pop     dx
79             pop     ax
80
81             ret
82
83      newLine ENDP
84
85      ;---------------------------------------------------------------
86
87      ;OFFSET of string to be printed must be on the stack
88      ; and the string must be null terminated
89
90      putStr PROC NEAR
91
92             push    bp
93             mov     bp, sp
94
95             push    ax
96             push    bx
97             push    dx
98
99             mov     bx, [bp + 4]            ;expects bx to point to string
100            mov     ah, 2h                  ;prepare to print a char with int 21h
101
102     nextChar:
103
104            cmp     BYTE PTR [bx], 0h       ;check for null
105            je      foundEnd                ;when found, exit
106            mov     dl, [bx]                ;print with int 21h
107            int     21h
108            inc     bx                      ;point to next char
109            jmp     nextChar
110
111     foundEnd:
```

Figure 5.4 cont.

```
112
113          pop      bx
114          pop      dx
115          pop      ax
116
117          pop      bp
118          ret      2
119
120  putStr ENDP
121
122  ;----------------------------------------------------------------
123
124  ;OFFSET of large enough buffer must have been pushed onto stack
125  ;string will be null terminated
126
127  getStr PROC NEAR
128
129          push     bp
130          mov      bp, sp
131
132          push     ax
133          push     bx
134
135          mov      bx, [bp + 4]        ;base address of string buffer
136          mov      ah, 01h             ;prepare to use function 01h
137                                       ; of int 21h
138  getLoop:
139
140          int      21h
141          cmp      al, CR              ;look for a CR in al
142          je       getEnd
143          mov      [bx], al            ;bx points to storage location
144          inc      bx
145          jmp      getLoop
146
147  getEnd:
148
149          mov      BYTE PTR [bx], 0    ;CR is converted to null term.
150
151          pop      bx
152          pop      ax
153
154          pop      bp
155          ret      2
156
157  getStr ENDP
158
159  ;----------------------------------------------------------------
160
161  END Start
```

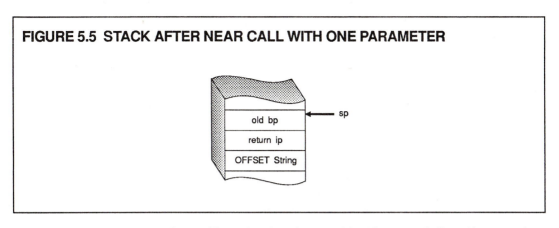

FIGURE 5.5 STACK AFTER NEAR CALL WITH ONE PARAMETER

detail in Chapter 6, we will see that there is a considerable range of allowable expressions that can legally be placed inside the square brackets.

At the moment, we need to know that [**bp**] is one of the legal indirect addressing expressions and that it behaves differently from [**bx**] in an important way. The expression [**bx**] produces machine code that uses the value in **bx** as the offset and by default uses the value in **ds** as the segment address. The expression [**bp**] still uses the value in **bp** as the offset but uses the value in **ss** as the segment address. In other words, the **bp** register is designed for the indirect addressing of quantities on the stack.

Another important fact about indirect addressing is that an expression of the form

```
[bp + displacement]
```

where displacement is a 16-bit immediate quantity, is also legal. It is interpreted as a reference to the data item whose offset is

```
(value of bp) + displacement
```

and whose segment address is in **ss**.

For example, if the value of **bp** is currently 80H and the value of **ss** is 123AH, then [**bp** + 6] represents the data item whose address is 123A:0086 and [**bp** − 6] represents the item with address 123A:007A.

With these observations in mind, it is time to explain line 130 of Figure 5.4. Since **sp** always points to the top of the stack, the effect of this instruction is to point **bp** to the top of the stack, and Figure 5.6 sums up the situation immediately after line 130.

In light of the preceding discussion, the words denoted by [**bp**], [**bp** + 2], and [**bp** + 4] give the values of old **bp**, return **ip**, and *OFFSET String*, respectively. This situation is summarized on the diagram by showing **bp**, **bp** + 2, and **bp** + 4 as "pointers" to those data items. Here, and in most similar contexts, [**bp**] and [**bp** + 2] are of no significance. The item of paramount importance is [**bp** + 4] because this is the expression that the procedure will use to access its data.

The central part of the code for *getStr* in Figure 5.4 is a direct translation of the corresponding section of the previous program. In that version, **bx** contained *OFFSET*

FIGURE 5.6 STACK AFTER SETTING THE BASE POINTER

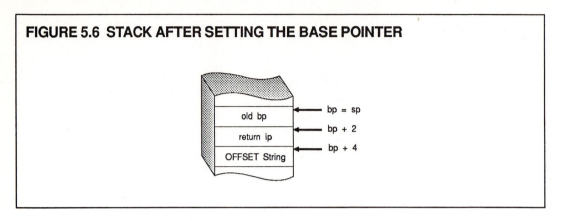

String. Here, *OFFSET String* is available using the expression [**bp** + 4]. To make the previous code work in the present context, we need only add the line

```
mov       bx, [bp + 4]
```

The programmer must correctly balance the pushes and pops that occur during the procedure. The processor expects that the return address will be on the top of the stack when the **ret** instruction is reached. If not, it will still interpret the value on top of the stack as a return address and transfer control there, inevitably resulting in disaster for the program. Of course, as part of this stack balancing act, stored values should be restored to their original locations, and so the pops must be done in reverse order to the pushes.

The *getStr* procedure shows three examples of balancing the stack.

First, instead of a simple **ret**, line 155 contains the instruction

```
ret       2
```

This instruction illustrates a convenient extension of the **ret** instruction, which uses the general syntax

```
ret       2n
```

where n is an integer. This form works just like **ret** except that it removes an extra 2n bytes from the stack. Its use here (and nearly always) is to remove the passed parameter(s) from the stack. Notice in particular that, since *OFFSET String* and the return address were pushed onto the stack first, they must be removed last and so the **ret 2** is correctly positioned.

As an aside, it should be pointed out that there is some ambiguity about which part of the program has responsibility for clearing the parameters from the stack. As this example indicates, the assembly language convention is that the callee should clear the stack (usually by means of a **ret 2n**). Unfortunately, some high-level languages use the convention that the caller should remove the parameters from the stack after control has returned from the procedure. This point will be discussed further in Chapter 14.

Second, the value of **bp** that was pushed onto the stack on line 129 is restored on line 154.

Third, **ax** and **bx** were pushed onto the stack on lines 132 and 133 and are restored in reverse order on lines 151 and 152. The reason for these pushes and pops is that **ax** and **bx** are changed by *getStr*. If this is to be a truly useful procedure, it should be callable from any point in a program with the assurance that it will not disrupt computations currently in progress. As mentioned earlier, the **int 21H** functions (with some necessary exceptions) behave in this way. The general policy in this book will be that all procedures (and, later, macros as well) must restore the registers that they use. The only exception to this rule is that procedures returning a value to the caller can most conveniently return this value in a register. A standard convention, which we will adopt, is that 16-bit values are generally returned in the **ax** register. For this reason, it will be unsafe for the user to make the blanket assumption that **ax** is preserved by our procedures (or by our macros).

In *newLine*, **bp** was not initialized to **sp** because it was never used.

PROG5_3 has shown how a single parameter is passed on the stack. The situation is analogous for any number of parameters. As an illustration, consider Figure 5.7. In this program fragment, we pretend that three parameters are required by a procedure named *procThree*. We assume, in this particular call, that the three passed values were defined in the data segment.

After execution of the instruction

```
mov      bp, sp
```

in *procThree*, the stack has the form shown in Figure 5.8.

On the basis of that diagram, we can make the following general observation:

- In the case of a **NEAR** call, the parameters are addressable as [**bp** + 4], [**bp** + 6], [**bp** + 8], ···, however many there are, and where the numbering is in reverse order in the sense that [**bp** + 4] is the parameter that was pushed last.

Suppose now that *procThree* is a **FAR** procedure rather than a **NEAR** procedure. The only difference in the use of the stack is that **cs** will now be pushed as well as **ip**. The corresponding stack picture changes slightly, as Figure 5.9 shows.

The resulting parameter list begins one word further down the stack. Hence we can make a statement that is totally analogous to the previous one:

- In the case of a **FAR** call, the parameters are addressable as [**bp** + 6], [**bp** + 8], [**bp** + 10], ··· , however many there are, and where the numbering is in reverse order in the sense that [**bp** + 6] is the parameter that was pushed last.

Of the two methods of parameter passing that we have introduced, in registers and on the stack, the method of using registers is certainly the traditional one. There are arguments that favor each:

- Passing parameters on the stack is slower. After all, those extra pushes and pops are not free. As well, it will be seen later that indirect addressing slows down access to data. For example, consider the instructions

```
mov      cx, ax
```

and

FIGURE 5.7 PASSING THREE PARAMETERS TO A PROCEDURE

```
                                    .
                                    .
                                    .
.DATA

        Num1    DW              ?
        Num2    DW              ?
        Num3    DW              ?
                                    .
                                    .
                                    .
.CODE

                                    .
                                    .
                                    .
;calling procThree
        push    Num1
        push    Num2
        push    Num3
        call    procThree
                                    .
                                    .
                                    .
procThree       PROC            NEAR

        push    bp
        mov     bp, sp
                                    .
                                    .
                                    .
        ;here the parameter Num3 is referred to as [bp + 4]
        ;                   Num2 is referred to as [bp + 6]
        ;                   Num1 is referred to as [bp + 8]
                                    .
                                    .
                                    .
        pop     bp
        ret     6           ;remove three parameters from the stack

procThree       ENDP
                                    .
                                    .
                                    .
```

```
        mov     cx, [bp + 4]
```

The first one might be used if a parameter had been passed in **ax** and the second if it had been passed on the stack. The second instruction turns out to require more clock cycles than the first. But there are many other factors that influence the speed of a program. For example, the **DOS** functions in **int 21H** receive their

FIGURE 5.8 STACK AFTER NEAR CALL WITH THREE PARAMETERS

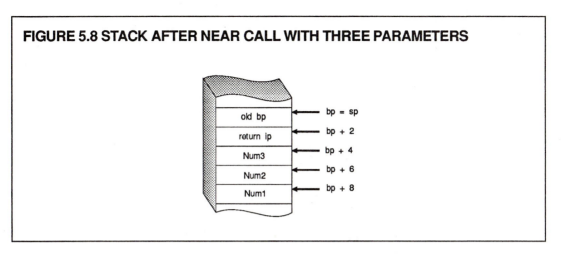

parameters in registers but are still notoriously slow. Try filling the screen with characters by using a loop of 2000 calls to **function 02H**!

- Registers are generally in short supply. Consequently, it is often necessary to free a register by saving its contents before it can be used. This will partly destroy the time advantage just mentioned. If there are many parameters, there will not be enough registers to hold them all. It is possible to circumvent this problem by placing all the parameters in a single block of memory, usually in the data segment, and then passing the offset of that block as a parameter. This works but, unfortunately, exacts another penalty. The callee must use indirect addressing to access the data items, so that another of the time advantages is lost.

- Programs that use the stack as the passing mechanism are easier to document and simpler to use. When parameters are passed on the stack, the user need only know the order in which to push the parameters. Contrast this situation with the irregularity of usage of the registers in the **int 21H** functions. If the offset of a string is needed, it is *usually* passed in **dx**, but there are enough exceptions to this rule to keep the programmer alert!

- To a person with the right cast of mind, assembly language programs are fun to write. But the economics of the modern programming world dictate that few large programs are written entirely in assembly language. It is probably a reasonable rule of thumb that an assembly language program will take ten times as long to write and be three times faster and three times smaller than a high-level language program that does the same job. But nowadays machines are fast, memory is cheap and plentiful, and programming time is very expensive. As a consequence, the trend is toward writing most code in a higher-level language (with C being the current favorite) and then *patching* with assembly language procedures to gain speed in those limited areas where it is imperative.

For this reason it is important, even in a beginning text such as this, to become aware of the conventions used in interfacing assembly language to high-level languages. In high-level languages, procedures generally receive their

FIGURE 5.9 STACK AFTER FAR CALL WITH THREE PARAMETERS

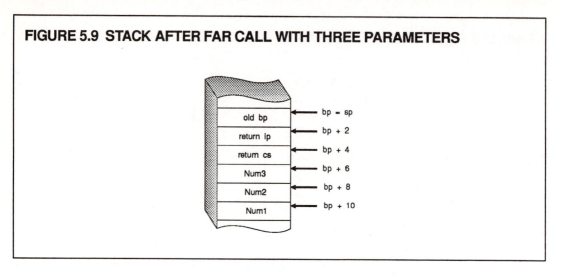

parameters on the stack, and so assembly language procedures that are destined to work with these high-level languages must do likewise.

Since the weight of these reasons seems to favor passing parameters on the stack, we chose this as our default passing mechanism. There are certainly circumstances under which registers should be used, and our procedures will do so when appropriate. For example, in a graphics procedure that draws a pixel on the screen and that may be called thousands of times, it is essential that every clock cycle be shaved, and so passing the coordinates of the pixel in registers would be the only reasonable technique.

A practical approach to the problem of parameter passing is to write the entire program using the stack to pass parameters and then to *profile* the execution of the program. This means that the program is run under the control of a *profiler*, which determines how much time the program spends in its various procedures, loops, etc. With this information available as a guide, the programmer can examine the code and try to find strategies for speeding up the sluggish sections, and these strategies might include passing parameters in registers, replacing procedure calls by macros (which we will discuss in Section 6 of this chapter), finding better algorithms, and making any other modifications that ingenuity suggests.

As one of the example programs in Chapter 15, we will develop a simple profiler, and will show how it can be used to analyze executing programs.

Exercise 5-7. Repeat Exercise 5-4 but use the stack to pass parameters

Exercise 5-8. Repeat Exercise 5-5 but use the stack to pass parameters.

Exercise 5-9. Repeat Exercise 5-6 but use the stack to pass parameters.

Exercise 5-10. Write a *swapChar* procedure that is passed the offsets of two byte-size locations in the data segment and swaps the contents of those locations. As usual, the procedure should be embedded in a short calling program that can be used to exercise it.

SECTION 5 LIBRARIES

Procedures are the main building blocks of assembly language programs, as is the case with most other programming languages.

Our plan of attack from this point on will be to produce fairly general-purpose procedures that will be reusable in a wide variety of situations and will ease the work of future programming.

The question immediately arises of how to organize these procedures. Where will they be stored? What mechanisms will be used to attach the procedures to the programs that use them?

An obvious answer to these questions is to physically include the code for a procedure with any program that uses it, just as we did in PROG5_4.ASM. This could be achieved by retyping the code for the procedure each time it is needed (madness!) or by using the file merge capabilities of a text editor (better).

In fact, **MASM** has its own built-in file-merging capability. Specifically, the directive

```
INCLUDE fileName
```

requests **MASM** to insert a copy of the disk file named *fileName* at the current position in the source code. *fileName* need not be in the current directory, although **MASM** checks there first. If it does not find *fileName* locally, it looks in the subdirectories listed under the environment variable named INCLUDE. For details on this and other environment variables, refer to the **MASM** manual.

We will find several uses for the **INCLUDE** directive, but it will not be used for the present purpose. The reason is that there is a far better way of storing and accessing procedures, namely by using libraries.

Before discussing libraries, let us quickly review the process of building an executable program. First the code is processed by **MASM**, which produces a .OBJ (*object*) file. **LINK** then "links" together one or more .OBJ files to produce the final .EXE file. This description perhaps suggests the "much better way." When the code for a new procedure is written, why not have **MASM** process it immediately and store it as a .OBJ file? In this way, it can be linked with other .OBJ files as needed, without the inefficiency of reassembling it each time. There are other reasons why this approach is especially enticing.

First, the .OBJ code is much, much smaller than the original .ASM file because the .OBJ code is basically just the final machine code with a modest amount of overhead information. (Check some examples on the disk to see the relative sizes of .OBJ files compared with the corresponding .ASM files.)

Second, **LINK** has an extremely useful ability in managing .OBJ files. It can work with specially formatted collections of .OBJ files, called *libraries*. **LINK** will search through one or more libraries looking for the procedures that a program requires and will adjoin the code for these procedures to the program. For example, a library may contain 100 procedures in .OBJ form, and a particular program may need three of these. **LINK** will then search the library, extract the code for only those three procedures, and attach that code to the program to form the final .EXE. This is a tremendously valuable technique and we naturally want to exploit it to the utmost.

Third, many suppliers of utility packages (graphics routines, for example) prefer to distribute their packages in .OBJ form in order to protect the privacy of their source code.

Telling **LINK** which libraries to search is easy. The **LINK** command line has the form

```
link listOfObjs, exeName, mapFileName, listOfLibs
```

Details can be found in the **LINK** manual. We will only point out that the list of libraries to be searched is entered in the last field of the **LINK** command line. The library names can be separated by spaces, for example. **LINK** requires libraries to be stored as disk files with extension .LIB, but the extension can be omitted on the command line. **LINK** assumes that all names appearing in the last field are libraries. Libraries need not be kept in the working directory. If the LIB environment variable is set, then **LINK** will look in the corresponding subdirectories for the listed libraries.

We have started a single library, USER.LIB, to be used in conjunction with this book. In most of our future batch files (and, later, in our **MAKE** files), this library will appear on the **LINK** command line.

Setting up a library is straightforward since the **MASM** package includes an easy-to-use utility called **LIB** (*the librarian*) whose purpose is to establish and maintain libraries. **LIB** responds to only a few commands, the three most useful of which we will now introduce.

To set up a library, type

```
lib libName;
```

LIB will respond that this library does not exist (assuming it doesn't) and ask whether it should be created. If the answer is 'y', **LIB** creates the library.

A second command is

```
lib libName +objFileName;
```

which has the obvious effect — it adds *objFileName* to the library called *libName*. Incidentally, a path name must be used to qualify *libName* if it is not in the local directory. The third command is rather nice:

```
lib libName -+objFileName;
```

This is the updating command. It removes a previous version of *objFileName* from the library and replaces it by the current (presumably updated) version from the disk.

Code to be added to a library must first be processed by **MASM**. We start with a procedure written in the minimal form that **MASM** will accept. This procedure is not destined to become a stand-alone executable program and so some corners can be cut. For example, it does not require a stack and need not contain the usual termination code.

Figure 5.10 shows the *getStr* procedure written in such a minimal form, and Figure 5.11 contains another version of our sample program, updated to use procedures from the library USER.LIB.

The source code for *getStr* starts with a *procedure header*, which contains basic archiving information about the source code and describes the procedure's input parameters and return value. Procedure headers are an essential item of documentation and we will include one with every procedure that is "important enough" to be stored in a library. The information in the header should allow the procedure to be used without further reference to the procedure code. The REMARKS field can be used to transmit miscellaneous information about the procedure, such as warnings about side-effects or other anomalies. In a more formal setting, the procedure headers would be combined into a separate library documentation manual.

This header shows another **MASM** comment convention, which is convenient for writing longer comments. **MASM** recognizes the reserved word **COMMENT** as introducing a block comment. The first character other than white space occurring after the word **COMMENT** plays the role of the comment delimiter: the comment continues until the end of the line containing the next occurrence of that character. We generally use '#' as the comment delimiter, although this choice is quite arbitrary.

Figure 5.10 needs little commentary. The **END** directive on line 55 is not of the standard form

```
END        Label
```

that we have always used before. It would be incorrect to write

```
END        getStr
```

since there should be only one entry point to a program, and certainly that entry point ought to be in the calling program and not in a library module. Unfortunately, if multiple entry points are absentmindedly incorporated into a program, no error message is emitted. The only result is that **LINK** may make the wrong choice for the starting address of the program, with consequences that will become painfully obvious at run time.

Anther point that should be discussed is line 19:

```
PUBLIC    getStr
```

This line must be explained in conjunction with line 18 of Figure 5.11:

```
EXTRN getStr:NEAR, putStr:NEAR, newLine:NEAR
```

These lines are directives that are of interest to both **MASM** and **LINK**. First of all, **MASM** assembles PROG5_4.ASM before the code for GETSTR.OBJ is linked to it. Hence an identifier such as *getStr* will appear to **MASM** to be undefined. Consequently, **MASM** must be told that *getStr* is, in fact, defined in another file and that detailed information about it will appear in due course (at link time). But this is not sufficient. **MASM** must generate correct code for each usage of the identifier and so must know what kind of object it is. Is it just a constant? Is it an item declared in a data segment in some other file? If it is a data item, is it a byte or a word or one of the other legal alternatives? Is it a procedure name? If

FIGURE 5.10 FORMAT FOR A LIBRARY PROCEDURE

```
 1   TITLE  getStr.asm
 2
 3   COMMENT      #   PROCEDURE HEADER
 4   TYPE:          NEAR            FILE:  getStr.asm      LIBRARY: user.lib
 5   PURPOSE:       Inputs an ASCIIZ string from keyboard.
 6   CALLED AS:     getStr(Buffer)
 7                  where Buffer is a large enough storage area to hold string
 8                  including null-terminator. Buffer must be in segment pointed
 9                  to by ds.
10   RETURNS:       Nothing.
11   REMARKS:       Expects offset of Buffer to be passed on stack.
12               #  Changes CR into null-terminator.
13
14   CR        EQU    0dh
15
16   DOSSEG
17   .MODEL SMALL
18
19   PUBLIC GetStr
20
21   .CODE
22
23   getStr PROC NEAR
24
25          push    bp
26          mov     bp, sp
27
28          push    ax
29          push    bx
30
31          mov     bx, [bp + 4]          ;base address of string buffer
32          mov     ah, 01h               ;prepare to use function 01h
33                                        ; of int 21h
34   getLoop:
35
36          int     21h
37          cmp     al, CR                ;look for a CR in al
38          je      getEnd
39          mov     [bx], al              ;bx points to storage location
40          inc     bx
41          jmp     getLoop
42
43   getEnd:
44
45          mov     BYTE PTR [bx], 0      ;CR is converted to null term.
46
47          pop     bx
48          pop     ax
49
50          pop     bp
51          ret     2
52
53   getStr ENDP
54
55   END
```

FIGURE 5.11 CALLING LIBRARY PROCEDURES

```
 1   TITLE Prog5_4.asm   Another Version. Using Preassembled Library Procedures.
 2
 3         LEN      EQU      80
 4
 5   DOSSEG
 6   .MODEL SMALL
 7
 8   .STACK 100h
 9
10   .DATA
11
12         Prompt1 DB   "Input a string:  ", 0
13         Prompt2 DB   "Do another?  ", 0
14         String  DB   (LEN + 1) dup(?)
15
16   .CODE
17
18   EXTRN getStr:NEAR, putStr:NEAR, newLine:NEAR
19
20
21   ;----------------------------------------------------------------
22
23   Start:
24
25         mov    ax, @DATA
26         mov    ds, ax
27
28   Begin:
29
30         mov    ax, OFFSET Prompt1
31         push   ax
32         call   putStr
33         call   newLine
34         call   newLine
35
36         mov    ax, OFFSET String
37         push   ax
38         call   getStr
39         call   newLine
40         call   newLine
41
42         mov    ax, OFFSET String
43         push   ax
44         call   putStr
45         call   newLine
46         call   newLine
47
48         mov    ax, OFFSET Prompt2
49         push   ax
50         call   PutStr
51
52         mov    ax, OFFSET String
53         push   ax
54         call   getStr
```

Figure 5.11 cont.

```
55          call  newLine
56          call  newLine
57
58          mov   bx, OFFSET String
59          cmp   BYTE PTR [bx], 'y'
60          je    Begin
61
62          mov   ax, 4c00h
63          int   21h
64
65   END Start
```

so, is it a **NEAR** or a **FAR** procedure? The **EXTRN** directive answers these questions for **MASM**. For example,

```
            EXTRN     getStr:NEAR
```

obviously informs **MASM** that *getStr* is the name of a **NEAR** procedure. **MASM** knows that it is a procedure because **NEAR** and **FAR** are only used in connection with procedure names. (This is not quite accurate. **NEAR** and **FAR** are actually used in connection with labels, and a procedure name is an example of a label. This point will be explored in Chapter 12.)

Some other versions of the **EXTRN** directive are

```
            EXTRN    Number: ABS
            EXTRN    wData : WORD
            EXTRN    bData : BYTE
```

The first says that *Number* is a constant (i.e., an **ABS**olute constant), the second says that *wData* is a word variable, and the third says that *bData* is a byte variable.

The **EXTRN**s can be listed several to the line as in Figure 5.11 or one to a line as in the preceding display. One important point is that each **EXTRN** must occur inside the correct segment. For example, in our present program *getStr* is defined in the segment denoted by **.CODE** in the library module, whence the **EXTRN** directive is in that segment in Figure 5.11.

The **PUBLIC** declaration is essentially the dual to **EXTRN**. **EXTRN** is like an import license: it says that the item in question will be imported from some other file. **PUBLIC**, on the other hand, is like an export license. We pointed out earlier that some of the desirable features of structured programming are available in this assembly language. One of these features is privacy of variables. Specifically, the default is that a variable has *scope* (i.e., is only known within) the file in which it was defined. Here a variable means any user-defined quantity: data variables, labels, and procedure names are examples. It is **LINK** that polices this scope restriction by not allowing variables defined in one .OBJ file to be used in any other .OBJ file. But there are times when this is not desirable, and the present situation is a case in point. *getStr*, for example, is defined in its own .OBJ module and then stored in the library, yet PROG5_4.OBJ must be empowered to use *getStr*. This runs counter to the preceding privacy rules.

The solution to this problem is to declare *getStr* to be **PUBLIC**, as was done in Figure 5.10. This overrides the default and tells **LINK** to make *getStr* available to all the files being linked. Stated differently, **PUBLIC** makes *getStr* into a global identifier: it is known throughout the entire program. In this sense, **PUBLIC** is like an export license that gives **LINK** authority to release information about the identifier. Notice also that the **PUBLIC** directive does not need a qualifier such as **NEAR**. The **PUBLIC** directive resides in the module in which the symbol is defined and all the facts about the symbol are already known in that module.

One point to bear in mind is that **LINK** does not type-check the use of **PUBLIC** and **EXTRN**. If a procedure is defined as a **PUBLIC NEAR** in one module and used as an **EXTRN FAR** in another the program will certainly crash.

Figure 5.11 makes it clear that we have made a good deal of progress toward getting the small-scale structure of assembly language under control. A comparison of Figure 5.1 with Figure 5.11 shows that the latter program accomplishes much more using the same amount of code and, almost as importantly, many of the technical details of the program have been hidden behind the scenes. In Section 5, we take one further step in this direction.

Before leaving this example and the subject of libraries, it is a worthwhile exercise to analyze PROG5_4 using **CODEVIEW**. Here are some things to watch for:

- In dealing with the code for procedures, the F10 key is a useful alternative to F8. F8 steps through the procedure code while F10 jumps past the procedure. As soon as a procedure is working reliably, use F10 to bypass it.

- To step through the code for a procedure from a separate module (in a library, for example) and display the trace in source mode, **CODEVIEW** must be able to find the source code for the procedure. If the source code is not in the local directory, **CODEVIEW** will prompt for the name of the directory that contains it.

- When stepping through PROG5_4, use a watch command of the form

```
ww  ss:f0 1 10
```

so that the stack can be monitored. The things to watch for are the results of the pushes, and especially the concealed pushes resulting from the calls.

The procedures in USER.LIB are intended for use in a learning situation and so are not the most efficient possible. For example, the procedures are always written "knowing what we know now" even if later developments could improve the quality of the code. In addition, the procedures were assembled with **MASM**'s /zi switch and so contain line-number information for **CODEVIEW**. This means that **CODEVIEW** will have its full power when used on these procedures, but this line number information adds considerably to the sizes of the .OBJ files.

We will end this section on a slightly negative note. Often the same procedures must be used as **FAR** in some cases and as **NEAR** in others. Generally, separate libraries are maintained, one containing **FAR** forms of the procedures and the other containing **NEAR** forms. The appropriate library can then be linked with any application. The double libraries are necessary because, among other things, the return statement means something different in each case, and because the locations of the parameters on the stack are different. For example, rather than building the single library USER.LIB, we might have constructed two libraries called USERN.LIB and USERF.LIB. However, to minimize the level of complexity and because **NEAR** calls are adequate for all our applications, we chose to maintain only a **NEAR** library.

Exercise 5-11. Add the procedures *toUpper* and *toLower* (from Exercise 5-7) to USER.LIB.

Exercise 5-12. The **LIB** utility will generate a listing of library contents, which contains the names of the procedures in the library, together with their offsets from the beginning of the library and the names of the **PUBLIC** quantities they contain. To generate a listing file, type the command line

```
lib libName
```

and respond to the *Operations* prompt with a CR. At the *List File* prompt, supply a name for the list file, followed by a semicolon and a CR. Construct a list file for USER.LIB and peruse its contents.

Exercise 5-13. We made the point that each **EXTRN** directive for a symbol must be in the segment in which the symbol is defined. What is the effect of violating this rule? Answering this question will require the construction of examples and the use of the .LST file. It will also be helpful to look up the term *segment override* in the index.

SECTION 6 AN INTRODUCTION TO MACROS

Figure 5.11 still involves a good deal of uninteresting, repetitive writing. For example, the basic sequence on lines 30-32,

```
mov     ax, OFFSET Prompt1
push    ax
call    putStr
```

is repeated with variations several times in the program. The way to avoid this mindless repetition is the same is assembly language as in high-level languages, or in any text processing application, for that matter: the use of macro substitutions.

The macro capability that **MASM** offers is sufficiently complex that we devote all of Chapter 13 to it. However, even the most basic macros will vastly improve our programs.

The general format of a **MASM** macro is

macroName   **MACRO**   *listOfReplaceableParameters*

```
                    (code for macro)
```

ENDM

MACRO is a reserved word that informs **MASM** that this is the beginning of a macro definition. **ENDM** flags the end of the definition. The definition must appear in the file before the first use of the macro. The *listOfReplaceableParameters* is just a collection of zero or more text strings that will generally be repeated at various points in the macro code. A macro named *Macro1* is used (*called* or *invoked*) in the assembly language source code by writing an invocation line of the form

```
        Macro1    listOfArguments
```

MASM replaces this line by a copy of the macro code with each occurrence of a replaceable parameter replaced by the corresponding argument.

An example may make this process clearer. Consider this macro definition:

```
inpStr MACRO Buffer

        push    ax
        mov     ax, OFFSET Buffer
        push    ax
        call    getStr
        pop     ax

    ENDM
```

The one replaceable parameter is *Buffer*. We have named the macro *inpStr* since its purpose is to call the *getStr* procedure to input a string from the keyboard.

If *inpStr* is called by a line of the form

```
        inpStr    Prompt1
```

then **MASM** replaces this invocation line with the following code:

```
        push    ax
        mov     ax, OFFSET Prompt1
        push    ax
        call    getStr
        pop     ax
```

Our macros will normally restore all the registers that they alter (when this is possible), and so we have included an extra **push/pop** pair to save and restore **ax**.

As is the case with procedures, macros that are of lasting importance should have descriptive headers. We use very similar formats for procedure and macro headers. Here is a suitable header for *inpStr*:

```
COMMENT       #   MACRO HEADER
```

```
MACRO NAME:          inpStr          FILE: console.mac
PURPOSE:             Calls getStr to input an ASCIIZ string
                     from keyboard.
CALLED AS:           inpStr    Buffer
                     where Buffer is a storage area for the
                     string. Buffer must be in the segment pointed
                     to by ds.
REMARKS:             Buffer must be long enough to hold input
              #      string and null terminator.
```

To conserve space, we will not always show headers for the macros that we develop in the text, although every macro should have one. The reader who checks the contents of CONSOLE.MAC will find that it contains somewhat more elaborate versions of the macros than we are presenting in this chapter. These discrepancies exist because we will later endow these early macros with extra capabilities and the code in CONSOLE.MAC shows them in their final form. It is safe to use the macros from CONSOLE.MAC since they behave identically to the versions from this chapter in the elementary contexts in which we are using them.

It is convenient to add an external declaration,

```
        EXTRN   getStr:NEAR
```

to the code for *inpStr*. Since *inpStr* calls the library procedure *getStr*, this external declaration must occur somewhere in the source file. Making the line a part of the macro code ensures that it will be included. Also, each macro invocation line appears in the code segment and so the external declaration occurs in the correct segment. Of course, if a given macro is invoked several times in a given source module, then the corresponding external declaration will be repeated that number of times, but this is of no consequence.

The macro definition must appear in the source code file so that **MASM** can make the translation. The easiest way to incorporate the macro code when needed is to keep macros in special files that are adjoined to the source code by means of the **INCLUDE** directive. There is one slight technical problem here, namely that the **INCLUDE** directive is not as intelligent as the **LINK** library search capability. When **LINK** searches a library, it includes only those .OBJ files that are actually needed in the current code module. But **INCLUDE** includes the entire text in the named macro file even if only a few (or none) of the macros are actually called. This is not a very serious problem. Its main effect is to slow the assembly process if the macro files are really huge.

Our partial solution to this problem is to store the macros in several files, according to their general function. This approach has other obvious benefits. Of the various macro files that we will develop, the only one of immediate interest is CONSOLE.MAC. As the name suggests, this file contains macros relating to keyboard input and screen output. Figure 5.12 shows a number of other macros that are contained in CONSOLE.MAC.

Some of these macros are temporary because, as mentioned in Section 1, **functions 01H** and **02H** will be replaced by superior functions in Chapter 8.

Most of the macro code in Figure 5.12 should be clear from our prior discussions. An exception is the directive **LOCAL**, which occurs in the *Skip* macro. To see why this directive is necessary, first recall how a macro is used. Each time the macro is called, a copy of the macro code is substituted in the text, with correct values for the replaceable parameters. Now consider what happens if the macro contains a label, as *Skip* does. If *Skip* is used more than once in a given source module, this label will be repeated, and repeating a label is illegal. The **LOCAL** directive tells **MASM** to circumvent this problem by using a different name for the label *skipLoop* each time it is used in a given module. The syntax here is delicate: **LOCAL** must occur on the line immediately following the macro name, without intervening empty lines. The actual function of *Skip* should be clear. The invocation

```
        Skip   n
```

for an integer n > 0 causes *newLine* to be called n times and hence "skips n lines."

Figure 5.13 is a version of our program that uses the elementary macros from CON-SOLE.MAC. It already shows the ability of macros to sweep a lot of the ugly detail of assembly language under the rug. By the judicious use of macros, much of the conciseness and readability that is associated with high-level languages can be achieved in assembly language programming. Of course, it is not possible to match the expressiveness of a good high-level language. This requires the interpretive ability of a compiler.

Macros offer an interesting alternative to procedures. They provide some speed advantages since there is no **call/ret** overhead and no loss of time in passing parameters. However, it would be remiss to close this discussion without mentioning some of their drawbacks. For example:

- A little earlier, we made the statement that macros "sweep the ugly details under the rug." Unfortunately, this hiding of information means that macros may make debugging difficult. The situation can become especially unpleasant if there are layers of macros calling other macros and a deeply nested macro has a long-dormant bug. Debugging is further complicated by the fact that **CODEVIEW** does not trace through macro code while in source mode — it treats the entire macro as one program step. One way around this problem is to manually substitute the source code for suspect macros before using **CODEVIEW**. Another approach is to temporarily switch to assembly mode, although this frequently makes it harder to follow the execution of the program.

- Macros can add unreasonable bulk to the code. For example, if a macro assembles to 20 bytes of machine code and is used 50 times, it will add 1000 bytes to the final .EXE file. A moral to be gleaned from this is that short macros are probably more useful than long ones.

- Macros may slow down code by introducing their own overhead. Consider the *inpStr* macro as a case in point. This macro calls a procedure and so does not save on the procedure overhead. In addition, **ax** is pushed and popped by *inpStr*, and again by *getStr*, thus introducing extra overhead. This duplication is really necessary to make *getStr* safe to use either directly or through *inpStr*. Whether this kind of waste is worth tolerating depends on the context. In the present example, it is of no significance since the machine is processing input from the keyboard, and this input arrives at a snail's pace by machine standards.

- If a procedure that needs local variables is replaced by a macro, then the macro will also need local variables. It is quite possible to set up local variable storage

FIGURE 5.12 SOME MACROS FROM CONSOLE.MAC

```
COMMENT           #       MACRO HEADER
MACRO NAME:               outStr          FILE: console.mac
PURPOSE:                  Calls putStr to print a null-terminated string to the screen
CALLED AS:                outStr Buffer
REMARKS:          #

outStr MACRO String

        EXTRN   putStr:NEAR
        push    ax
        mov     ax, OFFSET String
        push    ax
        call    putStr
        pop     ax

ENDM

;-------------------------------------------------------------

COMMENT           #       MACRO HEADER
MACRO NAME:               Skip            FILE: console.mac
PURPOSE:                  Prints multiple newlines to screen
CALLED AS:                Skip  N
                          where N is the number of newlines to print
REMARKS:          #       Prints 65536 newlines if N = 0.

Skip MACRO N
        LOCAL skipLoop

        EXTRN   newLine:NEAR
        push    cx
        mov     cx, N

skipLoop:

        call    newLine
        loop    skipLoop
        pop     cx

ENDM

;-------------------------------------------------------------

COMMENT           #       MACRO HEADER
MACRO NAME:               inpChar         FILE: console.mac
PURPOSE:                  Uses function 01h to get a character from keyboard; leaves
                          character in al.
CALLED AS:                inpChar
REMARKS:          #       Destroys value in ax.

inpChar MACRO

        mov     ah, 01h
        int     21h
```

```
ENDM

;-------------------------------------------------------------

COMMENT        #        MACRO HEADER
MACRO NAME:             outChar        FILE: console.mac
PURPOSE:                Uses function 02h to print a character to the screen
CALLED AS:              outChar C
                        where C can be a byte of data of any kind (memory, register,
                        or constant).

REMARKS:       #

outChar MACRO C

        push    dx
        push    ax
        mov     dl, C
        mov     ah, 02h
        int     21h
        pop     ax
        pop     dx

ENDM
```

for macros, and in fact we will do this later (in Chapters 8 and 13, for example). However, the techniques involved in doing so are fairly devious and so it is usually best to stick with procedures in such cases.

In spite of these very real problems, macros offer enormous advantages by helping the assembly language programmer to write robust, readable programs in the shortest possible time. We will be use them consistently throughout this book.

Exercise 5-14. Rewrite the *inpChar* macro so that it preserves the value of **ah**.

Exercise 5-15. The present version of *Skip* responds badly to an invocation line of the form

```
Skip 0
```

Make the appropriate correction to the macro code.

Remarks on the Next Few Exercises. A basic library of ASCIIZ string-handling functions should contain at least these four:

1. *strLeng* — computes the length of a string, excluding the null terminator.
2. *strComp* — compares two strings. Returns 0 if they are identical, returns a positive value if the first is later in terms of the ASCII collating scheme, and returns a negative value if the second is later. In plainer English, this means that it returns a positive value if, in the first position at which the strings differ, the character in the first string has bigger ASCII code than the character in the second string, with a similar explanation in the other case. This definition is awkward to state but easy to program!

FIGURE 5.13 A PROGRAM THAT USES MACROS

```
 1    TITLE Prog5_5.asm  Another Version, Using Macros.
 2
 3    INCLUDE console.mac     ;basic input/output macros
 4
 5    LEN      equ    80
 6
 7    DOSSEG
 8    .MODEL SMALL
 9
10    .STACK 100h
11
12    .DATA
13
14    Prompt1    DB     "Input a string:  ", 0
15    Prompt2    DB     "Do another?  ", 0
16    Message    DB     "The string was:  ", 0
17    String     DB     LEN, (LEN + 1) dup(?)
18
19    .CODE
20
21    Start:
22
23        mov    ax, @DATA
24        mov    ds, ax
25
26    Begin:
27
28        Skip   3
29        outStr Prompt1
30        inpStr String
31        Skip   2
32        outStr Message
33        outStr String
34        Skip   2
35        outStr Prompt2
36        inpChar
37        cmp    al, 'y'
38        je     Begin
39
40        Skip   2
41        mov    ax, 4c00h
42        int    21h
43
44        END    Start
45
```

3. *strCat* — concatenates two strings, which means joins the second onto the end of the first.
4. *strScan* — searches a string for the first occurrence of a specified symbol. It it doesn't find the symbol, it returns the value zero; if it does, it returns the offset of the first occurrence.

Exercise 5-16. Write procedures that implement the basic library functions. The procedures should receive their parameters on the stack and *strLeng* should return the length of the string in the **ax** register. In writing *strCat*, assume that the first string resides in a buffer that is long enough to hold the concatenated string without overflowing. In addition, write a short "test harness" that checks the correct operation of the basic library functions. At the very least, the test harness should do the following

- Prompt the user to input a string.
- Print the length of that string.
- Prompt the user to input a second string.
- Print the concatenated string.
- Prompt the user to input a character.
- Check whether the concatenated string contains that character.
- Give the user the opportunity to run the tests again.

Exercise 5-17. Repeat the previous exercise, but this time use macros rather than procedures.

Exercise 5-18. Since return addresses (and local variables, if any), are stored on the stack and parameters are passed on the stack, several procedure calls can be in progress simultaneously. Each call has its own *stack frame* containing the information that pertains to that call. In particular, procedures can call themselves, a phenomenon that is known as *recursion*.

Recall that the *factorial function* is defined for integers n ≥ 0 by

```
0! = 1
1! = 1
n! = n * (n - 1)! for n ≥ 2
```

From this definition, it is easy to check that, for n ≥ 1, n! is the product of the integers from 1 to n.

Pseudocode for the factorial is

```
if (n ≤ 0) fact(n) = 1
else fact(n) = n * fact(n - 1)
```

Finally, here is the statement of the problem: write an assembly language procedure that computes the factorial recursively.

In addition, write a small calling program to pass the factorial procedure its parameter n. After the program is running (even if it is not yet producing the correct results), analyze it carefully using **CODEVIEW**. A reasonable value for n is 3 or 4. In particular, observe how the stack frames are piled up on the stack and use the 'k' command at various points in the trace. 'k', the *stack trace* command, shows the chain of procedure calls that brought the program to its current state.

The preceding algorithm assigns the value 1 to n! if n < 0, rather than doing the correct thing, namely to report an error. The ambitious reader might want to incorporate this error reporting into the solution.

Exercise 5-19. Redo Exercise 5-16, but this time use recursive procedures.

Exercise 5-20. You may wish to review the definition of the **MS-DOS** environment before working on this problem, although it is not really necessary. The *environment* is a collection of strings, called *environment variables*, from which a program can receive information during run time. We have already encountered it in the text. For example, **LINK** checks the environment for an environment variable named LIB and, if it finds it, interprets its contents as paths that should be searched for libraries. Assume these facts:

1. The environment variables are stored as ASCIIZ strings and the last string in the environment has two null terminators.

2. An executing program can find the segment address of the environment at XXXX:002C, where XXXX is the common value of **ds** and **es** when the program begins — before the data segment has been initialized. In other words, if the word stored at address XXXX:002C is YYYY, then the environment begins at address YYYY:0000.

Write a program called GETENV that will print the environment strings to the screen, one to a line.

Remark. The **DOS** command SET, when used with no parameters, prints the environment to the screen and can be used to check your answer.

Exercise 5-21. Try out all the 50 or so **CODEVIEW** commands given in the **CODEVIEW** manual. The difficulty involved in exercising the various commands ranges from trivial to arduous to thought provoking. An example of the first kind is the '7' command. An example of the second kind is the /[*regExpr*] (*search for a regular expression*) command. If you are not familiar with the syntax of regular expressions, exploring this command can use up a few evenings! An example of the third kind is the **O** *Port Value* command (*send a byte to a port*). The challenge is to use this command in some way that produces an observable effect.

CHAPTER 6

ADDRESSING

SECTION 1 PREVIEW

Section 2 of this chapter is devoted to an analysis of addressing modes. The term *addressing mode* refers to how the operands in instructions are interpreted. As we know, these operands can be constants, registers, names of variables, or indirect addressing expressions. Only the last two of these categories are at all complex, and so they will receive most attention.

The complete determination of addresses is spread over the various stages of program preparation and execution, and this complicates the discussion of addressing. There are four different times during the history of a program when address computations are performed:

- At assembly time.

- At link time.

- At load time, or when the program is "loaded" from the disk to machine memory.

- At run time, or during program execution.

One of the aims of this chapter is to sort out these different contributions to the final addressing structure.

So far, it has been unnecessary to discuss the translation of assembly language into machine language. In Chapter 9, this process will be examined in detail. Unfortunately, some knowledge of the encoding is prerequisite to understanding the addressing computations done by **MASM** and **LINK**, and so the translation process will be previewed briefly in Section 2.

In Section 3, we finally relate the complete story on indirect addressing.

The simplified segment directives used so far mask some essential features of addressing, and therefore the traditional, more complicated segment directives must be introduced. These directives are discussed in Section 5, except for **ASSUME**. Since the complete explanation of this directive is fairly involved, we devote all of Section 6 to it.

LINK's contributions to the addressing structure are best studied in the context of programs in which the source code is submitted to **MASM** as several separate files (more accurately called *program modules*) that are assembled separately and then combined by **LINK** into a single executable file. These multi-module programs are the subject of Section 7.

Our penultimate task in this chapter is to write procedures for converting between one-word binary integers and their *alphanumeric representations*. By the alphanumeric representation of an integer, we mean the integer written out as an ASCIIZ string of decimal digits, preceded by an optional '+' or '−' sign. The necessary procedures are given in Section 8 and open the door to programs that do more elaborate numerical manipulations. Such programs frequently require a source of random numbers, and so a random integer generator is developed in Section 9.

Finally, in Section 10, we discuss stack frames and present an example of a recursive procedure.

SECTION 2 THE BASIC ADDRESSING MODES

The following terminology is used in classifying addressing modes:

1. *Immediate Mode*. This term refers to an operand that contains constant data. More precisely, the operand can be evaluated at assembly time. It may contain constants, symbolic constants, or items of these types combined by various arithmetic operations. As we will see in Chapter 13, **MASM** accepts a wide range of arithmetic directives and will do assorted arithmetic operations at assembly time. As an example, if NUM1 and NUM2 have been defined as symbolic constants then a line such as

```
mov     ax, NUM1 + NUM2 SHL 3
```

can be used, and the arithmetic will be done at assembly time. Here **SHL** is one of **MASM**'s many arithmetic directives. It means binary shift left, which of course gives multiplication by 2, so that SHL 3 corresponds to multiplication by 8.

2. *Register addressing*. This term is self-explanatory, and the reference to **ax** in the preceding instruction provides an example.

3. *Memory addressing*. This means that the operand refers to a memory location and, as we have seen, it is generally called a *memory reference*. Memory addressing is of two general types:

a. *Direct.* This term is used whenever the address of a memory operand can be computed prior to run time. In this chapter, we will show that the address is basically computed at link time, although the segment part is modified in a fairly trivial way (*relocated*) when the program is loaded.

If *wData* is defined by a **DW** statement, then the instruction

```
mov     ax, wData
```

is an example of direct addressing. The actual information that will be recorded in the machine form of the instruction is the offset of *wData*, and this offset is known at link time.

Another example of direct memory addressing is

```
mov     ax, wData[2],
```

even though it contains [ ]. It is direct because as soon as the offset of *wData* is known, the offset for *wData[2]* can be obtained by adding 2.

b. *Indirect.* This term is used if the address of the data cannot be determined until run time. The reason for the delay in knowing the address is always the same: the expression in square brackets contains one or more registers serving as pointers to the data, and these registers must be given their run-time values.

For example, an instruction such as

```
mov     ax, [bx]
```

uses indirect memory addressing since the appropriate offset depends on the dynamic value of **bx** when the instruction is about to be executed.

PROG6_1.ASM, shown in Figure 6.1, is a short program designed to illustrate these distinctions in a trivial setting. PROG6_1 is intended solely for execution from within **CODEVIEW**. If run from **DOS**, it will lock up the machine since the **jmp** on line 28 gives rise to an infinite loop.

A good starting point is to follow the execution of PROG6_1 in **CODEVIEW**, although this is one situation in which **CODEVIEW** cannot give the whole story since it only shows the program at run time. Later in this chapter, we will obtain information about the earlier life of a program by examining the .LST file provided by **MASM**. The .LST file reflects the situation after assembly but before linking.

For the remainder of this section, all numbers will be in hex. To match the **CODEVIEW** displays, we will write them without the trailing 'H'.

Figure 6.2 shows **CODEVIEW** in assembly mode. (Use F3 F3 to get there.) If the reader is following this discussion live in front of **CODEVIEW**, it is slightly more revealing to use the mixed mode. (Use a single F3 to get there.) Since *wData* is the first word in the data segment and since the data segment contains a total of four words, the command

```
wi &wData 1 4
```

should display the entire data segment. The watch commands default to **ds** so it is

FIGURE 6.1 ADDRESSING EXAMPLES

```
 1    TITLE   Prog6_1.asm   Demonstrating Addressing Modes
 2
 3    DOSSEG
 4    .MODEL SMALL
 5
 6    .STACK 100h
 7
 8    .DATA
 9
10       wData   DW    400
11       wAry    DW    500, 600, 700
12
13    .CODE
14
15    Start:
16
17         mov      ax, @DATA
18         mov      ds, ax
19
20         mov      ax, 20                  ;immediate
21         mov      bx, OFFSET wAry         ;immediate
22         mov      ax, bx                  ;register
23         mov      ax, wData               ;direct memory
24         mov      ax, wAry                ;direct memory
25         mov      ax, wAry[4]             ;direct memory
26         mov      ax, [bx]                ;indirect memory
27         mov      ax, [bx+800]            ;indirect memory
28         jmp      Start
29
30         mov      ax, 4c00h
31         int      21h
32
33         END      Start
34
```

unnecessary to write *ds:&WData*. The watch window shows that this command was successful and that the offset of *wData* is 04H. Since *wAry* occurs immediately after *wData* in memory, its offset is 06H.

Before proceeding, recall that the information at the left edge of Figure 6.2 represents the *segment:offset* at which the machine code is stored, followed by the actual machine code.

In PROG6_1.ASM, several instructions have the form

```
        mov      ax, immediateData
```

The machine code for each of these begins with the byte B8 and is followed by the value of *immediateData* written as a two-byte hex quantity, stored in memory with the least significant word at the lower memory location, as always. For example, the instruction

```
        mov      ax, 20
```

FIGURE 6.2 PROG6_1 IN CODEVIEW

```
#File  View  Search  Run  Watch  Options  Language  Calls  Help # F8=Trace F5=Go
############################### prog6_1.ASM ###################################
0)  &WData L 4  :  56B3:0004    400    500    600    700         # AX = 56B3
#############################################################################  # BX = 0000
START:                                                          # CX = 0000
56B0:0010 B8B356        MOV       AX,56B3                       # DX = 0000
56B0:0013 8ED8          MOV       DS,AX                         # SP = 0100
56B0:0015 B81400        MOV       AX,0014                       # BP = 0000
56B0:0018 BB0600        MOV       BX,0006                       # SI = 0000
56B0:001B 8BC3          MOV       AX,BX                         # DI = 0000
56B0:001D A10400        MOV       AX,Word Ptr [0004]            # DS = 56B3
56B0:0020 A10600        MOV       AX,Word Ptr [0006]            # ES = 56A0
56B0:0023 A10A00        MOV       AX,Word Ptr [000A]            # SS = 56B4
56B0:0026 8B07          MOV       AX,Word Ptr [BX]              # CS = 56B0
56B0:0028 8B872003      MOV       AX,Word Ptr [BX+0320]         # IP = 0015
56B0:002C EBE2          JMP       START (0010)                  #
56B0:002E B8004C        MOV       AX,4C00                       #   NV UP
56B0:0031 CD21          INT       21                            #   EI PL
56B0:0033 009001F4      ADD       Byte Ptr [BX+SI-0BFF],DL      #   NZ NA
56B0:0037 015802        ADD       Word Ptr [BX+SI+02],BX        #   PO NC
#############################################################################  #
Microsoft (R) CodeView (R)  Version 2.2                         #
(C) Copyright Microsoft Corp. 1986-1988.  All rights reserved.  #
wi &WData 1 4                                                   #
                                                                #
```

which appears in Figure 6.2 as

```
        mov       ax, 14
```

and, since the display defaults to hex, translates to B81400.

The first byte of the machine language encoding, which tells which operation is to be performed, is called the *operation code* or *op-code*. In some cases, part of the next byte is also used to help specify the operation.

Our observation can therefore be paraphrased as: the op-code for "moving a constant into **ax**" is B8, and the constant occupies the two succeeding bytes.

Likewise, looking at the machine encoding of

```
        mov       bx, OFFSET wAry
```

lets us conclude that the op-code for "moving a constant to **bx**" is BB.

The instructions

```
        mov       ax, wData
        mov       ax, wAry
        mov       ax, wAry[4]
```

appear as

```
56B0:001D A10400          MOV        AX,Word Ptr [0004]
56B0:0020 A10600          MOV        AX,Word Ptr [0006]
56B0:0023 A10A00          MOV        AX,Word Ptr [000A]
```

These encodings show that the op-code for "move a word-sized direct memory reference into **ax**" is A1 and that the offset of the memory variable occupies the second and third bytes of the machine code.

This observation is central to the present discussion. When an instruction contains a direct memory reference, the assembler records the corresponding offset as part of the instruction. This is the real reason for the name *direct addressing* — the offset is coded directly into the machine instruction.

Although it is not totally clear from the evidence of Figure 6.2, the encoding of

```
        mov     ax, bx
```

as 8BC3 results from these facts: 8B is the op-code for "a 16-bit move where at least one operand is a register," and C3 means that the source is the **bx** register and the destination is the **ax** register.

The instructions

```
        mov     ax, [bx]
        mov     ax, [bx+800]
```

are encoded as

```
56B0:0026 8B07            MOV        AX,Word Ptr [BX]
56B0:0028 8B872003        MOV        AX,Word Ptr [BX+0320]
```

To interpret these encodings, we use the information about the 8B op-code from an earlier paragraph. It now seems that if the second byte has value 07, then the instruction has operands **ax** and [**bx**]; if this byte is 87, then the indirect operand is replaced by [**bx**+displacement], and the value of displacement is contained in the next two bytes of machine code.

The reasonable generalization is that in indirect addressing, a byte is used to tell the nature of the indirect addressing (07 or 87 in the examples), including information about whether or not there is a displacement. Furthermore, if there is a displacement, its value occupies the succeeding bytes.

In a slightly different vein, consider the encoding of the **jmp** instruction:

```
56B0:002C EBE2            JMP        START (0010)
```

Here EB is the op-code for **jmp**. In interpreting the byte with value E2, remember that the target in a jump instruction is always treated as a signed offset. We leave it to the reader to check that E2 is the correct offset value in this case.

In Chapter 9, we will see that these tentative interpretations of the machine encodings are all correct and that there is not much more to the encoding scheme than these observations suggest.

The essential point of this section has been to clarify the distinctions between the different addressing on the machine-code level. Reiterating these distinctions:

- In immediate addressing, the value of the operand is part of the machine instruction.

- In direct addressing, the offset is part of the instruction.

- In indirect and register addressing, the instruction indicates the particular form of the addressing mode and possibly also contains an explicit displacement.

SECTION 3 INDIRECT ADDRESSING

Table 6.1 shows the entire list of addressing modes that are available in programming the **8088**. The table may look somewhat daunting but actually is very easy to memorize. First of all, the names assigned to the various modes are of little consequence and in fact are not completely standardized. Only a few basic principles are needed to understand the table:

1. Square-bracketed expressions represent offsets. If a square-bracketed expression contains a sum, then the offset is evaluated as the sum of the corresponding values. For example,

```
[bx + si + 10]
```

is an indirect reference to a data item whose offset is

```
(value in bx) + (value in si) + 10.
```

2. The indirect modes occupy the lower part of the table, beginning with *Indexed*. In an indirect mode, the square-bracketed expression can contain

- an optional base register (bx or bp)

- an optional index register (si or di)

- an optional displacement

By our terminology, the expression in the square brackets must actually contain at least one register to be considered an indirect mode. Notice that the expression cannot contain two base registers or two index registers. The displacement is interpreted as an 8- or 16-bit signed integer.

3. The square-bracketed expression gives an offset, but a complete address requires a corresponding segment. The **8088** assigns a default segment to each addressing expression. These defaults are easy to remember: if a **bp** occurs in the square brackets the default segment address is the value in ss; in all other cases it is the value in ds. This is consistent with

---

TABLE 6.1 THE 8086/8088 ADDRESSING MODES

NAME	OPERAND FORMAT	DEFAULT SEGMENT
Register	8- or 16-bit register	--
Immediate	8- or 16-bit constant	--
Direct	[disp] or label	ds
Indexed	[di]	ds
	[si]	ds
Based	[bx]	ds
	[bp]	ss
Indexed Displaced	[si + disp]	ds
	[di + disp]	ds
Based Displaced	[bx + disp]	ds
	[bp + disp]	ss
Based Indexed	[bx + si]	ds
	[bx + di]	ds
	[bp + di]	ss
	[bp + si]	ss
Based Indexed Displaced	[bx + si + disp]	ds
	[bx + di + disp]	ds
	[bp + di + disp]	ss
	[bp + si + disp]	ss
String Source	[si]	ds
String Destination	[di]	es

---

our previous examples and underlines the fact that **bp** is designed for working with the stack. The last line of Table 6.1 contains one slight exception to these rules, since it shows a case in which [**di**] defaults to **es**. This exception will be discussed in Chapter 10.

4. For the most part, the default segment assignment can be overridden by a *segment override*. For example, to force the expression

```
[bx + di - 479]
```

to represent the offset of an element in the segment pointed to by **es**, use the expression:

```
es:[bx + di - 479].
```

Some of the difficulties associated with the use of the different addressing modes stem from the fact that **MASM** is too liberal. It allows the programmer to use input formats that differ widely from those in Table 6.1 and performs the necessary translations.

We will now give some illustrations of the addressing modes and of the varied notations that are acceptable to **MASM**. Suppose that the machine is in the initial memory configuration shown in the diagrams in Figure 6.3.

Note that, contrary to our usual conventions, each box in the diagram of the data segment represents a word. The second diagram conveys the information that **bp** has been initialized

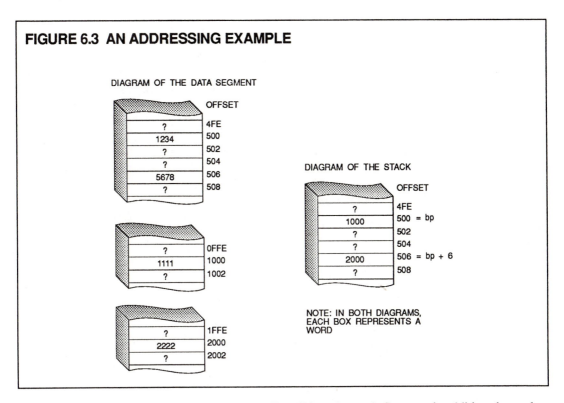

FIGURE 6.3 AN ADDRESSING EXAMPLE

to the value 500, so that it points to offset 500 on the stack. Suppose, in addition, that **ax** has been initialized to 1. Each diagram shows the hypothetical contents of a number of memory locations.

We imagine the changes in these pictures resulting from the execution of various instructions and assume that each of following eight modifications starts from the initial configuration, rather than occurring sequentially.

INSTRUCTION	RESULT
1. mov bp, ax	replaces the 500 by 1
2. mov [bp], ax	replaces the 1000 by 1
3. mov bp + 6, ax	syntax error
4. mov [bp + 6], ax	replaces the 2000 by 1
5. mov ds:[bp], ax	replaces the 1234 by 1
6. mov ds:[bp + 6], ax	replaces the 5678 by 1
7. mov bx, [bp]	
mov [bx], ax	replaces the 1111 by 1
8. mov bx, [bp + 6]	
mov [bx], ax	replaces the 2222 by 1

Of these eight examples, the last two are perhaps the most interesting since they represent situations that cause many beginning assembly language programmers grief.

The last configuration arises naturally in the following context. Suppose that a procedure expects its parameters on the stack and must compute a one-word answer, recording it at a specified location in the data segment. Assume that the offset of that location was passed in **bp** + 6 on the stack, that **ds** has been initialized to point to the data segment, and that the answer has already been computed and is contained in **ax**. How will the program return the answer to the given location?

It should certainly use indirect addressing with respect to one of the registers that default to **ds**. If **bx** is selected, the offset of the answer location should be moved into **bx** and then **ax** should be stored at this offset in the data segment. These are the steps performed in 8.

This example should be studied carefully. In particular, it is important to understand why 8 succeeds whereas 4 and 6 do something totally different.

MASM allows an array name to be incorporated as part of an indirect addressing mode. For example, if *Array* has been defined as an array of bytes, say by means of the definition

```
Array DB 100 DUP(?)
```

then byte number (**bx** + **di** + disp) in *Array* can be accessed as

```
Array[bx + di + disp].
```

Since *Array* was declared as a byte array, its type is recorded as BYTE in **MASM**'s symbol table and so this expression is interpreted as a BYTE reference, without the need for **BYTE PTR**.

Practically any ordering of the components in an indirect addressing mode will be accepted. For example, if the offset of *Array* is 10, then the instruction

```
        mov         BYTE PTR [bx + di + 13], -1.
```

will be generated by each of these lines of source code:

```
        mov         Array[bx + di + 3], -1
        mov         Array[bx][di][3], -1
        mov         Array[bx][di + 3], -1
        mov         [Array + bx + di + 3], -1
        mov         3 + Array[bx + di], -1
        mov         3[Array + bx + di], -1
        mov         3[Array][bx][di], -1
        mov         [Array][bx][di][3], -1
        mov         [Array + bx][di + 3], -1
        mov         BYTE PTR 3[OFFSET Array + bx + di], -1
```

Note that, in the last example, **BYTE PTR** is really needed because *OFFSET Array* is just a constant, and so **MASM** does not associate a type with the addressing expression, even though *Array* itself has a type.

Combinations with an unbracketed *Array* or a 3 at the end are not allowed, but taking into account the various permutations of the preceding examples — most of which are legal — there must be 100 different ways of writing this address information! Confusing?

Definitely. In this book, the first of the formats just listed will be used exclusively. We have pointed out the others since the reader will certainly come across them.

MASM allows this wide flexibility to make compiler construction somewhat easier. The compiler is not restrained to generating code in which the indirect addressing expressions have a strictly regimented form.

The second of the listed formats,

```
mov      · Array[bx][di][3], -1
```

is quite common but it seems a good idea to avoid it because it suggests a parallel with higher dimensional arrays which is not, in fact, correct. If *Ary2* designates a two-dimensional array then it is most emphatically *not* the case that *Ary2[bx][si]* represents the (*bx,si*) entry of *Ary2* in the sense that *Ary2[i][j]* represents the (*i,j*) entry of *Ary2* in some high-level languages.

To clarify this, suppose that *Ary2* will be interpreted as a two-dimensional array of bytes with N rows and M columns, where N and M are symbolic constants. **MASM** has no built-in formalism for working with such arrays, and so it is up to the programmer to decide how to store and access the elements of *Ary2*.

The most common method of storing the array elements is in *row-major form*, which is defined as follows. *Ary2* has the form

```
Ary2[0][0]     Ary2[0][1] ··· Ary2[0][j] ··· Ary2[0][M-1]
Ary2[1][0]     Ary2[0][1] ··· Ary2[1][j] ··· Ary2[1][M-1]
                                    .
                                    .
Ary2[i][0]     Ary2[i][1] ··· Ary2[i][j] ··· Ary2[i][M-1]
                                    .
                                    .
Ary2[N-1][0]   Ary2[N-1][1]···Ary2[N-1][j]···Ary2[N-1][M-1]
```

Starting the row and column indices with 0 is consistent with assembly language conventions. In row-major form, the elements of the array are stored sequentially in memory, starting with the elements from row zero, then the elements from the first row, and so on. A reference to the array element *Ary2[i][j]*, is in reality a reference to byte number M * i + j in the linearized array, since to get to this byte, it is necessary to scan over i rows of length M and pass j bytes in row i. (This shows how much better indexing works when the count starts from 0 rather than 1.) In terms of indirect addressing, an appropriate expression is

```
Ary2[bx + si]
```

where **si** plays the role of j but where **bx** *has value i * M*.

The moral of this example is

- In using based indexed addressing to represent two-dimensional arrays, the row index must be scaled by multiplication by the row length, which is equal to the number of columns.

Analogously, if the individual items in the array are of size bigger than one byte, both the row and column indices must be additionally scaled by multiplying them by the size of a single datum.

Exercise 6-1. In the preceding section, we made the statement that "100 variations must be possible." Is this an exaggeration? How many variations can you get **MASM** to accept?

SECTION 4 AN EXAMPLE: INSERTION SORT

As an illustration of indirect addressing, we will present a version of the *insertion sort* algorithm that sorts an array of integers into increasing order.

Insertion sort is probably the easiest to understand of the standard sorting algorithms. It is sometimes called the *cardplayer's sort* because it sorts in the way many cardplayers sort their cards: order the first two elements of the array, then position the third so that the first three are in order, and proceed in this way until the entire array is sorted.

Insertion sort makes an interesting assembly language program since it involves a nested double loop. Nested double loops can be implemented in a number of ways. For example, the programmer can maintain two loop counters (memory variables or registers) and control the loop logic using **inc**, **cmp**, and **jl** instructions.

We chose an alternative method for this program. The **loop** instruction was used for the inner loop, and a different counter (the **dx** register) was used for the outer loop. Since the inner loop is traversed many times more than the outer one and the **loop** instruction is faster than the **inc/cmp/jl** combination, this was obviously the best allocation of resources.

Yet another approach would be to use the **loop** instruction in both loops. This involves saving the outer loop value of **cx** (say by pushing it) when the inner loop is entered and then retrieving this value when exiting the inner loop.

Although insertion sort is included in USER.LIB, under the name INSERT.OBJ, it is of doubtful long-term value since it runs very slowly on even moderately large arrays. However, it does provide some sorting capability for use in examples until a faster sort is available. (Quicksort will be presented in Chapter 11.)

In Figure 6.4, the first thing of note is the pseudocode for the algorithm. In a tricky algorithm, it is a good idea to include pseudocode and use the notations of the pseudocode in the program comments. There is little to be gained from analyzing this pseudocode in detail in the text. Before studying the program code, the reader should verify that the pseudocode is nothing more than a formalization of the insertion sort algorithm as we described it. Here are a few observations on Figure 6.4:

Lines 3-18. The procedure header is written in the standard format that we introduced in the previous chapter. In a real-life environment, the pseudo-code would not be part of the procedure header.

Lines 32-33. If the size n of the array is 0 or 1, no sorting need be done, and so the procedure makes an immediate return. It would be disastrous to continue as far as *innerLoop* with either of these values of n. For example, if n = 1 then **cx** = 0 on entering *innerLoop*, and there is no **jcxz**! If n < 0 it would probably be better to print out an error message and abort the program but, again, this would increase the complexity of the program.

FIGURE 6.4 INSERTION SORT

```
 1   TITLE   Insert.asm. A Version of Insertion Sort
 2
 3   COMMENT      #    PROCEDURE HEADER
 4   TYPE:             NEAR    FILE: insert.asm    LIBRARY: user.lib
 5   PURPOSE:          Uses insertion sort to sort an array of 16-bity signed ints
 6                     into increasing order.,
 7   CALLED AS:        Insert(sizeAry(2), offsetAry(2))
 8   RETURNS:          Nothing
 9   REMARKS:          Array must be in segment pointed to by ds.
10   PSEUDOCODE:       Array named Ary is of size n. Uses the following
11                        algorithm:
12                        for (i = 1 to n-1)   ;Ary[0],..,Ary[i-1] already sorted
13                        {   save Ary[i] in the variable named temp
14                            for (j = i-1 to 0) ;find right spot to insert temp
15                            {  if(temp < Ary[j]) Ary[j+1] = temp, next i
16                                          Ary[j+1] = Ary[j] }
17                               Ary[0] = temp
18        #        }
19
20   PUBLIC      Insert
21
22   DOSSEG
23   .MODEL SMALL
24
25   .CODE
26
27   Insert        PROC    NEAR
28
29       push    bp
30       mov     bp, sp
31
32       cmp     WORD PTR [bp + 4], 1
33       jle     Done2                ;Do nothing unless n >= 2
34
35       push    ax
36       push    bx
37       push    cx
38       push    dx
39       push    di
40       push    si
41
42       mov     dx, 1                ;initialize outerLoop counter
43       mov     bx, [bp + 6]         ;point bx to array
44       mov     si , 0               ;point bx+si to Ary[i]; initially i
45                                    ;  should be 1 but it will be
46   outerLoop:                       ;    incremented before its first use
47
48       add     si, 2
49       mov     ax, [bx + si]        ;store Ary[i] in temp = ax
50       mov     cx, dx               ;initialize innerLoop counter to i
51       mov     di, si
52       sub     di, 2                ;point bx+di to Ary[j] in inner loop,
53                                    ;  starting with Ary[i-1]
54
```

Figure 6.4 cont.

```
55   innerLoop:
56
57        cmp       ax, [bx + di]          ;compare temp with Ary[j]
58        jl        shiftItRight
59        mov       [bx + di + 2], ax      ;Ary[j + 1] = temp
60        inc       dx
61        cmp       dx, [bp + 4]
62        jl        outerLoop              ;next i
63        jmp       SHORT Done1
64
65   shiftItRight:
66
67        push      [bx + di]
68        pop       [bx + di + 2]          ;Ary[j+1] <- Ary[j]
69
70        sub       di, 2
71        loop      innerloop              ;next j
72
73        mov       [bx], ax               ;if you get here temp is the smallest
74                                         ;  element of Ary seen to date
75        inc       dx
76        cmp       dx, [bp + 4]
77        jl        outerLoop              ;next i
78
79   Done1:
80
81        pop       si
82        pop       di
83        pop       dx
84        pop       cx
85        pop       bx
86        pop       ax
87
88   Done2:
89
90        pop       bp
91        ret       4
92
93   Insert    ENDP
94
95   END
```

Line 43. We point **bx** to the start of the array and will not change it throughout the procedure. This means that a reference such as

```
[bx + si]
```

will denote a data item **si** bytes beyond the start of the array. Since the array contains 16-bit integers, each one requiring two bytes of storage, **si** should have value 2*k in order to point to the k-th integer in the array (with the count starting at zero, as always).

Line 48. Going from one integer to the next involves adding 2 to **si**.

Line 63. The new wrinkle here is the assembler directive **SHORT**. We know that when the instruction

```
jmp        Target
```

is translated to machine code, *Target* is interpreted as an offset, and the actual value of this offset becomes part of the machine code. By default, **MASM** encodes this offset as a word unless *Target* is close enough to be reached by a one-byte signed displacement, i.e., unless *Target* is no further than 128 bytes backward or 127 bytes forward in the code. In the present situation, *Target* occurs later in the code than does the **jmp** instruction so that, when **MASM** is allotting space for the **jmp** instruction, the distance to *Target* is unknown, and **MASM** consequently makes the most conservative assumption, allocating a word for the offset. Such a configuration, in which an object is used before being defined, is known as a *forward reference*. In this instance, the only negative effect is that the resulting code is a byte longer than necessary. When **MASM** later discovers that a one-byte displacement would have sufficed, it prints a warning message to that effect.

The punctilious programmer should then replace the **jmp** instruction with a line having the form

```
jmp        SHORT Target
```

as we have done here. The directive **SHORT** instructs **MASM** to encode the **jmp** instruction with a one-byte offset.

Lines 67-68. *Ary[j]* must be moved to *Ary[j+1]*, and this is done using a **push/pop** sequence. The **push/pop** is actually slower than the more usual

```
mov        someReg, [bx + di]
mov        [bx + di + 2], someReg
```

The reason for using the **push/pop** here is that all the general-purpose registers are in use — a situation that comes up all too often in **8088** programs. The only free register at the moment is **es**. While the segment registers are not often used in general computations, **es** could certainly play the role of *someReg*. But no time would be saved because **es** would join the registers that are changed in the procedure, and so it should also be preserved by a **push/pop**.

One of the most important features of the **80286** microprocessor (and all later members of this family) is that they can operate in a new configuration called *protected mode*. In protected mode, segment registers cannot be used for performing incidental arithmetic. Since protected mode will become more and more important in future years, it is a good policy to minimize general-purpose use of segment registers, so that programs will be easier to convert to protected-mode environments.

Exercise 6-2. Rewrite insertion sort using the **loop** instruction in both the inner and the outer loops. At this point, testing the rewritten program will be somewhat awkward since we do not yet have procedures for input and output of integers. For the moment, the best approach is to define a small array (of size 6, say) by a **DW** and follow the sorting of this array in **CODEVIEW**.

SECTION 5 EXPLICIT SEGMENT STRUCTURE

As we explained earlier, the simplified segment directives supply default values for several parameters relating to segment structure. Since the simplified segment directives have been used in all our programs so far, we have paid relatively little attention to segment structure. With any set of defaults, there are circumstances under which they are not appropriate. In addition, we must learn some of the details of segment structure in order to understand how the segment parts of addresses are computed. For these reasons, we will now give a preliminary discussion of the segment structure of an assembly language program. Many points will be glossed over but will be analyzed in detail in Chapter 12.

A certain amount of overhead is required in writing programs that does not use the simplified segment directives, and Figure 6.5 shows a template that can be used to supply these overhead lines.

In Figure 6.5, each segment is declared explicitly. The essential components of a segment declaration are the directive **SEGMENT**, which marks the beginning of the segment, and the directive **ENDS** (*end segment*), which marks the end of the segment. Each of these directives is used in conjunction with a user-defined name for the segment. For example, the suggestive name *dSeg* was used for the data segment, with similar names for the stack and the code segment. The exact choice of names is up to the programmer and is of no significance to **MASM**.

In the case of the stack segment another directive must be used, namely **STACK**. This directive enables **LINK** to identify the stack segment, so that it can arrange for the correct initialization of **ss** and **sp**. A minor benefit resulting from writing out the segment structure explicitly is that the contents of the stack can be initialized, which is not possible if the simplified directives are used. Initializing the stack can be helpful in debugging. In Figure 6.5, we initialized the stack to contain repeats of the very distinctive pattern "STACK   ". Notice that the word "STACK" is padded with three spaces to give it length eight, so that two repeats of the pattern just fill one line of the output resulting from **CODEVIEW**'s *db* (*display bytes*) command. This is another example of using *tracks in the snow*: when the stack is viewed in **CODEVIEW**, the amount of the pattern that has been obliterated shows the high-water mark — the maximum amount of the stack that has been in use at any point in the program up to that time. (One weakness of this method is that the stack now contains initialized data and so will be stored as part of the disk image of the program. See Chapter 8 for an explanation of this point.)

The data segment has no keyword that is analogous to **STACK**. None is needed since the programmer is responsible for initializing **ds** within the program. An obvious question is why the data segment is not treated in the same way as the stack, thus eliminating the need for explicit initialization of **ds** in every program. The answer is that a program can have only one stack but can have many different data segments. The programmer has the flexibility of

FIGURE 6.5 EXPLICIT SEGMENT STRUCTURE

```
 1   TITLE : Template Showing Explicit Segment Structure
 2
 3   ;a good place for macros and equates
 4
 5   ;================================================================
 6
 7   sSeg SEGMENT STACK 'STACK'
 8
 9         db 16 DUP ("STACK    ") ;actual size depends on program
10
11   sSeg ENDS
12
13   ;================================================================
14
15   dSeg SEGMENT PUBLIC WORD 'DATA'
16
17         ;data go here
18
19   dSeg ENDS
20
21   ;================================================================
22
23   cSeg SEGMENT PUBLIC WORD 'CODE'
24
25         ASSUME cs:cSeg, ds:dSeg
26
27   ;----------------------------------------------------------------
28
29   Start:
30
31         mov ax, dSeg          ;initialize ds
32         mov ds, ax
33
34         ;entry code goes here
35
36         mov ax, 4c00h         ;termination
37         int 21h
38
39
40   ;----------------------------------------------------------------
41
42   Proc1 PROC   NEAR
43
44         ;code for Procedure1
45         ret
46
47   Proc1 ENDP
48
49   ;----------------------------------------------------------------
50
51   ;more procedures
52
53   ;----------------------------------------------------------------
54
```

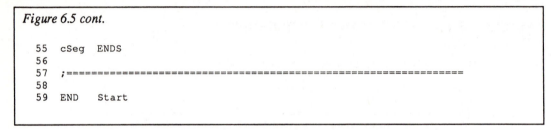

Figure 6.5 cont.

```
55   cSeg   ENDS
56
57   ;===================================================================
58
59   END     Start
```

initializing **ds** to point to any of the data segments, then later in the program changing it to point to a different data segment by repeating the basic two lines, using the name of the new segment. This process is frequently repeated many times in a program.

Likewise, no analog of the **STACK** keyword is present in the code segment header. A program can have several different code segments, but the template as written contains enough information to allow **LINK** to provide for the initialization of **cs** and **ip**. The segment containing *Label*, where *Label* is used in the

```
END      Label
```

directive, is used to initialize **cs** and, as discussed earlier, the offset of *Label* is used as the initial value of **ip**.

The headers for both *cSeg* and *dSeg* contain the directive **PUBLIC**. The exact meaning of this directive, and the other choices that can be substituted for it, need not concern us at the moment. Generally speaking, several segments (in the same program module or spread over several modules) can have the same name. If they have *combine class* **PUBLIC**, they are all joined, end to end, into a single segment, which is given the shared name.

Another directive appearing in the *cSeg* and *dSeg* headers is **WORD**. **WORD** is called the *alignment type* and informs **LINK** that each of these segments should be loaded into memory so that it starts on an even address, i.e., on a word boundary. Other options for alignment are **BYTE**, with the obvious meaning; **DWORD**, which means start on a multiple of 4; **PARAGRAPH**, which means start on an address that is a multiple of 16; and **PAGE**, which means start on an address that is a multiple of 256. A discussion of alignment types is best left until our major onslaught on directives in Chapter 12.

The names STACK, DATA, and CODEE occurring in single quotes in Figure 6.5 are examples of *class names*. An explanation of segment classes and other more technical items can also be safely postponed until Chapter 12.

SECTION 6 THE ASSUME DIRECTIVE

The one item from Figure 6.5 that must still be explained is the **ASSUME** directive, and this is one of the sticky points of the **8088** language.

For each variable or label that the user has declared in a program, the assembler includes an entry in its symbol table to record information about that object. An example of a symbol table will be shown in Section 7. At the moment, we only need to know that the symbol table entry for each identifier contains the name of the segment in which it was defined. Consequently, **MASM** has ready access to that segment name throughout the assembly process.

We will now explain how **MASM** determines which segment register contains the segment part of an address. Consider, for purposes of illustration, a case where the address in question is that of a data item, say *Var*, defined in *dSeg*. The programmer must include certain instructions that associate *dSeg* with a segment register, and we assume that these instructions have been included, with **ds** the chosen register. To find which segment register holds the segment part of the address of *Var*, **MASM** performs a two-step process: First, it looks in its symbol table and finds that *Var* was defined in *dSeg*. Second, it consults its records and finds that *dSeg* has been associated with the register **ds**. At this point, it knows that **ds** contains the segment part of the address.

To associate a segment register with a segment, two actions are actually required of the programmer:

1. Point a segment register at the desired segment.
2. Notify the assembler of this action.

Action 1 is accomplished by a slight variation on the standard two lines of code, such as

```
        mov     ax, dSeg
        mov     ds, ax
```

This differs from our previous usage only in that **@DATA** is replaced by the segment name *dSeg*.

The purpose of the **ASSUME** directive is to accomplish action 2. The word **ASSUME** should be interpreted literally. If **MASM** sees a line such as

```
        ASSUME      ds:dSeg
```

and needs to make use of the segment part of the address of an item defined in *dSeg*, it will *assume* that **ds** has been pointed to *dSeg*.

Suppose that a program contains the following information:

```
        dSeg1       SEGMENT     PUBLIC
            Var1 DW 10
        dSeg1       ENDS
```

and

```
        dSeg2       SEGMENT     PUBLIC
            Var2 DW 20
        dSeg2       ENDS
```

and that the instruction

```
mov        ax, Var1
```

appears in the program.

    The following examples are intended to clarify the assembler responses to a failure to do either 1 or 2 or both.

1. If neither the pointing nor the notifying is done before using the instruction, **MASM** emits an error message to the effect that the datum is in an inaccessible segment.

2. If the pointing is done but not the notifying, i.e., if the program contains these lines:

```
mov        ax, dSeg1
mov        ds, ax
mov        ax, Var1
```

the same error message results. **MASM** has not been notified that a segment register was pointed to *dSeg1* and so assumes that this was not done.

3. Suppose that the pointing was done, and instead of the notifying, a segment override was used:

```
mov        ax, dSeg1
mov        ds, ax
mov        ax, ds:Var1
```

    Because **MASM** is told which segment register to use, this is totally acceptable and generates correct code The only snag is that the segment override must be used for all references to variables in *dSeg1*. The purpose of the **ASSUME** is to enable **MASM** to make segment decisions automatically.

4. Suppose that **MASM** was notified but the pointing was done incorrectly (or not at all!):

```
mov        ax, dSeg2
mov        ds, ax
ASSUME     ds:dSeg1
mov        ax, Var1
```

    The assembler will not complain (even if the pointing was not done). However, it takes the assume at face value and so moves into **ax** the word at *ds:Var1*. It uses **ds** to address the segment (*dSeg2*) and refers to the symbol table to find the offset for *Var1* (0 in this case). The result is that the word at *dSeg2*:0, i.e., *Var2*, gets moved into **ax**!

    A more complicated situation occurs when there are several **ASSUME**s "out" on a given segment at the same time. For example, suppose that the program contains a line

```
ASSUME     es:dSeg1, ss:dSeg1
```

and the instruction

```
                    mov        ax, Var1
```

again occurs. Will **MASM** assemble this as

```
                    mov        ax, es:Var1
```

or as

```
                    mov        ax, ss:Var1
```

The answer is that it will use the second of these. This is a consequence of the following rule:

- If **ASSUME** directives indicate that more than one segment register points to a given segment, **MASM** gives precedence according to the following list:

```
            ds   ss   es   cs
```

That is, among the segment registers assumed to point to the given segment, **MASM** chooses the one occurring earliest in this list and uses it to generate segment overrides.

Two further examples may clarify this:

5. Suppose the code contains these statements:

```
            mov        ax, dSeg1
            mov        ds, ax
            mov        ax, dSeg2
            mov        es, ax
            ASSUME     ds:dSeg2, es:dSeg2
```

The assembler will interpret

```
            mov        ax, Var2
```

incorrectly as

```
            mov        ax, dSeg1:0
```

6. Given the statements

```
            mov        ax, dSeg1
            mov        ds, ax
            mov        ax, dSeg2
            mov        es, ax
            ASSUME     ds:dSeg1,es:dSeg1
```

the assembler will interpret

```
        mov      ax, Var1
```

correctly.

The reader may have noticed that Figure 6.5 contains **ASSUME**s for *dSeg* and *cSeg* but none for *sSeg*. It is quite correct to include an **ASSUME** of the form

```
        ASSUME    ss:sSeg
```

but such an **ASSUME** is seldom necessary. The reason is that, as is implicit in the preceding discussion, **MASM** uses an **ASSUME** only when associating segments with user-defined names, and named variables or labels rarely occur in the stack segment.

Exercise 6-3. If a program contains the line

```
        mov      ax, ds:[bx]
```

will **MASM** realize that no segment override is needed or will it generate one anyway?

Exercise 6-4. Write a minimal program to check the precedence rule stated in the preceding section.

Exercise 6-5. Suppose that a program is in the following configuration (all numbers are hex):

```
cs = 1000   ds = 2000   es = 3000   ss = 4000
dSeg is a segment that has been loaded at segment address 0500
eSeg is a segment that has been loaded at segment address 0600
Var is a variable defined at offset 4F in dSeg.
No ASSUMEs have yet been given.
```

If, at this point in the program, the instructions from the following groups occur, what will be the effect? (Assume that each group of instructions starts from the current configuration, not that the groups occur sequentially.) In each case, decide whether **MASM** will emit an error message and, if not, to what linear address the contents of **ax** will be moved.

```
a.      mov      Var, ax

b.      mov      es:Var, ax

c.      ASSUME   ds:eSeg
        mov      Var, ax

d.      mov      bx, dSeg
        mov      ds, bx
        mov      Var, ax

e.      ASSUME   ds:dSeg, ds:eSeg
        mov      ds, bx
```

```
        mov     Var, ax
```

Exercise 6-6. Suppose that

```
ds =1000  ss = 2000 bp = 0300  ss:[bp+4] = 0400
```

a. To what linear address will the instructions

```
    mov bx, [bp+4]
    mov [bx], ax
```

send the contents of **ax**?

b. Answer the same question for the instruction

```
    mov ds:[bp+4], ax
```

Exercise 6-7. The **8088** language is often criticized because it forces the user to write **ASSUME** directives as well as actually initializing segment registers. It would seem that **MASM** should be able to "deduce" the correct segment register to associate with each segment by the following simple scheme: For each segment, it should keep a list of registers that point to that segment, updating this list as needed. When it is necessary to associate a segment register with a segment, it should check the list corresponding to that segment. If the list contains a segment register, that segment register is used. (If the list contains more than one segment register, some precedence rule such as the one mentioned in the previous section would be used.) If the list is empty, an error message should be printed.

This method would slow the assembly process somewhat but, more significantly, it would not work. Why not?

SECTION 7 MULTI-MODULE PROGRAMS

Most large programs are composed of many different .OBJ modules that are linked together to form the final executable program. In general, some of these .OBJ modules will be in separate files and some will need to be extracted from libraries by **LINK**.

This process of building programs from several .OBJ modules has ramifications with regard to addressing, and so the discussion in this chapter would not be complete without an example to illustrate these extra complications and how they are resolved. Our real adventures with multi-module programming (other than through the use of libraries) will come much later in the book and so, for the moment, we will be content to present a simple example to demonstrate the basic principles. The example will be clearest if we use the explicit segment directives, and so we will follow the template of Figure 6.5.

Figure 6.6 and Figure 6.7 contain two separate assembly language source files, intended for separate assembly and subsequent linking into a single program, PROG6_2.EXE.

Before studying the code in Figure 6.6, we should mention the mechanics of turning

this program into a .EXE file. In later chapters, this process will be accomplished much more
deftly using the **MAKE** utility, but for the moment a simple batch file will suffice:

```
masm   /zi /z /w2 /Mx module1,,,;
if errorlevel 1 goto stop
masm   /zi /z /w2 /Mx module2,,,;
if errorlevel 1 goto stop
link   /co module1 module2, prog6_2,,user;
:stop
```

Note that the name PROG6_2 appears in the second parameter position on the **LINK**
command line and so will become the base name for the .EXE file.

Now consider the general structure of the program given in Figures 6.6 and 6.7. There
is a data segment called *dSeg1*, which is partly defined in each module. Both parts of *dSeg1*
are declared **PUBLIC**, hence they will be joined together by **LINK** to give a single segment
having the shared name. There is a second data segment named *dSeg2* defined entirely in
MODULE1. This segment is also declared as **PUBLIC**, but this is unimportant since there
are no other pieces of the same name.

The code segment also comes in two pieces, each **PUBLIC**. The actual code appearing
in the code segments resembles a standard program that has been unzipped in the middle,
the first part (including the *Start* label) having been placed in MODULE1, and the second
part (including the termination code) placed in MODULE2. This is quite unorthodox and
probably would never occur in a real program. The normal and reasonable approach is to
have a "complete" program in the first module, calling procedures residing in the other
modules. This rather bizarre example is intended to demonstrate how seamlessly **LINK** puts
the whole thing together. One observation: under normal circumstances, **CODEVIEW** has
no trouble with multi-module programs, but the curious construction of this one upsets it.
CODEVIEW will only trace the program successfully in assembly mode, which is sufficient
for our current purposes.

MODULE1 and MODULE2 show the **PUBLIC** and **EXTRN** directives in action once
again. *Var1* is defined in MODULE1 but is used in MODULE2; hence a **PUBLIC/EXTRN**
pair is required. The situation with *Var5* is similar. Notice that the **PUBLIC** declarations are
at the tops of the respective files, but the **EXTRN**s are in the correct segments, as is
mandated.

cSeg contains some features of note. The **ds** register is pointed to *dSeg1* and **es** to *dSeg2*,
each with the correct **ASSUME**. The *cSeg* pieces are each given **BYTE** alignment. This
ensures that they will be concatenated with no padding bytes added between them. (In one
of the exercises, the consequences of neglecting to use **BYTE** alignment in this example
will be examined.) The actual code is trivial. It consists of some **mov** instructions serving
to illustrate the handling of addresses.

Each module has an **END** directive, but only one contains a *Start* label. As stated earlier,
there should only be one

```
END      Label
```

directive, since more than one can confuse the linker.

FIGURE 6.6 MODULE 1 OF A TWO-MODULE PROGRAM

```
 1   TITLE  Module1.asm : First Module of Two-Module Program
 2
 3   PUBLIC  Var1
 4
 5   ;================================================================
 6
 7   dSeg1   SEGMENT  WORD PUBLIC 'DATA'
 8
 9       EXTRN   Var5:WORD
10
11      Var1  DW    1
12      Var2  DW    20 DUP(?)
13
14   dSeg1   ENDS
15
16   ;================================================================
17
18   dSeg2   SEGMENT  WORD PUBLIC  'DATA'
19
20       Var3  DW    3
21
22   dSeg2   ENDS
23
24   ;================================================================
25
26   sSeg    SEGMENT STACK 'STACK'
27
28      DB   32  DUP("STACK    ")
29
30   sSeg    ENDS
31
32   ;================================================================
33
34   cSeg    SEGMENT    BYTE PUBLIC 'TEXT'
35
36       ASSUME  cs:cSeg, ds:dSeg1, es:dSeg2
37
38
39   Start:
40
41      mov    ax, dSeg1
42      mov    ds, ax
43
44      mov    ax, dSeg2
45      mov    es, ax
46
47      mov    ax, Var5
48      mov    ax, Var2
49      mov    ax, Var3
50
51   cSeg        ENDS
52
53   ;================================================================
54
55      END    Start
```

FIGURE 6.7 MODULE 2 OF A TWO-MODULE PROGRAM

```
 1   TITLE   Module2.asm : Second Module of Two-Module Program
 2
 3   PUBLIC  Var5
 4
 5   ;==================================================================
 6
 7   dSeg1    SEGMENT  WORD PUBLIC  'DATA'
 8
 9       EXTRN    Var1: WORD
10
11       Var4  dw    4
12       Var5  dw    5
13
14   dSeg1    ENDS
15
16   ;==================================================================
17
18   cSeg     SEGMENT  BYTE  PUBLIC  'TEXT'
19
20       ASSUME   cs:cSeg, ds:dSeg1
21
22
23       mov     ax, OFFSET Var1
24       mov     ax, Var4
25
26       mov     ax, 4c00h
27       int     21h
28
29   cSeg         ENDS
30
31       END
```

The first thing to explore is how **MASM** treats each of these modules, and this requires examining the .LST files. The .LST file is known as a *listing file* and is constructed automatically by **MASM** as a byproduct of the assembly operation (unless its generation is suppressed). Figure 6.8 shows the .LST file that **MASM** created for MODULE1.ASM, after slight editing to remove a few lines not of current interest.

It should be reiterated that MODULE1.LST represents the state of the file MODULE1.ASM after **MASM** has processed it and before its transmission to **LINK**. To help the human reader, **MASM** includes the original source code. Here are some significant points:

1. The information toward the left, next to the line numbers, resembles the left side of the **CODEVIEW** screen in assembly mode, but with some obvious differences, which we will now delineate.

2. One difference is that while **CODEVIEW** lists segments and offsets, the .LST file lists only offsets, and in each segment the offsets start from zero.

3. The machine encodings also show some differences from **CODEVIEW**. Line 49 is unchanged, but look at line 48:

```
0000   B8 ---- R            mov    ax, dSeg1
```

Again the 0000H is the offset into *cSeg*, and the B8 is expected — it is the op-code for moving a constant into **ax**. What should come next in the machine code is the segment address of **ds**, rather than the ---- R that actually occurs.

    MASM uses the "----" to signify that *dSeg1* is unknown. Obviously, it won't be completely determined until load time. The 'R' means *relocation item* and flags this item so that **LINK** will process it further during the next stage of the address computations.

4. The philosophy behind lines 54 and 55 is similar. Line 54 is flagged 'E' for external and line 55 is again marked 'R'. This time the final values will be available at link time, which is different from the situation in 3. In such cases, instead of using "----," **MASM** fills in a tentative value for the operand. As in this example, when the flag is 'E' it fills in 0000H. When the flag is 'R' it fills in the offset into the segment. This last choice will turn out to be a good one.

5. Line 56 also looks strange:

```
0010   26: A1 0000 R        mov    ax, Var3
```

Var3 is defined in *dSeg2*, which is being addressed by **es**. Everything on this line makes sense as a result of our previous analysis, except for the 26:. To understand this, we must go back to first principles.

    Ultimately, the only information passed to the **8088** is the machine code. The information needed to determine offsets is hard-coded into the machine instructions. But how does the microprocessor know which segment register to use as the corresponding segment part of a complete address? The answer is that it uses a set of defaults that work most of the time. Specifically, if the instruction is an obvious code manipulation instruction (say, a **jmp** or a **call**), it uses **cs** for the segment, and if it is a data manipulation instruction (say, a **mov**), it uses **ds**, unless the instruction accesses the stack, either directly or indirectly using **bp**, in which case it uses **ss**.

    But the problem in line 56 is that we have a **mov**, and **es** rather than **ds** contains the segment value, whence the default gives the wrong segment register. The **ASSUME** won't help. This is used for communication between the programmer and **MASM** and does not appear directly in the final machine code. What **MASM** does is to code an extra byte into the machine instruction to tell the processor to use something other than the default segment register. This is the mysterious 26:. Of course, the ':' is just for the eyes of the reader — it is not part of the machine code.

    This extra byte is called, fittingly enough, a *segment override byte*. It is always inserted immediately before the instruction to which it applies and is encoded as follows:

FIGURE 6.8 LIST FILE FOR MODULE1

```
Microsoft (R) Macro Assembler Version 5.10                 6/22/90 18:13:55
Module1.asm : First Module of Two-Module Program           Page     1-1

     1                     TITLE   Module1.asm : First Module of Two-Module Program
     2
     3                     PUBLIC  Var1
     4
     5                     ;============================================================
     6
     7 0000               dSeg1    SEGMENT  WORD PUBLIC 'DATA'
     8
     9                         EXTRN    Var5:WORD
    10
    11 0000   0001          Var1  DW     1
    12 0002   0014[         Var2  DW     20 DUP(?)
    13        ????
    14        ]
    15
    16
    17 002A               dSeg1    ENDS
    18
    19                     ;============================================================
    20
    21 0000               dSeg2    SEGMENT  WORD PUBLIC  'DATA'
    22
    23 0000   0003          Var3  DW     3
    24
    25 0002               dSeg2    ENDS
    26
    27                     ;============================================================
    28
    29 0000               sSeg     SEGMENT STACK 'STACK'
    30
    31 0000   0020[          DB    32  DUP("STACK     ")
    32        53 54 41 43 4B
    33        20 20 20
    34        ]
    35
    36
    37 0100               sSeg     ENDS
    38
    39                     ;============================================================
    40
    41 0000               cSeg     SEGMENT    BYTE PUBLIC 'TEXT'
    42
    43                         ASSUME   cs:cSeg, ds:dSeg1, es:dSeg2
    44
    45
    46 0000               Start:
    47
    48 0000   B8 ---- R             mov     ax, dSeg1
    49 0003   8E D8                  mov     ds, ax
```

```
Microsoft (R) Macro Assembler Version 5.10              6/22/90 18:13:55
Module1.asm : First Module of Two-Module Program        Page     1-2


     50
     51 0005  B8 ---- R          mov      ax, dSeg2
     52 0008  8E C0              mov      es, ax
     53
     54 000A  A1 0000 E          mov      ax, Var5
     55 000D  A1 0002 R          mov      ax, Var2
     56 0010  26: A1 0000 R      mov      ax, Var3
     57
     58 0014 cSeg       ENDS
     59
     60     ;=================================================================
     61
     62  END    Start
Microsoft (R) Macro Assembler Version 5.10              6/22/90 18:13:55
Module1.asm : First Module of Two-Module Program        Symbols-1


Segments and Groups:

              N a m e            Length  Align  Combine Class

CSEG . . . . . . . . . . . . .   0014    BYTE   PUBLIC  'TEXT'
DSEG1 . . . . . . . . . . . .    002A    WORD   PUBLIC  'DATA'
DSEG2 . . . . . . . . . . . .    0002    WORD   PUBLIC  'DATA'
SSEG . . . . . . . . . . . . .   0100    PARA   STACK   'STACK'

Symbols:

              N a m e            Type    Value  Attr

START . . . . . . . . . . . . .  L NEAR  0000   CSEG

VAR1 . . . . . . . . . . . . .   L WORD  0000   DSEG1   Global
VAR2 . . . . . . . . . . . . .   L WORD  0002   DSEG1   Length = 0014
VAR3 . . . . . . . . . . . . .   L WORD  0000   DSEG2
VAR5 . . . . . . . . . . . . .   V WORD  0000   DSEG1   External
```

OVERRIDE BYTE	SEGMENT OVERRIDE
2Eh	cs:
3Eh	ds:
26h	es:
36h	ss:

At this point we can give a final interpretation of the **ASSUME** directive:

- The effect of the **ASSUME** directive is that **MASM** either allows the **8088** to use the default segment register, or else *automatically* generates the correct segment override byte.

A quick verification of this interpretation is possible. The obvious thing to try is deleting *es:dSeg2* from the list of **ASSUMEs** and changing *Var3* to *es:Var3* on line 56, with the hope of checking whether this alternate approach will generate the same segment override byte. Unfortunately, this won't work since **MASM** will notice that data are being addressed by name in *dSeg2* with no assume referencing that segment, and consequently will report an error.

A way around this is to change the *es:dSeg2* to *ds:dSeg2* and, as before, change the *Var3* to *es:Var3*. Now **MASM** will not automatically generate the override, but a direct check of the .LST file will reveal that the explicit override has the same effect and the generated code will look exactly like that in PROG6_4.

As mentioned earlier, classes will be discussed in Chapter 12. Nearly everything else in Figure 6.8 should be self-explanatory.

The last part of Figure 6.8 (beginning *Symbols*) contains the symbol table generated by **MASM**. The symbol table contains an entry for each name used in the program. A symbol entry consists of several fields:

1. The name field.

2. A type field giving the data type of the item. The type field contains descriptions such as **BYTE, WORD, DWORD, NUMBER, NEAR, FAR**, and a number of other choices, all with their usual significance. The symbol table shows once again that **MASM** views the names of data items as labels — a variable defined by a **DW** will appear in the symbol table as an "L NEAR", where the 'L' means label. A 'V' means that the item is external.

3. A value field. Again this field shows that named variables are treated as labels. In spite of its name, this field does not contain the actual value, even for an initialized variable — it contains the offset.

4. An attribute field containing the name of the segment in which the identifier was defined. The attribute field sometimes holds additional information, as the symbol table in Figure 6.8 shows.

In the case of an externally defined identifier, the offset is not yet known and the value field is padded with 0000.

The listing file for MODULE2.ASM has not been reproduced because it contains no new features.

The next item requiring discussion is **LINK**'s role in the program-building process. As indicated earlier, **LINK** glues MODULE1.OBJ and MODULE2.OBJ together to give a version of the program suitable for loading into machine memory. More exactly, **LINK** builds a *relocatable load module*. The word *relocatable* means that the module can be successfully loaded into machine memory at any available starting address. "Relocatable load module" is generally abbreviated to just "load module." To understand how the load module is constructed, we must consider the segment and offset parts of addresses separately, as usual.

LINK builds the load module with all the segment addresses correct, but under the assumption that the program will be loaded into memory starting at segment address 0000H (which, as we will see, *never* really happens.) The program will be a block of code, each segment following on the heels of the previous (except for possible alignment gaps), and any references to segments in the code (e.g., initialization of segment registers and jumps between segments) will have the correct values encoded, corresponding to the pretended starting location 0000H.

The correction that must be made when the program is loaded should be clear. If the program will be loaded at starting address *segAddr*:0000 rather than 0000:0000, every segment reference in the load module will need to have the quantity *segAddr* added to it in order that the relocated code will work correctly! Hence the load module needs to contain a list of all the locations in the machine code where segment register values occur. The load module does indeed contain such a list, called the *relocation pointer table*. The relocation pointer table is part of the *.EXE header*, which is prepended to the load module. We will discuss the .EXE header in detail in Chapter 9. For the moment it suffices to say that it is quite large (always a multiple of 512 bytes) but only takes up space in the disk image of the program — it is not loaded as part of the executing program.

LINK's duties in dealing with offsets should be fairly obvious. **MASM** has marked various items as relocatable, and **LINK** can totally resolve the ones relating to offsets. These factors must be considered:

1. **MASM** starts the numbering of offsets in each segment with 0000H. Even if a segment consists of only one piece, alignment requirements may make it necessary to position the first element of the segment at a positive offset, and **LINK** must make that adjustment.

2. If a segment is composed of several pieces from different modules, then clearly the later pieces must have appropriate values added to their offsets to account for the earlier segment contents that have suddenly materialized.

3. Information about external references must be filled in.

When **LINK** finishes, it provides the programmer with a file summarizing its results. This file is called a *map file*, and its default name is the base name of the .EXE program with the extension .MAP. Figure 6.9 shows a somewhat edited map file for PROG6_2.

The map file gives the sizes and ordering of the segments. As already discussed, this is an exact map of the final machine code under the assumption that it begins with segment address 0000H.

Having followed the process of program building in minute detail, we should now examine PROG6_2 in **CODEVIEW**, and Figure 6.10 shows a sample **CODEVIEW** screen.

Figure 6.10 indicates that **LINK** seems to have successfully grafted together the two sections of code into a single program. However, it is a worthwhile exercise to step through the code to double check whether everything is working as the source code intended. We leave this to the reader.

Exercise 6-8. In the discussion of PROG6_2, we stated that **BYTE** alignment was critical. Change the alignment to **WORD** and assemble and link the program. Go into **CODEVIEW** and get a screen similar to Figure 6.10. Find a *complete* explanation for the differences between your screen and Figure 6.10.

FIGURE 6.9 MAP FILE FOR PROG6_2

START	STOP	LENGTH	NAME
0000H	002DH	002EH	DSEG1
002EH	002FH	0002H	DSEG2
0030H	012FH	0100H	SSEG
0130H	014EH	001FH	CSEG

Exercise 6-9. In PROG6_2, we concentrated on how offsets of data items are pieced together in a multi-module program. Write a program analogous to PROG6_2, but designed to show how code labels and jumps in the second module are resolved by **LINK** when the code from the modules is joined.

Exercise 6-10. Build a two-module program having its "real" start label in MODULE1 and an "accidental" start label in MODULE2. Submit the program to **LINK** twice, first with the modules listed in the order {MODULE1, MODULE2} on the **LINK** command line and then in the opposite order. Examine both versions of the .EXE file in **CODEVIEW**.

SECTION 8 ALPHANUMERIC CONVERSION

To date, our numeric examples have been somewhat restricted because we have not formally presented procedures to perform input and output of integers. What we need are final implementations of Algorithms 1.1 and 1.2. Since ASCIIZ strings will be used exclusively, we really require:

- A procedure taking as input an ASCIIZ string representing a decimal integer and converting it to a one-word binary integer.

- The converse procedure: it starts with a one-word binary integer and converts it to an ASCIIZ string.

These procedures will be used in conjunction with *inpStr* and *outStr* (and their later replacements) to solve the input/output problem for decimal integers.

In line with our general philosophy, each of these procedures will receive its parameters on the stack, will be stored in the library for easy use, and will be accessible by means of a simple macro.

The procedure that performs the first task is called ASCBIN16.ASM and is shown in Figure 6.11.

Several points about ASCBIN16.ASM are worth mentioning. The procedure *ascBin16* is a straightforward implementation of Algorithm 1.1, but with a few enhancements. It allows the input decimal string to begin with an optional '+' or '−', which it processes in the reasonable way: a '+' is ignored and a '−' has the effect of negating the input. The procedure

```
FIGURE 6.10  PROG6_2 IN CODEVIEW

#File  View  Search  Run  Watch  Options  Language  Calls  Help # F8=Trace F5=Go
############################## Prog6_2.ASM ####################################
590F:0000 B8FC58        MOV     AX,58FC                        # AX = 0000
590F:0003 8ED8          MOV     DS,AX                          # BX = 0000
590F:0005 B8FE58        MOV     AX,58FE                        # CX = 0000
590F:0008 8EC0          MOV     ES,AX                          # DX = 0000
590F:000A A12C00        MOV     AX,Word Ptr [002C]             # SP = 0100
590F:000D A10200        MOV     AX,Word Ptr [0002]             # BP = 0000
590F:0010 26A10E00      MOV     AX,Word Ptr ES:[000E]          # SI = 0000
590F:0014 B80000        MOV     AX,0000                        # DI = 0000
590F:0017 A12A00        MOV     AX,Word Ptr [002A]             # DS = 58EC
590F:001A B8004C        MOV     AX,4C00                        # ES = 58EC
590F:001D CD21          INT     21                             # SS = 58FF
590F:001F 4E            DEC     SI                             # CS = 590F
590F:0020 42            INC     DX                             # IP = 0000
590F:0021 3030          XOR     Byte Ptr [BX+SI],DH            #
590F:0023 EA00000000    JMP     0000:0000                      #   NV UP
590F:0028 0000          ADD     Byte Ptr [BX+SI],AL            #   EI PL
590F:002A 0000          ADD     Byte Ptr [BX+SI],AL            #   NZ NA
590F:002C 0000          ADD     Byte Ptr [BX+SI],AL            #   PO NC
#############################################################################
                                                               #
Microsoft (R) CodeView (R)  Version 2.2                         #
(C) Copyright Microsoft Corp. 1986-1988.  All rights reserved.  #
                                                               #
```

does no bounds checking on the input. Since the output is stored as a 16-bit signed integer, the answer will be correct only if the input is in the range -32768 to +32767. For out-of-range inputs, the procedure still gives answers that are correct modulo 65536.

Before discussing the code for *ascBin16*, we will introduce the most basic of the *bit instructions*, although for the next few chapters we will only use them in very simple contexts. They are called bit instructions because they modify the individual bits in their first operand in specified ways. We will discuss them in detail in Chapter 10. Here are the instructions:

or Op1, Op2: Turns on exactly those bits in *Op1* that are on in either *Op1* or *Op2* or both.
and Op1, Op2: Turns on exactly those bits in *Op1* that are on in both *Op1* and *Op2*.
xor Op1, Op2 (*exclusive or*): Turns on exactly those bits in *Op1* that are on in either *Op1* or *Op2* but not on in both.

These instructions are very fast — they require as few as three clock cycles on the **8088**. Our main reason for previewing them at this juncture is that almost all assembly language programmers use them to perform certain basic programming tasks.

First, consider

```
    xor     Reg, Reg
```

A moment's thought should convince the reader that the effect of this instruction is to give *Reg* the value zero. In future, we will always use this instruction to zero registers.

Next, consider

```
and        Reg, Reg
```

On the surface, this seems a singularly pointless instruction — it has no effect whatsoever on the value of *Reg*. However, *it does affect the flags*. In particular, ZF is set after this instruction if and only if *Reg* = 0. Hence, this instruction gives a quick test for whether a register equals zero (or for any other property that can be discerned from the flags). Most programmers test using **and** (or **can** also be used), rather than using **cmp**, before a conditional jump.

For example, instead of

```
cmp        ax, 0
jne        shortTarget
```

most programmers would write

```
and        ax, ax
jne        shortTarget
```

Again, the advantage is that the **and** instruction is faster and generates less machine code than does the corresponding **cmp**. In future, we will use **and** (or **or**) to test register values.

Given an invalid input, *ascBin16* does not print an error message. Rather, it converts the largest initial portion of the input representing valid decimal integer data and then returns. For example, if the input string is "123abc," then the converted binary integer is 123_2 and if the input is "abc," then the converted form is 0_2.

At this point, most of the code in Figure 6.11 is self-explanatory, but here are a few specific observations that may be of interest:

Line 40. If the input is preceded by a '−', the "flag" **si** is given the value −1. The rest of the input is then processed normally and, toward the end of the procedure, **si** is checked and if it is found to have value −1, the result of the computation is replaced by its negative value. The answer is accumulated in **ax**, and the negation occurs on line 66.

Lines 50-52. To find out if a character is a digit, just check whether its ASCII code lies between the codes for '0' and '9'.

Line 66. For convenience, we have used a new instruction

```
neg        Operand
```

here. It does the obvious thing, namely replaces the contents of *Operand* by its two's complement. This instruction is convenient but certainly not necessary. The same effect could be achieved, more slowly and laboriously, by

```
xor        bx, bx
sub        bx, ax
mov        ax, bx
```

FIGURE 6.11 THE ASCBIN16 PROCEDURE

```
 1   TITLE ascBin16.asm
 2
 3
 4   COMMENT        #  PROCEDURE HEADER
 5   TYPE:              NEAR    FILE:ascBin16.asm          LIBRARY: user.lib
 6   PURPOSE:           Converts alphanumeric representation of integer in
 7                      ASCIIZ form into one-word binary
 8   CALLED AS:         ascBin16(offsetIntStr(2)
 9                      where IntStr holds the alphanumeric form and is pointed
10                      to by ds
11   RETURNS:      # Binary value in ax
12
13   PUBLIC ascBin16
14
15   .MODEL SMALL
16   .CODE
17
18   ascBin16 PROC NEAR
19
20       push   bp
21       mov    bp, sp
22
23       push   bx
24       push   cx
25       push   dx
26       push   di
27       push   si
28
29       xor    si, si              ;store sign in si, with 0 meaning +
30       mov    bx, [bp + 4]        ;point bx to input string
31       cmp    BYTE PTR [bx], '+'  ;check whether there is a + sign
32       jne    checkNeg            ;if not, check for - sign
33       inc    bx                  ;move to first digit
34       jmp    SHORT firstDigit
35
36   checkNeg:
37
38       cmp    BYTE PTR [bx], '-'
39       jne    firstDigit
40       mov    si, -1              ;-1 stored in si will mean input negative
41       inc    bx                  ;move to first digit
42
43   firstDigit:
44
45       xor    ax, ax
46       mov    di, 10
47
48   convertLoop:
49
50       cmp    BYTE PTR [bx], '0'  ;is it a digit?
51       jl     endConvert          ;also tests for null-terminator
52       cmp    BYTE PTR [bx], '9'
53       jg     endConvert
54       mul    di
```

Figure 6.11 cont.

```
55        xor     dx, dx
56        mov     dl, [bx]
57        sub     dl, '0'              ;convert from ASCII code to digit value
58        add     ax, dx
59        inc     bx
60        jmp     convertLoop
61
62   endConvert:
63
64        and     si, si
65        je      notNeg
66        neg     ax
67
68   notNeg:
69
70        pop     si
71        pop     di
72        pop     dx
73        pop     cx
74        pop     bx
75
76        pop     bp
77        ret     2
78
79   ascBin16 ENDP
80
81        END
```

Figure 6.12 shows the opposite conversion. This procedure will print out either an integer in the range 0 to 32767 with no sign or an integer in the range −1 to −32768 with a leading '−' sign. It is the responsibility of the programmer to ensure that the buffer designated to receive the decimal string is sufficiently long. Specifically, this buffer must have length at least seven, to allow for the possible minus sign and the null terminator.

Line 7 in the procedure header for *bin16Asc* introduces another convention that we will use throughout the book. We have displayed the calling syntax as

```
bin16Asc(offsetBuffer(2), Int(2))
```

Of course, this line relays the information that *bin16Asc* expects two arguments, *offsetBuffer* and *Int*, on the stack. The parenthesized numbers '2' indicate that each of these quantities should be of size two bytes. Finally, and very importantly, *the arguments should be pushed in right-to-left order: Int* first, so that it will be pointed to by **bp** + 6, followed by *offsetBuffer*, which will be pointed to be **bp** + 4. As we will see in Chapter 14, this usage conforms to the conventions of the **C** language, although other languages, such as **Pascal** and **FORTRAN**, push their parameters in left-to-right order.

An easy way to remember our convention is to think in physical terms: it is as though the right-hand parenthesis had been removed and the arguments "poured" onto the stack.

The following macros can be used to access these procedures:

```
aToI MACRO intStr
```

```
                EXTRN      ascBin16:NEAR
                push       bx
                lea        bx, intStr
                push       bx
                call       ascBin16
                pop        bx

        ENDM

        iToA MACRO intStr, N

                EXTRN      bin16Asc:NEAR
                push       ax
                lea        ax, N
                push       ax
                lea        ax, intStr
                push       ax
                call       bin16Asc
                pop        ax

        ENDM
```

These macros use a new instruction, **lea** (*load effective address*). In *aToI*, for example, the instruction

```
        lea bx, intStr
```

occurs where the instruction

```
        mov bx, OFFSET intStr
```

is expected. Both instructions have the same effect: *effective address* is a synonym for offset, and *lea* loads the offset of its second operand into its first operand. The reader may wonder why **lea** is needed, especially since its machine code requires one more byte than does the **mov** instruction. The reason for its importance is that the **lea** computations are performed entirely at run time, whereas the **OFFSET** computation is completed at assembly time. Consequently, **lea** can interpret indirect addressing operands correctly but the **mov** variant cannot.

For example,

```
        lea bx, Str1[bx]
```

will do the expected thing, namely move into **bx** the value

```
        OFFSET Str1 + bx
```

using the run-time value of **bx**. It is not possible to achieve the same result with a single instruction using **mov**.

We will favor **lea** in our macros since it allows them to accept indirect addressing expressions in their arguments.

FIGURE 6.12 THE BIN16ASC PROCEDURE

```
 1   TITLE bin16Asc.asm
 2
 3   COMMENT       # PROCEDURE HEADER
 4   TYPE:         NEAR       FILE: bin16Asc.asm    LIBRARY: user.lib
 5   PURPOSE:      Converts one-word binary integer to decimal equaivalent
 6                 which is stored in ASCIIZ format.
 7   CALLED AS:    bin16Asc(offsetBuffer(2), Int(2))
 8                 where Buffer holds converted Int; both in segment pointed
 9                 to by ds. Buffer must have length at least seven.
10   RETURNS:    #  Nothing
11
12   PUBLIC bin16Asc
13
14   .MODEL SMALL
15
16   .CODE
17
18   bin16Asc PROC NEAR
19
20       push    bp
21       mov     bp, sp
22
23       push    ax
24       push    bx
25       push    cx
26       push    dx
27       push    di
28       push    si
29
30       mov     ax, [bp + 6]           ;ax contains integer to convert
31       mov     bx, [bp + 4]           ;bx points to Buffer
32       and     ax, ax
33       jge     notNegative
34       neg     ax
35       mov     BYTE PTR [bx], '-'
36       inc     bx
37
38   notNegative:
39
40       push    ax                     ;preserve value of number
41       mov     di, 10                 ;operand for division
42       xor     cx,cx                  ;cx will hold number of digits
43
44   countDigits:
45
46       xor     dx, dx
47       inc     cx
48       div     di
49       and     ax, ax
50       jne     countDigits
51       pop     ax                     ;restore number
52
53   convert:
54
```

```
55        add     bx, cx
56        mov     BYTE PTR [bx], 0
57        dec     bx
58
59   convertLoop:
60
61        xor     dx, dx
62        div     di
63        add     dx, '0'              ;convert digit value to ASCII code
64        mov     [bx], dl
65        dec     bx
66        loop    convertLoop
67
68        pop     si
69        pop     di
70        pop     dx
71        pop     cx
72        pop     bx
73        pop     ax
74
75        pop     bp
76        ret     4
77
78   bin16Asc ENDP
79
80        END
```

The names of these macros are supposed to suggest their functions. For example, aToI does alphanumeric- (i.e., decimal string) to-integer (i.e., binary integer) conversion. Another point worth mentioning is that here, as in all similar contexts, the macro parameters appear in the order that matches the operand usage in the **8088** language. In other words, the normal form of a two-operand instruction is

```
inst  Dest, Source
```

and this ordering has been used for the macro parameters in *iToA*: *intStr* is the source and *M* is the destination. If this policy is used consistently, it eases the memory burden associated with macro usage.

Exercise 6-11. Write a program containing an instruction of the form

```
mov bx, OFFSET Str[bx]
```

How does **MASM** respond to the program? Look at the .LST file or run the program under **CODEVIEW** to determine what code is generated.

Exercise 6-12. Write a program that prints a nicely formatted table of powers of integers from 1 to 100, up to and including the fifth power. The format might look like this:

Integer	Square	Cube	Fourth	Fifth
1	1	1	1	1
2	4	8	16	32
3	9	27	81	243
		.		
		.		
		.		

Each row should contain only powers small enough to fit in a single precision signed integer, i.e., powers less than 32768. For example, the row of the table corresponding to the integer 10 should only contain the powers of 10 as far as 10^4.

SECTION 9 GENERATING RANDOM NUMBERS

It is convenient to have a source of random integers available for program testing. While truly random sequences of integers are hard to generate, it is very easy to obtain what are called *pseudo-random sequences*. These sequences behave quite erratically and, even though they repeat themselves eventually, the *period* (i.e., the number of terms with no repeats) can be quite large. In fact, it is easy to make the period have value 65536.

An especially easy way to generate such sequences is by means of a *linear congruence*. This means that we select constants, a MULTIPLIER and an ADDER, and an initial value to be used in generating the sequence, usually called the *seed*. The sequence is then defined iteratively by the formulas

```
r1    =    MULTIPLIER * seed + ADDER
rn+1  =    rn * MULTIPLIER + ADDER for each n ≥ 1
```

in which the arithmetic is done modulo 65536. With this method, it is easy to achieve maximum period length. The only requirements are that ADDER should be an odd integer, and MULTIPLIER should be of the form $1 + 4k$, where k is also an integer. Of course, to make the sequence "look" random, it is also a good idea to use a relatively large value for MULTIPLIER or ADDER; otherwise, the sequence increases steadily at first. For a complete discussion on this method and random number generation in general, see Chapter 3 in Volume 2 of [5].

Implementing the linear congruence method in assembly language is quite easy, and Figure 6.13 shows how it can be done.

We are now equipped with all the tools necessary to really test INSERT.ASM, the version of insertion sort developed in Section 4. INSTEST, the program in Figure 6.14, performs this test. The user decides on a seed for *Rand16*, and generates an array of random integers from this seed. The array is printed before and after sorting. The size of the array is set by an **EQUATE** and was made small in our trial run, so that the output could be printed in the text.

INSTEST requires little commentary. Since the array is printed twice, before and after sorting, we wrote a macro to do the printing.

Exercise 6-13. If RAND16.ASM is used with an array that will not fit on a single line when printed, the results look quite messy. Improve the code so that the integers in the array will be printed eight to a line, padded with enough spaces to begin in columns 0, 8, 16, ⋯.

Exercise 6-14. Another standard and easy sorting algorithm is *bubble sort*. Pseudocode for bubble sort has the form

```
for (i = n - 1 to 1)
    for (j = 0 to i - 1)
        if (Ary[j] > Ary[j + 1]) interchange them
```

Write a procedure that implements bubble sort. Test it using a slightly modified version of INSTEST.

Here are a few variants of **CODEVIEW** commands that you may find helpful:

ww Ary I 6	The advantage of ww rather than wi is that it displays the integers in the array in hex, which matches their appearance when they are displayed in registers.
w? wo bx+si	Gives WORD PTR ds:[bx+si].
w? wo bx+di	Similar.
w? wo ss:bp+4	To get WORD PTR ss:[bp+4] requires the explicit override. If you just use "w? wo bp+4" you (quite irrationally) are shown WORD PTR ds:[bp+4].
g Proc1.labelName	Takes you to labelName in Proc1. With the cursor starting on first instruction in a loop, each F7 gives one trip through the loop.

Exercise 6-15. A *Pythagorean number* is an integer n such that there exists a pair of integers r and s, with r and s both > 0, and satisfying

$$r^2 \quad + \quad s^2 \quad = \quad n^2$$

In other words, n is the hypotenuse of a right triangle with integer legs r and s. For example, 5 is a Pythagorean number, with r = 3 and s = 4, and 13 is Pythagorean, with r = 5 and s = 12.

Write a program that finds all the Pythagorean numbers that are no larger than 255. It should print them to the screen in this format: each line should contain a single Pythagorean number n followed by a corresponding r and s. For each Pythagorean number, just print the corresponding line in which r ≤ s. The first line will then look like

```
2    1    1
```

Exercise 6-16. Compute the primes between 1 and 10000. Recall that an integer n is prime if it is at least 2 and if it can't be divided evenly by any positive integers except 1 and itself. The list of primes begins

```
2, 3, 5, 7, 11, 13, 17, ⋯
```

FIGURE 6.13 GENERATING RANDOM NUMBERS

```
 1   TITLE  Rand16.asm
 2
 3   COMMENT       # PROCEDURE HEADER
 4   TYPE:         NEAR         FILE: rand.asm        LIBRARY: user.lib
 5   PURPOSE:      Fills Array with 16-bit pseudorandom numbers generated
 6                 using a linear congruence
 7   CALLED AS:    Rand(Seed(2), offset Array(2), sizeArray(2))
 8                 All data must be in segment pointed to by ds
 9   RETURNS:      Nothing
10   REMARKS:      #
11
12   PUBLIC    Rand16
13
14      MULTIPLIER    EQU    12345
15      ADDER         EQU    123
16
17   .MODEL SMALL
18
19   .CODE
20
21   Rand16    PROC    NEAR
22
23      push   bp
24      mov    bp, sp
25
26      push   ax
27      push   bx
28      push   cx
29      push   dx
30      push   si
31
32      mov    bx, [bp + 6]            ;point bx to array
33      mov    cx, [bp + 8]            ;number of ints to generate
34      mov    ax, [bp + 4]            ;the seed
35      mov    si, MULTIPLIER
36
37
38   randLoop:
39
40      mul    si
41      add    ax, ADDER              ;new = MULTIPLIER * old + ADDER
42      mov    [bx], ax
43      add    bx, 2                  ;advance one word into array
44      loop   randLoop
45
46      pop    si
47      pop    dx
48      pop    cx
49      pop    bx
50      pop    ax
51
52      pop    bp
53      ret    6
54
55   Rand16       ENDP
56
57      END
```

FIGURE 6.14 TESTING INSERTION SORT

```
 1   TITLE    InsTest.asm:  driver to test insertion sort
 2
 3        INCLUDE    console.mac
 4
 5        NUMBER    EQU  10
 6
 7   ;---------------------------------------------------------
 8
 9   aryPrint MACRO Message
10        LOCAL printloop
11
12        outStr    Message
13        SKIP      1
14        mov       cx, NUMBER                ;print this number of ints
15        mov       bx, OFFSET Ary            ;start at this address
16
17   printLoop:
18
19        iToA      intStr, [bx]
20        outStr    intStr
21        outChar   ' '
22        add       bx, 2
23        loop      printLoop
24        SKIP      1
25
26   ENDM
27
28   ;----------------------------------------------------
29
30   DOSSEG
31   .MODEL SMALL
32
33   .STACK 100h
34
35   .DATA
36
37        Ary       DW   NUMBER dup(?)
38        Prompt    DB   "Input seed for Rand16: ", 0
39        intStr    DB   6 dup(?)
40        Message1 DB   "Array as generated:", 0
41        Message2 DB   "Array after sorting:", 0
42
43   .CODE
44
45        EXTRN     Rand16:NEAR,  Insert:NEAR
46
47   Start:
48
49        mov       ax, @DATA
50        mov       ds, ax
51
52        mov       ax, NUMBER
53        push      ax
54        mov       ax, OFFSET Ary
```

Figure 6.14 cont.

```
55          push      ax
56          outStr    Prompt
57          inpStr    intStr
58          SKIP 1
59          aToI      intStr
60          push      ax
61
62          call      Rand16
63
64          aryPrint  Message1
65
66          mov       ax, OFFSET Ary
67          push      ax
68          mov       ax, NUMBER
69          push      ax
70          call      Insert
71
72          aryPrint  Message2
73
74          mov       ax, 4c00h
75          int       21h
76
77   END        Start
```

Print the table of primes to the screen in the nice format suggested in Exercise 6_12.
Suggestion: The easiest way of finding the primes is the *sieve of Eratosthanes*. With this method, start with an array containing the integers

```
2,  3,  4,  5,  6,  ··· ,  10000
```

2 is a prime but no multiple of 2 can be a prime, so delete 4, 6, 8, 10, ··· from the array. The next surviving array element after 2 is 3. 3 is a prime, but no multiple of 3 can be a prime, so delete the multiples of 3 that are still in the array: 9, 15, 21, ···. Repeat the process with the next surviving array element 5, and so on. When you are through, the list will contain only the primes. Here are two important implementation details:

a. It is impractical to physically "delete" an integer from the array. The easy thing to do is "mark" it as deleted by replacing it by 0.

b. Multiples of 2, then 3, then 5, then 7, and so on, must be deleted. Need this process be continued all the way to 10000 or can it stop sooner? A little thought should convince the reader that any non-prime less than 10000 is a multiple of some integer less than or equal to 100 (since 100 is the square root of 10000) and so the process can be stopped when all multiples of 100 have been deleted. The deletions can consequently be stopped with multiples of 97, since this is the biggest prime less than or equal to 100.

SECTION 10 STACK FRAMES AND RECURSION

The part of the stack used for a single procedure call is referred to as the *stack frame* associated with that call. We have already seen some of the uses of a stack frame: it stores the procedure return address and input parameters. Another important application of the stack frame, which we will use in some of our later examples, is to store *local variables* needed by the procedure. This term is used in the same sense as in high-level languages: local variables are intended for use by the procedure. Local variables are set up on entry to the procedure and cease to exist when control returns to the caller. As with most temporary data, they are stored on the stack.

To see where locals should most reasonably be stored on the stack, consider Figure 5.5 or 5.6 again. If our standard stack initializations have been performed, then **bp** presently points to the top of the stack, whence the first available position is [**bp** - 2]. Consequently, locals are stored sequentially at locations

$$[bp - 2], \ [bp - 4], \ \cdots$$

and, assuming they are word-size, can be addressed as

$$WORD \ PTR \ [bp - 2], \ WORD \ PTR \ [bp - 4], \ \cdots$$

For the obvious reason, this kind of usage is referred to as *negative stack addressing*.

When locals are stored on the stack, certain precautions must be taken: as it stands, **sp** = **bp** and so the next push onto the stack will occur at offset **bp** - 2, thereby overwriting any data stored there. Even if the procedure does not push data onto the stack, disaster will still almost definitely strike since an interrupt will likely make use of the stack.

An extra operation required is to *protect the storage area*, and this is very easy to do. Since the microprocessor interprets the value of **sp** as lowest offset on the stack currently in use, it is only necessary to decrement **sp** appropriately. For example, suppose that a hypothetical procedure needs two words of local storage. The procedure code should begin with

```
push    bp
mov     bp, sp
sub     sp, 4           ;protect 4 bytes of storage
                        ;  on the stack
```

As we will see later, it is customary to use equates to give the temporary variables more meaningful names than the rather bland

$$WORD \ PTR \ [bp - 2], \ WORD \ PTR \ [bp - 4], \ \cdots$$

Naturally, the stack must be balanced, i.e., the temporary storage must be released, as part of the procedure termination:

```
add     sp, 4
pop     bp
ret     2n
```

where n is, as always, the number of pararmeters passed to the procedure.

The present assembly language allows the nesting of procedure calls, which means that it is legal to call a procedure from within another procedure. In fact it is possible to have a chain of arbitrarily many procedures calls, with each procedure called by the previous one, the only limitation on the length of the chain being the amount of memory available for use as stack space.

We will say that a procedure is *active* if it has been called but the corresponding **ret** instruction has not yet been executed. To say that procedure calls can be nested is then equivalent to saying that more that one procedure can be simultaneously active, and this is possible because the stack frames are pushed onto the stack as needed. Indeed, the stack frames themselves are treated stack-fashion: as the calls in a nest are executed, the stack frames are pushed; the returns are encountered in reverse order, and so the frames are removed from the stack in last-in/first-out order.

Of course, in a nested chain of procedure calls, the procedures themselves may not all be different. The extreme case in which a procedure calls itself is called *simple recursion*. We gave an informal introduction to recursion in the exercises at the end of the previous chapter and now we will present the basic ideas in detail.

If the same procedure occurs twice in a nest of calls, then at some point program control reenters a procedure that is already active. For this reason, code that supports this kind of usage is called *reentrant*. Many of the difficulties involved in using the **MS-DOS** operating system stem from the fact that many of its internal procedures are not reentrant.

In general, a reentrant procedure must maintain separate copies of all pertinent information for each active call. Otherwise, later calls to the procedure will overwrite the information needed to complete the earlier calls. Normally, the only pieces of information that a procedure needs are its parameter values, its return address, and perhaps some local variables. The usual method of storing this information is in a stack frame, which is the model that we are primarily using in this book.

When we introduced the stack as a parameter-passing mechanism in Chapter 5, our stated reasons for adopting it instead of using registers were largely matters of expediency: it is an easier method to use and provides a standard interface with high-level languages. But we now see that there is also a basic structural reason why passing on the stack is superior to passing in registers:

- Code in which all the information about procedure calls (return address, local variables and local variables) is maintained in stack frames is reentrant. Code in which some of this information is stored in fixed buffers (including registers) will nearly always be non-reentrant.

The reason for the phrase "nearly always" rather than the expected "always" will emerge later in this section.

Figure 6.15 gives an example of a recursive procedure. To best illustrate the basic issues, we chose to write a procedure, ADDFIRST.ASM, that does a trivial computation: given a positive integer, called *highIndex* here and in the comments accompanying the code, *addFirst* computes the sum

```
1 + 2 + 3 + ... + highIndex
```

FIGURE 6.15 A SIMPLE RECURSIVE PROCEDURE

```
 1    TITLE addFirst.asm: demonstrates simple recursion
 2
 3    INCLUDE console.mac
 4
 5    DOSSEG
 6    .MODEL SMALL
 7
 8    .STACK  100h
 9
10    .DATA
11
12        Prompt1    DB    CR, LF, LF, "Input an Integer: ", 0
13        intStr     DB    6 DUP(?)
14        ansStr1    DB    CR, LF, "The sum of the integers from 1 to ", 0
15        ansStr2    DB    " is ", 0
16
17    .CODE
18
19    Start:
20
21        mov       ax, @DATA
22        mov       ds, ax
23
24    Again:
25
26        outStr    Prompt1
27        inpStr    intStr                ;value of highIndex
28        aToI      intStr
29
30        push      ax                    ;push parameter
31        call      addFirst              ;start recursive chain
32
33        outStr    ansStr1               ;print answer
34        outStr    intStr                ;   including value of highIndex
35        outStr    ansStr2
36        iToA      intStr, ax            ;reuse intStr for printing of answer,
37        outStr    intStr                ; which has been returned in ax
38        Skip      2
39
40        jmp       Again                 ;will need a CONTROL C to exit
41
42        mov       ax, 4c00h             ;these lines are never reached and
43        int       21h                   ;   so could be eliminated
44
45    ;-------------------------------------------------------------------
46
47    ;recursively adds 0 + 1 + 2 + ... + highIndex, returning answer in ax
48    addFirst    PROC    NEAR
49
50        push    bp                      ;establish base pointer for
51        mov     bp, sp                  ;   indirect addressing
52
53        cmp     WORD PTR [bp + 4], 0    ;is highIndex = 0? If so,
54        jne     Recurse                 ;   stop the recursion, but before
55        xor     ax, ax                  ;   doing so, record 0 as answer in
56        jmp     SHORT Done              ;      ax
```

Figure 6.15 cont

```
57
58   Recurse:                                ;here if recursion is necessary
59                                           ;  i.e., if highIndex >= 1
60        mov      ax, [bp + 4]             ;present value of highIndex
61        dec      ax                       ;decrement it for next call
62        push     ax                       ;push parameter for next call
63        call     addFirst                 ;the recursive call
64        add      ax, [bp + 4]             ;the actual computation: update
65                                          ; the answer in ax
66   Done:
67
68        pop      bp
69        ret      2
70
71   addFirst    ENDP
72
73   ;--------------------------------------------------------------------
74
75   END    Start
```

addFirst is passed the value of *highIndex* as a parameter on the stack. It leaves the answer to the computation in the **ax** register.

The pseudocode for *addFirst* is just the additive analog of the pseudocode for the factorial and so should be familiar to everyone:

```
if (highIndex = 0)
       return 0
else
       return (addFirst(highIndex-1) + highIndex)
```

(We are using the notation *addFirst(k)* informally to denote the action of calling *addFirst* with input parameter k. Of course, this notation is not acceptable to **MASM**.)

Figure 6.16 illustrates the steps involved in the recursive computation of

$$1 + 2$$

This computation involves three calls to *addFirst*: the calling program calls *addFirst(2)*, which calls *addFirst(1)*, which calls *addFirst(0)*. The corresponding control flow is shown in detail in Figure 6.16, and readers who are not entirely comfortable with recursion should study it very carefully indeed since it is typical of all recursive procedures.

The code for *addFirst* breaks into two parts: the *pre-call code*, which precedes the recursive call on line 63 and the *post-call code*, which comes after the call. As Figure 6.16 shows, the pre-call code for all the recursive calls is executed first, in the natural order. Afterwards, the post-call code for the procedure calls is executed, but in reverse order to the calls. In the case of *addFirst*, the pre-call code merely sets up the stack for the recursive call. In our example, the actual computation is done by the post-call code: it updates the sum in **ax** by adding the current value of *highIndex* to it.

Now that we have recognized the distinction between pre-call and post-call code we can explain the phrase "nearly always" used earlier in the section:

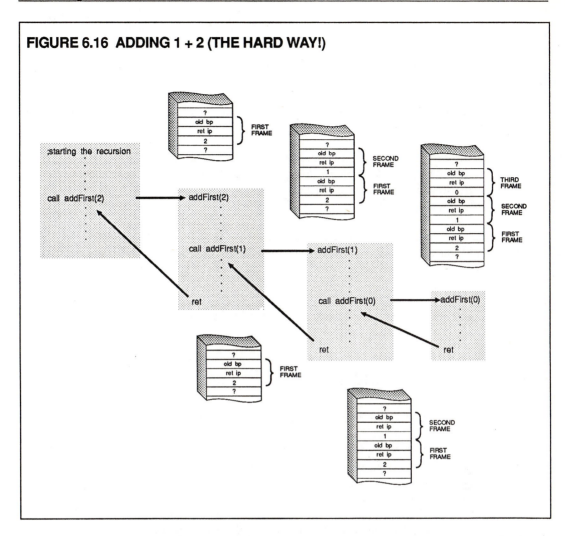

FIGURE 6.16 ADDING 1 + 2 (THE HARD WAY!)

- Recursive procedures can receive passed parameters in fixed storage areas (such as registers) under the following circumstances: either these parameters are used in the pre-call code only; or else they are not modified by the recursive invocations of the procedure.

An analogous observation can be made about reentrant code in general:

- A procedure that receives parameters in fixed buffers will still be reentrant under the following circumstances: either these parameters are not used again after control returns to this invocation of the procedure; or else they retain their values during the chain of calls that lead back to the original invocation.

Exercise 6-17. Write a recursive procedure that receives as input in **bp** + 4 the offset of an ASCIIZ string and computes its length, excluding the null terminator, returning the answer in **ax**. (Assume that **ds** points to the segment containing the string.)

Exercise 6-18. Write a recursive procedure that receives as input in **bp** + 4 the offset of an ASCIIZ string and counts the number of occurrences of the letter 'a' (lower case) in that string, returning the answer in **ax**. (Assume that **ds** points to the segment containing the string.)

Exercise 6-19. Rewrite *addFirst* so that the computations are done in the pre-code rather than in the post-code.

Exercise 6-20. A recursive procedure such as *addFirst* in which the computations are performed in the post-code is said to be *tail recursive*. Explain why a tail-recursive procedure can be directly transformed into a procedure that uses a loop to replace the recursion. Rewrite *addFirst* is this way.

Exercise 6-21. Write a recursive procedure that takes as input an integer n and prints its prime factorization to the screen. For example, given input 24, the procedure should print

2 * 2 * 2 * 3

Suggestion: The smallest factor of n that is ≥ 2 is a prime.

SECTION 11 ADDRESSING SUMMARY

The segmented architecture of the **8088** makes the whole problem of addressing especially cumbersome. In this chapter, we have tried to trace the building of the address structure of a program at all stages, from the original assembly of the source code to the final loading of the program into machine memory, and even to the dynamic computation of some offset values while the program is running. The picture is sufficiently complicated to justify summarizing our conclusions before moving on.

The data that enter into operands can be classed as immediate, register, or memory referencing. Memory-referencing expressions are further categorized as direct or indirect, depending on whether they contain registers. For example, [**si**] is an indirect memory reference.

MASM generates complete code for immediate and register operands at assembly time, even though the values contained in the registers are not determined until run time.

Code for direct memory references is partly generated by **MASM**, and the offset computations are completed by **LINK**. For direct memory references, the actual values of the offsets become part of the machine code.

With register addressing and indirect references, on the other hand, information about the kind of addressing becomes part of the machine code. The machine code may also contain an explicit displacement.

We will now turn to the handling of segments. On the assembler level, **MASM** always demands that an **ASSUME** be given before an item defined in a segment can be referenced by name. It addition, the programmer is responsible for pointing the correct segment register to the segment containing the datum.

The microprocessor assumes that **ds**, **ss**, and **cs** contain the segment addresses associated with data-type instructions, stack-accessing instructions, and code transfers, respectively. If a segment override byte is needed, it can be supplied manually by the programmer or inserted automatically by **MASM** with the help of the **ASSUME** mechanism.

Even if the programmer knows that a segment override byte is not needed, **MASM** still requires that an **ASSUME** be given, so that it can check on that fact for itself.

LINK will combine multi-module programs and will resolve references to offsets that were left incomplete by **MASM**. It builds a .EXE file consisting of a load module, which is a copy of the executable code but with all segment references based on start address 0000H, together with the .EXE header, which contains relocation information.

After the load module is transferred to machine memory, all occurrences of segment addresses are incremented by the value of the starting segment address.

One final note concerns how a program is loaded into memory. The **int 21H** functions are so central to the structure of **MS-DOS** that COMMAND.COM uses them in essentially the same way that our programs do. For example, **function 4BH** of **int 21H**, called the *EXEC function*, is used to load a program into memory and transfer control of the machine to that program. When the name of a program is typed at the **DOS** prompt, COMMAND.COM itself calls the EXEC function to load the program.

Exercise 6-22. Write double precision versions *ascDouble* and *doubleAsc* of *ascBin16* and *bin16Asc*, respectively. These should do the conversions between decimal integers in the range

$$-(2^{31} - 1) \text{ through } 2^{31}$$

and 32-bit binary integers that are stored at doubleword locations. Write a short driver to test the new procedures.

Exercise 6-23. (To be done after the previous exercise.) Extend the recursive factorial procedure so that it still takes its input n as a single precision integer but prints its output n! as a double precision integer. How big an n will this new version handle before it overflows?

Exercise 6-24. Suppose that there are 25 people in a room. What is the probability that some two of these people share a birthday? Use *Rand* to set up number of instances (perhaps 1000) of this problem and use the outcomes to get an approximate answer. If you are not familiar with the problem, you may be very surprised by the result!

Exercise 6-25. Use *strComp* to write a version of bubble sort that sorts an array of fixed-length strings into alphabetical order. Include a calling program that generates an array of random strings of the chosen length, submits it to the sorting procedure, and prints the array before and after sorting.

CHAPTER 7

THE 80286 AND THE 80386

SECTION 1 PREVIEW

In the chapter, we begin our investigation of the more recent members of the **8086** family, namely the **80186/80188**, the **80286**, the **80386** and the **80486**. Relatively little need be said about the **80186/80188** since the important advances arrived with the **80286**. Unfortunately, for most of its life the **80286** has not been supported by an operating system that simultaneously exploited its features and offered a large software base appealing to a wide class of users. Consequently, the really impressive features of the **80286** have always been slighted, and we will continue to slight them in this book. At this point in time, the **80386** is the most significant processor in the Intel family, and we will give it the lion's share of our attention. As we indicated in Chapter 2, the **80486** is nearly identical to the **80386** from an assembly-language viewpoint.

In Section 2, we give a general survey of the **80386** architecture, concentrating on those aspects that are of most importance in applications programming.

The **80386** offers many more indirect addressing formats than did its predecessors. We examine these formats in Section 3.

One of the main features of the **80386** is that it is a 32-bit processor: its registers are 32 bits wide and hence it does its "native-mode" operations on 32-bit data. In particular, it offers a complete array of 32-bit arithmetic operations. To exploit these extended capabilities requires writing 32-bit versions of our basic *ascBin16* and *bin16Asc* procedures, and we provide these procedures in Section 4.

Our intention in Section 5 is to demonstrate the power of the **80386** in dealing with large collections of data. We write a simple 32-bit random-number generator and use it to generate an array containing 500,000 32-bit integers. Consequently, this array contains 2 megabytes of data. We next write a version of the quicksort algorithm and use it to sort the array. The computations were done on a 33-megahertz machine. We invite the reader to guess how long it took to generate and sort the 500,000-element array. The answer is given at the end of the chapter.

SECTION 2 THE MORE ADVANCED PROCESSORS IN THE 8086 SERIES

The **8088** processor is extremely primitive in a number of ways. For example, it can address at most 1 megabyte of memory. By 1980 standards, this seemed like a huge amount for a personal computer. Of course, as we saw in Chapter 2, the memory actually available to applications programs running on the **IBM-XT** is much less — 640K minus the size of the various programs that have already been loaded. These programs include a part of the operating system itself (the *resident portion* of **MS-DOS**), the device drivers loaded as part of the boot process (see Chapter 16), and whatever other memory-resident programs (see Chapter 15) the user has chosen to load. The end result is that the typical **IBM XT** has somewhere in the neighborhood of 550K available for use by applications programs.

In these days, when major applications can involve more than 400K of source code, relatively little space may be available to hold the data generated by the application. Examples of such generated data are the text entered in a word processing program and the numerical and formatting information associated with a spreadsheet program. The solutions to this memory shortage are all woefully inefficient: they involve swapping parts of the data or even parts of the program code between machine memory and some alternate storage location, replacing information not currently needed either with newly generated data or with some section of program code. Swapping part of the executable code into and out of memory is called *program overlaying*. The alternate location in which information is stored can be either a mass-storage device such as a hard disk (very slow in this context) or, better, an expanded memory board. As we saw in Chapter 2, *expanded memory* is a technique for increasing the apparent range of addressable memory by switching four 16K-pages of memory so that they view blocks of physical memory selectable by the program.

Another signal weakness of the **8088** is its inability to protect sensitive areas of memory from corruption by programs that are, either deliberately or more often accidentally, trying to change them. The most obvious example of such an area is the operating-system code: altering it will cause the machine to behave erratically, at the very least. While software techniques can be used to protect specific areas of memory, the performance penalty is so enormous that this approach is seldom used. In response to the *tp* (*tracepoint*) command, **CODEVIEW** monitors a region of memory and breaks program execution when it is modified. Write-protect software would work in essentially the same way. The reader can check that the *tp* command can drastically degrade execution speed, often by a factor of 1000! Protecting areas of memory from illicit reading is even more difficult.

Memory protection is especially significant when the machine is used for *multitasking*, i.e., when it is used to run more than one program at the same time. An errant program must be restrained from interfering with other, correctly functioning programs, and it is especially important that programs be unable to jeopardize the correct functioning of the operating system. Granted, because of the memory limitations just discussed, this application of memory protection is hardly significant in the case of the **IBM-XT**. However, it becomes vital in considering more powerful processors having greater addressing capabilities.

The **80186/80188** processors represented the first step upward from the basic **8086/8088** members of this family of microprocessors. They were not widely used, and in fact the improvements they afforded were fairly minimal: a few new instructions were added and some existing instructions execute more quickly. Other than to introduce these new instructions in Chapter 11, we will not discuss the **80186/80188** processors further.

The next processor in the family, the **80286**, is used in the **IBM-AT**, and represents an enormous step forward. It provides a further increase in speed and more new instructions. It is available only with a 16-bit data bus — there has never been an **80288**.

The most important new feature of the **80286** is its ability to operate in two different configurations, with characteristics so different that it is almost like having two separate processors in one shell.

The first configuration is called *real address mode* or *real mode*. An **80286** operated in real mode closely emulates an **8086**, and in fact real mode was provided so that the new processor could run the enormous amount of existing **8088** software.

But the real excitement of the **80286** is associated with its second configuration, called *protected mode*, primarily for these two reasons:

- Under protected mode, the addressing space increases from the 1 megabyte of the **8088** to a very substantial 16 megabytes.

- As the name protected mode suggests, the memory space can be partitioned into areas that are easily protected from unauthorized use. A given region of memory can be written to or read from only with the permission of the operating system.

The details of how the extended memory addressing and protection mechanisms work are quite complicated. (It is probably a fair assessment to say that the **80286** architecture is an order of magnitude more difficult than the **8088**.) Even though we will not consider these mechanisms in detail until Chapter 18, it is important to appreciate the implications of the 16-megabyte addressing space.

One fact should be clear. Just as the **8088** requires individual addresses to be 20 bits wide in order to address 1 megabyte of data, the **80286** must surely be using 24-bit addresses to address 16 megabytes. This is indeed the case and, like the **8088**, the **80286** views each address as a *segment:offset*. But the technique used to recover an address from the segment and the offset is totally different in protected mode. The offset is actually handled quite similarly — it contributes the low 16 bits to the resulting address. However, the segment is interpreted in an entirely new way. Its numerical value is not used directly in the linear-address computation. Rather, it is an index into a table (called a *descriptor table*), and the entry of the table that it indexes determines (among other things) the remainder of the linear address. This description should already provide the reader with some insight into one aspect of the protection mechanism. A program that wishes to circumvent the operating system and write directly to a particular region of memory can only do so if it can find the address of that region. Having access to the *segment:offset* of the region is not sufficient since the segment part is just an index into a table. Of course, the next thing a marauding program might try is to read the descriptor table in order to find the high part of the address. However, if the region of memory is sensitive, the operating system will obviously not grant the program permission to read the descriptor table! This view of the protection mechanism is very much oversimplified. In particular, we have not explained why a critical memory area cannot be *accidentally* overwritten by a malfunctioning program.

The reason for our detour of the last paragraph is to emphasize how differently addresses are viewed in protected mode from their usual real mode interpretation. Unfortunately, the standard interpretation of addresses is an integral part of **MS-DOS** and so we are led to the inescapable conclusion that protected mode programs are totally incompatible with **MS-DOS**. We will see in Chapter 18 that there are other reasons why protected mode programs cannot be run under **MS-DOS**. For example, many **MS-DOS** (and ROM BIOS) functions directly write to or read from machine memory locations, and this is expressly forbidden by the protection mechanisms.

We have now explained the sad story of the first years of existence of the **80286**. It is a chip that can address 16 megabytes of protected memory, but the dominant operating system that controls it is totally incapable of exploiting these capabilities. Of course, there are other operating systems that go much further toward unleashing the power of the **80286** (notably **0S/2** and **UNIX**), as well as *DOS extenders*, which allow programs to use many of the advanced **80286** features while still allowing them to access **DOS** services.

The **80386** represents another huge leap forward in the evolution of our family of microprocessors. One of its many features is that, in a certain sense, it is even more compatible with the **8088** than is the **80286**. This added compatibility arises in *virtual 8086 mode*, which is a new configuration offered by the **80386** in addition to the real and protected modes that are analogous to the **80286** offerings. In virtual **8086** mode it is possible to partition off a megabyte (or less) of machine memory in which the **80386** will almost perfectly emulate an **8086**. Each such region is called a *virtual 8086 machine*. Virtual **8086** mode is a great advance over real mode because the **80386** can simultaneously support several virtual **8086** machines and can even run tasks in protected mode at the same time. Another important feature of virtual **8086** mode is that each virtual **8086** machine can use **MS-DOS** services.

The **80386** accepts a number of new instructions, allows many more addressing formats than the **8088**, and shows spectacular decreases in execution times for many instructions. But the single most significant feature of the **80386** is that it is a full-scale 32-bit processor: the general registers are all 32 bits wide and it is capable of manipulating 32-bit addresses. We will see in Chapter 18 that the **80386** still supports the *segment:offset* form of addressing, although it is also possible to work with 32-bit offsets only and so have what is called a *flat addressing space*.

We must introduce some new terminology to describe the addressing capabilities of the **80386**. Just as the names *kilobyte* and *megabyte* are used for 2^{10} and 2^{20} bytes, respectively, the term *gigabyte* denotes 2^{30} bytes and *terabyte* denotes 2^{40} bytes. In other words a gigabyte is about a billion bytes and a terabyte is about a trillion bytes. Since the **80386** allows 32-bit addresses, its addressing space is 4 gigabytes. In Chapter 18, we will show how the **80386** supports *virtual memory*. Using virtual memory, it is possible to view mass-storage devices as extensions of computer memory and so, in effect, to have much greater memory available than is physically present in the machine **RAM**. When this facility is used, memory can be partitioned into as many as 2^{14} segments, each as long as 2^{32} bytes, so that the amount of addressable memory is 2^{46} bytes. In other words, the **80386** can address 64 terabytes of virtual memory!

Computer programs can be divided into two types, systems programs and applications programs. The term *systems program* refers to a program that is a part of the operating system or is attached to it afterward and behaves as though it were integral with it. Systems programs may be invoked automatically as part of the functioning of the operating system or may be made available to the assembly language programmer through special instructions such as

```
        int n
```

Installable device drivers, which we will discuss in Chapter 16, are examples of systems programs. *Applications programs*, on the other hand, are programs intended for the final machine user and are generally invoked from the command line. Programs such as **MASM**, text editors, and the **DOS** DISKCOPY utility are examples of applications programs.

Because the **8088** is a totally unprotected system, there is little distinction between writing systems programs and writing applications programs. In particular, essentially all the facilities available to the operating system are also available to any applications program — there are no "protected" instructions that only the operating system can use and there are no special procedures residing at addresses visible only to the operating system.

On the other hand, when an **80286** or **80386** is operating in protected mode, under the control of an appropriate operating system, the distinction between systems programs and applications programs is vital. A number of instructions are intended solely for the use of the operating system and it is illegal for an applications program to even try to use them. In general, when an applications program is running it will only have access to its own code and data, while a systems program may very well need to have access to all of machine memory.

The entire architecture of the **80286** or **80386** breaks cleanly into two areas:

- Instructions and architectural features that are usable in all programming contexts, including the writing of applications programs.

- Instructions and capabilities used in writing systems programs. If the appropriate protection mechanisms are invoked, access to these features will be forbidden in applications programs.

As might be suspected, the systems programming aspects of the **80286** and **80386** are considerably more complex than the applications programming aspects. For this reason, we will postpone all discussion of the systems architecture of the chips until Chapter 18. In terms of applications programming, the **80286** contained relatively few advances over the **8088** — recall that the main improvement was the introduction of protected mode, and dealing with protected mode falls in the realm of systems programming. The big advances in applications programming arrived with the **80386** — the 32-bit registers and extended methods of addressing. Hence our decision to consider only applications programming at the moment has an immediate corollary: we will focus our attention entirely on the **80386** for the remainder of this chapter.

Our general scheme is therefore to present a leisurely introduction to the **80386**, beginning in the next section. The reader will soon see that, because of the improved addressing modes, the 32-bit registers, and various improvements in the instruction set, many aspects of applications programming are actually easier on the **80386** than on earlier processors. For the moment, we will discuss only a few **80386** instructions that will slightly expand our basic instruction set. In Chapter 11, we will return to the **80286** and **80386** and give a complete account of the applications instructions.

Since we will continue to use **MS-DOS** as the operating system throughout this book, we will not write many applications programs that actually run in protected mode. For the most part, our approach will be to make quick sortees into protected mode in order to set up various system parameters in rather exotic ways and then to return to real mode to execute our programs. We adopt this strategy so that we can employ the services of **MS-DOS**. This plan of attack will give us much more insight into the workings of the **80386** than would the more conventional approach of writing demonstration programs to run under a standard protected mode operating system such as **OS/2**. In particular, in Chapter 18 we will take a close look at the **80386** interrupt handling facilities and at virtual **8086** mode.

In discussing the **80286**, we pointed out that it interprets the offset part of a *segment:offset* address in essentially the same way as the **8088**. This statement is still basically true for the **80386**. However, the **80386** allows offsets to be 32 bits. It also allows segments to be as long as 4 gigabytes and so the range of offsets can span the longest segment. It is also possible to ask the **80386** to use only 16-bit offsets (and consequently to limit segment length to 64K); this is mandatory when writing programs to run under **MS-DOS**.

To start doing really interesting things with the **80386** immediately, we must "borrow" a pair of programs from Chapter 18. We will introduce these programs in Section 5 of the present chapter and will explain generally what they do. However, they involve a number of fairly advanced ideas, and so the reader is urged to take them on faith until we analyze them in detail in Chapter 18.

SECTION 3 THE 80386: REGISTERS AND ADDRESSING MODES

In designing the **80386**, Intel made every effort to ensure that it would be as compatible as possible with the earlier processors in the series. In particular, the 32-bit general-purpose registers were constructed so that they are natural extensions of the 16-bit general-purpose registers. Just as **al** is the lower half of **ax**, **ax** is itself the lower half of a new 32-bit accumulator, which is denoted **eax**, for *extended ax*. The other general-purpose registers and the index and pointer registers are extended in exactly the same way. The details of this scheme are illustrated in Figure 7.1, which shows only those registers used in routine applications programming. In addition, the **80386** has a number of debugging and control registers, which we will introduce in Chapter 18.

The segment registers are still 16 bits wide. They are used in a novel way in protected mode, and the 16-bit width is sufficient for that application. In real mode and in virtual **8086** mode, the segment registers are used in the old-fashioned **8088** way, and so the 16-bit width is again sufficient. Figure 7.1 also shows two new segment registers, **fs** and **gs**. These new registers have no special features. They are provided solely as a convenience to help minimize the switching of segment registers associated with programs using more than four different segments.

FIGURE 7.1 THE 80386 APPLICATIONS REGISTERS

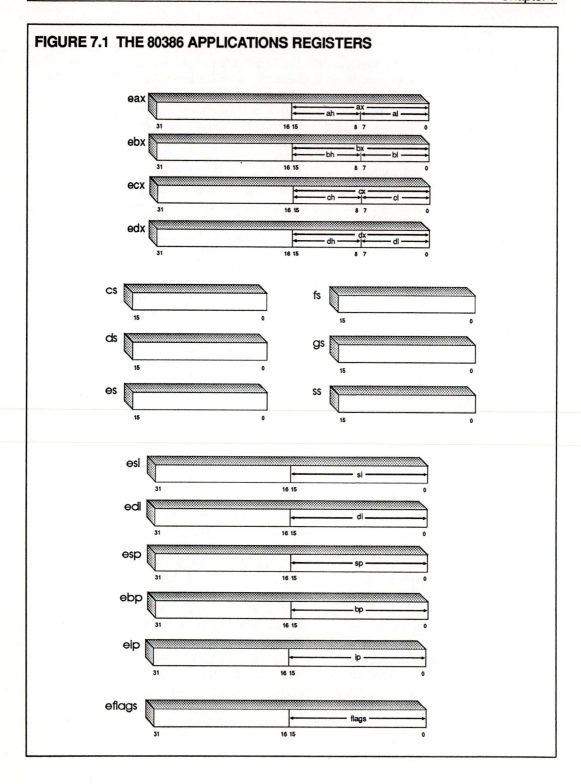

We are now ready for our first surprise: the artificial rules governing the form of indirect addressing expressions in **8088** programming have been abandoned. For example, recall that

```
mov     ax, [bx + si]
```

is legal, whereas

```
mov     ax, [cx + si]
```

is not. This situation has changed totally, provided that the *extended* registers are used for indirect addressing. An expression such as

```
mov     ax, [bx + si]
```

is still legal, as is

```
mov     ax, [ebx + esi]
```

and the second will have the same effect as the first if ebx and esi have the same values as **bx** and **si**. In other words, if the high 16 bits of **ebx** and **esi** are all equal to zero. But the exciting new item is that

```
mov     ax, [ecx + esi]
```

is also legal and it, too, will have the same effect, again provided that **ecx** and **esi** have appropriate values.

Figure 7.2 shows the indirect addressing options available with the **80386**. An indirect-addressing expression can contain up to two registers. As before, they are called the *base* and the *index*, but now each can be selected independently from the set of eight general-purpose registers — they can even be identical. The only restriction is that **esp** cannot play the role of the index.

The index can be given an optional *multiplicative scaling factor*, with allowed values 1, 2, 4, or 8. The reader should appreciate the utility of this new feature from our discussion in Chapter 6, where we pointed out the necessity of "scaling" by the size of a data element when indexing into an array.

As we noted in the previous section, the **80386** can use either 16-bit offsets or 32-bit offsets in a given program. The choice is called the *address size* and is made at assembly time. If the simplified segment directives are used, it is especially easy to communicate the desired value of the address size to **MASM**. To accept the complete range of **80386** applications instructions, **MASM** requires that the directive

```
.386
```

should appear in the source file. If this directive occurs *before* the

```
.MODEL Size
```

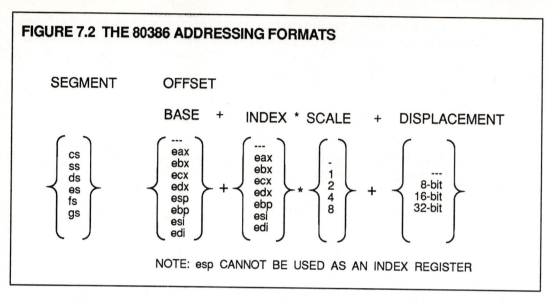

FIGURE 7.2 THE 80386 ADDRESSING FORMATS

SEGMENT   OFFSET

BASE + INDEX * SCALE + DISPLACEMENT

cs, ss, ds, es, fs, gs

eax, ebx, ecx, edx, esp, ebp, esi, edi

eax, ebx, ecx, edx, ebp, esi, edi

1 2 4 8

8-bit, 16-bit, 32-bit

NOTE: esp CANNOT BE USED AS AN INDEX REGISTER

directive, **MASM** will generate code using 32-bit offsets; in the contrary case, it will generate code using 16-bit offsets. Since we will normally use the **SMALL** model and 16-bit offsets, the following directive sequence is appropriate for our programs:

```
.MODEL SMALL
.386
```

It is important to realize that this choice affects only the default method used by the **80386** to compute addresses. In both 16-bit and 32-bit programs, it is legal to use the extended registers and the new addressing forms. We will see later that the initial choice of address size is not really restrictive: the **80386** recognizes a certain size-override byte (66H) as a request to change the prevailing address size for the following instruction. **MASM** automatically generates these override bytes even though, as we will soon see, it sometimes generates inappropriate warnings.

Mixing 16-bit registers with 32-bit registers in a single indirect addressing expression is illegal. For example,

```
mov     ax, [bx + esi]
```

is not allowed.

Even though it is legal to use all aspects of the 32-bit applications instructions in standard 16-bit real mode programs, certain structural restrictions must be observed. Consider, for example, the instruction

```
mov     eax, [ebx]
```

Syntactically, this instruction is legal — it will draw no complaint from **MASM**. But the run-time response of the machine to this instruction is dependent on the actual value of **ebx** when the instruction is encountered. In real mode, the size of a segment is 64K, unless special steps have been taken to modify this size, and the **80386** issues a *general protection fault* if an attempt is made to access a location beyond the end of the segment. By default, the machine halts in response to a general protection fault. Hence, this instruction will work correctly only if the run-time value of **ebx** is small enough that the referenced data item lies entirely in the segment pointed to by **ds**. Since this is a **mov** to a 4-byte destination, the implied size of **[ebx]** is four bytes. In order that a four-byte item fit entirely within the confines of a 64K segment, its last byte must have offset no larger than 0FFFFH, and so its base offset should be no larger than 0FFFCH. We conclude that this instruction will execute correctly in the standard real mode configuration provided **ebx** is less than or equal to 0FFFCH and will lock up the machine otherwise. The reader should try this and similar experiments. We will shed some more light on this strange phenomenon in Section 5, but the reader must wait until Chapter 18 to see a complete explanation.

We know that, in the **8088** architecture, the machine associates a default segment register with each indirect addressing expression, according to these rules: if the expression contains **bp**, the segment is assumed to be **ss**; otherwise, it is assumed to be **ds**. (The string instructions, which we have not yet discussed, cause a slight exception to these rules.) Since the **80386** allows more choices for the indirect addressing expression, the rules for determining the default segment are necessarily somewhat more involved. The basic rule is

- If the base register contained in an indirect addressing expression is either **ebp** or **esp**, then the default segment register is **ss**; otherwise, it is **ds**. Again, there is a small exception to this rule associated with the string instructions.

While this rule is clear enough on the surface, it does present a problem: how does **MASM** determine which part of the indirect addressing expression is the base? This may not be obvious, since the addends can be written in any order. Sometimes it is clear, as in

```
mov     ax, [edx*4 + ebp]
```

Since only the index can have a scaling factor, **ebp** must be the base, and so the default segment register is **ss**. But a case such as

```
mov     ax, [edx + ebp]
```

is ambiguous, and the intended choice of base register is critical since the candidates are associated with different segment registers.

The following additional rules, imposed by **MASM**, resolve all possible conflicts:

- If neither register in an indirect addressing expression uses scaling, the first is considered to be the base.

- If either register uses scaling, it is taken as the index.

- If only one register is present, it is considered to be the base. Of course, if it happens to be **esp**, it still cannot have a scaling factor.

A final important feature of indirect addressing on the **80386** is that the requisite computations are done in parallel with the other activities of the microprocessor. Consequently, the use of indirect addressing extracts no time penalty on the **80386**, in contrast with the **8088**.

The other registers in Figure 7.1 are mainly used in 32-bit programs and have the expected significance. For example, in a 32-bit program, **cs:eip** points to the current instruction and **ss:esp** points to the top of the stack. The **ebp** register is used in the same way that **bp** is used in 16-bit programs. The **eflags** register contains some new flags in its high 20 bits; we will examine them in Chapter 18.

Exercise 7-1. Check the statement made in this section about general protection faults resulting from the use of data lying too close to the end of a segment. Write test programs that deliberately situate word and dword data too close to the end of a segment and then attempt to access them.

SECTION 4 SOME 80386 INSTRUCTIONS

In this section, we will slightly extend our basic instruction set by introducing a few new instructions, some of which arrived with the **80386** and others of which go back as far as the **80186**.

Before doing this, we will give a short example to show how the extended addressing capabilities of the **80386** already make some computations more efficient.

Suppose that we have an array *Array1* of 16-bit integers, which we wish to move to a buffer named *Array2*. Let the size of the array be *Siz*, and assume that *Array1*, *Array2*, and *Siz* have all been defined in the segment pointed to by **ds**. The reader is probably aware that a block move can be treacherous if the source and destination happen to overlap. We will discuss this point in Chapter 10, but for the moment we will assume that no such complications arise. At first blush, it might seem natural to use the **loop** instruction. However, since we need a register, say **bx**, to index into the arrays, it is really more efficient to let this indexing register decrease and also use it as the iteration counter. Hence the **8088** code might look like this:

```
        mov     bx, Number
        dec     bx              ;bx = index of last array element
        add     bx, bx          ;convert to byte displacement

moveLoop:

        mov     ax, Array1[bx]
        mov     Array2[bx], ax ;move an element
        sub     bx, 2
        jge     moveLoop
```

Now let us consider how this code can be improved if written for the **80386**. First of all, the **loop** instruction works somewhat differently on the **80386**: in a 16-bit program it still uses **cx** as a counter, but in a 32-bit program it uses **ecx**. Since we planning to write 16-bit programs, this is not of much concern to us. However, in the present program we only wish to maintain one counter. Hence we will use **ecx** to measure the offsets into the arrays and its lower half **cx** as the loop counter. Since indirect-addressing computations basically cost nothing, they should contain as much of the computation as possible. With these ideas in mind, here is a reasonable **80386** version of the program fragment:

```
    mov       ecx, Siz
    jcxz      Done          ;do nothing if Array1 empty

moveLoop:

    mov       ax, Array1[ecx*2-2]
    mov       Array2[ecx*2-2],ax
    loop      moveLoop

    Done:
```

We have assumed that *Array1* is small enough to fit in a 16-bit segment. Hence, the

```
    mov       ecx, Siz
```

instruction really moved *Siz* into **cx**, as required for the **loop** instruction, and also zeroed the high half of **ecx**. We could equally well have used

```
    movzx     ecx, Siz
```

Since the size of *Array1* was in **cx**, **jcxz** gave an appropriate test for an empty array. Incidentally, there is also a

```
    jecxz     Target
```

instruction available under the **80386**.

The loop logic should be clear. We are again starting at the top end and proceeding downward. The starting value of **ecx*2** − 2 correctly indexes the high elements of the arrays.

This example already suggests the power of the **80386**, but the increase in speed is much greater than just counting instructions would indicate. For instance, a **mov** instruction between the accumulator and a memory location requires at least 10 clock cycles on the **8088** (even ignoring any indirect addressing penalty) but needs only 2 clock cycles on the **80386**. As a rough estimate, this code fragment therefore requires only about one-eighth as many clock cycles on the **80386** as on the **8088**.

Other aspects of the **80386** also result in faster execution times. For example, the clock speed of a basic **80386** machine is more than three times that of an **IBM-XT**. In our example, we chose to move the array a word at a time. But instead we could have moved a doubleword (i.e., two words) at a time by using the **eax** register rather than **ax**. Of course, this approach would have involved a small amount of additional overhead in checking whether the array contained an odd number of integers and, in case it did, performing a separate one-word move before or after the main loop. We ask the reader to implement this modification as an exercise.

The **80386** instruction set has many features designed to increase the efficiency of computations. For example, multiplication on the **8088** is sometimes awkward since one operand must be the accumulator and since multiplication by an immediate value is prohibited. These restrictions have been lifted in the case of multiplication, although unfortunately not in the case of division. Table 7.1 shows the various formats for multiplication and division that are accepted by the **80386.**

The most striking feature of Table 7.1 is the selection of new formats for **imul**, which now comes in 1-, 2-, and 3-operand varieties. The only enhancement of the 1-operand mode is a new option using the 32-bit registers: a 32-bit operand is multiplied by the implied accumulator **eax** and the 64-bit product ends up in **edx:eax.**

The new 2-operand versions are noteworthy for two reasons. The destination, which is the first operand, need no longer be the accumulator: it can be any 16- or 32-bit general-purpose register. The second operand can be memory, register, or immediate, and this last alternative is especially convenient. If the second operand is memory or a register, it must be the same size as the first; if it is immediate data, it must be no larger than the first.

There can be a loss of significant information in these forms of multiplication, since the number of bits retained is the size of the first operand. If such a loss occurs, the carry and overflow flags are set. Operations such as multiplication by 10 can now be done with a single instruction, such as

```
imul      bx, 10
```

These new versions are easier to write and generate fewer bytes of machine code. In addition, all types of multiplication are faster on the **80386.** For example, on the **8088** a typical **imul** requires about 90 clock cycles, whereas our preceding example requires only 10 clock cycles on the **80386.** One interesting architectural feature of the **80386** is that in performing an operation such as

```
imul      Reg, Immed
```

the size of the constant *Immed* is important. The *early-out multiplication algorithm* used by the **80386** multiplies *Reg* by the bits of *Immed*, starting with the low bit and terminating as soon as all non-zero bits have been used. Consequently, the multiplication is faster with small values of *Immed* than with high values. If *Reg* is 16 bits, the execution times obtained for different values of *Immed* range from 9 to 22 clock cycles.

The three-operand form of **imul** multiplies the second and third operands, using the first operand as the destination. Again, the first operand must be a 16- or 32-bit register. The second operand is a register or memory reference of size equal to the first, and the third operand is immediate data of size less than or equal to the first. Once more, the entire answer may not be retained.

Even though machine multiplication is very fast on the **80386,** it is often possible to use clever tricks to accomplish even faster multiplication. For example, consider this method of multiplying **eax** by 10:

```
lea       eax, [eax+eax*4]
shl       eax, 1
```

The first line effectively multiplies **eax** by 5, and the second line, of course, multiplies by 2. Each instruction requires 2 clock cycles, and the indirect addressing computation exacts no penalty. Hence this multiplication by 10 requires an incredible 4 clock cycles!

TABLE 7.1 80386 MULTIPLICATION AND DIVISION FORMATS

OPERATION	Op1	Op2	Op3	EFFECT		
mul Op1	r/m8			ax	<—	al * Op1
	r/m16			dx:ax	<—	ax * Op1
	r/m32			edx:eax	<—	eax * Op1
imul Op1	r/m8			ax	<—	al * Op1
	r/m16			dx:ax	<—	ax * Op1
	r/m32			edx:eax	<—	eax * Op1
imul Op1, Op2	r16	r/m16		Op1	<—	Op1 * Op2
	r16	i8/16		Op1	<—	Op1 * Op2
	r32	r/m32		Op1	<—	Op1 * Op2
	r32	i32/8		Op1	<—	Op2 * Op2
imul Op1, Op2, Op3	r16	r/m16	i16/8	Op1	<—	Op2 * Op3
	r32	r/m16	i32/8	Op1	<—	Op2 * Op3
div Op1	r/m8			al	<—	ax / Op1
				ah	<—	Remainder
	r/m16			ax	<—	dx:ax / Op1
				dx	<—	Remainder
	r/m32			eax	<—	edx:eax / Op1
				edx	<—	Remainder
idiv Op1	r/m8			al	<—	ax / Op1
				ah	<—	Remainder
	r/m16			ax	<—	dx:ax / Op1
				dx	<—	Remainder
	r/m32			eax	<—	edx:eax / Op1
				edx	<—	Remainder

KEY   1. '/' means "or"
      2. r = register, m = memory, i = immediate data
      3. 8, 16, and 32 means size in bits
      4. mul and div perform unsigned operations while imul and idiv
         perform signed operations
      5. the analogs of the second and third forms of imul are not
         required for mul since signed and unsigned multiplication have
         the same effect of the lower half of the product

Returning to Table 7.1, we note that there are no forms of **mul** that are analogous to the 2- and 3-operand forms of **imul**. The reason is that none are required because, in the context of these instructions, **mul** and **imul** do exactly the same thing. We will clarify this statement by considering how a fictitious analog **mul** of the 2-operand **imul** would work. To be specific, let us contemplate the imaginary instruction

```
        mul     Reg, Immed
```

where *Reg* is a 16-bit register. This operation will only produce a valid answer when the product does not overflow, i.e., if the unsigned product *Reg*Immed* fits in 16 bits. But, except for the trivial cases where *Immed* = 0 or *Immed* = 1, this size restriction requires that *Reg* have a 0 in the high bit. Similarly, *Immed* must have a 0 in its high bit unless *Reg* is 0 or 1. Consequently, if the trivial cases are ignored both operands must be positive when considered as signed bit patterns, and so the answer delivered by **imul** will equal the answer from our hypothetical **mul**.

Table 7.1 shows that, in contrast to the expanded **imul** offerings, the **80386** does not offer a greatly enhanced set of division operations. It does provide 32-bit extensions of the basic division instructions, and these work in the expected ways.

We have already encountered the problem of copying a byte of data into a word register. Using the **8088**, transferring the byte *varB* to **cx** requires a sequence such as

```
mov     cl, varB
xor     ch, ch
```

The **80386** provides instructions allowing this and similar operations to be performed in a single step. One such instruction,

```
movzx   Op1, Op2
```

is called *move with zero-extend*. *Op1* must be a register and *Op2* a register or memory reference of size strictly less than *Op1*. The effect is to move *Op2* to the low end of *Op2*, padding with zeroes on the high end. Our previous pair of instructions could therefore be replaced by

```
movzx   cx, varB
```

A similar instruction,

```
movsx   Op1, Op2
```

is named *move with sign-extend*. Its operation is identical with **movzx** except that it pads the high end of *Op1* with copies of the sign bit of *Op2*.

Another useful instruction is

```
pusha
```

which is called *push all*. It pushes the 8 general-purpose registers onto the stack, in the order **ax, cx, dx, bx, sp, bp, si**, and **di**. The *pop all* operation

```
popa
```

undoes the effect of **pusha**. The **pusha** instruction is certainly not used for its time efficiency: each **push** of a register on the **80386** requires 2 clock cycles, while **pusha** completes 8 pushes in 18 clock cycles! It does, however, save code space. Much more importantly, using **pusha** and **popa** ensures that the pops are done in reverse order to the pushes. This is a significant consideration since a lapse in this respect can cause sporadic and hard-to-diagnose bugs.

Another worthwhile improvement in the instruction set of the later processors is the

```
push    Immed
```

instruction. It is no longer necessary to perform a contortion such as

```
mov       ax, 100
push      ax
```

in order to push the constant 100 onto the stack. A simple

```
push      100
```

is legal and has the desired effect.

While we are discussing pushes and pops, we will point out an undesirable feature of Version 5.1 of **MASM**. We know that the **80386** can be operated either in 16-bit or 32-bit mode and that addresses that are not of the default address size must be prefaced by a size-override byte, which has value 66H. Similarly, the **80386** assumes that the default data size is the same as the default address size and requires that references to data items that are not of the default size be prefaced by a *data-size override byte* (67H). Like the address-size overrides, **MASM** generates the data-size overrides automatically.

Suppose that we are using 16-bit segments. Then here are some examples of the override bytes:

INSTRUCTION		OVERRIDE BYTES
mov	ax, [bx]	none
mov	ax, [ebx]	67h
mov	eax, 10	66h
mov	eax, [ebx]	67h 66h

The interested reader can check these and similar examples by building a simple program and examining the .LST file generated by **MASM**. It is also worthwhile to assemble such a program using 32-bit segments and to observe that the override bytes are needed in 32-bit mode precisely when they are not needed in 16-bit mode, and conversely.

In 16-bit mode the instruction

```
push      eax
```

requires a size override. **MASM** does indeed generate the size override but it also issues an unneeded warning message. It is possible to ignore this message. Unfortunately, some of our programs in Chapter 18 collect over 100 of these warnings, which completely obscure any important messages that may be emitted by **MASM**. One way to escape the problem is to turn off the warning messages (by assembling with a /w0 switch on the **MASM** command line). We emphatically do not recommend this practice. Generally, the warning messages are significant, and the underlying causes should be found and fixed. Our solution was to write a macro that manually inserts the size-override byte 67H and then recodes the **push** instruction so that it only involves a 16-bit object and hence provokes no warning. This macro is in CONSOLE.MAC. Since it involves macro machinery that we will not introduce until Chapter 13, we have not included it in the text. The reader should examine it after reading that chapter. The macro is named *pushEM* (for *push-extended macro*) and uses the calling syntax

```
pushEM    Op
```

where *Op* can be any 4-byte object: register, memory, or constant.

Since **popa** provokes the same warning as **pusha** when used with operands not having the default address size, we also wrote a *popEM* macro that is analogous to *pushEM*.

The 80386 offers a **pushad** (for *push-all-double*) instruction, which pushes all eight 32-bit general-purpose registers, in the same order as does **pusha**. The **popad** instruction has the inverse effect. Again, when either of these instructions in used in 16-bit mode, **MASM** emits an unnecessary warning message. We deal with this precisely as in the **push** and **pop** cases, namely by introducing macros that actually fabricate the machine code. These macros are named *pushadM* (since it is the macro form of **pushad**) and, analogously, *popadM*.

To utilize the 32-bit computational powers of the **80386** effectively, we need 32-bit analogs of the *ascBin16* and *bin16Asc* procedures introduced in Chapter 6. The 32-bit analog of *ascBin16* is called *ascBin32* and is shown in Figure 7.3. By comparing Figure 7.3 with Figure 6.11, the reader can check that our new program is a fairly direct translation of the original. We have made a number of improvements that take advantage of the new **80386** capabilities. Operationally, *ascBin32* is the exact analog of *ascBin16*: as input it expects a null-terminated string of decimal digits; it uses the basic "multiply by 10 and add the next digit" algorithm to compute the binary equivalent, which it stores in a doubleword; and conversion stops as soon as the null terminator or a non-digit is encountered in the input.

We have already covered all of the new **80386** features used in this code but, for the sake of review, here is a rundown of the salient points:

Line 4. So far, we have only written programs using the simplified segment directives. We know that, under these circumstances, **MASM** bases its choice of address size on the relative positions of the **.MODEL** and the **.386** directives in the source file. In Chapter 12 we will see that segments can be defined more generally, and **MASM** then makes a selection based on the appearance of either a **USE16** or a **USE32** directive. Since these two terms are also used throughout the Intel **80386** documentation, we decided to use them in our procedure headers.

Lines 18-19. Because the **.MODEL** directive occurs before the **.386** directive, **MASM** instructs the **80386** to use 16-bit as the default address size.

Line 33. As we discussed in Chapter 6, it is something of an assembly language tradition to use statements like

```
xor      si, si
```

to zero registers. When executed by the **8088**, this instruction is faster than say

```
mov      si, 0
```

However, in the case of the **80386**, the **mov** instruction is just as fast as the **xor** (2 clock cycles), although the **mov** instruction still generates one more byte of code than the **xor** (3 bytes versus 2). Since each **80386** instruction fetch returns 4 bytes, this extra byte will seldom have an effect of execution time. Hence there is no longer any strong reason to use the bit operations in contexts such as this one. It can even be argued that the **mov** version makes programs more readable. Nevertheless, we will continue to use the bit operations here and in similar contexts for consistency with our **8088** programs.

Line 57. Here we are using the 2-operand form of **imul**. Of course, **mul** is really needed here but, as explained earlier, **imul** does the job equally well.

Line 60. This is our first application of the **movzx** instruction. We are using it to move an 8-bit source to a 32-bit destination.

Line 69. As a general rule, instructions that work on 8- or 16-bit quantities extend in the natural way to 32-bit objects. The **neg** instruction is an example.

We also need a 32-bit analog of *bin16Asc*, the procedure that does the inverse transformation. In one of the exercises, we have asked the reader to make the required modifications to *bin16Asc* to produce an appropriate *bin32Asc*. USER.LIB contains ASCBIN32.OBJ and, even though we have not supplied the source code, it also contains a version of BIN32ASC.OBJ. As is our custom, we have written macros to facilitate using these conversion routines. These macros, *aToL* and *lToA*, are shown at the end of Figure 7.3 and are also contained in CONSOLE.MAC.

Exercise 7-2. Modify the code fragment from the preceding section so that it moves a doubleword at a time. It will be necessary to check first whether the array contains an even or an odd number of words. In the odd case, begin with a single one-word move and then process the remaining even number of integers as doublewords. Embed the fragment in a .386 program. Assemble and link this program and trace through part of it using **CODEVIEW**. Incidentally, **CODEVIEW** will display the extended **80386** registers: just make the *386* choice in the *Options* menu.

Exercise 7-3. In this section, we showed how to fabricate a really fast multiplication by 10 on the **80386**. For what other values of n ≤ 20 can you find a very fast multiplication by n?

Exercise 7-4. Translate *bin16Asc* to a 32-bit version, which should be named *bin32Asc*. Work by analogy with our translation of *ascBin16*. Write a small calling program to check the operation of the new procedure. It is best to structure this calling program as a loop that iterates these steps:

- Prompts the user to input a 32-bit integer in its alphanumeric form.
- Converts the input integer to binary form using ascBin32.
- Uses the new procedure to convert this binary back to alphanumeric form. Prints the result to the screen.

Of course, the final value should equal the input value in every case.

FIGURE 7.3 ALPHANUMERIC-TO-32-BIT BINARY CONVERSION

```
 1   TITLE    ascBin32.asm
 2
 3   COMMENT #  PROCEDURE HEADER
 4   TYPE:      NEAR 386 USE16    FILE: ascBin32.asm    LIBRARY: user.lib
 5   PURPOSE:   Converts null-terminated alphanumeric representation of
 6              decimal integer to 32-bit two's complement format
 7   CALLED AS: ascBin32(offsetAlphaNumeric(2))
 8              with buffer in segment pointed to by ds
 9   RETURNS:   32-bit value in eax
10   REMARKS:   Keeps converting input digit stream until non-digit
11              or null terminator is encountered. If input is outside
12              32-bit range, ascBin32 returns the value that is within
13          #   range and is correct modulo 2^32
14
15   INCLUDE console.mac
16   PUBLIC  ascBin32
17
18   .MODEL SMALL
19   .386
20
21   .CODE
22
23   ascBin32 PROC NEAR
24
25       push    bp
26       mov     bp, sp
27
28
29       push    bx
30       pushEM  edx
31       push    si
32
33       xor     si, si              ;store sign in si, 0 meaning +
34       mov     bx, [bp + 4]        ;point bx to input string
35       cmp     BYTE PTR [bx], '+'  ;check whether there is a + sign
36       jne     SHORT checkNeg      ;if not, check for - sign
37       inc     bx                  ;move to first digit
38       jmp     SHORT firstDigit
39
40   checkNeg:
41
42       cmp     BYTE PTR [bx], '-'
43       jne     SHORT firstDigit
44       not     si                  ;-1 in si means input minus sign
45       inc     bx                  ;move to first digit
46
47   firstDigit:
48
49       xor     eax, eax
50
51   convertLoop:
52
53       cmp     BYTE PTR [bx], '0'  ;is it a digit?
54       jl      SHORT endConvert    ;this test also catches end of string
55       cmp     BYTE PTR [bx], '9'
```

```
56          jg       SHORT endConvert
57          imul     eax,10
58          mov      dl, [bx]
59          sub      dl, 30h
60          movzx    edx, dl
61          add      eax, edx
62          inc      bx
63          jmp      convertLoop
64
65   endConvert:
66
67          and      si, si
68          je       SHORT notNeg
69          neg      eax
70
71   notNeg:
72
73          pop      si
74          popEM    edx
75          pop      bx
76
77
78          pop      bp
79          ret      2
80
81   ascBin32 ENDP
82
83   END
84
```

```
MACROS THAT CALL ascBin32 AND binAsc32

COMMENT     #  MACRO HEADER          FILE: console.mac
MACRO NAME:    aToL
PURPOSE:    Calls ascBin32 to convert ASCIIZ string to 32-bit integer
CALLED AS:     aToL intStr
REMARKS:    #  Returns 32-bit integer in eax

aToL    MACRO    intStr

    EXTRN    ascBin32:NEAR
    lea      ax, intStr
    push     ax
    call     ascBin32

ENDM


COMMENT     # MACRO HEADER           FILE: console.mac
MACRO NAME:    lToA
PURPOSE:    Calls bin32Asc to convert 32-bit integer to ASCIIZ format
CALLED AS:     lToA intStr, Int
REMARKS:    #

lToA    MACRO    intStr, Int

    EXTRN    bin32Asc:NEAR
    pushEM   eax
```

Figure 7.3 cont.

```
        pushem  Int
        lea     ax, intStr
        push    ax
        call    bin32Asc
        popEM   eax

        ENDM
```

SECTION 5 WORKING WITH LARGE ARRAYS

We are going to use the **80386** to generate an array of 500,000 randomly selected 32-bit integers and will sort these integers into increasing order using a version of the quicksort algorithm that will be developed in the present section. The array will reside entirely in one segment, and the program will execute under **MS-DOS**. The reader may find this puzzling since we have emphasized that **MS-DOS** is a 16-bit operating system and is only capable of controlling the **80386** in its 16-bit mode. The question then arises of how a single segment can be made long enough to hold an array of size 500,000 * 4 = 2 megabytes. We will answer this question later in this section.

We need a new version of our random-number generator, tailored to the generation of 32-bit random numbers. The code for this generator involves fairly minor modifications of the corresponding 16-bit random number generator presented in Figure 6.12. The 32-bit version is contained in the second part of Figure 7.4.

As we pointed out in Chapter 6, most random-number generators generate the same sequence of numbers each time they are started, unless they are given a different starting value, or *seed*, at the beginning of each run. In Section 6.9, we manually supplied different values of the seed. It is certainly more convenient to have the machine automatically provide a different value of the seed at each use, and the procedure *Seed32*, shown in the first part of Figure 7.4, accomplishes this end. The idea behind *Seed32* is simple: find some location in machine memory containing a constantly changing sequence of values and use the current value from that location as the seed. There are a number of candidates for such a location. We chose the doubleword at machine address 0040:006C. As we saw in Chapter 2, the area of machine memory starting at address 0040:0000 (i.e., at absolute address 400H) is called the *BIOS data area* and is used to hold various significant data items relating to the hardware configuration of the machine. One of these data items is called the *timer tick count*, and this is the quantity that we have chosen as the return value of *Seed32*. The timer-tick count is set to zero at midnight and is thereafter incremented at the approximate rate of 18.2 times per second. (The origin of the constant 18.2 will be explained in Chapter 15.) This is clearly a reasonable method of choosing the seed.

The code for *Seed32* is straightforward. In **8088** programming our convention is to return 16-bit values in the **ax** register. By analogy, we will return 32-bit values in the **eax** register when programming the **80386**. *Seed32* adheres to this convention.

To address data at 0040:006C, some segment register must be pointed to 40H. We chose **fs** rather than **ds** or **es**, just to emphasize the fact that the new segment registers can be used interchangeably with the old ones.

The code for *Rand32*, the 32-bit random-number generator, contains a few items of interest:

Line 6. We are planning to use *Rand32* to generate very large arrays. Since the projected sizes will be larger than 65535, it is necessary to use a 32-bit integer as the *arraySize* parameter. Likewise, as we will see later in this section, the array must be allowed to start at a very high offset into the current segment, and so the *offsetArray* parameter is also 32-bit.

Lines 34-36. *Seed* is a 32-bit value and hence occupies 4 bytes on the stack. Consequently, *offsetArray*, the next parameter, begins at offset **bp + 8** on the stack. Likewise, *offsetArray* is a 32-bit parameter and so *sizeArray* begins at offset **bp + 12**.

Line 40. Another use of the 2-operand **imul**, again really intended as a **mul**.

Line 42. We are once more making good use of the extended indirect addressing facilities of the **80386**. Here **ebx** points to the base of the array and **ecx** always contains the index of the current array location. The scaling factor "*4" is needed because each array element is four bytes long. Because of the "-4", the starting value *arraySize* of **ecx** corresponds to the highest array position. On each trip through the loop, **ecx** is decremented and the next lowest array element becomes the target of the indirect addressing expression.

Lines 43-44. The reader may wonder why this pair of lines appears, rather than the more efficient

```
        loop        randLoop
```

The reason is that in 16-bit mode **loop** uses **cx** as the counter and here (because of the potential size of the array) we have stored the size in **ecx**. If this were a 32-bit program, the **loop** instruction should certainly be used.

Line 50. The procedure received three 32-bit parameters, and so 12 bytes must be popped to clear the stack.

Our next step is to write a version of the quicksort algorithm that will sort an array of 32-bit integers into increasing order. For the sake of the reader who is not intimately acquainted with quicksort, we will begin with a brief discussion of the algorithm in general. We will then explain the register usage in our implementation.

Quicksort is a very easy algorithm to understand, although the implementation details are delicate. In the case we are considering, namely sorting an array into increasing order, the algorithm consists of the following three steps:

- Select an element of the array, traditionally called the *pivot*.

- Partially sort the array so that all the elements less than the pivot come first, then the pivot, and finally all the elements greater than or equal to the pivot. We will call the collection of elements less than the pivot A and the elements greater than or equal to the pivot, but excluding the pivot itself, B.

- Have the algorithm call itself recursively twice, once to sort A and once to sort B.

FIGURE 7.4 GENERATING 32-BIT RANDOM NUMBERS

```
 1   TITLE Seed32.asm
 2
 3   COMMENT   # PROCEDURE HEADER
 4   TYPE:       NEAR 386 USE16   FILE: Seed32.asm    LIBRARY: user.lib
 5   PURPOSE:    Selects 32-bit seed for random number generation
 6   CALLED AS:  Seed32()
 7   PARAMS:     None
 8   RETURNS:    Value of seed in eax
 9   REMARKS:  # Obtains seed value from BIOS timer tick count
10
11   DOSSEG
12   .MODEL SMALL
13   .386
14
15   PUBLIC   Seed32
16
17   .CODE
18
19   Seed32      PROC      NEAR
20
21       push    es
22
23       mov     ax, 40h                  ;point es to BIOS data area
24       mov     es, ax
25       mov     eax, es:[6ch]            ;BIOS timer tick count
26
27       pop     es
28       ret
29
30   Seed32      ENDP
31
32   END


 1   TITLE  Rand32.asm
 2
 3   COMMENT   #  PROCEDURE HEADER
 4   TYPE:       NEAR 386 USE16   FILE: Rand32.asm    LIBRARY: user.lib
 5   PURPOSE:    Fills array with random 32-bit integers
 6   CALLED AS:  Rand32(Seed(4), offsetArray(4), sizeArray(4))
 7   PARAMS:     Seed is the four-byte seed for the random number generator
 8               offsetArray is four-byte offset of array which will hold
 9               the 32-bit integers
10               sizeArray is the number of elements in Array
11   RETURNS:    Nothing
12   REMARKS:  #  Uses linear congruence. Note that offsetArray is 4 bytes long
13
14   INCLUDE   console.mac
15
16   PUBLIC    Rand32
17
18       MULTIPLIER    EQU   12345
19       ADDER         EQU   123
20
21   .MODEL SMALL
22   .386
```

```
23
24   .CODE
25
26   Rand32    PROC    NEAR
27
28       push    bp
29       mov     bp, sp
30
31       pushEM ebx
32       pushEM ecx
33
34       mov     ebx, [bp + 8]          ;point ebx to Array
35       mov     ecx, [bp + 12]         ;number of ints to generate
36       mov     eax, [bp + 4]          ;the seed
37
38   randLoop:
39
40       imul    eax, MULTIPLIER        ;uses immediate two-operand multiplication
41       add     eax, ADDER             ;new = MULTIPLIER * old + ADDER
42       mov     [ebx + ecx*4 - 4], eax ;uses new 386 addressing mode
43       dec     ecx                    ;to index previous element of Array
44       jne     randLoop
45
46       popEM ecx
47       popEM ebx
48
49       pop     bp
50       ret     12
51
52   Rand32    ENDP
53
54   END
```

Clearly, this technique really sorts the array: if A has been sorted and B has been sorted and the components of the array occur in the order {A, pivot, B}, then certainly the entire array has been sorted. The recursion also terminates nicely: when the size of the array has been reduced to 1, both A and B are empty and there is nothing further to do.

It turns out that the choice of the pivot has a critical effect on the efficiency of the algorithm. Ideally, the pivot should be chosen as the median element of the array, so that A and B have the same size. Of course, it is not possible to make such a choice efficiently when processing an unknown, unsorted array. Some implementations of the algorithm examine three or more elements of the array and choose the median of these elements as the pivot. This ensures that the pivot will not be an extreme value of the array, at least most of the time. In our implementation, we will do nothing as fancy as this, although we do ask the reader to do so as an exercise. Our approach is to use the centrally located element of the array as the pivot (or one of the two central elements if the array has even length). Of course, for a totally random array this is no better than choosing the first element as the pivot and does involve more work. However, for an array that is already partially sorted (and such arrays do arise) it does somewhat improve the performance of the algorithm.

Even though we will not select the first element of the array as the pivot, it turns out that the subsequent array operations are easier if the pivot occupies the first array position. Hence, immediately after we choose the pivot we swap it with the first element of the array.

The main computation of the algorithm consists of a single left-to-right scan of the array, in the course of which all the elements that are less than the pivot are brought to the left end of the array and the other elements to the right end. The configuration when this scan has been partially completed can be represented by a diagram like this:

```
plll...lllggg...ggg???...???
```

In this diagram, 'p' is the pivot (which has been brought to the start of the array), each 'l' is an array element that has already been examined and found to be less than the pivot, each 'g' is an element that has been found to be greater than or equal to the pivot, and each '?' is an element that must still to be inspected. The next element to be examined is the leftmost '?'. If it turns out to be a 'g', it can be left where it is. If it is an 'l', it must be moved over to join the other 'l' elements. This is most easily accomplished by swapping it with the leftmost 'g'. In both cases, this '?' is replaced by a 'g', and we should transfer our attention to the next '?' in line.

Upon completion of the scan, the array has the form

```
plll...lllggg...ggg
```

Reducing the array to its final form requires moving the pivot to a position between the last 'l' and the first 'g'. Again, this is most easily done by a swap, this time of 'p' and the rightmost 'l'.

It is now a fairly easy matter to translate this scheme into an assembly language program. We assign pointers into the array according to this diagram:

```
plll...lllggg...ggg???...???
^          ^         ^
ebx      ebx+edi*4 ebx+esi*4
```

In words, **ebx** always points to the base of the array, **edi** is kept updated so that **ebx+edi*4** points to the rightmost 'l', and likewise **ebx+esi*4** always points to the leftmost '?', which is the element currently being examined. Initially, **edi** should be given the value 0 and **esi** should have value 1.

The code for our quicksort procedure, *qkSort32*, is given in Figure 7.5. Here are some remarks on that program:

Lines 21-22. As soon as a program becomes at all complicated, it is a good idea to use equates such as these to increase readability.

Lines 26-32. Since there are three locations in the code where a pair of 32-bit elements must be swapped, it is worth writing a macro to do the job.

Lines 43-46. This is the "termination code" for the recursion, that is, the code that prevents it from running forever. In words, it says that when the array size has been reduced to 1, we should stop. Of course, the exact location of the termination code in the procedure is largely a matter of taste, but the author always finds it reassuring to position it at the start of the code.

Lines 53-54. We locate the central element of the array by dividing the number of elements (in **edi**) by 2. If the array has even size, we are actually selecting the rightmost of the central pair of elements.

Line 55. Swapping the central element with the initial element.

Lines 62-73. We scan the array, left to right, collecting the 'l' and 'g' elements at the correct ends of the array.

Line 75. Putting the pivot back where it belongs, between the 'l' and the 'g' elements.

Lines 77-87. Things become interesting here — we are setting up the stack for the recursive call. After the left-to-right scan has been completed and the pivot element has been repositioned, the array has this form:

```
lll......lllpggg......ggg
^            ^          ^
ebx       ebx+edi*4   ebx+esi*4
```

Since 'p' was swapped with the rightmost 'l', **ebx+edi***4 now points to 'p'.

It is unimportant whether the recursive call to sort A or the one to sort B is made first. We arbitrarily chose to sort B first. A call to *qkSort32* requires that the number of elements in the array and its offset be pushed onto the stack, in that order. The offset of B can be read directly from the diagram: its value is

```
ebx + edi*4 + 4
```

The size of B is almost as easy to find: it is the number of 'g' elements in the diagram. This number equals

```
ARYSIZ - (number of elements before the first 'g')
= ARYSIZ - (edi + 1)
= ARYSIZ - edi - 1
```

Line 89. Calling *qkSort32* recursively to sort B.

Lines 91-92. We are setting up the stack for the recursive call that will sort A. Since we have saved and restored the extended registers (lines 51 and 97), **ebx** and **ecx** have survived the call to *qkSort32* on line 90, and so still have the same values as on line 88. In our words, our diagram is still valid, so that **ebx** gives the offset of A and **edi** gives its size.

Before we can build an interesting application from the pieces constructed in this chapter, we must examine the **80386** view of segments a little more closely. The following discussion will be quite general and qualitative; the technical details must wait until Chapter 18.

In the **80386** architecture, a segment can be of virtually any length, from 1 byte to 4 gigabytes. (Long segments must actually have lengths that are multiples of 4K, but the

FIGURE 7.5 QUICKSORT FOR 32-BIT INTEGERS

```
 1   TITLE qkSort32.asm
 2
 3   COMMENT   # PROCEDURE HEADER
 4   TYPE:        NEAR  386  USE16    FILE: qkSort32.asm    LIBRARY: user.lib
 5   PURPOSE:     Sorts an array of 32-bit integers into non-decreasing order
 6   CALLED AS:   qkSort(offsetArray(4), sizeArray(4))
 7   RETURNS:     Nothing.
 8   REMARKS:     Uses recursive quicksort algorithm.
 9               Chooses middle array element as pivot, which it swaps to start
10               of array. ebx points to base of array, ebx+edi to the last
11               element currently known to be < the pivot, and ebx + esi points
12           #   to the element that is currently being examined.
13
14   INCLUDE console.mac
15   PUBLIC   qkSort32
16
17   DOSSEG
18   .MODEL SMALL
19   .386
20
21       ARYSIZ      EQU      DWORD PTR [bp + 4]
22       BASEADDR    EQU      DWORD PTR [bp + 8]
23
24   ;------------------------------------------------------------
25
26   Swap32 MACRO a, b               ;swaps 32-bit objects
27
28       mov     eax, a
29       xchg    eax, b
30       mov     a, eax
31
32   ENDM
33
34   ;------------------------------------------------------------
35
36   .CODE
37
38   qkSort32    PROC    NEAR
39
40       push    bp
41       mov     bp, sp
42
43       cmp     ARYSIZ, 1           ;is it a trivial case?
44       jg      SHORT toWork
45       pop     bp
46       ret     8
47
48   toWork:
49
50       pusmADM
51
52       mov     ebx, BASEADDR       ;point ebx to array
53       mov     edi, ARYSIZ         ;number of elements to sort
54       shr     edi, 1              ;point di to "middle" integer in Array
55       Swap32  [ebx], [ebx+edi*4]  ;middle element is pivot - put it first
```

```
56        mov     ecx, ARYSIZ
57        dec     ecx                 ;number of comparisons to be made
58        xor     edi, edi            ;point ebx + edi to pivot
59        mov     esi, 1              ;point ebx + esi to present element
60        mov     eax, [ebx]          ;always compare with eax = pivot
61
62   compLoop:
63
64        cmp     [ebx+esi*4], eax
65        jge     SHORT orderOK
66        inc     edi
67        Swap32  [ebx+esi*4], [ebx+edi*4] ;if present < pivot, then swap
68                                         ; present with leftmost 'g'
69   orderOK:
70
71        inc     esi
72        dec     ecx
73        jne     compLoop
74
75        Swap32  [ebx], [ebx+edi*4]      ;return pivot to correct place
76
77        mov     eax, edi                ;set up stack for recursive calls
78        shl     eax, 2
79        add     eax, ebx
80        add     eax, 4
81        pushEM  eax                     ; = offset of B = ebx+edi*4+4
82
83        mov     eax, ARYSIZ
84        mov     ecx, edi
85        sub     eax, ecx
86        dec     eax
87        pushEM  eax                     ; = size of B = ARYSIZ-edi-1
88
89        call    qkSort32
90
91        pushEM  ebx                     ; = offset of A = ebx
92        pushEM  edi                     ; = size of A = edi
93
94        call    qkSort32
95
96        popADM
97
98        pop     bp
99        ret     8
100
101  qkSort32   ENDP
102
103  END
```

reasons for this need not concern us at the moment.) A segment can begin at any memory address and can be designated as read-only or write-only. The **80386** then polices all segment use: it checks whether, in each *segment:offset* reference, the segment part refers to a "legal" segment; it also examines the offset value to be sure that the address references a location that is really within the segment limits; and it checks whether the use of the segment is compatible with its read/write permissions. When the machine is operating in protected mode, new segments can be set up and given characteristics appropriate to the task at hand.

In most **80386** systems, only operating system code would be empowered to perform operations of this kind.

When the **80386** is booted, it begins operating in real mode, and segments are given a default length. This default length is 64K, as is appropriate to the standard real-mode operating system. Although this fact is not well documented by Intel, it is possible to go into protected mode and change the segment limits and then to return to real mode while retaining these new limits. This is the technique that we have used in the program BIGARRAY.ASM, presented in Figure 7.6. Specifically, we change the segment limit on the data segment to 4G, the largest possible. Of course, no machine has that much memory, but the effect is that the segment has length equal to the total size of machine memory, whatever that may be. We left the code and stack segments at length 64K, only because there was no reason to change them. The procedure that performs the segment extension is called *expandSegs*. It is already in USER.LIB. The reader can either accept this procedure on faith or, in the face of insatiable curiosity, scan the first few sections of Chapter 18 to get a general idea of how it works.

It is important to realize immediately that this approach provides an experimental tool but should not be viewed as a serious way of overcoming the 640K limitation of **MS-DOS**. In particular, we are using memory without the knowledge of the operating system. Memory that has been reserved for a ramdisk or anything else can easily be overwritten by our program.

We have taken one precaution to help control the damage that this program might inflict. *expandSegs* increases the length of the data segment but does not change its base address. It is very convenient to leave the base address unchanged, so that the offsets of data items are not affected by *expandSegs*. All the memory areas used by the **IBM-XT** (resident portion of operating system, device drivers, ROM BIOS, video buffers, etc.) lie in the first megabyte of memory. Our precaution is to limit our non-standard uses of the data segment to locations with offsets at least 1M, so that we will not overwrite any of these standard memory areas. (It is possible to select a somewhat smaller "safe" starting offset — see the exercises)

Of course, this method only applies on machines with more than 1M of memory. The reader who is using a 1M machine must do something different. To begin with, only a relatively small amount of data (perhaps 400-500K) of data can be accommodated on such a machine. With the help of the memory map in Chapter 2, the reader can find a likely area in which to store this data. This choice may involve some trial and error.

Since we are radically altering the default configuration of the **80386**, it is important that we restore the internal parameters to their initial values before the program terminates. The *shrinkSegs* procedure (also contained in USER.LIB) performs this function.

At this point, little remains to be said about BIGARRAY. It will run in the given form only on an **80386** machine having somewhat more than 3M of memory, since the generated array has size 2M and begins at an address beyond 1M. Practically speaking, this really means that the machine must have at least 4M.

The loop in lines 52-58 makes the machine pause until the spacebar is pressed, to give the user time to read the on-screen message. We used **function 07H** of **int 21H**, rather than the *inpChar* macro, which uses **function 01H**, because **function 07H** does not echo the input character on the screen. In the present context, this means that accidental keypresses will not show up on the screen.

BIGARRAY.ASM gives an inkling of the power of the **80386**. When run on a 33-megahertz machine, it requires about 18 seconds. This is very impressive, considering the size of the array. Of course, it is also a tribute to the efficiency of quicksort.

Exercise 7-5.
a. Change *qkSort32* so that, instead of choosing the central array element as the pivot, it uses the alternate method mentioned in the text. Namely, it selects three elements from the array and uses the one with middle value as the pivot. Use the first, central, and last elements of the array as the three. Next write a small calling procedure that calls the new version, passing it the offsets and sizes of randomly generated arrays as inputs.
b. Compare the performance of our original version of *qkSort32* with the new version on a number of randomly generated arrays. Is there any detectable difference? To check the performance, borrow a pair of macros from Chapter 13. These macros are invoked by the commands

```
startTiming
```

and

```
endTiming
```

and do the obvious things: *endTiming* prints a message giving the elapsed time since the occurrence of the *startTiming* line.

Exercise 7-6. In BIGARRAY, we entered the array of 32-bit integers into memory at base address *segment:offset* where *segment* is the value in **ds** and *offset* has value 10000H. This strategy kept our newly generated data out of the basic megabyte used by the **IBM-XT**. Explain why 10000H could be replaced by the quantity

```
100000H - @DATA*16
```

without endangering the basic megabyte and implement a version of *bigArray* that does this.

Exercise 7-7. *qkSort32* would work equally well if the first recursive call, presently on line 89, were moved to line 95. Explain why this is true. Even though the execution times would be identical, we claim that the present version is definitely better. Why?

Exercise 7-8. Try to improve the execution speed of *qkSort32*. For example, pushing and popping only the essential registers rather than using *pushadM* and *popadM* will give a slight improvement. Study the code carefully with an eye toward further improvement.

Exercise 7-9. Write a 32-bit version of bubble sort and use it to sort a very large array. Compare the time required with the time taken by *qkSort32*.

FIGURE 7.6 USING EXTENDED SEGMENTS

```
 1   TITLE   bigArray.asm: builds and sorts an array of 500,000 32-bit integers
 2
 3   INCLUDE     console.mac
 4
 5   DOSSEG
 6   .MODEL    SMALL
 7   .386P
 8
 9   SIZ    EQU    500000
10   BASE   EQU    100000h
11
12   .STACK 100h
13
14   .DATA
15
16       intStr          DB     12   DUP(?)
17       infoString1     DB     CR, LF, LF
18                       DB     "Please wait. "
19                       DB     "After all, generating and sorting ", CR, LF
20       sizString       DB     11   DUP(?)
21       infoString2     DB     " integers does take a few seconds ...", 0
22       continueStr     DB     CR, LF, LF
23                       DB     "Press the spacebar to see the integers "
24                       DB     "(^S will pause ", CR, LF
25                       DB     "the scrolling and ^C "
26                       DB     "will terminate the program.) ", 0
27   .CODE
28
29   EXTRN expandSegs:NEAR, Seed32:NEAR, Rand32:NEAR, qkSort32:NEAR
30   EXTRN shrinkSegs:NEAR
31
32   Start:
33
34       mov     ax, @DATA
35       mov     ds, ax
36
37       outStr  infoString1
38       lToA    sizString, SIZ
39       outStr  sizString
40       outStr  infoString2
41
42       call    expandSegs              ;expand the segment length to 4G
43
44       pushEM  SIZ                     ;push the first two 32-bit parameters
45       pushEM  BASE                    ;  for Rand32
46       call    Seed32                  ;generate the random number seed
47       pushEM  eax                     ; and push it also
48       call    Rand32
49
50       pushEM  BASE                    ;push two 32-bit parameters
51       pushEM  SIZ                     ;  for qkSort32
52       call    qkSort32
53
54       outStr  continueStr
55
```

```
56  getLoop:
57
58
59      mov     ah, 07h                 ;unbuffered keyboard input
60      int     21h                     ;  without echo
61      cmp     al, ' '                 ;has spacebar been hit yet?
62      jne     getLoop
63
64      SKIP    2
65
66      mov     ebx, BASE               ;prepare to print the sorted
67      mov     ecx, SIZ                ;  array, from high end to low end
68
69  Print1:
70
71      mov     eax, [ebx + ecx*4 - 4]  ;addressing element with index ecx-1
72      lToA    intStr, eax             ;convert it to alphanumeric form
73      outStr  intStr                  ;  and print it
74      outChar ' '
75      dec     ecx
76      jne     Print1
77
78      call    shrinkSegs              ;restore the 64K segments
79
80      mov     ax, 4c00h
81      int     21h
82
83  END     Start
```

Exercise 7-10. Repeat the previous exercise using insertion sort rather than bubble sort.

Exercise 7-11. (Based on [31].) Write a "memory-browsing" program. This program should prompt the user to input a starting address and a size and should then display the contents of the block of machine memory with that starting address and size. The display should be in the traditional "hex-dump" format, i.e., 16 bytes to the line, displayed as hex codes on the left of the screen and as characters (if they are printable) on the right. Of course, this program must use *expandSegs* to access all of machine memory.

CHAPTER 8

FILE HANDLING

SECTION 1 PREVIEW

In Section 2 we discuss the file handling facilities that **MS-DOS** makes available through **int 21H** and in Section 3 construct macros to invoke the most basic of these functions.

Sections 4 through 6 are devoted to developing a fairly complicated application of the file handling macros. In these sections, we also discuss buffering of input and output and its effect on program speed.

Finally, in Section 7 we are ready to discard our macros *inpStr*, *outStr*, *inChar*, *outChar*, and *Skip* in favor of much improved versions.

SECTION 2 FILE HANDLING

MS-DOS provides two kinds of file handling functions, both available through **int 21H**. The first are called the *control block functions* and the second are called the *handle functions*.

The control block file functions were introduced with Version 1.0, the very first version of **MS-DOS**. In fact, they are patterned quite closely after the even earlier **CP/M** functions. They are fairly awkward to use since they require that the programmer manipulate data structures called *file control blocks*, which contain technical data pertaining to the physical organization of the file on the disk. File control blocks should really be managed by the operating system and be totally invisible to the applications programmer. This fact would be sufficient to cause most programmers to stay clear of the control block functions, but they have one additional drawback that makes them totally unsuitable for use in a modern computing environment: they cannot deal with tree-structured directories. Primarily for this last reason, we will discuss them no further in the present book. The reader interested in gaining a historical perspective on **MS-DOS** can read about these functions in many of the standard references.

Since the handle functions did not become available until Version 2.0 of **MS-DOS**, there was a lengthy period during which software developers felt that their products had to support both the control block functions and the handle functions. This kind of situation makes programmers' lives unpleasant, but by now it is only history. Few or none of the new software products support the control block functions.

The handle functions are patterned quite closely after the **UNIX** file functions. They accept the pathnames associated with tree-structured directories. To write to or read from a disk file, it must first be opened. The basic idea behind these functions is that each open file is assigned a *handle*. The handle is actually a small, positive integer used by all the functions wishing to access that file. To write to or read from an open file, it is only necessary to invoke the appropriate handle function and to supply it with the correct handle.

One of the most convenient features of these functions is that, as well as applying to disk files, they are also usable with devices. *Devices* include the obvious hardware devices: keyboard, screen, printer, and modem. But in fact a device can mean something totally different. For example, it is possible to partition **RAM** so that part of it represents what is called a *ram disk*. A ram disk behaves like a disk drive except that it has faster response than even a hard disk. The system views it as a device, and hence its input and output can be controlled by the handle functions. In Chapter 16, we write a program that installs a primitive ram disk in memory.

When a program takes control of the machine under **MS-DOS**, five standard devices are opened automatically and are assigned the lowest numbered handles. These devices are:

DEVICE NAME	HANDLE
STDIN (standard input)	0
STDOUT (standard output)	1
STDERR (standard error)	2
STDAUX (standard auxiliary)	3
STDPRN (standard printer)	4

In the next section, we will write a number of macros making file operations easier, and will store them in a macro file named FILE.MAC. As a small extra service, FILE.MAC contains **EQUATE**s for the five standard devices. Consequently, we will be able to refer to these devices by name in our code, rather than being forced to use their "magic" numbers.

By default, STDIN means the keyboard, although we shall see in the next paragraph that this default can be changed. In other words, a file-handle read with handle equal to STDIN, will actually take input from the keyboard. Likewise, STDOUT and STDERR default to the screen, STDAUX defaults to the first serial port (COM1, to which a modem is often connected), and STDPRN defaults to the first parallel port (LPT1, to which a parallel printer is frequently connected).

Another great convenience of the handle functions is their support of *redirection* and *piping*. Redirection of input means that STDIN can be changed so that it takes its input from some file or device other than from the keyboard. Specifically, if *progName* is an executable program written to receive its input from STDIN, then the command line

```
progName < deviceOrFileName
```

will cause the input for *progName* to come from *deviceOrFileName* instead. What is going on behind the scenes, of course, is that the operating system is juggling handles: *progName* reads its input from handle 0, so the operating system temporarily changes handle numbers and reassigns handle 0 to *deviceOrFileName*.

Redirection of output is similarly supported: the command line

```
progName > deviceOrFileName
```

causes output intended for STDOUT to be diverted to *deviceOrFileName*. Both input and output direction can occur on the same command line.

It is important to realize that output redirection introduced by the command line

```
progName > fileName
```

overwrites the existing contents of *fileName* with the output from the present program. To append the current output to the end of *fileName*, the redirection request should be written as

```
progName >> fileName.
```

The alert reader may be wondering why there are two handles, STDOUT and STDERR, assigned to the screen. The answer is that, while output sent to STDOUT can be redirected, output to STDERR cannot — it will always go to the screen. The rationale is that programs should always send their error messages to STDERR. Then, when errors occur, the messages appear immediately on the screen, rather than being buried in some disk file if redirection is in effect.

Piping is a useful variant of redirection. Suppose that *Prog1* sends its output to STDOUT and *Prog2* expects its input from STDIN. Frequently, we wish to cascade these programs so that the output of *Prog1* becomes the input of *Prog2*. The *pipe* symbol 'l' has this effect. More exactly, the command line

```
Prog1 | Prog2
```

will cause the output of the first program to become the input of the second.

Several programs can be piped together in this fashion. A judicious combination of redirection and piping can be very useful in building utilities from simpler pieces that happen to be at hand. We will return to this subject later in this chapter when we discuss filters.

A final important feature of the handle functions is their error reporting. Good error reporting is critical when dealing with files or devices. For example, a well written program should produce an error message when an attempt is made to read from a non-existent file.

The handle functions report such errors to the calling program in a way that is not only consistent among themselves but that is also used by many other **int 21H** functions. Here is the general scheme. If the requested operation is successful, the carry flag is cleared. If the operation is not successful, the carry flag is set. Hence, in those cases where the success of the operation is important, the calling program must check the carry flag to find out whether an error occurred. This is most conveniently done by means of the instruction

```
        jc          shortTarget
```

which will take the jump if the carry flag is set, or by

```
        jnc         shortTarget
```

which will jump if it is clear. If the carry flag is set after a file operation, indicating an error, the programmer may wish to find out more about the nature of the error, so that corrective action can be taken or, at the very least, an informative message can be printed (to STDERR, of course). More information can be found by examining **ax**, which will return a code indicating the nature of the error. Figure 8.1 contains a list of these standard error codes

It is good programming practice to check for errors at least when a file is created or opened. If the contents of the file are important, it may also be worthwhile to error check after every write to the file. Error checking is seldom necessary when reading from a file that has been successfully opened, although the careful programmer may wish to do this. In any case, error checking is done often enough to make it worthwhile to write a library procedure that will perform this task easily. To be really informative, such a procedure should print out a description of the error in words, rather than just the error number. "File not found" is certainly more user-friendly than "Error Number 2." Our error checking procedure, shown in Figure 8.1, produces reasonable error messages. It will be discussed in Section 3.

SECTION 3 THE FILE HANDLE FUNCTIONS

At the moment, we are interested in only the seven most basic of the file handle functions, and will write a macro to invoke each of them. Here they are:

1. **Function 3CH** is the *file create* function. As the name indicates, it will create a disk file with a desired directory name. Unfortunately, it is a somewhat dangerous function since if a file with the given name already exists, no error message is emitted. Instead, the file length is truncated to zero, and the present contents of the file are lost.

Our macro will invoke **function 3CH** in this rather dangerous form, because this behavior is frequently desired. However, as an exercise, we ask the reader to write an alternate *safCreat* macro that first checks whether the file already exists and, if it does, prints an error message and aborts, rather than destroying the present version of the file. The *safCreat* macro is unnecessary when programs are written to run only under Version 3.0 or later of **MS-DOS** because these versions provide a variant of the create function (**function 5BH**) that works in essentially this way.

The file create function requires several input parameters. Since it will set up a disk directory entry for the created file, it must be provided with a filename, which must be given as an **ASCIIZ** string, pointed to by **ds:dx**. (The fact that the name is an **ASCIIZ** string shows that we are dealing with one of the more modern areas of **DOS**.)

These functions work with tree-structured directories. For example, if the disk contains a subdirectory named \MASM\INCL and if **function 3CH** is given the filename \MASM\INCL\NEWFILE.MAC, then it will make the correct interpretation: it will create the file NEWFILE.MAC in the subdirectory \MASM\INCL. Since **DOS** allows the path specification of a file (i.e., the entire text string describing the file including the path prefix and the actual filename) to be as long as 79 characters and a space is needed for the null terminator, buffers which hold filenames must frequently be 80 bytes long.

As we discussed previously, when an error occurs **function 3CH** sets the carry flag and records an error number in **ax**. If no error occurs it clears the carry flag and automatically opens the new file, returning a handle in **ax**. This shows how important error checking is: the contents of **ax** represents something completely different in the error and non-error cases. Since **ax** sees frequent use, it is probably a good idea to set up some permanent storage for the handle. The handle is always a small positive integer and so can be stored in a single byte. However, it arrives in **ax** and is generally used in a word-size register. Hence, to save many byte-to-word conversions, most programmers waste a byte and store the handle in a one-word location. We will do this in the forthcoming macro.

The third input parameter that **function 3CH** requires is especially interesting since it shows how much access the assembly language programmer has to the substructure of **DOS**. This parameter is called the *attribute* of the file and describes the intended use of the file, using the following scheme:

BIT NUMBER	IF BIT IS ON
0	read-only file
1	hidden file
2	system file
3	volume label
4	subdirectory name
5	archived file

Function 3CH requires that the attribute be passed to it in the **cx** register. Note that the above list consists entirely of special features with which a file might be endowed. A "garden variety" file should have none of these properties, and so the normal value for the attribute is 0. It is hard to imagine any context in which a file would be created with the read-only bit set — it would be an empty file to which no one could write! After the file has been used the attribute can be changed and then, under various circumstances, it makes sense to change it to read-only.

The other bits in the attribute are not really important to us, but here is a brief description of their significance.

The term *hidden* is almost self-explanatory. A hidden file will not appear in a directory listing. It is also invisible to the various functions that copy files, although the **MS-DOS** DISKCOPY program makes an exact image of the disk and so will include any hidden files. A hidden executable file will still execute since the EXEC function can find it.

System files residing in the root directory of the boot disk are executed automatically when the machine boots. They generally contain initialization information relating to the machine configuration. Usually they are given the extension .SYS but this is not required.

The disk directory stores the *volume label* (if there is one) and subdirectory names in exactly the same format as filenames. The operating system can tell them apart from normal files only by means of the volume and subdirectory bits.

The *archive bit* is provided as a convenience to software that does backups of disk files. When a disk file is created or written to, its attribute bit is set. When backup software makes a backup of a file, it clears the archive bit. An efficient backup method is to make fresh backups of only those files that have changed since the last backup and the archive bit makes this easy to do: it is only necessary to make backups of those files whose archive bit is set. A backup of this kind is called *incremental*.

The following macro calls **function 3CH**:

```
Create MACRO fileName, Attribute, Handle

        push    cx
        push    dx
        lea     dx, fileName
        mov     cx, Attribute
        mov     ah, 3ch
        int     21h
        mov     Handle, ax
        pop     dx
        pop     cx

ENDM
```

This macro does not push and pop **ax** since the returned value from **function 3CH** uses that register. It is important to remember that this macro destroys the value of **ax**, as do most of the remaining file macros.

2. **Function 3DH**, the *open handle* function, opens an existing file. As input parameters, it requires the directory name, again presented as an **ASCIIZ** string pointed to by **ds:dx**, and another parameter called the *access mode*. The access mode is a one byte quantity, transmitted in **al**, and interpreted as follows:

ACCESS	MEANING
0	read-only
1	write-only
2	reading and writing

If the open is successful, the handle is again returned in **ax** and the macro invocation given below assigns the handle to a one word variable, which is assumed to be in the segment pointed to by **ds**.

Once again, this function is potentially dangerous. While the operating system is reading from or writing to a file, it maintains a *file pointer* to indicate the location in the file at which the next character will be read or written. When a file is opened using **function 3DH**, the file pointer is positioned at the start of the file. Hence if a file is opened and immediately written to, the present contents of the file will be overwritten and lost.

To avoid this potential catastrophe, the file pointer should be moved to the end of the file before writing, and this can be done using the *Lseek* macro given below. In one of the exercises, the reader is asked to supply a safe open macro. This macro should be called *Append* and must move the file pointer to the end of the file before writing.

Here is the *Open* macro:

```
Open MACRO fileName, Access, Handle

        push    dx
        lea     dx, fileName
        mov     al, Access
        mov     ah, 3dh
        int     21h
        mov     Handle, ax
        pop     dx

    ENDM
```

3. **Function 3EH**, the *close handle* function, closes an already open file. Since the file is open, it has been assigned a handle and that handle, rather than the directory name, must be used to access the file. The handle is the only argument required by the close function. It is seldom necessary to error check file closing. Technically, it is not usually necessary to close files at all since one of the tasks performed by the exit **function 4CH** is to close all open files. But in assembly language, as in all programming languages, it is considered good programming practice to explicitly close all open files.

There is one circumstance under which closing files is necessary. **DOS** places a limit on the number of simultaneously open files and devices. The default value of this limit is 8, which includes the five standard devices. Hence, in the default configuration, a program can have no more than 3 actual files open at the same time. It is possible to increase the maximum allowance of files and devices from 8 to any value n as high as 20 by placing the line

```
    FILES=n
```

in the CONFIG.SYS file. On rare occasions, even this may be insufficient. At that point, the only recourse is to close some files in order to open others.

The *Close* macro does not push and pop **ax** and so leaves open the possibility of error checking:

```
Close MACRO Handle

        push    bx
        mov     bx, Handle
        mov     ah, 3eh
        int     21h
        pop     bx

    ENDM
```

4. **Function 3FH**, the *read handle* function, allows a program to read a block of data into a buffer from a random position in a file. Here "random position" means relative to the present position of the file pointer, and this position can be modified by *Lseek*. Since the buffer must reside in some segment, it cannot be longer than 64K, which is therefore the maximum number of bytes that can be read in a single application of **function 3FH**. The read function automatically updates the file pointer so that consecutive calls will read contiguous blocks from the file.

The parameter usage in *Read* is completely analogous to that of the previous macros:

```
Read MACRO Handle, Number, Buffer

        push    bx
        push    cx
        push    dx
        mov     bx, Handle
        lea     dx, Buffer
        mov     cx, Number
        mov     ah, 3fh
        int     21h
        pop     dx
        pop     cx
        pop     bx

    ENDM
```

If the carry flag is clear after the function call, indicating that no error occurred, then **ax** contains the actual number of characters read. This is important, since if no error occurred and fewer characters were read than asked for, the only reasonable explanation is that end-of-file was reached. Hence this is the standard test for end-of-file: if, after the call, the carry flag is clear and **ax** < *Number*, then no more data remains in the file.

5. **Function 40H**, the *write handle* function, is treated like the previous function:

```
Write MACRO Handle, Number, Buffer

        push    bx
        push    cx
        push    dx
        mov     bx, Handle
        lea     dx, Buffer
        mov     cx, Number
        mov     ah, 40h
        int     21h
        pop     dx
        pop     cx
        pop     bx

    ENDM
```

The **function 40H** returned value is similar to that for **function 3FH**. If no error occurred, **ax** contains the actual number of characters that were written, and this number should be equal to the number requested. There is no particular reason to check the **ax** value in this case since, if less than the full number was written, an error must have occurred and the carry flag would be set.

6. **Function 41H**, the *unlink* function, deletes a disk file. Since an open file cannot be deleted, the candidate for deletion must be referred to by its filename and, as usual, this name should be an ASCIIZ string pointed to be **ds:dx**.

Here is the macro:

```
unLink MACRO fileName

        push    dx
        lea     dx, fileName
        mov     ah, 41h
        int     21h
        pop     dx

    ENDM
```

7. Finally, **function 42H** is the random access function, named *lseek*. It positions the file pointer at a chosen point within the file, ready for the next read or write. As input parameters, it requires a handle, a parameter called the *mode*, and a 32-bit *offset*. The function works by setting the file pointer at the given offset relative to a starting position determined by the value of mode, as follows:

MODE	STARTING POSITION
0	beginning of the file
1	current file pointer position
2	end of the file

Since files can be larger than 64K, large values of the offset are sometimes needed, which explains why the offset is a 32-bit quantity, and also explains the 'L' in *Lseek*: it means "long." The offset is generally written in the form *hiOffset:loOffset* but this is perhaps misleading since the offset is not interpreted as a *segment:offset*. It is a 32-bit signed number with low 16 bits in *loOffset* and high 16 bits in *hiOffset*.

Here is the macro formulation

```
Lseek MACRO Handle, Mode, hiOffset, loOffset
        push    bx
        push    cx
        mov     bx, Handle
        mov     al, Mode
        mov     cx, hiOffset
        mov     dx, loOffset
        mov     ah, 42h
        int     21h
        pop     cx
        pop     bx
    ENDM
```

Typical applications are

Go to beginning of file:	Lseek Handle, 0, 0, 0
Go to end-of-file:	Lseek Handle, 2, 0, 0
Jump ahead 100 bytes in file:	Lseek Handle, 1, 0, 100
Go backwards 100 bytes in file:	Lseek Handle, 1, −1, −100

The last example is noteworthy: To go backwards 100 bytes in the file, the offset should be −100. When −100 is stored in 32-bit two's complement form, the high 16 bits are all 1s and the low 16 bits give the 16-bit encoding of −100. This justifies the values assigned to *hiOffset* and *loOffset*. In most situations, the offset will be between −32768 and 32767 and so *hiOffset* will be −1 or 0.

The returned value from *Lseek* is also important. In no error occurs, the new offset of the file pointer relative to the start of the file is returned as a 32-bit quantity, with the high 16 bits in **dx** and the low 16 bits in **ax**. For that reason the macro does not try to preserve **dx** or **ax**.

The returned value makes the second of the above examples especially interesting. After an *Lseek* to the end of the file, **dx** and **ax** contain the file length as a 32-bit integer. This is the easiest way to find the length of a file in an assembly language program.

It is a good exercise to explore the results of deliberately misapplying *Lseek*. For example, what happens when an attempt is made to *Lseek* by a negative distance from the beginning of the file, or by a positive distance from the end of the file? The reader is asked to consider these questions in one of the exercises.

Figure 8.1 contains the code for ERRCHECK.ASM, the error-checking procedure mentioned in Section 2. ERRCHECK.ASM has a few features that are worth discussing.

It is the first of our library modules to require its own data, which consists mostly of the text of the error messages to be printed. In addition, the location of the data definitions differs from that of our previous programs — the data are defined within the code segment. Such placement of the data, though legal, is *not* recommended: a program that defines data should do so in a separate data segment, unless there is a compelling reason to proceed as we did here. Our "compelling reason" is that we want *errCheck* to be callable from any of the later programs in the book. Several of these later are in the so-called .COM format (defined in Chapter 9), which only allows one segment, and of course that segment must be the code segment.

We will now make some specific comments on the code in *errCheck*:

Lines 21-43. The various error messages are stored in memory so that they can be easily printed by the *Write* macro. Incidentally, these are the official **MS-DOS** descriptions associated with the returned error values in **ax**. For example **ax** = 3 means "Path not found." A perusal of the text of the error messages in ERRCHECK.ASM shows that many of them apply in contexts other than file handling. This reiterates a point made earlier, namely that the error reporting is uniform for a wide range of **int 21H** functions: if an error occurs, the carry flag is set, and **ax** contains an error code. From our point of view, this means that *errCheck* has potential uses that go beyond our present applications.

The next problem concerns the actual printing of the error messages. When the carry flag is set and **ax** contains 5, for example, *Write* must be passed the offset of *Error5* as one

FIGURE 8.1 AN ERROR-CHECKING PROCEDURE

```
 1   TITLE    errCheck.asm
 2
 3   COMMENT     #  PROCEDURE HEADER
 4   TYPE:          NEAR                    File: errCheck.asm       LIBRARY: user.lib
 5   PURPOSE:       Error checks various int 21h functions
 6   CALLED AS:     errCheck()
 7   RETURNS:       Aborts program if error occurs, setting ERROR LEVEL to 1.
 8   REMARKS:       The program data has been defined in _TEXT so that
 9              #  errCheck can be used with .COM programs
10
11      PUBLIC    errCheck
12      INCLUDE   file.mac
13
14  _TEXT    SEGMENT  WORD  PUBLIC   'CODE'
15
16      ASSUME cs:_TEXT
17
18      nLBuff    DB   CR, LF
19      errMess   DB   "Error: "
20
21      Error1    DB   "Invalid function number"
22      Error2    DB   "File not found"
23      Error3    DB   "Path not found"
24      Error4    DB   "Too many files open"
25      Error5    DB   "Access denied"
26      Error6    DB   "Invalid handle"
27      Error7    DB   "Memory control blocks destroyed"
28      Error8    DB   "Insufficient memory"
29      Error9    DB   "Invalid memory block address"
30      Error0a   DB   "Invalid environment"
31      Error0b   DB   "Invalid format"
32      Error0c   DB   "Invalid access code"
33      Error0d   DB   "Invalid data"
34      Error0e   DB    0          ;this error number is not used
35      Error0f   DB   "Invalid drive specified"
36      Error10   DB   "Attempted to remove current directory"
37      Error11   DB   "Not same device"
38      Error12   DB   "No more files"
39
40      errAry    DW   Error1, Error2, Error3, Error4, Error5, Error6
41                DW   Error7, Error8, Error9, Error0a, Error0b, Error0c
42                DW   Error0d, Error0e, Error0f, Error10, Error11, Error12
43                DW   errAry
44
45  errCheck    PROC    NEAR
46
47      jnc       errCheck1
48
49      push      cs
50      pop       ds                ;point ds to _TEXT, which contains the data
51      ASSUME    ds:_TEXT
52      push      ax                ; = the error code; necessary because
53      Write     STDERR, 2, nLBuff ;   the Write macro does not preserve ax
54      Write     STDERR, 2, nLBuff
55      Write     STDERR, 7, errMess
```

```
56          pop     ax                      ;recover error code
57          dec     ax                      ;decrement error number in al to index array
58          add     ax, ax                  ;because errAry is an array of words
59          mov     bx, ax
60          mov     si, errAry[bx]          ;offset of error message to be printed
61          mov     cx, errAry[bx+2]        ;offset of next error message
62          sub     cx, si                  ;difference = number of characters to print
63
64          Write   STDERR, cx, [si]
65          Write   STDERR, 2, nLBuff
66
67          mov     ax, 4c01h               ;set system error level to 1 to signal
68          int     21h                     ;   abnormal exit
69
70  errCheck1:
71
72          ret
73
74  errCheck    ENDP
75
76  _TEXT     ENDS
77
78  END
```

of its arguments. We accomplish this with the help of the array *errAry* defined on lines 40-43. *errAry* is initialized to contain the values *Error1*, *Error2*, ···. Remembering that to **MASM** the name of a variable (be it a scalar or a string) is just a synonym for its starting address, we see that *errAry* actually contains the *offsets* of the error message strings. Consequently, line 60 is pointing **si** to the appropriate error message.

As the reader might suspect, **MASM** supplies machinery that will automatically generate lists such as the data statements on lines 40-42. We will show how to do this in Chapter 13.

Lines 49-51. *Write* expects its data to be in the segment pointed to by **ds**, hence we must point **ds** to the code segment. We do this in lines 49 and 50. Line 51 is *very* interesting. We claim that *errCheck* will run equally well with or without it, and leave it for the reader to explain (in an exercise) why including it improves the program.

Lines 56-62. The remaining complications are minor: the error message numbering starts with one and array indexing starts with zero, which necessitates subtracting one from the error number (on line 57) to get the array index; array displacements are in bytes and so the array index must be doubled (on line 58) to advance by the right number of words. *Write* must be passed the length of the error message to be printed. This is computed on line 62: it equals the starting offset of the next error message minus the starting offset of the present one.

We will finish this section with a trivial program that checks the operation of the various macros and of the *errCheck* function. This program is presented in Figure 8.2, under the name PROG8_1.ASM.

As an exercise, the reader should trace through the program by hand to predict the contents of the file named "Data2" at program termination and then check the answer by actually running the program.

Here are a few general observations. First, it is unlikely that anyone would *ever* do this much error checking in a real program — we do it here only for demonstration purposes. It is probably worth repeating the general rules given earlier: *Creates* and *Opens* should always be error checked; *Reads* and *Writes* in important applications; the others, rarely.

When running this program under **CODEVIEW**, it is easy to set the carry flag artificially and place a selected value in **ax** in order to check the operation of *errCheck*. After line 29 is executed, for example, the **CODEVIEW** command

```
rf cy
```

will set the carry flag. Then the command

```
rax   n
```

where n is an integer will give **ax** the value n. At that point, an F10 will execute line 30 and an F4 will flip the screen. If all is well, error message number n should be displayed on the output screen.

Exercise 8-1. Write the *safCreat* and *Append* macros mentioned in the preceding section and try them out by means of a simple test program.

Exercise 8-2 Do some experiments do determine what happens when an attempt is made to *Lseek* beyond the limits of the file. For example, what happens if you try to *Lseek* a positive distance from the end of the file or a negative distance from the beginning? Reasonably speaking, the second attempt should have more gruesome consequences than the first. In the first case, the operating system might interpret the *Lseek* as a request to make the file longer and hence assign more sectors to it. But there is no mechanism in the operating system to grow a file longer in the backward direction!

Exercise 8-3. Write a program that does the following:

- Creates a file named *File1* in the local directory.
- Writes 10000 copies of the word "cat" to *File1*.
- Appends 5000 copies of the word "dog" to *File1*.
- Moves the file pointer in *File1* to a point 29950 bytes from the start of the file
- Prints 100 characters starting at this location in *File1* to the screen.
- Deletes *File1*.

Exercise 8-4. Write a program that prompts the user to input a filename and prints a message to the screen indicating whether or not that file exists.
Remark: The file-handle functions work with directory pathnames. In the present problem, for example, the program will interpret filenames as follows:

FIGURE 8.2 TESTING THE BASIC FILE MACROS

```
 1   TITLE Prog8_1.asm: Testing the Disk File Operations
 2
 3       INCLUDE console.mac
 4       INCLUDE file.mac
 5
 6   DOSSEG
 7   .MODEL SMALL
 8
 9   .STACK  100h
10
11   .DATA
12
13       F1          DB      "Data1", 0
14       F2          DB      "Data2", 0
15       Handle1     DW      ?
16       Handle2     DW      ?
17       inBuffer    DB      10 DUP('z')
18       outBuffer   DB      10 DUP('a')
19
20   .CODE
21
22       EXTRN   errCheck:NEAR
23
24   Start:
25
26       mov     ax, @DATA
27       mov     ds, ax
28
29       Create F1 0 Handle1
30       call    errCheck
31       Write   Handle1 10 outBuffer
32       call    errCheck
33       Close   Handle1
34       call    errCheck
35       Open    F1 0 Handle1
36       call    errCheck
37       Read    Handle1 10 inBuffer
38       call    errCheck
39       Create F2 0 Handle2
40       call    errCheck
41       Write   Handle2 10 inBuffer
42       call    errCheck
43       Lseek   Handle2 0 0 5
44       call    errCheck
45       Write   Handle2 10 inBuffer
46       call    errCheck
47       Close   Handle1
48       call    errCheck
49       Close   Handle2
50       call    errCheck
51       unLink F1
52       call    errCheck
53
54       mov     ax, 4c00h
55       int     21h
56
57   END     Start
```

233

fileName	A file in the local subdirectory.
Spec1\fileName	A file contained in the Spec1 subdirectory of the local subdirectory.
\Spec1\fileName	A file contained in the Spec1 subdirectory of the root directory of the current drive.
a:\Spec1\fileName	A file contained in the Spec1 subdirectory of the root directory of drive **a:**.

Exercise 8-5. Write a program that prompts the user to input two filenames. If the files exist, the program should concatenate them, i.e., adjoin the contents of the second to the end of the first. Otherwise, the program should print an error message and abort. Again, the program will automatically work with files contained in arbitrary subdirectories, with no special programming required.

Exercise 8-6. Write a filter that changes the lowercase letters in its input to uppercase, leaving all other characters unchanged.

SECTION 4 A DISASTROUS EXAMPLE

Among the most useful features of **functions 3FH** and **40H** is their ability to read from and write to devices as well as files and their correct handling of input and output redirection. As a consequence, they can be used to write *filters*. A filter is a program written to receive its input from STDIN and to send its output to STDOUT, but with the real intention of operating on files or devices by means of redirection. Generally, filters are written to perform some kind of text processing. As we will see in the next chapter, it is considerably more complicated to write a program that deals with files directly by receiving the filenames as parameters on the command line.

As our first example of a filter, we will write a program that adds line numbers to its input. The program, named PROG8_2, can be seen in Figure 8.3. In response to the command line

```
prog8_2
```

it does nothing very interesting: it just sits waiting for input from the keyboard. When a line of input is received (terminated by a carriage return) the program echoes it to the screen, preceded by a line number. The real utility of the program resides in the fact that it is usable with a command line of the form

```
prog8_2 < inputFile > outputFile
```

It responds by adding line numbers to *inputFile*, storing the line-numbered file on the disk under the name *outputFile*.

The program operates in the obvious way. It reads from STDIN, and writes to STDOUT, processing one character at a time. All characters read are echoed unchanged to the output. At end-of-file, the program terminates.

When a linefeed is read, the program inserts a new line number, but first checks whether the file contains any characters beyond that linefeed. Because of this check, a program that happens to end with a linefeed will not be printed with an extra, numbered, empty line at the end. (Of course, in some contexts this suppression of an empty trailing line may not be desirable.) The check for characters beyond the line feed is done on lines 46-48. Line 47 (and similarly the earlier line 34) checks whether **ax** = 0. Recall from our discussion of *Read* that the actual number of characters read is returned in **ax**, and that this number will be less than the number requested only when end-of-file has been reached. But in the present case there is not much maneuvering room. The number of characters requested was one, and **ax** less than one implies that **ax** = 0.

Before proceeding, we will say a few words about end-of-file in the **MS-DOS** environment. First of all, disk files do not need any particular "end-of-file sentinel." After all, the operating system knows the length of the file (from the disk directory) and must keep track of the current position of the file pointer in an open file at all times, consequently it knows when it has reached end-of-file. Some programs actually mark the end of a disk file with a byte having numeric value 26, which is the **ASCII** code for Control Z, but this is a somewhat old-fashioned convention.

Processing input from the keyboard is different. In that case the operating system has no prior knowledge of the intended length of the input, and so does need an end-of-input sentinel. In **MS-DOS** systems, Control Z is used to signal end-of-input from the keyboard.

Function 3FH makes the correct translations when used with redirection. When it is reading from the keyboard, it interprets Control Z as end-of-file; when it is reading from a file, the operating system informs it when the physical end-of-file has been reached.

It is very easy to check the operation of PROG8_2 using redirection. It performs its task flawlessly. However, when used on a long file, it is excruciatingly slow. The exact time required is clearly dependent on the hardware, but here is the result of one test. The machine was an **IBM-XT** clone with a **80286** accelerator board and the file contained about 1200 long lines. The time required to add line numbers was a dismal 138 seconds!

To give an idea of how bad this performance really is, we wrote a utility in **C**, given in Figure 8.4, that performs the same operation. An equivalent program can easily be written in **PASCAL**, or any language of the reader's choice. When the same 1200 line program was numbered using this C program, the operation required only 13 seconds — less than one-tenth as long! It is therefore no exaggeration to say that our assembly language example is a disaster.

What went wrong? The experienced reader probably knows already — the problem is that we performed single character reads and writes. The sample 1200 line file contained about 1200*80 = 96,000 characters. Transferring this file a character at a time required nearly 100,000 calls to the read function and the same number of calls to the write function. We will see in Chapter 16 that in response to a request to read or write even one character to a disk file, **MS-DOS** actually reads or writes a block of 512 characters. Hence we can state the problem in somewhat different terms: the present version of the program reads and writes nearly every character in the file 512 times. Assembly language may be fast, but it isn't that fast! The solution to our speed problem is to read and write in blocks that are larger than one character, and this is what the next version of our program will do.

It may seem puzzling that the C version of the utility also appears to read and write one character at a time since it is uses *getchar( )* and *putchar( )*, yet does not suffer the same speed degradation. The truth is that *getchar( )* and *putchar( )* are translated in the C language

FIGURE 8.3 FIRST VERSION OF LINE-NUMBERING UTILITY

```
 1    TITLE Prog8_2.asm: First Version of Line Numbering Utility
 2
 3    INCLUDE   console.mac
 4    INCLUDE   file.mac
 5
 6      LF     EQU      0ah
 7
 8    DOSSEG
 9    .MODEL SMALL
10
11    .STACK    100h
12
13    .DATA
14
15        lineNo          DW        1
16        lineNoStr       DB        5 DUP(' '), 0
17        charBuf         DB        ?
18        spaceChar       DB        ' '
19
20    .CODE
21
22    Start:
23
24        mov    ax, @DATA
25        mov    ds, ax
26
27        iToA   lineNoStr, lineNo         ;lineNo was initialized to 1
28        Write  STDOUT, 5, lineNoStr
29        Write  STDOUT, 1, spaceChar
30
31    nextChar:
32
33        Read   STDIN, 1, charBuf         ;read one character at a time
34        and    ax, ax                    ;checking for EOF
35        jne    jumpOver
36        jmp    Finish
37
38    jumpOver:
39
40        Write  STDOUT, 1, charBuf        ;here only if not yet EOF
41        cmp    charBuf, LF               ;time to start a new line?
42        jne    nextChar
43
44    ;prepare to print next line
45
46        Read   STDIN, 1, charbuf         ;before you print a new
47        and    ax, ax                    ; line number, first check
48        je     Finish                    ;  that the file has at
49        inc    lineNo                    ;   least one more char
50        iToA   lineNoStr, lineNo
51        Write  STDOUT, 5, lineNoStr
52        Write  STDOUT, 1, spaceChar
53        Write  STDOUT, 1, charBuf
54        jmp    nextChar
55
```

```
56  Finish:
57
58      mov    ax, 4c00h
59      int    21h
60
61  END    Start
```

into a form of input/output that is performed in sizable blocks. (The block size is frequently set at 512 bytes by the C compiler, in conformity with the **MS-DOS** convention mentioned previously.)

Exercise 8-7. Write a filter that removes all empty lines from its input.

Exercise 8-8. Write a filter that interchanges consecutive pairs of characters in its input. If the input has an odd number of characters, the last character should be left unchanged.

Exercise 8-9. Write a filter that replaces each horizontal tab character in its input with N spaces, where N is a symbolic constant defined in the code.

SECTION 5 A CONSIDERABLE IMPROVEMENT

In the next version of the line numbering utility, PROG8_4.ASM in Figure 8.5, each call to the read function procures a large number of bytes from the input file. We want the utility to work on arbitrarily long input files and so it is not possible to set up a "large enough buffer" to hold the entire file. Consequently, we must still embed the read calls in a loop.

We will show in Section 6 that the actual number of bytes read by each call to the read function is not important, as long as it is considerably bigger than one. To demonstrate the effect of the read-block size on program time, we have used a buffer named *inputBuf* of size BUFSIZE, where BUFSIZE is given by an **EQUATE** on line 25. Later, BUFSIZE will be varied so that its influence on program speed can be checked. Initially, BUFSIZE is assigned the very large value of 8000H. This equals 32K, or half a segment. Since the buffer must be contained in a segment, its maximum allowed size is 64K, and it could be this large only if it had a segment to itself.

Before proceeding, let us discuss the general operation of the program, and its ramifications with regard to input and output buffering. Ideally, the program should read its input a line at a time, but this is impractical since the individual lines cannot be found directly from the input. Hence the program just blindly fills *inputBuf* from the input file by means of a block read. It next scans *inputBuf* until it has seen a complete line, i.e., until it encounters a linefeed character. At that point, it prepends a line number to the line of text and sends the package to the output. This suggests that the natural output from the program should be a line at a time. Therefore, on line 38, we set up *lineBuf* of length MAXLEN + 6, where MAXLEN is given the value 100H by an **EQUATE** on line 26. This means that we are limiting the maximum length of any line in the input file to MAXLEN. Such a limitation on line length is quite natural since we are processing text files. The "+ 6" provides an allowance for the prepended line number: as many as five digits, and a trailing space character.

FIGURE 8.4 C LANGUAGE VERSION OF UTILITY

```
1    /* Prog 8_3.c: C language version of line numbering utility */
2
3    #include <stdio.h>
4    #include <stdlib.h>
5
6    void main(void)
7    {
8        int lineno = 1;    /* This C code looks clumsy because we do not */
9        int ch;            /* want to end up with a numbered empty line */
10
11       while (1)
12       {
13           /* check if next line is empty before printing line number */
14           if ((ch = getchar()) == EOF) exit(0);
15           ungetc(ch, stdin);
16
17           printf("%-5d ", lineno++);
18
19           /* print until newline or EOF */
20           while ((ch = getchar()) != '\n' && ch != EOF) putchar(ch);
21           if (ch == '\n') putchar('\n');
22       }
23   }
```

The line-oriented operation of the program has an effect on how *inputBuf* is used. When *inputBuf* is filled, it most likely will not end with a linefeed. In other words, *inputBuf* will end with part of a line, the remainder of which will arrive with the next refill of *inputBuf*. Some special code must be introduced to handle this dangling line. We adopt an especially simple strategy to deal with it. When most of *inputBuf* has been processed and there is the possibility of encountering such an incomplete line, the characters remaining in *inputBuf* are slid to the top of the buffer, which is then refilled with as many characters as it will hold. At what point is there danger of hitting an incomplete line in *inputBuf*? The most conservative answer is that a line that begins within MAXLEN characters of the end of *inputBuf* may be incomplete. Hence the code calls for a buffer refill as soon as the number of characters remaining in *inputBuf* falls as low as MAXLEN.

The approach of the last paragraph is not the only way of handling the refilling of buffers. For example, another common technique is to use a *split buffer*. This means that the program uses two input buffers, say *inputBuf1* and *inputBuf2*. First *inputBuf1* is filled and the program reads lines from it. When the end of *inputBuf1* is close, *inputBuf2* is filled, and code is invoked that reads a line partly from the end of *inputBuf1* and partly from the start of *inputBuf2*, and the program then proceeds to take its input from *inputBuf2*. Likewise, when the end of *inputBuf2* is close, *inputBuf1* is refilled and the program gets the next line partly from *inputBuf2* and partly from *inputBuf1*. The buffers are used alternately in this way, as many times as required.

PROG8_4 contains little else that is new. The comment at the beginning of the listing describes the use of the **si** and **di** registers. The essential operation of the program is to isolate a line of text from the input file, storing it beginning at location *lineBuf[6]*, then to write an

FIGURE 8.5 SECOND VERSION OF LINE-NUMBERING UTILITY

```
 1    TITLE Prog8_4.asm: Second Version of Line Numbering Utility
 2
 3    COMMENT # This version of the program buffers both the input and the
 4    output for faster execution.  The input is buffered in inputBuf of
 5    size BUFSIZE and the output is buffered in linebuf, which holds one
 6    line of text. The input buffer is updated by using chars from it
 7    until no more than MAXLEN (= maximum length of a text line) remain,
 8    and then sliding the residual chars to the beginning of the buffer
 9    and refilling the rest of it from the disk.  di and si are used to
10    index the current and next lines being addressed in InputBuf as
11    follows:
12
13                 si                              di
14                  |                               |
15                  |                               |
16                  v                               v
17          -----------------------------------------------------
18          | (current line)                    LF| (next line)
19    #     -----------------------------------------------------
20
21        INCLUDE console.mac
22        INCLUDE file.mac
23
24        LF               EQU      0ah      ;line feed character
25        BUFSIZE          EQU      8000h    ;size of input buffer
26        MAXLEN           EQU      100h     ;max allowed line length
27
28    DOSSEG
29    .MODEL SMALL
30
31    .STACK 100h
32
33    .DATA
34
35        lineNo           DW       0
36        charsLeft        DW       0
37        inputBuf         DB       BUFSIZE dup (?)
38        lineBuf          DB       (MAXLEN + 6) dup (' ')
39
40    .CODE
41
42    Start:
43
44        mov      ax, @DATA
45        mov      ds, ax
46
47        mov      di, OFFSET inputBuf      ;next line starts at head of inputBuf
48        mov      si, di                   ;initialize si for first buffer filling
49
50    refill:
51
52        mov      cx, charsLeft
53        mov      si, OFFSET inputBuf
54        jcxz     noCharsLeft
55
```

Figure 8.5 cont.

```
56   moveChars:
57
58       mov    al,   [di]
59       mov    [si], al
60       inc    si
61       inc    di
62       loop   moveChars
63
64   noCharsLeft:
65
66       mov    cx, BUFSIZE
67       sub    cx, charsLeft          ;number of chars needed for refill
68       Read   STDIN, cx, [si]
69       add    charsLeft, ax          ;update charsLeft
70       cmp    charsLeft, 0
71       je     Finish
72       mov    di, OFFSET inputBuf
73
74       mov    si, di                 ;update si to start of current line
75
76   nextLine:
77
78       mov    cx, charsLeft
79       dec    di                     ;compensate for the initial inc di
80
81   findNextLF:
82
83       inc    di                     ;di now points to next line
84       cmp    BYTE PTR [di], LF
85       loopne findNextLF
86       inc    di
87
88       mov    cx, di
89       sub    cx, si                 ;cx now contains no. of chars in line
90
91       push   cx                     ;because we will need it later
92
93       mov    bx, OFFSET lineBuf[6]   ;move current line of text to Linebuf
94
95   moveLine:
96
97       mov    al,   [si]
98       mov    [bx], al
99       inc    si
100      inc    bx
101      loop   moveLine
102
103      add    lineNo, 1
104      iToA   lineBuf, lineNo
105      mov    lineBuf[5], ' '        ;replace null terminator by space
106      pop    cx                     ;restore length of current line
107
108      sub    charsLeft, cx          ;update charsLeft
109      add    cx, 6
110      Write  1, cx, lineBuf         ;write the new line with line number
111      cmp    charsLeft, MAXLEN      ;if fewer than MAXLEN chars left in
```

```
112       jge      jumpOver                  ; inputBuf, we refill it
113       jmp      Refill
114
115   jumpOver:
116
117       jmp      nextLine
118
119   Finish:
120
121       mov      ax, 4c00h
122       int      21h
123
124   END   Start
```

incremented line number and a space character into the first six positions in *lineBuf*, and finally to send *lineBuf* to STDOUT.

If PROG8_4 is run with our 1200 line input file, things look much better indeed. The time required to process this file is about five seconds, which compares very favorably with the 13 seconds required by the C version of the program. This is about the expected time relationship between an assembly language program and a corresponding high-level language program. We will see later that the assembly language version can be further improved. (In all honesty, it should be pointed out that the C version can also be improved.)

Unfortunately, we are not quite through yet. Another feature of assembly language programs is that, when stored in disk files, they are generally much smaller than their high-level counterparts. While this is seldom as significant as the speed difference, it does affect the time required to load the program and, all other things being equal, it is certainly more satisfying to write a small program than a large program to do a given job.

Here are the .EXE sizes of the three versions of the utility, as given in the disk directory:

PROG8_2.EXE (first assembly language version):   1018 bytes
PROG8_3.EXE (C language version):   7945 bytes
PROG8_4.EXE (second assembly language version):   33974 bytes

In order to get true readings of the program sizes, the programs were all linked so that they do not contain **CODEVIEW** information. (That is, they were linked without the /**co** switch.)

The size relationship between PROG8_2.EXE and PROG8_3.EXE is reasonable: the assembly version is less that one seventh as big. But PROG8_4 is a monster, dwarfing even the C version.

The reason we made BUFSIZE as large as 32K was to make it obvious where the extra size in PROG8_4 came from. Notice that PROG8_4.EXE is almost exactly 32K bigger than PROG8_2.EXE, and it would be hard to believe that this is just a coincidence.

It is *not* coincidental, and is just a reflection of how **LINK** works. When **LINK** builds the disk image of the program, it includes all the data declared in the data segment .**DATA**. This certainly makes sense for initialized data items such as *lineNo*, because the initialization is done by the assembler and so must be stored as part of the program. But for uninitialized data items such as *inputBuf*, the source of our present difficulty, it is totally pointless. 32K of disk space is storing uninitialized "garbage." Happily, **LINK** provides a way around this problem, which we will present in the next section.

Exercise 8-10. In the preceding section, we mentioned an alternate method that is frequently used for buffering input, namely the use of a split buffer. Rewrite the appropriate sections of PROG8_5.ASM so that it uses a split buffer.

Exercise 8-11. Write a filter that find all integers in its input, echoing them to STDOUT, formatted in a reasonable way. Assume that each integer will consist of an optional '+' or '-' sign followed by no more than five digits.

SECTION 6 A FURTHER IMPROVEMENT

Simple experiments will convince the reader that **LINK** does not always store the entire contents of all the program segments on the disk. For example, take any program that we have written, check its .EXE size, change the stack allocation, and recheck the .EXE size. It will be unchanged. The stack contents are never stored as part of the disk image when the usual Microsoft ordering (**DOSSEG**) is used.

The general rule that **LINK** uses is the following:

- Segments that consist entirely of uninitialized data defined by **DUP** statements and that occur at the end of the list of program segments, in the ordering used by **LINK**, are not stored as part of the disk image. When the program is loaded into memory, these segments are of course allocated space.

For example, with the default ordering, the stack is such a segment. The method of solving our problem is now clear: we must break the data segment into two pieces, one for initialized data and one for uninitialized data, and contrive to have the uninitialized piece come at the end of the list of segments.

The general method of achieving this segment ordering will be discussed in Chapter 12, but if the simplified segment directives are used, the solution is trivial. As well as the **.DATA** directive, there is a **.DATA?** directive. If a segment contains only uninitialized data defined by the **DUP** directive and is introduced by the **.DATA?** directive, then **LINK** positions it toward the end of the list of segments (just before the stack) and so, by the above rule, it will not be stored as part of the disk image.

It is only reasonable to include *lineBuf* in this new segment in order to save another 100H bytes on the disk. After this change, *lineBuf* cannot be initialized by the assembler and so must be initialized dynamically by the program. As a matter of fact, only four bytes in *lineBuf* need be initialized: *lineBuf[1]*, *lineBuf[2]*, *lineBuf[3]*, and *lineBuf[4]*. *lineBuf[0]* already receives a character since each line number consists of at least one digit. *lineBuf[5]* is assigned the null-terminator by *iToA*, and this is subsequently overwritten by a space character. All later spaces in *lineBuf* receive the characters that are to be printed.

These four initializations can be done using just two instructions:

```
mov WORD PTR lineBuf[1], '  '  ;'  ' means two space
mov WORD PTR lineBuf[3], '  '  ;   characters
```

In general, **MASM** will let you initialize a one word location by using a "double character" as we did here. The size override **WORD PTR** is required since the declared data type of *lineBuf* is **BYTE**. Figure 8.6 shows the new version of our utility. Since it is essentially identical with the previous version, only the minor changes are shown.

The complete code for PROG8_5.ASM is on the Program Disk. One potentially puzzling feature is that the code is now divided between two data segments and yet, exactly as before, **ds** is initialized only once. How are we able to read alternately from two different data segments with one setting of **ds**? The answer to this question involves the **GROUP** directive and must wait until Chapter 12.

Checking the disk directory shows good news indeed: the size of the .EXE file has shrunk to 956 bytes. Hence our assembler version provides a two-and-one-half times gain in speed and an eight times improvement is size over the C version.

Now consider Figure 8.7, which contains the *map file* PROG8_5.MAP, constructed by **LINK**. A map file exhibits the ordering of the program segments in memory. Figure 8.7 shows that the code segment, with default name **_TEXT**, comes first. Next comes the initialized data segment, with default name **_DATA**. As expected, it length is only 4 bytes. Next comes the uninitialized data segment constructed in response to the **.DATA?** directive. For archaic reasons, this segment has default name **_BSS** (which is an abbreviation for *block structure segment*). Finally comes the stack, the other uninitialized segment.

The last item remaining for discussion in this section is the effect of the size of *inputBuf* on execution speed. By now, it should be clear to the reader that the rather large size of 8000H was chosen mainly for effect: it made the .EXE size absurdly large. Figure 8.8 shows the results of running PROG8_5 on our sample 1200 line file with a number of different sizes for *inputBuf*.

Recalling that the buffer is always refilled when it has fewer than 100H characters remaining in it, we see that the number of characters brought in at each read may be nearly 100H smaller than the size of *inputBuf*. In other words, performance does not fall off radically until the number of bytes per read approaches one.

In terms of the number of reads required to process the file this is completely reasonable. For instance, if each read brings in 10 bytes on the average then only one tenth as many reads are required as in the single byte per read case. This already represents a 90% improvement and so the headroom remaining for further improvement is quite limited. The conclusion is that larger buffer sizes don't save much time. **MS-DOS** itself frequently reads from and writes to disks in blocks of 512 bytes, which suggests that this is probably a good size to use.

Exercise 8-12. Write a filter that counts the number of non-empty lines in its input. To improve performance, it should buffer its input.

Exercise 8-13. Write a filter that counts the number characters, words, and lines in its input, printing suitable messages containing these statistics. Here a character means any character in the file, including punctuation and white space, characters (where a white space character means a space, carriage return, linefeed, formfeed, or tab). The easiest definition of *word* is a maximal (i.e. largest possible) block of characters not containing a punctuation or white space character. It will be necessary to look up the **ASCII** codes for the white space characters. By this definition, in the line

---

FIGURE 8.6 THIRD VERSION OF LINE-NUMBERING UTILITY

```
TITLE Prog8_5.asm: Third Version of Line Numbering Utility

    ;exactly as before

.DATA


    LineNo          DW          0
    CharsLeft       DW          0

.DATA?
    inputBuf        DB          BUFSIZE dup (?)
    lineBuf         DB          (MAXLEN + 6) dup (?)

    ;exactly as before


    ;initialize lineBuf

    mov WORD PTR lineBuf[2], ' '     ;' 'means two space
    mov WORD PTR lineBuf[4], ' '     ;  characters

    ;exactly as before
```

```
    Ahoy shipmates, all.
```

the words are "Ahoy", "shipmates,", and "all.". Again, the program should buffer its input.

SECTION 7 NEW STRING AND CHARACTER MACROS

Our *inpStr*, *outStr*, *inChar*, and *outChar* macros, are all based on the low numbered **int 21H** functions. These functions were introduced before redirection became an integral part of the operating system. In an upcoming exercise, we ask the reader to check on the effect of using redirection of input and output with these functions. The essential difficulty is that they do not respond appropriately when they reach the end of a disk file, and actually go into an infinite loop, hence locking up the machine.

From this point on, we will seldom use these functions or the macros based on them. Instead, we will write a new set of macros for input and output of strings and characters that are based on **function 3FH** and **function 40H**.

The first of the new macros, designed to replace *inpStr*, is

```
inAsc   MACRO   Buffer, Handle
    LOCAL loopLabel, Done

    push ax
```

FIGURE 8.7 MAP FILE FOR PROG8_5

START	STOP	LENGTH	NAME	CLASS
00000H	001B7H	001B8H	_TEXT	CODE
001B8H	001BBH	00004H	_DATA	DATA
001BCH	082C1H	08106H	_BSS	BSS
082D0H	083CFH	00100H	STACK	STACK

Origin	Group
001B:0	DGROUP

Program entry point at 0000:0010

```
        push   bx
        push   cx

        push   dx
        push   di

        IFB    <Handle>
            mov    bx, STDIN
        ELSE
            mov    bx, Handle
        ENDIF
        mov    cx, 1                  ;read 1 byte
        lea    dx, Buffer             ;   from location ds:dx
        mov    di, dx

LoopLabel:

        mov    ah, 3fh                ;handle read function
        int    21h
        cmp    BYTE PTR [di], CR
        je     Done                   ;stop when you reach the CR
        inc    di
        inc    dx
        jmp    LoopLabel

Done:

        mov BYTE PTR [di], 0          ;convert CR to null terminator
        mov    ah, 3fh                ;we must also get the LF that
        int    21h                    ;   results from using cooked mode

        pop    di
        pop    dx
        pop    cx
        pop    bx
        pop    ax

    ENDM
```

FIGURE 8.8 EFFECT OF BUFFER SIZE ON TIME IN PROG8_5

SIZE OF inputBuf	TIME REQUIRED
8000H	3.57 secs
4000H	3.68 secs
1000H	3.73 secs
750H	4.17 secs
500H	4.50 secs
400H	4.55 secs
300H	4.62 secs
200H	4.88 secs
110H	5.98 secs
100H	12.90 secs

The lines

```
IFB    <Handle>
       mov    bx, STDIN
ELSE
       mov    bx, Handle
ENDIF
```

are certainly the most interesting part of this macro. These lines contain our first example of *conditional assembly*, which is a mechanism allowing the programmer to control the code that is assembled, without physically changing the source code. The code actually processed by **MASM** can be made dependent on the values of designated quantities, or on the truth or falsity of certain expressions, or on any of a number of other parameters. The subject of conditional assembly will be presented in detail in Chapter 12; our examples in this chapter should be viewed only as an informal introduction to the subject.

To provide maximum convenience and utility, the macro is written so that it can be used in two ways. First, an invocation of the form

```
inAsc    Buffer
```

imports a string from STDIN. Second, using the form

```
inAsc    Buffer, Handle
```

where *Handle* holds the handle of an open file or device causes input to be read from that file or device. The conditional assembly directive **IFB** means *if this argument is blank*. The conditional assembly logic should now be clear: if the *Handle* parameter is not written, STDIN is used as the handle; if *Handle* is written, its value is used.

This example already demonstrates that conditional assembly can add considerably to the power of macro programming.

The remainder of the macro code should be self-explanatory except for one small point. When **function 3FH** reads from STDIN, it defaults to what is called *cooked mode*. In this mode, Control C is treated in the standard way (i.e., causes the program to abort) and, more importantly in the present context, a carriage return in the input is converted to a {CR, LF} pair. The *inAsc* macro is designed to replace the carriage return by a null terminator, and certainly wants no part of this extra line feed. Consequently, the macro code contains two lines of code that excise this spurious character.

Rather than use the default cooked mode, it is possible to change the operation of **stdin** (or of any file or device) to an alternative option, *raw mode*. In raw mode, the operating system does no extra processing of the input. For example, carriage returns are brought in unchanged, and Control C is not treated in any special way. Normally, files are operated in cooked mode, and we will generally do so in our examples. For more details on these modes, see [3] or [24].

The output analog of the previous macro, which replaces *outStr*, is:

```
outAsc   MACRO   Buffer, Handle
    LOCAL   looplabel, Done

        push   ax
        push   bx
        push   cx
        push   dx

        ;find length
        lea    dx, Buffer      ;for use with the function 40h
        mov    bx, dx          ;to index into Buffer
        xor    cx, cx          ;give cx the "biggest possible" value

loopLabel:

        cmp    BYTE PTR [bx], 0
        je     Done
        inc    bx
        loop   loopLabel

Done:

        neg    cx              ;length of string excluding terminator
        IFB    <Handle>
            mov    bx, STDOUT
        ELSE
            mov    bx, Handle
        ENDIF

        mov    ah, 40h         ;handle write function
        int    21h

        pop    dx
        pop    cx
        pop    bx
        pop    ax

ENDM
```

Again, we use conditional assembly to build a macro that will write to a handle if one is given, but which this time defaults to STDOUT if no handle is given.

Another point of interest in this macro is that, since it is possible to compute the length of the string in advance, the entire string can be printed with a single call to the write function, rather than using the slower option of printing one character at a time by repeated calls.

Finding the length of the string requires searching for the null terminator. If the **loop** instruction is used, **cx** should be made large enough to ensure that we do not fall out of the loop before the terminator is found. In practical terms, the largest value to which the counter **cx** can be initialized is -1, since this produces 65535 iterations of the loop. The instruction

```
mov       cx, -1
```

performs this initialization. Because **cx** starts as -1 and decreases by 1 for each character in the string, its final value will be

```
-1 -(length of string)
```

Therefore, recovering the length from **cx** requires the sequence

```
inc   cx
neg   cx
```

The reader who checks the contents of the file CONSOLE.MAC will discover that it contains a version of *outAsc* that is considerably more complicated than the one shown here. In Chapter 13, we return to this macro and extend its capabilities enormously. CONSOLE.MAC contains this final version.

The replacement for *inChar* is:

```
inCh   MACRO   Buffer, Handle

       push  ax
       push  bx
       push  cx
       push  dx

       IFB    <Handle>
            mov   bx, STDIN
       ELSE
            mov   bx, Handle
       ENDIF
       mov   cx, 1              ;read 1 byte
       lea   dx, Buffer         ; from ds:dx
       mov   ah, 3fh            ;read handle function
       int   21h

       pop   dx
       pop   cx
       pop   bx
       pop   ax

ENDM
```

We have again used conditional assembly to give the same flexibility as in the previous cases.

inCh has one somewhat unpleasant feature. If it is used to bring in a single character from the keyboard, this character is not processed by the operating system until a carriage return has been also been typed. To input an 'x', for example, the user must type the pair of characters {'x',CR}. Since STDIN operates in cooked mode, this pair is translated into the triple {'x',CR,LF}. The result is that, as well as the 'x', the two characters CR and LF find their way into the keyboard buffer. Depending on the circumstances, something may have to be done to prevent these characters from being received by the next calls to *inCh*. For example, it may be necessary to interpolate two extra calls to *inCh* to *flush* the keyboard buffer.

The new version of *outChar* is:

```
outCh   MACRO   Buffer, Handle

    push ax
    push bx
    push cx
    push dx

    IF ((.TYPE Buffer) AND 10100B)      ;if Buffer is reg. or immed.
        IFDEF _DATA
        isFirstUse outCh
            IF  firstUseFlagOutCh
                @CURSEG   ENDS
                _DATA  SEGMENT  PUBLIC WORD 'DATA'
                    outChBuf  DB ?
                _DATA ENDS
                _TEXT SEGMENT
            ENDIF
        ENDIF

        mov   BYTE PTR outChBuf, Buffer
        lea   dx, outChBuf          ;point ds:dx to char. to write
    ELSE
        lea   dx, Buffer            ;point ds:dx to char. to write
    ENDIF

    IFB   <Handle>
        mov   bx, 1                 ;handle 1 = stdout
    ELSE
        mov   bx, Handle
    ENDIF
    mov   cx, 1                     ;write 1 byte
    mov   ah, 40h                   ;write handle function
    int   21h

    pop   dx
    pop   cx
    pop   bx
    pop   ax

ENDM
```

outCh uses conditional assembly in a manner similar to the previous examples and also in a new and interesting way.

One limiting feature of **function 40H** is its requirement that **ds:dx** point to the characters to be printed. In particular, this function is designed to output data stored in memory: it cannot use immediate data or the contents of a register.

To be really useful, our macro should be applicable in any of these contexts:

```
outCh    byteAry[bx]
outCh    byteVar
outCh    al
outCh    'A'
```

The first and second formats will work automatically because of our use of **lea;** the other conditional assembly statements induce the macro to accept data in the third and fourth formats.

At this point, we will give the barest outline of how this is done and will supply the details in Chapter 13. One of the assembler directives is **.TYPE**. The expression

```
.TYPE Name
```

has as value a byte whose bits give information about the nature of the object *Name*. For example, if bit two of this value byte is set, *Name* is immediate data and if bit four is set it is a register.

```
Op1    AND    Op2
```

is an expression evaluated by **MASM** at assembly time. It is the assembly-time analog of the **and** instruction. The value of this expression is non-zero if both *Op1* and *Op2* have bit number k set for at least one value of k, and is zero otherwise.

Putting these facts together, we see that the expression

```
(.TYPE Buffer) AND 10100B
```

is non-zero only if the macro argument that is substituted for *Buffer* is immediate data or a register name.

The **IF** directive has the same significance as the "if" in high-level languages. In a sequence such as

```
IF    Expr
      Statements
ENDIF
```

the section of code labeled *Statements* is included with the code to be assembled only if *Expr* is true, i.e., has value different from zero.

At this point nearly everything should be clear: if the actual argument supplied for *Buffer* is a constant or a register, code is generated to set up a one-byte memory variable named *outChBuf* in the data segment and store the value of the argument there. The address of *outChBuf* is passed to **function 40H**.

There is only one remaining snag. If the macro is called more than once in a program, then the line

```
outChBuf   DB    ?
```

will be repeated in the source code and **MASM** will reject the program because of a duplicate data definition. What is needed is a mechanism that will generate this line the first time the macro is called, but not during subsequent calls.

That goal is accomplished by the lines

```
isFirstUse outCh
IF  firstUseFlagOutCh
    @CURSEG   ENDS
   _DATA   SEGMENT   PUBLIC WORD 'DATA'
          outChBuf   DB ?
   _DATA ENDS
   _TEXT SEGMENT
ENDIF
```

At the moment, we will only sketchily explain these lines, but will analyze equivalent constructions in detail in Chapter 13. *isFirstuse* is a macro that we will write in Chapter 13. The invocation

```
isFirstUse   outCh
```

will clear a flag named *firstUseFlagOutCh* if this is indeed the first time that *outCh* has been used in the present module and will set that flag in the contrary case. From this description, it should be clear that the conditional **IF** block does the correct thing: it defines a byte named *outChBuf* the first time *outCh* is used and does nothing on subsequent uses. The definition of *outChBuf* should be part of the data segment. Consequently, we temporarily close the code segment with the

```
_TEXT ENDS
```

directive and open the data segment with the

```
_DATA SEGMENT WORD PUBLIC 'DATA'
```

directive prior to writing the **DB** statement. Before finishing, we must close the data segment and reopen the code segment so that the assembly will continue in the normal way.

Another solution to the duplicate-definition problem would be to declare *outchBuf* as **LOCAL** in the macro definition. The buffer would then be given a different name at each use and so no error would result. Of course, this solution is wasteful of space. Why allocate several buffers when one is enough?

Before leaving this section, we present a new version of *Skip*, called *hSkip* (for *handle skip*). Again, it defaults to STDOUT but can be used to write to any handle. This time we leave the analysis of the macro logic to the reader.

```
hSkip    MACRO   Number, Handle
    LOCAL  hSkipLabel

    push  ax
    push  cx
    push  dx

    IFB    <Handle>
        mov   bx, STDOUT
    ELSE
        mov   bx, Handle
    ENDIF

    ISFIRSTUSE  hSkip
    IF firstUseFlagHSkip
        @CURSEG   ENDS
        _DATA    SEGMENT
            hSkipBuf  DB ?
        @CURSEG   ENDS
        _TEXT    SEGMENT
    ENDIF

    lea   dx, hSkipBuf
    mov   cx, Number

hSkipLabel:

    push  cx
    mov   cx, 1
    mov   ah, 40h
    mov   BYTE PTR hSkipBuf, 0dh
    int   21h
    mov   ah, 40h
    mov   BYTE PTR hSkipBuF, 0ah
    int   21h
    pop   cx
    loop  HSKIPLabel

    pop   dx
    pop   cx
    pop   ax

ENDM
```

These five macros are part of CONSOLE.MAC and, from this point on, we will use them instead of their predecessors.

SECTION 8 IS IT REALLY WORTH IT?

An unbiased observer who compares PROG8_3 (the C language version of the utility) with PROG8_5 (the buffered assembly language version) can only reach one conclusion:

the writing of the assembly language program required enormously more labor than did the C version. In fact, the relative lengths of the two programs probably does not accurately reflect the time differences involved in the construction of the two programs. The assembly language version is about 10 times longer. Although the author did not time the writing of the two programs, it is likely that the C version could be dashed off in 10 minutes, but the assembly language version probably represents half a day of programming. This suggests that the assembly language program may take 20 times as long to write as the C version. In fairness to assembly language, it should be pointed out that high-level languages fare especially well in comparisons that stress input and output formatting because of their extensive libraries. But, in general, assembly language programming will be slower by a factor ranging from a minimum of three or four up to a maximum that is almost unthinkable!

What are the advantages of programming in assembly language? In our present example, we attained a size advantage of about eight (usually not considered to be that important) and a speed advantage of about two and one-half times (generally conceded to be very important). But was it worth all the work?

The answer is surely dependent on the context. If a programmer is writing a utility for his or her personal use and this utility will only be run a few times a week, then it is probably much better to accept the slower, larger, but much more easily written high-level language version.

If the utility will be run several hundred times a week for many weeks then the situation becomes more debatable. It probably will ultimately pivot on how familiar the programmer is with assembly language and whether or not he or she enjoys working with it.

But if the utility is part of a commercial package that will be sold to hundreds of thousands of customers, and must compete successfully with packages from rival vendors, then the conclusion again seems clear. Small differences in quality are tremendously important in swaying customers (or reviewers) toward or away from a given product. If one software package consistently outperforms another by a factor of two then, all else being equal, the slower package will not be viable.

Unfortunately, the above description is quite simplistic since there are many other factors that operate in the marketplace. For example, the development time for software packages written in high-level languages, both in terms of original issue and in terms of updates, is much shorter than for corresponding assembler programs, and this obviously gives them a competitive advantage. In addition, the very complexity of large programs written in assembly language, even when they use the modular techniques that we are advocating in this book, makes them more prone to bugs.

Our final conclusion is that the "Is it worth it?" question has no easy, universal solution. It must be considered carefully on a case by case basis and, as indicated earlier, the usual answer with our present level of technology is that hybrid programs, consisting partly of assembly language but mostly of high-level language, seem to work best.

For example, PROG8_5, our best version of the line-numbering program, is small and fast. But some of the code in it is really quite clumsy since it uses our very restricted set of instructions. At several points of the program, blocks of data were moved or a particular character was searched for. These operations can be done much more elegantly and quickly using the *string instructions*, which we mentioned in an earlier chapter. We will see in a few chapters that the program will speed up appreciably when more appropriate instructions are used.

We have also seen that our macro technology is not up to the demands that we will need to place upon it. For example, a macro must accept its arguments in a variety of reasonable formats to be truly useful. We have seen, rather informally, that the **MASM** macro language can generate extremely powerful, decision-making macros, which will adapt themselves to the exact form of the input data. This fascinating subject will be explored in Chapter 13.

It may surprise the reader to learn that PROG8_5 can be made even smaller than its present size. As well as the .EXE programs that we have used so far, there is another kind of executable program. Since these programs are given the extension .COM, they are said to be in *.COM format*. We will see in a later exercise that when PROG8_5 is changed to this other format its disk image shrinks by a further 50%!

As well as developing the file-handle macros, we presented the macros *inAsc*, *outAsc*, *inCh*, *Outch*, and *hSkip*, which are superior to the old string and character input/output macros and will henceforth replace them. The main reasons for their superiority is that they can be used with any file or device handle, and they work perfectly with **DOS** redirection.

Exercise 8-14. Investigate the difficulties that arise when redirection is used with the low numbered **DOS** functions. This problem can be done either by using the functions (**function 01H**, **function 02H**, etc., of **int 21H**) directly, or by using some of our macros (*inChar*, *outChar*, etc.) that use them.

Exercise 8-15. In the text, we made the point that ERRCHECK.ASM will assemble and run with or without the **ASSUME** on line 51. Yet this assume plays an important role in the program. What is that role? If the answer to this question is not obvious to you, review the pertinent sections of Chapter 6. When you arrive at an answer compare the .LST files for versions of *errCheck* assembled with and without line 51 to be sure that you are correct.

CHAPTER 9

MISCELLANY

SECTION 1 PREVIEW

As the title suggests, this chapter is concerned with a number of disparate topics. Some of these items are intended as background information and will not be used in the remainder of the book.

In Section 2, we introduce the program segment prefix. This is a block of data attached to each executing program by the **DOS** loader. It contains information that can be important to the program, as well as information of interest to the operating system.

Section 3 is devoted to writing a useful utility program that prints out the contents of any file in hexadecimal and character formats.

Each .EXE file, when stored on the disk, is prefaced by an information block called the *.EXE header*. The structure of this header file is examined in detail in Section 4.

As well as the .EXE files that we have used exclusively to date, **MS-DOS** allows the construction of an alternate, simpler kind of executable file. These files have extension .COM, hence are usually called ".COM programs." They are discussed in Section 5. As an example, in Section 6, we will write a .COM program that gives a nicely formatted printout of a .EXE header.

In Section 7, we give a rather cursory introduction to the format and contents of .OBJ files. The information in this section is not needed elsewhere in the book, and we have included it largely for the sake of completeness. Since part of our philosophy is to try to explain all the basic software aspects of the **8088** environment, it would seem inconsistent

---

TABLE 9.1 CONTENTS OF THE PROGRAM SEGMENT PREFIX

ADDRESS	DATA
PSP:00H	Machine code for an int 20H instruction
PSP:02H	Segment address of last paragraph allocated to program
PSP:05H	Address of DOS function dispatcher
PSP:0AH	Address of int 22H interrupt handler
PSP:0EH	Address of int 23H interrupt handler
PSP:12H	Address of int 24H interrupt handler
PSP:2CH	Segment address of environment
PSP:50H	Machine code for int 21H and retf
PSP:5CH	First unopened FCB
PSP:6CH	Second unopened FCB
PSP:80H	Character count for unformatted parameter area
PSP:81H	The unformatted parameter area runs from here to offset 0ffH

---

to leave the structure of .OBJ files as a complete "black box."

In Chapter 6, we briefly considered the assembly process, i.e., the actual translation of assembly language into machine code. Our discussion there was quite tentative and incomplete; in Section 8, we return to that topic and this time paint a considerably more complete picture.

Finally, in Section 9, we look in more detail at the two-pass operation of **MASM**. The somewhat mysterious "phase error" grows out of **MASM**'s two-pass analysis, and is explained in Section 9.

SECTION 2 THE PROGRAM SEGMENT PREFIX

At this point, we are ready to answer a question raised in Chapter 4. In our first **CODEVIEW** experiments we noticed that, when a program was given control of the machine, the **ds** and **es** registers were initialized to point to a location 100H bytes earlier in memory than the start of the program, and wondered why.

The answer is that every executing program is assigned a 100H-byte block of memory, in addition to the memory required by the normal program structure, and the **es** and **ds** registers initially point to the start of this block. It is called the *program segment prefix* (*PSP*) and is situated just before the program, as our experiments in Chapter 4 indicated. The PSP contains certain data that the operating system wishes to pass to the program, and other information reserved by the system for its own use. Table 9.1 lists the areas of the PSP whose functions are documented by Microsoft. In Table 9.1, PSP means the segment address of the PSP, i.e., the initial value of the registers **ds** and **es**.

A number of the fields in the PSP are only of historic interest. They were inherited from **CP/M** and were used to ease the conversion of **CP/M** programs to the then new **MS-DOS** Version 1.0.

The **int 20H** instruction at offset 00H is a good example. A call to **int 20H** is the **CP/M** mode of terminating a program. **CP/M** programs consist of a single segment beginning with an **int 20H** instruction, and so to terminate a program it is sufficient to transfer control to offset zero in the code segment, which causes the **int 20H** to execute. When we discuss .COM programs later in this chapter, we will discover that the **int 20H** mode of termination is also available under **DOS**, although it is not recommended and we will never use it.

In examining the .EXE program header, we will see that a .EXE program is normally allocated all free memory when it is loaded (although this default can be changed). As a consequence, the programmer cannot use the *last-paragraph-allocated address*, which is located at offset 02H in the PSP, as an indication of where to go to get some more memory! In fact, the contents of this field do not find much application in everyday programming.

The *DOS function dispatcher* at offset 05H is another relic of CP/M. It gives an alternative address (*segment:offset* with offset occurring in the lower address, as always) that can be called to address the lower numbered **int 21H** functions. There is no reason to use this information and no one ever does.

Int 22H calls the procedure that should gain control when the present program terminates. (In most instances this procedure will be COMMAND.COM.) **Int 23H** is the *control break interrupt*, i.e., it calls the code that executes when Control C is pressed. **Int 24H** is the *critical error* interrupt, i.e., the corresponding handler executes when a critical error occurs. A *critical error* is what it sounds like: a serious error condition, usually of hardware origin. The addresses of the code corresponding to these three interrupts are contained in the PSP, but essentially for the convenience of the operating system, since applications programs do not call these interrupts directly. The first one occurs as part of the termination procedure, while the second and third are triggered by hardware events. These addresses are contained in the PSP to enable an executing program to pass control to (*spawn*) another program. If the *child program* wishes to change the code for one of these interrupts, it normally does so by substituting the address of the new interrupt code for the original interrupt code address. The operating system takes it upon itself to restore the address to its original value when the child program terminates. To do this, it uses the copy of the original address stored in the PSP.

The segment address of the *environment* occupies the word at offset 2CH. (See Exercise 5-20.) The environment is a collection of ASCIIZ strings, maintained by the operating system and containing information useful to executing programs. PATH is an example of an environment string found in most machine environments. But there are many others, and in fact any program can add strings to the environment for its own use. **MASM**, for example, makes quite heavy use of the environment. One of several strings that it will use, if it finds it in the environment, is INCLUDE. It interprets INCLUDE as giving a path to non-local files to be included by the **INCLUDE** directive. The end of the environment is signalled by two consecutive null terminators.

We will consider the environment further when we introduce the **MAKE** utility in Chapter 14.

The **int 21H** at offset 50H gives the programmer, in principle, another way of calling the **int 21H** functions. Instead of containing an **int 21H** instruction, the program can contain a line that says, in effect, "call PSP:50H," which causes this **int 21H** instruction to execute. But no one ever really does this — it is easier to just write "int 21H."

Before discussing the items at 5CH and 6CH, it is better to look first at the *unformatted parameter area (UPA)*, which begins at offset 80H. From the programmer's viewpoint, this is the most interesting part of the PSP.

Many programs expect to receive information on the command line when they are invoked. For example:

```
diskcopy a: b:
masm /Zi /Z /AM prog.asm
```

The information appearing after the program name on the command line is called the *command-line tail* or the *command-line parameters*. Normally, the executing program must have access to the command-line tail, and one of the services that **DOS** performs is to store a copy of it in the unformatted parameter area of the PSP. It is the responsibility of the program to *parse* the unformatted parameter area in order to extract whatever information it needs. Specifically, all the characters from the command-line tail, including the opening white space but excluding the terminating CR, are stored in the PSP starting at offset 81H. Consequently, the command-line parameters can have total length no greater than 7FH = 127 bytes, excluding the CR. In addition, **DOS** stores the actual character count of the command-line tail, excluding the CR, in the byte at PSP:80H. Hence, if the command-line tail is empty except for the CR, this byte has value zero.

- **WARNING. CODEVIEW** does something reprehensible in processing the command-line parameters. When a program is run under **CODEVIEW**, it modifies the command-line tail by reducing each block of white-space characters to a single space, and storing the result in the PSP in this modified form. Consequently, if a program parses the command-line tail improperly, it might work perfectly under **CODEVIEW** but fail under **DOS**.

Finally, let us say a few words about the unopened FCBs at offsets 5CH and 6CH. Since FCB means *file control block*, the reader can guess that these also harken back to **CP/M** days. But they do have a potential value in some situations. If the first command-line parameter (i.e., the first string occurring on the command line after the program name) can be interpreted as a legal filename, possibly prefaced by a drive designator such as **a:**, but with no path specifier allowed, then this name is entered into the first FCB. If no drive specifier was given, it is preceded by a '0' when it is recorded there; if **a:** was given as the drive specifier, it is preceded by a '1', and so on. The second FCB works identically, using the second command-line parameter. The programmer can sometimes use the FCBs to find the first two command-line parameters, without the trouble of parsing the command line. Of course, this cannot be done if these parameters are filenames containing path information.

The unformatted parameter area does double duty: it is additionally used as the *default DTA (disk transfer area)*, which is a storage area used by the FCB functions. As such, it does not concern us. (As a matter of fact, this area is not even used much by the FCB functions because it is too small to allow the transfer of large records and because this use can conflict with the storage of the command-line tail. Consequently, in using the FCB functions, it is customary to define a new, larger buffer to use as the DTA.) The DTA is used by only two of the file-handle functions, **function 4EH** (*find first file*) and **function 4FH**(*find next file*). Since we will not use these functions in the text, we refer the reader to Appendix 3 for details.

```
FIGURE 9.1  THE PSP IN CODEVIEW


#File  View  Search  Run  Watch  Options  Language  Calls  Help # F8=Trace F5=Go
############################## hexDump.asm ##################################
23:    .CODE                                                                    #
24:                                                                             #
25:    Start:                                                                   #
26:                                                                             #
###########################################################################
db 0 L 100                                                                     #
58EC:0000   CD 20 00 A0 00 9A F0 FE-1D F0 15 07 7B 27 D9 07  . ..........{'..  #
58EC:0010   7B 27 B5 0A 7B 27 6C 1E-01 03 01 00 02 03 01 04  {'..{'l.........  #
58EC:0020   05 FF FF FF FF FF FF FF-FF FF FF FF C3 58 68 CD  .............Xh.  #
58EC:0030   C1 46 14 00 18 00 EC 58-FF FF FF FF 00 00 00 00  .F.....X........  #
58EC:0040   00 00 00 00 00 00 00 00-00 00 00 00 00 00 00 00  ................  #
58EC:0050   CD 21 CB 00 00 00 00 00-00 00 00 00 00 49 4E 50  .!...........INP  #
58EC:0060   55 54 30 20 20 20 20 20-00 00 00 00 01 49 4E 50  UT0      .....INP #
58EC:0070   55 54 31 20 20 20 20 20-00 00 00 00 00 00 00 00  UT1      ........ #
58EC:0080   22 20 69 6E 70 75 74 30-20 61 3A 69 6E 70 75 74  " input0 a:input  #
58EC:0090   31 20 62 3A 69 6E 70 75-74 32 20 63 3A 69 6E 70  1 b:input2 c:inp  #
58EC:00A0   75 74 33 0D EB 06 7B 27-46 00 4D 5E 99 14 00 10  ut3...{'F.M^....  #
58EC:00B0   99 14 53 01 09 00 00 02-88 D4 99 14 53 11 09 00  ..S.........S...  #
58EC:00C0   00 00 99 14 01 3E 09 00-03 00 00 00 30 31 00 00  .....>......01..  #
58EC:00D0   12 CE C1 46 C1 46 EB 06-7B 27 86 00 FE 56 7C 1E  ...F.F..{'...V|.  #
58EC:00E0   86 02 2E CE 3F 26 7C 1E-09 00 00 00 99 14 00 00  ....?&|.........  #
58EC:00F0   00 00 00 00 00 00 0F 00-CD CE 40 CE E2 61 7C 1E  ..........@..a|.  #
                                                                               #
```

It is easy to inspect the PSP in **CODEVIEW**. As an illustration, we executed HEX-
DUMP (a program from the next section) under **CODEVIEW**, using the command line

```
cv hexDump  input0  a:input1  b:input2  c:input3   >>  output
```

In **CODEVIEW** we used the command

```
db 0 L 100
```

and then used Alternate G to make the dialog window bigger. The results are shown in Figure
9.1.

As a matter of fact, HEXDUMP requires only one command line parameter: the plethora
of parameters was written to demonstrate a number of points. Notice how the parameters
are brought into the unformatted parameter area in Figure 9.1. (The figure has been edited
so that all the documented fields of the PSP are printed in boldface.) The parameters were
deliberately written with multiple spaces between; **CODEVIEW** has replaced each block
of spaces with a single space. The character count, which is stored in the byte at PSP:0080H,
has value 22H. Also notice how the first two parameters are entered into the FCB areas.
They are always changed to upper case.

Another interesting observation is that the redirection information does not appear in
the PSP. This is a general fact. Redirection is completely transparent to a program. All

FIGURE 9.2 VIEWING THE ENVIRONMENT IN CODEVIEW

```
#Filer  View  Search  Run  Watch  Options  Language  Calls  Help # F8=Trace F5=Go
############################## Prog9_1.ASM ####################################
##############################################################################
dw 2c 1 1                                                                    #
58EC:002C   58C3                                                             #
db 58c3:0 L 100                                                              #
58C3:0000   50 41 54 48 3D 43 3A 5C-3B 44 3A 5C 3B 45 3A 5C   PATH=C:\;D:\;E:\  #
58C3:0010   55 53 52 5C 42 49 4E 3B-46 3A 5C 3B 44 3A 5C 53   USR\BIN;F:\;D:\S  #
58C3:0020   59 53 54 45 4D 5C 42 41-54 3B 44 3A 5C 53 59 53   YSTEM\BAT;D:\SYS  #
58C3:0030   54 45 4D 5C 55 54 49 4C-3B 44 3A 5C 4D 41 53 4D   TEM\UTIL;D:\MASM  #
58C3:0040   5C 42 49 4E 3B 44 3A 5C-4D 53 43 5C 42 49 4E 3B   \BIN;D:\MSC\BIN;  #
58C3:0050   44 3A 5C 4D 57 3B 44 3A-5C 59 41 43 43 5C 42 49   D:\MW;D:\YACC\BI  #
58C3:0060   4E 3B 44 3A 5C 4C 45 58-5C 42 49 4E 3B 44 3A 5C   N;D:\LEX\BIN;D:\  #
58C3:0070   4E 55 3B 5C 4D 54 4E 5F-54 41 50 45 3B 44 3A 00   NU;\MTN_TAPE;D:.  #
58C3:0080   43 4F 4D 53 50 45 43 3D-63 3A 5C 63 6F 6D 6D 61   COMSPEC=c:\comma  #
58C3:0090   6E 64 2E 63 6F 6D 00 49-4E 43 4C 55 44 45 3D 64   nd.com.INCLUDE=d  #
58C3:00A0   3A 5C 6D 73 63 5C 69 6E-63 6C 3B 64 3A 5C 6D 61   :\msc\incl;d:\ma  #
58C3:00B0   73 6D 5C 69 6E 63 6C 00-4C 49 42 3D 64 3A 5C 6D   sm\incl.LIB=d:\m  #
58C3:00C0   73 63 5C 6C 69 62 3B 64-3A 5C 6D 61 73 6D 5C 6C   sc\lib;d:\masm\l  #
58C3:00D0   69 62 3B 5C 66 6C 65 78-5C 6C 69 62 20 00 54 4D   ib;\flex\lib .TM  #
58C3:00E0   50 3D 66 3A 00 49 4E 49-54 3D 64 3A 5C 6D 61 73   P=f:.INIT=d:\mas  #
58C3:00F0   6D 5C 62 69 6E 00 45 41-53 59 46 4C 4F 57 2E 50   m\bin.EASYFLOW.P  #
db 58c3:240 1 10                                                             #
58C3:0240   49 4E 46 4F 09 C1 81 C1-41 41 81 C1 C1 C1 00 00   INFO....AA......  #
                                                                             #
```

redirection (and piping) information is stripped from the command line before it is forwarded to the PSP. In other words, a program does not know that its input/output is being redirected.

While in **CODEVIEW**, we also looked at the environment for this particular machine. The results are shown in Figure 9.2, and were obtained by the following steps. First the command

```
dw 2c L 1,
```

provided us with the segment address of the environment. This value was 58C3H, and so the command

```
db 58c3:0 L 100
```

displayed the first 100H bytes of the environment, as shown in Figure 9.2. For emphasis, the null terminators of the environment strings were printed in bold. Finally, a search command

```
s 58c3:0 L 400 00 00
```

(not shown) gave the position of the two null terminators marking the end of the environment, and the line containing these null terminators was displayed with another *db* command. This display in also shown in Figure 9.2, again with the null terminators in boldface.

FIGURE 9.3 A HEX DUMP OF HEXDUMP.MAP

```
0D 0A 20 53 74 61 72 74-20 20 53 74 6F 70 20 20      .. Start  Stop
20 4C 65 6E 67 74 68 20-4E 61 6D 65 20 20 20 20       Length Name
                        .
                        .
                        .
6E 74 72 79 20 70 6F 69-6E 74 20 61 74 20 30 30      ntry point at 00
30 30 3A 30 30 31 30 0D-0A                           00:0010..
```

Exercise 9-1. In Chapter 5, we noticed that location **ds**:0000 contains the character '=', where **ds** has its starting value, i.e., before it has been initialized by the program to point to the data segment. Explain this phenomenon.

Exercise 9-2. Write a program named *Add* that expects to receive two integers as command-line parameters. The program should extract the values of the input integers from the FCB fields of the PSP and add them, printing the sum to the screen.

SECTION 3 EXAMPLE: A HEX-DUMP UTILITY

It is sometimes useful to have a program that will produce a *hex dump* of a file, and we will now develop such a utility. A hex dump usually provides two views of the file: the left-hand part of the display shows the data from the file in hex, printed 16 bytes to a line; the right-hand side contains the alphabetic forms of the characters if they are printable, and is padded with the character '.' in positions where non-printing characters occur. Our utility, HEX-DUMP.ASM, is shown in Figure 9.4.

Figure 9.3 is excerpted from a hex dump produced by HEXDUMP. An interesting feature of HEXDUMP.ASM is that it obtains its input filename by reading the PSP. It is invoked by a command line of the form

```
hexDump  inFileName
```

When HEXDUMP is run using this command line, it sends its output to STDOUT, but can be used with redirection. For example, the command line

```
hexDump  inFileName  >  outFileName
```

sends the output to *outFileName*. To keep the program relatively simple, no page viewing or scrolling facilities were included. But recall that a program that writes to STDOUT can be piped through any other program that expects its input from STDIN.

One of the programs supplied with **DOS** is called MORE.COM and is of this latter type. MORE.COM is a filter that enables the user to move forward through the input a page at a

FIGURE 9.4 A HEX-DUMP UTILITY

```
1    TITLE    hexDump.asm
2
3        INCLUDE    console.mac
4        INCLUDE    file.mac
5
6        DOSSEG
7        .MODEL SMALL
8
9    .STACK    100H
10
11       EXTRN errCheck:NEAR
12
13   .DATA
14
15       errorMess    DB    CR,LF,LF,"Error: No Input File Name Given",CR,LF,0
16       Heading      DB    "  -- hex dump", CR, LF, LF, 0
17       Handle       DW    ?
18       Buffer1      DB    16 DUP(?)        ;buffer to receive input
19       Buffer2      DB    48 DUP(?), "   " ;to hold hex part of display
20       Buffer3      DB    16 DUP(?), CR, LF;character part of display
21       transTable   DB    "0123456789ABCDEF"
22
23   .CODE
24
25   Start:
26
27       mov    bx, 80h                ;PSP:80H is the character count
28       cmp    BYTE PTR [bx], 0
29       jne    InputOK
30       mov    ax, @DATA              ;point ds to data segment
31       mov    ds, ax
32       outAsc errorMess
33       mov    ax, 4c01h              ;error exit
34       int    21h
35
36   inputOK:
37
38       mov    cx, 80h                ;initialize loop counter
39
40   @@:                               ;find first non-blank on command line
41
42       inc    bx
43       cmp    BYTE PTR [bx], ' '
44       loope  @B
45       push   bx                     ;save its location
46
47       dec    bx                     ;find end of input file name
48
49   @@:
50
51       inc    bx
52       cmp    BYTE PTR [bx], CR      ;find CR at end of command tail
53       loopne @B
54       mov    BYTE PTR [bx], 0       ;null terminate the string
```

```
55
56        pop        bx                          ;start of input file name
57        Open       [bx], 0, ax                 ;can't send handle to its storage
58        call       errCheck                    ;   location now since ds does not
59                                                ;     yet point to data segment
60        hSkip      2
61
62        outAsc     [bx]
63
64        mov        cx, @DATA
65        mov        ds, cx
66        mov        Handle, ax                  ;send handle to its storage location
67
68        mov        bx, OFFSET Buffer2 + 2  ;initialize ' ' and '-' in Buffer2
69        mov        cx, 16
70
71   initLoop:
72
73        mov        BYTE PTR [bx], ' '
74        add        bx, 3
75        loop       initLoop
76        mov        Buffer2[23], '-'            ;get the '-' in the right place
77
78        outAsc     Heading
79        mov        bx, OFFSET transTable       ;as xlat requires
80
81   readLoop:                                    ;outer loop of nested double loop
82
83        Read       Handle, 16, Buffer1
84
85        xor        si,si                       ;to index into Buffer1 and Buffer3
86        xor        di,di                       ;to index into Buffer2
87        mov        dl, 16                      ;divisor for hex conversion
88        mov        cx, ax                      ;number of characters read - always 16
89                                               ;   except possibly on last read
90        and        cx, cx                      ;checking for end of file
91        jne        lineLoop                    ;   but too far for a jcxz Done
92        jmp        Done
93
94   lineLoop:                                    ;inner loop of nested double loop
95
96        mov        al, Buffer1[si]             ;present character from file
97        mov        Buffer3[si], '.'            ;guess it is not a printing character
98        cmp        al, ' '                     ;"lowest" printing character
99        jl         goodGuess
100       cmp        al, '~'                     ;"highest" printing character
101       jg         goodGuess
102       mov        Buffer3[si], al             ;correct the bad guess
103
104  goodGuess:
105
106       inc        si                          ;update si for next character
107       mov        ah, al                      ;copy current character to ah
108       shr        al, 1
109       shr        al, 1
110       shr        al, 1
111       shr        al, 1                       ;al now contains high only high 4 bits
```

Figure 9.4 cont.

```
112      xlat                                   ;convert these bits to a hex digit
113      mov     Buffer2[di], al               ;store the low hex digit
114      inc     di                            ;update di for next hex digit
115      mov     al, ah                        ;restore al from backup
116      and     al, 0fh                       ;only the 4 low bits will remain
117      xlat                                   ;convert these bits to a hex digit
118      mov     Buffer2[di], al               ;store the high hex digit
119      add     di, 2                         ;di inccmemented by two to account for
120                                            ;  this digit and a space
121
122      loop    lineLoop                      ;end of inner loop
123      cmp     si, 16                        ;was this a full 16 character read?
124      je      fullBlock
125
126      cmp     si, 8                         ;here if last read less than 16 chars
127      jg      @F                            ;first a fine point - if last line has
128      mov     Buffer2[23], ' '              ;  <= 8 entries, we suppress the '-'
129
130  @@:
131
132      mov     cx, 16
133      sub     cx, si                        ;      characters and pad Buffer2
134                                            ;        and Buffer3 with trailing blanks
135  padLoop:
136
137      mov     WORD PTR Buffer2[di], ' '  ;double blank
138      mov     Buffer3[si], ' '
139      add     si, 2
140      add     di, 2
141      loop    padLoop
142
143  fullBlock:
144
145      Write   STDOUT, 51, Buffer2           ;including the three trailing spaces
146      Write   STDOUT, 18, Buffer3
147
148      jmp     readLoop                      ;end of outer loop
149
150  Done:
151
152      Close   Handle
153
154      mov     ax, 4c00h
155      int     21h
156
157  END      Start
```

time, using the PGDN key. Hence we can impart this paging ability to HEXDUMP by using the command line

```
hexDump  inFileName  |  more
```

The HEXDUMP utility is useful in many situations. The *db* command of **CODEVIEW** gives a hex dump but only works for .EXE files. The older Microsoft debuggers such as **DEBUG** will give a hex dump of any file, but it is sometimes faster and more convenient to have a free-standing utility.

HEXDUMP reads from its input file in 16-byte blocks, depositing the data in *Buffer1*. The characters in *Buffer1* are processed one at a time. As each character is read, it is translated into two hex digits, which are entered at the correct positions in *Buffer2* and, depending on whether or not the character is printable, either the character itself or else a '.' is stored in the appropriate position in *Buffer3*. Finally, *Buffer2* and *Buffer3* are written to STDOUT, and the program loops back to refill *Buffer1*.

Here is a detailed commentary on some lines of the program:

Line 3. Rather than writing the standard **EQUATE**s for CR and LF in every source file, we have made them a part of CONSOLE.MAC.

Lines 27-34. The **ds** register has not yet been initialized by the program and so still points to the PSP. Recall that the byte at offset 80H in the PSP is the number of characters in the command-line tail, not counting the CR. Hence line 28 is a quick check on whether the user forgot to input a file name. If *BYTE PTR ds:[80H]* = 0, certainly no filename was input and so the program does an error exit. Before doing so, it really should print an error message, and we define a suitable message on line 15. But to print this using *outAsc*, **ds** must point to the data segment, and this explains lines 30-31.

Line 36. This is certainly an optimistic label. We arrive here only if the command-line tail contains *something* in addition to the carriage return. Whether it contains a legal filename will only emerge when we try to open it on line 57.

Lines 44, 53. **Loope** and **loopne** are two useful variants on the **loop** instruction.

The first of these instructions behaves exactly like **loop** except that it continues to loop only while ZF = 1. Frequently, it is preceded by a comparison and then the effect is to loop only while the comparison indicates equality. As in the present context, it can be used to find the first character in a string that is different from a given character.

The second instruction is identical except that it loops only while ZF = 0. Again, it is frequently preceded by a comparison and then continues only while the comparison shows inequality. Our application here is typical: it is frequently used to find the first occurrence of a specified character in a string.

Lines 40, 44. We are using a nice feature introduced with Version 5.1 of **MASM**. In most cases, it frees the programmer from the chore of inventing pointless label names. If a label is denoted by **@@**, it can be subsequently referred to as **@B**. When **MASM** sees this pair of characters in the code, it substitutes a unique label name for the **@@** and substitutes the same name for the **@B**. Here the 'B' connotes "back" since this is a backwards jump; the **@B** is associated with the closest preceding **@@**. **MASM** supplies the same facility for forward jumps — **@F** is used instead of **@B**. Lines 127 and 130 give an example of such usage. Of course, this method should be used only when an actual label name would not add to the clarity of the code.

Lines 38-54. Here we are extracting the filename from the command-line tail. We jump over the opening white space until **bx** points to the first character in the filename, at which point **bx** is pushed onto the stack; next we scan the filename looking for the terminating CR, which is changed to a null terminator.

Lines 56-62. The starting offset of the filename is popped from the stack and used in the *Open* macro. Since **ds** does not yet point to the data segment, it is inconvenient to store the handle in the variable named *Handle* at this point. Hence we keep the handle in **ax** for the moment. We have not yet switched **ds** since we want to print out the filename, and this printing is done on line 62.

Lines 64-66. Now it is convenient to point **ds** to the data segment and store the file handle.

Line 68. Notice the use of immediate arithmetic here. **MASM** views *OFFSET Buffer2* as a constant and so

```
OFFSET   Buffer2 + 2
```

is a sum of two constants, and this arithmetic is done at assembly time.

Lines 69-76. Every third character in *Buffer2* is a space, except that the central space should be replaced by a '-'. These initializations are done here.

Lines 85, 96. In indexing into *Buffer1*, for example, there is a choice of methods: either

```
xor       si, si
initialize si
refer to Buffer1[si]
```

or

```
mov       si, OFFSET Buffer1
initialize si
refer to BYTE PTR [si]
```

What are the advantages of each? The first one is more readable; the second is somewhat faster since an addressing mode of the form [si + disp] is slower than the corresponding [si]. (Check this in a table of instruction times or look ahead to Section 8 of this chapter.) Our main reason for using the first method here is that in a few lines we will be indexing into a total of *four* different arrays simultaneously (*Buffer1*, *Buffer2*, *Buffer3*, and *transTable*) and only three registers **si**, **di**, and **bx** can be used for indexing. We will see that *Buffer1* and *Buffer3* are traversed in synchronization and so **si** will do double duty in the expressions *Buffer1[si]* and *Buffer3[si]*.

Lines 98, 100. We want to identify the printing characters. As can be seen from an ASCII table, these have codes between ' '(20H) and '~' (7eH).

Lines 106-119. At this point, **al** contains the character whose ASCII code must be translated into two hex digits and stored in *Buffer2*. To accomplish the translation, we use the instruction **xlat** which was introduced in the exercises at the end of Chapter 4. Again, here is how **xlat** works: **ds:bx** should point to a "translation table," which is a table of bytes (here named *transTable*); if **al** contains the value k when **xlat** executes, then the value in **al** is replaced by the k-th byte from the translation table.

At this point, we are using another of the bit instructions, namely **shr** (*shift right*), which shifts the bit pattern of it 8- or 16-bit operand to the right. It can be used in either of these two forms:

```
shr     Op1, 1
shr     Op1, cl
```

In the first case, the bit pattern of *Op1* is shifted one bit to the right; in the second, it is shifted to the right by a number of bits equal to the value of **cl**. (The **cl** register *must* be used in the second form.) In both cases, the vacated high positions are filled with zeros. One curiosity of **shr** (and other related bit instructions) is that the first form is much faster than the second, especially when the required initialization of **cl** is taken into account. In fact, as we will see in Section 8 of this chapter, shifting right by three positions can usually be accomplished more quickly using a string of three **shr** instructions of the first form than by using the second form with **cl** = 3.

The **shr** instruction has an exact analog, **shl** (*shift left*), which shifts a bit pattern to the left. The preceding discussion applies equally to **shl**.

It should now be clear how the two hex digits are generated. First the four high bits in **al** are translated by **xlat** and stored in the correct position in *Buffer2*; then the four low bits are translated and stored in the next position. Since isolating the high four bits destroys **al**, we store a temporary copy of it in **ah**. A sequence of four

```
shr     al, 1
```

moves the four high bits to the low end, and pads the high end with four zeros — exactly what is needed. The reader may wonder why we used a sequence of four **shr** instructions of the first form rather than a single **shr** of the second form with **cl** = 4. The reason is that **cl** is already in use — **cx** is being used as the loop counter.

After the high hex digit from **al** has been translated and stored, we restore the original value of **al** from **ah**. At this point, the four high bits should be replaced with zeros, and this is accomplished by

```
and     al, 0fh
```

Lines 126-128. If the last line of the printout has eight or fewer characters, the separating '-' in the middle of the *Buffer2* printout looks peculiar and should be deleted.

Lines 126-141. Boundary conditions frequently require special consideration. If the last line doesn't contain a full 16 characters, then it must be padded with spaces; otherwise, the tail-end characters from the previous use of *Buffer2* will print out again. On line 137 we perform this padding operation using a double character.

Before leaving HEXDUMP.ASM, it is a good idea to look at its execution in **CODEVIEW**. We will not do this in the text but will be content to suggest some suitable instructions for the reader to try.

Here are some reasonable watch instructions:

```
wa   Buffer1 L 10
wa   Buffer3 L 10
wb   (&Buffer2)[di-3] L 3
```

If the **CODEVIEW** instruction

```
g  .126
```

is issued initially, control transfers immediately to the end of *lineLoop*, with one pass of *lineLoop* already completed. Since **di** has already been incremented three times, the value *di − 3* in the third watch instruction is exactly right to display the two hex digits and the space from the current position in *Buffer2*. A series of F7's (*go to the cursor*) is now appropriate. Each F7 will cause another iteration of *lineLoop*, which allows the translation process to be checked in detail.

Exercise 9-3. As written, HEXDUMP.ASM expects that the input file will be given as a command-line argument. Improve this program so that it will accept either command-line input or input by redirection. In other words, given a command line

```
hexDump  inputFile
```

it will accept *inputFile* as its input, and given the command line

```
hexDump < inputFile
```

it will still read its input from *inputFile*.

Exercise 9-4. An exercise in Chapter 8 asked the reader to write a program that checked whether a given file existed or not. Write a version of that program that allows the user to input the filename as a command-line parameter.

Exercise 9-5. Write a program that accepts the names of two files as command-line parameters and compares the contents of these files, printing a message to the screen indicating whether or not the files are identical.

Exercise 9-6. Write a procedure that mimics the C language *argc* and *argv* capability. In other words, the procedure should define and initialize two variables:

- An integer *Argc* to which it assigns a value equal to the number of command-line parameters (where the actual program name should count as a parameter for compatibility with **C**).

• An array *Argv* containing the starting addresses of locations where the command-line parameters are stored as ASCIIZ strings.

Suggestions: The standard **C** approach is to copy the command-line parameters to the stack. In this problem, it is easier to leave them in the PSP and null-terminate them in that position. The module containing this procedure should have a data segment in which it defines *Argc* and *Argv* (both **PUBLIC**). Unfortunately, the size of *Argv* cannot be determined in advance; the easiest thing is to define it as, say, size 10 and thereby restrict the program to that maximum number of parameters. *Argv* should be an array of doublewords, each of which stores the corresponding address in the form *segment:offset*. Of course, each *segment* value should equal the segment of the PSP and should be stored in the high half of the corresponding doubleword. Don't worry about initializing *argv[0]* to point to the program name.

SECTION 4 THE STRUCTURE OF THE .EXE HEADER

We will now take a close look at the .EXE header, which figured briefly in our discussion of addressing in Chapter 6. As the reader may remember, one of the items contained in the .EXE header is a table of *relocation vectors* giving the addresses relative to the start of the load module of items requiring *relocation* when the program is loaded into machine memory by the **DOS** loader.

Figure 9.5 shows the first few lines of a hex dump of HEXDUMP.EXE. (HEX-DUMP.EXE is included in the utilities section of the Program Disk.) Since the .EXE header is stored at the beginning of the disk image of the .EXE file, Figure 9.5 actually shows part of the header. Even though the .EXE header is always at least 512 bytes long, it turns out that Figure 9.5 contains all the interesting information in the present case. The header for HEXDUMP.EXE is exactly 512 bytes long, the later part consisting entirely of 00H's.

Figure 9.6 provides a much more informative display of the header. This table was produced by a utility that will be the example program of the next section. It can be used to produce a similar display of any entirely .EXE header, for purposes of detailed study. More precisely, there are presently two somewhat different kinds of .EXE files in use under **MS-DOS**: one kind contains special information needed by Microsoft Windows, and the other does not. This utility is intended for use with the second, more traditional, form of the header file. A quick comparison of Figure 9.5 with Figure 9.6 shows that all the essential information in the second display comes directly from the first, except for the prose descriptions of the data in the various fields. We will now give a brief explanation of these 14 basic fields.

The **DOS** loader uses the signature word at offset zero to verify that this is really a .EXE file. Every .EXE file has signature word equal to 5A4DH. (The standard explanation of this signature is that the corresponding characters, MZ, are the initials of Mark Zbikowski, one of the creators of **MS-DOS**.) The loader performs additional checks to ensure that it is a valid .EXE file.

The load module consists of a certain number of 512 byte *pages* and perhaps one final incomplete page. The word at offset 0004H gives the number of pages in the load module, counting the last incomplete page, if there is one, as a page. If there is an incomplete page,

---

FIGURE 9.5 HEX DUMP OF START OF HEXDUMP.EXE

```
4D 5A FB 00 04 00 03 00-20 00 11 00 FF FF 50 00     MZ...... .....P
00 01 CA 81 10 00 00 00-1E 00 00 00 01 00 19 00     ................
00 00 B5 00 00 00 9B 02-00 00 00 00 00 00 00 00     ................
00 00 00 00 00 00 00 00-00 00 00 00 00 00 00 00     ................
00 00 00 00 00 00 00 00-00 00 00 00 00 00 00 00     ................
00 00 00 00 00 00 00 00-00 00 00 00 00 00 00 00     ................
                       .
                       .
                       .
```

---

the word at offset 0002H gives its size in bytes. If this word equals zero, there is no incomplete page.

The word at offset 0006H is vital, since it tells how many relocation items are in the relocation table.

The word at offset 0008H gives the size of the header in 16-byte paragraphs. In the case of HEXDUMP.EXE, the header size is therefore 16*32 = 512 bytes, as stated previously.

The words at offsets 000AH and 000CH are called, respectively, *minAlloc* and *max-Alloc*. *minAlloc* is the minimum number of paragraphs of memory required to run the program, in addition to the actual size of the program. The *minAlloc* allowance includes the stack and other uninitialized segments that are not stored as part of the disk image. (Recall that we have used the simplified directive .**DATA?** to store such data in the segment named BSS.)

maxAlloc contains the maximum memory in paragraphs that the loader should assign to the program, if sufficient memory is available. The loader, by default, always assigns the largest available block of memory to the program, although this can be changed after the fact by using the **MS-DOS** utility **EXEMOD** (or, using our new knowledge, by just going to the disk file and changing the word stored at this location).

Offsets 0010H and 0014H contain the initial values of **sp** and **ip**. As we pointed out in Chapter 7, the values of **sp** and **ip** are known at link time and so these locations already contain their final values. On the other hand, the values of **ss** and **cs**, stored at offsets 000EH and 0016H, are only known relative to the start of the load module and, like all segment references, must have the *start address* added to them at load time.

The word at offset 0012H is used as a checksum to verify that the file has not been corrupted. According to [24], present versions of the **MS-DOS** loader do not actually check this sum, although this may change in the future.

Offset 0018H is also very important — it contains the starting offset of the relocation table.

The word at offset 001AH is used in connection with overlays. *Overlaying* is a technique that allows a computer to execute a program that is larger than available machine memory. Of course, the entire program cannot be present in memory at the same time. Instead, sections of the program are swapped from mass storage (generally a hard disk) so that at least the currently executing code is always present. There may be additional information about overlays starting at this point in the header, before the relocation table begins.

FIGURE 9.6 THE .EXE HEADER FOR HEXDUMP.EXE

INFORMATION IN .EXE HEADER

OFFSET	DATA	HEX VALUE	DECIMAL VALUE
0000	Signature	5A4D	23117
0002	Last Page Size	00FB	251
0004	No. of 512-Byte Pages	0004	4
0006	Number of Relocation Items	0003	3
008	Header Size in 16 Byte Pars.	0020	32
000A	minAlloc	0011	17
000C	maxAlloc	FFFF	-1
000E	Relative SS Value	0050	80
0010	Initial SP Value	0100	256
0012	Complemented Checksum	81CA	-32310
0014	Initial IP Value	0010	16
0016	Relative CS Value	0000	0
0018	Offset Reloc. Pointer Table	001E	30
001A	Overlay Number:	0000	0

RELATIVE OFFSETS OF RELOCATION ITEMS IN LOAD MODULE

0000:0019 0000:00B5 0000:029B

To finish this section, we will give a quick example that shows how relocation calculations are done. Suppose that HEXDUMP.EXE will be loaded into memory at address 1000:0000. (Programs are always loaded on a paragraph boundary.) Assume that the first relocation item occurs at offset 0019 into the load module. The loader always loads the program into memory and then fixes the relocation items. After loading, the first relocation item will be at address 1000:0019. To fix this item, the loader need only take the word (the segment part of an address) that is currently at address 1000:0019 and add 1000H to it.

SECTION 5 PROGRAMS IN .COM FORMAT

As the example in the last section demonstrates, the .EXE header can be very wasteful of disk space, and so it is natural to ask whether all programs require a header.

The answer to this question is no. The most important information contained in the .EXE header is the relocation table, and this information is only important in programs comprised of multiple segments. If a program consists of only one segment, containing the code, the data, and the stack, then the program can be loaded with all the segment registers pointing to the start address, and no relocation is necessary.

Single-segment programs of the type mentioned in the last paragraph are usually called *.COM programs* or are said to be in *.COM format*. When they are assembled and linked into executables, they are given the extension .COM, rather than the .EXE extension that we have seen so far. These .COM programs are not new. In fact, they are quite the opposite: their origins go back to the days when 64K seemed a large amount of memory on *any* computer.

By their very nature, .COM programs intermingle code and data, and this is not terribly good programming practice. It is likely that their days are numbered but, as of this writing, they are still an integral part of the **DOS** world. After all, even COMMAND.COM is itself a .COM program!

One of the weaknesses of **CODEVIEW** is its inadequate support of .COM programs. While it is possible to step through the code, **CODEVIEW** will not *symbolically debug* a .COM program. This means that the programmer cannot refer to the quantities in the program being debugged by name. To watch a data variable, for example, it is necessary to deduce its storage address from the assembled code, so that a watch can be placed on that address. How can an address be deduced? There are many ways of doing this.

Suppose, for example, that the variable is named *Var1*, and that the third **mov** instruction in the source code is

```
        mov     ax,   OFFSET Var1
```

In **CODEVIEW**, the programmer might observe that the third **mov** instruction appears as

```
        mov     ax,  [107]
```

The obvious conclusion is that *OFFSET Var1* equals 107H and so a suitable watch command would be

```
     w?   107,  d
```

assuming that *Var1* is an integer. This may sound unpleasant if several variables are simultaneously of interest, and indeed it is.

Debugging .COM programs using **CODEVIEW** is sufficiently arduous that many programmers, when faced with the task of writing a .COM program, prefer to write and debug it as an .EXE program, and then do the reformatting required to change it to .COM format.

Another difficulty with .COM programs is that they are basically limited to 64K total length, since they reside in a single segment. This is not strictly true, since **DOS** allows the use of overlaying with .COM programs. A more accurate characterization is that no more than 64K of a .COM program can be *simultaneously* present in machine memory.

In addition, it is not possible to use the simplified segment directives in a .COM program. This is not really a hardship since the overhead involved in writing out the traditional directives is minimal. After all, there is only one segment.

Programs in .COM format do have certain advantages. Since there is only one segment, the problems associated with switching segment registers do not arise. These programs contain no code relating to segment manipulation, and so are usually somewhat smaller than their .EXE counterparts. But notice that, when loaded into machine memory, a .EXE program is *not* larger than its .COM counterpart by an amount equal to the size of the .EXE header, since the .EXE header is not part of the load module.

Memory resident programs and interrupt handlers should be as small as possible, so the .COM format is favored for them. In particular, certain system programs called device drivers must be written in a manner closely resembling .COM format.

Figure 9.7 shows a reasonable template for use in building .COM files. As we stated previously, it is not possible to use the simplified segment directives. Although not essential, it is still a good idea to use the Microsoft default name, _TEXT, for the code segment, and we will always do so.

When a .COM program receives control of the machine all four segment registers point to the single program segment. This initialization is done automatically by the program loader, but we must still notify **MASM** where the registers will point by means of **ASSUME** directives, and on line 8 we have given a complete set of **ASSUME**s. As we indicated in Chapter 6, an **ASSUME** for the **ss** register is seldom necessary and so we could have omitted it from the list. Likewise, in many programs the **ASSUME** for **es** will be superfluous.

In a .EXE file, the PSP is given its own segment. In a .COM file, the PSP is stored in the first 100H bytes of the single segment, which explains the

```
ORG  100h
```

directive on line 10. **ORG** is a contraction of the word *origin* and tells the assembler to set its *location counter* to an origin 100H bytes inside the segment before it starts to generate code. In other words, the first 100H bytes should be left empty to store the PSP. Of course, the same effect could be achieved by beginning the segment with the line

```
DB   100H  DUP(?)
```

Data can reasonably be stored at a number of positions within the segment; we will consider the alternatives later in the present chapter. For the moment, the template suggests that data should be stored at the effective beginning of the segment, i.e., just after the **ORG** directive.

But there is a slight problem with this configuration. The microprocessor will begin code execution at offset 100H and, if data have been placed there, will try to execute the binary form of the data statements. This *always* has disastrous results. The standard solution is to include a **jmp** instruction whose only purpose is to "jump over the data." We do this on line 14, jumping to the *Begin* label on line 18.

When a .COM program is given control by the loader, here is how the most important registers are initialized:

- As we discussed earlier, the four segment registers point to the start of the segment.

- The **ip** register contains the value 100H, because this is always the entry of a .COM program.

- Since there is no .EXE header, there are no parameters *minAlloc* and *maxAlloc* to indicate how much memory the program should be given. The solution that the loader adopts is strange: even though, by its very nature, a .COM program cannot use more than 64K of memory, it is allocated all of available machine memory. Of course, this is exactly the default allocation method for a .EXE file,

FIGURE 9.7 GENERAL FORM OF A .COM PROGRAM

```
1    TITLE   comTemp.asm: template for a .COM source file
2
3    ;equates and macros go here
4
5
6    _TEXT SEGMENT 'CODE'
7
8        ASSUME CS:_TEXT, DS:_TEXT, ES:_TEXT, SS:_TEXT
9
10       ORG 100h          ;this line is essential in a .com file
11
12   Start:
13
14       jmp    Begin
15
16       ;data can be stored here
17
18   Begin:
19
20       ;code goes here
21
22       mov     ax, 4c00h
23       int     21h
24
25
26   _TEXT    ENDS
27
28   END      Start
```

but a significant distinction in that the default allocation cannot be overridden in the .COM case. Nevertheless, the loader knows that a .COM program can use only one segment and so also sets up the stack in that single segment. This is partly done by the initialization of **ss**. If at least 64K of memory is available for the program, **sp** is initialized so that the stack is at the very top of the segment. If less than 64K is available for the program, **sp** is initialized to the highest possible address in the segment. Immediately before control is passed to the program, the word 0000H is pushed onto the stack.

We will illustrate this last point in terms of specific numbers. Suppose that an entire segment is available for the program. The initial value of **sp** is then equal to 0000H, but a 0000H is pushed immediately so that, when the program gets control, **sp** has value 0FFFEH and the word stored at **ss**:FFFE is 0000H.

It is worth spending a few seconds in checking these assertions, using an actual .COM program such as XHDRDUMP.COM, the program given in Figure 9.8. For example, load XHDRDUMP.COM under **CODEVIEW** using the command

```
cv xHdrDump.com  <  hexDump.exe
```

CODEVIEW will load a .COM file only if the extension .COM is explicitly written
— it defaults to .EXE files. XHDRDUMP.COM gives a printout of the .EXE header, and
expects to receive its input from a .EXE file by redirection, which explains the rest of the
command line. Finally, from within CODEVIEW, take note of the initial register values,
and use the dump command

```
wd ss:sp L 1
```

to check that the top location on the stack really contains 0000H.

A natural question to ask is why the loader pushes 0000H onto the stack, and the answer
is that it provides compatibility with CP/M-style programs that use the following method
of program termination. When a program is ready to terminate, it presumably has balanced
its own use of the stack. Hence if the program ends with an extra return instruction, the
0000H pushed onto the stack by the loader will be popped as the return address. This will
cause control to transfer to cs:0000, i.e., to the start of the code segment. But remember that
the first item in the code segment (which, in a .COM program, is also the first element in
the PSP) is the machine code for an int 20H. Hence the machine will execute this instruction
and terminate. Notice that this termination would not work if cs did not point to the PSP at
the end of the program. Consequently, this kind of termination is better suited to .COM
programs than to programs containing multiple segments, although it can be adapted to such
programs easily enough by having the program itself push the PSP segment address at the
start and then terminate with a FAR return. In the case of a .EXE, the program need only
push the initial value of ds or es.

In any case, it is not advisable to terminate programs of either kind by this method since
Microsoft no longer approves the use of int 20H in any context.

The only remaining question is how to go about constructing a .COM program. The
answer is to build a .EXE first, exactly as we have always done (using MASM and LINK),
and then to submit this .EXE program to a "converter" utility named EXE2BIN. This utility
examines the program, looking for features that would make the conversion impossible. The
conversion might fail for reasons that are usually variations on the obvious theme: either
explicitly or implicitly, the program has defined or made reference to more than one segment.
Unfortunately, it is not always obvious why EXE2BIN cannot make the conversion, and its
error reporting is execrable. (The sole error message is "Program cannot be converted.")

The original .EXE file should be erased, since if the DOS loader finds a .EXE and a
.COM file with the same base name, it will give precedence to the .EXE.

Here is a simple batch file to use in constructing .COM files:

```
MASM /w2 /z %1;
if errorlevel 1 goto stop
LINK %1,,,user;
if errorlevel 1 goto stop
EXE2BIN %1.exe %1.com
if errorlevel 1 goto stop
del %1.exe
:stop
```

This batch file is on the Program Disk, under the name ALC.BAT. To assemble, link,
and convert the .COM source file PROGNAME.ASM, use the command line

```
         alc  progName
```

The reader may be wondering whether it is possible to dispense with line 12 and change lines 16 and 26 to a standard *Start* and *END Start* combination. This configuration passes the scrutiny of both **MASM** and **LINK** but, unfortunately, it is not acceptable to **EXE2BIN**. The problem is that a .COM program contains no header in which to store information such as the location of the program entry point. Consequently, the entry point to a .COM must always be the "official" beginning point, i.e., at offset 100H, immediately after the **ORG** directive.

SECTION 6 A .COM PROGRAM

In the next example program, we will need to print out a word as four hex digits. Since this operation comes up from time to time, it is a good idea to write a macro to do the conversion and printing. The following macro, *hexPrt*, is a somewhat smoother version of the code that did this computation in HEXDUMP.ASM.

```
hexPrt   MACRO   Buffer   ;prints a word as four hex digits
    LOCAL hexPrtLoop

    push    ax
    push    bx
    push    cx
    push    dx
    push    si

    IFDEF _DATA
        isFirstUse hexPrt
        IF firstUseFlagHexPrt
            @CURSEG   ENDS
            _DATA   SEGMENT
                hexTable   db   "01234567890ABCDEF"
            @CURSEG   ENDS
            _TEXT   SEGMENT
        ENDIF
    ENDIF

    mov     dx, Buffer
    lea     bx, hexTable
    mov     cl, 4
    mov     si, 4

hexPrtLoop:

    rol     dx, cl
    mov     al, dl
    and     al, 1111b
```

```
        xlat
        outCh     al
        dec       si
        jne       hexPrtLoop

        pop       si
        pop       dx
        pop       cx
        pop       bx
        pop       ax

ENDM
```

This macro uses a new bit instruction, namely **rol** (*rotate left*). The **rol** instruction is very much like **shl**, both in syntax and effect. The difference between the two is that, whereas **shl** shifts zero into the low-bit position, **rol** shifts the old high bit into the low-bit position. The four consecutive

```
        rol       dx, 1
```

instructions that occur in *hexPrt* clearly rotate the four high bits of **dx** into the four low bit positions. The instructions

```
        mov       al, dl
        and       al, 1111B
```

isolate these four bits as the entire contents of **al**, ready for translation by **xlat**.

This operation is repeated four times in the *shiftLabel* loop, whence the four hex digits are printed in the correct order.

Figure 9.8 shows our sample .COM program, XHDRDUMP.ASM. As we said earlier, it displays .EXE headers in the format shown in Figure 9.6. XHDRDUMP.ASM is written as a filter, receiving file input by redirection. Most of the code should be familiar, but there are a few features that merit elaboration:

Lines 23-25. Recall that the macro code for *hSkip*, *outCh*, and *hexPrt* contains conditional statements designed to set up variables in a segment named _DATA, if these variables have not already been defined. In the present context, it would be an error for a macro to introduce a data segment, since this is going to be a .COM program. The easiest way to block the execution of the conditional code is be sure that these variables have already been defined in the program. We define them on lines 22-24.

Line 27. CR and LF are used without any visible **EQUATE**s because they are now defined by **EQUATE**s that are a permanent part of CONSOLE.MAC.

Lines 70-71. We have used this trick before, but it is worth describing again. For each value of **si**, *hdrOffsets[si]* contains the address of the corresponding *Heading* string, and so the effect of line 70 is to point **di** to that string, all ready for printing on line 71.

Line 73. When a macro parameter contains spaces, such as

```
WORD PTR readBuf[si]
```

it should be encased in angled brackets, otherwise **MASM** thinks that the intended parameter ends at the first white space. The angled brackets constitute the *literal text operator*, which will be discussed more fully in **Chapter 13**.

Line 86. It may seem surprising that *Lseek* works with STDIN. It does indeed, when used with redirection, as in the present case, and does exactly the right things. *WORD PTR readBuf[18]* is the offset of the start of the relocation table and so we are advancing to that position in the input file.

Lines 88-91. A standard use of **shl**. Since **shl** gives multiplication by two, two of them give multiplication by four. This provides the requisite scaling since each relocation pointer (*segment:offset*) is four bytes long.

Lines 111-112. This is analogous to the previous situation. Two **shr** instructions give division by 4, which converts the number of bytes read into the number of relocation items.

Exercise 9-7.   Rewrite HEXDUMP.ASM as a .COM program.

SECTION 7 AN INTRODUCTION TO OBJECT FILES

The construction of object modules is very intricate and a detailed knowledge of their structure is needed only by specialists such as compiler or assembler writers. However, it is possible to give a brief overview of the formatting of object modules, and that is the goal of the present section. This section can also be viewed as an introduction to Article 19 of [24], which analyzes object modules in excruciating detail (57 pages of it). The information presented here is mainly provided to satisfy the curiosity of the reader, and will not be used in the rest of the book.

Before beginning, we will review the role played by object modules in program construction. When an assembler or compiler has finished processing a source file, certain pieces of information are missing and must be supplied before the file can be executed. These gaps stem from several sources. For example, the resulting executable file should be relocatable, i.e., should be loadable into any sufficiently large block of machine memory, whence all segment addresses occurring in the code must be flagged so that they can have the starting-segment address added to them. Offsets of various items may need to be fixed up in the final code, either because they were defined externally, or because relative offsets change when **LINK** puts together different pieces of the same segment originating in different modules. Of course, more than just addresses enter in. If an identifier is declared to be **EXTRN** or **PUBLIC** in a file, its name must be recorded in the object module so that it can be matched with its occurrences in other modules, in one of which it must be defined and declared to be **PUBLIC**.

FIGURE 9.8 A UTILITY THAT DUMPS THE .EXE HEADER

```
1    TITLE  XHdrDump.asm: XHdrDump.asm: displays contents of .EXE header
2
3        INCLUDE console.mac
4        INCLUDE file.mac
5
6   _TEXT SEGMENT WORD PUBLIC 'CODE'
7
8        ASSUME cs:_TEXT, ds:_TEXT, es:_TEXT, ss:_TEXT
9
10       EXTRN   errCheck:NEAR
11
12       ORG 100h                                  ;needed in a .com file
13
14   Start:
15
16     jmp    Begin
17
18     readBuf      DB    32 dup(?)                ;big enough to hold 8 double words
19     numBuf       DB    6 dup(?)                 ;to hold a null term. dec. integer
20     relocBytes DW    ?                          ;holds 4 * (no. of reloc. items)
21
22     hSkipBuf     DB    ?                        ;byte buffer for use by hSkip
23     outChBuf     DB    ?                        ;ditto for outCh
24     hexTable     DB    "0123456789ABCDEF"  ;for use by xlat
25
26     Banner0      DB    CR,LF,LF,"INFORMATION IN EXE HEADER", CR,LF,LF
27                  DB    "OFFSET          DATA                         HEX VALUE      "
28                  DB    "DECIMAL VALUE", CR, LF, 0
29
30     Banner1      DB    CR,LF,LF,LF, "RELATIVE OFFSETS OF RELOCATION"
31                  DB    " ITEMS IN LOAD MODULE"
32                  DB    CR, LF, 0
33     Spaces       DB    "            ", 0
34
35     Heading0     DB    "Signature                       ", 0
36     Heading1     DB    "Last Page Size                  ", 0
37     Heading2     DB    "No. of 512 Byte Pages           ", 0
38     Heading3     DB    "Number of Relocation Items      ", 0
39     Heading4     DB    "Header Size in 16 Byte Pars.    ", 0
40     Heading5     DB    "minAlloc                        ", 0
41     Heading6     DB    "maxAlloc                        ", 0
42     Heading7     DB    "Relative SS Value               ", 0
43     Heading8     DB    "Initial SP Value                ", 0
44     Heading9     DB    "Complemented Checksum           ", 0
45     Heading10    DB    "Initial IP Value                ", 0
46     Heading11    DB    "Relative CS Value               ", 0
47     Heading12    DB    "Offset Reloc. Pointer Table     ", 0
48     Heading13    DB    "Overlay Number:                 ", 0
49
50     hdrOffsets DW    Heading0,Heading1,Heading2,Heading3,Heading4,Heading5
51                DW    Heading6,Heading7,Heading8,Heading9,Heading10, Heading11
52                DW    Heading12,Heading13
53
54   Begin:
```

Figure 9.8 cont.

```
55
56      Read    STDIN, 28, ReadBuf          ;read the 14 basic information words
57
58
59      outAsc  Banner0
60
61      xor     si, si                      ;printLoop1 is jmp-controlled
62      mov     bx, OFFSET hexTable         ;   with si as counter since too
63                                          ;      too big a jump for a loop
64  printLoop1:
65
66      hSkip   1
67      hexPrt  si                          ;offset into load module
68      outAsc  Spaces
69
70      mov     di, hdrOffsets[si]          ;offset of corresponding Heading
71      outAsc  [di]                        ;print that heading
72
73      hexPrt  <WORD PTR readBuf[si]>      ;print value in hex
74      outAsc  Spaces
75
76      iToA    numBuf, <WORD PTR readBuf[si]>
77      outAsc  numBuf                      ;print same value as signed decimal
78      cmp     si, 26                      ;the headings are 0 thru 13, doubled
79      je      @F                          ;   for words
80      add     si, 2
81      jmp     printLoop1
82
83  @@:
84
85      outAsc  Banner1
86      Lseek   STDIN,0,0, <WORD PTR readBuf[018h]> ;to start of reloc. table
87      mov     ax, WORD PTR readBuf[06h]   ;number of relocation items
88      shl     ax, 1
89      shl     ax, 1
90      mov     relocBytes, ax              ;times 4 for bytes since each reloc.
91                                          ; item is an offset and a segment
92  readLoop:
93
94      cmp     ax, 32                      ;bytes to be read is either 32 or the
95      jle     @F                          ;   remaining value of relocBytes,
96      mov     ax, 32                      ;      whichever is smaller
97
98  @@:
99
100     sub     relocBytes, ax              ;update relocBytes by subtracting the
101     Read    STDIN, ax, readBuf          ;   number that are about to be read
102
103     and     ax, ax                      ;if none left, quit
104     jne     @F
105     jmp     Done
106
107   @@:
108
109     mov     si, OFFSET readBuf          ;printLoop2 prints line of 8 reloc.
```

```
110        hSkip    1                        ;addresses in form segment:offset
111        shr      ax, 1
112        shr      ax, 1                    ;items to print = (bytes to print)/4
113
114  printLoop2:
115
116        hexPrt   <[si + 2]>               ;do the printing of an address
117        outCh    ':'
118        hexPrt   [si]
119        cmp      si, OFFSET readBuf+28    ;suppress trailing space because it
120        je       @F                       ;  triggers an extra linefeed on the
121        outCh    ' '                      ;     on 80 column display or printer
122
123    @@:
124
125        dec      ax
126        and      ax, ax
127        je       @F
128        add      si, 4                    ;every address uses up four bytes
129        jmp      printLoop2
130
131    @@:
132
133        mov      ax, relocBytes           ;at top of loop, ax should contain
134        jmp      readLoop                 ;  updated value of relocBytes
135
136  Done:
137
138        hSkip    2
139
140        mov      ax, 4c00h
141        int      21h
142
143    _TEXT    ENDS
144
145  END      Start
```

As well as information on user-defined variables, object modules contain information about the names, alignment types, and other parameters relating to segment structure, allowing **LINK** to glue the whole thing together correctly.

An object module consists of a sequence of *records*. These records are of 14 different types. Some types of records may occur many, many times in a given object module, and not all the types need occur in every object module. The general format of a record is easy to explain. A record consists of

- A one-byte identification code.

- Two bytes giving the remaining length of the record.

- The data contained in the record.

- A one-byte checksum.

The 14 types, together with their identification bytes, their standard six-character name abbreviations, and their full names, are listed in Table 9.2.

The utilities section of the Program Disk contains a program named OBJDUMP.COM, which produces a dump of a .OBJ file in a format that makes it easier to study its contents. Since the source code for this utility is similar to that for HEXDUMP.ASM, which was presented in detail in Section 3, we have not included it here. Instead, one of the exercises at the end of this chapter asks the reader to write a version of OBJDUMP by adapting HEXDUMP.ASM. If the reader does not wish to work this exercise, and would like to see the source code for such a utility, a C version of a very similar utility can be found in Appendix N of [24]. We will be content to give an example of the output from OBJDUMP, and will use this to help explain the format of object file records.

Since the object module for even a short source file contains many records, it best suits our purposes to start with an unreasonably simple source module so that we will obtain an object file of manageable size. Figure 9.9 shows the selected source module.

Figure 9.10 and Figure 9.11 contrast the standard hex dump of PROG9_1.OBJ and the new .OBJ dump. The actual information in both files is of course identical, being just the contents of the disk file. The only difference is that the .OBJ dump is formatted to make it much easier to identify the different object records.

We will now give a quick survey of some of the 14 record formats, using Figure 9.11 to illustrate the discussion. As we stated earlier, the exact formatting of some of the records is quite involved, and it is certainly not appropriate for us to examine all of them in detail.

Looking at Figure 9.11, observe that the ASCII printout at the right begins with byte number three of each record (where the byte count starts with zero). As stated earlier, byte number zero gives the record identification code and is used to generate the correct heading (THEADR, etc.) in Figure 9.11. Likewise, the next two bytes give the record length, which our program prints as a two-byte hex number. Here is a partial analysis of Figure 9.11:

Line 1. THEADR. As the module name suggests, this record contains the name of the source module, PROG9_1 in this case. The format of the name consists of a byte giving the length (0BH here), followed by the text of the name. As in all records, the last byte is a checksum (which equals DBH in this instance).

Line 3. COMENT. The comment records do not relate to programmer comments in the source code, which have long since disappeared from the file. They refer to various pieces of information passed from the translator to **LINK**. In a COMENT record, byte number three is called the *attribute*, and is somewhat technical; byte number four gives the type of the COMENT. The first COMENT record has type 9EH which, according to [24], means that the assembler is requesting **LINK** to set the **DOSSEG** switch. A COMENT record can contain additional information after byte number four. In this case there is no extra information — just the always-present checksum.

Line 5. The second COMENT record relates to the transfer of **CODEVIEW** information.

Line 7. LNAMES. A record of this kind contains a list of names that can be referred to by subsequent SEGDEF and GRPDEF records. These records contain the usual three opening bytes and checksum closing byte. The list of names lies between, with the length of each name written before the name. There is generally an opening dummy name of length 00H,

TABLE 9.2 THE 14 TYPES OF OBJECT RECORDS

ID CODE	SHORT NAME	FULL NAME
80H	THEADR	Translator Header Record
88H	COMENT	Comment Record
8AH	MODEND	Module End Record
8CH	EXTDEF	External Names Definition Record
8EH	TYPDEF	Type Definition Record
90H	PUBDEF	Public Names Definition Record
94H	LINNUM	Line Number Record
96H	LNAMES	List of Names Record
98H	SEGDEF	Segment Definition Record
91H	GRPDEF	Group Definition Record
9CH	FIXUPP	Fixup Record
A0H	LEDATA	Logical Enumerated Data Record
A2H	LIDATA	Logical Iterated Data Record
B0H	COMDEF	Communal Names Data Record

as there is in this example. When later records reference this one, they refer to names by their position number in the LNAMES record, with the numbering starting with the dummy name as number 1. For example, here the name _TEXT is number 0BH.

Lines 13, etc. SEGDEF gives information about a segment. Byte number 3 (called the *ACBP byte*) includes information about segment alignment type and combine class (both of which have been discussed briefly in previous chapters and will be explained completely in Chapter 12.) These are in fact the 'A' and 'C' in ACBP. Bytes 4 and 5 give the size of the segment. Bytes 6, 7, and 8 give the segment name, the combine class name for the segment, and an overlay name for the segment. Each of these is recorded as an integer, representing the number of the corresponding name in the preceding LNAMES record. The overlay name is not used by **MS-DOS** and only references the dummy name 01H in LNAMES.

A quick check should convince the reader that the first SEGDEF record is concerned with the segment named _TEXT (the Microsoft default name for the code segment) and that this segment has class name CODE and length 0AH.

Similarly, the second and third SEGDEFs contain information about the data and stack segments.

Line 23. GRPDEF. This kind of record indicates which segments belong to which groups. (Groups will also be explained in Chapter 12). Byte 3 is the group name, again represented as an index into LNAMES. This time the name is DGROUP. There follows a list of pairs of hex digits, the first of each pair being 0FFH. The 0FFH indicates that the next digit represents the name of a segment that is part of this group. The second digit gives the number of this segment, using the listed ordering of the previous SEGDEFs. In this example, **LINK** is being told that DGROUP consists of the second and third segments occurring in the SEGREG list, namely _DATA and STACK.

FIGURE 9.9 A SHORT TEST PROGRAM

```
1    TITLE  Prog9_1.asm:  trivial program on which to test ObjDump
2
3    PUBLIC  pubVar
4
5    DOSSEG
6    .MODEL SMALL
7
8    .STACK 100H
9
10   .DATA
11
12           pubVar    DW   27
13
14   .CODE
15
16       EXTRN    extVar:BYTE
17
18   Start:
19
20           mov    ax, @DATA
21           mov    ds, ax
22
23           mov    ax, 4c00h
24           int    21h
25
26   END     Start
```

Line 25. EXTDEF. This contains information about the EXTRNs in the module. Again, the format is familiar. There can be a list of EXTRN names. Each has the format: length; the text of the name; coded type information. In our example there is only one EXTRN. The length of its name is 06H, the text of the name is *extVar*, and the type is represented by the bytes 80H and 84H.

Line 27. PUBDEF. Similar to EXTDEF.

Line 29. COMENT. This comment is of a class (0A2H) that is not documented by Microsoft.

Line 31. LEDATA. These records contain actual machine code, with various pieces of overhead data. The exact formatting is not worth going into here.

Line 35. FIXUPP. Records of these types, as the name indicates, contain the information that **LINK** needs to fix up incomplete segments and offset references. The content of these records is tremendously technical and it would be foolhardy to try to give the details in this modest survey.

Line 41. LINNUM. This one is easy to explain. It relates line numbers in the source code to locations in the machine code, so that **CODEVIEW**, for example, can highlight the

FIGURE 9.10 HEX DUMP OF PROG9_1.OBJ

```
PROG9_1.OBJ   --  hex dump

80 0D 00 0B 50 52 4F 47-39 5F 31 2E 41 53 4D 58   .......PROG9_1.ASMX
88 03 00 80 9E 57 88 06-00 00 A1 01 43 56 37 96   ........W......CV7.
45 00 00 06 44 45 42 53-59 4D 06 44 45 42 54 59   E..E...DEBSYM.DEBTY
50 06 44 47 52 4F 55 50-07 24 24 54 59 50 45 53   P.DP.DGROUP.$$TYPES
09 24 24 53 59 4D 42 4F-4C 53 04 44 41 54 41 04   .$$.$$SYMBOLS.DATA.
43 4F 44 45 05 53 54 41-43 4B 05 5F 44 41 54 41   CODCODE.STACK._DATA
05 5F 54 45 58 54 79 98-07 00 48 0A 00 0B 08 01   ._T._TEXTy...H.....
FB 98 07 00 48 02 00 0A-07 01 05 98 07 00 74 00   ....H.........t.
01 09 09 01 D9 98 07 00-60 0B 00 06 02 01 ED 98   ..........`.......
07 00 60 0C 00 05 03 01-EC 9A 06 00 04 FF 02 FF   ..`..`............
03 59 8C 0A 00 06 45 78-74 56 61 72 82 00 88 90   .Y..Y....ExtVar....
0E 00 01 02 06 50 75 62-56 61 72 00 00 80 85 04   ........PubVar.....
88 04 00 00 A2 00 D2 A0-06 00 02 00 00 1B 00 3D   ................=
A0 0E 00 01 00 00 B8 00-00 8E D8 B8 00 4C CD 21   .............L.!
41 9C 06 00 C8 01 15 01-01 7E A0 0F 00 04 00 00   A..A.......~......
0A 0B 00 00 00 05 53 54-41 52 54 A5 9C 06 00 C4   ......START.....
02 04 01 01 92 94 13 00-00 01 14 00 00 00 15 00   ................
03 00 17 00 05 00 18 00-08 00 F0 A0 10 00 05 00   ................
00 01 03 00 72 80 74 01-03 00 72 80 73 78 8A 07   ......r.t...r.sx..
00 C1 00 01 01 00 00 AC           8 8A 07   .......... . . x .
```

correct line of source code while an instruction is being executed. The formatting is direct. Bytes 3 and 4 refer to a group index and segment index for the information in question. The group-index field is not actually used — it is set to zero. The segment-index field refers to the number of the SEGDEF record going with the segment. In this case, there is only one code segment, whence this field contains 01H. Next there follows a number of four-byte fields. In these fields, the first two bytes give a line number and the last two give the offset into the segment at which the matching code is located. In the present example, the first line containing code is 0014H (= line 18) and the corresponding code is found at _TEXT:0000, and there are a total of four lines containing executable code. These facts can be corroborated from Figure 9.9.

Line 46. MODEND. Once more, the formatting is somewhat technical. Of course, MODEND signals the end of the object module. Byte 3 is especially interesting because, for example, bit 6 shows whether this module contains the start address for program execution. If it does, the module must contain information about the location of the start address and, in particular, whether it is a relocatable item.

One interesting record type not occurring in this particular example is LIDATA, the *logical iterated data record*. The word "iterated" refers to the **DUP** directive, since these records are used to store data that were defined using **DUP**.

Exercise 9-8. Write a utility that will print the contents of an object file, formatted like Figure 9.11. Use the .COM format for the utility. A good starting point is the XHDRDUMP.ASM, the corresponding utility that dumps .EXE headers.

FIGURE 9.11 OBJECT DUMP OF PROG9_1.OBJ

```
 1   Record 1: 80h THEADR
 2   80 000Dh 0B 70 72 6F 67 39 5F 31 2E 41 53 4D D8        .prog9_1.ASM.
 3   Record 2: 88h COMENT
 4   88 0003h 80 9E 57                                      ..W
 5   Record 3: 88h COMENT
 6   88 0006h 00 A1 01 43 56 37                             ...CV7
 7   Record 4: 96h LNAMES
 8   96 0045h 00 06 44 45 42 53 59 4D 06 44 45 42 54 59 50 06    ..DEBSYM.DEBTYP.
 9            44 47 52 4F 55 50 07 24 24 54 59 50 45 53 09 24    DGROUP.$$TYPES.$
10            24 53 59 4D 42 4F 4C 53 04 44 41 54 41 04 43 4F    $SYMBOLS.DATA.CO
11            44 45 05 53 54 41 43 4B 05 5F 44 41 54 41 05 5F    DE.STACK._DATA._
12            54 45 58 54 79                                     TEXTy
13   Record 5: 98h SEGDEF
14   98 0007h 48 0A 00 0B 08 01 FB                          H......
15   Record 6: 98h SEGDEF
16   98 0007h 48 02 00 0A 07 01 05                          H......
17   Record 7: 98h SEGDEF
18   98 0007h 74 00 01 09 09 01 D9                          t......
19   Record 8: 98h SEGDEF
20   98 0007h 60 0B 00 06 02 01 ED                          `......
21   Record 9: 98h SEGDEF
22   98 0007h 60 0C 00 05 03 01 EC                          `......
23   Record 10: 9Ah GRPDEF
24   9A 0006h 04 FF 02 FF 03 59                             .....Y
25   Record 11: 8Ch EXTDEF
26   8C 000Ah 06 65 78 74 56 61 72 82 00 68                .extVar..h
27   Record 12: 90h PUBDEF
28   90 000Eh 01 02 06 70 75 62 56 61 72 00 00 80 85 E4    ...pubVar.....
29   Record 13: 88h COMENT
30   88 0004h 00 A2 00 D2                                   ....
31   Record 14: A0h LEDATA
32   A0 0006h 02 00 00 1B 00 3D                             .....=
33   Record 15: A0h LEDATA
34   A0 000Eh 01 00 00 B8 00 00 8E D8 B8 00 4C CD 21 41    .........L.!A
35   Record 16: 9Ch FIXUPP
36   9C 0006h C8 01 15 01 01 7E                             .....~
37   Record 17: A0h LEDATA
38   A0 000Fh 04 00 00 0A 0B 00 00 00 05 53 54 41 52 54 A5    .........START.
39   Record 18: 9Ch FIXUPP
40   9C 0006h C4 02 04 01 01 92                             ......
41   Record 19: 94h LINNUM
42   94 0013h 00 01 14 00 00 00 15 00 03 00 17 00 05 00 18 00    ................
43            08 00 F0                                      ...
44   Record 20: A0h LEDATA
45   A0 0010h 05 00 00 01 03 00 72 80 74 01 03 00 72 80 73 78    ......r.t...r.sx
46   Record 21: 8Ah MODEND
47   8A 0007h C1 00 01 01 00 00 AC                          .......
48
49   There were 21 object records
```

SECTION 8 THE ASSEMBLY PROCESS

In Section 2 of Chapter 6, we introduced the basic ideas of machine code generation, and will now consider this subject in more detail. The information in this section is somewhat tangential to our main development, since it is seldom necessary to drop down to the machine code level in writing or debugging assembly language programs.

The encoding scheme used in converting assembly language to machine code is totally mechanical, but is tiresome to do by hand. Each assembly language instruction corresponds to one or more bytes of machine code. The first machine code byte is called the *op-code* and identifies the general class of the instruction: **mov**, **add**, etc. The op-code may also carry some specific information about the exact form of the instruction, for example, whether it uses byte- or word-size operands, and whether it uses registers or memory references for its source and/or destination operands.

The subsequent bytes of the machine encoding of an instruction, if there are any, contain information about the registers involved in the instruction, the form of addressing used for indirect operands, the actual offsets of direct memory operands, and the values of immediate data.

Table 9.3 gives the details of the encoding. Generally, each piece of information needed to interpret the instruction is stored in as few bits as possible.

For example, the information on whether the operands are bytes or words can be stored in a single bit which, following the usual conventions, is named *w* in Table 9.3. If a non-segment register is involved in the instruction, then the name of the register is encoded in the three-bit pattern called *reg*. The interpretation of reg depends on the value of the *w* bit. The *r/m* bit field (*register or memory*) gives information on the addressing form for memory operands. The *mod* field (*mode*) tells about the size of a displacement when there is one: 0, 1, or 2 bytes. The *sreg, d,* and *s* fields are self-explanatory.

The segment override byte has been discussed before. Recall that it is used as a prefix to indicate that an instruction should not use the default segment register.

Instructions using some subset of the *mod*, *reg*, and *r/m* fields incorporate them into a single byte of machine code called the *ModR/M byte*. This byte occurs immediately after the op-code.

Of course, translation to or from machine language requires having access to the op-codes and other pertinent data for the instructions in question. Our Appendix 1 contains such information for all the instructions accepted by the different members of the **8086** family, through the **80486**, presented in a format similar to that used in the Intel manuals. An especially useful reference in this context is [25], which is distributed as part of the **MASM** package. That booklet is compact, durably bound, and filled with important information. The instruction descriptions given in [25], which are in a format similar to Figure 9.12, are somewhat more detailed than our Appendix 1.

We will use the data from Figure 9.12 as the basis for our examples in this section. In particular, we will verify the machine encodings arrived at empirically in Chapter 6.

Parts of Figure 9.12 need elaboration. The *ODITSZAPC* appearing on the same line as the instruction name is a listing of the flag names: **O**verflow, **D**irection, etc. If any of these flags were changed by the instruction, an *x* or a checkmark or some other indication appears immediately below the flag letter. **Mov** does not alter any flags, and so no such symbols are shown.

The **mov** instruction has several different machine code forms, with corresponding op-codes, depending on the nature of the operands. The first form covers these cases:

```
mov      Reg, Reg
mov      Mem, Reg
mov      Reg, Mem
```

The corresponding machine encoding has the format

```
100010dw  mod,reg,r/m  disp(0 or 2)
```

The bit-fields *d, w, mod, reg,* and *r/m* are determined by the rules in Table 9.3. The first byte of the machine encoding is 100010*dw*, the second byte is the ModR/M byte, and there may or may not be two more bytes, depending on whether there is a memory operand containing a displacement. One potentially confusing point is that the bytes of the instruction are stored in the order shown, in the direction of increasing memory, except that two-word displacements (or data items) are reversed and stored (as always) in the order {low byte, high byte}.

The *Clocks* column gives the number of clock cycles required to execute the instruction. A parenthesized quantity such as (9,13) means that if the instruction has byte-size operands, 9 clock cycles are required, and if it has word-size operands, 13 are required. Of course, the time penalty incurred by the **8088** results from the 8-bit data bus. Each fetch of a byte from memory requires four clock cycles. Hence, in the word case the extra fetch adds four clock cycles to the time when this instruction executes on an **8088**.

In addition, indirect addressing modes such as [**bx**] or [**bx+si+disp**] cause the microprocessor to do extra computation, which requires more clock cycles. Obviously, the more complicated the addressing mode, the more clock cycles are needed. This extra time is accounted for by the "+ *EA*" term (meaning "+ effective address"). The number of clock cycles that must be added is given in Table 9.4.

One other feature in Figure 9.12 is worth pointing out. An instruction such as

```
mov      ax, Var1
```

where *Var1* is a direct memory reference, can be assembled in two ways: either by using the first form

```
mov      Reg, Mem
```

or by using the fourth form

```
mov      Accum, dirMem
```

Of these, the second is both shorter (three bytes instead of four) and faster (since the first form requires 19 clock cycles, including the *EA*, while the second requires only 14). It is to be expected that, faced with such an alternative, a good assembler will choose the more efficient alternative. There are many instructions in the **8088** set that have forms that are faster and/or shorter when one of the operands is the accumulator (either **ax** or **al**).

TABLE 9.3 INFORMATION USED IN MACHINE ENCODINGS

MOD		REG	w = 1	w = 0
00	if r/m = 110 means	000	ax	al
	direct memory operand	001	cx	cl
	else disp = 0, memory	010	dx	dl
	operand is indirect	011	bx	bl
01	indirect memory operand	100	sp	ah
	8-bit disp.	101	bp	ch
10	indirect memory operand	110	si	dh
	16-bit disp.	111	di	bh
11	two register inst.			
	reg field gives dest.			
	r/m field gives source			

R/M	
000	ds:[bx+si+disp]
001	ds:[bx+di+disp]
010	ss:[bp+si+disp]
011	ss:[bp+si+disp]
100	ds:[si+disp]
101	ds:[di+disp]
110	ds:[bp+disp]
111	ds:[bx+disp]

SREG		SEGMENT OVERRIDE BYTE	
000	es	2eh	cs
001	cs	3eh	ds
010	ss	26h	es
110	ds	36h	ss

SPECIAL BITS

d d = 1 means register or memory to register
   d = 0 means register to memory

w w = 1 means word operands
   w = 0 means byte operands

s s = 1 means sign extend 8-bit operands to 16-bits
   s = 0 means make unsigned extension (pad with 8 0's)

We will now check the correctness of some of the encodings that were deduced in Section 2 of Chapter 7. Our first example was

        mov   ax, 20

Since this has the form

        mov   Reg, Immed

it matches the third form of **mov** and so its encoding has the general form

        1011wreg data(1 or 2)

We wish to make it word size, so **w = 1**. The register in question is **ax** and so **reg = 000**. Hence the op-code is 1011 1000 = B8H.

FIGURE 9.12 MOV: A SAMPLE 8088 INSTRUCTION

mov   ODITSZAPC

```
100010dw   mod,reg,r/m   disp(0 or 2)
```
Form	Clocks
mov reg, reg	2
mov mem, reg	(9,13) + EA
mov reg, mem	(8,12) + EA

```
1100011w   mod,000,r/m   disp(0 or 2)   data(1 or 2)
```
Form	Clocks
mov mem, immed	(10,14) + EA

```
1011wreg   data(1 or 2)
```
Form	Clocks
mov reg, immed	4

```
101000dw   disp(0 or 2)
```
Form	Clocks
mov dirmem, accum	(10,14)
mov accum, dirmem	(10,14)

```
100011d0   mod,sreg,r/m   disp(0 or 2)
```
Form	Clocks
mov segreg, reg16	2
mov segreg, mem16	(8,12) +EA
mov reg16, segreg	2
mov mem16, segreg	(9,13) +EA

Since $w = 1$, the microprocessor will look for two bytes of data, coming next in the machine code. This means that we must encode 20_{10} as a two-byte hex number. The hex value is 0014H and when this is written in the form {low byte, high byte} and combined with the op-code, we get the machine encoding B81400.

Next, consider the example

```
mov       ax, bx
```

This matches the first form of **mov**:

```
100010dw   mod,reg,r/m   disp(0 or 2)
```

Schematically, the computation proceeds as follows:

```
100010dw   mod, reg, r/m   disp(0 or 2)
   ||        |    |    |         |
   11       10  dest src     nothing
                  |    |
                 000  011
```

TABLE 9.4 TIMES FOR EFFECTIVE ADDRESS CALCULATIONS

ADDRESS FORMAT	CLOCK CYCLES
disp	6
based or indexed	5
based displaced or indexed displaced	9
[bp+di] or [bx+si]	7
[bp+si] or [bx+di]	8
[bp+di+disp] or [bx+si+disp]	11
[bp+si+disp] or [bx+di+disp]	12
segment override	2

This translates as 8BC3, in agreement with our expectations from Chapter 6.

Next, consider

```
mov     ax, [bx]
```

This again matches the first **mov** format and the instruction derivation looks like this:

```
100010dw  mod, reg, r/m  disp(0 or 2)
   ||       |    |    |       |
   11       00  dest src   nothing
                 |    |
                000  011
```

We again get the expected result, namely 8B07.

Finally, consider

```
mov     ax, [bx + 800]
```

Once more this matches the first format, and the computation looks like this:

```
100010dw  mod, reg, r/m  disp(0 or 2)
   ||       |    |    |       |
   11       10  dest src    800₁₀
                 |    |       |
                000  111    0320h
```

After inverting the byte order in the displacement, we get 8B872003, which is again the correct result.

Before concluding this section, we should point out that timings based on the instruction times and the EA additions are not really reliable, since there is another, hard-to-compute factor that plays an important role.

Before explaining this other factor, we will briefly review the discussion of the internal structure of the **8088**, as presented in Chapter 2. We saw that the processing of an instruction really consists of two operations: the code and data for the instruction must first be fetched from machine memory, and then the code must be executed by the **8088**. We now know that each fetch of a byte from memory requires four clock cycles. To partly circumvent the degradation in machine performance resulting from this fetch time, the microprocessor maintains a prefetch queue which, in the case of the **8088**, can hold four bytes of code. Information is brought into the queue from memory by a part of the microprocessor (the BIU, or *bus interface unit*), that is entirely separate from the execution part of the **8088** (the EU, or *execution unit*). Hence, the filling and refilling of the queue do not steal computational time.

However, there are three problems. First, the bytes in the prefetch queue always contain code from the instructions lying immediately ahead in the code. Consequently, if there is a sudden need to execute some other instruction, the queue will not contain the correct information. This situation arises when there is any kind of jump in the code: as examples, a **jmp**, a **call**, a **ret**, or a conditional jump that is taken. When this happens, the queue is *flushed* and the microprocessor must wait until the information needed for executing the target instruction has been fetched. This means that every jump in the code actually slows down the program.

The second problem is that a number of consecutive, very fast instructions may empty the queue, and so again result in a forced pause while additional bytes are fetched. A standard example of this phenomenon is a sequence of shift instructions, say

```
shl     ax, 1
shl     ax, 1
shl     ax, 1
          .
          .
```

From the instruction tables in Appendix 1, each of these instructions occupies two bytes and executes in two clock cycles. Therefore, the time required to execute a sequence of three of these instructions ranges from 6 clock cycles (if the code for them is already in the queue) to 14 clock cycles (if the queue is empty at the beginning of the sequence).

On the other hand, the pair of instructions

```
mov     cl, n
shl     ax, cl
```

where n is an immediate value, has an execution time of 4 clock cycles for the first instruction and $8 + 4n$ for the second. From this it is clear that if n gets big enough, these instructions provide a faster multiple shift than would a corresponding sequence of single shifts when the time required to refill the buffer is taken into account.

In one of the exercises at the end of the chapter, the reader is asked to determine the "crossover" point at which the **cl** version of the instruction becomes the more efficient choice.

The third problem is that the *BIU* is in charge of bringing data to the microprocessor, as well as keeping the instruction queue filled. Hence in a section of the code involving a good deal of data manipulation, the instruction queue may empty.

The conclusion to be drawn from this discussion is that the actual execution times for individual instructions can be quite context dependent, and the timings from the instruction tables can only be used as an optimistic guide. There are actually two different times that might be assigned to an instruction:

- The execution time, computed from the instruction tables and modified as necessary by segment override and effective-address-computation penalties.

- The time required to fetch the instruction and its data from memory. In the case of the **8088**, this time equals

```
4*(instructionBytes + dataBytes)
```

where *instructionBytes* means the number of bytes in the machine language version of the instruction and *dataBytes* means the total number of bytes of data used by the instruction. The factor 4 appears because each memory fetch requires 4 clock cycles.

The relative importance of these times in the execution of a given instruction depends on the immediate context, and in particular on the state of the prefetch queue.

As a matter of general interest, we point out that the situation is somewhat better, but even more complicated, when the **8086** processor is used. Recall that the **8086** has a 16-bit data bus, which means that it transfers information in 16-bit pieces — some of the time. Specifically, if a word begins at an even memory address, it is brought in a single fetch, but if it begins at an odd address, it requires two fetches, one for the first byte and one for the second. In terms of fetching the code for a contiguous sequence of instructions, this behavior causes no problems. But immediately after a jump to an odd code address, a single byte of an instruction will be read. As with the **8088**, each read requires four clock cycles. The instruction queue of the **8086** is a somewhat more generous six bytes long.

Exercise 9-9. Compute the machine form for the following instructions:

```
1.    sub      cx, 1000
2.    mul      WORD PTR [bx + 10]
3.    mov      BYTE PTR [bx + si + 1], 100
4.    add      Ary[bp + di - 30], ax
```

where *Ary* is defined in the segment pointed to by **es** that has a correct **ASSUME** associated with it, and *Ary* begins at offset 20 in that segment.

It will be necessary to look up the op-codes and auxiliary data about the instructions in Appendix 1 or [25]. It is an easy matter to check on the correctness of your answers using **CODEVIEW** or the .LST file. Notice that (d) is especially interesting. The name *Ary* suggests to **MASM** that **es** should be used as a segment override prefix, but the occurrence of **bp** in the indirect addressing expression indicates that **ss** should be used instead. Which way does **MASM** jump? The answer that you find in this case holds in all similar situations: given an apparent conflict between symbol table information and an indirect addressing default, **MASM** always gives precedence to one of them, and the point of the exercise is to find out which one.

Exercise 9-10. Check using **CODEVIEW** or the .LST file that the encoding of an indirect addressing mode of the form **[bp]** needs one more byte of machine code than does **[bx]**. Then use the information in Table 9.3 to explain this phenomenon.

Exercise 9-11. Compare the time taken for the pair of instructions

```
mov     cl, n
shl     ax, cl
```

where n is an immediate value, with the time for the sequence of instructions

```
shl     ax, 1
shl     ax, 1
          .
          .
```

where the **shl** instruction is repeated n times. In particular, find the crossover point, i.e., the value of n at which the first approach becomes faster than the second. Assume that the **BIU** is able to give its entire attention to keeping the prefetch queue filled. The problem should really be done twice: once assuming that the prefetch queue is empty at the beginning of the instruction sequence, and once assuming it is full at the start. The typical, real-life configuration will lie somewhere between these extremes.

Exercise 9-12. Text to be displayed on an 80-column-by-25-row screen is stored as an 80-by-25 array of words in row major form. Hence the character that will occur at a given position (row,col) on the screen (with $0 \le row \le 24$ and $0 \le col \le 79$) is stored at word number

```
row * 80 + col
```

in the array. In particular, the operation of multiplication by 80 comes up frequently in this context. The obvious way to multiply by 80 is by some such instruction sequence as

```
mov     al, row
mov     cl, 80
mul     cl
```

A more subtle approach is to observe that $80 = 64 + 16$, so that multiplication by 80 can be synthesized from two left shifts and an addition. Work out timings for both methods. Ignore the fact that extra time will be needed if the instruction queue empties during the instruction sequence.

SECTION 9 THE TWO PASSES OF MASM

MASM is an example of a *two-pass assembler*. In other words, in the process of constructing a .OBJ file, **MASM** reads the input file twice. During the first reading (*Pass 1*), the symbol table is constructed and a preliminary version of the machine code is generated. During the second reading (*Pass 2*), the preliminary code is converted to its final form by resolving forward references. The term *forward reference* refers to the use of a name before it has been defined in the source code. *Resolving* a forward reference means filling in the information about that forward reference when it becomes available.

So far, our only examples of forward references have been to labels in the code, whenever a jump or call was made to some future location in the code. We will see in a moment that other kinds of forward references are legal, and that some forward references can cause **MASM** to make errors.

It is not strictly necessary that an assembler (or compiler) make two passes in order to resolve forward references. Many language translators just make a list of the locations of unresolved references and, when the first scan is complete, enter the necessary information at these locations.

We have already seen one instance where **MASM** needs some help in giving an optimal resolution of a forward reference. This occurs when the code contains an instruction of the form

```
jmp        forwardLabel
```

where *forwardLabel* is located no more than 127 bytes ahead in the code. During Pass 1, when **MASM** is constructing the preliminary version of the code, the distance to the target is not yet known. Since the **jmp** instruction can have a target that lies anywhere in the current segment, **MASM** must allocate two bytes of storage for the displacement to be safe. When *forwardLabel* is discovered to be quite close to the **jmp** instruction, **MASM** is stuck: the code up to the target location has already been written under the assumption that the **jmp** displacement requires two bytes. Theoretically, **MASM** could redo all this intermediate code, but this is not what it does. Instead, it changes the machine code for the **jmp** to the correct form for a one-byte displacement jump and pads the unused byte with a **nop** (*no operation*) instruction. It then emits a warning message, which gives the programmer the opportunity to resubmit the code with the original **jmp** instruction replaced by

```
jmp        SHORT forwardLabel
```

Another way of introducing forward references is to reorder the segments so that the code comes before the data. There are occasions in assembly language programming when this is desirable, and we will point out such a situation later in this section. If the segments are ordered in this way, then every occurrence of a data item in the code results in a forward reference.

Figure 9.13 is a short example of a program where code comes before data. It uses the explicit segment structure, although the simplified segment directives could equally well have been used. When the simplified directives are used, the directive **DOSSEG** tells **LINK** to order the segments in the standard Microsoft ordering, in which code precedes data. But in all cases the segments are processed by **MASM** in the exact order in which they appear in the source file.

The program in Figure 9.13 is constructed to demonstrate some of the pitfalls of forward references. If this program is submitted to **MASM**, it will produce an error message saying

---

FIGURE 9.13 A PHASE ERROR

```
1    TITLE   Prog9_2.asm:   Shows a Phase Error
2
3   _TEXT   SEGMENT WORD PUBLIC 'CODE'
4
5        ASSUME cs:_TEXT, es:_DATA
6
7   Start:
8
9        mov      ax, _DATA
10       mov      es, ax
11
12       jmp      SHORT Done
13
14       mov      ax, Var
15
16  Done:
17
18       mov      ax, 4c00h
19       int      21h
20
21  _TEXT        ENDS
22
23  _DATA SEGMENT WORD PUBLIC 'DATA'
24
25       Var     dw    10
26
27  _DATA    ENDS
28
29  END    Start
```

---

that a *phase error* occurred. This means that when **MASM** compared the preliminary version of the code that it generated in Pass 1 with the final version that it generated in Pass 2, it found that the offsets disagreed in some manner that was not readily fixable. Normally, this means that some extra bytes of code were needed in the second pass that **MASM** did not foresee in the first pass. If fewer bytes are needed in the second pass, **MASM** pads with **nop**s. It can also happen that **MASM** must substitute code of the same length in the second pass; it will generally do this without complaining.

In the present program, **MASM** discovered in Pass 2 that an extra byte of code was needed. *Var* is defined in the segment _DATA, which is pointed to by **es** and has the correct **ASSUME** in effect. In Chapter 6 we saw that when a data-type instruction is used with a memory operand, the default segment for the operand is assumed to be **ds**, unless a segment override byte is used. In this case the **es** segment override byte 26H must be used so that *Var* will be addressed by **es**. Unfortunately, when **MASM** is reading line 14 during Pass 1, it cannot know that *Var* is defined in _DATA. It might be defined in _TEXT or, later in the code, **ds** might be pointed to some entirely new data segment, with an appropriate **ASSUME**, and *Var* might be in that segment. So, lacking any specific information, **MASM** assumes that the default segment register is appropriate and uses no override. When the mistake

---

FIGURE 9.14 PASS 1 LISTING OF PROG9_2

```
                        TITLE   Prog9_2.asm:  Shows a Phase Error

0000                    _TEXT   SEGMENT WORD PUBLIC 'CODE'

                        ASSUME cs:_TEXT, es:_DATA

0000                    Start:

0000  A1 ---- R U              mov     ax, _DATA
PROG9__2.ASM(9): error A2009: Symbol not defined: _DATA
0003  8E C0                    mov     es, ax

0005  EB 00                    jmp     SHORT Done
PROG9_2.ASM(12): error A2009: Symbol not defined: DONE

0007  A1 0000 U                mov     ax, Var
PROG9_2.ASM(14): error A2009: Symbol not defined: VAR

000A                    Done:

000A  B8 4C00                  mov     ax, 4c00h
000D  CD 21                    int     21h

000F                    _TEXT       ENDS

0000                    _DATA SEGMENT WORD PUBLIC 'DATA'

0000  000A                     Var     dw    10

0002                    _DATA   ENDS

                        END   Start
```

---

is caught in Pass 2 and a segment override byte inserted, a phase error results. Once the source of the phase error is found, fixing it is trivial: use an explicit segment override, i.e., replace line 14 with

```
        mov     ax, es:Var
```

A reasonable question to ask here is why, when confronted with an ambiguous situation of this kind, **MASM** does not leave an empty byte to be filled in with the correct override on the second pass. This "worst-case assumption" would be the analog of leaving two bytes for each forward jump, as we discussed previously. The reason **MASM** does not do this is presumably just a matter of efficiency. In the case of a forward-referenced data segment that is ultimately addressed by **ds**, there could be a large number of unnecessary 3EH bytes (the **ds** segment override) in the code. The assembler writers (wisely) decided that it was better to force the programmer to fix his or her own code.

Phase errors do come up from time to time and there is a fairly easy way to find their origin. If **MASM** is run with the /D command line option, it will construct a Pass 1 listing, in addition to its usual .LST file, which is really a Pass 2 listing.

FIGURE 9.15 PASS 2 LISTING OF PROG9_2

```
 1                          TITLE   Prog9_2.asm    Shows a Phase Error
 2
 3 0000                     _TEXT   SEGMENT WORD PUBLIC 'CODE'
 4
 5                             ASSUME cs:_TEXT, es:_DATA
 6
 7 0000              Start:
 8
 9 0000  B8 ---- R            mov     ax, _DATA
10 0003  8E C0         mov    es, ax
11
12 0005  EB 03         jmp     SHORT Done
13
14 0007  26: A1 0000 R mov     ax, Var
15
16                    Done:
PROG9_2.ASM(16): error A2006: Phase error between passes
17
18 000A  B8 4C00              mov     ax, 4c00h
19 000D  CD 21         int    21h
20
21 000F                _TEXT         ENDS
22
23 0000                _DATA SEGMENT WORD PUBLIC 'DATA'
24
25 0000  000A                Var     dw    10
26
27 0002                _DATA    ENDS
28
29                     END   Start
```

Figures 10.14 and 10.15 contain the Pass 1 and Pass 2 listings for our example. In general, the Pass 1 listing will show a lot of "Symbol not defined" errors, one for each forward reference. These should normally be ignored. To find the source of the phase error, compare the two listings, noticing where the offsets start to drift apart. This gives the location of the error, and the underlying cause usually becomes apparent at this point.

As we said earlier, there are various instances where it is good to have the code precede the data, in spite of the possibilities of generating phase errors.

One important example of this is a .COM file. Referring to Figure 9.7, the only reason for the

```
        jmp       Begin
```

instruction on line 14 was to protect the data from execution. This effect could be obtained more elegantly by removing lines 14 and 18 and moving the data to the location of line 24. There, it will not be executed since it is beyond the program termination instruction. It is also inside a segment, which **MASM** requires. But, even in a .COM program, data placed at that location can result in phase errors if the code is not carefully written. This subject is explored in one of the exercises.

There is a more compelling reason for placing the data at the end of a .COM program than just getting rid of the jump over data. Recall that in a .EXE program, uninitialized data can be placed in the segment that is referenced with the directive **.DATA?**, so that it will not be stored as part of the disk image of the program. This option is certainly not available in a .COM program, which can only have one segment. Instead, it is usual to place the uninitialized data at the end of the program so that they are free to grow out into the unused portion of the segment.

Ideally, a .COM program should be structured so that the data occur first when seen by **MASM** but come last when seen by **LINK**. In Chapter 12, we will see how this goal can be accomplished.

Exercise 9-13. In the preceding section, we alluded to the possibility of phase errors arising in .COM programs when the data are defined after the code. Write a short .COM program that provokes phase errors of this type. Check by comparing a Pass 1 listing with the .LST file that you really understand the source of phase errors. Finally, use appropriate segment overrides to fix them.

CHAPTER 10

THE COMPLETE 8086/8088 INSTRUCTION SET

SECTION 1 PREVIEW

It is finally time for us to examine the entire **8088** instruction set. The instructions break naturally into various categories such as program control, data movement, and arithmetic types, and these are all explored in the following sections.

Some instructions, the binary coded decimal operations for example, are definitely of lesser importance. Nevertheless, for completeness, these are discussed in Section 6.

The string instructions are the most interesting group that we have not yet used. They are analyzed in detail in Section 8.

Rather than cluttering the discussion of each instruction with information about its effect on the flags, it seemed easier on the reader to include this information only when it was vital to the understanding of the instruction. The general effects of the different classes of instructions on the flags are presented in tabular form in Section 10.

SECTION 2 UNCONDITIONAL PROGRAM TRANSFER INSTRUCTIONS

We will first present the family of program control instructions, many of which we have seen and used already. The program control instructions break into two general groups: the

TABLE 10.1 UNCONDITIONAL PROGRAM TRANSFER INSTRUCTIONS

MNEMONIC	ALLOWED FORMATS	
call	call	[NEAR PTR] nearLabel
	call	[FAR PTR] farLabel
	call	Reg16
	call	[WORD PTR] Mem16
	call	[DWORD PTR] Mem32
ret	ret	[2n]
	retn	[2n]
	retf	[2n]
jmp	jmp	[SHORT] shortLabel
	jmp	[NEAR PTR] nearLabel
	jmp	[FAR PTR] farLabel
	jmp	Reg16
	jmp	[WORD PTR] Mem16
	jmp	[DWORD PTR] Mem32
int	int	Immed8
iret	iret	
into	into	

unconditional jumps, such as **call** and **jmp**, and the *conditional jumps* such as **je** and **jcxz**.

Table 10.1 shows the unconditional jumps, together with their allowable formats.

The **call** instruction should be very familiar. We know that it transfers program control to the target (which, until now, has generally been a procedure name) and pushes a two- or four-byte return address onto the stack.

The syntax for **call** is nearly identical to that for **jmp**, and so we will only discuss **jmp** in detail. One difference between the two is that **jmp** has an additional legal format (using **SHORT**). Another difference is that, by default, each forward **jmp** is assumed to be **NEAR** regardless of any **MODEL** directive that may be in effect, whereas in the case of **call** the default **NEAR** is overridden by a **MODEL** directive and the choice between **NEAR** and **FAR** that matches the particular model is used. The information in the next few paragraphs (except as it relates to the **SHORT** form) applies equally well to **call**.

The first three alternatives for **jmp** are of the general format

```
jmp     Label
```

We have seen that *Label* can be defined in the code in a number of ways: for example, by using the standard convention that an identifier followed by a colon is a label, or by the **PROC** directive. We will see in Chapter 12 that it is also possible to use the **LABEL** directive to specify code and data labels.

The **SHORT** modifier should be used when the target of the **jmp** is a forward reference, located no more than 127 bytes ahead.

Similarly, the modifiers **NEAR** and **FAR** need only be used in the case of forward references or where the labels are defined by **EXTRN**s. There are interesting distinctions between the machine encodings of the three forms of the

```
jmp          Label
```

instruction. In the **FAR** case, the target is stored as an actual address — not as an offset from the present code location. In the other two forms, the target is stored as a 8- or a 16-bit signed offset, in the **SHORT** and **NEAR** cases, respectively. This suggests that in the **NEAR** case the **jmp** should be limited to targets that are no further than 35768 bytes behind or 35767 bytes ahead in the segment. Luckily, this is not correct, and in fact a **NEAR jmp** can have as target any location in the current code segment. The reason is that **NEAR jmp**s use segment "wraparound" in determining their targets. In other words, if adding the displacement associated with the **jmp** to the starting offset produces an answer that is not between 0 and 64K, then the quantity 64K is added or subtracted from the answer to bring it within that range. Equivalently, if the segment is thought of as wrapped around a circle of circumference 64K, then any signed single-word displacement ends up at the correct place on the circle.

It might be expected that **SHORT jmp**s would work the same way. In other words, if the **jmp** instruction is located within 50 bytes of the end of the segment, for example, and the target is within 50 bytes of the beginning of the segment, then (using wraparound) the displacement is no more than 100 bytes in the forward direction, and so should be reachable by a **SHORT jmp**. There is probably no really good reason why the processor does not work this way — it just doesn't. Of course, this configuration occurs rather infrequently!

These observations are illustrated in the sample program of Figure 10.1 and in Figure 10.2, which contains parts of some **CODEVIEW** screens associated with that program.

In Figure 10.1, we have introduced lots of empty space into the code by using the **ORG** directive. Figure 10.2 shows that **MASM** fills these skipped areas of the code segment with zero bytes. The main points to be noticed in Figure 10.1 and Figure 10.2 are

Line 12. The op-code for **jmp** is 0E9H, and the rest of the machine encoding gives the relative displacement, as can be easily checked.

Line 14. The op-code is 0EAH this time but, since it is a **FAR jmp**, the machine code contains the target address 56D6:0510, rather than an offset.

Line 19. The **NEAR jmp** has displacement nearly the whole length of the segment and so works only because of wraparound. It is a good exercise to check the arithmetic and verify that the recorded displacement 0FADDH is really correct.

Line 24. This line is commented out because **MASM** would not accept it. It shows that wraparound does not work with **SHORT** jumps. Taking wraparound into account, the displacement would only be about 20 bytes.

Although we have not used the form

```
jmp          Reg16
```

FIGURE 10.1 EXAMPLES OF JUMPS

```
1     TITLE Prog10_1.asm: examples of jumping to a label
2
3     DOSSEG
4     .MODEL SMALL
5
6     .CODE
7
8      Start:
9
10         mov    ax, @DATA
11         mov    ds, ax
12         jmp    Target1            ;defaults to NEAR PTR -- machine code
13                                   ;   contains distance to be jumped
14         jmp    FAR PTR Target1    ;machine code contains actual address
15         org    500h               ;   of target so this is not a relative
16                                   ;      jump
17     Target1:
18
19         jmp    Target2            ;the distance to the target is  8000h
20         org    0ffe0h             ;   but it still works because of
21                                   ;      segment wraparound
22     Target2:
23
24         ;jmp   SHORT Target1      ;not everything works; including
25         mov    ax, 4c00h          ;   wraparound, this is about 20 bytes
26         int    21h                ;      from target, but it won't work
27
28     END Start
```

before, it is self-explanatory. The value of the 16-bit register *Reg16* is treated as the offset part of a target address. Here is a typical application of the register form of the **jmp**:

```
mov        ax,  OFFSET Code1
cmp        Something, 10
jne        @F
mov        ax,  OFFSET Code2

@@:

    jmp        ax

Code1:
    .
    .
    jmp        @F

Code2:
    .
    .
@@:
```

FIGURE 10.2 CODEVIEW SCREENS FROM PROG10_1

```
#File  View  Search  Run  Watch  Options  Language  Calls  Help # F8=Trace F5=Go
############################## Prog10_1.asm ###################################
START:                                                          # AX = 0000
10:        mov   ax, @DATA                                       # BX = 0000
56D6:0010 B8D566           MOV       AX,66D5                     # CX = 0000
11:        mov   ds, ax                                          # DX = 0000
56D6:0013 8ED8             MOV       DS,AX                       # SP = 0000
12:        jmp   Target1                      ;defaults to NEAR PT# BP = 0000
56D6:0015 E9F804           JMP       TARGET1 (0510)              # SI = 0000
14:        jmp   FAR PTR Target1              ;machine code contai# DI = 0000
56D6:0018 EA1005D656       JMP       56D6:0510                   # DS = 56C6
56D6:001D 0000             ADD       Byte Ptr [BX+SI],AL         # ES = 56C6
56D6:001F 0000             ADD       Byte Ptr [BX+SI],AL         # SS = 56D6



#File  View  Search  Run  Watch  Options  Language  Calls  Help # F8=Trace F5=Go
############################## Prog10_1.asm ###################################
TARGET1:                                                        # AX = 66D5
19:        jmp   Target2                   ;the distance to the# BX = 0000
56D6:0510 E9DDFA           JMP       TARGET2 (FFF0)              # CX = 0000
56D6:0513 0000             ADD       Byte Ptr [BX+SI],AL         # DX = 0000
56D6:0515 0000             ADD       Byte Ptr [BX+SI],AL         # SP = 0000



#File  View  Search  Run  Watch  Options  Language  Calls  Help # F8=Trace F5=Go
############################## Prog10_1.asm ###################################
TARGET2:                                                        # AX = 66D5
25:        mov   ax, 4c00h                ;  wraparound, this # BX = 0000
56D6:FFF0 B8004C           MOV       AX,4C00                     # CX = 0000
26:        int   21h                      ;   from target, bu# DX = 0000
56D6:FFF3 CD21             INT       21                          # SP = 0000
```

The code after label *Code1* is executed if *Something* = 10, and the code after label *Code2* is executed in the contrary case.

The various types of jumps and calls shown in Table 10.1 are sometimes referred to by the following names:

• Forms like

```
        call      nearLabel
```

that refer to an explicit code address are called *memory direct*.

• Forms such as

```
        jmp       Mem16
```

that jump to an address stored in a memory location are called *memory indirect*.

• Forms such as

```
call     Reg16
```

that jump to an address contained in a register are called *register indirect*.

The memory forms of the **jmp** instruction are very interesting since they can use any of the addressing modes. One nice application of these types is in the construction of jump tables. A *jump table* is just a generalization of the previous example. Suppose that instead of two choices, the result of a computation gives rise to one of a finite number of outcomes, and that corresponding to each of these outcomes, a different block of code must be executed. In **FORTRAN**, this construct is given the rather descriptive name *computed goto*.

We will build a somewhat more elaborate example to illustrate a jump table. Suppose that we are envisioning the possibility of four outcomes, say 0, 1, 2, and 3, from a computation, and that corresponding to each of these outcomes we will make a **FAR** jump to a certain block of code. In the data segment we might build an array as follows:

```
jumpTable     DD        Address0
              DD        Address1
              DD        Address2
              DD        Address3
```

We assume that the double word *Address0* has been initialized to contain the offset and segment, in that order, of the code to be executed in case 0, and so on.

Suppose that the prior code left the outcome of the computation in the **di** register. The **jmp** code can be written like this:

```
shl   di, 1        ;index into jumpTable -- must multiply
shl   di, 1        ; by 4 since it is a table of dwords
jmp   jumpTable[di]
```

An interesting sidelight is that this code will work as planned, whether the data precede the code or conversely. Of course, it is totally reasonable that it works if the data come first, since then **MASM** knows that *jumpTable* has type **DWORD**, and hence generates the right kind of **jmp** in Pass 1. But if the code comes first, it would seem that **MASM** would incorrectly use its default **WORD PTR** when generating the **jmp**, and then discover its mistake on the second pass. In fact, this is exactly what happens. But no phase error results, since both the **WORD PTR** and **DWORD PTR** forms of the instruction have the same length (four bytes). If the Pass 1 and Pass 2 listings are compared, it will be seen that **MASM** does actually correct the Pass 1 code during Pass 2.

It is important to remember when to use **NEAR** or **FAR**, as opposed to **WORD** or **DWORD**. **MASM** is quite consistent in its usage. The words **NEAR** and **FAR** are always used with reference to code labels, while **WORD** and **DWORD** are used with memory references. This distinction will be elaborated on when we talk about the **LABEL** directive.

The **ret** instruction is an old friend by now. It is nearly always used with the **call** instruction. It is seldom necessary to use the **retn** (*NEAR return*) or **retf** (*FAR return*) forms, since **MASM** automatically makes the choice that matches the **call**. An exception to this statement occurs when the programmer chooses to synthesize a **FAR** call from a **jmp** by writing

```
push    cs
push    ip
jmp     farTarget
```

where *farTarget* is not defined as a procedure. Under these circumstances it is necessary to return with an explicit **retf**, since using **ret** would cause **MASM** to generate a **retn**, by default.

The interrupt instruction, **int**, is used to call an *interrupt handler*. Hence **int** is rather like **call**. More precisely, here is what the

```
int     n
```

instruction does:

- Pushes the flags register.
- Clears the trap flag and the interrupt flag.
- Pushes **cs**.
- Pushes **ip**.
- Transfers control to address stored at 0000:4*n.

This means that an **int n** can be synthesized by the instructions

```
pushf
xor     ax, ax
mov     es, ax
call    DWORD PTR es:(4*n)
```

where n is a constant (or has been specified by an **EQUATE**), provided that clearing the trap and interrupt flags is not important. We will use this fact in Chapter 16. A complete discussion of **int** must wait until that chapter, but here are the basic ideas. There are convincing reasons why debuggers should not try to trace into certain interrupt code, and the clearing of the trap flag gives insurance against this happening accidentally. (It is easy to subvert this protection mechanism, if desired.) Likewise, it is sometimes important that interrupt code should not itself be interrupted by hardware interrupts, and this is why the interrupt flag is cleared. Before the flags register is changed, a copy is pushed onto the stack (by the **pushf** instruction) so that it can be restored afterwards. At this point, the **int** instruction acts like an indirect **FAR** call to the address stored at location 0000:4*n, where n is the number of the interrupt. This address is used because the addresses of the interrupt handlers are stored as *interrupt vectors* in low machine memory. Specifically, the address of the code executed by the instruction

```
int     n
```

is contained in the four bytes beginning at absolute address 0000:4*n.

Iret is the *return from interrupt* instruction. It performs the operations required to undo an **int**: first it pops **ip** and **cs** and does a **FAR** return, and then it pops the flags register to restore its original value.

The **into** instruction (*interrupt on overflow*) is basically a conditional jump to the **int 04H** code, since it triggers an **int 04H** if the overflow flag is set. A typical use of **into** involves lines such as

```
add       ax, bx
into
```

The effect of this code is to call **int 04H** if the **add** instruction produced a signed overflow. An obvious question to ask is exactly what happens when **int 04H** executes, and the answer is — nothing! The default **int 04H** code consists solely of an **iret** instruction. The programmer who wishes to use **into** for overflow detection must first substitute a new **int 04h** handler that will do the "correct thing." The nature of the "correct thing" depends on the circumstances: perhaps to abort the program, or possibly to invite the user to submit different input. The techniques used in writing interrupt handlers will be presented in Chapter 15.

Exercise 10-1. Check by hand calculation that the displacements on lines 12 and 19 of Figure 10.2 are correct.

Exercise 10-2. Write an integer calculator that can be used from the **DOS** command line. It should perform the four basic operations. For example, in response to the input

```
calc 4000 / 1000
```

it should give the answer

```
quotient = 4  remainder = 0
```

It should also warn of overflow. The main mechanism of the calculator should be a jump table that directs control to the correct operation, depending on whether '+', '-', '*', or '/' appears as the second command-line parameter.

Exercise 10-3. A **push** instruction occurring when **sp** = 0 signals the beginning of *stack overflow* on the **8088**. If a **push** instruction is executed when **sp** = 0, at what address are the data stored? The two obvious candidates are

```
ss:0000 - 2
```

or, if the processor uses wraparound,

```
ss:fffe
```

SECTION 3 CONDITIONAL PROGRAM TRANSFER INSTRUCTIONS

We have already had extensive experience with the conditional transfers, and so the list presented in Table 10.2 contains no surprises.

At first glance, the number of conditional jumps given in Table 10.2 may seem somewhat daunting, but it requires only a few minutes' study to get them under control.

To begin with, the first column lists alternate names for many of these jumps. These alternate names are quite reasonable. For example, the alternate name for **ja** (*jump if above*) is **jnbe** (*jump if not below or equal*). But the alternate names are frequently longer and do represent an extra memory burden and so we do not use them. Arguable exceptions to this policy are the alternate name **jz** (*jump if zero*) for **je** (*jump if equal*) and the corresponding pair **jne/jnz**. Depending on the context, one or other of the choices may better document the meaning of the instruction. Specifically, if used after a **cmp**, then the **je** form is probably better, while the **jz** form is marginally better after an arithmetic instruction. We do not consistently observe this usage.

The next general observation about Table 10.2 is that about one-fourth of the instructions contain an 'a' or a 'b' (**ja, jae,** ⋯) and about one-fourth are identical except that the 'a' or 'b' has been replaced by a 'g' or an 'l' (**jg, jge,** ⋯). The distinction here is that the 'a' and 'b' (standing for "above" and "below") refer to *unsigned* comparisons, while the 'g' and 'l' (meaning "greater than" and "less than") refer to *signed* comparisons. In other words, the 'a' and 'b' types are intended for use in unsigned arithmetic, while the 'g' and 'l' types are used in signed arithmetic. As a trivial example, consider

```
mov     ax, -1
mov     bx, 1
cmp     ax, bx
jb      Target1
jl      Target2
```

Since, with an unsigned interpretation, **ax** has value 65535, the jump to *Target1* will not be taken, but the jump to *Target2* will occur.

The final item of interest in Table 10.2 is the last-column, which shows flag values needed to trigger each of the jumps. While the programmer seldom need worry about the exact flag settings that induce a given conditional jump, it is nevertheless amusing to check on the correctness of some of these entries. Many are obvious, such as **jc**. Non-obvious examples are **jg, jge, jl,** and **jle**. Here is how one verifies the last column entries in these instances. We will just consider the 8-bit case, since it is easier to write out the details. The 16-bit case is analogous.

We begin by determining which pairs of values {*Op1, Op2*} will cause the jump to be taken in the sequence

```
cmp     Op1, Op2
jl      Target
```

The **jl** will occur provided *Op1* < *Op2* when *Op1* and *Op2* are interpreted as signed integers. Since *Op1* and *Op2* are in the 8-bit signed range, $-128 \le Op1$ and $Op2 \le 127$. Hence

```
-255 ≤ Op1 - Op2 < 0
```

This outcome allows only two possibilities:

TABLE 10.2 THE CONDITIONAL JUMPS

MNEMONIC	MEANING ("JUMP IF···")	CONDITION TESTED
ja/jnbe	above	CF = 0 and ZF = 0
jae/jnb	above or equal	CF = 0
jb/jnae	below	CF = 1
jbe/jna	below or equal	ZF = 1 or CF = 1
jc	carry	CF = 1
jnc	no carry	CF = 0
jg/jnle	greater than	SF = OF and ZF = 0
jge/jnl	greater than or equal	SF = OF
jl/jnge	less than	SF ≠ OF and ZF = 0
jle/jng	less than or equal	SF ≠ OF
jo	overflow	OF = 1
jno	no overflow	OF = 0
je/jz	equal	ZF = 1
jne/jnz	not equal	ZF = 0
jp/jpe	parity	PF = 1
jnp/jpo	no parity	PF = 0
js	sign	SF = 1
jns	no sign	SF = 0
jcxz	cx equals 0	CX = 0
loop	cx not 0	CX = 0
loope/loopz	cx not 0 and equality	CX = 0 and ZF = 1
loopne/loopnz	cx not 0 and not equality	CX = 0 and ZF = 0

1. If $-128 \leq$ Op1 $-$ Op2 < 0 then SF $= 1$ and OF $= 0$.
2. If $-255 \leq$ Op1 $-$ Op2 < -128 then SF $= 0$ and OF $= 1$.

This show that if a **jl** occurs, then SF $\neq$ OF. By an almost identical argument, the reader can show that if a **jge** occurs, then SF $=$ OF. Putting these pieces together will complete the verification, and the reader will be asked to do this in one of the exercises.

A final aspect of the conditional jumps, encountered many times already, is their limited range. Recall that in the machine encoding of an instruction such as

```
je      Target
```

the information about *Target* is stored as a one-byte signed offset from the present location in the code. This restricts the effective range to between 128 bytes in the backward direction and 127 bytes in the forward direction. In the event that *Target* is beyond the range of a conditional jump, **MASM** emits a very clear error message and the programmer must amend the code. The standard workaround that we have presented is the "jump over a jump."

We have chosen to place **loop** and its relatives, **loope** and **loopne**, with the conditional jumps. Even though they perform an additional task (decrementing **cx**), they do indeed make a conditional jump, and also suffer from the range limitation of the other conditional jumps.

The **loope** instruction is just like **loop**, except that it checks the zero flag as well as checking **cx**, and only continues to loop while ZF = 1 and **cx** ≠ 0. **Loopne** is identical, except that it requires ZF = 0 and **cx** ≠ 0 in order to loop.

A typical use of **loopne** is to control a loop containing a **cmp**. For example, **loopne** can be used in this way to find the first occurrence of a given character in a string. As an illustration, the following code fragment uses this technique to find the null terminator of an ASCIIZ string and leaves the length of the string in **cx**.

```
        xor     cx, cx  ;same effect as 65536
        xor     al, al  ;look for null terminator
        mov     bx, OFFSET Str - 1

@@:

        inc     bx
        cmp     [bx], al
        loopne  @B
        inc     cx
        neg     cx          ;cx now contains the length
```

We have already considered the logic underlying this computation (in Chapter 8) but, for the sake of review, we will outline it again. Since **cx** is the loop counter, it must be made large enough to ensure that the loop will not terminate before the null terminator is reached. Consequently **cx** is initialized to 0, which effectively sets it to 65536. **Cx** is decremented by one for each character in the string, including the null terminator; hence the last two lines modify **cx** correctly so that its final value is the string length.

The reader may wonder about the use of the two instructions

```
        xor     al, al
            .
            .
        cmp     [bx], al
```

rather than the single line

```
        cmp     BYTE PTR [bx], 0
```

They are used because this second form of the **cmp** instruction requires one more clock cycle than the first form. The loop will usually be traversed a number of times and so the one-cycle-per-iteration time saving from the faster form of **cmp** more than pays for the extra

```
        xor     al, al
```

instruction. Granted, the faster version requires several extra bytes of code, which might in rare instances swing the balance in favor of the slower form.

Another point is that the fragment initializes **bx** to *OFFSET Str – 1* and then increments **bx** before it is used in the **cmp** instruction, in order that **bx** will actually point to the first character in the string when the **cmp** is reached for the first time. The following fragment seems to achieve the same effect less clumsily:

```
                          mov       bx, OFFSET Str

              @:

                          cmp       [bx], al
                          inc       bx
                          loopne            @B
```

Why was this substitute code not used? The answer is that, as we shall see in Section 10, **inc** changes most of the standard flags, including ZF. Consequently, the second version would continue to loop until **bx = 0**.

The typical uses of **loope** are quite similar to the application of **loopne** in the previous example. It can be used to find the first character in a string that fails to match a specified character. As an exercise, the reader might write a fragment to find the first non-space character in an ASCIIZ string. (Doing this neatly requires computing the string length in advance, say by using the previous fragment.)

Exercise 10-4. Write a procedure that receives as an input the offset of a null-terminated buffer, which it searches for the first occurrence of the word *horse*. If the word occurs, the procedure should return the beginning offset in **ax**; otherwise, it should return 0.
Suggestion: Problems of this kind are most easily solved by means of a *transition diagram:*

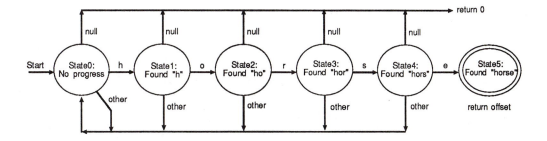

The basic idea of this transition diagram is that the *states* measure the progress that has been made toward identifying *horse*. For example, being in State0 means that we have made no progress, while being in State2 corresponds to "ho" having been identified. If an 's' is received in State2, we transfer to State 3; if the null terminator is received, we return the value 0; and if any other character is received, we start over, i.e., transfer to State0. State5 is the *final state*: we have found the entire word.

To solve the problem, implement the transition diagram with the help of a jump table.

Exercise 10-5. Repeat the previous exercise, but this time search for the string *abcabd*.

Exercise 10-6. Discuss the problem of translating the **Pascal** *case statement* or the **C** *switch statement* into assembly language and provide an example.
Suggestion: Use a jump table.

Exercise 10-7.
 a. Complete the arguments needed to verify that the flag settings given for **jg, jge, jl**, and **jle** in Table 10.2 are correct.
b. Provide the corresponding arguments to show that these flag settings are also correct in the 16- and 32-bit cases.

SECTION 4 DATA TRANSFER INSTRUCTIONS

The data transfer instructions are shown in Table 10.3. Again, many of these instructions have already been used repeatedly, and need not be reviewed here.

The first unfamiliar instruction in the list is **xchg**, which interchanges the values of its two operands. Of course, it obeys the standard restrictions on the allowable operand types in two-operand instructions. In particular, it cannot be used to directly interchange the contents of two memory locations. For instance, if *Var1* is a word-sized memory variable, then interchanging the values of *Var1* and *WORD PTR [bx + si + 2]* requires a sequence such as

```
mov       ax, Var1
xchg      ax, [bx + si + 2]
mov       Var1, ax
```

If this is done minimally with the **mov** instruction, it requires a total of four instructions and the use of two registers. On the other hand, each **mov** instruction is about twice as fast as an **exch** and so, even at that, the **mov** version is faster!

We have already used **xlat** a number of times. It provides an efficient way of translating an index into a table of byte-size data into the corresponding value from that table. It can be used to give a fast translation between different character sets (ASCII to EBCDIC, for example) or as the basis for simple substitution codes. The **xlat** instruction requires that **ds:bx** point to the byte array and replaces the value in **al** with the **al**-th element from the array.

The **8088** communicates with hardware devices by means of *ports*. A port is an address at which an input/output device is connected, and data are sent to the device by sending it to that port, or are input from the device by reading it from the port. A port address can be any value in the range 0000H to FFFFH. The **out** instruction is used to output data to a port and the **in** instruction reads data from a port. The syntax for both instructions is identical, except for the order of the operands, and so we will only consider **in**. There are two forms of this instruction:

```
in        Accum, Immed8
```

and

```
in        Accum, dx
```

```
TABLE 10.3  THE DATA TRANSFER INSTRUCTIONS


MNEMONIC                              OPERATION PERFORMED

mov                                   move a byte or a word
push                                  push a word onto the stack
pop                                   pop a word off the stack
xchg                                  exchange two bytes or two words
xlat                                  translate from a table

in                                    input a byte or a word from a port
out                                   output a byte or a word from a port

lea                                   load effective address
lds                                   load segment:offset using ds
les                                   load segment:offset using es

lahf                                  load 8080 flags from ah
sahf                                  save 8080 flags in ah
pushf                                 push the flags onto the stack
popf                                  pop the flags off the stack
```

The *Accum* operand must be either **al** or **ax**, and this choice determines whether a byte or a word is read. In the first case, *Immed8* means an 8-bit immediate value that is interpreted as the port address. In particular, the first form can only be used to read from ports 00H-0FFH. In the second form, the second operand must be the **dx** register, and its value is again interpreted as the port address. Hence, the second form can be used to read from any port. If the time required to load **dx** is ignored, the second form of the instruction is actually faster than the first.

We have already encountered the **lea** instruction in Chapter 6, but will briefly review it here. **Lea** means *load effective address*. Since the effective address of a datum is a synonym for its offset, the following two instructions are, to a first approximation, equivalent:

```
        mov     bx, OFFSET String
        lea     bx, String
```

There are a number of distinctions between them. First, the **lea** instruction generates code that is one byte longer and so, all other things being equal, the standard **OFFSET** form of the instruction is preferred.

But there are other factors involved. For example, we will see in Chapter 12 that when the **GROUP** directive is used, the **OFFSET** directive may not work as expected, and so there are circumstances under which it should be avoided.

But the most important distinction between the two instructions is that **OFFSET** is a directive to **MASM**, while **lea** is a machine instruction. Consequently, *OFFSET String* is evaluated by **MASM**, with later adjustments made by **LINK**. This means that the instruction

```
        mov     bx, OFFSET String
```

is transmitted to the microprocessor as an instance of the

```
mov     bx, Immed16
```

instruction. In particular, the value of *OFFSET String* is immutably set by run time. On the other hand, **lea** is executed by the machine, and so the value of the second operand that is ultimately loaded into **bx** will be the actual run-time value.

This distinction is not significant in the preceding example, but consider a case such as

```
lea     bx, String[di]
```

The microprocessor will successfully execute this instruction, using the run-time value of **di** and computing the corresponding value for the offset of *String[di]*. Of course, the **OFFSET** directive would not work here.

Neither **lds** nor **les** is an essential instruction. They give the programmer the capacity to load a two-word address using a single line of code. Suppose, for example, that the data segment contains the definition

```
farAddress   DD  ?
```

and that *farAddress* has been initialized to contain the *segment:offset* of some location in memory. As always, the offset should be stored in the low word and the segment in the high word. The instruction

```
lds     bx, farAddress
```

then loads the segment part of *farAddress* into **ds** and the offset part into **bx**. In other words, this single instruction is equivalent to the two instructions

```
mov     bx, WORD PTR farAddress
mov     ds, WORD PTR farAddress[2]
```

The **les** instruction is totally analogous.

The **lahf** and **sahf** instructions are relics of the past. In the early days of the **8088**, it was important that code written for the **8080** be easily ported to the new processors. These two instructions were provided to make this porting simpler. Respectively, they save a copy of the **8080** flags in **ah**, and restore these flags from **ah**. The **8080** flags are a subset of the **8088** flags, namely SF, ZF, AF, PF, and CF. These flags all reside in the low half of the flags register, and so **lahf** and **sahf** really load or restore the lower "half-flags" register in **ah**. We will see in Chapter 17 that **sahf** does have an interesting use in programming the numerical coprocessors.

The final two instructions are self-explanatory. The **pushf** instruction saves a copy of the flags register by pushing it onto the stack, while **popf** pops the top element of the stack into the flags register.

SECTION 5 BINARY ARITHMETIC INSTRUCTIONS

The **8088** binary arithmetic instructions are shown in Table 10.4. The **8088** also includes some supporting operations for a different kind of arithmetic, called binary coded decimal, which we will consider in the next section.

The first three instructions in Table 10.4 are variants of addition, and of these the only new one is **adc**, *add with carry*. The effect of

```
adc       Op1, Op2
```

is to replace *Op1* by

```
Op1 + Op2 + CF
```

The primary application of **adc** is in *multiple-precision arithmetic*, where decimal integers are stored in several words, rather than in a single word. For example, if the contents of a doubleword are interpreted as the unsigned bit pattern of a decimal integer, then that integer can be in the range

$$0 \text{ to } 4,294,967,295 \ (= 2^{32} - 1)$$

While this *double-precision* range is certainly more satisfactory for doing arithmetic than is the standard *single-precision* range of

$$0 \text{ to } 65535 \ (= 2^{16} - 1)$$

it is still inadequate for many applications, and so we must also consider *triple-precision integers*, which are stored in 48 bits; *quadruple-precision* integers, which are stored in 64 bits; and so on. In fact, it is customary to write multiple-precision procedures that will work in the general case, i.e., they manipulate multiple-precision integers of precision N, where N can be selected to suit the problem at hand. In Chapter 11, we will provide quite general multiple-precision routines, although they will take advantage of the 32-bit registers of the **80386** by using 32-bit arithmetic throughout.

In this chapter, we will just establish the basic principles in order to demonstrate the use of instructions such as **adc**. Consequently, the double-precision case will generally be sufficient. For the moment, we will refer to double-precision integers as DPIs.

In setting up a new structure, such as DPI, it is important to establish conventions that are as compatible as possible with the machine architecture. The **8088** always stores multi-byte quantities with the least significant part in the lowest memory address, and so we should use this convention in our double-precision arithmetic. Consequently, when an integer is stored in memory as 32 bits, the bits should be allocated to the two words according to the scheme depicted in Figure 10.3.

For example, the integer 1 will be stored with a 1 in the low word and a 0 in the high word, while 65536 will be stored with a 0 in the low word and a 1 in the high word.

Now contemplate the process of adding two of these DPIs. The basic algorithm should perform bit-by-bit addition starting with bit 0. In particular, if the low words are added using

---

TABLE 10.4 THE BINARY ARITHMETIC INSTRUCTIONS

MNEMONIC	OPERATION PERFORMED
add	add bytes or words
adc	add bytes or words with carry
inc	increment byte or word
sub	subtract bytes or words
sbb	subtract bytes or words with borrow
dec	decrement byte or word
mul	unsigned 8- or 16-bit multiply
imul	signed 8- or 16-bit multiply
div	unsigned 8- or 16-bit division
idiv	signed 8- or 16-bit division
neg	negate byte or word
cmp	compare bytes or words
cbw	sign extended conversion byte to word
cwd	sign extended conversion word to doubleword

---

the 16-bit **add** instruction, then the 16-bit answer will be the low word of the double-precision answer. The high word of the double-precision answer can likewise be obtained by adding the two high words *except* that the carry out of bit 15, if there is one, must be added to the high-word total. If the low-word addition generates a carry, the carry flag will be set and so it suffices to add the value of the carry flag when doing the high-word addition.

This means that our addition algorithm can be reformulated as

• Add the low words using the 16-bit add instruction.

• Before doing any other operation that will change the carry flag, perform an **adc** using the high words.

This shows how **adc** enters naturally into double-precision arithmetic (and analogously into arithmetic of higher precision). We will complete this discussion by writing a macro that does double-precision addition.

For concreteness in this and the ensuing examples, we assume that our DPIs are declared in the data segment with definitions of the form

```
        doubleInt    DW    2 DUP(?)
```

Rather than overwriting the first addend with the answer, our addition macro assigns the answer to a third DPI. We assume that all DPIs have been defined in the segment pointed to by **ds** and are passed as the macro arguments. Here is the macro:

```
doubAdd     MACRO    Answer, First, Second

    push    ax
```

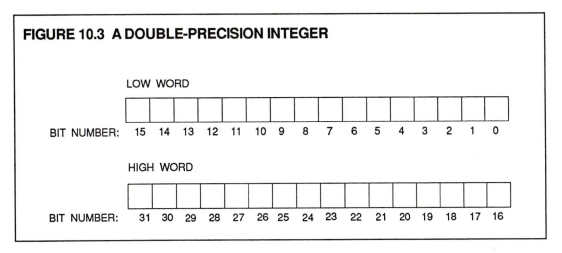

FIGURE 10.3 A DOUBLE-PRECISION INTEGER

```
push    bx
push    di
push    si

lea     di, First       ;point di to first DPI
lea     si, Second      ;point si to second DPI
lea     bx, Answer      ;point bx to Ans
mov     ax, [di]
add     ax, [si]
mov     [bx], ax
mov     ax, [di+2]
adc     ax, [si+2]
mov     [bx+2], ax

pop     si
pop     di
pop     bx
pop     ax
```

ENDM

There are two **mov** instructions between the **add** that deposits the carry out of bit 15 in the carry flag and the **adc** that uses it. This is not dangerous since **mov** instructions do not affect the flags. A typical high word is addressed as [**si** + 2] because displacements are always in bytes.

The reader may have realized that the testing of *doubAdd* presents certain problems. To submit test data easily to the macro, we need a routine that will accept an alphanumeric string such as 100000 and convert it to a DPI and, likewise, a routine that will convert a DPI back to an alphanumeric string. In other words, we need double-precision analogs of the *ascBin16* and *bin16Asc* procedures developed in Chapter 6. (One of the exercises at the end of Chapter 7 asked the reader to construct such procedures.) Later in this section and in the exercises we will also need input and output procedures for triple- and higher-precision integers. The program disk contains conversion procedures that work for arbitrary values of the precision. Since the code for these procedures is not very interesting — it consists of fairly obvious extensions of the *ascBin16* and *bin16Asc* code — we have not reproduced it in the text. The use of these procedures and of the macros that call them is discussed in the exercises at the end of this section.

The next three instructions are just the subtractive analogs of the three addition instructions. Again, the only new one is **sbb**, subtract with borrow.

```
sbb       Op1, Op2
```

leaves *Op2* unchanged and replaces *Op1* with

```
Op1 - Op2 - CF
```

Its use is exactly analogous to **adc**. When doing the high half of a double-precision subtraction, the high words of the operands are subtracted, but if there is borrow from bit 16 to bit 15, an extra one must be subtracted. If this borrow is needed, the carry flag will be set after the low-word subtraction, and so an **sbb** of the high words accounts for it. In one of the exercises, we ask the reader to implement a *doubSub* macro in this way.

We are already familiar with the various forms of the **mul** instruction. Recall that the 16-bit **mul** works as follows: the instruction

```
mul       Op
```

causes *Op*, a 16-bit operand bit operand, which must be a register or memory reference, to be multiplied by **ax**. The answer is computed as a double-precision integer, with its low word in **ax** and its high word in **dx**. The 8-bit **mul** has basically the same syntax: the instruction

```
mul       Op
```

multiplies *Op*, an 8-bit register or memory reference, by **al** and records the answer as a 16-bit integer in **ax**.

An important point to remember about **mul** is that it gives *unsigned* multiplication. In the 8-bit case, for example 0FFH multiplied by 0FFH using **mul** gives answer 255*255, not 1. The analogous instruction that does signed multiplication is **imul** (where the *i* connotes "integer"). The syntax of **imul** is exactly the same as that of **mul**. It, too, comes in 8- and 16-bit varieties. An 8-bit multiplication of 0FFH by 0FFH using **imul** *will* give 1 as an answer.

The situation for **div** precisely parallels that for **mul**. So far, we have used only the unsigned version, although we did discuss *idiv*, the signed version, in Chapter 7. The instruction

```
div       Op
```

divides *Op*, again a 16-bit register of memory reference, into the 32-bit double-precision integer whose low word is in **ax** and whose high word is in **dx**. The answer is recorded as a 16-bit integer in **ax**, and the remainder as a 16-bit integer in **dx**.

In the 8-bit case, the instruction

```
           div        Op
```

divides *Op*, this time an 8-bit register or memory reference, into **ax**, recording the quotient as an 8-bit integer in **al**, and the remainder as an 8-bit integer in **ah**.

Idiv is used in exactly the same way as **div**.

In Chapter 3, we pointed out an unpleasant aspect of **div** (which also holds for **idiv**). Namely, the answer may not fit in the register provided. For example, in the 8-bit case (signed or unsigned), **ax** might contain 1000 and *Op* have value 2, in which case the quotient would not fit in **al**, the appointed register. Under these circumstances, a type 00H interrupt will be generated. **Int 00H** is a hardware interrupt, which means that it is generated by a hardware event. In this case, the hardware event is that the quotient is too big. **Int 00H** is called *divide overflow*. The default **int 00H** interrupt handler prints a message that says "Divide overflow" and terminates the program by returning control to **DOS**. It is necessary, in many serious applications programs, to take over **int 00H** and replace its code with a new handler that responds in a more sympathetic manner.

We will now give an example of multiple-precision multiplication. Since **mul** already multiplies two 16-bit operands to give a double-precision answer, we must go to higher precision in order to accomplish something new. The next higher level is to multiply a double-precision integer by a single-precision integer to get a triple-precision answer, and that will be our example. For reasons that will be discussed in the exercises, two's complement notation does not work well with multiple-precision multiplication and division, and so for the moment we will always interpret multiple-precision integers as unsigned and use **mul** and **div** as the building blocks in the corresponding multiple-precision operations. When we write our full-scale multiple-precision arithmetic package in Chapter 11, we will adopt a somewhat different tack. Namely, we will store multiple-precision integers in two's complement form but, before submitting them to the multiplication or division operations, we will negate them when necessary, so that the operands will always be non-negative.

The algorithms for multiple-precision operations are most easily understood by making analogies with the usual decimal case. For example, the standard decimal analog of multiplying a double-precision by a single-precision is a computation such as 79 * 8. How is this done? This picture illustrates the very familiar process

```
         79
          8
       _____

         72
       56
       _____

       632
```

First, the low digit, 9, of the "double-precision" integer 79 is multiplied by the "single-precision" integer 8 to give a "double-precision" answer 72. Then the high digit, 7, of 79 is multiplied by 8 to give answer 56. 56 is moved one digit right (since its first factor was really 70 rather than 7) and added to the 72 to get the "triple-precision" answer 632.

Our multiple-precision multiplication is done in exactly the same way, except that "digit" now means "word." Stated differently, multiple-precision arithmetic is really arithmetic to base 2^{16}, rather than base 10. Taking into account the fact that our multiple-precision notation puts the low word on the right rather than on the left, the computation looks like

```
double prec:  LowWord     HighWord
single prec:  OnlyWord
             ─────────────────────────
             (LowWord * OnlyWord)
         0       (HighWord * OnlyWord)
             ─────────────────────────
(added with carries to give triple-precision answer)
```

The form of the macro call will be

```
         doubSingMul   Answer, First, Second
```

where *Answer* is a three-word buffer and *First* and *Second* are, respectively, the double-precision and single-precision factors. Here is the macro code:

```
doubSingMul   MACRO   Answer, First, Second

    push  ax
    push  bx
    push  di
    push  si

    lea   si, Second        ;point si to single-precision
    lea   ax, [si]          ;the single-precision int is now in ax
    lea   di, First         ;point di to double-precision
    mul   WORD PTR [di]     ;lowWord * onlyWord has been computed
    lea   bx, Answer        ;point bx to triple-precision
    mov   [bx], ax          ;deliver low word
    mov   [bx + 2], dx      ;deliver first part of middle word
    mov   ax, [si]          ;refresh ax
    mul   WORD PTR [di+2]   ;highWord * onlyWord has been computed
    add   [bx + 2], ax      ;deliver rest of middle word
    mov   WORD PTR [bx+4], 0 ;initialize this location to zero
    adc   [bx + 4], dx      ;deliver high word

    pop   si
    pop   di
    pop   bx
    pop   ax

ENDM
```

The code for *doubSingMul* should be comprehensible on account of our previous discussion. One point is worth mentioning. Since there may be a carry from *WORD PTR [bx + 2]* to *WORD PTR [bx + 4]*, an **adc** is used for the last **add**. Preparatory to using the

adc, it is important that *WORD PTR [bx + 4]* contain the value 0, and this explains the **mov** before the **adc**.

As an exercise, the reader will be asked to extend this example by writing a macro that multiplies two double-precision integers to give a quadruple-precision answer. The problem of multiple-precision division will also be explored in the exercises.

Of the four remaining arithmetic instructions, **neg** and **cmp** need no further discussion. The final two are **cbw** and **cwd**.

Cbw is *convert byte to word*. It uses **al** as its operand and sign-extends it to 16 bits, storing the answer in **ax**. Its primary uses are in arithmetic. For example, to do a 16-bit signed multiplication on an 8-bit quantity, move it to **al**, use **cbw**, and then perform a 16-bit **imul**.

Cwd, *convert word to double word*, is similar. It takes the quantity in **ax** and sign-extends it to 32 bits, leaving the low half in **ax** and storing the high half in **dx**. Of course, this might very well be used as a prelude to 16-bit signed division.

Remark on the Following Exercises. As we indicated in the preceding section, the Program Disk contains procedures and macros for the input and output of multiple-precision integers. The procedures have also been placed in USER.LIB. Since the macros are needed in the next few problems, we will now explain their use. The macros have the form

```
aToMp16    MACRO    mpInt, alphaNum
mp16ToA    MACRO    alphaNum, mpInt
```

aToMp16 converts the ASCIIZ string *alphaNum* to the multiple-precision *mpInt*, while *mp16ToA* does the reverse transformation. The rules for using these macros are simple:

- The source code must define a quantity named *Prec16* by means of an **EQUATE** and initialize it to the size of the multiple-precision integers (in words). All multiple-precision integers in the program should have precision equal to *Prec16*.

- The source code must also contain an **EQUATE** of the following form:

```
mp16Len    EQU    5*Prec16 + 1
```

A buffer of size *mp16Len* bytes is then large enough to hold the alphanumeric form of a multiple-precision integer of precision *Prec16*, including an optional sign but excluding the null terminator. To allow for the null terminator, each such buffer should be given minimal size *mp16Len + 1*.

- *Prec16* and *mp16Len* must be declared to be **PUBLIC** in the source file.

- To access the macros, the file CONSOLE.MAC must be included in the source file (using the **INCLUDE** directive).

The Program Disk also contains a short program named MPDEMO.ASM that demonstrates the use of these macros.

Exercise 10-8. Show by examples that even when multiple-precision integers are stored in two's complement form, **idiv** and **imul** cannot be used to fabricate multiple-precision multiplication and division operations.

Suggestion: It is sufficient to investigate what happens when a double-precision integer is multiplied or divided by a single-precision integer.

Exercise 10-9.
a. Write a *doubSub* analog of the *doubAdd* macro given in this chapter.
b. Write a test harness that prompts the user to input two double-precision integers and a choice of operation, '+' or '−' and prints the result of applying the given operation to these double-precision integers.

Exercise 10-10. Write a *doubDoubMult* analog of the *doubSingMult* macro given in the previous section. Of course, *doubDoubMult* should multiply two double-precision integers and store the answer as a quadruple-precision integer. Again, write a short calling program that can be used to test the new macro thoroughly.

Exercise 10-11. Write a *quadDoubDiv* macro that divides a quadruple-precision integer by a double-precision integer, storing the quotient and the remainder as double-precision integers. Note that this macro shares a problem with the machine **div** and **idiv** instructions: for some choices of the dividend and the divisor, the quotient will not fit in the allocated space. Once more, write a calling program to test this macro.

SECTION 6 BINARY CODED DECIMAL INSTRUCTIONS

The arithmetic instructions that were covered in Section 5 are certainly the most important. They use the intrinsic, fast, binary machine operations, and are central to nearly all applications calling for arithmetic manipulation.

However, the **8088** does provide a few instructions that support arithmetic to base 10. These are called the *BCD* (*binary coded decimal*) *instructions*, and come in two flavors, *unpacked* and *packed*.

The distinction between these types is that in unpacked BCD, decimal digits (0-9) are stored one per byte, while in packed BCD they are stored two per byte. Both kinds of arithmetic are quite dismally slow. In addition, the packed variety makes it unreasonably difficult (but not impossible) to do multiplication and division. The advantages of the packed variety are that they require less storage per digit and offer somewhat greater execution speed for addition and subtraction.

Most programmers do not find much use for these arithmetic operations. They do provide an easy way to implement arbitrary-precision arithmetic but, as we shall see, the speed penalty is high indeed. Since they allow multiple-precision arithmetic, they also allow a primitive kind or real-number arithmetic, called *fixed-point*. In fixed-point arithmetic, the programmer deals with real numbers having a fixed number of places after the decimal point, say six. The actual arithmetic computations in the program are done by treating the numbers as though they were integers, and the decimal point is only introduced in the input/output routines. For example, to add 128.111111 to 239.222222, the program would actually add

```
128111111
239222222
_____

367333333
```

but print the answer as 367.333333. Multiplication is somewhat more complicated: the integers representing the reals must be multiplied, with allowance being made to store the total number of digits contained in the product, then the decimal point must be inserted 12 places from the right end, and (usually) the answer rounded to six places before being output. Division is similar: the numerator must be padded with six (or perhaps seven to allow for rounding) zeroes before dividing.

The **8088** provides no real-number support, and fixed-point arithmetic is the easiest way to provide a program with the capability of doing some real-number computation. The preferred, but more involved, alternatives are to do *floating-point arithmetic* with the help of a numerical coprocessor such as the **8087**, as we will do in Chapter 17, or to write or otherwise obtain a *floating-point emulation library*, which mimics the **8087** capabilities in software.

In Chapter 11, we will develop a complete multiple-precision arithmetic package and use it for high-precision fixed-point computations.

Another reason why the programmer should have a passing acquaintance with the BCD instructions is that they are sometimes useful for quickly writing programs involving a modest amount of decimal integer arithmetic. We will give an example of such an application later in this section.

Our example programs will deal only with unpacked BCD, which is also known as *ASCII coded decimal*. Looking at Table 10.5, we see that the first four instructions, which help with unpacked BCD arithmetic, begin with the letter 'a', on account of this alternate name. Our procedures, macros, and constants that relate to unpacked BCD will be given the prefix *ACD*, again because of the alternate name.

First, we will look at the general techniques used in BCD arithmetic, and will see immediately that the existence of certain machine instructions would make the implementation of the BCD arithmetic operations easier. These desirable machine instructions will turn out to be precisely the ones listed in Table 10.4.

In unpacked BCD arithmetic, an integer is stored as an array of bytes, one digit per byte. Each digit is stored as its bit pattern, and so resides entirely within the low four bits of its byte. When we actually implement unpacked BCD arithmetic, we will assume that the representing byte arrays are all of the same length, given by the constant *ACDLen*, which has been set by an **EQUATE** to a value appropriate for the given application. In addition, we will store integers in byte arrays in the order that is consistent with everything else in this architecture, namely the least significant digit will be stored at the lowest address. For example, if *ACDLen* = 3, then the integer 123 would be stored in a byte array, say *Int*, in the form

```
Int[0] = 3
Int[1] = 2
Int[2] = 1
```

TABLE 10.5 THE BCD ARITHMETIC INSTRUCTIONS

MNEMONIC	OPERATION PERFORMED
aaa	ASCII adjust for addition
aas	ASCII adjust for subtraction
aam	ASCII adjust for multiplication
aad	ASCII adjust for division
daa	decimal adjust for addition
das	decimal adjust for subtraction

The question of storing negatives must also be resolved, and the situation is much the same as for binary arithmetic. We would like the same addition and subtraction operations to work for positive and for negative integers. In the binary case, this goal was achieved by using two's complement arithmetic. Analogously, the correct thing to do with BCD is to use ten's complement arithmetic. (Ten's complement arithmetic was introduced in Exercise 1-10.)

The *N digit ten's complement* of a decimal integer k is defined to be $10^N - k$. In the N digit ten's complement representation, integers k with $10^N/2 \le k < 10^N/2$ are stored using N decimal digits as follows:

(1) If $0 \le k < 10^N/2$, then k is stored as its decimal representation, left padded with as many zeros as necessary.

(2) If k satisfies $-10^N/2 \le k < 0$, then k is stored as its N digit ten's complement.

The reader should review the appropriate sections of Chapter 1 and verify the N-digit ten's complement analogs of the statements about two's complement given there. In particular, one way to compute the ten's complement is to take the *nine's complement* (subtract from 999···999, where there are N 9s), and then add 1.

Now consider the operation of adding arrays, say *Int1* and *Int2*, and leaving the sum in an array called *Answer*. The basic idea is to add byte by byte, from the low end of the arrays to the top, propagating carries as necessary. If, for example, *Int1[0]* = 3 and *Int2[0]* = 4 then we should make *Answer[0]* = 7. But what if *Int1[0]* = 6 and *Int1[0]* = 7? We cannot record the result as *Answer[0]* = 13, because 13 is not a legal value for a digit. Rather, we should let *Answer[0]* = 3, and arrange to carry a 1 to the *Answer[1]* position.

This is precisely what the **aaa** instruction, *ASCII adjust for addition*, does. The official description of **aaa** (in [12], for example) reads:

```
if ((al & 0fh) > 9 or AF = 1) then
{
     al <- al + 6
     ah <- ah + 1
     AF <- 1
}
CF <- AF
al <- al & 0fh
```

In this description, '&' is used to represent the bitwise *and* operator. The most interesting case is when the "if" condition is true. Since **al** & 0FH gives the value of the low four bits of **al**, this case covers situations like 6 + 7; because AF (the auxiliary flag) has value one when there is a carry out of bit number three, it also covers cases such as 9 + 9. When the "if" holds, **al** is replaced by **al** + 6. This is the correct thing to do since adding 6 is the same as subtracting 10 when working modulo 16. For example, if the low four bits contain 11, adding 6 will give the low four bits the value 17 (mod 16) = 1, exactly as required. The fact that **ah** is also incremented is not of interest at the moment; this feature is of importance in multiplication and will be considered later in this section. Finally, when the "if" holds, AF is set.

In all cases, the value of AF moved to CF. This means that CF will equal 1 precisely when **al** started with value greater than 9. Finally, the high four bits of **al** are zeroed, so that **al** is left with a legal value in the range 0-9. Hence, we can add our unpacked BCD arrays using a combination of the **aaa** and **adc** instructions.

Figure 10.4 shows a procedure, *ACDPlus,* that uses this technique to add two ASCII coded integers. Notice that it is written using the conventions introduced earlier: each array is assumed to have length equal to *ACDLen* and the integers are stored with the least significant digit in the lowest array position. The procedure will work equally well for adding positives or negatives, provided ten's complement is used in storing the operands.

Line 35 of *ACDPlus* shows a trick that we will use many times in the future. In the loop starting on line 37, we must perform an **add** in the first iteration and an **adc** in every succeeding iteration. It would be clumsy to make a special case of the **add** and use **adc** only in the later iterations. A neater approach is begin with CF = 0, and then use **adc** throughout the loop, even in the first iteration. Since CF = 0, the first **adc** behaves as though it were an **add**. The instruction **clc** (*clear the carry*) is used to clear CF.

To keep the examples as simple as possible, we have not worried about detection of signed or unsigned overflow. It turns out that unsigned overflow is easy. The most recent instruction to affect CF is the **aaa** encountered on the last traverse of the loop, and this sets CF if the "high digit" is bigger than 9. In other words, CF = 1 means that there was an unsigned overflow. Checking for signed overflow involves adding some code, since **aaa** leaves OF undefined. Even if OF were defined, it would not tell us anything useful in terms of our ten's complement representation.

We will not present the analogous *ACDMinus* procedure, although it is on the Program Disk. *ACDMinus* is almost identical to *ACDPlus*, except that it uses the **aas** instruction instead of **aaa** and **sbb** instead of **adc**. **Aas** is the obvious subtractive counterpart of **aaa**; the ambitious reader might want to write a description of **aas** corresponding to the official description of **aaa** given previously and then check the answer with [12].

Multiplication of unpacked BCD integers is more delicate. The best way to write a multiplication procedure is to work by analogy with standard multiplication. Consider how the multiplication

```
1234 * 5678
```

is performed. Basically, each of the four digits 1,2,3,4 is multiplied by each of the four digits 5,6,7,8 and the 16 partial answers are added together to give the final result. But when, say, the '3' is multiplied by the '6', it must be remembered that the '3' stands for 30 and the '6' stands for 600, and so this product adds 18000, not 18, to the total. This is accounted for by left-shifting the 18 three places before adding it. Stated differently, the '3' comes in position 1 (where the position count starts with 0 at the least significant end) and the '6' comes in position 2, whence the 18 must be left-shifted $1 + 2 = 3$ positions. In other words, in the final answer, the $3*6 = 18$ contributes an 8 to position 3 and a 1 to position 4. Generally, when the digit from position i is multiplied by the digit from position j, the result contributes to positions $i + j$ and $i + j + 1$ of the final answer.

Now apply these observations to ASCII coded decimal multiplication. Suppose that the byte arrays *Int1* and *Int2* are being multiplied to produce *Ans*. When the bytes *Int1[i]* and *Int2[j]* are multiplied, they produce a word, the low byte of which contributes to *Ans[i+j]* and the high byte to *Ans[i+j+1]*. But the situation is somewhat more complicated than this.

Suppose that we let $k = i + j$ for simplicity. All the products *Int1[i]*Int2[j]* must be computed, and the obvious mechanism for performing this computation is a double loop, looping over the values of i and j. It is not important which loop is chosen as the outer and which as the inner, so let us assume that the j-loop is the outer and the i-loop the inner (since this is how it is done in hand calculation and since our forthcoming procedure will also use this ordering).

Here is what is happening in the neighborhood of the *Int1[i]*Int2[j]* multiplication:

```
Int1[i-1] * Int2[j]  adds to Ans[k-1], Ans[k]
Int1[i]   * Int2[j]  adds to          Ans[k], Ans[k+1]
Int1[i+1] * Int2[j]  adds to                  Ans[k+1], Ans[k+2]
```

The product *Int1[i]*Int2[j]* will be computed using 8-bit multiplication and so will end up in **ax**. But if, for example, *Int1[i]* = 7 and *Int2[j]* = 8, then **al** will contain the value 56 and **ah** the value zero. It would be better if **al** contained the 5 and **ah** the 6, since then **al** could be added to *Ans[k]* and **ah** to *Ans[k+1]*. This is precisely the transformation of **ax** induced by the **aam** (*ASCII adjust for multiplication*) instruction. Specifically, **aam** takes the present value v in **ax** and replaces **ah** by v/10 and **al** by v mod 10.

The previous display reveals some other potential problems with the multiplication. For example, after the multiplication of *Int1[i]*Int2[j]* and the subsequent **aam** have been completed, **al** must be added to *Ans[k]* and **ah** to *Ans[k+1]*. But if the result of adding **al** to *Ans[k]* is bigger than 9, this value should be reduced to the legal range and a carry added to *Ans[k+1]*. Since **ah** is about to be added to *Ans[k+1]*, this carry can be made to **ah** instead. These effects can be obtained by inserting an **aaa** instruction at this point in the code — and this explains the extra 1 that **aaa** adds to **ah** in the "if" case of its pseudo-code!

One final complication is that when the **ah** part of the product is added to *Ans[k+1]*, it may again give an answer bigger than 9. This could also be fixed by an **aaa**. The overflowed 1 must be added to *Ans[k+2]*. But it is unfortunately not enough to make only this correction, because adding 1 to *Ans[k+2]* may make it bigger than 9, necessitating an addition to *Ans[k+3]*, and so on. In fact, the carry may propagate all the way to the highest byte of *Ans*. Since these carries are much too complicated to keep track of, a better solution is to postpone the fixing of *Ans[k+2]* until the product *Int1[i+1]*Int2[j]* is being computed. The information on whether a carry occurred is contained in CF and so can be stored on the stack, via a **pushf**, until after the next multiplication, at which point it can be recovered, using a **popf**, and accounted for by using an **adc**.

FIGURE 10.4 ASCII CODED DECIMAL ADDITION

```
 1    TITLE ACDPlus.asm: procedure which does ASCII coded decimal addition
 2
 3
 4    COMMENT        # PROCEDURE HEADER
 5    TYPE:          NEAR          FILE: ACDPlus.asm     LIBRARY: user.lib
 6    PURPOSE:       Adds two ASCII coded decimal integers
 7    CALLED AS:     ACDPlus(offsetFirst, offsetSecond, offsetAnswer)
 8    RETURNS:       Nothing
 9    REMARKS:       # Assumes all data in segment pointed to by ds.
10
11    EXTRN     ACDLen:ABS
12    PUBLIC    ACDPlus
13
14    DOSSEG
15    .MODEL    SMALL
16
17    .CODE
18
19    ACDPlus    PROC    NEAR
20
21        push   bp
22        mov    bp, sp
23
24        push   ax
25        push   bx
26        push   cx
27        push   di
28        push   si
29
30        mov    bx, [bp + 8]           ;offset of Answer
31        mov    di, [bp + 6]           ;offset first addend
32        mov    si, [bp + 4]           ;offset second addend
33
34        mov    cx, ACDLen             ;manifest constant -- defined by an EQU
35        clc                           ;so that the first adc is really an add
36
37    @@:
38
39        mov    al, [di]               ;aaa only works on al
40        adc    al, [si]
41        aaa
42        mov    [bx], al
43        inc    bx
44        inc    di
45        inc    si
46        loop   @B
47
48        pop    si
49        pop    di
50        pop    cx
51        pop    bx
52        pop    ax
53
54        pop    bp
```

Figure 10.4 cont.

```
55      ret    6
56
57 ACDPlus    ENDP
58
59 END
```

All these ideas were used in the program shown in Figure 10.5, which performs ASCII coded decimal multiplication.

Multiplication using ASCII coded decimal is extremely slow, and it is easy to explain why. Consider the multiplication problem

```
12345 * 12345
```

Using 16-bit binary, this requires one multiplication. Using ASCII coded decimal, it require 25 multiplications, 50 additions, and a great deal of other overhead!

As mentioned earlier, the BCD instructions can sometimes be used to do quick arithmetic, especially in cases where the form of the data is known in advance. For example, suppose that **al** contains an integer in the range 0-99 (perhaps an error code) and it is required to print it to the screen as two decimal digits. This code will do it:

```
aam
add     ax, '00'            ;convert to ASCII codes
outCh   ah
outCh   al
```

In this example, we again used a **MASM** double character, '00'. It is worth keeping the BCD instructions in mind for applications like this.

The fourth of the ASCII coded decimal instructions is **aad** (*ASCII adjust for division*). The algorithms for division of ASCII coded decimals, in cases where the divisor has more than one digit, are so slow and cumbersome that it is doubtful whether anyone ever uses them. If the divisor has one digit, it is a feasible method of division, and is discussed in the exercises. The **aad** instruction provides some help. It is basically the inverse of the **aam** instruction. The **aam** instruction is used after multiplication and unzips **al** into two digits which it stores in **ah** and **al**. The **aad** instruction is used before division and zips the digits in **ah** and **al** together, leaving the answer in **al**. In other words, it replaces **al** by 10 * **ah** + **al**, and **ah** by 0.

The Program Disk also contains basic input and output procedures for ASCII coded decimal integers. These procedures use the format mentioned previously. Namely, they store the integers in arrays of fixed-size *ACDLen* with the least significant digits coming first.

The various ASCII coded decimal procedures are accessed by means of macros that are stored in the file ACD.MAC. Here are the macros:

```
ACDIn     MACRO    Buffer, Handle
ACDOut    MACRO    Buffer, Handle
ACDNeg    MACRO    Buffer
```

```
ACDAdd    MACRO    Answer, First, Second
ACDSub    MACRO    Answer, First, Second
ACDMul    MACRO    Answer, First, Second
ACDMov    MACRO    Dest, Source
```

For the most part, the use of these macros is self-evident. We refer the interested reader to the source code for further information. One warning: *ACDMul* will not work if *Answer = First* or *Answer = Second*. In one of the exercises, the reader is asked to supply a version that works even in these cases.

Figure 10.5 shows a simple example of these macros in use. This program computes the factorial of any input integer. In preparation for computing the factorial of 100, the buffer length *ACDLen* was given the value 200, because

$$100! < 100^{100} = 10^{200}$$

and so 200 digits are more than sufficient to hold the value of 100!. The output from the program is shown at the end of Figure 10.6. This computation took 33 seconds on the particular machine being used.

The two remaining BCD instructions are used with packed representations, i.e., when the integers are stored two digits to the byte, one digit in the low four bits and one in the high four bits. Since we will not use these instructions, we refer the user to [12] for detailed descriptions. Generally speaking, **daa** and **das** make the corrections after addition and subtraction, respectively, that correspond to the actions of **aaa** and **aas** in the unpacked case.

Exercise 10-12. The *ACDMul* macro

```
ACDMul MACRO Answer, First, Second
```

calls a function *ACDMult* in order to multiply two unpacked BCD integers *First* and *Second*, assigning the answer to *Answer*. Fix the version of *ACDMult* that is presently on the Program Disk so that it produces correct answers when *Answer = First* or *Answer = Second* (or both).

Exercise 10-13. Write an *ACDDiv* macro

```
ACDDiv MACRO Quot, Num, Digit
```

that calls a procedure *ACDDivide* to divide an unpacked BCD integer, *Num*, by a *single digit* (1-9), storing the answer as an unpacked BCD in *Quot*. Of course, *ACDDivide* must also be written.

SECTION 7 BIT OPERATIONS

Of the bit operations listed in Table 10.6, the three most commonly used are **and, or,** and **xor.** These can be applied in a variety of interesting (and sometimes devious) ways, but they are commonly used in the general form

FIGURE 10.5 ASCII CODED DECIMAL MULTIPLICATION

```
 1   TITLE ACDMult.asm: procedure which does ASCII coded decimal mult.
 2
 3   COMMENT         # PROCEDURE HEADER
 4   TYPE:           NEAR         FILE: ACDMult     LIBRARY: user.lib
 5   PURPOSE:        Multiplies two ASCII coded decimal integers
 6   CALLED AS:      ACDMult(offsetFirst, offsetSecond, offsetAnswer)
 7   RETURNS:        Nothing
 8   REMARKS:        Assumes all data in segment pointed to by ds.
 9                   First[i]*Second[j] contributes to the bytes Answer[k] and
10                    Answer[k+1], where k=i+j. This notation is used in the
11                   # comments below.
12
13   EXTRN      ACDLen:ABS
14   PUBLIC     ACDMult
15
16   DOSSEG
17   .MODEL     SMALL
18
19   .CODE
20
21   ACDMult    PROC    NEAR
22
23       push   bp
24       mov    bp, sp
25
26       push   ax
27       push   bx
28       push   cx
29       push   dx
30       push   di
31       push   si
32
33       mov    bx, [bp + 8]            ;offset of Answer
34       mov    si, [bp + 6]            ;offset of First
35       mov    di, [bp + 4]            ;offset of Second
36
37       mov    cx, ACDLEN
38
39   @@:                                ;initialize Answer to 0
40
41       mov    BYTE PTR [bx], 0
42       inc    bx
43       loop   @B
44
45       mov    bx, [bp + 8]            ;offset of Answer, again
46       mov    cx, ACDLEN             ;counter for outer loop
47       mov    dx, bx
48       add    dx, cx
49       dec    dx                      ;upper limit of Answer array
50
51   outerLoop:
52
53       clc                            ;so that first adc is an add
54       pushf
```

```
55
56  innerLoop:
57
58       mov   al, [si]                  ;First[i]
59       mul   BYTE PTR [di]             ;  * Second[j]
60       aam                             ;puts low byte in al, high byte in ah
61       add   al, [bx]
62       aaa
63       mov   [bx], al                  ;add low byte to Answer[k]
64       cmp   bx, dx
65       jae   nextOuter
66       mov   al, ah                    ;here only if high byte to be added
67       popf                            ;recover CF from previous i
68       adc   al, [bx + 1]              ;prepare to update Answer[k+1]
69       aaa
70       pushf                           ;store CF for use with next i
71       mov   [bx + 1], al              ;actually update Answer[k+1]
72       inc   si                        ;update i
73       inc   bx                        ;update k
74       jmp   innerLoop
75
76  nextOuter:
77
78       popf                            ;to balance initial push
79       mov   si, [bp + 6]              ;reinitialize i
80       inc   di                        ;update j
81       mov   bx, [bp + 8]              ;reinitialize k
82       add   bx, di                    ;updating k: how many bytes the product
83       sub   bx, [bp + 4]              ;  word must be shifted
84       loop  oquterLoop
85
86       pop   si
87       pop   di
88       pop   dx
89       pop   cx
90       pop   bx
91       pop   ax
92
93       pop   bp
94       ret   6
95
96  ACDMult    ENDP
97
98  END
```

```
inst    Op, Mask
```

Mask is immediate data, and the choices of *Mask* and *inst* modify *Op* in some desired way. The name *Mask* is traditionally used by programmers for a constant that occurs in this context. Unfortunately, the word *Mask* cannot be used as an identifier in the source code, since it is a reserved word in this assembly language. In the next chapter we will see that its reserved meaning is similar to the present usage. We will now discuss the effect of this general form, used with various choices of *inst*.

First, consider the instruction

```
and      Op, Mask
```

Recall that **and** turns on those bits of its first operand that have value 1 in both operands, and turns off all other bits. In the present instruction, this means that the bits in *Op* corresponding to the 0s *Mask* are turned off, while the bits in *Op* corresponding to the 1s in *Mask* are left unchanged. Consequently:

- To turn off certain bits in an operand, **and** it with a *Mask* in which exactly those bits have value 0.

Second, consider the instruction

```
or       Op, Mask
```

We know that **or** turns on those bits in its first operand that have value 1 in either of its operands. In terms of the present instruction, this means that bits in *Op* corresponding to 0s in *Mask* are left unchanged, while bits corresponding to 1s in *Mask* are turned on. Hence:

- To turn on certain bits in *Op*, **or** it with a *Mask* in which exactly those bits have value 1.

Last, consider the instruction

```
xor      Op, Mask
```

The **xor** operation turns on those bits in its first operand that have value 1 in one operand and value 0 in the other operand. This means that the preceding instruction leaves unchanged those bits in *Op* that correspond to 0s in *Mask*, but toggles those bits in *Op* that correspond to 1s in *Mask*. *Toggle* means invert: if a bit is 1, it becomes 0; if it is 0, it becomes 1. This time our conclusion is

- To toggle certain bits in *Op*, **xor** it with a *Mask* in which exactly those bits have value 1.

Of course, we have already used these instructions in situations different from these canonical usages. For example, we routinely use

```
xor      Reg, Reg
```

to zero a register in the shortest possible time, and

```
and      Reg, Reg
```

to set the flags in order to establish whether *Reg* equals 0, or is negative, or to check any other property of *Reg* that is deducible from the flag settings.

The instruction

```
test     Op1, Op2
```

FIGURE 10.6 FACTORIALS USING ASCII CODED DECIMAL

```
 1   TITLE  Fact.asm
 2
 3   DOSSEG
 4   .MODEL SMALL
 5
 6       PUBLIC     ACDLen
 7       INCLUDE    console.mac
 8       INCLUDE    acd.mac
 9       ACDLen     EQU  200
10
11   .STACK 100H
12
13   .DATA
14
15       Prompt1      DB    "Input the value of n: ", 0
16       Heading      DB    "The value of n! is ", 0
17
18       intStr       DB    6              DUP(?)
19
20       ACDOne       DB    1, (ACDLen - 1) DUP (0)
21       ACDInt       DB    ACDLen         DUP(?)
22       oldFact      DB    ACDLen         DUP(?)
23       Fact         DB    ACDLen         DUP(?)
24
25   .CODE
26
27   Start:
28
29       mov   ax, @DATA
30       mov   ds, ax
31
32   Again:
33
34       hSkip   1
35       outAsc  Prompt1
36       inAsc   intStr
37       aToI    intStr
38       hSkip   1
39       outAsc  Heading
40
41       ACDMov  Fact, ACDOne
42       ACDMov  ACDInt, ACDOne
43       mov     cx, ax
44       cmp     cx, 1
45       jle     Done
46       dec     cx
47
48   Top:
49
50       ACDAdd  ACDInt, ACDInt, ACDOne
51       ACDMov  oldFact, Fact
52       ACDMul  Fact, oldFact, ACDInt
53       loop    Top
54
```

Figure 10.6 cont.

```
55   Done:
56
57         ACDout   Fact
58         hSkip    2
59         jmp      Again
60
61         mov      ax, 4c00h
62         int      21h
63
64   END   Start
```

SAMPLE OUTPUT

Input the value of n: 100

The value of n! is

9332621544394415268169923885626670049071596826438162146859296389521
7599993229915608941463976156518286253697920827223758251185210916864
00000000000000000000000000

is somewhat like **and**: it sets the flags in exactly the same way, but it does not modify either of its operands. Otherwise stated, **test** has the same relationship to **and** that **cmp** has to **sub**. **Test** is generally used in an instruction of the form

```
        test     Op, Mask
```

This instruction sets the flags corresponding to a non-zero result, i.e., clears ZF, under exactly the same conditions as would the corresponding **and** instruction. In other words, ZF is cleared provided some bit is simultaneously 1 in *Mask* and in *Op*.

This shows the standard use of **test**:

- To determine whether at least one of a given collection of bits in an operand has value 1, **test** the operand against a *Mask* having 1s in exactly those bit positions, and check ZF afterwards.

The **test** instruction is most often used to check whether a single bit is on. For example, the following fragment checks whether bit 3 in **ax** is on:

```
        test     ax, 1000b
        jne      itIsOn
;here if it is off
itIsOn:
;here if it is on
```

Note that **MASM** accepts binary constants, provided that they are flagged with a trailing 'b'.

We have already met the right shift operation in both its forms:

TABLE 10.6 THE BIT OPERATIONS

MNEMONIC	OPERATION PERFORMED
and	bitwise and
or	bitwise or
xor	bitwise exclusive or
test	test
not	one's complement
shr	shift right
sar	arithmetic shift right
shl	shift left
sal	arithmetic shift left
ror	rotate right
rol	rotate left
rcr	rotate right through the carry flag
rcl	rotate left through the carry flag

```
shr     Op, 1
shr     Op, cl
```

However, there are a number of features of the instruction that we have glossed over. For example, when the first form is used, the rightmost bit, which is shifted out, is not lost: it is stored in CF. When the second form is used, the machine basically implements it as a loop containing the correct number of repetitions of the first form. In particular, if **cl** is given a value such as −1, the result will not be a **shl**! Rather, it will induce a loop of 255 right shifts — a rather slow way of getting the value 0 into *Op*. Another consequence of this interpretation of the second form is that, after the instruction, CF contains the bit that was most recently shifted out of the rightmost position.

We have already used the fact that **shr** corresponds to integer division-by-2. That is, it divides by 2, rounding down in cases where the dividend is odd. Unfortunately, this division by 2 interpretation only holds in the unsigned case. If **ax** contains -2^{15} (which stores as 8000H) and the operation

```
shr     ax, 1
```

is performed, then **ax** contains 4000H. This is the correct quotient if an unsigned interpretation is made, but certainly not with a signed interpretation, since it does not even represent a negative number. The microprocessor gives the user a warning of this difficulty. If **shr** is used on an operand whose sign bit is 1, then OF is set.

This may be a useful service, but it is hard to imagine ever using it, since there is an alternate form of the shift-right instruction that is used in doing signed arithmetic. This alternate form is **sar** (for *arithmetic shift right*) and has the same syntax and behavior as **shr** except that, instead of always shifting 0 into the leftmost bit, it shifts in a copy of the sign bit. The result is that **sar** represents division by 2 when the dividend is interpreted as a signed integer. The answer is always *rounded down*. This means that positive answers are rounded toward zero but negative answers are rounded away from zero. For example, after performing a **sar** on an operand with value −1, the answer will have value −1, because the exact answer should be −1/2 and this rounds down to −1. In one of the exercises, the reader is asked to verify this rounding-down behavior of **sar** in the general case.

It is also worth noting that the rounding behavior of **sar** is different from **idiv**, since **idiv** always rounds toward 0. For example, if **idiv** is used to divide −1 by 2, the answer will be 0.

The **shl** (*shift left*) instruction has the same general behavior as **shr**. In this case, 0 is shifted into the rightmost position and the old leftmost bit is stored in CF. **Shl** corresponds to multiplication by 2, whether a signed or unsigned interpretation is made.

First, consider an unsigned interpretation. If the old high bit is zero, then the multiplication by 2 can be done without inducing unsigned overflow. On the other hand, if the old high bit is 1, then multiplication by 2 will cause an unsigned overflow. Hence we see that storing the old high bit in CF is an especially strategic thing to do: CF ends up being set precisely when there is an unsigned overflow.

Next we look at the signed case, and first assume that the operands are negative. If the old high bit is 1, then multiplication by 2 need not produce a signed overflow. For example, multiplying −1 by 2 certainly does not result in a signed overflow. What is important is how large in the negative direction the operand is, and this is determined by the bit immediately to the right of the sign bit. If this bit is 0, the quantity is "very negative" and so it cannot be multiplied by 2 without overflowing. The situation is quite analogous when a positive operand is considered: if the high bit is zero and the next bit is 1, using **shl** will result in a signed overflow. Summing up, multiplying an operand by 2 induces signed overflow if the sign bit differs from the bit immediately to the right of it.

But applying **shl** to such an operand results in either a carry into and no carry out of the sign bit, or the opposite. These are precisely the circumstances that cause the overflow flag to be set. Consequently, the overflow flag successfully monitors the possibility of signed overflow when **shl** is used to give multiplication by 2.

A reasonable conclusion is that, since **shl** works equally well to give multiplication by 2 in both the signed and unsigned cases, there is no need for a special **sal** version of the instruction. This is completely true, and the **sal** appearing in the list of bitwise instructions is not a new instruction. It is just another name for **shl**, introduced (? rather pointlessly) in order to "make the instruction set more symmetric."

The next instruction is **ror**, which means *rotate right*. **Ror** is similar, in syntax and behavior, to the shift operations. The difference is that the old rightmost bit is "wrapped around" and moved into the leftmost bit position. It is good to think geometrically and interpret **ror** as an 8- or 16-bit "circular shift." In addition to moving to the high position, the old rightmost bit is also copied to CF.

Ror can be used to move the bits in an operand sequentially to a given position, without destroying the operand. For example, the following fragment prints out the bits in **ax** in low-to-high order:

```
        mov        cx, 16

    loopLabel:
```

```
            test    ax, 1
            je      printZero
            outCh   '1'
            jmp     Next

    printZero:

            outCh   '0'

Next:

            ror     ax, 1
            loop    loopLabel
```

The advantage of using **ror** rather than **shr** is that ax returns to its original value after the complete cycle. Of course, instead of using **ror** to change **ax**, in this particular example the mask could be changed by an **shl** on each traverse of the loop.

Rol is the totally analogous left-rotation instruction.

The remaining bit operations are **rcr**, which is *rotate right through the carry*, and **rcl**, *rotate left through the carry*.

These again form a symmetric pair, and so we will only consider **rcr**. **Rcr** moves the bit pattern one position to the right, and shifts the rightmost bit into CF, in exactly the same way as the right shift. A new feature is that **rcr** shifts the old value of CF into the leftmost position. In other words, **rcr** should be interpreted as a 9- or 17-bit "circular shift," with CF used as the extra position.

One of the main applications of **rcr** (and likewise **rcl**) is to build shift operations in multiple-precision arithmetic.

As an example, consider the problem of building a triple-precision left shift. A triple-precision integer is stored as a low word, a middle word, and a high word. The low-word bits should be shifted one position to the left, and a **shl** can be used for this. This **shl** will leave the old bit 15 in CF. If an **rcl** is used on the middle word, things work beautifully: CF (the old bit 15) is shifted into bit 16, the bits in the middle word are shifted left, and old bit 31 is rotated into CF. Finally, another **rcl** on the high word completes the operation, leaving old bit 47 in CF. Assuming that the triple-precision integer is in the segment addressed by **ds**, here is a macro implementation of the left shift:

```
    tripleLeftShift     MACRO   triplePrec

        push    bx
        lea     bx, triplePrec
        shl     WORD PTR [bx], 1
        rcl     WORD PTR [bx+2], 1
        rcl     WORD PTR [bx+4],1
        pop     bx

ENDM
```

To do a left shift with arbitrary precision N, the individual **rcl** instructions should be replaced by a loop. It is best to replace the initial **shl** by another **rcl**, which can be accomplished by a trick that we have used before. If CF is first cleared (using **clc**), then **rcl** has exactly the same effect as **shl**.

Designing a multiple-precision right shift is similar. The only difference is that, while in the left-shift case it is necessary to start with the low word and proceed uphill, in the right-shift case the computation must begin with the high word and run downhill.

Exercise 10-14. Write and test a macro that prints the bits in a word to the screen in high-to-low order.

Exercise 10-15. Write a macro that inverts the bit order in a word. For example, given the input word with bit pattern

```
0000 1111 0101 0101
```

the macro should replace it by the word

```
1010 1010 1111 0000
```

Exercise 10-16. In the text, we showed an example in which **sar** rounded in the downward direction, and stated that this was always the case. Show that this statement is correct.

SECTION 8 STRING INSTRUCTIONS

The string instructions are very fast and very powerful. They perform the customary operations on blocks of data: moving, comparing, searching, and filling. They can be used when the data consist of a block of words or a block of bytes, and they provide the option of processing a block from lowest address to highest address or in the opposite order.

The list of **8088** string instructions is shown in Table 10.7. The usage of the various instructions is similar, and so we will only give the complete details on the first of them, **movs**, which of course means *move string*.

Movs is a direct memory-to-memory move. It moves the datum with address **ds:si** to location **es:di**. Si and di are given their usual names, *source index* and *destination index*, because of this application. Already we see that using **movs** involves a certain amount of overhead. Four registers, namely **di**, **si**, **ds**, and **es**, must be correctly initialized. The **8088** designers' choice of **es:di** rather than **ds:di** as the destination address was deliberate and significant: it allows **movs** to move data between different segments.

As we stated earlier, **movs** can move a byte or a word, and we must indicate which is required. This can be done in two different ways. First, the **movs** instruction has two variants, **movsb** and **movsw**, that can be used to convey the data size.

The second method of indicating which size data to move applies only to named data items. For example, if *sourceWord* and *destWord* are word-sized variables defined in possibly different segments, then the **movs** instruction can be used in the form

```
movs      destWord, sourceWord
```

to move the datum located at *sourceWord* to *destWord*. The only extra information communicated to the assembler by this expanded form of the instruction is the size of the operands, which it can now extract from its symbol table. The program must still explicitly initialize **di**, **si**, **ds**, and **es**. Since this form of the instruction involves considerably more writing than does the equivalent **movsw** (or **movsb** in the byte case), it sees relatively little use. Of course, it does have the additional advantage of being self-documenting. This form has one further advantage, which we will discuss later in this section.

A single **movs** instruction moves only one byte or one word. Obviously, considering the register-initialization overhead involved, it is a rather inefficient way to accomplish such an end. The real point of **movs** (and the other string instructions) is that they are designed to deal with blocks of memory, and this ability is built into the instructions. The assumption is that one **movs** will be followed immediately by another, and so each application of **movs** automatically sets up **di** and **si** for the next.

The exact meaning of "sets up" depends on the context. For example, if the operation is **movsb**, then presumably **di** and **si** should be incremented by 1 to prepare for the next **movsb**, whereas in the **movsw** case, they should be incremented by 2.

While this is basically correct, there is another parameter involved. The reader may be familiar with the fact that, in moving a block of data one item at a time, it can be important whether the move proceeds from low address to high address or conversely. This is usually significant only in cases where the source region overlaps the destination region.

This phenomenon is best illustrated by examples. Suppose that the six bytes beginning at **ds**:0006 are initialized to {1,2,3,4,5,6} and we wish to move them to the region beginning at **ds**:0009. If the move is conducted from high address to low address, it works perfectly; but if it is conducted from low address to high address, the pattern actually moved to **ds**:0009 is {1,2,3,1,2,3}. This outcome can be most easily verified by drawing a picture. Similarly, if the same six starting bytes are to be moved to the location starting at **ds**:0003, the move will work correctly only if done in the order from low address to high address. We leave it to the reader to formulate a general rule on how to conduct an overlapping move.

The microprocessor allows the programmer to specify whether a multiple-byte or multiple-word move should be performed from low address to high, or in the other order. The indicator that is used is DF, the *direction flag*. If DF is clear, the move proceeds in the uphill direction; if DF is set, it proceeds downhill. We can now give a complete answer to the meaning of the term "sets up," which was used a couple of paragraphs ago. After a **mov** instruction **di** and **si** are automatically updated according to this scheme:

	DF=0	DF=1
movsb	+1	−1
movsw	+2	−2

There is one potential problem associated with this dependence on DF. If, for example, the programmer expects a block move to occur in the uphill direction from the starting address, and if it happens that DF = 1, then the wrong block of data will be moved, presumably with dire consequences. The moral is that in dealing with the string functions, it is vital to know the value of DF at all times. The microprocessor actually makes this easy: the machine

TABLE 10.7 THE STRING INSTRUCTIONS

MNEMONIC	OPERATION PERFORMED
movs	move string
cmps	compare strings
scas	scan (search) a string
lods	load a string from the accumulator
stos	store a string item in the accumulator

THE REPEAT PREFIXES

rep	repeat a string operation while cx > 0
repe	repeat a string operation while cx > 0 and ZF = 1
repne	repeat a string operation while cx > 0 and ZF = 0

always comes on with DF = 0, and none of the instructions affect DF, except for two instructions that are specifically designed to change it. These instructions are **std** (*set the direction flag*) and **cld** (*clear the direction flag*). This behavior suggests the following strategy for monitoring DF:

- At all points in a program, assume that DF = 0. On those rare occasions when it is necessary to set DF using **std**, be sure to clear it at the earliest possible moment by using **cld**.

In all our examples, we will tacitly assume that DF = 0, so that the direction of iteration is upward. There is one circumstance under which a program cannot assume that DF is in a known state. Various programs, of which interrupt handlers and "pop-up utilities" are examples, have the power to take control of the machine at any time, interrupting whatever program is currently executing. Such a program must explicitly initialize DF before making use of it.

The ability of the string instructions to repeat is only really useful if there is an easy way to trigger their repetition. The instruction set provides a method for doing this, namely the **rep** prefix. It is called a prefix because it is not itself a separate instruction. Rather, it is written on the same line as the instruction to which it refers, as in

```
        rep        movsw
```

Just like a segment override prefix, **rep** generates a byte of machine code (0F2H) that precedes the machine code for **movsw**. This prefix byte causes the succeeding string instruction to iterate a number of times equal to the starting value of the **cx** register. **Cx** is adjusted automatically after each repetition. Unlike **loop**, **rep** does the reasonable thing if **cx** = 0 — the instruction iterates zero times. **Rep** has variants (**repe** and **repne**) that we will consider soon. They are not important in dealing with **movs**.

As a trivial example, suppose we want to move 100 words from *Ary1* to *Ary2*, where both are defined in the data segment. Suppose that at this point in the program, **ds** has already been pointed to the data segment, but **es** is not pointing there. Then this fragment will accomplish the move:

```
push    ds
pop     es
mov     si, OFFSET Ary1
mov     di, OFFSET Ary2
mov     cx, 100
rep     movsw
```

It is interesting to compare the time required for this sequence with the time for an equivalent sequence using **mov** and **loop**. From Appendix 1, for example, we can find the times for the individual instructions in the sequence. As we discussed in Chapter 9, times obtained in this way are only optimistic approximations, since the actual execution time depends on a number of other factors (such as the condition of the prefetch queue).

Using the times for the instructions in the fragment, we arrive at

```
15 + 12 + 4 + 4 + 4 + (9 + 17 * 100) = 1748 clock cycles
```

An equivalent sequence using **loop** and **mov** is

```
mov     cx, 100
mov     si, OFFSET Ary1
mov     di, OFFSET Ary2

loopLabel:

mov     ax, [si]
mov     [di], ax
add     si, 2
add     di, 2
loop    loopLabel
```

The time for this sequence is

```
4 + 4 + 4 + 100*((14 + 5) + (14 + 5) + 2*4)) + 99*5 + 17
= 4921 clock cycles
```

The parentheses have been included as clues to the reader who wishes to verify the correctness of this arithmetic. Our conclusion is that the **movs** version is faster by a factor of almost three in this case. This is fairly typical of the performance of the string instructions.

One final aspect of the use of the **rep** prefix should be mentioned. The **di** and **si** registers are automatically updated at each execution of **movs**. It is clear that the updating must be done *after* the data have been moved, since otherwise the wrong data would be moved. Consequently, when a block of data is moved using **movs**, **si** will end up pointing one data item beyond the last source item that was moved, and **di** will point one data item beyond the final destination item. Likewise, **cx** receives an extra adjustment. This phenomenon of "overshoot" is usually unimportant with **movs**, but it is shared by the other string instructions, and it is of critical importance when using **scas** (*string search*) and **cmps** (*string compare*), to which we now turn.

Cmps has essentially the same syntax as **movs**. It, too, has three forms, namely

```
cmpsb
cmpsw
cmps        Source, Dest
```

and, again, the third form in not often used. In general, **cmps** works like **cmp** in that it does an implied subtraction and sets the flags accordingly. Unfortunately, the use of the registers in **cmps** is inconsistent with their use with **cmp**.

The instruction

```
cmp        Dest, Source
```

does an internal subtraction

```
Dest  -  Source
```

and set the flags accordingly. But, no matter which form of **cmps** is used, the corresponding internal subtraction is

```
(item pointed to by ds:si)  -  (item pointed to by es:di)
```

which, by any reasonable interpretation, means

```
Source  -  Dest
```

At least, in the third form of **cmps**, this still translates as

```
(first operand)  -  (second operand)
```

This inconsistency does not present any real problems — as long as the programmer does not forget!

It is time for us to be more explicit about the exact behavior of the **rep** prefix. Most often, when comparing two blocks of data, we are interested in knowing whether or not they are identical. As soon as they disagree at a single location, we know the answer and do not need to continue the comparison any further. This is exactly how **rep** works in the line

```
rep        cmpsb
```

It causes **cmps** to iterate a maximum number of times equal to the value of **cx**, but only as long as the comparison gives "equal" as the answer. In other words, it continues only as long as ZF = 1. **Cmps** does the comparison before the zero flag is checked and hence it is not necessary to set ZF initially. Since **rep** always consults the zero flag, it is also known by the names **repe** and **repz** by analogy with **loope** and **loopz**. But we must emphasize — whereas **loop** is a different instruction from **loope/loopz**, the prefixes **rep**, **repe**, and **repz** are all identical (they all encode as the prefix byte 0F2H), the different names being used only to provide a measure of documentation. Of course, the exact effect of this prefix depends upon which string instruction follows it. If the instruction is **movs**, for instance, then the setting of the zero flag is ignored.

As a trivial example, suppose we compare blocks of byte data of length 100 named *Str1* and *Str2*. As before, assume that both are in the segment pointed to by **ds**. An appropriate code fragment is

```
        push    ds
        pop     es
        lea     si, Str1
        lea     di, Str2
        mov     cx, 100
        rep     cmpsb
        je      theyAreEqual
        ;do this if different
        jmp     Over

theyAreEqual:

        ;do this if identical

Over:
```

If the blocks are different, control will fall through the compare instruction at some point, with ZF = 0. On the other hand, if they are identical, ZF will have value 1 after each comparison, including the last one. Hence looking at ZF gives a foolproof test as to whether or not the blocks are identical.

Note that checking the final value of **cx** does not give a totally reliable test for equality. Certainly if **cx** > 0 after the **cmpsb** line, the strings are different. But if **cx** = 0, they may be identical or they may differ in the last byte.

In using **cmps**, the programmer is frequently interested in knowing the first offset at which the blocks differ. It is then important to remember the overshoot phenomenon. As a concrete example, let us consider the case of a byte comparison with DF = 0. When the repeated **cmps** terminates, **si** and **di** will each have been incremented once beyond the first point at which the blocks first disagree. Hence the first positions at which the blocks differ correspond to offsets **si** − 1 and **di** − 1, where **si** and **di** are the final values of these registers.

The byte and word forms of the string instructions have the same execution times. Consequently, this example will run nearly twice as fast if it is coded using 50 repetitions of **cmpsw** rather than the 100 repetitions of **cmpsb** that were used. The only weakness of this alternate scheme is that the final values of **si** and **di** would no longer give a precise indication of the first point at which the strings differ. Another slight complication would arise if the strings to be compared had odd length. However, it is a trivial matter to add a few extra instructions to resolve these problems. Even taking these added instructions into account, it should be clear that when dealing with even moderately sized blocks of data, the word forms of the string instructions will outperform the byte forms.

There is another variant of the **rep** prefix, called **repne** or **repnz**. Unlike **repe**, **repne** is really different from **rep**. It is the analog of **loopne**, and triggers a repetition only if ZF = 0, indicating inequality, and **cx** is not zero. **Repne** is more often used with **scas** (defined below) than with **cmps**. The instruction

```
        repne   cmpsb
```

can be used to compare two blocks of byte data and find the first position at which they agree.

The next string operation, **scas**, searches for a byte or a word in a block of data. It tries to match the byte in **al** in the **scasb** case, or the word in **ax** in the **scasw** case. There is only one block of data involved in the search, and it is indexed by **es:di**. Scas shares the automatic increment/decrement feature of the previous instructions, but this time it is applied only to **di**.

The **scas** instruction is used frequently, both with the **repe** prefix and with the **repne** prefix. We will now give examples of both usages.

In parsing the PSP, we have already dealt with the problem of jumping over the opening white space in the command-line tail. This can be done very neatly using **scasb** with the **repe** prefix and **al** = ' ', the space character. Recall that an executing program receives control with **ds** and **es** pointing to the PSP, that the byte at **ds:0080H** contains the length of the command-line tail, and that the actual text of the command-line tail begins at **ds:0081H**. This fragment will therefore locate the first non-space character:

```
mov     cl, ds:[80h]
xor     ch, ch  ;initialize cx
mov     di, 81h ;the starting offset
mov     al, ' ' ;the search character
repe    scasb
dec     di        ;to correct for overshoot
push    di      ;store it
```

The **scasb** instruction stops iterating as soon as the first non-space character is encountered, i.e., at the start of the first command-line parameter. But because of overshoot, **di** advances one position too far, and so must be decremented to compensate.

After finding the beginning of the first command-line parameter, it is frequently desirable to continue and find the first space character occurring after it. This space character can then be replaced by a null terminator, thereby turning the parameter into an ASCIIZ string. Taking up where the last example left off, **di** already points to the start of the first parameter, **al** still contains the space character, and **cx** has value one less than the remaining character count (because of overshoot). Hence all we need is

```
inc     cx        ;now cx = character count
repne   scasb
dec     di        ;to correct for overshoot
mov     BYTE PTR [di], 0  ;null terminate
pop     di        ;start of ASCIIZ string
```

Finding the subsequent parameters is equally easy. It involves more applications of **scasb**, alternating the prefixes **repe** and **repne**.

The two remaining string functions are best discussed together. They are **lods**, *load the accumulator*, and **stos**, store the accumulator. Of course, the accumulator refers to **al** or **ax**, in the byte or word case, respectively. If these instructions are thought of as "load from" and "store in," the register usage is easy to remember. In "load from," the string is the source and so is addressed as **ds:si**; in "store in," the string is the destination and so is addressed as **es:di**.

Obviously, **stos** can be used with the **rep** prefix to fill a block with copies of a given byte or word. In principle, **lodsb** can also be used with a **rep** prefix, but it is hard to see why one would want to do such a thing.

There is a standard context in which **lods** and **stos** are used as a pair but where the **loop** instruction, rather than the **rep** prefix, must be used. This situation arises because it is impossible to interrupt a **rep** prefix after every cycle to perform auxiliary processing. We will illustrate this observation with an example.

Suppose we need to move a block of data from one location to another and also to manipulate the data in some way as they are moved. To be specific, consider the problem of moving a byte string between locations *Ary1* and *Ary2* in the data segment and suppose that the string consists solely of lowercase letters and that these must be changed to uppercase as the string is moved. Assume, as usual, that **ds** points to the data segment but that **es** requires initialization, and let *Len* represent the length of *Ary1*. Here is a solution to the problem:

```
            push    ds
            pop     es
            mov     si, OFFSET Ary1
            mov     di, OFFSET Ary2
            mov     cx, Len

moveLoop:

            lodsb
            add     al, 'A'-'a'
            stosb
            loop    moveLoop
```

A variant of this situation arises in updating the video screen. In 80-column-by-25-row text mode, the information that appears on the screen is actually the contents of a certain 2000-word *video buffer*. Each word in the video buffer consists of the ASCII code of the character to be displayed, stored in the low byte, and a *video attribute* stored in the high byte. This video attribute controls how that character will look when displayed. It determines properties like the color of the character and its background on a color display and whether it is underlined or reverse video on a monochrome display. We will not discuss the various **IBM-XT** video systems further in this book but instead refer the reader to any of the standard references. ([9] contains an excellent introduction but unfortunately was written before the advent of the EGA or VGA; [11] is an encyclopedic treatment.) For the sake of the present example, we assume these facts: each character should be displayed with attribute value 07H; the starting address of the video buffer is B800:0000. These are perfectly reasonable defaults for most color displays.

Suppose that a 2000-byte buffer named *charBuf* contains text (one character per byte) that we wish to display on the video screen. Assume that *charBuf* is in the segment pointed to by **ds**. The following code moves the characters in *charBuf* to the video buffer, padding each with a copy of the video attribute to make it a word:

```
    mov    cx, 2000      ;number of characters to write
    mov    si, OFFSET charBuf
    mov    ax, 0b800h
```

```
        mov    es, ax       ;point es to the video buffer
        xor    di, di       ;start at offset zero therein
        mov    ah, 07h      ;video attribute

moveLoop:

        lodsb               ;loads byte at ds:si into al, incs. si
        stosw               ;stores ax at es:di, adds two to di
        loop    moveLoop
```

The only remaining aspect of the string instructions needing discussion is the question of segment overrides. Must the source always be addressed by **ds** and the destination by **es**, or can these defaults be altered? The answer is that the segment for the source can be overridden, but not the segment for the destination. This means that the source segment in **movsb** and **cmpsb** can be altered, as can the sole segment in **lodsb**, but that neither **scasb** nor **stosb** can receive an override.

To effect an override, the long form

```
        inst    Op1, Op2
```

must be used. For example, if *Data1*, *Data2*, and *Data3* are in the segments pointed to by **cs**, **es** and **ss**, respectively, then these segment overrides are all legal:

```
        movs    Data2, cs:Data1
        cmps    cs:Data1, Data2
        lods    ss:Data3
```

Instead of using an explicit override, it is possible to use an **ASSUME** and have **MASM** automatically generate the correct override. As an illustration, suppose that *Data3* in the previous display is in a segment called *Stack*. Then the **lods** example could be replaced by

```
        ASSUME  ss:Stack
        lods    Data3
```

But remember — when using the long form of any string instruction, it is still necessary to explicitly initialize whichever of **si**, **di**, **ds**, and **es** are used with that instruction.

There is an additional complication. If a segment override is used with a **rep** prefix, and if the string instruction is interrupted by a hardware interrupt, the microprocessor will forget the existence of the segment override when it resumes executing the code. There is an instruction, **cli**, that prevents hardware interrupts (except for the so-called non-maskable interrupt that we will discuss in Chapter 15). A corresponding instruction, **sti**, reenables the hardware interrupts. These instructions can be used to protect a string instruction from interruption, as follows:

```
        cli
        rep     movsb
        sti
```

The problem with this approach is that repeated string instructions can take a long time to execute (by machine standards) and it is not considered good policy to leave the interrupts disabled for too long a period. Hence the safest policy is to refrain from using segment overrides on string instructions.

Exercise 10-17. If **movs** is used when the source string overlaps the destination string, it will work correctly only if it is performed in the right direction (uphill or downhill). What happens when it proceeds in the wrong direction is also interesting — the result consists of repeats of a certain pattern. Investigate this phenomenon and use it to write a macro that uses **movs** to fill a given area with repeats of a chosen pattern of bytes or words.

Exercise 10-18. Write final versions of the string macros that were considered in the exercises at the end of Chapter 5. Naturally, these versions should use the string instructions and they should work correctly even if the source and destination strings overlap.

SECTION 9 THE REMAINING INSTRUCTIONS

Table 10.8 shows all the remaining **8088** instructions. The flag-setting instructions are self-explanatory and, for the most part, we have encountered them before.

The carry flag is obviously of special significance since it has three instructions dedicated to it. The **cmc** instruction, *complement the carry flag*, toggles CF — if set, it is cleared, and conversely. Even though not every flag has dedicated instructions that can be used to change it, any flag value can be easily modified. The bit operations cannot be used directly on the flags register. However, the flags register can be pushed/popped into some other register, changed using the bit operations, and then restored. As an example, suppose we want to set the trap flag, which occupies bit position 8. Here is the natural way to do it:

```
pushf
pop     ax
or      ax,  100000000b
push    ax
popf
```

As the name suggests, the external synchronization instructions are not needed in pure **8088** programming. They are used when the **8088** is working in conjunction with a coprocessor, most often the **8087** numerical coprocessor. We will not use these instructions until Chapter 17 but, for completeness, will briefly describe them here.

The **esc** (*escape to coprocessor*) instruction takes two operands: the first operand specifies a coprocessor instruction and the second operand is a datum, either a register or memory reference. The **8088** automatically puts the datum onto the data bus, where it can be accessed by the given coprocessor instruction. We will see in Chapter 17 that **MASM** automatically inserts the **esc** instruction when a coprocessor instruction is used.

Chips such as **8087** are called *coprocessors* because they execute concurrently with the **8088**. A potentially unpleasant aspect of this concurrency is that two processors may be

TABLE 10.8 MISCELLANEOUS INSTRUCTIONS

MNEMONIC   OPERATION PERFORMED

FLAG OPERATIONS

stc	set the carry flag
clc	clear the carry flag
cmc	complement the carry flag
std	set the direction flag
cld	clear the direction flag
sti	set the interrupt flag
cli	clear the interrupt flag

EXTERNAL SYNCHRONIZATION

hlt	halt until interrupt or reset
wait	wait for coprocessor
esc	escape to coprocessor
lock	lock bus during next instruction

NO OPERATION

nop	no operation

using, and changing, the same piece of data at the same time. **Hlt, wait,** and **lock** are designed to protect against this situation. The **hlt** instruction stops the processor until it receives a signal from the coprocessor (or, more generally, until an interrupt occurs). The **wait** instruction is similar, except that the processor will begin automatically as soon as the coprocessor finishes its current instruction. Finally, **lock** (which is actually a prefix rather than an instruction) denies other processors the use of the data bus for the duration of the current instruction.

The final instruction is **nop,** the *no operation* instruction. **Nop** leaves the system unchanged, including the settings of the flags. It consumes one byte of code space and requires three clock cycles. As an interesting aside, we point out that even though **nop** has its own mnemonic, it is not a new instruction: **MASM** encodes it as

```
xchg     ax, ax
```

The uses of **nop** are not terribly significant. A collection of **nop**s can be used to fill up space in the code segment, perhaps so that some code can be inserted later without changing the position of the existing code. **MASM** uses a **nop** as padding when it discovers that a forward **jmp** can be encoded as a **SHORT jmp.** A loop of **nop**s can be used as a do-nothing delay loop in a program. A series of **nop**s could be used to overwrite and hence delete code on the machine-language level, but this kind of application does not come up often.

TABLE 10.9 EFFECTS OF INSTRUCTIONS ON FLAGS

	OF	SF	ZF	AF	PF	CF
ADD AND SUB						
add adc sub sbb	x	x	x	x	x	x
cmp neg cmps scas	x	x	x	x	x	x
INC AND DEC						
inc dec	x	x	x	x	x	
MUL AND DIV						
mul imul	x	?	?	?	?	x
div idiv	?	?	?	?	?	?
BCD						
aaa aas	?	?	?	x	?	x
asm aad	?	x	x	?	x	?
daa das	?	x	x	?	x	?
BITWISE						
and or xor test	0	x	x	?	x	0
shl shr (by 1)	x	x	x	?	x	x
shl shr (by cl)	?	x	x	x	x	x
sar	0	x	x	?	x	x
rol ror rcl rcl (by 1)	x					x
rol ror rcl rcr (by cl)	?					

KEY	'x' means this flag is affected
	'?' means this flag is left in an indeterminate state
	'0' means this flag is assigned value 0
	blank means flag is not changed

SECTION 10 EFFECT ON THE FLAGS

We will conclude this chapter by summing up the effects of the various instructions on the flags. This information is easiest to remember if the instructions are considered in groups, as is done in Table 10.9. This diagram considers only the arithmetic instructions and other instructions for which the flag settings are either significant or not obvious.

In addition to the information in Table 10.9, it must be remembered that the data-moving instructions (including **mov, movs, xchg, push,** and **pop**) do not change any flags. Likewise, the program-control instructions (including **call, jmp, ret,** and the conditional jumps) do not change them. **Int** does change the interrupt and trap flags, but this is not usually important, since **iret** restores the original values.

As we pointed out previously, **inc** and **dec** do not change the carry flag, and this behavior is frequently useful in looping constructs.

We know in general that CF is set to signal unsigned overflow after an arithmetic operation, while OF is set to signal signed overflow. However, they are treated somewhat

FIGURE 10.7 A MYSTERY PROGRAM

```
1    TITLE    Myst1.asm : must be linked in order Myst2 then Myst1
2
3    DOSSEG
4    .MODEL SMALL
5    .STACK 100H
6
7    .DATA
8
9        Flag    DW    0
10
11   .CODE
12
13       EXTRN    Proc1:NEAR
14
15   Start:
16
17       mov     bx, @DATA
18       mov     ds, bx
19
20       or      Flag, 0
21       js      Beyond
22       not     Flag
23       mov     cx, 'Z'-'A'+1
24       mov     dl, 'A'-1
25       mov     ah, 02h
26
27   Beyond:
28
29       inc     dl
30       int     21h
31
32       call    Proc1
33
34       mov     ax, 4c00h
35       int     21h
36
37   END Start


1    TITLE    Myst2.asm
2
3    PUBLIC  Proc1
4
5    .MODEL SMALL
6    .STACK 100H
7
8    .CODE
9
10   Proc1   PROC    NEAR
11
12       loop    Done
13       pop     dx
14       pop     cx
15       pop     bx
16       pop     ax
```

```
17      pop     bx
18      pop     cx
19      pop     dx
20      jmp     ax
21
22  Done:
23
24  Proc1   ENDP
25
26  END
```

differently by **mul** and **imul**. In the 16-bit case, OF and CF are set when the answer is bigger than 16 bits. The use of OF and CF in the 8-bit case is analogous.

Div and **idiv** also behave differently. Here the flags are undefined. The division analog of overflow occurs when the quotient is too large for its allotted storage. This occurrence is called *divide overflow* and is signalled, not by flag settings, but by the triggering of the hardware interrupt number **int 00H**.

Exercise 10-19. (*Pell Equations*) A famous problem in mathematics asks for integers x and y that are solutions of an equation of the form

$$x^2 - d * y^2 = 1$$

where d is a fixed positive integer. The solution $x = 1$ and $y = 0$ is not allowed. For example, when $d = 2$, a solution is $x = 3$ and $y = 2$. It is quite easy to find solutions for $d = 3,5,6,7,8$, etc., by hand. It is a fact that if d is a perfect square $(1,4,9,\cdots)$ there are no solutions. Write a program that finds a solution of this equation for each value of $d < 100$ that is not a perfect square.

Suggestions: The size of the smallest solution varies radically for different values of d, and so it is necessary to use some kind of multiple-precision arithmetic. Using our macros for unpacked BCD is the best approach at this point. This is a very interesting programming problem because the solution appears to require a nested double loop (since there are two variables x and y), but using a double loop will result in an impractically slow program. With a little ingenuity, the double-loop algorithm can be replaced by a single loop.

Exercise 10-20. Figure 10.7 contains the code for a two-module mystery program. What does that program do? Answer the question by analyzing the code and then run the program to find out whether you were correct. (The source code is on the Program Disk.)

Exercise 10-21. Write a program that *consists of only one line* (in addition to the standard overhead lines), yet runs very differently under **DOS** and under **CODEVIEW**.

CHAPTER 11

APPLICATIONS INSTRUCTIONS ADDED WITH LATER PROCESSORS

SECTION 1 PREVIEW

We will now continue with the analysis of the **80286/80386** extensions to the instruction set that we began in Chapter 7. In the present chapter, we will complete our discussion of the application instructions, leaving those instructions that are primarily used in systems programming until Chapter 18.

Most of the new application instructions are examined in Section 2. However, the **enter** and **leave** instructions are quite specialized and require a good deal of elaboration. Consequently, we devote the optional Section 3 to them.

The remainder of the chapter contains sundry applications of the new instructions.

Section 4 opens with a version of the *sieve of Eratosthenes*, which is a classic method of finding prime numbers The sieve can be implemented very efficiently on the **80386** because of its bit-searching and testing capabilities. The next program in Section 4 is a general procedure that moves a bit string of arbitrary length and with arbitrary starting alignment to a destination again having arbitrary position and alignment. This procedure amply illustrates the complexities involved in bit-intensive programming. However, the **80386** was designed to be strong in this area precisely because it is of ever-increasing importance in applications programming. Bit-mapped graphics and proportionally spaced print are two especially significant applications.

The fast 32-bit arithmetic operations of the **80386** lend themselves well to the implementation of a multiple-precision integer arithmetic package, a project that we undertake in Section 5. As an application of our multiple-precision operations, we present a program that computes the factorial function of large integers. As written, this program will compute the factorial of any integer up to 10,000.

Finally, in Section 6 we consider the problem of high-precision real-number computations. The easiest approach to this problem is by using *fixed-point arithmetic*, which basically means treating the numbers in question as though they were integers but "remembering" to insert a decimal point at the correct location. Since we have multiple-precision integer routines available, it is only natural that we should use this approach. We will see that our multiple-precision integer package requires only a few extensions to allow its use in extended-precision real-number computations.

As soon as we have the capacity to do highly accurate real-number computations, we examine a problem that has fascinated mathematicians for the last 400 years and computer scientists for the last 40; namely, the computation of the number π. By using a famous formula discovered by the mathematician Ramanujan, we are able to compute π to over-1000-decimal-place accuracy — a computation requiring about 20 seconds!

SECTION 2 NEW APPLICATION INSTRUCTIONS

Table 11.1 shows the extra application instructions that became available with the later processors in the series. Some of these are totally new, while others are just old instructions used with new formats. In this section, we will make general observations on these instructions and illustrate how they are used.

Multiplication and Division. We examined the extended forms of **mul**, **imul**, **div**, and **idiv** quite completely in Chapter 7 and refer the reader to that discussion.

The New **80486** Arithmetic Instructions. For the sake of completeness, we have included the three new application instructions available under the **80486**. However, since the function of each can be duplicated using two or three earlier instructions, it is unlikely that many programmers will make their code **80486**-specific by using them.

Probably the most interesting of these instructions is **bswap**, which inverts the byte order in a 32-bit register by interchanging bytes 0 and 3 and interchanging bytes 1 and 2. We know that, in the architecture used by this family, multi-byte quantities are stored with the least significant byte at the lowest address. This format is sometimes called *little endian*. By contrast, many processors (such as the *68000* series) store data with the most significant byte at the lowest address, and this format is called *big endian*. This instruction eases the conversion between the two formats.

Data Extension. The **cwde** and **cdq** instructions are not really new. They are actually the 32-bit analogs of **cbw** and **cwd**, respectively. For example, **cbw** and **cwde** have exactly the same op-code (98H). In 16-bit mode, the machine interprets this op-code as **cbw** and in 32-bit mode as **cwde**. As always, the size-override byte 66H can be used to reverse the interpretation: in 16-bit mode the machine code

TABLE 11.1 INSTRUCTIONS ADDED WITH LATER PROCESSORS

INSTRUCTION	DESCRIPTION	INTRODUCED
ARITHMETIC		
mul, imul, div, and idiv in a variety of new formats	see Chapter 7	various
bswap	reverses byte order in 32-bit register	80486
cmpxchg r/m8,r8 r/m16,r16 r/m32,r32	compares dest with accumulator (al,ax,eax); if equal, source loaded into accumulator else dest loaded into accumulator	80486
cwde	converts word in ax to dword in eax by sign extension	80386
cdq	converts dword in eax to qword edx:eax by sign extension	80386
xadd r/m8,8 r/m16,16 r/m32,32	equivalent to add followed by xchg	80486
BIT INSTRUCTIONS		
rcl r/m, immed8	rotates r/m left through carry by distance given in immed8	80186
rcr r/m, immed8	rotates r/m right through carry by distance given in immed8	80186
rol r/m, immed8	rotates r/m left by distance given in immed8	80186
ror r/m, immed8	rotates r/m right by distance given in immed8	80186
sal r/m, immed8	same as shl r/m, immed8	80186
sar r/m, immed8	shifts r/m right by distance given in immed8, pads with zeros	80186
shl r/m, immed8	shifts r/m left by distance given in immed8, pads with zeros	80186
shr r/m, immed8	shifts r/m right by distance given in immed8, pads with sign bit	80186
bsf r16, r/m16 r32, r/m32	scans op2 starting at bit zero looking for first bit that is on; if one is found clears ZF and returns number in op1; else sets ZF	80386
bsr	same as bsf but scans in reverse direction	80386
bt r/m16, r16 r/m32, r32 r/m16, immed8 r/m32, immed8	stores bit number op2 of op1 in CF	80386
btc	same as bt but also complements given bit	80386

btr		same as bt but resets given bit	80386
bts		same as bt but sets given bit	80386
shld	r/m16,r16,immed8 r/m32,r32,immed8 r/m16,r16,cl r/m32,r32,cl	shifts op1 left by amount op3; pads with bits from op2	80386
shrd		same as shld but right instead of left	80386

DATA MOVEMENT

movsx	r16,r/m8 r32,r/m8 r32,r/m16	move op2 to op1 and sign-extend	80386
movzx		same as movsx except zero-extend	80386

MISCELLANEOUS

jcc	m16/m32	versions of all the conditional jumps with 16- or 32-bit displacements	80386
lfs	r16,m16:16 r32,m16:32	loads segment part of address into fs and offset into op1	80386
lgs		same as lfs but uses gs	80386
lss		same as lfs but uses ss	
setcc	r/m8	set op1 if condition cc holds; cc can be any conditional jump condition: a, ae, b, etc.	80386
bound	r16,m16&16 r32,m32&32	checks whether op1 within bounds set by both parts of op2; if not, calls int 05h	80186 80386
enter		sets up display when dealing with nested procedure definitions	80186
leave		reverses effect of enter	80186

STACK MANIPULATION

popa		pops all eight 16-bit general-purpose registers, but discards sp	80186
pusha		pushes all eight 16-bit general-purpose registers	80186
popad		analog of popa for 32-bit registers	80386
pushad		analog of pusha for 32-bit registers	80386
push	immed8 immed16 immed32	pushes immediate value	80186 80186 80386

Table 11.1 cont.

pop	immed8	pops immediate value	80186
	immed16		80186
	immed32		80386
pushfd		pushes eflags register	80386
popfd		pops eflags register but discards bits 16 and 17	80386

STRING INSTRUCTIONS

cmpsd		dword version of cmps	80386
lodsd		dword version of lods	80386
movsd		dword version of movs	80386
scasd		dword version of scas	80386
stosd		dword version of stos	80386
ins	r/m8, dx	inputs byte/word/dword from port dx to es:(e)di;	80186
	r/m16,dx	this is a new string function and works just like the others;	80186
	r/m32, dx	it is generally used with a rep prefix	80386
insb			
insw			
insd			
outs	dx, r/m8	outputs byte/word/dword pointed to by (e)si to port dx;	80186
outs	dx, r/m16	works like other string functions; segment override;	80186
outs	dx, r/m32	can be used on source generally used with rep prefix	80386
outsb			
outsw			
outsd			

is interpreted as a **cwde**, while in 32-bit mode it is interpreted as a **cbw**.

A potential point of confusion is the relationship between **cwde** and the standard **cwd** instruction, since both convert a word to a doubleword with sign extension. The difference is that **cwd** sign-extends **ax** to **dx:ax** while **cwde**, being the 32-bit analog of **cbw**, sign-extends **ax** to **eax**.

Shifts and Rotates. The most interesting fact here is that, beginning with the **80186**, the shifts and rotates can be used with constant shift values bigger than 1. For example, an instruction such as

```
shl      ax, 13
```

is now legal. Another interesting fact is that the time penalty involved in using shift counts larger than 1 in these instructions is quite modest; in fact, in the case of the **80386**, the time required is independent of the shift count — for any value of the shift count it is a miniscule

3 clock cycles when the first operand is a register and is 7 clock cycles when it is a memory reference. These times apply whether the second operand is immediate or is the **cl** register. Consequently, time-honored devices such as using

```
shl     ax, 1
shl     ax, 1
shl     ax, 1
```

to give a small speed advantage must fall by the wayside.

Bit-Scan Instructions. These very useful instructions are new to the **80386**. A bit-scan instruction will scan its second operand, a word or dword, either from low bit to high bit or in the opposite direction, looking for the first bit that is on. If such a bit is found, its number is returned in the first operand of the instruction and ZF is cleared. If the second operand is identically zero, ZF is set.

One feature of these instructions is that they are surprisingly slow: execution requires $10 + 3n$ cycles, where n is the number of zeros encountered before the first on-bit. If, for example, the first on-bit in a dword is bit number 20, then **bsf** requires 70 clock cycles to find it. Of course, using a bit-scan instruction is still much faster than, say, using **test** in a loop.

A real weakness of these instructions is that they will find only the first or last on-bit in an operand. Ideally, they should accept a starting bit number as a third operand, beginning the search at that point. The **bsf** instruction, for example, could then be used to sequentially find the first, second, ⋯, on-bit within an operand. As things stand, this can be done only by using a software loop involving the bit-test instructions, which we are going to discuss next.

The Bit-Test Instructions. These instructions are used to check whether a given bit of a register or memory operand is on. In addition, the various forms of the instruction will either set, reset, complement, or leave unchanged the bit in question. The register or memory reference is given as the first operand of the instruction and the bit number as the second operand. The value of the bit is returned in CF.

The most intriguing aspect of these instructions is their treatment of the second operand when it is larger than the bit size of the first operand. To be specific, consider the instruction

```
bt    Op1, ax
```

where *Op1* is of size 16 bits. If **ax** has value 100, then the machine interprets this instruction as a request to test the bit that is located 100 bits above the base address of *Op1*. In other words, this instruction is equivalent to

```
bt    Op1[12], 4
```

since adding 100 bits to the base address *Op1* has the effect of adding 12 bytes and then advancing a further 4 bits.

Because of this behavior, the bit-test instructions are extremely adept at dealing with bit arrays, and these bit arrays can be very large indeed in the 32-bit case. The basic idea is to keep the first operand constant, pointing to the base of the array, as in

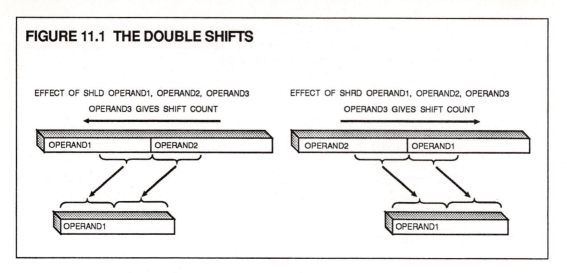

FIGURE 11.1 THE DOUBLE SHIFTS

```
bt    bitArray, eax
```

The second operand then gives the index into the array in bits. We will use this technique in the next section.

The Bit-Blt Instructions. This name is a contraction of *bit-block transfers*. The instructions in question, **shld** and **shrd**, are generally used to move bit strings quickly from one position to another. Of course, if the strings actually fill an integral number of bytes and begin on byte boundaries, then it is faster to use the string instructions. But there are two standard contexts in which nonaligned bit strings come up: on a bit-mapped graphics screen and in the manipulation of proportionally spaced text.

The **shld** and **shrd** instructions act like the usual shifts with multiple shift counts except that, instead of always shifting in 0s or 1s, they shift in bits from a register or memory operand. This action is depicted in Figure 11.1, which already strongly suggests how these instructions can be used to fabricate moves of bit-string data. We will illustrate this process in the next section.

The Data Movement Instructions. We have already used these in Chapter 7.

Miscellaneous Instructions. The short-range restriction (−127 to +128 bytes) has been removed from the conditional jumps (**ja, jae,**···). They actually come in three forms now: as well as the traditional configuration that uses a one-byte displacement, it is now permissible to use a word or a dword displacement. Hence the target of the conditional jump can be located anywhere in a 32-bit segment.

The **lfs** and **lgs** instructions are just the analogs of the old **lds** and **les** for use with the new segment registers. The **lss** instruction is used in the same way with the **ss** register. Of course, this instruction should always be used in the form

```
lss     sp, newStackData
```

Since the machine is in a vulnerable state when **ss** has been switched but not **sp**, it is reassuring to be able to change both values with a single instruction.

The *set byte on condition* instructions are used to set byte flags for later inspection. They come in varieties that match the conditional jumps: **seta, setae,···**. Here is a fragment illustrating how these instructions are used to set a flag:

```
cmp     Op1, Op2
setge   op1BiggerFlag
;change values of Op1 and Op2
```

Since *Op1* and *Op2* are about to be changed, the flag is necessary to record their original relative sizes. Later in the program, the following lines could be used to find out about the original sizes:

```
test    op1BiggerFlag, 1
jne     op1Bigger
;code to be executed if Op2 was originally bigger
op1Bigger:
;code to be executed if Op1 was originally bigger
```

The **bound** instruction is used in writing compilers. It checks whether its first operand is within the bounds given by the two parts of its second operand. Of course, it is designed for bounds checking of array references. It would probably find more use in assembly language programming if it signaled an out-of-bounds condition by some simple response such as setting the carry flag. Instead of doing this, it triggers an interrupt, **int 05H**, the *bounds check fault*. Consequently, even the casual use of the **bound** instruction involves taking control of this interrupt. (The reader may know that **int 05H** is generally described as the *shift-print-screen interrupt* and so may be puzzled by the preceding description. This apparent contradiction will be explained in Chapter 18.)

The **enter** and **leave** are also used in compiler writing. However, they are quite interesting and do give insight into the operation of a compiler. Hence we will look at them in some detail in Section 3.

The Stack Instructions. Most of these were introduced in Chapter 7. The only one that needs elaboration at this point is **popfd**. As we saw in Chapter 7, the flags register of the **80386** is 32 bits wide and contains the flags of the previous processors in their usual positions in its lower half. Bits 16 and 17 contain new flags that should only be changed by the operating system. As a result, even though applications programs can use the **popfd** instruction, it will have no effect on either of these bits. It will replace the flags with its stack image, except that these two bits will remain unchanged.

The String Instructions. As might be expected, there are dword analogs of all the standard string instructions (**cmpsd, lodsd, ···**). These work exactly as expected. An additional pair of string instructions, **ins** and **outs**, was introduced with the **80186**. These are the string versions of the standard **in** and **out** instructions which, respectively, input and output data from ports. These new instructions work in the same general way as the other string functions: they first came in byte and word forms, and a dword version was introduced with the **80386**.

SECTION 3 THE ENTER AND LEAVE INSTRUCTIONS

The **enter** and **leave** instructions are primarily of interest to compiler writers, and we include them mainly for the sake of completeness. Nothing from this section is used in the remainder of the book and so it may be safely omitted on a first reading. Before studying the present section, the reader should review Section 10 of Chapter 6. We will assume throughout this section that 16-bit segments are being used. However, the **enter** and **leave** instructions are sensitive to address size. In dealing with 32-bit segments, the obvious adjustments to our discussions must be made. For example, **bp** and **sp** should be replaced by **ebp** and **esp**.

Some programming languages allow *nesting of procedure definitions*, which means that a procedure definition can contain another procedure definition within it. **Pascal** is such a language, but **C** is not.

The first part of Figure 11.2 contains a **Pascal** fragment that illustrates nested procedure definitions: *Proc2* is defined within *Proc1* and *Proc3* is defined within *Proc2*. The most interesting feature of procedure nesting is its effect on the block structure of the language: the scope of a variable includes all procedures nested inside the procedure in which it is defined. In other words, a variable defined in a given procedure can be used by any procedure whose definition is contained within that procedure.

In terms of our **Pascal** fragment, this *scope* rule has the following consequences:

- The variables that can be used in *Proc1* are the argument values *parm1* and *parm2*, and the local variables *loc1* and *loc2*.

- *Proc2* has access to *parm1*, *parm2*, *loc1*, and *loc2*, as well as its own arguments *parm3* and *parm4* and its locals *loc3* and *loc4*.

- Similarly, *Proc3* can use any of *parm1*, *parm2*, *parm3*, *parm4*, *parm5*, *parm6*, *loc1*, *loc2*, *loc3*, *loc4*, *loc5*, and *loc6*.

The scope of the identifier *Proc2* is just *Proc1*. This means that the name *Proc2* is "visible" only inside *Proc1* and so *Proc2* can be called only as part of the code for *Proc1*. (This statement is really an over-simplification — the *present instance* of the identifier *Proc2* is local to *Proc1*. However, *Proc2* may be defined to mean something totally different elsewhere in the program.) Consequently, *Proc1* must be active when *Proc2* is called. There may be several versions of *Proc1* active at such a point, but the block structuring rules dictate that the most recent activation of *Proc1* will be associated with the present activation of *Proc2*. The same general comments can be made about *Proc2* and *Proc3*.

As a result, *Proc3* can only be called while there are active calls to both *Proc2* and *Proc1*. The inset in Figure 11.2 is intended to depict the stack configuration at such a point in the program: it shows the stack frame for the *Proc3* call, as well as the frames for the associated *Proc2* and *Proc1* calls.

This stack diagram reveals the essential problem: the quantities *loc1*, *loc2*, *loc3*, *loc4*, *var1*, *var2*, *var3*, and *var4* are buried quite deeply on the stack, yet *Proc3* can legally use them. How can their values be efficiently extracted from the stack? This is the problem that the **enter** and **leave** instructions are designed to solve.

Lines 22-47 show the assembly language code into which a hypothetical compiler might translate the **Pascal** fragment. These lines are not intended as a realistic depiction of compiler-generated code, even if the compiler produces assembly language output, which

FIGURE 11.2 THE ENTER AND LEAVE INSTRUCTIONS

```
1   {Pascal fragment A: shows nested procedure definitions}
2   procedure proc1(parm1, parm2: integer);
3       var loc1, loc2: integer;
4       procedure proc2(parm3, parm4: integer);
5           var loc3, loc4: integer
6           procedure proc3(parm5, parm6: integer);
7               var loc5, loc6: integer
8               begin;
9               {code for proc3}
10              end;
11          begin;
12          {code for proc2}
13          end;
14      begin;
15      {code for proc1}
16      end;
17
18  ;assembly language translation
19  ;   of nested procedures by
20  ;      hypothetical compiler
21
22  Proc1   PROC NEAR
23
24          enter  4, 1
25          ;code for Proc1
26          leave
27          ret     4
28
29  Proc1   ENDP
30
31  Proc2   PROC NEAR
32
33          enter  4, 2
34          ;code for Proc2
35          leave
36          ret     4
37
38  Proc2   ENDP
39
40  Proc3   PROC NEAR
41
42          enter   4, 3
43          ;code for Proc3
44          leave
45          ret     4
46
47  Proc3   ENDP
```

STACK CONFIGURATION DURING
ACTIVATION OF Proc3

FRAME FOR Proc3: loc6, loc5, frame ptr3, frame ptr2 (DISPLAY3: 3 FRAME POINTERS), frame ptr1, old bp (PRESENT BP = FRAME PTR3), return ip, var6, var5

FRAME FOR MOST RECENT Proc2: loc4, loc3, frame ptr2, frame ptr1 (DISPLAY2: 2 FRAME POINTERS), old bp (FRAME PTR2), return ip, var4, var3

FRAME FOR MOST RECENT PROC1: loc2, loc1, frame ptr1 (DISPLAY1), old bp (FRAME PTR1), return ip, var2, var1

it may not — it may generate object code only. Our only goal is to show the use of the **enter** and **leave** instructions. One observation is that the assembly language translation does not exhibit procedure nesting to reflect that of the original fragment. Of course, this would be illegal since procedure definitions cannot be nested in this assembly language.

Before describing the actions of the **enter** instruction precisely, let us look more closely at the stack frames in Figure 11.2. The only new feature that they exhibit is a region called the *display*. To understand the function of the display, consider how *Proc3* might access *var1*. The essential step is to recover the value that **bp** had when *Proc1* was activated. The present value of **bp** is certainly different and, in fact, **bp** may have changed many times since the activation of *Proc1*. The desired old value of **bp** is labeled "FRAME PTR1" on Figure 11.2 and the essential point is that this value is available as part of the current display. Hence to copy *var1* into **ax**, for example, the compiler need only generate code such as this:

```
mov     si, [bp+2]          ;point si to correct stack frame
mov     ax, ss:[si+4]       ;si+4 now points to var1
```

Similarly, to copy *loc4* into **ax**, the compiler might generate this code:

```
mov     si, [bp+4]          ;point si to correct stack frame
mov     ax, ss:[si-8]       ;si-8 now points to loc4
```

The content and use of a display should now be clear: it consists of pointers to the stack frames of the antecedents of the given procedure along the nesting chain, and these pointers are used to access data associated with the corresponding procedures. The main function of **enter** is to provide an updated display for each stack frame associated with a nested procedure definition. As extra services, **enter** also reserves storage for locals on the stack and saves and updates **bp**. In other words, **enter** performs the chores that are generally done by lines such as

```
push    bp
mov     bp, sp
sub     sp, 4      ;reserve space for locals
```

Consequently, these lines should be omitted when **enter** is used.
Here are the actual operations performed by **enter**:

- Pushes old **bp**.

- Moves **bp** to **sp**.

- Copies previous display to top of stack.

- Augments display by pushing present **bp**.

- Decrements **sp** to reserve space for locals.

To perform these operations correctly, **enter** requires two parameters: the present nesting depth, so that it knows how many old display items must be copied (i.e., one less than the nesting depth), and the number of bytes to reserve for locals. This explains the syntax

enter *nestingDepth, bytesToReserve*

The reader can now check that the assembly language code on lines 22-47 of Figure 11.2 does indeed represent a reasonable translation of the nesting structure of the **Pascal** fragment, and that it generates the corresponding stack frames.

There is a variant form of **enter**. If the first parameter is given the value 0, then the same services are performed, except those that relate to the display. This form is appropriate for use in contexts (or languages) where nesting of procedure definitions is not used.

The action of the **leave** instruction needs little explanation: it undoes the effects of the corresponding **enter** and so is used to "clean house" at the procedure exit point.

SECTION 4 SOME EXAMPLES

The classical *sieve of Eratosthenes* is a technique for generating prime numbers and is familiar to most students of computer science. (See Exercise 6-16.) We will now implement the sieve using the **80386** bit-scan and bit-test instructions, and will find all the primes less than 500,000, printing a few of them to the screen.

For the sake of the reader who is unfamiliar with the sieve, here is how it is used to find all the primes less than N, for a given integer N:

- Begin with an array of N elements, each initialized to 1.

- Modify the array by changing all entries with non-prime index to 0, so that the primes will be precisely the set of indices with corresponding array entry equal to 1.

The non-primes can be identified by making a number of passes through the array:

- First, 0 and 1 are not prime, so these array entries should be made 0.

- The number 2 is prime, but its multiples 4, 6, ⋯ are not, hence these entries should also be made 0.

- The next number after 2 with non-zero entry is 3. This is prime but its multiples 6, 9, 12, 15, ⋯ are not, so the corresponding entries should be made 0. (Of course, some are already 0.)

- Repeat the process with the next index k corresponding to a non-zero entry, namely k = 5: this is a prime, hence its entry is retained, but all its multiples are made 0.

- Continue this search-and-delete operation with increasing values of k, terminating as soon as k reaches the square root of N.

In this description, we have not been specific about the *kind* of array that should be used. Since each array element need only take on values 0 and 1, it suffices to use an array of *bits*. Even without resorting to the segment-expansion technique introduced in Chapter 7, we can use an array of size nearly 64K bytes. In the **SMALL** model, the total size of the data and stack segments together cannot exceed 64K, consequently the array must be somewhat smaller than 64K. However, it can be made large enough to hold over 500,000 bits, as we did in our demonstration program PRIMES.ASM, which is shown in Figure 11.3.

The **80386** is the first processor in the series that provides instructions for the efficient manipulation of bit arrays. The most important of these instructions are the bit tests: **bt**, **bts**, **btr**, and **btc**. In Section 2, we pointed out a very important feature of these instructions: if the first operand is initialized to the base address of an array then the second operand represents an index into the array, *measured in bits*. We used this feature in PRIMES.ASM.

FIGURE 11.3 SEARCHING FOR PRIMES

```
 1   TITLE    Primes.asm: demonstrates the bit test instructions
 2
 3   COMMENT  #  Generates the primes in the range 2 - 15700*32 and prints those
 4            #  that lie within 1000 of the end of the range
 5
 6   INCLUDE console.mac
 7   DOSSEG
 8   .MODEL SMALL
 9   .386
10
11       Len            EQU   15700          ;chosen so that numberOfBits > 500,000
12       numberOfBits   EQU   Len*32
13
14   .STACK 100h
15   .DATA
16
17       longStr     DB      12  DUP(?) ;in the present case, 7 dups would do
18       bitArray    DD      NOT 11B, (Len-1) DUP(-1) ;because 0 and 1 not primes
19       mpInt       DD       ?
20
21   .CODE
22
23   Start:
24
25       mov     ax, @DATA
26       mov     ds, ax
27
28   startTiming
29
30       mov     edx, numberOfBits       ;find upper bound for square root
31       bsr     ecx, edx                ;  of numberOfBits
32       inc     ecx                     ;net result of these three lines:
33       inc     ecx                     ;   if ecx is even add 1
34       and     ecx, NOT 1              ;   if ecx is odd add 2
35       sar     ecx, 1                  ;now divide it by two
36       mov     edx, 1
37       shl     edx, cl                 ;edx is now upper bound for square root
38
39       mov     eax, 1                  ;when incremented, will give first prime
40
41   findNextPrime:
42
43       inc     eax
44       cmp     eax, edx                ;edx contains the square root bound
45       je      SHORT printThem
46       bt      bitArray, eax           ;checks whether present bit is already 0
47       jnc     findNextPrime           ;if so, search further for next prime
48
49       mov     ebx, eax                ;at this point, eax contains next prime
50
51   removeMultiples:
52
53       add     ebx, eax                ;ebx will contain multiples of the prime
54       cmp     ebx, numberOfBits       ;  in eax, up to bitArray limit
55       jae     findNextPrime
```

```
56        btr     bitArray, ebx            ;replaces ebx bit in bitArray with 0
57        jmp     removeMultiples
58
59  printThem:
60
61  endTiming
62
63        mov     eax, numberOfBits-1000   ;starting point for range to print
64
65  printLoop:                             ;find and print primes in chosen range
66
67        inc     eax
68        cmp     eax, numberOfBits        ;stop when you reach end of bitArray
69        je      Done
70        bt      bitArray, eax            ;test whether bit is one -- if not, it
71        jnc     printLoop                ;   ia not a prime, so try the next one
72        mov     mpInt, eax               ;if it
73        lToA    longStr, mpInt           ;   is --
74        outAsc  longStr                  ;      print it,
75        outCh   ' '                      ;         nicely
76        outCh   ' '                      ;            aligned
77        jmp     printLoop
78
79  Done:
80
81        mov  ax, 4c00h
82        int  21h
83
84  END   Start


Elapsed time was: 1.71 seconds

501401  501409  501419  501427  501451  501463  501493  501503  501511  501563
501577  501593  501601  501617  501623  501637  501659  501691  501701  501703
501707  501719  501731  501769  501779  501803  501817  501821  501827  501829
501841  501863  501889  501911  501931  501947  501953  501967  501971  501997
502001  502013  502039  502043  502057  502063  502079  502081  502087  502093
502121  502133  502141  502171  502181  502217  502237  502247  502259  502261
502277  502301  502339  502393
```

Here are some specific comments on the code:

Line 11. *Len* is the length of the array of dwords. The value of *Len* was chosen so that the number of bits was bigger than 500,000 but small enough to leave room for the other data and the stack.

Lines 30-37. This is a quick way of getting a reasonable upper bound for the square root of an integer. Ideally, we should compute the exact integer square root of 15700*32 and use it as the termination point in the sieve algorithm. Although we suggest a method for doing this in the exercises, we chose not to do it in the text in order to conserve space. Rather, we use this obvious approximation:

• For an integer N suppose that the leftmost '1' in its binary representation occurs in bit k, and define r to be equal to k+1 if k is odd and k+2 otherwise. Then $2^{r/2}$ is an upper bound for the square root of N.

In lines 30-37, we perform the computations delineated in this approximation.

Line 56. Notice how well the bit-test instructions are tailored to this kind of computation. The **ebx** register contains the index of the bit to be zeroed. The **btr** instruction zeroes this bit directly, without the overhead of dividing **ebx** by 32 to generate an offset and a bit index into a dword.

We have used the timing macros that we will develop in Chapter 13 to check the performance of this program. These macros, *startTiming* and *endTiming*, have the obvious effect: the time required for execution of the sandwiched portion of the program in printed to the screen.

The last part of Figure 11.3 shows the program output and also gives the execution time (excluding printing time) when the program is run on a 33-megahertz machine. The execution time was an impressive 1.71 seconds, and even this time can be improved upon by using a better approximation for the square root.

Our next example demonstrates some of the tedious complications that can afflict assembly language programs — it is probably the ugliest program in the entire book! The problem is to write a procedure that will perform a general bit-string move. This means that both the source and the destination can have arbitrary bit alignment, i.e., each can begin at a designated bit number within its starting dword, and the length of the string (in bits) can also be specified as a parameter. Here are some of the difficulties with which the code must contend:

- The source string may overlap the destination. In an earlier version of the program (which does not appear in the book), we actually checked for occurrence of the

  "bad" overlap case, i.e., when the strings overlap and the destination lies "uphill" from the source. This is the only configuration that would cause difficulties since we are going to move the data in low-to-high order. However, checking for overlap required so much code (try it!) that we rewrote the program under the pessimistic assumption that overlap always occurs: the code automatically builds a copy of the source string on the stack and works with this copy. If the user is primarily interested in run-time efficiency (rather than program bulk), a better solution would be to distinguish cases: if the source location is lower than that of the destination, use the code as written; otherwise, transfer control to an analogous code block that implements the move in high-to-low order.

- The fact that the source and destination can begin at arbitrary bit offsets considerably complicates the code. Our solution is to begin by moving a partial dword to reduce to the case in which the destination begins on a dword boundary.

- Since the bit string can have any length, there will likely be some bits left over after the dword-by-dword move of the main part of the string. It is therefore necessary to provide special code to deal with the tail of the string.

- It will turn out that the situation where the string is short enough to fit entirely in one dword of the destination requires special treatment. To make matters worse, even this case breaks into two subcases: a very short string might originate within

FIGURE 11.4 WORKING WITH BIT STRINGS

```
 1   TITLE bitStr.asm: general bit string move procedure
 2
 3   COMMENT   # PROCEDURE HEADER
 4   TYPE:        NEAR 386  USE 16        FILE: bitStr.asm       LIBRARY: user.lib
 5   PURPOSE      Moves bit string with arbitrary alignment
 6   CALLED AS:   bitStrMov(destOffset(2), destStartBit(2), sourceOffset(2),
 7                     sourceStartBit(2), bitStrLen(2))
 8   PARAMS:      destOffset and sourceOffset have the obvious meanings
 9               destStartBit is the starting bit number of source bit string
10               in the dword with offset destOffset. sourceStartBit is similarly
11               defined. bitStrLen is the length of the source string in bits.
12               These quantities are abbreviated D, S, and L in the sequel
13   RETURNS:     Nothing
14   REMARKS:     Assumes ds points to segment of source string and es points to
15          #  segment of destination string
16
17   INCLUDE   console.mac
18   .SALL
19
20   ;------------------------------------------------------------
21
22   ;Replaces bits a through b-1 of inDword with corresponding bits from Source.
23   ;  Overwrites inDword. At least one of inDword, outDword must be a register.
24   ;    For efficiency does not restore ebx or cl.
25   Insert   MACRO  outDword, inDword, b, a
26
27       mov    ebx, -1              ;start building a mask in ebx
28       mov    cl, b
29       neg    cl
30       shl    ebx, cl              ;shift left by 32-b
31       add    cl, a
32       shr    ebx, cl              ;shift right by a+(32-b)
33       mov    cl, a
34       shl    ebx, cl              ;shift left by a
35       and    inDword, ebx
36       not    ebx
37       and    outDword, ebx
38       or     outDword, inDword
39
40   ENDM
41
42   ;------------------------------------------------------------
43
44   .MODEL SMALL
45   .386
46   PUBLIC  bitStrMov
47
48       destOffset     EQU     WORD PTR [bp+4]
49       D              EQU     [bp+6]                ;destStartBit
50       sourceOffset   EQU     WORD PTR [bp+8]
51       S              EQU     [bp+10]               ;sourceStartBit
52       L              EQU     [bp+12]               ;bitStrLen
53
54   .CODE
55
```

Figure 11.4 cont.

```
56  bitStrMov        PROC     NEAR
57
58      push    bp
59      mov     bp, sp
60
61      pushadM
62
63      mov     si, sourceOffset
64      mov     di, destOffset
65
66      mov     cx, L
67      shr     cx, 5                    ;number of dwords in Source, rounded down
68      add     cx, 2                    ;max. number of dwords holding Source bits
69
70      mov     dx, cx                   ;make a copy of it
71      shl     dx, 2                    ;max. number of bytes needed Source copy
72      sub     sp, dx                   ;protect space on stack for copy of Source
73      push    dx                       ;store this number to use in releasing space
74
75      push    es                       ;we will restore it later
76      push    ss
77      pop     es                       ;prepare to copy Source to stack
78
79      mov     si, sourceOffset
80      mov     ax, sp
81      add     ax, 4                    ;start of storage for Source copy
82      mov     di, ax                   ;register are all set for movsd
83      rep     movsd                    ;copy cx dwords from Source to stack
84
85      ;We must now point ds to stack and return es to original value
86      pop     es                       ;restore its entry value
87      push    ds                       ;to restore it later
88      push    ss
89      pop     ds                       ;so that ds is pointing to the temporary
90                                       ;  copy of Source on the stack
91
92      mov     si, sp
93      add     si, 4                    ;point si to copy of Source on stack
94      mov     di, destOffset           ;point di to Dest
95      mov     edx, [si]                ;edx is "low dword" for shrd
96      add     si, 4
97      lodsd                            ;eax is "high dword" for shrd
98
99      ;Check whether L <= 32-D, so that Dest lies entirely in one dword
100     mov     cl, 32
101     sub     cl, D                    ;cl = no. of bits of Dest
102     cmp     L, cl                    ;  lying in first dword
103     ja      SHORT moreThanOneDestDword
104
105     ;Here if Dest fits in a single dword
106     mov     cl, D
107     cmp     S, cl
108     jg      SHORT rightShiftNeeded
109
110     ;Here if S <= D and Source and Dest each entirely contained in one dword
111     sub     cl, S                    ;do a left shift by D-S
```

```
112         shl     edx, cl
113         jmp     SHORT @F
114
115     rightShiftNeeded:                   ;shrd by S-D
116
117         ;Here if S > D -- Source may span two dwords but Dest is a single dword
118         mov     cl, S
119         sub     cl, D
120         shrd    edx, eax, cl
121
122     @@:
123
124         mov     ch, D
125         add     ch, L                   ;Source occupies bits D
126                                         ;   through ch-1 in edx
127         Insert  es:[di], edx, ch, D
128         jmp     Done
129
130     moreThanOneDestDword:
131
132         ;We will first reduce to the case D=0 by moving initial 32-D bits
133         mov     cl, D
134         sub     cl, S
135         jl      SHORT SBigger
136
137         ;Here D >= S: we can get the 32-D bits to move entirely from edx
138         shl     edx, cl                 ;cl = D - S
139         Insert  es:[di], edx, 32, D     ;move 32-D bits to dest
140         mov     edx, [si-8]             ;refresh damaged edx
141         add     di, 4                   ;we have filled an entire dword of Dest
142         mov     bx, S
143         cmp     bx, D
144         jne     SHORT @F
145         mov     edx, eax                ;old "high dword" becomes new "low dword"
146         lodsd                           ;update "high dword"
147
148     @@:
149
150         jmp     SHORT updateParams
151
152     SBigger:
153
154         neg     cl                      ;S-D bits to be moved to first dword of
155         shrd    edx, eax, cl            ;   Dest come from first two dwords of Source
156         Insert  es:[di], edx, 32, D
157         mov     edx, eax                ;old "high dword" becomes new "low dword"
158         lodsd                           ;update "high dword"
159         add     di, 4                   ;we have filled an entire dword of Dest
160
161     updateParams:
162
163         mov     cx, 32                  ;number of bits moved = 32-D
164         sub     cx, D
165         sub     L, cx                   ;number remaining: L = L-(32-D)
166
167         mov     cx, D
168         sub     S, cx
169         jae     SHORT @F                ;computing new value for S:
170         add     BYTE PTR S, 32          ;   = S-D if S >= D
```

Figure 11.4 cont.

```
171                                   ;    = S-D+32 if S < D
172   @@:
173
174       mov     WORD PTR D, 0        ;the new value of D
175
176   middleWords:
177
178       ;D = 0 for the remainder of the code
179       mov     bx, L
180       shr     bx, 5               ;number of complete dwords to move
181       je      SHORT lastDword
182       mov     cl, S
183
184   moveLoop:
185
186       shrd    edx, eax, cl        ;edx contains new dest. dword
187       xchg    edx, eax            ;old eax is new "high dword"
188       stosd                       ;store in dest. dword
189       lodsd                       ;new "high dword" for next shrd
190       dec     bx                  ;one fewer to do
191       jnz     moveLoop
192
193   lastDword:
194
195       ;Move the final partial dword
196       mov     cl, S               ;for the upcoming shrd
197       shrd    edx, eax, cl        ;final partial dword now in low
198                                   ;  end of edx
199
200       mov     ecx, L
201       and     ecx, 1fh            ;remainder mod 32, i.e., number of
202                                   ;  bits in final, incomplete move
203       Insert  es:[di], edx, cl, 0
204
205   Done:
206
207       pop     ds                  ;because we changed it earlier
208       pop     dx                  ;size of temporary storage block on stack
209       add     sp, dx              ;release temporary storage
210       popadM
211       pop     bp
212       ret     10                  ;clear five two-byte parameters
213
214   bitStrMov       ENDP
215
216       END
```

one dword in the source or might be partly contained in each of two dwords —
even a bit string as short as two bits can span two dwords.

The extent to which these boundary issues complicate the code can best be appreciated
by counting lines: the complete procedure as presented in Figure 11.4 runs to some 200 lines,
but moving the main part of the string requires only thirty or so lines (lines 176-191, together
with various initializations performed earlier).

Before getting to the details of the coding, we will state the general mechanism that the program uses. The bits that end up in a given dword in the destination string originate in two contiguous dwords in the source string. In the comments, we call these the "high dword" and the "low dword." The basic moving strategy consists of the following steps:

- Transfer the low dword to **edx** and the high dword to **eax**.

- Perform a **shrd** with the correct shift count to collect in **edx** the bits needed for a dword of the destination.

- Move **edx** to the correct location in the destination.

Here are some line-by-line remarks on the code as presented in Figure 11.4:

Lines 6,14. For example, the procedure call

```
bitStrMov(1000,5,2000,10,76)
```

would move 76 bits starting with bit number 10 of the dword beginning at offset 2000 to the location starting with bit 5 of the dword at offset 1000. As the comment on line 14 indicates, it is the responsibility of the programmer to initialize **ds** to the segment containing *Source* and **es** to the segment containing *Dest*. We have chosen to make the length parameter L a word. Of course, this limits the maximum length string that can be moved to 2K dwords. This seems totally reasonable, considering the likely applications of this procedure. However, in Exercise 11-4 we ask the reader to write a modified version of the procedure in which this parameter is a dword.

Lines 22-40. This macro is useful from time to time. It transfers the bits numbered a through $b - 1$ of *inDword* to the corresponding positions in *outDword*, leaving the rest of *outDword* unchanged. To gain some speed, this particular version of the macro fails to fix the damage it inflicts on various registers and on *inDword*. The code has only one notable feature. The comment attached to line 30 indicates that the instruction

```
shl     ebx, cl
```

shifts **ebx** left by $32 - b$ bits, yet at that point the value in **cl** is $-b$, not $32 - b$. This shows a difference in how shifts and rotates are executed by the **80386** compared with previous processors. Unlike its predecessors, the **80386** interprets a shift or rotate count modulo 32. The advantage of this approach is that it is sometimes unnecessary to add or subtract multiples of 32 to the shift count to generate the correct code, this being a case in point. Line 32 shows another example of this phenomenon.

Lines 66-68. Computing the maximum number of dwords of *Dest* that can possibly hold bits of *Source*.

Lines 88-93. We want **ds:si** to point to the copy of *Source* on the stack and so point **ds** to the stack. Two words (**dx** and **ds**) were pushed after space was reserved on the stack for the copy and so **si** must be initialized to **sp** + 4.

Lines 95-97. Loading the first two dwords containing bits of *Source* into **edx** and **eax**.

Lines 99-128. The special case in which *Source* is so short that it fits entirely in the first dword of *Dest*.

Lines 132-174. Here we are moving enough bits to *Dest* to fill the first partial dword. Consequently, the remaining part of the string should be moved to the next dword, beginning at $D = 0$. Hence we have effectively reduced to the case $D = 0$.

Lines 178-191. Moving the main part of the string, 32 bits at a time.

Lines 193-203. Moving the final incomplete dword, if there is one. The number of bits to be moved is just the previous value of L reduced modulo 32, and this value is computed on lines 200 and 201. Since we have already left-aligned these bits in **edx** (lines 196-197), the application of *Insert* on line 203 completes the move.

Now that we have *bitStrMov*, it is reasonable to inquire how fast it is and, in particular, whether it is practical for use in bit-mapped graphics. It is a simple matter to simulate such an application. For example, the author timed *bitStrMov* with a bit string of length 640 (the bit width of an EGA screen) and found that a 33-megahertz machine completed approximately 26,000 calls per second. The EGA screen has 350 scan lines and is redrawn 60 times per second. Consequently, using *bitStrMov* to "keep up with the hardware" would require about 20,000 calls per second, which is under the attained limit. Of course, the snag is that this computation assumes that the processor can devote its time entirely to executing calls to *bitStrMov*, which is highly unlikely. On the other hand, it is also unlikely that every scan line will need to be updated with every screen refresh. If we decide (fairly arbitrarily) that, on average, we will update each scan line once for every three refreshes, then the coprocessor would spend about one-fourth of its time on calls to *bitStrMov*. Under most circumstances, this would probably be acceptable.

When we develop our execution profiler in Chapter 16, we will use it to examine *bitStrMov*, with an eye toward improving its performance.

Exercise 11-1. As written, the program PRIMES.ASM prints those primes that are contained among the last 1000 integers in its range. Modify the program so that, instead, it prints the last 1000 primes that it finds.

Exercise 11-2. The search-and-replace loop in PRIMES.ASM can terminate when k reaches the square root of N, but in our implementation, we used only a very rough approximation to the square root. Of course, the program will run considerably faster if this approximation is replaced by the true value of the square root.

Here is an algorithm for computing the square root of a 32-bit integer N:

```
s = 15, Old = 0, oldSq = 0, sqRt = 0
while (1)
{
```

```
        while ((Temp = oldSq + (sqRt SHL (s+1)) + (1 SHL (2*s)))> N)
            s=s-1
        if (s = -1) stop
        oldSq = Temp
        sqRt = sqRt + (1 SHL s)
}
```

a. Explain why this algorithm works.

Suggestion: The algorithm finds the on-bits in the square root starting with bit number 15 and working downward. Verify and make use of this formula:

$$(m + (1\ \mathrm{SHL}\ t))^2 = m^2 + (m\ \mathrm{SHL}\ (t+1)) + (1\ \mathrm{SHL}\ (2*t))$$

b. Write a procedure that uses this algorithm to find square roots and use it to speed up PRIMES.ASM.

Exercise 11-3. At the moment, the number of primes computed by PRIMES.ASM is limited by the 64K segment length. Rewrite the program so that it uses the *expandSegs* and *shrinkSegs* procedures from Chapter 7 to overcome this limitation. The new version should define an array above the 1M boundary and fill it with primes. The choice of array size is up to you — perhaps 1M. It would be even more interesting to run the program for a variety of sizes to see how the time required varies as a function of size.

Exercise 11-4. We wrote *bitStrMov* using a word-size length parameter *L* and so limited the maximum string length to 2000 dwords. Rewrite it using *L* of size one dword.

Exercise 11-5. If speed is not a primary concern, then **bt**, **bts**, and **btr** can be used to write a much shorter version of *bitStrMov*. The method is simple: just treat *Source* and *Dest* as bit arrays and move through them in tandem, testing each bit in *Source* using **bt** and copying it to *Dest* using **bts** or **btr**. Write such a version.

Exercise 11-6. *bitStrMove* is just one of a family of useful bit-string manipulation procedures. The other family members are *bitStrIns*, *bitStrDel*, *bitStrCmp*, and *bitStrCat*, where these perform the obvious operations. Implement some or all of these procedures. To keep the amount of labor within bounds, you might want to sacrifice speed and use the bit-test instructions whenever possible, in the manner suggested in Exercise 11-5.

SECTION 5 MULTIPLE-PRECISION INTEGER ARITHMETIC

In Chapter 10, we stated the general principles used in writing multiple-precision arithmetic routines and we will now present the implementation details of such a package. Our routines differ from the suggestions made in Chapter 10 in only one major way: in order to utilize the capabilities of the **80386** to the fullest, we represent a multiple-precision integer as an array of dwords, rather than as an array of words.

We implemented the multiple-precision routines as macros rather than procedures, mainly to minimize the number of text pages required to present the package. However, some of the macros are lengthy (as long as 200 lines) and so, if they are to be used several times in a single program, it would be worthwhile to recode them as procedures.

The size of a multiple-precision integer will be given by the quantity *Prec*, which we assume to be a one-word memory variable. Note that *Prec* cannot be given by an **EQUATE** — a number of the macros require that it be a variable. We chose to define *Prec* as a variable rather than by an **EQUATE** primarily because it eases the conversion of the macros to procedures that can be stored in a library.

Unfortunately, it is often desirable to have the value of *Prec* available at assembly time, especially for use in specifying buffer lengths. In our implementation, we will solve this problem by the very clumsy expedient of introducing another parameter *Mprec* by means of an **EQUATE**, where *Mprec* has the same value as *Prec*. In other words, *Mprec* will be nothing more than a copy of *Prec* whose value is usable at assembly time. Of course, it must be given a different name.

In conformity with the **8086** conventions, we will also store multiple-precision integers in memory with the least significant bits occupying the lowest dwords. In addition, we will always store multiple-precision integers in two's complement format. This means that the biggest value that a multiple-precision integer with precision equal to *Prec* can hold is

$$2^{32*\text{Prec} - 1} - 1$$

and the smallest value is

$$-2^{32*\text{Prec} - 1}$$

For input and output of multiple-precision arithmetic integers, we must provide routines that convert them to and from alphanumeric form. Our package contains macros that make these conversions (*aToMp* and *mpToA*). Following our usual convention, we store our alphanumeric strings in ASCIIZ format. In making the conversion from multiple-precision to binary, the string buffer must be long enough to hold the decimal digits, as well as a potential minus sign and the null terminator. Deciding on the length for such a buffer requires knowing the maximum number of decimal digits that can result from the conversion of a multiple-precision integer of given precision. Since it is awkward to give an exact answer to this question, we will be content to find a "safe" upper bound for this number and use it to size our buffers. In Exercise 11-7, the reader is asked to verify that a buffer of size

$$(9\ 2/3)*\text{Prec} + 3$$

will be big enough, for any value of *Prec*. Unfortunately, as *Prec* gets large, this estimate becomes increasingly inaccurate and results in the waste of a good deal of storage space. Nevertheless, we assume in our macros that this buffer length has been used. Specifically, the macros expect that the calling program contains a one-word memory variable named *mpLen* that has been initialized to this value.

Headers for our multiple-precision macros are shown in Table 11.2. The code for these macros is in the file MP.MAC on the Program Disk. They perform most of the basic functions needed in doing multiple-precision arithmetic. Note that, as well as providing macros that do the standard arithmetic operations using pairs of multiple-precision integers, we have also provided macros to cover the case where one operand is a multiple-precision integer and one operand is a 32-bit integer. While these latter macros are not strictly necessary, they do add considerably to the efficiency of the package. One operation is missing from the package as it stands: there is no multiple-precision division macro. In Exercise 11-8, we ask the reader to provide such a macro and make suggestions for writing it in a reasonably efficient way.

The macro headers given in Table 11.2 and the notes at the end of that table should suffice for making routine applications of the macros. However, it will be necessary to look at the source code to check on the legality of substituting registers or indirect addressing expressions for the operands.

Since the code for the macros is mostly quite routine and is also fairly repetitive, we have chosen to illustrate only a few of them in the text. Specifically, Figure 11.5 shows the code for three of the macros, which are representative of the package.

The first macro shown, *mpShl*, shifts a multiple-precision integer left by a variable shift count. The code for *mpShl* should be clear. It provides a very natural application of **shld**, the double shift left. Since *mpShl* is a left shift, it must proceed uphill from the low dword to the high dword. It uses a loop of *Prec − 1* repetitions of **shld** to deal with the main part of the shift, and then uses a plain **shl** on the high dword.

The second macro is *mpMul*, the multiple-precision multiplication. This version of multiplication records the answer only to the precision of the factors; that is, it keeps just the "low half" of the answer. (*mpDoubMul* works similarly except that it keeps the entire answer, i.e., it records the result with precision equal to 2*Prec*.)

mpMul performs its multiplication by the obvious algorithm. Using a double loop, each dword of the first factor is multiplied by each dword of the second factor, the products being added to *Answer* as they are computed. The only interesting part of the computation is the treatment of potential carries from one multiplication to the next. Specifically, when the high half of one product (i.e., the **edx** part) is added to *Answer*, a carry may be generated and if so, it must be propagated to the next multiplication. This propagated carry is captured and used by a strategically placed **pushf** and **popf** pair.

The third macro in our set is *mpIntDiv*. It divides a multiple-precision integer by a 32-bit integer using the technique that is familiar from elementary arithmetic. Namely, the 32-bit integer is divided into the multiple-precision integer a dword at a time, starting at the high end and working downward. The dividend for each division beyond the first is really made up from the old remainder and the new dword. Because our applications require it, we allow some flexibility in the arguments accepted by *mpIntDiv*. It can be invoked with optional third and fourth arguments: the third argument can be a 32-bit variable or the **eax** register and, when used, returns the remainder after the division; the fourth parameter can be a 16-bit variable or the **cx** register and, if it appears, its value is used as the precision, rather than the default *Prec*.

mpIntDiv does contain one new notational feature, which we have borrowed from the next chapter. Lines 124 and 131 contain an application of the **SHL** assembly-time operator. This operator has the obvious effect: it is just the assembly-time equivalent of the **shl** instruction. Its use can enhance the readability of the source code considerably, the present

TABLE 11.2 MULTIPLE-PRECISION MACROS IN MP.MAC

UTILITY MACROS

COMMENT	#	MACRO HEADER	
MACRO NAME:		mpMov	FILE: mp.mac
PURPOSE:		Moves multiple-precision integer	
CALLED AS:		mpMov Mp1(Prec dwords), Mp2(Prec dwords)	
REMARKS:		Assumes Mp1 in segment pointed to by es and Mp2 in	
	#	segment pointed to by ds	

COMMENT	#	MACRO HEADER	
MACRO NAME:		mpShl	FILE: mp.mac
PURPOSE:		Multi-bit left shift on multiple-precision integer	
CALLED AS:	#	mpShl Mp1(Prec dwords), NoOfBits(4)	

COMMENT	#	MACRO HEADER	
MACRO NAME:		mpShr	FILE: mp.mac
PURPOSE:		Multi-bit right shift on multiple-precision integer	
CALLED AS:		mpShr Mp1(Prec dwords), Mp2(Prec dwords)	
REMARKS:		Assumes Mp1 in segment pointed to by es and Mp2 in	
	#	segment pointed to by ds	

COMMENT	#	MACRO HEADER	
MACRO NAME:		mpIntInit	FILE: mp.mac
PURPOSE:		Initializes a multiple-precision integer to a 32-bit value	
CALLED AS:	#	mpIntInit Mp(Prec dwords), Int(4)	

COMMENT	#	MACRO HEADER	
MACRO NAME:		mpCmp	FILE: mp.mac
PURPOSE:		Compares two multiple-precision integers	
CALLED AS:		mpCmp Mp1(Prec dwords), Mp2(Prec dwords)	
REMARKS:		Assumes Mp1 in segment pointed to by es and Mp2 in	
	#	segment pointed to be ds. Sets flags appropriately.	

CONVERSION MACROS

COMMENT	#	MACRO HEADER	
MACRO NAME:		aToMp	FILE: mp.mac
PURPOSE:		Converts alphanumeric string to multiple-precision integer	
CALLED AS:	#	aToMp Mp(Prec dwords), mpStr(ASCIIZ)	

COMMENT	#	MACRO HEADER	
MACRO NAME:		mpToA	FILE: mp.mac
PURPOSE:		Converts multiple-precision integer to alphanumeric form	
CALLED AS:		mpToA MpStr, Mp(Prec dwords)	
REMARKS:		mpStr should be buffer of size (9 2/3)*Prec+3 bytes	
	#	In addition, MPTOA uses 4*Prec bytes of stack space	

ARITHMETIC MACROS

COMMENT	#	MACRO HEADER	
MACRO NAME:		mpNeg	FILE: mp.mac

```
PURPOSE:              Takes two's complement of a multiple-precision integer
CALLED AS:      #     mpNeg  Mp(Prec dwords)


COMMENT         #     MACRO HEADER
MACRO NAME:           mpIntAdd                    FILE: mp.mac
PURPOSE:              Adds a 32-bit integer to a multiple-precision integer
CALLED AS:      #     mpIntAdd  Mp(Prec dwords), Int(4)


COMMENT         #     MACRO HEADER
MACRO NAME:           mpIntSub                    FILE: mp.mac
PURPOSE:              Subtracts a 32-bit integer from a multiple-precision integer
CALLED AS:      #     mpIntSub  Mp(Prec dwords), Int(4)


COMMENT         #     MACRO HEADER
MACRO NAME:           mpIntMul                    FILE: mp.mac
PURPOSE:              Multiples multiple-precision by 32-bit integer
CALLED AS:      #     mpIntMul  Mp(Prec dwords), Int(4)


COMMENT         #     MACRO HEADER
MACRO NAME:           mpIntDiv                    FILE: mp.mac
PURPOSE:              Divides multiple-precision integer by 32-bit integer
CALLED AS:            mpIntDiv  Mp(Prec dwords), Int(32), Remainder(32), PrecParam(32)
REMARKS:             Remainder can be returned in an optional third parameter, which
                     can be either a dword variable or eax. It will use either the
                     global value of Prec, or a custom value can be passed as an
                #    optional fourth parameter, either as a word variable or in cx.


COMMENT         #     MACRO HEADER
MACRO NAME:           mpAdd                       FILE: mp.mac
PURPOSE:              Adds two multiple-precision integers
CALLED AS:      #     mpAdd  Mp1(Prec dwords), Mp2(Prec dwords)


COMMENT         #     MACRO HEADER
MACRO NAME:           mpSub                       FILE: mp.mac
PURPOSE:              Subtracts two multiple-precision integers
CALLED AS:      #     mpSub  Mp1(Prec dwords), Mp2(Prec dwords)


COMMENT         #     MACRO HEADER
MACRO NAME:           mpMul                       FILE: mp.mac
PURPOSE:              Multiplies two multiple-precision integers
CALLED AS:            mpMul  Answer(Prec dwords), First(Prec dwords),
                                   Second(Prec dwords)
REMARKS:        #    Only records low Prec dwords of result


COMMENT         #     MACRO HEADER
MACRO NAME:           mpDoubMul                   FILE: mp.mac
PURPOSE:              Multiples two multiple-precision integers
CALLED AS:            mpDoubMul  Answer(2*Prec dwords), First(Prec dwords),
                                   Second(Prec dwords)
REMARKS:             Records entire product and so Answer must be large
                #    enough to store 2*Prec dwords
```

GENERAL USAGE

1. The macros are unsophisticated in the sense that they expect all data
to be in the segment pointed to by ds and will not reliably accept

Table 11.2 cont.

register or indirect addressing operands. Some exceptions are noted in
the remarks.
2. The calling program should define variables Prec and mpLen as words.
Prec should have value >= 2 and mpLen should be the safe buffer size
for the alphanumeric form of a multiple-precision integer of this
precision, i.e., mpLen = (9 2/3)*Prec+3.
3. A number of the macros are quite long and so, if they are to be used
repeatedly in a single program, might well be converted to procedures.

application being a case in point. The obvious alternative to the expression *1 SHL 31* would
be the rather clumsy *80000000H.*

As an application of the multiple-precision macros, we present a program, BIG-
FACT.ASM, which computes large factorials. BIGFACT.ASM is shown in Figure 11.6. As
written, it will compute the factorial of any integer up to 10,000 (actually, somewhat beyond
this value). This limit is not intrinsic to our macros — it is used so that both the buffer holding
the binary version of the factorial and the buffer holding the ASCIIZ version will fit in a
single data segment. It turns out that the computation of 10,000! requires precision of nearly
4,000, so that the binary form needs almost 16,000 bytes. Consequently, by our standard
formula for *mpLen*, the alphanumeric version of 1000! requires about 39,000 bytes. The
combined length of 65,000 bytes basically fills a segment. The sample output at the end of
Figure 11.6 shows that our estimated digit count is somewhat on the high side. It turns out
that 10,000! contains only 35,660 digits.

As we pointed out in the macro header for *mpToA* in Table 11.2, this macro makes
extensive use of the stack. A quick review of the standard ASCIIZ-to-binary conversion
algorithm reveals why this is the case. This algorithm involves repeated division of the binary
version by 10 and so, when implemented directly, destroys the original binary value. Since
it seems undesirable that *mpToA* should damage its second argument, we make a temporary
copy from which to restore the original. In this implementation, we chose to make this
temporary copy on the stack, whence *mpToA* uses 4**Prec* bytes of stack space.

But now we recognize yet another problem. When *bigFact* is run with precision 4000,
the last paragraph indicates that it needs at least 16,000 bytes of stack space, in addition to
its 65,000 bytes of data. *This means that the SMALL model cannot be used in this program.*
For this reason, we have chosen to write the program using the traditional segment directives.
This is a worthwhile endeavor in any case since it illustrates the **USE16** directive, which
specifies that 16-bit segments be used.

Before briefly examining the details of the code, let us say a few more words about the
segment structure. Recall from Chapter 8 that segments (for instance the stack) containing
only uninitialized data defined by **DUP** statements and appearing at the end of the list of
segments (as seen by **LINK**) do not become part of the disk image of the program. Hence
our positioning of the stack to the end of the source file ensures that it will not become part
of the stored **.EXE** file, and so shrinks this file size by 5000H bytes. Unfortunately, the
program as written still has a giant **.EXE** file (about 91,000 bytes) since all the buffers from
_DATA are stored on the disk. The reader may be wondering why we have not also moved

FIGURE 11.5 SAMPLES OF MULTIPLE-PRECISION MACROS

```
 1   COMMENT     #   MACRO HEADER
 2   MACRO NAME:   mpShL                  FILE: mp.mac
 3   PURPOSE:      Multi-bit left shift on multiple-precision integer
 4   CALLED AS: #  mpShL  Mp1(Prec dwords), noOfBits(32)
 5
 6   mpShL    MACRO   Mp, noOfBits
 7       LOCAL   shiftLoop, Done
 8
 9       pushEM  ebx
10       pushEM  edx
11
12       lea     ebx, Mp                  ;point ebx to Mp
13       mov     edx, Prec                ;left shift must proceed
14       dec     edx                      ;   in high-to-low direction
15
16   shiftLoop:
17
18       and     edx, edx                 ;stop when edx = 0
19       je      SHORT Done
20       mov     eax, [ebx+edx*4-4]       ;low dword for shld
21       shld    DWORD PTR [ebx+edx*4], eax, noOfBits
22       dec     edx
23       jmp     shiftLoop
24
25   Done:
26
27       shl     DWORD PTR [ebx+edx*4], noOfBits   ;the final dword
28
29       popEM   edx
30       popEM   ebx
31
32   ENDM
33
34   ;-------------------------------------------------------------
35
36   COMMENT     #   MACRO HEADER
37   MACRO NAME:   mpMul                  FILE: mp.mac
38   PURPOSE:      Multiplies two multiple-precision integers
39   CALLED AS:    mpMul  Answer(Prec dwords), First(Prec dwords),
40                           Second(Prec dwords))
41   REMARKS:   #  Only records low Prec dwords of result
42
43   mpMul   MACRO   Answer, First, Second
44       LOCAL outerLoop, innerLoop, nextOuter
45
46       pushadM
47
48       mpIntInit   Answer, 0            ;initialize answer to 0
49
50       xor     esi, esi                 ;index into First
51       xor     edi, edi                 ;index into Second
52       xor     ebx, ebx                 ;index into Answer
53
54       mov     ecx, Prec
55
```

Figure 11.5 cont.

```
56   outerLoop:
57
58       clc                                      ;so that second popf below finds
59       pushf                                    ;  no propogated carry
60
61   innerLoop:
62
63       mov      eax, First[esi*4]               ;implied operand for mul
64       mul      DWORD PTR Second[edi*4]
65       add      Answer[ebx*4], eax              ;low dword of product
66       pushf                                    ;for use when adding high dword
67       inc      ebx
68       cmp      ebx, Prec                       ;keep only Prec dwords of product
69       jae      SHORT nextOuter
70       popf                                     ;was there a carry from low dword?
71       adc      edx, 0
72       popf                                     ;  or a propagated carry from last mult?
73       adc      Answer[ebx*4],edx
74       pushf                                    ;will be popped at next iteration as
75       inc      esi                             ;  propogated carry
76       jmp      innerLoop
77
78   nextOuter:
79
80       add      sp, 4                           ;equivalent to discarding two pops --
81       inc      edi                             ;  needed to balance the stack
82       xor      esi, esi                        ;reinitialize esi
83       mov      ebx, edi                        ;  and ebx
84       loop     outerLoop
85
86       POPADM
87
88   ENDM
89
90   ;------------------------------------------------------------
91
92
93   COMMENT    #  MACRO HEADER
94   MACRO NAME:   mpIntDiv              FILE: mp.mac
95   PURPOSE:      Divides multiple-precision integer by 32-bit integer
96   CALLED AS:    mpIntDiv  Mp(Prec dwords),Int(32),Remainder(32),precParam(32)
97   REMARKS:      Remainder can be returned in an optional third param., which
98                 can be either a dword variable or eax. It will use either the
99                 global value of Prec, or a custom value can be passed as an
100            #  optional fourth parameter, either as a word variable or in cx.
101
102  mpIntDiv   MACRO   Mp, Int, Remainder, precParam
103      LOCAL   signFlag, mpPositive, startDivision, divLoop, Done
104
105      signFlag EQU    <WORD PTR [bp]>
106
107      pushEM ebx                               ;pushadM not used to allow the
108      pushEM ecx                               ;  possibility of returning
109      pushEM edx                               ;    Remainder in eax
110      pushEM esi
111      pushEM edi
```

```
112
113     mov     esi, Int
114
115     sub     sp, 2                   ;reserve space on stack for signFlag
116     and     signFlag, 0             ;tentatively assume answer positive
117
118     IFNB <precParam>                ;works correctly whether or not
119           movzx   ecx, precParam    ;  precParam is specified as a
120     ELSE                            ;      parameter
121           movzx   ecx, Prec
122     ENDIF
123     lea     ebx, Mp
124     test    DWORD PTR [ebx+ecx*4-4], 1 SHL 31 ;is Mp negative?
125     jz      SHORT mpPositive
126     MPNEG   Mp                      ;macro that takes two's complement
127     not     signFlag                ;take account of a minus sign
128
129  mpPositive:
130
131     test    esi, 1 SHL 31           ;is Int negative?
132     jz      SHORT startDivision
133     neg     esi
134     not     signFlag                ;take account of another minus sign
135
136  startDivision:
137
138     xor     edx, edx                ;high dword of implied dividend
139
140  divLoop:
141
142     mov     eax, [ebx+ecx*4-4]      ;low dword of implied dividend
143     div     esi
144     mov     [ebx+ecx*4-4], eax      ;the quotient
145     dec     ecx
146     jne     Divloop
147
148     IFNB    <Remainder>             ;if the user want to have the
149           mov     Remainder, edx    ;  remainder returned ...
150     ENDIF
151
152     test    signFlag, -1            ;is a two's complement needed?
153     jz      SHORT Done
154     MPNEG   Mp
155
156  Done:
157
158     add sp, 2                       ;release reserved storage
159
160     popEM   edi
161     popEM   esi
162     popEM   edx
163     popEM   ecx
164     popEM   ebx
165
166  ENDM
```

FIGURE 11.6 COMPUTING LARGE FACTORIALS

```
 1    TITLE    bigFact.asm: computes very large factorials
 2
 3    ;==============================================================
 4
 5    .386
 6
 7    INCLUDE      console.mac
 8    INCLUDE      mp.mac
 9    .SALL
10
11    maxPrec     EQU     4000                ;max. precision allowed
12    maxLen      EQU     29*maxPrec/3+3
13
14    ;==============================================================
15
16    _DATA SEGMENT DWORD USE16 PUBLIC 'DATA'
17
18        Fact      DD     maxPrec DUP(?)    ;holds binary form of n!
19        Integer   DD     ?                 ;the n that is input
20        Prec      DW     ?                 ;actual precision used
21        mpLen     DW     ?                 ;corresponding length
22        intStr    DB     6      DUP(?)     ;holds alphanumeric form of n
23        lenStr    DB     6      DUP(?)
24        mpStr     DB     maxLen DUP(?)     ;holds alphanumeric form of Fact
25        digitCnt  DD     ?                 ;number of digits in previous
26
27    _DATA ENDS
28
29    ;==============================================================
30
31    _TEXT SEGMENT DWORD USE16 PUBLIC 'CODE'
32
33        ASSUME cs:_TEXT, ds:_DATA, ss:STACK
34
35    Start:
36
37        mov       ax, _DATA
38        mov       ds, ax
39
40    Again:
41
42        outAsc    NL, NL, NL, "Input an integer <= 10000: "
43        inAsc     intStr
44
45        aToL      intStr
46        mov       Integer, eax            ;store it
47
48        mov       ecx, eax                ;find appropriate value of precision
49        bsr       eax, ecx                ;  using the bound
50        mul       ecx                     ;    n*MSB(n)/32+1 where MSB(n)
51        shr       eax, 5                  ;      means most significant bit
52        add       eax, 2                  ;        number in n
53        mov       Prec, ax
54        cmp       Prec, maxPrec           ;under no circumstances accept
55        jbe       SHORT @F                ;  Prec > maxPrec
```

```
56       mov     Prec, maxPrec              ;if this happens, replace Prec by
57                                          ; maxPrec
58   @@:
59
60       movzx   eax, Prec                  ;find corresponding value of Mplen
61       imul    eax, 29                    ;  by formula (9 2/3)*Prec+3
62       xor     edx, edx
63       mov     ecx, 3
64       div     ecx
65       add     ax, 3
66       mov     mpLen, ax
67
68       startTiming
69
70       mov     ecx, 1                     ;initialize multiplier for factLoop
71       mpIntInit  Fact, 1                 ;initialize Fact
72
73   factLoop:
74
75       cmp     ecx, Integer               ;this is a count-up loop with Integer
76       jae     Complete                   ;  as cut-off
77       inc     ecx
78       mpIntMul Fact, ecx                 ;do the multiplication
79       jmp     factLoop
80
81   Complete:
82
83       endTiming                          ;time only the binary computation
84
85       outAsc  "The value of ", intStr, "! is ", NL, NL
86       mpToA   mpStr, Fact                ;convert answer to alphanumeric form
87
88       outAsc  mpStr, NL, NL
89
90       xor     eax,eax
91       strLen  Mpstr                      ;returns string length in ax
92       mov     digitCnt, eax              ;we use LTOA rather than ITOA since
93       lToA    lenStr, digitCnt           ;  ITOA limited to +32767
94       outAsc  "Number of digits = ", lenStr, NL, NL
95
96       jmp     Again                      ;get new input from user
97
98       mov     ax, 4c00h
99       int     21h
100
101  _TEXT ENDS
102
103  ;===============================================================
104
105  STACK SEGMENT PARA USE16 STACK 'STACK'
106
107      DB 05000h DUP (?)                  ;the mpToA macro uses the stack heavily
108
109  STACK ENDS
110
111  ;===============================================================
112
113  END     Start
```

Figure 11.6 cont.

```
SAMPLE OUTPUT

Input an integer <= 10000: 10
Elapsed time was: 0.0 seconds
The value of 10! is

3628800

Number of digits = 7


Input an integer <= 10000: 100
Elapsed time was: 0.0 seconds
The value of 100! is

93326215443944152681699238856266700490715968264381621468592963895217599
99322991560894146397615651828625369792082722375825118521091686400000000
0000000000000000

Number of digits = 158


Input an integer <= 10000: 1000
Elapsed time was: 0.55 seconds
The value of 1000! is

40238726007709377354370243392300398571937486421071463254379991042993851
23986290205920442084869694048004799886101971960586316668729948085589013
2382966 ... (output truncated)

Number of digits = 2568


Input an integer <= 10000: 10000
Elapsed time was: 79.10 seconds
The value of 10000! is

28462596809170545189064132121198688901480514017027992307941799942744113
40003764443772990786757784775815884062142317528883004233994015351873905 2
4211613 ... (output truncated)

Number of digits = 35660
```

_DATA to the end of the program, thereby ensuring that it too is excluded from the disk image. The answer is that this would not work because, unfortunately, _DATA actually contains some initialized data, placed there by the present version of *outAsc*. (Recall that a number of our other macros — *hSkip* is another example — also make use of the data segment in this way.) Consequently, _DATA will be stored in the disk image, no matter where in the program it is located. If it were placed after STACK, it would also cause the stack bytes to be stored on the disk. Our problem has a very simple solution: it is only necessary to break _DATA into two pieces: a tiny section containing the initialized data and a huge section containing only uninitialized data. The uninitialized section can then be moved to the end of the program. We have not made this change since doing so neatly requires accessing two different data segments simultaneously with one setting of the **ds** register. In Chapter 12, we will learn how to do this using the **GROUP** directive. In one of the exercises in Chapter 12, the reader will be asked to make this modification to *bigFact* and will find that the disk image shrinks to about 6,000 bytes.

Here are some line-by-line observations on *bigFact*:

Lines 11,12. *bigFact* is used interactively to compute the value of n!. If the value of n input by the user is small, it is foolish to perform the computation using *Prec* = 4000. Consequently, the program uses the input value of n to compute an appropriate value of *Prec* and a corresponding value of *mpLen*. If the computed value of *Prec* is less than *maxPrec*, then these computed values are used; otherwise, *maxPrec* = 4000 and the matching value of *maxLen* are used. The buffers in _DATA are sized to work in this maximum case.

The reader may also be concerned about the validity of the assembly-time computation on line 12,

```
maxLen    EQU 29*maxPrec/3+3
```

when *maxPrec* has a value as large as 4000. With such a value for *maxPrec*, the intermediate result 29*maxPrec* certainly will not fit in 16 bits, even though the final value for *maxLen* is a 16-bit quantity. By default, **MASM** does assembly-time arithmetic only to 17-bit precision. However, the appearance of a **.386** directive changes this default to 33-bit. Consequently, our computation is valid but would not be if we moved the **.386** directive from line 5 to, say, line 13. Under those circumstances, **MASM** would not even print a warning message — it would just produce an incorrect answer, namely the correct answer reduced modulo 65536.

Line 42. This line gives a preview of a development from Chapter 13, the main macro chapter. There we will write the final version of our *outAsc* macro. That version will accept multiple parameters and is being used here. Each parameter can be of any of three types: the name (or address) of an ASCIIZ string; a string in double quotes (i.e., a "string literal"); or the string *NL* (written without quotes). In each of the first two cases, *outAsc* will print the string in question; in the third case it will print a newline. Hence the effect of line 42 is to print three newlines followed by the text of the quoted string. Lines 85, 88, and 94 also show the new *outAsc* at work.

Lines 48-53. Here the program chooses a value of *Prec* corresponding to the input Integer. It uses the formula

```
Prec = n*MSB(n)/32 + 1
```

where n is the value of Integer and MSB(n) is the number of the most significant bit in n. That is, it is the bit number of the highest on-bit in n, where the bit count starts, as always, with number zero at the low end. In Exercise 11-9, the reader is asked to verify that this is a reasonable value to use for *Prec*.

Lines 54-56. As we indicated previously, the value of *Prec* is limited to a maximum value of *maxPrec*.

Lines 68, 83. We are again borrowing the timing macros from Chapter 13.

Lines 70-79. The main code is so simple that it is something of an anticlimax: *Fact* is initialized to 1, and a loop of *mpIntMul* is used to compute the factorial.

Before leaving *bigFact*, we should briefly mention the program output, shown at the end of Figure 11.6. The timing macros produce answers in increments of approximately 1/18 of a second and so the time for 100! should be taken with a grain of salt. The announced time proves only that the 100! computation required less than 1/18 of a second. The times for 1000! and 10000! underline an obvious fact — the time required to compute n! is highly non-linear in n.

Exercise 11-7. In the multiple-precision macros, we used the value

$$\text{mpLen} = (9\ 2/3) * \text{Prec} + 3$$

as a safe buffer length for holding the alphanumeric form of a multiple-precision integer with precision *Prec*. Verify that this is indeed an adequate length for any value of *Prec*. **Suggestion:** The quantity $32 * \log_{10} 2$ has value approximately 9.63.

Exercise 11-8. We have not supplied a procedure or macro to divide two multiple-precision integers. Write such a macro (or procedure if you prefer). It should accept four parameters

```
mpDiv   Quotient, Dividend, Divisor, Remainder
```

where *Divisor* and *Remainder* have precision *Prec* and the others have precision 2**Prec*. *mpDiv* should compute the quotient to its full precision. That is, it should not truncate *Quotient* to precision *Prec*.
Suggestion: It would be disastrously slow and also quite difficult to fabricate *mpDiv* from machine divisions. Instead, use the following algorithm:

```
s = 64*Prec, Quotient = 0
while (1)
{
    while ((Divisor MPSHL s) > Dividend)
        s = s - 1
    if (s = -1) stop
    Dividend = Dividend - (Divisor MPSHL s)
    Quotient = Quotient + (1 MPSHL s)
}
```

We are using the obvious notation *Mp MPSHL r* to denote the result of left-shifting the multiple-precision integer *Mp* by *r* bits. Of course, you will need to understand how the algorithm works before you can implement it successfully.

Exercise 11-9. In BIGFACT.ASM we used the value

```
Prec = n*MSB(n)/32 + 1
```

where MSB(n) is the number of the highest on-bit in n, and claimed that this value was large enough for use in computing n!. Verify this claim.
Suggestion: $n! < n^n$ if $n > 1$. How many bits are needed to store n^n?

Exercise 11-10. The Pell equation was introduced in Exercise 10-19. The only multiple-precision arithmetic that we had available then was the outrageously slow unpacked BCD. Rework Exercise 10-19 using the new macros. It is possible to push the upper limit considerably above the 100 that was previously suggested. How far can you get?

SECTION 6 HIGH-PRECISION REAL-NUMBER ARITHMETIC

Now that we have a reasonable collection of multiple-precision arithmetic routines, it is a relatively simple matter to use them for high-accuracy real-number computations. We use *fixed-point binary arithmetic*, which means that each binary representation will carry with it an implied binary point position. This binary point will not play a very great role in actual computations: it will necessitate certain adjustments after multiplication or division, and must be accounted for in converting to or from decimal format.

More precisely, we use mixed binary expansions of the form

$$d_n d_{n-1} \cdots d_1 d_0 . c_1 c_2 \cdots c_m$$

where the binary point is not stored as part of the number. (The reader might wish to review Exercise 1-8 for the definition of a mixed binary expansion.) Rather, the program keeps an independent record of its position. We will refer to such a binary representation, together with an implied position for the binary point, as a *fixed-point real*. Each fixed-point real number of the preceding format requires a total of $n + 1 + m$ bits of storage. The portion of the binary expansion to the left of the binary point is called the *integer part* and the portion to the right is called the *fractional part*. The format shown previously (with $n + 1$ places before the binary point and m places after it) is referred to as the *standard form*.

We will always store bit patterns representing fixed-point reals in the ordering that is consistent with **8086** architecture. Namely, the least significant information will always occur at the lowest address. Hence, the individual bits will be stored in memory in the reverse order to that shown in the standard form.

Adding or subtracting two such numbers is trivial since it just involves adding or subtracting their bit patterns. Normally, the total bit count $n + 1 + m$ will be greater than 32 and so the arithmetic operations will be done using our multiple-precision package rather than the primitive machine operations. An important observation is that the position of the binary point does not change during addition or subtraction.

Multiplication and division are somewhat more complicated. Consider multiplication first. When two fixed-point reals in standard form are multiplied, the answer involves $2*(n + 1 + m)$ bits. (Indeed, this is why we introduced the *mpDoubMul* macro.) To further complicate matters, the position of the implied decimal point in the product has shifted: there are now $2*(n + 1)$ bits in the integer part and $2*m$ bits in the fractional part. In other words, the answer has the form

$$e_{2*n+1}e_{2*n}\cdots e_1e_0.f_1f_2\cdots f_{2*m}$$

To convert this to standard form requires ignoring the first $n + 1$ and the last m bits. Recalling that the bit pattern is stored in reverse order, these operations can be implemented by shifting the answer m bits to the left and then "truncating" it after $n + 1 + m$ bits. This renormalization must be done after each multiplication and we will provide a macro (*fxpMulNorm*) that does it.

Since we have left the implementation of fixed-point division as an exercise to the reader, we also leave the analysis of the required renormalization after division.

Because we wished to integrate the fixed-point package as seamlessly as possible with the multiple-precision macros, we chose to use *Prec* dwords to store each fixed-point real. The result is that our basic arithmetic macros are directly applicable to the fixed-point case. *Prec* dwords of storage yield $32*Prec$ bits, and so we must decide on values of n and m satisfying

```
n + 1 + m = 32*Prec
```

Many of the algorithms are easier if the integer and fractional parts each exactly fill one or more dwords. Since we have no need for reals with very large integer parts, we chose to maximize m and so selected

```
n + 1 = 32
m     = 32 * (Prec - 1)
```

In other words, the most significant dword represents the integer part and everything else gives the fractional part.

There are two other important considerations involved in using this fixed-point package. First, as we discussed previously, products must be collected to twice the working precision, so that they can be renormalized. This means that any buffer destined to hold a product must be allocated length $2*Prec$. Rather than carefully tabulating which fixed-point reals might hold the answers to multiplications at some time during a program, it is much easier (although somewhat wasteful) to allocate all fixed-point buffers of length at least $2*Prec$, and this is what we generally do.

The second potential pitfall relates to the conversion from fixed-point real to alphanumeric form. Looking at the standard form of a fixed-point real again, we see that the obvious conversion to alphanumeric form involves these steps: treat the stored number as a multiple-precision integer and convert it to binary using *mpToA*; divide the answer by 2^m to account for the position of the implied binary point. Unfortunately, this is *totally* impractical.

If the conversion to alphanumeric is done first, then each division by 2 is performed on the alphanumeric string and so is excruciatingly slow: it must be implemented by the elementary arithmetic technique of dividing 2 into the digits of the dividend one at time, making appropriate use of the remainder after each division. What makes it really impossible, of course, is that this division must be performed m times, where m can be very large indeed — 3808 in our upcoming application, for example.

Since converting to alphanumeric form before doing the arithmetic is disastrous, the operations must be performed in the other order. This involves multiplying by 5^m before converting to alphanumeric form. The answer is then too big by a factor of 10^m and hence the final adjustment involves a trivial shift of the decimal point position in the alphanumeric string. Consequently, our conversion macro (*fxpToA*) multiples the fixed-point number by 5^m *before* changing it to decimal, and so both the buffer that holds the fixed-point real and the buffer that holds the converted form must be suitably large. In Exercise 11-13, we ask the reader to verify that sizes 4*Prec and 4*mpLen, respectively, are sufficient.

Let us now sum up the salient points from this discussion:

- Fixed-point arithmetic is performed using *Prec* dwords, the most significant of which holds the integer part, while the others hold the fractional part.

- Each fixed-point real should be allocated a buffer of length at least 2*Prec dwords.

- If a fixed-point real serves as the source of the *fxpToA* macro, it should be allocated a buffer of length at least 4*Prec dwords; a string that is to be the destination of *fxpToA* must have length at least 4*MpLen.

Table 11.3 shows the headers for the fixed-point macros contained in MP.MAC. The general usage of these macros is similar to the other macros in MP.MAC. Indeed, a number of these macros do little more than call the corresponding multiple-precision macros. For the most part, the functioning of these macros should be clear from our previous discussions. However, the last pair, *fxpRecip* and *fxpSqRt*, require explanation, and this will be our next topic.

As we noted earlier, we have not supplied a fixed-point division routine. The primary reason for this omission is that fixed-point division is very slow. There is, however, a fast algorithm for the computation of reciprocals: given a non-zero fixed-point real x, this algorithm computes 1/x. Combining the reciprocal algorithm with multiplication then provides a reasonable substitute for division.

Our reciprocal algorithm is based on a technique in numerical analysis called *Newton's Method*. In Section 9 of Chapter 17 we will discuss Newton's Method in general but, for the moment, will be content to state some formulas that it provides. These formulas are easy to understand and, if the reader is willing to accept them at face value, can be used without any particular knowledge of Newton's method.

The first set of formulas generates a sequence of better and better approximations to 1/x, where x is a non-zero real number. The formulas are

```
x₀ = initApprox
xₙ = xₙ₋₁ * (2 - xₙ₋₁ * x) for each n ≥ 1
```

TABLE 11.3 FIXED-POINT ARITHMETIC MACROS IN MP.MAC

```
COMMENT        #         MACRO HEADER
MACRO NAME:              fxpMov                        FILE: mp.mac
PURPOSE:                 Multiplies two binary fixed-point reals
CALLED AS:               fxpMov  Dest(2*Prec), Src(2*Prec)
REMARKS:                 Will check whether either Dest or Src contains an explicit
                         segment override prefix and, if so, act upon it. Otherwise,
                         assumes Dest and Src are, resp., in segments pointed to
               #         by es and ds.


COMMENT        #         MACRO HEADER
MACRO NAME:              fxpToA                        FILE: mp.mac
PURPOSE:                 Converts fixed-point binary to ASCIIZ
CALLED AS:               fxpToA  FxpStr(4*MpLen), Fxp(4*Prec dwords)
REMARKS:                 Note the sizes of the operands: the conversion
               #         process requires a great deal of working space


COMMENT        #         MACRO HEADER
MACRO NAME:              fxpInit                       FILE: mp.mac
PURPOSE:                 Initializes binary fixed-point real to 32-bit integer value
CALLED AS:     #         fxpInit    Fxp(2*Prec dwords), Int(32)


COMMENT        #         MACRO HEADER
MACRO NAME:              fxpMul                        FILE: mp.mac
PURPOSE:                 Multiplies two binary fixed-point reals
CALLED AS:               fxpMul  Answer(4*Prec dwords), First(2*Prec dwords),
                                        Second(2*Prec dwords)
REMARKS:       #         Computes answer to same precision as factors


COMMENT        #         MACRO HEADER
MACRO NAME:              fxpMulNorm                    FILE: mp.mac
PURPOSE:                 Normalizes answer after fixed-point multiplication
CALLED AS:               fxpMulNorm  Mp(4*Prec dwords)
REMARKS:                 Normalization requires shifting left by Prec-1 dwords
               #         and zeroing the upper half of answer


COMMENT        #         MACRO HEADER
MACRO NAME:              fxpRecip                      FILE: mp.mac
PURPOSE:                 Computes 1/Src for a fixed-point input Src
CALLER AS:               fxpRecip    oneOverx(2*Prec dwords), Src(2*Prec dwords),
                                        Init(2*Prec dwords)
REMARKS:                 Uses Newton's method. To work reliably, the initial approx.
                         Init should be of the same sign as Src and of smaller
               #         absolute value than Src


COMMENT        #         MACRO HEADER
MACRO NAME:              fxpSqRt                       FILE: mp.mac
PURPOSE:                 Computes the square root of fixed-point number Src
CALLED AS:               fxpSqRt sqrtX(2*Prec dwords), Src(2*Prec dwords),
                                 sqrtInit(2*Prec dwords), recipInit(2*Prec dwords),
                                        Epsilon(2*Prec dwords)
REMARKS:                 Uses Newton's method. Should be called with the initial approx.
                         sqRtInit larger than the true square root and with recipInit
               #         smaller than 1/sqRtInit.
```

Again, as n gets larger and larger, the corresponding value x_n gets closer and closer to $1/x$. The Program Disk contains a procedure, RECIP.ASM, that implements this algorithm, and the *fxpRecip* macro calls this procedure. The choice of *initApprox* is actually fairly delicate. It should be selected to lie between $1/x$ and 0. We have not included the code for RECIP.ASM in the text since it is similar to, but simpler than, the next procedure to be discussed. The code for RECIP.ASM is on the Program Disk.

Our second application of Newton's Method is the computation of the square root of a fixed-point number. This time the formulas are

$$x_0 = \text{InitApprox}$$
$$x_n = (1/2) * (x_{n-1} + x/x_{n-1}) \text{ for each } n \geq 1$$

where x is the number whose square root we wish to compute. Our implementation of the square-root algorithm is shown in Figure 11.7.

Most of the code in this algorithm is quite direct. However, here are a few extra comments:

Lines 25-44. We need space for an extra fixed-point number to hold intermediate results during the computation. Rather than burdening the user with the chore of setting up such a buffer in the data segment, we chose to allocate space for it on the stack (*Temp* on line 35). Instead of performing our computations using some data from locations in the data segment and some from the stack, with the consequent segment register-switching, we copied all the input data onto the stack and used these copies for the computations. Lines 25-44 provide convenient **EQUATE**s for the copies of the data on the stack. Note that each fixed-point needs $2*Prec$ dwords = $8*Prec$ bytes.

Lines 68-78. We are copying the data to the stack.

Lines 87-90. This is the basic iteration step: we are using the name *New* for x_n and the name *Old* for x_{n-1}.

Lines 93-95. As one of its parameters, the algorithm is passed a measure of closeness, here named *cutOff*. When consecutive approximations are within distance *cutOff*, the iteration stops and the current value of *New* is accepted as the square root. In most of our applications, the calling program defines the measure of closeness and gives it the name *Epsilon*. The definition of *Epsilon* has the general form

```
Epsilon    DD    -1, (Prec-1) DUP(0)
```

(Of course, the **DUP** repetition factor cannot be written in exactly this way in the program — it must be an assembly-time constant.) In other words, *Epsilon* has 1s in its 32 least significant binary digits and 0s everywhere else. If *Prec* is reasonably large, *Epsilon* is a very small quantity.

The caller passes a pointer to *Epsilon* to *squareRoot*, which builds a local copy under the name *cutOff*.

FIGURE 11.7 THE SQUARE ROOT OF A FIXED-POINT NUMBER

```
 1   TITLE Sqrt.asm : computes multiple-precision square root iteratively
 2
 3   COMMENT  #  PROCEDURE HEADER
 4   TYPE:       NEAR 386  USE 16        File: sqrt.asm        LIBRARY: none
 5   PURPOSE:    Computes the square root of a fixed-point number
 6   CALLED AS:  Sqrt(offsetSqrt(2), offsetX(2), offsetInitApprox(2),
 7                     offsetRecipInit(2), offsetEpsilon(2)
 8   PARAMS:     Each parameter must be of size at least 2*Prec dwords. Sqrt
 9               receives the answer; X is the input whose square root will be
10               extracted; InitApprox is the beginning approx. in Newton's
11               method; RecipInit is the beginning approx. that will be used in
12               Recip; and Epsilon is the smallness measure -- iteration stops
13           #  when consecutive approximations vary by no more than Epsilon
14
15   PUBLIC squareRoot
16
17   INCLUDE    console.mac
18   INCLUDE    mp.mac
19   .SALL
20
21   .MODEL SMALL
22   .386
23
24   ;Each fixed-point number should be allocated a double-length buffer
25       ;We will stop when Diff <= Cutoff
26       Cutoff         EQU   <DWORD PTR [ebp-56*MPREC]>
27
28       ;Diff will hold the difference between consecutive approximations
29       Diff           EQU   <DWORD PTR [ebp-48*MPREC]>
30
31       ;Initializer for the FXPRECIP
32       recInit        EQU   <DWORD PTR [ebp-40*MPREC]>
33
34       ;Extra working Space
35       Temp           EQU   <DWORD PTR [ebp-32*MPREC]>
36
37       ;The new approximation
38       New            EQU   <DWORD PTR [ebp-24*MPREC]>
39
40       ;The old approximation
41       Old            EQU   <DWORD PTR [ebp-16*MPREC]>
42
43       ;The input value whose square root has been requested
44       X              EQU   <DWORD PTR [ebp-8*MPREC]>
45
46       ;These addresses have been passed on the stack
47       sqRtXPtr       EQU   <WORD PTR [bp+6]>
48       srcPtr         EQU   <WORD PTR [bp+10]>
49       initPtr        EQU   <WORD PTR [bp+14]>
50       recipInitPtr   EQU   <WORD PTR [bp+18]>
51       epsilonPtr     EQU   <WORD PTR [bp+22]>
52
53   .CODE
54
55       EXTRN Reciprocal:NEAR
```

```
56          EXTRN Prec:WORD
57
58   squareRoot  PROC  NEAR
59
60       pushEM  ebp
61       mov     ebp, esp
62
63       pushadM
64
65       sub     esp, 56*Mprec          ;protect working space on the stack
66
67       movzx   esi, srcPtr
68       fxpMov  ss:X, [esi]            ;copy X onto stack
69
70       movzx   esi, initPtr          ;copy initial approximation to
71       fxpMov  ss:Old, [esi]         ;   square root onto stack
72
73       movzx   esi, recipInitPtr     ;copy initial approximation
74       fxpMov  ss:recInit, [esi]     ;   for taking reciprocals onto stack
75
76       movzx   esi, epsilonPtr       ;copy the "close enough" value
77       fxpMov  ss:CutOff, [esi]      ;   onto the stack
78
79       push    ds
80       push    es
81       mov     ax, ss
82       mov     ds, ax                ;point ds and es to the stack
83       mov     es, ax
84
85   sqRtLoop:                         ;the main approximation loop
86
87       fxpRecip Temp, Old, recInit   ;Temp = 1/Old
88       fxpMul  New, X, Temp          ;New = X/Old
89       mpAdd   New, Old              ;New = Old + X/Old
90       mpShR   New, 1                ;New = 1/2*(Old + X/Old)
91
92       mpMov   Diff, Old
93       mpSub   Diff, New             ;Diff = Old - New
94       mpCmp   Diff, CutOff
95       jbe SHORT Done                ;stop if Diff <= CutOff
96
97       fxpMov  Old, New              ;make New the Old for the next iteration
98
99       jmp sqRtLoop
100
101  Done:
102
103      pop     es
104      pop     ds
105
106      movzx   edi, sqRtXPtr         ;copy final New back to data segment
107      fxpMov  [edi], ss:New         ;   as the answer
108
109      add     esp, 56*Mprec         ;release local storage
110
111      popadM
112      popEM   ebp
113
114      ret     20
```

```
Figure 11.7 cont

115
116   squareRoot      ENDP
117
118   ;-------------------------------------------------------------
119
120   END
```

As an application of the fixed-point package, we will now perform a computation that is of enduring interest to mathematicians and computer scientists: we will compute the number π to a large number of decimal places. Our computation uses a spectacular formula discovered by the Indian mathematician Ramanujan early in this century:

$$\frac{1}{\pi} = \frac{\sqrt{8}}{9801} \sum_{n=0}^{\infty} \frac{(4n)! \ (1103 + 26390n)}{(n!)^4 * 396^{4n}}$$

(To mathematicians the single most wonderful thing about this formula is the appearance of numbers such as 9801 and 1103 which, on the surface, seem to bear no relationship whatsoever to π — or to anything else in mathematics!)

The reader with a moderate knowledge of calculus can check that this series converges remarkably quickly. The ratio of consecutive terms is about 10^{-8} (this is easy to verify) and so each term of the series provides approximately eight more correct digits than the previous one. Hence, adding together the first 125 or so terms of the series gives about 1000-place accuracy. The reader without knowledge of calculus should just take this last statement on faith.

Notice that computing π to 1000 decimal places using this formula requires knowing the square root of 8 to 1000 decimal places, and also necessitates taking the reciprocal of a high-precision fixed-point. This was the motivation for our development of the *fxpRecip* and *fxpSqRt* macros.

PI.ASM, shown in Figure 11.8, uses Ramanujan's formula to approximate π. To build a complete working program, the modules PI.ASM, SQRT.ASM, and RECIP.ASM should be assembled separately and linked together to form the final PI.EXE. We specified the **EQUATE** value of *Mprec* by defining it on the **MASM** command line. As we indicated earlier, the value of *Mprec* must then be transferred to *Prec* within the program, which occurs on line 44. This approach has two advantages: we can use the *Mprec* to size statically allocated buffers — *Prec* cannot be used in this way because it is a variable; and we can run the program with different values of *Prec* just by reassembling with a new value of *Mprec* on the **MASM** command line. The commands need to build this program with, say, *Prec* = 120 are

```
masm /DMprec=120 /zi /z /W2 pi,,,;
masm /DMprec=120 /zi /z /W2 sqrt,,,;
masm /DMprec=120 /zi /z /W2 recip,,,;
link /Co pi sqrt recip,,,user;
```

FIGURE 11.8 COMPUTING PI TO 1000 DECIMAL PLACES

```
 1   TITLE pi.asm : computing pi to high precision
 2
 3   PUBLIC  Prec
 4   PUBLIC  answerStr
 5
 6   INCLUDE    console.mac
 7   INCLUDE    mp.mac
 8   .SALL
 9
10   IF  Mprec   EQ   2                    ;these lines are necessary only
11       Padding EQU <>                    ;   because a data declaration
12   ELSE                                  ;      cannot contain "0 DUP(0)"
13       Padding EQU <(Mprec-2) DUP(0),>
14   ENDIF
15
16   ;------------------------------------------------------------
17
18   DOSSEG
19   .MODEL SMALL
20   .386
21
22   .STACK 6000H
23
24   .DATA
25
26       Sum         DD      (Mprec-1) DUP(0), 1103, (Mprec) DUP(0) ; = 1103.0
27       Term        DD      (Mprec-1) DUP(0), 1   , (Mprec) DUP(0) ; = 1.0
28       fxpZero     DD      2*Mprec DUP(0)
29       Index       DD      1
30       U1          DD      2                        ;the U's are the factors
31       U2          DD      12                       ;   that enter into the
32       U3          DD      1103+26390               ;      numerator of Term
33       L1          DD      1                        ;likewise, the L's are
34       L2          DD      396*396                  ;   the factors that enter
35       L3          DD      1                        ;      into the denominator
36
37       sqRtInit    DD      (Mprec-1) DUP (0), 3, Mprec DUP(0)   ; = 3.0
38       recipInit   DD      Padding  1 SHL 30, (Mprec+1) DUP(0) ; = 0.25
39       Temp        DD      (Mprec-1) DUP(0), 8, Mprec DUP(0)    ; = 8.0
40       sqRt8       DD      2*Mprec DUP(?)
41       Epsilon     DD      -1, (2*Mprec-1) DUP(0)                ; = very small
42
43       Pi          DD      4*Mprec DUP(?)        ;double the normal fixed-point
44       Prec        DW      Mprec                 ;   length for use by fxpToA
45       mpLen       DW      9*Mprec+2*Mprec/3+3
46
47       answerStr   DB      4*(9*Mprec+2*Mprec/3+3)  DUP(?) ;quadruple mpLen for
48       Buffer      DB      7 DUP(?)                        ;   use by fxpToA
49
50   .CODE
51
52       EXTRN Reciprocal:NEAR
53       EXTRN squareRoot:NEAR
54
55   Start:
```

Figure 11.8 cont.

```
56
57      mov     ax, @DATA
58      mov     ds, ax
59      mov     es, ax
60
61      startTiming
62
63  PiLoop:
64
65      mpIntMul    Term, U1            ;updating Term by
66      mpIntMul    Term, U2            ;   separately updating
67      mpIntMul    Term, U3            ;     the numerator and
68      mpIntDiv    Term, L1            ;        the denominator
69      mpIntDiv    Term, L2
70      mpIntDiv    Term, L2
71      mpIntDiv    Term, L3
72
73      mpCmp       Term, fxpZero       ;keep going until Term = 0
74      je          SHORT Done
75
76      mpAdd       Sum, Term           ;update Sum
77      mov         eax, Index          ;update Index
78      shl         eax, 5              ;  by multiplying by 32
79      add         U1, eax             ;now
80      sub         U1, 4               ;  update
81      add         U2, eax             ;    the U's
82      add         U2, 12              ;      and the L's
83      mov         eax, U3
84      mov         L3, eax
85      add         U3, 26390
86      inc         Index               ;update Index again
87      mov         eax, Index
88      mul         Index
89      mul         Index
90      mul         Index
91      mov         L1, eax             ;L1 = Index^4
92
93      jmp         PiLoop
94
95  Done:
96
97      ;The following macro call returns with sqRt8 = sqrt(8)
98      fxpSqRt    sqRt8, Temp, sqRtInit, recipInit, Epsilon
99      fxpMul     Temp, sqRt8, Sum     ;Temp = Sum * sqrt(8)
100     mpIntDiv   Temp, 9801           ;Temp = Temp * 9801
101     fxpRecip   Pi, Temp, recipInit  ;Pi = 1/Temp
102
103     endTiming
104
105     fxpToA  answerStr, Pi
106     mov     bx, Mplen
107     and     answerStr[bx-16], 0     ;null-terminate so that
108     outAsc  answerStr               ;  meaningless digits
109                                     ;    at end won't print
110     mov     ax, 4c00h
111     int     21h
```

```
   112
   113        END Start

Elapsed time was: 19.22 seconds

3.
141592653589793238462643383279502884197169399375105820974944592307816406
286208998628034825342117067982148086513282306647093844609550582231725359408128481117450284102701938521105559644622948954930381964428810975665
933446128475648233786783165271201909145648566923460348610454326648213393
607260249141273724587006606315588174881520920962829254091715364367892590
360011330530548820466521384146951941511609433057270365759591953092186
117381932611793105118548074462379962749567351885752724891227938183011949
129833673362440656643086021394946395224737190702179860943702770539217176
29317675238467481846766940513200056812714526356082778577134275778960917
36371787214684409012249534301465495853710507922796892589235420199561121
290219608640344181598136297747713099605187072113499999983729780499510
597317328160963185950244594553469083026425223082533446850352619311881710
10000313783875288658753320838142061717766914730359825349042875546873115
95628638823537875937519577818577805321712268066130019278766111959092164
201989380952572010654858632788659361533818279682303019520353018529689957
736225994138912497217752834791315155748572424541506959508295331168617278
5588907
```

The code in PI.ASM needs only slight additional commentary at this point:

Lines 10-14. One of **MASM**'s eccentricities is that it will not accept a **DUP** statement with a zero repetition count. We would like line 38 to begin with (*Mprec–2*) *DUP(0)*. Unfortunately, if the user attempts to assemble the program with *Mprec* = 2 (useful in debugging, for example) this would reduce to a zero **DUP** count. These lines contain our artifice for circumventing this problem.

Lines 29-33. In the program, the general term in the Ramanujan series is stored in the variable named *Term*. *Term* must be computed for n = 0,1,2⋯. Rather than starting the computation from scratch each time, it is faster to modify the value of *Term* for a given n so that it becomes the value for the next n. The variables on these lines are used to update *Term*. The updating process occupies lines 66-72.

Lines 37-38. We need to compute the square root of 8, and the initial approximation to the square root should be chosen larger than the true value. In line 37 this initial approximation, *sqRtInit*, is given the value 3.0.

Likewise, we need a starting point for various applications of *fxpRecip*, which is used in *fxpSqRt* and in PI.ASM. In the first case, we are taking the reciprocal of a number near the square root of 8 and, in the second case, of a number near π. The initial approximation for *fxpRecip* should be smaller than the actual reciprocal. Hence, 0.25 is a good starting value to use in both our applications. The reader should check from the definitions that line 38 does indeed initialize *recipInit* to the value 0.25.

Lines 78-91. Here we are updating the parameters from lines 29-35 for their use in the next traverse of the loop.

Lines 99-102. The final steps in the computation. The comments say exactly what is happening.

Line 108. Remember that *fxpToA* works with a very long output string, most of which contains information that is beyond the range of accuracy of the computation. Of course, we do not want to print these meaningless digits as part of the answer. The easiest way to suppress them is to drop a null terminator into the string.

Exercise 11-11. Check on the correctness of our fixed-point square root algorithm by writing a program that solicits input from the keyboard, extracts the square root of this input, then squares the square root so that the answer can be compared with the original. Of course, this program will also check on the functioning of *mpMul*. At the moment, only integers can reasonably be input to the program, via *fxpIntInit*, since we do not yet have an *aToFxp* macro. Exercise 11-14 remedies this situation.

Exercise 11-12. Another basic mathematical constant, e, the base of the natural logarithms, is given as the sum of the series

$$ e = \sum_{n=0}^{\infty} \frac{1}{n!} $$

Compute e to 1000 decimal places.

Exercise 11-13. As part of the conversion process, the *fxpToA* macro multiplies its input by 5^m, where m is the number of places after the binary point in the standard form, before making the conversion to alphanumeric form. Consequently, as we pointed out in the text, both the input and the output buffers must be made especially large, to hold these bloated numbers. Verify that our choices of 4*Prec and 4*mpLen for these sizes is sufficient. **Suggestion:** $5 < 8$.

Exercise 11-14. Write an *aToFxp* macro.
Suggestion: Carefully examine the *fxpToA* macro in MP.MAC.

Exercise 11-15. (To be done after Exercise 11-8.) Supply an *fxpDiv* macro that is analogous to the *mpDiv* macro of Exercise 11-8. In fact, the *mpDiv* macro should do the major part of the computation.
Suggestion: The main new component needed is an *fxpDivNorm* analog of the *fxpMulNorm* macro. Look at the code for *fxpMul* and *fxpMulNorm* and review the discussion of *fxpMulNorm* in the text.

CHAPTER 12

THE ASSEMBLER DIRECTIVES

SECTION 1 PREVIEW

In this chapter, we undertake a fairly detailed study of the assembler directives. We do not attempt to be encyclopedic, nor do we pay equal attention to all the different categories of directives. In particular, we lavish most care on those directives relating to segment structure, because understanding them is an essential prerequisite to understanding the structure of any program, assembled or compiled, in the **MS-DOS** world.

Since it was impractical to include complete details on all the directives, we have followed the general ordering used in the corresponding chapters of the **MASM** *Programmer's Guide*. For the most part, each section of the present chapter corresponds to a chapter in that book. This will make it somewhat easier for the reader to find expanded versions of the discussions given here.

SECTION 2 THE SEGMENT DIRECTIVES

We will begin by looking at the so-called *traditional segment directives*. Even though the newer, *simplified segment directives* are easier to use and should be used in most normal programming, there are several good reasons why the traditional directives must be com-

---

TABLE 12.1 OPTIONS FOR SEGMENT ALIGNMENT

TYPE	MEANING
BYTE	Segment begins at next available address
WORD	Segment begins at next available word (even) address
DWORD	Segment begins at next available doubleword (multiple of 4) address
PARA	Segment begins at next available paragraph (multiple of 16) address
PAGE	Segment begins at next available page (multiple of 256) address

---

pletely understood:

- When things go wrong, especially in contexts that involve interfacing different languages, the programmer must be prepared to investigate what is happening behind the scenes.

- In many interfacing problems, the default names supplied by the simplified directives are not applicable, and so the traditional directives must be used.

- In other contexts, for example the writing of .COM programs, the simplified directives do not supply the correct defaults, and so the programmer must again resort to the traditional directives.

Later in this section, we will examine the simplified directives more closely than we have done to date.

THE TRADITIONAL SEGMENT DIRECTIVES

The general form of a traditional segment definition is

Name **SEGMENT** [*alignType*] [*combineType*] ['*className*']

.
.
.

Name **ENDS**

In this definition, *Name* is a user-defined name, and **SEGMENT** and **ENDS** are reserved words, with the latter obviously signaling the end of the segment.

alignType determines whether the segment will be loaded at an arbitrary starting address, or at a starting address that is a multiple of two, or of four, etc. The choices for *alignType* are shown in Table 12.1. If *AlignType* is omitted from a segment definition, **MASM** uses **PARA** as the default. In normal **8088** programming, the exact choice of *alignType* is not terribly significant. However, a program that will be run on the **8086** (or any of the more advanced processors in the family) will execute slightly faster if the segments have at least **WORD** alignment.

TABLE 12.2 OPTIONS FOR SEGMENT COMBINE TYPE

TYPE	MEANING
PUBLIC	Combine into a single segment by concatenation
COMMON	Combine into a single segment by overlapping
STACK	Like PUBLIC, but also causes initialization of **ss** and **sp**
AT Address	Allows a memory region to be considered as a segment

---

The reason was given in Chapter 9. Recall that the **8086** data bus is designed so that a word beginning at an even address is brought in one fetch, while one beginning at an odd address requires two fetches. Giving a data segment **WORD** alignment does not automatically give **WORD** alignment to all the items contained in it — an odd number of byte-size items will throw off the later alignment. For example, here are two sample data segments:

```
dSeg1     SEGMENT    WORD

    Char1    DB    ?
    wAry1    DW    100 dup(?)

dSeg1     ENDS

dSeg2     SEGMENT    WORD

    wAry2    dw    100 dup(?)
    Char2    db    ?

dSeg2     ENDS
```

At first glance they may seem equivalent, but when used on an **8086** machine the second version is considerably better, since every array reference, say *wAry1[bx]*, will require two fetches, while a corresponding reference *wAry2[bx]* will require only one.

The easiest rule to follow when writing programs for the **8086** is that segments should be given at least **WORD** alignment and that single-byte data items should be defined after larger items. In passing, we will point out that while **WORD** alignment suffices for programs designed for the **8086** or the **80286**, programs that will run on the **80386** should have segments with at least **DWORD** alignment since the **80386** has a 32-bit data bus, which means that it can receive information from memory four bytes at a time, provided that the information begins on a dword boundary.

In **8086** programs, it is especially important that the stack be given at least **WORD** alignment. A normal data access to the stack (a **push** or a **pop**) involves a word, whence if the stack happens to start on an odd address, then each and every use of the stack from that point on will be out of phase!

The next parameter occurring in a segment definition is *combineType*. It governs how segments with the same name will be combined. A single source file may contain several such segments, or they may occur in different modules that are to be combined by **LINK**. *combineType* indicates whether identically named segments should be kept totally separate, or whether some or all of them should be combined into one segment having the common name, and, if so, exactly how they should be combined. Table 12.2 shows the options for *combineType*.

As well as these explicit options, the default value of *combineType*, **PRIVATE**, keeps each of the identically named segments separate from all the others. This outcome can only be obtained by leaving *combineType* blank — the word **PRIVATE** is not a recognized option.

Segments having the same name and *className* (see below) and with *combineType* **PUBLIC** are combined into a single segment by concatenating them, i.e., placing them end to end, so that the final length of the segment is the sum of the lengths of the pieces. Of the various options for *combineType*, **PUBLIC** is clearly the most useful. Generally, it is best to combine as much as possible of the data in a program into a single segment, so that it can be referenced with one setting of **ds**, without the need for switching segment registers. **COMMON** is a less frequently used option that can provide an easy method for sharing data between different modules. When **LINK** combines **COMMON** segments of the same name, it gives them all the same starting address, so that they are overlaid in memory, and the total length of the resulting segment is the maximum of the lengths of any of the components. If a datum at a given offset is changed in any of the constituent pieces, the data at this offset in all the other segments automatically change to match it.

STACK is a convenient, though not strictly necessary, value of *combineType*. It behaves like **PUBLIC**, in that it concatenates pieces of the same name, but in addition the loader initializes **ss** to point to this segment and initializes **sp** to its length. If **PUBLIC** were used instead of **STACK**, the program would have to explicitly initialize **ss** and **sp**.

The **AT** option allows the programmer the advantage of viewing a fixed area of memory as though it were a segment. A segment register can then be pointed to this area, and the objects residing there can be accessed by means of the standard memory addressing modes. **AT** is most often used in interfacing with the machine hardware. Perhaps the two most common uses of **AT** are in dealing with the BIOS data area and in writing directly to the video buffer.

As an example, we will consider the BIOS data area. Recall that this is a region of low memory beginning at address 0000:0400 and containing various data buffers and flags holding information about the hardware configuration. One of the most interesting items in the BIOS data area is the *keyboard buffer*, which is a block of 18 words that can store as many as 15 characters input from the keyboard, while they await processing by the system. The detailed workings of the keyboard buffer will be presented in Chapter 15. For our present example, it suffices to know that the keyboard buffer begins at address 041AH and contains two one-word "pointers," conventionally called *Head* and *Tail*, followed by a 16-word buffer area. Here is how **AT** can be used to address the keyboard buffer:

```
biosSeg    SEGMENT AT 40h

    ORG    1ah
    Head   dw    ?
    Tail   dw    ?
    Buffer dw    16  dup(?)

biosSeg    ENDS
```

The starting address of *biosSeg* and the value of **ORG** are chosen so that *Head* occurs at address 0040:001A = 041AH. Pointing a segment register at *biosSeg* makes it possible to refer to its constituents by name, as in this fragment:

```
mov     ax, biosSeg
mov     es, ax
ASSUME  es:biosSeg
mov     bx, Tail
cmp     bx, Head
je      Empty
mov     ax, es:[bx]
```

MASM is quite permissive in its rules regarding segment definitions. For example, a given **PUBLIC** segment can be partly defined in each of several modules, and any given module can have several disjoint pieces of the segment, each starting with *Name SEGMENT* and ending with *Name ENDS*.

It is only necessary to list the parameters of a segment the first time its definition occurs. Thereafter, **MASM** assumes that the parameters are the same as they were on its first appearance. Of course, it is incorrect to give the segment conflicting parameters on subsequent uses. However, different parts of a **PUBLIC** segment need not have the same *alignType*. For example, an initial part of a segment might be given **BYTE** alignment, while a later part has **WORD** alignment.

The next segment definition parameter is *className*. className must be written in single quotes, and gives the programmer some control over the order in which the various segments of the program are loaded into machine memory. Specifically, segments with the same *className* are loaded contiguously, so that they always appear as one continuous region of memory, except for possible alignment gaps.

There are a number of reasons why selected segments should occur together. For example, it is most logical to have all the code segments together and all the data segments together. If certain parts of the program are to be loaded into ROM, it will probably be essential that they occur together or, at most, are separated by minimal alignment gaps. Another use of *className* relates to the important **GROUP** directive, which will be discussed presently. We will see that segments can be placed in the same group even if they have gaps between them, but that the entire span from the start of the first segment to the end of the last segment in a given group cannot be more than 64K. Hence such segments must not be too far apart when they are loaded, and putting them in the same class is one way to ensure this.

The question of segment ordering has a number of aspects, of which *className* is only one. **MASM** always reads the input file from start to finish, and so will see the segments in the order in which they are written. The programmer must keep this in mind when considering the question of forward references. But the programmer has some control over the order in which **MASM** places the segments in the completed .OBJ file. If the directive **.SEQ** (or the **MASM** command-line switch **/S**) is used, the segments will appear in the .OBJ file in the order of their first appearance in the source file; if the directive **.ALPHA** (or the command-line switch **/A**) is used, the segments will occur in alphabetical order in the .OBJ file. If no directive or switch is used, the default is in order of first appearance.

In a multi-module program, the final ordering of classes and segments in the **.EXE** file will also depend on the order in which the .OBJs are listed on the **LINK** command line. For example, here is how the class that will occur first in the load module is determined: **LINK** takes the first segment from the first .OBJ on its command line, then searches the .OBJs, looking for other segments that belong to this class. The order in which it finds these segments depends on how **MASM** constructed the .OBJ files and on the ordering of the .OBJs on **LINK**'s command line.

There are two easy ways to get a guaranteed segment ordering in the executable file. The first is to use the simplified segment directives, which we will discuss later. The second method is to be sure that **LINK** first sees the segments in the order in which they should occur in memory. This can be accomplished by starting the source file that will become the first .OBJ on the **LINK** command line with a "dummy" list of segments:

```
firstName     SEGMENT   [Parameters]
firstName     ENDS
secondName    SEGMENT   [Parameters]
secondName    ENDS
thirdName     SEGMENT   [Parameters]
thirdName     ENDS
```

Here *firstName*, *secondName*, *thirdName*, ⋯ must of course be replaced by the actual names of the segments that should occur first, second, third, ⋯ in the executable file. As we mentioned earlier, the segment parameters need not be repeated with the later occurrences of these segments. If this approach is used, it is not necessary to use the *className* parameter. However, according to the Microsoft documentation, **CODEVIEW** expects code segments to have class name "CODE," hence it is certainly advisable to use at least this class.

As we know, a feature of the present assembly language is the necessity of pointing a segment register at a segment before that segment can be accessed. Many times a program needs several code and/or data segments, which may require switching segment registers between segments. This can occur in even a relatively small program. As an example, consider our line-numbering program in Chapter 8. In order to have large, uninitialized buffers that were not stored as part of the disk image of the program, it was necessary to put these buffers in a special segment consisting of only uninitialized data, and then to place that segment, together with other uninitialized segments (such as the stack) at the high end of the executable file. Since the program also had initialized data, two data segments were needed.

Ideally, in cases such as this, where the data have total size less than 64K but are necessarily spread over several segments, there should be a mechanism by which all the data can be reached with a single initialization of a segment register. Such a mechanism exists, and it is activated by the **GROUP** directive.

The syntax used with the **GROUP** directive is

Name **GROUP** *Segment* {, *Segment* }

The effect of this directive is to assign *Name* to the *group* consisting of the listed segments. The same segment may occur in several different groups. As mentioned previously, the segments in a group need not be contiguous, but the total distance in memory spanned by the segments in a group cannot exceed 64K.

An example of the **GROUP** directive is

```
dGroup    GROUP    dSeg1, dSeg2, dSeg3
```

The **GROUP** directive is usually used with a variant of **ASSUME**, which in this example would have the form

```
ASSUME ds:dGroup
```

This directive tells **MASM** that we will use **ds** to address all the segments in *dGroup* simultaneously. Of course, we are responsible, as always, for actually pointing the **ds** register, this time to *dGroup*:

```
mov       ax, dGroup
mov       ds, ax
```

Now if our program contains a line such as

```
mov       ax, Var2
```

where *Var2* is a variable in *dSeg2*, for example, **MASM** will generate the correct code. The address for *Var2* will be built using the segment address of *dGroup* and using the distance of *Var2* from the start of *dGroup* as the offset.

Only the **OFFSET** operator fails to perform perfectly in this context. Suppose that *Var2* has offset 10 bytes relative to the start of *dSeg2*, but has offset 110 bytes relative to the start of *dGroup*. When the line

```
mov       bx, OFFSET Var2
```

is written, what is presumably wanted is the offset of *Var2* relative to the start of *dGroup*, 110 in this case. What is actually moved into **bx** is the offset relative to the start of *dSeg2*, or 10. Getting the "right" answer of 110 requires writing

```
mov       bx, OFFSET dGroup:Var2
```

We will see later that using the group name as a segment override is usually unnecessary when the simplified segment directives are used.

A nice application of the **GROUP** directive is in the construction of .COM programs. Earlier, we stated that a basic requirement for a .COM program is that it consist of a single segment. As a matter of fact, the interpretation of "one segment" made by **EXE2BIN** is quite liberal. The real requirement is that all the segments in the program should be addressable by one setting of a segment register. In other words, it is sufficient that the program consist of one group. Of course, various items are forbidden in a .COM file. For example, no segment of combine type **STACK** is permitted, and no reference to a segment name, such as

```
mov      ax, dSeg
```

is allowed. Each of these will draw an error from **EXE2BIN**. Figure 12.1 shows a template for building .COM files using **GROUP**.

Many advantages accrue from using this template. Code and data are divided into separate logical segments, which is always desirable. When **MASM** reads the source file, the data precede the code and so there is no potential difficulty with forward references. Lines 5-10 ensure that the data come after the code in the load module and, in particular, that the uninitialized data segment loads highest and so is not part of the disk image. Finally, all the segment registers are initialized to the same value (since this will be a .COM file), this common address being the start of the group. Consequently, any of the segment registers can be used to access any location in the program. The most important ramification of this fact is that **ds** and **es** can each be used to refer to both data segments. In using the string instructions, it is sometimes helpful that **ds** and **es** also point to the stack.

THE SIMPLIFIED SEGMENT DIRECTIVES

As we have known since Chapter 4, the simplified segment directives supply a reasonable set of defaults for segment names and other parameters, and provide matching values for the **ASSUME** directive. One of the main reasons for using the simplified directives is that the defaults they give are compatible with those enforced by the compilers supplied with the other Microsoft languages, and with the languages supplied by many other vendors who (wisely) choose to be consistent with these conventions. Consequently, even if the traditional directives are used, it is generally a good idea, with an eye toward future interfacing, to use the default segment names and parameters. Since additional segments of the programmer's choice can be introduced into a program that uses the simplified directives, there is usually no loss involved in using them.

So far, we have always used the directive **.MODEL SMALL** in our programs that used the simplified directives. It selects the **SMALL** model for the structure of the program, but this is just one of a number of alternatives. Each of the Microsoft family of languages supports some subset of the following five models:

a. The **SMALL** model. In this model, there can be only one code segment (although, as pointed out in Chapter 7, overlaying is possible) and at most 64K of data and stack combined. In assembly language, a separate stack segment is usually declared, and this is combined with the data segments into a group named DGROUP. In terms of execution speed and program size, **SMALL** is the most efficient model since all addresses can be stored or referenced in terms of their offsets alone. In particular, all procedure calls can be **NEAR**.

b. The **COMPACT** model. Here there can only be 64K of code but there can be an arbitrary amount of data, up to the limits of machine memory. This configuration is obviously useful when the program code is of modest size, but a lot of data must be manipulated. Of course, all procedure calls can again be **NEAR**.

FIGURE 12.1 A NEW TEMPLATE FOR .COM FILES

```
 1    TITLE    Prog12_1.asm: alternate template for .COM files
 2
 3    comGrp    GROUP   dSeg1, dSeg2, cSeg
 4
 5    cSeg    SEGMENT WORD 'CODE'
 6    cSeg    ENDS
 7    dSeg1    SEGMENT WORD PUBLIC 'DATA'
 8    dSeg1    ENDS
 9    dSeg2    SEGMENT WORD PUBLIC 'DATA'
10    dSeg2    ENDS
11
12    dSeg1    SEGMENT
13
14        ;initialized data here
15
16    dSeg1 ENDS
17
18    dSeg2  SEGMENT
19
22        ;uninitialized data here
21
22    dSeg2  ENDS
23
24    cSeg    SEGMENT
25
26        ASSUME  cs:comGrp, ds:comGrp, es:comGrp, ss:comGrp
27
28        ORG    100h
29
30    Start:
31
32        ;code here
33
34        mov    ax, 4c00h
35        int    21h
36
37    cSeg    ENDS
38
49    END    Start
```

c. The **MEDIUM** model. There can be as much code as memory permits, but no more than 64K of data and stack combined. Calls can be **NEAR** or **FAR**, and data are efficiently addressed by means of near pointers, i.e., by using offsets only.

d. The **LARGE** model. Both code and data can be as large as machine memory allows.
e. The **HUGE** model. This is just like the **LARGE** model except that it is possible to define single arrays of data that are larger than 64K, i.e., that span more than one segment.

MASM supports all five models, although its support of the huge model is only for notational convenience in interfacing with high-level languages. Unlike **C**, it offers no

FIGURE 12.2 SIMPLIFIED SEGMENT DIRECTIVES

```
TITLE    Prog12_2.asm: default segments with simplified directives

DOSSEG
.MODEL LARGE

.STACK
.DATA
.DATA?
.CONST
.FARDATA  InitFarData    ;name optional — default is FAR_DATA
.FARDATA? UninitFarData ;name optional — default is FAR_BSS
.CODE                    ;name of FAR code segment is moduleName_TEXT
Start:
END Start
```

particular support for huge arrays — the assembly language programmer must explicitly define such arrays so that they span several segments and supply code to manipulate them.

Figure 12.2 shows the different segment types that are available when the simplified directives are used. A number of segment types are supplied primarily for the use of compilers (**FARDATA, FARDATA?,** and **CONST**) but can also be used in assembly language programs. **FARDATA** and **FARDATA?** allow optional names. The name for the **CODE** segment in the **LARGE** and **COMPACT** models is always _TEXT prefaced by the directory name of the assembly module. Also, the **FAR** segments are not used in the **SMALL** and **MEDIUM** models. **CONST** is generally used to hold data that will not be changed at run time. The '?' at the end of **FARDATA?** has the same significance as in **DATA?** — the segment "loads high" and is not stored as part of the disk image.

Figure 12.3 is an expurgated version of the list file for PROG12_2.ASM. It was assembled using **MASM's /LA** (*list all generated code*) option, and shows the results of using the simplified directives. It merits detailed study. To save space, we have not included a Pass 1 listing, but that is also worth perusing. Here are some observations on Figure 12.3:

1. It shows the default name, *alignType, combineType,* and *className* for each of the standard segments. Notice that _DATA, STACK, _BSS, and CONST are all part of DGROUP, but the **FAR** data segments are not.

2. For each of the standard segments, there is a predefined equate, such as @code or @fardata, evaluating to the name of that segment. The exception is that @data evaluates to the group name DGROUP. Hence the automatic **ASSUME**s associate **cs** with the code segment and **ds** and **ss** with DGROUP.

3. @curseg is a predefined equate evaluating to the name of the current segment. It works even when the traditional segment definitions are used.

4. If no size is specified for the stack, the default size (as in this example) is 400H.

FIGURE 12.3 LIST FILE FOR PROG12_2

```
TITLE    Prog12_2.asm: default segments with simplified directives

                DOSSEG
                .MODEL LARGE
                assume cs:@code,ds:@data,ss:@data

                .STACK
0000            STACK segment 'STACK'
0400            @CurSeg ends
                .DATA
0000            _DATA segment 'DATA'
                .DATA?
0000            @CurSeg ends
0000            _BSS segment 'BSS'
                .CONST
0000            @CurSeg ends
0000            CONST segment 'DATA'
                .FARDATA  initFarData    ;name optional — default is FAR_DATA
0000            @CurSeg ends
0000            INITFARDATA segment 'FAR_DATA'
                .FARDATA? uninitFarData ;name optional — default is FAR_BSS
0000            @CurSeg ends
0000            UNINITFARDATA segment 'FAR_BSS'
                .CODE              ;name optional — default is _TEXT
0000            @CurSeg ends
0000            CSEG segment 'CODE'
0000            Start:
                END Start
0000            @CurSeg ends

Segments and Groups:

N a m e                  Length   Align   Combine Class

DGROUP  .  .  .  .  .  .          GROUP
  _DATA  .  .  .  .  .   0000     WORD    PUBLIC  'DATA'
  STACK  .  .  .  .  .   0400     PARA    STACK   'STACK'
  _BSS  .  .  .  .  .  . 0000     WORD    PUBLIC  'BSS'
  CONST  .  .  .  .  .   0000     WORD    PUBLIC  'DATA'
INITFARDATA  .  .  .     0000     PARA    NONE    'FAR_DATA'
PROG12_2_TEXT  .  .      0000     WORD    PUBLIC  'CODE'
UNINITFARDATA  .  .      0000     PARA    NONE    'FAR_BSS'
```

5. The exact ordering resulting from the use of **DOSSEG** is somewhat complicated, but here it is, in essence: segments from class "CODE" come first; next the segments that are not part of DGROUP; finally, the segments in DGROUP, with classes BSS and STACK last. If a main module calls subsidiary modules, the **DOSSEG** directive need only appear in the main module. Likewise, if assembly language modules are destined to be called from a high-level language, they need not contain the **DOSSEG** directive, since they will inherit it.

There is one final, minor advantage that results from using the simplified directives. We pointed out earlier that, under the traditional directives, the **OFFSET** operator presents a slight difficulty when used with groups. Namely,

```
OFFSET    varName
```

evaluates to the offset of *varName* relative to the start of the containing segment, rather than relative to the start of the group, which is generally needed. Circumventing this difficulty requires writing an explicit override, such as

```
OFFSET    grpName:varName
```

When the simplified directives are used, this problem does not arise with respect to DGROUP. In that case,

```
OFFSET    varName
```

will automatically evaluate to the offset of *varName* relative to the start of DGROUP.

Exercise 12-1. In this section, we stated that the **MASM OFFSET** directive does not work as expected when groups are used with the traditional segment directives. Construct an example to illustrate this problem.

Exercise 12-2. Rewrite our best version of the line-numbering utility (from Section 6 of Chapter 8), improving it in any way you can. For example: it should be written as a .COM program to minimize the size of the disk image; it should use the new .COM template; and it should use the string instructions to parse the PSP and move data within the buffers.

Exercise 12-3. (For **80386** users.) Use the **GROUP** directive to rewrite *bigFact* (from Section 5 of Chapter 11) so that the uninitialized data are not stored as part of the disk image.

SECTION 3   VARIABLES AND LABELS

So far, we have associated variable names with objects in the data segment and labels with locations in the code segment. But as far as **MASM** is concerned, there is no real distinction between variable names and labels.

There are actually two species of labels, data and code, and **MASM** treats a variable name as a special case of a data label. The essential difference between the two kinds of labels is that, in the symbol table, a data label has a size (**BYTE, WORD, ···**) associated with it, while a code label has a distance (**NEAR** or **FAR**) associated with it.

A variable is defined by means of a *defining directive*, the choices for which are listed in Table 12.3.

Of the defining directives, only the first three need concern us at the moment. **DF** is used mainly in storing addresses for the **80386**; when we study the numerical coprocessors in Chapter 17, we will use the **DQ** and **DT** directives.

TABLE 12.3 THE DEFINING DIRECTIVES

DIRECTIVE	MEANING
DB	define BYTE
DW	define WORD
DD	define DWORD (doubleword or four bytes)
DF	define FWORD (farword or six bytes)
DQ	define QWORD (quadword or eight bytes)
DT	define TBYTE (ten-byte word)

The syntax used by the defining directives is quite familiar by now. If *defDir* is one of these directives, then

[*varName*]   *defDir initVal* { , *initVal* }

allocates and initializes the requested number of contiguous bytes. *initVal* represents an expression that must be known at assembly time. If *varName* is used, it can be used to reference this region of memory. More precisely, it is a label with value equal to the initial offset of the defined data block. As we saw in Chapter 6, **MASM** stores this value in the symbol table, along with type information (**BYTE, WORD,**···) and an attribute, which records the segment in which the item is defined.

A data label can be defined by the **LABEL** directive:

Name **LABEL** *Type*

where *Type* can be either **BYTE, WORD, DWORD, FWORD, QWORD,** or **TBYTE,** these words having the same significance as in Table 12.3, or can be any previously defined structure or record name. (Structures and records will be introduced in the next section.) Data labels have *exactly* the same meaning to **MASM** as do variable names. The only difference is that **LABEL** declarations do not cause memory to be allocated. Since **MASM** stores all its information about named objects in the symbol table, it is easy to verify that it does not distinguish between data labels and variable names. Define a data label and a data object of the same type at the same location in the data segment. Check the symbol table descriptions of these two items — they will be identical, showing that **MASM** does not even know which mode of definition was used.

A standard application of a data label is to "alias" a given location in memory, i.e., to provide two different names, usually with different characteristics, for this location.

Suppose, as an example, that we wish to set up storage for a full address, both segment and offset, in the data segment, and we will sometimes need to access the entire address (as a double word), but would also like to access the segment and offset portions separately. This fragment will accomplish these goals:

```
fullAdr      LABEL   DWORD
offsetAdr    DW      offsetVal
segmentAdr   DW      segmentVal
```

Of course, if the initializers *offsetVal* and *segmentVal* are included, they must be values that are computable at assembly time. Loading the offset into **bx** and the segment into **ds** can be effected by the instructions

```
mov      bx, offsetAdr
mov      ds, segmentAdr
```

or, using the alias for more efficiency, by the single instruction

```
lds      bx, fullAdr
```

An essential point here is that **lds** requires a double word as its operand. The operation could also be completed in a single line, without using **LABEL**, by using a size override:

```
lds      bx, DWORD PTR offsetAdr
```

However, this method is quite ugly and does not provide the self-documentation that comes with the **LABEL** approach.

We will encounter another application for data labels in Chapter 15. In dealing with memory-resident programs, it is important to minimize program size, and one standard technique for doing this is to store data in the **PSP**. This is usually accomplished by assigning names to the storage locations, using the **LABEL** directive.

As we stated earlier, code labels differ slightly from data labels since each code label has a distance associated with it, rather than a size. The distance is either **NEAR** or **FAR** and is entered in the symbol table as the *type* of the label. We have encountered the words **NEAR** and **FAR** several times before, and they always have the same significance. If the target of a program transfer instruction is a **NEAR** label, code is generated for an *intrasegment transfer*, i.e., a transfer within the present code segment, so that **ip** is adjusted but **cs** is left unchanged. In the case of a **FAR** label, code appropriate to an *intersegment transfer* is generated, which means a transfer to a different segment, with the result that both **ip** and **cs** are adjusted.

Code labels can be declared in three ways: by introducing them as identifiers followed by colons, as we have done many times; as procedure names using the **PROC** directive; and by using the **LABEL** directive.

We have already seen the general rules that determine the distances of labels defined by the first two methods. Any label defined as an identifier followed by a colon is **NEAR**. A label defined by a **PROC** directive can have its distance explicitly named as **NEAR** or **FAR**. If the distance is not explicitly named, then it is **NEAR** if the traditional segment directives are used and has the value appropriate to the current model if the simplified directives are used.

The syntax used when defining code labels with the **LABEL** directive is similar to that used when defining data labels:

Name **LABEL** *Distance*

Code labels defined in this way see relatively little use. Any definition of a **NEAR** label using the **LABEL** directive can be replaced, more succinctly, by a label name followed by a colon. **FAR** labels are generally the entry points to **FAR** procedures and are best coded as such. An occasional use of **FAR** labels is to provide alternate entry points to procedures. For example:

```
Proced    PROC    FAR
          .
          .
altProced    LABEL    FAR
          .
          .
     ret

Proced        ENDP
```

Note that the **LABEL** directive cannot be replaced by another **PROC** directive, since **MASM** insists that every **PROC** have a matching **ENDP**. (Why won't it work to make that replacement and, in addition, interpolate the line

```
altProced    ENDP
```

between the last two lines?)

There are a few other directives relating to data definition. We have used **DUP** many times. Perhaps the most significant fact about **DUP** that has not yet been mentioned is that (as of Version 5.1 of **MASM**), **DUP**s can be nested to a maximum depth of 17! We are also well acquainted with the **ORG** directive. To review quickly, its syntax is

    ORG *Exp*

where *Exp* is an expression whose value must be known during the first assembly pass (and

so cannot contain forward references). The effect of this directive is to set **MASM**'s "location counter" to the value of *Exp*. The **ORG** directive is generally used to leave gaps in the code. Perhaps the single most important application of **ORG** is the line

```
ORG       100h
```

which is placed in a file destined to become a .COM program, the object being to leave space for the PSP.

Two other directives that are somewhat related to **ORG** are

    EVEN

which sets the location counter to the next even address, and

    ALIGN *Constant*

which sets the location counter to the next address that is a multiple of *Constant*. Here *Constant* must be a power of two.

By virtue of our previous discussions, the applications of **EVEN** and **ALIGN** should be clear: they can be used to minimize the number of fetches from memory in programs intended for the more advanced processors in the family. These directives are not used much in **8088** programming.

Exercise 12-4. Write a program that uses the **LABEL** directive to store data in the UPA of the PSP. One possibility is to use *Rand16* to generate an array of 64 integers, store the integers in the UPA, and then print them to the screen.

SECTION 4   STRUCTURES AND RECORDS

This assembly language permits the use of *structures*, which are like arrays except that their elements need not all be of the same size. These structures are quite analogous to the structures used in **C** and the records used in **PASCAL**, both in general syntax and in usage. In particular, the use of a structure usually involves two steps: declaring a *structure template*, and actually allocating memory to hold copies of the structure. The structure template assigns a name to the structure and notifies **MASM** of the form of the structure elements. It does not cause memory to be allocated for actual copies or *instances* of the structure. The structure elements, which are called members in C and **PASCAL**, are called *fields* in the present context. The declaration of a structure template uses the following syntax:

> *structName* **STRUC**
> > *fieldDeclarations*
> *structName* **ENDS**

STRUC and **ENDS** are reserved words, with **ENDS** meaning "end of structure." The field declarations are just standard data declarations (involving **DB**s, **DW**s, etc., and **DUP**s, if necessary). An identifier cannot be used both as a variable and as a structure field name in the same module, or as a field name in two different structure templates within the same module. Also, structure template declarations cannot be nested — it is illegal to use a structure template as a field declaration. The field declarations in the template may include initializers.

As an example, here is a structure representing a rather simplified employee record:

```
Employee     STRUCT
      Name   DB      40 DUP (?)
      SSN    DB      9  DUP (?)
      telNo  DB      "0000000"
      strAdr DB      40 DUP (?)
      City   DB      20 DUP (?)
Employee     ENDS
```

Notice that the telephone number field has been initialized to *0000000*. Consequently, each instance of the structure will, by default, have its telephone number field initialized to that value, unless the default is overridden explicitly when the instance is defined. The use of the initializer *0000000* rather than the somewhat more readable *7 DUP('0')* may seem strange, but is necessitated by a curious restriction placed by **MASM**. If an initializer in a template is multiple in the sense that it is a comma-separated list or contains a **DUP**, then it cannot be overridden when an instance is defined!

The telephone field was initialized for a practical reason. If the employee has a telephone, then this field will be explicitly initialized when the instance for that employee is defined. If not, this field will contain the "impossible" telephone number 000-0000, indicating that the employee has no telephone.

Definitions of actual instances of a structure can only occur after the template declaration. They use this syntax:

[*instanceName*]   *structName* < [*fieldInit* {*,fieldInit*}] >

If *instanceName* is left blank, memory is allocated for an unnamed instance of *struct-Name*. The *fieldInit* entries are optional initializers for the fields of the instance of the structure. Any subset of the fields can be initialized and, if necessary, commas should be used to enable **MASM** to associate each initializer with its appropriate field. Even if no initializers are supplied in the instance definition, the angle brackets are still required.

For example, the definition

```
Emp1    Employee    <"John Doe",,,,"Anytown" >
```

allocates space for one instance of our structure, explicitly initializes the first and last fields, and of course the telephone field inherits the default initialization from the structure template. If an initializer were supplied for the telephone field, it would replace the default.

The **OFFSET** directive has a new meaning when applied to the fields in a structure. If *fieldName* is the name of a structure field, then

```
OFFSET    fieldName
```

means the offset of *fieldName* relative to the start of the structure, i.e., the number of bytes preceding *fieldName* in the structure. In our example,

```
OFFSET    Name  = 0
OFFSET    SSN   = 40
OFFSET    telNo = 49
```

The individual fields of a given instance of a structure can be accessed using a '.' notation quite similar to that used in C and **PASCAL.** If *fieldName* is the name of a structure field, then an expression of the form

```
baseAdr.fieldName
```

is translated by **MASM** into the form

```
baseAdr + OFFSET fieldName
```

where *OFFSET fieldName* is interpreted as in the previous paragraph. This means that the

'.' notation works as expected, provided that *baseAdr* evaluates to the beginning or "base" address of the structure instance. For example, *Emp1.Name* refers to the *Name* field in the instance *Emp1*.

A more realistic application of our *Employee* structure might involve constructing an array of, say, 100 instances, which can be done as follows:

```
Emps    Employee    100 DUP(<>)
```

This defines *Emps* as an array of structures of type *Employee* and gives each the default initialization. The employees will now have a natural numbering 0-99, corresponding to their positions in the array. Suppose that we have already initialized this array with appropriate data about the 100 employees, and wish to recover some information about the employee whose number is contained in **ax**.

A useful assembler operator in this context is **TYPE**. We will look at **TYPE** more closely later but, for the moment, the salient fact is that if *Ident* is the name of a variable or structure, then the value of the expression

```
TYPE      Ident
```

equals the size of *Ident* in bytes.

The code fragment

```
mov     cx, TYPE Employee
mul     cx
mov     bx, ax
```

sets **bx** equal to the offset of the correct instance of the structure relative to the start of the array *Emps*. Hence the information fields for the employee whose number is in **ax** lie at offsets

```
Emps[bx].Name, Emps[bx].SSN, ···
```

relative to the start of the segment. It would now be a simple matter to print out these items.

If we wished to do the same computation for a particular employee, and if the number of that employee, say 29, happened to be known at assembly time, then our fragment would be unnecessary. The name field, for example, of this employee can be referenced by the single line

```
Emps[29 * TYPE Employee].Name
```

or by the line

```
Emps.Name[29 * TYPE Employee]
```

In a number of our previous programs we have used equates to assign names to parameters passed to procedures, in order to improve the readability of our code. In Chapter

14, we will discuss the new interfacing conventions introduced with Version 5.1 of **MASM**, which provide an alternate mechanism for assigning names to parameters passed to a procedure.

There is yet another method of associating names with passed parameters, which uses structure notation. We will outline this technique since it provides an interesting example of the use of structures. In particular, it shows that it is not always necessary to define an explicit instance of a structure. It sometimes suffices to declare a structure template and then to establish a base address directly.

Suppose, for purposes of illustration, that three parameters have been passed on the stack and that we are dealing with a **NEAR** call, so that the parameters reside at offsets **bp** + 4, **bp** + 6, **bp** + 8, and that we wish to refer to them as *Var1*, *Var2*, and *Var3*. We set up a structure template, which is traditionally named *DSAStruc* (where *DSA* stands for *dynamic stack allocation*):

```
DSAStruc    STRUC
    oldBP   DW    ?
    retIp   DW    ?
    Var1    DW    ?
    Var2    DW    ?
    Var3    DW    ?
DSAStruc    ENDS
```

The fields in *DSAStruc* have been given names corresponding to the stack contents at offsets **bp** through **bp** + 8, after entry to the procedure. The remaining chore is to position a copy of *DSAStruc* so that these fields actually reference the correct words on the stack, and this can be accomplished by including the line

```
DSA    EQU    [bp]
```

at the start of the source file. When **MASM** encounters an expression such as

```
DSA.Var1
```

it replaces it by

```
[bp].Var1
```

This is of the correct form for a ".". structure reference since [**bp**] is a memory reference. **MASM** further translates it as

```
[bp] + 4
```

since the offset of *Var1* (in the structure sense) is 4. But this is just an alternate form for [*bp* + 4], which is indeed an indirect reference to *Var1*. Since the register entering into the indirect reference is **bp**, **ss** is used as the default segment register, which is correct in the present situation. The only weakness of this scheme is that *Var1* must be referred to using the somewhat clumsy *DSA.Var1*, and *Var2* and *Var3* must be similarly treated.

Geometrically, we can view the process of the last paragraph as "superimposing" the structure template at a chosen position in memory.

This notation extends naturally to the use of local variables, which are accessed at negative offsets relative to **bp**. Let us extend the previous example and assume that, in addition, we wish to have two local variables *Local1* and *Local2*, each of size one word, available to the procedure. The structure template should be replaced by

```
DSAStruc   STRUC
     Local1  DW    ?
     Local2  DW    ?
     oldBP   DW    ?
     retIp   DW    ?
     Var1    DW    ?
     Var2    DW    ?
     Var3    DW    ?
DSAStruc   ENDS
```

A line of the form

```
DSA   EQU   [bp - 4]
```

will serve to superimpose this template correctly on the stack. The number 4 must be subtracted to allow four bytes before the *oldBp* field for the locals. The reader is encouraged to check that this equate results in the locals and parameters falling at the correct locations.

Rather than using the preceding equate for *DSAStruc*, it is much better to use

```
DSA   EQU   [bp - OFFSET oldBp]
```

to accomplish the superposition. This certainly gives the same result, since *OFFSET oldBp* = 4. But it has the advantage that, should the number of locals be changed at a later date, **MASM** will automatically adjust the *OFFSET oldBp* value. For example, if a third local is added, the number 4 should be changed to 6. This is the kind of detail that can be easily overlooked when code is updated. Consequently, this second form of the equate is a good example of "defensive programming."

As we pointed out earlier, when local space is allocated on the stack, it is important to protect these locals by decrementing **sp** by the correct amount. In the present situation, the best way to accomplish this is by using the instruction

```
sub   sp, OFFSET OldBp
```

at the appropriate point in the code, and, as always, making a later compensation by means of the line

```
add   sp, OFFSET OldBp
```

or, if **bp** has not changed during the procedure,

```
mov   sp, bp
```

MASM also supports a data structure called a *record*. These records are akin to the bit fields used in **C**. They are not used often and so we will describe them fairly briefly. We will find applications for them in Chapter 18.

The basic idea is that records allow a byte or a word to be divided into named collections of bits, and certain operators are provided for manipulating these bits.

The syntax for using records is similar to that for structures. In particular, setting up records is usually a two-step process: declaring a template and defining instances. Depending on the circumstances, it may not be necessary to define instances.

A declaration of a record template has the form

> *recordName* **RECORD** *Field* {, *Field*}

Each *Field* has the format

> *fieldName:Width*[=*Exp*]

Here *fieldName* is just an identifier, *Width* is an integer, and *Exp* is an (optional) initializer, which must be computable at assembly time. There are actually three different ways of initializing the record fields: if an initializing expression is supplied in the record template, it becomes the default applying to all instances of the record; we will see later that when instances are defined, they can be initialized, and this initialization overrides any initialization supplied in the template; if no initialization of a field is specifically requested, the field is automatically initialized to 0.

If the sum of the field widths is less than or equal to 8, objects defined by *recordName* have size one byte. The various fields are stored in this byte from high bit to low bit, in the order written, but padded with enough zero bits on the high end so that they occupy the lowest possible bits. Likewise, if the sum of the widths is greater than 8 but no greater than 16, a word of storage is used. If the sum of the widths is greater than 16, **MASM** prints an error message. (In programs written for the **80386**, records can be as wide as 32 bits.)

The objects defined by *recordName* are of two types, constants and variables. A constant of type *recordName* is written as

> *recordName* <[*fieldInit*, {, *fieldInit*}] >

where each *fieldInit* is a constant expression and the general conventions are the same as in the structure case. The definition of a variable of type *recordName* follows the same general pattern as for structures:

> [*instanceName*] *recordName* [*fieldInit*, {, *fieldInit*}]

As an illustration, we will consider the date and time stamps on disk files. As part of the directory information about each file, **DOS** records the date and time at which the file was most recently changed. When a file is written to, this information is automatically updated. Sometimes it is convenient to be able to read this information (or even to change it) from within a program. For example, this situation occurs in connection with the **MAKE** utility, to be discussed in Chapter 14: it is often desirable to give a source file a recent time stamp, without actually changing the file contents, in order to trigger the updating of some collection of target files.

Function 57H of int 21H can be used to read or modify the time and date of a disk file. The file must be open and bx must contain the file handle. If al = 0, function 57H returns the time information in cx and the date information in dx; if al = 1, the function interprets the contents of cx as time information and the contents of dx as date information and uses these values to update the time and date stamps for the given file.

Records work naturally in conjunction with function 57H because DOS uses bit fields to format the time and date information. The time is stored in a single word with the hours (0-23) in the five highest bits, the minutes (0-59) in the next six bits, and seconds divided by two (0-29) in the low five bits. Of course, this means that the time is only recorded in multiples of two seconds. The natural RECORD corresponding to this format is

```
timeRec   RECORD  hourFld:6, minFld:5, secFld:5
```

In setting the time stamp to 12:00:00, for example, a natural step would be

```
        mov     cx, timeRec <12,,>
```

Similarly, the date is stored in a word with the quantity (year − 1980) stored in the high seven bits, the month (1-12) in the next four bits, and the date (1-31) in the low five bits. A corresponding record is

```
dateRec   RECORD  yearFld:7, mnthFld:4, dayFld:5
```

A program that sets the date stamp to Jan 1, 2000, could contain a instruction such as

```
        mov     dx, dateRec <20,1,1>
```

MASM supplies some operators to support the RECORD directive. These can make computations involving bit manipulation easier and, probably more important, they provide a measure of self-documentation in programs that use them.

The first such operator is

MASK *fieldName* | *recordname*

where *fieldName* is a field in a record. This operator has as value a mask (of appropriate 8- or 16-bit size) with ones in the bit positions occupied by *fieldName*, or in the positions actually used by *recordName*, and zeros in all other positions.

The second operator is

WIDTH *fieldName* | *recordName*

with *fieldName* again being a record field. It returns the number of bits occupied by *fieldName* or *recordName*.

With *fieldName* once more meaning a record field, MASM performs a third useful service: if *fieldName* is used in an instruction, it is interpreted as an expression whose value is the bit number of the rightmost bit occupied by *fieldName*. For example,

```
        mov     cl, yearFld
```

is translated as

```
        mov     cl, 9
```

As an easy example, the following fragment will print out the directory time stamp for a file. We assume that the file has been opened, that its handle is stored in **bx**, and that *intStr* is a buffer that has already been defined in the segment pointed to by **ds**.

```
mov     ax, 5700h        ;ah = 57h, al = 0
int     21h              ;Get time and date
mov     ax, cx           ;store working copy of time info in ax
and     ax, MASK hourFld
shr     ax, hourFld      ;ax now has hourFld in its low bits
iToA    intStr, ax
outAsc  intStr
outCh   ':'
mov     ax, cx           ;put a new copy of time info in ax
and     ax, MASK minFld
shr     ax, minFld       ;ax now contains minFld in its low bits
iToA    intStr, ax
outAsc  intStr
outCh   ':'
mov     ax, cx           ;put another copy of time info in ax
and     ax, MASK secFld
shr     ax, secFld - 1   ;ax now has secFld as its low bits
iToA    intStr, ax
outAsc  intStr
```

Exercise 12-5. The **MS-DOS** TIME and DATE utilities allow the user to get/set the system time and date. Write your own versions of these utilities. For example, *fixTime* could be written so that, when invoked without a command-line parameter, it will print the time to the screen, but will interpret a command line such as

```
        fixTime 02:23:16
```

as a request to set the system time.

Exercise 12-6. Write a primitive version of the TOUCH utility, which is available under the **UNIX** system and as part of many **MS-DOS** utility packages. This utility should accept the name of a file as a command-line parameter and replace its date and time stamps with the present time and date obtained from the system clock.

Exercise 12-7. Write a procedure that uses the *DSAStruc* notation to access its parameters and local variables. Although it is somewhat contrived, one simple possibility is to write a

---

TABLE 12.4 EXTRN TYPE SPECIFIERS

TYPE	MEANING
NEAR, FAR, PROC	distance specifier for code labels
BYTE, WORD, DWORD, FWORD, QWORD, TBYTE	size specifier for data items
ABS	(i.e., absolute) a constant

Swap procedure that receives two parameters on the stack and uses a local variable as the temporary in swapping them.

SECTION 5 THE PUBLIC AND EXTRN DIRECTIVES

We have already explained these directives in some detail and have used them many times. A few details of their usage must still be discussed.

A **PUBLIC** declaration uses a line of the form

> **PUBLIC** *symbolName* {, *symbolName*}

An important effect of using **PUBLIC** is that the corresponding symbols are actually recorded by **MASM** in the .OBJ file, so that they can be matched with occurrences in other assembly modules (where they should, of course, be declared **EXTRN**). It then becomes a responsibility of **LINK** to assign addresses to these symbols. On the other hand, if a symbol defined in a module is not declared **PUBLIC**, its name is not recorded in the .OBJ file. As we saw in Chapter 6, **MASM** assigns a tentative address to it, and flags this as an item requiring a fixup by **LINK**. In particular, symbol names that are not **PUBLIC** are local to the assembly module in which they are defined.

An **EXTRN** declaration has the form

> **EXTRN** *symbolName:Type* {, *symbolName:Type*}

where *Type* is any of the choices listed in Table 12.4.

One delicate aspect of the use of **EXTRN** is its exact placement in a module. The general rules are: for **NEAR** code labels (including **NEAR** procedures), an **EXTRN** declaration must occur in the segment in which it is used; for **FAR** code labels and **ABS** declarations, there are no restrictions on the **EXTRN** placement; for a data item, the **EXTRN** must occur in a segment with the same name and attributes as the segment in which the item is defined, even if this involves introducing a dummy segment in the module.

By default, **MASM** converts all **PUBLIC** and **EXTRN** symbols to uppercase before storing them in the .OBJ file, and this practice can wreak havoc in modules that interface with case-sensitive languages such as **C**. The standard practice in such cases is to assemble using either the /**ML** option (which makes all names case sensitive) or the /**Mx** option (which makes all **PUBLICs** and **EXTRNs** case sensitive).

The same general effect resulting from using the **PUBLIC/EXTRN** directives can be achieved in another way, namely by using the **COMM** (*communal*) directive. To use this mechanism, the symbols are declared to be communal in all source modules (perhaps by means of a **COMM** directive contained in an **INCLUDE** file). The general syntax of **COMM** is similar to **EXTRN**. This method is less flexible than is the use of **PUBLIC/EXTRN** since it does not permit the initialization of variables and since special segment names must be used. We will not make use of the **COMM** directive in this book and leave it to the interested reader to read about it in the **MASM** *Programmer's Guide*.

SECTION 6   OPERANDS AND EXPRESSIONS

MASM allows the operands in instructions and directives to be rather complicated expressions. These expressions can contain various arithmetic operators and other directives involving computations performed by **MASM** at assembly time. It is clearly desirable to have as much computation as possible done by **MASM**, rather than by the programmer or by the machine at run time. Of course, **MASM** can only be asked to do computations involving quantities known at assembly time. Table 12.5 contains a list of operators used by **MASM** in assembly-time computations.

The details and syntactic restrictions governing the use of these operators are quite involved and so we will be content to discuss only the high points and provide a number of examples, again referring the reader to the **MASM** *Programmer's Reference* for the very technical details.

First of all, the arithmetic operators generally require constants, or expressions evaluating to constants, as their operands. They actually do 17-bit two's complement arithmetic, so that they can work successfully with operands in the range from −65536 to 65535. However, a returned answer is always truncated to 16 bits (by ignoring the high bit). (When the **80386** is used in 32-bit mode, 33-bit two's complement arithmetic is used for assembly-time computations.)

The binary '+' and '−' are exceptional in that one of the operands can be a memory reference, and the result of the computation can then be used as a memory reference. In the case of '−', both operands are permitted to be memory references, but the result is only usable as a constant.

The demonstration program in Figure 12.4 shows some of the operators in action. It is important to realize that all the operand computations were done by **MASM** at assembly time. The values for the second operand in lines 24-35, shown in the comments, were actually obtained from the .**LST** file — no .**EXE** file was ever constructed.

Figure 12.4 is intended to show some standard constructions used in assembly-time arithmetic and some of its limitations. Specifically:

Line 24. NOT −1 gives the expected value.

Line 25. NOT (NOT −1) also gives the expected value, but **MASM** will not accept NOT

TABLE 12.5 SOME MASM OPERATORS

```
OPERATOR        SYNTAX              OPERATION

+               +Exp                Unary plus
-               -Exp                Unary minus
*               Exp1 * Exp2         Multiplication
/               Exp1 / Exp2         Division
MOD             Exp1 MOD exp2       Modulus: remainder from Exp1 / Exp2
+               Exp1 + Exp2         Addition
-               Exp1 - Exp2         Subtraction

NOT             NOT Exp             Bitwise complement
AND             Exp AND Exp         Bitwise and
OR              Exp OR Exp          Bitwise inclusive or
XOR             Exp XOR Exp         Bitwise exclusive or
SHR             Exp SHR Count       Shift right
SHL             Exp SHL Count       Shift left

EQ              Exp1 EQ Exp2        -1 if Exp1  = Exp2; 0 otherwise
NE              Exp1 NE Exp2        -1 if Exp1 != Exp2; 0 otherwise
LT              Exp1 LT Exp2        -1 if Exp1 < Exp2; 0 otherwise
LE              Exp1 LE Exp2        -1 if Exp1 <= Exp2; 0 otherwise
GT              Exp1 GT Exp2        -1 if Exp1 > Exp2; 0 otherwise
GE              Exp1 GE Exp2        -1 if Exp1 >= Exp2; 0 otherwise

.               Var.Field           Returns offset of a structure field
[ ]             [Exp]               Index operator: has same effect as +
$               $                   Returns present value of location counter

:               SegExp:Exp          Modifies default segment
PTR             Type PTR Exp        Exp considered to be of type Type
                Dist PTR Exp        Exp considered to have distance Dist
SHORT           SHORT Label         Label reachable by one-byte displacement
THIS            THIS Type           Used with EQU or =; defines new object with
                                    same attributes as Type
HIGH            HIGH Exp            Returns high byte of Exp
LOW             LOW Exp             Returns low byte of Exp
SEG             SEG Exp             Returns segment part of address of Exp
OFFSET          OFFSET Exp          Returns offset part of address of Exp
.TYPE           .TYPE Exp           Returns information about Exp in byte
                                    described in Table 12.6
TYPE            TYPE Exp            Returns number of bytes in single item from Exp
LENGTH          LENGTH Var          Returns repetition count in outer DUP in Var
                                    or 1 if no DUPs involved
SIZE            SIZE Var            Returns TYPE Var * LENGTH Var
```

NOT −1 (without parentheses). In order for this to work as expected, NOT would need tobe right associative, and, in fact, this is the associativity given to unary operators in most languages. However, the **MASM** reference manual does say that all of the **MASM** operators are left associative. This statement is not completely correct since, for example, ++10 is a legal expression. The implications are that the implementation of some of the operators is not optimal and that the documentation is somewhat murky.

FIGURE 12.4 USING SOME OF THE ASSEMBLER OPERATORS

```
 1  TITLE   opTest.asm
 2
 3  DOSSEG
 4  .MODEL SMALL
 5  .STACK 100h
 6
 7  endAry   EQU  Ary + TYPE Ary * (LENGTH Ary - 1)
 8
 9  .DATA
10
11      ORG 100h
12      Ary  DW  10  DUP(7)
13      Var  DW  ?
14      Str  DB  "Hello, World",0
15      strLen   EQU  $ - Str
16
17  .CODE
18
19  Start:
20
21      mov   ax, @DATA
22      mov   ds, ax
23
24      mov   ax, NOT -1                    ;0
25      mov   ax, NOT (NOT -1)              ;1
26      mov   ax, (0ffffh + 0ffffh) / 2    ;07FFF
27      mov   ax, SEG Var                   ;——R
28      mov   ax, Ary                       ;0100R
29      mov   ax, Ary + 10                  ;010AR
30      mov   ax, SIZE Ary                  ;0014
31      mov   ax, endAry                    ;0112R
32      mov   ax, Var - Ary                 ;0014
33      mov   ax, strLen                    ;000D
34      mov   Var + 10, 20                  ;20
35      jmp   $ + 2
36
37      mov   ax, 4c00h
38      int   21h
39
40  END   Start
```

Line 26. Although the documentation does not say so, no error message is produced when overflow occurs. Overflow did occur in this case, which explains the answer.

Line 27. The operators deal intelligently with relocatable items, passing the appropriate relocation information to **LINK**. This is also demonstrated by lines 28, 29, and 31.

Line 28. Note that, as always, a variable name is interpreted as an address by **MASM**, and not as a value.

Line 29. Shows that a memory reference added to a constant is interpreted as a memory reference.

Line 30. *SIZE Ary* evaluates to the size of *Ary* in bytes.

Line 31. This line really shows the utility of assembly-time arithmetic. *endAry* points to the last word in *Ary*. It is defined by the fairly complicated equate on line 7 and shows, in particular, that **MASM** can handle forward references in the context of assembly-time arithmetic.

Line 32. Shows that the difference between memory references is a constant — the value is the expected 14H and it is not relocatable, since it is a number.

Line 33. This is a favorite application of **$**. The equate on line 15 does indeed evaluate to the length of the string.

Line 34. Shows again that a memory reference added to a constant can be used as a memory reference. Of course, an alternate to *Var + 10* is *Var[10]*, and we find this latter choice more readable.

Line 35. At first blush, this seems to be a singularly pointless line. It jumps two bytes ahead in the code, and the length of the instruction

```
jmp      $ + 2
```

is exactly two bytes. Hence the result of this instruction is to proceed to the next instruction. However, this line is sometimes used because of one or other of its two side effects: it introduces a slight delay into the program since its execution uses up a few clock cycles and, since it is a jump instruction, it empties the prefetch queue.

The **.TYPE** operator, which we discussed briefly in Chapter 8, is especially interesting. When applied to an expression, **.TYPE** returns a byte as its value, and various bits of this byte give information about the nature of the expression. The exact interpretation of these bits is given in Table 12.6.

The main uses of **.TYPE** are in conditional assembly and in macros, as we saw in Chapter 8. For example, macros should often generate code that depends on the exact form of the arguments, and **.TYPE** makes such case distinctions possible. Probably the most useful information deducible from the use of **.TYPE** is whether an instruction operand is a constant, a register, or a memory reference. Unfortunately, it is not possible to use **.TYPE** to determine the size of an indirect memory reference. Later in this chapter, after we have discussed conditional assembly, we will present a short program showing some applications of **.TYPE**.

The precedences of the various operators are given in Table 12.7.

TABLE 12.6 THE RETURN VALUE FROM .TYPE Exp

BIT NUMBER	CORRESPONDING INFORMATION ABOUT Exp
0	1 if program related; 0 if not
1	1 if data related; 0 if not
2	1 if a constant value; 0 if not
3	1 if direct addressing mode; 0 if not
4	1 if a register; 0 if not
5	1 if defined; 0 if not
7	1 if external; 0 if local or public

REMARKS: 1. If Exp is not a valid expression, .TYPE return 0.
  2. If bits 2 and 3 are both zero, Exp involves a register-indirect expression.

SECTION 7 CONDITIONAL ASSEMBLY

Conditional assembly was introduced in Chapter 8. To review briefly, the basic idea behind conditional assembly is that the code presented to **MASM** for assembly can be different from run to run, depending on the values of certain parameters, without the awkwardness of "commenting out" or otherwise altering the source code. This ability to easily generate different versions of the .OBJ file is invaluable in many contexts. As examples: debugging code used during program development can remain in the source code but be excluded from the assembly of the final, production version of the program; a program can be configured to match different models (e.g., **SMALL** or **LARGE**) or to match different operating environments or even different machines; as we saw earlier, macros can be tailored to accept different kinds or numbers of parameters.

There are many conditional assembly directives available. Probably the most basic is

> **IF** *Cond*
>   *Statements*
> { **ELSEIF** *Cond*
>   *Statements* }
> [**ELSE**
>   *Statements*]
> **ENDIF**

Here {} and [] have their usual meanings: there can be any number of **ELSEIF**s, including none, and the **ELSE** is optional. **IF**, **ELSEIF**, **ELSE**, and **ENDIF** are used exactly as in high-level languages. *Cond* represents a constant expression whose value must be known at assembly time. (We will elaborate on this in a later paragraph.) If the *Cond* appearing after **IF** is true, i.e., has non-zero value, then the corresponding *Statements*

TABLE 12.7 OPERATOR PRECEDENCES

PRECEDENCE	OPERATORS
1	LENGTH, SIZE, WIDTH, MASK , (), [],
2	.
3	:
4	PTR, OFFSET, SEG, TYPE, THIS
5	HIGH, LOW
6	unary +, -
7	*, /, MOD, SHL, SHR
8	binary +. -
9	EQ, NE, LT, LE, GT, GE
10	NOT
11	AND
12	OR, XOR
13	SHORT, .TYPE

REMARK: Listed from highest to lowest; operators on the same line have
            equal precedence.

---

are included in the assembly process, after which the assembler passes to the code immediately beyond the **ENDIF**. If this *Cond* is false, i.e., has value zero, then the condition going with the first **ELSEIF** is similarly checked, and if found to be true, the appropriate *Statements* are assembled. The analysis proceeds in this way, the **ELSE** statement being the "default" that is used if all the previous conditions fail. In the extreme case, if no **ELSEIF**s and no **ELSE** appear and the **IF** condition is false, then no code between the **IF** and the **ENDIF** is assembled.

Since **MASM** is relatively insensitive to formatting, it places no restrictions on the indentation of conditional statements. However, readability can be enormously enhanced by the use of a reasonable style of indentation. We have indented carefully in the previous examples, and will unfailingly do so in future.

Perhaps the simplest example of conditional assembly is a fragment such as

```
IF 0
    Statements
ENDIF
```

Since the expression 0 is always false, the code labeled *Statements* is omitted from the assembly process. This is the best method of temporarily deleting a section of code.

Here is a another simple example. Suppose that we have an assembly language module containing two types of debugging code and we wish to make it easy to assemble the module so that it contains the code of neither, either, or both of these kinds. One approach is to define a symbol, say *DEBUG*, to which we will assign arbitrarily chosen values 0, 1, 2, or 3, to denote the choices: include no debugging code; include code of the first kind; include code of the second kind; include code of both kinds. The easiest way to assign a value to *DEBUG* is by using the **/D** switch on the **MASM** command line:

TABLE 12.8 CONDITIONAL ASSEMBLY DIRECTIVES

DIRECTIVE	SYNTAX	ASSEMBLY OCCURS IF
IF	IF Exp	Exp is TRUE (!= 0)
IFE	IFE Exp	Exp is FALSE (= 0)
IF1	IF1	Only during PASS 1
IF2	IF2	Only during PASS 2
IFDEF	IFDEF Name	Name has been defined
IFNDEF	IFNDEF Name	Name has not been defined
IFB	IFB <Arg>	Arg is blank
IFNB	IFNB <Arg>	Arg is not blank
IFDIF	IFDIF <Arg1>,<Arg2>	Arg1 different from Arg2
IFDIFI	IFDIFI <Arg1>,<Arg2>	(Case-insensitive version of previous)
IFIDN	IFIDN <Arg1>,<Arg2>	If Arg1 identical to Arg2
IFIDNI	IFIDNI <Arg1>,<Arg2>	(Case-insensitive version of previous)

REMARKS: 1. "Defined" means defined as a variable or label, or by
EQUATE or '='., or by the /D switch on the MASM command
line.
2. "Arg" means macro argument, and so the conditional
directives that use Arg are only used in macros.
3. Each of these directives has a corresponding ELSEIF,
ELSEIFE, ELSEIF1, ELSEIF2, ELSEIFDEF, ...
4. Each of directives can be followed by optional ELSEIFs of
varying kinds and an optional ELSE.
5. The angled brackets are required where written.

```
/DDEBUG=Val
```

where *Val* denotes one of 0, 1, 2, or 3.

Each section of debugging code of the first kind should be embedded in a conditional block of the form

```
IF DEBUG EQ 1 OR DEBUG EQ 3
    ;debugging code of first kind
ENDIF
```

with the second kind of debugging code treated similarly.

The only slight inelegancy here is that, in the case where no debugging code is desired, it is still necessary to use the command line switch

```
/DDEBUG=0
```

Otherwise, when **MASM** comes to an expression such as

```
DEBUG EQ 1
```

it will generate a "symbol not defined" error and abort. It would be better if we could cause

FIGURE 12.5 USING .TYPE

```
 1   TITLE   dotTYPE.asm
 2
 3   Aardvark  = 100
 4
 5   IF (.TYPE Aardvark) AND 20H
 6       %OUT Aardvark is defined
 7   ELSE
 8       %OUT Aardvark is not defined
 9   ENDIF
10
11   IF (.TYPE Var1) AND 20H
12       %OUT Var1 is defined
13   ELSE
14       %OUT Var1 is not defined
15   ENDIF
16
17   IF (.TYPE ANIMAL) AND 20H
18       %OUT Platypus is defined
19   ELSE
20       %OUT Platypus is not defined
21   ENDIF
22
23   DOSSEG
24   .MODEL SMALL
25
26   .STACK    100h
27
28   .DATA
29
30       Var1   dw   ?
31
32   .CODE
33
34   Start:
35
36       mov    ax, @DATA
37       mov    ds, ax
38
39       mov    ax, .TYPE ax     ;ax = 30h - bits 4, 5 on
40       mov    ax, .TYPE 123    ;ax = 24h - bits 2, 5 on
41       mov    ax, .TYPE @DATA  ;ax = 20h - bit 5 on
42       mov    ax, .TYPE Start  ;ax = 21h - bits 0, 5 on
43       mov    ax, .TYPE Var1   ;ax = 2ah - bits 1, 3, 5 on
44       mov    ax, .TYPE [bx]   ;ax = 20h - bit 5 on
45
46       mov    ax, 4c00h
47       int    21h
48
49   END    Start

ASSEMBLY-TIME OUTPUT :

Aardvark is defined
Var1 is not defined
```

```
Platypus is not defined
Aardvark is defined
Var1 is defined
Platypus is not defined
```

the debugging code to be excluded just by failing to define "DEBUG" at all on the command line. We will soon see how to accomplish this gracefully.

The exact circumstances under which **MASM** views a quantity as *defined* are interesting. Specifically, a quantity is *defined* as soon as it is entered into the symbol table, which happens when **MASM** encounters it for the first time. This means that a quantity that is used at some point before its definition (i.e., is used as a forward reference) is undefined at that point in the assembly during Pass 1 but is defined during Pass 2. The reader can easily verify this statement by comparing a Pass 1 listing with a Pass 2 listing. The programmer can define quantities by any of these methods: as a variable or label; by an equate or an '=' definition; by the /D option on the command line.

As well as the basic **IF, ELSEIF, ELSE,** and **ENDIF,** there are many other conditional assembly directives available, and these are listed in Table 12.8. Particularly notice Remark 3 of that table: each directive in the table has a corresponding form prefixed by **ELSEIF** and having the obvious interpretation. We will give several examples of conditional assembly in the next two chapters. In particular, see Section 8 of Chapter 13 and Section 5 of Chapter 14.

We can now improve on our last example. Consider the fragment

```
IFDEF DEBUG
    IF DEBUG EQ 1 OR DEBUG EQ 3
        ;debugging code of first kind
    ENDIF
ELSEIF DEBUG EQ 2 OR DEBUG EQ 3
        ;debugging code of second kind
    ENDIF
ENDIF
```

This will still have the desired effect if "DEBUG" is defined to have values 0, 1, 2, or 3 on the assembler command line. In addition, neglecting to define "DEBUG" on the command line results in the exclusion of all the debugging code, without causing an assembler error.

Figure 12.5 contains a program demonstrating some of the conditional assembly directives and illustrating the use of **.TYPE.**

Sometimes the debugging process must be carried back to the assembly stage. If **MASM** refuses to even generate a .OBJ file, then **CODEVIEW** is certainly of no use. As an aid to debugging the assembly process, the *conditional error directives* are provided. They can be used to monitor the progress of the assembly operation and, in particular, to check that the arguments passed to macros are of the correct types.

Specifically, these directives can be used to check whether various quantities that are of significance at assembly time are defined, whether they are zero or non-zero, whether

---

TABLE 12.9 THE CONDITIONAL ERROR DIRECTIVES

DIRECTIVE	SYNTAX	ERROR NUMBER
.ERR	.ERR	89
.ERR1	.ERR1	87
.ERR2	.ERR2	88
.ERRE	.ERRE Exp	90
.ERRNZ	.ERRNZ Exp	91
.ERRDEF	.ERRDEF Name	93
.ERRNDEF	.ERRNDEF Name	92
.ERRB	.ERRB <Arg>	94
.ERRNB	.ERRNB <Arg>	95
.ERRIDN	.ERRIDN <Arg1>,<Arg2>	96
.ERRIDNI	.ERRIDNI <Arg1>,<Arg2>	96
.ERRDIF	.ERRDIF <Arg1>,<Arg2>	97
.ERRDIFI	.ERRDIFI <Arg1>,<Arg2>	97

REMARKS
1. The meanings of the names and the general usage are identical with the corresponding directives in Table 13.8.
2. When one of these directives occurs, and its condition holds, the error number and an error message are printed.

---

certain pairs are equal or not, and various other alternatives. They operate by printing error messages under circumstances that the programmer can select. The list of conditional error directives is shown in Table 12.9.

Exercise 12-8. The following fragment prints the uppercase alphabet to the screen:

```
        mov     cx, 26
        mov     al, 'A'
printLoop:
        outCh   al
        loop    printLoop
```

Use the **MASM $** operator to write an equivalent loop that does not contain a label. Embed the replacement fragment in a small test program.

SECTION 8 THE CONTENTS OF THE .LST FILE

The .LST file that **MASM** generates as part of the assembly process is an extremely valuable resource. In learning assembly language, the programmer should, ideally, use an editor that allows the simultaneous editing of two files and permits calling the assembler from within the editor. The source file and the .LST file can then both be loaded into the editor. When a change is made to the source code, the new version can be assembled and the updated .LST file inspected immediately to determine **MASM**'s response to the change.

TABLE 12.10 CONTROLLING CONTENTS OF THE .LST FILE

DIRECTIVE   EFFECT

GENERATION OF .LST FILE

.LIST   Include subsequent code lines in .LST file
.XLIST   Exclude subsequent code lines from .LST file

LISTING OF CONDITIONAL BLOCKS

.SFCOND   Suppress listing of false conditional blocks from .LST file
.LFCOND   List false conditional blocks
.TFCOND   Toggle listing of false conditionals

LISTING OF MACRO EXPANSIONS

.LALL   List all lines of macro expansions
.XALL   List only the lines of macro expansions that generate code or data
.SALL   Suppress all listing of macro expansions

CROSS REFERENCE LISTING

.XCREF   Exclude symbols from cross listing and from .LST file
.CREF   Include symbols in cross listing and in .LST file

REMARKS: 1. Defaults are .LIST, .SFCOND, .LALL, and .CREF.
                         2. Conditional block listing also toggled by /x command line switch.
                         3. /N command line switch excludes all tables from listing file.

One problem with the .LST file is that it can become unreasonably large unless special steps are taken, especially when very large macro files are included as part of the source code. For example, some of the programs occurring later in this book can give rise to .LST files that are nearly a megabyte long! These long .LST files present a number of problems: generating them and writing them to the disk slow the assembly process considerably; they use up an unreasonable amount of disk space; and, by far most important, they are hard to read.

Fortunately, **MASM** provides a number of directives that tailor the content of the .LST file to the needs of the moment. These directives are shown in Table 12.10.

First, there are the **.LIST** and **.XLIST** directives, which have the obvious effect: when **.XLIST** appears in the input, **MASM** ceases to make additions to the .LST file until a **.LIST** directive is encountered. The author generally uses **.XLIST** to suppress the inclusion of macro source code in the .LST file. For example, the lines

```
.XLIST
```

```
INCLUDE console.mac
.LIST
```

ensure that the voluminous CONSOLE.MAC code does not appear in the .LST file and also restart generation of the list file, so that the later code will appear. When a macro file has "stabilized," it is better to transfer the **.XLIST** and **.LIST** directives to the file itself rather than writing them in each and every program that includes the macros.

The next group of directives shown in Table 12.10 relates to conditional assembly. Normally, the conditional directives result in the generation of one of several alternate blocks of code, depending on the values of certain parameters. It is usually sufficient to include the conditional branches that are true, i.e., that actually generate code or data, in the .LST file. The directives in this group give the programmer control of whether or not to list "false conditionals."

Likewise, when a macro is called, some macro lines may generate code or data and some may not. The next group of directives allows the programmer to specify whether all lines in macro expansions should appear in the .LST file, or only those that generate code or data, or even whether no macro expansion lines whatsoever should appear. On the whole, the author is inclined to use the third alternate, in order to simplify the .LST file as much as possible. Of course, when a new macro is being developed, it is essential to view the code and data it generates. In such a case, expansion listing can be turned on temporarily by means of a "sandwich" such as

```
.LALL
;new macro invocation
.SALL
```

The directives in Table 12.10 relating to the cross-reference listing file do not directly pertain to the .LST file. However, when generation of the cross reference file is inhibited with the **.XCREF** directive, **MASM** also refrains from placing symbols in the symbol table listing at the end of the .LST file. Again, some of our symbol tables become rather unwieldy, whence this can be a useful device. Note, however, that the complete exclusion of all tabular material from the .LST file can be ordered by using the **/N** command line switch.

CHAPTER 13

MACROS

SECTION 1 PREVIEW

In this chapter, we look closely at the **MASM** macro language, and develop a number of macros that will be used in many of our later programs.

MASM makes available three types of macro capability, which are accessed by the =, **EQUATE**, and **MACRO** directives. Section 2 outlines the basic rules for using each of these kinds of macro, and, as examples, introduces macros that are useful in measuring program execution times.

Several operators, such as **&**, the substitution operator, and **%**, the expression operator, are used primarily with macros. These operators are discussed in Section 3, where we also provide examples that point out some of their subtleties.

Version 5.1 of **MASM** introduced new directives allowing the easy assembly-time manipulation of strings defined by the **EQUATE** directive. We examine these in Section 4, and use them to write macros for the management of assembly-time stacks.

In Section 5, we discuss the directives **REPT**, **IRPC**, and **IRP**, which are sometimes useful in defining repetitive blocks of data. As an application, in Section 6 we construct convenient macros for saving and restoring registers.

In Section 7 we make some quite serious applications of the macro language. Our goal is to write fairly general macros that provide assembly language implementations of such structured programming concepts as *While/Wend* loops and the *If/elseIf/Else/endIf* control structures. It is important that these control structures support nesting, and this is achieved by the careful use of an assembly-time stack.

Finally, in Section 8 we present the code for our last version of the *outAsc* macro. This version accepts a variable number of parameters, which can include memory references and string literals.

SECTION 2 MACRO DEFINITIONS

Of the three directives provided by **MASM** for defining macro substitutions, = is the most restricted. The general format for using = is

> *Name = Exp*

where *Exp* must be an *assembly-time constant*, i.e., an assembly-time expression that evaluates to a numerical constant. *Exp* can involve constants, assembler operators, numerical quantities defined by other uses of =, and one- or two-character string constants. It cannot be a string of length greater than two (except in the **.386** mode, where four-character string constants are also legal). A significant feature of quantities defined by the = directive is that they can be redefined by reusing this directive. Hence they are called *redefinable numeric equates*.

Consider the trivial example

```
Len = 10
Wid = 20
Hgt = 30
Vol = Len * Wid * Hgt
```

It is important to realize that **MASM** does not store the text on the right-hand side of the *Vol* definition. Rather, it evaluates the right-hand side immediately and stores the value 6000. Consequently, if later in the file the line

```
Len = 20
```

appears, the value of *Vol* is not updated to 12000. Modifying *Vol* to match the new *Len* requires repeating the line

```
Vol = Len * Wid * Hgt
```

or performing some equivalent computation.

The **EQUATE** directive has two quite distinct uses. First, it can be used in a manner analogous to the = directive. The syntax is

> *Name* **EQU** *Exp*

Again, *Exp* must evaluate to an assembly-time constant. The difference between the =

directive and this form of the **EQUATE** is that constants defined by the **EQUATE** cannot be redefined — any attempt to do so will cause a syntax error. For this reason, constants defined by an **EQUATE** are called *non-redefinable numeric equates*. It is also illegal to attempt using an **EQUATE** to redefine a quantity that has been previously defined by the = directive.

The other use of **EQUATE** follows the syntax

Name   **EQU**   [<] *String* [>]

The result is that the text of *String* is assigned to *Name*, so that each occurrence of *Name* in the source file is replaced by the text of *String*. (This statement is somewhat inaccurate. For example, an occurrence of *Name* on the right-hand side of another **EQU** will not be automatically replaced. In the next section, we will discuss this phenomenon in the context of the expression operator.) Text substitutions defined by the **EQUATE** mechanism are called *text macros*. They can be redefined as often as needed by repeated use of **EQU**.

If the angled brackets are used, they represent the *literal text operator* and must occur as a pair. Even though they are frequently superfluous, it is a good idea to use them always. We will discuss the significance of the literal text operator in the next section.

Finally, and most importantly, there is the **MACRO** directive, which is used to define macros with replaceable parameters. The macro definition syntax is

Name   **MACRO**   [*Param* { , *Param* }]
    Statements
ENDM

Param represents a macro *parameter*. The parameters can be separated by commas, spaces, or tabs, and must all appear on a single line. However, since **MASM** will ignore a newline character that is immediately preceded by a \ (the *line-continuation character*), judicious use of this character effectively allows a macro parameter list to span more than one line. Just as with a procedure, there are two steps involved in using a macro of this kind, namely *defining* it and *calling* or *invoking* it. One interesting difference between these macros and procedures is that, contrary to the case for procedures, each macro definition must appear in the source code before its first call. An important point, which sometimes causes odd results, is that a macro definition is not read by **MASM** until the macro is actually called. Of course, it is this behavior that makes it reasonable for us to keep our macros in rather large macro files. If a macro is not called, the only wasted assembly-time overhead is the reading of the macro file from the disk and the construction of a longer list file (assuming that macro listing has not been suppressed by the **.XLIST** directive).

The macro calling syntax is

Name   [*Arg* { , *Arg* }]

where *Arg* represents a macro *argument*. When **MASM** reads this line, it inserts a copy of the macro definition at the corresponding location in the file, with each occurrence of a parameter in the *Statements* replaced by the corresponding argument. This process is just text substitution. Like the parameters, all the arguments must fit on a single line, and can be separated by commas, spaces, or tabs, but again this restriction can be overcome by using the line-continuation character. However, if the arguments are complicated expressions or involve other operators, it is advisable, and sometimes even mandatory to use the comma as separator. Each argument can be arbitrary text — it is blindly substituted for the corresponding parameter. Of course, the resulting code will later be scrutinized during the assembly process. The number of arguments need not exactly match the number of parameters. If there are more arguments, the extras are ignored; if there are more parameters, the later ones are replaced by the empty string, and **MASM** prints a warning message.

Macro definitions can be nested, as can macro calls. The initial definition of a macro can be modified during the reading of the input file, and in fact a macro can even modify itself.

Here is a very simple example of a macro that calls itself recursively, in order to compute the factorial function:

```
Fact    MACRO   N
        IF  (N EQ 1)
            mov         ax, 1
            EXITM
        ENDIF
        Fact    N-1
        mov     bx, N
        mul     bx
ENDM
```

This macro is quite primitive. It expects an immediate value N as its argument, and stores the resulting value of the factorial in the **ax** register. Since the computation is single-precision, the allowed range for N is unusably small. Finally, the macro overwrites the **bx** register. The **EXITM** directive has the obvious effect: it terminates the execution of the macro immediately. (To be more precise, **EXITM** transfers control to the point immediately beyond the smallest containing macro or repeat block. We will define repeat blocks later in this chapter.)

It is also worthwhile to write a program that calls *Fact*, say using the macro call

```
Fact    5
```

and then to examine the corresponding .LST file. Here is an excerpt from such a .LST file:

```
484                                     Fact 5
485 0005   B8 0001                      5   mov     ax, 1
486 0008   BB 0002                      4   mov     bx, 5-1-1-1
487 000B   F7 E3                        4   mul     bx
488 000D   BB 0003                      3   mov     bx, 5-1-1
489 0010   F7 E3                        3   mul     bx
490 0012   BB 0004                      2   mov     bx, 5-1
491 0015   F7 E3                        2   mul     bx
492 0017   BB 0005                          1       mov     bx, 5
493 001A   F7 E3                        1   mul     bx
```

Once again, these lines show the brute-force nature of macro substitution. The actual code for the macro is repeated each time the macro is called. Incidentally, the numbers 5, 4, 4, ⋯ appearing to the left of the instructions indicate that the corresponding code was generated from a macro call at that nesting depth.

Many macros logically consist of two parts, an initialization section that should only be executed the first time the macro is called, and a main section that should be executed at every call. For example, consider a macro that needs to allocate space in the data segment. Normally, such a macro would allocate space on its first call, and then reuse this space on later calls. Of course, if the macro uses named variables, any attempt to reallocate the space on later calls will result in a repeated identifier error, unless the **LOCAL** directive is used or some other precaution is taken.

The most direct way of ensuring that the initialization section is only executed once is to define a flag during the first call, and include the initialization code only if the flag has not yet been defined. Here is the simplest method of setting up such a flag:

```
macroName    MACRO  Param1, Param2, ⋯
       IFNDEF isFirstUseFlag
             isFirstUseFlag  =  0
             ;code to be executed only during the
             ;   first call to the macro should
             ;      appear here
       ENDIF
       ;code to be executed during every call
       ;    should appear here
   ENDM
```

Unfortunately, the *isFirstUse* flag must be monitored more carefully than this fragment indicates or phase errors will result. This difficulty is discussed in one of the exercises at the end of this section. Our method of controlling this flag (which we already used in Chapter 8) is through the use of a separate macro named *isFirstUse*, and a macro using this approach should have the form

```
macroName   MACRO  Param1, Param2, ⋯
       isFirstUse       macroName
       IF firstUseFlag
             ;code to be executed only during the
             ;   first call to the macro should
             ;      appear here
       ENDIF
       ;code to be executed during every call
       ;    should appear here
   ENDM
```

Basically, the *isFirstUse* macro sets the flag named *firstuseFlag* to 1 if this is the first use of *macroName*; otherwise, it clears the flag. The code for *isFirstUse* will be presented in the next section (as an illustration of the & operator).

A more elegant way of ensuring that the initialization code is only executed once is to have the macro modify itself, so that when called for the first time in any module it includes the initialization code, but in subsequent calls the initialization code is missing.

If this method is used, the macro code might look like

```
macroName      MACRO        Param11, Param12, ···
        ;Initialization code
        ;Main code
macroName      MACRO        Param21, Param22,···
        ;Main code
    ENDM
    ENDM
```

When *macroName* is first called, **MASM** looks for its definition and finds the entire block, from the first occurrence of *macroName* to the matching **ENDM**. In response to the first call, the operations contained in the body of the macro are performed: a copy of the initialization code and a copy of the main code are inserted into the source file, and the original definition of *macroName* is overwritten by the new one. In subsequent calls, only the new definition is available. Of course, it is unfortunate that two different copies of the main code must be included in the macro definition, but this does not affect run-time efficiency. (In an exercise at the end of this section, the reader is asked to verify that the inclusion of both copies of the main code is indeed necessary.)

Because redefining a macro does involve duplication of code, we generally use the alternate approach and call the *isFirstUse* macro to automatically attend to the flag-setting details. *isFirstUse* is used in the first of the pair of macros, *startTiming* and *endTiming*, that are presented in Figure 13.1. If these macros are used in a configuration such as

```
startTiming
        Statements
endTiming
```

then a message is printed giving the time required for the execution of the code labeled *Statements*.

Recall from Chapter 7 that the machine stores the elapsed time since midnight in the dword at absolute address 0040:006C. This elapsed time is stored in *timer ticks*, where there are approximately 18.2 timer ticks per second. The *startTiming* and *endTiming* macros use the timer tick count in the obvious way: *startTiming* stores the value at the beginning of the interval to be timed; *endTiming* subtracts this initial value from the value at the end of the interval. The difference is divided by 18.2 to give an answer in seconds.

To keep the code reasonably short, we have cut various corners. For example, 18.2 is not the precise divisor that should be used (see Section 6 of Chapter 16). We have also ignored the possibility of the day changing during the timing interval. This latter eventuality can be accounted for by using **function 2BH** of **int 21H**, which returns the current date.

The code in Figure 13.1 is quite direct. The macro prints the elapsed time in seconds, written as a real number with two digits after the decimal point. Of course, it is somewhat optimistic to record the answer to hundredths of a second since the basic method is only accurate to about one-eighteenth of a second. The output was obtained using integer

FIGURE 13.1 THE TIMING MACROS

```
1    COMMENT      #    MACRO HEADER
2    MACRO NAME:       startTiming              FILE: console.mac
3    PURPOSE:          Initializes interval timer
4    CALLED AS:        startTiming
5    REMARKS:     #    Can be used repeatedly in given module
6
7    startTiming   MACRO
8
9        isFirstUse startTiming               ;is this first call in present module?
10       IF firstUseFlag                      ;if so, allocate buffers ...
11          @curseg      ENDS
12          _DATA  SEGMENT
13              lowTickCount     DW      ?
14              highTickCount    DW      ?
15              eTIntStr         DB      6 dup(?)
16              timeString       DB      "Elapsed time: ", 0
17          _DATA        ENDS
18          _TEXT        SEGMENT
19       ENDIF
20
21       push    es
22       push    ax
23       mov     ax, 40h                      ;point es to BIOS data area
24       mov     es, ax
25       cli                                  ;in case of rollover
26       mov     ax, es:[6ch]                 ;copy ETT (elapsed timer ticks since
27       mov     lowTickCount, ax             ;   midnight) from DWORD PTR 0040:006c
28       mov     ax, es:[6eh]                 ;     to allocated buffer
29       mov     HightickCount, ax
30       sti
31       pop     ax
32       pop     es
33
34   ENDM
35
36   ;-------------------------------------------------------------
37
38   COMMENT      #    MACRO HEADER            FILE: console.mac
39   MACRO NAME:       endTiming
40   PURPOSE:          Stops interval timer and prints elapsed time
41   CALLED AS:   #    endTiming
42
43   endTiming    MACRO
44
45       push    ax
46       push    cx
47       push    dx
48       push    si
49       push    di
50       push    es
51
52       mov     ax, 40h                      ;again, point es to BIOS data area
53       mov     es, ax
54       cli
```

Figure 13.1 cont.

```
55        mov     ax, es:[6ch]              ;  and get ETT
56        mov     dx, es:[6eh]
57        sti
58
59        sub     ax, lowTickCount          ;compute DETT (difference of elapsed
60        sbb     dx, highTickCount         ;  timer ticks and leave it in dx:ax
61        push    dx                        ;save high word of DETT
62        mov     cx, 1000
63        mul     cx                        ;dx:ax = (low word of DETT) * 1000
64        mov     si, ax
65        mov     di, dx                    ;store it in di:si
66        pop     ax                        ;high word of DETT
67        mul     cx
68        mov     dx, ax                    ;= (high word of DETT) * 1000
69        add     dx, di
70        mov     ax, si                    :dx:ax = DETT * 1000
71        mov     cx, 182
72        div     cx                        ;ax = (elapsed seconds) * 100
73        xor     dx, dx                    ;to prepare for next division
74        mov     cx, 100
75        div     cx                        ;ax = integer part of elapsed secs
76                                          ;dx = decimal part in hundredths of sec
77        hSkip   2, STDERR                 ;write output to STDERR
78        outAsc timeString, STDERR
79        iToA    eTIntStr, ax
80        outAsc eTIntStr, STDERR           ;the whole seconds
81        outCh   '.', STDERR               ;the decimal point
82
83        iToA    eTIntStr, dx
84        outAsc eTIntStr, STDERR           ;hundredths of a second
85        hSkip   2, STDERR
86
87        pop     es
88        pop     di
89        pop     si
90        pop     dx
91        pop     cx
92        pop     ax
93
94  ENDM
```

arithmetic by multiplying the timer count by 1000, then dividing it by 182, and finally printing out the answer with a decimal point interpolated before the final two digits. The integer arithmetic was done to 32-bit precision.

Exercise 13-1. Write a trio of macros named *Prolog*, *Middle*, and *Epilog* that make it easier to incorporate the basic overhead lines into an assembly language program. When these macros are used, the input to **MASM** would have this form:

```
        TITLE progName.asm
        Prolog          ;inserts overhead lines
                        ;  through the .DATA line
        ;actual data statements
```

```
        Middle          ;inserts lines through
                        ;   mov  ax, @DATA
        ;actual code statements
        Epilog          ;inserts lines from
                        ;   mov   ax, 4c00h to END Start
```

Exercise 13-2. Rewrite the *Fact* macro so that it computes its answer to double precision, storing the low 16 bits of the answer in **ax** and the high 16 bits in **dx**. Of course, this still does not extend the domain of the factorial by very much.

Exercise 13-3. Rewrite the *outCh* macro so that it allocates buffer space during its first call but then modifies itself and does not allocate space during later calls. Start with the version given in Section 7 of Chapter 8.

Exercise 13-4. Why is it necessary to include the "Main code" twice in a self-modifying macro? Is it possible to avoid physically including two copies of this code? (**Suggestion:** Call another macro.) Redo the previous exercise so that the new solution does not contain repeated code.

Exercise 13-5. In the fragment illustrating our discussion of macro redefinition, we gave different names to the parameters used in each definition. Explain why this is necessary and show by example that your explanation is correct.

Exercise 13-6. In the text, we showed a "simple" method of controlling the *isFirstFlag* and claimed that it would not work. Show by example that it can result in phase errors.
Suggestion: The problem grows out of the two-pass operation of **MASM**. To illustrate the difficulty, rewrite some macro, say *outCh*, so that it uses the "simplified" method and then compare the Pass 1 and Pass 2 listings produced by **MASM**. (To generate a Pass 1 listing, use the /**D** command line switch on the **MASM** command line.)

    One interesting aspect of this problem is that, even though *outCh* is the source of the phase error, the error will not occur every time *outCh* is used. In fact, it will only show up in a context such as

```
        outCh       'x'
        hSkip       2
```

involving a subsequent allocation of memory. Explain this curious phenomenon.

Exercise 13-7. Use **function 2BH** of **int 21H**, as suggested in the text, to improve the timing macros so that they will give a correct answer if the date changes during the timed interval. Appendix 3 contains the information needed for using **function 2BH**.

SECTION 3   SOME MACRO OPERATORS

Table 13.1 lists several operators designed especially for use with macros.

TABLE 13.1 THE MACRO OPERATORS

OPERATOR   DEFINITION

;;   Macro comment operator
!   Literal-character operator
<>   Literal text operator
= &   Substitution operator
%   Expression operator

The *macro comment operator* ;; provides an alternate way of marking comment text in a macro. The usual comment delimiter **;** can also be used within macros. The distinction between the two kinds of comment markers is that comments introduced by **;** are reproduced in the listing file both when the original macro text is included and each time the macro text is substituted after a macro call, while comments introduced by **;;** are reproduced only with the original macro text.

The *literal character operator* **!**, which is also used in contexts other than macros, turns off any special interpretation of the character immediately following. For example, writing "!;" instructs **MASM** to interpret the ';' as just a semicolon character, rather than as a comment delimiter. The usefulness of the literal character operator is limited by the fact that it does not work in either single- or double-quoted strings. For instance, the line

```
    outCh        ' ! ' '
```

will not print a single quote — it will draw a syntax error. (The line

```
    outCh        " ' "
```

will print a single quote.)

We have already encountered **<>**, the *literal text operator*. As the name suggests, it instructs **MASM** to interpret the characters within the angled brackets as a literal string. For example, **MASM** will interpret 3 + 4 as the constant with value 7, but will interpret <3 + 4> as the string "3 + 4." The literal text operator must be used in slightly extended form in the case of nested macro calls. Each time **MASM** processes a macro call, it removes one set of angled brackets from the argument strings. Hence, if an argument that figures in a nested collection of macro calls requires protection by the literal text operator, it should be encased in the correct number of sets of angled braces so that they have all been used up by the time the argument is evaluated.

As an example, we will show how the literal text operator works when used with the **%OUT** directive. **%OUT** is used in the format

```
    %OUT      String
```

and its effect is to send the actual text of *String* to STDOUT. The following rather contrived triple of macros demonstrates the use of the literal text operator in nested macro calls:

```
Level1  MACRO  Param
    Level2  Param
ENDM

Level2  MACRO  Param
    Level3  Param
ENDM

Level3  MACRO    Param
    %OUT     Param
ENDM
```

An argument passed to *Level1* passes through three nested macro calls before it is printed by **%OUT**. Now consider the effect of each of the following calls to *Level1*:

```
IF1
    Level1  Hello, World
    Level1  <Hello, World>
    Level1  <<Hello, World>>
    Level1  <<<Hello, World>>>
    Level1  <<<<Hello, World>>>>
ENDIF
```

The **IF1** conditional block is not essential to the present example. However, either an **IF1** or an **IF2** conditional is often used with **%OUT** since it will otherwise produce two copies of its output, one for each assembly pass. The output from our macro calls is

```
Hello
Hello
Hello
Hello, World!
<Hello, World!>
```

The reason for this output should be clear to the reader: a set of angled brackets is stripped from the macro argument at each macro call. If all angled brackets have disappeared before the *Level3* call, for example, then this call has the form

```
Level3   Hello, World!
```

which **MASM** interprets as a macro call in which there are more arguments (two) than parameters and so (without issuing a warning) it discards the second argument.

The *substitution*, or *concatenation*, operator, **&**, is used either to indicate that a substring of a longer string represents an occurrence of a macro parameter or text equate, or that some text inside a quoted string should be treated as a macro parameter or text equate. Suppose, for example, that the macro parameter *Param* should be replaced by *Arg* in a macro call. The following examples show the results of using or failing to use the substitution operator:

```
MACRO TEXT          REPLACED BY

abcParam            abcParam
```

```
        abc&Param            abcArg
        ab&Param&cd          abArgcd
        "Param"              "Param"
        "&Param&"            "Arg"
```

Similarly to the case of the literal text operator, **MASM** strips away an **&** from each group of **&**'s when a macro call is processed, and does not substitute the argument value for the parameter until the last **&** is removed. This mechanism can be used to delay the actual substitution process. We will see examples of this phenomenon in Section 5.

Figure 13.2 shows the code for the *isFirstUse* macro, which was used in the last section. Recall that the macro invocation

```
        isFirstUse      macroName
```

sets *isFirstFlag* to 1 during the first use of *macroName* in the current source module, and sets *isFirstFlag* to 0 during all subsequent uses. Our typical application of *isFirstUse* occurs when we wish to allocate data during the first use of a macro but not during later uses. But such data-defining sections of code must be included during *both* Pass 1 and Pass 2 of the assembly process; otherwise, a phase error results. (See Exercise 13-6.) If, for example, *macroName* is called three times in a source file, then *isFirstFlag* should have values {1,0,0} during the three readings of the macro code occurring during Pass 1, and again should have values {1,0,0} during the three Pass 2 readings.

Consequently, *isFirstUse* must keep a record of the **MASM** pass number (which it does in *passNumber*) and of the number of times that *macroName* has been called so far in Pass 1 and in Pass 2. This latter information is kept in the variables *firstPassUse&Name* and *secondPassUse&Name*. Note the use of the **&** operator: we have used it to "customize" these names so that they apply only to the macro in question.

The *expression operator*, **%**, is used in two slightly different ways. First, suppose that a macro argument has the form

```
        %Exp
```

where *Exp* is an assembly-time expression, which may include numeric equates. The result of using the **%** operator is that the *value* of *Exp*, rather than the *string* "Exp" itself, is passed to the macro as the argument. Recalling that arguments are always passed to macros as strings, we see that what gets passed to the macro is the value of *Exp*, as a string.

It is important to realize that the expression operator only works in this way when applied to macro arguments, and this restriction sometimes requires circuitous constructions.

As an example, consider the **%OUT** directive. (The use of the '**%**' character in the name **%OUT** is not ideal — it does not signify the **%** operator in this context.) A problem with **%OUT** is that it will only interpret its argument as literal text — if the argument is an expression or equate, there is no *direct* way to induce **%OUT** to print the corresponding value.

Specifically, suppose we have the lines

```
        Val1    =       10 + 10
        Val2    EQU     20
```

FIGURE 13.2 THE isFirstUse MACRO

```
 1   COMMENT        #    MACRO HEADER
 2   MACRO NAME:        isFirstUse                  FILE: console.mac
 3   PURPOSE:          Checks whether this is first use of a given macro in
 4                     present program module
 5   CALLED AS:        isFirstUse  macroName
 6   RETURNS:          Sets redefinable numeric equate firstUseFlag to 1 if this
 7                     is the first use and to 0 otherwise
 8
 9   isFirstUse      MACRO    Name
10
11       firstUseFlag = 0              ;= 1 only while this macro is being
12       IFNDEF firstPassuse&Name      ;   called during Pass 1 or Pass 2
13           firstPassuse&Name = 0     ;number of appearances in Pass 1
14           secondPassUse&Name = 0    ;number of appearances in Pass 2
15       ENDIF
16       IF1
17           firstPassuse&Name = firstPassuse&Name + 1
18           passNumber = 1                ;passNumber equals 1 during Pass 1 and
19       ENDIF                             ;  equals 2 during Pass 2
20       IF2
21           secondPassUse&Name = secondPassUse&Name + 1
22           passNumber = 2
23       ENDIF
24       IF  firstPassuse&Name EQ 1 AND passNumber EQ 1 OR\
25           secondPassUse&Name EQ 1 AND         nber EQ 2
26           firstUseFlag = 1
27       ENDIF
28
29   ENDM
```

```
Str     EQU   ABC
```

and we want to print out the values of *Val1*, *Val2*, and *Str*. The obvious thing to try is

```
%OUT   Val1
%OUT   Val2
%OUT   Str
```

It doesn't work — the output is just the three strings "Val1", "Val2", and "Str".
After a little thought, we might decide to try using the expression operator:

```
%OUT   %Val1
%OUT   %Val2
%OUT   %Str
```

Unfortunately, this still will not work, because the expression operator only computes a value when applied to a macro argument. This time the output consists of the three strings "%Val1", "%Val2", and "%Str" — a small step in the wrong direction!

To achieve our goal, we must resort to trickery. The idea is to introduce a special macro whose only function is to trigger the evaluation of the expressions. Here is the macro:

```
printIt MACRO Arg
      %OUT    Arg
ENDM
```

Now we use the commands

```
printIt    %Val1
printIt    %Val2
printIt    %Str
```

This time, we succeed: the strings "20", "20", and "ABC" are printed. Consider in detail what happens in the first case. Since *Val1* is a macro argument, *%Val1* evaluates to the number 20. The number 20, being a macro argument, is interpreted as a string. Finally, **%OUT** is passed the string "20", which it prints.

The macro file CONSOLE.MAC on the Program Disk contains the following pair of macros which work even better than *printIt*:

```
prePrint    MACRO   Exp, Val
      %OUT    Exp = Val
ENDM

printExp    MACRO    Exp
      prePrint    <Exp>, %&Exp
ENDM
```

The directive

```
printExp Val1
```

will cause the line

```
Val1 = 20
```

to be printed, with similar output in the other cases. In our present examples, the angle brackets in the argument *<Exp>* are not needed, but if *Exp* is a more complicated expression (perhaps containing embedded spaces), they guarantee that it is interpreted as a literal string and that the entire string is used as the argument. Notice the use of the expression operator &. Without it, **MASM** would not be able to identify the parameter *Exp* within the string "%Exp".

A minor point, but one that can cause bizarre behavior, is that if the expression operator is used in a macro argument, then this argument must be separated from its successor by a comma. The usual white space alternatives to the comma will not work.

There is the second use of the substitution operator. This variant relates to a point alluded to in the last section, namely that **MASM** does not always evaluate text **EQUATE**s without some additional prodding. A simple example will help to clarify this. Suppose that our code contains these lines:

```
firstEqu    EQU    <abcde>
secondEqu   EQU    <firstEqu>
```

A check of the .LST file will reveal that **MASM** has recorded the values

```
FIRSTEQU     TEXT      abcde
SECONDEQU    TEXT      firstEqu
```

in its symbol table. In other words, **MASM** has computed the correct value for *firstEqu* but not for *secondEqu*. The essential difficulty is that **MASM** scans each **EQU** line only once (during each assembly pass). It records the fact that each occurrence of *secondEqu* should be replaced by *firstEqu*, without taking note of the fact that *firstEqu* is itself a text macro that should be replaced. The second use of **%** provides a mechanism that forces **MASM** to rescan lines looking for text macros. Specifically, if a line opens with the substitution operator followed by at least one space or tab, then all text macros on that line are replaced by their values. If any new text macros are introduced by these substitutions, these in turn are evaluated, and so on until no text macros remain.

If we now replace the second of the preceding **EQUATE**s by

```
% secondEqu    EQU    <FirstEqu>
```

and check the .LST file, we find the desired line:

```
SECONDEQU    TEXT     abcde
```

This new equate for *secondEqu* replaces the old one, which no longer appears in the .LST file.

The astute reader may realize that, since **MASM** continually rescans until no text macros are found, the process does not stop here. After all, the line

```
secondEqu    EQU    abcde
```

still contains the name *secondEqu*, which has a corresponding text equate. **MASM** does in fact do one more scan, replacing SecondEqu by "abcde". The proof of this assertion can again be found in the .LST file: it contains the (useless) text macro

```
ABCDE    TEXT                abcde
```

An important point to remember is that only text macros are evaluated by this use of **%**. Other kinds of expressions remain unchanged. Returning to our earlier example, for instance, suppose we now try

```
%    %OUT  Val1
%    %OUT  Val2
%    %OUT  Str
```

The resulting output is "Val1", Val2", and "ABC".

Exercise 13-8. Compare **MASM**'s response to the following **EQUATE**s:

```
ABCDE     EQU     ABCDE
ABCDE     EQU     <ABCDE>
```

Do you think that the different responses are deliberate or are they symptomatic of a bug in **MASM**? (This example was assembled using Version 5.1 of **MASM**. The outcome of this comparison may be different and less interesting if a different version is used.)

Exercise 13-9. Write a macro named *compTextMacs* that compares its two arguments, which may be either text macros or string literals. If they are equal, it assigns the value 1 to a flag name *isEqual* (which it defines); otherwise, it assigns the value 0 to the flag.

SECTION 4 THE STRING DIRECTIVES

Starting with Version 5.1, **MASM** includes some interesting directives designed for the manipulation of text macros. These new directives, called the *string directives*, are listed in Table 13.2.

The string directives give alternate, more readable methods of doing a variety of assembly-time computations. For example, suppose we already have an equate

```
firstEqu     EQU     <labelNumber>
```

and we wish to generate another equate with value "labelNumber1000" (say as part of a sequence of labels). One way of doing this is by writing

```
% secondEqu     EQU     <firstEqu&1000>
```

However, the same computation can be expressed much less cryptically as

```
secondEqu     CATSTR     firstEqu, <1000>
```

Of course, the string directives also permit constructions that would be very difficult or impossible without them. For example, suppose we wish to modify *firstEqu* to produce a text macro with value "Label1000". We could proceed as follows:

```
thirdEqu     SUBSTR     firstEqu, 5
thirdEqu     CATSTR     thirdEqu, <1000>
```

In passing, we point out an apparent bug in **SUBSTR**, at least in the implementation distributed with Version 5.1 of **MASM**. The documentation indicates that **SUBSTR** is callable in the format

```
textLabel    SUBSTR    textLabel, Start [, Length]
```

i.e., with identical input and output strings. This usage is analogous to our application of **CATSTR** in the last example. However, when used with **SUBSTR**, this configuration draws a syntax error. The obvious method of circumventing this problem (which we use later in this section) is to assign the returned value of **SUBSTR** to a temporary name, and then to assign this temporary value to *textLabel*.

We will now use the string directives to implement an assembly-time stack. In other words, we will develop a mechanism for storing text strings or numbers used during the assembly process, so that we can retrieve them in the standard last-in/first-out stack ordering. Here are two immediate applications for such a stack. Macros that generate instructions to save and restore groups of registers on the stack should write the pop instructions in reverse order to the pushes, and this interchange can be handled neatly using a stack. Macros that implement the *While/Wend* control structure must cope with the problem of nested loops. As the program goes deeper and deeper into a nest of loops, the "break addresses" should be stacked, so that they can be retrieved in reverse order as the loops are exited.

The stack macros, listed in Figure 13.2, demonstrate one unpleasant notational feature: the names *Push* and *Pop* cannot be used for these operations on our stacks since they are reserved words in the **MASM** language. The solution that we adopt conforms to that used with the "official" macros supplied with **MASM**. Whenever we wish to use a reserved word as a macro name, we prefix it with an '@'. This problem will occur again in the next section.

An interesting observation is that *@Pop* need not check for stack underflow. This check occurs automatically because, as soon as the stack is empty, **INSTR** returns the value 0, so that **SUBSTR** is passed a −1 as its final operand, causing it to print an "out of range" error message.

The temporary variable *Temp* is used in *@Pop* because of the bug in **SUBSTR** mentioned earlier.

getTop is sometimes useful. It allows the user to inspect the top element on the stack without removing it.

Using the string directives, the implementation of an assembly-time stack is quite easy. The stack is constructed as a string, i.e., as a text macro. Elements are pushed onto the stack by concatenating them to the beginning of this string, and are separated by commas to make it easy to identify the end of a given element during an *@Pop* operation. Of course, in contexts where the comma is an important lexical element, some other character should be used as the separator.

The stack macros are shown in Figure 13.3, which also shows a typical dialog with **MASM** making use of these macros. Our real applications of the assembly-time stack will begin in Section 6.

Exercise 13-10. In dealing with stacks, it is frequently useful to have a *Dup* operation to push a copy of the present top-of-stack element onto the stack, and a *Swap* operation to interchange the two elements at the top of the stack. Implement these operations for our assembly-time stacks. Test the new operations by means of an appropriate assembly-time dialog with **MASM**.

TABLE 13.2 THE STRING DIRECTIVES

textLabel **SUBSTR** String, Start, **[** *Length* **]**
Inputs: *String* is a previously defined string. *Start* is an integer giving a starting position within *String*.
Length is the length of the substring to be computed. If this parameter is missing, length to end of string
is used.
Returns: *textLabel* becomes a text macro equated to the selected substring of *String*.

textLabel **CATSTR** String **{,** *String* **}**
Inputs: *Strings* to be concatenated.
Returns: *textLabel* becomes a text macro equated to the concatenated string.

Number **SIZESTR** *String*
Input:*String*.
Returns: The number of characters in *String*.

Number **INSTR** **[** *Start* **]**, *String1, String2*
Inputs: *String1* is a string to be searched for the first occurrence of *String2*, starting from position *Start*.
If *Start* is not given, the default value is 1.
Returns: The position (an integer) of the beginning of the first copy of *String2* in *String1*, if it actually oc-
curs; otherwise, it returns 0.

REMARKS:

1. Each input string can be defined by a text equate or can be a constant string.
2. Each input number can be a numeric equate or a constant expression.
3. The position count within a string starts with 1.

SECTION 5 DEFINING REPEAT BLOCKS

Among the **MASM** directives are several designed to facilitate the writing of source code
containing repeated elements of various kinds. They are called *repeating-block directives*.
We will discuss them, both for completeness and since they provide some insight into the
workings of **MASM**. However, it has been our experience that in most day-to-day programming, the time (and ingenuity) required to fabricate customized macros using these directives far exceeds any possible time saved in avoiding repetitive typing.

The first of the repeating block directives is **REPT**, repeat block. It is used in the form

    REPT *Exp*
     Statements
    ENDM

Exp must evaluate to an assembly-time constant. The **REPT** directive causes the block
labeled *Statements* to be repeated a number of times equal to the value of *Exp*. As a simple
example of **REPT**, here is a macro that prints out the bit pattern of an input word:

```
bitPrt    MACRO    Buffer     ;prints a word as 16 bits
```

```
                    push      ax
                    push      dx
                    ;the next line make immediate inputs acceptable
                    mov       dx, Buffer
                    REPT 16
                         rol      dx, 1
                         mov      al, dl
                         and      al, 1
                         add      al, '0'
                         outCh    al
                         ENDM
                    pop       dx
                    pop       ax
          ENDM
```

How practical is this macro? The 16 repetitions could be replaced by a loop instruction, at a small cost in running time. To save this modest loop overhead, the macro incorporates the code from the **REPT** block 16 times, and so even a single call to this macro bloats the machine code by over 500 bytes!

Hence the first moral is that repeating blocks are perhaps not ideal in executable code, and in fact **REPT** (and the other repeating block directives) are used most often in simplifying data definitions.

As a more typical application, suppose that we wish to initialize 1000 words using the **DW** directive, so that the first word contains 0, the second 1, etc. This fragment will generate the correct data definitions:

```
          Counter = 0
          REPT 1000
               DW    Counter
               Counter = Counter + 1
          ENDM
```

The next repeating block directive is **IRPC**, *indefinite repeat with characters*. The general syntax for **IRPC** is

IRPC *Param, String*
   Statements
ENDM

The block labeled *Statements* is repeated once for each character in *String*. Each occurrence of *Param* in *Statements* in replaced by the first character in *String* during the first repetition, by the second character during the second repetition, and so on.

As an example, suppose that we wish to print a series of **DB** statements having the form

```
          ASCIIa   DB    'a'
          ASCIIb   DB    'b'
          ASCIIc   DB    'c'
```

FIGURE 13.3 THE STACK MACROS

```
 1   COMMENT       #        MACRO HEADER
 2   MACRO NAME:            @Push                FILE: console.mac
 3   PURPOSE:              Pushes element onto assembly-time stack
 4   CALLED AS:  #         Push     Element, Stack
 5
 6   @Push    MACRO  Element, Stack
 7
 8      Stack    CATSTR    <Element>, <,>, Stack
 9
10   ENDM
11
12   ;-------------------------------------------------------------
13
14   COMMENT       #        MACRO HEADER
15   MACRO NAME:            @Pop                 FILE: console.mac
16   PURPOSE:              Pops element from assembly-time stack
17   CALLED AS:  #         Pop      Element, Stack
18
19   @Pop   MACRO   Element, Stack
20
21      firstCommaPos    INSTR    Stack, <,>
22      Element          SUBSTR   Stack, 1, firstCommaPos-1
23      Temp             SUBSTR   Stack, firstCommaPos+1
24      Stack            SUBSTR   Temp, 1
25
26   ENDM
27
28   ;-------------------------------------------------------------
29
30   COMMENT       #        MACRO HEADER
31   MACRO NAME:            @getTop              FILE: console.mac
32   PURPOSE:              Returns top element from assembly-time stack
33   CALLED AS:  #         getTop     Element, Stack
34
35   getTop  MACRO    Element, Stack
36
37      firstCommaPos    INSTR    Stack, <,>
38      Element          SUBSTR   Stack, 1, firstCommaPos-1
39
40   ENDM


SAMPLE INPUT:

@Push          1, stackName
printExp       stackName
@Push          2, stackName
printExp       stackName
getTop         topOfStack, stackName
printExp       topOfStack
@Pop           Temp, stackName
printExp       stackName
@Pop           Temp, stackName
printExp       stackName
```

```
@Pop          Temp, StackName

CORRESPONDING OUTPUT:

stackName = 1
stackName = 2,1,
topOfStack = 2
stackName = 1,
stackName =
stackName = 1,
stackName = 2,1,
topOfStack = 2
stackName = 1,
stackName =
stack.ASM(47): error A2050: Value out of range
stack.ASM(47): error A2009: Symbol not defined: FIRSTCOMM
stack.ASM(47): error A2050: Symbol not defined: FIRSTCOMMAPOS
```

In other words, we want a collection of named bytes, associated with certain letters, and initialized to the **ASCII** codes for those letters. The following macro will produce the required output:

```
ascInit  MACRO   x
    IRPC  w, x
           ASCII&&w  DB  '&w'
    ENDM
ENDM
```

Generating the three desired **DB** statements requires only the macro call

```
ascInit   <abc>
```

Perhaps the most interesting aspect of this macro is the use of the substitution operator **&**. First of all, it is necessary to use an ampersand in "ASCII&w" to notify **MASM** that 'w' is a macro parameter. As we mentioned in the last section, repeated appearances of **&** can be used to delay the substitution of an argument value for a macro parameter, and it is being used here for that reason. We wish to print the line

```
ASCIIw   DB  'w'
```

three times, with both occurrences of 'w' replaced sequentially by 'a', 'b', and 'c'. Consequently, it is necessary to delay the evaluation of the 'w' in *ASCIIw* until after 'x' has been replaced by "abc". That is, until the outer macro *ascInit* has been processed. This delay is accomplished by using a doubled **&**. The general rule is that using k contiguous copies of **&** will delay parameter substitution until nesting depth k has been reached.

Although the **MASM** documentation does not enunciate this fact, the last rule apparently does not apply inside quoted strings. Here it seems that parameter substitution is always deferred as long as possible. So, for example, *&w* is used in the previous example, rather than the more consistent *&&w*. The interested reader is urged to work with variants of this macro to better understand how the substitution operator works.

A related directive is **IRP**, indefinite repeat with parameters, which is used with the syntax:

> **IRP** *Param, < Arg, {, Arg} >*
>   Statements
> **ENDM**

In this case, the number of repeats equals the number of different choices of *Arg*, and in each repeat, the appearances of *Param* are replaced by one of the values of *Arg*. Each *Arg* can be a string or a numeric constant.

Consider the example

```
Alloc    MACRO    x, y
        IRP    z, y
                &x&&z    DB    z
        ENDM
ENDM
```

The macro call

```
Alloc Var, <1,2,3,4,5>
```

produces the output

```
Var1    DB    1
Var2    DB    2
Var3    DB    3
Var4    DB    4
Var5    DB    5
```

Likewise, in the example

```
twoAlloc    MACRO  x
        IRP    a, <0,1,2,3,4,5,6,7,8,9>
                IRP    b, <0,1,2,3,4,5,6,7,8,9>
                        x&&a&&b    DB    a&&b
                ENDM
        ENDM
ENDM
```

the call

```
twoAlloc Var
```

produces output

```
Var00    DB    00
Var01    DB    01
Var02    DB    02
```

```
                          .
              Var10    DB   10
              Var11    DB   11
              Var12    DB   12
                          .
                          .
```

which continues for a total of 100 lines.

Again, the most intriguing aspect of these last two examples is the use of the **&** operator.

Exercise 13-11. Write a *threeAlloc* macro that is analogous to *twoAlloc*, but produce 1000 **DB** definitions of the general form

```
              Var129    DB   129
```

The actual text that will be printed in place of *Var* should be specified as a macro argument.

Exercise 13-12. Write an *nAlloc* version of *threeAlloc*, but rather than fixing the range of postscript values as 0-9, allow it to be specified as an argument. For example, in response to an invocation of the form

```
              nAlloc    varName, 5, 4
```

the macro should produce 4^5 data definitions, a specimen of which is

```
              varName32201 DB        32201
```

Specifically, the second parameter should specify the number of integers that are appended to the name and the third parameter indicates the range of those values (0-3 in this case).

Exercise 13-13. Redo the *nAlloc* example using the string directives.

Exercise 13-14. When the present version of *hSkip* is called to produce code that will skip n lines, it makes n calls to **function 40H** of **int 21H**. Rewrite *hSkip* so that such a request requires only a single call to **function 40H**.

SECTION 6 MACROS FOR SAVING AND RESTORING REGISTERS

As our first application of the assembly-time stack, we present two macros that are adaptations of a pair found in the **MASM** manual. These macros are given in Figure 13.4. The first is

```
              pushRegs Param  {, Param}
```

It will save the registers listed as its parameters by generating instructions to push them, in the order given, onto the run-time stack. The companion macro

```
popRegs
```

generates instructions to pop the registers, in the opposite order, to restore their original values.

But the most interesting feature of the macros is that several calls to *pushRegs* can be made without intervening calls to *popRegs*. The only requirement is that, ultimately, the same number of *pushRegs* calls as *popRegs* calls should appear in the code. Each *popRegs* call is associated with the most recent *pushRegs* not yet having a matching *popRegs*. In other words, the calls to *pushRegs* and *popRegs* are themselves governed by a standard stack discipline.

To make the macro code look nicer, we have also included a pair of macros that increment and decrement numeric equates. Only the increment is needed here; the decrement will be used later. Again, these macros were given names prefixed with an @ to avoid conflict with reserved words.

Each group of registers saved by a call to *pushRegs* is stored on the assembly-time stack named *regStack*; the register groups corresponding to different calls are separated by a '#' character.

Typically, these macros might be called as in the following example, although with other code intervening between the macro calls:

```
pushRegs     ax,bx,cx,dx
printExp     regstack
pushRegs     bx,di
printExp     regstack
popRegs
printExp     regstack
popRegs
printExp     regstack
pushRegs     ax, bx, cx
popRegs
```

Of course, the calls to *printExp* are included only for purposes of illustration. In response to this input, **MASM** will produce the following output at assembly time:

```
regStack = dx,cx,bx,ax,#,
regStack = di,bx,#,dx,cx,bx,ax,#,
regStack = dx,cx,bx,ax,#,
regStack =
```

Actually, unless the calls to *printExp* are encased in **IF1/ENDIF** pairs, **MASM** will print two copies of this output, one during each assembly pass.

These calls to *pushRegs* and *popRegs* will generate the following executable code:

```
push    ax
push    bx
push    cx
push    dx

push    bx
```

FIGURE 13.4 MACROS THAT SAVE AND RESTORE REGISTERS

```
 1
 2   COMMENT      #        MACRO HEADER
 3   MACRO NAME:           @Inc              FILE: console.mac
 4   PURPOSE:              Increments redefinable equate
 5   CALLED AS:  #         @Inc   Arg
 6
 7   @Inc   MACRO   Arg
 8
 9       Arg = Arg + 1
10
11   ENDM
12
13   ;------------------------------------------------------------
14
15   COMMENT      #        MACRO HEADER
16   MACRO NAME:           @Dec              FILE: console.mac
17   PURPOSE:              Decrements redefinable equate
18   CALLED AS:  #         @Dec      Element, Stack
19
20   @Dec   MACRO   Arg
21
22       Arg = Arg - 1
23
24   ENDM
25
26   ;------------------------------------------------------------
27
28   regStack    EQU     <>
29
30   COMMENT      #        MACRO HEADER
31   MACRO NAME:           pushRegs          FILE: console.mac
32   PURPOSE:              Generates code to push group of registers onto stack
33   CALLED AS:            pushRegs    Register {, Register}
34   REMARKS:     #        No more than 9 registers can be pushed by a given call
35
36   pushRegs    MACRO    r1,r2,r3,r4,r5,r6,r7,r8,r9
37
38       @PUSH  <#>, regStack
39       IRP    reg, <r1,r2,r3,r4,r5,r6,r7,r8,r9>
40           IFNB   <reg>
41             push   reg
42             @PUSH  reg, regStack
43           ELSE
44              EXITM
45           ENDIF
46       ENDM
47
48   ENDM
49
50   ;------------------------------------------------------------
51
52   COMMENT      #        MACRO HEADER
53   MACRO NAME:           popRegs           FILE: console.mac
54   PURPOSE:              Undoes the effect of pushRegs
55   CALLED AS:            popRegs
```

Figure 13.4 cont.

```
56   REMARKS:              Several calls to pushRegs can come before a call to
57                         popRegs. The succeeding popRegs calls then undo the
58               #         pushRegs calls in inverse order.
59
60   popRegs MACRO
61
62   %   IRP    reg, <regStack>
63          IFDIF <reg>, <#>
64              pop    reg
65              @POP Temp, regStack
66          ELSE
67              EXITM
68          ENDIF
69      ENDM
70      @POP    Temp, regStack
71   ENDM
```

```
                    push    di

                    pop     di
                    pop     bx

                    pop     dx
                    pop     cx
                    pop     bx
                    pop     ax

                    push    ax
                    push    bx
                    push    cx

                    pop     cx
                    pop     bx
                    pop     ax
```

SECTION 7 MACROS FOR STRUCTURED PROGRAMMING

We will now discuss the problem of translating the standard program control structures used in structured programming into assembly language. It is fairly trivial to make this translation in the case of a single *While* loop, for example, but in the case of doubly or even more deeply nested loops, the assembly language code is unpleasant to write and is usually extremely difficult to read.

Macros can be used to ease the burden of writing structured assembly language code and, especially in cases involving nested control structures, they tend to produce code that is self-documenting. As is generally the case with macros, there is a certain deterioration in performance associated with the structured programming macros. But probably these macros should only be used, and in fact are most needed, when the loops in question contain a considerable amount of code. In such cases, the extra loop overhead will amount to only a few percent.

In the present section, we will first consider *While* loops, implementing them through a series of macros of increasing sophistication. Later in the section we will discuss the *If/elseIf/Else/endIf* control structures in some detail, and look at some other control structures more briefly. The reader will find an interesting, alternative discussion of this topic in [9].

To review, the basic *While* loop has the general form

```
While(Expression)
      Statements
Wend
```

Each time control reaches the top of the loop, *Expression* is tested. If it is true, i.e., has non-zero value, then the code contained in *Statements* is executed and control returns to the top of the loop. If *Expression* is false, i.e., has value zero, control transfers to the point beyond the *Wend*. It would certainly be best if the loop could be written without an explicit *Wend* to mark the loop end, but this would be difficult using only the available macro machinery. Notice that, since the *While* and *Wend* statements occur at separated locations in the resulting code, it is necessary to implement them as separate macros.

Among other issues, we must decide on the permitted formats for *Expression*, and how to implement nested loops. Initially, we will only allow *Expression* to have a form that makes the instruction

```
cmp Expression, 0
```

legal. In other words, *Expression* can be either a register or a memory reference. If it is a memory reference, it must have an unambiguous size associated with it, which means that it may be necessary to include a size directive such as **WORD PTR** or **BYTE PTR** as part of *Expression*.

Here are our first, very simple-minded versions of the *While* and *Wend* macros:

```
While1   MACRO    Exp
    topOfWhile:
         cmp    Exp, 0
         jne    $ + 5
         jmp    endWhile
ENDM

Wend1    MACRO
         jmp    topOfWhile
     EndWhile:
ENDM
```

These macros already contain some points of interest. If *Exp* = 0, we wish to jump to the end of the *While* loop. This would be done most directly by the sequence

```
cmp    Exp, 0
```

```
        je    endWhile
```

However, in the most useful applications, the distance to the end of the loop will be too large for a **SHORT** jump, so that a "jump over a jump" is called for. Since the instruction

```
        jmp   endWhile
```

involves a forward reference, **MASM** will by default encode it as a **NEAR** jump, which requires three bytes of machine code. In addition, the instruction

```
        jne   $ + 5
```

itself requires two bytes, so that this instruction does indeed result in a jump over the *jmp endWhile* instruction. It is obviously unsafe to use the **MASM @F** formalism within macros.

The initial versions of our macros suffer from a fatal flaw. They cannot be used twice within the same source module, since this would cause a repeated definition of the *topOfWhile* and *endWhile* labels. The obvious resolution of this difficulty is to make these labels **LOCAL** to the *While1* macro. But, alas, this will not work because each *Wend1* macro call needs to have access to the label names defined in the matching *While1* call.

The most practical solution to our problem is to build custom labels for use in each application of the macros. This can be accomplished easily using the string directives, and gives the second version of our macros:

```
whileCounter = 0


While2   MACRO   Exp
    whileCounter = whileCounter + 1
    topOfWhile   CATSTR   <topOfWhile>, %whileCounter
topOfWhile:
    cmp    Exp, 0
    jne    $ + 5
    endWhile    CATSTR   <endWhile>, %whileCounter
    jmp    endWhile
ENDM


Wend2   MACRO
    jmp    topOfWhile
    endWhile:
ENDM
```

CATSTR concatenates the literal text *topOfWhile* with the values 1,2, ···, of *whileCounter* to produce the sequence of labels *topOfWhile1*, *topOfWhile2*, ···, and similarly for the *endWhile* labels.

This form will allow the sequential use of *While*, but most emphatically will not support nesting of *While* loops. The pseudocode that corresponds to a minimal, doubly nested loop has the form

```
    topOfWhile1:
        if (Exp1 = 0) goto endWhile1
```

```
topOfWhile2:
    if (Exp2 = 0) goto endWhile2
    Statements
    goto topOfWhile2
endWhile2:
    goto topOfWhile1
endWhile1:
```

When our present version of the *While* macro is used in an attempt to generate these nested loops, the code produced deviates from this pseudocode in one small but critical feature. Since *whileCounter* is never reset, the final *endWhile1* label will actually be replaced by a repetition of the *endWhile2* label.

In general, it is clear how the numbers should be assigned to nested *topOfWhile* and *endWhile* labels. Of course, each time a new *While* is encountered, the next value of *whileCounter* is assigned to its labels. But these values of *whileCounter* should be assigned in reverse order to the corresponding labels in *Wend*. The obvious scheme for implementing this ordering is to store the values of *whileCounter* on a stack as they are generated, and then pop a value from the stack each time a *Wend* is encountered.

As we stated earlier, one of the motivations for setting up an assembly-time stack was to make it easy to handle the labels in these nested *While* loops, and this application is made in WHILE3.ASM, which is shown in Figure 13.5.

WHILE3.ASM also shows the macros in action, including their use in a triply nested loop. To improve readability, it is certainly a good idea to indent the code for nested loops, as we have done there and as is customary in high-level languages. We have used memory variables for the loop counters, but of course registers could be used to improve performance somewhat.

The basic idea behind these macros is that the current *While* loop is indexed by the integer *whileCounter*. The labels marking the beginnings and ends of *While* loops are built by concatenating the string constants *topOfWhile* and *endWhile* with the current value of *whileCounter*. The values of *whileCounter* are controlled by incrementing and pushing them onto the assembly-time stack named *whileStack* on entry to *While* loops, and popping them at the corresponding loop exits.

Figure 13.6 shows the code that is generated from WHILE3.ASM, but with the *outCh* lines commented out. The most significant feature of Figure 13.6 is that the *endWhile* labels match the *topOfWhile* labels, but in reverse order.

While, our final version of the *While* macro, allows the user somewhat more flexibility in choosing the controlling expression *Exp*. It is impossible to achieve the flexibility associated with high-level languages, but it is a relatively simple matter to allow the use of simple relational operators. We will extend the permitted form for the controlling expression so that, in addition to the format used previously, the calling syntax

```
While    Arg1    Arg2    Arg3
```

will be accepted, with *Arg1*, *Arg2*, and *Arg3* as follows:

- *Arg1* and *Arg3* are registers, constants, or memory references, but with the restriction that, if they are both memory references, than they must both refer to word-size locations.

FIGURE 13.5 THIRD VERSIONS OF While/Wend MACROS

```
 1    TITLE   While3.asm
 2
 3    INCLUDE    console.mac
 4
 5    whileCounter = 0
 6    whileStack EQU  <>
 7
 8    While3   MACRO   Exp
 9        @Inc whileCounter
10        @Push   %&whileCounter, whileStack
11        topOfWhile   CATSTR   <topOfWhile>, %whileCounter
12        topOfWhile:
13            cmp   Exp, 0
14            jne   $ + 5
15        endWhile  CATSTR   <endWhile>, %whileCounter
16        jmp   endWhile
17    ENDM
18
19    Wend3    MACRO
20        @Pop    topOfStack, whileStack
21        topOfWhile   CATSTR   <topOfWhile>, %topOfStack
22        jmp   topOfWhile
23        endWhile    CATSTR   <endWhile>, %topOfStack
24        endWhile:
25    ENDM
26
27    DOSSEG
28    .MODEL SMALL
29    .STACK   100h
30
31    .DATA
32
33        Counter1   dw   ?
34        Counter2   dw   ?
35        Counter3   dw   ?
36
37    .STACK    100h
38
39    .CODE
40
41    Start:
42
43        mov   ax, @DATA
44        mov   ds, ax
45
46        mov   Counter1, 4
47        While3   Counter1
48            outCh 'a'
49            mov   Counter2, 3
50            While3 Counter2
51                outCh 'b'
52                mov   Counter3, 2
53                While3 Counter3
54                    outCh 'c'
```

```
55                    dec    Counter3
56               Wend3
57               dec Counter2
58          Wend3
59          dec    Counter1
60     Wend3
61
62     mov    ax, 20
63     While3    ax
64       outCh 'd'
65       dec    ax
66     Wend3
67
68          mov    ax, 4c00h
69          int    21h
70
71  END    Start

PROGRAM OUTPUT:

abccbccbccabccbccbccabccbccbccabccbccbccdddddddddddddddddddddd
```

• *Arg2* can be any of the "relational" operators from the following list.

OPERATOR	MEANING
E	equals
G	greater than
GE	greater than or equal to
L	less than
LE	less than or equal to
A	above
AE	above or equal
B	below
BE	below or equal

Each of these operations can also be used with an 'N' prepended, with the obvious meaning.

For example, in this version, the controlling expression can have any of these forms:

```
Var1 EQ 10
Var2 LE ax
[bx + si - 10] NE [di + 17]
Var1 GE Var2
```

The only real restriction is that, in the last two forms, all the quantities that enter in must have size one word.

The code for *While* is shown in the program WHILE.ASM, contained in Figure 13.7. WHILE.ASM also shows elementary applications of the *While/Wend* macros, as well as showing some of their limitations. Here are a few observations on the program:

FIGURE 13.6 CODE GENERATED BY WHILE3.ASM (EDITED)

```
START:
5544:0010 B85155          MOV        AX,5551
5544:0013 8ED8            MOV        DS,AX
5544:0015 C70608000400    MOV        Word Ptr [0008],0004
TOPOFWHILE1:
5544:001B 833E080000      CMP        Word Ptr [0008],+00
5544:0020 7503            JNZ        _edata+25 (0025)
5544:0022 E98400          JMP        ENDWHILE1 (00A9)
5544:0040 C7060A000300    MOV        Word Ptr [000A],0003
TOPOFWHILE2:
5544:0046 833E0A0000      CMP        Word Ptr [000A],+00
5544:004B 7503            JNZ        _edata+50 (0050)
5544:004D EB53            JMP        ENDWHILE2 (00A2)
5544:004F 90              NOP
5544:006B C7060C000200    MOV        Word Ptr [000C],0002
TOPOFWHILE3:
5544:0071 833E0C0000      CMP        Word Ptr [000C],+00
5544:0076 7503            JNZ        _edata+7b (007B)
5544:0078 EB22            JMP        ENDWHILE3 (009C)
5544:007A 90              NOP
5544:0096 FF0E0C00        DEC        Word Ptr [000C]
5544:009A EBD5            JMP        ͟   ͟WHILE3 (0071)
ENDWHILE3:
5544:009C FF0E0A00        DEC        Word Ptr [000A]
5544:00A0 EBA4            JMP        TOPOFWHILE2 (0046)
ENDWHILE2:
5544:00A2 FF0E0800        DEC        Word Ptr [0008]
5544:00A6 E972FF          JMP        TOPOFWHILE1 (001B)
ENDWHILE1:
5544:00A9 B81400          MOV        AX,0014
TOPOFWHILE4:
5544:00AC 3D0000          CMP        AX,0000
5544:00AF 7503            JNZ        _edata+b4 (00B4)
5544:00B1 EB1F            JMP        ENDWHILE4 (00D2)
5544:00B3 90              NOP
5544:00CF 48              DEC        AX
5544:00D0 EBDA            JMP        TOPOFWHILE4 (00AC)
ENDWHILE4:
5544:00D2 B8004C          MOV        AX,4C00
5544:00D5 CD21            INT        21
```

Lines 9-11. A macro call of the form

```
        While    Arg1
```

generates the original, simple conditional test

```
    cmp    Arg1, 0
```

Notice again that if *Arg1* is an anonymous memory reference, then an explicit size override will be required.

FIGURE 13.7 FINAL VERSIONS OF While/Wend MACROS

```
 1   TITLE  While.asm
 2
 3   INCLUDE   console.mac
 4
 5   ;-----------------------------------------------------------------------
 6
 7   @genJump   MACRO   Arg1, Arg2, Arg3
 8
 9       IFB <Arg2>
10           cmp  Arg1, 0
11           jne  $ + 5
12       ELSE
13           isReg = (.TYPE Arg1) AND 00010000B
14           isConst =  (.TYPE Arg3) AND 00000100B
15           IF ((isReg EQ 0) AND (isConst EQ 0))
16               push  ax
17               mov   ax, Arg1
18               cmp   ax, Arg3
19               pop   ax
20           ELSE
21               cmp  Arg1, Arg3
22           ENDIF
23               j&Arg2 $ + 5
24       ENDIF
25   ENDM
26
27   ;-----------------------------------------------------------------------
28
29   whileCounter = 0
30   whileStack EQU  <>
31
32   While   MACRO   Arg1, Arg2, Arg3
33       @Inc   whileCounter
34       @Push  %&whileCounter, whileStack
35       topOfWhile   CATSTR   <topOfWhile>, %whileCounter
36       topOfWhile:
37       @genJump   Arg1, Arg2, Arg3
38       endWhile   CATSTR   <endWhile>, %whileCounter
39       jmp   endWhile
40   ENDM
41
42   ;-----------------------------------------------------------------------
43
44   Wend   MACRO
45       @POP  TopOfStack, whileStack
46       topOfWhile     CATSTR   <topOfWhile>, %TopOfStack
47       jmp   topOfWhile
48       endWhile       CATSTR   <endWhile>, %TopOfStack
49       endWhile:
50   ENDM
51
52   ;-----------------------------------------------------------------------
53
54   DOSSEG
```

Figure 13.7 cont.

```
55    .MODEL SMALL
56    .STACK    100h
57
58    .DATA
59
60        Counter1    dw    ?
61        Counter2    dw    ?
62        Counter3    dw    ?
63
64    .CODE
65
66    Start:
67
68        mov    ax, @DATA
69        mov    ds, ax
70
71        mov    si, OFFSET Counter1
72        ;WORD PTR [si] is now an alias for Counter1
73        mov    WORD PTR [si], 0
74        mov    di, OFFSET Counter2
75        ;  and WORD PTR [di] is an alias for Counter2
76        mov    Counter2, 10
77        While    [si] LE [di]
78            OUTCH 'a'
79            mov    Counter3, 0
80            While Counter3 GE -20
81                OUTCH 'b'
82                dec Counter3
83            Wend
84            inc WORD PTR [si]
85        Wend
86
87            mov    ax, 4c00h
88            int    21h
89
90    END    Start
```

Lines 13-14. Recall from Chapter 12 that the directive

```
.TYPE Expression
```

returns a one-byte value, in which bit four is on if *Expression* is a register and bit two is on if *Expression* is a constant. Hence line 15 can be paraphrased as: "If *Arg1* is not a register and *Arg3* is not a constant ···."

An example of this configuration is when both *Arg1* and *Arg3* are memory references. The easiest way to treat such cases is by copying *Arg1* into a register, which is then used in the **cmp** instruction. The generated code does exactly this. It is the choice of register size here that necessitates the restriction to word-sized data items, in cases where both *Arg1* and *Arg3* are data references. Ideally, it should be possible to test after line 15 to find out whether these memory references are words or bytes, so that a byte register, say **al**, could be used in the byte case instead of **ax**. As we pointed out in Chapter 12, the **.TYPE** directive cannot be used to distinguish bytes from words when dealing with indirect memory references.

Line 23. Here we fabricate the correct conditional jump, based on the form of *Arg2*. The macro would be cleaner if it were possible to write, for example,

```
While    Var1  <=    Var2
```

instead of the somewhat more cryptic

```
While    Var1  LE    Var2
```

Unfortunately, this second form is required since **MASM** balks when asked to accept a macro argument such as "<=".

Lines 71-85. These lines show some rather artificial uses of the macros. The main point is that memory references, even indirect ones, can occur as both *Arg1* and *Arg3*.

The *While/Wend* macros are especially useful since some of the other standard control structures can be fabricated easily in terms of them.

For example, consider a basic case of the **C** language *for* loop, corresponding to the following pseudocode:

```
for (Counter = Start; Counter < End; Counter += Increment)
    Statements
```

This immediately translates into the *While/Wend* loop given by this pseudocode:

```
        Counter = Start
        While Counter L End
            Statements
            Counter = Counter + Increment
        Wend
```

One essential control structure that cannot be fabricated easily in terms of *While/Wend* is *If/elseIf/Else/endIf*. The program IFTEST.ASM, shown in Figure 13.8, shows a direct, macro implementation of this control structure.

The ideas behind our *If/elseIf/Else/endIf* macros are similar to the *While/Wend* pair. In particular, the standard convention that each *elseIf* or *Else* should be associated with the closest unmatched *If* requires that the appropriate labels should again be stacked. This time two separate stacks, *ifStack* and *elseStack*, are used. *ifStack* measures the *If* nesting depth, while *elseStack* administers the label numbers for the *elseIf* and *Else* jump targets. Figure 13.9 gives an example of code produced by these macros.

The macros that we have developed in this section are contained in the file CONSOLE.MAC on the Program Disk. Although the author uses these macros regularly, they will not be used in the remainder of this book, in order to minimize the inter-chapter dependencies.

FIGURE 13.8 THE If/elseIf/Else/endIf MACROS

```
 1    TITLE   ifTest.asm
 2
 3    INCLUDE    console.mac
 4
 5    ifCounter = 0
 6    ifStack   EQU  <>
 7    elseCounter = 0
 8    elseSTack EQU <>
 9
10    ;------------------------------------------------------------------
11
12    @If   MACRO    Arg1, Arg2, Arg3
13
14        @Inc      ifCounter
15        @Push     %&ifCounter, ifStack
16        @genJump  Arg1, Arg2, Arg3
17        @Inc      elseCounter
18        @Push     %&elseCounter, elseSTack
19        elseLab   CATSTR   <elseLab>, %elseCounter
20        jmp   elseLab
21
22    ENDM
23
24    ;------------------------------------------------------------------
25
26    @Else   MACRO
27
28        getTop   Top  ifStack
29        pastElse   CATSTR   <pastElse>, %Top
30        jmp pastElse
31        @POP Top  elseSTack
32        elseLab   CATSTR   <elseLab>, %Top
33        elseLab:
34        @Inc  elseCounter
35        @Push %&elseCounter, elseSTack
36
37    ENDM
38
39    ;------------------------------------------------------------------
40
41    @elseIf   MACRO   Arg1, Arg2, Arg3
42
43        @Else   Arg1, Arg2, Arg3
44        elseLab   CATSTR   <elseLab>, %elseCounter
45        @genJump  Arg1, Arg2, Arg3
46        jmp   elseLab
47
48    ENDM
49
50    ;------------------------------------------------------------------
51
52    @endIf   MACRO
53
54        @Pop  Top   elseSTack
```

```
55       elseLab     CATSTR <elseLab>, %Top
56       elseLab:
57       @Pop  Top  ifStack
58       pastElse    CATSTR <pastElse>, %Top
59       pastElse:
60
61   ENDM
62
63   ;-----------------------------------------------------------------
64
65   DOSSEG
66   .MODEL SMALL
67   .STACK   100h
68
69   .DATA
70
71       Counter1    dw   10
72       Counter2    dw   ?
73       Counter3    dw   ?
74
75   .CODE
76
77   Start:
78
79       mov   ax, @DATA
80       mov   ds, ax
81       @If Counter1 LE bx
82           @If cx LE dx
83               outCh 'c'
84           @elseIf  si LE di
85               outCh 'd'
86           @Else
87               outCh 'e'
88           @endIf
89       @endIf
90       mov   ax, 4c00h
91       int   21h
92
93   END   Start
```

Exercise 13-15. In the text, we pointed out that *While2* does not support nesting of *While* loops since it does not print the correct sequence of *endOfWhile* labels. In the example shown, the correct result would be obtained if *whileCounter* were decremented after the printing of each *endOfWhile* label. Why would this not work in general?

Exercise 13-16. Rewrite insertion sort, the code for which is shown in Figure 6.4, so that it uses the structured programming macros.

Exercise 13-17. Redo Exercise 6-14 (writing a bubblesort procedure) using the structured programming macros.

FIGURE 13.9 CODE GENERATED BY IFTEST.ASM (EDITED)

```
START:
5B6E:0010 B8715B          MOV        AX,5B71
5B6E:0013 8ED8            MOV        DS,AX
5B6E:0015 50              PUSH       AX
5B6E:0016 A10A00          MOV        AX,Word Ptr [000A]
5B6E:0019 3BC3            CMP        AX,BX
5B6E:001B 58              POP        AX
5B6E:001C 7E03            JLE        _edata+21 (0021)
5B6E:001E EB15            JMP        ELSELAB1 (0035)
5B6E:0020 90              NOP
5B6E:0021 3BCA            CMP        CX,DX
5B6E:0023 7E03            JLE        _edata+28 (0028)
5B6E:0025 EB04            JMP        ELSELAB2 (002B)
5B6E:0027 90              NOP
5B6E:0028 EB0B            JMP        ELSELAB1 (0035)
5B6E:002A 90              NOP
ELSELAB2:
5B6E:002B 3BF7            CMP        SI,DI
5B6E:002D 7E03            JLE        _edata+32 (0032)
5B6E:002F EB04            JMP        ELSELAB1 (0035)
5B6E:0031 90              NOP
5B6E:0032 EB01            JMP        ELSELAB1 (0035)
5B6E:0034 90              NOP
ELSELAB1:
5B6E:0035 B8004C          MOV        AX,4C00
5B6E:0038 CD21            INT        21
```

SECTION 8 THE AUTHOR'S FAVORITE MACRO

The **MASM** macro language is powerful enough to use in building a quite general string output routine, and we will now show how this can be done. Our starting point is the *outAsc* macro, and our requirements are as follows:

- The output routine must accept several arguments as part of as single call, as in

```
outAsc    Str1, Str, Str3
```

- Any ASCIIZ string, whether specified by a direct or indirect memory reference, should be usable as a parameter. Of course, even our earlier version of *outAsc* has this capability.

- The output routine should accept string literals as parameters, without their being predefined by means of **DB** statements. For example, the call

```
outAsc    "Hello, World!"
```

should do the expected thing.

FIGURE 13.10 THE FINAL FORM OF THE outAsc MACRO

```
 1   TITLE    outAsc.asm
 2
 3   INCLUDE CONSOLE.MAC
 4
 5   COMMENT      #       MACRO HEADER
 6   MACRO NAME:          outAsc              FILE: console.mac
 7   PURPOSE:             Prints ASCIIZ strings, newlines, and string literals
 8                        to a file or device
 9   CALLED AS:           outAsc Param { , Param }
10   INPUTS:              Each Param can be of one of four types:
11                            a memory reference to an ASCIIZ string
12                            a string literal in double quotes
13                            the non-quoted string NL indicating a newline
14                            a handle designator -- either one of the standard
15                            names (stdin, etc.) or an integer in range 0-19 or
16                            the name of a one-word storage location for a handle
17                            that begins with the substring "Handle"; if a handle
18                            is passed, it must be in the last parameter position;
19                            if no handle is passed, stdout is used as the default
20   RETURNS:             Nothing
21   REMARKS:             At the moment, outAsc accepts a max. of 10 parameters;
22                        it will not print a string whose name begin with
23                        "Handle" and that occurs as the last parameter since it
24               #        assumes that this is a file handle designator
25
26   outAsc      MACRO  Par1,Par2,Par3,Par4,Par5,Par6,Par7,Par8,Par9,Par10
27
28       pushRegs    ax, cx, dx, si, bx  ;note that bx was pushed last
29
30       mov    bx, STDOUT              ;assume STDOUT as default
31       ;Find actual number of parameters and store last one as text equate
32       Count = 0
33       IRP Str, <Par1,Par2,Par3,Par4,Par5,Par6,Par7,Par8,Par9,Par10>
34           IFNB    <Str>
35               @INC Count             ;Count = actual number of params
36               lastParm     EQU    <Str> ;lastParm will be last param
37           ELSE
38               EXITM
39           ENDIF
40       ENDM
41       ;Is lastParm a handle?
42       isHandle = 0                   ;assume not
43       IRP  Handle, <STDOUT,STDIN,STDERR,STDAUX,STDPRN,0,1,2,3,4,5,6,7,8,9,10,\
44                    11,12,13,14,15,16,17,18,19>
45 %        IFIDNI  <lastParm>, <Handle>
46               isHandle = 1           ;set flag indicating that lastParm is a
47               mov    bx, Handle      ;  handle and initialize bx to value
48               EXITM                  ;     of handle
49           ENDIF
50       ENDM
51
52       IF isHandle EQ 0               ;if we still have not recogized a handle...
53           ;Is lastParm of the form "Handle..."?
54           lastParmLEN SIZESTR    lastParm
55           IF lastParmLEN GE 6
```

Figure 13.10 cont.

```
56                     possibleHandle  SUBSTR lastParm, 1, 6   ;first 6 letters of Str
57    %              IFIDNI <possibleHandle>, <Handle>
58                    isHandle = 1
59    %                  mov     bx, lastParm   ;if Str begins "Handle..." assume
60                    ENDIF                    ;  that it is a handle designator
61           ENDIF
62       ENDIF
63
64       printCount = 0
65       IRP   Str, <Par1,Par2,Par3,Par4,Par5,Par6,Par7,Par8,Par9,Par10>
66           @Inc printCount
67           IF printCount GT Count-isHandle  ;if the last parameter represents
68               EXITM                         ;  a handle, do not try to print
69           ENDIF                             ;      it
70           outSingle    Str                  ;print strings one at a time
71       ENDM
72
73       POPREGS
74
75    ENDM
76
77    ;-------------------------------------------------------------------
78
79    COMMENT      #       MACRO HEADER
80    MACRO NAME:          outSingle          FILE: console.mac
81    PURPOSE:             Prints an ASCIIZ string, newline, or string literal
82                         to a file or device
83    CALLED AS:           outSingle Par
84    INPUTS:              Par can be of any of the three types
85    REMARKS:             Written to be called by OUTASC, which initializes the
86                 #       file handle and saves the register used by outSingle
87
88    outSingle    MACRO   Buffer
89       LOCAL immedBuf, newLineBuf
90
91       IFIDNI   <Buffer>, <NL>
92
93           @CURSEG    ENDS
94           _DATA   SEGMENT
95               newLineBuf    DB  0dh, 0ah, 0
96           @CURSEG  ENDS
97           _TEXT    SEGMENT
98           lea  dx, newLineBuf
99       ELSE
100
101           immedFlag    =    0
102           immedStr            EQU      <Buffer>
103           immedStrFirstChar   SUBSTR   immedStr, 1, 1
104   %       IFIDN <immedStrFirstChar>, <"">      ;look for opening '"' as first
105                                                ;  check for immediate string
106               immedStrLen          SIZESTR   immedStr
107               immedStrLastChar     SUBSTR    immedStr, immedStrLen
108   %           IFIDN <immedStrLastChar>, <"">  ;look for closing '"' as second
109                   immedFlag = 1               ;  check for immediate string
110                   @CURSEG   ENDS
111                   _DATA SEGMENT
112   %                   immedBuf    DB  Buffer, 0
```

```
113                    @CURSEG    ENDS
114                 _TEXT SEGMENT
115                    lea    dx, immedBuf
116              ENDIF
117           ENDIF
118         IF (immedFlag EQ 0)
119             mov    ax, bx                    ;save handle value
120             pop    bx                        ;restore entry bx in case used
121             lea    dx, Buffer                ;  in indirect address by Buffer
122             push   bx
123             mov    bx, ax                    ;restore handle
124           ENDIF
125       ENDIF
126
127     mov    si, dx                 ;point si to data buffer
128     strLen [si]                   ;STRLEN returns length in ax
129     mov    cx, ax                 ;= length
130     ;bx already contains the file handle
131     mov    ah, 40h                ;handle write function
132     int    21h
133
134   ENDM
135
136   ;-------------------------------------------------------------
137
138   DOSSEG
139   .MODEL SMALL
140   .STACK    100h
141
142   .DATA
143
144       Buffer1   DB    "This is immediate data" , 0
145
146   .CODE
147
148   Start:
149
150       mov   ax, @DATA
151       mov   ds, ax
152
153       outAsc "Hello, !!@@,,;::;;; World!", NL, STDERR
154       outAsc NL, Buffer1, " First"," Second"," Third", NL
155       outAsc Buffer1, NL, "HELLO,", " WORLD", NL, STDERR
156       outAsc "THIS IS A SOMEWHAT LONGER STRING", NL, \
157               "THIS IS A SOMEWHAT LONGER STRING", NL, \
158               "THIS IS A SOMEWHAT LONGER STRING", NL, \
159               "THIS IS A SOMEWHAT LONGER STRING", NL
160
161       mov   ax, 4c00h
162       int   21h
163
164   END    Start
```

PROGRAM OUTPUT

WHEN RUN WITH COMMAND LINE outasc

OUTPUT TO SCREEN:
Hello, !!@@,,;::;;; World!

Figure 13.10 cont.

```
This is immediate data First Second Third
This is immediate data
HELLO, WORLD
THIS IS A SOMEWHAT LONGER STRING
THIS IS A SOMEWHAT LONGER STRING
THIS IS A SOMEWHAT LONGER STRING
THIS IS A SOMEWHAT LONGER STRING


WHEN RUN WITH COMMAND LINE outasc > tempfile


OUTPUT TO SCREEN:
Hello, !!@@,,;:::;;; World!
This is immediate data
HELLO, WORLD


OUTPUT TO tempfile:
This is immediate data First Second Third
THIS IS A SOMEWHAT LONGER STRING
THIS IS A SOMEWHAT LONGER STRING
THIS IS A SOMEWHAT LONGER STRING
THIS IS A SOMEWHAT LONGER STRING
```

- It must be easy to output newlines. A suitable format would be

```
outAsc    NL, "Hello, World!", NL
```

- The output routine must support redirection. Again, our more primitive implementation of *outAsc* does this, but it is clearly harder to identify the redirection target when it is part of an invocation line containing a number of other arguments in diverse formats.

The final version of *outAsc*, which is shown in Figure 13.10, satisfies these criteria. The version that we show will accept no more than ten arguments, although this limit can easily be increased. If no handle is given on the invocation line, *outAsc* prints to STDOUT. If a handle is given, it must be the last argument on the argument list, and can be in any of three formats: either one of the predefined handles STDOUT, etc.; or an integer in the range 0-19; or the name of a one-word storage location reserved for the handle. In the last case, the name must begin with the substring *Handle*. The only real restriction in using *outAsc* is that the last argument cannot be an actual string whose name begins with the substring *Handle*, since then the macro code interprets this argument as a handle, and a syntax error results.

The code for *outAsc* (and the dependent *outSingle* macro) applies a good deal of what we have learned in this chapter. Here are some additional observations on Figure 13.10:

Line 30. We give **bx** the default value of STDOUT. This value will be changed if a handle is included on the macro invocation line. In any case, the final value of **bx** is passed to *outSingle*, which is responsible for printing the actual printable strings, one with each call.

Lines 32-40. The number of arguments in the given call to *outAsc* is assigned to *Count* and the last parameter is assigned to *lastParm*.

Lines 42-50. The *isHandle* flag will ultimately have the value 1 if a handle was specified on the invocation line. On lines 45-49 we are looking for a handle specified by one of the default names or by an integer in the range 0-19. Notice that we do a case-insensitive compare (**IFIDNI**) so that we pick up inputs like *stdout* or *stdOut*.

Lines 52-62. If no handle has yet been found, we check whether *lastParm* has the form *Handle···*, in which case it is interpreted as the name of a one-word storage location for a handle. Again, we have used **IFIDNI**.

Lines 64-71. *outSingle* does the actual printing. Notice line 67 in particular: if *isHandle* = 0 all the arguments should be printed; if *isHandle* = 1 the last argument is a handle designator and so one less than the total number of arguments should be printed.

Lines 102-118. We check on whether *Buffer* is a string literal by seeing whether it starts and ends with a double quote. If so, we use all of *Buffer*, including the double quotes, on the right-hand side of the **DB** statement on line 112.

Line 153. Sometimes things work out better than can be reasonably expected. Note that *outAsc* accepts, and prints correctly, strings that contain characters such as ';' that have special operator significance. (Such characters are usually called *meta-characters*.) The explanation is presumably that, when **MASM** is scanning a string, i.e., after it has seen the opening double quote but has not yet seen the matching closer, it goes into a special "string-scanning" mode. In this special mode, most characters are interpreted as ASCII characters with no operator significance.

Exercise 13_18. Which meta-characters cannot be used in string literals that are to be printed by *outAsc*? What is the easiest way of printing such characters?

Exercise 13_19. Modify *outAsc* so that when it encounters "TAB" as an argument it will print a tab character, and, similarly, when it encounters the argument "FF" it will print a form-feed.

Exercise 13_20. Improve *outAsc* so that it accepts string literals encased in single quotes as well as those in double quotes. It will then be possible to use a string containing a double quote as a single argument.

Exercise 13_21. At the moment, *outAsc* checks only its last parameter to find whether it is a handle. Modify the code so that handles can occur anywhere on the invocation line. For example,

```
outAsc    "abc", Str1, STDPRN, "def", Handle2
```

will send the first two strings to STDPRN and the string "def" to *Handle2*. Of course, after this modification, no string name can begin with the substring *Handle*.

CHAPTER 14

INTERFACING WITH HIGH-LEVEL LANGUAGES

SECTION 1 PREVIEW

One of the professed goals of this book is to present assembly language from a contemporary viewpoint, and achieving this goal certainly requires that attention be paid to interfacing assembly language with high-level languages. We have already laid the groundwork for easily calling assembly language procedures from high-level languages by establishing the stack as the default parameter passing mechanism.

It is now time to start writing programs that are hybrid in the sense that they consist of assembly and high-level language modules. Since the most prevalent situation in the programming world is where C plays the role of the high-level language, we will use this configuration in the examples in the text. However, the basic ideas can be quite readily adapted to other high-level languages, provided that the high-level language compilers in question are sufficiently well documented.

As well as containing information needed in calling various high-level languages from assembly language, the present chapter discusses the problem of calling C library procedures from assembly language and introduces the reader to the C compiler initialization code. For the most part, we use the simplified segment directives and assume that the high-level languages conform to the Microsoft segment naming and model conventions, since this makes the interfacing problem much easier.

The conventions used when high-level languages call assembly language procedures differ considerably from language to language. In Section 2, we outline the general

478

interfacing rules used by the languages in the Microsoft family.

Our primary emphasis throughout the chapter is the case where C calls assembly language or conversely. Section 3 contains our first example of a C program calling an assembly language procedure.

In Section 4, we discuss the substantial improvements in the procedure definition mechanism introduced with Version 5.1 of **MASM**. These enhancements make it relatively simple to deal with the interface between assembly language and the high-level languages in the Microsoft family.

One of the most vexing problems encountered in interfacing is that the non-uniformity of the interfacing conventions imposed by the different high-level language compilers necessitates assembling multiple versions of assembly language. In Section 5, we show by example how this bookkeeping can be partially automated through the use of macros.

Section 6 contains a number of examples showing how to call C library functions from assembly language. Although this technique can be useful for getting a preliminary version of a program running quickly, we have included it mainly because it sheds light on the interface between a high-level language and assembly language.

Finally, in Section 7 we introduce the **MAKE** utility and use it to automate the production of multi-module programs and to prepare multiple .OBJ versions of a program for use in different interfacing situations.

SECTION 2 GENERAL OBSERVATIONS

Before giving our first example, we will comment on the interfacing problem in general, and review how parameter passing and returned values from procedures are handled by various high-level languages. The discussion will be directed toward the Microsoft versions of these languages, although most of the information will apply equally well to compilers from other vendors, except that the segment and group names may differ, in which case the simplified segment conventions cannot be used.

As we saw in Chapter 13, each of the Microsoft languages supports some subset of the five models **SMALL**, **COMPACT**, **MEDIUM**, **LARGE**, and **HUGE**. Both **MASM** and the Microsoft C compiler support all five memory models. Starting with Version 2.0, the Microsoft **QuickC** compiler also supports all five models. **FORTRAN** supports the **MEDIUM**, **LARGE**, and **HUGE** models only. **Pascal** basically uses the **MEDIUM** and **LARGE** models since code pointers are always far (i.e., consist of a segment and an offset) while data pointers can be either near (i.e., offset only) or far. **BASIC** uses far code pointers and near data pointers and so is using the **MEDIUM** model.

As an introductory example, suppose that a high-level language program wishes to call a procedure named *proc1*, which is written in assembly language. Assume that *proc1* requires three arguments *a*, *b*, and *c*, so that the appropriate statement in the high-level language might be

```
proc1(a,b,c)
```

or

FIGURE 14.1 STACK AFTER FAR CALL BY LEFT-PUSHER

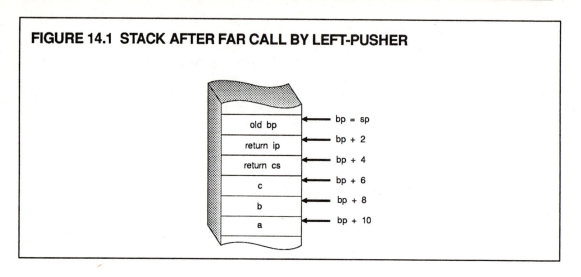

```
call proc1(a,b,c)
```

depending on the particular high-level language.

We will also assume in our initial discussion that *a, b,* and *c* have size no bigger than one word and that the high-level compiler generates code to push the values of *a, b,* and *c* onto the stack, save the return address, and transfer control to the first instruction in *proc1*.

The compiler controls whether this is a **FAR** or **NEAR** call. Of the Microsoft high-level languages, **FORTRAN, BASIC,** and **PASCAL** always make **FAR** calls, while C can make both **NEAR** and **FAR** calls. If the C code is compiled using the **SMALL** or **COMPACT** model, the call will be **NEAR**; if compiled using the **MEDIUM, LARGE,** or **HUGE** model, it will be a **FAR** call. Of course, the assembly language module should be assembled with the **NEAR** or **FAR** attributes of its procedures matching the corresponding values in the high-level module.

An important question is exactly where *proc1* will find its arguments on the stack, and the answer depends significantly on which high-level language is being used. In generating code for a procedure call such as *proc1(a,b,c)*, some high-level languages push the arguments onto the stack in the order first *a,* then *b,* then *c,* while some push the arguments in the reverse order. If a language is of the first kind (a *left-pusher*) and if, for example, the compiler is generating code for a **FAR** call, then the stack will have the general form shown in Figure 14.1. If the language is of the second kind (a *right-pusher*), then the stack will look like Figure 14.2.

Of the standard Microsoft languages, **FORTRAN, BASIC,** and **PASCAL** are left-pushers, while C is a right-pusher. With assembly language, the distinction is meaningless. Depending on the order in which the programmer lists the parameters in the documentation, **MASM** can be made to look like a left-pusher or a right-pusher. Since we have written our assembly language procedures so that they could be called naturally from C as well as from assembly language, we have always ordered the arguments in the procedure headings to make **MASM** look like a right-pusher.

Right-pushing does offer one advantage over left-pushing. With right-pushing it is easy to write a procedure that can be called with a variable number of arguments (such as C's

FIGURE 14.2 STACK AFTER CALL BY RIGHT-PUSHER

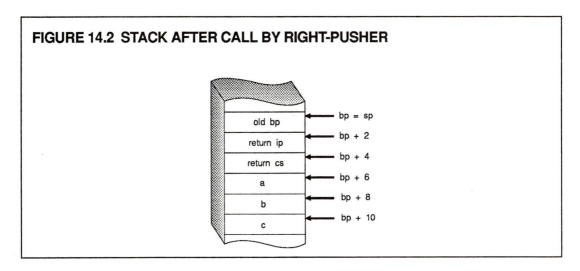

printf( ) and *scanf( )*). The first argument need only contain information about the total number and sizes of the arguments involved in that particular call (which is the approach used by *printf( )* and *scanf( )*). With a right-pusher, the location of the first argument is known (at **bp** + 4 or **bp** + 6 on the stack or, as we shall see later, sometimes at **bp** + 8) and so the called procedure can extract the information needed to isolate the remaining arguments.

Another important question is how procedures return values to the calling program, and the conventions again vary from language to language.

In C, if the returned value needs four or fewer bytes, it is by default returned in registers: if it is one or two bytes long, it is returned in **ax**; if it is a three- or four-byte object, then the low word is returned in **ax** and the high byte or word in **dx**. If the returned value requires more than four bytes, then the called procedure is expected to store it in some address (in a data segment, for example) and to return the offset and segment parts of that address in **ax** and **dx**, respectively.

In **FORTRAN**, **BASIC**, and **PASCAL**, short returned values (no longer than four bytes) are handled in the same way as in **C** but longer returned values are treated differently. If a longer returned value is needed, then the calling program must push the offset part of the address to which the value is to be returned onto the stack after the return address and before the first argument. Consequently, if the call involves a long returned value in any of these three languages, our example stack really looks like Figure 14.3, where *rvo* means *returned-value offset*. It is the responsibility of the called procedure to record the returned value starting at address **ds**:*rvo*. Note that the presence of a returned-value offset on the stack displaces the first parameter by two bytes.

One final inconsistency must be allowed for in interfacing. In assembly language, we have used the convention that the caller pushes the procedure arguments onto the stack, while the responsibility for balancing the stack by removing these arguments lies with the called procedure. For example, if three values were pushed before the call, then our typical assembly language procedure would end with

```
ret 6
```

which has the effect of removing the pushed values and hence balancing the stack.

FIGURE 14.3 STACK WITH RETURNED-VALUE OFFSET

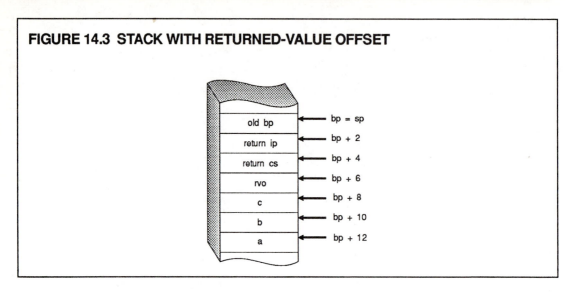

Unfortunately, high-level languages are divided on their view of whether the caller or the called procedure should have responsibility for balancing the stack. In the case of the Microsoft languages, **FORTRAN, BASIC,** and **PASCAL** use the same convention as assembly language, namely that the called procedure must clear the stack. In other words, if our hypothetical procedure is to be called by one of these three languages, it should still end with

```
ret 6
```

Once again, **C** differs from the other high-level languages: the **C** convention is that the caller must clear the arguments from the stack as soon as it regains control after the call. This approach facilitates the compilation of functions accepting a variable number of arguments. Certainly the caller, which has just pushed the arguments onto the stack, knows how many bytes were pushed and can easily generate the correct number of pops. While the called program could deduce the number of bytes to pop by analyzing the first passed argument, this would obviously add to the complexity of the code. As we point out in one of the exercises at the end of this section, this second method can also convert simple programming errors into stack imbalances.

In practical terms, the consequence of the **C** convention is that the compiler will (invisibly to the programmer) generate code to remove the required number of bytes from the stack, so that if our hypothetical procedure is to be called from **C**, it should end with a simple

```
ret
```

These differences between the calling conventions imposed by the different high-level languages are awkward because they require assembling different versions of an assembly language module procedure for each language from which it will be called. However, we will soon see that the construction of these customized versions can be automated by the use of simple macros.

Exercise 14-1. Suppose that C conformed to the other languages in requiring that the called procedure should clear the arguments from the stack. Explain why a programming error such as

```
printf("%ld", x);
```

where x is an integer would result in a stack imbalance. Even an ANSI C compiler would not catch the type mismatch contained in this *printf( )* statement. Why not?

SECTION 3 CALLING ASSEMBLY LANGUAGE FROM C

We will now illustrate the basic principles by writing an assembly language procedure and calling it from a C program.

Even in this simple application, it seemed worthwhile to provide C with a capability not directly available in the standard C libraries. The example chosen provides a function

```
void placeStr(char *, unsigned, unsigned)
```

that allows the user to select row and column coordinates on the screen (the unsigned parameters) and prints a string at that location (the char * parameter).

Figure 14.4 shows the calling program, written in C, and Figure 14.5 gives the first version of the assembly language program. The C module must be compiled, the assembly language module assembled, and the pair linked together. If the **QuickC** compiler is used, then these command lines will do the requisite operations:

```
masm /Mx /W2 /Zi /Z prog14_2,,,;
qcl /c /AS prog14_1.c
link /NOI prog14_1 prog14_2,,,user;
```

Notice the use of the **/Mx** switch on the MASM command line. This directs **MASM** to preserve the case of all **PUBLIC** and **EXTRN** identifiers rather than converting them to uppercase, which is its default. The use of this switch is important in interfacing with C since C is a case-sensitive language. Likewise, the **/NOI** (*no ignore case*) option on the **LINK** command line notifies **LINK** to observe differences between uppercase and lowercase. The **/AS** on the **QuickC** command line is not really necessary. It is included as a reminder that the C module should be compiled using the **SMALL** model, but this is actually the default if no model is specified.

The only feature of Figure 14.4 requiring comment is line 5. The meaning of *extern* in C programs is exactly the same as **EXTRN** in assembly language programs — only the spelling is different. It tells the C compiler that the code for the function named *placeStr* will become available at link time.

Figure 14.5 shows the assembly language procedure that will actually do the printing of the string. It uses **int 10H**, which is one of the ROM BIOS interrupts, known as the *video interrupt*. Like **int 21H**, it gives access to various functions, and the number of the requested function is transmitted in the **ah** register.

FIGURE 14.4 CALLING ASSEMBLY LANGUAGE FROM C

```
 1   /* Prog14_1.c:  Example caller  written in C */
 2
 3   #include <stdio.h>
 4
 5   extern void placeStr(char *, unsigned, unsigned);
 6
 7   void main(void)
 8   {
 9       int n;
10       for (n = 10; n < 20; ++n)
11           placeStr("This is the string", n, 45);
12   }
```

We will not discuss the video setup of the **IBM-XT** is detail, but will briefly indicate the significance of the functions that are being used in this program. It would be a good idea for the reader to read the description of **int 10H** in Appendix 2 at this point.

The first function called in PROG14_2.ASM, **function 0FH** of **int 10H**, returns the number of the *active video page* in the **bh** register. To understand this example, it is sufficient to know that the **XT** can store several different screenfuls of information, called *pages*, in memory simultaneously. Any one of these pages can be displayed on the screen. The page currently displayed is called the *active page* and, by default, this will be page zero, unless the program in control has changed it.

We must call **function 0FH** to find the number of the active page, because **function 02H**, which sets the cursor position, will display it on any chosen page, and we certainly want the cursor to be on the currently visible page since the string will be printed starting at the cursor position. **Functions 0FH and 02H** work well together: 0FH returns the active page number in **bh**, and 02H requires that the active page number be input in **bh**. **Function 02H** must also be passed the row and column coordinates at which the cursor should be placed. The upper left corner of the screen has coordinates row = 0, column = 0; the row coordinate increases in the downward direction and the column coordinate increases in the rightward direction. As the comments in PROG14_2 indicate, **function 02h** expects to receive the row number in **dh** and the column number in **dl**.

The actual code in PROG14_2 should be self-explanatory, except for one requirement enforced by the C compiler. Notice that the procedure is named *_placeStr*, rather than *placeStr*, because **C** compilers preface all external variables with an underscore. Hence the compiler translates the *placeStr* on line 5 of Figure 14.5 to *_placeStr*, and so **LINK** must find a **PUBLIC** of that name in one of the modules.

Of the standard Microsoft languages, only **C** has this slightly awkward feature. When writing assembly language code to interface with any of the other languages, do not prepend the underscore. Since C is a right-pusher, **bp + 4** points to the string to be printed, **bp + 6** contains the value of n, the row number, and **bp + 8** contains 45, the column number.

Finally, note that line 35 does not contain

```
ret 6
```

FIGURE 14.5 PROG14_2: THE PROCEDURE CALLED BY PROG14_1

```
 1    TITLE Prog14_2.asm: written to be called by Prog14_1
 2
 3        PUBLIC    _placeStr
 4        INCLUDE   console.mac
 5
 6    .MODEL SMALL
 7    .CODE
 8
 9    _placeStr    PROC
10
11        push      bp
12        mov       bp, sp
13        push      ax
14        push      bx
15        push      dx
16
17        mov       ah, 0fh ;get current page — returns in bh
18        int       10h
19
20        mov       dl, [bp + 8]
21        mov       dh, [bp + 6]
22        mov       ah, 02h              ;set cursor position
23        int       10h
24
25        mov       bx, [bp + 4]         ;point si to string
26        outAsc    [bx]
27
28        pop       dx
29        pop       bx
30        pop       ax
31        pop       bp
32
33        ret
34
35    _placeStr    ENDP
36
37        END
```

as would normally be expected at this point. In the previous section, we saw that the C calling convention requires the caller to balance the stack, hence the 6 is not needed.

Exercise 14-2. Write an assembly language module containing a single, trivial procedure that takes two integers passed to it on the stack and adds them, returning the answer in the **ax** register. Assemble two versions of this module, one suitable for calling from assembly language and one from your choice of high-level language. Write small calling programs in assembly language and in the high-level language you are using. Put the pieces together and verify that everything works.

Exercise 14-3. Basically the same exercise as the previous one, but this time experiment with call by reference. For example, pass the procedure the addresses (i.e., offsets if you use the **SMALL** or **MEDIUM** model) of two integers on the stack and include code in the procedure to swap the values of the integers. Finally, have the calling program print out the values of the integers before and after swapping to check that they were really interchanged.

Exercise 14-4. Again, the same kind of exercise but this time the point is to show that long data items are really handled by the compiler using the method explained in Section 2. The easiest approach is to have the procedure return a real number (double in C so that it is longer than four bytes), and then to follow the call/return process in **CODEVIEW** to see that things are happening as they should. A slight difficulty is that reals are formatted in a complicated way and so it is hard to build a correctly formatted and identifiable real in the assembly language program.

A simple solution to this problem is to have **MASM** do the work for you. If the assembly language module has a data segment containing a definition of the form

```
        realVar    DQ 10.0
```

then **MASM** will initialize the eight-byte storage area *realVar* to the bit pattern representing the real number 10.0 in the format used by most contemporary languages. (This is the so-called *IEEE double-precision real number format* and will be analyzed in detail in Chapter 17.)

SECTION 4 SIMPLER INTERFACING WITH VERSION 5.1 OF MASM

Beginning with Version 5.1 of **MASM**, Microsoft introduced certain conventions that substantially reduce the amount of writing required in interfacing assembly language to high-level languages. Figure 14.6 shows the program in Figure 14.5 rewritten to take advantage of these new features.

First, consider line 8 of this listing. The beginning of the line is standard: it is just the declaration of *placeStr* as a **PROC**, which is **NEAR** because of the **SMALL** model declaration on line 5. A new item on line 8 is the phrase

```
        USES    ax bx dx
```

This is a nice convenience. It notifies **MASM** that these three registers are used in the procedure, and so should be pushed at the start of the procedure and popped at the end. **MASM** will consequently generate the three pushes and the three pops at the correct places in the code.

The remainder of the line,

```
        String:WORD, Row:BYTE, Col:BYTE
```

is even more interesting. It tells **MASM** that this procedure will receive three arguments on the stack, of the sizes stated. Since **C** is a right-pusher, these arguments would normally be referenced, in the order given, as

FIGURE 14.6 PROG14_3: ANOTHER VERSION OF PROG14_2

```
 1   TITLE Prog14_3.asm:  Written to be called by Prog14_1
 2
 3        INCLUDE   console.mac
 4
 5   .MODEL SMALL, C
 6   .CODE
 7
 8   placeStr PROC USES ax bx dx, String:WORD, Row:BYTE, Col:BYTE
 9
10       mov      ah, 0fh   ;get current page — returns in bh
11       int      10h
12       mov      ah, 02h              ;set cursor position
13       mov      dh, Row
14       mov      dl, Col
15       int      10h
16
17       mov      bx, String           ;print string
18       outAsc   [bx]
19
20       ret
21
22   placeStr     ENDP
23
24       END
```

```
WORD PTR [bp + 4]
BYTE PTR [bp + 6]
BYTE PTR [bp + 8]
```

The appearance of *String:WORD* actually causes **MASM** to generate an equate of the form

```
String  EQU  WORD PTR [bp + 4]
```

(check the .LST file) and similarly for the other two arguments. Hence the arguments can be referred to by name throughout the code, which certainly makes the program easier to write, as well as improving readability. Note carefully that the ordering of the arguments on line 8 is exactly the same as the ordering of the arguments in the function call

```
placeStr(str, row, col)
```

In other words, the **C** function call can be thought of as naturally translating into

```
placeStr(String, Row, Col)
```

in the assembly language discussion.

The general syntax for these parameter declarations is

varName[: [[**NEAR | FAR**] **PTR**] *Type*]

Type can be any of the usual data types (**BYTE**, **WORD**, etc.), or any structure or record type. If it is omitted, the assumed default is **WORD**. If **PTR** is used, **MASM** interprets *varName* as a pointer and in this case the optional *Type* is ignored by **MASM** although it is used by **CODEVIEW**. **MASM** does not generate any code to dereference the pointer — the program code must do that. It does generate an equate using a size override appropriate to a pointer of the given size. If neither **NEAR** nor **FAR** appears, the size of the pointer agrees with the current model; if **NEAR** or **FAR** does occur, it will override the default model size. The three possible pointer sizes correspond to the size overrides **WORD PTR** (near pointers), **DWORD PTR** (far pointers), and **FWORD PTR** (for the 48-bit pointers used with the **80386**).

Next, observe that line 5 contains a new form of the **.MODEL** directive:

```
.MODEL SMALL, C
```

This is an example of the extended use of the **.MODEL** directive, which has the syntax

.MODEL *Mdl, Lang*

where *Mdl* can be any of the usual five choices (**SMALL**, etc.) and *Lang* any of the standard Microsoft languages. This extended form of **.MODEL** causes **MASM** to generate appropriate code for an assembly language module designed to be called from the high-level language given in *Lang* and using the **MODEL** given by *Mdl*. Here are the effects of using the extended model directive:

- Since the arguments will be indirectly addressed using **bp**, these lines are *automatically* generated by **MASM**:

```
push    bp
mov     bp, sp
        .
        .
        .
pop     bp
```

- **PUBLIC** declarations are generated for all procedure names.

- The assembly language module need only contain a simple **ret** instruction, no matter which language is going to call it. **MASM** generates code to remove the passed arguments from the stack, if *Lang* is any language other than C.

- **MASM** makes the correct right- or left-pusher interpretation of the passed arguments, again based on the choice of *Lang*.

- If *Lang* is C, all **PUBLIC** and **EXTRN** names in the assembly language module are prefixed with a '_', as the C compiler requires.

If, instead of line 5, we had written

```
.MODEL LARGE, Pascal
```

then **MASM** would have generated the correct code so that *placeStr* could be called from **Pascal**.

The easy way to see the exact code produced by **MASM** from Figure 14.6 is to assemble the program with the **/LA** (*list all*) command-line flag. When this directive is used, the .LST file contains all the code generated by **MASM**.

Another significant new directive is **LOCAL**, which allows the definition of variables that are local to a procedure. The syntax is

LOCAL   varDef, { ,*varDef* }

where each *varDef* has the form

Name [[*Count*] : [[**NEAR** | **FAR**] **PTR**] *Type*]

The optional *Count* gives the number of items to be allocated. If used, *Count* must be written in square brackets (e.g., [20]); if *Count* is not specified, the default value is 1. The rest of the syntax is similar to the corresponding syntax for parameter declarations.

The effect of the **LOCAL** directive is to reserve space for the named variables using negative stack addressing. These locals can be accessed by name in the procedure in which they are declared.

Exercise 14-5. Rewrite the programs INSERT.ASM and RAND.ASM of Chapter 7 as separate modules using the new interfacing directives, and assemble them so that they can be called from the high-level language of your choice. Then write a calling program in the high-level language that declares an array of 100 integers, which it initializes using calls to *Rand*. It should then print the values of the integers to the screen, sort them by a call to *Insert*, and print the sorted array. Build and run the three-module program.

Exercise 14-6. Int 10H contains many interesting video functions in addition to the ones we used in *placeStr*. Write procedures analogous to *placeStr* that activate some of these other functions. For example, one of the **int 10H** functions initializes a rectangular window on the screen with a given video attribute (e.g., with given color or in reverse video) and scrolls text in this window up a specified number of lines. (Another function scrolls down.) To write text to the window, you might want an enhanced version of *placeStr* that will print text with a given attribute, and will "wrap" when it hits the right edge of the window and scroll up when it hits the bottom of the window. A real word-wrapping function, which wraps at the beginning of the first word that is too long to fit in the window, is considerably harder to write. As well as reading about **int 10H** in Appendix 2, you will need to consult a table of video attributes. Finally, the procedures must be tested by calling them from a high-level language. The reader should be warned that, while these **int 10H** functions are quite flexible, they are also notoriously slow.

SECTION 5 INTERFACING WITH SEVERAL LANGUAGES

As the discussion in Section 3 shows, it is necessary to assemble different versions of an assembly language source module in order to call it from several languages. We will now show that it is not actually necessary to write different versions of the assembly language module since the differences between the calling conventions imposed by the various high-level language compilers can be accommodated through the use of conditional assembly directives. Granted, each procedure must be assembled several times and the different .OBJ versions kept in separate libraries for use with their designated languages. Fortunately, all of this housekeeping can be easily automated.

Figure 14.7 contains a new version of the called procedure, containing conditional assembly directives on lines 65-84. Before proceeding, we will briefly review the subject of conditional assembly.

Referring to Table 12.8, the conditional directive **IFNDEF** (*if not defined*) refers to whether a quantity has or has not been defined. As noted in Table 12.8, a quantity can be defined either in the source module or by means of a switch, such as

```
/DSymbol=Value
```

on the **MASM** command line. The conditional directive **IFIDNI** (*if identical, case-insensitive*) refers to the outcome of a comparison of text-equate strings. A % (*expression operator*) occurring at the start of a line (and followed by at least one space or tab) causes each text-macro on the line to be replaced by its value.

The conditional code on lines 66-83 now has the obvious interpretation: if the symbol LANG has not been defined, then the directive on line 67 should execute. As we saw in Chapter 13, the line

```
%OUT String
```

requests **MASM** to send a copy of *String* to STDOUT. Hence, the effect of line 67 is to print a reminder that LANG must be defined.

The structure and purpose of the later conditional assembly code is analogous. For example, the **ELSEIFIDNI** directive on line 68 sets the value of MDL to **MEDIUM** in the case where LANG = BASIC, line 70 prints an appropriate message, and line 83 includes the line

```
.MODEL MEDIUM, BASIC
```

in the assembled code.

The complete structure of the conditional assembly code should now be clear except for lines 65 and 84. Recall that **MASM** makes two passes. The **IF1** on line 65 is a directive to **MASM** to process the ensuing "IF block" only during Pass 1. The "IF block" goes as far as the matching **ENDIF** directive — line 84 in this case. Many times **IF1** (or the corresponding **IF2**) is included merely for efficiency. Most macro code need only be read by **MASM** on one of its two passes. Generally, this should be done on Pass 1 since the macro code must nearly always be available during this pass. But the **IF1** directive plays a much more important role in this instance. If it is not included, then line 83 will be executed on both passes, producing two copies of the **MODEL** directive in the source code, and a consequent syntax error. Try it!

FIGURE 14.7 CALLING A PROCEDURE FROM SEVERAL LANGUAGES

```
 1   TITLE Multiple.asm:  Can be called from various languages
 2
 3       INCLUDE   console.mac
 4
 5   ;-------------------------------------------------------------------
 6
 7   COMMENT     #   MACRO HEADER
 8   MACRO NAME:     getVal                    FILE: interfac.mac
 9   PURPOSE:        Retrieves passed parameter from stack, using pass
10                   by value or near or far reference, whichever is
11                   appropriate for the language in question.
12   CALLED AS:      getVal  Reg, Name
13   REMARKS:        Defaults: By value for C and Pascal; by far reference for
14           #       FORTRAN; by near reference for BASIC
15
16   getVal  MACRO   Reg, Name
17
18   %   IFDIFI <LANG>, <C>              ;if not C or Pascal, assume that
19   %       IFDIFI <LANG>, <Pascal>     ;  param was passed by either:
20               IF @datasize            ;     far reference
21                   les  bx, Name
22                   mov  Reg,es:[bx]     ;or
23               ELSE                    ;     near reference
24                   mov  bx, Name
25                   mov  Reg, [bx]
26               ENDIF
27               EXITM
28           ENDIF
29       ENDIF
30           mov  Reg, Name              ;if C or Pascal, assume param
31                                       ;  passed by value
32   ENDM
33
34   ;-------------------------------------------------------------------
35
36   COMMENT     #   MACRO HEADER
37   MACRO NAME:     getPtr              FILE: interfac.mac
38   PURPOSE:        Retrieves a pointer from the stack.
39   CALLED AS:      getPtr  Reg16, Name
40   REMARKS:        When used with compact, large, or huge model, it transfers
41           #       the pointer to ds:Reg16.
42
43   getPtr  MACRO   Reg, Name
44
45       IF @datasize
46           lds  Reg, Name
47       ELSE
48           mov  Reg, Name
49       ENDIF
50
51   ENDM
52
53   ;-------------------------------------------------------------------
54
```

Figure 14.7 cont.

```
55   COMMENT      #   MACRO HEADER
56   MACRO NAME:      selectModel            FILE: interfac.mac
57   PURPOSE:         Sets up MODEL directive in form
58                          .MODEL  LANG, SIZE
59                    using LANG entered on MASM command line (/DLANG=???)
60   CALLED AS:       selectModel
61   REMARKS:     #   Sets SIZE to default values shown in code below
62
63   selectModel    MACRO
64
65       IF1                              ;so that .MODEL only occurs once
66          IFNDEF LANG
67             %OUT MUST SPECIFY A LANGUAGE NAME
68   %      ELSEIFIDNI   <LANG>, <BASIC>
69             MDL    EQU    <MEDIUM>
70             %OUT TO BE CALLED FROM BASIC
71   %      ELSEIFIDNI  <LANG>, <C>
72             MDL    EQU    <SMALL>
73             %OUT TO BE CALLED FROM C
74   %      ELSEIFIDNI  <LANG>, <FORTRAN>
75             MDL    EQU    <LARGE>
76             %OUT TO BE CALLED FROM FORTRAN
77   %      ELSEIFIDNI   <LANG>, <PASCAL>
78             MDL    EQU    <MEDIUM>
79             %OUT TO BE CALLED FROM PASCAL
80          ELSE
81             %OUT  BAD LANGUAGE NAME
82          ENDIF
83   %         .MODEL MDL, LANG
84       ENDIF
85
86   ENDM
87
88   ;-------------------------------------------------------------------
89
90   selectModel
91   .CODE
92
93   % IFIDNI <LANG>, <C>
94       placeStr  PROC    USES ax bx dx, String:WORD, Row:BYTE, Col:BYTE
95   % ELSE   ;assume LANG is BASIC, FORTRAN, or Pascal
96       placeStr  PROC    USES ax bx dx, String:PTR WORD, \
97                              Row:PTR BYTE, Col:PTR BYTE
98      ENDIF
99
100     mov    ah, 0fh    ;get current page -- returns in bh
101     int    10h
102
103     mov    ah, 02h             ;set cursor position
104     getVal dh, Row
105     getVal dl, Col
106     int    10h
107
108     getPtr bx, String
109     outAsc [bx]                  ;print string
```

```
110
111      ret
112
113 placeStr      ENDP
114
115 ;-------------------------------------------------------------------
116
117      END
```

It is now easy to sum up the effects of the conditional assembly code. For each choice of LANG, the code will be assembled with a corresponding value of MDL. The chosen values of MDL are

```
.MODEL   MEDIUM, BASIC
.MODEL   SMALL, C
.MODEL   LARGE, FORTRAN
.MODEL   MEDIUM, Pascal
```

The reader can check that these are reasonable defaults, based on the discussion of memory models given in Section 2.

The next problem we must confront is that the different languages have different default parameter-passing conventions:

- **BASIC** passes all arguments by near reference, i.e., passes only the offset parts of addresses.

- C passes scalars by value and arrays by reference (which, in our **SMALL** model context, really means that arrays are passed by near reference).

- **FORTRAN** passes all arguments by far reference, i.e., passes both the segment and offset parts of the address.

- **Pascal** passes arguments by value, unless they are declared as **VAR** or **CONST**, in which case they are passed by near reference, or **VARS** or **CONSTS**, in which case they are passed by far reference.

To further complicate matters, these languages provide various mechanisms to override the parameter-passing defaults (**BASIC's BYVAL**, for example).

The version of our assembly language program given in Figure 14.7, MULTIPLE.ASM, is designed to be called by any of the four Microsoft high-level languages, where each language has used its default parameter passing technique.

To obtain four versions of MULTIPLE.OBJ, suitable for calling from **BASIC**, **C**, **FORTRAN**, or **Pascal**, respectively, we need only run **MASM** four times, using these command lines:

```
masm /DLANG=BASIC multiple, multb,,;
masm /DLANG=C /Zi /Z /W2 /Mx multiple, multc,,;
masm /DLANG=FORTRAN /Zi /Z /W2 multiple, multf,,;
masm /DLANG=Pascal /Zi /Z /W2 multiple, multp,,;
```

We will end up with four .OBJ versions of *Multiple*: MULTB.OBJ will be suitable for calls from **BASIC** using the **MEDIUM** model; MULTC.OBJ will be correct for calls from **C** using the **SMALL** model; MULTF.OBJ will be appropriate for calls from **FORTRAN** using the **LARGE** model; and MULTP.OBJ will be appropriate for calls from **PASCAL** using the **MEDIUM** model.

The code in MULTIPLE.ASM needs only a few additional comments before we leave it:

Lines 7-32. This macro retrieves the value of the passed argument *Name* and stores it in *Reg*, assuming that the argument was passed using the default method for the language in question. For example, if the language is C or **Pascal**, then the conditional macro code on lines 20-26 is omitted and line 30 is included, i.e., the argument is interpreted as a value. In the contrary case, **MASM** examines the code on lines 20-26, and makes a further distinction based on the value of @datasize, which is a built-in variable kept by **MASM**. It has value 0 for those models using near reference by default (**SMALL** and **COMPACT**), has value one for the **MEDIUM** and **LARGE** models, and has value two for the **HUGE** model. This conditional code also does the correct things in the **FORTRAN** and **Pascal** cases.

Lines 36-51. This macro is used to recover a variable passed by reference, even in the **C** or **Pascal** cases where the default is to pass by value. It is needed, for example, in dealing with the *String* parameter in the present program. The only reasonable way to pass an array in *any* language is by reference, and this is, in fact, the C default for passing arrays.

Lines 93-102. Since the different callers push differing numbers of bytes onto the stack before the call, **MASM** needs help in setting up the text equates used to access the arguments. In general, this necessitates using a separate procedure heading for each language, although in the present case it is possible to use a common heading for **BASIC**, **FORTRAN**, and **Pascal**. For example, line 94 informs **MASM** that each of *String*, *Row*, and *Col* occupies two bytes on the stack, while lines 96-97 relay the information that each argument occupies either two or four bytes, depending on the current model.

Exercise 14-7. Since the high-level enhancements provided with Version 5.1 of **MASM** are so useful, we would like to use them in pure assembly language programs as well. By pure assembly language we mean programs written 100% in assembly language, i.e., where both the caller and the called procedures are in assembly language modules. Because our high-level examples use **C**, it would probably be best if our conventions could be set up so that the same .OBJ version that is constructed for calling from C could also be called from assembly language. State some reasons why this is impractical. Explain why the version of the extended model directive coming closest to our needs is

```
.MODEL Pascal, SMALL
```

Notice that, technically, this directive should not even be legal since all procedure calls from **Pascal** are **FAR**. However, **MASM** will accept it. Write a version of PROG14_2.ASM using this form of the model directive and the other new interfacing features and write an assembly language program that successfully calls this new version.

SECTION 6 CALLING C FROM ASSEMBLY LANGUAGE

Many students of assembly language have looked longingly at the treasures contained in the standard C libraries. For example, these libraries contain

- Functions that input and output data in nearly any format.

- Functions that perform almost any operation imaginable on strings.

- Functions that do real-number arithmetic, including the computation of most standard mathematical functions such as *sin* and *exp*, and even such esoterica as the *Bessel functions*!

This list is only a tiny sampling of the over 300 functions contained in the typical C library.

As well as providing access to the library functions, the C run-time environment offers other services, notable among which are easy access to the command-line parameters (through the *argc* and *argv* variables) and special code formatting that utilizes a numerical coprocessor (such as the **8087**) when one is present and calls functions from an emulation library when there is no coprocessor.

Of course, any one of these functions or facilities can be easily duplicated by the reader of this book, but in the aggregate they represent many thousands of programming hours. It is often advantageous to "borrow" one or more functions from the C library. The author does this on occasion, in order to concentrate on the more central parts of a project. It is generally worthwhile, at some later point, to replace the C library functions with custom assembly language versions, since many of the library functions are general purpose and, consequently, are relatively slow and bulky. The *scanf( )* and *printf( )* functions are notorious examples of this kind: each of these functions adds over 4K to the size of a program that uses it to process even a single character.

In this section, we will show how to access any of the C library functions or compiler-supplied services from an assembly language program.

Fairly elaborate initialization procedures must be performed before the C library functions or other run-time amenities can be used. Consequently, the essential problem in calling C from assembly language is how to perform these initializations efficiently. The initialization code is supplied as part of the compiler package and, in the course of building a normal C program, it is combined with the program's .OBJ modules at link time. Here are some of the tasks performed by the initialization code:

- Suppose that, as in our case, the **SMALL** model is being used. Then the initialization code combines the data and stack into a DGROUP and points **ds**, **es**, and **ss** to that group. In addition, it initializes **sp**.

- The initialization code parses the command line and initializes the standard parameters to *main( )* (conventionally named *argc* and *argv*).

- If any of the C modules involved in the program uses floating-point arithmetic, the initialization code allocates various buffers and arranges for the linking of the floating-point routines from the standard C library.

These are by no means the only steps involved in the initialization process — they are just the ones of interest to us at the moment. Nowadays, most C compiler vendors supply the complete source code for the initialization routines, and it makes interesting reading for the student of assembly language. (Unfortunately, Microsoft does not supply this source code with **QuickC**, although it does supply it with the Microsoft C Compiler.) In order to call C from assembly language, it is necessary to mimic the initialization code, and this is generally done by editing the official version so that only the sections of immediate use remain, and then assembling and linking this residual code with the assembly language code.

To minimize the level of complexity (and for other rather obvious reasons relating to Microsoft copyrights), we will not present an example of this modification process in the text, but will be content to link in the entire initialization code with our assembly language module. Of course, this corner-cutting makes the final assembly language programs much larger than they have to be.

The skeptical reader is probably wondering at this point whether it is really worth all the trouble — would it not be easier to just start with a small C calling program, instead of insisting on calling from assembly language? The answer is yes, it would be easier, and in most contexts this is how it should be done. But the approach used in this section provides real insight into the workings of a compiler — insight that is hard to obtain in any other way. For example, to develop a machine-level understanding of how *qsort( )* receives its arguments, there is no substitute for actually writing the code that passes it a pointer to a comparison function, the size of an array element, the size of the array, and the offset of the array, all of this done while adhering to the C parameter passing and return conventions. The later programs in this section should be viewed mainly as an attempt to illuminate some of the darker corners of the interface between C and assembly language, rather than as a guide to practical action.

The program CALLC1.ASM, shown in Figure 14.8, illustrates a few elementary applications of the C library functions. In CALLC1.ASM we deal only with integers. We call the C function *srand( )* to seed the library random-number generator *rand( )*, then make a series of calls to *rand( )* to fill an array with non-negative integers and, most interestingly, call the library function *qsort( )*, which uses the quicksort algorithm to sort the array. Finally, we use *printf( )* to print the contents of the array, both before and after sorting. CALLC1 contains the minimum amount of overhead required to interface with the C library. In the following discussion, we will specifically comment on these interfacing lines and explain their significance. Here is a brief analysis of CALLC1:

Line 9. The entry point to the user-supplied code called by the C initialization module must be a function named *main( )*. Since the identifier *main* is global, the standard C protocol prefixes it with an underscore before passing it to the linker.

Lines 12-30. This macro encapsulates a C function call of the form

```
printf("%s", String)
```

The significant features of the macro code are

- The parameter named *String* is pushed first since C is a right-pusher.

- *strFormat*, the formatting string, is defined and space allocated for it during its first use in the current assembly module. Note that *strFormat* is null-terminated, as are all strings in C.

FIGURE 14.8 CALLING C FROM ASSEMBLY LANGUAGE

```
 1   TITLE    Callc1.asm:  calling functions in the C library
 2
 3   INCLUDE console.mac
 4
 5   arySiz  EQU   40
 6   LF      EQU   0ah
 7   Seed    EQU   1234
 8
 9   PUBLIC  _main
10   ;-------------------------------------------------------------------
11
12   COMMENT     #      MACRO HEADER        FILE: callc.mac
13   MACRO NAME:         printString
14   PURPOSE:            Prints an ASCIIZ string to STDOUT using the C library
15                      function printf() with the "%s" formatting string.
16   CALLED AS:  #       printString  String
17
18   printString  MACRO  String
19
20       EXTRN   _printf:NEAR
21       allocFirst  strFormat, <strFormat DB "%s", 0>
22
23       lea     ax, String
24       push    ax                         ;push offset of String
25       mov     ax, OFFSET DGROUP:strFormat
26       push    ax                         ;push offset of format string
27       call    _printf
28       add     sp, 4                      ;caller must clear args from stack
29
30   ENDM
31
32   ;-------------------------------------------------------------------
33
34   COMMENT     #      MACRO HEADER        FILE: callc.mac
35   MACRO NAME:         printArray
36   PURPOSE:            Prints elements of array of integers in "%8d" format.
37   CALLED AS:          printArray  Array, Size
38   REMARKS:    #       Relies on "screen-wrap" to print integers ten to a line.
39
40   printAry    MACRO  Array, Size
41       LOCAL   printLoop
42
43       EXTRN   _printf:NEAR
44       allocFirst  printArray, <intFormat    DB      "%8d", 0>
45
46       push    si                         ;the C convention is that si and di
47                                          ;  should be preserved by function calls
48       lea     si, Array
49       mov     cx, Size
50
51   printLoop:
52
53       push    cx                         ;because printf() changes it
54       push    [si]                       ;push integer to be printed
```

Figure 14.8 cont.

```
55      mov     ax, OFFSET DGROUP:intFormat
56      push    ax                          ;push offset of format string
57      call    _printf
58      add     sp, 4                       ;caller must clear args from stack
59      inc     si
60      inc     si                          ;point to next array element
61      pop     cx                          ;restore loop counter
62      loop    printLoop
63
64      pop     si                          ;restore si
65
66  ENDM
67
68  ;---------------------------------------------------------------------
69
70  .MODEL SMALL
71
72  .DATA
73
74      Prompt1         DB      LF,LF, "The unsorted array is:", LF, LF, 0
75      Prompt2         DB      LF, LF, "The sorted array is:", LF, LF, 0
76      Array           DW      arySiz DUP(?)
77
78  .CODE
79
80      EXTRN   __astart:NEAR
81      EXTRN   _rand:NEAR, _srand:NEAR, _qsort:NEAR
82
83  _main   PROC    NEAR                    ;C compiler initialization code
84                                          ;   expects program entry point
85      mov     ax, Seed                    ;     to be named main
86      push    ax
87      call    _srand                      ;seed random-number generator
88      add     sp, 2                       ;caller clears arg after return
89
90      mov     cx, arySiz
91      lea     si, OFFSET Array
92
93  fillLoop:                               ;fill Array with random integers >= 0
94
95      push    cx                          ;because C functions do not preserve
96      call    _rand                       ;   registers except for si and di
97      mov     [si], ax
98      inc     si
99      inc     si
100     pop     cx                          ;restore the loop counter
101     loop    fillLoop
102
103     printString Prompt1
104     printAry    Array, arySiz
105
106     mov     ax, OFFSET Compare
107     push    ax                          ;pointer to the Compare function
108     mov     ax, 2
109     push    ax                          ;size of array element = 2 bytes
```

```
110         mov     ax, arySiz
111         push    ax                              ;number of array elements
112         mov     ax, OFFSET Array
113         push    ax                              ;offset of Array
114         call    _qsort
115         add     sp, 8                           ;caller removes 4 args from stack
116
117         printString Prompt2
118         printAry    Array, arySiz
119
120         ret                                     ;_main has no arguments in this case
121                                                 ;  but even if it did this would be
122  _main  ENDP                                    ;     a plain ret since it must use
123                                                 ;        the C convention
124  ;-------------------------------------------------------------------
125
126  Compare PROC    NEAR                            ;must satisfy qsort() requirements:
127                                                 ;  returns pos. value if [bp+4] bigger
128         push    bp                              ;  returns neg. value if [bp+6] bigger
129         mov     bp, sp                          ;  returns zero if inputs equal
130
131         mov     bx, [bp+4]
132         mov     ax, [bx]
133         mov     bx, [bp+6]
134         sub     ax, [bx]                        ;return [bp+4] - [bp+6] since this
135                                                 ;  satisfies the requirements
136         pop     bp
137         ret                                     ;written to be called by qsort(), and
138                                                 ;  so uses the C convention that
139  Compare ENDP                                    ;     caller clears the stack
140
141  ;-------------------------------------------------------------------
142
143         END     __astart
```

```
OUTPUT:

The unsorted array is:

    4068       213     12761      8758     23056      7717     15274     24508      4056     13304
   19945     16918     24771      3983     11618     13621      6668     22019      1112     11675
   17469     31624      3264     31167     16127     16370     10925     17075     20273     21625
    2828         4     21303      3769      6801     25314      4501     19709     26865     31872

The sorted array is:

       4       213      1112      2828      3264      3769      3983      4056      4068      4501
    6668      6801      7717      8758     10925     11618     11675     12761     13304     13621
   15274     16127     16370     16918     17075     17469     19709     19945     20273     21303
   21625     22019     23056     24508     24771     25314     26865     31167     31624     31872
```

- After the call to *printf( )*, the caller clears the stack, in compliance with the C conventions.

- Since the various C models use a DGROUP, we compute the offset relative to DGROUP by using an explicit DGROUP override. Technically, this is not needed in the present program since we are using the simplified segment directives. With the traditional directives, **OFFSET** used without an override evaluates to the offset relative to the start of the segment. In our later examples, we will use the traditional directives and will always include an explicit DGROUP override when the **OFFSET** directive is appears in such a context.

- As is our custom with macro arguments, we use **lea** since this works correctly with respect to groups and since it allows the argument to contain an indirect addressing expression.

The file CALLC.MAC on the Program Disk contains these macros, as well as the later ones that relate to calling **C** from assembly language.

Lines 34-66. This macro calls *printf( )* to print the elements of the array to the screen in the *%8d* format. The standard **C** convention is that the only general-purpose registers that function calls must preserve are **si** and **di**. We observe this convention by saving and restoring **si**. The *printf( )* function does not preserve the value of **cx**, our loop counter, and so we push and pop it during each traverse of the loop.

Line 70. As we have seen earlier, each of the Microsoft high-level languages supports some subset of the basic models. Even when a program uses one of the standard models, it may introduce segments in addition to the standard ones — and the **C** initialization code does this with a vengeance. As the reader can verify from the .MAP file, the assembled version of CALLC1 contains over 20 segments (many of which are empty in the current example). In this vein, notice that this source module contains no stack segment. The **C** initialization code actually defines a stack segment, of default size 2048 bytes. The easiest way of changing the default size is to use the

```
/ST:size
```

switch on the **LINK** command line.

Lines 74-76. These strings will be printed by *printf( )*. We have not written *Prompt1* in the form

```
Prompt1    DB   "\n\nThe unsorted array is:\n\n", 0
```

as is customary in **C** programs. The reason is that escape characters are not interpreted properly when C functions are called from assembly language. We ask the reader to explain why in an exercise at the end of this section.

Line 80. The official entry point of the C initialization code is labeled _astart. Since it is a global identifier, it must be prefixed with an underscore and so — note carefully — we have written it with *two* underscores: __astart. Since we want __astart to also be the entry point of the program, it is used on line 153 in association with the **END** directive. This is the first example we have seen in which the entry point is external to the module containing the **END** directive.

Line 81. We will call these three C library functions in this module. Of course, **LINK** must be able to find these functions (and _astart as well), and so the standard C library must be listed on the **LINK** command line. The choice of library depends on the model being used and on whether **8087** emulation routines are needed. In our examples, the library SLIBCE.LIB is a good choice.

Lines 85-88. This is a typical call to a C library function. As the name suggests, *srand( )* seeds the random-number generator. It expects to receive one argument, the seed, on the stack. On line 88, we remove this argument from the stack, since the C convention requires the caller to clear the stack.

Lines 90-101. Each call to *rand( )*, the random-number generator, returns a non-negative integer in **ax**. We use a loop to fill *Array* with these integers. As we mentioned previously, under the C conventions functions need preserve only two of the general-purpose registers, namely **si** and **di**. Consequently, we must protect our loop counter **cx** from being changed by the calls to *rand( )*, just as we did earlier in the case of *printf( )*.

Lines 106-115. We are going to call the library function

```
void qsort(void *Address, unsigned arySiz, unsigned eltSiz,
           int (*compFunction)(void *, void *))
```

and so must push the four function arguments onto the stack. The most interesting argument is the rightmost one, namely a pointer to a comparison function. Later, we define an appropriate comparison function and push its offset. Again, the caller must clear the stack, this time by removing eight bytes.

Lines 126-137. The comparison function used by *qsort( )* must receive *pointers* to the elements to be compared as inputs, and return a positive answer if the first element is bigger, 0 if the elements are equal, and a negative answer if the second element if bigger. The code for *Compare* was written to satisfy these requirements.

Line 137. Since *Compare* is intended for calling from **C** (i.e. called by *qsort( )*), it also adheres to the C convention that the caller clear the stack.

Our next example program, CALLC2.ASM, is shown in Figure 14.9 and illustrates the use of C library functions to perform floating-point computations.

A very important addition to this program is the new external declaration

```
EITRN   __fltused:NEAR
```

on line 100. The C initialization code performs extensive floating-point initialization, but does so only if at least one module of the program actually does floating-point computation. Including an external declaration for *_fltused* triggers these floating-point initializations. If this declaration is not included, a run-time error will occur and the error message "Floating-point not loaded" will be printed. Again, note the use of a double underscore.

Here are some remarks on CALLC2.ASM:

FIGURE 14.9 CALLING C FLOATING-POINT FUNCTIONS

```
 1    TITLE callc2.asm: calling C library floating-point functions
 2
 3    INCLUDE    console.mac
 4    INCLUDE    callc.mac
 5
 6    ;----------------------------------------------------------------------
 7
 8    COMMENT      #        MACRO HEADER
 9    MACRO NAME:           pushEight              FILE: CALLC.mac
10    PURPOSE:              Pushes eight contiguous bytes onto stack.
11    CALLED AS:            pushEight   memRef
12    REMARK:      #        Mainly used to push a double-precision real onto stack.
13
14    pushEight    MACRO     memRef
15
16        push    WORD PTR memRef[6]
17        push    WORD PTR memRef[4]
18        push    WORD PTR memRef[2]
19        push    WORD PTR memRef
20
21    ENDM
22
23    ;----------------------------------------------------------------------
24
25    COMMENT      #        MACRO HEADER
26    MACRO NAME:           getDouble              FILE: CALLC.mac
27    PURPOSE:              Calls scanf() to input a double-precision real from
28                         STDIN.
29    CALLED AS: #          getDouble  Double
30
31    getDouble    MACRO   Double
32
33        EXTRN   _scanf:NEAR
34        allocFirst  dblFormat, <dblFormat   DB   "%lf", 0>
35
36        lea     ax, Double
37        push    ax
38        mov     ax, OFFSET DGROUP:dblFormat
39        push    ax
40        call    _scanf
41        add     sp, 4
42
43    ENDM
44
45    ;----------------------------------------------------------------------
46
47    COMMENT      #        MACRO HEADER          FILE: CALLC.mac
48    MACRO NAME:           printDouble
49    PURPOSE:              Calls printf() to print a double-precision real to
50                         stdout
51    CALLED AS: #          printDouble  Double
52
53    printDouble  MACRO   Double
54
```

```
55      EXTRN    _printf:NEAR
56      allocFirst    fltFormat, <fltFormat    DB    "%f", 0>
57
58      pushEight  Double
59      mov    ax, OFFSET DGROUP:dblFormat
60      push   ax
61      call   _printf
62      add    sp, 10
63
64  ENDM
65
66  ;------------------------------------------------------------------
67
68  PUBLIC  _main
69
70  DGROUP  GROUP _DATA
71
72  ;------------------------------------------------------------------
73
74  _DATA   SEGMENT  WORD PUBLIC 'DATA'
75
76      Double        DQ      ?
77
78      Prompt        DB      "Input a real number: ", 0
79      ansFormat     DB      "%s(%f) = %f", 0
80
81      funcName0     DB      "sin", 0
82      funcName1     DB      "cos", 0
83      funcName2     DB      "tan", 0
84      funcName3     DB      "exp", 0
85      funcName4     DB      "sqrt", 0
86
87      jumpTable     DW      _sin, _cos, _tan, _exp, _sqrt
88
89      nameOffsets   DW      funcName0, funcName1, funcName2
90                    DW      funcName3, funcName4
91
92  _DATA   ENDS
93
94  ;------------------------------------------------------------------
95
96  _TEXT   SEGMENT  WORD PUBLIC 'CODE'
97
98      ASSUME cs:_TEXT, ds:DGROUP, ss:DGROUP
99
100     EXTRN __astart:NEAR, __fltused:NEAR   ;declaring __fltused as an EXTRN
101                                           ;  causes the floating-point
102                                           ;    initializations to occur
103                                           ;notice the double underscores
104     EXTRN _sin:NEAR, _cos:NEAR, _tan:NEAR, _exp:NEAR, _sqrt:NEAR
105
106 _main   PROC  NEAR                        ;C compiler initialization code
107                                           ;  expects program entry point to
108                                           ;    be named _main
109     printString Prompt
110     getDouble    Double
111     outAsc  NL
```

Figure 14.9 cont.

```
112
113        mov     ax, OFFSET DGROUP:funcName0
114        sub     ax, nameOffsets         ;ax = discrepancy between the offsets
115                                         ;   relative to _DATA and the offsets
116        mov     cx, 5                   ;      relative to DGROUP
117        xor     bx, bx
118
119    @@:
120
121        add     nameOffsets[bx], ax     ;it is necessary to do manual fixups
122        add     bx, 2                   ;  of the entries in the array
123        loop    @B                      ;    nameOffsets
124
125        xor     si, si                  ;use si to index into jumpTable --
126                                         ;  this is a better choice than bx
127    callLoop:                           ;    since it is preserved by C
128                                         ;      functions
129        pushEight Double
130        call    jumpTable[si]           ;the called library function returns
131                                         ;  a pointer to Answer in ax
132        add     sp, 8                   ;caller clears 8 bytes = 1 double
133
134        ;Recall that when a C function returns a long data item it actually
135        ;   returns it by reference. In the SMALL model, this means that
136        ;    it returns the offset in ax. Consequently,
137        mov     bx, ax                  ;points bx to Answer
138
139        pushEight [bx]                  ;push Answer
140        pushEight Double                ;push input argument
141        mov     ax, nameOffsets[si]     ;push pointer to name
142        push    ax                      ;  of function that was called
143        mov     ax, OFFSET DGROUP:ansFormat
144        push    ax
145        call    _printf
146        add     sp, 20                  ;caller clears 20 bytes = 2 eight-byte
147        outAsc  NL                      ;  and two two-byte quantities
148        add     si, 2
149
150        cmp     si, 10                  ;allow for five iterations of callLoop
151        jl      callLoop
152
153        ret                             ;_main has no args in this case but even
154                                         ;  if it did this would be a plain ret
155    _main      ENDP                     ;    to conform to the C convention
156
157    _TEXT      ENDS
158
159    ;------------------------------------------------------------------
160
161    END     __astart
```

SAMPLE OUTPUT

Input a real number: 3.0

```
sin(3.000000) = 0.141120
cos(3.000000) = -0.989992
tan(3.000000) = -0.142547
exp(3.000000) = 20.085537
sqrt(3.000000) = 1.732051
```

Lines 8-19. Pushing a double onto the stack requires pushing a total of eight bytes. Since this operation must be done frequently, it is worth writing a macro to handle it.

Lines 25-64. These macros invoke *scanf( )* and *printf( )*, respectively, to input a double from STDIN or send one to STDOUT. The *scanf( )* function uses an address (i.e., an offset in this context) as its second parameter while *printf( )* requires that the value be passed as the second parameter. Consequently, the *printf( )* call uses the *pushEight* macro, but the *scanf( )* call does not. Each macro ends with the correct adjustment of the stack (lines 41 and 62).

Lines 70, 96, 98. In this program we are using the traditional segment directives. The **SMALL C** model uses a DGROUP consisting of many segments (see the .MAP file). We mention DGROUP (on line 98) and so must define it (on line 70). However, the only segment from DGROUP that is used explicitly in the present module is _DATA and hence we need only give a partial description of DGROUP. Finally, in the **SMALL C** model, **ss** and **ds** both point to DGROUP, and this dictates the form of the assumes on line 98.

Line 87. The program applies the C library functions *sin( )*, *cos( )*, *tan( )*, *exp( )*, and *sqrt( )* to a real value input by the user of the program. The table on line 87 contains the offsets of these functions and so is an "array of (near) pointers to functions."

Lines 113-123. The computation done on these lines seems very clumsy, but it is not clear how to do it more cleanly. An array of the type defined on lines 89-90 actually contains the offsets of the named items. Unfortunately, these offsets are computed relative to the containing segment (_DATA) and the C library functions use offsets relative to DGROUP. We do the required "fixup" at this point in the code: in lines 113-114, we compute the difference between the offset relative to DGROUP and the offset relative to _DATA for the *funcName0* and, on lines 116-123, we add this difference to each element of *nameOffsets*.

Line 137. C functions return values longer than four bytes by reference. In the present context, this means that the offset of such an item is returned in **ax**.

One of the curiosities of calling **C** from assembly language is that it is comparatively hard to access the standard arithmetic operations +, -, *, and / for floating-point numbers. Part of the difficulty is that these operations are performed by explicitly writing the operation in the C code, rather than by calling a named function. In other words, the C code would contain a line such as

$$x + y$$

rather than a line like

```
dubAdd(x, y)
```

Another aspect of the problem is that the **C** initialization code can configure the run-time environment to use a math coprocessor (an **8087**, for example) if one is present or, if no coprocessor is present, code from an *emulation library* will be called to perform the operations. Since the emulation code is much slower than the coprocessor, we would obviously like to take advantage of this flexibility.

We will now sketch briefly how the **C** initialization code sets up the run-time environment in order to make this choice at run time, and in the program CALLC3.ASM, shown in Figure 14.10, apply the method in an assembly language program. It is also possible to have **MASM** attend to some of the details automatically (by using the /E command-line switch — see Section 2 of Chapter 17).

Completely understanding the techniques used by the initialization code and by CALLC3.ASM requires some familiarity with the material from the beginnings of Chapters 15 and 17. However, the following outline should convey the general ideas.

First of all, the Intel numerical processors use an *operand stack* in performing arithmetic operations. Here is a typical sequence of coprocessor instructions:

```
fld  Op1 ;loads Op1 onto coprocessor stack
fadd Op2 ;replaces Op1 on coprocessor stack with Op1 + Op2
fstp Op3 ;pops sum from coprocessor stack and stores
         ;  it in location given by Op3
```

To perform a floating-point addition, we must incorporate such a triple of instructions into the code. The macros on lines 16-72 of CALLC3.ASM accomplish this task, not just for addition, but for all four basic operations. As well as the basic triple of instructions, the macros arrange for an **fwait** instruction (lines 40-46). Understand the significance of this instruction is not important at the moment.

The trick used to make the run-time decision on whether to use a coprocessor or emulation code involves the use of self-modifying code. Here is the approximate sequence of events:

- A coprocessor instruction occurring in the machine code causes a certain interrupt handler to be called.

- That interrupt has been taken over by the initialization code.

- The exact function performed by this interrupt is determined at run-time and depends on whether or not a coprocessor is present. If no coprocessor is present, the interrupt invokes code from an emulator library. If a coprocessor is present, the interrupt handler passes control to the coprocessor.

The **CODEVIEW** screens in Figure 14.11 show the details of this process. The machine code contains the correct code bytes for the coprocessor instruction, but the beginning of the instruction has been overwritten with the code for the interrupt in question (that happens to be CD39, or **int 39H** in the example). If a coprocessor were not present, the **int 39H** code would not modify the damaged instruction. Rather, it would call the emulation code and then return control to the next instruction — the line

```
INT 38 ;FADD
```

FIGURE 14.10 FLOATING-POINT EMULATION

```
1   TITLE   Callc3.asm:  emulating the floating-point arithmetic operations
2
3   INCLUDE   console.mac
4   INCLUDE   callc.mac
5
6   ;-------------------------------------------------------------------
7
8   COMMENT       #       MACRO HEADER        FILE: CALLC.mac
9   MACRO NAME:           floatOp, flAdd, flSub, flMul, flDiv
10  PURPOSE:              Generate code that calls the 8087 if it is present and
11                        calls emulator routines if it is not.
12  CALLED AS:            flAdd  doubleAns, doubleFirst, doubleSecond
13                        and similarly for the others.
14  REMARK:       #       Generates self-modifying code.
15
16  floatOp  MACRO   Op,  Answer, First, Second
17      LOCAL   Begin, End
18
19      Begin1 =        $
20      fld     First                   ;generate machine code for this instruction
21      End     =       $
22      ORG     Begin1
23      int     39h                     ;overwrite the first two bytes of above
24      ORG     End                     ;  instruction with code for int 39h
25                                      ;    (i.e., with CD39H)
26      Begin   =       $
27      Op      Second                  ;repeat previous sequence but this time
28      End     =       $               ;  use the input value of Op and
29      ORG     Begin                   ;    int 38h
30      int     38h
31      ORG     End
32
33      Begin   =       $
34      fstp    Answer                  ;again, repeat with the indicated
35      End     =       $               ;  modifications
36      ORG     Begin
37      int     39h
38      ORG     End
39
40      Begin   =       $
41      nop                             ;once more, essentially the same operation
42      fwait                           ;this time, the fwait code is only one byte
43      End     =       $               ;  and so the nop is required to make space
44      ORG     Begin                   ;    for the int 3dh
45      int     3dh
46      ORG     End
47
48  ENDM
49
50  flAdd   MACRO Answer, First, Second
51
52      floatOp  fadd, <Answer>, <First>, <Second>
53
54  ENDM
```

Figure 14.10 cont.

```
 55
 56  flSub   MACRO Answer, First, Second
 57
 58      floatOp  fsub, <Answer>, <First>, <Second>
 59
 60  ENDM
 61
 62  flDiv   MACRO Answer, First, Second
 63
 64      floatOp  fdiv, <Answer>, <First>, <Second>
 65
 66  ENDM
 67
 68  flMul   MACRO Answer, First, Second
 69
 70      floatOp  fmul, <Answer>, <First>, <Second>
 71
 72  ENDM
 73
 74  ;----------------------------------------------------------------------
 75
 76  DGROUP   GROUP  _DATA
 77
 78  PUBLIC   _main
 79
 80  ;----------------------------------------------------------------------
 81
 82  _DATA    SEGMENT  WORD PUBLIC 'DATA'
 83
 84      Answer       DQ      0.0
 85      First        DQ      5.0
 86      Second       DQ      8.0
 87
 88  _DATA    ENDS
 89
 90  ;----------------------------------------------------------------------
 91
 92  _TEXT    SEGMENT  WORD PUBLIC 'CODE'
 93
 94      ASSUME cs:_TEXT, ds:DGROUP, ss:DGROUP
 95
 96      EXTRN __astart:NEAR, __fltused:NEAR
 97
 98  _main   PROC  NEAR
 99
100      flAdd Answer, First, Second
101      printDouble First
102      outAsc " + "
103      printDouble Second
104      outAsc " = "
105      printDouble Answer
106      outAsc NL
107
108      flSub Answer, First, Second
109      printDouble First
```

```
110         outAsc " - "
111         printDouble Second
112         outAsc " = "
113         printDouble Answer
114         outAsc NL
115
116         flMul Answer, First, Second
117         printDouble First
118         outAsc " * "
119         printDouble Second
120         outAsc " = "
121         printDouble Answer
122         outAsc NL
123
124         flDiv Answer, First, Second
125         printDouble First
126         outAsc " / "
127         printDouble Second
128         outAsc " = "
129         printDouble Answer
130         outAsc NL
131
132         ret
133
134  _main        ENDP
135
136  _TEXT        ENDS
137
138  ;-------------------------------------------------------------
139
140  END     __astart


OUTPUT:

5.000000 + 8.000000 = 13.000000
5.000000 - 8.000000 = -3.000000
5.000000 * 8.000000 = 40.000000
5.000000 / 8.000000 = 0.625000
```

on our **CODEVIEW** screen. If a coprocessor is present, the **int 39H** handler "repairs" the coprocessor instruction and returns control to that point in the code so that the coprocessor instruction executes. This is the situation illustrated in our sample **CODEVIEW** screens: the top view shows the damaged coprocessor instruction and the bottom view shows it after it has been repaired.

The code in CALLC3.ASM needs little additional commentary. One small point concerns lines 84-86. If a datum is defined by a **DQ** and given an initializer containing a decimal point, then **MASM** will initialize it to the bit pattern representing that real value in the standard IEEE encoding of double-precison real numbers (which we will define in Chapter 17).

Exercise 14-8. Fix the *printAry* macro in CALLC1 so that it does not rely on screen-wrap to supply newlines. Check that your repair works by running the program with output redirected to a file that you later view using a text editor.

FIGURE 14.11 GENERATION OF EMULATION CODE

```
#File  View  Search  Run  Watch  Options  Language  Calls  Help # F8=Trace F5=Go
############################# callc3.ASM #############################
0)  first  :  5.0000000000000                                       # AX = 120D
1)  second :  8.0000000000000                                       # BX = 1258
2)  answer :  0.00000000000000                                      # CX = 0022
####################################################################### DX = 0026
118:        FLADD Answer, First, Second                             SP = 124C
531C:001B CD39064A00     INT      39 ;FLD      QWord Ptr [004A]     # BP = 124C
531C:0020 CD38065200     INT      38 ;FADD     QWord Ptr [0052]     # SI = 0082
531C:0025 CD391E4200     INT      39 ;FSTP     QWord Ptr [0042]     # DI = 127C
531C:002A CD3D           INT      3D ;FWAIT                         # DS = 5803
119:        PRINTDOUBLE First                                       # ES = 5803
531C:002C FF365000       PUSH     Word Ptr [0050]                   # SS = 5803
531C:0030 FF364E00       PUSH     Word Ptr [004E]                   # CS = 531C
531C:0034 FF364C00       PUSH     Word Ptr [004C]                   # IP = 001B
531C:0038 FF364A00       PUSH     Word Ptr [004A]                   #
531C:003C B85A00         MOV      AX,005A                           #   NV UP
531C:003F 50             PUSH     AX                                #   EI PL
531C:0040 E81D09         CALL     _PRINTF (0960)                    #   ZR NA
531C:0043 83C40A         ADD      SP,+0A                                PE NC
#######################################################################
>w? first                                                          DS:004A
>w? second                                                         #  00000000
>w? answer                                                         #
>

#File  View  Search  Run  Watch  Options  Language  Calls  Help # F8=Trace F5=Go
############################# callc3.ASM #############################
0)  first  :  5.0000000000000                                       # AX = 120D
1)  second :  8.0000000000000                                       # BX = 1258
2)  answer :  0.00000000000000                                      # CX = 0022
####################################################################### DX = 0026
118:        FLADD Answer, First, Second                             SP = 124C
531C:001B 90             NOP                                        # BP = 124C
531C:001C DD064A00       FLD      QWord Ptr [004A]                  # SI = 0082
531C:0020 CD38065200     INT      38 ;FADD     QWord Ptr [0052]     # DI = 127C
531C:0025 CD391E4200     INT      39 ;FSTP     QWord Ptr [0042]     # DS = 5803
531C:002A CD3D           INT      3D ;FWAIT                         # ES = 5803
```

Exercise 14-9. CALLC2 has an intriguing bug. When the input is a relatively short file and the output is redirected, all the newlines get printed before any of the text.

a. Explain this phenomenon.

b. Fix the bug the easy way, namely by using *printf( )* rather than *outAsc* to print the newlines.

c. (Harder) Fix the bug the interesting way, namely by interpolating a call to an appropriate function from the C library that will ensure that the code, as written, will execute correctly.

Exercise 14-10. Rewrite CALLC1.ASM so that it sorts an array of doubles rather than an array of integers.

Exercise 14-11. In the text we make the point that C functions called from assembly language will not correctly interpret escape sequences. Explain why this is the case.

Exercise 14-12. Rewrite our line-numbering utility (PROG8_5.ASM) so that, instead of parsing the command line itself, it uses the C language *argc* and *argv* variables.

Exercise 14-13. Run CALLC3 under **CODEVIEW** on a machine with a coprocessor and again on a machine without a coprocessor. Trace through enough of the **int 39H** code to see that different handler code is executed in each case. Check that, while the original source code is indeed modified as shown in the text in the coprocessor case, it is left unchanged when no coprocessor is present.

SECTION 7 THE MAKE UTILITY

The operations involved in building a program consisting of a sizable number of modules can be quite tedious. **MASM, LINK,** various compilers, and perhaps other utilities must be called, all with their correct (and usually impossible to remember) command line syntax.

When some of the constituent modules are changed, it is desirable to carry out the minimum number of reassembly and other operations needed to bring the whole system up to date. For example, if a single assembly language module is changed in a system made up of 100 separate modules, then it would be ludicrous to go through the reassembling and recompiling steps for all 100 modules. Obviously, it suffices to reassemble the single changed module and relink it with the 99 unchanged modules to produce an updated version of the entire program.

But this idea of minimal updating of a system of modules can be fraught with danger. For example, what if an **INCLUDE** file is changed that happens to be used in 17 **MASM** modules? It is important that all 17 of these be reassembled. Depending on the circumstances, forgetting to update one of them, so that 16 of the modules are in the new form and one is still in the old form, can introduce a really subtle bug into the program.

What is needed, of course, is a means of automatically performing the minimum set of updating operations, and this is precisely the service that the **MAKE** utility performs.

The principle of operation of **MAKE** is simple. The programmer must provide a specially formatted file called a *makefile*, or *dependency file*, that gives **MAKE** information about which program modules depend on which others and what should be done to update a dependent module when one of the modules on which it depends is changed. **MAKE** determines when a file was most recently changed by consulting the time stamp that the operating system keeps as part of the directory entry for each file (see Section 3 of Chapter 16). If module B depends on A and module A has a more recent time stamp than B, then B is considered to be out of date with respect to A, and **MAKE** does all the operations needed to update B.

We will not give the detailed syntax used in makefiles, especially since we will shortly present a utility to construct them automatically. Figure 14.12 is an example of a makefile that can be used to build the version of our program consisting of the modules PROG14_1.C, PROG14_2.ASM, and the include file CONSOLE.MAC.

FIGURE 14.12 A SIMPLE MAKEFILE

```
1    #Prog14_1 : A Primitive Makefile for Building prog14_1.exe
2
3    Prog14_1.obj :   prog14_1.c
4                     qcl /c /AS /W3 /Zi $*.c
5
6    Prog14_2.obj :   prog14_2.asm \masm\incl\console.mac
7                     masm /Zi /Z /W2 /Mx $*,,,;
8
9    Prog14_1.exe : prog14_1.obj prog14_2.obj
10          link /Co /NOI prog14_1.obj prog14_2.obj,,,user;
```

Here is a quick survey of the information in Figure 14.12. A block such as lines 6 and 7 is called a *dependency*. Line 6 says that PROG14_2.OBJ depends on PROG14_2.ASM and \MASM\INCL\CONSOLE.MAC. (**MAKE** must be given the complete path specification for includes.) Line 7 gives the operation needed to update PROG14_2.OBJ. The text "$*" is an example of a **MAKE** macro. This particular macro, which is built into **MAKE**, means the base name of the target, i.e., PROG14_2. Hence line 7 translates as a standard call to **MASM**. Lines 3 and 4 are analogous: they contain the information that PROG14_1.OBJ depends on PROG14_1.C and the operation needed to update PROG14_1.OBJ with respect to PROG14_1.C is a call to the **QuickC** compiler. Lines 9 and 10 are interpreted similarly, except that on line 10, the built-in **MAKE** macros "$**" and "$@" are used. "$**" means the complete list of sources, i.e., PROG14_1.OBJ and PROG14_2.OBJ, and "$@" means the name of the target of the dependency rule, or PROG14_1.EXE. Remembering that the name entered as the second parameter on the **LINK** command line becomes the name of the constructed .EXE file, we see that line 10 is just a standard call to **LINK**.

Since the makefile will be stored on the disk, it must be given a filename. Many people just name it *MAKEFILE*, but it is probably better to give it a name that associates it with the .EXE file being built. One reasonable convention, which we adopt, is to give the makefile the base name of the .EXE file (with no extension).

The command-line syntax for **MAKE** is simply

MAKE *makeFileName*

which, if our naming convention is used for *makeFileName*, becomes

```
make prog14_1
```

in the present example.

The reader should execute this command before reading further. If the working directory contains PROG14_1.C, PROG14_2.ASM, and the makefile PROG14_1, and if it does not contain either of the .OBJ files (so that all the operations in the makefile must be performed), then the preceding command line should result in **MASM**, the **QuickC** compiler, and **LINK** each being called once, and PROG14_1.EXE should be constructed. As **MAKE** calls the various utilities, it reports its progress on the screen.

Figure 14.13 shows three versions of the makefile needed for the construction of PROG14_1.EXE, but this time replaces PROG14_2.ASM by MULTIPLE.ASM, which is shown in Figure 14.7.

The makefile named Version1 in PROG14_1 shows the requisite calls to **QuickC**, **MASM**, and **LINK**. **MASM** is called with the command-line switch (/DLANG=C) that is needed to trigger the assembly of the correct C-to-assembly-language interface code.

The makefile named Version2 demonstrates the definition and use of user-defined macros. The form of a **MAKE** macro is

macroName = String

Everything on the line after the '=', beginning with the first character other than white space, is part of the macro substitution string. If only white space occurs on the line after the '=', then the substitution string is considered to be the empty string (no characters at all). Whenever **MAKE** sees an occurrence of the text *$(macroName)*, it substitutes a copy of the macro substitution string.

Three macros are defined in Version2. The macro *MFLAGS* contains various command-line switches to be used by **MASM**. *MDEFS* provides a value for *DLANG*. Finally, *MINC* gives **MAKE** the path specification for **INCLUDE** files. Although the names of these macros are arbitrary, they seem as mnemonic as any, and we will always use them.

Version2 is purely transitional. It involves much more writing than Version1 and offers no extra capabilities. However, it does pave the way for Version3. One of the most interesting things about **MAKE** macros is that, when faced with a macro invocation such as *$(macroName)*, **MAKE** looks for the definition of *macroName* in three places:

- On the **MAKE** command line.

- In the makefile.

- As a string in the machine environment.

The search is conducted in the order given, and when **MAKE** finds one definition of *macroName*, it looks no further. An important ramification of this search order is that *macroName* can be initialized using an environment string, and this initialization can be overridden either in the makefile or from the command line, or both. If it is overridden in both locations, the command-line override carries the day. Incidentally, if **MAKE** finds no definition of *macroName* in any of these three places, it substitutes the empty string.

To use **MAKE**'s search technique to best advantage, the desired defaults should be placed in the environment. The easiest way to do this is by including these lines in the AUTOEXEC.BAT file:

```
set MFLAGS=/Zi /Z /W2 /Mx
set MDEFS=
set MINC=\masm\incl
set QFLAGS=/AS /Zi /W3
set QDEFS=
set LFLAGS=/CO
```

FIGURE 14.13 THREE MORE MAKEFILES

```
prog14_1: Version1

 1   # MAKEFILE FOR PROG14_1.EXE
 2
 3   multiple.obj:  multiple.asm \masm\incl\console.mac
 4           masm /Zi /Z /W2 /Mx /DLANG=C $*,,,;
 5
 6   prog14_1.obj:  prog14_1.c
 7           qcl /c /Zi /W3 $*.c
 8
 9   prog14_1.exe:  prog14_1.obj multiple.obj
10           link /CO /NOI $**,$@,,user;


prog14_1: Version2

 1   # MAKEFILE FOR PROG14_1.EXE
 2
 3   MFLAGS      =/Zi /Z /W2 /Mx
 4   MDEFS       =/DLANG=C
 5   MINC        =\masm\incl
 6
 7   QFLAGS      = /c /Zi /W3
 8   QDEFS       =
 9
10   LFLAGS      =/CO /NOI
11
12   multiple.obj:  multiple.asm $(MINC)\console.mac
13           masm $(MFLAGS) $(MDEFS) $*,,,;
14
14   prog14_1.obj:  prog14_1.c
16           qcl $(QFLAGS) $(QDEFS) $*.c
17
18   prog14_1.exe:  prog14_1.obj multiple.obj
19           link $(LFLAGS) $**,$@,,user;


prog14_1: Version 3

 1   # MAKEFILE FOR PROG14_1.EXE
 2
 3   multiple.obj:  multiple.asm $(MINC)\console.mac
 4           masm $(MFLAGS) $(MDEFS) $*,,,;
 5
 6   prog14_1.obj:  prog14_1.c
 7           qcl /c $(QFLAGS) $*.c
 8
 9   prog14_1.exe:  prog14_1.obj multiple.obj
10           link $(LFLAGS) $**,$@,,user;
```

Notice that we have left "MDEFS" empty, so that the default action causes **MASM** to generate object modules that are correct for use in pure assembly language programs. Of course, the exact form of the defaults will depend to some extent on the user's preferences, and on the C compiler being used.

If "MDEFS" is defaulted to be the empty string, as we are suggesting, then the use of Version3 of the makefile necessitates assigning a value to "MDEFS" by one of the other two methods: either by using a command line of the form

```
make MDEFS=/DLANG=C prog14_1
```

(which, incidentally, shows the syntax used to set a macro definition from the **MAKE** command line) or else by including a line such as

```
DLANG    EQU    <C>
```

in the source file.

It is probably clear by now that the construction of a makefile for a multi-module program is not a terribly pleasant task. The labor can be lessened by the judicious use of macros and *generic dependencies*, which we will introduce presently. General information can also be made available to **MAKE** by storing it in the file TOOLS.INI. For a discussion of this file, we refer the reader to the **MAKE** documentation.

We have personally found it easier to write a utility that will automatically build makefiles. This utility is called MMF (*makeMakeFile*) and a copy is on the Program Disk. It builds makefiles that are somewhat more elaborate than the one discussed previously. Figure 14.14 contains an example of a makefile produced by MMF.

During the construction of the makefile in Figure 14.14, MMF automatically copied lines 5-10 from the environment. MMF was constructed up to operate in this fashion since it is frequently desirable to temporarily change one or more of these default macros. Making changes in the macros by altering the AUTOEXEC.BAT is slow, especially since AUTOEXEC must then be rerun to permit the operating system to record the changes. In addition, since the changes are temporary, AUTOEXEC.BAT will ultimately need to be restored to its original form. The changes can be made on the command line, but if the makefile is run many times during the development of a program, this can be quite arduous. The best solution is to copy these macros into the makefile, as MMF does, and then to customize the makefile as needed by hand-editing it.

Lines 14-17 are included as documentation. Line 18 also serves as documentation, but in addition it is used on line 28.

The file @MAKEFILE.LNK appearing on line 29 has nothing to do with **MAKE**. It shows an example of a *linker response file*, which is used to circumvent the **MS-DOS** 127-character command-line limit. From time to time, it is necessary to link a list of .OBJ files that is so long that this command-line length limit is exceeded. The linker response file provides a (very clumsy) method of coping with this situation. Clearly, the response file is not necessary in this example, but in writing MMF, it was easier to have it generate such a file by default, rather than making the requisite analysis in each case to find out whether one is really needed. For the details on response files, see the **LINK** documentation. It is not necessary to know about them in order to use MMF.

FIGURE 14.14 MAKEFILE CONSTRUCTED BY MMF

prog14_1: Makefile for prog14_1.exe Generated by the MMF Utility

```
 1   # MAKEFILE FOR PROG14_1
 2
 3   # FLAGS FROM ENVIRONMENT
 4
 5   MFLAGS  =   /Zi /Z /W2/Mx
 6   MDEFS   =
 7   MINC    =   \masm\incl
 8   QFLAGS  =   /AS /Zi /W3
 9   QDEFS   =
10   LFLAGS  =   /CO /NOI
11
12   # PROGRAM COMPONENTS
13
14   INCS    =   $(MINC)\console.mac
15   SRCS    =   multiple.asm prog14_1.c
16   ASMS    =   multiple.asm
17   CS      =   prog14_1.c
18   OBJS    =   multiple.obj prog14_1.obj
19
20   # DEPENDENCY LINES
21
22   multiple.obj  : $(MINC)\console.mac
23
24   prog14_1.obj  :
25
26   # TARGETS
27
28   prog14_1.exe : $(OBJS)
29        link /Co @makefile.lnk, $@, $*.map, user;
30
31   # BUILTINS
32
33   .c.obj :
34        qcl /c $(QFLAGS) $(QDEFS) $*.c
35
36   .asm.obj :
37        masm    $(MFLAGS) $(MDEFS) $*,,,;
38
39   .exe.com :
40        exe2bin $*.exe $@
41        del $*.exe
```

Lines beginning with '#' are comments in the makefile and are, of course, included only as documentation.

Finally, blocks such as lines 33-34 are called *generic dependencies*. MAKE interprets lines 33 and 34 as follows: given a pair of files FILENAME.C and FILENAME.OBJ having the same basename, then FILENAME.OBJ depends on FILENAME.C and the updating process is delineated on line 34. This generic dependency makes it unnecessary to record with the .OBJ form of each .C file the information that it depends on the corresponding .C

— the generic dependency says it once and for all. Compare the dependencies in Figure 14.14 with those in Figure 14.13.

Lines 39-41 give another example of a generic dependency, showing how to build a .COM file from a .EXE. This dependency is not needed in the present makefile, but when MMF sees a .ASM in the SRC list (the sources) it prints all its generic dependencies relating to .ASM files. MMF handles its generic dependencies associated with C modules in an analogous way.

Constructing makefiles with MMF is very easy. Here are the basic rules:

- Default values for MFLAGS, MDEFS, etc., should be set in the environment.

- The system time and date should be correct.

- Each multi-module program should be constructed in its own subdirectory. This local subdirectory should contain all the .ASM and .C modules entering into this program, and should contain no other files with these extensions. All C header files included with the directive

```
#include "fileName"
```

should also be in the local directory. All files that MASM will include using

```
INCLUDE fileName
```

should be on the path given by the environment variable MINC.

- The command line

MMF *execBaseName* > *makeFileName*

causes MMF to build a makefile. MMF assumes that all local .ASM's and .C's are intended as modules in the completed program. It searches these files, looking for occurrences of **INCLUDE** and #include directives and makes the included files part of the dependency lists. (MMF does not call itself recursively and so misses "nested includes," i.e., files that are included by means of **INCLUDE** directives that are themselves contained in include files.) It names the final target file EXECBASENAME.EXE and names the makefile MAKEFILENAME. Hence, an appropriate MMF command line for our present example is

```
mmf prog14_1 > prog14_1
```

- As soon as the makefile has been constructed, **MAKE** can be called using the command line

MAKE [*Options*] [*Defines*] *MakefileName*

FIGURE 14.15 RUNNING MAKE WITH THE /N SWITCH

```
Microsoft (R) Program Maintenance Utility  Version 4.07
Copyright (C) Microsoft Corp 1984-1988.  All rights reserved.

MAKE : warning U4000: 'multiple.obj' : target does not exist

   masm   /Zi /Z /W2 /Mx /DLANG=C multiple,,,;
MAKE : warning U4000: 'prog14_1.obj' : target does not exist

   qcl /c /Zi /W3  prog14_1.c
MAKE : warning U4001: dependent 'multiple.obj' does not exist; target
'prog14_1.exe' not built
```

In our present example, this becomes

```
make MDEFS=/DLANG=C prog14_1
```

The reader should consult the **MAKE** documentation for a list of the available options. One option worth remembering is /N (*no execution*). It causes **MAKE** to list the commands that it would issue without actually calling any utilities and is very useful in debugging recalcitrant makefiles.

For example, in the present context, if we use the command line

```
make /N MDEFS=/DLANG=C prog14_1
```

and if neither of the .OBJ files has yet been constructed, then **MAKE** produces the output shown in Figure 14.15.

The warnings about targets not existing on the first run of **MAKE** are normal. In Figure 14.15, **MAKE** also refuses to build the .EXE file since the corresponding .OBJ files do not exist — the commands to build these components were just listed, not executed.

It can be argued that none of the multi-module programs in this book is complicated enough to really require the services of **MAKE**. But **MAKE** is one of the most powerful weapons available to the programmer — it is surely one of the most significant programming utilities ever written — and so every programmer should be well acquainted with it. The best way to learn the quirks of **MAKE** is to begin using it in relatively uncomplicated situations. When combined with MMF, the overhead in using **MAKE** is minimal.

Clearly, if a program consists of a single file, it is fairly pointless to use **MAKE**. But our recommendation is that every program that consists of at least two modules should be built in its own subdirectory and constructed with the help of MMF and **MAKE**.

CHAPTER 15

INTERRUPT HANDLERS AND MEMORY-RESIDENT PROGRAMS

SECTION 1 PREVIEW

In this chapter we will study the interrupt system of the **IBM-XT** in detail and, in the process, come to understand much more clearly how the machine works.

We begin, in Section 2, by clarifying the distinction between processor exceptions and hardware and software interrupts, and go on to discuss the Programmable Interrupt Controller.

In Section 3, we present macros that can be used to "take over" an interrupt and provide an example of this process.

Many of the difficulties involved in programming the **IBM-XT** stem from the failure of **MS-DOS** to build separate stack frames when various interrupts and **int 21H** functions are simultaneously active. This situation, which we examined in Section 10 of Chapter 6, is usually referred to as the *reentrancy problem*. A number of fairly successful techniques are available to help solve this problem, and these are discussed in Section 4. In addition, Section 4 contains a major example in the form of a memory-resident program that changes the operation of the Shift-PrtSc key combination so that, instead of performing its default action of dumping the screen to the printer, it sends a copy of the screen to a disk file. This example must circumvent the reentrancy problem.

Section 5 gives another example, this time of the "pop-up" variety. It is again a memory-resident program and it responds to the press of a particular key combination by displaying on the screen the contents of an information file that is kept stored in memory.

Our last example, contained in Section 6, is a rudimentary execution profiler. This program is especially interesting for a number of reasons: it involves programming the hardware in a non-trivial way; it is a very natural two-module hybrid using C and assembly language; and it provides a utility that can be used to analyze and improve the operation of other programs.

SECTION 2 THE INTERRUPT STRUCTURE OF THE IBM-XT

The term *interrupt* is used in three rather different contexts:

- The *software interrupts*, of which **int 21H** is the most familiar example, provide a mechanism whereby the programmer can use the **int** instruction to access blocks of code that already exist and are resident in machine memory.

- The *hardware interrupts* are triggered by hardware events external to the microprocessor, rather than resulting from an **int** or any other instruction.

- The *exceptions* are also of hardware origin, but these originate within the microprocessor itself.

Hardware interrupts normally represent requests for service by external devices such as disk drives. Exceptions are frequently triggered by some anomalous event within a program, such as an attempt to divide by zero or, in the case of the **80286** or **80386**, by a violation of the protection mechanism.

Software interrupts and exceptions result from particular instructions within an executing program or from the state of the microprocessor during program execution. Consequently, if the program is executed again, they will reoccur exactly as before and, for this reason, they are usually said to be *synchronous*. Since hardware interrupts originate outside the program and the microprocessor, their occurrence is, to a degree, independent of the executing program, whence they may not repeat with the same pattern when the program is rerun. For this reason, hardware interrupts are said to be asynchronous. The term *asynchronous* should be interpreted with caution. For example, the interrupt that updates the system clock is totally independent of the executing program, while the interrupts relating to the disk drives are generally instigated by program instructions and are therefore normally synchronous with the program execution.

In Table 15.1, the exceptions are **int 00H**, **int 01H**, **int 03H**, and **int 04H**. Here are brief descriptions:

As we have seen already, **int 00H** is the *divide-overflow interrupt*. It occurs whenever an attempt is made to divide by zero, or when the microprocessor detects that the answer produced by a division operation would be too large to fit in its allotted register. The default interrupt handler for **int 00H** aborts the executing program.

Int 01H, the *single-step interrupt*, is used by debuggers. If the trap flag is set, the microprocessor executes a single instruction and then generates an **int 01H**. The default interrupt handler is just an **iret** (return from interrupt), and so does nothing. A debugger must "take over" this interrupt, replacing the default handler with a new one that will do the things a debugger should: print information, such as the register values, to the screen, and allow user input, before allowing another instruction to execute.

TABLE 15.1 EXCEPTIONS AND HARDWARE INTERRUPTS

INTERRUPT NUMBER	INTERRUPT NAME
00H	Divide by zero
01H	Single step
02H	Non-maskable interrupt
03H	Breakpoint trap
04H	Overflow trap
05H	Print screen
06H	Unused
07H	Unused
08H	Timer tick (IRQ0)
09H	Keyboard (IRQ1)
0AH	Reserved (IRQ2)
0BH	COM2 (IRQ3)
0CH	COM1 (IRQ4)
0DH	Fixed disk (IRQ5)
0EH	Floppy disk (IRQ6)
0FH	Printer (IRQ7)

Int 03H, the *breakpoint trap*, is also used by debuggers. Whereas the other interrupts are represented by two bytes of machine code, **int 03H** translates into a single machine code byte, namely 0CCH. At any location in the code where a breakpoint has been requested, the debugger replaces the existing byte of code with 0CCH. When the microprocessor encounters this special byte, it activates **int 03H**. Again, the default handler for **int 03H** consists only of an **iret**, and so must be replaced with a handler designed to take appropriate action.

Int 04H is called the *overflow interrupt*. It is executed whenever the overflow flag is set *and* an **into** instruction is encountered. This allows *trapping* instances of overflow. By placing an **into** instruction at any location in the code, the programmer can arrange to have control transfer to **int 04H** if overflow occurs at that point. Once again, the default handler consists of an **iret** instruction. Of course, the programmer should decide on the required overflow response in a given program, and replace the standard **int 04H** handler with a new one delivering this result. In Section 3, we will show how to replace an interrupt handler, using **int 04H** as an example.

The hardware interrupts are of two types, the non-maskable interrupt and the maskable interrupts.

The *non-maskable interrupt* (*NMI*), which is **int 02H**, occurs when a particular pin (number 17) on the **8088** goes high. It is used to signal some hardware catastrophe, and the default response is to halt the machine. In the standard **IBM-XT** architecture, **int 02H** is initiated by a memory parity-check error, although it is sometimes put to additional uses by the vendors of peripheral cards. In a few paragraphs, we will explain why this interrupt is called non-maskable.

All other hardware interrupts in the **IBM-XT** are referred to as *maskable*. The maskable interrupts are those numbered 08H-0FH in Table 15.1, and their names indicate their uses.

The maskable interrupts are administered by the **8259A** *programmable interrupt controller* (*PIC*) *chip*. Many aspects of the PIC behavior can be controlled by the programmer. For example, it is possible to "mask off" any subset of the interrupts that the PIC controls, so that these will be ignored. This is, of course, the genesis of the name maskable interrupts. Likewise, it explains why the non-maskable interrupt is called by that name: it is not under the control of the PIC, and cannot be masked. For information on programming the PIC, we refer the reader to [19].

The devices that the PIC services connect to it by means of *interrupt request lines*, and these are given names IRQ0-IRQ7. Table 15.1 indicates which lines are associated with which devices.

Here is a general description of how a device connected to the PIC obtains interrupt service:

- It signals the PIC using its IRQ line.

- The PIC checks on whether this line is "masked off" and, if so, ignores the request.

- If the line is not masked off, the PIC signals the **8088** that it requires service by causing the voltage on a certain pin (INTR, for *interrupt request*) to go high.

- The **8088** checks whether the interrupt flag is set, i.e., whether interrupts are enabled. If not, it ignores the request; if so, it processes the request by calling the appropriate interrupt handler.

There are many other important aspects to the servicing of interrupts. For example, if data are arriving at a communications port, say **COM2**, at a rapid rate, then each byte must be processed before the next one arrives; otherwise, data will be lost. Consequently, the interrupt handler associated with **COM2** must be fast enough to keep up with the incoming data. But there is another potential problem, namely that interrupts can themselves be interrupted by other interrupts. Even if our hypothetical **COM2** handler were very fast, it might still be interrupted by a slow floppy disk handler, with resulting loss of data.

The **8259A** partially solves this problem by *prioritizing* the interrupts. This means that the interrupts controlled by the PIC are given priorities, with a lower-number interrupt always having higher priority than a higher number one. A higher-priority interrupt can interrupt a lower-priority one but not conversely. In Table 15.1, the lower numbers in the range 08H-015H are generally associated with situations where the handler must respond more quickly.

In addition, it is possible to inhibit the maskable interrupts by clearing the interrupt flag. But remember — the interrupt flag affects only the maskable interrupts. There are various reasons why the interrupt flag should not be left cleared for too long a period. For example, one of the maskable interrupts is the clock interrupt, **int 08H**. This interrupt occurs approximately 18.2 times per second and is responsible for maintaining the system clock. Consequently, one effect of leaving the interrupt flag cleared is that the system clock will run slow.

Another interesting aspect of the interrupt structure relates to instructions that **mov** or **pop** a segment register. After such an instruction, the **8088** will not recognize an interrupt until another instruction has been executed. This protective mechanism is built into the **8088** for the following reason. There are times when a program must change to a temporary stack, and such a change is easily accomplished by changing **ss** and **sp** to point to the new stack location. Suppose that **ss** had already been changed, but not **sp**, when an interrupt occurred. The interrupt mechanism saves the return address by pushing it onto the stack and the interrupt handler itself will almost certainly try to make use of the stack (to save registers, for example). But, at this point, **ss** would contain the new stack segment address, while **sp** would still contain the old stack offset location, and so disaster would inevitably result. The protective mechanism renders this situation impossible *provided* the programmer remembers this rule:

- When changing **ss** and **sp** to point to a new stack, always change **ss** first and change **sp** in the immediately following instruction.

An appropriate sequence of instructions is

```
mov    ax, newSS
mov    ss, ax
mov    sp, newSP
```

This protective mechanism has an amusing manifestation that can be observed when **CODEVIEW** is being used. For example, suppose the code under analysis contains the instruction sequence

```
mov    ax, 40h
mov    ds, ax
mov    bx, 31h
mov    ax, [bx]
```

If this code is executed in **CODEVIEW** using the trace (F8) command, the third instruction appears to be omitted. In other words, immediately after executing the second instruction, **CODEVIEW** seems to jump directly to the fourth instruction. The reason is that the interrupts, including **int 01H**, are inhibited after the second instruction, and consequently **CODEVIEW** does not regain control until one instruction later.

As we pointed out in Chapter 2, the **IBM-XT** can support as many as 256 different interrupts, although the number actually used is much smaller. Appendix 2 contains descriptions of representative software interrupts.

Invoking an interrupt causes the corresponding interrupt handler code to execute, and it is interesting to ask where this handler code is stored in machine memory. The answer is that, when the machine is booted, as many as 256 *interrupt vectors* are initialized. Each of these interrupt vectors is four bytes long and contains a far pointer to the handler for that interrupt. The interrupt vectors are stored, in order, in the first 1024 bytes of machine memory, so that the offset of the code for **int n** is contained in the word at address 0000:4*n, and the corresponding segment is stored in the word at 0000:4*n+2.

It is a simple matter to examine the handler for any particular interrupt, with the help of **CODEVIEW**. Suppose, for example, that we wish to look at the handler for **int 23H**, the *Control C interrupt*. As the name indicates, this code executes when Control C is pressed. First, from within **CODEVIEW**, the command

```
dd 0:4*0x23 1 1
```

will display the interrupt vector in the form *segment*:offset. Assume that this vector turns out to be 1EFE:07D9. (This address will be machine dependent.) The **CODEVIEW** command

```
u 0x1efe:0x07d9
```

(*unassemble*) will then display the beginning of the handler code.

One consequence of this discussion is that it seems easy to replace a default interrupt handler with a customized version written by the programmer. It is only necessary to overwrite the interrupt vector with the address of the substitute code. When the interrupt is called, the interrupt vector then points to the new handler, which will be executed. While this approach is feasible (and has been used), it is not recommended. The proper method for making such a replacement will be discussed in the next two sections.

Exercise 15-1. In the text, we asserted that the default handlers for several of the early interrupts consist only of an **iret**. Use **CODEVIEW** to check the correctness of this claim.

Exercise 15-2. The code for most of the interrupts is difficult to trace. One exception is **int 05H**, the Shift-PrtSc interrupt. Use **CODEVIEW** to disassemble the **int 05H** code and analyze it thoroughly. You will need to refer to the table of interrupts in Appendix 2 to determine exactly what the handler code is doing.

SECTION 3 REPLACING AN INTERRUPT HANDLER

When we speak of replacing an interrupt handler, we can mean one of two things. It may be appropriate to incorporate a replacement handler as part of some executing program. The new handler will only be effective while that program is executing and the default handler will be restored when the executing program terminates. This is the kind of example with which we will be concerned in the present section.

Another approach to replacing an interrupt handler is to make the new handler a permanent part of machine memory, so that it will affect all future executing programs. Of course, the word *permanent* must be interpreted reasonably. The handler will (normally) become a part of machine RAM and will evaporate when the machine is shut down. But it is a simple matter to include an installation program for the substitute handler in the AUTOEXEC.BAT file, thereby ensuring that the substitute handler is always present. This approach to interrupt handlers brings us into the domain of *memory-resident programs*, which is the subject of the next section.

Returning to the present topic, we intend to incorporate our replacement handler as part of a larger program. Logically, this operation involves two parts: we must substitute the new handler for the old one at the start of the program, and we must restore the original handler at the end of the program.

As we pointed out in the last section, these operations are conceptually very simple. To make the substitution we need only replace the original interrupt vector with the address of the new handler. It is important to store a copy of the original interrupt vector, in order to restore it at the end of the program. The only problem with this approach is that we are making the replacement "behind the back" of the operating system, since it does not know that the substitution is taking place. Under present versions of **MS-DOS**, this will have no dire consequences. However, Microsoft strongly discourages the direct overwriting of interrupt vectors because it may not work under future versions of **MS-DOS**, and certainly would not work under **OS/2**. One difficulty stems from the fact that more advanced operating systems allow *multi-tasking*. That is, they allow several programs to execute simultaneously on the same machine. If, under those circumstances, a program changed an interrupt vector without notifying the operating system, then another executing program would get a surprise if it tried to use that interrupt! Of course, if the operating system has been notified of the modification of the interrupt vector, it can make the appropriate adjustment when it is "switching tasks."

The end result is that more sophisticated operating systems will not allow a program to "poke" new values into the interrupt vectors. Rather, some mechanism is provided by which the program can request the operating system itself to make such changes. **MS-DOS** has such a mechanism, and we will always use it to change interrupt vectors.

Specifically, **function 25H** of **int 21H** is used to request the replacement of an interrupt vector. As inputs, it requires that the interrupt number be passed in **al** and that **ds:dx** point to the new handler code. The following macro can be used to call **function 25H**. It has only one interesting feature. Programs that change interrupts are frequently in .COM format, and so (since, for the most part, **ds = cs** in these programs) **ds** will probably already contain the segment address of the new handler. In such cases, it is unnecessary to pass the *Segment* argument, and the macro responds correctly when the *Segment* parameter is blank.

```
;install new interrupt vector
;if Segment parameter not passed, it is assumed to be ds
setInt   MACRO  Number, Offset, Segment

    pushRegs  ax, dx
    mov    dx, Offset
    IFNB <Segment>
        push  ds                  ;to preserve it
        mov   ax, Segment
        mov   ds, ax
    ENDIF
    mov   al, Number
    mov   ah, 25h                  ;set interrupt vector
    int   21h
    IFNB <Segment>
        pop ds                     ;to restore it
    ENDIF
    popRegs

ENDM
```

The old interrupt vector must be stored for later restoration. **Function 35H** of **int 21H** can be used to determine the value of the interrupt vector before it is changed. It requires that the interrupt number be input in **al** and it returns the segment and offset of the interrupt vector in **es and bx**, respectively. The following macro implements this function, taking as parameters the interrupt number and one-word storage locations for the offset and segment parts of the vector.

```
;store old interrupt vector — destroys ax, bx, es
getInt MACRO  Number, Offset, Segment

    mov   al, Number
    mov   ah, 35h              ;get interrupt vector
    int   21h
    mov   Offset, bx
    mov   Segment, es

ENDM
```

We are finally ready for our example, which is shown in Figure 15.1. This program demonstrates the use of the *getInt* and *setInt* macros to replace and restore the handler for **int 04H**, the divide-overflow interrupt.

We have chosen to write the program in .COM format, but there was no compelling reason to do this. However, several of the later programs in this chapter are memory-resident, and it is traditional to write memory-resident programs in .COM format, since this tends to minimize program size.

NEW04H.ASM uses the **GROUP** directive and the format introduced in Section 2 of Chapter 12. Recall the advantages of this approach: when **MASM** reads the source file, the data occur first; consequently, phase errors are avoided without the use of explicit segment overrides. Lines 7-11 ensure that, when the program is linked, code precedes data, a requirement for the program to be convertible to .COM format.

For the most part, the mechanics of the program are straightforward:

Lines 33-37. We store the old interrupt vector and replace it with the address of the substitute handler, the procedure *New04H*. Since **ds = cs**, the third argument was not needed in *setInt*.

Lines 39-46. A few trivial tests of the functioning of the new handler.

Line 49. Restoring the original handler.

Lines 56-75. The code for the replacement handler.

Lines 60-62. These lines show the inelegance of the *inCh* macro. A single character is expected from STDIN (presumably 'y' or 'n'), but this character arrives followed by a CR. In cooked mode, the CR is converted to a {CR, LF} pair and so three calls to *inCh* are required to clear the input buffer.

Line 69. The procedure must end with an **iret** rather than a **ret**. After all, this handler is called, not by a **call**, but by an **int**. Consequently, the flags register has been pushed onto the stack and needs the **iret** to remove it. (Of course, just as an **int** can be fabricated from a **pushf** and a **FAR call**, an **iret** can be constructed from a **retf** and a **popf** or, if the flag values are not of interest, by a **retf 2**.)

Lines 72-73. In this case no **iret** is needed — we are just transferring control back to the operating system.

FIGURE 15.1 A NEW HANDLER FOR INT 04H

```
1   TITLE   New04h.asm: a new handler for int 04h
2
3       INCLUDE console.mac
4
5   ;--------------------------------------------------------------
6
7       DGROUP   GROUP  _TEXT, _DATA
8       _TEXT   SEGMENT WORD PUBLIC 'CODE'
9       _TEXT   ENDS
10      _DATA   SEGMENT WORD PUBLIC  'DATA'
11      _DATA   ENDS
12
13  ;--------------------------------------------------------------
14
15  _DATA  SEGMENT
16
17      Warning db  CR,LF,"Overflow occurred. Do you wish to abort? ",CR,LF,0
18      old04hOffset  dw   ?
19      old04hSegment dw   ?
20
21  _DATA  ENDS
22
23  ;--------------------------------------------------------------
24
25  _TEXT   SEGMENT
26
27      ASSUME   cs:DGROUP, ds:DGROUP
28
29      ORG    100h
30
31  Start:
32
33      ;store old int04h vector
34      getInt 04h, old04hOffset, old04hSegment
35
36      ;replace with address of new interrupt handler
37      setInt   04h, <OFFSET New04h>
38
39      mov al, 50
40      add al, al
41      into                ;doesn't call int 04h since OF = 0
42      mov al, 100
43      add al, al
44      into                ;calls int 04h
45      mov al, 100
46      add al, al          ;this overflow is missed since no into
47
48      ;restore original interrupt handler
49      setInt   04h, old04hOffset, old04hSegment
50
51      mov   ax, 4c00h
52      int   21h
53
54  ;--------------------------------------------------------------
55
```

```
Figure 15.1 cont.

56   New04h  PROC  NEAR
57
58      outAsc Warning
59
60      inCh  al
61      inCh  ah              ;to catch the CR
62      inCh  ah              ;  and the LF
63
64      cmp   al, 'y'
65      je    Abort
66      cmp   al, 'Y'
67      je    Abort
68      iret
69
70   Abort:
71
72      mov  ax, 4c01h
73      int  21h
74
75   New04h   ENDP
76
77   ;------------------------------------------------------------
78
79   _TEXT  ENDS
80
81   ;------------------------------------------------------------
82
83   END    Start
```

Int 04H was chosen as the subject of our first example mainly because it is easy to invent a substitute handler that could actually be used under certain circumstances. For example, this handler might appear as part of a calculator program. When overflow occurs, the user might wish to abort the program, or, alternatively, to continue and obtain an answer that is correct modulo 2^{16}. The reader should be warned, however, that few programmers would bother to write a new handler for **int 04H**, since the same effects can be obtained by judicious use of the **jo** and **jno** instructions.

SECTION 4 THE REENTRANCY PROBLEM

As we saw in Chapter 6, code that utilizes the stack the storage of procedure return addresses, parameters, and local variables is *reentrant*. In particular, such a procedure can be interrupted in mid-execution by a call to itself. The parameters and locals for the new copy of the procedure will be located in a new frame "higher" on the stack and so will not overwrite the data for the original call. Consequently, such a procedure can call itself recursively as many times as the size of the stack will allow.

One of the major inconveniences of programming the **IBM-XT** is that many of the ROM BIOS and **MS-DOS** interrupts, including most of the functions available under

int 21H, are not reentrant. Even worse, many of these interrupts share buffers or stack space, so that a call to one of them while another is active will frequently spell disaster. Since a number of the basic services that it provides are non-reentrant, **MS-DOS** is said to be a *non-reentrant operating system*.

In terms of the original design objective of **MS-DOS**, namely to be a single-user operating system, this appeared to be quite reasonable. After all, in the forward flow of a single application program, there seems no way that a **DOS** function call, for example, can "break in" on the same or a different **DOS** call that is executing.

But the program presented later in the present section shows that this can really occur. The forthcoming program will supply a new handler for hardware interrupt **int 05H**, the *print screen interrupt*, which is triggered by the Shift-PrtSc key combination and sends a copy of the video screen to the printer. We propose to modify the handler for **int 05H** so that, instead of sending a screen dump to the printer, it sends it to a disk file. The natural way to transmit this information to the diskfile is by using **function 40H** of **int 21H**, the write handle function (or our macro *Write* that is based on it).

The problem is that we want our substitute interrupt handler to execute each time the Shift-PrtSc key combination is pressed, even in the middle of some application program. At the exact instant when Shift-PrtSc is pressed, a sensitive **int 21H** function may be in progress — exactly the kind of interruption that **MS-DOS** will not tolerate.

If we decided to activate our substitute handler only at the **DOS** prompt (which would make it rather worthless!), the problem would still not be avoided. As a matter of fact, while **DOS** is "idle," i.e., is waiting for input and only presenting the **DOS** prompt on the screen, it is in an "active" state because it is executing a loop of calls to **function 0AH** (*buffered keyboard input*). If our substitute handler tried to execute under those circumstances, it would almost certainly cause the machine to lock up.

The designers of **MS-DOS** did supply certain facilities that, to a large extent, circumvent the reentrancy problem:

- **DOS** keeps a one-byte flag, which is usually called the *inDOS flag* or the *DOS Active Byte*. The value of this flag at any instant equals the number of calls to **int 21H** functions that are currently active. In particular, if the value is zero, no **DOS** function is presently active and **DOS** functions can be safely called. Finding the value of the inDOS flag is easy: a call to **function 34H** of **int 21H** returns the address of the flag in **es:bx**.

- This mechanism is not helpful if we wish to activate our substitute handler at the **DOS** prompt. As we stated earlier, **DOS** is active then, and the inDOS flag has a non-zero value. But even when **DOS** is busy, it may not be executing a non-interruptible section of code. During such "safe" periods, **DOS** makes regular calls to **int 28H**. By checking directly (using **CODEVIEW**), the reader can verify that **int 28H** does nothing — the code consists only of an **iret**. The sole reason for its existence is to provide the programmer with another method for determining whether it is safe to execute **DOS** functions: if **int 28H** is active, **DOS** is in a safe condition. A number of the traditional **DOS** functions (01H-0CH) must wait for user input and, during such waiting periods, they call **int 28H** repeatedly. In particular, a program that needs to execute a **DOS** function call while **DOS** is active should monitor **int 28H** and, as soon as that interrupt becomes active, can safely make the call.

Our replacement handler for **int 05H** is contained in the program SAVESCR.ASM, shown in Figure 15.2. Before looking at the code in detail, we will make some general comments on the structure of the program.

Unlike the program of Figure 15.1, which was *transient*, SAVESCR.ASM is a *memory-resident program (MRP)*. MRP's are also known as *terminate-and-stay-resident programs (TSR's)*. These terms are used to describe programs containing code that remains in memory after the program has executed. These resident sections can then be rerun without reloading the program from the disk.

More precisely, SAVESCR.ASM consists of two sections: the portion of the program up to and including line 159 is called the *resident code*, and will remain in memory after program termination; the part of the program after line 159 is called the *transient code* and will not remain in memory. The transient code is only executed once. It replaces various interrupt vectors, does other housekeeping chores, and finally terminates, using a special terminate function (**function 31H** of **int 21H**) that leaves the resident code in memory. The resident code, on the other hand, can be executed many times — each time the Shift-PrtSc key combination is pressed, in the present example.

In general, here is how the resident code in SAVESCR.ASM operates. When Shift-PrtSc is pressed, the variable named *Request* is set to 1 to indicate that a request for a screen dump is pending. Since this screen dump uses the disk functions, it should be performed only when **DOS** is in a safe condition. Specifically, it should only be done when either the inDOS flag is zero, or else while **int 28H** is executing.

The second option is easy to implement. It is just a question of taking over **int 28H** and, each time it is called, checking whether *Request* = 1. If so, the screen is saved to the disk file and *Request* is reset to 0. If *Request* = 0, nothing is done.

Checking the inDOS flag is harder. A mechanism must be found for performing this check at regular, quite frequent intervals, in the hope that **DOS** will soon be caught at an idle moment. This situation, where an action must be repeated at frequent intervals, comes up quite often in programming, and was provided for by the designers of the **IBM-XT**.

The technique that is used involves **int 1cH**, the *user timer interrupt*. **Int 1cH** is called by **int 08H**, the timer interrupt, and consequently, like **int 08H**, it executes 18.2 times per second. The default handler consists only of an **iret**, because **int 1cH** is provided entirely as a convenience to the user. Since any code placed in a new **int 1cH** handler will execute 18.2 times per second, it is ideal for such chores as building displays requiring continual updating or, as in our present case, *polling* repeatedly to find out whether some quantity has a desired value.

In many cases, we need to augment an interrupt handler, so that it performs some extra operations in addition to the functions of the old handler. Normally, this is accomplished by *chaining* to the original interrupt, which means that the new handler contains the code to do the additional processing and also calls the original handler to complete the standard operations.

The reader may wonder why it is necessary to chain to the old handler in the present case, since the default **int 1cH** handler consists only of an **iret**. The reason is that our program may not be the first to chain to **int 1cH**. It may already be in use by one or more other programs, and we must allow any extensions that these programs may have made to the handler code to execute.

FIGURE 15.2 A NEW HANDLER FOR INT 05H

```
 1    TITLE   saveScr.asm: changes Shift PrtScr so that it writes to a disk file
 2
 3    ;uses int 28h and int 1Ch as "hooks"
 4    ;============================================================
 5
 6    INCLUDE console.mac
 7    INCLUDE file.mac
 8
 9    ;============================================================
10
11    _DATA SEGMENT WORD PUBLIC 'DATA'
12
13        orig05hVector       LABEL       DWORD
14        orig05hOffset       DW          ?
15        orig05hSegment      DW          ?
16
17        orig1CHVector       LABEL       DWORD
18        orig1CHOffset       DW          ?
19        orig1CHSegment      DW          ?
20
21        orig28hVector       LABEL       DWORD
22        orig28hOffset       DW          ?
23        orig28hSegment      DW          ?
24
25        inDOSAdr            LABEL       DWORD           ;address of DOS ACTIVE BYTE
26        inDOSOffset         DW          ?
27        inDOSSegment        DW          ?
28
29        Request             DW          0               ;non-zero if Shift PrtScr
30                                                        ; request pending
31        Handle1             DW          ?               ;storage for file handle
32        dataFile            DB          'Data', 0       ;file name
33        scrBuf              DB          2050 dup(?)     ;temporary storage for screen
34        bufLen              DW          2050
35
36        Notice      DB  CR, LF, 'NEW PRT_SCR RESIDENT MODULE INSTALLED'
37                    DB  CR, LF, 0
38
39    _DATA   ENDS
40
41    ;============================================================
42
43    _TEXT SEGMENT WORD PUBLIC 'CODE'
44
45            ASSUME cs:_TEXT, ds:_DATA
46
47    ;------------------------------------------------------------
48
49    New05h PROC FAR
50
51        pushRegs  ax, ds                ;preserve interrupted ds
52        mov     ax, _DATA               ;so that resident data
53        mov     ds, ax                  ;  can be addressed
54        mov     Request, 1              ;notification of request
```

Figure 15.2 cont.

```
55      popRegs                         ;restore interrupted ds
56      iret
57
58  New05h ENDP
59
60  ;-------------------------------------------------------------
61
62  New1Ch  PROC FAR                    ;usr timer interrupt
63
64      pushRegs ax, bx, ds, es
65      mov     ax, _DATA
66      mov     ds, ax
67      pushf
68      cli
69      call    orig1CHVector
70
71      sti                             ;turn on interrupts
72      cmp     Request, 0              ;if no request
73      je      Done1                   ;  pending -- exit
74      mov     ax, inDOSSegment        ;else get DOS ACTIVE BYTE
75      mov     es, ax
76      mov     bx, inDOSOffset
77      cmp     BYTE PTR es:[bx], 0
78      jne     Done1                   ;if DOS is busy -- wait until next time
79      call    saveScreen              ;  if not, get screen now
80      mov     Request, 0              ;request has been dealt with
81
82  Done1:
83
84      popRegs
85      iret
86
87  New1Ch ENDP
88
89  ;-------------------------------------------------------------
90
91  New28h  PROC FAR                    ;if here, DOS is safe
92
93      pushRegs ax, ds
94
95      mov     ax, _DATA
96      mov     ds, ax
97      pushf
98      cli
99      call    orig28hVector           ;chain to old one, in case another
100                                     ;  application is also using it
101     cmp     Request, 0              ;if no request pending, exit
102     je      Done2
103     call    saveScreen              ;else get the screen
104     mov     Request, 0              ;  and signal that request fulfilled
105
106 Done2:
107
108     popRegs
109     iret
```

```
110
111  New28h  ENDP
112
113  ;------------------------------------------------------------------
114
115  saveScreen PROC NEAR
116
117      pushRegs ax, bx, dx, di, si, ds, es
118      mov    ax, _DATA
119      mov    es, ax
120      push   es
121
122      mov    ax, 0b800h                 ;0b000h for mono screen
123      mov    ds, ax
124      xor    si, si                     ;ds:si points to video buffer
125      mov    di, OFFSET scrBuf          ;es:di points to the scrBuf
126
127      mov    cx, 25                     ;number of lines to move
128
129  nextLine:
130
131      mov    dx, 80                     ;number of characters per line
132
133  nextChar:
134
135      lodsw                             ;load ASCII code and attribute byte
136      stosb                             ;store only the ASCII code
137      dec    dx
138      jnz    NextChar
139      mov    ax, (LF SHL 8) OR CR       ;terminate each line with {CR,LF} pair
140      stosw
141
142      loop   nextLine
143
144      pop    ds
145      Open   dataFile 2 Handle1         ;open for appending if it exists
146      jnc    Exists
147      Create dataFile 0 Handle1         ;else create
148
149  Exists:
150
151      Lseek  Handle1 2 0 0
152      Write  Handle1 bufLen scrBuf
153      Close  Handle1
154      mov    Request, 0                 ;signal that task is complete
155
156      popRegs
157      ret
158
159  saveScreen ENDP
160
161  ;------------------------------------------------------------------
162
163  Start:
164
165      mov    ax, _DATA
166      mov    ds, ax
167
168      push   es                         ;save segment of PSP
```

Figure 15.2 cont.

```
169
170        ;get original int 05h vector
171        getInt 05h, orig05hOffset, orig05hSegment
172
173        ;replace with new int 05h vector
174        setInt 05h, <OFFSET New05h>, cs
175
176        ;get original int 1Ch vector
177        getInt 1ch, orig1CHOffset, orig1CHSegment
178
179        ;replace with new int 1ch vector
180        setInt 1ch, <OFFSET New1ch>, cs
181
182        ;get original int 28h vector
183        getInt 28h, orig28hOffset, orig28hSegment
184
185        ;replace with new int 28h vector
186        setInt 28h, <OFFSET New28h>, cs
187
188        mov    ah, 34h      ;find address of DOS ACTIVE BYTE
189        int    21h
190        mov    inDOSSegment, es        ;save it
191        mov    inDOSOffset, bx
192
193        ;free environment space
194
195        pop    es
196        mov    es, es:[2ch]             ;segment address of environment
197        mov    ah, 49h                  ;free memory block
198        int    21h
199
200
201        outAsc Notice                   ;installation notice
202
203        mov    dx, _TEXT                ;dx = starting paragraph of code
204        sub    dx, _DATA                ;dx = number of paragraphs in _DATA
205        add    dx, 10h                  ;extra paragraphs for the PSP
206        add    dx, ((Start - New05h) + 15)/16 ;dx = total paragraphs to remain
207                                        ;   resident
208        mov    ax, 3100h
209        int    21h                      ;terminate and stay resident
210
211  _TEXT      ENDS
212
213  ;=============================================================
214
215  Stack   SEGMENT   STACK 'STACK'
216
217          DW 100 DUP (?)
218
219  Stack ENDS
220
221  ;=============================================================
222
223        END Start
```

The *New1Ch* code on lines 62-87 gives an example of chaining: lines 67-69 call the old handler (by simulating an **int** instruction), while lines 72-80 provide the new processing. The new handler that we chain to **int 1cH** actually does nothing unless *Request* = 1. If so, it checks the inDOS flag and, only if it is 0, it then saves the screen to disk.

Here are some detailed comments on SAVESCR.ASM:

Line 49. *New05h* is the replacement handler for **int 05H**. We have rather arbitrarily made this a **FAR** call. In the present case it does not matter whether it is **NEAR** or **FAR**. It is never accessed by a **call** — only as a result of a hardware interrupt — and so there is never a question of what kind of return address to load onto the stack. Likewise, it contains no **ret** instruction — only an **iret** — and so **MASM** does not need the **NEAR/FAR** information to determine the return-address size. Nevertheless, conceptually, it seems better to label it as **FAR** since it will be called via a hardware interrupt, and hence both the segment and the offset will be changed.

Lines 51-53. These lines, innocuous as they may seem, are vital to understanding how hardware interrupts work. First of all, we know that hardware interrupts are asynchronous, which means they occur at times that are unpredictable by the programs they are interrupting. When the interrupt handler is given control, only the **cs** and **ip** registers are changed to match the code of the handler. Later, these are restored by the **iret** instruction. The other registers still contain the values they had when the previous program was interrupted. To make an orderly return from the handler to the interrupted program, these values must be preserved. Hence:

- An interrupt handler must save and restore all registers that it changes.

The **flags** register is an exception to this rule since it is saved by the **int** instruction (whether it occurs explicitly in the code or corresponds to a hardware event) and is restored by the **iret** instruction.

Continuing with this train of thought, **ds** presumably contains a value relating to the interrupted program, but the handler code requires that **ds** point to the handler's data (on line 54, for example). This is one of the basic problems in writing interrupt handlers: how do they find their data?

There are two standard solutions. One is to write the handler as a .COM program, which will consist of a single segment (or **GROUP**); when the handler gains control, **cs** will point to this segment (or **GROUP**), and hence it suffices to set **ds** equal to **cs**.

The other method is to "hard code" the value of **ds** into the interrupt code, and we have done this on line 52. Of course, lines 52 and 53 can be viewed as the "standard two lines" that initialize **ds**, but it is important to realize why they are really needed here:

- If an interrupt handler refers to data, it must take appropriate steps to ensure that it can find those data at run time, since only the values of **cs** and **ip** are passed to it.

Lines 67-69. We chain to the original **int 1cH** handler.

Line 71. At this point, we can safely enable the maskable interrupts.

Lines 72-80. If *Request* = 1, we check whether the inDOS flag is 0. The address of the inDOS flag was found and stored during the installation code (lines 188-191), and on line 77 we check its value. If **DOS** is inactive, we call the function *saveScreen*, which performs the actual capture of the screen, on line 79.

Lines 101-104. The second "hook." This time, we are inside a call to **int 28H,** and so **DOS** is definitely in a safe condition. Hence, we need only check whether *Request* = 1, and call *saveScreen* if it is.

Line 115. *saveScreen* is declared to be a **NEAR** procedure, and here there is no choice. It is called (twice) from this code, and ends with a **ret.**

Lines 118-119. **Es** is pointed to the data segment since we are going to perform a block move using the string instructions, with the data segment as destination.

Line 120. We save the address of the data segment, so that it can be popped into **ds** on line 144.

Line 122. As we have mentioned earlier, the actual information displayed on the screen is the contents of a particular area of machine memory, called the *video buffer*. The starting address of the video buffer depends on the kind of video board installed, as indicated in the comments. Rather than force the programmer to make a choice of address for the video buffer, it would be much better to query the hardware at run time, and so have the program configure itself automatically to run with any video board. For information on how to do this, see [11], for example.

Lines 127-142. We move the contents of the video buffer to the temporary memory buffer named *scrBuf*, using a double loop: a traverse of the inner loop moves an 80-character line, and the outer loop causes the inner loop to execute 25 times, thereby moving all the lines on the standard 25-line screen. A {CR, LF} pair is appended to each line as it is moved, so that the file that is later generated will print out with appropriate newlines when displayed using a standard text editor.
   Notice line 139, in particular: by using immediate arithmetic, it is possible to move both the CR and the LF using a single instruction. Of course, this could also be done using the ASCII codes directly:

```
mov ax, 0a0dh
```

This nested double loop is certainly a natural candidate on which to use our *While/Wend* macros. However, we refrained from using them for two reasons: as we pointed out during the development of these macros, they add a large percentage of time overhead when used in very short loops (which these are); and we want this memory-resident code to be as compact as possible. Nevertheless, as an exercise, we do ask the reader to rewrite this section of the program using the *While/Wend* macros.
   Finally, to understand lines 134-135 it is necessary to recall how characters are stored in the video buffer. This subject was covered briefly in Chapter 10, and here it is, again, in

a nutshell. The characters displayed on the screen are stored in the video buffer in row-major order, one to a word. The word corresponding to a character has the ASCII code in the low byte and an *attribute* in the high byte. The attribute determines how the character will look when it is displayed on the screen. In the present context, we have no interest in storing this attribute byte in the disk file and so, even though we must read from the video buffer a word at a time, we only store the low bytes in *scrBuf*. This explains lines 135 and 136.

A good deal of effort could be saved here by using a single *Write* to save the entire 2000 word video buffer. This would give a disk image that could be nicely redisplayed on the screen by sending it back to the video buffer, but that would not be correctly printed or displayed by a text editor. Try it.

Lines 144-147. This **pop** matches the **push** on line 119, and so reinitializes **ds** to point to _DATA, which is necessary because of the references to named variables in the succeeding lines. Lines 145-147 are basically a *safCreat* macro: if the file exists, it is opened for appending; otherwise, it is created.

Line 163. The resident code has been completed and the transient code begins here. Recall that the transient part of the code is only executed once, to initialize and install the resident section, and does not itself remain permanently in memory. Line 163 is the entry point of the program, as can be checked by looking at line 223.

Lines 170-186. We are taking over various interrupts.

Lines 188-191. Function 34H of **int 21H** returns the address of the inDOS flag in **es:bx**. We immediately store this address in the appropriate data containers.

Lines 193-198. Every executing program is provided with its own copy of the machine environment by the **DOS** loader, whether it needs it or not. This one does not — it never needs to refer to PATH or any other environment string. This copy of the environment needlessly increases the size of the resident program, by an amount equal to the size of the environment (about 300 bytes on the machine on which this program was developed) and by an additional 16 bytes constituting a *memory control block*. (**DOS** manages the blocks of memory that it has allocated as a linked list, and each block has a 16-byte control block containing necessary linkage pointers and size information about the block.) It is easy to release this block of memory by using **function 49H** of **int 21H**, which is designed specifically to release an allocated block of memory. **Function 49H** must be passed the starting address of the block to be released in the **es** register. Recall from Chapter 9 that the starting segment address of the environment is given in PSP:002C. We had the foresight to **push** the PSP segment address on line 168. Now it can be popped into **es**, and line 196 completes the initialization of **es**.

Lines 208-209. We now need to terminate the program and leave resident the section ending on line 159. To accomplish this, **DOS** provides **function 31H** of **int 21H**, the *terminate-and-stay-resident* function. Like **function 4CH, function 31H** will set the system error level to the value passed to it in **al**. As an additional input parameter, it must be told the size, in paragraphs, of the block that is to remain resident, and this number should be passed in **dx**. The length is given in paragraphs so that blocks of size larger than 64K can be handled with one call to the function. The block that remains resident starts at the beginning of the memory image of the program, i.e., at the start of the PSP.

In our case, this block must be made large enough to hold the PSP and the machine code corresponding to lines 1-159. The question arises of how to enter the appropriate number of paragraphs (rounded up, if necessary) into **dx**, and one solution is shown in lines 203-206.

The code in these lines certainly merits some elaboration. First, there are three contributions to the paragraph count: the number of paragraphs in _DATA; 10H paragraphs for the PSP; and the number of paragraphs in the code segment corresponding to lines 42-159.

The second item is trivial. The first and third are interesting because they give insight into the limitations of assembly-time arithmetic. Consider the first one. Since _TEXT is interpreted by **MASM** as a constant whose value is the corresponding segment address and _DATA is similarly interpreted, it would seem reasonable that the instruction

```
mov     dx, _TEXT - _DATA
```

could be used to initialize **dx** to the number of paragraphs in _DATA, rather than our having to resort to the two lines 203-204. But **MASM** can only do assembly-time arithmetic on quantities that are known at assembly time, and neither _TEXT nor _DATA is such a quantity — their final values are not known until load time. Hence **MASM** declines to accept the preceding single instruction.

Next, consider line 206, namely

```
add     dx, ((Start - New05h) + 15)/16
```

We want to discuss why **MASM** will accept this particular version, but not other, simpler variants of it. First of all, here is how **MASM** interprets the second operand in this instruction: *Start* and *New05h* are labels, and **MASM** replaces each by its offset, hence their difference is the number of bytes in the code block that interests us. Converting to paragraphs requires dividing by 16. Since this division discards the remainder, if any, we first add 15 to bring the size beyond the next multiple of 16. Effectively, this rounds the quotient up.

The thing that is interesting about this formula is that *New05h* has value zero and so does not contribute to the numerical answer. In that case, why is it included? (The reader might check that **MASM** will not accept line 209 without the "- *New05h*" term.) The reason is, again, that **MASM** will only deal with quantities known at assembly time. Granted, neither *Start* nor *New05h* is actually known at assembly time — each may have a constant added at link time. But if this happens, each will have the *same* constant added, and hence the difference will not change! Hence, **MASM** is quite happy to accept the difference as an assembly-time quantity.

Another approach that can be tried is to substitute the instruction

```
add     dx, (OFFSET Start + 15)/16
```

Again this is unacceptable. What is perhaps puzzling here is that a line such as

```
add     dx, OFFSET Start
```

would be acceptable to **MASM** (if it were of any use in the present context). The point is that *OFFSET Start* is a relocatable item: it is marked as requiring fixup by **LINK**. In the second instruction this causes no problem. But in the first it is impossible: if **MASM** has done the addition and division requested in this instruction using the provisional value of *OFFSET Start*, there is no way that it can "go back" and fix the computation when the final value is provided by **LINK**.

This aside has been lengthy but seems worthwhile because of the insight it gives. In particular, it engenders a certain respect for the astuteness of **MASM** (or, more accurately, the astuteness of the writers of **MASM**!)

The only remaining point to be made before we leave our discussion of the specifics of SAVESCR.ASM concerns the ordering of the components of the program. This ordering is basically dictated by how **function 31H** works: the resident part of the program must come before the transient part. In particular, we could not use the simplified segment directives, since the **DOSSEG** ordering places the code before the data.

SAVESCR.ASM gives a reasonably robust utility, but it is certainly not "bomb-proof." There are a number of circumstances under which it can lock up the machine. Writing a truly solid utility that will *never* succumb to the non-reentrancy of **DOS** is quite an arduous endeavor. For more complete information, we refer the reader to [24].

We will conclude by pointing out a few of the weaknesses of our version of the utility, with corresponding suggestions for improving it:

1. As an experiment, the reader might replace line 31 by

```
dataFile    DB    'a:\Data', 0
```

thereby associating the data file with drive **A:**, and then run the program with no disk in **A:**, or with the drive door open. In either case, **int 24H**, the *critical error handler*, will be triggered. The default action of the **int 24H** is to print to the screen the familiar message

```
Not ready error reading drive A
Abort, Retry, Ignore?
```

Try the "Abort" alternative. Nothing will happen. Then attempt to exit the program by using Control C. Still nothing will happen. In fact, the only way to extricate yourself is by rebooting the machine. The difficulty is that **DOS** does not know that the transient part of *saveScr* is in control — it assumes that the interrupted program is still in control, and this is what it attempts to abort. That attempt unfortunately does not have the effect of terminating *saveScr*.

The best solution to this particular problem is not clear. For example, it seems rather presumptuous to have *saveScr* try to abort the interrupted program in such circumstances. The approach that is usually adopted is to ignore the problem, leaving it up to the user to close the disk door or whatever is required. This is accomplished by having the resident program take over the three interrupts that cause the kind of difficulty we have been discussing: **int 24H**, the critical error interrupt; **int 23H**, the Control C interrupt; and **int 1BH**, the control break interrupt, which is basically the ROM BIOS counterpart of the **int 23H**. The resident program should therefore replace each of these handlers by an **iret**. As an exercise, the reader is asked to make these modifications to *saveScr* and then to repeat the experiment that we described previously.

2. It is a general rule that disk operations should not be interrupted. One reason is that some disk operations involve time-critical sequences, which, if disrupted, will result in errors. Another reason, in the case of the **IBM-XT**, is that all **MS-DOS** disk operations ultimately use **int 13H**, the ROM BIOS *disk interrupt*, and the **int 13H** handler is not reentrant. Although it is somewhat difficult to simulate this kind of problem, *saveScr* is certainly vulnerable to it. The interrupted program might well be doing a disk operation when *saveScr* takes control. Fortunately, this situation is easy to deal with. The resident program supplies a new **int 13H** handler having the following additional features:

- It introduces a flag that will have non-zero value whenever the interrupt is active.

- It contains code to test this flag and declines to reactivate **int 13H** if it is already active.

In one of the exercises, we ask the reader to make this change to *saveScr*.

3. As *saveScr* is written, more than one copy of it can be installed in memory at the same time. While this does not affect its operation, it is certainly wasteful of system resources and should not be allowed. It turns out to be surprisingly difficult for a memory-resident program to detect whether or not it has already been installed. We suggest one approach to this problem in the exercises.

4. A number of other things can go wrong if a memory-resident program takes control at the wrong time.

For example, many programs of this type (including *saveScr*) do not define their own stacks, but instead use the stack belonging to the interrupted program. This approach obviously carries an element of danger. If the resident program makes extensive use of the stack, it should certainly define its own stack and transfer to it immediately. The interrupted **ss** and **sp** must be saved, of course.

Even the opening of files can be hazardous. **DOS** limits the number of files that can be opened simultaneously in any program. What if *saveScr* is given control in a program that is using the maximum allowed number of files? A file error will occur!

How can this be avoided? Although this fact is not documented by Microsoft, **MS-DOS** keeps the information about opened files in the program's PSP. As presently written, *saveScr* shares the PSP of the interrupted program and consequently it shares the file allotment of that program since, after all, **DOS** does not even know when *saveScr* becomes active. The solution to our problem is therefore easy: give *saveScr* a new PSP when it takes control, and change back to the old PSP when it retires. These changes of PSP can be accomplished using **function 50H** (*set PSP*) and **function 51H** (*get PSP*) of **int 21H**.

5. As it stands, *saveScr* uses a large amount of machine memory: about 2650 bytes. Approximately 350 bytes of this is the actual code and 256 bytes is the PSP. (Unfortunately, every program has one.) But the lion's share of the memory is used by *scrBuf* (2050 bytes), and it is possible to reclaim this memory.

The reader is probably familiar with the fact that memory can be allocated *dynamically* in most high-level languages. In other words, it is possible to ask for a block of memory only while it is of use, at run time, and then to return this memory to the system when it is no longer needed. As might be guessed, it is also possible to do this in an assembly language program, using functions available through **int 21H**. In fact, we have already met **function 49H**, which releases a block of memory, in the code for *saveScr*. In order to minimize the size of the resident portion of *saveScr*, it seems tempting to dynamically allocate space for *scrBuf*. But this will not work. Remember that, by default, **DOS** assigns all of available machine memory to an executing program. In particular, if *saveScr* asked for a memory allocation after it had interrupted another program was resident, it would likely be told that there was no memory available! Since there is no practical method by which *saveScr* can safely manipulate the memory allocation of another program, this approach does not appear to be feasible.

A technique that will work is to have *saveScr* write the screen contents directly to the data file, without using a buffer. Of course, it will be necessary to write one line at a time to the file, following each line with a {CR, LF} pair, which will slow the program considerably. In one of the exercises at the end of this section, we ask the reader to make this modification to the program.

In a similar vein, the installation message on lines 35 and 36 is only used at the end of the initialization process and so need not become resident. The easiest way to exclude it from the resident portion is to define a new data segment, coming right after the code segment, and place the message in this new segment. If this segment is placed in a group that also contains the present data segment, then no switching of **ds** will be needed. In addition, there will be no problem with forward references, since the default register assignment, namely **ds**, that is associated with the expansion of line 201 will be correct.

Exercise 15-3. Rewrite the nested double loop in SAVESCR.ASM using the *While/Wend* macros from Chapter 13.

Exercise 15-4. In our discussion of *saveScr*, we made the point that it responds badly to occurrences of these interrupts: **int 24H**, the critical error interrupt; **int 23H**, the Control C interrupt; and **int 1BH**, the ROM BIOS control break interrupt. The easiest way to improve the situation is to have *saveScr* take over each of these interrupts, replacing its handler with an **iret**. Of course, the replacement handlers should only operate while *saveScr* is active: the original handlers should be reinstalled each time *saveScr* goes to sleep. Make these changes to *saveScr* and check that it then responds more reasonably to **int 24H**.

Exercise 15-5. Following the method suggested in the text, add code to SAVESCR.ASM to ensure that whenever a call to **int 13H** is in progress when Shift-PrtSc is pressed, no action will be taken until the completion of the **int 13H** call.

Exercise 15-6. Modify *saveScr* so that, if it is already resident and an attempt is made to reinstall it, a message will be printed and the program will not be reinstalled.
Suggestion: Embed a "signature" into the *saveScr* code. This signature should consist of a block of characters (of length perhaps 20) that is not likely to appear elsewhere in machine memory. As part of the installation process, *saveScr* should search for this distinctive pattern and, if it is found, decline to reinstall itself. It is not necessary to search all of machine memory for the pattern — consult the memory map in Chapter 2 for guidance. Of course, this method is not totally foolproof.

Exercise 15-7. Modify *saveScr*, as suggested in the text, so that it sends the screen contents directly to the disk file without using a buffer.

Exercise 15-8. Implement the scheme outlined in the text for introducing a second data segment into SAVESCR.ASM.

SECTION 5   A POP-UP UTILITY

We will now give an example of a kind of program that has become known as a *pop-up utility*. Such programs are installed permanently in memory (generally by the use of **function 31H** of **int 21H**) and are activated by a *hot-key sequence*. This means that, when the appropriate sequence of keys is pressed, control passes to the resident utility, which performs its appointed task and then returns control to the interrupted program. Clearly, these programs are conceptually identical to our *saveScr* program of the last section.

Our demonstration program, shown in Figure 15.4, is called FILEPOP.ASM. It stores the contents of a selected file in RAM and displays it on the screen at the press of a hot key. The user can move through the file, using the cursor keys, and return to the interrupted program at any time. Obviously, this is a useful utility for constructing "on-line" help files. As an example, the Program Disk contains a help file for **CODEVIEW**, which the user can augment or modify in any way, before installing it as the information file to be displayed by *filePop*. We arbitrarily selected Alternate 5 as the hot key that activates the utility. It is entirely feasible to have several versions of the utility simultaneously resident in memory, each having a different hot-key sequence and each allowing access to a different file of information.

Before looking at the code for FILEPOP.ASM, we must consider the operation of the **IBM-XT** keyboard. The keyboard is a rather complicated device containing, among other components, a 4-bit microprocessor. The precise functioning of the keyboard circuitry is not of much interest in normal programming. The lowest-level information generally needed is that the keyboard is connected to the **8255** chip (*PPI* or *Programmable Peripheral Interface*). The **PPI** has three 8-bit registers, named A, B, and C, which are accessed at port addresses 60H-62H (using the **in/out** instructions). Of these three registers, the first two are used in connection with the keyboard, as well as having other uses.

When a key on the keyboard is pressed or released, two events take place:

- An 8-bit scan code is deposited in register A of the **PPI**.

- An **int 09H** hardware interrupt (the *keyboard interrupt*) is generated on the IRQ1 line of the PIC chip.

The *scan code* is a one-byte code associated with each key on the keyboard, so that each key is assigned a different code. For example, the right and left shift keys have distinct scan codes. For a list of the scan codes, see [20]. The scan codes are actually stored in the low 7 bits of Port A, and the high bit relays another piece of information. The preceding two events occur each time a key is released, as well as when a key is pressed. If a key press is being signaled, bit 7 of Port A is 0; if a key release, it is 1. Clearly, Port A provides the programmer with very complete information about keyboard activity.

The **int 09H** interrupt handler (which is contained in the ROM BIOS), is responsible for getting the scan code from Port A of the PIC, sending an acknowledgement to the PIC that it has done so, and translating the scan code into the form in which it is stored in the BIOS data area.

Recall that the BIOS data area is a region of low memory, beginning at address 0040:0000, which is used to store flags and other information about the state of the machine. For example, the two bytes beginning at address 0040:0017 consist of 1-bit flags telling the present state of the various shift and toggle keys: right and left shift, alternate, control, shift lock, etc. For further information on these flags, see [20], for example. Part of the function of **int 09H** is to update these flags, as necessary.

But the most important duty of **int 09H** is to relay information to the *keyboard buffer*. As the name suggests, the keyboard buffer stores information from the keyboard while it awaits processing by the system. The keyboard buffer endows the **XT** with its limited "type-ahead" ability. It is an 18-word-long storage area in the BIOS data area, beginning at address 0040:001A.

Despite its 36-byte length, the keyboard buffer will only allow 15 characters to be typed ahead, for reasons that we will now explain.

First of all, each key press is stored in the buffer as a word. The exact contents of this word are dependent on which key or combination of keys is pressed. The so-called *normal characters* are stored with the ASCII code for the character in the low byte and the scan code in the high byte. Additionally, there are *extended codes* corresponding to special keys, such as the cursor keys. For such keys, 00H is stored in the low byte and a special code is stored in the high byte. Some of these special codes are enumerated in Figure 15.4 (lines 88-95). It is always possible to tell a normal code from an extended code since 00H is not used as an ASCII code.

Next, the beginning two words in the buffer are not used for key-press storage, but instead hold near pointers. These pointers are usually called *Head* and *Tail*. *Head* points to the oldest character in the buffer, i.e., to the character that arrived first and that should be processed first. *Tail* points to the first available location in the buffer, i.e., to the word immediately beyond the most recent arrival.

Finally, the keyboard buffer is operated as a *circular buffer* by **int 09H**. This means that, as soon as the last position in the buffer has been filled, the filling algorithm "wraps around" and starts again at the beginning of the buffer. If the buffer happens to be full when the result of a new key press arrives, **int 09H** generates a "bell" character (07H), which causes the speaker to beep. The information about that key press is lost.

The configuration in which *Head* = *Tail* is interpreted as meaning that the buffer is empty. We now see why the buffer can only hold information on 15 key presses, even though it has 16 storage locations (excluding *Head* and *Tail*). The point is that the distance from *Head* to *Tail* tells how many key presses are in the buffer. For each position of *Head*, *Tail* can only assume 16 positions, and these correspond to counts of 0, 1, 2, ···, 15.

The keyboard buffer is illustrated in Figure 15.3.

We will begin our discussion of *filePop* by outlining its general operating principles, and will then look at the code in more detail.

Like our last example, *filePop* consists of a resident section, which ends with line 263, and a transient portion, which begins on line 267 and installs the resident portion. For variety, we have chosen to write this program in the "classical" .COM format: it consists of a single segment, the data are defined in that segment, and it does not use the **GROUP** directive.

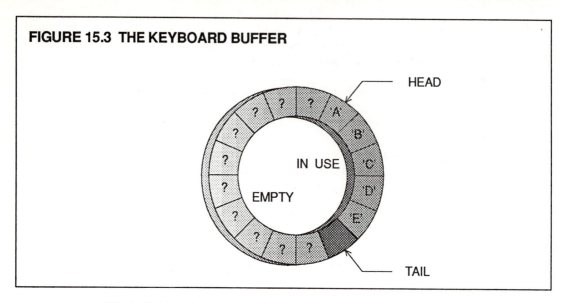

FIGURE 15.3 THE KEYBOARD BUFFER

The basic idea of the program is simple. It maintains a flag called *opMode*, which has value −1 whenever the resident section of *filePop* is in control, and has value 0 whenever *filePop* is "asleep."

The program operates by taking over **int 09H**. Since the original **int 09H** code is extremely complicated, it would certainly be ill-advised to try to replace it. Rather, the new **int 09H** chains itself to the old one. The only new processing involves examining the key presses to find out whether they are intended for *filePop*.

Specifically, if *filePop* is asleep (*opMode* = 0), the new **int 09H** passes all key presses on to the application presently in control, except for the hot key, Alternate 5. This key is used to activate *filePop* and is also removed from the keyboard buffer. If *filePop* is active (*opMode* = −1), it ignores Alternate 5 and, in fact, ignores all keys except those listed on lines 89-95. The ignored keys are deleted from the keyboard buffer. The cursor keys scroll the screen appropriately. The escape key deactivates *filePop* and returns control to the interrupted application.

There are actually two methods of taking over **int 09H**. First, as we did here, it is possible to let the old **int 09H** deposit all key-press information in the keyboard buffer and then to directly manipulate the buffer. We used this method so that we could demonstrate very explicitly the operation of the keyboard buffer.

Another method, which turns out to be somewhat simpler to program, is to examine the key presses while they are still at Port A of the **PPI**, before the old **int 09H** has had a chance to process them. In those cases where they are intended for *filePop*, they can be dealt with directly, without calling the old **int 09H**. If they are not intended for *filePop*, control should be passed to the old **int 09H**, which will process them in the normal way. In an exercise at the end of this section, the reader is asked to work out the details of this alternate method.

Recall that *filePop* displays the contents of an information file on the screen. In order that this file display quickly, its entire contents are kept resident in memory. While this can require a good deal of memory if the information file is large, it lets the program respond

FIGURE 15.4 A POP-UP UTILITY

```
 1    TITLE   filePop.asm: MRP giving screen display of a chosen file
 2
 3    INCLUDE   console.mac
 4
 5    ;------------------------------------------------------------
 6
 7    ;clear screen
 8    clrScr   MACRO
 9
10        mov    ax, scrSeg              ;es points to screen
11        mov    es, ax
12        xor    di, di
13        mov    ax, 700h               ;replace with 00h, attribute 07h
14        mov    cx, 2000
15        rep    stosw
16
17    ENDM
18
19    ;------------------------------------------------------------
20
21    Scroll   MACRO   Key, Increment, Target
22
23        cmp    inWord, Key            ;inWord is current position in
24        jne    @F                     ;  keyboard buffer
25        IFNB <Increment>
26           add    firstLine, Increment ;if scrolling
27        ELSE
28           mov    firstLine, Target   ;if jumping
29        ENDIF
30        jmp    SHORT beginPrint
31        @@:
32
33    ENDM
34
35    ;------------------------------------------------------------
36
37    ;assumes that String is in segment pointed to by ds and that es:di
38    ;  points to location on screen where String is to be printed
39    ;expects first byte in string to contain character count of string
40    ;string should not be terminated (by NULL or CR)
41
42    Print MACRO offsetString
43
44        pushRegs ax, cx
45        mov    ah, 07h                ;normal attribute byte
46        mov    si, offsetString       ;point si to start of line
47        xor    cx, cx
48        mov    cl, [si]               ;init. si to number of chars to print
49        jcxz   endPrint               ;in case of empty lines
50        inc    si                     ;point si to first char to print
51
52    nextChar:
53
54        lodsb
```

Figure 15.4 cont.

```
55      stosw
56      loop nextChar
57
58  endPrint:
59
60      popRegs
61
62  ENDM
63
64  ;------------------------------------------------------------
65
66  ;prints the screen with given starting line number
67  ;destroys ax,bx,cx,and di
68  printScreen MACRO lineNo
69
70      xor    di, di
71      mov    bx, lineNo                ;line number in DataFile that
72      shl    bx, 1                     ;  should print at top of screen
73      mov    cx, 25
74      xor    ax, ax                    ;ax holds offset into video buffer
75
76  nextLine:
77
78      Print  Line[bx]                  ;bx is current line to print --
79      add    bx, 2                     ;  it is an index into a word array
80      add    ax, 160                   ;add 160 to video array index line
81      mov    di, ax                    ;di is used as the video array index
82      loop   nextLine
83
84  ENDM
85
86  ;------------------------------------------------------------
87
88  Alt5      EQU    7c00h               ;the first seven keys are "extended"
89  cursDn    EQU    5000h               ;Alt5 = Alternate 5, is the
90  cursUp    EQU    4800h               ;  arbitrarily selected "hotkey"
91  pgDn      EQU    5100h
92  pgUp      EQU    4900h
93  homeKey   EQU    4700h
94  endKey    EQU    4f00h
95  escKey    EQU    011bh               ;high byte is scan code, low is ASCII
96  scrSeg    EQU    0b800h              ;for color or EGA; b000 for mono
97
98  Active    EQU    -1                  ;equate value for active state of
99                                       ;  pop-up program
100
101 ;============================================================
102
103 biosSeg SEGMENT AT 40h               ;"formal" segment for addressing
104
105     ORG 1ah
106     Head      DW    ?                ;pointer to next character to use
107     Tail      DW    ?                ;pointer to most recent character
108     Buffer    DW    16 dup(?)        ;number of positions in buffer
109     bufferEnd LABEL DWORD
```

```
110
111   biosSeg  ENDS
112
113   ;===============================================================
114
115   _TEXT SEGMENT WORD PUBLIC 'CODE'
116
117       ORG   80h                     ;some data defined in the PSP
118                                       ;  to save space -- it is certainly
119       orig09hVector   LABEL    DWORD ;    safe to use the UPA since no command
120       orig09hOffset  DW  ?           ;       line paramets used and no use made
121       orig09hSegment DW  ?           ;          of default DTA
122       opMode         DW  ?           ;-1 if resident utility is active
123       firstLine      DW  ?           ;number of first line to display
124       inWord         DW  ?           ;holds present word in keyboard buffer
125
126       ORG   100h
127
128           ASSUME cs:_TEXT, ds:_TEXT, es:biosSeg
129
130   ;---------------------------------------------------------------
131
132   Start:
133
134       jmp Begin
135
136   Main  PROC  FAR
137
138       pushRegs ax,bx,cx,dx,di,si,ds,es
139
140       push  cs
141       pop   ds                        ;point ds to _TEXT
142
143       pushf
144       cli
145       call  orig09hVector             ;simulate an int
146
147       mov   ax, biosSeg               ;prepare to address biosSeg
148       mov   es, ax                    ;  using es -- ASSUME already in effect
149       mov   bx, Tail
150       cmp   bx, Head                  ;Tail = Head if buffer is empty
151       je    ToDone                    ;if so, clean up and exit
152
153       cmp   bx, OFFSET Buffer         ;get here if buffer not empty
154       jne   notAtStart                ;Tail = OFFSET Buffer means wraparound
155       lea   bx, buff·                 ;  occurred, and so most recent character
156                                       ;     is actually at end of buffer
157   notAtStart:
158
159       sub   bx, 2                     ;if no wraparound, most recent character
160                                       ;  is one word back from Tail
161
162       mov   ax, es:[bx]               ;in both cases, bx now points to most
163       mov   inWord, ax                ;  recent character, now stored in inWord
164       cmp   ax, Alt5                  ;if not Alt5 has arrived, check whether
165       jne   checkOpMode               ;  utility is active
166
```

Figure 15.4 cont.

```
167        mov     Tail, bx              ;here if it is Alt5 -- delete it
168        cmp     opMode, Active        ;if utility is already active,
169        je      ToDone                ;   it ignores Alt5, else it treats it
170                                       ;     as cue to activate
171        not     opMode                ;set flag to indicate active mode
172
173        mov     ax, scrSeg
174        mov     ds, ax                ;ds now points to video buffer
175        xor     si, si
176
177        ;store screen
178        mov     ax, cs
179        mov     es, ax                ;es now points to _TEXT
180        lea     di, scrBuf
181        mov     cx, 2000
182        rep     movsw                 ;store video buffer contents in scrBuf
183
184        jmp     beginPrint            ;fill video buffer from DataFile
185
186   checkOpMode:                        ;here whenever a keystroke other than
187                                       ;   Alt5 received
188        cmp     opMode, Active         ;if not in active mode, pass the
189        je      @F                     ;   keystroke on to the previous
190                                       ;       application in the int 09h
191   toDone:                             ;         chain
192
193        jmp     Done
194
195   @@:
196
197        mov     ax, biosSeg           ;address biosSeg with es -- the es
198        mov     es, ax                ;   ASSUME was never changed
199        mov     ax, Head              ;delete character
200        mov     Tail, ax
201
202        ;the Scroll macro adjusts firstLine before the screen is displayed
203        Scroll cursDn, 1
204        Scroll cursUp, -1
205        Scroll pgUp, -25
206        Scroll pgDn, 25
207        Scroll homeKey,, 0
208        Scroll endKey,, maxFirstLine
209
210        cmp     inWord, escKey
211        jne     toDone
212
213        ;here if escKey was pressed and we were in active mode -- appropriate
214        ;  action is to enter inactive mode
215        mov     Opmode, NOT Active
216        mov     ax, scrSeg
217        mov     es, ax
218        lea     si, scrBuf            ;start restoring screen
219        xor     di, di
220        mov     cx, 2000
221        rep     movsw
```

```
222      jmp     SHORT Done              ;end of restoring screen
223
224  beginPrint:                         ;print data from DataFile to screen
225
226      clrScr
227
228      mov     ax, cs                  ;to access DataFile, which is in _TEXT
229      mov     ds, ax
230
231      cmp     firstLine, 0            ;to avoid overshooting the start of
232      jge     @F                      ;  DataFile
233      mov     firstline, 0
234      jmp     SHORT PrintIt
235
236  @@:
237
238      cmp     firstLine, maxFirstLine ;to avoid overshooting the end of
239      jle     PrintIt                 ;  DataFile
240      mov     firstLine, maxFirstLine
241
242  PrintIt:
243
244      printScreen firstLine
245
246  Done:
247
248      popRegs
249
250      iret
251
252  Main ENDP
253
254  ;-------------------------------------------------------------
255
256  scrBuf dw 2000 dup(?)
257
258  INCLUDE dataFile                    ;specially formatted data
259
260  Notice   db   CR,LF,LF,'Alt5 Keyed Resident Module Installed'
261           db   CR, LF, 0
262
263  pgmLen  EQU  $ - Start
264
265  ;-------------------------------------------------------------
266
267  Begin:                              ;initialization code
268
269      getInt  09h, orig09hOffset, orig09hSegment
270      setInt  09h, <OFFSET Main>
271
272      mov     opMode, NOT Active      ;these cannot be statically initialized
273      mov     firstLine, 0           ;  since they were defined in the PSP
274
275      outAsc  Notice
276
277      mov     dx, ((pgmLen + 15) / 16) + 10h  ;reallocate program length
278      mov     ax, 3100h                        ;TSR exit
279      int     21h
280
```

```
      Figure 15.4 cont.

      281   _TEXT ENDS
      282
      283   ;=============================================================
      284
      285   END Start
```

much faster than would the alternative of accessing a disk file each time the screen display changes. In addition, since we are not using any **DOS** functions or interrupts while *filePop* is active, we do not need to worry about the reentrancy problem here. Of course, it is possible to rewrite *filePop* so that it gets its data from a disk file, coping with the reentrancy issue exactly as we did in the previous example.

To minimize the size of the resident data file, it is formatted in a special way, which we will discuss later in this section. This specially constructed file is called DATAFILE and is included among the data of the program by means of the **INCLUDE** directive on line 256.

We will now give some detailed commentary on the *filePop* code:

Lines 7-84. These macros are used in *filePop*.

clrScr clears the screen by writing directly to the video buffer. It writes 0700H to each word, thereby assigning attribute byte 07H (normal attribute) and character value 00H to each screen position. The value 00H prints as a blank.

Scroll is used to scroll the displayed file up or down. The variable *firstLine* is the number of the line in the file that will show at the top of the screen. Hence, adding 1 to *firstLine* has the effect of scrolling one line downward in the file, and similarly for subtracting 1 or adding or subtracting 25. The required change in *firstLine* is transmitted in the *Increment* argument.

We will see later that in the special formatting of DATAFILE it is convenient to store each line with the character count occupying the first byte, followed by the actual characters in the line, excluding the CR and LF. No null terminator is used. This format is used because each line is displayed on the screen by sending it directly to the video buffer with a **stosw** instruction. To do this, **cx** must be initialized to the line length. Performance would suffer unreasonably if the length had to be recomputed each time a line was displayed. The *Print* macro is responsible for displaying a line on the screen. To fill the screen requires printing 25 lines. *printScreen* accomplishes this by making 25 calls to *Print*.

Lines 88-95. These are one-word codes used for various key combinations. Line 95 represents a normal key, with the scan code in the high byte and the ASCII code in the low byte while line 88, for example, represents a special key, with an extended code in the high byte and 00H in the low byte.

Lines 103-111. This is an example of the **AT** directive, as discussed in Section 2 of Chapter 12. Recall that it allocates no memory, but merely provides a formal mechanism by which we can assign names to specific items in an area of memory and refer to them using segment nomenclature. In particular, if we initialize a segment register to point to *biosSeg*, and use the appropriate **ASSUME**, MASM will generate the correct segment references, and we can use the names *Head* and *Tail* to produce the corresponding offsets. Of course, it would also be possible to use the **AT** directive to set up the video buffer as a segment but this would not be helpful unless we wanted to give names to some particular locations. Here we were content to supply an **EQUATE** for the start of the video buffer, *scrSeg*, on line 96. As in the last example, it would be better to include code to make the program adapt itself automatically to different video display types.

The programming would have been easier if *biosSeg* and _TEXT could have been placed in a single group in order to minimize the switching of segment registers. But an essential restriction of the **GROUP** directive is that the segments in a group cannot span more than 64K, and _TEXT will certainly be loaded into memory further than that distance from *biosSeg* (as can be seen from the memory map in Chapter 2).

Lines 112-131. Line 126 sets the code origin at 100H, as is required in all .COM programs.

One of the annoyances of **MS-DOS** is that all .EXE and .COM programs are assigned a PSP of length 100H, no matter how little use they may make of it. One way of salvaging some of this memory is to use it for something else in the program. It is frequently used to store data, as in the present program. But if this strategy is used, a few points must be borne in mind. First, the PSP is intended for other purposes and hence data stored there cannot be initialized. Indeed, any initial values will be overwritten by the "official" contents of the PSP at run time. Next, the early parts of the PSP are used by the operating system, invisibly (and sometimes in undocumented ways) to the programmer, and so should not be interfered with. It is probably safe to reuse any part of the PSP starting with the first FCB (byte 5CH). Of course, if sections of the program use command-line parameters, or invoke **int 21H** functions that use the default DTA, then these parts of the program must be complete before it is safe to overwrite the UPA (starting at 80H) section of the PSP. In lines 114-121, we have arranged to store 5 words of uninitialized data in the UPA.

Since this is a .COM program, line 125 contains **ASSUME**s associating both **cs** and **ds** with the code segment, _TEXT. We also associate **es** with *biosSeg*. Even though **ds** and **es** must be pointed to different segments when we use the string instructions, these **ASSUME**s will not need to be changed for the duration of the program.

In order that the initialization code not remain resident, it must occur at the end of the code segment. However, **EXE2BIN** insists that the entry point to the code occur at offset 100H in the code segment. The only solution is to use a **jmp** instruction, as we have done on line 134. Note that the actual machine code for this instruction remains resident and wastes a few bytes of space, but this seems unavoidable.

We could have located the remaining data at the present line 135, rather than at the end of the resident code, as we chose to do (lines 258-261). It really doesn't matter — since **cs** = **ds** at run time (see the next paragraph), **MASM** need not compensate for the fact that the data is in _TEXT by generating **cs:** segment overrides.

Lines 140-141. These are critical lines. Since we did not make **MASM** generate **cs:** overrides on data references, we must be sure that **ds** also points to _TEXT. This is just a variation on a theme mentioned earlier: when a memory-resident program is given control, only the contents of **cs** and **ip** relate to this program. In particular, some provision must be made to ensure that it will address its data correctly.

Lines 149-150. It can happen that a key press occurred but the keyboard buffer is empty. This happens when a shift or toggle key is pressed or released. The result of such activity is stored in the two status bytes beginning at 0040:0017. The test for an empty buffer consists of checking whether *Head = Tail*.

Lines 153-160. This is probably the most interesting aspect of controlling the keyboard buffer. The problem is to find the location of the most recent key press, and the solution is slightly complicated by the fact that we are dealing with a circular buffer (look at Figure 15.3 again). The value of *Tail* gives the answer: if *Tail* points to the start of the buffer, then wraparound has just occurred, and so the most recent key press can be found at the end of the buffer; otherwise, it can be found in the word immediately preceding the one pointed to by *Tail*.

Lines 177-182. Our resident utility overwrites the present screen with the information from the data file. Of course, it must first save the present screen contents, so that the screen can be restored afterwards. In these lines, the screen is saved in *scrBuf*. As in our last example, the old screen data could be saved in a disk file in order to reduce the size of the resident code.

Line 193. At a number of points in the code, instructions of the form

```
        conditionalJump    Done
```

are needed. Unfortunately, at several of these locations, the target *Done* is beyond the range of a conditional jump. An efficient expedient in such cases is to introduce a new label, *toDone* in our present example, that is positioned within **SHORT** range of as many of these locations as possible. The conditionals are then given *toDone* as target, and only a single

```
        jmp    Done
```

instruction is needed, as on line 193.

Lines 202-208. *filePop* is in control at this point, and these lines give its responses to the use of the cursor keys. The only noteworthy item is that the *Scroll* macro (lines 21-33) makes a case distinction based on whether its second argument is blank, and in the macro call the blankness of the second argument can be communicated by using consecutive commas, as on line 207:

```
        Scroll homeKey,, 0
```

Lines 231-240. We do not want to scroll backward beyond the beginning of the file, or forward beyond the end of the file. These requirements can be phrased in terms of the variable *firstLine*, which holds the number of the line occupying the topmost position on the screen. Our requirements are that *firstLine* must be ≥ 0 and $\leq$ *maxFirstLine*, where *maxFirstLine* has value equal to

```
        (total number of lines in file) - 24
```

FIGURE 15.5 FORMAT OF DATA FILE FOR FILEPOP

```
INFORMATION FILE TO BE STORED AND VIEWED

Short line.
This is a longer line.

And so on.

CORRESPONDING DATAFILE

Line0        DB      11,83,104,111,114,116,32 ,108,105,110,101,46
Line1        DB      22,84,104,105,115,32 ,105,115,32 ,97 ,32 ,108,111,110
             DB      103,101,114,32 ,108,105,110,101,46
Line2        DB      0
Line3        DB      10 ,65 ,110,100,32 ,115,111,32 ,111,110,46

Line         DW      Line0, Line1, Line2, Line3

MAXFIRSTLINE    EQU    0
```

The code starting at line 231 ensures that *firstLine* is within the allowed range. Incidentally, *maxFirstLine* is set by an **EQUATE** in DATAFILE.

We should also point out that there is one context in which *filePop* does not perform satisfactorily. Namely, *filePop* will always display 25 lines, even if the information file has fewer than this number of lines. In that situation, it will display "garbage" on the remainder of the screen. As an exercise, we ask the reader to fix this problem.

Line 258. DATAFILE is a specially formatted version of the information file. A specimen information file and the corresponding DATAFILE are shown in Figure 15.5.

DATAFILE assigns names *Line0*, *Line1*,⋯ to the lines of the input file. Each line is stored, using one or more **DB** directives, as a byte giving the character count on the line, followed by a list of the ASCII codes of the characters on this line. For example, line 2 is empty and hence is stored as

```
Line2 db 0
```

where the '0' is the character count. The advantage of this format is that each line is stored in a number of bytes that equals its length, plus one overhead byte, rather than allocating perhaps 80 bytes to very short lines. The result is a sizable saving in memory. A disadvantage is that the screen must be printed a line at a time, rather than by using a single block move.

The remainder of DATAFILE consists of an array giving the offsets at which the lines begin, and the **EQUATE** for *maxFirstLine*.

An immediate question is how DATAFILE is generated, and of course the only reasonable answer is that a program must be written to do the job. As we have pointed out before, this is the kind of task for which assembly language is not well suited — programming that involves interpreting and creating special formats is quite unpleasant in assembly language. For this reason, we wrote a utility in C, CONVERT.C, that does the conversion.

CONVERT.EXE can be found on the Program Disk. In response to the command line

```
convert  infile outfile
```

it will take the information file named INFILE and convert it to our special format, labeling the resulting file as OUTFILE. Of course, in the present context, the name DATAFILE should be used for OUTFILE. The source code for CONVERT.EXE is also on the Program Disk. The interested reader might wish to write an equivalent utility in **Pascal** or, as a more strenuous exercise, even in assembly language.

Exercise 15-9. In both *saveScr* and *filePop*, we saw examples of the process of *chaining* to an interrupt, which means that the substitute handler performs some auxiliary operations, and also calls the original handler to allow it to do its normal processing. There are two different methods of chaining to an interrupt:

- *Early chaining* means that the substitute does its auxiliary processing first, and then calls the original handler.

- *Late chaining* means the opposite: the substitute handler calls the original handler first and, after the return, does the auxiliary processing.

The distinction between the two methods becomes very interesting when several different programs take over the same interrupt. To be specific, consider the keyboard interrupt and suppose that a number of memory-resident programs simultaneously want to use Alternate 5 as a hot key. In terms of early and late chaining, and the order in which these utilities were installed in memory, discuss which of them will actually obtain access to the chosen hot key. (A certain well-known commercial memory-resident program used to chain itself on repeatedly to the interrupts that were important to it, to ensure that it was always at the "head of the chain.")

Exercise 15-10. Rewrite *filePop* so that it stores its information file in a disk file, rather than in memory. In addition, it should save the present screen contents in a temporary disk file rather than in a buffer, and the temporary file should be deleted after use. Of course, this version will have to contend with the reentrancy problem, using the same techniques that we used in SAVESCR.ASM.
Suggestion: One interesting question is how to name the temporary file so that its name does not conflict with the name of an existing file. If *filePop* is run only under **DOS** Version 3.0 or later, then **function 5AH** of **int 21H** can be used to *Create a Temporary File*. The advantage of using this function is that the temporary file is guaranteed to have a "unique" name, i.e., a name that is different from the name of any existing file. But it is probably unwise to make such an assumption about the **DOS** version. Instead, invent a temporary file name that has minimal chance of being used in any other context.

Exercise 15-11. We chose to manipulate the keyboard buffer directly in *filePop*. Another method is to use the **in** instruction to obtain the characters directly from the keyboard or, more accurately, from port address 60H, which is Port A of the **8255** chip. (See the discussion at the beginning of this section.) Here is the general technique that should be employed in this alternate approach:

a. Take over **int 09H**, just as we did in the original version.

b. The new handler should use the **in** instruction to find out whether a key press is intended for *saveScr* or not. If so, the high bit of the input must also be checked to be sure that it is a key press and not a release. If the key press is intended for *saveScr*, it should not be transmitted to the keyboard buffer. In the contrary case, it should be sent on by transferring control to the original **int 09H.** Note that key presses corresponding to extended keys require two **in** instructions: the first returns 0 and the second returns the special code. Normal key presses only require one **in** and this returns the scan code.

c. In cases where the key press is intended for *saveScr*, it will be necessary to send an acknowledgement to the keyboard, informing it that the key press has been received. This is done by changing the value at Port B of the **8255** (port address 61H) to 1 and then immediately changing it back to 0. It is important that no other bits at Port B be changed. If, for example, bit 6 is accidentally cleared, the keyboard will be disabled.

Rewrite the appropriate parts of SAVESCR.ASM so that it receives its keyboard input in this alternate way.

Exercise 15-12. In our discussion of *filePop*, we mentioned a bug: the program as written will always display 25 lines, even if the file contains fewer than that number of lines. Consequently, when very short files are used, the display will contain some lines of "garbage." Fix this problem.

Exercise 15-13. For the truly dedicated assembly language programmer: study the code for our conversion utility CONVERT.C and write an assembly language version.

Exercise 15-14. Write a memory-resident program that will display the contents of the keyboard buffer (as words in hex) on the screen, at the press of a hot key. Repeated use of the hot key should toggle the display on and off. Probably the program should remove the hot key from the buffer, to prevent its appearance as part of the display. It is important to continually update the display, to keep it fixed even when the screen scrolls.

SECTION 6 AN EXECUTION PROFILER

In Chapter 5, we introduced the notion of *profiling*, which means determining how much time a program spends on various parts of its code, with an eye toward improving performance. In the present section, we will actually construct a simple profiler, and, toward the end of the section, give some suggestions for its use.

At first blush, it seems that writing a profiler would be a very difficult undertaking. After all, a profiler must somehow monitor the program being profiled (the *profilee*) and keep a running tally of where this program is spending its time. In fact, this aspect of the profiler code turns out to be fairly trivial. First of all, the profiler does not *continuously* monitor the profilee; rather, it *samples* the execution at frequent intervals, recording the values of **cs** and **ip** at each sampling. Of course, the rate at which sampling should occur depends on the profilee. If the profilee runs for two or three minutes, a sampling rate of perhaps 20 or 30 times per second might be reasonable, while a program that runs for only a second or so should probably be sampled at a rate of several hundred times per second.

The exact technique used to collect the **cs** and **ip** values is marvelously simple. Each time an interrupt occurs, the **cs** and **ip** for the interrupted program are pushed onto the stack. The profiler can therefore collect its samples by arranging to have the profilee interrupted at the desired sampling frequency and, during each interrupt, read the **cs** and **ip** from the stack and store them for future analysis. The only question is how to interrupt the profilee frequently, and we already have a partial answer: the timer interrupt, **int 08H**, occurs 18.2 times per second. Hence, if we take over this interrupt and reprogram it to deposit the **values** of **cs** and **ip** in a safe place during each occurrence, we already have the basis for a fixed-sampling-rate profiler. To attain our goal, we will also change the frequency with which **int 08H** occurs, and have the new rate be selectable by the user of the profiler.

It will turn out that the bulk of the programming labor involved in writing a profiler relates to record keeping and output: the profiler must collect and store many values of **cs** and **ip**, later presenting them to the user in a variety of informative formats. In fact, the output requirements of this program are sufficiently involved that it makes an excellent hybrid program, and we have chosen to write it partly in C and partly in assembly language.

Our program is very loosely based on one developed in [30]. While the basic principles used in the two profilers are the same (as they are for nearly all profilers), the implementation details are very different. In particular, the output procedures in [30] are written in **Pascal**, and so we especially recommend that article to readers who wish to see an example written in that language.

Before presenting our profiler code, we must make a short detour and consider yet another hardware topic, namely the operation of the **8253** timer chip. The **8253** contains three timers, which perform a variety of functions essential to the functioning of the **IBM-XT**. Even though these three timers are identical in construction, they have different capabilities when they are used in the **XT** context, since their outputs are connected in different ways.

The **8253** receives its main timing pulse from a crystal on the system board that vibrates at a frequency of 14.31818 Mz. This frequency is divided by 12 before being sent to the **8253**, and so the basic timing pulses arrive at the timer chip with a frequency of 1.19318 Mz.

The three timers on the **8253** are called *Timer0*, *Timer1*, and *Timer2*. Each of these timers has a 16-bit counter associated with it, and these can be given initial values, say *initial-Count0*, *initialCount1*, and *initialCount2*. At each timing pulse, the values of these counters are decremented. When the counter for a timer has reached zero, that timer places a signal on the corresponding output pin of the **8253** and the counter returns to its original value, so that the cycle can repeat.

Each of the three timers has a different, dedicated function:

- Timer0 is connected to the IRQ0 line of the **8259 PIC**, hence hardware interrupt **int 08H** is triggered each time it has counted down to zero. The ROM BIOS initialization routine gives initialCount0 the value 0, which, in terms of countdown to 0, is equivalent to giving it value 65536. Consequently, the output signal from Timer0 occurs $(1.19318 * 10^6) / 65536 = 18.206482$ times per second. We now see why **int 08H** occurs at the approximate rate of 18.2 times per second.

- The RAM chips must be *refreshed* frequently or they will "forget" their contents. The output of Timer1 is connected to this refresh circuitry. While it is possible to change the programming parameters for Timer1, there is never any good reason to do so, and attempts to do so will nearly always cause the system to crash.

- Timer2 is connected to the speaker and so can be used to generate sound effects. Since only the duration and frequency (i.e., pitch), and not the volume, of the sounds produced can be controlled, the effects produced are somewhat limited.

It is clear from this brief discussion that only Timer0 is of use to us in our present example, since we must have an interrupt occur at the end of each timer cycle. Our basic strategy will be to reprogram Timer0 to cause the corresponding interrupt to occur at a variable, software-controlled rate. A profiler would rarely sample less often than 18.2 times per second, hence we will only be concerned with speeding up the timer rate. But it is important to do this speedup carefully, ensuring that, even though **int 08H** may occur more frequently, the standard functions associated with this interrupt (relating to the system clock and the floppy disks) will still occur at the standard rate.

While the technicalities involved in the operation of the **8253** are fairly involved, its basic programming is simple. The **8253** is accessed through four 8-bit registers, named *Timer0*, *Timer1*, *Timer2*, and the *Control Word Register*, located at port addresses 40H, 41H, 42H, and 43H, respectively.

Each **8253** command must be prefaced by sending a byte to the Control Word Register. The format of this byte is

```
Bit Name  SC1  SC0  RL1  RL0  M2  M1  M0  BCD
Bit No.    7    6    5    4    3   2   1   0
```

The SC1 and SC0 bits contain the number (in binary) of the timer with which we wish to communicate. RL1 and RL0 indicate whether we will send one or two bytes. In our case, we will send a word, and the appropriate bit values are 11. Bits M2, M1, and M0 represent the *mode*. Each timer can operate in one of six modes (0-5), and the choice of mode basically determines the form of the output pulse from the timer. This becomes somewhat technical and we refer the reader to [19] for details. Mode 3, which generates a "simple square wave" and is the one used by the ROM BIOS, is satisfactory for our application. Each timer can either act as a binary counter, counting down from a maximum of 65536, or as a decimal counter, counting down from a maximum of 10000. These two alternatives correspond to the BCD bit having value 0 or 1, respectively. Hence, we will assign value 0 to this bit.

Immediately after the control byte is sent to the Control Word Register, the new value of the initial count should be sent to the appropriate timer. In our case, this means sending two bytes to Port 40H.

As we indicated earlier, our profiler is a hybrid program, consisting of a module in **C** and a module in assembly language. Figure 15.6 shows the **C** module and Figure 15.7 the assembly language module. Part of the **C** code consists of fairly easy printing and formatting functions and so, to save space, these are not shown in Figure 15.6. The complete source code is on the Program Disk.

FIGURE 15.6 THE C MODULE OF THE PROFILER

```
1   /* profile.c -- a primitive execution profiler        */
2   /* externs are defined in companion module, NewTimer.asm  */
3
4   #include <stdio.h>
5   #include <process.h>
6   #include <stdlib.h>
7   #include <graph.h>
8   #include <conio.h>
9   #include <string.h>
10
11  #define  WAIT    {while (!getch());}
12  #define  CR      ('\015')
13  #define  MAXSEGS 20              /* maximum number of segments permitted */
14                                  /* in program being profiled            */
15  typedef struct
16  {
17      unsigned offset;
18      unsigned segment;
19  }  ADDRESS;                     /* Holds a segmented address */
20
21  ADDRESS *addressArray;          /* Points to array that holds "hits" --    */
22                                  /* sample addresses collected by profiler  */
23
24  typedef struct
25  {
26      unsigned address;    /* Holds the segment(paragraph) address of segment */
27      unsigned startPos;   /* Index where first seen in sorted addressArray  */
28      unsigned hits;       /* Number of times code executing found in segment */
29      unsigned minOffset;  /* Minimum offset found in this segment           */
30      unsigned maxOffset;  /* Maximum offset found in this segment           */
31      unsigned len;        /* = maxOffset - minOffset + 1                    */
32  }  SEGMENT;
33
34      SEGMENT segments[MAXSEGS];
35
36  typedef struct              /* A segment is divided into bins. Each    */
37  {                           /* bin consists of the range of offsets    */
38      unsigned offset;        /* between minOffset and maxOffset.        */
39      unsigned hits;          /* A hit occurs in a bin when the code is  */
40      unsigned minOffset;     /* executing there when interrupted by     */
41      unsigned maxOffset;     /* int 08h.                                */
42  }  BIN;
43
44      BIN  *bins;
45
46  extern unsigned codeSegment;
47
48  /* Prototypes */
49  extern void changeTimer(unsigned);      /* Takes over int 08h        */
50  extern void restoreTimer(void);         /* Restores int 08h          */
51  int compFunction(ADDRESS *, ADDRESS *); /* Compares addresses for Qsort */
52  void segmentPrint(char *);
53  void binPrint(unsigned);
54  void constructBins(unsigned,unsigned,double);
55  void findSegments(unsigned);            /* Initializes segments array   */
```

```
56
57  unsigned ArraySiz;                               /* Size to allocate addressArray  */
58                                                   /* Equal 4 * numberSamples        */
59  void main(int argc, char **argv)
60  {
61      unsigned speedupFactor;                      /* To speed up clock -- argv[1]   */
62      unsigned numberSamples;                      /* Max. number of samples to take */
63      unsigned currentSegAdr;
64      unsigned index, temp;
65      unsigned segNumber, numberBins, totalHits;
66      int ch, counter;
67      double binSiz;
68
69      if (argc < 4)
70      {
71          puts("Usage: profile numberSamples speedupFactor ProgName Args");
72          exit(1);
73      }
74
75      numberSamples = (unsigned)atoi(argv[1]); /* Used to calloc addressArray */
76      speedupFactor = (unsigned) atoi(argv[2]);/* Used to change timer rate    */
77      ArraySiz      = numberSamples << 2;       /* Each address = 4 bytes       */
78
79      if (!(addressArray = calloc(numberSamples, sizeof(ADDRESS))))
80      {
81          puts("\n\nError allocating memory for numberSamples.\n\n");
82          exit(1);
83      }
84      changeTimer(speedupFactor);
85
86      /* spawnvp is a C version of the exec function. The 'v' means that the    */
87      /* spawned program is passed an argument vector (here argv + 3); the 'p'  */
88      /* means that spawn will search the PATH to find the program to spawn     */
89      if (spawnvp(P_WAIT, argv[3], argv + 3) == -1)
90      {
91          puts("\nProblem spawning.");
92          restoreTimer();                     /* If aborting, fix timer first */
93          exit(1);
94      }
95
96      /* Restore original timer countdown value as soon as possible           */
97      restoreTimer();
98
99      /* totalHits = number of non-zero locations in addressArray             */
100     for (totalHits = 0; (addressArray[totalHits].segment
101             || addressArray[totalHits].offset) && totalHits < numberSamples;
102                 ++totalHits);
103
104     /* The rest of the program runs more efficiently if addressArray is      */
105     /* sorted lexicographically with respect segment first, then offset      */
106     qsort((void *)addressArray, totalHits, sizeof(ADDRESS),
107                     (int (*) (const void *, const void *)) compFunction);
108
109     /* Initialize the segments array by finding minimum and maximum          */
110     /* offsets and starting indices in addressArray for each segment         */
111     findSegments(totalHits);
112
113     while(1)
```

Figure 15.6 cont.

```
114        {
115             segmentPrint(argv[3]);    /* send name of profilee as parameter */
116             printf("\nTo analyze a particular segment, input its number,");
117             printf("\nor to exit the profiler, press RETURN:  ");
118             fflush(stdin);
119             if ((ch = getche()) == CR) break;
120             ungetc(ch, stdin);
121             scanf("%u", &segNumber);
122             printf("Into how many bins should segment number %d be divided? ",
123                     segNumber);
124             scanf("%u", &numberBins);
125             fflush(stdin);  /* Get the CR that scanf misses */
126             printf("Only non-empty bins will be printed.\n");
127             if (numberBins > segments[segNumber].len)
128             {
129                 puts("\nToo many bins for length of segment.");
130                 puts("Press any key to try again.");
131                 WAIT
132                 continue;
133             }
134             if (!(bins = calloc(numberBins, sizeof(BIN))))
135             {
136                 puts("\n\nError allocating memory for bins.\n\n");
137                 exit(1);
138             }
139             binSiz = (double)segments[segNumber].len / numberBins;
140
141             /* Subdivide segment into bins of nearly equal size, record the   */
142             /* number of hits in each.                                        */
143             constructBins(segNumber,numberBins,binSiz);
144             binPrint(numberBins);
145             free(bins);
146             puts("\n\nPress any key to continue.");
147             WAIT
148             fflush(stdin);
149        }
150   }
151   /* Sorts by value of segment and, in case of ties, by value of offset.    */
152   /* Returns +1, -1, 0 as Qsort requires                                    */
153   int compFunction(ADDRESS *ptr1, ADDRESS *ptr2)
154   {
155        if (ptr1 -> segment > ptr2 -> segment) return 1;
156        if (ptr1 -> segment < ptr2 -> segment) return -1;
157        if (ptr1 -> offset > ptr2 -> offset) return 1;
158        if (ptr1 -> offset < ptr2 -> offset) return -1;
159        return 0;
160   }

/* the code for the following functions is on the Program Disk */

162   void segmentPrint(char *progName)

182   void binPrint(unsigned numberBins)

194   void constructBins(unsigned segNumber, unsigned numberBins, double binSiz)

216   void findSegments(unsigned totalHits)
```

Although we will not analyze PROFILE.C as minutely as our assembly language programs, we must devote some attention to it in order to fully appreciate the workings of the profiler. The reader who is not familiar with C should still understand the general outlines, based on the remarks on the source code for PROFILE.C and our comments in the next few pages.

Here are some detailed observations:

Lines 15-21. *ADDRESS* is a structure intended to hold the segment and offset parts of an address. It could just as easily have been defined as an array of two unsigned integers, but it is more self-documenting when defined as a structure. On line 21, *addressArray* is defined as a pointer to *ADDRESS*. It will be initialized to point to a dynamically allocated block of memory (on line 79). The size of this block is determined by how many sample addresses must be stored, and this information is input by the user as one of the command-line parameters. To increase the efficiency of the searches occurring later in the program, the array of addresses is sorted (using the *qsort( )* library function), so that the segments occur in increasing order and, for each segment value, the offsets occur in increasing order.

Lines 24-34. The structure named *SEGMENT* contains all the necessary information about a segment: its address; *startPos*, the index at which it first occurs in the sorted array of addresses; *Hits*, the number of times it was found to be the active segment when the code was interrupted; *minOffset* and *maxOffset*, the minimum and maximum offsets found when the code was executing in that segment; and *Len*, the apparent length of the segment, as computed from *minOffset* and *maxOffset*. Of course, *Len* may be less than the true segment length since the range of offsets determined by *minOffset* and *maxOffset* may not be complete: if some locations in the segment did not execute often, they may not have been active during a sample, hence will not occur in the array of addresses. On line 34, the symbolic constant *MAXSEGS* (which is defined on line 13) is used to assign a size to the array *Segments*. This array could also have been defined dynamically, but it did not seem worthwhile to do so since the given size (20) is sufficient for nearly any application and is certainly not profligate with memory.

Lines 36-44. As soon as the list of active segments has been determined, the user is invited to inspect them, one at a time, in detail. This inspection consists of dividing the observed range of offsets in the segment (from *minOffset* to *maxOffset*) into a number of "bins" and computing how many of the hits fell in each bin. The structure *BIN* contains the important information relating to a bin. The user chooses the number of bins, and memory is allocated for this number (on line 134). The pointer variable named *Bins*, which is defined on line 44, is pointed to this block of memory.

Line 46. The code segment of the profiler itself will very likely appear on the list of sampled segments (unless the sampling rate is low enough to miss it). It is certainly a good idea to flag this segment since it really has nothing to do with the execution time for the profilee. Hence it is necessary to find and record the code segment of the profiler. The **QuickC** compiler provides a standard mechanism for reading segment values, but in a hybrid program such as this it is easier to have the assembly language part of the program record the **cs** value in the data segment. In the assembly language module (see Figure 15.7), we provide a storage location, named *codeSegment*, for the **cs** value. On line 46, it is declared to be an *extern*, as the **C** compiler requires.

Lines 48-55. This program is written to conform to ANSI **C** requirements and so, in particular, all functions are prototyped. Note that the functions *changeTimer* and *restoreTimer* on lines 48 and 49 are declared to be *extern*, since they are defined in the assembly language module.

Line 57. The variable *arraySiz* gives the size of *addressArray*, the array of sample addresses. The user selects this value as a command-line parameter.

Line 59. A correct command for invoking the profiler has the form

```
profile numberSamples speedupFactor progName Args
```

where: *numberSamples* sets the size of the array of addresses, and so determines the maximum number of sample addresses that can be stored; the value of *speedUpFactor* is used to set the sampling rate to (18.2 * *speedUpFactor*); *progName* is the name of the profilee to be profiled; and *Args* means any command-line arguments that are to be passed to *progName*. Lines 69-71 make a preliminary check on the correctness of the command line.

Line 84. Calls the assembly language procedure that speeds up the timer.

Lines 88-92. *spawnvp( )* is one of the **C** library functions implementing the **int 21H EXEC** function. In the "spawnvp" version, the 'v' means that "spawn" will look for command-line arguments for the program to be spawned in a vector (here *argv + 3*) and the 'p' means that it will look for the program to be spawned (*argv[3]*) on the PATH, if necessary.

Line 97. As soon as the sampling is completed, the timer should be restored, and here we are calling the assembly language procedure that does the restoring. In this context, line 92 is also important. If *spawnvp( )* is unsuccessful, so that the program should abort, the timer must still be reset.

Lines 100-102. Since the array of addresses was initialized to contain 0s by *calloc( )*, it is easy to determine the total number of hits by counting the non-zero locations in the array.

Line 106. As mentioned earlier, we sort the array of addresses using *qsort( )* in order to make later searches more efficient. The *qsort( )* function requires a special comparison function, which is supplied on lines 151-160.

Line 115. Prints the information from the segment array to the screen.

Lines 116-133. Standard user dialog, asking the user to specify a segment to examine and the number of bins into which to divide that segment.

Lines 139-145. Constructing and printing the information about the bins.

Lines 162-end. These functions are concerned with various formatting and printing chores that are not central to the operation of the profiler. To save space, we have not reproduced this code in the text.

We will now turn our attention to Figure 15.7, which contains the code for NEW-TIMER.ASM, the assembly language module of the profiler. Because of our previous discussion, NEWTIMER.ASM should hold few mysteries. However, there are several points that might profit from review or elaboration:

Line 5. We are using the extended form of the **.MODEL** directive, although it is not of great consequence in this example. The only procedure that takes parameters is *changeTimer*, and it only requires one of them, so that the distinction between "left-pusher" and "right-pusher" is nonexistent! However, because of line 29, we are able to refer to the parameter by the name *speedUpFactor*.

Line 15. These are **EXTRN** declarations for quantities defined in PROFILE.C. The only interesting point is that *addressArray* was defined to be a pointer, which has size one word since we are using the **SMALL** model.

Lines 33-34. We are storing the value of the profiler's **cs** so that it can be printed out by the appropriate function in the **C** module.

Lines 35-38. We wish to speed up the 18.2 ticks per second of Timer0 by a multiplicative factor equal to the value of *speedUpFactor*. This means that *initialCount* for Timer0 should have value

```
65536 / speedUpFactor
```

In these lines, this quotient is computed and stored in **bx**.

Lines 40-45. First we send a byte with value 36H to the Control Word Register at Port 43H to keep Timer0 in mode 3 and prepare it to receive the new value of *initialCount* in two bytes. The value of **bx** is then sent to Timer0 at Port 40H, a byte at a time, by using two **out** instructions.

Lines 47-48. We are invoking our usual macros to store the original **int 08H** vector and substitute our new handler.

Lines 57-71. There is nothing new here — the value of Initialcount0 is being reset to 0.

Line 77. Since we are using the extended form of the **.MODEL** directive, the reader might expect to see

```
USES ds, ax, bx, bp
```

on line 75, rather than the use of *pushRegs* on the present line. Unfortunately, USES will not work in this context. The macro that it invokes apparently needs to see a **ret** at the end

FIGURE 15.7 ASSEMBLY LANGUAGE MODULE OF THE PROFILER

```
1    TITLE   newTimer.asm
2
3
4    DOSSEG
5    .MODEL SMALL, C
6
7    PUBLIC   codeSegment
8
9    INCLUDE console.mac
10
11   ;===========================================================
12
13   .DATA
14
15   EXTRN   arraySiz:WORD, addressArray:WORD
16
17   origTimerCountdown    DW   0   ;effectively counts down from 65536
18   arrayOffset           DW   0
19   codeSegment           DW   ?
20
21   orig08hVector         LABEL DWORD
22   orig08hOffset         DW   ?
23   orig08hSegment        DW   ?
24
25   ;===========================================================
26
27   .CODE
28
29   changeTimer   PROC   speedUpFactor:WORD
30
31       cli                     ;mask interrupts while changing timer
32
33       mov    ax, @CODE
34       mov    codeSegment, ax
35       mov    ax, 0          ;initialize dx and ax to original timer countdown
36       mov    dx, 1          ;   starting point in preparing for 16-bit division
37       div    speedUpFactor
38       mov    bx, ax         ;bx now contains new starting point for
39                             ;   timer countdown
40       mov    al, 36h        ;place timer 0 in mode 3
41       out    43h, al        ;send control byte to timer
42       mov    al, bl         ;relay new starting point for countdown
43       out    40h, al        ;   to timer by sending it a byte at a time
44       mov    al, bh         ;      to port 40h
45       out    40h, al
46
47       getInt 08h, orig08hOffset, orig08hSegment
48       setInt 08H, <OFFSET New08h>, cs
49
50       sti                     ;restore maskable interrupts
51       ret
52
53   changeTimer   ENDP
54
```

```
 55   ;------------------------------------------------------------
 56
 57   restoreTimer    PROC    NEAR
 58
 59       cli                         ;mask interrupts while changing the timer
 60       setInt  08h, orig08hOffset, orig08hSegment
 61
 62       mov    al, 36h        ;send control word to timer --
 63       out    43h, al        ;  we still want timer 0, mode 3,
 64       mov    al, 0          ;    but now we want to restore the
 65       out    40h, al        ;       original countdown value of 0
 66       out    40h, al
 67
 68       sti                         ;restore interrupts
 69       ret
 70
 71   restoreTimer        ENDP
 72
 73   ;------------------------------------------------------------
 74
 75   New08h          PROC
 76
 77       pushRegs  ds, ax, bx, bp
 78       mov    bp, sp
 79
 80       mov    ax, @DATA
 81       mov    ds, ax
 82
 83       mov    ax, arraySiz        ;when addressArray is full, sampling
 84       cmp    arrayOffset, ax     ;   should be discontinued
 85       jae    skipSampling
 86
 87       mov    bx, addressArray    ;point bx to addressArray
 88       add    bx, arrayOffset     ;   and add offset to present entry
 89       mov    ax, [bp+8]          ;the segment that int 08h pushed
 90
 91       mov    [bx], ax            ;store it in addressArray
 92       mov    ax, [bp+10]         ;the corresponding offset
 93       add    bx, 2
 94       mov    [bx], ax            ;store this as well
 95       add    arrayOffset, 4      ;point to the next DWORD location
 96
 97   skipSampling:                  ;call orig08h only 18.2 times per second
 98
 99       dec    origTimerCountdown  ;mimic the ROM BIOS countdown procedure
100       cmp    origTimerCountdown, 0
101       jne    skipOrig08h         ;call only after count from 65536 to 0
102       mov    origTimerCountdown, 0 ;when finally called, reinitialize
103
104       pushf
105       cli
106       call   orig08hVector       ;mimic an int instruction
107
108   skipOrig08h:
109
110       mov    al, 20h             ;acknowledge receipt of interrupt to
111       out    20h, al             ;   8259 -- only necessary if Orig08h
```

Figure 15.7 cont.

```
112      popRegs                        ;      call was not made
113      iret
114
115  New08h      ENDP
116
117  ;===============================================================
118
119  END
```

of the procedure in order to operate correctly, and the present procedure ends with an **iret**. Not everything works the way one would like it to!

Lines 83-85. This is an item of defensive programming. If the profilee should run for too long a period or if the value of *speedUpFactor* is too large, more sample addresses would be collected than the array of addresses can hold. These extra addresses would overwrite other memory, probably with disastrous results. Consequently, we stop collecting sampling information as soon as the address array is full.

Lines 87-88. *addressArray* points to the start of the array of addresses and *arrayOffset* is kept updated so that it always represents the offset into the array of addresses of the first unused space (see lines 18 and 95). Hence, after line 88, **bx** points to the location at which the next address sample should be recorded.

Lines 89-97. This is the interesting part. After **int 08H** occurs, we need to locate the **cs** and **ip** of the interrupted program in order to store them in the array of addresses. Figure 15.8 shows the stack at this point in the program, and should completely explain lines 89-94.

Lines 97-102. It is important that the standard **int 08H** operations be executed with their normal frequency, hence the original **int 08H** handler code should be called at the correct intervals. This end is most easily achieved by keeping a counter that duplicates the action of the original Timer0, which is exactly the purpose of *origTimerCountdown*.

Lines 110-111. Part of the protocol of using the **8259** is that each interrupt request that it transmits must be acknowledged by outputting the byte 20H to Port 20H. Previously, we have not needed to send this acknowledgement since our handlers for the maskable interrupts have jumped to or called the original handler at some point, and hence have executed the acknowledgement that is always part of that code. In the present case, though, the original code is not executed whenever the jump on line 101 is taken.

Since the profiler is a two-module program, it affords us an opportunity to use MMF and **MAKE**. Recall that MMF constructs a makefile, which contains the information needed by **MAKE** in building PROFILE.EXE. If we are working in a directory containing only PROFILE.C and NEWTIMER.ASM, and if we wish to name the makefile PROFILE and the executable file PROFILE.EXE, then these two command lines suffice:

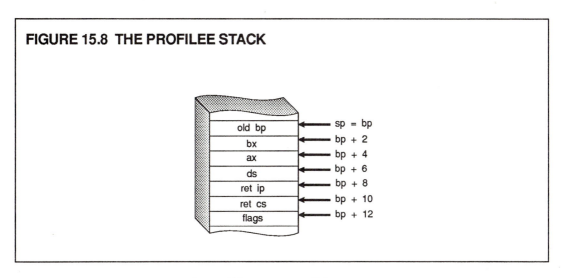

FIGURE 15.8 THE PROFILEE STACK

```
mmf profile  >  profile
make profile
```

Because we generally use the profiler to examine programs of modest size, it was built using the **SMALL** model. But each *ADDRESS* requires 4 bytes of storage and each *BIN* requires 8, and so the numbers of *ADDRESSes* and *BINs* will need to be kept down to the low thousands. More headroom would be obtained by using the **LARGE** model, or possibly even the **HUGE** model so that the array of *BINs* could be larger than 64K.

We will conclude this section with an example and a brief discussion of the use of the profiler. As the profilee in our example we chose the HEXDUMP program from Chapter 9. This choice was made since HEXDUMP is relatively long, uses **int 21H** functions, and needs command-line parameters. To invoke profile, we must select values for the command-line parameters *numberSamples* and *speedUpFactor*. We frequently, quite arbitrarily, use 2000 for *numberSamples*. To make use of this allocated memory, *speedUpFactor* should then be selected so that the number of samples taken during the execution of the profilee is less than, but reasonably close to, 2000. Naturally, the value of *speedUpFactor* will depend on the choice of profilee, as well as on the speed of the machine being used. A reasonable value of *speedUpFactor* can be selected by doing a trial run and using ratio and proportion, as we will now illustrate.

To run HEXDUMP, we must supply the name of the file to be dumped as a command-line parameter. Since HEXDUMP sends its output to STDOUT, it is a good idea to select a short file for these experiments. If the reader is using **MAKE**, as suggested previously, the current directory will contain an appropriately short file, namely the makefile PROFILE. This file was used in our example. If *speedUpFactor* is tentatively selected to be 10, the profile command line becomes

```
profile 2000 10 hexdump profile
```

Again, recall that the parameters occurring after the profilee name are interpreted as the command-line parameters for the profilee. When this version of profile was run, the actual

FIGURER 15.9 SAMPLE OUTPUT FROM THE PROFILER

```
EXECUTION PROFILE OF HEXDUMP

Segments found (code segment for profile.exe: 1616):

Segment   0:  address=0070  hits=0011  minOffset=00c6  maxOffset=0c3b  len= 2934
Segment   1:  address=02c1  hits=0063  minOffset=14ad  maxOffset=6768  len=21180
Segment   2:  address=0a68  hits=0009  minOffset=07ac  maxOffset=0fe9  len= 2110
Segment   3:  address=0e24  hits=0052  minOffset=241e  maxOffset=25bf  len=  418
Segment   4:  address=1616  hits=0001  minOffset=2ef0  maxOffset=2ef0  len=    1
Segment   5:  address=c000  hits=1344  minOffset=0562  maxOffset=2409  len= 7848
Segment   6:  address=f000  hits=0231  minOffset=9b83  maxOffset=c9df  len=11869


INFORMATION FOR SEGMENT 5 USING 100 BINS.

Bin    0:  Offsets   562- 5af  hits= 327
Bin    1:  Offsets   5b0- 5fd  hits=  45
Bin   24:  Offsets   cbd- d0b  hits=  71
Bin   33:  Offsets   f7f- fcd  hits= 123
Bin   34:  Offsets   fce-101b  hits=   9
Bin   39:  Offsets  1156-11a4  hits=  99
Bin   40:  Offsets  11a5-11f2  hits=  36
Bin   45:  Offsets  132d-137b  hits= 321
Bin   69:  Offsets  1a89-1ad6  hits=  86
Bin   70:  Offsets  1ad7-1b25  hits=  80
Bin   85:  Offsets  1f70-1fbe  hits=  62
Bin   99:  Offsets  23bb-2409  hits=  85


INFORMATION FOR SEGMENT 1 USING 20 BINS.

Bin    0:  Offsets  14ad-18cf  hits=   6
Bin    1:  Offsets  18d0-1cf2  hits=   2
Bin    2:  Offsets  1cf3-2115  hits=  12
Bin    9:  Offsets  39e8-3e0a  hits=  11
Bin   10:  Offsets  3e0b-422d  hits=   2
Bin   11:  Offsets  422e-4650  hits=   1
Bin   12:  Offsets  4651-4a73  hits=  13
Bin   13:  Offsets  4a74-4e96  hits=   2
Bin   14:  Offsets  4e97-52b9  hits=   6
Bin   16:  Offsets  56dd-5aff  hits=   4
Bin   17:  Offsets  5b00-5f22  hits=   1
Bin   18:  Offsets  5f23-6345  hits=   1
Bin   19:  Offsets  6346-6768  hits=   2
```

number of samples was somewhat over 100. This indicated that a *speedUpFactor* of 150 would be more reasonable, since that would bring the number of samples to somewhere between 1500 and 2000. The actual number of samples will vary somewhat from run to run. A suitable command line was therefore

```
profile 2000 150 hexdump profile
```

Figure 15.9 shows the frequencies of segment usage found by profile, as well as the (slightly edited) output resulting from some additional dialog.

Looking at Figure 15.9, we see that HEXDUMP spends most of its time in segment C000, with segment F000 being the runner-up. The memory map in Chapter 2 shows that these are, respectively, the locations of the EGA BIOS and ROM BIOS. Hence, HEXDUMP spends the vast majority of its time writing to the screen or accessing routines in the ROM BIOS.

Segments 0-3 are in the area of low memory in which **DOS** resides. We will soon see that these particular segments correspond to the locations of certain of the installable device drivers for this particular machine. An installable device driver is a special kind of memory-resident program that is normally used for interfacing the machine to external hardware devices. We will study them extensively in the next chapter.

The code segment for profile received only one hit, which suggests that the profiler is adding negligible overhead to the execution process. This is, unfortunately, incorrect. The real overhead added by the profiler results from **int 08H**: it occurs more frequently and contains extra code. This overhead does not show in our profile, because interrupts are masked while our extension of **int 08H** is executing, and so no samples are collected then. In an exercise at the end of the section, we investigate the overhead that is really inflicted by the profiler.

The later parts of Figure 15.9 show how profile can be used to examine particular segments. The middle display illustrates the activity in the EGA BIOS segment. From that display, it would seem that the activity at the offsets corresponding to Bins 0 and 45 are likely associated with the *Writes* to the screen. This can be checked, somewhat indirectly, by commenting out the *Writes* in the source code for HEXDUMP, then reassembling it and profiling the new version. The activity at these offsets will have decreased markedly. This technique of "commenting out" can be used to associate "hot spots" in the profile with areas of the original code.

Of course, if the entire source code is available, it is a simple matter to find the exact locations in the code corresponding to particular bins, either by using the .LST file or by using **CODEVIEW**. The mechanics of this process are discussed in one of the exercises that follow.

Exercise 15-15. The point of the present exercise is to get an idea of how much overhead the profiler is actually adding to execution time. One approach is to start with a program that takes a modest amount of time to execute (say a few seconds) and incorporate our timing macros (from Chapter 13) into its source code. Then run the program with larger and larger values of *speedUpFactor*, noting the degradation in speed. At what approximate value of *speedUpFactor* is the overhead 50%, i.e., when does the execution time required about double? When does the overhead approach 100%?

Exercise 15-16. Run the profiler on one or more programs for which you have the source code. After you get the timing information, use either **CODEVIEW** or the .LST file and try to understand why the program is spending time where it does. Especially since the .LST can be rather clogged with macro expansions and other extraneous items, we have found that **CODEVIEW** seems to work best in this kind of analysis. The easiest approach is to find the section of code that interests you while in source mode and then to switch to assembly mode so that you are seeing only the bare essentials — the instructions and their offsets.

Suggestion: Look at programs containing loops. A good starting point is program WHILE3.ASM, shown in Figure 14.4. Increase the sizes of the inner loops and see how much time is spent there.

Exercise 15-17. (For **80386** users.) In Section 4 of Chapter 11, we developed *bitStrMov*, a general-purpose procedure to move bit strings. Simulate a graphics application by writing a short program that uses *bitStrMov* to move 350 bit strings of length 640 bits, and analyze the performance of the program using the profiler.

CHAPTER 16

INSTALLABLE DEVICE DRIVERS

SECTION 1 PREVIEW

In this chapter, we will examine installable device drivers, which are among the most important features of **MS-DOS**. In Section 2, we outline the main ideas that underlie device drivers, and explain why their introduction constituted a really significant improvement to the operating system.

Device drivers come in two varieties, called character drivers and block drivers, and to understand the latter it is necessary to review some aspects of the structure of disks, as they are formatted under **MS-DOS**. This necessitates our again taking a slight detour from our main path, and this detour is the substance of Section 3.

The code for a device driver breaks rather cleanly into two parts. The first part can be structured so that it is identical for all device drivers, and we present that code in Section 4.

Section 5 is devoted to a discussion of the actual commands used in device drivers.

Sections 6 and 7 contain a pair of examples illustrating the device-dependent code in both the character- and block-driver cases. In addition, the examples in these sections provide us with a pair of potentially useful utilities. In Section 6, we write a driver that will work with most Postscript laser printers that can be connected to a parallel port. In Section 7, we give an example of the very common ramdisk program.

SECTION 2 INSTALLABLE DEVICE DRIVERS

Adding a new input or output device to a computer system involves two steps:

- Installing an interface card to perform the actual communication with the new device by sending data to it in the required format and/or interpreting data received from it.

- Setting up some system by which applications programs wishing to use the new device can communicate with the interface. Device interfaces, like the devices themselves, must be sent information in special formats and using protocols that vary widely depending on the nature of the device.

In the early days of **MS-DOS** (before Version 2.0), the operating system provided no particular assistance in completing either of these steps. Since the device and its interface normally function as though they were a single hardware unit, there is no particular reason why the operating system should be involved in the first step. On the contrary, such involvement would run counter to the basic design premise that **MS-DOS** should contain only portable, hardware-independent code usable on a wide variety of machines.

But the failure of the operating system to help with the second step presented a considerable hardship to the installers of new devices. As well as supplying the device interface, it was necessary to supply a *device driver*, which in those early days meant a program that would modify **DOS** (perhaps by taking over one or more interrupts) to allow it to communicate with the new device interface. This approach had a number of weaknesses:

- The installation of a new I/O device involved "patching" the operating system.

- Some of the code contained in these patches to the operating system was very "low-level," in the sense that it dealt directly with hardware devices, and so its inclusion contradicted the hardware-independence principle referred to previously.

- The patches supplied by different hardware purveyors did not always work harmoniously together.

Of course, one way of sidestepping the second of these objections was to have the device driver modify the ROM BIOS, rather than **MS-DOS**. But this approach entailed modifying the source code for the BIOS, reassembling it, and "burning" it into new ROM chips. With a little luck, when the new ROMs were installed, the replacement device driver performed flawlessly. But the real problem with this solution was that *everyone* who needed to use the new device driver had to obtain new ROM chips, a rather impractical expedient!

Version 2.0 introduced a radically different approach. The operating system now comes with built-in "generic" functions, which perform the standard operations required by most I/O devices: opening or closing a device, reading from a device, writing to a device, and a number of others, which we will introduce in this chapter. When a new device is installed, it is only necessary to supply a memory-resident program to translate these generic functions into the form required by the device interface. A translation program of this kind is called an *installable device driver*.

The file-handle functions, which we studied in Chapter 9, are actually examples of generic functions, usable by any installable device driver. This is the *real* reason that they work with any file or device. For example, a file handle read or write request causes **DOS** to call the device driver code, which translates the request into a form appropriate for the given device interface.

Under this new scheme, every device is totally integrated into the system and inherits all the perquisites of the existing devices: its name or letter designation can be used in any context where an existing device can be used. To illustrate, when we install our device driver RAMDISK later in this chapter, and assuming it is assigned the drive designation **F:** (as it was in our case), then the following commands are legal:

```
copy fileName f:
dir f:
chkdsk f:
```

They do the expected things.

The basic idea behind installable device drivers is that the operating system neither knows nor cares about the hardware details of input or output devices. The only requirement is that each I/O device have a unique name or other unique designation. When **DOS** receives a request from an application program to make use of an I/O device (perhaps to perform a read or a write), it formats this request in a special way (using a data packet called a *request header*) and transmits it to the corresponding device driver for execution. If it is a write, for example, the contents of the request header are (almost) independent of whether the data are written to PRN or to drive **C:**. Of course, a different device driver is called in each case.

It is therefore only a slight exaggeration to say that, to **MS-DOS**, a printer looks exactly like a disk drive! We will now discuss the nature of this "slight exaggeration."

DOS recognizes two kinds of device drivers, called *character device drivers* and *block device drivers*, and these names suggest the distinction being made. The first kind of driver is associated with devices that generally perform I/O one character at a time: the keyboard, the screen, and the printer are examples. The second kind is used for devices that read or write in larger blocks: disk drives, magnetic tapes, and CD ROMs are examples.

Of course, large blocks of data are sometimes sent to the screen and single characters are sent to a disk file, and so the preceding characterizations are not terribly precise. When we look at the device driver commands in detail in the later sections of this chapter, we will see that the real distinction is based on exactly which commands we wish to have the driver execute and what background services we desire from **DOS**. For example, **DOS** writes to a block device in blocks of size at least one "sector." While the size of a sector could be as small as one byte, it is frequently taken to be 512 bytes, which shows that block devices are generally used when large data transfers are anticipated.

The code for a device driver is written essentially in .COM format. The only difference is that there will be no **PSP** and so the code should begin at the start of the code segment — the *ORG 100* used in .COM files must be omitted.

As the reader probably knows, installable devices are installed at boot time by placing invocation lines in the CONFIG.SYS file. Device drivers are generally given the extension .SYS (although this is not required). To install the driver named DRIVER1.SYS, the CONFIG.SYS file should contain the line

```
DEVICE=DRIVER1.SYS
```

FIGURE 16.1 EXAMPLE LIST OF DEVICE DRIVERS

BASE ADDRESS	TYPE	NAME/UNITS
0006:2BF8	CHARDEV	NUL
10D2:0000	BLOCKDEV	1 UNIT
10A5:0000	CHARDEV	LASR
0FE2:0000	BLOCKDEV	2 UNITS
0C26:0000	CHARDEV	SMARTAAR
09A5:0000	CHARDEV	MS$MOUSE
0070:0BB3	CHARDEV	CON
0070:0C68	CHARDEV	AUX
0070:0D17	CHARDEV	PRN
0070:0E15	CHARDEV	CLOCK$
0070:0EE5	BLOCKDEV	3 UNITS
0070:0C7A	CHARDEV	COM1
0070:0D29	CHARDEV	LPT1
0070:2071	CHARDEV	LPT2
0070:2083	CHARDEV	LPT3
0070:2095	CHARDEV	COM2

13 CHARDEVs, 3 BLOCKDEVs

As well as installable device drivers, **DOS** comes with certain built-in *resident device drivers*. The resident drivers service the keyboard, the screen, the real-time clock, the parallel printer, the serial port, and at least one disk drive (so that the machine can boot). In addition, there is a resident driver named NUL which, as the name suggests, does nothing.

The device drivers are stored in memory as a linked list, where the first doubleword in each driver is a far pointer to the next driver in the list. The NUL device serves as the list header (which is one reason for its existence), the resident drivers are entered prior to the installed ones, and the last driver is the list has its pointer set to FFFF:FFFF.

When **DOS** adds new entries to the list, they are not always added at the beginning. However, the list is constructed in such a way that new character devices appear ahead of old ones. In this way, if a new character device named PRN, say, is added, it will be the one found first by **DOS** when traversing the list, and so will replace the original **PRN**. On the other hand, block devices are not assigned names, but rather consecutive letters A:, B:, C:,···, and these letters reflect the order in which the drivers were installed. Since new block devices are given different letters, they never replace previous block devices. Of course, if a block device is installable, it can be removed from CONFIG.SYS, but if it is resident, it is unchangeable.

Figure 16.1 shows the list of device drivers, resident and installed, in a typical machine. Most of the information in Figure 16.1 should be understandable. One new item is that, in the case of block devices, it is possible to install several "units" with one device driver. For example, if the last letter used by a previous block driver was **D:** and the number of units is three, then the new units would be designated **E:**, **F:**, and **G:**.

In one of the exercises at the end of the section we make suggestions for writing a utility to produce a listing of devices on the host machine, formatted like Figure 16.1.

Now that we have explored the general ideas underlying device drivers, it is time to study the device driver format in detail. The code for a device driver splits neatly into two parts: the first part is common to all drivers, and we will examine it in Section 4; the second part is specific to the driver, and we will illustrate it with two examples, a minimal laser printer driver, called LASR, in Section 6, and a ramdisk driver in Section 7. Both of these drivers can be seen in the list in Figure 16.1. (The ramdisk is the 1-unit block driver.)

Unfortunately, in order to understand the functioning of installable device drivers completely, it is first necessary to consider some aspects of the structure and formatting of disks under **MS-DOS**, and we will look at this topic in the next section.

The reader who is solely interested in writing character device drivers or who is willing to take a few things on faith can safely omit Section 3.

SECTION 3 THE FORMAT OF MS-DOS DISKS

We will only look at those aspects of disk structure used in the present chapter: the nature of the Bios Parameter Block, the structure of the File Allocation Table, and the general form of a directory entry. The exercises at the end of this section are intended to help the reader in exploring these ideas. We do not need to know about the physical structure of the disk, which involves such things as the number of tracks and heads and the interleave factor. For a discussion of these matters, and for more details on the aspects that we do discuss, we refer the interested reader to [3] or [24].

Every disk formatted under **DOS** is divided into *sectors*. A sector is just a contiguous storage area on the disk of a size that must be a power of two and is chosen when the disk is formatted. The standard sector size for **MS-DOS** disks is 512 bytes.

The first few sectors on a disk are used to store various records telling the system exactly how the disk is formatted and enabling it to locate the data stored on the remainder of the disk. In particular, the first sector (sector 0) is called the *boot sector*. It contains information on the disk format and a short program (the *boot program*) that is run if an attempt is made to boot the system using that disk. Of course, if the disk does not contain the standard system files (named IO.SYS and MSDOS.SYS in the Microsoft version of **MS-DOS** — see Chapter 2), any attempt to boot from the disk will fail. Figure 16.2 shows a hex dump of the first few paragraphs of the boot sector of a typical 360K **MS-DOS** floppy.

The boot sector always begins with a **jmp** instruction, which is a jump to the boot code and is allocated the first three bytes on the disk. Sometimes this is encoded as a **SHORT** jump, which only requires two bytes of machine code, and it is then followed by a **nop** to pad the length to three bytes. This is the configuration shown in Figure 16.2. In other cases, the first three bytes are encoded as a **NEAR** jump, which uses three bytes with no **nop** being necessary. In our example, the displacement contained in the **jmp** is 34H, and so the target is actually 36H. As an exercise, we ask the reader to disassemble the boot code on a floppy and attempt to decipher its meaning.

The next eight bytes are reserved for the machine manufacturer to insert an identification code.

From our point of view, the next 19 bytes are the most interesting part of the boot sector. They constitute the *Bios Parameter Block*, or *BPB*, and have been highlighted on the first

---

FIGURE 16.2 THE BEGINNING OF A BOOT SECTOR

HEXDUMP

```
2088:0000  EB 34 90 49 42 4D 20 20-33 2E 32 00 02 02 01 00   k4.IBM  3.2.....
2088:0010  02 70 00 D0 02 FD 02 00-09 00 02 00 00 00 00 00   .p.P.}..........
2088:0020  00 00 00 00 00 00 00 00-00 00 00 00 00 00 00 0F   ................
2088:0030  00 00 00 00 01 00 FA 33-C0 8E D0 BC 00 7C 16 07   ......z3@.P.|..
2088:0040  BB 78 00 36 C5 37 1E 56-16 53 BF 2B 7C B9 0B 00   ;x.6E7.V.S?+|9..
2088:0050  FC AC 26 80 3D 00 74 03-26 8A 05 AA 8A C4 E2 F1   |,&.=.t.&..*.Dbq
2088:0060  06 1F 89 47 02 C7 07 2B-7C FB CD 13 72 67 A0 10   ...G.G.+|{M.rg .
(THE BPB OCCUPIES THE RANGE OF OFFSETS 0BH-1D)
```

THE FIELDS OF THE THE BPB

OFFSETS	VALUE	MEANING
00h-02h	-----	Machine code for a short jmp and a nop
02h-0bh	-----	Text: vendor and version number
0bh-0ch	0200h	Bytes per sector
0Dh-0dh	02h	Sectors per cluster
0eh-0eh	0001h	Reserved sectors
10h-10h	02h	Number of FATs
11h-12h	0070h	Number of root directory entries
13h-14h	02d0h	Total sectors on disk
15h-15h	fdh	Media descriptor byte
16h-17h	0002h	Sectors per FAT
18h-19h	0090h	Sectors per track
1ah-1bh	0002h	Number of heads
1ch-1dh	0000h	Number of hidden sectors

(THE BPB OCCUPIES THE RANGE OF OFFSETS 0BH-1DH)

---

display in Figure 16.2. These bytes contain information about the structure of the disk, and are shown again on the second part of Figure 16.2, along with their meanings. We will explain those BPB fields that are most important to us.

First of all, sectors are organized into contiguous groups called *clusters*. The number of sectors in a cluster must be a power of two, and any file on the disk will be allocated a whole number of clusters. For instance, if (as here) the cluster size is 2 and the sector size is 512, then any file, no matter how small, will use at least 1024 bytes of disk space. If a file contains 1025 bytes, it will use 2048 bytes of space on the disk.

Although it is peripheral to our main theme, we will briefly discuss the significance of cluster size in efficient disk usage. The numbers in the last paragraph already suggest a weakness of large cluster size: it can be wasteful of space, especially when many small files are stored on the disk. But, on the other hand, we will see that when a file is stored in several clusters on the disk, these clusters may not be contiguous and the operation of finding the correct "next" cluster involves a non-trivial computation. Hence, small cluster size tends to slow disk access whenever large files are being used. A general guideline for selecting cluster size is that large hard disks will likely be used to store large files and so it is probably safe

TABLE 16.1 FORMAT OF A 32-BYTE DIRECTORY ENTRY

OFFSETS	CONTENTS
00h-07h	Filename
08h-0ah	Extension
0bh-0bh	Attribute
0ch-15h	Reserved
16h-17h	Time file most recently changed
18h-19h	Date file most recently changed
1ah-1bh	Starting cluster number
1ch-1fh	Filesize (double precision integer)

to give them large cluster size. For a different reason, to be discussed below, it turns out that large disks *must* be given a large cluster size.

It is possible to reserve any number of sectors (at the start of the disk) to store specialized information or for any other reason. The boot sector is considered to be a reserved sector and most disks have no others. Hence the normal value for the number of *reserved sectors* is one.

Each file stored on the disk must have a *directory entry*. In addition, the volume label and subdirectory names are stored as directory entries. A directory entry requires 32 bytes of disk storage and is formatted as shown in Table 16.1.

The interpretation of some of the fields in a directory entry can be quite technical, and we refer the reader to [3] or [24] for details. For example, we have already encountered the formats used for the date and time fields. (See Section 4 of Chapter 12.) One item of interest to us is that the directory entry for a file contains the starting cluster number of the file, which enables the operating system to find the beginning of the file on the disk. Figure 16.3 contains a dump of the first part of a disk directory.

A **DOS** disk can contain many subdirectories, each of which has its own directory entry. Whether a given directory entry represents a file or a subdirectory or a volume label is communicated by the value of its *attribute*. (The attribute was defined in Section 3 of Chapter 8.) In general, a **DOS** directory can contain an arbitrary number of entries: the list of entries in the directory just grows longer, as needed. The only exception to this rule is the root directory, which has a maximum number of entries that is recorded in the BPB. In our example, this number is 70H = 112. Since **DOS** knows this number and also knows that each directory entry requires 32 bytes, it can easily compute how many sectors are required for the root directory. In this case we get 112 * 32 / 512 = 7.

These sectors are allocated near the start of the disk, but behind another important storage area, the *file allocation table*. The file allocation table (known as the FAT) is so important that most **DOS** disks contain more than one copy of it, with two being the normal number. When the FAT is updated, all copies are changed. In principle, if one copy of the FAT becomes corrupted, it is possible to recover the vital information that it contains from one of the backup copies. There is good reason to keep at least one backup of the FAT, since without it the disk is virtually worthless. The disk whose boot record is shown in Figure 16.2 contained two copies of the FAT but, unfortunately, present versions of **MS-DOS** do not make any use of extra copies of the FAT.

TABLE 16.2 MEANINGS OF THE FAT ENTRIES

12-BIT FAT VALUE	16-BIT FAT VALUE	MEANING
000h	0000h	Cluster not in use
001h	0001h	This value is not used
ff0h - ff6h	fff0h-fff6h	Reserved
ff7h	fff7h	Bad cluster
ff8h-fffh	fff8h-ffffh	Last cluster in a file
Any other value	Any other value	Link to the next file cluster

As we pointed out previously, the directory entry for a file contains the number of its starting cluster. The FAT contains the "linkage" enabling the operating system to find the remaining clusters constituting the file. Of course, since the directory entry contains the file size, it is a trivial matter to determine how many clusters the file occupies. But the snag is that these clusters do not always occur contiguously on the disk.

Here is how the FAT is used to find the clusters corresponding to a given file. First, the clusters are numbered sequentially throughout the data area of the disk, and the FAT contains an entry corresponding to each cluster. The directory entry for the file contains the first cluster number, say N_1, for the file. The N_1-entry in the FAT then contains the second cluster number, say N_2, the N_2-entry in the FAT contains the third cluster number, and so on. The process continues until all the clusters have been found. Recall that the operating system knows in advance how many clusters there will be but, as a double check, the FAT entry with index equal to the last cluster number contains a special code to indicate that the end of the file has been reached. The values of this and other special codes are shown in Table 16.2.

Two different sizes are used for FAT entries: "small" disks generally have FAT entries of size 12 bits, while "large" disks have FAT entries of size 16 bits. We will examine the small case more closely. Because each cluster number must have a corresponding FAT number, and since $2^{12} = 4096$, it follows that a disk with a 12-bit FAT is restricted to a maximum size of about 4000 clusters. Since we are now talking about a (relatively) small disk, it would seem reasonable to limit the cluster size to two sectors, or 1024 bytes, using the standard **DOS** sector size. Hence the disk size would be limited to about 4 megabytes. **DOS** is actually somewhat more liberal than this: it uses a 12-bit FAT if the disk has fewer that 20740 sectors and a 16-bit FAT otherwise. In any case, it is clear that most hard disks use a 16-bit FAT.

Finally, we can check that a reasonable number of sectors has been allocated to each copy of the FAT in the example in Figure 16.2. According to Figure 16.2, there are 02D0H = 720 sectors, or 360 clusters. Hence the FAT requires 360 12-bit entries. In addition, we will see that the FAT contains a few overhead entries, and so this translates to about 550 bytes per FAT, whence each FAT should be allocated two sectors, as was done.

The only remaining item of interest to us in Figure 16.2 is the *media descriptor byte*, which, as the name suggests, is a code telling **DOS** whether the disk is a hard disk or a floppy of any of various sizes or densities. Table 16.3 contains a list of the most important values taken by this byte, and their interpretations.

FIGURE 16.3 EXAMPLE: DIRECTORY AND 12-BIT FAT

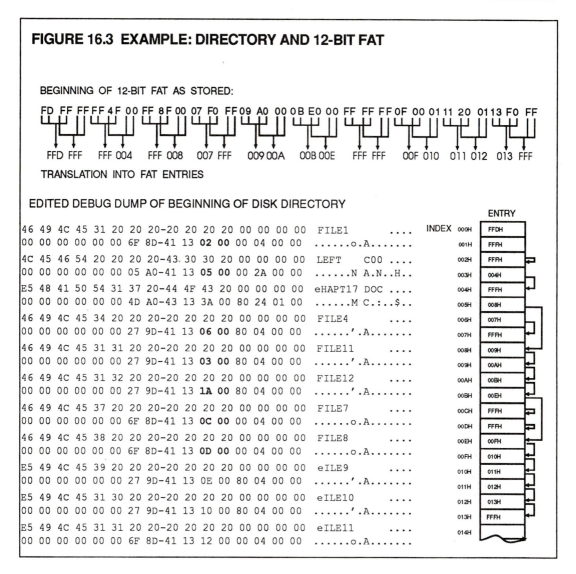

BEGINNING OF 12-BIT FAT AS STORED:

FD FF FF FF 4F 00 FF 8F 00 07 F0 FF 09 A0 00 0B E0 00 FF FF FF 0F 00 01 11 20 01 13 F0 FF

FFD FFF   FFF 004   FFF 008   007 FFF   009 00A   00B 00E   FFF FFF   00F 010   011 012   013 FFF

TRANSLATION INTO FAT ENTRIES

EDITED DEBUG DUMP OF BEGINNING OF DISK DIRECTORY

```
                                                              ENTRY
46 49 4C 45 31 20 20 20-20 20 20 20 00 00 00 00   FILE1       ....   INDEX 000H    FFDH
00 00 00 00 00 00 6F 8D-41 13 02 00 00 04 00 00   ......o.A..         001H    FFFH
4C 45 46 54 20 20 20 20-43.30 30 20 00 00 00 00   LEFT     C00 ....   002H    FFFH
00 00 00 00 00 00 05 A0-41 13 05 00 00 2A 00 00   ......N A.N..H..    003H    004H
E5 48 41 50 54 31 37 20-44 4F 43 20 00 00 00 00   eHAPT17 DOC ....    004H    FFFH
00 00 00 00 00 00 4D A0-43 13 3A 00 80 24 01 00   ......M C.:..$..    005H    008H
46 49 4C 45 34 20 20 20-20 20 20 20 00 00 00 00   FILE4       ....    006H    007H
00 00 00 00 00 00 27 9D-41 13 06 00 80 04 00 00   ......'.A.......    007H    FFFH
46 49 4C 45 31 31 20 20-20 20 20 20 00 00 00 00   FILE11      ....    008H    009H
00 00 00 00 00 00 27 9D-41 13 03 00 80 04 00 00   ......'.A.......    009H    00AH
46 49 4C 45 31 32 20 20-20 20 20 20 00 00 00 00   FILE12      ....    00AH    00BH
00 00 00 00 00 00 27 9D-41 13 1A 00 80 04 00 00   ......'.A.......    00BH    00EH
46 49 4C 45 37 20 20 20-20 20 20 20 00 00 00 00   FILE7       ....    00CH    FFFH
00 00 00 00 00 00 6F 8D-41 13 0C 00 00 04 00 00   ......o.A.......    00DH    FFFH
46 49 4C 45 38 20 20 20-20 20 20 20 00 00 00 00   FILE8       ....    00EH    00FH
00 00 00 00 00 00 6F 8D-41 13 0D 00 00 04 00 00   ......o.A.......    00FH    010H
E5 49 4C 45 39 20 20 20-20 20 20 20 00 00 00 00   eILE9       ....    010H    011H
00 00 00 00 00 00 27 9D-41 13 0E 00 80 04 00 00   ......'.A.......    011H    012H
E5 49 4C 45 31 30 20 20-20 20 20 20 00 00 00 00   eILE10      ....    012H    013H
00 00 00 00 00 00 27 9D-41 13 10 00 80 04 00 00   ......'.A.......    013H    FFFH
E5 49 4C 45 31 31 20 20-20 20 20 20 00 00 00 00   eILE11      ....    014H
00 00 00 00 00 00 6F 8D-41 13 12 00 00 04 00 00   ......o.A.......
```

A FAT always begins with two overhead entries: a 12-bit FAT opens with the byte pattern

```
        mediaDescriptor, 0FFH, 0FFH
```

which exactly fills 24 bits = 2 FAT entries; a 16-bit FAT starts with

```
        mediaDescriptor, 0FFH, 0FFH, 0FFH
```

which again exactly fills 32 bits = 2 FAT entries.

The first part of Figure 16.3 shows the initial 30 bytes of the FAT of a floppy disk, and how the 20 corresponding FAT entries are obtained from these bytes.

TABLE 16.3 THE VALUES OF THE MEDIA DESCRIPTOR BYTE

VALUE	DISK TYPE	BEGINNING DOS VERSION
Of8H	Fixed disk	2.0
Of0H	3.5 inch, 2-sided, 18-sector	3.2
Of9H	3.5 inch, 2-sided, 9-sector	3.2
Of9H	5.25 inch, 2-sided, 15-sector	3.0
Ofch	5.25 inch, 1-sided, 9-sector	2.0
Ofdh	5.25 inch, 2-sided, 9-sector	2.0
Ofeh	5.25 inch, 1-sided, 8-sector	1.0
Offh	5.25 inch, 2-sided, 8-sector	1.1

Immediately below this display is a dump of the start of the disk directory. This information was obtained using **DEBUG**, one of the older Microsoft debuggers, and the technique for obtaining such a display is discussed in the exercises at the end of this section. As Table 16.1 shows, a directory entry begins with the filename and, at offsets 1AH and 1BH, contains the starting cluster number of the file. When a file is deleted, **DOS** replaces the first letter in its name with the special byte 0E5H, as well as marking all its assigned clusters with value 000H (or 0000H in the 16-bit case) to indicate that they are free. A number of deleted files can be seen in the directory in Figure 16.3.

The reader should check the accuracy of the FAT diagram at the right of Figure 16.3. For each file that has not been erased, we have printed the starting cluster number in bold. Starting with this number, it is a simple matter to "follow the FAT chains" to find the locations of the later clusters in the file. As a final check, it should be noted that the size of each file (bytes 1CH-1FH) is consistent with the number of clusters in its chain.

Note on the Following Exercises. The object of the next few exercises is to explore the structure of disks written in the standard **DOS** format, and a word of caution may be in order at this point. When writing programs that examine disk structure, and especially programs that write to disks, it is only sensible to do all development work using a floppy with expendable data as the target. Before experimenting with such a utility on a hard disk, be sure to make a backup.

In order to study the structure of a disk, it is necessary to read its contents first, and this is one area in which **CODEVIEW** is weaker than its predecessors **DEBUG** and **SYMDEB**. Either of these earlier debuggers can be asked to read from or write to particular sectors of a disk, but **CODEVIEW** cannot. This weakness of **CODEVIEW** is not really serious since most programmers have a copy of **DEBUG** (which comes free with **MS-DOS**).

For anyone familiar with **CODEVIEW**, the earlier debuggers are easy to use. To enter either **DEBUG** or **SYMDEB**, just type its name at the **DOS** prompt. To load a file into either debugger, give its name as a command-line parameter. Any kind of file, executable or not, can be loaded, and will be found at the location appropriate for a .COM file, namely at cs:0100. Both debuggers have (very primitive) on-line help, accessed from the command line by the command '?'. The main command that we care about is 'L', for *load*. As well as the

L *fileName*

option, which works like the corresponding **CODEVIEW** menu command, there is an

L *Address Drive Start Number*

option, which loads sectors from a disk drive. *Address* is the address (*segment:offset*) at which they will be loaded. If the segment is not specified, the default is **cs**. *Drive* is the designator of the drive to load from, where 0 means **A:**, etc. *Start* is the starting sector number, and *Number* is the number of sectors to load. The correct command to load the boot sector of **A:** at **cs**:0100 is therefore

```
L 100 0 0 1
```

Once the data from the boot sector are in memory, it is probably a good idea to store them on disk. This requires three commands:

n *fileName*

which supplies a filename for the forthcoming write,

rcx *Number*

which places the number of characters to write in the **cx** register, and

w *Address*

which writes the prescribed number of characters, starting at *Address*, to *fileName*. Again if no segment is specified in *Address*, the default is **cs**.
In the present case, the commands might look like

```
n bootSect
rcx 200
w 100
```

The first 100H bytes in the sector can be displayed on the screen exactly as in **CODEVIEW:**

```
d 100 L 100
```

If the user does not wish to see these bytes on the screen, but only have them available in a file, then all the previous operations can be accomplished in one line, using redirection of output:

```
L 100 0 0 1; > bootSect; d 100 L 100; > con
```

The **u** (*unassemble*) command works like the **CODEVIEW** version. Studying our example in Figure 16.2 for a moment shows that the actual boot code begins at offset 36H (the target of the initial jump) and ends at offset 16DH (since everything after that is just text). A reasonable u-command in that case would be

```
u 36 16d
```

It is also a good idea to save the unassembled listing to disk, and this is most easily done using redirection:

```
> bootSect; u 36 16d;  > con
```

Finally, we can state the problems.

Exercise 16-1. Start with any bootable **DOS** disk and make an unassembled listing of the boot code, as outlined previously. Then trace through the code by hand. It should be possible to make sense of nearly all of it. Repeat the process with a non-bootable disk.

Exercise 16-2. Write a procedure (perhaps for installation in USER.LIB) that will read a chosen number of sectors from a disk into a buffer, beginning with any desired sector number. **Suggestion:** Use either **DOS int 25H** or **BIOS int 13H**. These interrupts are both described in Appendix 2. However, **int 13H** requires some more explanation.

A disk drive contains a number of *platters*, or separate disks, each divided into concentric *tracks*, and each track is further divided into *sectors*. In most modern disk formats, data is recorded on both sides of the platters, hence each platter has two *heads* associated with it. In the description of **int 13H**, the word *cylinder* is used as a synonym for track. A double-sided floppy disk format then corresponds to one platter and two heads.

In the ROM BIOS terminology, the head and cylinder numbering begin with 0, but the track numbering begins with 1! (In the **MS-DOS** numbering system, the sector numbering starts with 0 and increases linearly throughout the disk.) If we represent the disk drive parameters as C/H/S (cylinders/heads/sectors), then a 360K floppy is a 40/2/9, a 720K floppy is an 80/2/9, a 1.2M floppy is an 80/2/15, a 1.44M floppy is an 80/2/18, and many hard disks have the form ?/?/17. To translate the **MS-DOS** linear sector numbering into the ROM BIOS C/H/S form, it is also necessary to know the order in which the sectors are accessed. The order used corresponds to 'S' varying most rapidly and 'C' varying least rapidly.

Exercise 16-3. In the first display in Figure 16.2 we gave a primitive hex dump of the start of the boot sector and in the second display we showed a nicely formatted listing of the various fields of interest. Write a utility that will produce output of this second type for any **DOS** formatted disk.

Exercise 16-4. In Section 3, we outlined the structure of a FAT. The only way to really understand that discussion is to trace through part of one, as we did in Figure 16.3. This is much easier to do in the 16-bit FAT case than in the 12-bit case.
a. Write a utility that will read a 12-bit FAT from a disk and convert the entries into hexadecimal integers, formatting the results as a column whose typical entry has the form

```
FAT entry number: value contained in this entry.
```

b. Prepare a floppy containing a badly "fragmented" file as follows. Begin with a freshly formatted floppy, and fill it with small files. Randomly erase some of these files so that the disk data have "holes." Then write a large text file to the disk. Use a text file so that, at the end of the exercise, you will know whether you have successfully found its data.

c. Using the utility written in part a, find the sequence of cluster numbers for the text file. The special meanings associated with some FAT values were given in Table 16.2.

d. Read the data from these clusters into another file, or a sequence of files, and check that you have indeed found all of the original text file.

Exercise 16-5. (A lengthy problem!) Write a utility that will attempt to recover deleted files from a disk. In response to the command line

```
undel fileName
```

it should do its best to find the data from the deleted file named *fileName* and restore its directory entry and cluster linkage in the FAT. It is sufficient to write the program so that it works with 12-bit FATs on floppies, but it is easier, more useful, and also more dangerous to develop it using 16-bit FATs so that it will work on hard disks. The choice is yours — perhaps you would like to do a version that can handle both sizes of FAT.

Suggestions: Recall from our discussion of Figure 16.3 that a directory entry is not erased until it is reused. With luck, it will still be there, intact, except that the first byte will have been changed to 0E5H. Hence it is (relatively) easy to find the directory entry and fix the first letter. At this point, we will also have access to the starting cluster number and the file size, which tells us the total number of clusters. The next step seems unreasonably optimistic, and its only justification is that it works most of the time. Assume that the clusters whose entries in the FAT contain zero (i.e., are available) and that follow the starting cluster and are closest to it contained the remainder of the file. Patch these FAT entries so that they have the correct linkage and hope for the best.

If you feel especially industrious, it is possible to improve the utility by giving it a "manual" mode in which it makes a screen dump of each promising cluster, letting the user decide whether to include it or look further.

SECTION 4 THE DEVICE-INDEPENDENT CODE

The structure of installable device drivers is quite strictly mandated by **DOS**. On the one hand, this means that the programmer must know the rules completely in order to write a working driver but, on the other hand, many parts of the driver are trivial to write, since the coding amounts to little more than following a template.

Although it is not strictly necessary, we prefer to split the code for a device driver into two parts. The first part contains code that is the same for all device drivers, and so need not be rewritten for each new driver. The easiest way to combine this code with the second, device-dependent code is by means of **MASM's INCLUDE** directive. Figure 16.4 shows our version of the device-independent code.

Before talking about the code in Figure 16.4 in detail, we will briefly discuss the general structure of device drivers, keying our discussion to the definitions given in Figure 16.4.

First, as mentioned in Section 2, device drivers are basically .COM programs, except that they begin at offset zero in the code segment. They are written and prepared like other

.COM programs: they must consist of a single segment (or group), execution must begin at the beginning of that segment (or group), and they must be processed by **EXE2BIN**.

If a hardware device is associated with an installable device driver, it can automatically be controlled by a number of the **int 21H** functions. The file handle functions are probably the most important, but there are others. Examples are the disk directory functions (if it is a block device) and **function 44H** of **int 21H**, which is called *I/O Control for Devices* and will be discussed later.

When an application program uses an **int 21H** function to access a device, **DOS** encapsulates the essential information about the function call in a data structure called a *Request Header* and calls the *Strategy Routine* of the device driver (starting on line 106 of Figure 16.4). The Strategy Routine is passed the address of the Request Header in **es:bx** and should save that address.

Next **DOS** calls the *Interrupt Routine* (starting on line 116 of the driver code). The Interrupt Routine is basically a switching station that directs the service request to the correct *device driver command* and returns a completion code afterward.

The name "Interrupt Routine" is not well chosen — it suggests that perhaps calls to this procedure are asynchronous in the same way that hardware interrupts are. This is not the case because this procedure is called by **DOS** when required. Since the two routines, Strategy and Interrupt, are always called sequentially, it may seem artificial to make them separate procedures, and indeed it is. The standard explanation is that the formalism is set up in this way so that, should **DOS** ever become multi-tasking, the Strategy Routine is already in place to do something more useful, namely, to arbitrate in the scheduling of overlapping calls to the Interrupt Routine.

The actual commands to which the device driver may respond are listed on lines 74-98. As the comments indicate, some of these commands are intended for character devices and some for block devices. In fact, a typical device driver will support a relatively small subset of these commands. The next section will be devoted to a discussion of the most important (from our viewpoint) of the device driver commands.

Now we will look at some of the coding details of Figure 16.4:

Line 1. The semicolon before the **TITLE** directive is *not* a typo. We are going to **INCLUDE** this code as part of another module and consequently the present line 1 will occur at a later position in the combined file. However, **MASM** only allows the **TITLE** directive to occur on line 1 and so the simplest expedient was to comment it out.

Line 9. In all the device driver commands, **es:di** points to the Request Header, and we can make the code more readable by supplying a suggestive name for this quantity by means of an **EQUATE**. The only weakness of this approach is that *reqHdr*, the chosen name, is an anonymous reference and so, depending on the other operand of an instruction, may require a size override. It is not practical to supply a size override as part of the **EQUATE** name since it is sometimes used as a byte and sometimes as a word.

Lines 11-30. Each device driver has an *attribute word* (defined later by a **DW**), and these **EQUATE**s explain the meanings of the significant bits in that word. Notice that the early bits are set only for the various resident drivers. The middle bits indicate whether or not a driver supports some particular functions. Bit 15 is obviously important.

FIGURE 16.4 THE DEVICE-INDEPENDENT CODE

```
1    ;TITLE devIndep.asm -- code that is common to all device drivers.
2
3    COMMENT #   This code should be present in all installable device drivers.
4                The easiest way to incorporate it is to INCLUDE it at the
5            #   beginning of the code that is particular to the given driver.
6
7        INCLUDE     console.mac
8
9        reqHdr          EQU     es:[di]
10
11   ;Attribute Definitions
12
13       STDINDEV        EQU     01h     ;bit 0  -- 1 means current std. input
14       STDOUTDEV       EQU     02h     ;bit 1  -- 1 means current std. output
15       NUL             EQU     04h     ;bit 2  -- 1 means current NUL device
16       CLOCK           EQU     08h     ;bit 3  -- 1 means current clock device
17       RESERVED        EQU     10h     ;bit 4  -- use undocumented by Microsoft
18       GENIOCTL_GSLD   EQU     40h     ;bit 6  -- 1 if DOS 3.2 Generic IOCTL &
19                                       ;           Get/Set Logic. Dr. supported
20       OPCLREM         EQU     800h    ;bit 11 -- 1 means DOS 3.0 Open/Close/
21                                       ;           Removable Media Supported
22       NOIBM_OUB       EQU     2000h   ;bit 13 -- Block Device: 1 means non-IBM
23                                       ;           format Char. Device: 1 means
24                                       ;           Output Until Busy Supported
25       IOCTLWR         EQU     4000h   ;bit 14 -- 1 means IOCTL Read and Write
26                                       ;           supported
27       CHARDEV         EQU     8000h   ;bit 15 -- 1 means character device, 0
28                                       ;           means block device
29       BLOCKDEV        EQU     00H     ;just an EQU that can be or'ed with
30                                       ;   others when describing block devices
31
32   ;Request Header Status Word: Bits 0-7 contain error code if bit 15 is set
33
34       DONE            EQU     100h    ;bit 8
35       BUSY            EQU     200h    ;bit 9
36       ERROR           EQU     8000h   ;bit 15
37
38   ;Device Driver Error Codes -- always accessed as reqHdr[3]
39
40       DISKCHANGE      EQU     0fh     ;DOS 3.0
41       GENERALFAIL     EQU     0ch
42       READFAULT       EQU     0bh
43       WRITEFAULT      EQU     0ah
44       OUTOFPAPER      EQU     09h
45       SECTORNOTFOUND  EQU     08h
46       UNKNOWNMEDIA    EQU     07h
47       SEEKERROR       EQU     06h
48       BADREQSTRLEN    EQU     05h
49       CRCERROR        EQU     04h
50       UNKNOWNCOMMAND  EQU     03h
51       NOTREADY        EQU     02h
52       UNKNOWNUNIT     EQU     01h
53       WRITEPROTECT    EQU     00h
54
55   ;==============================================================
```

Figure 16.4 cont.

```
56
57    _TEXT    SEGMENT    PARA    PUBLIC    'CODE'
58
59        ASSUME cs:_TEXT, ds:NOTHING, es:NOTHING
60
61    ;Device Driver Header
62
63        deviceHeader    DD      -1
64                        DW      ATTRIBUTE
65                        DW      Strategy
66                        DW      Interrupt
67        devNameOrNo     DB      8 DUP(?)
68
69    ;Jump table: contains spaces for all commands that can be supported by
70    ;different kinds of device drivers. No single driver will support all the
71    ;commands. The comments indicate the kinds of device to which each command
72    ;applies, and the minimal DOS version with which it can be used
73
74        commandTable    DW      Initialize       ;BOTH       -- 2.0
75                        DW      mediaCheck       ;BLOCKDEV   -- 2.0
76                        DW      buildBPB         ;BLOCKDEV   -- 2.0
77                        DW      IOCTLRead        ;BOTH       -- 2.0
78                        DW      Read             ;BOTH       -- 2.0
79                        DW      nonDestRead      ;CHARDEV    -- 2.0
80                        DW      inputStatus      ;CHARDEV    -- 2.0
81                        DW      flushInputBuf    ;CHARDEV    -- 2.0
82                        DW      Write            ;BOTH       -- 2.0
83                        DW      writeVerify      ;BOTH       -- 2.0
84                        DW      outputStatus     ;CHARDEV    -- 2.0
85                        DW      flushOutputBuf   ;CHARDEV    -- 2.0
86                        DW      IOCTLWrite       ;BOTH       -- 2.0
87                        DW      Open             ;BOTH       -- 3.0
88                        DW      Close            ;BOTH       -- 3.0
89                        DW      removMedia       ;BLOCKDEV   -- 3.0
90                        DW      outputUntilBusy  ;CHARDEV    -- 3.0
91                        DW      numberNotUsed
92                        DW      numberNotUsed
93                        DW      genIOCTLReq      ;BOTH       -- 3.2
94                        DW      numberNotUsed
95                        DW      numberNotUsed
96                        DW      numberNotUsed
97                        DW      getLogicalDevice;BLOCKDEV   -- 3.2
98                        DW      setLogicalDevice;BLOCKDEV   -- 3.2
99
100   reqHdrAddr      LABEL    DWORD
101   reqHdrOff       DW       ?
102   reqHdrSeg       DW       ?
103
104       ;------------------------------------------------------------
105
106   Strategy    PROC    FAR
107
108       mov     reqHdrOff, bx      ;initialize es:bx to point to
109       mov     reqHdrSeg, es      ;  the request header
110       ret
111
```

```
112    Strategy    ENDP
113
114    ;------------------------------------------------------------
115
116    Interrupt    PROC    FAR
117
118        pushRegs ax,bx,cx,dx,si,di,ds,es,bp
119
120        les    di, reqHdrAddr        ;point es:di to the request header
121
122        mov    bl, reqHdr[02h]       ;command code
123        xor    bh, bh
124        cmp    bx, MAXCOMMAND        ;is command code in correct range?
125        jle    goodCommand
126        call   numberNotUsed
127
128    goodCommand:
129
130        shl    bx, 1                ;index into table of words
131        call   commandTable[bx]
132
133        les    di, reqHdrAddr        ;in case called function changed es or di
134        or     ax, DONE             ;signal completion of command
135        mov    reqHdr[03h], ax      ;record status word in request header
136
137        popRegs
138        ret
139
140    Interrupt ENDP
141
142    ;------------------------------------------------------------
143
144    numberNotUsed    PROC    NEAR
145
146        mov    ax, ERROR OR UNKNOWNCOMMAND    ;signal error
147        ret
148
149    numberNotUsed    ENDP
150
151    ;============================================================
152
153    ;DEVICE SPECIFIC CODE COMES HERE
```

Lines 32-53. When the driver has completed a task, it must return a *status code* to **MS-DOS**. Normally, the DONE bit is set to signal completion and, if an error occurred, the ERROR bit is set, in which case the low 8 bits will also contain an error code, as listed on lines 40-53.

Line 59. The directive

```
ASSUME ds:NOTHING, es:NOTHING
```

deactivates any **ASSUME**s that may be in effect for **ds** and **es**. In the present context, it has no effect since there are no active **ASSUME**s. We have included them only as documentation, to emphasize the fact that we definitely do not want the **ASSUME** statements

```
ASSUME ds:_TEXT, es:_TEXT
```

to occur in our versions of device drivers. At a number of points in the program, the segment registers are pointed to different regions of memory. Recall from Chapter 6 that if several segment registers have **ASSUME**s associating them with the same segment, then **MASM** gives precedence to **ds** and **es** over **cs** when referencing a named variable in that segment. This can easily lead to addressing errors. In one of the exercises, the reader is asked to rebuild our first example, LASR, incorporating these extra **ASSUME**s, and then to explain the outcome.

Lines 63-67. Every device driver has a *driver header*, which must occur first thing — at offset zero — in the code segment. The first entry in the header is a doubleword, which should be initialized to −1 (= 0FFFFFFFFH). When the driver is installed, **DOS** will overwrite this entry with a pointer to the next device in the linked list (unless, of course, this is the last device in the list). The next item is the *Attribute* word, which is initialized to a symbolic-constant value ATTRIBUTE, to be supplied in the second module of the device driver. Next come near pointers (offsets only) to the driver's Strategy and Interrupt Routines. Finally, there is an 8-byte storage area which, in the case of a character device, should be initialized to the device name (padded on the right with spaces), and, in the case of a block device, should be initialized to the number of units the device will support.

Lines 74-98. This jump table contains all possible commands supported by any device driver running under **DOS**. Notice that the later commands only work with the more recent versions of **DOS** and so should not be implemented in device drivers intended for general use. The comments in the table also indicate whether each command is meant to be used in a character driver or a device driver or both. The commands will be discussed in the next section.

Lines 100-102. We are setting up storage for the address of the Request Header, which is passed to the driver by **DOS**.

Lines 106-112. The Strategy Routine. The only operation required of this routine is to store the address of the Request Header, which is passed to it in **es:bx**.

Lines 116-140. The Interrupt Routine first points **es:di** to the Request Header, retrieving the address stored there by the Strategy Routine. **DOS** has passed, as the byte at address *reqHdr[02H]*, the number of the device driver command to be called. The Interrupt Routine uses this number to index into the jump table, and makes the correct call on line 131. The driver is expected to return a completion code in **ax**. (Possibly an error number in the low 8 bits and bit 15 set to indicate an error, for example.) The Interrupt Routine then **or**s this completion code with DONE, returning the answer to *reqHdr[03H]*, as required by **DOS**.

Line 153. At this point, the device-specific part of the driver code begins. This consists mostly of the code for the particular driver commands supported by the driver. Later in the chapter, we will give concrete examples.

Exercise 16-6. Write a utility that generates a listing of the device drivers for any machine, formatted like Figure 16.1.

Suggestion: The hardest thing is to find NUL, the start of the device driver chain. In all versions of **DOS**, this is installed somewhere after 0006:0000 and so the simplest approach is to search through memory, upward from this starting address, looking for the string "NUL." After this driver is found, it is easy to follow the chain of pointers, ending when the device with pointer FFFF:FFFF is reached.

SECTION 5 THE DEVICE DRIVER COMMANDS

Table 16.4 contains a list of all the commands currently supported by installable device drivers. Most of these commands have been available since installable drivers were introduced with Version 2.0 of **MS-DOS**, but four new commands were introduced with Version 3.0 and three further commands with Version 3.2. The last column of Table 16.4 shows the minimum **DOS** version with which each command is usable. Of course, it is nearly always desirable to write drivers that will run under **DOS** versions earlier than 3.0 and so it is common to ignore the later commands or, at least, to check the **DOS** version at run time and use the later commands only when it is legal to do so. In our discussion, we will concentrate on the main features of the most basic of the commands, referring the reader to [3] or [24] for additional information.

Some of the device driver commands are intended for character devices only, some for block devices only, and some for any kind of device. This information about the commands is contained in the "DEVICE TYPE" column of Table 16.4.

The general usage of the commands is similar: each receives its inputs at certain offsets in the Request Header, and is expected to return its results at prescribed offsets in the Request Header. For the most part, the locations in the Request Header used by the various commands are arbitrary, and must be looked up for each command. However, some of the usage is constant throughout the collection of commands. As examples, during input the number of the command being called is always found as the byte at offset 02H, while each command is expected to record the "return status" as the word at offset 03H.

We will always access the inputs and return values as indicated in the last section: when any command is sent to the driver, **es:di** points to the Request Header, and so introducing an **EQUATE** of the form

```
reqHdr    EQU   es:di
```

allows the data item at offset k in the Request Header to be referred to as *reqHdr[k]*.

We will now discuss the 20 device commands. In some cases, it is possible to discuss several of these commands at once, and in other cases they must be handled singly. Here are the commands:

COMMAND 00H: DRIVER INITIALIZATION (ALL)

INPUTS:
reqHdr[00H] (BYTE)   Request header length
reqHdr[02H] (BYTE)   Command code (=00H)

TABLE 16.4 DEVICE DRIVER COMMANDS

NUMBER	NAME	DEVICE TYPE	DOS VERSION
00h	Initialize	All	2.0
01h	Media Check	Block	2.0
02h	Build BPB	Block	2.0
03h	I/O Control Read	All	2.0
04h	Read	All	2.0
05h	Non-destructive Read	Character	2.0
06h	Input Status	Character	2.0
07h	Flush Input Buffers	Character	2.0
08h	Write	All	2.0
09h	Write With Verify	All	2.0
0ah	Output Status	Character	2.0
0bh	Flush Output Buffers	Character	2.0
0ch	I/O Control Write	All	2.0
0dh	Open	All	3.0
0eh	Close	All	3.0
0fh	Removable Media	Block	3.0
10h	Output Until Busy	Character	3.0
13h	Generic IOCTL Request	All	3.0
17h	Get Logical Device	Block	3.2
18h	Set Logical Device	Block	3.2

reqHdr[12H] (DWORD)   Pointer to first byte after the '=' on
                          the CONFIG.SYS line for this driver

RETURNS:
reqHdr[03H] (WORD)   Return status
reqHdr[0DH (BYTE)   Number of units supported (block devices only)
reqHdr[0EH] (DWORD)   Break address, i.e., address of first free memory
                          above this driver
reqHdr[12H] (DWORD)   BPB pointer array (block devices only)

This command is unique in that it is only called once, when the device driver is installed during the boot process. Hence, it need not remain resident in memory, and, consequently, we will put the code for the *Initialization* command last in our source file and arrange that the resident portion of the driver ends where this code begins.

It is possible to pass parameters to a device driver on its "invocation line." For example, the line in the CONFIG.SYS file that installs a ramdisk program might have the form

```
DEVICE=RAMDISK.SYS /128
```

where the 128 indicates that the disk should have size 128K. It would then be a duty of the *Initialization* command to parse this invocation line, find the size, 128, and then to proceed with whatever setup was required to initialize a ramdisk of this size. To parse the invocation line, the driver code must be able to find it, and this is the reason for the input in *reqHdr[012H]*. It contains a pointer to the region of memory where the invocation line is stored. More precisely, it contains a far pointer to the byte following the '=' on the invocation line.

Each command, including *Initialization*, must return a *status code* in *reqHdr[03H]* to indicate success or failure. To save repetition in the code, it is customary to have each command return a completion code (we return it in **ax**) to the Interrupt procedure, which **or**s it with DONE and then records it in the Request Header.

The *Initialization* command is also responsible for setting the *break address*, which means the address at which free memory begins above the device driver code. Generally, this will be the address immediately above the memory needed by the resident portion of the driver, although it may also be necessary, as in our ramdisk example, to reserve additional buffer space for use by the driver.

The other return values are used only for block devices, and relate to the Bios Parameter Blocks. In the case of a block driver, it is actually possible to install several *supported units* using the same driver, and the *Initialization* command must transmit the number of units in the byte *reqHdr[0DH]*.

Each supported unit must be assigned a BPB, and an array must be built using pointers to these BPBs. There must be at least one entry in the *BPBPtrArray* for each supported unit, although the entries need not be different. That is, the same BPB can be used for several (or all) units. The base address of the *BPBPtrArray* must be returned in *reqHdr[12H]*.

As an aside, here is an interesting use that **DOS** makes of the array of BPBs. When information is read from or written to a block device, the data are moved in blocks containing at least one sector, and an auxiliary buffer is used during the move. To decide on the size for this auxiliary buffer, **DOS** scans the list of **BPS**s for all block devices in order to find the largest sector size, and uses this to set the buffer size. Since the built-in **DOS** block devices use a sector size of 512 bytes, the buffer will always be at least this large.

The other duties performed by the *Initialization* command are device-dependent. It may do whatever initialization a particular hardware device requires, or it may take over interrupt vectors, to name only two possibilities that come up in our later examples.

COMMAND 01H: MEDIA CHECK (BLOCK)

INPUTS:

reqHdr[00H] (BYTE)	Request header length
reqHdr[01H] (BYTE)	Unit number
reqHdr[02H] (BYTE)	Command code (=01H)
reqHdr[0DH] (BYTE)	Media descriptor byte

RETURNS:

reqHdr[03H] (WORD)	Return status
reqHdr[0DH] (BYTE)	Media change code:
	-1 if disk has been changed
	0 if unsure
	1 if disk has not been changed
reqHdr[0FH] (DWORD)	Pointer to previous volume ID, if all of these
	conditions hold:
	MS-DOS Version is at least 3.0;
	attribute bit 11 is set, indicating that commands
	0DH-0FH are supported;
	the disk has been changed

The *Media Check* command should return information to **DOS** on whether the disk in the current drive has been changed since its last use. It is called automatically by **DOS** before executing a command that accesses the driver, other than a read or write. Problems arise, both in the implementation of this command and in the use that **DOS** should make of the information that is returned by the command.

First, it is difficult for a program to determine whether a disk has actually been changed. If each disk in the system had a unique volume ID, then it would be easy, but this is seldom the case in a typical **MS-DOS** installation. One partial solution is to notice that if a short enough time has elapsed since the last access to the disk (two seconds has been suggested), then the disk could not possibly have been changed. But obviously this criterion is of rather limited usefulness.

The second difficulty concerns the response **DOS** should make to an "unsure" return. If the disk has not been changed, an appropriate action is to flush any buffers containing data to be written to the disk, thereby bringing the disk contents up to date. If the disk has been changed, such data should be discarded since writing them to the wrong disk will almost definitely corrupt the data already on that disk. In addition, if the disk has been changed, **DOS** should prepare to work with the new disk: the BPB should be found (using command number 02H, which we discuss below), and the FAT and directory should be read.

What **DOS** does in the "unsure" case is a compromise: if the write buffers are not empty, it is assumed that no change took place; if they are empty, then the actions appropriate to a disk changed are performed, since this will have no bad effects.

If bit 11 of the device attribute word is set, indicating that the *Open/Close/Removable Media* commands are implemented, then the operating system will make a further check on whether the disk has been changed. If the *Media Check* command returns −1, to indicate that the disk has been changed, and also returns the address (*segment:offset*) of the volume ID for the previous disk, then **DOS** will actually check to find out whether the volume IDs agree. If the previous volume had no ID, then the *Media Check* command can return a pointer to some dummy name.

COMMAND 02H: BUILD BIOS PARAMETER BLOCK (BLOCK)

INPUTS:
reqHdr[00H] (BYTE)	Request header length
reqHdr[01H] (BYTE)	Unit number
reqHdr[02H] (BYTE)	Command code (=02H)
reqHdr[0DH] (BYTE)	Media ID byte
reqHdr[0EH] (DWORD)	Address of buffer containing first sector of FAT (if IBM format)

RETURNS:
reqHdr[03H] (BYTE)	Return status
reqHdr[12H] (DWORD)	Address of BPB

The *Build BPB* command is called each time **DOS** suspects that a new disk may have been inserted and **DOS** knows that it will not lose or corrupt data by making this call. Specifically, this happens when either the *Media Check* command returns "medium changed" or when it returns "unsure" and the output buffers do not need to be flushed.

If bit 13 of the device attribute word is 0, indicating that this is an IBM format (i.e., standard **DOS** format) disk, then the buffer pointed to by *reqHdr[0EH]* contains the first segment of the FAT and must not be overwritten; otherwise, it is available as an auxiliary workspace.

In the event that the present unit supports a variety of disk formats, the *Build BPB* command should use the media ID byte to determine which is the appropriate BPB to use and return a pointer to it.

COMMAND 03H: IOCTL READ (ALL)
COMMAND 04H: READ (ALL)
COMMAND 08H: WRITE (ALL)
COMMAND 09H: WRITE WITH VERIFY (ALL)
COMMAND 0CH: IOCTL WRITE (ALL)
COMMAND 10H: OUTPUT UNTIL BUSY (CHAR)

INPUTS:

reqHdr[00H] (BYTE)	Request header length
reqHdr[01H] (BYTE)	Unit number (for block devices)
reqHdr[02H] (BYTE)	Command code (=02H,04H,08H,09H,0CH,10H)
reqHdr[0DH] (BYTE)	Media descriptor byte (commands 04H,08H,09H starting with DOS 3.0)
reqHdr[0EH] (DWORD)	Address of transfer buffer
reqHdr[12H] (WORD)	Byte/sector count
reqHdr[14H] (WORD)	Starting sector number (for block devices)

RETURNS:

reqHdr[03H] (WORD)	Return status
reqHdr[12H] (WORD)	Actual bytes or sectors transferred
reqHdr[10H) (DWORD)	Address of volume ID (commands 04H,08H,09H starting with DOS 3.0, if error 0FH)

The only commands from the preceding group that we will use in our examples are the most elementary ones: *Read*, *Write*, and *Write With Verify*.

The use of these commands is straightforward. The *Write* command, for example, should transfer the number of bytes (for a character driver) or sectors (for a block driver) requested in *reqHdr[12H]*. In the case of a block device, the sector number on the disk at which the writing should begin is given in *reqHdr[14H]*. The data to write will be found in a buffer whose address is given in *reqHdr[0EH]*. The *Write* command must contain the code that does the transfer: in our forthcoming printer example it must send the characters to the printer; in our RAMDISK example it must record the characters in the region of memory that represents the disk; in the case of a driver for a real disk drive, it would need to communicate with the drive controller and arrange to transmit the correct amount of data. After completion of the task, the command must record, in *reqHdr[12H]*, the number of bytes (or sectors) that were transferred.

The *Read* command works in a totally analogous fashion. The *Write With Verify* command may optionally contain some extra code. Specifically, it is called when the system "verify flag" is set, say by means of the **DOS** command

```
verify on
```

Ideally, in that case, each data transfer should be double-checked for errors by comparing the transferred data with the original. This kind of verification is obviously most reasonable in the case of block devices. In our examples, we will merely make *Write With Verify* a "dummy" command that actually calls *Write*.

Output Until Busy is a rather specialized command intended to support print spoolers. A *print spooler* is a resident program that buffers data to be printed and does the printing as a "background process" while other programs are executing.

The *IOCTL Read* and *IOCTL Write* commands are very important in the construction of many device drivers. So far, our discussion of device drivers would seem to indicate that they are immutable — once they have been installed, they cannot be changed in any way without rebooting the machine and installing a different version of the driver.

This view is not correct. One of the most important, and certainly the most complicated, of the **int 21H** functions is number **44H**, which is called *I/O Control For Devices (IOCTL)*. **Function 44H** enables an application program to communicate with a device driver: to query the driver about some of its parameters, to actually change some of these parameters, or even to directly execute some of the driver commands. Of the many subfunctions available through **function 44H**, these are probably the most important:

SUBFUNCTION 02H: Receive Control Data from a Character Device
SUBFUNCTION 03H: Send Control Data to a Character Device
SUBFUNCTION 04H: Receive Control Data from a Block Device
SUBFUNCTION 05H: Send Control Data to a Block Device

When either of these *Send* subfunctions is executed, device driver command 03H executes, and similarly either *Receive* subfunction causes driver command 0CH to execute. These functions will transfer a buffer of data to or from the driver, just like the other read and write functions. Even from this general description, it should be quite clear that, if device driver commands 03H and 0CH are coded appropriately, an applications program can exercise a good deal of control over a device driver.

We will not pursue this matter further in the text, but will include a concrete example in one of the exercises. Specifically, we will construct a driver for a parallel printer in the next section. However, this driver is rather rigid in its performance: it prints on the page with fixed margins, fixed number of lines per page, and in a fixed font. In an exercise at the end of the next section, the driver will be modified to allow these parameters to be changed at will using the IOCTL function.

COMMAND 05H: NON-DESTRUCTIVE READ (CHAR)

INPUTS:
reqHdr[00H]   Request header length
reqHdr[02H] (BYTE)   Command code (=05H)

RETURNS:
reqHdr[03H] (WORD)   Return status
reqHdr[0DH] (BYTE)   Character

This command allows **DOS** to "look ahead" one character into the input, without actually removing a character from the input buffer. If the input buffer is empty, the command must set the BUSY bit (bit 9) in the status word. If there are characters in the input buffer, it must clear the BUSY bit and return the next character in *reqHdr[0DH]*, but without disturbing the input.

COMMAND 06H: INPUT STATUS (CHAR)
COMMAND 07H: FLUSH INPUT BUFFERS (CHAR)
COMMAND 10H: OUTPUT STATUS (CHAR)
COMMAND 11H: FLUSH OUTPUT BUFFERS (CHAR)

INPUTS:
reqHdr[00H] (BYTE)   Request header length
reqHdr[02H] (BYTE)   Command code (=06H,07H,10H,11H)

RETURNS:
reqHdr[03H] (WORD)   Return status

The general operation of these commands is clear from their names. *Input Status* returns BUSY if there are characters in the input buffer and *Output Status* returns BUSY if a write operation is in progress. The two *Flush* commands have the obvious effect. Since we will not need any of these commands, we refer the reader to the standard references for more details.

COMMAND 0DH: DEVICE OPEN (ALL)
COMMAND 0EH: DEVICE CLOSE (ALL)

INPUTS:
reqHdr[00H] (BYTE)   Request header length
reqHdr[01H] (BYTE)   Unit code (block devices)
reqHdr[02H] (BYTE)   Command code (=0DH,0EH)

RETURNS:
reqHdr[03H] (WORD)   Return status

These are the commands called when a file or device is opened or closed. Again, since we do not need them, we leave it to the reader to look up the details of their usage.

COMMAND 0FH: REMOVABLE MEDIA (BLOCK)

INPUTS:
reqHdr[00H] (BYTE)   Request header length
reqHdr[01H] (BYTE)   Unit code
reqHdr[02H] (BYTE)   Command code (=0FH)

RETURNS:
reqHdr[03H] (WORD)   Return status

This command supplies the driver support for **subfunction 08H** of the **int 21H** IOCTL function.

COMMAND 13H: GENERIC IOCTL (ALL)

INPUTS:

reqHdr[00h] (BYTE)	Request header length
reqHdr[01H] (BYTE)	Unit code (block devices)
reqHdr[0DH] (BYTE)	Category code
reqHdr[0EH] (BYTE)	Command code
reqHdr[0FH] (WORD)	si register value
reqHdr[11H] (WORD)	di register value
reqHdr[13H] (DWORD	Address of IOCTL data packet

RETURNS:

reqHdr[03H] (WORD)	Return status

This command supplies the driver support for **subfunctions 0CH** and **0DH** of the **int 21H** IOCTL function. Be warned that **subfunction 0DH** is rather labyrinthine.

COMMAND 17h: GET LOGICAL DEVICE (BLOCK)
COMMAND 18H: SET LOGICAL DEVICE (BLOCK)

INPUTS:

reqHdr[00H] (BYTE)	Request header length
reqHdr[01H] (BYTE)	Unit code
reqHdr[02H] (BYTE)	Command code (=17H,18H)

RETURNS:

reqHdr[02H] (BYTE)	Last device referenced
reqHdr[03H] (WORD)	Return status

This command supplies the driver support for **subfunctions 0EH** and **0FH** of the **int 21H** IOCTL function.

The device driver commands are called by **MS-DOS**, and so by their very nature must be written to cope with reentrancy. With the exception of the *Initialization* command, this is not normally much of a problem since, after all, a device driver is supposed to perform low-level operations, and so usually works directly with the hardware or with the ROM BIOS.

As we saw, *Initialization* is called only once for each driver, at a well-defined time during the boot process. Consequently, **DOS** "knows" which **int 21H** functions can be safely called by the *Initialization* command, and here is the official Microsoft rule:

- The *Initialization* command can safely call **int 21H functions 00H-0CH** (the traditional console functions), **35H** and **25H** (*Get and Set Interrupt Vectors*), and **30H** (*Get DOS Version Number*), and no others.

SECTION 6 A CHARACTER DEVICE DRIVER

In this section, we present a primitive driver for a Postscript laser printer. The primary motivation for our example is that Postscript printers require specially formatted input files. If a Postscript printer is connected to **LPT1**, then **DOS** commands such as

```
copy fileName LPT1
```

or

```
dir > LPT1
```

will not have the desired effect since the special formatting required by the Postscript interpreter is missing.

Our example driver, named LASR, will accept as input any standard ASCII file and transmit it to the laser printer, automatically supplying the extra formatting. Consequently, commands such as the ones used in the previous paragraph will work perfectly if LPT1 is replaced by LASR.

We assume that the printer is connected to the first parallel port and use **int 17H** to access the printer. In the exercises, we discuss the problem of programming the printer directly by writing to the appropriate port addresses.

To use the present version of the driver with a serial printer connected to a COM1, use the **DOS MODE** command. The following commands initialize COM1 and redirect the printer output to it:

```
mode com1:9600,n,8,1
mode lpt1:=com1
```

For details on using the MODE command, we refer the reader to any **DOS** manual.

Although this example may seem rather specialized, the amount of code specific to the laser printer is quite limited. It would be an easy matter for the reader to remove this special code and hence end up with a driver for any parallel printer, which could be used as a basis for further experimentation.

Our driver does not begin to tap the abilities of a laser printer. It merely provides speedy printing of program listings and other ASCII files, and this is how it is used by the author. It prints in a single font (a condensed Courier monotype), with fixed margins and a maximum of 54 lines per page. The typeface was chosen because it looks good for program listings, and allows about 85 characters per line, enough for a line number followed by as many as 80 characters of text.

Before we look at the driver code, we will say a few words about the format of Postscript files and the technique used by LASR to generate them. From our point of view, a Postscript input file is made up of three sections:

- A prolog, which is a "control string" that selects the font to be used, defines certain Postscript functions, and tells the printer where on the page to start printing.

- The main part of the file, which contains the actual text to be printed, but with several minor modifications made to it. First, the characters '\', '(', and ')' have special operator significance in the Postscript language and so must be "escaped."

This means that each occurrence of one of these characters must be prefaced by the character '\': they must be transmitted to the printer as "\\", "\(", and "\)", respectively. In addition, this part of the file contains control strings telling the printer when it should go to a new line and when it should print a page.

- An epilog, which is a control string notifying the printer to print the last, usually incomplete, page and also transmitting a Control d, the end-of-file sentinel in the Postscript language.

The printing of the prolog and the main file is easy. Our program maintains a flag having the values INACTIVE, CONTROL, and PRINTING.

When LASR is not engaged in a printing job, this flag has value INACTIVE. When the device driver command *Write* is called, it checks the flag. If it finds the value to be INACTIVE, it prints the prolog and sets the flag to PRINTING before fulfilling the write request.

During the main printing, the program manipulates the values of this flag: it is set to PRINTING when printing text requiring the insertion of escape characters and to CONTROL when control strings, which do not require extra escapes, are being printed.

Surprisingly, the hardest problem is to arrange for the printing of the epilog, which should be printed following the text. But how does the program know when all the text has been printed? After all, **MS-DOS** does not send a standard termination character to the printer at the end of the file.

The strategy used in the program is to assume that whenever a long enough period of time elapses during which the printer is capable of receiving characters to print (i.e., its input buffer is not full) but does not actually receive any characters, then the input file has been completely exhausted and so the epilog should be printed. The actual time that the printer must wait before deciding that no more input is forthcoming was selected empirically and is about 15 seconds. This seems quite reasonable on a printer that prints four or five pages a minute, since after this period a page will have been printed and the printer will certainly have space for more input in its buffer. (Note that our simple-minded scheme will not work for input files that slow the printer because they contain graphics.)

The approximately-15-second time period is measured by taking over **int 1CH**, the user timer interrupt and having it increment a counter, *idleCount*, maintained by the program. *idleCount* is reset to 0 after each character is printed, and when it reaches 300, the epilog is sent to the printer.

The source code for LASR is shown in Figure 16.5, and here are some line-by-line comments:

Line 3. It is necessary to include the device-independent code.

Line 17. Setting the value of the device *Attribute* word. CHARDEV was given the value 8000H by an **EQUATE** in the DEVINDEP.ASM.

Lines 18-21. This is an interesting application of the **ORG** directive. We wish to initialize the *deviceNameOrNo* field of the Device Header in DEVINDEP.ASM without having to go back and physically alter the code there. Line 19 "rolls back" **MASM**'s location counter to the value of *deviceNameOrNo*, hence the **DB** statement on line 20 stores the name at that

FIGURE 16.5 PRIMITIVE DRIVER FOR A POSTSCRIPT PRINTER

```
 1   TITLE Laser.asm -- character device driver for laser printer
 2
 3   INCLUDE devIndep.asm
 4
 5   ;DEVICE SPECIFIC CODE
 6
 7       ;equates for flag settings
 8       CLEAR               EQU     0
 9       SET                 EQU     1
10
11       ;equates for describing present operation of LASR driver
12       INACTIVE            EQU     0           ;no job in progress
13       CONTROL             EQU     1           ;printing a Postscript control string
14       PRINTING            EQU     2           ;printing data from the input file
15
16
17       ATTRIBUTE           EQU     CHARDEV
18       CURRENTORG          EQU     $
19           ORG             OFFSET devNameOrNo
20                           DB "LASR    "
21           ORG             CURRENTORG
22       MAXCOMMAND          EQU     18h         ;if all device driver functions incl.
23                                               ;  Vers 3.2 of DOS are included
24       PRINTERNUMBER       EQU     0           ;= LPT1
25
26       MAXLINES            EQU     54          ;maximum number of lines on a page
27       TIMEOUTVAL          EQU     300
28       FF                  EQU     0CH         ;form feed
29
30   ;------------------------------------------------------------r
31       origInt1chVector    LABEL   DWORD
32       origInt1chOffset    DW      ?
33       origInt1chSegment   DW      ?
34
35       errorFlag           DB      CLEAR
36       IdleCount           DW      0
37       lineCount           DB      ?
38       printMode           DW      INACTIVE
39
40       initMessage         DB      CR, LF, LF
41                           DB      "LASR Device Driver Installed"
42                           DB      CR, LF, LF, '$'
43
44       Prolog              DB      "/newline "              ;define a newline --
45                           DB      "{ currentpoint 12.5 "   ; dec. y-coord by
46                           DB      "sub exch pop 72 "       ;  12.5 pts., set
47                           DB      "exch moveto } def "     ; x-coord = 72 pts.
48                           DB      "/Courier findfont "     ;print using Courier
49                           DB      "[9 0 0 11 0 0] "        ; 11-point height
50                           DB      "makefont setfont "      ; but with width
51                           DB      "72 720 moveto ("        ;   of 9 point
52       PROLOGLEN           EQU     $-Prolog
53
54       Epilog              DB      ") show "                ;use up dangling '('
55                           DB      "showpage 4"             ;to print the last
```

Figure 16.5 cont.

```
56                                                              ; page, and a Ctrl d
57                                                              ;  for end of file
58      EPILOGLEN          EQU       $-Epilog
59
60      newLineStr         DB        ") show newline ("      ;')' closes previous
61      NEWLINESTRLEN      EQU       $-newLineStr            ; string and '('
62                                                           ;  starts next one
63      newPageStr         DB        ") showpage 72 720 "    ;print page and go
64                         DB        "moveto ("              ; to start position
65      NEWPAGESTRLEN      EQU       $-newPageStr            ;  on next one
66
67      ;-------------------------------------------------------------
68
69   sendString MACRO    Str              ;sets up the registers for a call
70                                        ;  to printString
71        pushRegs cx, si, ds
72        mov    cx, Str&Len              ;note the use of the macro concatenation
73        mov    si, OFFSET Str           ;  operator
74        call   printString
75        popRegs
76
77        ENDM
78
79      ;-------------------------------------------------------------
80
81   printString    PROC   NEAR        ;prints a string by calls to int 17h
82
83        mov    printMode, CONTROL      ;only used while printMode = CONTROL
84        push   cs                      ;because printChars requires that ds:si
85        pop    ds                      ;  point to the buffer containing chars
86        call   printChars              ;    to print; here the buffer is in _TEXT
87        mov    printMode, PRINTING     ;prepare printMode for its next use
88        ret
89
90   printString    ENDP
91
92      ;-------------------------------------------------------------
93
94   newInt1ch      PROC      NEAR
95
96        sti
97        cmp    printMode, INACTIVE    ;nothing need be done in INACTIVE mode
98        je     Finish
99
100       test   errorFlag, SET
101       jz     Continue               ;if an error occurred, don't increment
102       mov    idleCount, 0           ;  idleCount -- in fact, restart count
103       jmp    SHORT Finish
104
105  Continue:
106
107       inc    idleCount
108       cmp    idleCount, TIMEOUTVAL
109       jne    Finish                 ;when we have timed out, the Epilog
110                                      ;  should be printed
111
```

```
112         mov     idleCount, 0
113         sendString  Epilog            ;print the Epilog
114         mov     printMode, INACTIVE  ;LASR'S current job is complete
115
116  Finish:
117
118         jmp     origInt1chVector
119
120  newInt1ch   ENDP
121
122  ;-----------------------------------------------------------
123
124  writeVerify  LABEL   NEAR            ;notice that this procedure has two names
125  Write        PROC    NEAR
126
127         cmp     printMode, INACTIVE  ;is it the start of a new printing job?
128         jne     printIt              ;if not, we are already in PRINTING mode
129         sendString  Prolog           ;if so, we must start with the Prolog
130         mov     lineCount, MAXLINES  ;because we will count down to zero using
131                                      ;   lineCount
132  printIt:                            ;at this point printMode = 2
133
134         mov     cx, reqHdr[12h]      ;number of characters to print
135         lds     si, reqHdr[0eh]      ;point ds:si to input buffer
136         jmp     SHORT printChars
137         ret
138
139  Write       ENDP
140
141  ;-----------------------------------------------------------
142
143  printChars      PROC    NEAR         ;ds:si should point to start of buffer
144                                       ;cx should contain the count to print
145  printOne:
146
147         lodsb
148         cmp     printMode, PRINTING
149         jne     normalPrint          ;no special treatment of Prolog and Epilog
150         cmp     al, '\'              ;'\', '(', and '(' must be escaped in
151         je      printEscape          ;   PRINTING mode before being sent to
152         cmp     al, '('              ;      the Postscript interpreter
153         je      printEscape
154         cmp     al, ')'
155         jne     checkFF              ;FF is formfeed
156
157  printEscape:
158
159         push    ax                   ;save character while '\' being printed
160         mov     al, '\'
161         xor     ah, ah               ;prepare to use FUNCTION 00h of int 17h
162         mov     dx, PRINTERNUMBER
163
164  Again1:
165
166         int     17h                  ;use it
167         test    ah, 01h OR 08h OR 20h;these are the three standard error codes
168                                      ;  returned by int 17h and mean not ready,
169                                      ;   write fault, and out of paper, resp.
```

Figure 16.5 cont.

```
170        jz      @F                    ;if no error
171        mov     errorFlag, SET
172        jmp     Again1
173
174   @@:
175
176        mov     errorFlag, CLEAR
177        pop     ax                    ;restore the character to print (in ah)
178        jmp     SHORT normalPrint
179
180   checkFF:
181
182        cmp     al, FF                ;check for formfeed
183        je      printPage
184        cmp     al, LF                ;check for linefeed
185        jne     checkCR
186        sendString  newLineStr
187        dec     lineCount
188        jne     errorFree             ;jump if page is not full
189
190   printPage:
191
192        cmp     lineCount, MAXLINES ;if equal, this page is empty, hence don't
193                                    ;  really need to print a formfeed
194        je      errorFree
195        sendString  newPageStr        ;print newPageStr
196        mov     lineCount, MAXLINES
197        jmp     SHORT errorFree
198
199   checkCR:
200
201        cmp     al, CR                ;if it is, don't print it
202        je      errorFree
203
204   normalPrint:
205
206        xor     ah, ah                ;prepare to use FUNCTION 00h of int 17h
207        mov     dx, PRINTERNUMBER
208        int     17h                   ;use it
209        test    ah, 29h
210        jz      errorFree
211        mov     errorFlag, SET        ;if an error occurred --
212        jmp     normalPrint           ;  set the flag and try again
213
214   errorFree:
215
216        mov     idleCount, 0
217        mov     errorFlag, CLEAR
218        dec     cx                    ;because a character has been printed
219        je      @F
220        jmp     printOne              ;if no error, print the next character
221
222   @@:
223
224        xor     ax, ax                ;successful completion
225        ret
```

```
226
227   printChars        ENDP
228
229   ;---------------------------------------------------------------
230
231   outputStatus    PROC    NEAR
232
233       mov     ah, 02h                      ;FUNCTION 02H of int 17h returns
234       mov     dx, PRINTERNUMBER            ;   a status code in ah
235       int     17h
236       and     ah, 80h                      ;isolate the printer busy bit
237       not     ah                           ;in returned word, 0 means busy and we
238                                             ;   we want to invert this
239       xor     al, al
240       shr     ax, 1                        ;move the printer busy bit as bit 9,
241       shr     ax, 1                        ;   as Device Header Word requires
242
243       ret
244
245   outputStatus    ENDP
246
247   ;---------------------------------------------------------------
248
249   notUsed              LABEL      NEAR      ;this procedure has a lot of names!
250   mediaCheck           LABEL      NEAR
251   IOCTLRead            LABEL      NEAR
252   buildBPB             LABEL      NEAR
253   Read                 LABEL      NEAR
254   nonDestRead          LABEL      NEAR
255   inputStatus          LABEL      NEAR
256   flushInputBuf        LABEL      NEAR
257   flushOutputBuf       LABEL      NEAR
258   IOCTLWrite           LABEL      NEAR
259   Open                 LABEL      NEAR
260   Close                LABEL      NEAR
261   removMedia           LABEL      NEAR
262   outputUntilBusy      LABEL      NEAR
263   genIOCTLReq          LABEL      NEAR
264   getLogicalDevice     LABEL      NEAR
265   setLogicalDevice     PROC       NEAR
266
267
268       xor     ax, ax                       ;signal successful completion
269       ret
270
271   setLogicalDevice    ENDP
272
273   ;---------------------------------------------------------------
274
275   endOfRes    EQU    $                     ;beginning offset of free memory
276
277   ;---------------------------------------------------------------
278
279   Initialize   PROC    NEAR                 ;es:di points to request header
280
281       mov     ah, 01h                      ;initialize the printer port
282       mov     dx, PRINTERNUMBER            ;   using function 01h of int 21h
283       int     17h
```

Figure 16.5 cont.

```
284
285     mov     WORD PTR reqHdr[0eh], OFFSET EndOfRes   ;offset of free memory
286     mov     reqHdr[10h], cs         ;segment of free memory
287
288     GETINT 1ch, origInt1chOffset, origInt1chSegment ;replace int 1ch, the
289
290     SETINT 1cH, <OFFSET newInt1ch>                  ;   USER TIMER INTERRUPT
291
292     mov     dx, OFFSET initMessage
293     mov     ah, 09h
294     int     21h                     ;print it
295
296     xor     ax, ax                  ;successful completion
297     ret
298
299 Initialize   ENDP
300
301 ;-------------------------------------------------------------
302
303 _TEXT     ENDS
304
305 ;=============================================================
306
307 END
```

location. Line 21 repositions the location counter to the current location, which was saved on line 18.

Line 22. We are allowing the possibility that all the device driver commands through Version 3.2 of **DOS** might be supported. If this is definitely not needed, a few bytes of memory can be saved by removing the later lines from *commandTable* in DEVINDEP.ASM, and making the corresponding changes in the neighborhood of line 265 of the present code.

Line 26. LASR prints a maximum of 54 lines to the page. However, if the input file has formfeeds and is set up to print no more than 54 lines to the page, LASR will use those formfeeds and not introduce its own.

Lines 44-51. This is the prolog, which should be sent to the printer before the text of the file to be printed.

Lines 69-90. The macro *sendString* calls *printString*, which is the procedure used to print control strings. It sets *printMode* to CONTROL, so that these strings will be printed without the interpolation of extra escape characters.

Lines 94-120. The replacement **int 1CH** handler. While the printer is not in an error condition and no characters are being printed, it increments *idleCount*. When *idleCount* has reached TIMEOUTVAL, it calls for the printing of the epilog.

Lines 124-139. In the case of a printer, there is no practical way of verifying the correctness of a write, and the only reasonable thing to do is to interpret a *writeVerify* request as a *Write* request. Notice that line 136 contains a **jmp** rather than a **call**. Although either would work, the **jmp** is slightly better since the **call** would cause the **ret** on line 225 *and* the **ret** on line 137 to execute, while the **jmp** will only cause the second of these returns to execute. The correct status code is also being returned: line 224 causes zero to be returned to the Interrupt Routine, which **ors** it with DONE.

Lines 143-227. This is the basic printing function. In lines 148-155, it prepends escapes to appropriate characters in PRINTING mode. The loop on lines 164-172 checks the **int 17H** error return in **ah**: the three important bits are shown on line 167 and their significance is explained in the comment. The program loops as long as **int 17H** continues to signify the occurrence of an error.

Lines 231-245. The Output Status command is supposed to return the value 1 in the BUSY bit if the printer is presently occupied. This information is obtained here by means of **function 02H** of **int 17H**.

Lines 249-271. The unimplemented commands should return the value DONE. Again, this is achieved by returning 0 to the Interrupt Routine, which will always **or** the return value with DONE.

Line 275. Since *Initialize* is only called when the driver is installed, there is no reason to leave it resident in memory. Hence the offset part of the break address is set just before the beginning of the *Initialization* procedure.

Lines 279-299. There are no surprises in the *Initialization* procedure code. On lines 281-283, it initializes the parallel port by calling the appropriate **int 17H** function. Technically, this is not necessary since LASR is installed after the resident driver for LPT1, and so the parallel ports have already been initialized. The two important items accomplished by this code are taking over **int 1cH** and returning the break address to *reqHdr[0EH]*.

Exercise 16-7. Do the experiment with the **ASSUME** suggested is this section. That is, rebuild LASR with the **ASSUME** line replaced by

```
ASSUME cs:_TEXT, ds:_TEXT, es:_TEXT
```

and explain the results.

Exercise 16-8. Rewrite LASR, but program the parallel port directly rather than using **int 17H**.
Suggestions: You should use **out** and **in** instructions, with the port addresses appropriate to LPT1. Here is the needed information:

- Each of LPT1, LPT2, and LPT3 has a *base address*. These are port addresses and are stored at offsets 8, 10, and 12, respectively, in the BIOS data area.

- Each parallel printer port has an associated *output data register* with address equal to the corresponding base address. To send a byte of data to a parallel printer, send it to its output data register (using an **out** instruction).

- After sending a byte of data, pulse the *strobe* bit of the *output control register* for that printer on and off. The output control register has port address equal to the base address plus 2, and the strobe bit is number 0.

- Each parallel printer port also has an *input data register*, with port address equal to its base address plus one. Bit 6 of the input data register is called the *acknowledge bit*. It normally has value 1 and is pulsed to 0 to acknowledge receipt of the byte of data. After the strobe bit has been pulsed, a program must monitor the acknowledge bit and should not send another byte until the previous one has been acknowledged.

- The program should also check bit 3 of the input data register after each byte is transmitted. This is the *error bit* and has value 0 if an error occurred.

Exercise 16-9. Write a version of LASR in which the IOCTL function can be used to change the default settings of lines per page, etc. Consult Appendix 3 for information on the IOCTL function.

Exercise 16-10. Write a replacement for the CON driver supplied with **MS-DOS**. The new driver should be written to give faster screen response by writing directly to the video buffer. It should accept the base address of the video buffer as a command-line parameter on the *DEVICE=* installation line, so that it will work on both monochrome and color systems. Of course, if you wish, you can also have the driver accept IOCTL commands that configure it to different numbers of rows and columns or to different color preferences.
Suggestions: Unfortunately, the CON driver also controls keyboard input, hence the new driver must do the same. Since the keyboard is of no particular interest at the moment, it should probably be dealt with in the simplest possible manner, namely by using **function 00H** of the ROM BIOS **int 16H**.

SECTION 7 A BLOCK DEVICE DRIVER

For the sake of the reader who is not familiar with ramdisks, we will briefly review their structure and use. A ramdisk program reserves and initializes a region of computer RAM, and **DOS** treats this region exactly as though it were a disk drive. The ramdisk has all the features of a real disk drive: it is assigned a letter designation; all reads and writes directed toward the designated letter are actually read from or written to the allocated region of memory; it is given a standard **DOS** disk directory; and the usual commands such as DIR and CHKDSK will work as expected when applied to it.

The biggest advantage of a ramdisk is that, since the reads and writes are to machine memory, the response is much faster than any "real" disk drive. The biggest disadvantage is that the memory is volatile. The information contained in the ramdisk is lost unless it is transferred to permanent storage before the machine is shut off.

A ramdisk is especially useful for storing the temporary files constructed by compilers or assemblers. In the case of **MASM**, for example, it is possible to assign a pathname to the TMP environment variable, and this will be used for the storage of temporaries. The assembly process is speeded up considerably if this variable is initialized to point to a ramdisk.

From the preceding discussion it should be clear how to set up a ramdisk. Since it must behave just like a disk drive, it should be controlled by a block device driver. The initialization code should reserve an appropriate block of memory. The read and write functions need only work with this region of memory.

Most block device drivers are used to interface with complicated devices such as disk drives or tape drives and the actual interfacing details are so involved that they obscure the basic ideas involved. Hence these examples are not well suited to a basic text such as this one. The only common example of a block device driver that really makes use of the important functions and can still be discussed in a few pages is the ramdisk program, and that is why we chose it as our example.

The code for our ramdisk is shown in Figure 16.6, and nearly everything in the listing should be clear at this point. The reader might wish to review the details of the structure of disks, as surveyed in Section 3.

Here are a few extra remarks on the ramdisk code:

Lines 152-189. In order to look like a real disk drive to **DOS**, a ramdisk must have all the trimmings: a boot sector, one or more FATs, and sufficient space for the root directory. We have selected 512 bytes (line 9) as the sector size, in conformity with the **DOS** standard. In the case of a block device, the reads and writes occur in blocks that are multiples of a sector, and hence of a paragraph, and so things work best if each sector is chosen to begin on a paragraph boundary. This explains line 148.

As our ramdisk code is written, it only allows 62K for storage of data since the first 2K are given over to the various overhead sectors. Technically, this is not necessary. If desired, we could have the disk memory buffer occupy the 128 sectors starting after the directory (i.e., at line 188 in the listing). This would give 2K more usable space on the disk, but would of course remove that much more machine memory from general use.

We did not do this because it seemed pointless — even with an extra 2K, the disk is still too small to be practical. In order to make the disk into a worthwhile utility, two major changes are required:

- The disk must be made considerably bigger, preferably of a size selectable by the user. The disk will then span more than one segment, but the reads and writes must be done more carefully since they may cross segment boundaries.

- If the disk is made appreciably larger, it will take too much memory away from the basic 640K that **DOS** allows, and so should be moved to expanded memory.

The first of these changes is discussed in the exercises at the end of this section. The modifications required in moving the disk to expanded memory are too complicated for us to analyze here. However, the interested reader can see one method of accomplishing such a move by examining the code for VDISK.ASM. This is the "official" ramdisk program distributed with various versions of **DOS**. (The source code is included with some releases.)

FIGURE 16.6 A SIMPLE RAMDISK

```
 1    TITLE  ramDisk.asm:  example of block device driver
 2
 3    INCLUDE devIndep.asm
 4
 5    ;=============================================================
 6
 7    ;DEVICE DEPENDENT CODE
 8
 9    SECSIZE         EQU    512      ;bytes/sector, IBM-compatible media
10    MAXCOMMAND      EQU    24       ;max driver command code
11    ATTRIBUTE       EQU    BLOCKDEV
12    CURRENTORG      EQU    $
13       ORG            OFFSET devNameOrNo
14                   DB     1        ;number of devices
15       ORG            CURRENTORG
16
17    diskDataBase    DW     ?        ;start of "disk" storage area ( = Sector 4)
18    transferAddr    LABEL  DWORD    ;address of transfer buffer
19    transferOff     DW     ?
20    transferSeg     DW     ?
21    currentSector   DW     ?        ;current sector to transfer
22    numberDone      DW     ?        ;number of sectors actually transferred
23    totalToDo       DW     ?        ;number of sectors to transfer
24
25    BPBPtrArray     DW     BPB      ;array of pointers to BPB's -- one BPB
26                                    ;  pointer for each unit
27    commandCode     DB     ?
28
29    ;-------------------------------------------------------------
30
31    mediaCheck   PROC    NEAR
32
33        mov    BYTE PTR  reqHdr[0eh],1 ;code for "not changed"
34        xor    ax,ax                   ;indicate success
35        ret
36
37    mediaCheck    ENDP
38
39    ;-------------------------------------------------------------
40
41    BuildBPB    PROC    NEAR
42
43        mov    WORD PTR reqHdr[12h], OFFSET BPB ;return address of BPB
44        mov    reqHdr[14h], cs
45        xor    ax, ax                          ;indicate success
46        ret
47
48    BuildBPB    endp
49
50    ;-------------------------------------------------------------
51
52    initCxDsSiEsDi   MACRO           ;initializes ds,si,es,di,cx for a
53                                     ;  Read or Write
54        mov    ax, currentSector     ;present starting sector for transfer
55        mov    si, SECSIZE/16        ;paragraphs per sector
```

```
56        mul     si                      ;ax now contains starting offset relative to
57                                        ;   start of "disk" in paragraphs
58
59        add     ax, diskDataBase        ;ax:0 now gives the starting address for
60                                        ;   the transfer
61        mov     cx, SECSIZE/2           ;words per sector
62
63        cmp     commandCode, 4          ;is it a Read or a Write?
64        je      itsARead
65                                        ;here if a Write/Verify
66        lds     si, transferAddr        ;set source buffer address
67        xor     di, di                  ;   and destination address
68        mov     es, ax                  ;     for movsb
69        jmp     SHORT @F
70
71  itsARead:                             ;here if a Read
72
73        xor     si, si                  ;source address
74        mov     ds, ax                  ;   and destination
75        les     di, transferAddr        ;      buffer address for movsb
76
77  @@:
78
79        ENDM
80
81  ;-------------------------------------------------------------
82
83  Read            LABEL   NEAR
84  writeVerify     LABEL   NEAR
85  Write           PROC    NEAR
86
87        mov     al, reqHdr[02h]
88        mov     commandCode, al         ;tells whether a Read or a Write
89        mov     numberDone, 0           ;running count of sectors already moved
90        mov     ax, reqHdr[12h]         ;count of sectors to Read/Write
91        mov     totalToDo, ax           ;save for check at end of transfer
92        mov     ax, reqHdr[14h]         ;starting sector number on "disk" for Read/
93        mov     currentSector, ax       ;   Write -- used to initialize currentSector
94        mov     ax, reqHdr[0eh]
95        mov     transferOff, ax
96        mov     ax, reqHdr[10h]
97        mov     transferSeg, ax
98
99  transferLoop:
100
101       mov     ax, numberDone          ;done with all sectors yet?
102       cmp     ax, totalToDo
103       je      WrapUp                  ;jump if done
104
105       initCxDsSiEsDi
106
107       cld
108       rep     movsw                   ;transfer data in SECSIZE blocks
109       inc     currentSector           ;we have moved one sector
110       add     transferOff, SECSIZE    ; or, equivalently, SECSIZE bytes
111       inc     numberDone
112       jmp     transferLoop
113
```

Figure 16.6 cont.

```
114   WrapUp:                            ;transfer complete
115
116       les    di, reqHdrAddr         ;record sectors transferred
117       mov    ax, numberDone         ;   in request header
118       mov    reqHdr[12h], ax
119       xor    ax, ax                 ;indicate success
120       ret
121
122   Write   ENDP
123
124   ;-----------------------------------------------------------
125
126   IOCTLRead           LABEL     NEAR
127   nonDestRead         LABEL     NEAR
128   inputStatus         LABEL     NEAR
129   flushInputBuf       LABEL     NEAR
130   outputStatus        LABEL     NEAR
131   flushOutputBuf      LABEL     NEAR
132   IOCTLWrite          LABEL     NEAR
133   Open                LABEL     NEAR
134   Close               LABEL     NEAR
135   removMedia          LABEL     NEAR
136   outputUntilBusy     LABEL     NEAR
137   genIOCTLReq         LABEL     NEAR
138   getLogicalDevice    LABEL     NEAR
139   setLogicalDevice    PROC      NEAR
140
141       xor    ax, ax                 ;indicate success
142       ret
143
144   setLogicalDevice    ENDP
145
146   ;-----------------------------------------------------------
147
148   ALIGN 16
149
150   STARTOFDISK    EQU    ($-DeviceHeader)/16 ;paragraph address of "disk"
151   ;-----------------------------------------------------------
152   ;Sector 0: Boot Sector                                      ; |
153   BOOTRECORD    EQU    $                                      ; |
154                                                               ; |
155           jmp   $               ;these three bytes mimic the jmp   ; |
156           nop                   ;   instruction that comes at the  ; |
157                                 ;    start of the boot sector      ; |
158           DB    '??????'        ;OEM field                    ; |
159                                                               ; |
160   ;BIOS Parameter Block (BPB)                                 ; |
161   BPB     DW    SECSIZE         ;00h - bytes per sector       ; |
162           DB    1               ;02H - sectors per cluster    ; |
163           DW    1               ;03H - reserved sectors       ; |
164           DB    1               ;05H - number of FATs         ; |
165           DW    32              ;06H - root directory entries ; |
166           DW    128             ;08H - sectors = 64 KB / SECSIZE ; |
167           DB    0f8h            ;0AH - Media Descriptor       ; |
168           DW    1               ;0BH - sectors per FAT        ; |
169                                                               ; |
```

```
170             ORG     BOOTRECORD+SECSIZE                              ;|
171  ;----------------------------------------------------------------|
172  ;Sectors 1 and 2: File Allocation Table -- 12 bit                ;|
173                                                                   ;|
174          DB      0f8h, -1 ,-1      ;begins with Media Descriptor   ;|
175          DB      (SECSIZE-3) dup (0)                              ;|
176  ;----------------------------------------------------------------|
177  ;Sector 3: Directory                                            ;|
178                                                                   ;|
179  Volname DB      'RAMDISK     '       ;volume name for RAMdisk     ;|
180          DB      08h               ;attribute byte                ;|
181          DB      10 dup (0)        ;reserved area                 ;|
182          DW      0000h             ;time                          ;|
183          DW      1 OR 10 SHL 5 OR 9 SHL 9 ;date                   ;|
184          DB      6 dup (0)         ;reserved area                 ;|
185  IDENTLEN EQU    $-Volname                                        ;|
186          DB      (2*SECSIZE-IDENTLEN) dup(0)                      ;|
187  ;----------------------------------------------------------------|
188  ;Sectors 4-0fffh: Storage Area                                  ;|
189  ;----------------------------------------------------------------|
190
191  Initialize   PROC   NEAR
192
193      mov     ax, cs                  ;paragraph address of code segment
194      add     ax, STARTOFDISK         ;paragraph address of beginning of "disk"
195      mov     diskDataBase, ax        ;record beginning address for future use
196      add     ax, 1000h               ;paragraph addr. of end of "disk," which
197      mov     reqHdr[10h],ax          ; is also the beginning segment addr. of
198      mov     WORD PTR reqHdr[0eh],0   ;  free memory, with corres. offset 0
199      mov     BYTE PTR reqHdr[0dh], 1  ;number of units = 1
200      mov     word ptr reqHdr[12h], OFFSET BPBPtrArray ;address of BPBPtrArray
201      mov     reqHdr[14h], cs
202
203      call    printInitMess
204
205      xor     ax, ax                  ;indicate success
206      ret
207
208  Initialize      ENDP
209
210  ;-------------------------------------------------------------
211
212  startMess    DB   CR, LF, LF, '64 KB RAMDISK INSTALLED$'
213  driveMess    DB   ': ACCESSED AS DRIVE '
214  driveDesig   DB   ?
215  endMess      DB   CR, LF, LF, '$'
216
217  ;-------------------------------------------------------------
218
219  printInitMess   PROC   NEAR
220
221      mov     dx, OFFSET startMess
222      mov     ah, 09h
223      int     21h
224
225      mov     dx, OFFSET endMess    ;assume DOS Version 2.?
226      mov     ah, 30h               ;check assumption by getting DOS version
227      int     21h
```

Figure 16.6 cont.

```
228      cmp     al, 3                    ;returns "major" number (2 or 3) in al
229      jb      guessedright
230      mov     al, reqHdr[16h]          ;here if at least Version 3, in which case
231      add     al, 'A'                  ;   assigned drive designator is available
232      mov     driveDesig, al           ;    but must be converted to ASCII
233                                        ;       and stored in the printing string
234      mov     dx, OFFSET driveMess     ;to correct our guess
235
236  guessedRight:
237
238      mov     ah, 09h
239      int     21h
240      ret
241
242  printInitMess    ENDP
243
244  ;-----------------------------------------------------------------
245
246  _TEXT    ENDS
247
248  ;=================================================================
249
250  END
```

Lines 83-122. The *Read* and *Write* commands both use **movsw**. Consequently, they behave identically, except for the initialization of **ds**, **si**, **es**, and **di**. We have therefore combined these commands into a single *Read/Write* procedure, and a call to the macro on line 52 sets the registers for the correct option.

Lines 219-242. *printInitMess* is called by *Initialize* to print a message to the screen when the ramdisk is installed. The only new wrinkle is contained in lines 228-232. Under Version 3.0 or later of **DOS**, the block device designator assigned to the first (and, in this case, only) unit is returned as the byte in *reqHdr[16H]*, with 0 meaning 'A', 1 meaning 'B', and so on. If the ramdisk is being installed with Version 3.0 or later, it is a nice touch to make the device designator available to the user as part of the installation message. **Function 30H of int 21H** returns the "major **DOS** version number" (the 'x' in Version x.y) in **al** and the "minor **DOS** version number" (the y) in **ah**. Lines 228-232 test for the version number and make use of the major version in the obvious way whenever it is at least 3.

Exercise 16-11. Run the **DOS** CHKDSK utility on the installed RAMDISK. Why does it say that there is a hidden file?

Exercise 16-12. As written, RAMDISK has size less than 64K and so is virtually worthless. Modify the code to allow RAMDISK to be given a variable size specified by an **EQUATE** in the source code. If it makes things easier, you may require that the size be a multiple of 64K.

Exercise 16-13. Modify the version of RAMDISK produced in the last exercise so that its size can be specified on the invocation line, rather than by an **EQUATE**. For example, the invocation line

```
DEVICE=RAMDISK.SYS/128
```

should cause RAMDISK to be installed with data size 128K.

Exercise 16-14. As an aid in investigating how **DOS** uses device drivers, it is worthwhile to write a utility that will tell us which device commands are actually called in the course of performing various operations. For example, exactly what sequence of commands does **DOS** issue when a block device is performing a read of 10 sectors? Write a procedure to be included with the device driver code (or installed in USER.LIB) and which, when called from the device Interrupt Routine, prints the name of the device command that is about to be executed. Of course, it is necessary to have the source code for the device driver in order to use this utility.

Suggestion: Because of the reentrancy problem, the utility should print to the screen by writing directly to the video buffer.

CHAPTER 17

THE NUMERICAL COPROCESSORS

SECTION 1 PREVIEW

So far, only a small percentage of machines using the **8086/8088** series microprocessors have been equipped with numerical coprocessors. But applications software is becoming more complex and computationally demanding and so, especially considering the newly emerging graphics interfaces, it seems likely that the use of coprocessors will become much more widespread. One piece of evidence supporting this viewpoint is that the numerical coprocessor is actually an integral part of the new **80486** chip. It therefore seems important to give a reasonably detailed description of the workings of the numerical coprocessors, and that is the goal of the present chapter.

In Section 2 we begin by discussing coprocessor emulation libraries. From our point of view, the most significant aspect of emulation libraries is that they allow the programmer to write and test coprocessor code without having access to a machine with a coprocessor. This is especially interesting since emulation libraries are quite common. In fact, the run-time libraries distributed with most high-level language compilers include emulation libraries but, unfortunately, the **MASM** package does not.

The numerical coprocessors perform their computations entirely in eight 80-bit data registers. These data registers are introduced in Section 3, where examples of their use are also given.

Even though the coprocessors do their calculations in an extended-precision real-number format, they perform input and output in a variety of integer and real-number formats, which are described in Section 4.

In Section 5, we take a close look at coprocessor I/O. We introduce the basic I/O instructions and show how **MASM** facilitates the input of assembly-time constants in the different coprocessor formats using **DW**, **DD**, **DQ**, and **DT** data-defining directives. In addition, we write a pair of I/O procedures for use with one of these formats, ten-byte packed binary.

As well as the eight basic data registers, the numeric coprocessors have a number of registers that hold control and status information. While some uses of these registers fall beyond the scope of our introductory account, they are also used in straightforward applications programming. Section 6 contains a brief account of the entire "coprocessor environment."

Section 7 presents the complete coprocessor instruction set. The coprocessor offers a full complement of standard arithmetic instructions; a reasonable array of transcendental functions, including logarithms, exponentials, and trigonometric functions; and a very fast square-root function.

In Section 8, we return to the I/O problem and write procedures that perform coprocessor I/O in any of the allowed formats. We manage to do this very efficiently by using conditional assembly and by building on the basic procedures written in Section 5.

Section 9 contains two numerical examples, the more interesting of which is an implementation of Newton's Method. This procedure can be incorporated in a library and can be used interactively.

SECTION 2 USING AN EMULATION LIBRARY

Most high-level language compiler packages for the **8086/8088** family of machines include an *emulation library*, which contains routines that interpret each of the coprocessor instructions in software. A compiled high-level language program will use a coprocessor if one is present and will use the emulation routines otherwise. In Section 6 of Chapter 15 we showed how this switch is accomplished by a typical C compiler. Of course, it is preferable to use an actual coprocessor, since it is faster than the emulation routines, often by a factor of a hundred times.

Code can therefore be written to take advantage of a coprocessor but will still be usable on machines that do not have one. For the readers of this book who do not have access to a coprocessor, there is another advantage. Programs can be written using the coprocessor instructions and tested using an emulator. Even though they are much slower, the emulation routines require the same input as the corresponding coprocessor instructions, and so it is quite practical to learn to program the coprocessor by this method.

The only real disadvantage of this approach is the difficulty of calling the emulation code from an assembly language program. Indeed, as we saw in Chapter 14, all the library functions associated with a high-level language depend on certain compiler initialization code being run before they are called. We refer the reader to Chapter 14 for a discussion of this initialization process and how to trigger it from an assembly language program. In the present chapter, we avoid these complications by starting with a small C calling program.

FIGURE 17.1 USING AN EMULATION LIBRARY

```
 1    /* Emulate1.c: the C module */
 2
 3    #include <stdio.h>
 4
 5    double Product(double, double, double*);
 6
 7    void main(void)
 8    {
 9        double x = 1.39;
10        double y = 3.24;
11        double Answer;
12
13        Product(x,y, &Answer);
14        printf("\n\nThe product of %.2lf and %.2lf is %.4lf", x, y, Answer);
15
16    }
```

```
 1    TITLE    Emulate2.asm : the assembly language module
 2
 3    .MODEL SMALL, C
 4
 5    .CODE
 6
 7    Product       PROC USES bx,   X:QWORD, Y:QWORD, ansPtr:WORD
 8
 9        fld     X                       ;push X onto coprocessor stack
10        fld     Y                       ;then push Y
11        fmul                            ;pop X and Y and push X*Y
12        mov     bx, ansPtr              ;point bx to Answer
13        fst     QWORD PTR [bx]          ;store X*Y from top of stack in Answer
14        ret
15
16        Product       ENDP
17
18        END
```

```
OUTPUT:

    The product of 1.39 and 3.24 is 4.5036

COMMANDS FOR BUILDING THIS PROGRAM WITH MMF AND MAKE:

    mmf emulate > emulate
    make  mdefs=/E emulate
```

Figure 17.1 shows an example of this technique and also gives a very brief preview of the operation of the coprocessor. EMULATE1.C is the C calling program. It performs the trivial computation of multiplying two doubles and printing the answer. But the actual multiplication is done by an assembly language procedure, *Product*, contained in the module EMULATE2.ASM. *Product* receives three parameters on the stack: the factors to be multiplied and the address at which to leave the answer. We have used the extended

.MODEL directive and some of the new high-level language conventions from Chapter 14.

It is not important to understand the details of the EMULATE2.ASM module at this time. They will be clarified as the chapter proceeds, and the mixed-language use of the coprocessor will be shown again in later examples and explored further in the exercises. But, generally, here is how the code in EMULATE2.ASM should be interpreted. On line 7, "X" and "Y" are defined to be qwords. Therefore, each is eight bytes long — the size of a double in C. One of the modes of operation of the coprocessor is as a *classical stack machine*. When operating in this mode, it expects to find the operands on the top of a stack. In completing the operation, it pops the operands from the stack and replaces them by the answer. **Fld** is a push operation and **fmul** means multiplication. The meaning of lines 9-11 should now be fairly clear. Finally, the **fst** operation stores the top element of the stack in the given memory location, and hence has the effect of returning the answer to the data segment.

MASM must be run with the /E command-line flag in order to generate emulation code. We have used this flag on the **MAKE** command line.

Exercise 17-1. Trace through EMULATE1.EXE in **CODEVIEW.** After line 9 in EMULATE1.ASM executes, use the **CODEVIEW** '7' command, which displays the coprocessor stack. At this point not everything in the display will make sense. However, X will have been pushed onto the stack. Use the '7' command again after executing line 10 and again after line 11, convincing yourself that the "stack machine" operates as described in the text.

SECTION 3 THE COPROCESSOR DATA REGISTERS

In Intel literature, a numerical coprocessor in the **8087/80287/80387** series is often referred to as an "FPU" (for *floating point unit*). We will use this terminology in the sequel.

An FPU contains eight data registers, each 80 bits wide. These registers hold real numbers in a special high-precision format, which will be analyzed in the next section. At the moment, we will only discuss the general layout and use of the data registers.

As shown in Figure 17.2, the data registers are named **R0-R7**, although these names are never used in assembly language code. Rather, the registers are operated as a stack, and are given numbers relative to the top of the stack. Specifically, the top of the stack is referred to as **st** or **st(0)**. Initially, **st** is the physical register **R7**, but becomes, sequentially, **R6**, **R5**, etc., as more data are pushed onto the register stack. For any given position of **st**, the remaining registers are then labeled as **st(1)**, **st(2)**, ···, **st(7)**, proceeding down the stack from **st** and wrapping to physical register **R0** when **R7** is reached. This rather ornate numbering scheme is illustrated in Figure 17.2, where we assume that **st** is **R4**. From a programming viewpoint, this system has advantages and disadvantages.

On the positive side, we will see that the coprocessor can be operated in either of two modes: as a stack machine in which operations are always performed on the one or two operands at the top of the stack and the answer left on the stack and as a set of eight separately addressable registers. In dealing with procedure parameters, **st** frequently plays the same role in coprocessor arithmetic that **bp** plays in the basic processor.

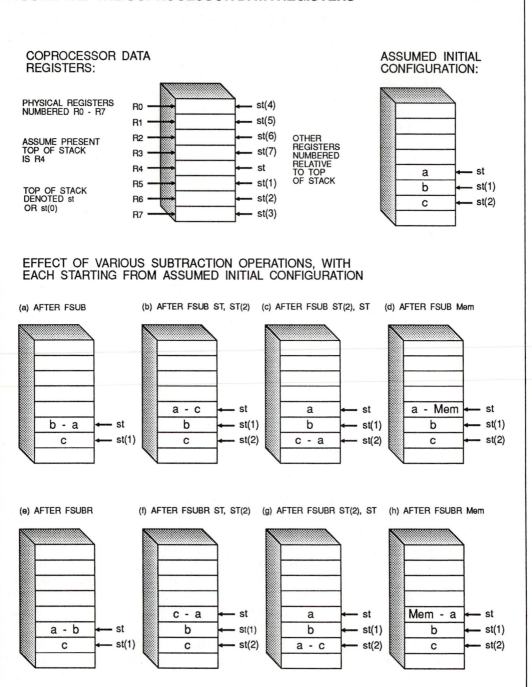

FIGURE 17.2 THE COPROCESSOR DATA REGISTERS

On the negative side, keeping track of data on the stack can be frustrating. To illustrate, suppose that there are several data on the stack and another datum is pushed. The datum previously in **st** will now be in **st(1)**, the old **st(1)** datum will now be in **st(2)**, and so on. This fluidity of names can be confusing in a complicated program. In practice, it is necessary to draw lots of pictures.

Attempting to push an item onto an FPU stack that is already "full," i.e., already contains eight data items, is an error. Likewise, trying to pop an item from an empty stack is an error. These errors are called, reasonably enough, *stack overflow* and *stack underflow*. When either of these situations occurs, a certain exception handler decides what to do next. We will discuss exception handling in some detail in Section 6. For the moment, we merely point out that the default handler continues the computation, almost definitely producing nonsensical results, and no external indication of the error occurs. Therefore, it is essential to be ever-vigilant in guarding against FPU stack overflow or underflow!

Although the instruction set will not appear formally until Section 5, we will now discuss the general usage of the registers and illustrate this discussion with a particular instruction.

Coprocessor instructions can have two, one, or zero operands. Most instructions requiring operands come in versions in which the operands are written explicitly and have variants involving one or more implicit operands.

First, consider a typical two-operand instruction, say **inst**. It will be usable in any of these formats:

```
inst Reg, Reg
inst Mem
inst
```

In the first form, each *Reg* must be an **st(i)**, and at least one of them must be **st = st(0)**. In conformity with the main processor notation, the first *Reg* is interpreted as the destination and the second as the source. The source is left unchanged while the destination is modified in the manner dictated by **inst**. Since nothing is pushed or popped from the register stack, the **st(i)**-indexing is not disturbed by this form of the instruction.

In the second form, *Mem* is a memory variable, defined in one of the formats introduced in the next section. It plays the role of source, while the implied operand **st** plays the role of destination. Again, the stack indexing remains unchanged.

The third form is usually referred to as the *classical stack machine* format. Here the implied operands are **st** as source and **st(1)** as destination. As well as making the expected change in **st(1)**, this form of the instruction pops the register stack, whence the destination becomes the new **st**. Of course, the indexing of the stack is modified.

One-operand instructions do not offer the same range of choices. Many of them use **st** as an implied operand: it functions both as the source and the destination. Others use a single memory or register operand. Whether it is the source or destination depends on the instruction.

Fsub, the coprocessor version of subtraction, is a representative two-operand instruction. It is used in Figure 17.2 to illustrate many of the available instruction formats.

In our discussion of Figure 17.2, we assume that data items *c*, *b*, and *a* have been loaded onto the coprocessor register stack, in that order, and that the top of the stack is presently

R4. This starting configuration is shown at the upper right in Figure 17.2. The eight remaining views of the register stack show the effects of variants of the **fsub** instruction, where we assume that each modification is applied to the initial configuration.

(a) in Figure 17.2 shows the classical stack form, (b) and (c) show register forms, and (d) shows a memory form.

The asymmetric arithmetic operations, subtraction and division, also have "reversed" forms in which the operands are used in reverse order. The reversed form of **fsub** is called **fsubr**. It works in precisely the same way as **fsub** except that *Dest* is replaced by *Source − Dest*, rather than by *Dest − Source*. The reversed forms of (a)-(d) are shown in (e)-(f).

SECTION 4 DATA FORMATS

Even though the coprocessors perform all their internal arithmetic using real numbers in an 80-bit high-precision format, they will accept input and generate output in a variety of integer, packed-decimal, and real-number formats. The seven formats allowed for input and output are shown in Figure 17.3. The instructions used to transfer data in these different formats will be introduced later in this section.

The first three formats need little discussion. They are just two's complement encodings of integers stored in 2, 4, or 8 bytes. The fact that the coprocessor can perform I/O operations on 8-byte integers already suggests that it performs its operations to higher precision than the main processor.

The fourth format accepted by the coprocessor is *ten-byte BCD (binary code decimal)*. This format uses the packed BCD form, introduced in Chapter 10, in which each byte holds two decimal digits in the range 0-9 — one in the low 4 bits and one in the high 4 bits. Even though this is a ten-byte format, it holds only 18 decimal digits, since the high byte is used to hold the sign of the number. Only the high bit of this byte is used and is set to indicate that the stored number is negative and clear otherwise.

The remaining three formats all represent real numbers, and are by far the most complex. Basically, each of them stores a real number as its mixed binary expansion (which was introduced informally in the exercises at the end of Chapter 1).

The *mixed binary expansion* of a real number x can be defined as

$$d_n d_{n-1} \cdots d_1 d_0 . c_1 c_2 \cdots c_m$$

where

$$d_n d_{n-1} \cdots d_1 d_0$$

is the binary representation of the integer part of x and $c_1, c_2, c_3, \cdots$ are selected, in this order, so that c_m is the largest integer satisfying

$$d_n * 2^n + d_{n-1} * 2^{n-1} + \cdots + d_1 * 2^1 + d_0 * 2^0 + c_1 * 2^{-1} + c_2 * 2^{-2} + \cdots + c_{m-1} * 2^{-(m-1)} \leq x$$

In an exercise at the end of this section, we ask the reader to verify that this forces each

FIGURE 17.3 COPROCESSOR DATA FORMATS

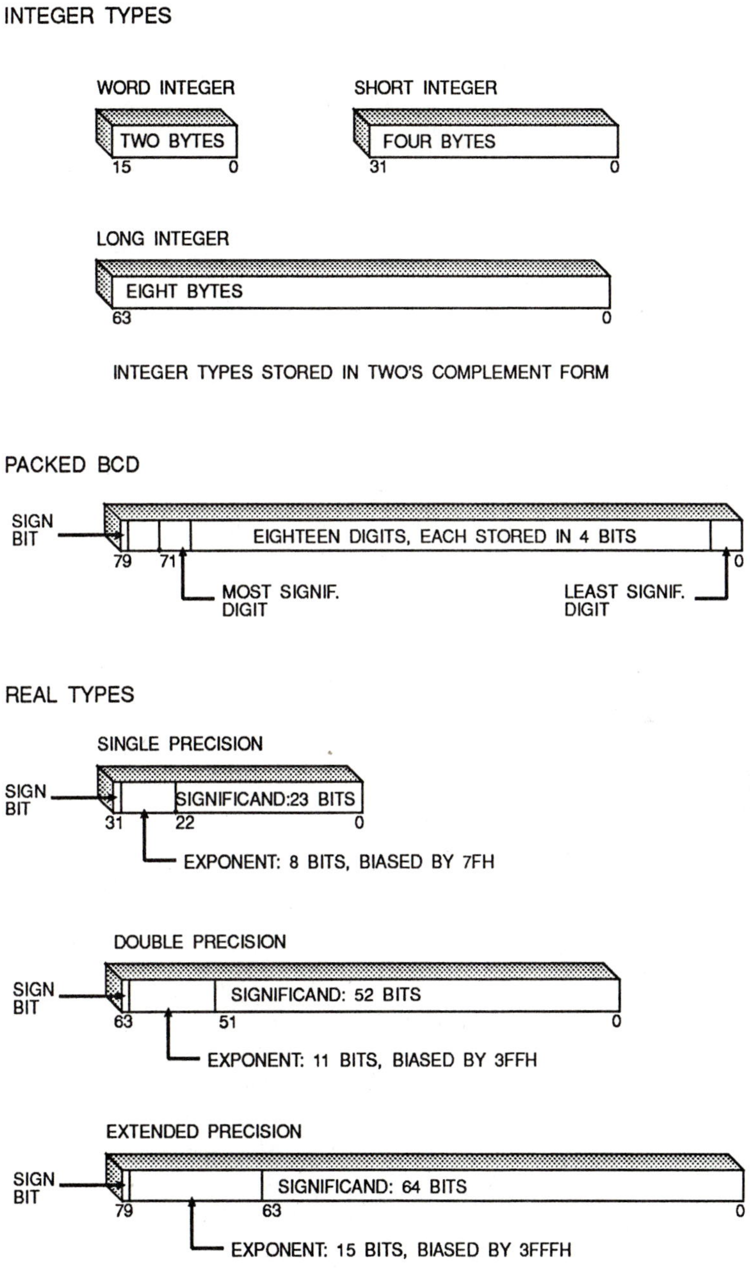

INTEGER TYPES

WORD INTEGER

TWO BYTES

15   0

SHORT INTEGER

FOUR BYTES

31   0

LONG INTEGER

EIGHT BYTES

63   0

INTEGER TYPES STORED IN TWO'S COMPLEMENT FORM

PACKED BCD

SIGN BIT

EIGHTEEN DIGITS, EACH STORED IN 4 BITS

79 71   0

MOST SIGNIF. DIGIT

LEAST SIGNIF. DIGIT

REAL TYPES

SINGLE PRECISION

SIGN BIT

SIGNIFICAND: 23 BITS

31 22   0

EXPONENT: 8 BITS, BIASED BY 7FH

DOUBLE PRECISION

SIGN BIT

SIGNIFICAND: 52 BITS

63 51   0

EXPONENT: 11 BITS, BIASED BY 3FFH

EXTENDED PRECISION

SIGN BIT

SIGNIFICAND: 64 BITS

79 63   0

EXPONENT: 15 BITS, BIASED BY 3FFFH

c_m to be 0 or 1, and that the sums in the last display get arbitrarily close to x as m gets large. As the examples at the end of Chapter 1 already show, some real numbers have a *finite binary expansion* (i.e., the c_m are all zero from some point on) and some do not, just as in the case of decimal expansions. These questions are also explored in the exercises.

Of course, when a real number is stored in one of the three real-number formats, it must be stored as a finite binary expansion. Depending on the circumstances, this finite expansion may be arrived at by truncation (*chopping*) or by rounding up.

Since the three real formats are quite similar, we will examine only the first of them, *single-precision real*, in detail. As a running example, we will convert −18.625 to this format. Here are the steps required to compute the single-precision real representation of x:

- Compute the first 24 digits in the binary expansion of x, ignoring the '−' sign, if there is one. (Of course, a point may be reached beyond which all digits are zero.) In our example,

$$18.625 = 1*2^4 + 0*2^3 + 0*2^2 + 1*2^1 + 0*2^0 + 1*2^{-1} + 0*2^{-2} + 1*2^{-3}$$

and so the binary expansion is 1001.101.

- Reposition the binary point to obtain a *normalized real number*, i.e., a number between 1 and 2, multiplied by a power of 2. In our example, this decomposition is

$$1.001101 * 2^3$$

- Delete the opening 1 from the normalized number. The remaining 23 digits are called the *significand* of x and are stored as bits 0-22 in the single-precision form. Our example has

        001 1010 0000 0000 0000 0000

as its significand.

- Bits 23-30 of the single-precision form hold the exponent on the power of 2 as computed previously, but *biased* by adding 7FH to it. In our case, the biased exponent is

        10000011

- The high bit in the single-precision representation gives the sign of x — set if x is negative and clear otherwise. This bit should have value 1 in our example.

Fitting the pieces together shows that the single-precision representation of −18.625 is

        1100 0001 1001 1010 0000 0000 0000 0000 = 0C1950000H

The reason for deleting the opening 1 in the normalized form is clear: it gives an extra bit of precision in the allotted space. Of course, the number zero has no opening 1 in its binary expansion and so must be handled specially. A single-precision representation in which bits 0-30 are all 0 is assumed to represent the number zero. Hence the coprocessor actually admits the existence of two different zeros — +0 and −0.

Biasing is used to make size comparisons easier. To compare the sizes of two non-negative single-precision reals, it is only necessary to make an unsigned comparison of their bit patterns.

The *double-precision representation* of x is computed in the same way except that the significand is stored in the low 52 bits and the exponent is biased by adding 3FFH before being stored in bits 52-63. Here is how the arithmetic for our example looks:

- The significand is 0010 0101 0000 ⋯ (total of 52 bits)
- The biased exponent is 100 0000 0011
- The sign bit is 1

Hence the double-precision representation of −18.625 is

        C032A00000000000H

In the *extended-precision* case, the significand is stored in 64 bits and the exponent in 15 bits. In this case, the opening 1 of the normalized form is also stored, the rationale being that the precision is already high enough to make an extra bit unnecessary, and storing the opening 1 simplifies the computational algorithms that use the extended-precision format. The latter consideration is important since the coprocessor uses the extended real representation for all its internal computations. The steps involved in finding the extended form of our sample real number are

- The significand is 1001 0010 1000 ⋯ (total of 64 bits)
- The biased exponent is 100 0000 0000 0011
- The sign bit is 1

It follows that the extended-precision representation of −18.625 is

        C0039500000000000000H

Even though the coprocessor uses the extended real format for all its computations, it accepts input and delivers output in any of the seven formats enumerated previously. In particular, the extended real format can be used for I/O. Nevertheless, this format is intended primarily for internal use by the coprocessor. In doing real-number arithmetic, data are normally input in double-precision format and answers returned in the same form. The enormous amount of extra precision used by the coprocessor effectively shields the data from the inevitable rounding errors that accumulate when chain computations are performed. Writing numerical algorithms to minimize accumulated error is a difficult and painstaking job. Under many circumstances, somewhat carelessly written algorithms will still give precise results when run on an FPU because of the extra precision with which the intermediate computations are performed.

The packed BCD format is frequently used in financial computations, where amounts must balance "to the penny," and so no roundoff error is permitted.

TABLE 17.1 SIZES AND RANGES OF DATA TYPES

FORMAT PARAMETERS FOR REAL TYPES

	BITS OF PRECISION	EXPONENT WIDTH IN BITS	E_{max}	E_{min}	EXPONENT BIAS
SINGLE-PREC. REAL	24	7	+127	-126	+127
DOUBLE-PREC. REAL	53	11	+1023	-1022	+1023
EXTENDED-PREC. REAL	64	15	+16383	-16382	+16383

SIZES AND RANGES OF ALL TYPES

TYPE	SIZE (BYTES)	SIGNIFICANT DIGITS	APPROXIMATE RANGE
WORD INTEGER	2	4	$32767 <= x <= +32768$
SHORT INTEGER	4	9	$2*10^9 <= x <= 2*10^9$
LONG INTEGER	8	18	$9*10^{18} <= x <= +9*10^{18}$
PACKED DECIMAL	10	18	$999...99 <= x <= +999...99$
SINGLE-PREC. REAL	4	15-16	$1.18*10^{-38} <= |x| <= 3.40*10^{+38}$
DOUBLE-PREC. REAL	8	15-16	$2.33*10^{-308} <= |x| <= 1.80*10^{308}$
EXTENDED-PREC. REAL	10	19	$3.30*10^{-4932} <= |x| <= 1.21*10^{+4932}$

The first part of Table 17.1 lists the formatting parameters for the real types. Because the implicit '1' bit is not stored, the precision for a single-precision real is given as 24 bits, even though only 23 bits are stored, and similarly for the double-precision form. E_{max} and E_{min}, respectively, give the highest and lowest values of the binary exponent used with each format. Note that in each case the exponent range is shorter than expected. In the single-precision case, for example, this range is from -126 to $+127$, rather than covering the full signed byte range of -128 to $+127$. The ranges are restricted in this way to reserve some bit patterns for holding special numeric values and non-numeric information. We will return to this subject in Section 6. The second part of Table 17.1 lists the sizes and ranges of the seven data types. In one of the exercises, we ask the reader to verify that the ranges given for the reals are compatible with the limits listed in the first part of Table 17.1.

Exercise 17-2. Convert 3.375 to single, double, and extended-precision formats. Use **MASM** to check your answers.

Exercise 17-3. In the text, we claimed that if the c_m are selected in order, and each is taken to be as large as possible while satisfying the stated inequality, then each c_m necessarily has value 0 or 1. Explain why this is true.
Suggestion: If $c_{m+1} \geq 2$, would it not have been possible to select a larger value for c_m?
Show that our other claim, namely that the sums get closer and closer to x, is also true.
Suggestion: If the sums did not get arbitrarily close to x, then there would be some value of t such that they did not get within distance $1/2^t$ of x. But in that case, would it not be possible to replace c_t by c_t+1?

Exercise 17-4. In the exercises in Chapter 1, we gave examples that showed that mixed binary expansions are sometimes finite (i.e., have only a finite number of d_m-terms) and are sometimes infinite (i.e., have infinitely many such terms). It is actually very easy to give a general answer to the question of which real numbers have finite mixed binary expansions and which have infinite ones:

- Only real numbers that can be written as fractions of the form $r/2^s$, for some pair of integers r and s, have finite mixed binary expansions.

Why is this true?

Exercise 17-5. Check that the real ranges in the first part of Table 17.1 are compatible with the limits given in the second part.

SECTION 5 COPROCESSOR INPUT AND OUTPUT

We will now examine the FPU input and output instructions. A natural starting point is to consider the amenities provided by **MASM**, which allows the user to define assembly-time constants in any of the seven FPU formats. Unfortunately, it is still necessary to write or otherwise acquire procedures to perform input and output of variables in the various formats. The easiest way of acquiring such procedures is by linking with a high-level language library containing them.

The **MASM DW**, **DD**, **DQ** (*define quadruple-word*), and **DT** (*define ten-byte data type*) directives can be used to define and initialize constant data for the FPU. In the **DW** case, the size alone shows that the contents must represent a word integer. In the other cases, there is potential ambiguity. For example, a data item defined by a **DD** directive may ultimately hold a short integer or a single-precision real. Of course, this ambiguity is of no concern to **MASM** unless it is called upon to initialize the data location. **MASM** will accept any reasonable clue about whether to initialize with an integer or real format: if the number contains a decimal point or an *e* or *E* (indicating scientific notation), then **MASM** interprets it as a real; otherwise, as an integer. Figure 17.4 shows some definitions of constant numeric data and **MASM**'s reactions to them. In the cases that are labeled "incorrect" **MASM** emits an error message and refuses to accept the input.

There are a few surprises in Figure 17.4. For example, while **MASM** rejects an input that overflows the data type, it does accept inputs that underflow, i.e., are too small to be represented by the data type. *doublePrec3* is an example. **MASM** merely "rounds down" to zero without even producing a warning. Another potential pitfall is that when a real number is input in hex format, as is *singlePrec4*, the input pattern is interpreted as representing the ultimate binary encoding and not the actual value of the real. Hence *singlePrec4* is not interpreted as "−1 viewed as a real number" but rather as "the quantity whose single-precision encoding has 1 is each bit." We will see later that this particular bit pattern does not even represent a bona fide real number. It is an example of a NaN — a "not-a-number." These are special patterns used to relay error messages and other information.

We now turn our attention to the FPU input and output instructions. The three primary input instructions are

---

FIGURE 17.4 USING MASM TO DEFINE NUMERICAL CONSTANTS

```
wordInt1     DW   12345
wordInt2     DW   0abcdh

shortInt1    DD   1234567899
shortInt2    DD   0abcdabcdh

singlePrec1 DD   1234.567899                    ;correct    -- loses precision
singlePrec2 DD   -1234E5                         ;correct    -- scientific notation
singlePrec3 DD   -1234E56                        ;incorrect -- overflows
singlePrec4 DD   0ffffffffr                      ;correct    -- 'r' makes it a real

longInt1     DQ   -123456789123456789            ;correct    -- in range
longInt2     DQ   0abcdabcdabcdabcdh             ;correct    -- in range
longInt3     DQ   0abcdabcdabcdabcdabh           ;incorrect -- overflows

doublePrec1 DQ   123456789123456789123456789.0 ;correct    -- loses precision
doublePrec2 DQ   1E400                           ;incorrect -- overflows
doublePrec3 DQ   1E-400                          ;correct    -- equals zero
doublePrec4 DQ   0abcdabcdabcdabcdr             ;correct    -- 'r' makes it a real

tenByteInt1 DT   -123456789123456789            ;correct    -- in range
tenByteInt2 DT   -1234567891234567891           ;incorrect -- overflows
tenByteInt3 DT   0abcdabcdabcdabcdabcdh         ;correct    -- BCD integer
extendPrec1 DT   0abcdabcdabcdabcdabcdr         ;correct    -- 'r' makes it a real
extendPrec2 DT   1E4000                          ;correct    -- in range
```

```
              fld memR          fbld memB          fild memI
```

The "ld" in each of these instructions denotes "load," because each pushes the designated memory operand onto the register stack. They change the **st(i)**-indexing of items already on the stack.

Fld, **fbld**, and **fild** interpret their operands as, respectively, real numbers, ten-byte BCDs, and integers. In the **fld** and **fild** cases the exact form of the operand is determined by **MASM**, based on its defined size or, in the case of an anonymous reference, using the size override that will be demanded. For example, if *sVar* is defined by a **DD** directive, then the instruction

```
              fld        sVar
```

will treat the contents of *sVar* as the encoding of a single-precision real.

In all cases, data loaded onto the FPU stack are converted to extended real format. Consequently, the load instructions include built-in data conversions. In addition to these primary input instructions, several instructions are provided to load constant data. These will be introduced in Section 7.

The FPU output instructions are analogous to the input instructions:

```
              fst memR                         fist memI
              fstp memR        fbstp memB      fistp memI
```

The "st" in these instructions indicates that they "store" data. Each instruction copies the present top of the FPU register stack to the designated memory location. The instructions with a 'p' in their mnemonics pop the top of the stack, while those without a 'p' do not. The presence of an 'i' or 'b' in the mnemonic has the same significance as with the load instructions: 'i' means that the output should be formatted as an integer; 'b' means as a ten-byte BCD; if neither occurs, the output is formatted as a real. For the integer and real options the exact form of the output is again determined by **MASM**, using the defined type of the destination or a size override.

The instruction set is not quite symmetric, since there is only one 'b' form of the store instruction. A number of instructions such as "store ten-byte real without popping the stack" were omitted from the instruction set because there was not enough room in the *op-code space* for them. In other words, there were not enough bit patterns available to give different machine encodings of all possible instructions, without unreasonably lengthening the machine code. There are many other gaps in the instruction set. For example,

```
fst   memR
```

is invalid when *memR* is an extended-precision real — it can only be used with single- and double-precision operands — whereas the **fstp** version is valid with all real formats. Similarly, the **fist** instruction cannot be used with long integer operands. We will present the entire instruction set, with all valid options listed, in Section 7.

But there are ways of synthesizing missing instructions. For example, there is another form of the load instruction,

```
fld       Reg
```

which does not do I/O. Instead, *Reg* refers to one of the FPU registers **st(i)**, which is pushed onto the register stack. The instruction sequence

```
fld       st
fbstp     memB
```

has the same effect as the missing "fbst."

Fbstp is one of the slowest instructions in the FPU instruction set, requiring about 500 clock cycles on all processors prior to the **80486**. Even on the **80486**, it requires about 175 clock cycles.

Figure 17.5 contains a sample program illustrating the data-conversion features of the FPU I/O instructions. On line 7, *Input* is defined as a short integer. It is loaded onto the FPU stack and later is output in each of the seven formats. The program uses the non-popping versions of the store instructions whenever they are legal. In the other cases, we interjected an extra

```
fld       st
```

to leave a copy of the input number on the stack.

The **CODEVIEW** display and watch commands provide excellent monitoring of the FPU data types. On the other hand, there is minimal support for the FPU itself, since only

FIGURE 17.5 FPU FORMAT CONVERSION

```
 1    TITLE     Formats.asm: examples of the coprocessor formats
 2    DOSSEG
 3    .MODEL SMALL
 4    .STACK 100H
 5    .DATA
 6
 7            Input    DD  -18.625          ;stored as real because of decimal point
 8            wInt     DW  ?                ;storage for a one-word int
 9            sInt     DD  ?                ;storage for a short int
10            lInt     DQ  ?                ;storage for a long int
11            BCD      DT  ?                ;storage for a packed decimal
12            singleP  DD  ?                ;storage for a single-precision real
13            doubleP  DQ  ?                ;storage for a double-precision real
14            extendP  DT  ?                ;storage for an extended-precision real
15
16    .CODE
17
18    Start:
19
20            mov      ax, @DATA
21            mov      ds, ax
22
23            fld      Input                ;load Input onto coprocessor stack
24            fist     wInt                 ;store Input as a one-word int
25            fist     sInt                 ;and as a short int
26            fld      st                   ;push extra operand that next inst. pops
27            fistp    lInt                 ;store Input as a long int
28            fld      st                   ;push extra operand that next inst. pops
29            fbstp    BCD                  ;store Input as a packed decimal
30            fst      singleP              ;store Input as a single-precision real
31            fst      doubleP              ;and as a double-precision real
32            fld      st                   ;push extra operand that next inst. pops
33            fstp     extendP              ;store Input as extended-precision real
34
35            mov      ax, 4c00h
36            int      21h
37
38            END      Start
```

the '7' command is tailored specifically to it. The '7' command displays the present state of the FPU, including the values of those registers presently in use. Unfortunately, it is not possible to watch the FPU stack dynamically during program execution — the '7' instruction must be used repeatedly to keep the display up to date.

Figure 17.6 contains a **CODEVIEW** display of our present program just after program termination. The watch window shows the results of the various store instructions and can be used to check the computations made in Section 4. Coincidentally, −18.625 was also the number used there to illustrate the different real-number formats!

The lower third of the display shows the effect of the **CODEVIEW** '7' command. At the close of the program, one of the FPU registers is occupied because of the final **fld** on line 34 in Figure 17.5. Its contents are shown both in extended real format and in equivalent

FIGURE 17.6 EXECUTING FORMATS.EXE UNDER CODEVIEW

```
#File  View  Search  Run  Watch  Options  Language  Calls  Help # F8=Trace F5=Go
############################# formats.ASM ###############################
0)  WInt 1 2   :  52AC:0006  ED FF ..                              # AX = 4C00
1)  SInt 1 4   :  52AC:0008  ED FF FF FF ....                      # BX = 0000
2)  LInt 1 8   :  52AC:000C  ED FF FF FF FF FF FF FF ........      # CX = 0000
3)  BCD  1 a   :  52AC:0014  19 00 00 00 00 00 00 00 00 80 ......  # DX = 0000
4)  SingleP 1 4 : 52AC:001E  00 00 95 C1 ....                      # SP = 0100
5)  DoubleP 1 8 : 52AC:0022  00 00 00 00 00 A0 32 C0 ......2.      # BP = 0000
6)  ExtendP 1 a : 52AC:002A  00 00 00 00 00 00 00 95 03 C0 ......# SI = 0000
############################################################### DI = 0000
6:        .DATA                                                   # DS = 52AC
7:                                                                # ES = 5297
8:        InPut    DD   -18.625          ;stored as real because of de# SS = 52B0
9:        wInt     DW   ?                ;storage for a one-word int # CS = 52A7
10:       sInt     DD   ?                ;storage for a short int  # IP = 0051
11:       lInt     DQ   ?                ;storage for a long int   #
############################################################### NV UP
7                                                                 # EI PL
cControl 037F  (Projective closure, Round nearest, 64-bit precision) # NZ NA
                  iem=0 pm=1 um=1 om=1 zm=1 dm=1 im=1            # PO NC
cStatus  3820  cond=0000 top=7 pe=1 ue=0 oe=0 ze=0 de=0 ie=0    #
cTag     3FFF  instruction=52AB8  operand=52AC2  opcode=D906    # DS:0000
Stack          Exp  Mantissa           Value                   #         21
cST(0) valid   C003 9500000000000000 = -0.18625E+2             #
```

real-number format. The "valid" entry indicates that this is a valid real-number entry (as opposed to such choices as NaN and infinity, which we will consider later). The 'c' before the **ST(0)** means that the program was running with an actual FPU. If an emulation library were used instead, the 'c' would be replaced by an 'e'.

The *Control* and *Status* entries reflect the contents of certain FPU non-data registers that we have not yet discussed. The only item of interest at the moment is "round nearest." The method used by the FPU in shortening data to fit in a lower-precision location is under programmer control. The choices are to *round nearest, round down, round up,* or *round toward zero*, with the first being the default. In Section 6, we will discuss how this default can be changed. Because the round nearest option is in effect, when -18.625 is output as a one-word integer, for example, it is rounded to -19.

In Chapter 6, we developed the procedures *ascBin16* and *bin16Asc*, which translate between the alphanumeric representations of integers and the corresponding one-word binary values. A complete I/O package should have analogous pairs of procedures to translate between the alphanumeric representations of each of the seven data types and their coded formats.

Since it is impractical to discuss all seven conversions in detail at this point, we have chosen to begin with the conversions for the ten-byte BCD format. There were a number of reasons for this choice. First, the procedures are comparatively easy to write. Second, they provide a platform on which to do relatively high-precision integer arithmetic (18 digits) with speed and ease. Third, this data type is not supported by the high-level languages (C in particular) and so the high-level language libraries do not contain routines of this type. Lastly, we will see in Section 8 that the BCD routines are natural building blocks for the construction of the more complicated conversions.

To elaborate slightly on the third point, one of the many advantages of calling FPU code from high-level languages is that most of the I/O routines are already in place. In **C**, for example, they are accessed through *scanf( )* and *printf( )*. The %f format specifier corresponds to single-precision reals, the %lf to double-precision, the %d to word integers, and the %ld to short integers. The use of the phrase "short integer" in the present context is unfortunately in conflict with the standard C language usage.

Our procedure, which translates an eighteen-digit decimal integer to ten-byte BCD format, is called *ascTBCD* and is shown in the first part of Figure 17.7. Since *TBCDAsc*, the routine performing the inverse translation, is quite similar to *ascTBCD*, we have not reproduced it in the text. However, it is on the Program Disk. ASCTBCD.ASM is in the correct form to be assembled and included in a library. In fact, both ASCTBCD.OBJ and BCDTASC.OBJ are contained in USER.LIB. As usual, the procedures are most easily accessed by means of corresponding macros, which appear at the end of Figure 17.7 and are also contained in the macro file CONSOLE.MAC.

The code for *ascTBCD* is straightforward. The procedure will accept an optional '+' or '−' sign at the start of the input. If there is a '−' sign, the sign bit in the ten-byte BCD representation is set. The main part of the code consists of packing input digits "two-for-one" into the nine lowest bytes of the ten-byte representation.

ascTBCD responds to input errors in a reasonable way. If an input string contains too many digits, it is truncated after the first 18 digits have been processed. In addition, *ascTBCD* will stop processing when it encounters an illegal character in the input. In other words, it interprets any non-digit beyond the possible opening '+' or '−' sign as the end of the input number. (This is the same mode of operation as *ascBin16*.)

SECTION 6 FPU ARCHITECTURE

As well as the data registers introduced in Section 3, the FPU contains five other registers, which hold control parameters, status information, and information important in the handling of error conditions. The data registers sometimes contain bit patterns not representing valid numeric data. This situation can arise because of program error and because such patterns are deliberately placed in the registers for signalling purposes. The FPU recognizes six distinct *exception conditions* and has built-in handlers to deal with each of these. It is also possible to replace these handlers with customized versions supplied by the programmer. We will discuss these aspects of the FPU structure in the present section.

THE OTHER REGISTERS

Figure 17.8 shows the five additional registers of the FPU.

FIGURE 17.7 ASCIIZ-TO-TEN-BYTE CONVERSION

```
 1   TITLE      ascTBCD.asm
 2
 3   COMMENT # Converts ASCIIZ string of decimal digits to the standard ten-byte
 4           packed decimal representation. Expects offsets of ten-byte buffer
 5           and input string to be pushed onto stack. If more than 18 digits
 6           are input, it will ignore the excess. Will stop conversion if it
 7       # encounters a non-digit beyond a possible opening '+' or '-'/
 8
 9   INCLUDE      console.mac
10
11   rangeCheck  MACRO     Char        ;checks whether Char is the ASCII
12                                     ;   code for a decimal digit
13       cmp      Char, '0'
14       jl       Done
15       cmp      Char, '9'
16       jg       Done
17
18       ENDM
19
20   ;-------------------------------------------------------------
21
22   PUBLIC      ascTBCD
23
24   .MODEL SMALL
25
26   .CODE
27
28   ascTBCD     PROC          NEAR
29
30       push     bp
31       mov      bp, sp
32
33
34       pushRegs    ax, cx, dx, si, di, ds, es
35       mov      di, [bp + 6]            ;initialize BCD to 0
36       mov      cx, 5
37       push     ds
38       pop      es                     ;preparing to use stosw
39       xor      ax, ax
40       rep      stosw
41
42       sub      di, 10                 ;reinitialize di
43       mov      si, [bp + 4]           ;point si to AscStr
44
45       cmp      BYTE PTR [si], '-'     ;look for opening minus sign
46       jne      notNeg                 ;here if negative, so
47       or       WORD PTR [di + 8], 1 SHL 15 ;   set the sign bit
48       inc      si                     ;to point to first digit
49       jmp      SHORT pastSign
50
51   notNeg:
52
53       cmp      BYTE PTR [si] , '+'    ;look for opening plus sign
54       jne      pastSign
```

Figure 17.7 cont.

```
55      inc     si                              ;here if a '+' sign -- ignore it
56
57  pastSign:
58
59      mov     di, si                          ;point di to first digit in AscStr
60      mov     cx, 19                          ;search for end of AscStr, but
61      xor     al, al                          ;  accept a maximum of 18 digits
62      repne   scasb
63      sub     cx, 18
64      neg     cx                              ;cx now contains digit count of AscStr
65      jcxz    Done                            ;if no digits, record answer as 0 in BCD
66      dec     di
67      dec     di
68      mov     si, di                          ;si points to the last digit in AscStr
69      mov     di, [bp + 6]                    ;  and di points to low byte in BCD
70
71  packDigits:
72
73      xor     al, al                          ;zero al
74      mov     al, [si]                        ;current digit
75      rangeCheck  al
76      sub     al, '0'                         ;ASCII to digit value conversion
77      dec     cx
78      jz      outOfDigits                     ;if an odd number of digits
79      dec     si                              ;point si to previous digit
80      mov     ah, [si]
81      rangeCheck  ah
82      sub     ah, '0'                         ;ASCII to digit value conversion
83      shl     ah, 1
84      shl     ah, 1
85      shl     ah, 1
86      shl     ah, 1                           ;move it to four high bit positions
87      or      al, ah                          ;combine two digits in one byte
88      mov     [di], al                        ;store the byte
89      inc     di                              ;point to next byte in BCD
90      dec     si                              ;  and previous one in AscStr
91      dec     cx
92      jnz     packDigits
93      jmp     SHORT Done
94
95  outOfDigits:
96
97      mov     [di], al                        ;deals with last of an odd
98                                              ;  number of digits
99  Done:
100
101     popRegs
102     pop     bp
103     ret     4
104
105 ascTBCD     ENDP
106
107     END
```

```
MACRO FOR INVOKING ascTBCD:

aToTBP  MACRO TBCD, ascStr

    EXTRN    ascTBCD:NEAR
    push     ax
    lea      ax, TBCD
    push     ax
    lea      ax,ascStr
    push     ax
    call     ascTBCD
    pop      ax

    ENDM

MACRO FOR INVOKING TBCDAsc:

TBPToA  MACRO ascStr, TBCD

    EXTRN    TBCDAsc:NEAR
    push     ax
    lea      ax, TBCD
    push     ax
    lea      ax, ascStr
    push     ax
    call     TBCDAsc
    pop      ax

    ENDM
```

The *status word* is a 16-bit register showing various aspects of the current state of the FPU:

Bits 0-5 contain the *exception flags*. These relate to the six exception conditions mentioned previously. When one of these conditions occurs, the FPU sets the corresponding exception flag. The exception flags are *sticky* in the sense that, once set, they remain set until explicitly cleared. As we will see in the next section, three instructions can be used to clear the exception flags: **fclex**, **frstor**, and **fldenv**.

Bit 6 is the *stack fault bit* and is only available with the **80387** and **80486**. Recall that both FPU stack overflow and stack underflow are errors. Bit 6 is set if either of these conditions occurs. The C_1 condition code (defined later) can be used to distinguish the two cases: $C_1 = 1$ means overflow and $C_1 = 0$ means underflow.

Bit 7 is called the *exception summary bit*. It is set if any of the exception bits corresponding to an *unmasked* exception is set. We will explain the significance of unmasked exceptions when we discuss the control register.

Bits 8, 9, 10, and 14 are called the *condition codes*, and are analogous to certain of the main processor flags. In the next section, we will see that there is a natural way of mapping these codes into the main processor flags register. When this is done, the condition codes correspond to specific main processor flags, as shown in Figure 8.8.

Bits 12-14 give the *top of the stack*: they hold the bit pattern of the integer j such that **Rj** is currently the top of the FPU stack. As we saw earlier, the **st(i)**-indexing begins with **st** = **st(0)** being the top of the stack.

FIGURE 17.8 THE OTHER FPU REGISTERS

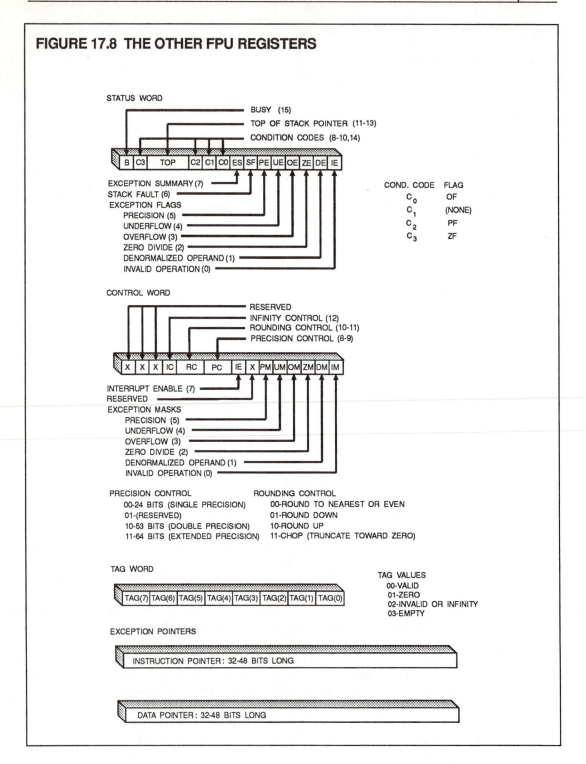

STATUS WORD

BUSY (15)
TOP OF STACK POINTER (11-13)
CONDITION CODES (8-10,14)

B	C3	TOP	C2	C1	C0	ES	SF	PE	UE	OE	ZE	DE	IE

EXCEPTION SUMMARY (7)
STACK FAULT (6)
EXCEPTION FLAGS
    PRECISION (5)
    UNDERFLOW (4)
    OVERFLOW (3)
    ZERO DIVIDE (2)
    DENORMALIZED OPERAND (1)
    INVALID OPERATION (0)

COND. CODE	FLAG
C_0	OF
C_1	(NONE)
C_2	PF
C_3	ZF

CONTROL WORD

RESERVED
INFINITY CONTROL (12)
ROUNDING CONTROL (10-11)
PRECISION CONTROL (8-9)

X	X	X	IC	RC	PC	IE	X	PM	UM	OM	ZM	DM	IM

INTERRUPT ENABLE (7)
RESERVED
EXCEPTION MASKS
    PRECISION (5)
    UNDERFLOW (4)
    OVERFLOW (3)
    ZERO DIVIDE (2)
    DENORMALIZED OPERAND (1)
    INVALID OPERATION (0)

PRECISION CONTROL
    00-24 BITS (SINGLE PRECISION)
    01-(RESERVED)
    10-53 BITS (DOUBLE PRECISION)
    11-64 BITS (EXTENDED PRECISION)

ROUNDING CONTROL
    00-ROUND TO NEAREST OR EVEN
    01-ROUND DOWN
    10-ROUND UP
    11-CHOP (TRUNCATE TOWARD ZERO)

TAG WORD

TAG(7)	TAG(6)	TAG(5)	TAG(4)	TAG(3)	TAG(2)	TAG(1)	TAG(0)

TAG VALUES
    00-VALID
    01-ZERO
    02-INVALID OR INFINITY
    03-EMPTY

EXCEPTION POINTERS

INSTRUCTION POINTER: 32-48 BITS LONG

DATA POINTER: 32-48 BITS LONG

Bit 15 is called the *busy* bit. With the **8087/80287**, it is set to indicate that the FPU is presently executing an instruction; with the **80387/80486**, this information is unnecessary and the busy bit always has value equal to bit 7.

The *control word* is another 16-bit register. As the name implies, it holds information controlling some aspects of FPU execution. Various bits are of interest:

Bits 0-5 are the *exception masks*. If an exception mask is set, the FPU will invoke a built-in default handler in response to the corresponding exception; otherwise, it will use a specially written handler, which must be supplied either as part of the system programs or with the application program. We will consider these bits in more detail later in the present section.

Bits 8-9 give the *internal precision control*. As we know, the FPU normally performs its computations to 64 bit precision. However, it is occasionally desirable to do computations to lower precision, say to obtain results compatible with those obtained by other, lower-precision processors. For such applications, the FPU precision can be reduced to 24 or 53 bits (single- or double-precision). The reduction in precision only applies to the four basic arithmetic operations and to the square-root instruction.

Bits 10-11 set the *rounding mode* of the FPU. The choices are shown in Figure 17.9. *Round to nearest or even* is the default and is also the most interesting. Rather than introduce a systematic error by always rounding quantities ending with 5 in the upward direction, this mode rounds in the direction making the last non-zero digit even.

Bit 12 is the *infinity control* bit. As we will see later, certain bit patterns are interpreted by the FPU as representing plus infinity ($+\infty$) and minus infinity ($-\infty$). The **8087/80287** coprocessors will do arithmetic in either of two ways: in a *projective* mode, in which there is only one value for infinity, i.e., $+\infty = -\infty$, and in an *affine mode*, in which there are two infinities, i.e., $+\infty \neq -\infty$. These modes correspond to bit 12 being clear or set, respectively, with the former being the default. On the **30387/80486** the value of this bit is ignored since the affine mode is always used.

The *tag register* is a 16-bit register whose contents indicate which FPU registers are occupied and the kinds of elements they contain. The encoding is shown in Figure 17.8. The tag register is mainly used by exception handlers.

The *instruction* and *data pointers*, also referred to as the *exception pointers*, are likewise used by exception handlers. As the names indicate, they contain the addresses of the current FPU instruction and of its memory operand, if it has one. We will explain below why they are needed. While these registers are part of the **8087/80287**, they are actually located on the **80386** rather than the **80387**, although they are still treated as part of the FPU in this case.

The *environment* of the FPU is a data block containing the five FPU registers introduced in this section. The size and formatting of the environment block differs in the 16- and 32-bit modes. The interested reader can find the details in [17], for example. In the next section we will list FPU instructions that save the environment block to memory and restore it.

Likewise, the *state* of the FPU is a data block that can be saved or restored using certain provided instructions. The state consists of the environment together with copies of the eight data registers.

SYNCHRONIZATION

The FPU is called a *coprocessor* for good reason: it is possible for the CPU (i.e., the *central processing unit*, which is a synonym for the main processor) and the FPU to execute instructions *simultaneously*. While this behavior can add greatly to the efficiency of coprocessor programs, it does introduce certain hazards.

The rules governing the *synchronization*, or concurrent operation, of the CPU and FPU are unfortunately somewhat different for the **8087** than for the **80287/80387/80486**. Specifically:

- When the CPU finds an FPU instruction in the input stream, its response is different for different coprocessors in the family. When the coprocessor is an **80287** or a later family member, the CPU waits until the coprocessor is idle before requesting it to execute the new instruction; in the **8087** case, the CPU does not, unfortunately, automatically wait for the coprocessor to finish before presenting the new instruction.

- The situation where an FPU instruction immediately precedes a CPU instruction is handled identically for all the coprocessors: the CPU begins execution without waiting for completion of the FPU instruction.

Because the **8087** fails to wait for the FPU in the first instance, an explicit instruction must be included in **8087** code to force an appropriate pause. **Fwait** is such an instruction. **Fwait** is actually an alternate name for the **wait** instruction which, as we saw in Chapter 10, makes the CPU stop until it receives a signal from the FPU indicating that it has completed an instruction. The programmer does not need to explicitly encode these **fwait** instructions:

- When **MASM** generates code for the **8087**, it inserts an **fwait** instruction before every FPU instruction.

Incidentally, when **MASM** encounters FPU code, its default is to generate **8087** code. Code for the more recent coprocessors will be generated only if either the **.287** or the **.387** directive is used.

The configuration in which an FPU instruction precedes a CPU instruction that uses the same data can cause grief with any of the coprocessors in the family. In this case, problems can arise even if there are several other CPU instructions between the critical pair. For example, the sequence

```
fst     wVar
inc     cx
inc     cx
mov     ax, wVar
```

will not work as designed. Of course, the difficulty is that the value of **wVar** will be used by the CPU before it has been updated by the FPU. Situations of this kind are especially treacherous since coprocessor data-storing instructions require a long time to complete (by machine standards) and it may require the execution of fifteen or twenty CPU instructions before a CPU access to a location modified by an FPU will yield valid data. The solution to this problem is entirely the responsibility of the programmer:

- If a memory location is modified by the FPU and used soon after by the CPU, be sure that either an **fwait** or some FPU instruction lies between these two critical instructions.

One exception to this synchronization rule is that certain of the control instructions (which will be introduced in the next section) always modify memory before the next CPU instruction accesses it. These instructions are **fstsw/fnstsw, fstcw/fnstcw, fldcw, frstor**, and **fldenv**.

Another aspect of synchronization concerns error trapping. If an exception is unmasked, the FPU notifies the CPU when the corresponding exception condition occurs. However, the CPU does not act on this notification until it encounters an **fwait** or FPU instruction. By this time, the CPU may have raced ahead in the input stream, and hence the present **cs:ip** is of no help in locating the instruction that led to the exception. This shows the real use of the FPU exception registers: they hold the addresses of the problem instruction and its datum so that this information is available to the exception handler.

NON-NUMERIC VALUES

Since the highest and lowest values of the biased exponent, $111\cdots111$ and $000\cdots000$ respectively, are not used to store numeric data (except for $+0.0$ and -0.0), bit patterns with these exponent fields are available to store non-numeric data. We will briefly introduce these other classes of data. Again, since this information quickly becomes very technical, we refer the reader to [17] for a complete discussion. Here are some of the non-numeric "data types" manipulated by the FPU:

Infinity, which has 1s throughout its exponent field and $1000\cdots000$ as its significand. The sign bit can be 0 or 1, giving $+\infty$ and $-\infty$. These are treated as different in the affine mode but not in the projective mode. The default FPU exception handlers do the correct things with infinities. For example, in the affine case

$$+\infty \ + \ +\infty \ = \ +\infty$$

and

$$-\infty \ + \ -\infty \ = \ -\infty$$

whereas attempted computations such as

$$+\infty \ + \ -\infty$$

or

$$+\infty \ * \ +0.0$$

raise the Invalid Operation exception.

Denormal reals are reals that are too small to be stored in the chosen real-number format. As we have seen, reals use a normalized format in which the significand has the form 1.???···. Of course, whether or not the '1' is actually stored depends on the choice of real format. As the name implies, denormal reals are stored in a format corresponding to the significand having the form 0.???···. This permits the storage of non-zero reals of smaller absolute value than the format would otherwise allow. The encoding is done in the obvious way. For example, -1023 is the smallest possible value for an 11-bit exponent, but 2^{-1025}, for example, can be stored in denormalized form by adding two to the exponent and moving the '1' in the significand two places to the right. In other words, it can be stored with exponent 000···000 and significand 001000···. There is a trade-off involved in the use of denormals: the smaller the denormalized real becomes, the less will be its precision since each leading zero effectively decreases the precision by one. Denormals are easy to recognize: only denormals and $+0.0$ and -0.0 have the lowest possible value for the biased exponent, namely 000···000.

The reader should consult [17] for information on why denormals are really useful. The essential point is that zero is surrounded by a large "gap" containing no real numbers that are exactly representable in the FPU formats, and the denormals diminish that gap.

The *NaN*s (*Not-a-Number*s) form another interesting class of quantities represented by various bit patterns in the real formats. These have the largest possible biased exponent 111···111. If the most significant bit of its significand is 0, a NaN is called *signalling*; otherwise, it is called *quiet*. These names already suggest some of the uses of NaNs: quiet NaNs are frequently produced by the FPU to indicate some error condition; signalling NaNs are introduced by the programmer to carry non-numeric information.

There are a number of other kinds of bit patterns recognized by the FPU. Some of these are used by the **8087/80287** but are no longer needed by the **80387/80486**. The reader who studies [12], [13], and [17] will learn of such exotica as *indefinites, pseudozeros, pseudo-NaNs, pseudoinfinities,* and *unnormal numbers.*

EXCEPTION HANDLERS

The FPU recognizes six types of exceptions and has default mechanisms for dealing with them. As we stated earlier, these default mechanisms are used when the corresponding exception control masks of the control word are set. Most numeric programming can be done using these default handlers since they are able to cope reasonably well with the standard error conditions occurring in routine numeric programming. Here are the six standard exception conditions to which the FPU responds:

Invalid Operation. This results from an FPU stack fault (i.e., overflow or underflow) or an incorrect operand or combination of operands in an arithmetic operation. The default response is to tag the results of the computation as *indefinite* rather than using the *valid* tag associated with numeric values, and to proceed with the computation.

Division by Zero. The default response is to record the answers as $+\infty$ or $-\infty$ and to proceed with the computation.

Denormal Operand. The default response is to continue the computation, making use of the denormal.

Overflow. With the **8087/80287**, the default response is the same as for division by zero. With the **80387/80486**, the default response depends on the present rounding control mode. If the rounding control is set for rounding toward zero, the result is recorded as the largest positive or negative (whichever is appropriate) number in the given format.

Underflow. The default response is to use denormals insofar as possible and, ultimately, to produce a zero answer if necessary.

Inexact. This exception condition can hardly be viewed as representing an error. It occurs whenever an operand cannot be exactly represented in the given format and hence arises frequently in most computations. The default handler does the obvious thing: it replaces the answer by the number that is exactly representable in the given format and best approximates it, in the sense dictated by the setting of the rounding control.

The exceptions are listed in decreasing order of seriousness and this is how the FPU treats them: if an instruction induces two of these exceptions, then the action appropriate to the more serious one is taken. The reader can find more information on the default handler responses in [12], [13], or [17].

If the programmer wishes to take an action different from the default when any of the exception conditions occur, it is only necessary to unmask the appropriate exception bit in the control register and provide the correct interrupt handler. When an unmasked exception occurs, the FPU signals the host processor and this action triggers **int 16H**, the *processor extension interrupt*. Consequently, handler code for the FPU should be written to service this interrupt.

Since the Invalid Operation exception covers the most serious errors, it is usual to unmask it and replace it with a custom handler. This handler should deal with such situations as FPU stack overflow and underflow. The standard method of dealing with stack overflow is to build a software-controlled extension of the FPU stack in memory, introducing new registers **st(8)**, **st(9)**,···, and using them whenever the FPU stack overflows. While this may be a useful service in certain contexts, it certainly should not be used indiscriminately. Obviously, the operation of the software stack is much slower (probably by a factor of 10) than the real hardware stack.

The reader who wishes to see such a software stack in action can easily do so. When FPU code is called from a Microsoft **C** program, a default handler is substituted, and this handler provides an extension of the FPU stack.

Exercise 17-6. If two resistances with values R_1 and R_2 are placed in parallel in an electrical circuit, then the equivalent resistance R_0 is given by the formula

$$1/R_0 = 1/R_1 + 1/R_2$$

where this formula remains correct when any of the quantities appearing has value 0 or ∞, provided it is interpreted in the obvious way. By using appropriate values for R_1 and R_2 in a short program, show that the coprocessor handles infinities and divisions by zero sufficiently well to always produce the "correct" answer from this formula.

Exercise 17-7. The initialization check code supplied with any C compiler substitutes a new handler for the invalid op-code exception. Investigate the responses of the substitute handler for **QuickC** (or any compiler of your choice) by subjecting it to a variety of errors designed to invoke the invalid op-code exception.

SECTION 7 THE INSTRUCTION SET

Table 17.2 shows the entire instruction set for the **8087/80287/80387** series of processors. Some instructions are new to the **80387** and these are so indicated in the table. A few instructions are used by the earlier processors but are not needed by the **80387** and hence are ignored by it. These instructions are also marked in the table. The coprocessor instruction set for the **80486** is identical to that of the **80387**.

The table also shows the operand choices for each instruction. For example,

```
        fst         store real                      /MemR4/MemR8/Reg/
```

means that **fst** will store the number presently at the top of the stack as a 4- or 8-byte real or in an FPU register. Recall that **fst** cannot be used to store data in the extended real format. Two consecutive slashes, "//", denotes the classical stack format — there are no explicit operands. *Reg* always means an FPU register. With the exception of the explicit occurrence of **ax** in the **80387/80486** instructions,

```
        fstsw         ax
        fnstsw        ax
```

the main processor registers can *never* be used in coprocessor instructions. When the pair *Reg,Reg* occurs, the first *Reg* is the destination and the second is the source, and at least one *Reg* must be **st**.

LOAD AND STORE INSTRUCTIONS

We have already covered most of the load and store instructions quite thoroughly. It is important to remember that there are gaps in the store-with-no-pop instructions: they will not work with long or packed BCD integers or with extended-precision reals. Storing data in these formats requires using the store-with-pop option.

We have not yet mentioned **fxch**, the exchange instruction. **Fxch** cannot be used to interchange **st** with memory — it will only interchange two registers. It can be used either with one explicit register, the implicit one being **st**, or in the classical stack form.

TABLE 17.2 THE COPROCESSOR INSTRUCTION SET

MNEMONIC	OPERATION	FORMATS
DATA TRANSFER INSTRUCTIONS		
REAL TRANSFERS		
fld	load real	/Mem/Reg/
fst	store real	/MemR4/MemR8/Reg/
fstp	store real and pop	/MemR/Reg/
fxch	exchange registers	/ /Reg/
INTEGER TRANSFERS		
fild	integer load	/MemI/
fist	integer store	/MemI2/MemI4/
fistp	integer store and pop	/MemI/
PACKED DECIMAL TRANSFERS		
fbld	packed decimal load	/MemBCD/
fbstp	packed decimal store and pop	/MemBCD/
LOAD CONSTANT INSTRUCTIONS		
fldz	load +0.0	/ /
fld1	load +1.0	/ /
fldpi	load pi	/ /
fldl2e	load $\log_2 e$	/ /
fldl2t	load $\log_2 10$	/ /
fldlg2	load $\log_{10} 2$	/ /
fldln2	load $\log_e 2$	/ /
NON-TRANSCENDENTAL INSTRUCTIONS		
ADDITION		
fadd	add real	/ /Reg,Reg/MemR/
fiadd	integer add	/MemI/
faddp	add real and pop	/Reg,st/
SUBTRACTION		
fsub	subtract real	/ /Reg,Reg/MemR/
fisub	integer subtract	/MemI/
fsubp	subtract real and pop	/Reg,st/
fsubr	subtract real reversed	/ /Reg,Reg/MemR/
fisubr	integer subtract reversed	/MemI/
fsubrp	subtract real reversed and pop	/Reg,st/

Table 17.2 cont.

MULTIPLICATION

fmul	multiply real	/ /Reg,Reg/MemR/
fimul	integer multiply	/MemI/
fmulp	multiply real and pop	/Reg,st/

DIVISION

fdiv	divide real	/ /Reg,Reg/MemR/
fidiv	integer divide	/MemI/
fdivp	divide real and pop	/Reg,st/
fdivr	divide real reversed	/ /Reg,Reg/MemR/
fidivr	integer divide reversed	/MemI/
fdivrp	divide real reversed and pop	/Reg,st/

OTHER OPERATIONS

fsqrt	square root	/ /
fscale	scale	/ /
fprem	partial remainder	/ /
fprem1[3]	IEEE standard partial remainder	/ /
frndint	round to integer	/ /
fxtract	extract exponent and significand	/ /
fabs	absolute value	/ /
fchs	change sign	/ /

COMPARISON INSTRUCTIONS

fcom	compare real	/ /Reg/MemR4/MemR8/
ficom	compare integer	/MemI2/MemI4/
ftst	test	/ /
fcomp	compare real and pop	/ /Reg/MemR4/MemR8/
ficomp	compare integer and pop	/MemI2/MemI4/
fcompp	compare real and pop twice	/ /
fucom	unordered compare real	/ /
fucomp	unordered compare real and pop	/ /
fucompp	unordered compare real and pop twice	/ /
fxam	examine	/ /

TRANSCENDENTAL INSTRUCTIONS

fsin[3]	sine	/ /
fcos[3]	cosine	/ /
fsincos[3]	sine and cosine	/ /
fptan	tangent	/ /
fpatan	arctangent of st(1)/st	/ /
f2xm1	$2^x - 1$	/ /
fyl2x	$y * \log_2 x$ where y is st(1) and x is st	/ /
fyl2xp1	$y * \log_2(x + 1)$ where y is st(1) and x is st	/ /

PROCESSOR CONTROL INSTRUCTIONS

finit/fninit	initialize coprocessor	/ /
fldcw	load control word	/Mem2/
fstcw/fnstcw	store control word	/Mem2/
fstsw/fnstcw	store status word	/Mem2/
fstsw ax/fnstsw ax	store status word in ax	/ax/
fclex/fnclex	clear exceptions	/ /
fstenv/fnstenv	store environment	/Mem14/
fldenv	load environment	/Mem14/
fsave/fnsave	save state	/Mem94/
frstor	restore state	/Mem94/
fincstp	increment stack pointer	/ /
fdecstp	decrement stack pointer	/ /
ffree	free register	/Reg/
fnop	no operation	/ /
fwait	CPU wait	/ /
fdisi/fndisi[0]	disable interrupts	/ /
feni/fneni [0]	enable interrupts	/ /
fsetpm[2]	set protected mode	/ /

KEY: / / means no operands
        Reg means one of the coprocessor registers st(i)
        MemI means integer memory operand of any size (2,4, or 8 bytes)
        MemIk means k-byte integer memory operand
        MemR means real memory operand of any size (4,8, or 10 bytes)
        MemRk means k-byte real memory operand
        Memk means k-byte memory buffer
        Superscript (0) means 8087 only
        Superscript (2) means 80287 only
        Superscript (3) means 80387 only

The only remaining load instructions push various constants onto the stack: +0.0, +1.0, π, $\log_{10}2$, $\log_2 10$, and $\log_e 2$. These instructions are used without operands. We will explain the significance of the logarithmic constants a little later.

NON-TRANSCENDENTAL ARITHMETIC INSTRUCTIONS

In Section 3 we illustrated the use of **fsub**, the subtraction instruction, in some detail. The usage and allowable formats for **fdiv**, the division instruction, are identical to those for **fsub**. **Fadd**, addition, and **fmul**, multiplication, are also identical except they do not have (or need) reversed forms.

Fsqrt takes no operands and replaces **st** by its square root. Its speed is remarkable — on the **80387**, for example, it takes about as long as four multiplications.

Fscale, the *scaling* instruction, is used to multiply or divide by powers of 2. Specifically, it rounds **st(1)** down to an integer (if necessary) and adds this value to the exponent of **st**. Note that the direction of rounding is not affected by the rounding control setting.

Fprem, the *partial remainder* instruction, divides **st** by **st(1)** and leaves the remainder in **st**, where the remainder is chosen to have the same sign as **st**. In other words, **fprem** finds an integer Q and a real number R satisfying

```
st = Q*st(1) + R
```

and such that $0 \le R < st(1)$ if **st(1)** > 0 and **st(1)** < R ≤ 0 if **st(1)** < 0. R replaces **st** and Q is discarded. We will see applications of **fprem** when we discuss the transcendental functions.

Fprem is called the *partial* remainder instruction because it does not always compute the remainder in a single application. It actually computes the remainder by successive subtractions so that, if the dividend is large and the divisor small, it may take a long time indeed. Since interrupts cannot be processed until the executing instruction is complete, it is necessary to limit the number of subtractions done by a single **fprem** instruction in order to control the interrupt latency. In general, a single call to **fprem** will never reduce the exponent of **st** by more than 63. Consequently, producing the final remainder may require a loop of **fprem** calls. If a call to **fprem** has not produced a remainder that is smaller than the divisor, the condition code C2 of the FPU status word is set; otherwise, it is cleared. Hence C2 can be used to control a loop of **fprem** calls to arrive at a complete reduction.

Fprem1 was introduced with the **80387** and is similar to **fprem**, except that it computes the remainder R slightly differently, to conform to the IEEE standard. Whereas **fprem** always chooses R to have the same sign as the divisor, **fprem1** chooses it to have the smallest possible absolute value: the remainder R always satisfies

$$-|st(1)|/2 \le R \le |st(1)|/2$$

In case |R| = |st(1)|/2, there are obviously two possible values of Q, one giving R = −|st(1)|/2 and the other giving R = |st(1)|/2. **Fprem1** uses the value making Q even, in order to randomize the sign of the roundoff error.

Code written only for **80387**-equipped or **80486** machines should use **frpem1**, but code that might be run on earlier machines must use **fprem**.

Frndint rounds the value in **st** to an integer. The direction in which rounding occurs is controlled by the rounding control bits.

Fxtract breaks **st** apart into its exponent and significand fields. The exponent replaces **st** and the significand is pushed onto the stack, with the same sign as the original value and with exponent 0 (biased by 3FFF). Consequently, the exponent can be accessed as **st(1)** and the significand as **st**.

Fabs replaces **st** with its absolute value. In other words, it clears the sign bit.

Fchs replaces **st** by its negative by toggling the sign bit.

COMPARISON INSTRUCTIONS

For the most part, the FPU comparison instructions work like the comparison instructions of the main processor. Just as in **8088** programming the results of comparisons are

---

TABLE 17.3 CONDITION CODES AFTER COMPARISON OR FTST

OUTCOME	C3(ZF)	C2(PF)	C0(CF)	COND.JMP
>	0	0	0	ja
<	0	0	1	jb
=	1	0	0	je
UNORDERED	1	1	1	jp

---

stored in the **flags** register, the results of FPU compares are stored in the condition codes of the FPU status word.

A basic compare instruction is **fcom**, which compares the implicit operand **st** with an explicit operand that can be either a four- or eight-byte real in memory or a register. As is normal with one-operand instructions, **st** plays the role of destination, the other operand being the source, and the condition codes are set according to the value of

```
Destination - Source
```

Table 17.3 shows how the condition codes are set to reflect the possible outcomes of comparisons. Notice that one of the possible outcomes of a comparison is UNORDERED. This outcome indicates that something went wrong in the comparison: either one of the operands was a NaN or was undefined, or else a stack fault occurred. Under these circumstances, an Invalid Operation exception also occurs.

Of course, performing a comparison is futile unless the outcome can be used. In the case of the main processor, the conditional jumps are provided for this reason, but there are no analogous FPU instructions. Instead, a clever trick is used. The condition codes C3, C2, and C0 are positioned in the status word so that if the high byte of this word is copied to the low byte of the flags register, their values overwrite ZF, PF, and CF. (Compare Figures 2.6 and 17.8.) Consequently, after this copying, the FPU comparison outcomes

```
'>',   '<',   '=',   'UNORDERED'
```

correspond to the conditional jumps

```
ja, jb, je, jp
```

as can be verified from Table 10.2. This information is summarized in Table 17.3.

The remaining point needing discussion is how to most conveniently transfer the FPU status word to the flags register, and the answer involves looking ahead in the instruction set. An essential intermediate step is to move the status word to the **ax** register. The **80387** provides a new instruction

```
fstsw     ax
```

that does this in one step. On earlier coprocessors, the two steps

TABLE 17.4 CONDITION CODES AFTER FXAM

C3	C2	C1	C0	TYPE OF ST
0	0	0	0	+UNSUPPORTED
0	0	0	1	+NAN
0	0	1	0	-UNSUPPORTED
0	0	1	1	-NAN
0	1	0	0	+NORMAL
0	1	0	1	+INFINITY
0	1	1	0	-NORMAL
0	1	1	1	-INFINITY
1	0	0	0	+0
1	0	0	1	+EMPTY
1	0	1	0	-0
1	0	1	1	-EMPTY
1	1	0	0	+DENORMAL
1	1	1	0	-DENORMAL

```
fstsw    memW
mov      ax, memW
```

are required, where *memW* is a one-word memory location.

Once the status word is stored in **ax**, the instruction

```
sahf
```

completes the task.

Fcomp operates precisely like **fcom**, but it also pops the stack. **Fcompp** also acts the same way, but it pops the stack twice and can be used only in the classical stack format.

Ficom and **ficomp** are similar, except that in this case the source operand is a 2- or 4-byte integer.

Fucom, fucomp, and **fucompp** work like the corresponding variants of **fcom** except that these will accept NaNs as operands without reporting an Invalid Operation.

Ftst also works like **fcmp** except that it compares the top of the stack with 0.0. It records its results as shown in Table 17.3, precisely like **fcmp**.

Fxam examines **st** and reports its type by setting the control codes appropriately. The FPU recognizes these alternatives: positive or negative; NaN; denormal; normal; zero; infinity; unsupported; and empty. We gave details on some of these categories in Section 6. The condition code settings are shown in Table 17.4.

TRANSCENDENTAL FUNCTIONS

Fcos, which is available only on the **80387/80486**, replaces **st** by cos(**st**). Here, and in the other trigonometric functions, **st** must be expressed in radians and the input value of **st**

must satisfy $|st| < 2^{63}$. Of course, to all intents and purposes, this means that the input argument is unrestricted in size.

However, the FPU does allow the computation of the trigonometric functions with extremely large arguments. First, if a trigonometric function is used with too large an argument, the C2 condition code is set. At that point, **fprem** (or **fprem1**) should be used to reduce the size of the argument to the allowed range. The obvious way of doing this is by using the periodicity of the trigonometric functions, i.e., applying either of the partial remainder functions with $st(1) = 2*\pi$. However, the official Intel recommendation is that the reduction be done using $st(1) = \pi/4$. This process is discussed in an exercise at the end of the next section.

Fsin, which again is available only on the **80387/80486**, computes the sine of **st** and is completely analogous to **fcos**.

Fsincos, yet another instruction introduced with the **80387**, also operates like **fcos** except that it replaces **st** by sin(**st**) and in addition pushes cos(**st**) onto the stack. In other words, **fcos** removes the input argument from the stack and leaves its cosine as **st** and its sine as **st(1)**.

Fptan behaves in a somewhat curious fashion. Of course, as the name suggests, it is intended for computing the tangent function. In the **8087/80287**, **fptan** pops the input argument and replaces it by two numbers, which are results of its internal computations and themselves of no significance, but whose ratio **st(1)/st** yields the tangent of the input argument. This means that **fptan** must be followed by **fdiv** in order to complete the computation. This approach is used so that the same function can be used for computing tangent and cotangent: to obtain the cotangent, just replace the **fdiv** by an **fdivr**.

The **30387/80486** achieves the same flexibility in a somewhat more rational manner. For compatibility with the previous FPUs, **fptan** still leaves two numbers on the stack with the property that **st(1)/st** gives the tangent of the input argument. However, in this case **st(1)** is the value of the tangent and **st** = 1. In other words, an **fdivr** will still give the cotangent, while an ultra-fast

```
      fstp      st
```

will bring the tangent to the top of the stack.

On the **8087/80287**, the input **st** must be in the range $0 \le st \le \pi/4$, a restriction that causes a certain amount of grief and is examined in the exercises. With the **80387/80486**, the allowed input values are the same as for the other trigonometric functions: $|st| < 2^{63}$.

Fpatan, the *partial arctangent function*, computes arctan(**st(1)/st**). On the **8087** and **80287**, **st** and **st(1)** must satisfy $0 \le st(1) \le st$, but there is no restriction with the later processors. The two input parameters are popped and replaced by the answer. One slight problem with this instruction is that, in the **80387/80486** case, it does not produce the "principle value" of the arctangent. The range of values of the output depends in a rather arbitrary way on the signs of the inputs **st** and **st(1)**, as shown in Table 17.5.

Since **fpatan** incorporates a division **st(1)/st** as part of its processing, it is easy to compute the other inverse trigonometric functions, using formulas such as

```
arcsin(x)  =  arctan(x/(1 - x²)^1/2)
arccos(x)  =  arctan((1 - x²)^1/2/x)
```

TABLE 17.5 VALUES OF FPATAN

SIGN OF y	SIGN OF x	RELATIVE SIZES	RANGE OF VALUES
+	+	$\|y\| < \|x\|$	$0 < \arctan(y/x) < \pi/4$
+	+	$\|y\| >= \|x\|$	$0 < \arctan(y/x) < \pi/2$
-	+	$\|y\| >= \|x\|$	$\pi/2 < \arctan(y/x) < 3^*\pi/4$
-	+	$\|y\| < \|x\|$	$3^*\pi/4 < \arctan(y/x) < \pi$
+	-	$\|y\| < \|x\|$	$-\pi/4 < \arctan(y/x) < 0$
+	-	$\|y\| >= \|x\|$	$-\pi/2 < \arctan(y/x) < -\pi/4$
-	-	$\|y\| >= \|x\|$	$-3^*\pi/4 < \arctan(y/x) < -\pi/2$
-	-	$\|y\| < \|x\|$	$-\pi < \arctan(y/x) < -3^*\pi/4$

F2xm1 computes $2^x - 1$, where x denotes the input value of **s(t)**. On the **8087/80287**, x must be in the range $0 \le x \le 0.5$, but on the **80387/80486** the allowable range has been increased to $-1.0 \le x \le +1.0$. Of course, in either case the range limitation necessitates the frequent use of **fprem** or **fprem1**.

This function is provided mainly as a means of computing 2^x and delivers the value $2^x - 1$ only to increase the precision of the computation for values of x close to zero.

As an example, consider the computation of $2^{0.0000001}$. The extended real value delivered by **f2xm1** is

```
+0.6931472045825965E-7
```

and the extended real value of $2^{0.0000001} - 1$ is

```
+1.00000006931472E+1
```

(This information was copied from a **CODEVIEW** '7' display and so shows only 16 digits, even though the internal computations are done to greater precision.)

Because of the zeros occurring in the second result, the first effectively gives many more digits of precision. Naturally, this extra information is only helpful if the quantity $2^x - 1$, rather than 2^x, can be used at this point in the computation.

Fyl2x replaces **st** and **st(1)** by $y*log_2x$, where the 'x' denotes **st** and the 'y' denotes **st(1)**. The parameter 'x' must satisfy the requirement $0 < x$ (which is a restriction resulting from the nature of the logarithm function rather than from the FPU) and 'y' can be arbitrary.

The function **fyl2x** can be used to compute logarithms to other bases, using the formula

```
logbx = (log2b)⁻¹*log2x
```

It is primarily on account of this application that **fyl2x** is designed to accept two input parameters.

Fyl2xp1 computes $y*log_2(x + 1)$, where again 'x' means **st** and 'y' means **st(1)**. As in **fyl2x**, the inputs are popped from the stack and replaced by the answer. Using "x + 1" rather than 'x' in computing the logarithm gives more precision when computing log_2z for values of z close to one.

CONTROL INSTRUCTIONS

Many of the processor control instructions come in two forms, a *no-wait* form, which has an 'n' immediately following the opening 'f' in the mnemonic, and a *wait* form, which is missing the 'n'. For example, the initialization instruction is available in both forms, with mnemonics **finit** and **fninit**. The distinction between the two forms of a control instruction is that the no-wait form ignores unmasked exception conditions.

Finit/fninit is used to return the FPU to its default initial state. This means that the stack is emptied and all registers are returned to their default values. These instructions are not very useful in writing code that might be called by various compilers since these normally configure the FPU differently from the Intel defaults. Consequently, our procedures generally restore the FPU to its state at the procedure entry point. In most programs, this only involves popping leftover items from the FPU stack.

Fldcw replaces the FPU control word with the instruction operand, which should be a one-word memory reference.

Fstcw/fnstcw stores the FPU control word in its operand, which should again be a one-word memory reference.

Fstsw/fnstsw stores the contents of the status word in a one-word memory location.

Fstsw ax/fnstsw ax is a convenient addition to the 80387/80486 instruction set. Recall that in dealing with the compare instructions, we stored the status word in memory, then transferred it to **ax**, and finally loaded **ah** into the flags register by using **sahf**. These gyrations allowed the use of conditional jumps as responses to the condition bit settings. This new instruction combines the first two of the preceding steps by storing the status word directly in **ax**.

Fclex/fnclex clears the exception flags, the exception status flag, and the busy flag.

Fstenv/fnstenv stores the FPU environment in the instruction operand, which must be a sufficiently large memory buffer. It is the responsibility of the programmer to provide a large enough buffer for this function: 14 bytes are sufficient unless the 80387/80486 is operating in 32-bit mode, in which case 28 bytes are required.

Fldenv inverts the previous functions: it updates the FPU environment with the data from the memory block given as the function operand.

Fsave/fnsave saves the present state of the FPU to a memory buffer provided as its operand. This buffer must be at least 94 bytes long and, when the 80387/80486 is operating in 32-bit mode, must be at least 108 bytes long.

Frstor is just the inverse to the previous function: it restores the FPU state from the memory buffer given as its operand.

Fincstp adds one to the stack top pointer. Referring back to the first illustration in Figure 17.2, this means that if, for example, physical register **R4** was the top of the stack, **R5** will assume the role. The subscript arithmetic is done modulo 8 and so the successor to **R7** is **R0**. The only effect of **finstp** is to change the value of the top-of-stack field in the status word, which changes the st(i)-numbering of the physical registers. *It does not have the same effect as popping the stack*, since that would also require marking the vacated register as empty in the tag word.

Fdecstp is the decreasing analog of the previous instruction.

Ffree takes a register as its parameter and marks that register as empty.

Fnop is the FPU analog of **nop**: it performs no action but does use up code space (two bytes) and time (12 clock cycles on the **80387**).

Fdisi/fndisi disables interrupts by setting the interrupt disable mask in the **8087** control word. It is not used with the **80287** or later coprocessors since they employ other mechanisms for dealing with interrupts.

Feni/fneni enables interrupts by reversing the effect of the previous instruction, and the same comments apply to both instructions.

Fsetpm is used only with the **80287**, which it sets to protected mode operation. It is not needed and is ignored by the **80387/80486**.

Fwait is not an FPU instruction. It is an alternate mnemonic for the instruction **wait**, which was introduced in Chapter 10 and discussed in Section 6 of this chapter.

SECTION 8 ASCIIZ-TO-REAL CONVERSIONS

Rather than building a set of ASCIIZ-to-real conversion routines from scratch, we will start with the ASCIIZ-to-ten-byte BCD routines developed in Section 5. The basic idea is to make the FPU do as much of the work as possible. For example, the ASCIIZ-to-double-precision conversion performs the following computations:

- Takes the input real number and rewrites it as a ten-byte BCD times a power of ten, using CPU instructions.

- Uses the ten-byte BCD and the exponent of the power of ten as inputs to the FPU. The ten-byte BCD part is input using the Section 5 routine; the exponent is just a one-word integer.

- Reconstitutes the input real number by multiplying the ten-byte BCD by the appropriate power of 10, again using FPU instructions. Outputs the result in double-precision format.

A total of six conversion procedures is required for performing input and output conversions in the single-, double-, and extended-precision formats. We will only show the details of the input conversions in the text, since the output conversions are analogous. However, the output routines are on the Program Disk.

Figure 17.9 contains the code for the input routines. Because they so similar, it was practical to write a single .ASM file and use conditional assembly directives to configure it for each of the three cases.

Before looking at the code in detail, we will say a few general words about the use of these routines. They accept an optional decimal point and an optional exponential part, prefaced by an 'E' or 'e'. For example,

```
-1796.4321E-279
```

is a valid input.

Since they use the *TBCDAsc* procedure to input the base and *ascBin16* to input the exponent, they respond in the same general way to incorrect inputs as do those procedures.

FIGURE 17.9 ASCIIZ-TO-REAL CONVERSIONS

```
1    TITLE  ascToRe.asm: converts ASCIIZ formatted real to any real FPU format
2
3    COMMENT # Converts the alphanumeric representation of a real number to the
4                standard IEEE formats. To generate the conversion routines
5                this file should be assembled three times, with SINGLE,
6                DOUBLE, and EXTEND defined on the MASM command line, and using
7                ascToSp, ascToDp, and ascToEP as the basenames of the generated
8                .obj files. The routines expect a pointer to the ASCIIZ string
9                containing the input and a pointer to the output buffer to have
10        # been pushed onto the stack in that order.
11
12   INCLUDE console.mac
13
14   IFDEF    SINGLE                           ;generate single-prec. conversion
15       ascToRe        EQU    <ascToSP>     ;  routine
16       PUBLIC         ascToSP
17       SIZEOVERRIDE   EQU    <DWORD PTR>
18       IF1
19           %OUT    Assembling single-precision version
20       ENDIF
21   ELSEIFDEF    DOUBLE                        ;generate double-prec. conversion
22       ascToRe        EQU    <ascToDP>     ;  routine
23       PUBLIC         ascToDP
24       SIZEOVERRIDE   EQU    <QWORD PTR>
25       IF1
26           %OUT    Assembling double-precision version
27       ENDIF
28   ELSEIFDEF    EXTEND                        ;generate extended-prec. conversion
29       ascToRe        EQU    <ascToEP>     ;  routine
30       PUBLIC         ascToEP
31       SIZEOVERRIDE   EQU    <TBYTE PTR>
32       IF1
33           %OUT    Assembling extended-precision version
34       ENDIF
35   ELSE
36       IF1
37           REPT    10
38               %OUT    ******Must specify precision******
39           ENDM
40       ENDIF
41   ENDIF
42
43   .MODEL SMALL
44
45   DSAStruc       STRUC
46
47       newCtrlWord    DW     ?            ;holds new control word
48       oldCtrlWord    DW     ?            ;stores old control word
49       tenByteBuf     DT     ?            ;holds TBCD part of input after it is
50                                          ;  rewritten in form TBCD * 10^Exp.
51       tempBuf        DB     20   DUP(?)  ;stores input real after '.' and
52                                          ;  exponential part have been removed
53       Exponent       DW     ?            ;holds Exponent in above decomposition
54       oldBp          DW     ?
```

Figure 17.9 cont.

```
55      returnIP        DW      ?
56      outputPtr       DW      ?
57      inputPtr        DW      ?
58
59  DSAStruc    ENDS
60
61  DSA     EQU     [bp - OFFSET oldBp]   ;sets up base address of structure
62
63  ;============================================================
64
65
66  .CODE
67
68
69  ascToRe     PROC    NEAR
70
71      push    bp
72      mov     bp, sp
73
74      sub     sp, OFFSET oldBp    ;protect DSA area of stack
75      pushRegs    ax, si, di, ds, es
76
77      mov     DSA.Exponent, 0     ;initialize exponent value
78
79      lea     di, DSA.tempbuf     ;point di to tempbuf
80      mov     si, DSA.inputPtr    ;point si to input real number
81      push    ss
82      pop     es                  ;point es to stack for use with string inst.
83      cmp     BYTE PTR [si], '-'
84      jne     @F
85      mov     BYTE PTR ss:[di], '-';insert '-' sign in tempbuf
86      inc     di                  ;point to position for first digit
87      inc     si                  ;advance to first digit in input real
88      jmp     SHORT moveDigits
89
90  @@:
91
92      cmp     BYTE PTR [si], '+'  ;check for a '+' sign
93      jne     moveDigits
94      inc     si                  ;if there is one, ignore it
95
96  moveDigits:
97
98      cmp     BYTE PTR [si], '.'  ;check for a decimal point
99      je      atDecimalPoint
100     cmp     BYTE PTR [si], 'E'  ;check for an exponential part
101     je      atExponent
102     cmp     BYTE PTR [si], 0    ;end of input?
103     je      Finished
104     movsb                       ;move a digit to the TBCD storage area
105     jmp     moveDigits
106
107 atDecimalPoint:
108
109     inc     si                  ;discard the decimal point
```

```
110
111   pastDecimalPoint:
112
113        cmp     BYTE PTR [si], 'E'    ;check for an exponential part
114        je      atExponent
115        cmp     BYTE PTR [si], 'e'
116        je      atExponent
117        cmp     BYTE PTR [si], 0      ;end of input?
118        je      Finished
119        movsb                         ;move a digit to the TBCD storage area
120        dec     DSA.Exponent          ;decimal point must be shifted once more
121        jmp     pastDecimalPoint
122
123   atExponent:
124
125        inc     si                    ;discard the 'E' or 'e'
126        aToI    [si]                  ;convert the exponent to a binary int
127        add     DSA.Exponent, ax      ;   and add it to the accumulated exp.
128
129   Finished:
130
131        push    ds                    ;because we will need it again
132        push    ss
133        pop     ds                    ;point ds to stack
134        mov     BYTE PTR [di], 0      ;null terminate
135        lea     si, DSA.tempBuf
136        lea     di, DSA.tenByteBuf
137        aToTBP  [di], [si]           ;this macro requires that both operands
138                                      ;   be in the segment pointed to by ds
139        lea     di, DSA.tenByteBuf
140        fbld    DSA.tenByteBuf        ;push BCD form of input onto FPU stack
141        fild    DSA.Exponent         ;push the base 10 exponent of input real
142        fldl2t                        ;push log base 2 of 10
143        fmul                          ;mult. these last items to get base 2 exp.
144        fld     st                    ;duplicate previous item
145        fstcw   DSA.oldCtrlWord      ;store old control word
146        fstcw   DSA.newCtrlWord      ;   and copy it to newCtrlWord
147        mov     ax, 1 SHL 11
148        not     ax                    ;mask to turn off bit 11 in newCtrlWord
149        and     DSA.newCtrlWord, ax
150        or      DSA.newCtrlWord, 1 SHL 10 ;set new control word to round down
151        fldcw   DSA.newCtrlWord      ;load the new control word
152        frndint                       ;st contains integer part of base 2 exponent
153        fldcw   DSA.oldCtrlWord      ;restore default control word
154        fld     st                    ;duplicate int. part of base 2 exp. on stack
155        fxch    st(2)                ;mov exponent to the top of the stack
156        fsubr                         ;st now contains fract. part of base 2 exp.
157        f2xm1                         ;computes 2^(fract. part of base 2 exp.) - 1
158        fld1                          ;load the constant 1.0
159        fadd                          ;st contains 2^(fract. part of base 2 exp.)
160        fscale                        ;multiply by 2^(integer part of base 2 exp.)
161        fld     st(2)                ;get the TBCD part on top of stack
162        fmul                          ;multiply TBCD times 2^(base 2 exp.)
163
164        pop     ds                    ;restore input ds value
165        mov     di, DSA.outputPtr    ;store result at memory location of
166        fstp    SIZEOVERRIDE [di]    ;   size set by conditional assembly code
```

Figure 17.9 cont.

```
167
168       fstp    st                    ;clean
169       fstp    st                    ;  up the
170                                      ;    FPU stack
171
172       POPREGS
173
174       mov     sp, bp                ;release stack area reserved for DSA
175       pop     bp
176       ret     4
177
178   ascToRe      ENDP
179
180   ;================================================================
181
182       END


SAMPLE INVOCATION MACRO:

aToTSP  MACRO SP, ascStr

    EXTRN    ascToSp:NEAR
    push     ax
    lea      ax, ascStr
    push     ax
    lea      ax, BCD
    push     ax
    call     ascToSP
    pop      ax

ENDM
```

In the case of *TBCDAsc*, conversion stops as soon as the maximum capacity of 18 digits has been reached, or when a non-digit is encountered (after the optional opening sign). The *ascBin16* conversion is similar, except that on overflow it records the answer modulo 65536.

Since the *TBCDAsc* conversion is exact (for numbers with no more than 18 digits) and since the FPU parts of the conversion are done to extended precision, the routines give exact results in the single- and double-precision cases. *However, they do suffer from roundoff error in the extended-precision case*. The reader who needs exact extended-precision routines will need to write them from the ground up. But it is not clear that this would ever be worthwhile, since FPU extended-precision computations themselves introduce roundoff error.

A major weakness of our output routines is that they only deal with real numbers: they ignore the fact that the FPU registers may contain such quantities as infinity or NaNs. When called upon to output a quantity that is not a bona fide real, these output routines should print some informative message.

Here is an analysis of the code for the input conversions, as they are presented in Figure 17.9:

Lines 14-41. This is the conditional assembly code used to generate the three input conversion routines. This file should be submitted to **MASM** three times, with command lines of the following general forms:

```
masm /Zi /z /W2 /Mx /DSINGLE ascToRe, ascToSP,,user;
masm /Zi /z /W2 /Mx /DDOUBLE ascToRe, ascToDP,,user;
masm /Zi /z /W2 /Mx /DEXTEND ascToRe, ascToEX,,user;
```

The generated files ASCTOSP.OBJ, ASCTODP.OBJ, and ASCTOEX.OBJ should then be added to USER.LIB. (The version of USER.LIB on the Program Disk already contains these three files, as well as the output analogs SPTOASC.OBJ, DPTOASC.OBJ, and EXTOASC.OBJ).

The attentive reader may wonder why it was necessary to repeat the **PUBLIC** directive on lines 16, 23, and 30. It would be much more reasonable to remove these lines and replace them with a single directive, say

```
PUBLIC ascToRe
```

situated on the present line 42. The author tried unsuccessfully to do this. The problem is that the operand of the **PUBLIC** directive cannot be given by an **EQUATE**.

Lines 45-59. We are going to use the elegant structure notation to access data on the stack, and will use the traditional name *DSA* (for dynamic stack allocation) for the base address of the structure instance that is erected on the stack. In addition to the definition of the structure template on lines 45-59, the essential ingredients are the setting of the structure base address on line 61, the protection of the local variable space on the stack on line 74, and the release of this stack space on line 174.

Lines 77-138. This is just main processor code to break the input into ten-byte BCD and exponent parts and stores them in their respective stack locations.

For example, if our hypothetical input is again

```
-1796.4321E-279
```

then, as of line 122, *DSA.tempBuf* contains

```
-17964321
```

and *DSA.Exponent* has value -4, indicating that *DSA.tenByteBuf* must be multiplied by 10^{-4} to equal the input significand. By line 128, the input exponent -279 has been added to the -4, so that *DSA.Exponent* now has value -283.

Line 137. *aToTBP* is the macro that calls the ASCIIZ-to-TBCD conversion routine. Hence we are converting *DSA.tempBuf* to TBCD format and storing it in *DSA.tenByteBuf*.

Lines 139-162. This is the FPU part of the code, which rebuilds the input real from its TBCD and exponent parts.

Lines 145-153. Our program requires the FPU to *round down* when converting the base 2 exponent to an integer on line 152. As we saw in Section 6, the direction of rounding is controlled by bits 10 and 11 in the control word and that values 1 and 0, respectively, correspond to rounding down. Since we do not know the present values of these bits, we must give them the correct values. (The default values correspond to rounding to nearest.) But, in line with our observations in Section 6, we should restore the control word to its previous value before leaving the procedure. These operations are performed on lines 145 and 153.

We chose this method primarily to demonstrate the saving and restoring of the control word. The computations can actually be done more quickly using **fprem** or **fprem1**. Starting with the exponent (call it E2) in **st** and **st(1)** = 1 and using either of these instructions will produce a value R in **st** such that $|R| < 1$ and

```
E2 = Q*1 + R
```

where Q is an integer. In other words, R can be used as the fractional part of the exponent and the integer part Q can be computed as E2 − R.

Lines 165-166. To generate the correct store instruction, **MASM** must be given a size override. On line 166 we do this, making a final application of the conditional assembly code.

Exercise 17-8. (For **80387** users.) Evaluate $\cos 10^{100}$, where the argument is given in radians, by using **fprem1** to reduce the argument to the range used by **fcos**. Reduce using $\pi/4$ as the divisor.

Exercise 17-9. Write a coprocessor program to compute n factorial. The program should use the packed BCD format and should print the values of the factorial to the screen. What is the biggest value of n for which it can compute the corresponding factorial without overflowing?

Exercise 17-10. Write a program that prompts the user for a real number and prints the cube root of that number to the screen. The program should use double-precision arithmetic. **Suggestion:** $\log_{10} x^{1/3} = 1/3 * \log_{10} x$.

Exercise 17-11. Write a "command-line calculator" named CALC. In response to a command line of the form

```
calc Operand1 Operand2 Operation
```

it should print the result of combining the double-precision reals *Operand1* and *Operand2* using the requested *Operation*, which can be any one of '+', '−', '*', or '/'. For example, the command line

```
calc 10.0  2.5 /
```

should produce the answer 4.0.

Exercise 17-12. Compute tan x, for x = 2, 3, 4, and 5, where x is given in radians. Even if you are working with an **80387**, assume that the code will be run on an **8087** so that the value of x must be reduced to the range $0 \le x \le \pi/4$ before applying **fptan**.

Exercise 17-13. Compute arctan 1.2, arcsin 0.5, and arccos 0.001. Use the formulas given in Section 7 to do the last two computations.

SECTION 9 SOME EXAMPLES

Our first numeric application of the FPU, shown in Figure 17.10, is a program that solves quadratic equations using the standard quadratic formula. We chose to write a calling module in C, QUAD1.C, which calls an assembly language module, QUAD2.ASM, to do the actual computations.

The code requires only a few comments. To increase readability, we have used the same symbolic constants in both modules, defined appropriately in each language: by #defines in the C module and by **EQUATE**s in the assembly language module. The assembly language procedure, *solveQuad*, leaves the answers in the array *Ary*: if there is a repeated real root, it is stored in *Ary[0]*; a pair of unequal real roots is stored in *Ary[0]* and *Ary[1]*; if the roots are complex, their real and imaginary parts are stored in *Ary[0]* and *Ary[1]*, respectively. In addition, *solveQuad* returns a value in **ax** (following the standard C convention) indicating whether the roots are EQUAL, REAL, or COMPLEX. As always, we have taken care to balance the FPU stack.

The procedure *solveQuad* in QUAD2.ASM exhibits several potential synchronization problems. For example, the **fstp** on line 46 stores a value that is later referenced by the CPU. However, another FPU instruction occurs on line 47, and so the line 46 instruction will have been completed before the CPU instruction can occur. The reader should check that the program, exactly as presented, is free of synchronization problems.

Coprocessor code is considerably harder to read than normal **8088** assembly language because it is difficult to remember the exact FPU stack contents from line to line. The easiest solution to this problem is to construct a new stack drawing corresponding to each program line in which the stack changes. The author does this in a quite formal way, using printed sheets containing multiple representations of the stack. As the program code is being written (or frequently even before the code is written), the stack contents are recorded after each stack-changing instruction. These entries should be made in pencil to allow for the inevitable changes of strategy. The diagrams are kept as part of the permanent documentation of the program.

Figure 17.11 shows a sample page of the diagrams that should accompany QUAD2.ASM. This approach is slightly awkward when branching occurs in the program: then it is necessary to maintain several sets of diagrams, corresponding to the different branch paths.

FIGURE 17.10 SOLVING QUADRATIC EQUATIONS

```c
1   /* quad1.c: driver for the quadratic equation solving procedure */
2
3   #include <stdio.h>
4
5   #define     EQUAL      0
6   #define     REAL       1
7   #define     COMPLEX   -1
8
9   extern int solveQuad(double, double, double, double*);
10
11  void main(void)
12  {
13      double a, b, c;
14      double Roots[2];
15      int ch;
16
17      do
18      {
19          printf("\n\nInput coefficients a, b, and c of a quadratic:  \n");
20          scanf("%lf %lf %lf", &a, &b, &c);
21          switch(solveQuad(a,b,c,Roots))
22          {
23              case EQUAL:
24
25                  printf("\n\nThe equation has a repeated real root %lf.\n",
26                      Roots[0]);
27                  break;
28
29              case REAL:
30
31                  printf("\nThe roots are %lf and %lf.", Roots[0], Roots[1]);
32                  break;
33
34              case COMPLEX:
35
36                  printf("\nThe roots are %lf + i%lf and %lf - i%lf.",
37                      Roots[0], Roots[1], Roots[0], Roots[1]);
38          }
39          printf("\n\nDo another? (y or n)  ");
40          scanf("%d",&ch);
41      }
42      while ((ch = getchar()) == 'y' || ch == 'Y');
43  }
```

```asm
1   TITLE  Quad2.asm: the FPU procedure that solves quadratics
2
3   COMMENT # Expects the coefficients a, b, and c to be pushed onto the stack
4           as doubles, in that order, followed by the address aryAdr of an
5         # array Ary of two doubles, used as indicated below.
6
7   ;values returned by solveQuad in the ax register:
8   EQUAL       EQU     0   ;equal root case: Ary[0] holds the root
9   REAL        EQU     1   ;unequal real roots: Ary[0] and Ary[1] hold them
```

```
10   COMPLEX     EQU     -1    ;complex roots: Ary[0] and Ary[1] hold real and
11                             ;   imaginary parts
12
13   .MODEL      SMALL, C
14   .CODE
15
16   solveQuad   PROC    USES bx, A:QWORD, B:QWORD, C:QWORD, aryAdr:WORD
17                       LOCAL statusWord:WORD
18
19       mov     bx, aryAdr        ;point bx to answer location
20       fld1                      ;push 1.0
21       fadd    st, st            ;double it
22       fld     st                ;duplicate it
23       fadd    st(1), st         ;double it again, so that st contains 4
24       fld     A                 ;push A
25       fmul                      ;replace st by 2*A
26       fld1
27       fdivr                     ;st = 1/(2*A)
28       fld     st                ;duplicate st
29       fld     B                 ;push B
30       fchs                      ;st = -B
31       fmul    st(1),st          ;st(1) = -B/(2*A)
32       fmul    st, st            ;st = B*B
33       fld     A                 ;push A
34       fmul    st, st(4)         ;st = 4*A
35       fld     C                 ;push C
36       fmul                      ;st = 4*A*C
37       fsub                      ;st = B*B-4*A*C
38       ftst
39       fstsw   statusWord        ;to check the result of the ftst
40       mov     ax, statusWord
41       sahf
42       jb      complexCase       ;since the roots will be complex
43       ja      realCase          ;there will be two real, unequal roots
44       mov     ax, EQUAL         ;set return value for real, equal roots
45       fstp    st                ;discard B*B-4*A*C, so that st = -B/2*A
46       fstp    QWORD PTR [bx]    ;store st
47       fstp    st                ;pop the FPU stack
48       jmp     SHORT Done
49
50   complexCase:
51
52       mov     ax, COMPLEX       ;set return value for complex roots
53       fchs                      ;because st is negative
54       fsqrt                     ;st = sqrt(4*A*C - B*B)
55       fmulp   st(2), st         ;st = sqrt(4*A*C - B*B)/(2*A)
56       fstp    QWORD PTR [bx]    ;store the imaginary part
57       fstp    QWORD PTR [bx+8]  ;store the real part
58       jmp     SHORT Done
59
60   realCase:
61
62
63       mov     ax, REAL          ;set return value for unequal real roots
64       fsqrt                     ;st = sqrt(B*B - 4*A*C)
65       fmul    st, st(2)         ;st = sqrt(B*B - 4*A*C)/(2*A)
66       fld     st                ;duplicate it
```

Figure 17.10 cont.

```
67      fadd    st,st(2)         ;compute first root
68      fstp    QWORD PTR [bx]   ; and store it
69      fsubp   st(1), st        ;compute second root
70      fstp    QWORD PTR [bx+8];and store it
71      fstp    st               ;pop the FPU stack
72
73  Done:
74
75      fstp    st               ;finish clearing the FPU stack
76
77      ret
78
79  solveQuad    ENDP
80
81      END
```

Our second example is an implementation of *Newton's Method* for finding a root of an equation. Given a function f(x), Newton's Method attempts to find a number r such that f(r) = 0, by making a series of approximations. The initial approximation X_0 is supplied by the user and, for each $n \geq 1$, new approximations are defined by the formula

$$X_n = X_{n-1} - f(X_n) / f'(X_n)$$

where f'(x) means the derivative of f(x). Using only the most basic ideas from calculus, it is easy to verify that this formula should generate a sequence of "reasonable" approximations to a root r, provided the starting X_0 is not too far from r.

Figure 17.12 contains the code for Newton's Method. It is written in our standard library module form, and in fact has been added to USER.LIB. Here are some comments on NEWTON.ASM:

Lines 63-64. NEWTON.ASM expects that the caller will have pushed two items onto the run-time stack: a near pointer to the derivative f'(x) followed by a near pointer to f(x). This is very easy to implement in assembly language. Lines such as

```
mov    ax, OFFSET funcName
push   ax
```

have the effect of pushing a near pointer to the procedure named *funcName* onto the stack, while an instruction like line 64 of the present program

```
call   [bp+4]
```

executes an "indirect near call" to the procedure whose offset is passed as [**bp**+4] on the stack. **MASM** resolves the anonymous reference by using **WORD PTR**, i.e., as a **NEAR** call, since this is the default when the **SMALL** model is used.

FIGURE 17.11 DIAGRAMMING THE FPU STACK IN QUAD2.ASM

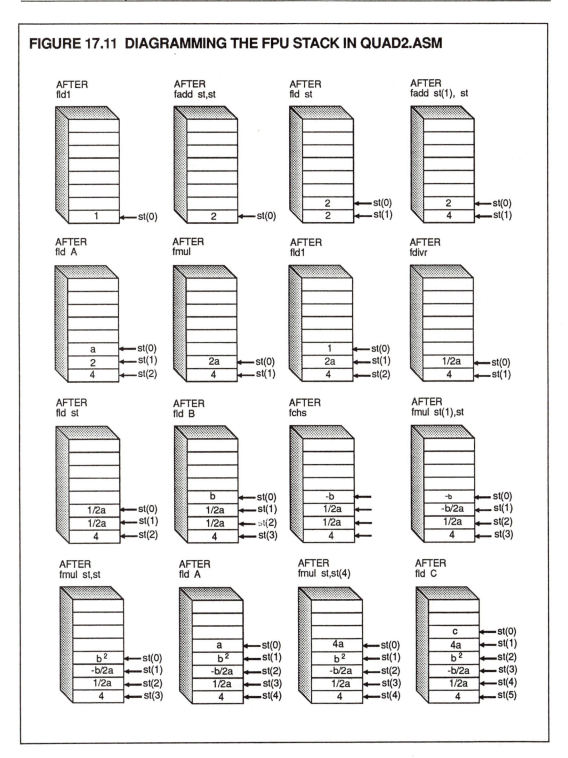

FIGURE 17.12 NEWTON'S METHOD

```
 1    TITLE   Newton.asm: implements Newton's method
 2
 3    COMMENT  # PROCEDURE HEADER
 4    TYPE:     NEAR      FILE: Newton.asm          LIBRARY: user.lib
 5    PURPOSE:   Interactive implementation of Newton's method
 6    CALLED AS: Newton(offsetDeriv(2), offsetFunct(2))
 7               where Funct is the function whose root is to be found and Deriv
 8               is its derivative
 9    RETURNS:   Coordinate of root of Funct
10
11    COMMENT     Searches iteratively for a root of f(x) = 0. Prompts for input of
12                initial approximation X0. Expects near pointers to f(x) and f'(x)
13                to be pushed onto stack, in that order. The code for f(x) and f'(x)
14                should be written to receive the input parameter x on the top of
15                the FPU stack and replace it with the computed value of f(x) or
16                f'(x). The code for these functions should not disturb the prior
17                contents of the FPU stack and can use a maximum of seven stack
18            # positions
19
20    PUBLIC    Newton
21
22    INCLUDE console.mac
23
24    ITERATIONS      EQU    <10>
25
26    .MODEL SMALL
27
28    ;=============================================================
29
30    .DATA
31
32        Real        DQ      ?
33        strBuf      DB      20    DUP(?)
34        statusWord  DW      ?
35
36    ;=============================================================
37
38    .CODE
39
40    Newton      PROC      NEAR
41
42        push    bp
43        mov     bp, sp
44
45        pushRegs   ax, bx, cx, dx
46        xor     dx, dx                         ;counter for total iterations
47
48    newReal:
49
50        outAsc   NL,NL,"Input value of X0: " ;ask for
51        inAsc    strBuf                       ;   starting
52        aToDP    Real, strBuf                 ;     value X0
53        fld      Real                         ;push X0 onto FPU stack
54
55    Another:
```

```
56
57      mov      cx, ITERATIONS
58
59   Iterate:
60
61      inc      dx                            ;increment iterations counter
62      fld      st
63      fld      st                            ;st = st(1) = st(2) = Xn-1
64      call     [bp + 4]                      ;call the test function
65      fld      st(1)                         ;push another copy of Xn-1
66      call     [bp + 6]                      ;call derivative of test function
67      fdiv                                   ;compute Xn =
68      fsub                                   ;   Xn-1 - f(Xn-1)/f'(Xn-1)
69      fxch                                   ;st = Xn, st(1) = Xn+1
70      fcomp
71      fstsw    statusWord
72      mov      ax, statusWord
73      sahf
74      jne      @F                            ;jump if Xn still not equal to Xn-1
75      jmp      foundIt
76
77   @@:
78
79      loop     Iterate
80
81   GetInput:
82
83      hSkip
84      outAsc   "After "                      ;print
85      iToA     strBuf, dx                    ;   total
86      outAsc   strBuf                        ;      number of
87      outAsc   " iterations: "               ;         iterations
88
89      fst      Real                          ;store answer
90      fwait                                  ;  and synchronize
91      outAsc   "Xn = "                       ;print
92      DPToA    strBuf, Real                  ;   value
93      outAsc   strbuf                        ;      of Xn
94
95      ;Ask what the user wants to do next
96      outAsc   NL,NL,"Press  c to continue  a to abort  n to choose new X0: "
97
98      inAsc    strBuf                        ;collect user response
99      cmp      strBuf, 'c'                   ;continue with present sequence?
100     jne      @F
101     jmp      Another
102
103  @@:
104
105     cmp      strBuf, 'a'                   ;abort?
106     jne      @F
107     jmp      Done
108
109  @@:
110
111     cmp      strBuf, 'n'                   ;choose a new X0?
112     jne      @F
113     jmp      newReal
114
```

Figure 17.12 cont.

```
115   @@:
116
117       jmp       GetInput                  ;if use response not correct,
118                                            ;  repeat until it is
119   FoundIt:
120
121       hSkip                                ;print total
122       iToA      strBuf, dx                 ;  number of
123       outAsc    "After "                   ;    iterations
124       outAsc    strBuf                     ;      required
125       outAsc    " iterations: "
126
127       fstp      Real                       ;store final answer
128       fwait                                ;  and synchronize
129       outAsc    "root has value "          ;print
130       DPToA     strBuf, Real               ;  final
131       outAsc    strbuf                     ;    answer
132       hSkip     2
133
134   Done:
135
136       popRegs
137
138       pop       bp
139       ret       4
140
141   Newton        ENDP
142
143   ;================================================================
144
145   END
```

The *Newton* procedure assumes that the code for f(x) and f'(x) has been written so that each will get its input parameter from the FPU stack, and will subsequently replace it with the corresponding functional value.

The FPU stack provides a fast and convenient parameter passing mechanism for procedures using the FPU. The only disadvantage is that whenever procedure A calls procedure B with both using the FPU stack, the number of stack positions available for use by B is decreased by whatever number are already in use by A. In the present case, there are only six FPU stack positions available for use by the code for f(x) and seven available for f'(x).

Line 90. We have separated lines 89 and 92 by a synchronizing **fwait**. This is not really necessary in the present situation and was done only as a reminder. The **fwait** can be omitted since the *outAsc* macro call hides an **int 21H** function call, which is much slower than the **fst** on line 84. A similar comment applies to the **fwait** on line 128.

The program TANXEQX.ASM of Figure 17.13 demonstrates the use of Newton's method. The problem is to find solutions of tan x = x or, equivalently, to find solutions of f(x) = 0 where f(x) = tan x − x. For this function f(x), we have f'(x) = $\sec^2 x - 1$, and Figure 17.13 contains code to compute f(x) and f'(x).

FIGURE 17.13 AN APPLICATION OF NEWTON'S METHOD

```
 1    TITLE   tanXEqX.asm: implements Newton's method for tan x = x
 2
 3    COMMENT  # Uses the Newton approximation to find a root of tan x = x
 4             # This version is written for the 386/387
 5
 6    INCLUDE console.mac
 7
 8    DOSSEG
 9    .MODEL SMALL
10
11    .386                        ;accept 386 mnemonics but use 16-bit registers
12                                ;   since this directive occurs after .MODEL
13    .387                        ;accept 387 mnemonics - can't be used unless
14                                ;   .386 directive already given
15    .STACK  100h
16
17    ;===========================================================
18
19    .CODE
20
21    Start:
22
23        mov     ax, @DATA
24        mov     ds, ax
25
26        mov     ax, OFFSET secSqM1          ;inputs to Newton procedure are
27        push    ax                          ;  near pointers to the derivative
28        mov     ax, OFFSET tanXEqX          ;    of the function and to the
29        push    ax                          ;       function itself
30        call    Newton
31
32        mov     ax, 4c00h
33        int     21h
34
35    ;-----------------------------------------------------------
36
37    tanXEqX    PROC    NEAR             ;computes the function
38                                        ;  f(x) = tan x - x
39        fld     st                      ;expects to find x on
40        fptan                           ;  top of FPU stack and
41        fstp    st                      ;    replaces it by f(x)
42        fsubr
43        ret
44
45    tanXEqX    ENDP
46
47    ;-----------------------------------------------------------
48
49    secSqM1       PROC    NEAR          ;computes the derivative of f(x),
50                                        ;  namely f'(x) = c x) - 1
51        fcos                            ;expects to find x on
52        fmul    st, st                  ;  top of FPU stack and
53        fld1                            ;    replaces it by f'(x)
54        fdivr
55        fld1
56        fsub
```

```
Figure 17.13 cont.

 57     ret   58
 59  secSqM1          ENDP
 60
 61  ;==============================================================
 62
 63  END    Start

OUTPUT FROM FIRST RUN OF tanXEqX

Input value of X0: 4.5
After 5 iterations: root has value +0.44934094579E1

OUTPUT FROM SECOND RUN OF tanXEqX

Input value of X0: 4.9
After 37 iterations: Xn = +0.23636911110E20

Press  c to continue   a to abort   n to choose new X0: n
Input value of X0: 4.8
After 35 iterations: root has value +0.14359639006E20
```

Notice lines 11 and 13 in Figure 17.13: we chose to write this as a program for the **80387** rather than for the **8087**. The reason is one of efficiency: the **8087** will only compute tan x for $0 \leq x \leq \pi/4$. Obtaining tan x for general x requires using **frem** and trigonometric reductions. Of course, we are also cutting corners by assuming implicitly that the arguments for the trigonometric functions will never be as large as 2^{63}.

Finally, at the end of Figure 17.13 we include some sample output from the program. This is interesting since it shows the potential instability of Newton's Method when applied to a wildly undulating function such as the present f(x). As can be easily checked from a rough sketch, tan x = x has infinitely many solutions, one of which is close to x = 4.5. If the initial approximation is close enough to the answer (say, 4.5), the computation quickly closes in on the correct answer. But if the initial guess is mildly off (say, 5.0) then a dramatically "wrong" solution is obtained — the answer obtained is very large indeed. It is educational to search for different solutions using different choices of the initial approximation. A good starting point is to try to find the solution that is close to 7.5.

Exercise 17-14. Another standard method for finding roots of equations is known as the *bisection method* and works in the following way. (This description can be most easily followed by drawing a diagram.) To find a root of f(x), start with a pair of numbers a and b with f(a) < 0 and f(b) > 0. If f(x) is a reasonable function, then, by a standard fact from calculus, it will have a root between a and b. Let c be the midpoint of the interval from a to b. If f(c) = 0, we have found the root. If f(c) > 0 then, again by the standard fact, there is a root between a and c. If f(c) < 0 then, for the same reason, there is a root between c and b. In each of the last two cases we have found an interval half as long as the original containing a root. Iterating this process finitely many times generates an arbitrary close approximation to the root. Use this method to find some of the roots of tan x = x and check the answers against those found by Newton's method.

CHAPTER 18

PROTECTED-MODE PROGRAMMING

SECTION 1 PREVIEW

In this chapter, we will finally do justice to the **80386**. In earlier chapters, we treated it essentially as a glorified **8088** — a great deal faster and offering an improved instruction set and much more reasonable addressing modes. In Chapter 11, we did get an inkling of some of its more exotic capabilities when, by "magic," we were able to change the sizes of segments from the previously immutable 64K.

Now it is time to study some of the advanced features of the **80386** very closely. We will see that segment addresses are computed in a new and extremely flexible way; that segments can be tailored, in terms of length and other parameters, to suit the program at hand; and that the **80386** is capable of multitasking, i.e., controlling several programs so that they appear to be running simultaneously.

Unfortunately, it is not possible to cover all aspects of the **80386** in a single chapter, and so we were forced to confine ourselves to brief descriptions of some features such as paging, hardware debugging, and virtual **8086** mode.

In Section 2, we discuss one of the major differences between the **80386** (and **80286**) and earlier processors in the series, namely the protected-mode interpretation of segment addresses. In protected mode, the segment address is interpreted as an index into a descriptor table, and the corresponding entry in that table, called a descriptor, gives the physical location (and other properties) of the segment in question.

We use our new-found knowledge, in Section 3, to write the *expandSegs* and *shrinkSegs* procedures introduced in Chapter 7 to change the sizes of real-mode segments.

Interrupts and exceptions are handled very differently in protected mode, and Section 4 discusses the differences. In addition, the use of protected-mode interrupts on an **IBM-AT**-style machine requires modification of some of the hardware initializations performed by the **BIOS** at boot time. These changes are also discussed in this section.

In Section 5, we build a very basic protected-mode operating system kernel. We assume that the machine will be booted under **MS-DOS** and then switched to protected mode. In protected mode, we set up an interrupt system and provide for minimal input and output by writing a keyboard interrupt handler and sending output directly to the video buffer. Here we make one of the major compromises of the chapter: the kernel uses 16-bit code, so that we can more easily call various procedures in USER.LIB.

Section 6 takes a careful look at the **80386** protection mechanisms. There, we are mainly concerned with privilege levels and how they are used to limit the access of untrustworthy programs to code and data.

Multitasking is certainly one of the central features of the **80386**. We examine it in Section 7 and, in Section 8, add basic multitasking features to our kernel.

In Section 9, we fill in some of the gaps in our prior discussions of the systems registers and the instructions and, to round out our discussion, touch on the various **80386** features that have not played a prominent role in the chapter.

SECTION 2 SEGMENT DESCRIPTORS AND SELECTORS

We will begin by describing some of the basic ideas behind protected-mode programming. This preliminary description is quite incomplete and is presented only to motivate the definitions appearing in the next few sections.

A guiding principle underlying protected-mode programming is that a given computer will be called upon to run code of widely varying quality and making different demands of the system.

At one extreme, there is the operating system code. By its very nature, this code must be given access to all the system resources. For example: it must be able to load and terminate other programs; it must interpret and act upon input/output requests from executing programs; and it must be empowered to administer system resources to other programs, in the sense that **MS-DOS** makes available the **int 21H** functions upon request. Of course, the operating system code has been thoroughly debugged and so can be trusted to function flawlessly(!) under all circumstances.

On the other hand, a typical computer is called upon to execute a variety of "client" programs. Advanced operating systems can effectively run several such programs at the same time by multitasking. *Multitasking* means that the operating system cycles the processor between the various clients, so that each receives some portion of the machine's computational power. Depending on how this *timesharing* is administered by the operating system, it can appear as though the programs are executing simultaneously. Of course, each runs at decreased speed.

Some of the clients will surely be of indifferent quality and, in extreme cases, can misbehave so badly that they overwrite their own code or data, or the code or data of other programs with which they are timesharing, or even the code or data of the operating system, thereby potentially bringing the entire machine to its knees.

An essential aspect of protected-mode programming is to prevent this kind of damage by severely limiting the access of less trusted programs to machine memory and other resources. The extent to which this access is restricted is basically determined by the design of the operating system and, as we will see, the structure of the **80386** allows a good deal of flexibility in matters of this kind. As an extreme example, the operating system can forbid a client to even read from its own code segments — much less write to them. (Of course, the **80386** must still be able to read the code in order to execute it.) Likewise, the operating system can structure a client program so that it cannot write to any of its data segments.

Normally, the operating system will not go to the extremes mentioned in the last paragraph. More typically, a program running in a protected-mode environment will face these restrictions:

- It cannot *write* to any of its code segments, and therefore cannot modify its own code, either accidentally or deliberately.

- It cannot access memory — either to read from or write to — that is not contained in one of its declared segments. In particular, it is unable to alter code or data belonging to the operating system or to any program with which it may be multitasking.

- Any attempt to access operating system services must be directed to the operating system, just as is the case with **MS-DOS**. But a protected-mode operating system will scrutinize each such request to determine whether it is appropriate and may decline to honor it.

- The indiscriminate use of **in** and **out** instructions, and even changing the interrupt flag with a **cli** or **sti**, can wreak havoc in a multitasking system. Consequently, a typical client program will not be permitted to use these instructions.

As we will see in Section 7, the **80386** allows the creation of programs with four different levels of privilege, ranging from Level 0, which represents the most trusted code, to Level 3, which corresponds to the least trusted. The **80386** architecture is sufficiently flexible that an operating system need not make use of all four privilege levels, and to date no operating system has done so. (**UNIX** systems use only privilege Levels 0 and 3; **OS/2** uses Levels 0, 2, and 3.)

This very brief introduction should already convince the reader that segments intended for use in protected-mode programs must be described more completely than is customary in real-mode programs. For instance, each segment must have a precisely defined length, to permit attempts to read or write beyond the segment end to be caught. It might be argued that **LINK** can determine the sizes of segments just by counting bytes but, nonetheless, the protection mechanisms require that every segment be given a formal description consisting of a number of segment parameters, of which the length is one.

The protected-mode description of a segment is contained in a data structure called, fittingly enough, a *segment descriptor*. In addition to segment descriptors, there are other varieties of descriptors, and these will be introduced later in this chapter.

Figure 18.1 shows the general formats of 80386 segment descriptors. Each segment descriptor is an eight-byte data structure. Since the meanings of some of the data fields are different for descriptors in the code segment and data segment cases, we have illustrated

FIGURE 18.1 FORMATS OF SEGMENT DESCRIPTORS

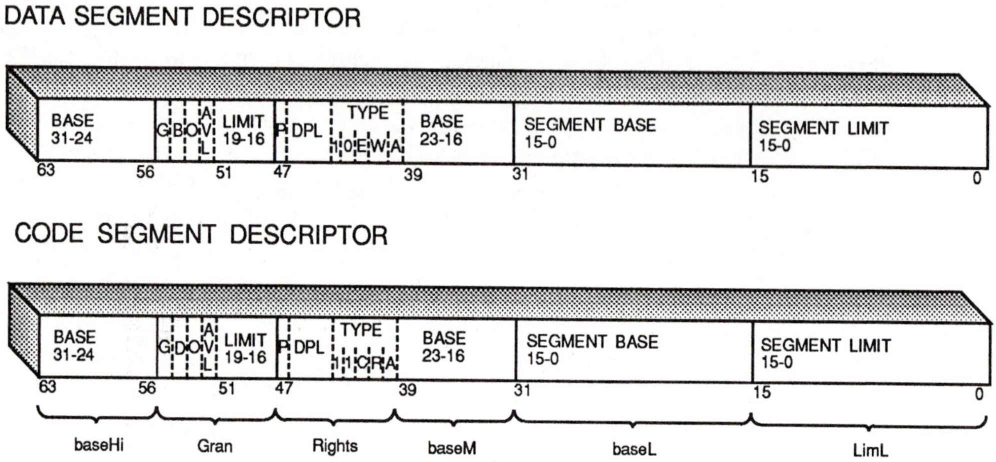

DATA SEGMENT DESCRIPTOR

CODE SEGMENT DESCRIPTOR

KEY:

A	-	ACCESSED
AVL	-	AVAILABLE FOR PROGRAMMER USE
B	-	BIG
C	-	CONFORMING
D	-	DEFAULT
DPL	-	DESCRIPTOR PRIVILEGE LEVEL
E	-	EXPAND-DOWN
G	-	GRANULARITY
P	-	SEGMENT PRESENT
R	-	READABLE
W	-	WRITABLE

both in Figure 18.1. We will now explain the different fields shown in these descriptor diagrams.

A descriptor contains the base address of the segment that it describes, but not presented in the obvious format. An **80386** segment can begin anywhere in the 4G memory space and so, in general, its base address requires 32 bits. In the descriptor, the low 24 of these bits occur, in the logical order, starting with the lowest bit in position 16. Unfortunately, the high 8 bits of the address occupy bit positions 56 to 63. We will explain this peculiar ordering presently.

The 20-bit limit field basically contains the length of the segment. More precisely, the limit field contains the maximum legal offset in the segment. Consequently, if the segment length is L, then the limit field contains the value $L - 1$. Of course, this method of storage saves a bit in case L is a power of two. Since $L - 1$ is limited to 20 bits, it would seem that segments are therefore limited to length 2^{20}, or 1M. However, this is not the case because another parameter, the G-bit, or *granularity* bit (bit number 55), affects the segment length:

if $G = 0$, the segment size is measured in bytes, but if $G = 1$, it is measured in multiples of $2^{12} = 4K$. Consequently, segments can be given arbitrary lengths up to 1M, and lengths that are multiples of 4K from 1M through 4G.

Bit number 54 has a different name and significance in data and code segments. In a code segment it is called the D-bit, or *default* bit. The value of the D-bit determines whether the segment will use 16-bit or 32-bit addressing: value zero corresponds to 16-bit addressing, and value one means 32-bit addressing. Consequently, we can now discern the real meaning of the **USE16** and **USE32** assembler directives. The **USE16** directive tells **MASM** to construct a segment with the D-bit clear, and **USE32** defines a segment with the D-bit set. In the case of a code segment, bit 54 is called the B-bit, or *big* bit. Its use is somewhat technical and so we refer the reader to [14] for a complete description. It is only significant with segments of length greater than 64K and of a type known as "expand-down." These special segments are sometimes used for stacks because they make it easier for the operating system to replace the stack by a larger one in case of stack overflow.

The next bit, which we call the O-bit, is reserved by Intel, and must be given the value zero.

Bit number 52, which we label the AVL-bit, is not used by the **80386** and so is available for use by the programmer.

The P-bit, or *present* bit, is used to flag whether or not a segment is present in memory: $P = 1$ means the segment is present, while $P = 0$ means that it is not. Any attempt to access a segment with $P = 0$ results in a program error. While the P-bit can be used to temporarily deny access to a given segment, its real use is in connection with the virtual memory capabilities of the **80386**, which we will discuss in Section 9. The basic idea behind virtual memory is that not all program segments need simultaneously reside in machine memory. If a segment is not present (say is only available in mass storage), then its P-bit is given value zero. An attempt to access this segment will trigger an interrupt and a handler can be supplied that will load the missing segment into memory, swapping out some other, unneeded segment, if necessary.

The 2-bit DPL-field contains the *descriptor privilege level*. This is the privilege level of the segment contents in the sense introduced earlier: 0 means highest privilege and 3 means lowest privilege. Although we will discuss the privilege mechanisms in Section 7, we will not use them in our example programs. Rather, we will give all our segments privilege level 0 and so, effectively, will circumvent this aspect of the protection mechanism.

We have now explained the entire contents of the segment descriptors, except for the 5-bit *type* field, and here the meanings of some of the bits are different in the data and code cases. First, the highest bit (number 44) has the value 1 in both cases. It is sometimes called the *segment bit* because it distinguishes segment descriptors from other descriptors to be introduced later: these will all have segment bit equal to zero. The next bit (bit number 43) distinguishes data descriptors from code descriptors: it has values 0 and 1, respectively, in the two cases.

In the data case, bit number 42 is called the E-bit, or *expand-down* bit. $E = 0$ in a "normal" (*expand-up*) segment and $E = 1$ in one of the special expand-down segments mentioned previously. In the code case, bit number 42 is called the C-bit, or *conforming* bit. A segment with $C = 1$ is called *conforming*. We will explain the significance of conforming segments in Section 7. For the moment, we will take $C = 0$ in our code segments.

Bit number 41 is called the W-bit, or *writable* bit, in the data case, and is called the R-bit, or *readable* bit, in the code case. This bit shows just how rigidly protection mechanisms

---

TABLE 18.1 TYPES OF NON-ACCESSED SEGMENTS

TYPE	CHARACTERISTICS
10h	data, expand-up, non-writable
12h	data, expand-up, writable
14h	data, expand-down, non-writable
16h	data, expand-down, writable
18h	code, non-conforming,non-readable
1ah	code, non-conforming, readable
1ch	code, conforming, non-readable
1fh	code, conforming, readable

---

can be enforced on the **80386**. Unless the W-bit of a data segment is set, it is not possible for a program to write to that segment. In other words, the segment contains "constant" data, in the sense of some high-level languages. Likewise, unless the R-bit is set in a code segment, a program cannot read data from that segment. In other words, it would not be worthwhile to store even constant data in such a segment since it could not be accessed by the program!

For completeness, we should point out that these restrictions can be circumvented, although the protection mechanisms make it impossible to do this in any illegal way. A legal method of, say, writing to a read-only segment, is to *alias* the segment. To alias a segment means to introduce another segment referring to the same physical memory (i.e., with base and limit chosen so that the new segment contains the old one). In the present case, the alias should be defined as a segment having write-permission. Of course, a write to the second segment is effectively a write to the first one.

The lowest bit of the type field is called the A-bit, or *accessed* bit. When the descriptor is set up, this bit should be given the value 0. As soon as the segment is accessed, the **80386** changes the value of the bit to 1. It is of no significance to us in this chapter but can be polled by an operating system to obtain statistics about the frequency of use of various segments.

For convenient reference, Table 18.1 lists the standard types of data and code segments. There is nothing new in this table: the type values can be constructed easily from the descriptions of the various bits already given.

Before moving on, we will explain why the limit and base fields of segment descriptors are stored in their peculiar, non-contiguous formats. The reason is purely historical. Protected mode was introduced with the **80286**. Considering the address size and other capabilities of the **80286**, six bytes would have been sufficient to store a segment descriptor. However, Intel looked ahead to the future **80386** and realized that **80386** descriptors would need to be eight bytes long and that, ideally, the **80286** descriptor format should be made upwardly compatible with the **80386**. Consequently, they decreed that an **80286** descriptor should be eight bytes long, but with the two high bytes being zero. When the **80386** descriptor format was designed, the extra bits needed for the base and limit were stored in the two high bytes. (Of course, they *could* have distributed the zero bits in the **80286** selector so that the fields in the **80386** format would be contiguous. One also wonders whether the G-bit was introduced because eight bytes turned out to be not quite long enough.) The positive result is that **80286** protected-mode code will run on the **80386**.

The **80286/80386** permits a protected-mode program to access a region of memory only if the region is described by a segment descriptor, and the access must use the descriptor in a special way, which we will soon describe. For example, if a program wishes to read from or write directly to the video buffer, then the video buffer must be part of a segment given by a descriptor, and similarly for the BIOS data area. This simple observation has momentous consequences for protected-mode programming. Nearly all the ROM BIOS and **MS-DOS** interrupts read from or write to regions of memory that were obviously not described by descriptors. Merely introducing descriptors retroactively to cover these regions is of no avail since, as we will see, the **80386** requires that memory references use the descriptors in an essential way. Therefore, our conclusion is

- Adapting the ROM BIOS and **MS-DOS** interrupt routines (including the **int 21H** functions) to run in protected mode would involve massive rewriting. Such a rewriting has not been undertaken, nor is it likely that it ever will be.

Stated differently, our conclusion is that the **80286/80386** in protected mode requires an entirely new operating system. As we have mentioned earlier, two such systems are **UNIX** and **OS/2** (although, to date, **OS/2** is actually a protected-mode **80286** operating system).

In Section 5, we take some small steps toward setting up a "protected-mode operating system kernel," and use it to demonstrate how the **80286/80386** handles interrupts.

It is natural to use **MASM**'s structure and record capabilities to simplify the definition of descriptors. As the chapter progresses, we will encounter a number of other fairly involved data structures used in protected-mode programming. We have collected these structures, together with a number of **EQUATE**s and macros, in a file named PROT.MAC.

Figure 18.2 shows the structure template used to define a segment descriptor, as well as some records that are helpful in initializing the various bit-fields.

An array whose elements are descriptors, either segment descriptors or descriptors of other kinds to be introduced later, is called a *descriptor table*. Descriptor tables come in three varieties: *global*, *local*, and *interrupt*. We will not make use of local descriptor tables, although we will indicate their significance in Section 8. A typical protected-mode program has one global descriptor table and one interrupt descriptor table. Since only a global descriptor table is needed in the example program of the next section, we will postpone discussing interrupt descriptor tables until Section 4.

Recall that, in protected mode, only areas of memory described by segment descriptors can be accessed. Generally, code, data, and physical memory locations that the operating system must access are described in the global descriptor table. A global descriptor table must contain at least two descriptors: a code descriptor establishing the active code segment on entry to protected mode, and a data descriptor allowing access to data. In addition, the **80286/80386** architecture demands that a global descriptor table begin with a dummy descriptor, all of whose fields are initialized to zero. Consequently, in terms of the structure and record definitions given in Figure 18.2, a minimal global descriptor table might look like:

```
Members:          LimL     BaseL BaseM Rights      Gran            BaseH

Dummy    SEGDESC <0000h,   0000h, 00h, PDT<0,0,0>,  GXOAL<0,0,0,0,0>,  00h>
smlCDesc SEGDESC <0ffffh,      ,     ,PDT<1,0,1ah>, GXOAL<0,0,0,0,0>,  00h>
bigDDesc SEGDESC <0ffffh,      ,     ,PDT<1,0,12h>, GXOAL<1,0,0,0,0>,  00h>
```

This table provides two present, non-accessed segments. *smlCDesc* describes a segment of type 1AH, i.e., a non-conforming, readable code segment. The G-bit is 0 and the given

FIGURE 18.2 EXCERPT 1 FROM THE FILE PROT.MAC

```
 1   ;structure template for segment descriptor
 2
 3   segDesc STRUC
 4
 5       limL        DW    ?          ;low 16 bits of segment limit
 6       baseL       DW    ?          ;low 16 bits of segment base address
 7       baseM       DB    ?          ;next 8 bits of segment base address
 8       Rights      DB    ?          ;segment present, dpl, and type fields
 9       Gran        DB    ?          ;granularity, misc., and high 4-bit limit fields
10       baseH       DB    ?          ;high 4 bits of base address
11
12   segDesc ENDS
13
14   ;-------------------------------------------------------------------------
15
16   ;records used to initialize descriptor fields
17
18   PDT     RECORD        Pres:1, descPrivLev:2, Type:5
19   GXOAL   RECORD        Granul:1, X:1, O:1, Avail:1, limitMed:4
20
21   ;-------------------------------------------------------------------------
22
23   COMMENT      #    MACRO HEADER
24   MACRO NAME:       setBaseDesc
25   PURPOSE:          Initializes descriptor base fields in terms of usual
26                     real mode segment and offset.
27   CALLED AS:        setDescBase  descName, Offset, Segment
28   RETURNS:     #    Nothing
29
30   setDescBase    MACRO  DescName, Offset, SegMent
31
32       mov     ax, Segment
33       movzx   eax,ax
34       shl     eax, 4
35       add     eax, Offset
36       mov     descName.baseL, ax
37       shr     eax, 16
38       mov     descName.baseM, al
39
40   ENDM
```

segment limit is 0FFFFH, so that the segment has length 64K. The high four bits of the base have been initialized to zero, but the 20 low bits of the base have not yet been initialized. *bigDDesc* describes a segment of type 12H, i.e., an expand-up writable data segment. The segment base has been initialized to 0H. The segment limit is set to 0FFFFH and the G-bit to 1, so that the segment length is the maximum possible, namely, 4G.

When the **80386** is booted, it starts operating in real mode. If the **80386** is operating under the control of a protected-mode operating system, it is a responsibility either of the boot code or of the operating system itself to switch the microprocessor to protected mode. We will show how to do this in the next section. In our examples, the **80386** will be operating under **MS-DOS** when we make the switch. Under these circumstances, the machine will be operating in a real-mode code segment and it will be convenient to set up a segment

FIGURE 18.3 FORMAT OF SEGMENT SELECTOR

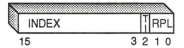

INDEX   T RPL

15   3 2 1 0

TI - TABLE INDICATOR (GLOBAL OR LOCAL)

RPL - REQUESTOR'S PRIVILEGE LEVEL

descriptor for this physical segment so that the machine can legally continue operating in this segment when it enters protected mode. Similarly, it is often convenient to include descriptors for the real-mode data and stack segments in the global descriptor table.

This explains why we neglected to statically initialize the base of *smlCDesc* in our example: the base of this descriptor should be chosen at run time to agree with the physical location of the code segment in memory. In other words, the base should have value 16*(value in **cs**). This operation of "pointing a descriptor" to a real segment comes up often enough that we have supplied a macro to do it easily. The macro in question, *setDescBase*, is shown in Figure 18.2.

The **80386** stores the length and location of the global descriptor table in a special register, called the *global descriptor table register*, or *GDTR*. Initializing the GDTR, which is an essential step in the switch to protected mode, is accomplished by the special instruction **lgdt** (*load global descriptor table*). The syntax for **lgdt** is

```
lgdt lgdtBuf
```

where *lgdtBuf* is a 6-word memory buffer containing the limit (i.e., maximum offset) of the global descriptor table, followed by its base address.

The segment registers are used in a totally new way in protected-mode programming. A segment register contains a *selector*, which is a word structured as shown in Figure 18.3. The high 13 bits in a selector contain an index into a descriptor table: if this 13-bit field has value 0, the segment register "points" to the segment given by the initial descriptor in the table; if it has value 1, the register points to the segment associated with the next descriptor; and so on. The next bit, the *table indicator* or *TI-bit*, tells whether the descriptor in question lies in the global descriptor table or in a local descriptor table, with TI = 0 meaning the global descriptor table. Finally, the two low bits give the *requestor's privilege level*, or *RPL*. This parameter relates to the protection mechanisms and will be discussed in Section 7.

In this chapter, we will always use a global table so that TI = 0 and will always take RPL = 0. Since the *Index* field begins with bit 3 in the selector, the index must be multiplied by 8 before being assigned to the selector. By a pleasant coincidence, each descriptor also has size 8 bytes, so that the value to be assigned to the selector is numerically equal to the offset of the descriptor from the start of the descriptor table (again, provided that TI = RPL = 0, as we are now assuming).

Recall that the GDT begins with a dummy descriptor, initialized to zero. This null descriptor plays a role somewhat analogous to the NULL pointer in C. It is legal to load a selector for the null descriptor into a segment register, but using (i.e., "dereferencing") that segment register gives an error. (This kind of error is called a "general-protection violation" and will be discussed in Section 4.)

Exercise 18-1. Check the correctness of the segment types given in Table 18.1.

SECTION 3 CHANGING THE LIMITS OF REAL-MODE DESCRIPTORS

As we saw in Chapter 7, some aspects of the **80386** protection mechanisms are active even when the processor is executing in real mode. For instance, an attempt to write to a segment location whose offset is larger than 0FFFFH causes a general-protection violation. This happened, for example, when we tried to write a dword to a segment beginning with offset 0FFFDH or greater.

When the **80386** boots in real mode, it is equipped with a collection of default segment descriptors. These are called *pseudo-descriptors* in the Intel manuals, because they are not members of any descriptor table accessible to the programmer. The characteristics of these pseudo-descriptors seem completely natural for real-mode segments: granularity zero and limit 0FFFFH, present, expand-up, D-bit and B-bits equal to zero, privilege level zero, and the code segments are readable and the data segments are writable. In [31], Roden pointed out a fact that is not well documented in the Intel literature: it is possible to actually change some of the default characteristics of the real-mode pseudo-descriptors. An especially interesting change is to increase the segment limits, giving them values as large as 4G. Of course, performing calculations in these large segments requires using 32-bit offsets. This is the mechanism used by our *expandSegs* procedure of Chapter 7, and we are finally in a position to show exactly how the technique works. At this point, we should give a word of warning: real-mode segment expansion is basically an undocumented feature of the **80386** processor and so there is no guarantee that future processors in the series will behave in the same way.

Since the pseudo-descriptors can only be changed when the **80386** is running in protected mode, the upcoming program will also show how to change from real to protected mode (and back again). But before discussing the transition to protected mode, we must detour to examine a pair of hardware topics.

First, during a change between real and protected mode, the processor is in an unstable state and so all interrupts should be inhibited. Switching off the maskable interrupts is trivial — it just requires a **cli** instruction. But it is also important to disable the NMI, or non-maskable interrupt. The reader may wonder whether this is really necessary. After all, in the traditional **IBM-XT** and **IBM-AT** designs, the NMI is used to signal a cataclysmic hardware failure, and it hardly seems that the magnitude of the disaster would increase if it should chance to occur in the middle of a switch to protected mode. But the NMI is sometimes put to other uses by the makers of peripheral cards and so may occur at rather frequent intervals. Consequently, it is indeed important to disable it during the switch and, luckily, this is easy to do. Disabling the NMI is accomplished by turning off a certain bit in one of the bytes in memory corresponding to the CMOS BIOS. Recall that the CMOS BIOS stores various system parameters in **IBM-AT**-type machines. Disabling the NMI involves clearing bit 7 of the byte accessible through Port 70H, and reenabling it requires resetting that bit.

The second hardware topic involves a curiosity of the **IBM-AT** architecture. The **8086** and the **8088** wrap addresses at the 1-megabyte boundary. In other words, these microprocessors do address arithmetic "modulo 1 megabyte." For example, they interpret the address FFFF:FFFF as 0000:FFEF. This behavior is totally natural in terms of their structure: the address bus consists of 20 lines, conventionally called A0 through A19, and any address bit that overflows from line A19 is lost. (See Figure 2.3.) The **80286** and the **80386** behave differently. The **80286** has 24 address lines and performs exact address arithmetic on addresses up to size 16M − 1, while the **80386** has 32 address lines and manipulates addresses up to 4G − 1. However, in designing the **IBM-AT**, IBM wished to mimic the behavior of the early processors as closely as possible and therefore introduced extra hardware to "turn off the A20 address line," so that these machines would simulate the address wrapping of the **8086/8088**. This circuitry is also used by the designers of **IBM-AT** clones, including **80386** machines.

In order to address memory beyond 1M limit, it is essential to turn on the A20 address line. Happily, this is also comparatively easy to do. The state of the A20 line is governed by a certain bit in the output port of the **8042** keyboard controller. In the program to be presented in Figure 18.4, we include a procedure that enables or disables the A20 line.

In our sample program, we will be content to expand the data segment, leaving the stack and code segments with their default lengths. Since expanding the real-mode data segment leaves the **80386** in an unnatural state, it is important for programs using this expansion technique to restore the segment parameters to their default values before terminating. Figure 18.4 shows the procedures, *expandSegs* and *shrinkSegs*, that perform the segment expansion and subsequent restoration.

Perhaps the most interesting features of the code in Figure 18.4 are the entry to protected mode and the subsequent return to real mode. The reader should be warned that, in general, entry to protected mode requires several additional steps, which we were able to ignore in this example. These steps will be explained in Section 5.

Function 89H of **int 15H** (one of the ROM BIOS interrupts) can be used to change the processor to protected-mode operation. We chose not to use **function 89H** for a number of reasons: using this function is not much easier than performing the switch directly; the function hides a number of details that we should be discussing; it requires setting up specific segment descriptors, some of which are extraneous to our examples; and it can only be used to switch to protected mode — not to switch back to real mode. This last restriction is related to what is generally considered as the single greatest weakness of the **80286**. While the **80286** can be easily switched to protected mode, Intel provided no method for switching it back to real mode, short of rebooting the machine. Somewhat arcane methods have been devised for effecting this backwards switch, but these really involve a partial reboot, and are slow by machine standards. In any case, the **IBM-AT** ROM BIOS was written for **80286** machines and so does not provide a BIOS function for switching to real mode.

Here are some line-by-line comments on the programs in Figure 18.4:

Lines 21-28. As we indicated in the previous section, the global descriptor table must always begin with a dummy descriptor. Since we do not intend to change the limit on the code descriptor, we have not defined a large version of it. We have provided two descriptors for the data segment. The *smlDDesc* is only needed when *shrinkSegs* restores the data segment to its default value.

FIGURE 18.4 ADJUSTING REAL-MODE SEGMENT SIZE

```
 1    TITLE    fixSegs.asm
 2
 3    INCLUDE   console.mac
 4    INCLUDE   prot.mac
 5
 6    ;-------------------------------------------------------------------------
 7
 8    DOSSEG
 9    .MODEL SMALL
10    .386P
11
12    PUBLIC expandSegs, shrinkSegs, gateA20, empty8042
13
14    ;=========================================================================
15
16    .DATA
17
18    ;#########################################################################
19    ;GLOBAL DESCRIPTOR TABLE                                                ;#
20                                                                           ;#
21    GDT      LABEL    WORD                                                 ;#
22                                                                           ;#
23    ;Members:          limL    baseL baseM Rights         Gran        baseH;#
24                                                                           ;#
25    Dummy    SEGDESC < 0000h, 0000h, 00h, PDT<0,0,0>,   GXOAL<0,0,0,0,0>,   00h>;#
26    codeDesc SEGDESC <0ffffh,      ,     , PDT<1,0,1ah>, GXOAL<0,0,0,0,0>,   00h>;#
27    smlDDesc SEGDESC <0ffffh,      ,     , PDT<1,0,12h>, GXOAL<0,0,0,0,0>,   00h>;#
28    bigDDesc SEGDESC <0ffffh, 0000h, 00h, PDT<1,0,12h>, GXOAL<1,0,0,0,0fh>, 00h>;#
29                                                                           ;#
30    ;-------------------------------------------------------------------------;#
31                                                                           ;#
32        GDTRData        LABEL    FWORD            ;for lgdt                ;#
33        GDTLimit        DW       $ - GDT - 1                               ;#
34        GDTLinAddr      LABEL    DWORD                                     ;#
35                        DW       GDT                                       ;#
36                        DW       0                                         ;#
37                                                                           ;#
38    ;#########################################################################
39
40    ;=========================================================================
41
42    .CODE
43
44    COMMENT      #   PROCEDURE HEADER     NAME: expandSegs
45    TYPE:            NEAR 386 USE16    FILE: fixSegs.asm    LIBRARY: User.lib
46    PURPOSE:         Changes the default 386 pseudo-descriptors so that the
47                     registers ds, es, fs, and gs can be used to address the
48                     entire 4G addressing space
49    CALLED AS:       expandSegs()
50    RETURNS:         Nothing
51    REMARKS:         Turns on the A20 gate; disables the NMI while switching
52             #       to/from protected mode
53
54    expandSegs  PROC  NEAR
55
```

```
56
57     setDescBase codeDesc, 0, cs              ;set descriptor base
58     setDescBase smlDDesc, 0, ds              ;  addresses
59
60     pushRegs ds, es, fs, gs, ss              ;save them
61
62  ;fix up base address of GDT
63
64     mov     ax, ds
65     movzx   eax, ax
66     shl     eax, 4
67     add     GDTLinAddr, eax                  ;it already contains the offset
68     lgdt    GDTRData                         ;initialize GDTR
69
70     turnA20  ON                              ;enable the A20 address line
71     turnNMI OFF                              ;disable the NMI
72     cli                                      ;  and the maskable interrupts
73
74  ;**********ENTER PROTECTED MODE*********************************************
75
76     mov     eax, cr0                         ;enter protected mode
77     or      al, 1                            ;  by setting protection
78     mov     cr0, eax                         ;    enable bit in cr0
79
80     jmp     SHORT protMode1                  ;flush pre-fetch queue
81
82  protMode1:
83
84     mov     ax, bigDDesc-GDT                 ;change ds,es,fs, and g
85     mov     ds, ax                           ;  so that they point to
86     mov     es, ax                           ;   4G segment
87     mov     fs, ax
88     mov     gs, ax
89
90  ;**********LEAVE PROTECTED MODE*********************************************
91
92     mov     eax, cr0                         ;leave protected mode
93     and     al, NOT 1                        ;  by clearing PE enable
94     mov     cr0, eax                         ;    bit in cr0
95
96     jmp     SHORT realMode1                  ;to clear the pre-fetch queue
97
98  realMode1:
99
100    popRegs                                  ;restore them
101
102    sti                                      ;enable maskable interrupts
103    turnNMI  ON                              ;  and the NMI
104
105    ret
106
107 expandSegs     ENDP
108
109 ;-------------------------------------------------------------------------
110
111 COMMENT #  PROCEDURE HEADER      NAME: shrinkSegs
112 TYPE:      NEAR 386 USE16    FILE: fixSegs.asm    LIBRARY: User.lib
113 PURPOSE:   Restores the default 386 pseudo-descriptors, thereby undoing
114            the effect of expandSegs.
```

Figure 18.4 cont.

```
115   CALLED AS: shrinkSegs()
116   RETURNS:    Nothing
117   REMARKS:    Turns off the A20 gate; disables the NMI while switching to/from
118          #   protected mode
119
120   shrinkSegs  PROC   NEAR
121
122       setDescBase    codeDesc, 0, cs            ;set descriptor base
123       setDescBase    smlDDesc, 0, ds
124
125       pushRegs  ds, es, fs, gs, ss              ;save them
126
127       turnNMI  OFF                              ;disable the NMI
128       cli                                       ;  and the maskable interrupts
129
130   ;**********ENTER PROTECTED MODE*********************************************
131
132       mov      eax, cr0                         ;enter protected mode
133       or       al, 1                            ;  by setting protection
134       mov      cr0, eax                         ;     enable bit in cr0
135
136       jmp      SHORT protMode2                  ;to clear the pre-fetch queue
137
138   ProtMode2:
139
140       mov      ax, smlDDesc-GDT                 ;change ds, es, fs, and gs
141       mov      ds, ax                           ;  so that they index a
142       mov      es, ax                           ;    descriptor with parameters
143       mov      fs, ax                           ;      appropriate to a real
144       mov      gs, ax                           ;        "pseudo-descriptor"
145
146   ;**********LEAVE PROTECTED MODE*********************************************
147
148       mov      eax, cr0                         ;leave protected mode
149       and      al, NOT 1                        ;  by clearing protection
150       mov      cr0, eax                         ;     enable bit in cr0
151
152       jmp      SHORT realMode2                  ;to clear the pre-fetch queue
153
154   RealMode2:
155
156       popRegs                                   ;restore them
157
158       sti                                       ;enable maskable interrupts
159       turnNMI  ON                               ;  and the NMI
160       turnA20  OFF                              ;disable the A20 address line
161
162       ret
163
164   ShrinkSegs    ENDP
165
166   ;-------------------------------------------------------------------------
167
168   COMMENT #  PROCEDURE HEADER      NAME: gateA20
169   TYPE:      NEAR 386 USE16    FILE: fixSegs.asm    LIBRARY: User.lib
170   PURPOSE:   Enables or disables the "1 megabyte wrap" by masking or unmasking
```

```
171                the A20 line.
172  CALLED AS:  gateA20(Param)
173                where Param = 0dfh turns off the A20 mask, thus enabling
174                1 megabyte wrap, while Param = 0ddh has the opposite effect.
175  RETURNS:    al = 00h if successful and al = 02h if unsuccessful.
176       #
177
178  gateA20    PROC      NEAR
179
180     and     esp, 0ffffh                   ;to ensure high 16 bits are zero
181     push    cx
182     cli
183     call    empty8042                     ;8042 input buffer must be empty
184     jnz     Failed                        ;   before a command will be
185     mov     al, WRITEOUTPUTPORT           ;      accepted
186     out     STATUSPORT, al
187     call    empty8042
188     jnz     Failed
189     mov     ax, [esp+4]
190     out     PORTA, al
191     call    empty8042
192     jnz     Failed
193
194  Failed:
195
196     pop     cx
197     ret     2
198
199  gateA20    ENDP
200
201  ;-------------------------------------------------------------------------
202
203  ;Support function called by gateA20 to check status of 8042 input buffer
204  empty8042       PROC       NEAR
205
206     xor     cx, cx                        ;try 65536 times
207
208  keepTrying:
209
210     in      al, STATUSPORT
211     test    al, INPUTBUFFULL              ;will = 0 if input buffer empty
212     loopne  keepTrying
213
214     ret                                   ;ZF = 1 if failed to empty
215
216  empty8042       ENDP
217
218  ;=======================================================================
219
220     END
```

Lines 32-35. The global descriptor table register must be initialized to contain the limit and address of the GDT. This information is most conveniently presented in the format shown. Since the label *GDT* on line 35 is interpreted as an offset by **MASM**, the effect is to initialize the address of the GDT to equal the offset part of the complete linear address. At run time, the segment contribution must still be added. This extra computation will be done on lines 64-68.

Lines 57-58. Recall from Figure 18.2 that the *setDescBase* macro initializes the base fields of a descriptor, using the offset and segment parts of its address as parameters.

Line 60. After entering protected mode, we will replace the contents of the segment registers with segment selectors. But after returning to real mode, we certainly want to restore them to their original real-mode values, and so must store these values.

Lines 64-68. This is the completion of the GDT linear address computation. It requires multiplying the **ds** contents by 16, adding the result to the GDT offset, which is already stored in *GDTLinearAddr*.

Line 70. We are using the macro *turnA20*, given in Figure 18.5, to enable the A20 address line. The *turnA20* macro calls a procedure, *gateA20*, the code for which appears later in this program. Depending on the value of the parameter passed to it (notice the **EQUATE**s on lines 44 and 45 of Figure 18.5), *gateA20* either enables or disables the A20 address line. We will comment on the *gateA20* code a little later.

Line 71. The macro *turnNMI*, also shown in Figure 18.5, is being used to turn off the nonmaskable interrupt. The *turnNMI* code should be almost self-explanatory: enabling the A20 line requires turning on bit 7 of the CMOS byte, accessed through Port 70H (and given by the **EQUATE** *cmosAddr* in the macro code); disabling A20 requires turning bit 7 off.

Line 72. As we know, the maskable interrupts must be disabled during the transition to protected mode. In Section 4, we will see that extensive preparations are needed before interrupts can be enabled in protective mode. Since we do not undertake these preparations in the present program, the interrupts must remain masked for the duration of our stay in protected mode.

Lines 76-78. After the somewhat involved initializations required for a successful switch to protected mode, the switch itself is quite trivial. As we will see in Section 9, the **80386** contains a number of control and debugging registers. Of course, we have already encountered one of these, the **gdtr**. Another such register is the 32-bit *control register zero*, which is denoted **cr0**. Whether the **80386** is operating in real or protected mode is determined by the value of bit 0 in **cr0**: if bit 0 is off, the **80386** is in real mode; otherwise, it is in protected mode. Consequently, lines 76-78 place the **80386** in protected mode.

Lines 80-82. These lines are perhaps somewhat mysterious in the present context. The point is that the machine code formatting of instructions can be different in real and protected mode. Hence, it is important to clear the prefetch queue of any lingering real-mode instructions now that we have entered protected mode. A jump instruction has this effect. In later programs, we will need to replace the present **SHORT** jump with a **FAR** jump, because this will force the initial **cs** value (a real-mode segment address) to be replaced by the value that is appropriate for protected mode, namely the selector for the code segment. The protected-mode portion of the present program contains no instructions requiring the **80386** to manipulate the **cs** register and so its value is never checked.

Lines 84-88. Here we "point" **ds**, **es**, **fs**, and **gs** to *bigDDesc* in the protected-mode sense, by initializing each with the selector of *bigDDesc*. As we indicated in the previous section,

FIGURE 18.5 EXCERPT 2 FROM PROT.MAC

```
 1   ;keyboard controller equates
 2   STATUSPORT       EQU     64h
 3   PORTA            EQU     60h
 4   INPUTBUFFULL     EQU     10b
 5   WRITEOUTPUTPORT EQU      0d1h
 6
 7   ;-----------------------------------------------------------------------
 8
 9   COMMENT     #    MACRO HEADER
10   MACRO NAME:      turnNMI
11   PURPOSE:         Enables or disables non-maskable interrupts
12   CALLED AS:       turnNMI  Param
13                    where Param = "ON" enables the NMI and Param = "OFF"
14                    disables it
15   RETURNS:    #    Nothing
16
17   cmosAddr    EQU      70h
18   turnNMI MACRO Param
19
20       push    ax
21       in      al, cmosAddr
22       IFIDNI  <Param>, <OFF>
23          or      al, 1 SHL 7              ;turn bit 7 on to disable
24       ELSEIFIDNI <Param>, <ON>
25          and     al, NOT 1 SHL 7          ;turn bit 7 off to enable
26       ELSE
27          %OUT    BAD PARAMETER FOR turnNMI
28       ENDIF
29       out     cmosAddr, al
30       pop     ax
31
32   ENDM
33
34   ;-----------------------------------------------------------------------
35
36   COMMENT     #    MACRO HEADER
37   MACRO NAME:      turnA20
38   PURPOSE:         Enables or disables the A20 address line
39   CALLED AS:       turnA20  Param
40                    where Param = "ON" enables the A20 line and Param = "OFF"
41                    disables it
42   RETURNS:    #    Nothing
43
44   onGateA20        EQU      0dfh
45   offGateA20       EQU      0ddh
46   turnA20 MACRO Param
47
48       IFIDNI  <Param>, <ON>
49          push    onGateA20
50       ELSEIFIDNI  <Param>, <OFF>
51          push    offGateA20
52       ELSE
53          %OUT BAD PARAMETER FOR turnA20
54       ENDIF
55       call    gateA20
56   ENDM
```

this value is equal to the offset of *bigDDesc* from the start of the GDT, and so is given numerically by

```
bigDDesc - GDT
```

Lines 92-94. Since the only reason for entering protected mode was to point the four data segment registers to *bigDDesc*, we are ready to return to real mode. These lines accomplish the return.

Lines 96-98. Again, we flush the prefetch queue, this time to replace any protected-mode detritus with instructions formatted for real mode.

Lines 100-103. We restore the original register values and turn on the interrupts, including the NMI. Of course, we leave the A20 line enabled.

Lines 120-164. The *shrinkSegs* procedure undoes the work of *expandSegs*. Since the operations are virtually identical, it should require no further explication. Note that it does turn off the A20 line, in order to return the machine to its default state.

Lines 178-199. This procedure enables or disables the A20 line. To change the A20 state, it is necessary to send the appropriate byte value to PORTA of the **8042** keyboard controller. The byte values are given on lines 44-45 of Figure 18.5 and the actual output occurs on line 190 of the present program. Unfortunately, such a write must be prefaced by sending a particular byte to the STATUSPORT, which occurs on lines 185-186. To further complicate matters, the **8042** will only accept data when its input buffer is empty and the state of the input buffer is tested by checking a particular bit in the STATUSPORT byte, as on lines 210-211. The *empty8042* procedure on lines 203-216 loops repeatedly, checking whether the input buffer is yet empty. The *gateA20* procedure calls *empty8042* before each write, and only attempts to complete the write if the input buffer is indeed empty.

   As this brief outline indicates, the programming of the **8042** controller is fairly complicated. For more information, we refer the interested reader to [21], where it is discussed in some detail.

Exercise 18-2. With the help of *expandSegs* and *shrinkSegs*, write a better version of DISKCOPY than the one distributed with **MS-DOS**. Assuming that the host machine has at least 2M of memory, the new version, say NEWCOPY, should execute a command such as

```
newcopy a: a:
```

on any floppy of size up to 1.44M without requiring multiple insertions of the source and destination disks.
Suggestion: Use the ROM BIOS functions available through **int 13H.**

SECTION 4 INTERRUPTS AND EXCEPTIONS

As we indicated in the previous section, most of the **MS-DOS** and ROM BIOS interrupt handlers contain code that will not run in protected mode. But it turns out that the differences between real and protected-mode interrupt handling are considerably deeper than we have so far indicated, and so a substantially different set of interrupt handlers must be supplied.

Before we begin, recall the distinction between exceptions and interrupts made in Chapter 16: an exception originates either within the microprocessor or as a result of a program instruction, while an interrupt originates with some external source. Exceptions are *synchronous*, in the sense that the same exceptions will always occur at the same points in the program, no matter how often it is run, while interrupts are frequently *asynchronous*, in that their occurrences may vary radically from one run of a given program to the next.

The **80286/80386** processors distinguish between three different kinds of exceptions, depending on the general response anticipated from the corresponding handler:

- A *fault* is an exception resulting from a condition that is potentially repairable by the interrupt handler. If such a repair is possible (and desirable), the handler can then restart the interrupted program at the instruction causing the fault. To facilitate such a restart, the microprocessor pushes the address of the problem instruction as the return address.

- A *trap* is an exception arising in a context making it undesirable or impossible to repeat the instruction that triggered the exception. Consequently, the microprocessor pushes the address of the next instruction as the return address. A trap frequently corresponds to some task that the machine must perform. After its completion, it should not be repeated but, instead, execution should proceed with the next instruction.

An *abort* is an exception of a sufficiently serious nature to make it impractical to restart the interrupted program.

These definitions have a curious corollary: a software interrupt, such as **int 21H**, is not an interrupt at all — it is an exception. More precisely, it should be treated as a trap rather than a fault — unless you want an infinite loop of calls to **int 21H**!

Just as is the case with the **8088**, the **80286** and **80386** support a maximum of 256 interrupts and exceptions, which carry numbers from 00H through 0FFH. Intel has reserved the numbers 00H-1FH for its own use. Of these, only **int 00H - int 11H** are actually used at the moment. Table 18.2 gives more information on the interrupt structure.

A quick perusal of Table 18.2 reveals yet another hardware problem with which we must cope. For example, Intel has assigned **int 08H** to an exception called the double fault, yet we know that in the standard **IBM-XT/AT** architecture, **int 08H** is the timer hardware interrupt. Comparing Table 18.2 with Table 15.1 will reveal several other inconsistencies. This problem arises because IBM chose to use some interrupt numbers that were reserved for future use by Intel. In principle, it is possible to live with the situation as it is. For example, it is feasible to provide an **int 08H** handler with code to examine a service request and deduce whether it originated with the timer or as a double-fault exception. But there is an easier way of dealing with the problem.

It turns out that the **PIC** can be reprogrammed to associate the maskable interrupts under its control with any eight consecutive numbers. In the standard **XT** configuration, the

TABLE 18.2 EXCEPTIONS AND INTERRUPTS RESERVED BY INTEL

NUMBER	DESCRIPTION	TYPE	ERROR CODE		TRIGGERED BY
00h	Divide error	Fault	Yes		div, idiv
01h	Debug exception	Varies	Varies		Any instruction
02h	NMI	---	---		
03h	Breakpoint	Trap	No		int 03h
04h	Overflow	Trap	No		into
05h	Bounds check	Fault	Yes		bound
06h	Invalid opcode	Fault	Yes		Any illegal inst.
07h	Coprocessor not available	Fault	Yes		esc, wait
08h	Double fault	Abort	Yes		Instructions that generate exceptions
09h	Coprocessor segment overrun	Abort	No		esc operand wrapping at end of segment
00ah	Invalid TSS	Fault	Yes		jmp, call, iret, or any interrupt
00bh	Segment not present	Fault	Yes		Modification of segment register
00ch	Stack exception	Fault	Yes		Use of ss
00dh	General protection	Fault	Yes		Memory reference or code fetch
00eh	Page fault	Fault	Yes		Memory reference or code fetch
00fh	Reserved				
010h	Coprocessor error	Fault	Yes		esc, wait
011h	Alignment Check	Fault	Yes		(80486 only) Memory operation
012h-0ffh	Available for HW and SW use	---	---	...	Hardware event or int

interrupts appearing on IRQ0-IRQ7 are mapped to the numbers 08H-1FH. To resolve the ambiguity resulting from multiple uses of the same interrupt vector, it is only necessary to remap the hardware interrupts out of "Intel territory."

In the case of an **IBM-AT** type machine, the situation is slightly more complicated than the last paragraph indicates, because these machines actually *cascade* two interrupt controllers, in order to support more than eight maskable interrupts. (When the interrupt controllers are cascaded, one of the IRQ lines of the first becomes the input to the second, so that there are really only 15 interrupt levels available.)

In the default **IBM-AT** configuration, the interrupt controllers are associated with vectors 08H-0FH and 70H-7FH. There is no compelling reason to remap the second set. However, it seems tidier to have the maskable interrupts occur as a contiguous block, hence, in our forthcoming program, we remap them all to the range 30H-3FH. PROT.MAC contains a macro that performs the remapping. This particular macro is shown in Figure 18.6 and, once again, we refer the interested reader to [19] for more details on programming the **PIC**.

Many of the interrupts and exceptions listed in Figure 18.2 are either familiar to us from the **8088** or else their functions are clearly described by their names. However, some do merit further description:

Debug Exception. **Int 01H** is the gateway to one of the more intriguing aspects of the **80386**, namely, its hardware debugging capabilities. We will describe the hardware debugging features of the **80386** in somewhat more detail in Section 9, but, briefly, here they are. The **80386** contains certain debugging registers that allow the programmer to *use the hardware* to monitor attempts to access regions of the code or data. This ability is similar to **CODEVIEW**'s watch commands, but is hundreds or even thousands of times faster. Perhaps even more important, it enables the program to be monitored "in its natural state," i.e., in real time and not under the control of a debugger. As the reader may have already observed, many programs behave radically differently when run on their own instead of under the protective wing of **CODEVIEW**. **Int 01H** is triggered by the hardware debugging mechanisms.

Double Fault. **Int 08H** can arise when an exception occurs while the microprocessor is processing another exception. Under most circumstances, the **80386** handles this situation by processing the exceptions serially, but there are cases where this is impossible, and it is these cases that lead to an **int 08H**. These bad cases correspond to the first exception being one of **int 00H**, **int 09H**, **int 0AH**, **int 0BH**, **int 0DH** and the second being any one of these or an **int 0EH**.

Invalid TSS. The "TSS" referred to in the **int 0AH** description is a "task state segment." We will define task state segments in Section 6.

General-Protection Fault. **Int 0DH** is the exception that the programmer will probably encounter most frequently. It is triggered by any violation of the protection rules not specifically covered by the other exceptions. This covers a wide variety of problems, such as:

- Loading an invalid selector into a segment register.
- Reading from or writing to a segment not having the appropriate permission.
- Exceeding the limit of a segment.
- Trying to access a segment using a segment register containing the NULL selector. (However, it is legal to load the NULL selector into a segment register.)
- Loading **ss** with the descriptor of an executable or read-only segment.
- Any violation of the privilege rules that we will delineate in Section 7.

This is only a partial listing of the offences inducing a general-protection fault. For a longer (but still incomplete) list, we refer the reader to [14].

Page Fault. Like **int 01H**, **int 0EH** is associated with an exciting feature of the **80386**, in this case its paging capabilities, which are used in implementing virtual memory. When the paging mechanisms are activated and a needed "page" of code or data is not present in memory, the microprocessor triggers an **int 0EH**. The **int 0EH** handler is responsible for bringing the missing page into physical memory. Since **int 0EH** is a fault, control returns to the faulting instruction, and the program continues as though nothing had happened!

Alignment Check (**80486** only). As we know, data fetches are more efficient when data is appropriately aligned in memory. **Int 11H** is designed to trap memory references failing

FIGURE 18.6 EXCERPT 3 FROM PROT.MAC

```
 1   ;Structure template for gate descriptor
 2   gateDesc        STRUC
 3
 4       gdOffLo     DW  0
 5       gdSel       DW  0
 6       gdMisc      DB  0
 7       gdRights    DB  0
 8       gdOffHi     DW  0
 9
10   gateDesc        ENDS
11
12   ;--------------------------------------------------------------------
13
14   COMMENT      #   MACRO HEADER
15   MACRO NAME:      remapInts
16   PURPOSE:         Changes the interrupt vectors to which the AT hardware
17                    interrupts are assigned.
18   CALLED AS:       remapInts  Level, Start
19                    where Level (= 1 or 2) is the interrupt level to be remapped
20                    and Start is the starting vector number after remapping.
21   RETURNS:     #   Nothing
22
23   remapInts  MACRO  Level, Start
24
25       IFIDNI <Level>, <1>
26           prtA = 20h                              ;port addresses for
27           prtB = 21h                              ;  Level 1 interrupts
28           Var = 04h
29       ELSE
30           prtA = 0a0h                     ;port addresses for
31           prtB = 0a1h                     ;  Level 2 interrupts
32           Var = 02h
33       ENDIF
34
35       mov    al, 11h
36       out    prtA, al
37       jmp    $ + 2                        ;gives times delay
38
39       mov    al, Start
40       out    prtB, al
41       jmp    $ + 2
42
43       mov    al, Var
44       out    prtB, al
45       jmp    $ + 2
46
47       mov    al, 01h
48       out    prtB, al
49       jmp    $ + 2
50
51   ENDM
```

to have the optimal alignment. It works in conjunction with the *Alignment Check flag* (*AC flag*, which is bit 18 of **eflags**) and the *Alignment Mask* (*AM bit*, which is bit 18 of **cr0**). These bits are defined only with the **80486** and **int 11H** is triggered when all of the following conditions hold: both AM and AC are set; the code is executing at Level 3; a non-aligned data access occurs.

Int 12H-0FFH. These interrupt numbers are available for the systems programmer and the applications programmer. Since a typical interrupt represents a request for a service to be performed, these would normally be traps rather than faults. Indeed, by default the **int** instruction works in that way.

As Table 18.2 shows, some exceptions return an *error code*, which is 16 bits long. (In the 32-bit case, it is padded to 32 bits, with the actual error code occupying the low 16 bits.)

The error code is pushed onto the stack after the return address; hence, it can be accessed from within the handler as the top-of-stack element. For exceptions arising from a problem with a particular segment, the high 14 bits of the error code are equal to the high 14 bits of the selector for the segment in question. Bit number 1 is clear if this selector refers to the global descriptor table and is set if it refers to the interrupt descriptor table (which will be defined in the next paragraph). Bit 0 is set if the exception was triggered by an event external to the program. In cases where the exception cannot be associated with a particular segment, the error code is zero.

As the reader might already suspect, the protected-mode analog of the real-mode interrupt vector table does not contain the addresses of the interrupt handlers. Rather, it contains a descriptor associated with each interrupt handler, and so is called an *interrupt descriptor table (IDT)*. The descriptors that we have previously encountered described segments. The descriptors in an IDT are different: they are called *gate descriptors* and, naturally, they give the locations of the interrupt handlers.

Figure 18.7 shows the general formats of gate descriptors. Three varieties of gate descriptors are illustrated. The *call gate descriptor*, shown in the third diagram, cannot actually occur in an IDT. It is included here for completeness and will be discussed in Section 6. The *task gate descriptor*, shown second, can occur in an IDT, but will not be discussed until Section 7.

The descriptors in an IDT are most often *trap gates* or *interrupt gates*, both of which have the format shown in the first diagram. Trap gates and interrupt gates, like all descriptors, are data structures of length eight bytes. Their exact format is given by the *gateDesc* structure in Figure 18.6. The content of the structure members should be self-explanatory: the selector and offset for the handler code and a rights byte have the same format as in the segment descriptor case. (See Figure 18.1.) We will discuss the general significance of the DPL field of the rights byte in Section 7.

Trap gates and interrupt gates are almost identical, the only difference being that interrupt gates automatically clear the interrupt flag while trap gates do not. For this reason, interrupt gates are commonly used for hardware interrupts and trap gates for software interrupts and exceptions. The table of types contained in Figure 18.7 shows that the **80386** distinguishes between **80286** gates and **80386** gates. The reason is the obvious one: in terms of control flow, a gate is similar to a **FAR** call and so must push the correct 16- or 32-bit size return-address offset onto the stack. The choice is based on the declared type of the gate.

The structure of the IDT is analogous to that of the GDT, except that the IDT does not begin with a dummy selector. The IDT need not contain 256 entries — it only requires entries for the interrupts that will actually be used. More precisely, the microprocessor locates each interrupt descriptor by its offset from the beginning of the table. Consequently, if, for

FIGURE 18.7 FORMATS OF GATE DESCRIPTORS

INTERRUPT AND TRAP GATE DESCRIPTORS

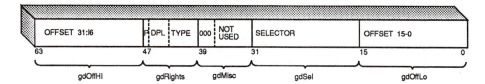

TASK GATE DESCRIPTOR

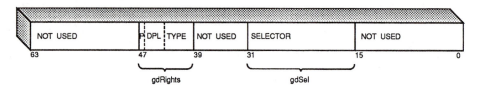

CALL GATE DESCRIPTOR

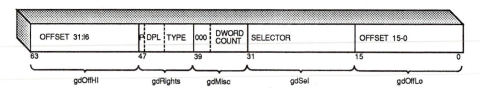

SYSTEM AND GATE DESCRIPTOR TYPES

TYPE	DESCRIPTION
00h	reserved
01h	available 286 TSS
02h	LDT
03h	busy 286 TSS
04h	call gate
05h	task gate
06h	286 interrupt gate
07h	286 task gate
08h	reserved
09h	available 386 TSS
0Ah	reserved
0Bh	busy 386 TSS
0Ch	386 call gate
0Dh	reserved
0Eh	386 interrupt gate
0Fh	386 trap gate

example, **int 27H** will be used but not **int 26H**, it will be necessary to pad the table with eight bytes to keep the indexing correct.

Finally, the **80286/80386** must be given the location and extent of the IDT. This information is relayed exactly as in the case of the GDT. The analog of the **gdtr** is the **idtr** (*interrupt descriptor table register*). It, too, requires as an initializer a six-byte block of data containing the limit (two bytes) and linear address (four bytes) of the table in question.

SECTION 5 A PROTECTED-MODE KERNEL

In this section we will develop a very limited protected-mode operating system kernel for the **80386**. We will present code allowing the machine to begin in real mode under the control of **MS-DOS** and then to transfer to protected mode. In protected mode, we provide programs with primitive "eyes and ears": they will be able to write directly to the video buffer and receive input from the keyboard. Perhaps the most significant compromise involved in this package is its restriction to 16-bit segments. While this is not strictly necessary, it does allow us to use many of our library functions and macros in protected-mode programs. Our kernel contains a skeletal protected-mode **int 21H**, and we were careful to give the protected-mode version the same number as the real-mode version so that our standard macros that call **int 21H** functions could be used unchanged. Unfortunately, we have only implemented **function 3FH** (the read handle function) and **function 40H** (the write handle function) and even these are implemented in a very limited sense. **Function 3FH** always reads from the keyboard, no matter what handle is used; similarly, **function 40H** always sends its output to the video buffer. Nevertheless, these functions give us access to our *inCh*, *outCh*, *inAsc*, and *outAsc* macros, and to several others. Our restriction to 16-bit code also allows us to use library functions such as *ascBin16* and *bin16Asc* so that, in addition, we can use the *iToA* and *aToI* macros that call them.

The kernel permits a program to run in the protected-mode environment and, when the program terminates, provides for an orderly return to real mode and **MS-DOS**. Later, in Section 8, we will add multitasking capabilities to the kernel.

FIXSEGS, the program presented in Section 3, takes the **80386** from real mode to protected mode and back again. However, the transitions presented in FIXSEGS skirted some of the essential issues because we did not need to use any interrupts while in protected mode.

Here is a complete list of the steps that should be executed in transferring from real to protected mode:

- Set up the global descriptor table.

- Initialize the global descriptor table register.

- Set up an interrupt descriptor table for use in protected mode. This table need only contain descriptors for those interrupts or exceptions that will actually be used (although, as we saw in the previous section, it may require padding so that each descriptor falls at the correct offset).

- Initialize the interrupt descriptor table register.

- If the **80386** paging mechanisms will be used, enable paging by turning on bit 31 of the **cr0** register. We will not incorporate paging into our programs.

- Enable the A20 address line.

- Disable the interrupts, including the NMI.

- Remap the hardware interrupts vectors so that they do not conflict with the reserved Intel numbers.

- Enter protected mode by turning on bit 0 of the **cr0** register.

- In protected mode, do a **FAR jmp** or **call** to flush the prefetch queue and load the **cs** register with the code segment selector.

- Initialize **ss** and the other segment registers that will be used, using selectors of the correct kinds.

- Enable interrupts, including the NMI.

- If multitasking is used, initialize the task register. (We will discuss this process in Section 8.)

The return from protected mode involves essentially the same sequence of steps, with the obvious modifications.

Our protected-mode kernel consists of three modules, which are linked with a module containing the user code. The first of these modules, INTMOD.ASM, is shown in Figure 18.8. It contains the protected-mode interrupt vector table and our interrupt handlers. Here are some comments on the code:

Lines 13-27. The interrupt descriptor table contains descriptors for handlers corresponding to interrupts 00H-3fH. We were able to write this table very succinctly by making careful use of the **IRPC** directive.

As we have seen, 00H-1FH are used or reserved by Intel, and so we remap the maskable interrupts to the range 30H-3FH. Our **int 21H** plays the same role as the **MS-DOS int 21H**, and it is the only interrupt in the range 21H-3FH that we actually use.

The interrupts in the range 00H-1FH are given by **80286** trap gates, while those in the range 31H-3FHh are defined as **80286** interrupt gates. This can easily be checked from the table of gate types given in Figure 18.7. Recall from the previous section that the only distinction between interrupt gates and trap gates is that the former disable the interrupt flag while the latter do not. This can be significant during the processing of hardware interrupts, and so we chose interrupt gates to be safe. **Int 30H** is unique in our table — it is given by a task gate. In Section 8, we will see the significance of task gates and will explain why a task gate was used in the **int 30H** slot of the table.

Lines 29-33. These lines contain the six-byte buffer used to initialize the **idtr**. It is still necessary to adjust the linear address at run time. Since this correction is done in another module, the various **idtr** data items must be declared as **PUBLIC** (line 3).

Lines 37-53. Our error handlers for the basic exceptions are minimal: they print an error message, perform a register dump, and abort the program. These lines contain part of the text of the error messages.

Lines 55-60. The keyboard handler is also fairly minimal. The keyboard buffer has length one — it is defined on line 55 — and only characters in the array on lines 57-60 are translated. If a given position k in this array has a non-zero entry, then that entry is the lowercase

FIGURE 18.8 PROTECTED-MODE INTERRUPT MODULE

```
 1   TITLE intMod.asm
 2
 3   PUBLIC  idtLimit, idtLinAddr, idtrData, Handler30h, tskGt30
 4
 5   .386P
 6   .SALL
 7   INCLUDE    prot.mac
 8   INCLUDE    console.mac
 9
10   _DATA SEGMENT USE16 WORD PUBLIC 'DATA'
11
12   ;###########################################################################
13   ;INTERRUPT DESCRIPTOR TABLE                                               ;#
14                                                                            ;#
15   IDT       LABEL    WORD                                                  ;#
16                                                                            ;#
17   IRPC A, <012>                                                            ;#
18    IRPC B, <0123456789abcdef>                                              ;#
19     trpGt&A&&B gateDesc <Handler&A&&B&&h, 08h, NOTUSED, PDT<1,0,07h>, 00h> ;#
20    ENDM                                                                    ;#
21   ENDM                                                                     ;#
22                                                                            ;#
23       tskGt30 gateDesc <NOTUSED,     , NOTUSED, PDT<1,0,05h>, NOTUSED>     ;#
24                                                                            ;#
25   IRPC B, <123456789abcdef>                                               ;#
26       intGt3&B gateDesc <Handler3&B&h, 08h, NOTUSED, PDT<1,0,06h>, 00h>   ;#
27   ENDM                                                                     ;#
28                                                                            ;#
29   IDTRData             LABEL    FWORD              ;for lidt               ;#
30       IDTLimit         DW       $ - IDT - 1                                ;#
31       IDTLinAddr       LABEL    DWORD                                      ;#
32                        DW       IDT                                        ;#
33                        DW       0                                          ;#
34                                                                            ;#
35   ;###########################################################################
36
37       intHeading00h    DB       "Divide Fault", 0
38       intHeading01h    DB       "Debug Exception", 0
39       intHeading02h    DB       "Non-Maskable Interrupt", 0
40       intHeading03h    DB       "Breakppoint Trap", 0
41       intHeading04h    DB       "Overflow Trap" , 0
42       intHeading05h    DB       "Bounds Fault", 0
43       intHeading06h    DB       "Invalid Opcode Fault", 0
44       intHeading07h    DB       "Coprocessor Not Available Exception", 0
45       intHeading08h    DB       "Double Fault", 0
46       intHeading09h    DB       "Coprocessor Segment Overrun Exception", 0
47       intHeading0ah    DB       "Invalid TSS Fault", 0
48       intHeading0bh    DB       "Segment Not Present Fault", 0
49       intHeading0ch    DB       "Stack Exception", 0
50       intHeading0dh    DB       "General Protection Fault", 0
51       intHeading0eh    DB       "Page Fault", 0
52       intHeading0Fh    DB       "Not Used", 0
53       intHeading10h    DB       "Coprocessor Fault", 0
54
55       kbBuffer         DB       0
```

Figure 18.8 cont.

```
 56
 57      toASCII          DB        0, ESCAPE, 13 DUP(0)
 58                       DB        0, "qwertyuiop[]", CR
 59                       DB        0, "asdfghjkl", 0, 0, 0
 60                       DB        0, 0, "zxcvbnm"
 61
 62  _DATA ENDS
 63
 64  ;============================================================================
 65
 66  _TEXT SEGMENT USE16 WORD PUBLIC 'CODE'
 67
 68      ASSUME cs:_TEXT, ds:_DATA
 69
 70      EXTRN         abortProgram:NEAR
 71
 72  ;----------------------------------------------------------------------------
 73
 74  IRPC B, <0123456789abcdef>                  ;interrupts 00h -- 0fh
 75
 76  Handler0&B&h:
 77
 78      outAsc NL, "Interrupt 0&B&h:", intHeading0&B&h, NL
 79
 80      isErrorCode      INSTR    <8abcdef>, <B>  ;these are the exceptions
 81      IF  isErrorCode NE 0                      ;   that push error codes
 82          outAsc "Error Code: "                ;      onto the stack
 83          pop     ax
 84          hexPrt  ax
 85          outAsc  NL
 86      ENDIF
 87
 88      jmp Common                               ;the code labeled Common is
 89                                               ;   executed by all exceptions
 90  ENDM                                         ;      in the range 00h - 0fh
 91
 92  Common:
 93
 94      IRP Reg, <eax, ebx, ecx, edx>       ;print the values of 13
 95          printReg32    Reg                ;  registers
 96      ENDM
 97      outAsc  NL
 98      IRP Reg, <esi, edi, ebp, esp>
 99          printReg32    Reg
100      ENDM
101      outAsc  NL
102      IRP Reg, <ds, es, fs, gs, ss>
103          printReg16    Reg
104      ENDM
105      outAsc  NL
106
107      outAsc  " return cs:ip = "          ;print the return cs:ip
108      pop     ax
109      pop     bx
110      hexPrt  bx
111      printChar ':'
```

```
112     hexPrt  ax
113
114     add     sp, 2                   ;for the flags
115     jmp     abortProgram            ;abort the program
116
117 ;-------------------------------------------------------------------------
118
119 Handler21h:                         ;interrupt 21h -- analogous to the
120                                     ;  MS-DOS interrupt with that number
121     push    cx
122     pushEM  edx
123     and     edx, 0ffffh             ;use only low 16 bits as offset
124     cmp     ah, 40h                 ;is it a function 40h call?
125     je      SHORT function40hLoop
126     cmp     ah, 3fh                 ;is it a function 39h call?
127     je      function3fhLoop
128
129     outAsc  NL, "UNSUPPORTED INT21H FUNCTION CALL", NL   ;only functions 39h
130     jmp     SHORT handler21hEnd                         ;  and 40h have been
131                                                         ;    implemented
132 function40hLoop:
133
134     printChar [edx]                 ;send to video buffer, starting at
135     inc     edx                     ;  offset passed in dx
136     loop    function40hLoop         ;dispatch cx characters
137     jmp     handler21hEnd
138
139 function3fhLoop:
140
141     cmp     kbBuffer, 0             ;wait for a key press
142     je      function3fhLoop        ;  to arrive in kbBuffer
143     mov     al, kbBuffer           ;move the character
144     mov     [edx], al              ;  to the caller's buffer
145     inc     edx                    ;update pointer to caller's buffer
146     mov     kbBuffer, 0            ;remove key from kbBuffer
147     loop    function3fhLoop        ;repeat cx times
148
149 handler21hEnd:
150     popEM   edx
151     pop     cx34
152     iret
153
154 ;-------------------------------------------------------------------------
155
156 Handler30h:                         ;interrupt 30h -- the timer interrupt
157
158     mov     al, 20h                ;send EOI (end of interrupt)
159     out     20h, al                ;  acknowlegement to PIC
160     iret
161     jmp     Handler30h
162
163 ;-------------------------------------------------------------------------
164
165 Handler31h:
166                                     ;interrupt 31h -- the keyboard
167     pushRegs    ax, bx             ;  interrupt
168
169     in      al, 60h                ;get scan code
170     mov     ah, al                 ;store scan code in ah
```

Figure 18.8 cont.

```
171     in      al, 61h                      ;send
172     or      al, 1 SHL 7                  ; acknowlegement
173     out     61h, al                      ;    to
174     and     al, NOT 1 SHL 7              ;       keyboard
175     out     61h, al                      ;          controller
176
177     cmp     ah, 01h                      ;is it the ESC key?
178     jne     isItAKeypress
179     jmp     abortProgram
180
181  isItAKeypress:
182
183     cmp     ah, 0f0h                     ;on AT class machines, this byte
184     jne     itsAKeypress                 ;   prefaces key releases
185
186     ;Discard scan code of released key, send acknowledgement
187
188     in      al, 61h                      ;send
189     or      al, 1 SHL 7                  ; acknowledgement
190     out     61h, al                      ;    to
191     and     al, NOT 1 SHL 7              ;       keyboard
192     out     61h, al                      ;          controller
193
194     jmp     endHandler31h                ;discard info about key release
195
196  itsAKeyPress:
197
198     cmp     ah, 50                       ;the max. scan code we are using
199     ja      endHandler31h
200     mov     al, ah                       ;get scan code back in al
201     lea     bx, toASCII                  ;translate scan code
202     xlat    toASCII                      ;  to ASCII code
203     mov     kbBuffer, al                 ;store ASCII code in keyboard buffer
204     printChar   al                       ;echo input character to screen
205
206  endHandler31h:
207
208     mov     al, 20h                      ;send EOI (end of interrupt)
209     out     20h, al                      ;  acknowledgement to PIC
210
211     popRegs
212     iret
213
214  ;-----------------------------------------------------------------------
215
216  IRPC B, <23456789abcdef>                 ;interrupts 32h -- 3fh
217     Handler3&B&h:
218
219     mov     al, 20h                      ;send EOI (end of interrupt)
220     out     20h, al                      ;  acknowledgement to PIC
221
222     iret
223
224  ENDM
225
226  ;-----------------------------------------------------------------------
```

```
227
228  IRPC B, <0123456789abcdef>              ;interrupts 10h -- 1fh
229      Handler1&B&h:
230
231          iret
232
233  ENDM
234
235  ;------------------------------------------------------------------------
236
237  IRPC B, <023456789abcdef>               ;interrupts 20h -- 2fh
238      Handler2&B&h:
239
240          iret
241
242  ENDM
243
244  ;------------------------------------------------------------------------
245
246  _TEXT ENDS
```

character corresponding to scan key k on the keyboard. Consequently, this array can be used with the **xlat** instruction to convert scan codes to lowercase letters. This is the application we will make of it, and it already indicates the limitations of our keyboard handler: it will translate only the lowercase characters shown in the array, and completely ignores the shift, alternate, and control keys.

Lines 74-115. These are the handlers for the interrupts in the range 00H-0FH. They make use of the *outAsc* macro, and so we need a substitute for **function 40H** of **int 21H**.

After a heading is printed on line 78, the **INSTR** string directive is used on line 80 to neatly select those interrupts returning an error code. The actual printing of the error codes for those handlers is handled on line 84 by our old *hexPrt* macro.

The macro code before line 88 is different for each handler (because the argument *B* is different and because not all exceptions push an error code). The code from that point on is shared by all the handlers. It consists of a dump of 13 general-purpose and segment registers, followed by the values of **cs** and **ip**.

Lines 119-152. This is our version of **int 21H**. Again, we were careful to choose the number 21H for our "function dispatcher" and to implement **functions 3FH** and **40H**, so that we would have access to our standard macros and library procedures that use these functions.

The implementations of the two functions are trivial since we channel each request to the screen or the keyboard. In both functions, **ds:dx** must point to the data buffer and **cx** should contain the character count. Since we index the data buffer indirectly using **edx**, we must be sure that the high half of **edx** contains zero, which explains line 123.

The essential code for **function 40H** (lines 132-137) consists of a loop of calls to a function named *directPrint*, which will be defined in the next module. This function sends a character to the video buffer, while keeping track of details such as updating the "cursor position" and scrolling the screen when necessary.

Our version of **function 3FH** occupies lines 139-147. Each traverse of this loop is analogous to the MS-DOS **function 01H** "wait for a character from the keyboard." Our convention is that *kbBuffer* should contain the zero byte to indicate that it is empty and should contain an ASCII code otherwise. On lines 139-142, we poll the keyboard repeatedly (i.e., wait for a character). As soon as a character arrives and is sent to the data buffer (lines 144-145), zero is moved to *kbBuffer* to indicate that it is now empty.

Lines 156-161. As we noted earlier, *Handler30h*, the remapped timer interrupt, is controlled by a task gate and will be discussed in Section 7, since it will be an important component of our multitasking kernel. For the moment, there are two points of interest. Lines 158-159 are a necessary part of all handlers for interrupts controlled by the **PIC**. They acknowledge receipt of the interrupt. (The **PIC** will not process another interrupt until the previous one has been acknowledged.) The other interesting aspect of this code is line 161, which must surely seem to the reader to be an error. It is, in fact, quite correct, but can only be explained in terms of the multitasking features of the **80286/80386**.

Lines 165-212. This is our version of the keyboard interrupt, **int 09h**, which has been remapped out of the Intel reserved range. We outlined the operation of the keyboard interface in connection with Exercise 15-11 and refer the reader to that discussion. However, we were then focusing on the **IBM-XT** keyboard, and there is a significant difference between that and the **IBM-AT** keyboard, which we will now explain. Recall that in the **XT**, key presses are distinguished from key releases on the basis of the high bit of the byte transmitted from the keyboard: if this bit is zero, it is a press; otherwise, it is a release. The **IBM-AT** keyboard works differently. In all cases, the high bit is 0, and a key release is signalled by being preceded by the special byte with value 0F0H. The low seven bits always give the scan code for the key in question. These observations should explain the **int 30H** code up to line 196.

The remainder of the code discards the key press if it is not in our limited range, and otherwise uses the translation table (lines 57-60) and the **xlat** instruction to convert the scan code to the corresponding **ASCII** code.

Lines 216-240. These handlers are provided essentially as padding in the interrupt descriptor table. Note that the handlers for the maskable interrupts send the requisite acknowledgements to the **PIC**.

The next module in our kernel, VIDMOD.ASM, is shown in Figure 18.9. Most of the procedures contained in it are quite direct and so we will not discuss them at length. Figure 18.10 shows the headers for macros that call these procedures. Here are some general observations about the usage of these procedures and macros:

- They expect **gs** to point to the video buffer. In our protected-mode environment, the GDT should contain a data descriptor initialized to the linear address and limit of the video buffer and **gs** should contain a selector for that descriptor. The segment address and limit of the video buffer are defined by **EQUATE**s in PROT.MAC. (See Figure 18.10.)

- The variables *rowNo*, *colNo*, *charPos* (lines 15-17) refer to the "cursor position," i.e., to the position of the next character to be printed. The first two have the obvious meanings, while *charPos* means the offset in words of the cursor position from the base of the video buffer. In other words, in the case of an 80-column screen

```
charPos = 80*rowNo + colNo
```

FIGURE 18.9 DIRECT CONTROL OF VIDEO BUFFER

```
1    TITLE vidMod.asm
2
3    PUBLIC  directPrint, directPrint16, directPrint32
4    PUBLIC  scrollUp, clearScreen, rowNo, colNo, charPos
5
6    .386
7    .SALL
8    INCLUDE prot.mac
9    INCLUDE console.mac
10
11   ;==============================================================================
12
13   _DATA SEGMENT USE16 WORD PUBLIC 'DATA'
14
15       rowNo        DD  0
16       colNo        DD  0
17       charPos      DD  0
18
19   _DATA   ENDS
20
21   ;==============================================================================
22
23   _TEXT SEGMENT USE16 WORD PUBLIC 'CODE'
24
25       ASSUME cs:_TEXT, ds:_DATA
26
27   ;------------------------------------------------------------------------------
28
29   ;Expects to receive Char to print in al
30   ;  and that gs points to screen
31   ;Prints Char at present charPos and updates chapPos, rowNo, and
32   ;  colNo appropriately
33
34   directPrint     PROC    NEAR
35
36       ;The code for directPrint is fairly long and not interesting.
37       ;It is on the Program Disk.
38
39   directPrint     ENDP
40
41   ;------------------------------------------------------------------------------
42
43   ;Prints 16-bit data item directly to screen in hex at present charPos.
44   ;Item must be pushed onto stack
45
46   directPrint16   PROC    NEAR
47
48       push    ax
49       and     esp, 0ffffh
50       mov     ax, ss:[esp+2]
51       hexPrt  ax
52       pop     ax
53       ret     2
54
55   directPrint16   ENDP
```

Figure 18.9 cont.

```
 56
 57    ;-----------------------------------------------------------------------
 58
 59    ;Prints 32-bit data item directly to screen in hex at present charPos.
 60    ;Item must be pushed onto stack
 61
 62    directPrint32    PROC    NEAR
 63
 64        push    ax
 65        and     esp, 0ffffh
 66        mov     ax, ss:[esp+4]
 67        hexPrt  ax
 68        mov     ax, ss:[esp+2]
 69        hexPrt  ax
 70        pop     ax
 71        ret     4
 72
 73    directPrint32    ENDP
 74
 75    ;-----------------------------------------------------------------------
 76
 77    ;Scrolls the screen upward one line, updating charPos, rowNo, and colNo
 78
 79    scrollUp    PROC    NEAR
 80
 81        pushRegs    eax, cx, si, di, es, ds
 82
 83        mov     ax, gs
 84        mov     ds, ax
 85        mov     es, ax
 86        mov     cx, (SCRLIM-2*MAXCOLS) SHR 2    ;the number of dwords to move
 87        mov     si, 2*(MAXCOLS+1)
 88        xor     di, di
 89        rep     movsd                          ;DF = 0 is OK for this move
 90                                               ;  even though there is overlap
 91        mov     cx, (MAXCOLS+1) SHR 1          ;number of dwords in a row
 92        mov     eax, gs:[di-4]                 ;to determine video attribute
 93        and     eax, 0FFH SHL 24 OR 0FFH SHL 8 ;blank last line but
 94        or      eax, ' ' SHL 16 OR ' '         ;  preserve video attribute
 95        rep     stosd
 96
 97        popRegs
 98
 99        sub     charPos, MAXCOLS+1
100        dec     rowNo
101
102        ret
103
104    scrollUp    ENDP
105
106    ;-----------------------------------------------------------------------
107
108    ;Clears the screen, setting the attribute of the entire screen to the value
109    ;  it finds as the attribute in the initial screen position
110
111    clearScreen     PROC    NEAR
```

```
112
113        pushRegs   eax, cx, di, es
114
115        push    gs
116        pop     es                                      ;for use with stosd
117
118        mov     cx, (SCRLIM+1) SHR 2
119        xor     edi, edi
120        mov     eax, gs:[edi]
121        and     eax, 0FFH SHL 24 OR 0FFH SHL 8   ;preserve video attribute
122        or      eax, ' ' SHL 16 OR ' '          ;   while filling screen with
123        rep     stosd                           ;      space characters
124
125        popRegs
126
127        ret
128
129 clearScreen       ENDP
130
131 ;-------------------------------------------------------------------------
132
133 _TEXT     ENDS
134
135 ;=========================================================================
136
137 END
```

These variables are updated automatically by the various procedures that manipulate the video buffer.

- In our forthcoming multitasking example, we want the different tasks to display their outputs on the screen using distinct values of the video attribute. To facilitate these attribute changes, the *clrScr* macro accepts, as an optional parameter, a new value for the attribute, which it uses when it clears the screen. In a similar vein, the *scrollUp* procedure (line 79 of Figure 18.9) assigns the current screen attribute to the characters in the new line that it introduces at the bottom of the screen.

The next module in our protected-mode kernel, STRTMOD1.ASM, is shown in Figure 18.11. Nearly everything of interest in it has been discussed already, except those aspects relating to tasks and task gates. For completeness, here are a few additional comments:

Lines 30-36. The only unexplained feature of the GDT is the pair of descriptors given on lines 35-36. As we will see in Section 8, the descriptors specify task state segments.

Lines 46-47, 103-106, 140-141. Likewise, these lines all relate to the task state segment structures, and will be examined in Section 7.

Lines 49-55. These labels provide the targets for the indirect **FAR** jumps used to flush the prefetch queue and initialize **cs** when entering or leaving protected mode. Note that the segment part of *protModeAddr* contains a selector for the code segment, as is appropriate for protected mode, while the segment part of *realModeAddr* contains the segment address of _TEXT, as is needed for real-mode initialization.

FIGURE 18.10 EXCERPT 4 FROM PROT.MAC

```
 1   SCRBAS         EQU      0b800h        ;use 0b000h for mono screeen
 2   SCRLIM         EQU      3999          ;for
 3   MAXROWS        EQU      24            ;   25 rows by
 4   MAXCOLS        EQU      79            ;      80 cols
 5
 6   ;-----------------------------------------------------------------
 7
 8   COMMENT      #    MACRO HEADER
 9   MACRO NAME:       printChar
10   PURPOSE:          Sends a character to the video buffer
11   CALLED AS:        printChar Char
12   RETURNS:          Nothing
13   REMARKS:          Calls directPrint; assumes that gs points to video buffer
14   RETURNS:     #    Nothing
15
16   ;-----------------------------------------------------------------
17
18   COMMENT      #    MACRO HEADER
19   MACRO NAME:       printReg16
20   PURPOSE:          Given a 16-bit register, it prints the register name,
21                     followed by value written as four hex digits.
22   CALLED AS:        printReg16 regName
23   REMARKS:          Calls directPrint16; assumes that gs points to video buffer
24   RETURNS:     #    Nothing
25
26   ;-----------------------------------------------------------------
27
28   COMMENT      #    MACRO HEADER
29   MACRO NAME:       printReg32
30   PURPOSE:          Given a 32-bit register, it prints the register name,
31                     followed by value written as eight hex digits.
32   CALLED AS:        printReg32 regName
33   REMARKS:          Calls directPrint32; assumes that gs points to video buffer
34   RETURNS:     #    Nothing
35
36   ;-----------------------------------------------------------------
37
38   COMMENT      #    MACRO HEADER
39   MACRO NAME:       clrScr
40   PURPOSE:          Clears screen, optionally changing the attribute
41   CALLED AS:        clrScr  Attrib
42                     where Attrib becomes the new attribute if it is non-blank,
43                     otherwise the attribute remains unchanged
44   REMARKS:          Calls clearScreen; assumes that gs points to video buffer
45   RETURNS:     #    Nothing
```

Lines 61-74. We begin execution in *realSeg* (see line 185) and then transfer to _TEXT, the main segment used in the program, by means of a **FAR** jump. While this is not strictly necessary, it can be convenient to have the extra segment *realSeg* available for various initializations. We have reserved the name _TEXT for the main segment since our library functions and a number of our macros can only be called from a segment having that name.

FIGURE 18.11 ENTERING AND LEAVING PROTECTED MODE

```
 1    TITLE strtMod1.asm: setup required for entering and leaving protected mode
 2
 3    .386P
 4    .SALL
 5    INCLUDE prot.mac
 6    INCLUDE console.mac
 7
 8    PUBLIC  abortProgram
 9
10    ;========================================================================
11
12    STACK SEGMENT USE16 PARA  STACK 'STACK'
13
14        DB  1000h DUP(?)
15
16    STACK ENDS
17
18    ;========================================================================
19
20    _DATA SEGMENT USE16 WORD PUBLIC 'DATA'
21
22        EXTRN       idtLimit:WORD, idtLinAddr:DWORD, idtrData:FWORD
23        EXTRN       tskGt30:QWORD
24
25    ;#############################################################################
26    ;GLOBAL DESCRIPTOR TABLE                                                    ;#
27                                                                               ;#
28    GDT     LABEL   WORD                                                       ;#
29                                                                               ;#
30    Dummy     segDesc < 0000h, 0000h, 00h, PDT<0,0,0>,  GXOAL<0,0,0,0,0>, 00h> ;#
31    codeDesc  segDesc <0ffffh,      ,    , PDT<1,0,1ah>,GXOAL<0,0,0,0,0>, 00h> ;#
32    stakDesc  segDesc <0ffffh,      ,    , PDT<1,0,12h>,GXOAL<0,0,0,0,0>, 00h> ;#
33    smlDDesc  segDesc <0ffffh,      ,    , PDT<1,0,12h>,GXOAL<0,0,0,0,0>, 00h> ;#
34    vidDesc   segDesc <SCRLIM, 8000h, 0bh, PDT<1,0,12h>,GXOAL<0,0,0,0,0>, 00h> ;#
35    mTskDesc  segDesc <  103,        ,    , PDT<1,0,09h>,GXOAL<0,0,0,0,0>, 00h> ;#
36    int30Desc segDesc <  103,        ,    , PDT<1,0,09h>,GXOAL<0,0,0,0,0>, 00h> ;#
37                                                                               ;#
38    GDTRData              LABEL   FWORD                   ;for lgdt            ;#
39        GDTLimit          DW      $ - GDT - 1                                  ;#
40        GDTLinAddr        LABEL   DWORD                                        ;#
41                          DW      GDT                                          ;#
42                          DW      0                                            ;#
43                                                                               ;#
44    ;#############################################################################
45
46        mTsk        TSS     <>
47        int30Tsk    TSS     <>
48
49        ProtModeAddr    LABEL   DWORD               ;used for far jump
50            DW  protMode                            ;  to protected mode
51            DW  codeDesc-GDT
52
53        RealModeLabel   LABEL   DWORD               ;used for far jump
54            DW  realMode                            ;  back to real mode
55            DW  _TEXT
```

Figure 18.11 cont.

```
56
57   _DATA ENDS
58
59   ;==============================================================================
60
61   realSeg    SEGMENT USE16 WORD PUBLIC 'CODE'
62
63       ASSUME cs:realSeg
64
65   Start:
66
67       jmp    FAR PTR Begin                        ;jump to _TEXT
68
69   dosExit:                                        ;target of far jump back from
70                                                   ;  _TEXT
71       mov    ax, 4c00h
72       int    21h
73
74   realSeg    ENDS
75
76   ;==============================================================================
77
78   _TEXT SEGMENT USE16 WORD PUBLIC 'CODE'
79
80       ASSUME cs:_TEXT, ds:_DATA, ss:STACK
81
82
83       EXTRN        testCode:NEAR, Handler30h:NEAR
84
85   Begin:
86
87       mov    ax, _DATA
88       mov    ds, ax
89       mov    ax, SCRBAS                           ;point gs to video buffer
90       mov    gs, ax                               ;  in real-mode sense
91
92       pushRegs   ds, es, fs, gs, ss               ;save segment registers
93
94       setDescBase  codeDesc, 0, cs                ;set descriptor bases
95       setDescBase  stakDesc, 0, ss
96       setDescBase  smlDDesc, 0, ds
97       setDescBase  mTskDesc, <OFFSET mTsk>, ds
98       setDescBase  int30Desc, <OFFSET int30Tsk>, ds
99
100
101      mov    tskGt30.gdSel, int30Desc - GDT  ;initialize selector for int30h
102                                             ;  task gate
103      ;Initialize int30Tsk
104      initTask int30Tsk,<codeDesc-GDT>, <smlDDesc-GDT>,<smlDDesc-GDT>,\
105                    <smlDDesc-GDT>, <vidDesc-GDT>, <stakDesc-GDT>,\
106                    <OFFSET Handler30h>, sp
107
108      mov    ax, ds                               ;set up address for gdtr
109      movzx  eax, ax
110      shl    eax, 4
111      add    GDTLinAddr, eax
```

```
112        lgdt     GDTrData                        ;load gdtr
113
114        cli                                      ;turn off all
115        turnNMI      OFF                         ;  interrupts
116
117        add      idtLinAddr, eax                 ;set up address for idtr
118        lidt     idtrData                        ;load idtr
119
120   ;********ENTER PROTECTED MODE**************************************************
121
122        mov      eax, cr0
123        or       eax, 01                         ;turn on protection
124        mov      cr0, eax                        ;  enable  bit
125
126        jmp      protModeAddr                    ;far jump to flush prefetch
127                                                 ;  queue and change cs to
128   protMode:                                     ;     protected-mode value
129
130        mov      ax, vidDesc-GDT                 ;point the segment registers
131        mov      gs, ax                          ;  to the correct segments
132                                                 ;    in the protected-mode sense
133        mov      ax, smlDDesc-GDT
134        mov      ds, ax
135        mov      fs, ax
136        mov      es, ax
137        mov      ax, stakDesc-GDT
138        mov      ss, ax
139
140        mov      ax, mTskDesc-GDT                ;load the mTsk selector into
141        ltr      ax                              ;  the task register
142
143        remapInts 1, 30h                         ;remap the maskable interrupts
144        remapInts 2, 38h
145        sti                                      ;enable all
146        turnNMI      ON                          ;  interrupts
147
148   ;The setting up of the protected-mode environment is now complete. We can
149   ;  now run an application that makes use of our primitive interrupts.
150
151        call testCode                            ;run the user code
152
153   abortProgram:                                 ;come here for a quick exit
154
155        cli                                      ;disable all
156        turnNMI      OFF                         ;  interrupts
157
158   ;********LEAVE PROTECTED MODE**************************************************
159
160        mov      eax, cr0
161        and      eax, NOT 1                      ;turn off protection
162        mov      cr0, eax                        ;enable bit
163
164        jmp      realModeLabel                   ;far jump to flush prefetch
165                                                 ;  queue and change cs to
166   realMode:                                     ;     real-mode value
167
168        mov      idtLimit, 3ffh                  ;load idtr with correct
169        mov      idtLinAddr, 0                   ;  parameters for real-
170        lidt     idtrData                        ;     mode interrupt table
```

```
Figure 18.11 cont.

171
172        popRegs                                       ;restore segment registers
173
174        remapInts 1, 08h                              ;remap maskable interrupt
175        remapInts 2, 70h                              ;   vectors to their default
176        turnNMI    ON                                 ;      values and turn on
177        sti                                           ;          all interrupts
178
179     jmp  FAR PTR    dosExit                          ;jump to realSeg
180
181   _TEXT ENDS
182
183   ;===========================================================================
184
185        END     Start
```

Line 151. Our kernel is set up to run a protected-mode program, which is supplied as a separate user module, and whose entry point is a procedure named *testCode*. Since the user module is also expected to use _TEXT as the name of its code segment, *testCode* is declared to be **NEAR** in the **EXTRN** declaration on line 83.

In Figure 18.12, we present a trivial sample program demonstrating our **int 21H** functions and showing the interrupt handlers in action. On lines 26-28, this program requests the user to input a string and echoes it to the screen. On lines 31-32, the program deliberately provokes a general-protection fault by attempting to load an illegal value into the **ds** register. Figure 18.12 also shows the output from this program.

Since this program consists of four separate modules, it is certainly worth using **MMF** and **MAKE** to build it. For purposes of review, here are the essential steps:

- Start with a subdirectory containing INTMOD.ASM, VIDMOD.ASM, STRTMOD1.ASM, and USERMOD.ASM, but containing no other .ASM or .C files.

- Be sure that CONSOLE.MAC and PROT.MAC are in the subdirectory pointed to by the MINC environment variable, and that the system time and date are correct.

- Use the command line

```
      mmf  testmod > testmod
```

to construct a makefile named TESTMOD, which will direct **MAKE** to build an executable name TESTMOD.EXE.

- Run **MAKE** with the command

```
      make testmod
```

Exercise 18-3. The occurrences of 08H on lines 19 and 26 of Figure 18.8 are clumsy. These are references to the offset of *codeDesc* into the GDT in Figure 18.11. Since they are "hard

FIGURE 18.12 A TRIVIAL TEST PROGRAM

```
 1    TITLE    userMod.asm: code that will run in our protected-mode environment
 2
 3    PUBLIC       testCode
 4
 5    .386
 6    INCLUDE      prot.mac
 7    INCLUDE      console.mac
 8
 9    ;========================================================================
10
11    _DATA    SEGMENT USE16 WORD PUBLIC 'DATA'
12
13        inputBuf    DB     11 DUP(?)
14
15    _DATA    ENDS
16
17    ;========================================================================
18
19    _TEXT    SEGMENT USE16 WORD PUBLIC 'CODE'
20
21    ASSUME   cs:_TEXT, ds:_DATA
22
23    testCode    PROC    NEAR
24
25        clrScr  57h                              ;make screen a garish color
26        outAsc  NL, "Input 10 or fewer characters: ", NL  ;test int 21h
27        inAsc   inputBuf                         ;    functions 39h
28        outAsc  NL, inputBuf                     ;       and 40h
29        outAsc  NL, "Hit a letter key to continue"
30        inCh    al
31        clrScr  07h                              ;return to a reasonable color
32
33        mov     ax, 177h                         ;deliberately provoke a general
34        mov     ds, ax                           ; protection fault to see the
35                                                 ;    the handler in action
36    testCode    ENDP
37
38    ;========================================================================
39
40    _TEXT    ENDS
41
42        END
```

PROGRAM OUTPUT

```
(On garish screen)
Input 10 or fewer characters:
abcde
abcde
Hit a letter key to continue
```

Figure 18.12 cont.

```
(On normal screen)
Interrupt 0dh: General Protection Fault
Error Code: ????
eax = 000D0D4B  ebx = 00000D80   ecx = 00EE0DA4   edx = 180A0DD8
esi = 000D0E4A  edi = 10000E74   ebp = 08820EA3   esp = 0EDD0ED7
ds = 1049  es= 10A0  fs = 10A0   gs = 10D4  ss = 1117
return cs:ip = 0000:16AA
```

coded," they must be manually updated if the ordering of segments in the GDT is changed. Fix this problem, using appropriate **PUBLIC** and **EXTRN** declarations.

Exercise 18-4. Elaborate on the last part of the program in Figure 18.12. Instead of just provoking a general-protection fault, introduce lines of code to deliberately induce as many of the other exceptions as you can.

Exercise 18-5. The invalid op-code exception is interesting because it does not occur as often as you might expect. Which one-byte op-codes are accepted as legal by the **80386**? Checking with Appendix 1 will show that some of these legal op-codes are undocumented. It is interesting (and, of course, much harder) to determine what, if anything, these undocumented op-codes do.

Exercise 18-6. The program in Figure 19.8 does not react correctly when it encounters an **int 10H**. Repair it.

Exercise 18-7. In Figure 19.8, we implemented only two of the **int 21H** functions. Add implementations of our old friends, **function 09H** and **function 0aH**.

Exercise 18-8. Augment our keyboard handler so that it recognizes digits (0-9) and uppercase letters.

Exercise 18-9. Include an input buffer in our keyboard handler to give it type-ahead capability.
Suggestion: It is probably best to use a circular buffer.

SECTION 6 MULTITASKING

Figure 18.13 shows some data structures used in preparing the **80286/80386** for multitasking. The first part of Figure 18.13 illustrates a *task state segment*, or *TSS*. When a task switch is performed, pertinent information about the old task must be saved so that it can be restored when that task is again given control of the machine, and the TSS is the storage area used by the **80286/80386**.

Although the microprocessor will automatically update the TSS of the outgoing task at each task switch, it is the responsibility of the programmer (or operating system) to set up and initialize a TSS for each task. When control is first passed to a task, the registers are

FIGURE 18.13 DATA STRUCTURES USED IN MULTITASKING

MINIMAL TASK STATE SEGMENT

31	15	0	
0 0 0 0 0 0 0 0 0 0 0 0 0 0 0 0	BACK LINK TO PREVIOUS TSS		00H
ESP0			04H
0 0 0 0 0 0 0 0 0 0 0 0 0 0 0 0	SS0		08H
ESP1			0CH
0 0 0 0 0 0 0 0 0 0 0 0 0 0 0 0	SS1		10H
ESP2			14H
0 0 0 0 0 0 0 0 0 0 0 0 0 0 0 0	SS2		18H
CR3 (PDBR)			1CH
INSTRUCTION POINTER (EIP)			20H
EFLAGS			24H
EAX			28H
ECX			2CH
EDX			30H
EBX			34H
ESP			38H
EBP			3CH
ESI			40H
EDI			44H
0 0 0 0 0 0 0 0 0 0 0 0 0 0 0 0	ES		48H
0 0 0 0 0 0 0 0 0 0 0 0 0 0 0 0	CS		4CH
0 0 0 0 0 0 0 0 0 0 0 0 0 0 0 0	SS		50H
0 0 0 0 0 0 0 0 0 0 0 0 0 0 0 0	DS		54H
0 0 0 0 0 0 0 0 0 0 0 0 0 0 0 0	FS		58H
0 0 0 0 0 0 0 0 0 0 0 0 0 0 0 0	GS		5CH
0 0 0 0 0 0 0 0 0 0 0 0 0 0 0 0	LDT		60H
I/O MAP BASE	0 0 0 0 0 0 0 0 0 0 0 0 0 0 0 T		64H

NOTE. LOCATIONS MARKED WITH 0 ARE RESERVED BY INTEL.

TSS SELECTOR

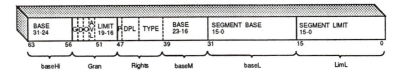

initialized to the values that have been placed in the TSS. We will discuss most of the fields of the TSS now, but a few must wait until the next section:

We will soon see that tasks can be invoked by the **call** instruction and can be *nested*, in the obvious sense: Task1 can call *Task2*, which can call *Task3*, and so on. To facilitate returns from such **calls**, each TSS stores a "return address" in its BACK LINK field. Of course, this return address will just be a selector pointing to the calling task.

As the names suggest, the fields ESP0, SS0, etc., can hold the stack pointers and segments for as many as three stacks. They are needed only when privilege levels are changed. We will explain their significance in the next section.

The only control register that we have met so far is **cr0**. We will see in Section 9 that there are actually four such registers, named **cr0-cr3**. The **cr3** register is known, more descriptively, as the *page directory base register*, or **pdbr**, because it holds the linear address of the active page directory. Since we will not use paging in any of our examples, this register will not concern us greatly.

The INSTRUCTION POINTER field must be initialized correctly. It determines the offset part of the address at which execution will begin after the first switch to the task. As part of the task-switching regimen, the microprocessor updates the INSTRUCTION POINTER field of the old task to point to the next instruction within the task. This simple mechanism ensures that, after the next return to the task, execution will resume where it left off.

We will not examine the **eflags** register in detail until Section 9, but the EFLAGS field is obviously used to store its value. In particular, the initialization of the EFLAGS field determines the value of **eflags** on first entry to the task. Generally, we allow EFLAGS to have the default initial value zero that it acquires from the structure template, which is shown in Figure 18.14. Giving all flags the value zero is usually appropriate in our examples. Notice, however, that this gives **IF** the value zero when the task is first entered and, depending on the circumstances, may require an **sti** instruction to enable the maskable interrupts.

The next fields hold the general-purpose registers. Only those general-purpose registers requiring guaranteed values on first entering the task need be initialized.

Among the fields containing segment registers, at least **cs** must be initialized to a selector for an executable segment, so that **cs:eip** points to the entry point to the task code. Of course, any other segment register used by the task must be initialized before its first use, either in the TSS, or within the task itself; otherwise, a general-protection fault results.

So far, we have encountered two kinds of descriptor tables, the GDT and IDT. There is a third kind, the *local descriptor table*, or *LDT*. Local descriptor tables are yet another aspect of the **80286/80386** protection mechanisms, since they can contain descriptors for segments intended for use by a single task. They are used in the same way as GDTs (although they do not need to begin with a dummy segment): the six bytes of relevant data about the active LDT are stored in the *local descriptor table register*, or *LDTR*, by using the **lldt** instruction.

FIGURE 18.14 EXCERPT 5 FROM PROT.MAC

```
 1   ;Structure template for task state segment
 2   TSS     STRUC
 3
 4       backLink    DW      0       ;Initialized defensively -- actual value
 5                   DW      0       ;  filled in by system when needed.
 6
 7       esp0        DD      0       ;Addresses of stacks for levels 2, 1, and 0.
 8       ss0         DW      0       ;Only needed when task switch involves a
 9                   DW      0       ;  change in privilege level. The stacks
10       esp1        DD      0       ;    that are actually used in such cases
11       ss1         DW      0       ;      must be explicitly initialized by
12                   DW      0       ;        the program.
13       esp2        DD      0
14       ss2         DW      0
15                   DW      0
16
17       cr3Reg      DD      0       ;These values are filled in by the system
18       eipReg      DD      0       ;  when a task switch occurs.  However, initial
19       eflagsReg   DD      0       ;    values must be given to those fields that
20       eaxReg      DD      0       ;      will be used by the program.
21       ecxReg      DD      0       ;The fields that must be initialized include
22       edxReg      DD      0       ;  cs and eip and, virtually always, ss, esp,
23       ebxReg      DD      0       ;    and ds.
24       espReg      DD      0
25       ebpReg      DD      0
26       esiReg      DD      0
27       ediReg      DD      0
28       esReg       DW      0
29                   DW      0
30       csReg       DW      0
31                   DW      0
32       ssReg       DW      0
33                   DW      0
34       dsReg       DW      0
35                   DW      0
36       fsReg       DW      0
37                   DW      0
38       gsReg       DW      0
39                   DW      0
40
41       ldtReg      DW      0       ;If used, must be initialized in program.
42                   DW      0
43       debugTrap   DW      0       ;Debug Trap Bit (0) must be init. in program.
44       ioMapBase   DW      0       ;If used, must be initialized in program.
45
46   TSS     ENDS
47
48   ;-------------------------------------------------------------------
49
50   COMMENT      #   MACRO HEADER
51   MACRO NAME:      initTask
52   PURPOSE:         Initializes cs, ds, es, fs, gs, ss, and eip fields of TSS.
53   CALLED AS:       setDescBase  taskName and 6 selectors and an offset.
54   REMARKS:         It may be necessary to manually initialize various other
55                    fields in the TSS, notably the eflags.
```

Figure 18.14 cont.

```
56   RETURNS:     #    Nothing.
57
58   initTask MACRO taskName, csSel, dsSel, esSel, fsSel, gsSel, ssSel, eipVal
59
60        mov      taskName.csReg,  csSel
61        mov      taskName.dsReg,  dsSel
62        mov      taskName.esReg,  esSel
63        mov      taskName.fsReg,  fsSel
64        mov      taskName.gsReg,  gsSel
65        mov      taskName.ssReg,  ssSel
66        mov      taskName.eipReg, eipVal
67        mov      taskName.espReg, espVal
68
69   ENDM
```

If a task uses an LDT, then its linear address is stored in the LDT field of the TSS, and the GDT should contain a descriptor for each LDT. As Figure 18.7 shows, LDT descriptors have type 02H.

For obvious reasons, a multitasking operating system must be able to control the use of the i/o ports. As we will soon see, the **80386** can exert this control on a task-by-task basis, and part of the control mechanism is a bit-array called the i/o permission map, which can be attached to the end of the TSS. When a permission map is used, the I/O MAP BASE field holds its offset relative to the start of the TSS.

The T-bit, or *debug trap bit*, is the low bit in the word at offset 64H in the TSS. It is a useful adjunct to the debugging capabilities of the microprocessor since, when set, it triggers a debug exception (**int 03H**) each time control is switched to this task.

In Figure 18.13, we labeled the first diagram as a *minimal* TSS, and we have seen previously that a TSS can be larger because it may contain an i/o permission map. But the TSS may be larger for other reasons. After all, the TSS as we have described it does not always contain *all* the important information about a task. As examples: the task may be engaged in a file operation when it is switched out, and information must be stored to ensure the correct resumption of this operation; if the task is using the screen, then presumably a copy of the screen buffer should be saved so that it can be restored when the task regains control. Consequently, it is frequently necessary to store the "software state" of a task, and this can be done by augmenting the TSS. If an i/o permission map is also used in such a circumstance, then the map must occur as the last item in the enlarged TSS.

The **80286/80386** views a TSS as a segment (technically, a *system segment*) and, as such, it requires a segment descriptor, which must be contained in the GDT. The second part of Figure 18.13 shows a TSS descriptor. It is similar in format to the normal segment descriptors given in Figure 18.1. The values usable in the type field are shown in Figure 18.7. Bit number 1 in the five-bit type field is noteworthy. It is called the *B-bit*, or *busy bit*, and is set if the task is busy, and clear otherwise. A task is considered busy even if it has been interrupted by another task, or an exception or interrupt. The busy bit is required because tasks are not *reentrant*: the same task cannot occur twice in a nested chain of tasks. (It is obvious that a task cannot be reentrant — after all, it stores its data in a fixed buffer, namely the TSS, rather than on a stack!) Trying to execute a task whose busy bit is set results in a general-protection fault.

There is another kind of descriptor associated with tasks, namely the *task gate*. The format of a task gate is illustrated in Figure 18.7. A task gate is "pointed" to a task by initializing its selector field to contain a TSS selector.

Having examined the general structures associated with multitasking, we must look at the mechanisms used to produce task switches. These are easily explained: a task switch can be accomplished by a **jmp** or **call** instruction that has a TSS descriptor or a task gate as its target, or by an exception or interrupt that references a task gate in the IDT, or by an **iret** instruction.

The alternatives given in the last paragraph show that the **jmp**, **call**, **int**, and **iret** instructions are *overloaded*, in the sense that they have different meanings depending on the context. It is clear how the assembler knows that a **jmp**, **int**, or **call** should result in a task switch: precisely when the target is a TSS descriptor or task gate. But it may seem mysterious how the machine knows whether an **iret** should be interpreted in the old-fashioned procedure sense, or as a request for a task switch. The answer is that yet another parameter is needed to make this determination. The **eflags** register contains a bit called the *nested task bit*, or *NT*. As the name implies, NT is set if the presently executing task is nested. When NT is set, the microprocessor assumes that an **iret** is a request for a task switch, and so switches to the task pointed to by the back link of the current task.

Two of the conclusions reached in the previous paragraphs are worth reiterating:

- No matter whether a task switch was invoked by a **call**, a **jmp**, an **int**, or a hardware interrupt or exception, the correct way to return to the interrupted task is by means of an **iret**.

- When control returns to a task, execution always recommences at the instruction immediately beyond the point at which it was interrupted.

The only remaining multitasking issue requiring elaboration is how to start the whole process. When the first task switch is made, the microprocessor requires a TSS in which to store the current execution environment. It is frequently convenient to provide a "dummy" TSS to play this role. Of course, as is the case in our examples, it may also be convenient to return to the initial task at the end of multitasking. A system register, named the *task register*, holds the TSS selector for the task presently in control. The task register is automatically updated on each task switch, but it must be explicitly initialized to the initial task. This is accomplished using the **ltr** (*load task register*) instruction.

Our protected-mode kernel already illustrates some multitasking features, because we implemented **int 30H** (the remapped timer interrupt) as a separate task. First, consider the multitasking aspects of INTMOD.ASM (Figure 18.8):

Line 23. The **int 30H** entry in the IDT is defined as a task gate. The value of the type, namely 05H, is correct, as can be seen from Figure 18.7.

Lines 156-161. *Handler30h* is designed as a separate task, which explains the bizarre line 161. A given call to the handler terminates with the **iret** on line 160. Consequently, on the next return to the interrupt handler, execution begins on line 161 and the **jmp** instruction immediately transfers control to the ʼ ʼntry point of the code.

Next, look at STRTMOD1.ASM (Figure 18.11):

Lines 35-36. These are minimal-length TSS descriptors for the initial task, *mTsk*, and the **int 30H** handler task, *int30Tsk*.

Lines 46-47. The actual TSSs.

Lines 97-98. Initializing the TSS descriptor bases.

Line 101. Initializing the selector field in the **int 30h** task gate.

Lines 104-106. Using the *initTask* macro from Figure 18.14 to initialize the essential fields in *int30Tsk*.

Lines 140-141. Initializing the task register to point to *mTsk*.

SECTION 7 PRIVILEGE CHECKING

The **80286/80386** recognizes four *privilege levels* at which code or data can be defined. These levels are referred to as Level 0, Level 1, Level 2, and Level 3, and can be visualized diagrammatically as in Figure 18.15. Because diagrams of this kind are universally used to illustrate privilege mechanisms, the levels are also referred to as Ring0 through Ring3. Operating systems are set up so that the most trusted code — the operating system code itself, for example — runs at Level 0, and increasing level corresponds to decreasing trustworthiness of the code. Generally, the user programs in a multitasking system run at Level 3. As we indicated earlier, operating systems need not use all four available privilege levels. It is somewhat unfortunate that, numerically speaking, the direction of increasing privilege is the direction of decreasing privilege level. To avoid potential confusion, we will consistently use the terms "more privileged" and "less privileged" in our discussions, rather than the synonymous "having lower privilege level" and "having higher privilege level."

Figure 18.15 also shows the basic restrictions on access to code and data imposed by processors using this approach to protection:

- Code executing at a given privilege level can only call code that is equally privileged or more privileged. In other words, it is only legal to "call in" from a given ring.

- Code executing at a given privilege level can only address data that are equally privileged or less privileged. That is, it is only legal to "address out" from a given ring.

These statements, especially the second, require considerable amplification.

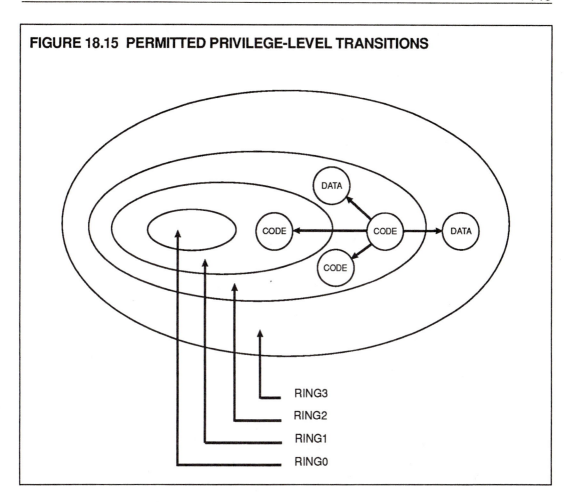

FIGURE 18.15 PERMITTED PRIVILEGE-LEVEL TRANSITIONS

In the definitions of selectors and descriptors, we have already encountered privilege levels but have glossed over the precise definitions until now. The **80286/80386** actually keeps track of three different measures of privilege:

- The DPL, or *descriptor privilege level*, is defined as part of each descriptor. It should be viewed as the "official" privilege level associated with that object.

- The RPL, or *requestor's privilege level*, is defined in the segment selector. (See Figure 18.3.) As the name suggests, it is supposed to measure the privilege level of the code requesting access to some resource. Its purpose may seem somewhat mysterious since the requestor can seemingly set the RPL to any desired value (zero, for example) before loading the selector. As we will see later, the RPL is primarily used by the operating system. For the moment, the reader should always assume that it has value zero, in which case it actually has no effect in privilege computations.

- The CPL, or *current privilege level*, is the privilege level of the presently executing code. With one exception, which we will discuss later, the CPL is equal to the DPL of the code segment containing the current code. When a new selector is loaded into **cs**, the microprocessor always updates the RPL field to contain the new value of CPL.

Checks of privilege level are made by the microprocessor only when a selector is loaded into a segment register. This happens when a segment register addresses a data segment or stack for the first time, when an intersegment **call**, **jmp**, **int**, hardware interrupt or exception, **ret**, or **iret** occurs, or as part of a task switch.

The rules governing all these transitions are shown in Figure 18.16. A quick survey of these rules corroborates the points we have already made: if RPL is assumed to have value zero (as we are presently recommending), then it has no effect in determining the legality of transitions; data can only be addressed in the current ring, or a less privileged one; and code transfers are legal only if the target resides in the current ring or in a more privileged one. In these statements, the current ring means the ring corresponding to the value of CPL.

We will now give a more careful analysis of Figure 18.16, with explanations of why some of these privilege rules are set up as they are:

1. The microprocessor allows no flexibility in privilege level when **ss** is loaded: the DPL of the new selector must match the current CPL. Of course, this explains why a TSS must maintain separate stacks for each privilege level that will be used. Incidentally, this is the one circumstance in which our primitive convention of always setting RPL = 0 can cause trouble, since RPL must also agree with the target DPL.

2. This rule is entirely reasonable. Code in a given ring should not have direct access to data from a more privileged ring, and this restriction prohibits such access.

3. The configuration given here should perhaps be viewed as the "default" behavior of the **80286/80386**: code in a given ring can only access code lying in the same ring. Checking through the remainder of the table shows that this rule can be broken only through the use of certain special devices. To see why this rule must be breakable, just think in terms of **MS-DOS** and, say, **int 21H**, which contains operating system code, and so should be in Ring0. But such operating system services must be available to programs that run in any ring. Of course, rather than allowing calls between rings, it is feasible to maintain four copies of the operating system services, one for each ring, but this would be a rather clumsy solution.

4. The first mechanism allowing *interlevel* **calls** or **jmps** is the *conforming segment*. Of course, a conforming segment means one with the conforming bit set in its segment descriptor. The significance of a conforming segment is that it has no intrinsic privilege level — it conforms to the level of its caller. In other words, code from a conforming segment executes with the same CPL as its caller. Earlier, we stated that the CPL always equals the DPL of the executing segment, with one exception, and this is the exception. Note that, if there is a change, the CPL must decrease to match the caller, and so we still have CPL ≤ DPL.

5. As we have already seen, the call gate gives another mechanism for performing interlevel jumps and calls. The name *gate* is well chosen because a call gate limits the callers allowed through, because only callers who are at least as privileged as the gate itself can use it. When a call gate is used as the target of a **jmp** instruction, the target privilege level cannot change.

FIGURE 18.16 PRIVILEGE-LEVEL CHECKS ON 80286/80386

	OPERATION	NECESSARY CONDITIONS	REMARKS
1.	Loading ss	CPL = RPL = DPL(targetSeg)	
2.	Loading ds,es,fs,or gs	Max{ CPL, RPL } <= DPL(targetSeg)	
3.	Jmp or call to a non-conforming executable segment	DPL(targetSeg) <= RPL DPL(targetSeg) = CPL	
4.	Jmp or call to a conforming executable segment	DPL(targetSeg) <= CPL	Target inherits CPL of caller; stack not copied even if CPL changed
5.	Jmp through a call gate to a non-conforming segment	max{ CPL, RPL } <= DPL(gateDesc) and DPL(targetSeg) = CPL	
6.	Call through a call gate to a non-conforming segment or call or jmp to a conforming segment	max{ CPL, RPL } <= DPL(gateDesc) and DPL(targetSeg) <= CPL	Stack copied if targetSeg non-conforming and CPL changed
7.	Far return	CPL(Caller)>= CPL	CPL(Caller) can be found in RPL of popped cs
8.	Task switch through TSS descriptor using jmp or call	max{ CPL, RPL } <= DPL(TSSDesc)	CPLs of tasks are independent
9.	Task switch through gate descriptor using jmp or call	max{ CPL, RPL } <= DPL(gateDesc)	DPL(TSSDesc) not used; CPLs of tasks independent
10.	Task switch using iret	None	
11.	Int instruction using trap or interrupt gate	CPL <= DPL(gateDesc) and DPL(targetSeg) <= CPL	
12.	Int instruction using task gate	CPL <= DPL(gateDesc)	
13.	Hardware interrupt or exception using trap or interrupt gate	DPL(targetSeg) <= CPL	
14.	Hardware interrupt or exception using task gate	None	

6. When a call gate is used as the target of a **call** instruction, then the privilege level *can* change but, as always, only in the more privileged direction. Call gates have an important advantage over conforming segments in implementing interlevel calls: a call gate allows entrance only at a specific entry point in the called code, rather than allowing the blanket access associated with a conforming segment. Of course, this is vital in the case of operating system code where, at most, a client should be given access to a few, well-defined operating system procedures.

Interlevel calls have another interesting facet. An interlevel call must transfer control from less privileged to more privileged code and so, if only the standard stack methodology were used, the more privileged code would depend on the stack of the less privileged code to maintain its parameters and return address. This is considered so undesirable that, as part of any interlevel call, the operating system copies the appropriate parts of the caller's stack to a new stack of the same privilege level as the called code. Of course, this means that the program must supply such stacks, and explains the ESP0, SS0, ... fields in the TSS. In particular, a special Level 3 stack is never needed and, in fact, the TSS structure does not even provide for one. If a program will make interlevel calls, then it must set up a stack for each of the target privilege levels, and store these stack locations in the TSS. It is only necessary to set up stacks for those levels that actually appear as interlevel targets. If a program uses several TSSs, then each must be endowed with the stacks it needs (although the stacks for different TSSs need not be distinct).

The data packet copied from stack to stack includes the return address and the number of parameters specified in the DWORD COUNT field of the call gate descriptor. (See Figure 18.7.) In the 16-bit case, the DWORD COUNT field contains the number of 16-bit words to be copied. A number of technicalities enter here that the interested reader should pursue in [14]. For example, the DWORD COUNT field is only 5 bits wide and so allows a maximum parameter count of 31. In the rare cases when this is insufficient, something else must be done.

7. Basically, the privilege check involved in a **FAR** return is just the inverse to that for a **call**. Since it is only possible to "call in," it is only legal to "return out." To enforce this rule, the microprocessor must be able to recover the caller's CPL, and it can do so because it was stored in the **cs** value that was pushed as part of the return address. The obvious privilege condition translates into the formula shown in 7 of Figure 18.16.

The reader may have wondered about the prohibition against "calling out." At first blush, it would seem that granting programs the ability to call less privileged code could have no dire consequences. However, our discussion of the **ret** instruction shows why this would be a dangerous practice. If it were legal to "call out," then it would necessarily be legal to "return in." But it is always possible to concoct a "reverse" call by pushing the target address onto the stack and performing a **ret**. If a "return in" were legal, programs of malicious or inquisitive intent could use this mechanism to gain access to the operating system at arbitrary entry points, rather than being restricted to those offered by call gates.

Here is a final interesting aspect of the interlevel return protocol. The more privileged code may have been using the segment registers to manipulate privileged data and may have (carelessly) left the corresponding selectors in the registers. Knowing these selectors could (in principle) provide the less privileged code with entry points to forbidden segments. To eliminate this possibility, as part of the return protocol from an interlevel transition the microprocessor always zeros segment registers containing selectors that are more privileged than the caller.

8. When a task switch references a TSS descriptor directly, only the DPL of the descriptor is used in the privilege check. The TSS descriptor is used in exactly the same way as a gate is used, namely its DPL represents a threshold level and only callers at least that privileged can use it. In general, there is no relationship between the CPL of the caller and the CPL of the target.

9. A problem with using the TSS descriptor for task switching is that it is too democratic: it must be in the GDT, and any caller who is privileged enough can use it. Task gates introduce another level of indirection into the task-switching process. The TSS descriptor can be in Ring0, consequently most callers will not be able to effect a task switch. To allow less privileged code in a given task to switch to this task, just give this code access to a task gate for the given task (say, in an LDT) and be sure that the privilege level of this gate is low enough. This scheme works because the DPL of the TSS descriptor is not consulted in this kind of task switch.

10. Since task switches place no restrictions on the CPLs of the caller and the callee, the **iret** need do no checking.

11. A software **int** (or **into**) through a trap or interrupt gate works just like a **call** through a call gate, except that the value of the RPL is not considered.

12. Again, a software **int** (or **into**) using a task gate is like any other task switch through a task gate, except that RPL is ignored.

13. This rule is analogous to number 11, except that, by any reasonable interpretation, the "caller" resides in Ring0, and so the first condition is automatically satisfied.

14. Likewise, this rule is the analog of number 12.

Figure 18.17 shows illustrates the privilege-checking operations occurring during calls to segment selectors or through gates.

An operating system must sometimes manipulate privilege mechanisms in somewhat indirect ways. We will now present two examples of this kind.

As a first example, consider a situation in which the operating system must call code provided by a less privileged program. One context in which this arises is when the operating system allows an application to supply a custom interrupt handler. Such a call is of the forbidden "call out" species. One way that an operating system can solve this problem is to perform a "reverse call" as we described it previously (by preparing the stack and making a **FAR** return). The called procedure can then return control to the operating system by means of a call gate.

Our second example relates to a possible method that might be used to breach the protection scheme. First, we will give an example of the potential difficulty, and then state the problem in general. Most operating systems contain procedures that will send data to a

FIGURE 18.17 EXAMPLES OF PRIVILEGE CHECKING

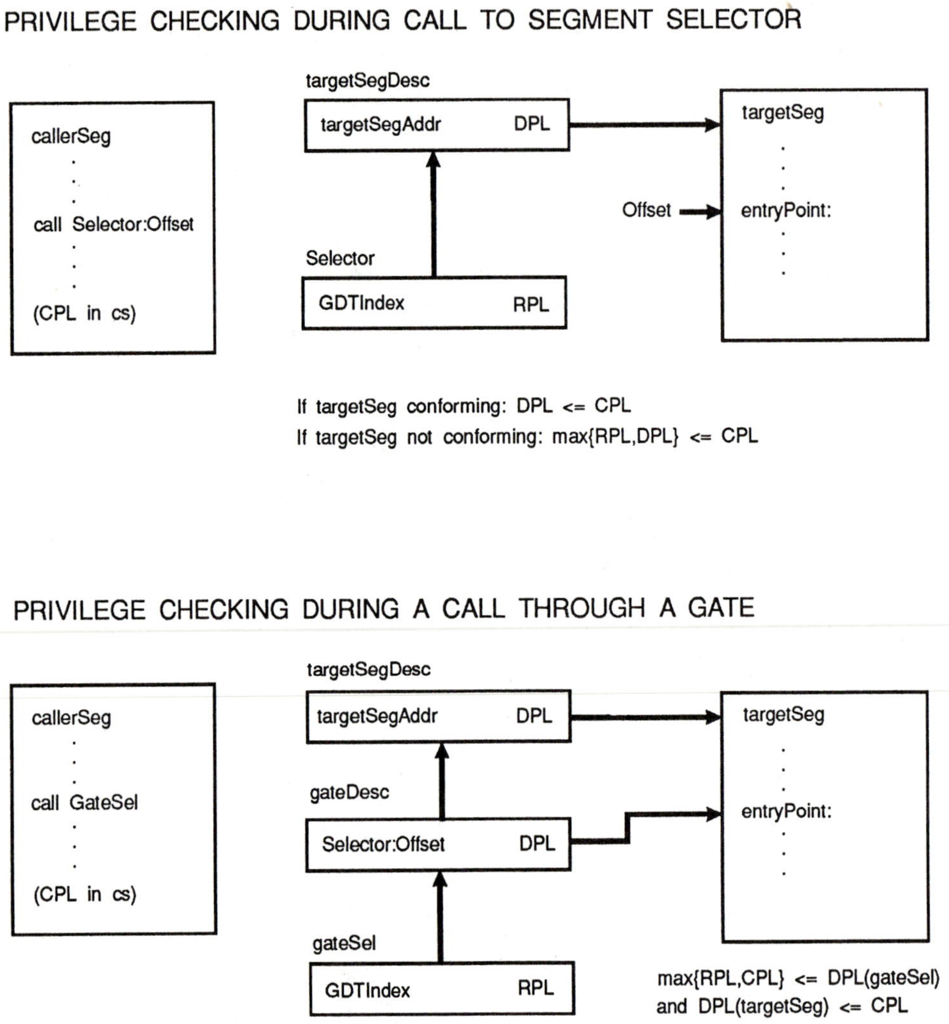
PRIVILEGE CHECKING DURING CALL TO SEGMENT SELECTOR
targetSegDesc
callerSeg
call Selector:Offset
(CPL in cs)
targetSegAddr
DPL
Selector
GDTIndex
RPL
Offset
targetSeg
entryPoint:
If targetSeg conforming: DPL <= CPL
If targetSeg not conforming: max{RPL,DPL} <= CPL
PRIVILEGE CHECKING DURING A CALL THROUGH A GATE
targetSegDesc
callerSeg
call GateSel
(CPL in cs)
targetSegAddr
DPL
gateDesc
Selector:Offset
DPL
gateSel
GDTIndex
RPL
targetSeg
entryPoint:
max{RPL,CPL} <= DPL(gateSel)
and DPL(targetSeg) <= CPL

disk file. Usually, such a procedure will require, as parameters, a pointer to the data to be written and various other obvious information items. Such a write procedure will almost definitely operate in Ring0, so that it can be called by code in all rings. Now suppose that the write procedure is called by Ring3 code and passed a pointer to a block of Ring0 data. And how might Ring3 code find a valid Ring0 data pointer? This could happen at least two ways. It might be an accident — a programming error produced an incorrect pointer value that just happened to point to a bona fide Ring0 data address. Alternately, it might result from a systematic search. Various values for the selector could be tried. For each selector value, an offset of zero is a good starting point. Whatever the origin of the pointer, this scenario results in a block of supposedly protected information being copied to the disk file.

It is easy to state the problem in general. A pointer was passed from less privileged to more privileged code, and the more privileged code was able to use this pointer in a manner that would have been forbidden to the less privileged code. This potential loophole in a protection scheme is known by various names, such as the *Trojan horse problem*. The **80286/80386** provides a very efficient solution to it, and this solution uses the RPL in a vital way.

In our example, the obvious thing to do is to tag the write request as originating with Ring3 code. Then, even though the write procedure that ultimately executes the request is in Ring0, access to the Ring0 data could be denied. The RPL field of the selector is used to tag the originator of the request, which explains the name *requestor's privilege level*.

The precise mechanism used to keep the RPL field correctly updated relies on the **arpl** (*adjust requestor's privilege level*) instruction. The **arpl** instruction has the syntax

```
arpl    Dest, Source
```

where *Dest* is a 16-bit register or memory reference and *Source* is a 16-bit register. Both *Dest* and *Source* should be selectors, and the effect of the instruction is to set the RPL of *Dest* to the maximum of the RPLs of *Dest* and *Source*. If the RPL of *Dest* is actually modified, then ZF is set; otherwise, it is cleared.

In our example, **arpl** could be used as follows:

```
;Calling code in Ring3
        .
        .
    ;push various parameters
    push      dataSel:dataOff  ;push a pointer to the data to write
    call      ring0WriteProc
        .
        .
;Validation code in Ring0:
        .
        .
    mov   ax, [bp+4]    ;move RPL = 3 of caller's cs into ax
    arpl  [bp+6],ax     ;stamp dataSel with caller's RPL= 3
    ;code to access dataSel:dataOff
        .
        .
```

At this point, *dataSel:dataOff* can be legally accessed only if

```
        max { CPL, RPL} <= DPL of segment pointed to by dataSel
```

If, as we are assuming, CPL = DPL = 0 and RPL = 3, this condition fails and a general-protection fault results.

This example also suggests the need for instructions that perform additional legality checks. Instead of blindly trying to dereference the pointer and risking a general-protection fault, the write procedure should first check whether such dereferencing is legal, and, if not, abort the caller's program with a stern message.

The instructions

```
verr   Operand
```

and

```
verw   Operand
```

facilitate such checking. **Verr** (*verify for reading*) takes a selector as parameter and determines whether a read from the segment pointed to by that selector is legal in the current context. If the answer is yes, it sets ZF, and clears it in the contrary case. **Verw** (*verify for writing*) is completely analogous.

One last check is required to ensure that a pointer can be legally dereferenced — its offset must be small enough to refer to data lying entirely within the segment. The instruction **lsl** (*load segment limit*) can be used to verify this condition. Its syntax is

```
lsl   Dest,  Source
```

where *Dest* is a register and *Source* is a register or memory reference. *Source* should contain a selector; the value of the limit will be returned in *Dest*. *Dest* and *Source* should have the same size, 16 bits or 32 bits, where the 32-size is needed to hold large **80386** segment limits, since the instruction always records the limit in byte-granular form. One interesting sidelight of **lsl** is that it cannot be used to elicit forbidden information from the machine. Unless *Source* is legally accessible from the present segment, i.e.,

```
max {CPL, RPL} <= DPL(Source)
```

the instruction leaves Dest unchanged and clears ZF to signal failure.

These checks on the correctness of pointers passed by less trustworthy code are usually called *pointer validation*, and are an important part of many operating system procedures. The **80386** makes pointer validation speedy and relatively painless by providing the correct machine instructions for the task, rather than forcing programs to incorporate cumbersome procedures to do the checking.

Our example shows how **arpl** stamps a pointer when a single code transfer is used. But, obviously, if **arpl** is used after each call, a pointer can be tracked through any number of control transfers, and will always be limited by the CPL of its originator.

The last aspect of privilege checking that we will consider is input/output. We have already made the point that indiscriminate use of the **in** and **out** instructions in a multitasking environment cannot be tolerated. The **80386** offers two different mechanisms to control access to such instructions.

First, the instructions **in, out, ins, outs, cli,** and **sti** are designated as *sensitive*, and the **eflags** register contains a two-bit field called IOPL. A sensitive instruction can be legally executed only if CPL ≤ IOPL. In other words, IOPL contains a threshold privilege level, and only code that is at least that privileged can use sensitive instructions. Since each task has its own copy of **eflags**, some tasks can be granted permission to use sensitive instructions while others are denied this permission.

The second method used to control input/output is more specific, since it may give tasks the capacity to use particular i/o ports, while forbidding them the use of others. If a task attempts to use an **in, out, ins,** or **outs** instruction, the microprocessor first checks whether CPL ≤ IOPL and, if so, grants permission without checking further. But if this test fails, the microprocessor examines the *i/o permission map* for the task. The i/o permission map is an optional item appearing in the TSS. If present, it must occur at the end of the TSS and its beginning offset must be recorded in the I/O MAP BASE field of the TSS. Since it extends to the end of the TSS, its final offset equals the value of the TSS limit. The i/o permission map is interpreted as a bit field, where bit k being clear means that the task can legally access i/o port number k, and bit k being set has the opposite meaning. In principle, the i/o permission map may need to be as long as 8K bytes but, in practice, this is usually unnecessary since the **80386** uses the convention that any bit position not occurring in the map has value 1. Consequently, it is only necessary to include a map containing positions for those ports that will actually be accessed.

As an example, suppose we want to give a task access to the first 100H ports. The i/o permission map should then be 20H bytes long, with each byte having value 0. Consequently, the TSS limit value should equal I/O MAP BASE + 1FH.

As a final point, consider the role of the **popf** instruction in these proceedings. First, it would seem that a task could easily subvert this protection mechanism by pushing an appropriate new value for **eflags** with IOPL = 3 onto the stack and then performing a **popf**. A task can indeed perform these operations, but the **80386 popf** instruction is designed so that IOPL will remain unchanged *unless* CPL = 0. In other words, only Ring0 code can change IOPL. If less privileged code attempts to change IOPL, it does not produce a fault — IOPL just remains unchanged. In a similar vein, a program could attempt to change IF by using **popf**. Again, there will be no effect unless the program is privileged enough. In this case, the requirement is not that the code be in Ring0, but only that CPL ≤ IOPL.

The reader will find more detailed information on the privilege-checking mechanisms in [14].

SECTION 8 ADDING MULTITASKING TO THE PROTECTED-MODE KERNEL

Using the basic principles laid out in Section 7, it is a fairly straightforward matter to add limited multitasking capabilities to our kernel. We have restricted the kernel to running two tasks simultaneously, although it is easy enough to increase this limit. In order to keep the programs as interactive as possible, task switching is controlled from the keyboard. The choice of keys is totally arbitrary: the '[' key switches between the two tasks and the ESCAPE key terminates multitasking and returns control to **MS-DOS**. This setup can be easily modified so that it uses the more traditional *preemptive time-slicing* approach, where each task is allotted a certain period of time before control automatically passes to another task. In the exercises, we outline a method for making this modification.

To minimize the complexity, we did not incorporate privilege levels into the multitasking code. All code and data are used with RPL = DPL = 0.

The INTMOD and VIDMOD modules of Section 5 will be used unchanged, although we will need to take over **int 30H** (the remapped timer interrupt) and replace it with a *multitasking dispatcher*, i.e., with the code that actually performs the task switches.

Because of our thorough discussion of task switching in Section 7, most of the code in the new start module, named STRTMOD2.ASM and shown in Figure 18.18, should seem entirely reasonable. The main item requiring explanation is the dispatcher. Here are some remarks on Figure 18.18:

Lines 38-41. These are descriptors for minimal length TSSs. Notice that *tsk2Desc* is slightly different from the others — its busy bit has value 1. (See Figure 18.13.) This difference will be explained when we discuss the dispatcher.

Lines 63-66. The declarations of the TSSs.

Lines 66-68. To make the screen displays as clear as possible, we have arranged for each task to have its own screen colors. In addition, each task "remembers" where it was when it last had control of the machine, and continues writing to the screen where it left off. This requires that each task have its own set of screen variables {*rowNo*, *colNo*, *charPos*}, and these are most conveniently stored in a structure, which we call *scrVars*. This structure template and the macros controlling it are in PROT.MAC. The template and macros (headers only) are shown in Figure 18.19. Of course, each task should really save its entire screen, and restore it when it regains control. In an exercise, we invite the reader implement such an improvement, using an extension of the task's TSS to store the screen and the screen variables.

Lines 85-88. Although it is not really necessary, one of our task switches uses a jump to a task gate, just for purposes of illustration.

Lines 128-144. Here we are using the *initTask* macro to initialize the critical fields of the TSSs. We are letting them all use the same stack, but are assigning them different initial **esp** values, so that they use different stack areas. Lines 138-141 are especially significant: we are substituting a new task for **int 30H**, with entry point *newHandler30h*. In other words, we are taking over this interrupt and replacing our originally supplied handler with a new one.

Lines 199-204. Here we make the first stack switch, by jumping through a task gate. We also switch the screen parameters. The task register has been initialized to point to *mTsk* (lines 196-197), and so the current task information is stored in the TSS for *mTsk*.

Line 206. When control ultimately returns to *mTsk*, execution will begin where it left off, i.e., at this location in the code. We proceed to restore the screen and make an orderly exit.

Lines 237-274. Since **int 30H** is the timer interrupt, it occurs about 18 times per second. Our replacement handler performs these operations:

- Checks the keyboard buffer to find whether a keypress has arrived. It ignores all keypresses except '[' and ESCAPE.

- If it finds that ESCAPE has been pressed, it jumps to *mTsk* (line 246). This transfers control to line 206, thereby effectively aborting the program.

- If '[' has been pressed, it invokes a task switch, from whichever of *Task1* and *Task2* is active to the one that is inactive.

FIGURE 18.18 START MODULE FOR MULTITASKING KERNEL

```
 1   TITLE strtMod2.asm
 2
 3   .XCREF
 4   .SALL
 5   INCLUDE console.mac
 6   INCLUDE prot.mac
 7   .386P
 8
 9   PUBLIC   abortProgram
10
11   ;===========================================================================
12
13   STACK SEGMENT USE16 PARA  STACK 'STACK'
14
15       DB   1000h DUP(?)
16
17   STACK ENDS
18
19   ;===========================================================================
20
21   _DATA SEGMENT USE16 WORD PUBLIC 'DATA'
22
23       EXTRN                idtLimit:WORD, idtLinAddr:DWORD, idtrData:FWORD
24       EXTRN                kbBuffer:BYTE, tskGt30:QWORD
25       EXTRN                rowNo:DWORD, colNo:DWORD, charPos:DWORD
26
27   ;###########################################################################
28   ;GLOBAL DESCRIPTOR TABLE                                                  ;#
29                                                                            ;#
30   GDT      LABEL   WORD                                                    ;#
31                                                                            ;#
32   Dummy    segDesc < 0000h, 0000h, 00h, PDT<0,0,0>,  GXOAL<0,0,0,0,0>,00h> ;#
33   codeDesc segDesc <0ffffh,      ,    , PDT<1,0,1ah>,GXOAL<0,0,0,0,0>,00h> ;#
34   stakDesc segDesc <0ffffh,      ,    , PDT<1,0,12h>,GXOAL<0,0,0,0,0>,00h> ;#
35   smlDDesc segDesc <0ffffh,      ,    , PDT<1,0,12h>,GXOAL<0,0,0,0,0>,00h> ;#
36   vidDesc  segDesc <SCRLIM, 8000h, 0bh, PDT<1,0,12h>,GXOAL<0,0,0,0,0>,00h> ;#
37                                                                            ;#
38   mTskDesc segDesc <   103,      ,    , PDT<1,0,09h>,GXOAL<0,0,0,0,0>,00h> ;#
39   tsk1Desc segDesc <   103,      ,    , PDT<1,0,09h>,GXOAL<0,0,0,0,0>,00h> ;#
40   tsk2Desc segDesc <   103,      ,    , PDT<1,0,0bh>,GXOAL<0,0,0,0,0>,00h> ;#
41   int30Desc segDesc <   103,      ,    , PDT<1,0,09h>,GXOAL<0,0,0,0,0>,00h> ;#
42                                                                            ;#
43   tsk1Gate gateDesc <NOTUSED, tsk1Desc-GDT, NOTUSED, PDT<1,0,05h>, NOTUSED> ;#
44                                                                            ;#
45   gdtrData             LABEL   FWORD               ;for lgdt              ;#
46       GDTLimit         DW      $ - GDT - 1                                ;#
47       GDTLinAddr       LABEL   DWORD                                      ;#
48                        DW      GDT                                        ;#
49                        DW      0                                          ;#
50                                                                            ;#
51   ;###########################################################################
52
53       protModeAddr    LABEL   DWORD               ;addresses for jumps to and
54           DW  protMode                            ;   from protected mode
55           DW  codeDesc-GDT
```

Figure 18.18 cont.

```
 56
 57     realModeaddr    LABEL    DWORD
 58         DW   realMode
 59         DW   _TEXT
 60
 61     mTsk          TSS      <>              ;allocate space for instances
 62     Tsk1          TSS      <>              ;  of STRUC TSS
 63     Tsk2          TSS      <>
 64     int30Tsk      TSS      <>
 65
 66     scrVars0    scrVars  <>                ;allocate space for instances
 67     scrVars1    scrVars  <>                ;  of STRUC scrVars
 68     scrVars2    scrVars  <>
 69
 70     tsk1Addr    LABEL    DWORD             ;addresses for jumping to tasks
 71
 72         tsk1Offset    DW    NOTUSED
 73         tsk1Selector  DW    tsk1Desc - GDT
 74
 75     tsk2Addr  LABEL    DWORD
 76
 77         tsk2Offset    DW    NOTUSED
 78         tsk2Selector  DW    tsk2Desc - GDT
 79
 80   mTskAddr  LABEL    DWORD
 81
 82         mTskOffset    DW    NOTUSED
 83         taskSelector  DW    mTskDesc - GDT
 84
 85     tsk1GateAddr    LABEL    DWORD         ;address for jumping to a
 86                                           ;  task through a task gate
 87                     DW    NOTUSED
 88                     DW    tsk1Gate - GDT
 89
 90     strBuf      DB      6 DUP(?)           ;to hold alphanumeric form
 91                                           ;  of 16-bit integer
 92 _DATA ENDS
 93
 94 ;==========================================================================
 95
 96 realSeg   SEGMENT USE16 WORD
 97
 98     ASSUME cs:realSeg
 99
100 Start:
101
102     jmp   FAR PTR Begin                    ;jump to _TEXT
103
104 dosExit:                                   ;target of far jump back from
105                                            ;  _TEXT
106     mov   ax, 4c00h
107     int   21h
108
109 realSeg   ENDS
110
111 ;==========================================================================
```

```
112
113    _TEXT SEGMENT USE16 WORD PUBLIC 'CODE'
114
115        EXTRN       Task1:NEAR, Task2:NEAR
116
117        ASSUME cs:_TEXT, ds:_DATA, ss:STACK
118
119    Begin:
120
121        mov     ax, _DATA
122        mov     ds, ax
123        mov     ax, SCRBAS              ;point gs to video buffer
124        mov     gs, ax                 ;  in real-mode sense
125
126        pushRegs   ds, es, fs, gs, ss     ;save segment registers
127
128        ;Initialize the Task1 TSS
129        initTask   Tsk1,<codeDesc-GDT>, <smlDDesc-GDT>,<smlDDesc-GDT>,\
130                   <smlDDesc-GDT>, <vidDesc-GDT>, <stakDesc-GDT>,\
131                   <OFFSET Task1>, 100h
132
133        ;Initialize the Task2 TSS
134        initTask   Tsk2,<codeDesc-GDT>, <smlDDesc-GDT>,<smlDDesc-GDT>,\
135                   <smlDDesc-GDT>, <vidDesc-GDT>, <stakDesc-GDT>,\
136                   <OFFSET Task2>, 200h
137
138        ;Initialize the int30h TSS
139        initTask   int30Tsk,<codeDesc-GDT>, <smlDDesc-GDT>,<smlDDesc-GDT>,\
140                   <smlDDesc-GDT>, <vidDesc-GDT>, <stakDesc-GDT>,\
141                   <OFFSET newHandler30h>, 300h
142
143        ;Initialize selector for int30h task gate
144        mov     tskGt30.gdSel, int30Desc - GDT
145
146
147        ;Set descriptor base addresses
148        setDescBase  codeDesc, 0, cs
149        setDescBase  stakDesc, 0, ss
150        setDescBase  smlDDesc, 0, ds
151        setDescBase  tsk1Desc, <OFFSET Tsk1>, ds
152        setDescBase  tsk2Desc, <OFFSET Tsk2>, ds
153        setDescBase  mTskDesc, <OFFSET mTsk>, ds
154        setDescBase  int30Desc, <OFFSET int30Tsk>, ds
155
156        ;Fix up linear address for gdtr
157
158        mov     ax, ds
159        movzx   eax, ax
160        shl     eax, 4
161        add     GDTLinAddr, eax
162        lgdt    gdtrData                   ;load gdtr
163
164        cli                                ;turn off all
165        turnNMI    OFF                     ;  interrupts
166
167        ;Fix up linear address for the idtr
168        add     idtLinAddr, eax
169        lidt    idtrData                   ;load idtr
170
```

Figure 18.18 cont.

```
171    ;********ENTER PROTECTED MODE********************************************
172
173        mov     eax, cr0
174        or      eax, 01             ;turn on protection
175        mov     cr0, eax            ; enable  bit
176
177        jmp     protModeAddr        ;far jump flushes prefetch
178                                    ; queue and initializes cs
179    protMode:
180
181        mov     ax, vidDesc-GDT     ;point the segment registers
182        mov     gs, ax              ; to the correct segments in
183                                    ;   the protected-mode sense
184        mov     ax, smlDDesc-GDT
185        mov     ds, ax
186        mov     fs, ax
187        mov     es, ax
188        mov     ax, stakDesc-GDT
189        mov     ss, ax
190
191        remapInts 1, 30h            ;remap maskable interrupt
192        remapInts 2, 38h            ;  vectors and turn on
193        sti                         ;    all interrupts
194        turnNMI    ON
195
196        mov     ax, mTskDesc - GDT  ;load the mTsk selector
197        ltr     ax                  ;  into the task register
198
199        clrScr  57h                 ;change screen to garish color
200        storeScrData    scrVars0    ;store main screen parameters
201        restoreScrData scrVars1     ;make screen parameters zero
202        jmp     tsk1GateAddr        ;jump to Task1 through a
203                                    ; task gate
204    abortProgram:
205
206        restoreScrData   scrVars0   ;restore main screen parameters
207        clrScr  07h                 ;  and more reasonable colors
208        cli                         ;turn off all
209        turnNMI    OFF                  interrupts
210
211    ;********LEAVE PROTECTED MODE********************************************
212
213        mov     eax, cr0
214        and     eax, NOT 1          ;disable protection by turning
215        mov     cr0, eax            ; off PE bit
216
217        jmp     realModeaddr        ;far jump flushes prefetch
218                                    ; queue and initializes cs
219    realMode:
220
221        mov     idtLimit, 3ffh      ;load idtr with correct
222        mov     idtLinAddr, 0       ; parameters for real-
223        lidt    idtrData            ;   mode interrupt table
224
225        popRegs                     ;restore segment registers
226
```

```
227          remapInts 1, 08h                    ;remap maskable interrupt
228          remapInts 2, 70h                    ;   vectors to their default
229          turnNMI     ON                      ;      values and turn on
230          sti                                 ;         all interrupts
231
232      jmp  FAR PTR   dosExit                  ;jump to realSeg
233
234  ;-------------------------------------------------------------------------
235
236  ;This is our multitasking dispatcher
237  newHandler30h:
238
239          mov     al, 20h                     ;acknowledgement to PIC
240          out     20h, al
241
242          cmp     kbBuffer, ESCAPE            ;check for ESCAPE character
243          jne     @F                          ;if equal, terminate
244          jmp     mTskAddr
245
246  @@:
247
248          cmp     kbBuffer, '['              ;check for '['
249          jne     Done
250
251          cmp     int30Tsk.backLink, tsk1Desc - GDT
252          je      switchTo2
253
254          ;Should switch to task 1
255          storeScrData    scrVars2
256          restoreScrData scrVars1
257          clrScr  57h
258          mov     int30Tsk.backLink, tsk1Desc - GDT
259          jmp     Done
260
261  switchTo2:
262
263          storeScrData    scrVars1
264          restoreScrData scrVars2
265          clrScr  75h
266          mov     int30Tsk.backLink, tsk2Desc - GDT
267
268  Done:
269
270          mov     kbBuffer, 0
271
272          iret
273          jmp     newHandler30h              ;every call to the handler after
274                                             ;  the first one comes here
275  ;-------------------------------------------------------------------------
276
277  _TEXT ENDS
278
279  ;=========================================================================
280
281      END     Start
```

FIGURE 18.19 EXCERPT 6 FROM PROT.MAC

```
 1   scrVars    STRUC
 2
 3   Row    DD    ?
 4   Col    DD    ?
 5   Pos    DD    ?
 6
 7   scrVars    ENDS
 8
 9   ;-------------------------------------------------------------------
10
11   COMMENT      #    MACRO HEADER
12   MACRO NAME:       storeScrData
13   PURPOSE:          Stores copies of rowNo, colNo, and charPos that are local
14                     to a task; uses copy of structure scrVars for the storage.
15   CALLED AS:        storeScrData scrVarStruct.
16   RETURNS:     #    Nothing.
17
18   ;-------------------------------------------------------------------
19
20   COMMENT      #    MACRO HEADER
21   MACRO NAME:       retoreScrData
22   PURPOSE:          Restores copies of rowNo, colNo, and charPos that have
23                     been stored by previous call to storeScrData.
24   CALLED AS:        restoreScrData scrVarStruct
25   RETURNS:     #    Nothing.
26
```

- An **iret** is used to produce a task switch. Recall that **iret** will cause a task switch to the task pointed to by the *backLink* field of the current task, but only if the task pointed to by the *backLink* is busy (i.e., has its busy bit set). The initial switch to *Task1* is performed on line 202. When the first ']' is received by **int 30h**, control should switch to *Task2*. In preparation for this switch, the *backLink* of *Task1* is pointed to *Task2*. But *Task2* has not yet been active, and so its busy bit has not been set by the microprocessor. This explains why we set the busy bit statically when we defined the TSS (on line 40).

- Note that it was not important to set the busy bit in *Task1*. On the contrary, *Task1* was first activated by the **jmp** on line 202, and so setting the busy bit statically would have produced a TSS fault, since it is illegal to **jmp** to a busy task.

Figure 18.20 shows the module, TASKMOD.ASM, containing the actual task code. We have chosen to run the same code in both tasks, partly to save space in the text and partly to illustrate the point that even though tasks cannot be nested, they can share code.

The code shared by the two tasks occupies lines 57-139. It implements a very inefficient algorithm for generating primes. The inefficiency is not significant here; on the contrary, it was still necessary to pad the algorithm with a substantial delay loop (lines 70-72) so that the results would print slowly enough on the screen to be read!

We will not spend time analyzing this code. The *findPrimes* procedure finds and prints to the screen all primes lying between a pair of limits that are passed to it on the stack.

FIGURE 18.20 SAMPLE TASKS FOR THE MULTITASKER

```
 1    TITLE taskMod.asm
 2
 3    PUBLIC  Task1, Task2
 4
 5    .XCREF
 6    .SALL
 7    INCLUDE console.mac
 8    INCLUDE prot.mac
 9    .386P
10
11    ;==============================================================================
12
13    _DATA SEGMENT USE16 WORD PUBLIC 'DATA'
14
15        EXTRN rowNo:DWORD, colNo:DWORD, charPos:DWORD
16
17        numStr  DB  6 DUP(?)
18
19    _DATA  ENDS
20
21    ;==============================================================================
22
23    _TEXT SEGMENT USE16 WORD PUBLIC 'CODE'
24
25        ASSUME cs:_TEXT, ds:_DATA
26
27    ;------------------------------------------------------------------------------
28
29    Task1   PROC  NEAR
30
31        sti
32        push    2                       ;lower limit for prime search
33        push    200                     ;upper limit for prime search
34        call    findPrimes
35
36        jmp     $ - 2                   ;task ends with infinite loop
37
38    Task1   ENDP
39
40    ;------------------------------------------------------------------------------
41
42    Task2   PROC    NEAR
43
44        sti
45        push    10001                   ;lower limit for prime search
46        push    10200                   ;upper limit for prime search
47        call    findPrimes
48
49        jmp     $ - 2                   ;task ends with infinite loop
50
51    Task2   ENDP
52
53    ;------------------------------------------------------------------------------
54
55    ;Finds primes between lower limit passed as [bp+6] and upper limit passed
```

Figure 18.20 cont.

```
56  ;  as [bp+4]
57
58  findPrimes    PROC   NEAR
59
60      push    bp
61      mov     bp, sp
62      pushRegs cx, edx
63
64      mov   cx, [bp+6]                 ;lower search limit
65
66  findLoop:
67
68      mov   edx, 100000               ;delay loop so that output
69      dec   edx                       ;  can be viewed on screen
70      jne   $-4
71
72      ITOA  numStr, cx                ;print integer
73      outAsc NL, numStr               ;  value
74      push  cx
75      call  isPrime                   ;check primality
76      jnc   notAPrime
77      ;Here if cx is prime
78      outAsc " is prime"              ;print message
79      jmp   Next
80
81  notAPrime:
82
83      outAsc  " is not prime"   ;  as appropriate
84
85  Next:
86      inc   cx
87      cmp   cx, [bp+4]                 ;exit when upper limit
88      jne   findLoop                  ;  is reached
89
90      popRegs
91      pop   bp
92      ret   4
93
94  findPrimes    ENDP
95
96  ;-----------------------------------------------------------------------
97
98  ;Checks whether integer n passed as [bp+4] is prime
99  ;  and returns appropriate isPrime value in the carry flag
100
101 isPrime    PROC   NEAR
102
103     push    bp
104     mov     bp, sp
105     pushRegs ax, cx, dx
106
107     mov    cx, [bp+4]               ;the n to be tested
108     dec    cx                       ;first divisor is n-1
109
110 divideLoop:
111
```

```
112        cmp     cx, 1
113        je      noDivisors
114        mov     ax, [bp+4]              ;always use n as dividend
115        xor     dx, dx                  ;zero high half of dividend
116        div     cx
117        and     dx, dx                  ;check whether remainder is 0
118        je      notPrime                ;if so, n is not a prime
119        dec     cx
120        jmp     divideLoop
121
122  noDivisors:                           ;here if n is a prime
123
124        stc
125        jmp     Done                    ;   so send back a yes answer
126                                        ;       to the caller
127  notPrime:
128
129        clc                             ;send back a no answer
130
131  Done:
132
133        popRegs
134        pop     bp
135        ret     2
136
137  isPrime    ENDP
138
139  ;-------------------------------------------------------------------
140
141  _TEXT     ENDS
142
143  ;===================================================================
144
145  END
```

Task1 prints the primes between 2 and 200, and ends with an infinite loop (line 38). The code for *Task2* is essentially identical to that for *Task1*, but with different limits.

Exercise 18-10. Modify the task dispatcher in Figure 19.18 by using calls instead of jumps.

Exercise 18-11. Change the task dispatcher by having it control six tasks instead of two. To test it, you can either run six copies of our basic task, or supply some other simple code. Again, it is probably best to have each task run in a different color.

Exercise 18-12. We implemented the task dispatcher as part of the code for the timer interrupt, but it is more common to implement it as a separate task. Make this modification to the multitasker.

Exercise 18-13. Ideally, each task should own its own copy of the screen, which replaces the contents of the current screen buffer when the task takes over and is stored when the task goes to sleep. Change our multitasker by including storage for a copy of the video buffer in each TSS.

Exercise 18-14. Modify the multitasker to provide *preemptive* task switching. In other words, the switching should be automatic, controlled by the kernel, rather than being dependent on a keypress.

Suggestion: Program the timer interrupt to do the switching. In the case of a real operating system, each *process* receives only a fraction of a second as its *time slice*. However, in this problem you should give each task a second or two, so that the switching can be observed more easily.

SECTION 9 80386 ARCHITECTURE

In this chapter, we have looked in detail at a number of aspects of systems programming on the **80386** microprocessor, but our account has by no means been complete. This section has three goals: to give a more formal introduction to the systems registers of the **80386**, a number of which we have been using throughout this chapter; to complete our listing of **80386** instructions even though most of them have already been introduced in the course of this chapter; and to pinpoint those features of the **80386** that we have not covered elsewhere in this book.

Figure 18.21 shows the 32-bit **80386** flags register, called **eflags**, for *extended flags*. As is required for **8086/8088** compatibility, the contents of the low 12 bits of **eflags** correspond exactly to those positions in the standard **flags** register. Among the high 20 bits of the **80386** **eflags**, all but four fields are reserved by Intel (and should be zeroed). Among these four fields, NT (*nested task*) and IOPL (*i/o privilege level*) are already familiar to us. RF (*resume flag*) is part of the hardware debugging apparatus, and VM (*virtual mode*) indicates whether the microprocessor is operating in virtual **8086** mode. Later in this section, we will briefly discuss hardware debugging and virtual **8086** mode. The **80486** also uses bit 18 of **eflags** as a new flag, *alignment check* (AC). We mentioned this flag in connection with the **int 17H**, the Alignment Check fault.

Figure 18.21 shows a group of four 32-bit registers called the *control registers* and named **cr0-cr3**. Of course, we are already acquainted with **cr0**. Only six fields in **cr0** are used on the **80386**:

PE (*protection enable*). As we know, the PE bit is set when the microprocessor is running in protected mode, and is clear when it is in real mode.

MP (*monitor coprocessor*). This bit is set if a coprocessor is attached to the **80386**, and is cleared otherwise. It is used as part of a protocol to ensure that, after a task switch, the context of the coprocessor matches the current task. See [17] for details.

EM (*emulate*). If this bit is set, it means that an emulation library should be used instead of a coprocessor. When the microprocessor executes an **esc** instruction (which always precedes a coprocessor instruction), it checks the EM bit. If it finds that this bit is set, it triggers an **int 07H**. The handler for this exception must transfer control to the emulation code.

FIGURE 18.21 OTHER 80386 REGISTERS

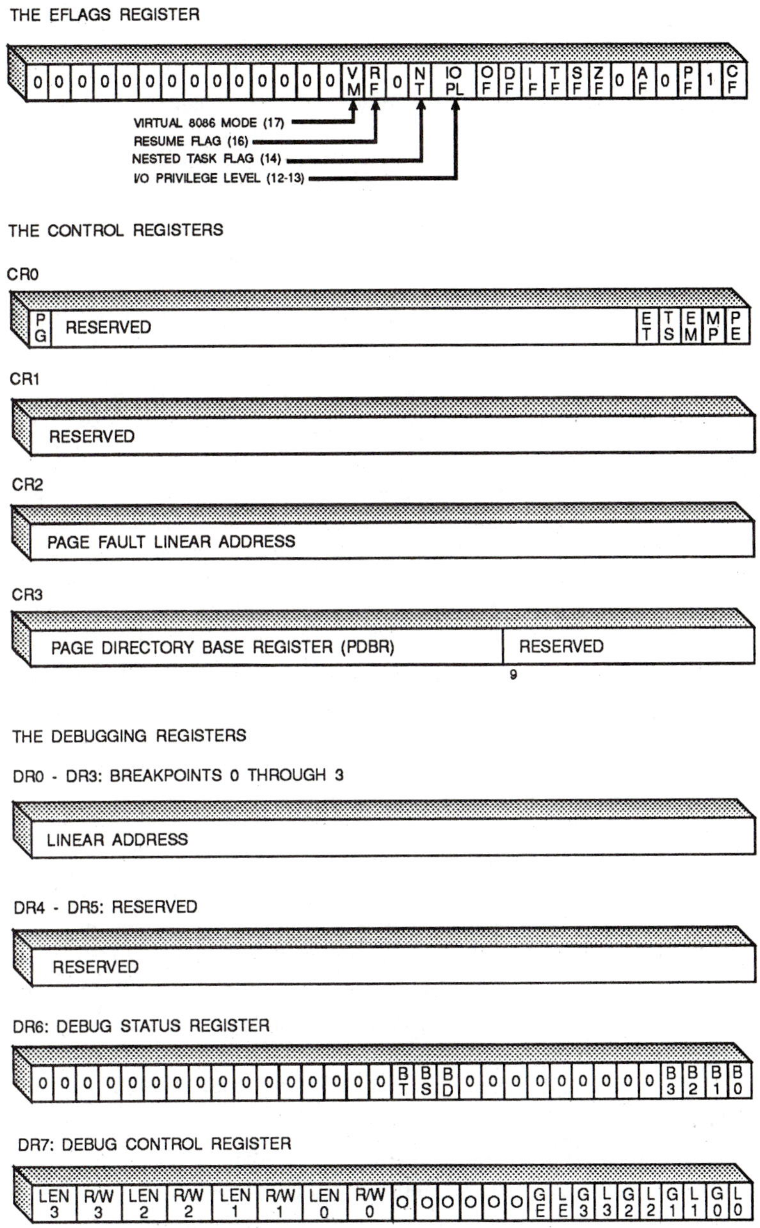
THE EFLAGS REGISTER
0 0 0 0 0 0 0 0 0 0 0 0 0 0 VM RF 0 NT IOPL OF DF IF TF SF ZF 0 AF 0 PF 1 CF
VIRTUAL 8086 MODE (17)
RESUME FLAG (16)
NESTED TASK FLAG (14)
I/O PRIVILEGE LEVEL (12-13)
THE CONTROL REGISTERS
CR0
PG RESERVED ET TS EM MP PE
CR1
RESERVED
CR2
PAGE FAULT LINEAR ADDRESS
CR3
PAGE DIRECTORY BASE REGISTER (PDBR) RESERVED
9
THE DEBUGGING REGISTERS
DR0 - DR3: BREAKPOINTS 0 THROUGH 3
LINEAR ADDRESS
DR4 - DR5: RESERVED
RESERVED
DR6: DEBUG STATUS REGISTER
0 0 0 0 0 0 0 0 0 0 0 0 0 0 0 0 BT BS BD 0 0 0 0 0 0 0 0 0 B3 B2 B1 B0
DR7: DEBUG CONTROL REGISTER
LEN 3 R/W 3 LEN 2 R/W 2 LEN 1 R/W 1 LEN 0 R/W 0 0 0 0 0 0 0 GE LE G3 L3 G2 L2 G1 L1 G0 L0

NOTE. THESE REGISTERS ARE ALL 32 BITS WIDE.

TS (*task switched*). The processor sets this flag whenever a task switch occurs. It is used with the MP bit (described previously) in controlling a coprocessor. The **clts** instruction is provided for clearing the TS flag.

ET (*extension type*). This bit tells the **80386** which kind of coprocessor is attached, if any: set means an **80387**, while clear means an **80287**.

PG (*paging*). The PG bit is set whenever the paging mechanisms are activated. (See below.)

The **cr1** register is reserved by Intel, while **cr2** and **cr3** are part of the **80386** *paging* machinery. Paging is used in the implementation of *virtual memory*. The **80486** has five more bits defined in **cr0** (including the Alignment Mask, which we have already encountered) and two defined bits in **cr3**. Most of these newly introduced bits deal with the management of the **80486** memory cache, and we refer the interested reader to [18] for more information. We will not cover paging and virtual memory in detail in this book, but here are the basic ideas.

The **80386** admits two basic kinds of memory blocks: segments and *pages*. Whereas a segment can be of (almost) any length, each page must be of length 4K. A decomposition of memory into pages can be independent of its decomposition into segments: a given segment might reside within a single page or span several, while a single page might contain parts of several segments. Complete information about pages is stored in special data structures called *page directories* and *page tables*. Paging is enabled by setting the PG bit in **cr0**. Paging essentially introduces another level of indirection into the process of translating a segmented address into a physical address. First, the segmented address is translated into a linear address with the help of a descriptor table, in the usual way. But the linear address is interpreted differently: it is comprised of an index into a page directory, an index into a page table, and an offset. The page directory index points to an entry describing a page table. Within that page table, the page table index entry points to a page. This is the page containing the physical address, and the offset is interpreted as the offset into this page. The address of the page directory is stored in **cr2**.

A page table contains an entry for each page, and each entry has a bit called the *present bit*. The present bit has the obvious significance: the operating system must ensure that, when a page is present in memory, its present bit is set, and that the bit is clear when the page only exists in mass storage. When the system is called upon to read from or write to a page whose present bit is clear, it issues an **int 0EH** (*page fault*). The exception handler must then bring the requested page into memory (by trading another page out, if necessary) and restart the program. Of course, **cr2** is helpful here, since it holds the linear address of the faulting instruction, which is the restart address.

Pages are more suitable than segments for the implementation of virtual memory for two reasons:

- Since all pages have the same length, swapping a page out of memory creates a "hole" that is of exactly the right size to hold a page when one is swapped in.

- Making the page size a multiple of the disk cluster size increases the efficiency of disk transfers.

The next registers shown in Figure 18.21 are the debugging registers. These registers allow the programmer to set *hardware-controlled breakpoints*, which are breakpoints controlled by the microprocessor rather than by software. We have already stated their advantages over software-controlled breakpoints: their presence does not slow program execution; unlike software breakpoints, they do not substantially alter the environment in which the test program is running; and they can monitor for events such as memory *reads* that are difficult to trap with software. The use of the debugging registers is easy. As many as four breakpoints can be set at a given time by placing the breakpoint addresses in registers **dr0-dr3**. When one of these breakpoints is taken, **int 01H** is triggered. The exception handler should be programmed to perform an appropriate postmortem based on the state of the machine when the breakpoint was taken.

The debugging registers **dr4** and **dr5** are reserved, and **dr6** and **dr7** provide control and status information during the debugging process. First, consider **dr6**, the *debug status register*:

The bits L0-L3 and G0-G3 are called, respectively, the *local enable* and *global enable* bits. If a local enable bit is set, it means that the corresponding breakpoint is local to a task. It will be taken only while that task is executing, and the bit will be reset at the first switch out of the task, so that the breakpoint becomes inactive. If a global enable bit is set, the breakpoint will remain active, regardless of task switches.

The bits LE and GE are called the *exact data breakpoint match* bits, and, of course, the first is task specific (i.e., is cleared at the first task switch), while the second is not. They are used in dealing with data breakpoints and slow the microprocessor sufficiently that it can report the exact address of the instruction causing the breakpoint.

The R/W fields (*read/write fields*) allow the user to specify the precise circumstances that will trigger the breakpoint, as follows:

00   break on instruction execution
01   break on data writes only
10   not used
11   break on data reads or writes, not on
     instruction fetches

The LEN fields (*length fields*) control the length of the data item to be checked, using this encoding:

00   one byte
01   two bytes
10   not used
11   four bytes

If the R/W field is given value zero (break on instruction execution), then LEN must also be given value zero.

The *debug control register*, **dr7**, can be read by the exception handler after a breakpoint is taken. It contains this information:

TABLE 18.3 INSTRUCTIONS USED IN SYSTEMS PROGRAMMING

INSTRUCTION		DESCRIPTION	REMARKS
POINTER VALIDATION			
arpl	r/m16,r16	adjust RPL	
lar	r16,r/m16	load access rights	
	r32,r/m32		
verr	r/m16	verify for reading	
verw	r/m16	verify for writing	
lsl	r16,r/m16	load segment limit	
	r32,r/m32		
LOCAL AND GLOBAL DESCRIPTOR TABLES			
lldt	m48	load LDT register	P
sldt	m48	store LDT register	
lgdt	m48	load GDT register	P
sgdt	m48	store GDT register	
MULTITASKING			
ltr	r/m16	load the task register	P
str	r/m16	store the task register	
COPROCESSING			
clts		clear TS flag in cr0	P
esc	immed6,r/m	escape	
wait		wait for coprocessor	
lock		lock the data bus	
INPUT AND OUTPUT			
in	various	input	S
out	various	output	S
ins	various	string input	S
outs	various	string output	S
INTERRUPT CONTROL			
cli		clear interrupt flag	S
sti		set interrupt flag	S
lidt	m48	load IDT register	P
sidt	m48	store IDT register	
MISCELLANEOUS			
mov	various	special system uses with control, debug, and test registers	P
SYSTEM CONTROL			
lmsw	r/m16	load MSW (machine status word)	P

smsw r/m16	set MSW	
hlt	halt processor	P
CACHE CONTROL (80486 ONLY)		
invlpg m	invalidate TLB entry	
invd	invalidate cache	
wbinvd	write-back and invalidate cache	
NOTE: P means privileged; S means sensitive		

One of bits B0-B3 (*breakpoint number*) will be set, indicating which breakpoint was taken.

The BT-bit will be set if the T-bit was set in the TSS of the task in control when the breakpoint occurred.

The BS-bit will be set if the TF flag was set, i.e., if single stepping was in effect when the breakpoint occurred.

The BD-bit is used in connection with an Intel hardware debugging device called the *in-circuit emulator* (ICE).

A final aspect of the **80386** that we will touch briefly upon is *virtual 8086 mode*. Running in virtual **8086** mode is a prerogative of individual tasks: if a task has the VM-bit set in its copy of **eflags**, then it will run in virtual mode; otherwise, it will not. It is entirely possible for the **80386** to run several tasks in virtual mode and to simultaneously control several tasks that are not. The significance of virtual mode is that the **80386** almost perfectly mimics the operation of the **8086/8088**. In particular, addresses are computed in the old-fashioned way (using address = 16*segment + offset), and segments have their usual size restrictions. Virtual tasks still have access to the extended **80386** applications instruction set and the 32-bit registers and addressing modes.

Perhaps the biggest attraction of virtual mode is that it offers the opportunity to multitask several **MS-DOS** programs. However, doing this successfully requires fairly extensive preparations. To begin with, **MS-DOS** programs expect to run in the lowest megabyte of physical memory. Using paging, it is easy to "trick" programs, so that each believes that it is using this low megabyte, while, in actuality, the paging mechanism is mapping the program's memory space to some convenient physical address in the machine.

The next important issue is that **MS-DOS** programs require operating system services and, as we well know, most **MS-DOS** services will not run in protected mode. However, they do run in virtual mode, because the environment is essentially that of a real-mode **8086/8088**. But still there are problems. For example, multitasking programs should not be allowed use of instructions such as **in** and **out**. The **80386** deals with this difficulty by declaring a general-protection fault whenever a virtual task uses a sensitive instruction, or even when it uses an **int** instruction, since many **MS-DOS** interrupt handlers themselves use sensitive instructions. When control transfers to the general protection fault handler, it decides what to do. In the case of a sensitive instruction, it can choose to execute the instruction or not, as it sees fit. In the case of an **int** instruction, it might "emulate" the appropriate function in protected mode, or "reflect" the interrupt back to a copy of the **MS-DOS** COMMAND.COM that it is also running as a task!

The virtual-memory, debugging, and virtual-mode features of the **80386** are all very exciting, and we have not begun to do justice to them in our brief survey. As always, we refer the reader to [14] for the complete story.

Table 18.3 contains a listing of those **80386** instructions used primarily in systems programming. Many of these instructions have either been examined in this chapter, or else can be readily understood from their names and descriptions. The last group, the *cache control instructions*, are new with the **80486** and relate to the paging mechanism and the maintenance of the on-board memory cache with which the **80486** is equipped.

Exercise 18-15. Write a program showing the debug registers in operation.
Suggestion: Set up an array of size 100K and start filling it randomly with integers. Monitor four arbitrarily chosen locations in the array and have the program terminate when one of these is changed. Before terminating, the program should read the debug registers and find the value of the integer in the monitored location. It should also contain code to check that this was, indeed, the integer most recently added to the array.

SECTION 10 PARTING THOUGHTS

Throughout this chapter, we have dealt almost exclusively with the segmentation-related features of the **80386**. This approach seemed reasonable since we are viewing the **80386** as a natural extension of the earlier processors in the family. In addition, we have seen that many of the most interesting of the protection mechanisms only become available when segmentation is used. For example, it is easy to trap references falling beyond the legal limits of an array by declaring the array in its own segment, with length equal to the array size.

There are, however, two schools of thought concerning the wholesale use of **80386** segmentation. The arguments against segmentation are the obvious ones:

- The rules governing the use of segments in protected mode are certainly very complicated, and would add greatly to the complexity of any operating system. Depending on the goals of the operating system, it may be able to achieve adequate levels of protection by simpler means.

- Programs using many segments run more slowly. For instance, if an array is given its private segment as suggested previously, then references to the array will result in extra segment-register switching. As we have seen, such switching is relatively slow in protected mode because of the validity checks performed on the new segment.

- Since the **80386** allows 32-bit offsets, it is entirely possible to fix the segment registers once and for all and work with a flat 4G addressing space.

It is certainly not clear at this time whether or not segmentation will continue to be used extensively by operating systems written for the **80386** and its successors. One indicator is that Version 2.0 of OS/2 (the first version written specifically for the **80386**) will use a flat addressing space.

BIBLIOGRAPHY

The following list, while by no means exhaustive, does constitute a solid reference library for the Intel **80XXX** microprocessors. It includes all the publications that I used heavily while writing this book and a few others that should be a part of every programmer's library.

BOOKS

[1] Abrash, Michael, *Zen of Assembly Language*, Volume 1, Glenview, Illinois: Scott, Foresman, and Company, 1989

[2] Brooks, Frederick P. , *The Mythical Man-Month*, Reading, Massachusetts: Addison-Wesley, 1975

[3] Duncan, Ray, *Advanced MS-DOS Programming,* 2nd Ed., Redmond, Washington: Microsoft Press, 1988

[4] Jourdain, Robert, *Programmer's Problem Solver*, New York, NY: Brady Books, 1986

[5] Knuth, D., *The Art of Computer Programming*, Vols. 1-3, Reading, Massachusetts: Addison-Wesley, 1973

[6] Morse, Stephen P., *The 8086/8088 Primer,* 2nd Ed., Hasbrouck Heights, New Jersey: Hayden Book Company, 1984

[7] Morse, Stephen P., and Douglas J. Albert, *The 80286 Architecture*, New York, NY: Wiley, 1986

[8] Morse, Stephen P., Eric J. Isaacson, and Douglas J. Albert, *The 80386/80386 Architecture*, New York, NY: Wiley, 1987

[9] Rollins, Dan, 8088 *Macro Assembler Programming*, New York, NY: Macmillan

[10] Sargent, Murray and Richard L. Shoemaker, *The IBM Personal Computer from the Inside Out*, Reading, Massachusetts: Addison-Wesley, 1984

[11] Wilton, Richard, *Programmer's Guide to PC and PS/2 Video Systems*, Redmond, Washington: Microsoft Press, 1987

MANUALS

[12] *iAPX 86/88, 186/188 User's Manual*, Santa Clara, CA: Intel, 1985

[13] *80286 and 80287 Programmer's Reference Manual*, Santa Clara, CA: Intel, 1987

[14] *80386 Programmer's Reference Manual*, Santa Clara, CA: Intel, 1986

[15] *80386 System Software Writer's Guide*, Santa Clara, CA: Intel, 1987

[16] *386 Microprocessor Hardware Reference Manual*, Santa Clara, CA: Intel, 1988

[17] *80387 Programmer's Reference Manual*, Santa Clara, CA: Intel, 1987

[18] *i486 Microprocessr Programmer's Reference Manual*, Osborne McGraw, 1990

[19] *Microprocessor and Peripheral Handbook* Vol. 1-2, Santa Clara: Intel, 1987

[20] *IBM-XT Technical Reference*, Boca Raton, Florida, 1984

[21] *IBM-AT Technical Reference*, Boca Raton, Florida, 1985

[22] *Disk Operating System Technical Reference*, Version 3.1, Boca Raton, Florida: IBM, 1985

[23] *System BIOS for IBM PC/XT/AT Computers and Compatibles* (*Phoenix Technologies*), Reading, Massachusetts: Addison-Wesley, 1989

[24] *The MS-DOS Encyclopedia*, Redmond, Washington: Microsoft Press, 1988

The following five items constitute the **MASM** Version 5.1 documentation.

[25] *Microsoft Assembler 5.1 Reference*, Redmond, Washington: Microsoft Press, 1987

[26] *Microsoft Assembler 5.1 Programmer's Guide*, Redmond, Washington: Microsoft Press, 1987

[27] *Microsoft Assembler 5.1 Version 5.1 Update*, Redmond, Washington: Microsoft Press, 1987

[28] *Microsoft Assembler 5.1 Microsoft CodeView and Utilities*, Redmond, Washington: Microsoft Press, 1987

[29] *Microsoft Assembler 5.1 Mixed-Language Programming Guide*, Redmond, Washington: Microsoft Press, 1987

ARTICLES

[30] Brickner, Ralph G., "An Execution Profiler for the PC," *PC Tech Journal* 4:11, November, 1986

[31] Roden, Thomas, "Four Gigabytes in Real Mode," *Programmer's Journal* 7:6, November/December, 1989

THE COMPLETE INSTRUCTION SET

This appendix contains an alphabetical listing of the entire **8086** family instruction set. For example, the information about the **dec** instruction is displayed as follows:

DEC								O	D	I	T	S	Z	A	P	C
decrement by 1								X				X	X	X	X	
FE /1	dec r/m8	8086	3/15	2/7	2/6	1/3										
FF /1	dec r/m16	8086	3/15	2/7	2/6	1/3										
FF /1	dec r/m32	80386			2/6	1/3										
48 + rw	dec r16	8086	3	2	2	1										
48 + rw	dec r32	80386			2	1										

The name of the instruction and its effect on the flags are given across the top of the display. The five following columns contain:

- The machine codes for all allowed formats of the instruction in question.
- The assembly language equivalents of these formats.
- The earliest processor in the family with which the format can be used.
- The approximate numbers of clock cycles required for execution on the applicable subset of the **8086, 80286, 80386,** and the **80486.**
- Additional information needed to interpret the instruction.

The following notations are used in the listings:

Effect on Flags. Changes in the flag values are represented as follows:

Blank means that the flag is unchanged.

'X' means that it is changed in a meaningful way.

'?' means that the value is meaningless after the instruction.

'0' and '1' have the obvious meanings.

Machine Code. Each machine code is shown as a sequence of hex bytes, with certain abbreviations. Here are the meanings of the non-obvious notations:

ib, iw, and id: Immediate byte, word, or doubleword, respectively.

/r: The ModR/M byte of the instruction contains information about both a register operand and an r/m operand.

/digit: The ModR/M byte uses the r/m field in the normal way but the reg field contains this digit, which serves as an extension of the instruction opcode rather than as a register code.

cb, cw, cd, and cp: Used in code transfer instructions to show that the next 1, 2, 4, or 6 bytes represent a code offset, possibly together with a new **cs** value.

+i: Used with FPU instructions and means that i is added to the preceding code byte to indicate that st(i) is one of the operands.

+rb,+rw, and +rd: A quantity that is added to the preceding code byte to determine which register should be used, using the scheme shown in the following diagram.

	0	1	2	3	4	5	6	7
rb	al	cl	dl	bl	ah	ch	dh	bh
rw	ax	cx	dx	bx	sp	bp	si	di
rd	eax	ecx	edx	ebx	esp	ebp	esi	edi

Another important feature of the **80386/80486** is the *SIB byte* (*scaled index byte*). This is an extra byte that appears after the ModR/M byte when one of the new addressing modes is used. A number of the parameters in Figure 9.12 are also interpreted differently in the 32-bit case. We refer the reader to [14] or [25] for details.

Clock Cycles. We have listed the **8086** times but not the **8088** times. Recall that the 16-bit versions of instructions run slower on the **8088** because each word is transferred from memory using two fetches, which requires 4 extra clock cycles per word. In addition, times for effective address calculations must be added in the **8086/8088** cases. The following notations are also used in the clock cycles column:

{time}: Means that this is the time required for execution in protected mode.

ts: Additional time required for task switch: it is about 200 cycles on the **80486** and in the 200- to 300-cycle range on the **80386**.

AAA				O	D	I	T	S	Z	A	P	C
adjust for ASCII addition				?				?	?	X	?	X
37	aaa	8086	8 3 4 3									

AAD				O	D	I	T	S	Z	A	P	C
adjust for ASCII division				?				X	X	?	X	?
D5 0A	aad	8086	60 14 19 14									

AAM				O	D	I	T	S	Z	A	P	C
adjust for ASCII multiplication				?				X	X	?	X	?
D4 0A	aam	8086	83 16 17 15									

AAS				O	D	I	T	S	Z	A	P	C
adjust for ASCII subtraction				?				?	?	X	?	X
3F	aas	8086	8 3 4 3									

ADC						O	D	I	T	S	Z	A	P	C
add with carry						X				X	X	X	X	X
14 ib	adc al, i8	8086	4	3	2	1							
15 iw	adc ax, i16	8086	4	3	2	1							
15 id	adc eax, i32	80386			2	1							
80 /2 ib	adc r/m8, i8	8086	4/17	3/7	2/7	1/3							
81 /2 iw	adc r/m16, i16	8086	4/17	3/7	2/7	1/3							
81 /2 id	adc r/m32, i32	80386			2/7	1/3							
83 /2 ib	adc r/m16, i8	8086	4/17	3/7	2/7	1/3							
83 /2 ib	adc r/m32, i8	80386			2/7	1/3							
10 /r	adc r/m8, r8	8086	3/16	2/7	2/7	1/3							
11 /r	adc r/m16, r16	8086	3/16	2/7	2/7	1/3							
11 /r	adc r/m32, r32	80386			2/7	1/3							
12 /r	adc r8, r/m8	8086	3/9	2/7	2/6	1/2							
13 /r	adc r16, r/m16	8086	3/9	2/7	2/6	1/2							
13 /r	adc r32, r/m32	80386			2/6	1/2							

ADD						O	D	I	T	S	Z	A	P	C
adds operands						X				X	X	X	X	X
04 ib	add al, i8	8086	4	3	2	1							
05 iw	add ax, i16	8086	4	3	2	1							
05 id	add eax, i32	80386			2	1							
80 /0 ib	add r/m8, i8	8086	4/17	3/7	2/7	1/3							
81 /0 iw	add r/m16, i16	8086	4/17	3/7	2/7	1/3							

81 /0 id	add r/m32, i32	80386			2/7	1/3
83 /0 ib	add r/m16, i8	8086	4/17	3/7	2/7	1/3
83 /0 id	add r/m32, i8	80386			2/7	1/3
00 /r	add r/m8, r8	8086	3/16	2/7	2/7	1/3
01 /r	add r/m16, r16	8086	3/16	2/7	2/7	1/3
01 /r	add r/m32, r32	80386			2/7	1/3
02 /r	add r8, r/m8	8086	3/16	2/7	2/6	1/2
03 /r	add r16, r/m16	8086	3/16	2/7	2/6	1/2
03 /r	add r32/ r/m32	80386			2/6	1/2

AND								O	D	I	T	S	Z	A	P	C
bitwise and								0				X	X	?	X	0
24 ib	and al, i8	8086	4	3	2	1
25 iw	and ax, i16	8086	4	3	2	1
25 id	and eax, i32	80386			2/7	1
80 /4 ib	and r/m8, i8	8086	4/17	3/7	2/7	1/3
81 /4 iw	and r/m16, i16	8086	4/17	3/7	2/7	1/3
81 /4 id	and r/m32, i32	80386			2/7	1/3
83 /4 ib	and r/m16, r8	80386	3/16	2/7	2/7	1/3
83 /4 ib	and r/m32, i8	80386			2/7	1/3
20 /r	and r/m8, r8	8086	3/16	2/7	2/7	1/3
21 /r	and r/m16, r16	8086	3/16	2/7	2/7	1/3
21 /r	and r/m32, r32	80386			2/7	1/3
22 /r	and r8, r/m8	8086	3/9	2/7	2/6	1/2
23 /r	and r16, r/m16	8086	3/9	2/7	2/6	1/2
23 /r	and r32, r/m32	80386			2/6	1/2

ARPL				O	D	I	T	S	Z	A	P	C
adjust requested privilege level									X			
63 /r	arpl r/m16, r16	80286	10/11	20/21	9/9

BOUND				O	D	I	T	S	Z	A	P	C
check array bounds												
62 /r	bound r16, m16&16	80286	13	10	7
62 /r	bound r32, r32&32	80286	13	10	7

BSF				O	D	I	T	S	Z	A	P	C
bit scan forward									X			
OF BC	bsf r16, r/m16	80386	10 + 3n on 80386 6-42/7-43 on 80486	n=number of leading zero bits

OF BC	bsf r32, r/m32	80386	10 + 3n on 80386 6-42/7-43 on 80486	

BSR					O	D	I	T	S	Z	A	P	C
bit scan reverse										X			
OF BD	bsr r16, r/m16	80386	10 + 3n on 80386 6-103/7-104 on 80486	n=number of trailing									
OF BD	bsr r32, r/m32	80386	10 + 3n on 80386 6-103/7-104 on 80486	zero bits									

BSWAP				O	D	I	T	S	Z	A	P	C
swap byte pattern in dword												
OF C8 /r	bswap r32	80486	1									

BT					O	D	I	T	S	Z	A	P	C
test bit value													X
OF A3	bt r/m16, r16	80386	3/12	3/8									
0F A3	bt r/m32, r32	80386	3/12	3/8									
OF BA /4 ib	bt r/m16, i8	80386	3/6	3/3									
0F BA /4 ib	bt r/m32,i8	80386	3/6	3/3									

BTC					O	D	I	T	S	Z	A	P	C
test bit and complement													X
OF BB	btc r/m16, r16	80386	6/13	6/13									
0F BB	btc r/m32, r32	80386	6/13	6/13									
OF BA /7 ib	btc r/m16, i8	80386	6/8	6/8									
OF BA /7 ib	btc r/m32,i8	80386	6/8	6/8									

BTR					O	D	I	T	S	Z	A	P	C
test bit and reset													X
OF B3	btr r/m16, r16	80386	6/13	6/13									
OF B3	btr r/m32, r32	80386	6/13	6/13									
OF BA /6 ib	btr r/m16, i8	80386	6/8	6/8									
OF BA /6 ib	btr r/m32, i8	80386	6/8	6/8									

BTS					O	D	I	T	S	Z	A	P	C
test bit and set													X
OF AB	bts r/m16, r16	80386	6/13	6/13									

0F AB	bts r/m32, r32	80386			6/13	6/13	
0F BA /5 ib	bts r/m16, i8	80386			6/8	6/8	
0F BA /5 ib	bts r/m32, i8	80386			6/8	6/8	

CALL call procedure								O	D	I	T	S	Z	A	P	C
EB cw	call rel16	8086	19	7+	7+	3	Call near, direct
FF /2	call r/m16	8086	16/21	7	7+	5/5	Call near, indirect
9A cd	call ptr16:16	8086	28	13+	17+	18{20}	Call far, direct
9A cd	call ptr16:16	8086		41	52+	35	Call gate, same privilege
9A cd	call ptr16:16	80286		82	96+	69	Call gate, more priv, no params
9A cd	call ptr16:16	80286		86+4x	94+	77+4x	Call gate, more priv, x params
9A cd	call ptr16:16	80286		182	ts	37+ts	Call to task
FF /3	call m16:16	8086	37	16/29	22+	17{20}	Call far, indirect
FF /3	call m16:16	80286		44	56+	35	Call gate, same privilege
FF /3	call m16:16	80286		83	90+	69	Call gate, more priv, no params
FF /3	call m16:16	80286		90+4x	98+4x+	77+4x	Call gate, more priv, x params
FF /3	call m16:16	80286		180	5+ts	37+ts	Call to task
E8 cd	call rel32	80386			7+	3	Call near, direct
FF /2	call r/m32	80386			7+	5/5	Call near, indirect
9A cp	call ptr16:32	80386			17+	18{20}	Call far, direct
9A cp	call ptr16:32	80386			52+	35	Call gate, same privilege
9A cp	call ptr16:32	80386			86+	69	Call gate, more priv, no params
9A cp	call ptr32:32	80386			94+4x+	77+4x	Call gate, more priv, x params
9A cp	call ptr16:32	80386			ts	37+ts	Call to task
FF /3	call m16:32	80386			22+	17{20}	
FF /3	call m16:32	80386			56+	35	Call gate, same privilege
FF /3	call m16:32	80386			90+	69	Call gate, more priv, no params
FF /3	call m16:32	80386			98+4x+	77+4x	Call gate, more priv, x params
FF /3	call m16:32	80386			5+ts	37+ts	Call to task

CBW/CWDE convert byte to word, word to doubleword								O	D	I	T	S	Z	A	P	C
98	cbw	8086	2	2	3	3	
98	cwde	80386			3	3	

CLC clear carry flag								O	D	I	T	S	Z	A	P	C
																0
F8	clc	8086	2	2	2	2	

CLD								O	D	I	T	S	Z	A	P	C
clear direction flag									0							
FC	cld	8086	2	2	2	2										

CLI								O	D	I	T	S	Z	A	P	C
clear interrupt flag										0						
FA	cli	8086	2	3	3	5										

CLTS								O	D	I	T	S	Z	A	P	C
clear task switched flag																
0F 06	clts	80286		2	5	7										

CMC								O	D	I	T	S	Z	A	P	C
complement carry flag																X
F5	cmc	8086	2	2	2	2										

CMP								O	D	I	T	S	Z	A	P	C
compare operands								X				X	X	X	X	X
3C ib	cmp al, i8	8086	4	3	2	1										
3d iw	cmp ax, i16	8086	4	3	2	1										
3d id	cmp eax, i32	80386			2	1										
80 /7 ib	cmp r/m8, i8	8086	4/10	3/6	2/5	1/2										
81 /7 iw	cmp r/m16, i16	8086	4/10	3/6	2/5	1/2										
81 /7 id	cmp r/m32, i32	80386			2/5	1/2										
83 /7 ib	cmp r/m16, i8	8086	4/10	3/6	2/5	1/2										
83 /7 ib	cmp r/m32, i8	80386			2/5	1/2										
38 /r	cmp r/m8, r8	8086	3/9	2/7	2/5	1/2										
39 /r	cmp r/m16, r16	8086	3/9	2/7	2/5	1/2										
39 /r	cmp r/m32, r32	80386			2/5	1/2										
3A /r	cmp r8, r/m8	8086	3/9	2/7	2/6	1/2										
3B /r	cmp r16, r/m16	8086	3/9	2/7	2/6	1/2										
3b /r	cmpr32, r/m32	80386			2/6	1/2										

CMPS/CMPSB/CMPSW/CMPSD								O	D	I	T	S	Z	A	P	C
compare string operands								X				X	X	X	X	X
A6	cmps m8, m8	8086	22	8	10	8										
A7	cmps m16, m16	8086	22	8	10	8										
A7	cmps m32, m32	80386			10	8										
A6	cmpsb	8086	22	8	10	8										
A7	cmpsw	8086	22	8	10	8										
A7	cmpsd	80386			10	8										

CMPXCHG			O	D	I	T	S	Z	A	P	C
compare and exchange			X				X	X	X	X	X

0F A6 /r	cmpxchg r/m, r8	80486	6/7 if comparison succeeds, else 6/10
0F A7 /r	cmpxchg r/m16, r16	80486	6/7 if comparison succeeds, else 6/10
0F A7 /r	cmpxchg r/m32, r32	80486	6/7 if comparison succeeds, else 6/10

CWD/CDQ			O	D	I	T	S	Z	A	P	C
convert word to doubleword, doubleword to qword											

99	cwd	8086	5	2	2	3
99	cdq	80386		2	3	

DAA			O	D	I	T	S	Z	A	P	C
decimal adjust after addition			?				X	X	X	X	X

27	daa	8086	4	3	4	2

DAS			O	D	I	T	S	Z	A	P	C
decimal adjust after subtraction			?				X	X	X	X	X

2F	das	8086	4	3	4	2

DEC			O	D	I	T	S	Z	A	P	C
decrement by 1			X				X	X	X	X	

FE /1	dec r/m8	8086	3/15	2/7	2/6	1/3
FF /1	dec r/m16	8086	3/15	2/7	2/6	1/3
FF /1	dec r/m32	80386			2/6	1/3
48 + rw	dec r16	8086	3	2	2	1
48 + rw	dec r32	80386		2	1	

DIV			O	D	I	T	S	Z	A	P	C
unsigned divide			?				?	?	?	?	?

F6 /6	div r/m8	8086	80/86	14/17	14/17	16/16
F7 /6	div r/m16	8086	144/150	22/25	22/25	24/24
F7 /6	div r/m32	80386			38/41	40/40

ENTER			O	D	I	T	S	Z	A	P	C
unsigned divide											

C8 iw 00	enter i16, 0	80286	11	10	14	
C8 iw 01	enter i16, 1	80286	15	12	17	
C8 iw ib	enter i16, i8	80286	286: 12 + 4(n-1)			n = nesting depth
			386: 15 + 4(n-1)			
			486: 17 + 3n			

F2XM1 computes 2^x - 1							O	D	I	T	S	Z	A	P	C
D9 F0	f2xm1	8086	310-630	310-630	211-476	140-279									

FABS absolute value							O	D	I	T	S	Z	A	P	C
D9 E1	fabs	8086	10-17	10-17	22	3									

FADD/FADDP/FIADD addition							O	D	I	T	S	Z	A	P	C
D8 /0	fadd m32real	8087	90-120	90-120	24-32	8-20									
DC /0	fadd m64real	8087	95-125	95-125	29-37	8-20									
D8 C0 + i	fadd st, st(i)	8087	70-100	70-100	23-31	8-20									
DC C0 + i	fadd st(i), st	8087	70-100	70-100	26-34	8-20									
DE C0 + i	faddp st(i), st	8087	75-105	75-105	23-31	8-20									
DE C1	fadd	8087	70-100	70-100	23-31	8-20									
DA /0	fiadd m32int	8087	108-143	108-143	57-72	19-32									
DE /0	fiadd m16int	8087	102-137	102-137	71-85	20-35									

FBLD load binary coded decimal							O	D	I	T	S	Z	A	P	C
DB /4	fbld m80dec	8086	290-310	290-310	266-275	70-103									

FBSTP store binary coded decimal and pop							O	D	I	T	S	Z	A	P	C
DF /6	fbstp m80dec	8086	520-540	520-540	512-534	172-176									

FCHS change sign							O	D	I	T	S	Z	A	P	C
D9 E0	fchs	8087	10-17	10-17	24-25	6									

FCLEX/FNCLEX clear exceptions							O	D	I	T	S	Z	A	P	C
9B DB E2	fclex	8087	2-8	2-8	11	10+									
DB E2	fnclex	8087	2-8	2-8	11	7									

FCOM/FCOMP/FCOMPP compare reals							O	D	I	T	S	Z	A	P	C
D8 /2	fcom m32real	8087	60-70	60-70	26	4									
DC /2	fcom m64real	8087	65-75	65-75	31	4									
DB D0+i	fcom st(i)	8087	40-50	40-50	24	4									

D8 D1	fcom	8087	40-50	40-50	24	4
D8 /3	fcomp m32real	8087	63-73	63-73	26	4
DC /3	fcomp m64real	8087	67-77	67-77	31	4
D8 D8+i	fcomp st(i)	8087	42-52	42-52	26	4
D8 D9	fcomp	8087	42-52	42-52	26	4
DE D9	fcompp	8087	45-55	45-55	26	5

FCOS cosine								O	D	I	T	S	Z	A	P	C
D9 FF	fcos	80387			123-772	193-279										

FDECSTP decrement stack pointer								O	D	I	T	S	Z	A	P	C
D9 F6	fdecstp	8087	6-12	6-12	22	3										

FDIV/FDIVP/FIDIV division								O	D	I	T	S	Z	A	P	C
D8 /6	fdiv m32real	8087	215-225	215-225	89	73										
DC /6	fdiv m64real	8087	220-230	220-230	94	73										
D8 F0+i	fdiv st, st(i)	8087	193-203	193-203	88	73										
DC F8+i	fdiv st(i), st	8087	193-203	193-203	91	73										
DE F8+i	fdivp st(i), st	8087	197-207	197-207	91	73										
DE F9	fdiv	8087	193-203	193-203	88	73										
DA /6	fidiv m32int	8087	224-238	224-238	136-140	73										
DE /6	fidiv m16int	8087	230-243	230-243	120-127	73										

FDIVR/FDIVRR/FIDIVR reverse division								O	D	I	T	S	Z	A	P	C
D8 /7	fdivr m32real	8087	216-226	216-226	89	70										
DC /7	fdivr m64real	8087	221-231	221-231	94	70										
D8 F8+i	fdivr st, st(i)	8087	194-204	194-204	88	70										
DC F0+i	fdivr st(i), st	8087	194-204	194-204	91	70										
DE F0+i	fdivrp st(i), st	8087	198-208	198-208	91	70										
DE F1	fdivr	8087	194-204	194-204	88	70										
DA /7	fidivr m32int	8087	225-239	225-239	135-141	70										
DE /7	fidivr m16int	8087	231-245	231-245	121-128	70										

FENI/FNENI enable interrupts							O	D	I	T	S	Z	A	P	C
									1						
DB E0	feni	8087	(8087 only)	2-8											
9B DB E0	fneni	8087	(8087 only)	2-8											

FFREE							O	D	I	T	S	Z	A	P	C
free FPU register															
DD C0+i	ffree st(i)	8087	9-16	9-16	18	3									

FICOM/FICOMP							O	D	I	T	S	Z	A	P	C
compare integers															
DE /2	ficom m16int	8087	72-86	72-86	71-75	16-20									
DA /2	ficom m32int	8087	78-91	78-91	56-63	15-17									
DE /3	ficomp m16int	8087	74-88	74-88	71-75	16-20									
DA /3	ficomp m32int	8087	80-93	80-93	56-63	15-17									

FILD							O	D	I	T	S	Z	A	P	C
load integer															
DF /0	fild m16int	8087	46-54	46-54	61-65	13-16									
DB /0	fild m32int	8087	52-60	52-60	45-52	9-12									
DF /5	fild m64int	8087	60-68	60-68	56-67	10-18									

FINCSTP							O	D	I	T	S	Z	A	P	C
increment stack pointer															
D9 F7	fincstp	8087	6-12	6-12	21	3									

FINIT/FNINIT							O	D	I	T	S	Z	A	P	C
initialize FPU															
DB E3	finit	8087	2-8	2-8	33	20+									
9B DB E3	fninit	8087	2-8	2-8	33	17									

FIST/FISTP							O	D	I	T	S	Z	A	P	C
store integer															
DF /2	fist m16int	8087	80-90	80-90	82-95	29-34									
DB /2	fist m32int	8087	82-92	82-92	79-93	28-34									
DF /3	fistp m16int	8087	82-92	82-92	82-95	29-34									
DB /3	fistp m32int	8087	84-94	84-94	79-93	29-34									
DF /7	fistp m64int	8087	94-105	94-105	80-97	29-34									

FLD							O	D	I	T	S	Z	A	P	C
load real															
D9 /0	fld m32real	8087	38-56	38-56	20	3									
DD /0	fld m64real	8087	40-60	40-60	25	3									
DB /5	fld m80real	8087	53-65	53-65	44	6									
D9 C0+i	fld st(i)	8087	17-22	17-22	14	4									

FLD1/FDL2T/FLDL2E/FLDPI/FLDLG2/FLDLN2/FLDZ
load real

			O	D	I	T	S	Z	A	P	C

D9 E8	fld1	8087	15-21	15-21	14	4
D9 E9	fldl2t	8087	16-22	16-22	40	8
D9 EA	fldl2e	8087	15-21	15-21	40	8
D9 EB	fldpi	8087	16-22	16-22	40	8
D9 EC	fldlg2	8087	18-24	18-24	41	8
D9 ED	fldln2	8087	17-23	17-23	41	8
D9 EE	fldz	8087	11-17	11-17	24	4

FLDCW
load control word

			O	D	I	T	S	Z	A	P	C

D9 /5	fldcw	8087	7-14	7-14	19	4

FLDENV
load NPX environment

			O	D	I	T	S	Z	A	P	C

D9 /4	fldenv	8087	35-45	35-45	71	34-44

FMUL/FMULP/FIMUL
multiply

			O	D	I	T	S	Z	A	P	C

D8 /1	fmul m32real	8087	110-125	110-125	27-35	11
DC /1	fmul m64real	8087	154-168	154-168	32-57	14
D8 C8+i	fmul st, st(i)	8087	130-145	130-145	46-54	16
DC C8+i	fmul st(i), st	8087	130-145	130-145	29-57	16
DE C8+i	fmulp st(i), st	8087	134-148	134-148	29-57	16
DE C9	fmul	8087	130-145	130-145	46-54	16
DA /1	fimul m32int	8087	130-144	130-144	61-82	22-24
DE /1	fimul m16int	8087	124-138	124-138	76-87	22-24

FNOP
no operation

			O	D	I	T	S	Z	A	P	C

D9 D0	fnop	8087	10-16	10-16	12	3

FPATAN
arctangent

			O	D	I	T	S	Z	A	P	C

D9 F3	fpatan	8087	250-800	250-800	314-387	289

FPREM
partial remainder

			O	D	I	T	S	Z	A	P	C

D9 F8	fprem	8087	15-190	15-190	74-155	70-138

FPREM1 partial remainder							O	D	I	T	S	Z	A	P	C
D9 F5	fprem1	80387		95-185	72-167										

FPTAN partial tangent							O	D	I	T	S	Z	A	P	C
D9 F2	fptan	8087	30-540	30-540	191-497	200-273									

FRNDINT round to integer							O	D	I	T	S	Z	A	P	C
D9 FC	frndint	8087	16-50	16-50	66-80	21-30									

FRSTOR restore FPU state							O	D	I	T	S	Z	A	P	C
DB /4	frstor m94/104byte	8087	197-207	(*)	308	120-131	(*) not meaningful								

FSAVE/FNSAVE store FPU state							O	D	I	T	S	Z	A	P	C
9B DD /6	fsave m94/108byte	8087	197-207	(*)	375-376	146+	(*) not meaningful								
DD /6	fnsave m94/108byte	8087	197-207	(*)	375-376	143-154									

FSCALE scale							O	D	I	T	S	Z	A	P	C
D9 FD	fscale	8087	32-38	32-38	67-86	30-32									

FSIN sine							O	D	I	T	S	Z	A	P	C
D9 FE	fsin	80387		122-771	193-279										

FSINCOS sine and cosine							O	D	I	T	S	Z	A	P	C
D9 FB	fsincos	80387		194-809	243-329										

FSQRT square root							O	D	I	T	S	Z	A	P	C
D9 FA	fsqrt	8087	180-186	180-186	122-129	83-87									

FST/FSTP store real							O	D	I	T	S	Z	A	P	C
D9 /2	fst m32real	8087	84-90	84-90	44	7									

DD /2	fst m64real	8087	96-104	96-104	45	8
DD D0+i	fst st(i)	8087	15-22	15-22	11	3
D9 /3	fstp m32real	8087	86-92	86-92	44	7
DD /3	fstp m64real	8087	98-106	98-106	45	8
DB /7	fstp m80real	8087	52-58	52-58	53	6
DD D8+i	fstp st(i)	8087	17-24	17-24	12	3

FSTCW store control word							O	D	I	T	S	Z	A	P	C
9B D9 /7	fstcw m2byte	8087	12-18	12-18	15	6+									
D9 /7	fnstcw m2byte	8087	12-18	12-18	15	3									

FSTENV store FPU environment							O	D	I	T	S	Z	A	P	C
9B D9 /6	fstenv m14/28byte	8087	40-50	40-50	103-104	70+-59+									
D9 /6	fstenv m14/282byte	8087	40-50	40-50	103-104	56-67									

FSTSW/FNSTSW store status word							O	D	I	T	S	Z	A	P	C
9B DF /7	fstsw m2byte	8087	12-18	12-18	15	6+									
9B DF E0	fstsw ax	80287		10-16	13	6+									
DF /7	fnstsw m2byte	8087	12-18	12-18	15	3									
DF E0	fnstsw ax	80287		10-16	13	3									

FSUB/FSUBP/FISUB subtraction							O	D	I	T	S	Z	A	P	C
D8 /4	fsub m32real	8087	90-120	90-120	24-32	5-17									
DC /4	fsub m64real	8087	95-125	95-125	29-37	5-17									
D8 E0 + i	fsub st, st(i)	8087	70-100	70-100	29-37	5-17									
DC E8 + i	fsub st(i), st	8087	70-100	70-100	26-34	5-17									
DE E8 + i	fsubp st(i), st	8087	75-105	75-105	26-34	5-17									
DE E9	fsub	8087	70-100	70-100	23-31	5-17									
DA /4	fisub m32int	8087	108-153	108-143	57-82	5-17									
DE /4	fisub m16int	8087	102-137	102-137	71-83	5-17									

FSUBR/FSUBRP/FISUBR reverse subtraction							O	D	I	T	S	Z	A	P	C
D8 /5	fsubr m32real	8087	90-120	90-120	25-33	5-17									

DC /5	fsubr m64real	8087	95-125	95-125	29-37	5-17
D8 E8 + i	fsubr st, st(i)	8087	70-100	70-100	29-37	5-17
DC E0 + i	fsubr st(i), st	8087	70-100	70-100	26-34	5-17
DE E0 + i	fsubrp st(i), st	8087	75-105	75-105	26-34	5-17
DE E1	fsubr	8087	70-100	70-100	23-31	5-17
DA /5	fisubr m32int	8087	109-144	109-144	58-83	5-17
DE /5	fisubr m16int	8087	103-139	103-139	72-84	5-17

FTST							O	D	I	T	S	Z	A	P	C
test															
D9 E4	ftst	8087	38-48	38-48	28	4									

FUCOM/FUCOMP/FUCOMPP							0	D	I	T	S	Z	A	P	C
unordered real comparison															
DD E0+i	fucom st(i)	80387			24	4									
DD E1	fucom	80387			24	4									
DD E8+i	fucomp st(i)	80387			26	4									
DD E9	fucomp	80387			26	4									
DA E9	fucompp	80387			26	4									

FWAIT							O	D	I	T	S	Z	A	P	C
wait															
9B	fwait	8087	4	3	6	1-3									

FXAM							O	D	I	T	S	Z	A	P	C
examine															
D9 E5	fxam	8087	12-23	12-23	30-38	8									

FXCH							O	D	I	T	S	Z	A	P	C
exchange															
D9 C8+i	fxch st(i)	8087	10-15	10-15	18	4									
D9 C9	fxch	8087	10-15	10-15	18	4									

FXTRACT							O	D	I	T	S	Z	A	P	C
extract exponent and significand															
D9 F4	fxtract	8087	27-55	27-55	70-76	16-20									

FYL2X							O	D	I	T	S	Z	A	P	C
y * (log base 2 of x)															
D9 F1	fyl2x	8087	900-1100	900-1100	120-538	196-329									

FYL2XP1
y * (log base 2 of (x+ 1))

								O	D	I	T	S	Z	A	P	C

D9 F9	fyl2xp1	8087	700-1000	700-1000	257-547	171-326

HLT
halt

O	D	I	T	S	Z	A	P	C

F4	hlt	8086	2	2	5	4

IDIV
signed division

O	D	I	T	S	Z	A	P	C
?				?	?	?	?	?

F6 /7	idiv r/m8	8086	101-118	17/20	19	19/20
F7 /7	idiv r/m16	8086	165-190	25/28	27	27/28
F7 /7	idiv r/m32	80386			43	43/44

IMUL
signed multiplication

O	D	I	T	S	Z	A	P	C
X				?	?	?	?	X

F6 /5	imul r/m8	8086	80-98/86-104	12/16	9-14/12-17	13-18/13/18
F7 /5	imul r/m16	8086	128-154/134-160	21/24	9-22/12-25	13-26/13-26
F7 /5	imul r/m32	80386			9-38/12/41	12-42/13-42
OF AF /r	imul r16, rm16	80386			9-22/12-25	13-26/13-26
OF AF /r	imul r32, r/m32	80386			9-38/12-41	13-42/13-42
6B /r ib	imul r16, r/m16, i8	80386			9-14/12-17	13-26/13-26
6B /r ib	imul r32, r/m32, i8	80386			9-14/12-17	13-42/13-42
6B /r ib	imul r16, i8	80386			9-14/12-17	13-26
6B /r ib	imul r32, i8	80386			9-14/12-17	13-42
69 /r iw	imul r16, r/m16, i16	80886			9-22/12-25	13-26/13-26
69 /r id	imul r32, r/m32, i32	80386			9-38/12/41	13-42/13-42
69 /r iw	imul r16, i16	80386			9-22/12-25	13-26/13-26
69 /r id	imul r32, i32	80386			9-38/12-41	13-42/13-42

IN
input from port

O	D	I	T	S	Z	A	P	C

E4 ib	in al, i8	8086	10	5	12{6,26}	8-28	In prot mode,
E5 lb	in ax, i8	8086	10	5	12{6,26}	8-28	smaller if CPL <= IOPL,
E5 ib	in eax, i8	80386			12{6,26}	8-28	larger if CPL > IOPL
EC	in al, dx	8086	8	5	13{7,27}	8-28	
ED	in ax, dx	8086	8	5	13{7,27}	8-28	
ED	in eax, dx	80386			13{7,27}	8-28	

INC
increment by 1

O	D	I	T	S	Z	A	P	C
X				X	X	X	X	

FE /0	inc r/m8	8086	3/15	2/7	2/6	1/3

FF /0	inc r/m16	8086	3/15	27/7	2/6	1/3	
FF /6	inc r/m32	80386			2/6	1/3	
40+rw	inc r16	8086	3	2	2	1	
40+rd	inc r32	80386			2	1	

INS/INSB/INSW/INSD						O D I T S Z A P C
input from port to string						
6C	ins r/m8, dx	80286	5	15,{9,29}	10-32	In prot mode,
6D	ins r/m16, dx	80286	5	15,{9,29}	10-32	smaller if CPL <= IOPL
6D	ins r/m32, dx	80386		15,{9,29}	10-32	bigger if CPL > IOPL
6C	insb	80286	5	15,{9,29}	10-32	
6D	insw	80286	5	15,{9,29}	10-32	
6D	insd	80386		15,{9,29}	10-32	

INT/INTO							O D I T S Z A P C
interrupt							_ _ _ 0 0 _ _ _ _
CC	int 3	8086	52	23+	33	26	Debugger trap
CC	int 3	80286		40+	59	44	Prot mode, same priv
CC	int 3	80286		78+	99	71	Prot mode, more priv
CC	int 3	80386			119	82	From V86 mode to PL 0
CC	int 3	80286		167	ts	37+ts	Prot mode, via task gate
CD /ib	int i8	8086	51	23+	37	30	Interrupt
CD /ib	int i8	80286		40+	59	44	Prot mode, same priv
CD /ib	int i8	80286		78+	99	71	Prot mode, more priv
CD /ib	int i8	80386			119	86	From V86 mode to PL 0
CD /ib	int i8	80286		167	ts	37+ts	Prot mode, via task gate
CE	into	8086	53	3-24+	3	3-28	Interrupt on overflow
CE	into	80286		3-24	59	46	Prot mode, same priv
CE	into	80286		3-24	99	73	Prot mode, more priv
CE	into	80386			119	84	From V86 mode to PL 0
CE	into	80286		3-24	ts	39+ts	Prot mode, via task gate

INVD				O D I T S Z A P C
invalidate cache				
0F 08	invd	80486	4	

INVLPG				O D I T S Z A P C
invalidate TLB entry				
0F 01 /7	invlpg m	80486	12	

IRET/IRETD							O	D	I	T	S	Z	A	P	C
return from interrupt							X	X	X	X	X	X	X	X	X
CF	iret	8086	32	17{31}	22-38	15	Interrupt return								
CF	iret	80286		55	82	36	To lesser privilege								
CF	iret	80286		169	ts	ts+32	To different task								
CF	iretd	80386			22-38	15	Interrupt return								
CF	iretd	80386			82	36	To lesser privilege								
CF	iretd	80386			60	15	To V86 mode								
CF	iretd	80386			ts	ts+32	To different task								

Jcc							O	D	I	T	S	Z	A	P	C
jump if condition is met															
77 cb	ja rel8	8086	16,4	7,3	7,3	3,1									
73 cb	jae rel8	8086	16,4	7,3	7,3	3,1									
72 cb	jb rel8	8086	16,4	7,3	7,3	3,1									
76 cb	jbe rel8	8086	16,4	7,3	7,3	3,1									
72 cb	jc rel8	8086	16,4	7,3	7,3	3,1									
E3 cb	jcxz rel8	8086	16,4	7,3	8,3	8,5									
E3 cb	jecxz rel8	80386			8,3	8,5									
74 cb	je rel8	8086	16,4	7,3	7,3	3,1									
7F cb	jg rel8	8086	16,4	7,3	7,3	3,1									
7D cb	jge rel8	8086	16,4	7,3	7,3	3,1									
7C cb	jl rel8	8086	16,4	7,3	7,3	3,1									
7E cb	jle rel8	8086	16,4	7,3	7,3	3,1									
73 cb	jnc rel8	8086	16,4	7,3	7,3	3,1									
75 cb	jne rel8	8086	16,4	7,3	7,3	3,1									
71 cb	jno rel8	8086	16,4	7,3	7,3	3,1									
7B cb	jnp rel8	8086	16,4	7,3	7,3	3,1									
79 cb	jns rel8	8086	16,4	7,3	7,3	3,1									
70 cb	jo rel8	8086	16,4	7,3	7,3	3,1									
7A cb	jp rel8	8086	16,4	7,3	7,3	3,1									
78 cb	js rel8	8086	16,4	7,3	7,3	3,1									
0F 87 cw/cd	ja rel16/32	80386			7,3	3,1									
0F 83 cw/cd	jae rel16/32	80386			7,3	3,1									
0F 82 cw/cd	jb rel16/32	80386			7,3	3,1									
0F 86 cw/cd	jbe rel16/32	80386			7,3	3,1									
0F 82 cw/cd	jc rel16/32	80386			7,3	3,1									
0F 84 cw/cd	je rel16/32	80386			7,3	3,1									
0F 8F cw/cd	jg rel16/32	80386			7,3	3,1									
0F 8D cw/cd	jge rel16/32	80386			7,3	3,1									
0F 8C cw/cd	jl rel16/32	80386			7,3	3,1									

0F 8E cw/cd	jle rel16/32	80386			7,3	3,1	
0F 83 cw/cd	jnc rel16/32	80386			7,3	3,1	
0F 85 cw/cd	jnerel16/32	80386			7,3	3,1	
0F 81 cw/cd	jno rel16/32	80386			7,3	3,1	
0F 8B cw/cd	jnp rel16/32	80386			7,3	3,1	
0F 89 cw/cd	jns rel16/32	80386			7,3	3,1	
0F 80 cw/cd	jo rel16/32	80386			7,3	3,1	
0F 8A cw/cd	jp rel16/32	80386			7,3	3,1	
0F 88 cw/cd	js rel16/32	80386			7,3	3,1	

REMARK. The times correspond to the jump being taken or not.

JMP								O	D	I	T	S	Z	A	P	C
jump																
EB cb	jmp rel8	8086	15	7	7+	3		Jump short
E9 cw	jmp rel16	8086	15	7	7+	3		Jump near
FF /4	jmp r/m16	8086	11/18	7/11	7+/10+	5/5		Jump near indirect
EA cd	jmp ptr16:16	8086	15	11{23}	12+{27+}	17{19}		Jump 4-byte immediate
EA cd	jmp ptr16:16	80286		38	45+	32		Jump to call gate
EA cd	jmp ptr16:16	80286		175	ts	42+ts		Jump via TSS
EA cd	jmp ptr16:16	80286		180	ts	43+ts		Jump via task gate
FF /5	jmp m16:16	8086	24	15/{26}	31+{43+}	13{18}		Jump memory indirect
FF /5	jmp m16:16	80286		41	49+	31		Jump to call gate, same priv
FF /5	jmp m16:16	80286		178	5+ts	41+ts		Jump via TSS
FF /5	jmp m16:16	80286		183	5+ts	42+ts		Jump via task gate
E9 cd	jmp rel32	80386			7+	3		Jump near
FF /4	jmp r/m32	80386			7+{10+}	5/5		Jump near indirect
EA cp	jmp ptr16:32	80386			12+{27+}	13{18}		Jump 6-byte immediate
EA cp	jmp ptr16:32	80386			45+	31		Jump to call gate, same priv
EA cp	jmp ptr16:32	80386			ts	42+ts		Jump via TSS
EA cp	jmp ptr16:32	80386			ts	43+ts		Jump via task gate
FF /5	jmp m16:32	80386			31+{43+}	13{18}		Jump memory indirect
FF /5	jmp m16:32	80386			49+	31		Jump to call gate, same priv
FF /5	jmp m16:32	80386			5+ts	41+ts		Jump via TSS
FF /5	jmp m16:32	80386			5+ts	42+ts		Jump via task gate

LAHF							O	D	I	T	S	Z	A	P	C
load flags into ah register															
9F	lahf	8086	4	2	2	3									

LAR							O	D	I	T	S	Z	A	P	C
load access rights byte												X			
0F 02 /r	lar r16, r/m16	80286		14/16	15/16	11/11									
0F 02 /r	lar r32, r/m32	80386			15/16	11/11									

LEA							O	D	I	T	S	Z	A	P	C
load effective address															
8D /r	lea r16, m	8086	2	3	2	1									
8D /r	lea r32, m	80386			2	1									

LEAVE						O	D	I	T	S	Z	A	P	C
high-level procedure exit														
C9	leave	80286	5	4	5									

LGDT/LIDT						O	D	I	T	S	Z	A	P	C
load global/local descriptor table register														
0F 01 /2	lgdt m16&32	80286	11	11	11									
0F 01 /3	lidt m16&32	80286	12	11	11									

LGS/LSS/LDS/LES/LFS								O	D	I	T	S	Z	A	P	C
load far pointer																
C5 /r	lds r16, m16:16	8086	16	7-21	7-22	6/12										
C5 /r	lds r32, m16:32	80386			7-22	6/12										
0F B2 /r	lss r16, m16:16	80386			7-22	6/12										
0F B2 /r	lss r32, m16:32	80386			7-22	6/12										
C4 /r	les r16, m16:16	8086	16	7-21	7-22	6/12										
C4 /r	les r32, m16:32	80386			7-22	6/12										
0F B4 /r	lfs r16, m16:16	80386			7-25	6/12										
0F B4 /r	lfs r32, m16:32	80386			7-25	6/12										
0F B5 /r	lgs r16, m16:16	80386			7-25	6/12										
0F B5 /r	lgs r32, m16:32	80386			7-25	6/12										

LLDT						O	D	I	T	S	Z	A	P	C
load local descriptor table register														
0F 00 /2	lldt r/m16	80286	17/19	20/24	11/11									

LMSW						O	D	I	T	S	Z	A	P	C
load machine status word														
0F 01 /6	lmsw r/m16	80286	3/6	10/13	13/13									

LOCK — lock the bus

			O D I T S Z A P C
F0	lock	8086	2 0 0 1

LODS/LODSB/LODSW/LODSD — load string operand

Flags: O D I T S Z A P C

Opcode	Instruction	CPU				
AC	lods m8	8086	12	5	5	5
AD	lods m16	8086	12	5	5	5
AD	lods m32	80386			5	5
AC	lodsb	8086	12	5	5	5
AD	lodsw	8086	12	5	5	5
AD	lodsd	80386			5	5

LOOP/LOOPcond — loop control with cx as counter

Flags: O D I T S Z A P C

Opcode	Instruction	CPU				
E2 cb	loop rel8	8086	17,5	8,4	11+m	9,6
E1 cb	loope rel8	8086	18,6	8,4	11+m	9,6
E0 cb	loopne rel8	8086	19,5	8,4	11+m	9,6

Remark. The smaller value corresponds to the jump not being taken.

LSL — load segment limit

Flags: O D I T S Z A P C   (X under Z)

Opcode	Instruction	CPU				
0F 03 /r	lsl r16, r/m16	80286	14/16	20/21	10/10	Byte granular
0F 03 /r	lsl r32, r/m32	80386		20/21	10/10	Byte granular
0F 03 /r	lsl r16, r/m16	80286	14/16	25/26	10/10	Page granular
0f 03 /r	lsl r32, r/m32	80386		25/26	10/10	Page granular

LTR — load task register

Flags: O D I T S Z A P C

Opcode	Instruction	CPU			
0F 00 /3	ltr r/m16	80286	17/19	23/27	20/20

MOV — move data

Flags: O D I T S Z A P C

Opcode	Instruction	CPU				
88 /r	mov r/m8, r8	8086	2/9	2/3	2/2	1
89 /r	mov r/m16, r16	8086	2/9	2/3	2/2	1
89 /r	mov r/m32, r32	80386			2/2	1
8A /r	mov r8, r/m8	8086	2/8	2/5	2/4	1
8B /r	mov r16, r/m16	8086	2/8	2/5	2/4	1
8B /r	mov r32, r/m32	80386			2/4	1

8C /r	mov r/m16, Sreg	8086	2/9	2/3	2/2	3/3	
8E /r	mov Sreg, r/m16	8086	2/8	2/5{17/19}	2/5{18/19}	3/9	
A0	mov al, moffs8	80386			4	1	
A1	mov ax, moffs16	8086	10	5	4	1	
A1	mov eax, moffs32	80386			4	1	
A2	mov moffs8, al	8086	10	3	2	1	
A3	mov moffs16, ax	8086	10	3	2	1	
A3	mov moffs32, eax	80386			2	1	
B0 + rb	mov reg8, i8	8088	4	2	2	1	
B8 + rw	mov reg16, i16	8088	4	2	2	1	
B8 + rd	mov reg32, i32	80386			2	1	
C6	mov r/m8, i8	8088	4/10	2/3	2/2	1	
C7	mov r/m16, i16	8088	4/10	2/3	2/2	1	
C7	mov r/m32, i32	80386			2/2	1	

MOV					O	D	I	T	S	Z	A	P	C
move to/from special registers													
0F 22 /r	mov cr0, r32	80386		10	16								
0F 20 /r	mov r32, cr0/cr1/cr2	80386		10/4/5	4								
0F 22 /r	mov cr2/cr3, r32	80386		4/5	4								
0F 21 /r	mov r32, dr0-3	80386		22	10								
0F 21 /r	mov r32, dr6/dr7	80386		14	10								
0F 23 /r	mov dr0-3, r32	80386		22	11								
0F 23 /r	mov dr6/dr7, r32	80386		16	11								
0F 24 /r	mov r32, tr4-7	80386		12	4								
0F 26 /r	mov tr4-7, r32	80386		12	4								
0F 24 /r	mov r32, tr3	80386		12	3								
0F 26 /r	mov tr3, r32	80386		12	6								

MOVS/MOVSB/MOVSW/MOVSD						O	D	I	T	S	Z	A	P	C
load string operand														
A4	movs m8, m8	8086	18	5	7	7								
A5	movs m16, m16	8086	18	5	7	7								
A5	movs m32, m16	80386			7	7								
A4	movsb	8086	18	5	7	7								
A5	movsw	8086	18	5	7	7								
A5	movsd	80386			7	7								

MOVSX							O	D	I	T	S	Z	A	P	C
move with sign-extend															
0F BE /r	movsx r16, r/m8	80386			3/6	3/3									
0F BE /r	movsx r32, r/m8	80386			3/6	3/3									
0F BE /r	movsx r32, r/16	80386			3/6	3/3									

MOVSZ							O	D	I	T	S	Z	A	P	C
move with zero-extend															
0F B6 /r	movsz r16, r/m8	80386			3/6	3/3									
0F B6 /r	movsz r32, r/m8	80386			3/6	3/3									
0F B6 /r	movsz r32, r/16	80386			3/6	3/3									

MUL								O	D	I	T	S	Z	A	P	C
unsigned multiplication								X					?	?	?	?	X
F6 /4	mul r/m8	8086	70-77/76-83	13/16	9-14/12-17	13-18/13-18										
F7 /4	mul r/m16	8086	118-133/124-139	21/24	9-22/12-25	13-26/13-26										
F7 /4	mul r/m32	80386			9-38/12-41	13-42/13-42										

NEG								O	D	I	T	S	Z	A	P	C
two's complement								X				X	X	X	X	
F6 /3	neg r/m8	8086	3/16	2/7	2/6	1/3										
F6 /7	neg r/m16	8086	3/16	2/7	2/6	1/3										
F6 /7	neg r/m32	80386			2/6	1/3										

NOP							O	D	I	T	S	Z	A	P	C
no operation															
90	nop	8086	3	3	3	1									

NOT							O	D	I	T	S	Z	A	P	C
one's complement															
F6 /2	not r/m8	8086	3/16	2/7	2/6	1/3									
F7 /2	not r/m16	8086	3/16	2/7	2/6	1/3									
F7 /2	not r/m32	80386			2/6	1/3									

OR							O	D	I	T	S	Z	A	P	C
bitwise or							0				X	X	?	X	0
0C ib	or al, i8	8086	4	3	2	1									
0D iw	or ax, i16	8086	4	3	2	1									
0D id	or eax, i32	80386			2	1									
80 /1 ib	or r/m8, i8	8086	4/17	3/7	2/7	1/3									

81 /1 iw	or r/m16, i16	8086	4/17	3/7	2/7	1/3	
81 /1 id	or r/m32, i32	80386			2/7	1/3	
83 /1 ib	or r/m16, i8	80386			2/7	1/3	
83 /1 ib	or r/m32, i8	80386			2/7	1/3	
08 /r	or r/m8, r8	8086	3/16	2/7	2/6	1/3	
09 /r	or r/m16, r16	8086	3/16	2/7	2/6	1/3	
09 /r	or r/m32, r32	80386			2/6	1/3	
0A /r	or r8, r/m8	8086	3/9	2/7	2/7	1/2	
0B /r	or r16, r/m16	8086	3/9	2/7	2/7	1/2	
0B /r	or r32, r/m32	80386			2/7	1/2	

OUT							O	D	I	T	S	Z	A	P	C
output to port															

E6 ib	out i8, al	8086	10	3	10{4,24}	16{11,31}	In prot mode:
E7 lb	out i8, ax	8086	10	3	10{4,24}	16{11,31}	smaller if CPL <= IOPL
E7 ib	out i8, eax	80386			10{4,24}	16{11,31}	larger if CPL > IOPL
EF	out dx, al	8086	8	3	11{5,25}	16{10,30}	
EF	out dx, ax	8086	8	3	11{5,25}	16{10,30}	
EF +	out dx, eax	80386			11{5,25}	16{10,30}	

OUTS/OUTSB/OUTSW/OUTSD						O	D	I	T	S	Z	A	P	C
output string to port														

6E	outs r/m8, dx	80286	5	14{8,28}	17{10,32}	In prot mode:
6F	outs r/m16, dx	80286	5	14{8,28}	17{10,32}	smaller if CPL <= IOPL
6F	outs r/m32, dx	80386		14{8,28}	17{10,32}	larger if CPL > IOPL
6E	outsb	80286	5	14{8,28}	17{10,32}	
6F	outsw	80286	5	14{8,28}	17{10,32}	
6F	outsd	80386		14{8,28}	17{10,32}	

POP						O	D	I	T	S	Z	A	P	C
pop a word from stack														

8F /0	pop m16	8086	17	5	5	6
8F /0	pop m32	80386			5	6
58 + rw	pop r16	8086	8	5	4	4
58 + rd	pop r32	80386			4	4
1F	pop ds	8086	8	5{20}	7{21}	3
07	pop es	8086	8	5{20}	7{21}	3
17	pop ss	8086	8	5{20}	7{21}	3
0F A1	pop fs	80386			7{21}	3
0F A9	pop gs	80386			7{21}	3

POPA/POPAD			O	D	I	T	S	Z	A	P	C
pop all general registers											
61	popa	80286	19	24	9						
61	popad	80386		24	9						

POPF/POPFD			O	D	I	T	S	Z	A	P	C
pop stack into flags or eflags											
9D	popf	80286	8	5	5	9{6}					
9D	popfd	80386		5	9{6}						

PUSH			O	D	I	T	S	Z	A	P	C
push operand onto the stack											
FF /6	push m16	8086	16	5	5	4					
FF /6	push m32	80386		5	4						
50+ /r	push r16	8086	11	5	2	1					
50 +/r	push r32	80386		2	1						
6A	push i8	80286	3	2	1						
68	push i16	80286	3	2	1						
68	push i32	80386		2	1						
0E	push cs	8086	10	3	2	3					
16	push ss	8086	10	3	2	3					
1E	push ds	8086	10	3	2	3					
06	push es	8086	10	3	2	3					
0F A0	push fs	80386		2	3						
0F A8	push gs	80386		2	3						

PUSHA/PUSHAD			O	D	I	T	S	Z	A	P	C
push all general registers											
60	pusha	80286	17	18	11						
60	pushad	80386		18	11						

PUSHF/PUSHFD			O	D	I	T	S	Z	A	P	C
push flags or eflags onto stack											
9C	pushf	8086	10	3	4	4(3)					
9C	pushfd	80386		4	4(3)						

RCL/RCR/ROL/ROR								O	D	I	T	S	Z	A	P	C
rotate								X								X
D0 /2	rcl r/m8, 1	8086	2/15	2/7	9/10	3/4										
D2 /2	rcl r/m8, cl	8086	8+4pb	5/8	9/10	8-30/9/31										
C0 /2 ib	rcl r/m8, i8	80286		5/8	9/10	8-30/9-31										
D1 /2	rcl r/m16, 1	8086	2/15	2/7	9/10	3/4										
D3 /2	rcl r/m16, cl	8086	8+4pb	5/8	9/10	8-30/9-31										
C1 /2 ib	rcl r/m16, i8	80286		5/8	9/10	8-30/9-31										
D1 /2	rcl r/m32, 1	80386			9/10	3/4										
D3 /2	rcl r/m32, cl	80386			9/10	8-30/9-31										
C1 /2 ib	rcl r/m32, i8	80386			9/10	8-30/9-31										
D0 /3	rcr r/m8, 1	8086	2/15	2/7	9/10	3/4										
D2 /3	rcr r/m8, cl	8086	8+4pb	5/8	9/10	8-30/9-31										
C0 /3 ib	rcr r/m8, i8	80286		5/8	9/10	8-30/9-31										
D1 /3	rcr r/m16, 1	8086	2/15	2/7	9/10	3/4										
D3 /3	rcr r/m16, cl	8086	8+4pb	5/8	9/10	8-30/9-31										
C1 /3 ib	rcr r/m16, i8	80286		5/8	9/10	8-30/9-31										
D1 /3	rcr r/m32, 1	80386			9/10	3/4										
D3 /3	rcr r/m32, cl	80386			9/10	8-30/9-31										
C1 /3 ib	rcr r/m32, i8	80386			9/10	8-30/9-31										
D0 /0	rol r/m8, 1	8086	2/15	2/7	3/7	3/4										
D2 /0	rol r/m8, cl	8086	8+4pb	5/8	3/7	3/4										
C0 /0 ib	rol r/m8, i8	80286		5/8	3/7	3/4										
D1 /0	rol r/m16, 1	8086	2/15	2/7	3/7	3/4										
D3 /0	rol r/m16, cl	8086	8+4pb	5/8	3/7	3/4										
C1 /0 ib	rol r/m16, i8	80286		5/8	3/7	2/4										
D1 /0	rol r/m32, 1	80386			3/7	3/4										
D3 /0	rol r/m32, cl	80386			3/7	3/4										
C1 /0 ib	rol r/m32, i8	80386			3/7	3/4										
D0 /1	ror r/m8, 1	8086	2/15	2/7	3/7	3/4										
D2 /1	ror r/m8, cl	8086	8+4pb	5/8	3/7	3/4										
C0 /1 ib	ror r/m8, i8	80286		5/8	3/7	3/4										
D1 /1	ror r/m16, 1	8086	2/15	2/7	3/7	3/4										
D3 /1	ror r/m16, cl	8086	8+4pb	5/8	3/7	3/4										
C1 /1 ib	ror r/m16, i8	80286		5/8	3/7	2/4										
D1 /1	ror r/m32, 1	80386			3/7	3/4										
D3 /1	ror r/m32, cl	80386			3/7	3/4										
C1 /1 ib	ror r/m32, i8	80386			3/7	3/4										

NOTE. pb means per bit. In those cases the 8088 needs 20+4pb.

REP/REPE/REPNE					O	D	I	T	S	Z	A	P	C
repeat string operation										X			

Opcode	Instruction	Proc				
F3 6C	rep ins r/m8, dx	80286		5+4cx	13+6(e)cx {7+6(e)cx}[1]/ {27+6(e)cx}[2] vm=29+8(e)cx	16+8(e)cx {10+8(ecx)}[1] {30+8(e)cx}[2]
F3 6D	rep ins r/m16, dx	80286		5+4cx	13+6(e)cx {7+6(e)cx}[1]/ {27+6(e)cx}[2]	16+8(e)cx {10+8(e)cx)}[1] {30+8(e)cx}[2] vm=29+8(e)cx
F3 6D	rep ins r/m32, dx	80386			13+6(e)cx {7+6(e)cx}[1]/ {27+6(e)cx}[2]	16+8(e)cx {10+8(e)cx)}[1] {30+8(e)cx}[2] vm=29+8(e)cx
F3 A4	rep movs m8,m8	8086	5+17cx	5+4cx	5+4(e)cx	5[3],13[4],12+3(e)cx[5]
F3 A5	rep movs m16,m16	8086	5+17cx	5+4cx	5+4(e)cx	5[3],13[4],12+3(e)cx[5]
F3 A4	rep movs m32,m32	80386			5+4(e)cx	5[3],13[4],12+3(e)cx[5]
F3 6E	rep outs dx, r/m8	80286		5+4cx	5+12(e)cx {6+5(e)cx}[1]/ {26+5(e)cx}[2]/	17+5(e)cx {11+5(ecx)}[1] {31+5(e)cx}[2] vm=30+5(e)cx
F3 6F	rep outs dx, r/m16	80286		5+4cx	5+12(e)cx {6+5(e)cx}[1]/ {26+5(e)cx}[2]	17+5(e)cx {11+5(ecx)}[1] {31+5(e)cx}[2] vm=30+5(e)cx
F3 6F	rep outs dx, r/m32	80386			5+12(e)cx {6+5(e)cx}[1] 26+56(e)cx}[2]	17+5(e)cx {11+5(ecx)}[1] {31+5(e)cx}[2] vm=30+5(e)cx
F2 AC	rep lods m8	8086	9+13cx	4+3cx	5+5cx	5[3], 7+4(e)cx[6]
F2 AD	rep lods m16	8086	9+13cx	4+3cx	5+5cx	5[3], 7+4(e)cx[6]
F2 AD	rep lods m32	80386			5+5cx	5[3], 7+4(e)cx[6]
F3 AA	rep stos m8	8086	9+10cx	4+3cx	5+5cx	5[3], 7+4(e)cx[6]
F3 AB	rep stos m16	8086	9+10cx	4+3cx	5+5cx	5[3], 7+4(e)cx[6]
F3 AB	rep stos m32	80386			5+5cx	5[3], 7+4(e)cx[6]
F3 A6	repe cmps m8	8086	9+22cx	5+9cx	5+9cx	5[3], 7+4(e)cx[6]
F3 A7	repe cmps m16	8086	9+22cx	5+9cx	5+9cx	5[3], 7+4(e)cx[6]
F3 A7	repe cmps m32	80386			5+9cx	5[3], 7+4(e)cx[6]
F3 AE	repe scas m8	8086	9+13cx	5+8cx	5+8cx	5[3], 7+4(e)cx[6]
F3 AF	repe scas m16	8086	9+13cx	5+8cx	5+8cx	5[3], 7+4(e)cx[6]
F3 AF	repe scas m32	80386			5+8cx	5[3], 7+4(e)cx[6]

F2 A6	repne cmps m8	8086	9+22cx	5+9cx	5+9cx	$5^3, 7+4(e)cx^6$
F2 A7	repne cmps m16	8086	9+22cx	5+9cx	5+9cx	$5^3, 7+4(e)cx^6$
F2 A7	repne cmps m32	80386			5+9cx	$5^3, 7+4(e)cx^6$
F2 AE	repne scas m8	8086	9+15cx	5+8cx	5+8cx	$5^3, 7+4(e)cx^6$
F2 AF	repne scas m16	8086	9+15cx	5+8cx	5+8cx	$5^3, 7+4(e)cx^6$
F2 AF	repne scas m32	80386			5+8cx	$5^3, 7+4(e)cx^6$

Notes. 1 if CPL <= IOPL; 2 if CPL > IOPL; 3 if (e)cx = 0;
4 if (e)cx = 1; 5 if (e)cx > 1; 6 if (e)cx > 0

RET							O	D	I	T	S	Z	A	P	C
return from procedure															
C3	ret	8086	16	11	10+	5	Near return
CB	ret	8086	26	15+{25}	18+{32+}	13{18}	Far return, same priv
CB	ret	80286		55	{68}	13{33 }	Far return, lesser priv
C2 iw	ret i16	8088	20	11	10+	5	Near return
CA iw	ret i16	8086	25	15{25}	18+{32+}	14{17}	Far return, same priv
CA iw	ret i16	80286		55	{68}	14{33}	Far return, lesser priv

SAHF							O	D	I	T	S	Z	A	P	C
store sh in flags															
9E	sahf	8086	4	2	3	2									

SAL/SAR/SHL/SHR							O	D	I	T	S	Z	A	P	C
shift							X				X	X	?	X	X
D0 /4	sal r/m8, 1	8086	2/15	2/7	3/7	3/4
D2 /4	sal r/m8, cl	8086	8+4pb	5/8	3/7	3/4
C0 /4 ib	sal r/m8, i8	80286		5/8	3/7	2/4
D1 /4	sal r/m16, 1	8086	2/15	2/7	3/7	3/4
D3 /4	sal r/m16, cl	8086	8+4pb	5/8	3/7	3/4
C1 /4 ib	sal r/m16, i8	80286		5/8	3/7	2/4
D1 /4	sal r/m32, 1	80386			3/7	3/4
D3 /4	sal r/m32, cl	80386			3/7	3/4
C1 /4 ib	sal r/m32, i8	80386			3/7	2/4
D0 /7	sar r/m8, 1	8086	2/15	2/7	3/7	3/4
D2 /7	sar r/m8, cl	8086	8+4pb	5/8	3/7	3/4
C0 /7 ib	sar r/m8, i8	80286		5/8	3/7	2/4
D1 /7	sar r/m16, 1	8086	2/15	2/7	3/7	3/4
D3 /7	sar r/m16, cl	8086	8+4pb	5/8	3/7	3/4
C1 /7 ib	sar r/m16, i8	80286		5/8	3/7	2/4

D1 /7	sar r/m32, 1	80386			3/7	3/4
D3 /7	sar r/m32, cl	80386			3/7	3/4
C1 /7 ib	sar r/m32, i8	80386			3/7	2/4
D0 /4	shl r/m8, 1	8086	2/15	2/7	3/7	3/4
D2 /4	shl r/m8, cl	8086	8+4pb	5/8	3/7	3/4
C0 /4 ib	shl r/m8, i8	80286		5/8	3/7	2/4
D1 /4	shl r/m16, 1	8086	2/15	2/7	3/7	3/4
D3 /4	shl r/m16, cl	8086	8+4pb	5/8	3/7	3/4
C1 /4 ib	shl r/m16, i8	80286		5/8	3/7	2/4
D1 /4	shl r/m32, 1	80386			3/7	3/4
D3 /4	shl r/m32, cl	80386			3/7	3/4
C1 /4 ib	shl r/m32, i8	80386			3/7	2/4
D0 /5	shr r/m8, 1	8086	2/15	2/7	3/7	3/4
D2 /5	shr r/m8, cl	8086	8+4pb	5/8	3/7	3/4
C0 /5 ib	shr r/m8, i8	80286		5/8	3/7	2/4
D1 /5	shr r/m16, 1	8086	2/15	2/7	3/7	3/4
D3 /5	shr r/m16, cl	8086	8+4pb	5/8	3/7	3/4
C1 /5 ib	shr r/m16, i8	80286		5/8	3/7	2/4
D1 /5	shr r/m32, 1	80386			3/7	3/4
D3 /5	shr r/m32, cl	80386			3/7	3/4
C1 /5 ib	shr r/m32, i8	80386			3/7	2/4

NOTE. pb means per bit. In those cases the 8088 needs 20+4pb.

SBB							O	D	I	T	S	Z	A	P	C
subtract with borrow							X				X	X	X	X	X
1C ib	sbb al, i8	8086	4	3	2	1									
1D iw	sbb ax, i16	8086	4	3	2	1									
1D id	sbb eax, i32	80386			2	1									
80 /3 ib	sbb r/m8, i8	8086	4/17	3/7	2/7	1/3									
81 /3 iw	sbb r/m16, i16	8086	4/17	3/7	2/7	1/3									
81 /3 id	sbb r/m32, i32	80386			2/7	1/3									
83 /3 ib	sbb r/m16, i8	8086	4/17	3/7	2/7	1/3									
83 /3 ib	sbb r/m32, i8	80386			2/7	1/3									
18 /r	sbb r/m8, r8	8086	3/16	2/7	2/6	1/3									
19 /r	sbb r/m16, r16	8086	3/16	2/7	2/6	1/3									
19 /r	sbb r/m32, r32	80386			2/6	1/3									
1A /r	sbb r8, r/m8	8086	3/9	2/7	2/7	1/2									
1B /r	sbb r16, r/m16	8086	3/9	2/7	2/7	1/2									
1B /r	sbb r32, r/m32	80386			2/7	1/2									

SCAS/SCASB/SCASW/SCASD							O	D	I	T	S	Z	A	P	C
load string operand							X				X	X	X	X	X
AE	scas m8	8086	15	7	7	6									
AF	scas m16	8086	15	7	7	6									
AF	scas m32	80386			7	6									
AE	scasb	8086	15	7	7	6									
AF	scasw	8086	15	7	7	6									
AF	scasd	80386			7	6									

SETcc						O	D	I	T	S	Z	A	P	C
set byte on condition														
0F 97	seta r/m8	80386		4/5	4/3									
0F 93	setae r/m8	80386		4/5	4/3									
0F 92	setb r/m8	80386		4/5	4/3									
0F 96	setbe r/m8	80386	4/5		4/3									
0F 92	setc r/m8	80386		4/5	4/3									
0F 94	sete r/m8	80386		4/5	4/3									
0F 9F	setg r/m8	80386		4/5	4/3									
0F 9D	setge r/m8	80386	4/5		4/3									
0F 9C	setl r/m8	80386		4/5	4/3									
0F 9E	setle r/m8	80386	4/5		4/3									
0F 93	setnc r/m8	80386	4/5		4/3									
0F 95	setne r/m8	80386	4/5		4/3									
0F 91	setno r/m8	80386	4/5		4/3									
0F 9B	setnp r/m8	80386		4/5	4/3									
0F 99	setns r/m8	80386		4/5	4/3									
0F 90	seto r/m8	80386		4/5	4/3									
0F 9A	setp r/m8	80386		4/5	4/3									
0F 98	sets r/m8	80386		4/5	4/3									

SGDT/SIDT						O	D	I	T	S	Z	A	P	C
store global/interrupt descriptor table register														
0F 01 /0	sgdt m	80286	11	9	10									
0F 01 /1	sidt m	80286	12	9	10									

SHLD						O	D	I	T	S	Z	A	P	C
double-precision shift left						?				X	X	?	X	X
0F A4	shld r/m16, r16, i8	80386		3/7	2/3									
0F A4	shld r/m32, r32, i8	80386		3/7	2/3									
0F A5	shld r/m16, r16, cl	80386		3/7	3/4									
0F A5	shld r/m16, r16, cl	80386		3/7	3/4									

shrd						O	D	I	T	S	Z	A	P	C
double-precision shift right						?				X	X	?	X	X
0F AC	shrd r/m16, r16, i8	80386	3/7	2/3										
0F AC	shrd r/m32, r32, i8	80386	3/7	2/3										
0F AD	shrd r/m16, r16, cl	80386	3/7	3/4										
0F AD	shrd r/m16, r16, cl	80386	3/7	3/4										

SLDT						O	D	I	T	S	Z	A	P	C
store local descriptor table register														
0F 00 /0	sldt r/m16	80286	2/3	2/2	2/3									

SMSW						O	D	I	T	S	Z	A	P	C
store machine status word														
0F 01 /4	smsw r/m16	80286	2/3	2/2	2/3									

STC						O	D	I	T	S	Z	A	P	C
set carry flag														1
F9	stc	8086	2	2	2	2								

STD						O	D	I	T	S	Z	A	P	C
set direction flag							1							
FD	std	8086	2	2	2	2								

STI						O	D	I	T	S	Z	A	P	C
set interrupt flag								1						
F13	sti	8086	2	2	3	5								

STOS/STOSB/STOSW/STOSD						O	D	I	T	S	Z	A	P	C
load string operand														
AA	stos m8	8086	11	3	4	5								
AB	stos m16	8086	11	3	4	5								
AB	stos m32	80386			4	5								
AA	stosb	8086	11	3	4	5								
AB	stosw	8086	11	3	4	5								
AB	stosd	80386			4	5								

STR				O	D	I	T	S	Z	A	P	C
store task register												
0F 00 /1	strw r/m16	80286	2/3	23/27	2/3							

SUB						O	D	I	T	S	Z	A	P	C
subtracts operands						X				X	X	X	X	X
2C ib	sub al, i8	8086	4	3	2	1								
2D iw	sub ax, i16	8086	4	3	2	1								
2D id	sub eax, i32	80386			2	1								
80 /5 ib	sub r/m8, i8	8086	4/17	3/7	2/7	1/3								
81 /5 iw	sub r/m16, i16	8086	4/17	3/7	2/7	1/3								
81 /5 id	sub r/m32, i32	80386			2/7	1/3								
83 /5 ib	sub r/m16, i8	8086	4/17	3/7	2/7	1/3								
83 /5 ib	sub r/m32, i8	80386			2/7	1/3								
28 /r	sub r/m8, r8	8086	3/16	2/7	2/6	1/3								
29 /r	sub r/m16, r16	8086	3/16	2/7	2/6	1/3								
29 /r	sub r/m32, r32	80386			2/6	1/3								
2A /r	sub r8, r/m8	8086	3/9	2/7	2/7	1/2								
2B /r	sub r16, r/m16	8086	3/9	2/7	2/7	1/2								
2B /r	sub r32, r/m32	80386			2/7	1/2								

TEST						O	D	I	T	S	Z	A	P	C
logical compare						0				X	X	?	X	0
A8 ib	test al, i8	8086	4	3	2	1								
A9 iw	test ax, i16	8086	4	3	2	1								
A9 id	test eax, i32	80386			2	1								
F6 /0 ib	test r/m8, i8	8086	5/11	3/6	2/5	1/2								
F7 /0 iw	test r/m16, i16	8086	5/11	3/6	2/5	1/2								
F7 /04 id	test r/m32, i32	80386			2/5	1/2								
84 /r	test r/m8, r8	8086	3/9	2/6	2/5	1/2								
85 /r	test r/m16, r16	8086	3/9	2/6	2/5	1/2								
85 /r	test r/m32, r32	80386			2/5	1/2								

VERR/VERW						O	D	I	T	S	Z	A	P	C
verify a segment for reading or writing											X			
0F 00 /4	verr r/m16	80286	14/16	10/11	11/11									
0F 00 /5	verw r/m16	80286	14/16	15/16	11/11									

WAIT								O	D	I	T	S	Z	A	P	C
wait for coprocessor																
9B	wait	8086	3+5n	3	6	1-3										

WBINVD					O	D	I	T	S	Z	A	P	C
write-back and invalidate the cache													
0F 09	wbinvd	80486		5									

XADD					O	D	I	T	S	Z	A	P	C
exchange and add					X				X	X	X	X	X
0F C0 /r	xadd r/m8, r8	80486		3/4									
0F C1 /r	xadd r/m16, r16	80486		3/4									
0F C0 /r	xadd r/m32, r32	80486		3/4									

XCHG								O	D	I	T	S	Z	A	P	C
exchange register/memory with register																
90 + r	xchg ax, r16	8086	3	3	3	3										
90 + r	xchg r16, ax	8086	3	3	3	3										
90 + r	xchg eax, r32	80386			3	3										
90 + r	xchg r32, eax	80386			3	3										
86 /r	xchg r/m8, r8	8086	4/17	3/5	3/5	3/5										
86 /r	xchg r8, r/m8	8086	4/17	3/5	3/5	3/5										
87 /r	xchg r/m16, r16	8086	4/17	3/5	3/5	3/5										
87 /r	xchg r16, r/m16	8086	4/17	3/5	3/5	3/5										
87 /r	xchg r/m32, r32	80386			3/5	3/5										
87 /r	xchg r32, r/m32	80386			3/5	3/5										

XLAT/XLATB								O	D	I	T	S	Z	A	P	C
table look-up translation																
D7	xlat m8	8086	11	5	5	4										
D7	xlatb	8086	11	5	5	4										

SELECTED ROM BIOS AND MS-DOS INTERRUPTS

Note. We have included those ROM BIOS and **MS-DOS** interrupts needed in the text or exercises and some others of special interest. In cases where the IBM implementation of an interrupt differs from the Intel default, we have listed the IBM version. For complete descriptions of the available BIOS and **MS-DOS** interrupts, see [3] or [24]. In all cases where function numbers are needed, they are transmitted in the **ah** register.

INT	FUNCTION	DESCRIPTION
00h	None	**Divide Overflow** - triggered by quotient being too large for destination Inputs: None Returns: Nothing
01h	None	**Single step** - occurs when trap flag set Inputs: None Returns: Nothing
02h	None	**NMI -** triggered by parity check error or other hardware-dependent events Inputs: None Returns: Nothing
03h	None	**Breakpoint** - taken when byte with value 0cch occurs in code Inputs: None Returns: Nothing
04h	None	**Overflow** - triggered by **into** instruction provided that OF = 1 Inputs: None Returns: Nothing
05h	None	**Print screen** - triggered by Shift PrtScr key combination Inputs: None Returns: Nothing
08h	None	**Timer interrupt** - occurs about 18.2 times per second Inputs: None

INT	FUNCTION	DESCRIPTION

Returns: Nothing

09h   None   **Keyboard interrupt** - sends information about key presses or releases to keyboard buffer and updates shift key status flags

Inputs: None

Returns: Nothing

10h   **Video interrupt**

Note. Upper left corner of screen has coordinates (0,0). The x-coordinate increases horizontally and the y-coordinate increases vertically.

00h   Initialize video mode

Inputs: Required mode, transmitted in al
Of the 16 modes, al = 3, which gives 80 x 25 text and al = 4, which gives 320 x 200 4-color graphics, are commonly used.

Returns: Nothing

01h   Set cursor type

Inputs: Starting scan line of cursor in low 4 bits of ch
Ending scan line of cursor in low 4 bit of cl

Returns: Nothing

02h   Set cursor position

Inputs: bh = video page
dh and dl = row and column numbers

Returns: Nothing

03h   Find cursor position

Inputs: bh = video page

Returns: (dh,dl) = (x,y)-coordinates of cursor
(ch,cl) = starting and ending scan lines of cursor

05h   Set video display page

Inputs: page number (0-7 for EGA mode 3)

Returns: Nothing

06h   Initialize or scroll window up

Inputs: al = number of lines to scroll (if 0, window cleared)
bh = attribute for cleared area
ch and cl = (x,y)-coordinates of upper left corner of window
dh and dl = (x,y)-coordinates of lower right corner of window

Returns: Nothing

07h   Initialize or scroll window down

Inputs: The same as function 06h

Returns: Nothing

08h   Read character and attribute at cursor

This function does not update the cursor position

Inputs: bh = page number

Returns: ah = attribute
al = character

09h   Write character and attribute at cursor

Inputs: al = character
bh = page number

INT	FUNCTION	DESCRIPTION

<table>
<tr><td></td><td></td><td>bl = attribute in text modes, color in graphics modes
cx = number of times to write the character</td></tr>
<tr><td></td><td></td><td>Returns: Nothing</td></tr>
<tr><td></td><td>0ah</td><td>Write character at cursor using current attribute
This function does not update the cursor position.</td></tr>
<tr><td></td><td></td><td>Inputs: al = character
bh = page number
bl = color (in graphics modes only)
cx= number of times to write the character</td></tr>
<tr><td></td><td></td><td>Returns: Nothing</td></tr>
<tr><td></td><td>0bh</td><td>Set background or border for 320 x 200 4-color graphics modes or border for text modes</td></tr>
<tr><td></td><td></td><td>Inputs: In text modes, bh = 00h and bl = color
In graphics modes, bh = 01h and bl = palette number
The palette number can be 0 or 1 and gives choices of {background,green,red,yellow} or {background,cyan,magenta,white} for the colors.</td></tr>
<tr><td></td><td></td><td>Returns: Nothing</td></tr>
<tr><td></td><td>0ch</td><td>Write graphics pixel</td></tr>
<tr><td></td><td></td><td>Inputs: al = pixel value
bh = page number
cx and dx = graphics x- and y-coordinates</td></tr>
<tr><td></td><td></td><td>Returns: Nothing</td></tr>
<tr><td></td><td>0dh</td><td>Read graphics pixel</td></tr>
<tr><td></td><td></td><td>Inputs: Same as function 0ch</td></tr>
<tr><td></td><td></td><td>Returns: al = pixel value</td></tr>
<tr><td></td><td>0eh</td><td>Write character in teletype mode
Updates the cursor position automatically</td></tr>
<tr><td></td><td></td><td>Inputs: al = character
bh = page number
bl = foreground color (graphics modes only)</td></tr>
<tr><td></td><td></td><td>Returns: Nothing</td></tr>
<tr><td></td><td>0fh</td><td>Get video mode</td></tr>
<tr><td></td><td></td><td>Inputs: None</td></tr>
<tr><td></td><td></td><td>Returns: ah = width of screen
al = display mode
bh = active page number</td></tr>
<tr><td>13h</td><td></td><td>Disk services
(Usage discussed in Exercise 16_2)</td></tr>
<tr><td></td><td>00h</td><td>Reset disk system</td></tr>
<tr><td></td><td></td><td>Inputs: dl < 80h - resets floppy controller
dl >= 80h - resets floppy and hard disk controllers</td></tr>
<tr><td></td><td></td><td>Returns: If successful, CF = 0, else CF = 1 and ah contains error code, as in function 01h below</td></tr>
</table>

INT	FUNCTION	DESCRIPTION

    01h   Get disk status
Inputs: None
Returns: al contains status of previous disk operation, as follows:

00h	no error
01h	invalid command
02h	address mark not found
03h	write attempted on write-protected disk
04h	sector not found
05h	reset failed
06h	floppy disk removed
07h	bad parameter table
08h	DMA overrun
09h	DMA crossed 64K boundary
0ah	bad sector flag
0bh	bad track flag
0ch	media type not found
0dh	invalid number of sectors on format
0eh	control data address mark detected
0fh	DMA arbitration level out of range
10h	uncorrectable CRC or ECC error
11h	ECC corrected data error
20h	controller failed
40h	seek failed
80h	time out
aah	drive not ready
bbh	undefined error
cch	write fault
e0h	status register error
ffh	sense operation failed

02h   read disk sectors
03h   write disk sectors
04h   verify disk sectors

On floppy, reset using function 00h and retry three times. This ensures that floppy motor has reached operating speed.

Inputs: al = number of sectors
              ch = cylinder number
              cl = sector number
              dh = head number
              dl = drive number
              es:bx = buffer address (not needed when ah = 02h)

Returns: CF set if error, in which case ah = error code, as above

14h   **Serial port services**

    00h   Initialize serial port

Inputs: al = parameters = bit pattern BBBPPSCC
              where BBB = 000, ..., 111 correspond to
              110,150,300,600,1200,2400,4800,9600 baud

INT	FUNCTION	DESCRIPTION

S = 0 or 1 means 1 or 2 stop bits
PP = 00,01,10,11 correspond to parity
none, odd, none, even
CC = character size (10 is 7-bit;11 is 8-bit)
dx = serial port number (0 = COM1, etc.)
Returns: ax = status information (see [3] or [24])

01h   Send a character
Inputs: al = character
dx = serial port number (0 = COM1, etc.)
Returns: ah is error status: 00h means no error; see
[3] or [24] for complete error information

02h   Receive a character
Inputs and Returns are like function 01h except
character is returned in al.

03h   Get port status
Inputs: dx = port number
Returns: As in function 00h

16h   **Keyboard services**

00h   Read next character
Inputs: None
Returns: If standard character: ah = scan code,
al = ASCII code
If extended character: ah = special code,
al = 00h

01h   Report if character waiting
Inputs: None
Returns: ZF clear if character waiting, in which case
ah and al are as in function 00h

02h   Get shift status
Inputs: None
Returns: al = shift status code, as follows:
           01h   right shift active
           02h   left shift active
           04h   control key active
           08h   alternate key active
           10h   scroll lock active
           20h   num lock active
           40h   caps lock active
           80h   insert state active
Inputs: al = byte to print
dx= printer number (0 = LTP1, etc.)
Returns: ah = status, as follows:
           01h   time out

17h   **Printer services**

00h   Send byte to printer
Inputs: dx = printer number (0 = LPT1, etc.)
al = character
Returns: ah = status, as follows:

INT	FUNCTION	DESCRIPTION

		01h time out
		08h i/o error
		10h printer selected
		20h out of paper
		40h printer acknowledgement
		80h printer not busy (0 if busy)
	01h	Initialize printer
		Inputs: dx = printer number (0 = LPT1, etc.)
		Returns: ah = status, as in function 00h
	02h	Get printer status
		Inputs: dx = printer number (0 = LTP1, etc.)
		Returns: ah = status, as in function 00h
1ah		**Get/set time/date**
	00h	Read current clock count
		Inputs: Nothing
		Returns: al = midnight signal (0 means time has not passed midnight since last read)
		cx = high word of tick count
		dx = low word of tick count
	01h	Set current clock count
		Inputs: cx = high word of tick count
		dx = low word of tick count
		Returns: Nothing
	02h	Read real-time clock
		Inputs: Nothing
		Returns: CF set if clock stopped
		ch = hours in BCD form
		cl = minutes in BCD form
		dh = seconds in BCD form
	03h	Set real-time clock
		Inputs: ch = hours in BCD form
		cl = minutes in BCD form
		dh = seconds in BCD form
		dl = 00h for standard time, 01h for daylight saving time
		Returns: Nothing
	04h	Read date from real-time clock
		Inputs: None
		Returns CF set if clock stopped
		ch = century in BCD form (19 or 20)
		cl = year in BCD form
		dh = month in BCD form
		dl = day in BCD form
	05h	Set date in real-time clock
		Inputs: ch = century in BCD form (19 or 20)
		cl = year in BCD form
		dh = month in BCD form
		dl = day in BCD form
		Returns: thing

INT	FUNCTION	DESCRIPTION
20h	**None**	**Terminate** - obsolete program termination Inputs: None Returns: Nothing
21h		**Function dispatcher** - see Appendix 3
25h	**None**	**Absolute disk read** - reads sectors from logical disk Important Note: May destroy all registers except segment registers. Neglects to remove the copy of flags pushed onto stack by the int instruction and so requires an extra popf after return to balance the stack Inputs: al = drive number (0 = A:, etc.) cx = number of sectors to read dx = starting sector number ds:bx = pointer to storage buffer Returns: Standard error reporting, but with special error codes in al and ah, for which we refer the reader to [3] or [24]
26h	**None**	**Absolute disk write** - write sectors to logical disk Important Note: Same as int 25h Inputs: al = drive number (0 = A:, etc.) cx = number of sectors to write dx = starting sector number ds:bx = pointer to data buffer Returns: Standard error reporting, but with special error codes in al and ah, for which we refer the reader to [3] or [24]

SELECTED INT 21H FUNCTIONS

Note. We have included those functions needed in the text or exercises and a few others of special interest. For a complete listing, see [3] or [24]. In all cases, the function number must be transmitted in the **ah** register.

In the following descriptions, the phrase "standard error reporting" means using the carry flag and **ax** to convey error information, as we discussed in Chapter 8: if CF is clear, no error occurred; if CF is set, then an error did occur and **ax** contains an error code, as shown in Figure 8.1.

FUNCTION	DESCRIPTION

00h   **Terminate** - obsolete termination for .COM program
          Inputs: None
          Return: Nothing

01h   **Character input with echo** - waits for character from keyboard
          Responds to Control C
          Inputs: None
          Returns: al = character

02h   **Output a character to video screen**
          Inputs: dl = character

03h   **Auxiliary input** - reads character from first serial port (COM1)
          Inputs: None
          Returns   al = character

04h   **Auxiliary output** - sends character to first serial port (COM1)
          Inputs: dl = character
          Returns   Nothing

05h   **Printer output** - sends character to first printer (LPT1 or PRN)
          Inputs: dl = character
          Returns: Nothing

06h   **Direct console i/o** - reads and writes all characters
          No special treatment of Control C
          Two calls required to read special characters, the first call returning 0
          Inputs: dl = ffh means input a character

FUNCTION   **DESCRIPTION**

dl < ffh means output the characterr in dl
Returns: If called with dl = ffh, returns nothing
            Else:
                    If character waiting, ZF = 0 and al = character
                    Else ZF = 1

09h   **Display string** - sends string to video screen
            Inputs: ds:dx = pointer to string
                        String must be '$' terminated
            Returns: Nothing

0ah   **Buffered keyboard input** - inputs string from keyboard
            Inputs: ds:dx = pointer to storage buffer
                        Buffer format: {maxCount,?, Storage}
                        where Storage can hold string including CR and
                        maxCount does not include CR
            Returns: After call, Buffer contains:
                        {maxcount, actualCount (excl. CR), characters read}

25h   **Set interrupt vector** - replaces interrupt vector
            Inputs: al = interrupt number
                        ds:dx = pointer to replacement handler
            Returns: Nothing

2ah   **Get date** - reads system date
            Inputs: Nothing
            Returns: cx = year-1980
                        dh = month (1 to 12)
                        dl = day (1 to 31)
                        al = day of week (0 = Sunday, etc.)

2bh   **Set date** - sets system date
            Inputs: dh = month (1 to 12)
                        dl = day (1 to 31)
                        al = day of week (0 = Sunday, etc.)
            Returns: al = 00h if successful
                           = ffh otherwise

2ch   **Get time** - reads system time
            Inputs: Nothing
            Returns: ch = hours (0 to 23)
                        cl = minutes (0 to 59)
                        dh = seconds (0 to 59)
                        dl = hundredths of second (0 to 99)

2dh   **Set time** - sets system time
            Inputs: ch = hours (0 to 23)
                        cl = minutes (0 to 59)
                        dh = seconds (0 to 59)
                        dl = hundredths of second (0 to 99)
            Returns: al = 00h if successful
                           = ffh otherwise

31h   **Terminate and stay resident**
            Inputs: al = return code
                        dx = amount of memory to reserve

FUNCTION	DESCRIPTION

35h
Returns: Nothing
Get interrupt vector - find present value of interrupt vector
Inputs: al = interrupt number
Returns: es:bx = value of interrupt vector

39h
Create directory - create directory with given drive and pathname
Inputs: ds:dx = pointer to ASCIIZ pathname (including
                 optional drive)
Returns: Standard error reporting

3ah
Delete directory - delete directory with given drive and pathname
Directory must be empty
Inputs and Returns: same as function 39h

3bh
Set current directory - changes to specified drive and pathname
Inputs and Returns: same as function 39h

3ch
Create file - creates and opens file with given name, which may
include a path designation
If file exists, it is truncated to length zero
Inputs: cx = attribute, with bits defined by:
                 0   read-only
                 1   hidden
                 2   system
                 3   volume label
                 4   reserved (directory bit - should be made 0)
                 5   archive
                 6-15 reserved (should be made 0)
                 ds:dx pointer to ASCIIZ pathname of file
Returns: Standard error reporting

3dh
Open handle - opens a file or device
Inputs: al = access mode, with bits defined by:
                 0-2 define the access:
                      000   read only
                      001   write only
                      010   read/write
                 3   reserved (should be 0)
                 4-6   sharing mode (MS-DOS Ver 3.0 or greater)
                      000   compatibility mode
                      001   deny all
                      010   deny write
                      011   deny read
                      100   deny none
                 7   inheritance flag (MS-DOS Ver 3.0 or greater)
                      0   child process can inherit handle
                      1   child process cannot inherit
Returns: Standard error reporting

3eh
Close handle - closes a file or device
Inputs: bx = handle
Returns: Standard error reporting

3fh
Read handle - reads from file or device

FUNCTION	DESCRIPTION

Inputs: bx = handle
cx = number of bytes to read
ds:dx = pointer to storage buffer
Returns: Standard error reporting
If function successful, ax = number of bytes read

40h   **Write handle** - write to file or device
Inputs: bx = handle
cx = number of bytes to write
ds:dx = pointer to data buffer
Returns: Standard error reporting
If successful, ax = number of bytes written

41h   **Unlink** - deletes file
Inputs: ds:dx = ASCIIZ pathname of file
Returns: Standard error reporting

42h   **Lseek** - set file pointer
Inputs: al = mode, defined by
           00h relative to start of file
           01h relative to present position in file
           02h relative to end of file
bx = handle
cx = high word of offset
dx = low word of offset
Returns: Standard error reporting
If successful, dx = high word of final file pointer position
                              ax = low word of final file pointer position

43h   **Get or set file attributes**
Inputs: al = 00h to get attributes
al = 01h to set attributes
cx = attribute value in the case al = 01h (see function 3ch
for bit meanings; bit 3 must equal 0)
ds:dx = pointer to ASCIIZ filename
Returns: Standard error reporting
If function successful in the al = 00h case, then cx =
file attribute

44h   **IOCTL - I/O control for devices**
Note. This function is very complex. For the most part, we have just
listed the names of the subfunctions to give an idea of the
available options, and refer the reader to [3] or [24] for complete
information. We have included descriptions of some subfunctions
that might be used in the exercises.
Subfunction 00h Get device information
Subfunction 01h Set device information
Subfunction 02h Read control data from character-device driver
Inputs: al = 02h (i.e., subfunction number)
bx = handle
cx = number of bytes to read
ds:dx = buffer to hold information
Returns: Standard error reporting

FUNCTION   **DESCRIPTION**

                      If successful, ax = number of bytes read
          Subfunction 03h Write control data to character-device driver
          Inputs: al = 03h (i.e., subfunction number)
                      bx = handle
                      cx = number of bytes to write
                      ds:dx = address of buffer containing data
          Returns: Standard error reporting
                      If successful, ax = number of bytes written
          Subfunction 04h Read control data from block-device driver
          Inputs: al = 04h (i.e., subfunction number)
                      bl = drive code (0 = default, 1 = A:, 2 = B:, etc.)
                          cx = number of bytes to read
                          ds:dx = address of buffer to hold information
          Returns: Standard error reporting
                          If successful, ax = number of bytes read
          Subfunction 05h Write control data to block-device driver
          Inputs: al = 05h (i.e., subfunction number)
                      bl = drive code (0 = default, 1 = A:, 2 = B:, etc.)
                      cx = number of bytes to write
                      ds:dx =address of buffer containing data
          Returns: Standard error reporting
                      If successful, ax = number of bytes written
          Subfunction 06h Check input status
          Subfunction 07h Check output status
          Subfunction 08h Check if block device is removable
          Subfunction 09h Check if block device is remote
          Subfunction 0ah Check if handle is remote
          Subfunction 0bh Change sharing retry count
          Subfunction 0ch Generic I/O control for character devices
                      Subfunction 0dh Generic I/O control for block devices
          Subfunction 0eh Get logical drive map
          Subfunction 0fh Set logical drive map

48h   **Allocate memory block**
          Inputs: bx = number of paragraphs of memory to allocate
          Returns: Standard error reporting
                      If successful, ax = segment address of allocated block
                      If unsuccessful, bx = size of largest available block (in
                      paragraphs)

49h   **Release memory block**
          Inputs: es = segment address of block to be released
          Returns: Standard error reporting

4ah   **Resize memory block**
          Inputs: bx = desired new size (in paragraphs)
                      es = segment address of block
          Returns: Standard error reporting
                      If unsuccessful, bx = maximum size available (in paragraphs)

4ch   **Terminate process**
          Inputs: al = return code

FUNCTION	DESCRIPTION

Returns: Nothing

4eh   **Find first file** - searches for first file matching given specification
            Inputs: cx = search attribute (see function 3ch)
                        ds:dx = pointer to ASCIIZ string giving search pathname
            Returns: Standard error reporting
                        If successful, results returned at following offsets in
                        current DTA (default DTA is PSP:80h):

15h	attribute of matched file
16h-17h	file time stamp (format as in function 57h)
18h-19h	file date stamp (format as in function 57h)
1ah-1dh	file size
1eh-2ah	ASCIIZ filename and extension, with '*' and '?' wildcards allowed

4fh   **Find next file** - call as often as needed after a successful call to
            function 4eh
            Inputs: Assumes DTA unchanged from previous call to function 4eh
                        or 4fh
            Returns: Same as function 4eh

57h   **Get or set file date and time**
            Inputs: To get date/time al = 00h
                        To set date/time al = 01h
                        bx = handle
                        If al = 01h:
                            cx = time, with bits encoded as follows:
                                00h-04h = seconds, in two-second increments
                                05h-0ah = minutes (0 to 59)
                                0bh-0fh = hours (0 to 23)
                            dx = date, with bits encoded as follows:
                                00h-04h = day (0 to 31)
                                05h-08h = month (1 to 12)
                                09h-0fh = year-1980
            Returns: Standard error reporting
                        If called with al = 00h and successrul, cx and dx contain
                        the time and date information formatted as in the al = 01h
                        case

Index